VIRGINIA WOOLF

HERMIONE LEE

Chatto & Windus

LONDON

First published in 1996

1 3 5 7 9 10 8 6 4 2

First published in Great Britain in 1996 by
Chatto & Windus Limited
Random House, 20 Vauxhall Bridge Road,
London SW1V 2SA

Random House Australia (Pty) Limited
20 Alfred Street, Milsons Point, Sydney
New South Wales 2061, Australia

Random House New Zealand Limited
18 Poland Road, Glenfield
Auckland 10, New Zealand

Random House South Africa (Pty) Limited
PO Box 337, Bergvlei, South Africa

Random House UK Limited Reg. No. 954009

A CIP catalogue record for this book
is available from the British Library

ISBN 0 7011 6507 3

Typeset by Deltatype Ltd, Birkenhead, Merseyside
Printed in Great Britain by
Mackays of Chatham PLC, Chatham, Kent.

For John Barnard

'I meant to write about death, only life came breaking in as usual.'

Diary, 17 February 1922

CONTENTS

PART III: 1919–1929

PART IV: 1929–1941

ILLUSTRATIONS

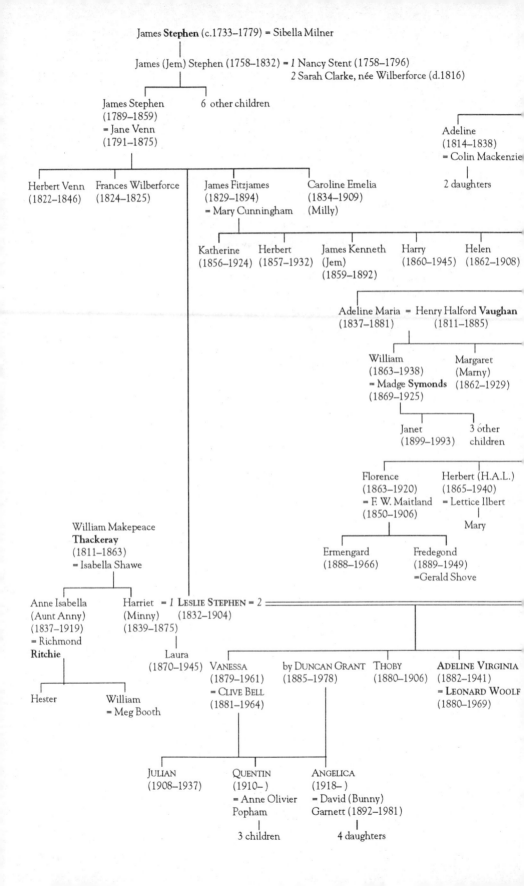

James **Stephen** (c.1733–1779) = Sibella Milner

James (Jem) Stephen (1758–1832) = *1* Nancy Stent (1758–1796)
                                      2 Sarah Clarke, née Wilberforce (d.1816)

James Stephen (1789–1859) = Jane Venn (1791–1875)   6 other children

Adeline (1814–1838) = Colin Mackenzie
    2 daughters

Herbert Venn (1822–1846)

Frances Wilberforce (1824–1825)

James Fitzjames (1829–1894) = Mary Cunningham

Caroline Emelia (1834–1909) (Milly)

Katherine (1856–1924)

Herbert (1857–1932)

James Kenneth (Jem) (1859–1892)

Harry (1860–1945)

Helen (1862–1908)

Adeline Maria (1837–1881) = Henry Halford **Vaughan** (1811–1885)

William (1863–1938) = Madge **Symonds** (1869–1925)

Margaret (Marny) (1862–1929)

Janet (1899–1993)

3 other children

Florence (1863–1920) = F. W. Maitland (1850–1906)

Herbert (H.A.L.) (1865–1940) = Lettice Ilbert

Mary

Ermengard (1888–1966)

Fredegond (1889–1949) = Gerald Shove

William Makepeace **Thackeray** (1811–1863) = Isabella Shawe

Anne Isabella (Aunt Anny) (1837–1919) = Richmond **Ritchie**

Harriet (Minny) (1839–1875) = *1* Leslie **Stephen** = *2* (1832–1904)

Hester

William = Meg Booth

Laura (1870–1945)

Vanessa (1879–1961) = **Clive Bell** (1881–1964)

by **Duncan Grant** (1885–1978)

Thoby (1880–1906)

Adeline Virginia (1882–1941) = **Leonard Woolf** (1880–1969)

Julian (1908–1937)

Quentin (1910–) = Anne Olivier Popham

3 children

Angelica (1918–) = David (Bunny) Garnett (1892–1981)

4 daughters

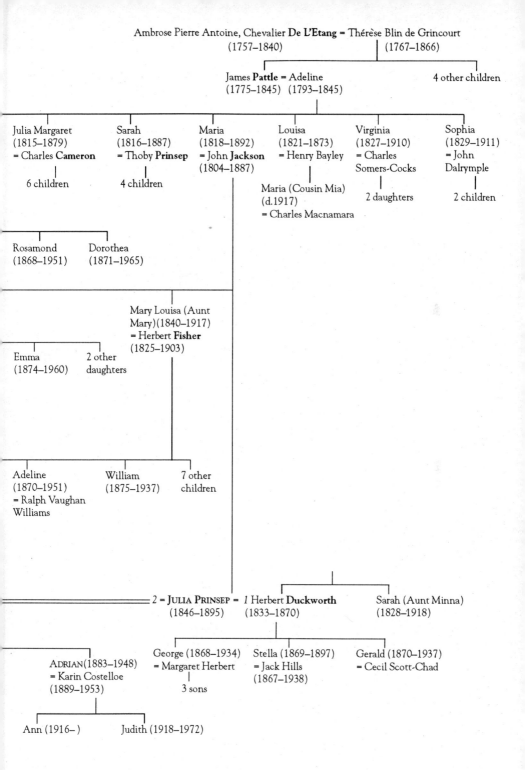

Ambrose Pierre Antoine, Chevalier **De L'Etang** = Thérèse Blin de Grincourt
(1757–1840)   (1767–1866)

James **Pattle** = Adeline   4 other children
(1775–1845) (1793–1845)

Julia Margaret   Sarah   Maria   Louisa   Virginia   Sophia
(1815–1879)   (1816–1887)   (1818–1892)   (1821–1873)   (1827–1910)   (1829–1911)
= Charles **Cameron** = Thoby **Prinsep** = John **Jackson** = Henry Bayley   = Charles   = John
                                     (1804–1887)   Somers-Cocks   Dalrymple

6 children   4 children   Maria (Cousin Mia)   2 daughters   2 children
                                                      (d.1917)
                                                      = Charles Macnamara

Rosamond   Dorothea
(1868–1951)   (1871–1965)

                              Mary Louisa (Aunt
                              Mary)(1840–1917)
                              = Herbert **Fisher**
Emma   2 other   (1825–1903)
(1874–1960)   daughters

Adeline   William   7 other
(1870–1951)   (1875–1937)   children
= Ralph Vaughan
Williams

                              2 = **JULIA PRINSEP** = 1 Herbert **Duckworth**   Sarah (Aunt Minna)
                                  (1846–1895)   (1833–1870)   (1828–1918)

                      George (1868–1934)   Stella (1869–1897)   Gerald (1870–1937)
ADRIAN(1883–1948)   = Margaret Herbert   = Jack Hills   = Cecil Scott-Chad
= Karin Costelloe   (1867–1938)
(1889–1953)   3 sons

Ann (1916–)   Judith (1918–1972)

PART I

1882–1904

ONE

Biography

'My God, how does one write a Biography?'[1] Virginia Woolf's question haunts her own biographers. How do they begin? 'Virginia Woolf was a Miss Stephen.'[2] 'Virginia Woolf was a sexually abused child: she was an incest-survivor.'[3] 'Was Virginia Woolf "insane"?'[4] 'Was Virginia Woolf mad?'[5] 'Virginia Woolf said that "if life has a base" it is a memory.'[6] Or: 'Yet another book about Bloomsbury.'[7]

The different openings suggest some of the choices for Virginia Woolf's biographers. They can start at source, with her family history, and see her in the context of ancestry, country, class. They can start with Bloomsbury, fixing her inside her social and intellectual group and its reputation. They can start by thinking of her as a victim, as someone who is going to kill herself. They can start with her own words about her own sense of the past. They can start with a theory or a belief and see her always in terms of it, since, like Shakespeare, she is a writer who lends herself to infinitely various interpretation. What no longer seems possible is to start: 'Adeline Virginia Stephen was born on 25 January 1882, the daughter of Sir Leslie Stephen, editor of the *Dictionary of National Biography*, and of Julia Stephen, née Jackson.'

There is no such thing as an objective biography, particularly not in this case. Positions have been taken, myths have been made. I have noticed that in the course of any conversation about this book I would, without fail, be asked one or more of the same four questions: Is it true that she was sexually abused as a child? What was her madness and why did she kill herself? Was Leonard a good or a wicked husband? Wasn't she the most terrible snob? It began to seem that everyone who reads books has an opinion of some kind about Virginia Woolf, even if derived only from the title of Albee's play, *Who's Afraid of Virginia Woolf?*

There are many times, writing this, when I have been afraid of Virginia Woolf. I think I would have been afraid of meeting her. I am afraid of not being intelligent enough for her. Reading and writing her life, I am often afraid (or, in one of the words she used most about her mental states, 'apprehensive') *for* her.

3

And her remains are fearsome, too. It's one of the peculiarities of her posthumous reputation that the full, immense extent of her life's work has only revealed itself gradually, changing the twentieth-century perception of her from the delicate lady authoress of a few experimental novels and sketches, some essays and a 'writer's' diary, to one of the most professional, perfectionist, energetic, courageous and committed writers in the language. Even in a year broken by illness (such as 1925) she would finish revising and publish one novel and a collection of essays, write eight or so short stories, start work on another novel, publish thirty-seven review articles, keep a full diary, read a great number of books and write a great number of letters.

Periodic attacks of archive-faintness overcame me, as I contemplated the transatlantically scattered hoards of manuscripts and letters, diaries and notebooks, which would allow a really uncompromising biographer to make a record of what Virginia Woolf said, felt, did and wrote on almost every day of her life. And this is to say nothing of the editions of her works and the hundreds of books and articles, reviews and conference papers on Virginia Woolf.

Yet for all this vast mass of material, I am also afraid of presuming. All readers of Virginia Woolf's diaries (even those who have decided to dislike her) will feel an extraordinary sense of intimacy with the voice that is talking there. They will want to call her Virginia, and speak proprietorially about her life. She seems extremely near, contemporary, timeless. But she is also evasive and obscure (there are a number of important things she never does talk about in the diaries), and, obviously, increasingly distant from us in time. If you listen to the only surviving recording of her,[8] you hear a voice from another century, which to us sounds posh, antiquated, class-bound, mannered. She was born over a hundred years ago; she lived through a period of the most rapid and dramatic changes in human history. Virginia Woolf's 'Orlando', in her 'biography', lives for centuries; so does – so will – 'Virginia Woolf'. Meanwhile, as for Orlando, everything changes. Virginia Woolf herself looks back, from her fifties to her childhood, with amazement, feeling both near to and utterly distant from her own past.

If she sometimes feels strange to herself, how much stranger is she to us! Biographers are supposed to know their subjects as well as or better than they knew themselves. Biography sets out to tell you that a life can be described, summed up, packaged and sold. But Virginia Woolf spent most of her life saying that that idea of biography is – to use a word she liked – poppycock. In her essays and diaries and fiction, in her reading of history, in her feminism, in her politics, 'life-writing', as she herself called it, was a perpetual preoccupation.

*

4

Virginia Woolf was an autobiographer who never published an autobiography; she was an egotist who loathed egotism. It's one of the words she most often uses, whether she is writing about herself or other people. Many of the letters she writes contain apologies – not always entirely sincere – for their egotism. And yet, 'How I interest myself!' she will say, happily, to herself.⁹ She is always trying to work out what happens to that 'myself' – the 'damned egotistical self' – when it is alone, when it is with other people, when it is contented, excited, anxious, ill, when it is asleep or eating or walking, when it is writing. 'Sydney comes & I'm Virginia; when I write I'm merely a sensibility. Sometimes I like being Virginia, but only when I'm scattered & various & gregarious.'¹⁰ 'I meet somebody who says "youre this or that", and I dont want to be anything when I'm writing.'¹¹

What does 'not being anything' mean? Perhaps it is being more concentrated, less externalised: 'I thought, driving through Richmond last night, something very profound about the synthesis of my being: how only writing composes it: how nothing makes a whole unless I am writing; now I have forgotten what seemed so profound.'¹²

She knows that the process of trying to explain the relation between 'myself' and the writing self risks being just self-absorbed, rather than profound. But she must take herself seriously: she is like a singer attending to the state of her vocal cords. 'Myself', for the writing self, is both material and instrument. Not for nothing did Freud, on the only occasion when they met, in 1939, give her a narcissus.

Egotism is often the subject of the diary. She is much concerned with how she writes it, and what it's for. And its uses vary: it is a 'barometer' of her feelings, a storehouse for memories, a record of events and encounters, a practice-ground for writing, a commentary on work in progress, and a sedative for agitation, anger, or apprehension. In the mid-1920s, she has a self-conscious debate with herself about whether it is a diary of facts, or a diary of 'the soul'. (At the same time she is working out how much the 'damned egotistical self' should get into her fiction.) She seems to have promised herself that the diary would be about 'life' rather than 'the soul' – perhaps as a way of keeping 'egotism' under control: 'Did I not banish the soul when I began? What happens is, as usual, that I'm going to write about the soul, & life breaks in.'¹³ Later she will 'cancel that vow against soul description': she wants to describe 'the violent moods of my soul'. But then, 'How describe them?'¹⁴ It is difficult to 'write directly about the soul. Looked at, it vanishes.'¹⁵ So the sense we get from Virginia Woolf's diaries of knowing everything about her is, perhaps, illusory.

Often she doesn't want to write about the soul or 'myself' at all, but about other lives, history, meetings, events. Sometimes – during the General

Strike, for instance – she takes herself to task for not writing more about historical events, and makes herself do so, even if these accounts may bore her later. Those bits of 'life', she suspects, might turn out to be the most interesting parts of the diary after all.

Clearly the diaries are intended for use. 'Oh yes, I shall write my memoirs out of them, one of these days.'[16] When their last house in London is bombed in the war, and Virginia and Leonard Woolf go up to take their valuables away to the country, she makes sure, first, of the twenty-four volumes of diaries: 'a great mass for my memoirs'.[17] When she does start writing her memoirs, they incorporate all her thoughts about life-writing. In her 'Sketch of the Past', which she began in the last two years of her life, she insists that in biography and autobiography there must be a relation between the obscure areas of personality – the 'soul' – and forces like class and social pressures; otherwise 'how futile life-writing becomes'.[18]

The life-writer must explore and understand the gap between the outer self ('the fictitious V.W. whom I carry like a mask about the world')[19] and the secret self. In her diaries and memoirs and fiction, she is always insisting on the difficulty of knowing people: 'She would not say of anyone in the world now that they were this or were that.'[20] The diary spends as much time trying to get inside other people as it does discussing the 'soul'. And the 'egotism' of the letters is always generously and curiously diffusing itself into the needs of her correspondents.

For this legendary egotist is also an empathiser of extraordinary powers. When people who knew her describe their conversations with Virginia Woolf, they remember two kinds of behaviour. One was her amazing flights of fancy, her wonderful performances in conversation, spinning off into fantastic fabrications while everyone sat round and, as it were, applauded. The other kind, though, was her attentive, detailed questioning. (Stephen Spender said that the reason she asked people questions about their lives all the time was because she didn't have enough life of her own to use for material.) Sometimes these two kinds of behaviour overlap, and the questions fuel the fantasy, as at a tea-party at Charleston in 1936, recorded by Virginia Woolf's niece Angelica Bell for her brother Julian:

Yesterday the Woolves came to tea. Virginia was in high fettle. She sat by Dorothy [Bussy] all the time and simply fired out questions at her.

'Now Dorothy tell me all your London news, as Clive would say – what did you have for breakfast? What parties have you been to? What was it like at the Clarks the other night? Mary Hutch went with you? What did she wear? I expect she looked like one of those drawings by a Frenchman – I forget his name – but you know – with a fountain of hair and a pencil-like oyster satin dress, done with a dash – Was it not?' Somebody pointed out that Mary hadnt got a fountain of hair but that didnt seem to matter to Virginia who fell back onto the oyster coloured satin and described the complete dress. Then Dorothy told us what it was really like – just plain black, high necked in front with no back to it, but oyster-coloured sleeves (at which V was immensely pleased).[21]

In that account (which has the advantage of being written at the time, rather than years later) Virginia Woolf isn't waiting for the answers to her questions. Among her friends she often got into trouble for being an unreliable witness. The letters are full of exaggeration and invention, and so too, sometimes, is the diary. She excites herself and amuses other people by 'doing her owl' (as she called it). But she is also constantly trying, via her own 'performances', to get inside other people.

Virginia Woolf is very interested in Boswell, the first great biographer. She wrote about him more than once, sympathetically evoking his vanity, his curiosity and exuberance, 'his intense consciousness of himself' and his capacity to notice everything – all qualities she shares. Her own biographer might want to echo this:

> It is strange how one wonders with an inquisitive kind of affection, what Boswell felt; it always seems possible with him as with living people that if one watches closely enough one will know. But when we try to say what the secret is, then we understand why Boswell was a genius.[22]

Whenever she mentions Boswell in the diary, she says she would like to write down what people say and the way they talk, as he did.[23] 'I told Lytton I should try to write down his talk – which sprang from a conversation about Boswell.'[24] She often does write down whole chunks of conversation, complaining all the time how difficult it is. But she does it because it releases her from herself. It may be true, she remarks, writing on Gibbon, 'that friends are chosen partly in order to live lives that we cannot live in our own persons'.[25] Sometimes this fails to release her from herself, and provokes melancholy or rivalrous comparisons.[26] Egotism and observation are always related.

Boswell was an egotist who was also a hero-worshipper. He believed in greatness: that was why it was worthwhile writing down everything Dr Johnson said. Virginia Woolf inherited this historical impulse to record the talk and behaviour of 'great men' from her parents' world. And her concept of traditional life-writing was derived from her father's major life's work, the *Dictionary of National Biography*. The last page of her 'Sketch of the Past' remembers the 'great men' who used to come to tea in her childhood, and how eccentric and remote that idea of greatness now seems: 'something that we are led up to by our parents and is now entirely extinct'.[27] She never quite loses that extinct idea, but she turns it to her own subversive biographical ends. Though she still takes every opportunity in the diary to write biographical sketches of 'great men' (much more frequently than of great women) – Keynes, Eliot, Sickert, Yeats, Arnold Bennett, Thomas Hardy, H.G. Wells[28] – these sketches are irreverent, personal, revealing, quite the opposite from the *DNB*. She questions the idea of 'greatness', and she looks behind public faces. Her diary, like her essays and stories and novels, blurs the lines between history, biography and fiction.

Fiction is often her version of biography. *Orlando* makes an explicit game out of this relationship, and suggests to her the possibility of more such fictive biographies.[29] Orlando's biographer is written in as a character in pursuit of his/her subject, always self-consciously referring back to the conventions, which are not always adequate for the task in hand: 'For that was the way his mind worked now, in violent see-saw from life to death, stopping at nothing in between, so that the biographer must not stop either, but must fly as fast as he can and so keep pace.'[30] The struggle of the biographer to keep pace is more painful in *Jacob's Room*, where s/he is always in pursuit of the vanishing hero, who can only be known through unfinished glimpses. In the earlier *Night and Day*, the heroine is burdened by her famous grandfather's papers and his unfinishable Life, while she tries to find a different language for her own life. And the desperate efforts of the six characters in *The Waves* to dispense with a biographer and to speak their own autobiographies collapses into the voice of the writer who has difficulty in telling his own story, let alone theirs.

When Virginia Woolf is working out in the 1910s and 1920s what kind of novelist she wants to be and what she thinks modern fiction ought to be doing, she always talks about how to get at the essence of personality. She makes up imaginary biographies ('An Unwritten Novel', 'Mr Bennett and Mrs Brown') to show how she wants to write fiction. And she attacks traditional biography in the same way that she criticises Edwardian fiction – as in this review of a new life of Christina Rossetti:

Here is the past and all its inhabitants miraculously sealed as in a magic tank; all we have to do is to look and to listen and to listen and to look and soon the little figures – for they are rather under life size – will begin to move and to speak, and as they move we shall arrange them in all sorts of patterns of which they were ignorant, for they thought when they were alive that they could go where they liked; and as they speak we shall read

8

into their sayings all kinds of meanings which never struck them, for they believed when they were alive that they said straight off whatever came into their heads. But once you are in a biography all is different.[31]

Why should being in a biography be so 'different' from being alive? The argument keeps pace with her discussion of why the representation of character in fiction needs to change. In both art-forms, she is aware of writing in a period of transition: and she herself partly makes that transition take place. She begins her writing life in the era of what she calls 'the draperies and decencies' of Victorian biography:[32] censored, reverential, public Lives of 'great men', such as Frederic Maitland's life of her father, which left out any hint of his domestic behaviour.

These 'Mausoleum Books' (as the life-story her father wrote for his children came to be called) were 'dominated by the idea of goodness', and written under the supervisory eyes of widows, friends, surviving relatives and admirers. They produced something that looked like 'the wax figures now preserved in Westminster Abbey, that were carried in funeral processions through the street'.[33] So Mr Green, an imaginary biographer of an imaginary ship-owner from Birkenhead called Thomas Watson (b.1868), has difficulty in telling the truth about his subject:

> For one thing, Mrs Watson has forbidden Mr Green the biographer to tell the truth about her husband's temper – Mr Watson used to throw the plates at her head if his porridge was cold. But that has to be left out. Then there is this difficulty: very few people write good letters or good diaries. Thomas Watson's letters were like this: 'Dear Jemma. Just a line to let you know that I arrived safely. The train was 10 minutes late, wh. considering the weather, is not bad. Unfortunately owing to Ellen's carelessness my sponge was packed still wet, and has I fear utterly spoilt my new dress waistcoat. Unless she will undertake to be more careful in future, I do not see how we can possibly keep her . . . I must insist that you give the girl notice or *supervise the packing yourself*.' There are probably 3,000 letters like that.[34]

In her lifetime, psychoanalysis, wars, social changes and the reaction against nineteenth-century habits of mind meant a revolution in biography and memoir-writing. By the end of her life Virginia Woolf was reading Gide's explicitly homosexual journals, with some amazement at their frankness. Of course Lytton Strachey's debunking of his eminent Victorians was a key moment in the pulling down of the draperies. But Virginia Woolf is not a Stracheyan clone. She had reservations about his tactics – she detested *Elizabeth and Essex* – and about 'the new biography' in general.

Her own ideas are worked out independently from Strachey, and she is more generous to the past.

For her the crucial problem in the biographies that her generation has inherited is the tug between fact and fiction and the difficulty of getting to the 'soul'. She admires Boswell's 'obstinate veracity',[35] but is appalled at the gap between the necessary facts of a life-story, and its hidden truth.

> The biographer is doing 2 incompatible things. He is providing us with sterile & fertile. Things that have no bearing upon the life. But he has to provide them. He does not know what is relevant. Nobody has yet decided. A bastard, an impure art.[36]

> Since a life has to begin with birth and to continue through the years these facts must be introduced in order. But have they anything to do with him [the subject of the biography]? That is where doubt begins; the pen trembles; the biography swells into the familiar fungoid growth. . . . Facts have their importance.
> —But that is where the biography comes to grief. The biographer cannot extract the atom. He gives us the husk. Therefore as things are, the best method would be to separate the two kinds of truth. Let the biographer print fully. completely, accurately, the known facts without comment; Then let him write the life as fiction.[37]

She often asks herself why she feels the need for biography. While she reads, she begins to be curious about the writer's life and personality. But how can curiosity be satisfied? In 'A Talk about Memoirs', two women friends, Ann and Judith, are exchanging views on what they get out of those 'great swollen . . . dropsical' Victorian memoirs – a life, for instance, of Lady Georgiana Peel, daughter of Lord John Russell, born in 1836. Ann describes Lady Georgiana's visit to Woburn.

> *Ann:* . . . And what d'you think they did there? They threw mutton chops out of the window 'for whoever cared to pick them up'. And each guest had a piece of paper by his plate 'in which to wrap up an eatable for the people waiting outside'. *Judith:* Mutton chops! people waiting outside! *Ann:* Ah, now the charm begins to work.[38]

The 'charm' works through these sorts of odd details and vivid scenes, moments when the wax figures begin to move. If you put Virginia Woolf's scattered writings on biography together, you can see her making up some rules. There must be these sharp moments, caught from the context, the subject's social world. But also there must be movement and change:

generalisations, fixed attitudes, summings-up, are fatal. A good biography 'is the record of the things that change rather than of the things that happen'.[39] Gradually, imperceptibly, we alter. 'A self that goes on changing is a self that goes on living': so too with the biography of that self.[40] And just as lives don't stay still, so life-writing can't be fixed and finalised. Our ideas are shifting about what can be said, our knowledge of human character is changing. The biographer has to be a pioneer, going 'ahead of the rest of us, like the miner's canary, testing the atmosphere, detecting falsity, unreality, and the presence of obsolete conventions'.[41] So 'There are some stories which have to be retold by each generation.'[42] She is talking about the story of Shelley, but she could be talking about her own life-story.

Reading other peoples' biographies or autobiographies – like talking to her friends – makes her think of herself. 'When one reads a life one often compares one's own life with it.'[43] But as soon as she compares her life with any life-writing, she is brought up against the gap between what she knows about herself and what she reads about other people. 'Why are all one's events so perfectly irrational that a good biographer would be forced to ignore them entirely?'[44]

So, when it comes to having biography written about *her*, she is equivocal. Her dealings with Winifred Holtby, who included a biographical chapter in the first English book written about Virginia Woolf, in 1932, are defensive. And whenever she reads about herself – in William Rothenstein's memoirs, for instance, where 'Vanessa, Stella and Virginia Stephen figure, most inaccurately' – she sees the same ludicrous gap between other people's versions and her own memory. 'Do you think' (she asks Clive Bell) 'that all memoirs are as mendacious as this – Every fact I mean, all on one side?'[45]

But she has mixed feelings about 'mendacity' versus privacy. Certainly she would have hated to read a 'life' about herself, in her life-time, which gave her secrets away. She is horrified at the thought that Ethel Smyth might be thinking of publishing her letters or writing about her. The desire for anonymity, one of the crucial themes of her later years, involves a violent detestation of all journalistic intrusions on her life.[46]

Yet she resents the censorship her generation has inherited. 'Well whats to be done about our "lives" I wonder? The EMF. Goldie thing to me quite futile,'[47] she says, referring to Forster's expurgated life of Goldsworthy Lowes Dickinson, which left out his homosexuality. She wants them all, eventually, to have honest, uncensored 'lives'. When the publication of Lytton's extremely candid letters is under discussion in her circle, she is all for it. There is some talk of her writing his biography after she has finished doing Roger Fry's, and she comments: 'I'm glad, I think, that there should be a full & outspoken life. Only not as a reply to criticism. And then the buggery?'[48] 'The buggery' is always a problem. While she is writing her life of Roger Fry she has a correspondence with Katherine Furse, the daughter of J.A. Symonds, who is trying, with great difficulty, to get her father's embargoed letters out of the London Library. She wants to write a more 'open' life of him than the censored version by Horatio Brown, who entirely omitted Symonds's homosexuality. Virginia Woolf writes to her approvingly – 'I'm glad to think that now we needn't hush up so much'.[49]

Virginia Woolf and her contemporaries are poised on the edge of the revolution which has turned biography into the iconoclastic, gossipy artform it is now, when the only taboo is censorship. She could see this coming, with some trepidation, and she is one of the people who made its coming possible. (And she and her friends, family and acquaintances became some of the main subjects of open, modern biography.)

But she herself can only half open the door to this flood of uncensored life-writing. When she comes to write her biography of Roger Fry, she finds herself as constricted as the Victorians. Biography, which she so loves to read, turns out to be the most terrible 'grind' to write.[50] She starts full of ideas for sabotaging the traditional form: she might begin at the end and work backwards? or give lots of 'specimen days'? or have it 'written by different people to illustrate different stages?'[51] But she ends up frustrated by the need for discretion, and by the clash between the facts and her 'vision'. 'How can one cut loose from facts, when there they are, contradicting my theories?'[52] She envies the painters, particularly Walter Sickert. He is, she says, a great biographer, able to penetrate through his portraits to 'the complexity and intrigue of character' without having to fall into 'the three or four hundred pages of compromise, evasion, understatement, overstatement, irrelevance and downright falsehood which we call biography'.[53]

Her thoughts on biography are comparable to the work being done by the painters she knew, particularly the portraits by Vanessa Bell, Duncan Grant and Carrington: domestic, impressionistic, irreverent, informal portraits which sought the essence of character through colour and form. A purple triangle, Lily Briscoe tells Mr Bankes in *To the Lighthouse*, can represent a mother and child in the new portraiture – if it suggests the essential 'self'. So, in Virginia Woolf's idea of biography – reacting against tradition as the artists were reacting against old Academy styles – the relationship would be uncovered between public and private, official and secret lives.

The breaking down of these divisions was one of the features of her circle. This could produce the impression of cosiness and élitism which has caused, retrospectively, much reproach. But it was also a way of crossing genres and exploring new forms. When Virginia Woolf and her friends and family read autobiographical papers to each other; when Quentin Bell and his aunt wrote comic sketches about their relations and neighbours for home entertainments; when Virginia Woolf's play about her family, *Freshwater*, was performed to an invited audience; when she wrote reviews for the *Nation* while her husband was the literary editor; when her books and pamphlets were published by their own press; when she sat for family portraits, or wrote prefaces to her sister's exhibition of paintings, or had Vanessa Bell regularly design her book-covers, or wrote *Orlando* as a private message for Vita Sackville-West, she was laying herself open to charges of élite practices. But she was also making the kind of connections between the public and the private which she wanted for biography and autobiography.

Virginia Woolf has a passion for 'lives of the obscure', and for marginal, unvalued literary forms like memoirs, letters, and journals.[54] These lives are, mostly, women's. When she writes about biography, she is also writing about feminism. She says to Vita Sackville-West, when the first idea for *Orlando* comes to her: 'it sprung upon me how I could revolutionise biography in a night.'[55] Orlando is the hero who turns into a heroine, in a biography which turns out to be a fiction. For Virginia Woolf, a revolution in biography is also a sexual revolution.

She is always writing to her women friends urging them to write their life-stories.[56] She wants them to fill a gap: 'Very few women yet have written truthful autobiographies. It is my favourite form of reading'.[57] While she is writing her own memoirs in 1940, she says to Ethel Smyth (herself an inveterate autobiographer): 'I was thinking the other night that there's never been a womans autobiography. Nothing to compare with Rousseau. Chastity and modesty I suppose have been the reason.'[58] The inhibitions and censorships of women's life-writing is one of her most urgent subjects. It was still possible for her to say, in 1927, out of her reading of history and biography, 'Very little is known about women.'[59]

Virginia Woolf's feminist programme, coming into its fullest and most explicit expression in her fifties, is above all a literary one. It is inextricably bound up with her desire to 'revolutionise biography'. She wants to find new forms for 'women's as yet unnarrated lives'.[60] She does this from the moment she starts to write. At twenty she starts a comical character sketch of her friend Violet Dickinson, as 'Aunt Maria', and goes back to it again in 1907. Virginia Stephen calls herself Violet's 'Bio- or mytho-grapher',[61] and *Friendship's Gallery* is a spoof love-letter-cum-biography,[62] an early *Orlando*. Its jokes (some purely personal) are about what you do as a biographer 'when you are writing the life of a woman'. The semi-serious attempts to describe 'the flight of her mind' ('Did she reason or only instincticise?') dissolve into a fairy-tale set in Japan about two magical princesses, a female story told to make a child sleep.

Friendship's Gallery is connected to 'The Journal of Mistress Joan Martyn' (1906),[63] which invents a middle-aged female historian who has been having some arguments about the rival merits of archival and imaginative research. Among the patriarchal archives of a Norfolk farmer's family, she comes upon the journal of a twenty-five-year-old country girl for the year 1480. The female biographer-historian disappears inside the pseudo-medieval journal's voice, the voice of a girl whose passion for experience and freedom – at a time of great social upheaval – is circumscribed by her mother's traditional ideas about women's roles. Her writing stops when she gets married. And in 'Memoirs of a Novelist', written three years later, the true life of a Victorian woman novelist, Miss Willatt, is uncovered beneath the surface of the official, censored life written by her woman friend, which gives us 'a wax work as it were of Miss Willatt preserved under glass'.[64] There is a lot of veiled autobiography in these early stories, and there are the beginnings – firmly, vividly, and quickly established – of the kind of biography that will shape itself to women's lives.

In later, published essays, this creative interplay between the biographer or historian and the dead subject is marvellously developed: Virginia Woolf's essays must be the envy of any biographer. And she makes the dead come most alive in her essays on the 'great women of their time', where she pours her energies into imagining her subjects from their archives.

Here for example is Mary Wollstonecraft – you can tell from her face, 'at once so resolute and so dreamy, so sensual and so intelligent', that her life 'was bound to be tempestuous'. 'Every day she made theories by which life should be lived; and every day she came smack against the rock of other people's prejudices. Every day too – for she was no pedant, no cold-blooded theorist – something was born in her that thrust aside her theories and forced her to model them afresh.'[65]

Here, by contrast, is Dorothy Wordsworth, from whose 'homely narrative' ('rapt but controlled, free yet strictly ordered') you can see her repressing her melancholy agitations, keeping 'her faculties forever on the stretch', 'searching into the lives of the poor as if they held in them the same secret as the hills'. She and Coleridge and Wordsworth go tramping hour after hour in foul weather because they knew 'there was some waterfall to be enquired into'. 'At last they reached the waterfall. And then all Dorothy's powers fell upon it. She searched out its character, she noted its resemblances, she defined its differences, with all the ardour of a discoverer, with all the exactness of a naturalist, with all the rapture of a lover. She possessed it at last – she had laid it up in her mind for ever.'[66] It is what Virginia Woolf does with her human subjects.

These intuitive biographical portraits come from a close acquaintance with the literary and historical source materials. They belong to a period when such emotional, anecdotal manners in essay-writing were more acceptable than they are now. But they go beyond the conventions of the time. They prove the case that her first woman biographer-historian was trying to make in 'The Journal of Mistress Joan Martyn', that the imagination can have historical authority.

In *A Room of One's Own*, she watches a 'very ancient lady' crossing the road with her daughter, with all her memories latent and untapped within her, and feels 'the pressure of dumbness, the accumulation of unrecorded life' piled up from 'all these infinitely obscure lives'[67] that remain to be recorded. Both Virginia Woolf's feminist essays, *A Room of One's Own* and the later *Three Guineas*, are also essays on life-writing. The climax of *A Room of One's Own* is, famously, a 'fascinating and masterly biography'[68] of Shakespeare's imaginary sister, as much of a genius as her brother, but doomed by her sex to a life of exploitation, pain and failure. Like so much of Virginia Woolf's feminist writing, this biographical fantasy is at once historical and Utopian, a tragic description of what women's lives have been like and an empowering fantasy of how they might become different.

In *Three Guineas*, the word 'biography' is constantly repeated. Biographies are read here – particularly the 'rich and revealing' Victorian biographies – to find one story hidden under another. 'Let us go on looking – if not at the lines, then between the lines of biography.'[69] Biography here is like an oracle, a cryptic text from which a hidden and very important message has to be decoded. Lurking inside it is the evidence of male attitudes to women (fathers' 'infantile fixations' on their daughters, for instance, or assumptions that all women should marry), of women's struggle for education, their attitudes to war, their attempt to enter the professions. There are good jokes about biography in the essay (we need a female biography of God, she says, since it looks as if a male biography of the Deity 'would resolve itself into a Dictionary of Clerical Biography'). But it mainly derives from its reading of biographies a furious analysis of patriarchal discrimination and censorship.

In Virginia Woolf's thinking on feminism and biography, in her novel-writing and in her thoughts about autobiography, she deals repeatedly with censorship. When she begins to write her memoirs in the late 1930s, she says: 'I have been thinking about Censors. How visionary figures admonish us.'[70] All writers, she feels, are aware of these admonishing figures; but women most of all are under their shadow, and have as a result felt unable to tell their stories truthfully. How truthful, then, could Virginia Woolf's own autobiography be?

Her intention to use the diaries for an autobiography was curtailed by her death. And the piecemeal history of her posthumous publications has meant that, until recently, her autobiographical writings – some of her finest work – are not as well known as her novels, her diaries and her letters. But she does write several versions of her autobiography, one as a letter for Vanessa's children, some as talks for the Memoir Club, the last as the beginnings of a book which she intended to publish. And in doing so, she is acutely aware that the sort of life-writing that might be appropriate for a public figure cannot 'fit' her. One of her papers for the Memoir Club begins, not entirely jokingly, with this disclaimer. It is unfair of Molly MacCarthy, she says, to ask *her* to contribute.

> I am not the most widely lived or the most richly memoried. Maynard, Desmond, Clive and Leonard all live stirring and active lives; all constantly brush up against the great; all constantly affect the course of history one way or another . . . Who am I that I should be asked to read a memoir? . . . My memoirs, which are always private, and at their best only about proposals of marriage, seductions by half-brothers, encounters with Ottoline and so on, must soon run dry.[71]

'My memoirs, *which are always private*.' So were most women's. Under the joking mask she wears here for her clever, intimate audience, Virginia Woolf is defining the difference she perceives between female and male autobiography. It was an inevitable difference, attributable to social history as much as to 'gender identity'.[72] Virginia Woolf's *curriculum vitae* is, in public terms, full of gaps. She did not go to school. She did not work in an office. She did not belong to any institution. With rare exceptions, she did not give public lectures or join committees or give interviews. And in private terms her life-story is sensational only for her breakdowns and suicide attempts. She did not have children. Her sexual life, though unusual, was not dramatic or notorious. She was not the subject of any public scandals or law cases. She did not engage in hazardous sports or bizarre hobbies. She never flew in an aeroplane, or travelled outside Europe. Her exploits and adventures are in her mind and on the page. And here too, in her writing life, she is intensely private.

But her disclaimer is also ironical and misleading. Ironical because she felt that the really important life was 'within'; misleading because she did, also, have an uninstitutionalised public life. She knew an enormous number of people and met many of the exceptional figures of her time. She listened to, and participated in, a huge amount of political discussion. She was a publisher, who worked with her husband as a business partner in the Hogarth Press. She was a close and observant analyst of the world she lived in. And she was one of the century's most insatiable readers.

To others, she may look like an 'insider' – inside a family, inside a group, inside a class. To herself, she feels like an 'outsider'. The autobiography of an insider can be filled with the facts of a profession, the trajectory of a mental career, the story of a personal development in the context of history. (See the autobiographies of Bertrand Russell, H.G. Wells – or Leonard Woolf.) But what is the autobiography of an outsider to consist of? Emotions, secret thoughts, and recollections of childhood? If so, an 'outsider's' autobiography necessitates self-revelation and confession. And this challenges her perpetual fear of egotistical self-exposure.

There is a personal basis to her published work which Virginia Woolf is at pains to conceal. Her life-story enters and shapes her novels (and her essays); she returns again and again to her family, her parents, her sister, the death of her mother, the death of her brother. 'In fact I sometimes think only autobiography is literature – novels are what we peel off, and come at last to the core, which is only you or me.'[73] She is one of the most self-reflecting, self-absorbed novelists who ever lived. Yet she is also one of the most anxious to remove personality from fiction. 'Autobiography it might be called', she says when she begins to work on what will become *The Waves*. But then: 'this shall be Childhood; but it must not be my childhood.'[74]

Her self-protectiveness is very strong in the feminist essays. This partly derives from a shrewd political sense of her audience's resistance to a woman's special pleading: she thinks her argument will have more impact if it is not perceived as a personal complaint. But it also shows a profound fear of exposing emotions like self-pity, sentimentality, or vanity.[75] In *A Room of One's Own*, the essay in which she chooses not to state her own personal case, she is very dubious about the 'modern' genre of confessional autobiography.[76] And she cancels from the final version of that essay a passage on Florence Nightingale's autobiography *Cassandra*, a painful expression of the thwarted lives of nineteenth-century women: 'It is hardly writing, it is more like screaming.'[77] Screams of rage and pain are not what she wants to hear from other women, or what she allows herself.

If this diary were a diary of the soul I could write at length of the 2nd meeting of the Memoir Club. Leonard was objective & triumphant; I subjective & most unpleasantly discomfited. I dont know when I've felt so chastened & out of humour with myself – a partner I generally respect & admire. 'Oh but why did I read this egotistic sentimental trash!' That was my cry, & the result of my sharp sense of the silence succeeding my chapter. It started with loud laughter; this was soon quenched; & then I couldn't help figuring a kind of uncomfortable boredom on the part of the males; to whose genial cheerful sense my revelations were at once mawkish & distasteful. What possessed me to lay bare my soul![78]

This diary entry for 1920 tells us everything about Virginia Woolf's difficulties with self-presentation: her fear of exposing the 'soul', her self-denigration, her horror of being laughed at, her turning of that male laughter and boredom on to herself, her determination to wear a mask rather than humiliate herself again. (And what had she been telling them? Why were the men so discomfited, and why, in a group renowned for its openness, was there so much difficulty in speaking frankly?)

Whenever after this she exposed painful recollections to others, she did so in a deliberately self-restrained, jocular way. In her surviving Memoir Club papers ('22 Hyde Park Gate', 'Old Bloomsbury', and 'Am I a Snob?'), she turns her life-story into witty, stylish performances, carefully avoiding sentiment and guaranteed to please the likes of Maynard Keynes. 'The Memoir Club was fearfully brilliant – I mean I was . . .'[79] Accordingly, the revelations in these narratives need to be handled with care.

And there is reserve even in her most intimate letters. It was only in the 'Sketch of the Past', begun in the late 1930s (and clearly intended for publication), that she began to speak openly about her own sexual history: and even then still hesitatingly, darkly. The whole of this uncompleted fragment of life-writing is marked by hiatuses and stoppages: 'Here I come to one of the memoir writer's difficulties . . . They [memoirs] leave out the person to whom things happened.'[80] The elusiveness of the self almost becomes the subject. In its refusal to make any pretence at a polished, coherent presentation of the 'self', 'Sketch of the Past' begins to look like that new kind of women's life-writing she has been recommending for so long.

It is the very opposite of 'Reminiscences',[81] written in 1908 in the form of a letter about her sister, addressed to her sister's firstborn son. Complicated and painful feelings about Vanessa, her husband Clive Bell and her new baby gave rise to this memoir, and it is an awkward hybrid. It makes a fierce critique of patriarchal behaviour, but it inherits, and imitates, a nineteenth-century patriarchal tradition of the autobiography written as a letter to one's children. (It is one of the painful aspects of 'Reminiscences' that Virginia

18

Stephen was not writing it for her own children.) Her great-grandfather had left such a narrative, and so had her father, in the memoir of his wife, which he wrote after her death 'for my darling Julia's children' and which they called the 'Mausoleum Book'. Virginia Stephen takes a leaf out of these fathers' books – while trying to avoid their egotism and emotionalism – to write the story of the women in the Stephen family – Julia, Stella, Vanessa and (by implication) herself. But she locks this story inside a formal language and structure, meant for suppressing sentiment.

Inside this shell, another kind of narrative is struggling to get out, and at times expresses its frustration, as when she tries to recall her mother's way of speaking:

> Written words of a person who is dead or still alive tend most unfortunately to drape themselves in smooth folds annulling all evidence of life. You will not find in what I say, or again in those sincere but conventional phrases in the life of your grandfather, or in the noble lamentations with which he fills the pages of his autobiography, any semblance of a woman whom you can love.[82]

And so her mother is entombed in the draperies of traditional life-writing, and it will be years before her daughter can get her out.

Three years before these 1908 'Reminiscences', Virginia Stephen wrote her first published biographical piece. It was an anonymous contribution ('by one of his daughters') to Frederic Maitland's *Life* of Leslie Stephen. She wrote it in 1905, a year after his death, and it was published in 1906. This 'Note' – respectful, affectionate, censored – places her in a traditional handmaid's role: the young woman writer dedicating herself to the life of the famous father.[83]

At exactly the same time that she is writing the 'Note on Father' (and having it approved by her brother), she writes in her diary (in January 1905) that she has gone back to her father's house, her childhood home (the Stephen children had moved out that year) and seen all the empty rooms. 'Saw my old room – so strange with the ink splashes & shelves as of old. I could write the history of every mark & scratch in that room, where I lived so long.'[84] The coincidence of that diary entry with her contribution to the *Life* of Sir Leslie sets up the conflict between private and public – and between the daughter's writing and the father's inheritance – which will be one of the main subjects of her writing life.

The 'history' she *could* write, at twenty-three, of the secret significance of every 'mark on the wall' of her childhood room, is not the 'history' she *can* write at that time. Instead, she writes the official history of her father. To arrive at the point of the late memoir, the 'Sketch of the Past', where this family story is told again, but differently, she has made the life's journey which I am about to trace. But her subject matter has come round full circle. At fifty-nine, she can write the true history of what went on in that room, and the true story of what her father was like: not just as she remembers him, but as he must have been as a young, daughterless man, independent of her feelings for him.

The 'Sketch of the Past' has the depth and experience of her whole writing life behind it, and is able to make a profound, detailed analysis of how she writes about herself. She has often thought about how memory works: 'I can only note that the past is beautiful because one never realises an emotion at the time. It expands later, & thus we don't have complete emotions about the present, only about the past.'[85] She has often tried to recuperate her past:

> To freshen my memory of the war, I read some old diaries. How close the tears come, again & again; as I read of L. & me at the Green . . . The sense of all that floating away for ever down the stream, unknown for ever; queer sense of the past swallowing so much of oneself.[86]

The 'Sketch of the Past' rescues herself from time's swallowing maw, and explains how she does so, by the same process that makes biography come alive: making lives vivid through scenes and moments. But, in her autobiography, 'scene making' is not a device. It is something she receives, something that happens to her. 'Representative scenes' from her life seem to endure as 'realities', waiting for their moment to 'flood in' to her consciousness. So 'scene making is my natural way of marking the past.' This, she tells us, is how her autobiography is written. Again and again, she marks the past by returning to the same scenes, the rooms, the landscapes, the figures of her life, like the ghosts revisiting their haunted house in her story of that name. Back she goes to the scenes of childhood: the blind tapping on the window of the bedroom at St Ives, the lighthouse beam going round, the sound of the waves breaking on the shore.

TWO

Houses

In the summer of 1905, the year after their father's death, the four orphaned Stephens – Vanessa, Thoby, Virginia, Adrian – all in their twenties, rented a house in Carbis Bay, a village outside St Ives. They had not been to Cornwall since the summer before their mother died ten years before. On the night they arrived, after the long train journey from London, they walked up the hill – a couple of miles – from Carbis Bay to Talland House, where they had spent all their childhood summers between 1882, the year of Virginia Stephen's birth, and 1894. Next day, Virginia turned this strange experience into a carefully written diary entry:

> It was dusk when we came, so that there still seemed to be a film between us & the reality. We could fancy that we were but coming home along the high road after some long day's outing, & that when we reached the gate at Talland House, we should thrust it open, & find ourselves among the familiar sights again. In the dark, indeed, we made bold to humour this fancy of ours further than we had a right to; we passed through the gate, groped stealthily but with sure feet up the carriage drive, mounted the little flight of rough steps, & peered through a chink in the escalonia [*sic*] hedge. There was the house, with its two lighted windows; there on the terrace were the stone urns, against the bank of tall flowers; all, so far as we could see was as though we had but left it in the morning. But yet, as we knew well, we could go no further; if we advanced the spell was broken. The lights were not our lights; the voices were the voices of strangers. We hung there like ghosts in the shade of the hedge, & at the sound of footsteps we turned away.[1]

'It was a ghostly thing to do,' she said in a letter to her friend Violet Dickinson.[2] It's possible to imagine the four 'ghosts', tall, silent, similar, rather shabbily dressed, in their walking shoes, standing in a row with their heads poking through the hedge at their lost childhood, rather like those characters in Tennyson's poems – *Maud, Enoch Arden* – lurking at the bottom of gardens or coming back in secret to the home that is theirs no more. Virginia Woolf made many other returns to Cornwall, but this is the symbolic one, that gathers up her feelings about her childhood. This revisiting would, twenty years later, be the source of the emotion and the plot of *To the Lighthouse*, the novel that comes from this house. Already, in the twenty-three-year-old's diary entry, the novel is being begun. The return to the lost house and garden, the lost parents, will be its story. In *To the Lighthouse*, Lily Briscoe, the painter, returning to the house ten years after the death of Mrs Ramsay, tries to work her way back through her painting into the past, and seems for a moment to be able to summon up the figure of Mrs Ramsay as she was, ten years ago:

> 'Mrs Ramsay! Mrs Ramsay!' she cried, feeling the old horror come back – to want and want and not to have. Could she inflict that still? And then, quietly, as if she refrained, that too became part of ordinary experience, was on a level with the chair, with the table. Mrs Ramsay – it was part of her perfect goodness to Lily – sat there quite simply, in the chair, flicked her needles to and fro, knitted her reddish-brown stocking, cast her shadow on the step. There she sat.[3]

Like Lily Briscoe conjuring up Mrs Ramsay, we can superimpose, on to the image of the four young Stephens standing outside the hedge in the dusk, the image of summers of twenty years before. We can take the ghosts, turning them back into children, through the escallonia hedge, up through the little divided gardens that sloped down from Talland House towards the sea, and back into the 1880s. The sun comes out, the house and garden are full of children and adults in Victorian clothes – family, visitors – walking and playing cricket and picking flowers and talking and reading. Julia Stephen is sitting there, casting her shadow on the step.

But what it's harder to do is to separate the actuality of those childhood summers from Virginia Woolf's idealised retrospect. 'When we were children the summers were always really hot.'[4] Talland House became, in Virginia Woolf's imagination and in the minds of her readers, something more than just a large square building near the sea in Cornwall. It is where she sites, for the whole of her life, the idea of happiness. (When she first rented her own house in Sussex she called it 'Little Talland House'). Happiness is always measured for her against the memory of being a child in that house. The images she uses to describe that memory are pleasurable and consolatory, images of fullness, rhythm and light. When she begins her memoirs with 'the most important of all my memories' (one of *two* equally important first memories, in fact) you can hear her enchanting herself with the process of writing it down. It is, for good reasons, the most quoted passage of her autobiography:

If life has a base that it stands upon, if it is a bowl that one fills and fills and fills – then my bowl without a doubt stands upon this memory. It is of lying half asleep, half awake, in bed in the nursery at St Ives. It is of hearing the waves breaking, one, two, one, two, and sending a splash of water over the beach; and then breaking, one, two, one, two, behind a yellow blind. It is of hearing the blind draw its little acorn across the floor as the wind blew the blind out. It is of lying and hearing this splash and seeing this light, and feeling, it is almost impossible that I should be here; of feeling the purest ecstasy I can conceive.[5]

So she 'conceives' her first sense of herself, gives birth to herself, out of that room, half a century away. She wasn't born there, but she was six months old when she was first taken there, and she lost the place suddenly when she was thirteen. Because of that drastic break in her life, the place retrospectively seemed to contain her childhood as in 'a bowl', separate and inviolable. The desire to get back inside that bowl, to write not just about childhood but *as if a child,* is one of the most powerful impulses in her writing. Whenever she writes about the childhood in Cornwall (disguising it thinly as Scarborough or Scotland) she tries to get back that first feeling.

The novel of her childhood in Talland House, and of its loss, is *To the Lighthouse.* But, though the best known, it is not the first or the last version of this story. A few years before it, she did a vivid, rapid sketch of life in Talland House, as a dreamy post-impressionist painting, in a single chapter of *Jacob's Room* (1922):

Opposite him were hazy, semi-transparent shapes of yellow and blue. Behind them, again, was the grey-green garden, and among the pear-shaped leaves of the escallonia fishing-boats seemed caught and suspended. A sailing ship slowly drew past the women's backs. Two or three figures crossed the terrace hastily in the dusk. The door opened and shut. Nothing settled or stayed unbroken.[6]

Hidden in the cancelled beginning of this novel – in a draft written in 1920 – is a first try at her first memory. The child Jacob takes a sheep's jawbone he has found on the beach into bed with him. He is falling asleep.

The blind was thin yellow; curved out, for the nursery window was open. It curved fuller, & then was sucked in. At the same time the sea made that dull noise; then the water was drawn back; then it made the dull noise again. Now the blind was filled with more yellow; & the dull noise sounded further away. On the chest of drawers Jacob could just see the big flowers in the white jar – or it might be the jawbone. Oh no, that was hard at the bottom of the bed. The little trailing noise that the knob on the blind cord made as it was drawn along the floor made him open his eyes. The purple petals were falling from the flower on the chest-of-drawers – it fell down – down . . . he saw a line; and following it up, came to a bulging white shape never seen by day; and following that up, came to purple things. Oh these were the flowers that mother picked; the one purple thing floated out and missed the chest-of-drawers and fell down – down – [7]

The same memory resurfaces in *The Waves* (1931) but this time in a more abstract form (and with memories of Cornwall coloured by her visits to Vanessa's family house in the South of France). It's like a painter making repeated versions of the same subject (Monet's Rouen Cathedral, or his haystacks, for instance) which become increasingly stylised and less naturalistic. In the original draft of *The Waves*, begun two years after *To the Lighthouse* is published, an observer is looking at the house by the sea full of children, at dawn, and speaks in the first person: 'I am telling myself the story of the world from the beginning,' she says.[8] In the second draft, this 'I' disappears. Instead, in her notes to herself, she says that she wants to tell 'the story of the world from the beginning' through the children's waking perceptions:

> the beginning shd. go like this.
> A description of dawn – & the sea – breaking on a
> beach.
> Then each child wakes & sees something
>   a globe: an object: Says something.
>   a face.   a spoon.
> The sea again
>   The garden . . .
> The light quickens –
> The garden
> The garden . . .[9]

In the final version of *The Waves*, she prefaces the children's perceptions with a disembodied descriptive passage – the first of several 'interludes' in the novel – which contains, again, her first memory:

> *The sun sharpened the walls of the house, and rested like the tip of a fan upon a white blind and made a blue finger-print of shadow under the leaf by the bedroom window. The blind stirred slightly, but all within was dim and unsubstantial. The birds sang their blank melody outside.*[10]

In all these fictional versions of her childhood – in *Jacob's Room*, *To the*

Lighthouse, and *The Waves* – she makes sure that her deepest memory is disguised or displaced: 'This shall be Childhood: but it must not be <u>my</u> childhood',[11] as she says of *The Waves.* She goes in fear of sentimentality and self-exposure. She knows that she idealises those childhood summers. 'When we were children the summers were always really hot.' *To the Lighthouse* is partly *about* the sentimentalising of the past. But it is full, too, of regret and longing. This tone makes it hard to separate that magical, mythologised garden, where (as she describes it in a story called 'Ancestors')[12] the parents are always loving and the servants are always good and the summer stars are always shining, from a real place and time.

Even at the time Talland House seemed to the Stephen family 'full of romance'.[13] Leslie Stephen found it in 1881 on one of his marathon walking tours, 'down at the very toe-nail of England',[14] and he bought the lease from the Great Western Railway,[15] justifying his own pleasure in the landscape with the advantages for his growing family. In 1881 this consisted of a 'backward' eleven-year-old daughter, Laura, by his first marriage to Minny Thackeray; the three children from his second wife Julia's previous marriage to Herbert Duckworth, George, Stella, and Gerald (then aged thirteen, twelve and eleven), and the two babies of his second marriage, Vanessa, aged two, and Thoby, aged one. Julia was pregnant with Virginia, the third of their four children. 'The children will be able to run straight out of the house to a lovely bit of sand and have good air and quiet', he wrote to her after he had decided to take the house. All the children would learn to swim, the boys would get boating and fishing, and he would be able to go off on his great walks with bread and cheese in his pocket. At first he was a little anxious that in taking the house he might be making Julia travel too far from her sick mother,[16] and there were some initial problems with the water supply and the cesspool which she was going to have to sort out. But 'it will really be a charming little place, when you have brought the magic of the womans eye to bear upon it.'[17] It would be very convenient for shopping in Penzance, and they would get a donkey-cart so that Julia would be able to explore the region.[18]

The house he found for their summers was a substantial mid-nineteenth-century house, with enough rooms for nurseries and dining-room and guest bedrooms and servants, just outside St Ives. (Though some of the guests, like Henry James, stayed in the grand Tregenna Castle Hotel up the hill.) It overlooked the station (the branch line from St Erth had opened in the 1870s to accommodate the beginnings of the Cornish tourist industry), the bay and the Godrevy lighthouse, built in 1859. The little fishing town of St Ives[19] was, then as now, a steep, 'windy, noisy, fishy, vociferous, narrowstreeted town' with 'no architecture; no arrangement'. There was the granite church, the houses with flights of steps up to the doors and thick walls, the fish-market, the old Sloop Inn, all 'like a bunch of rough shellfish clustered on a grey wall together'. There was no pleasure pier, only the 'Malakoff' (built after the Crimean War) an octagonal 'gravelly patch of ground, set with a few stone seats upon which retired fishermen in their blue jerseys smoked and gossiped' and where the band would play during the annual summer Regatta. There were tents for swimmers and, at the fishing end of the beach, the pilchard boats being tarred and the 'Hewer' with his telescope at the lookout point waiting for a rare sighting of pilchards in the bay. Only once in Virginia's childhood did a shoal come past St Ives, and she didn't see them actually being caught until 1905, when she gave a dramatic description of the great event: the cry going up, the boats loading and dropping their nets, the megaphone directions from the Hewer 'roaring like foghorns' as the boats tried to enclose the shoal, the suspense when the shoal – a thousand pounds worth of fish – seemed to have evaded the seines, the final closing in on water seething with iridescent fish, leaping in the air and lashing their tails, the lowering of the baskets and emptying out into the boats of a 'bubbling mass' of seemingly inexhaustible catch.

In the absence of the long-awaited pilchards, the fishermen caught dabs and gurnards and sold them on the beach. There was poverty and disease in the town. Like Mrs Ramsay, Julia, often with her daughter Stella, spent a great part of the summers going about visiting the poor and tending the sick: 'like a Good Angel to the poor of St Ives', as her children put it.[20] When the Stephen children returned in 1905 they found that they, and particularly Julia, were fondly remembered by many people in the town: and many years later the older inhabitants of St Ives still recalled them. A very old lady wrote down, in the 1960s, 'my recollections of the Leslie Stephens: Mrs Leslie Stephen wearing a mushroom hat tied under the chin, and a black cloak which she wore to the water's edge, and cast off when bathing. They were all tall and fair, never mixing with the other children, almost like Gods and Goddesses.'[21] Another regular visitor remembered seeing Leslie Stephen and his children at the beach: 'We watched with delight his naked babies running about the beach or being towed into the sea between his legs, and their beautiful mother.'[22]

Like other Victorian families who moved their entire way of life – maids, cooks, pets, visitors, books, clothes – into their country home for three or four months a year,[23] the Stephen family, though not rich, made a difference to the local economy. They brought their own servants, but St Ives people – whose names would recur in the novels – came up to the house as washerwomen, gardeners, carpenters and providers of chickens, milk, eggs and live lobsters. And there were regular treats at the big stationery store, Lanham's, and at Curnow's, the town's main café and bakery.

Old traditions persisted in the town, limpet-like. A town crier, who once 'cried' a Stephen visitor's lost brooch, still 'shuffled along the front swinging a muffin bell and crying "Oyez, oyez, oyez." ' At the annual Regatta there were flags, music, swimming and boat races. Every five years the citizens of St Ives would dance round the Knills Monument (one of Julia's favourite spots), a granite steeple just west of Carbis Bay built in 1782 in memory of a smuggler turned Mayor, and the couple who danced longest would be given a shilling. But the town was changing in the 1880s and 1890s. Mrs Durrant in *Jacob's Room* – an earlier sketch for Mrs Ramsay – laments it: 'Her eyes glazed as she looked at the view. "A little village once," she said, "and now grown . . ." '[24] A new class of tourists were beginning to come. Even before Julia's death, the family had decided to give up the house because in 1893 a huge hotel (the Porthminster) went up directly in their view of the bay. When the children went back in 1905 the old man who used to keep the bathing tents lamented 'the melancholy decline of St Ives bathing since our day . . . how the working classes bathe, where only people of good family were wont to use that privilege'.[25]

And, from the early 1880s – long before the town had been made famous by its associations with Alfred Wallis, Bernard Leach, Barbara Hepworth or Patrick Heron – painters were arriving, drawn by the soft Mediterranean light and the seascapes and the picturesque fishing community. Whistler – with his assistant Walter Sickert (who told Vanessa years later how impressed he had been by the sight of Leslie and Julia)[26] – painted delicate beach-scenes of St Ives, with busy groups of colourful, windswept little figures, in 1883, just after the Stephens had taken their house. After him came Adrian Stokes, Julius Olsson, and a great many others. In 1886 the American painter Howard Russell Butler converted the first of his sail lofts into studios; James Lanham opened a gallery over his shop in 1887 and used to have artistic soirées in his house, which Leslie Stephen attended; and in 1890 Louis Grier founded the St Ives Arts Club in an old granite and timber warehouse. The late-nineteenth-century fashions in water-colours are ironically described in *To the Lighthouse*:

> But now, she said, artists had come here. There indeed, only a few paces off, stood one of them, in Panama hat and yellow boots, seriously, softly, absorbedly, for all that he was watched by ten little boys, with an air of profound contentment on his round red face, gazing, and then, when he had gazed, dipping; imbuing the tip of his brush in some soft mound of

green or pink. Since Mr Paunceforte had been there, three years before, all the pictures were like that she said, green and grey, with lemon-coloured sailing-boats, and pink women on the beach.[27]

And Julia Stephen strikes a similarly ironic note in one of her stories written for her children in the 1880s, 'The Wandering Pigs', where three pigs who live on the cliffs above the sea go down to the bay. Here there are boats with brown sails and fishermen and 'a long pier which ran out to sea and far off, rising straight out of the sea was a white lighthouse on whose windows the sun was burning fiercely'. And here they see 'a monkey painting'.

> Curly, who was never shy, went up to see what was going on. He was quite surprised to see, on the bit of board before the monkey, the boats and their brown sails and blue sea running into the little harbour. 'Dear me, you are very clever,' said Curly.
>
> 'You are very polite,' said the monkey, looking round for a minute. 'Are you an art critic?'[28]

Painting overlaps with remembering in *To the Lighthouse*, and Virginia Woolf – like Lily Briscoe redoing her painting of the Ramsays' house and garden – spent a lifetime making and remaking her own 'views' of St Ives. When they went back in 1905 she made her first attempt, in a stiffly formal style, to write that luminous scenery of cliffs and rocks, and moorland with innumerable little footpaths, and streams, and granite walls with blocks sticking out for steps. She recorded all the walks they went on, the walks which they had taken eleven years before – sometimes grumpily and reluctantly – with Leslie, and now with a kind of 'melancholy' pleasure. When she comes to Mrs Ramsay, exclaiming 'Oh, how beautiful!' at the sight of the bay, she has given herself plenty of practice:

> For the great plateful of blue water was before her, the hoary Lighthouse, distant, austere, in the midst; and on the right, as far as the eye could see, fading and falling, in soft low pleats, the green sand dunes with the wild flowing grasses on them, which always seemed to be running away into some moon country, uninhabited of men.[29]

When Virginia Woolf describes Talland House in her memoirs she does it like a picture: she says it looked 'like a child's drawing of a house; remarkable only for its flat roof, and the crisscrossed railing that ran round the roof; again, like something a child draws'. Two french bay windows with three stone steps going down from them opened on to the garden; above them, the second floor windows had balconies with canopies edged with little pediments, and between the bays was a blind arch, as for a statue – a motif repeated on the side walls of the house. In the Stephens' time a profuse, disorderly flowerbed rampaged around these bay windows, with climbers and passion flowers 'with great starry blossoms' growing up to the second floor balconies. 'My mother would come out onto her balcony in a white dressing gown.'[30] There were attic dormer windows (since replaced) in the roof.

The inside of the house was always (like the house in *To the Lighthouse*) rather shabby – chintz wallpaper and ornaments and pictures and photographs and big sofas and tables, but nothing grand. When she went back to it again in 1914 she remarked on how much smarter it had become: 'wonderfully done up and spick and span . . . very unlike what it was in our day.'[31] The whole point of the house was the garden. Leslie Stephen described it with enthusiasm in his letters. One of the first things he noticed, when he bought it, was that there were 'quantities of new potatoes' and 'grapes and strawberries and peaches'.[32] And although Virginia Woolf describes Mr Ramsay as being too far-sighted to notice the flowers in the garden which his wife plants, Leslie wrote delightedly to Julia, when he went down to Cornwall in the spring of 1883, of seeing 'lots of primroses and bluebells and anemones'.[33] The view was wonderful: 'It is so clear' (Leslie wrote in the summer of 1884) 'that we see thirty miles of coast as plainly as we see the back of Queen's Gate from our drawing-room window in London. We have a little garden, which is not much to boast of, and yet it is a dozen little gardens each full of romance for the children – lawns surrounded by flowering hedges, and intricate thickets of gooseberries and currants, and remote nooks of potatoes and peas, and high banks, down which you can slide in a sitting posture, and corners in which you come upon unexpected puppies – altogether a pocket-paradise with a sheltered cove of sand in easy reach (for 'Ginia even) just below. Also there is a railway station between us and the said cove.'[34]

More nostalgic versions were given in his *Mausoleum Book* and in his daughter's 'Sketch of the Past'. The mood of the two retrospects is similar:

> Every corner of the house and garden is full of memories for me – I could hardly bear to look at it again, I think. We made what we called a 'lawn tennis' ground on the most level bit, where the children delighted in playing small cricket every evening. I can see my Julia strolling among her beloved flowers; sitting in the 'loo corner', a sheltered seat behind the grape-house, or the so-called 'coffee garden', where on hot days she would be shaded by the great escallonia hedge; and, still oftener, in the porch from which we used to watch the cricket. These words represent for me a long series of scenes of intense domestic happiness.[35]

It stood in a garden that ran downhill; and had formed itself into separate gardens, surrounded by thick escallonia hedges, whose leaves, pressed, gave out a very sweet smell. It had so many angles cut off, and lawns surrounded, that each had a name; there was the coffee garden; the Fountain – a basin with a funnel that dripped, hedged with damp evergreens; the cricket lawn; the Love Corner, under the greenhouse, where the purple jackmanii grew – where Leo Maxse proposed to Kitty Lushington . . . then there was the kitchen garden; the strawberry beds; the pond . . . and the big tree. All these different, cut off places were contained in that one garden of not more than two or three acres. One entered by a large wooden gate, the sound of whose latch clicking was one of the familiar sounds; up the carriage drive one went, under the steep wall of rock, sprinkled with the fleshy leaves of the mesembryanthemums; and then came to the Lookout place, between the clumps of pampas grass . . . From the Lookout place one had, then, a perfectly open view across the Bay.[36]

In an earlier and differently phrased version of this description, she wrote: 'You entered Talland House by a large wooden gate, the sound of whose latch clicking comes back.'[37] It is a Proustian phrase, and Virginia Woolf's earliest memories 'come back' to her rather like Marcel's 'vast structure of recollections'[38] ignited by the taste of the madeleine. Like Virginia Woolf, Marcel remembers himself as the child half-asleep looking at the indistinct shapes of the furniture in the bedroom, or hearing the sound of the bell tinkling on the garden door to announce the arrival of M. Swann.

She too can call up a 'miscellaneous catalogue' of real sounds, smells and sights which act as pointers to childhood – like 'little corks that mark a sunken net'.[39] The click of the garden gate, the creak of the gardener's mowing machine as the gardener's pony in its rubber overshoes went round and round, the sound of cricket on the lawn, the cawing of the rooks, the boom of the buoy, the murmur of voices talking on the terrace, the humming of bees; the smell of flowers and apples and seaweed and sea air; the lights of the little town at night, or the colours of the bay: this 'miscellaneous catalogue' of memories is consolatory. When she sums up the experience of St Ives, writing fifty years later, in war-time and in depression, she rocks herself into an appeasing chant of pleasure. The very names of the places make her feel better.

To have our own house; our own garden; to have the Bay; the sea; the moors; Clodgy; Halestown Bog; Carbis Bay; Lelant; Trevail; Zennor; the Gurnard's Head; to hear the waves breaking that first night behind the yellow blind; to dig in the sand; to go sailing in a fishing boat; to scrabble over the rocks and see the red and yellow anemones flourishing their antennae; or stuck like blobs of jelly to the rock; to find a small fish flapping in a pool; to pick up cowries; to look over the grammar in the dining room and see the lights changing on the bay; the leaves of the escallonia grey or bright green; . . . I could fill pages remembering one thing after another. All together made the summer at St Ives the best beginning to life conceivable.[40]

What good fortune, she adds somewhat snootily, to have these memories and not inferior ones: 'Suppose I had only Surrey or Sussex or the Isle of Wight to think about when I think about my childhood.'

This timeless idyll had its routines. There would be lessons with Julia in the morning and walks with Leslie in the afternoon. As in all middle-class Victorian families, there were a great number of hobbies: cricketing (Virginia was known as the demon bowler), boating, swimming, billiards, botany, bugs, photography, astronomy, album-making, family journals and plays. Fishing, too, though Leslie didn't like catching fish. He did not forbid the children to do it, but let them know his own feeling: as a result, 'I ceased to wish to catch fish'.[41] The family dogs – particularly a large hairy Skye terrier called Shag (short for Shaggy) – took up a lot of attention and affection. There were always visitors to be fetched from the station and taken on expeditions. On many evenings – as in *To the Lighthouse* – there would be fifteen or more for dinner. At nights when the 'grown-ups' were eating, the children (whose nursery was immediately over the kitchen) would lower a basket on a string in the hopes that the cook would fill it with something from the grown-ups' dinner. When she was in a bad mood, she cut the string. 'I can remember the sensation of the heavy basket, and of the light string.'[42]

Of all these family rituals, night-time moth hunting – which began at St Ives and went on for some time afterwards, into the Stephen children's teens – was one which most haunted her imagination. She associated it with Thoby, whose great passion it was, and who appointed her the 'name finder' of their Entomological Society; many hours were spent 'hunting up our catches' in the pages of Francis Orpen Morris's books on butterflies and moths, given to the children by Stella's suitor, Jack Hills (and consulted in *Jacob's Room*). Jack Hills, too, taught the children how to 'sugar'. A flannel rag would be soaked in a compound of rum and treacle and this would be pinned to the bark of the trees so that the sticky mixture ran down and attracted the moths. After dark the procession of children would set out with a glass jar – the 'poison pot' – butterfly nets and a lamp. The little lamp linked them together in the 'unknown world' of the dark trees. When they set it down, beetles and other insects would flock towards the light. As quietly as possible they would approach the 'sugared' trees and play the light on the drunken moths, sucking away like opium addicts, choose the species they wanted, and knock them into the jar. She would always remember the catching of a great red underwing:

> By the faint glow we could see the huge moth – his wings open, as though in ecstasy, so that the splendid crimson of the underwing could be seen – his eyes burning red, his proboscis plunged into a flowing stream of treacle. We gazed one moment on his splendour, & then uncorked the bottle. I think the whole procession felt some unprofessional regret when, with a last gleam of scarlet eye & scarlet wing, the grand old moth vanished.

This is a later, post-St Ives memory, but the experience of 'bug-hunting' – a mixture of intense pleasure, excitement, and some fear and disgust – went back to earliest days. Always she remembered the smell of seaweed mixed with the smell of camphor from the butterfly boxes.[43]

Fortunately the summer life of the family is not entirely bathed in idealised retrospect, but filters through the letters and diaries of the time. On their first summer there Leslie describes them all having an early dinner and sitting out under their apple tree 'with George and Gerald playing cricket and the babies kicking up their little heels on the grass'.[44] When he was there with the children and without Julia in 1893 he wrote to tell her about their goings-on: 'The children are always in the garden bug-hunting or up in the tree or playing cricket.'[45] Julia's sad fussy old mother Maria Jackson wrote daily black-edged wistful letters imagining them all at 'dear little St Ives with its blue waters and its peaceful shore'. To Stella, arriving at St Ives in 1889: 'The little ones no doubt were awake [when you arrived]; if not you had them at your door betimes in the morning. Now you are all in the drawing room. The room filled with the fragrance of the flower beds. Father in his big chair . . . You in your black dress with your amethysts on yr dear neck that I love to kiss. Mother in her tea gown. Perhaps she is writing her letters but no I think not.' Mrs Jackson was less than delighted by the descent of the painters on the town. 'I do not like this onslaught of Artists for the honour of painting you,' she wrote to Julia. 'I am sure something horrid will be the result and it will be as tedious to you to sit to them.'[46] And she was always worried about their health: Gerald must wear a vest under his cricket shirt, Leslie must be careful when he goes boating, the girls must watch the sun: 'At this hour you have all done luncheon and you are perhaps sitting on the dining room steps and Leslie strolling about with the children and my Stella in and out without her hat to which I object considering her complexion.'[47] Stella, in her diary for 1893, recorded the life of the family – but not whether she was wearing her hat:

9 August: Photographed – developed. 15 August: Children bathed. Cricket. 16 August: Ginia Thoby and Adrian went off to fish (caught nothing). 17 August: Very hot. Mother bathed with children. Cricket after tea. Photographed group. 18 August: Wild cricket. 19 August: 98 in the shade. 21 August: Children began lessons. Ginia did her music. Then Ginia, Adrian and I went to town to buy rum, muslin [the rum was for bug-hunting, not for drinking]. 23 August: Deathshead moth. Father sailed after lunch. 23 August: Photographed cricket. 24 August: Father took a boat. Nessa Mother and I settled down to paint in the rose garden. [And so on through the hot summer]: swimming races . . . water polo . . . tea . . . cricket . . . tried some Beethoven sonatas . . . tremendous storm . . . Father and George went off by 11 o'clock train to see wrestling . . . new gardener came . . . mounted photographs . . . packing . . .[48]

A more comical and elaborate record of the family's Cornish summers was kept in the St Ives' sections of the Stephen children's collaborative newspaper, *The Hyde Park Gate News*. In the summer of 1892, family arrivals are greeted with spoof outbursts of joy: 'Old and young stopped to admire the touching spectacle.' Farcical events are leapt on with glee. There are photographic mishaps, with plates broken or overexposed or the cook unwilling to have her photograph taken until called to order by Mrs Stephen, 'the head of the house'. (A visitor's list is compiled by photographing everyone who comes into 'the palatial residence'.) Stella rescues a rat in a trap from Shag. Mr Stephen takes them for walks on which he points out rare plants and 'the interesting sight of a raven pursuing a hawk'. There are carriage drives and trips to Land's End. Thoby, as usual, gets a splendid display of fireworks for his birthday, which go off 'rippingly'. (Oh, do be careful of the fireworks, warns Julia's mother.) There is cake and they play charades and the children are 'super-exuberant'. On another evening 'tableaus' are performed, which set off more bursts of laughter.

On one Saturday morning there is a disappointment for the youngest member of the family:

On Saturday morning Master Hilary Hunt and Master Basil Smith came up to Talland House and asked Master Thoby and Miss Virginia to accompany them to the light-house as Freeman the boatman said that there was a perfect tide and wind for going there. Master Adrian Stephen was much disappointed at not being allowed to go. On arriving at the light-house Miss Virginia Stephen saw a small and dilapidated bird standing on one leg on the light-house. Mrs Hunt called the man and asked him how it had got there. He said that it had been blown there and they then saw that its eyes had been picked out. On the way home Master Basil Smith spewed like fury.

But later in the summer Master Adrian does get his boat trip:

> On Monday Mr Stephen with his youngest son and daughter went down to the pier and there looked about for a boat. After a long time of waiting a man appeared. They were soon out and sailing merrily along. There was a good breeze and it not being too calm the party was in high spirits . . . The sail ended hapily [sic] by seeing the sea pig or porpoise.

Master Adrian's disappointment would be remembered. Pain and grief would enter into the mood of *To the Lighthouse*, as well as pleasure. There are sinister elements to this childhood – fear, shame, jealousy, rage, nightmare – which would make part of the memories and the fictional versions of Cornwall. In spite of this, her dominant images of childhood in St Ives were of light, freedom, pleasure, and space.

But this was only half of childhood. The outdoor section of her life was framed, every year, by two enormous all-day train journeys from Paddington to St Ives, and from St Ives to Paddington.[49] In the second or third week of October, as the weather began to turn, preparations started for the long journey back. People from the town came up to say goodbye; Stella and Julia packed up the baskets of apples and pears and left instructions for the winter upkeep of the house. The return journey, on a fine day in 1892, is recorded in *The Hyde Park Gate News*:

> While Mrs Stephen was with all the despatch of womankind settling all minor matters Mr Stephen sat with his children in a third-class carriage entranced by the effusive washerwoman . . . The Stephens thought of the many happy days which had been passed in laziness but it is only in going that we find out what might have been done and then it is no use.[50]

Sometimes on these annual journeys the engine would break down and the train be an hour or more late. And always by the time they got to Paddington night would have fallen, as if going back to London took them into the dark of winter.

In Virginia Woolf's memoirs, two first memories compete for precedence. One is of waking up at St Ives. The other is of 'red and purple flowers on a black ground – my mother's dress; and she was sitting either in a train or in an omnibus, and I was on her lap . . . Perhaps we were going to St Ives; more probably, for from the light it must have been evening, we were coming back to London.'[51] Either way, it is this journey that she forever associates with her first child's sense of being in her mother's lap.

At the other end of the journey was a house with as powerful associations as Talland House. But they were of an opposite nature: 22 Hyde Park Gate embodied darkness, solid objects, interiors, constriction. The tall narrow house, six floors high, with a flight of steps up to the front door and a small back garden, was the place where Virginia was born and where she lived, with up to seventeen other people (family and servants) for twenty-two years. Her memory of her life here as a child became overlaid with later feelings. When she described it in memoirs and fictions it came to stand for all of Victorian domestic life and for the whole of her family history: 'the place seemed tangled and matted with emotion'.[52]

Hyde Park Gate was (and is) a narrow cul-de-sac off Kensington Road – 'the great high road running from Hammersmith to Piccadilly' – between Palace Gate and Queen's Gate. Number 22 was down towards the bottom end of the cul-de-sac, on the left; you could only hear the traffic of the main road as a distant roar. Kensington in the 1880s and 1890s still had the last vestiges of a village atmosphere. At its centre were the formal eighteenth-century gardens with their mild, plain, ordered green spaces, gentle slopes, neatly radiating gravel paths, avenues of trees, and decorous landmarks: the Speke Monument, the Round Pond, the horseman ('Statue of Physical Energy', by G.F. Watts, a family friend) gazing towards Kensington Palace. The area was characterised too by its grandiose, confident Victorian structures: the Albert Memorial and the Albert Hall, and the cluster of mid-Victorian educational buildings in dark red Gothic masterminded by Henry Cole, whose territory spread from Kensington Gore down Exhibition Road to the Cromwell Road: the South Kensington Museum (later the Victoria & Albert), the Science Museum, the Natural History Museum. As for all middle-class children who grow up in South Kensington, these museums played an important part in the young Stephens' lives, and Virginia's early diaries are scattered with visits to 'the mechanical part of the SKM' or to 'the insect room' of the Natural History Museum, which she did not feel 'sufficiently student like' to enter.[53]

Kensington had been the family's village for over half a century. Leslie's father bought a house in Kensington Gore in 1829 (later renumbered as 42 Hyde Park Gate) where Leslie was born in 1832. (So he would die within a few minutes' walk of his birthplace.) He remembered Kensington as it was in his childhood:

The Kensington of those days was still distinctly separate from London. A high wall divided Kensington Gardens from the Hounslow Road; there were still deer in the gardens, cavalry barracks close to Queen's Gate, and a turnpike at the top of the Gloucester Road. The land upon which South Kensington has since arisen was a region of market gardens, where in our childhood we strolled with our nurse along genuine country lanes.[54]

Meanwhile, his future sister-in-law, Thackeray's daughter Anny, was growing up with her father and her sister Minny in Young Street, Kensington. She would wax eloquent about those early memories of 'Old Kensington', when 'hawthorn spread across the fields and market-gardens that lay between Kensington and the river' and there were untouched country corners and strawberry-beds and venerable elms.[55] Farther west at Little Holland House (in what became Melbury Road), the young Julia Jackson was receiving an education in Pre-Raphaelite paintings, in music and poetry, at her Uncle Thoby Prinsep's artistic salon.

When Leslie married his first wife Minny Thackeray in 1867, they lived in Onslow Gardens, close to many of their relatives. 'We all live within a few minutes' walk of each other' (he wrote to Oliver Wendell Holmes) 'and with sundry cousins we form a little colony in the neighbourhood of the South Kensington Museum.'[56] After Minny's tragic death in 1875, he moved, in 1876, to live in 11 Hyde Park Gate South, the house next door to the widowed Julia Duckworth at Number 13. He remarked on 'the intrinsic calm of this little backwater of a street . . . almost like the country'.[57] In 1884, Number 13 was renumbered 22 Hyde Park Gate, and this was the house which Leslie moved into when he and Julia married, in which they brought up their family, and in which both he and Julia died. Julia's first husband's sister, Sarah Duckworth, known as 'Aunt Minna', lived for a very, very long time in the same street, with her 'perennial parrot and her perennial Italian manservant',[58] until she died at the age of ninety.

No wonder that in Virginia Woolf's later life 'Kensington' was thickly imbued with the memory of family, and that 'the breath of South Kensington' is often used to sum up the spirit of 'respectable mummified humbug' she associated with her relatives and their friends, on the other side of the gulf from Bloomsbury.[59]

But in her childhood Kensington was her terrain and her routine. In 'the little sealed loop' of Hyde Park Gate, 'everybody knew everybody, and everything about everybody'.[60] The child Virginia shrank back in nervous anticipation of having to 'stop or at least smile' at the familiar adult figures whose footsteps could be heard tapping down the road towards her: perhaps the ancient Mrs Redgrave in her bath chair, like 'a museum specimen preserved under glass', or the rich American Mrs Biddulph Martin, 'somehow infamous' because of her suffragette sympathies, or the Stephens' neighbour, the fashionable and pretty Mrs Ashton Dilke, also 'tainted' in Julia Stephen's eyes by her 'connection with women's rights'. (In spite of this the Stephen children went to Miss Sybil Dilke's birthday party in 1892, and were amused by the ventriloquist.) In the middle of the street lived the disreputable Maude family, who kept a large and frightening dog which once attacked Virginia. The Hyde Park Gate 'villagers' brought an action against them and Virginia had to give evidence at the police court, an event written up (with an eye for detail) in *The Hyde Park Gate News*:

> Virginia Stephen went with her mother to the Police-court to bear testimony that the dog had flown at her ... She stated that the dog had run at her and bitten her cloak besides knocking her up against the wall ... Mr Mackenzie's maid next was called up and stated that the dog had *flown* at her. Whereupon the magistrate desired to know what was meant by 'flown'. The maid got very red and remained silent. The case ended by the magistrate saying the dog must either be killed or kept under proper control.[61]

All the houses were different, some like country houses, some, nearer the main road, more pompous and 'pillared': one house in the 1890s still had 'a carriage and pair with a coachman and footman who wore powdered wigs, and yellow plush knee breeches and silk stockings'. Many of the households kept or hired a carriage from Hobbs's livery stable with its great yard opening off the mews behind the street. At night – as well as church bells and the occasional evenings of dance music from a neighbouring party – the horses could be heard shifting in their stables. The Stephens did not keep a carriage or hire a hansom or a fourwheeler from the rank. They took the omnibus 'into town', though they might sometimes get a hansom or a four-wheeler back home. The Underground, with stations at Gloucester Road and Kensington High Street, 'a sulphur smelling steam clouded tunnel', was too far away to start out from. Julia Stephen was an 'omnibus expert' and did all her 'immense rounds' of 'shopping, calling, visiting hospitals and workhouses' by bus. So, mostly, did the children as they grew up. On the way home from the dressmaker's once, Vanessa and Virginia bought bath buns from an ABC and, pleasurably, ate 'the bath buns driving down Oxford St. on the top of the bus'.[62] Virginia would always be very proud of changing buses (or of 'undergrounding') successfully on her way home. In *Mrs Dalloway*, Elizabeth Dalloway is pleased with her pioneering journey on a strange bus into the City.

The main road that had to be crossed to get into Kensington Gardens was a roar of horse traffic – buses, cabs, carriages with cockaded footmen and coats of arms, fourwheelers, carts – interspersed with intrepid cyclists and little boys dashing in to scoop up the horse dung. Virginia found the streets terrifying. 'The horses kicked and reared and neighed. Often they ran away. Carriages crashed together I remember in High Street; horses went sprawling; they shied; they reared; wheels came off.'[63] Her first surviving diaries are full of sightings of lady cyclists being run over, a hansom overturned, 'a man in the course of being squashed by an omnibus', a runaway horse stampeding into the door of a Kensington High Street confectioner's. She is always expecting this to happen to her: we came back, she says wrily on one occasion, 'in a four wheeler, which, strange to say, carried us home safely'.[64]

Kensington Gardens was then a self-contained park separated from Hyde Park. In Julia Stephen's stories for children, it is always a delightful place. The children get a new boat, and exclaim: 'What fun it will be sailing it, in the Round Pond.' In summer 'the flower walk full of nurses and nursemaids is a refuge'. And even in bad weather it is tremendously healthy: 'Helen and Harry raced along the wet paths of Kensington Gardens, laughing when a gust of wind blew the rain drops from the trees onto their faces. The dead leaves gave out a pleasant fresh smell, and by the time they reached Lancaster Gate the children's cheeks shone like rosy apples.'[65]

Julia's improving versions did not describe four bored children trailing round the gardens monotonously, twice a day, every day. But although Virginia remembered the walks in Kensington Gardens as dull, these routines had their points of interest and moments of pleasure and adventure. Like Marcel's two walks, Swann's Way and the Guermantes Way, the walks took their character from the two entrances to the Gardens. At Queen's Gate, almost opposite Hyde Park Gate and along from the Albert Memorial, an old woman with a pockmarked face who rather reminded Virginia of her grandmother sold nuts and boot laces and was thought to be the worse for wear for drink. At the Gloucester Road entrance another, more appealing old woman sold desirable red and purple penny balloons. Inside, rituals attached to each route. The Broad Walk sloping up to Kensington Palace seemed ridiculously flat when they came back from St Ives, much steeper by the end of the London year. Next to Kensington Palace was the white house where a woman sold sweets. Once a week they would buy *Tit-Bits* and sit in the grass eating their chocolate (divided into fours which they called 'Frys') and reading the correspondence columns and the jokes. The Flower Walk was often littered with little ribbed shells which they would crunch underfoot. Behind the Flower Walk was a boggy patch where Vanessa and Thoby once found the skeleton of a dog.

They made up stories, and sailed boats on the Round Pond. One of the dramas of Virginia's early childhood was the sinking of her boat, the 'Fairy' ('my Cornish lugger') in the middle of the Round Pond and its rediscovery, months later, by the man who was dredging the pond of duckweed: a moment celebrated in the *News* as an 'Astounding Event!!' When the park thermometer dropped below freezing – especially in the great winter of 1894–5 - they skated: one of the intense pleasures of childhood, saved up for *Orlando*. Memorable encounters broke up the monotony: with 'the queer female who parades in Kensington Gardens every morning at about 12 o'clock dressed in a dirty white robe over which is a still dirtier wash-leather cloak (or rather dressing-gown)'; or with the terrifying 'idiot boy' who 'sprang up', begging for the children's toffees. Or they might encounter neighbours or literary acquaintances: 'In the afternoon Stella & I went out in to the gardens, & sat under the trees; & as we were going away Mr James came up, & walked with us part of the way home.' Often, Virginia would walk on her own with Leslie: 'In the afternoon Father & I went out together. When we arrived at the Serpentine we lazily sat down in 2 arm chairs; and lolled there for half an hour, watching the river, & the peacocks on the other banks.'[66]

In *The Years*, the little girl growing up in the Kensington family house is given a nightmarish encounter with a man standing by the pillar box at the end of the road, when she runs out of the house to the corner-shop after dark. But though that novel makes a dark reading of her childhood memories, it treats the Gardens tenderly, as a scene of 'primal innocence', shimmering in lozenges of light like a painting by Seurat:

> The sun dappling the leaves gave everything a curious look of insubstantiality as if it were broken into separate points of light . . . The size of the human figure seemed to have shrunk. Instead of full-grown people, children were now in the majority. Dogs of all sorts abounded. The air was full of barking and sudden shrill cries. Coveys of nursemaids pushed perambulators along the paths.

From a seat by the Round Pond, the scene – with the white statue of Queen Victoria, the red brick of the old palace and the pool of blue – makes an admirably composed picture. And outside this quiet place, 'the roar of London' encloses it 'in a ring of distant but complete sound'.[67]

At night inside the house, the family was quite sealed off from the 'roar of London'. *The Years* relives the feeling of seclusion and occlusion once the lamps were lit and the curtains were drawn:

They slid with a familiar click along the brass rod, and soon the windows were obscured by thick sculptured folds of claret-coloured plush. When she had drawn the curtains in both rooms, a profound silence seemed to fall upon the drawing-room. The world outside seemed thickly and entirely cut off.[68]

Inside, the house was a jumble of 'innumerable small oddly shaped rooms built to accommodate not one family but three'.[69] When they needed more space, Julia Stephen sketched an extension on a sheet of notepaper 'to save the architect's fees'. First a study for Leslie was added at the back, and then he was moved upstairs when an extra two floors, in Dutch gabled style, were built on top. (All the arrangements for moving his study were of course made by Julia; he writes to thank her, but has one criticism: 'Only one thing I want – I don't know how to express it delicately – a something which will enable me to refrain from going all the way to my dressing room and back, whenever a necessity arises.')[70]

The house was dark. This was partly due to the narrowness of the street (looking across at the intimate details of people's lives in the houses opposite was a potent memory, to be used in *Mrs Dalloway*), and partly to Julia's taste. 'My mother who had been brought up in the Watts-Venetian-Little Holland House tradition had covered the furniture in red velvet and painted the woodwork black with thin gold lines upon it.' The black folding doors of the drawing room were picked out in raspberry red. There were 'mounds of plush, Watts' portraits, busts shrined in crimson velvet'.[71] There was no electric light. Vanessa, too, remembered the sombre black paint, the dull blue walls absorbent of light, and the evening meals lit by candles when 'faces loomed out of the surrounding blackness like Rembrandt portraits'.[72]

The darkest room was the basement where Sophie Farrell cooked and the seven maids had their sitting-room. Sophie's kitchen 'must have been almost always dark. In winter a little fan of gas was always burning. In summer a curtain of creeper made the room like a green wave.'[73] When the family house is being sold in *The Years* and the older daughter goes back to say goodbye to the faithful old family cook, she is ashamed to realise 'how dark, how low' the basement was which had been Crosby's home 'for forty years'.[74] Virginia Woolf often looked back on the life of this Victorian household as it must have felt to the servants. Her description of the Carlyles' house in Cheyne Row, which had no running water, sums up her feelings about the labour-intensiveness of Victorian domestic life:

The high old house without water, without electric light, without gas fires, full of books and coal smoke and four-poster beds and mahogany cupboards, where two of the most nervous and exacting people of their time lived, year in year out, was served by one unfortunate maid. All through the mid-Victorian age the house was necessarily a battlefield where daily, summer and winter, mistress and maid fought against dirt and cold for cleanliness and warmth . . . the scene of labour, effort and perpetual struggle.[75]

The maids who carried out these labours in Hyde Park Gate had a sitting-room in the basement with a vast cracked portrait of Julia's parents and a shiny black sofa and a dim view, through the iron trellis of the window, on to 'the little, dust-smelling, patchy square of wall-circled back garden'. In the passage outside there was the wood-cupboard, where a wild cat used to lurk. When one of the maids dared to complain to Julia about their 'dark insanitary' conditions ('It's like hell,' she burst out) she was banished 'behind the red plush curtains, which, hooped round a semi-circular wire, and anchored by a great gold knob, hid the door that led from the dining room to the pantry'.

The dining-room was 'a very Victorian dining-room' which always smelt slightly of wine, cigars and food. It had a 'long baize covered table' where Julia gave the children their lessons; a 'heavily carved sideboard', a skylight with a loose pane of glass which made Virginia anxious; engravings by Reynolds; the mottled eyeless bust in yellow marble of the first Sir James Stephen; and a set of carved oak chairs with red plush panels. In the evening the dinner table, with its candles and silver and napkins, had a grand, festive look. In *The Years* we see it through the servant's eyes:

> The silver paid for polishing, she thought. Knives and forks rayed out round the table. The whole room, with its carved chairs, oil paintings, the two daggers on the mantelpiece, and the handsome sideboard – all the solid objects that Crosby dusted and polished every day – looked at its best in the evening. Meat-smelling and serge-curtained by day, it looked lit up, semi-transparent in the evening.[76]

A twisting staircase led into the hall. Like the landing outside the dining-room at St Ives, this in-between space evoked some of Virginia Woolf's strongest feelings about her childhood. Looking back at it from 1939 she remembers – in great detail – a collection of relics which signified the social and domestic habits of an extinct way of life, and had come to have a peculiar charm:

> In the hall lay a dog, beside him a bowl of water with a chunk of yellow sulphur in it. In the hall facing the front door stood a cabinet with blue

china; and on it a gold faced clock. In the hall was a three-cornered chair; and a chest in which rugs were kept; and on this chest was a silver salver deep in visiting cards; and a plush glove for smoothing the silk of George's and Gerald's top hats; and I also remember nailed over the fire place a long strip of chocolate coloured cardboard on which was written: 'What is to be a gentleman? It is to be tender to women, chivalrous to servants . . .' – what else I cannot remember; though I used to know it by heart. What innocence, what incredible simplicity of mind it showed – to keep this cardboard quotation – from Thackeray I think – perpetually displayed, as if it were a frontispiece to a book – nailed to the wall in the hall of the house.[77]

Off the hall was the double drawing-room, divisible by those black folding doors, so essential to the crises and intimacies of a large Victorian family. The back half, overshadowed by Virginia creeper, where emotional scenes often took place, was 'dark and agitated', while the front half, facing the street and comparatively light, could be cheerful enough. Here Leslie led visitors up to his Watts portrait, and Julia and Stella presided at the tea-table (an oval table supplemented by a small folding one) with – on Sundays – its pink shell plates full of brown spiced buns and thin slices of brown and white bread and butter. There was a grand piano and a writing table. *Night and Day* begins with the daughter of the house, 'in common with many other young ladies of her class', pouring tea for elderly visitors at just such a tea-table. In *The Years*, the daughters of the family feel as if they have spent their whole life sitting around this table, waiting for 'the old-fashioned brass kettle, chased with a design of roses that was almost obliterated', to boil on its brass bowl.[78] Making an anthropological survey, in her memoir, of her family as a specimen Victorian tribe, Virginia Woolf calls the tea-table the sacred spot in the house, the centre of life, much as 'savages, I suppose, have some tree, or fire place, round which they congregate'.[79]

Off the back drawing-room was a little side room, which was handed over to Virginia and Vanessa, and which Vanessa remembered as 'a cheerful little room, almost entirely made of glass' with a skylight, windows looking on to the back garden, and a window cut in the wall between it and the drawing-room. 'Also another door by which one could retreat to the rest of the house.' 'In this room we used to sit, I painting and she reading aloud. We read most of the Victorian novelists in this way & I can still hear much of George Eliot & Thackeray in her voice. From this room too we could spy on the grown-ups.'[80] Virginia remembered overhearing, in a tumult of emotions, the love-making of Stella and Jack Hills, 'in my covert, behind the folding doors'.[81]

Above the drawing-rooms, on the first floor, was the bedroom (with a dressing-room off it) which was the other life centre – 'the birth centre, the death centre' – of the house. It was not a large room, filled with its family portraits and mirrors and dressing-table and four-poster bed, but 'its walls must be soaked . . . of all that makes the most private being, of family life.' Four children were conceived and born there; both her parents died there. On the same floor was the bedroom that Julia's invalid mother used to live in when she was staying with the family; Vanessa remembered her dressing up there in her shawls and brooches to receive company 'by that cosy fireside with the curtains drawn and the street outside as quiet as any country lane.'[82]

The two floors above were mostly bedrooms: George's, Gerald's and Stella's on the second floor (and later, bedrooms for Adrian and Thoby), the day and night nurseries on the third floor. In the night nursery, 'we four children and a nurse slept & had our baths & did all else in what I think must by modern standards have been a very unhealthy atmosphere', Vanessa recalled. 'Was the window ever open at night? I doubt it. There was a lovely bright fire to go to bed by; coal, food, hot water & babies being carried up many times a day; we were very snug if stuffy & of course told stories in bed.'[83] The night nursery became Virginia's bed-sitting room when she was fifteen. 'There she had a curious high desk at which she stood to write, & many books, & white walls & bright blue curtains.'[84] Virginia described the two halves of the room, the 'living' half with her wicker chair and the writing table which had been Stella's, stained green and decorated with brown leaves (in a style 'much the rage' then), and the 'sleeping' half with the long imitation Chippendale looking-glass, the washstand, and the bed under the window. 'How often I was in a rage in that room; and in despair; and in ecstasy . . .' Anyone reading her books and looking back on her there would have to say, 'This room explains a great deal'.[85]

As small children in the nursery they would hear Leslie chanting and groaning on his way upstairs to his study, and the thud of books dropped on the floor as he wrote 'in the large room with three long windows at the top of the house'. In this book-lined room with its Watts portrait of Minny, its view of Kensington, its stack of alpenstocks in the corner and its smell of tobacco from his short clay pipe, Leslie sat recumbent in his old rocking chair, wearing a fez, his feet in the air, a writing board across him 'with the sheets of foolscap always folded down the middle, so that he could make corrections in the margin', and his fine steel pen and 'curious china inkpot' at the side. This was 'the brain of the house'.[86]

Above him, carpets and pictures ran out, and the servants' bedrooms were shabby enough for Julia to be embarrassed when a visitor ran up there to help mend a burst pipe. Lower down was the water closet, 'with all the brass hot water cans standing by a sink'; on another landing was 'the solitary family bath'. 'My father all his life washed in a yellow tin bath with flat ears on which the soap stood.' The entire family had 'one bathroom and three water-closets between them'.[87] This would make it an undesirable property when they put it on the market after the war, in 1919 – a detail used in *The Years*, when Eleanor Pargiter is trying to sell the house:

> Mr Grice turned to her as they went downstairs.
> 'The fact is, our clients expect more lavatory accommodation nowadays', he said, stopping outside a bedroom door.
> Why can't he say 'baths' and have done with it, she thought.[88]

Eleanor Pargiter goes on down the stairs to the empty drawing-room. 'There . . . were marks on the wall, where the bookcase had stood, where the writing-table had stood.' For thirty years Virginia Woolf remembered going back to the emptied house at Hyde Park Gate after the orphaned Stephens had left it, and seeing the marks on the walls where her childhood had been spent. Like the night-time return to Talland House, it was a return which haunted her. When Virginia Woolf turned Hyde Park Gate into fiction, she embodied the 'spirit of the age' – patriarchal, Victorian – in the solid objects which filled it and without which it looked so strange. *Night and Day*, her earliest version of the house, merges Hyde Park Gate with memories of her aunt Anny Ritchie's house, a 'religious temple . . . crowded with relics' of her father Thackeray. The ceremonial objects of the house lovingly and stiflingly enclose its daughter: ' Dear things! ' exclaims Mrs Hilbery (the novel's fictional – and recognisable – Anny Ritchie), looking at her drawing-room. ' Dear chairs and tables! How like old friends they are! ' In her struggle with the past Katharine Hilbery wants to go outside, find bare rooms, escape from these 'dear things'. But they speak to her like voices, and seem to set a standard for living which it is extremely hard to reformulate:

> Like all people brought up in a tradition, Katharine was able, within ten minutes or so, to reduce any moral difficulty to its traditional shape and solve it by the traditional answers. The book of wisdom lay open, if not upon her mother's knee, upon the knees of many uncles and aunts. She had only to consult them, and they would at once turn to the right page and read out an answer exactly suited to one in her position . . . but in her case . . . the traditional answer would be of no use to her individually. Yet it had served so many people, she thought, glancing at the rows of houses on either side of her, where families, whose incomes must be between a thousand and fifteen-hundred a year lived, and kept, perhaps, three

servants, and draped their windows with curtains which were always thick and generally dirty, and must, she thought, since you could only see a looking-glass gleaming above a sideboard on which a dish of apples was set, keep the room inside very dark. But she turned her head away, observing that this was not a method of thinking the matter out.[89]

But looking at houses and their solid objects is, in fact, an eloquent method of 'thinking the matter out', the 'matter' of what use the traditional Victorian answers – the old mental furniture – can be for the next generation. In *The Years*, the whole story of the middle-class daughter's servitude to her father and her brothers is embodied in the objects on the writing-table which she has inherited from her mother:

> It'll be my table now, she thought, looking at the silver candlestick, the miniature of her grandfather, the tradesmen's books – one had a gilt cow stamped on it – and the spotted walrus with a brush in its back that Martin had given his mother on her last birthday.[90]

The walrus-brush takes on a recurring life, turning up in the novel long after the house has been emptied and left. In *Flush*, the device of telling Elizabeth Barrett Browning's story from the vantage point of her spaniel gives the Victorian household in Wimpole Street a comically thick solidity. The dog's narrative registers the physical sensations of living in a house very like Hyde Park Gate:

> Mr Barrett, the seven brothers, the two sisters, the butler, Wilson and the maids, Catiline, Folly, Miss Barrett and Flush all went on living at 50 Wimpole Street, eating in the dining-room, sleeping in the bedrooms, smoking in the study, cooking in the kitchen, carrying hot-water cans and emptying the slops from January to December. The chair-covers became slightly soiled; the carpets slightly worn; coal dust, mud, soot, fog, vapours of cigar smoke and wine and meat accumulated in crevices, in cracks, in fabrics, on the tops of picture-frames, in the scrolls of carvings.

Flush takes in the house through his nose:

> Mixing with the smell of food were further smells – smells of cedarwood and sandalwood and mahogany; scents of male bodies and female bodies; of men servants and maid servants; of coats and trousers; of crinolines and mantles; of curtains of tapestry, of curtains of plush; of coal dust and fog; of wine and cigars. Each room as he passed it – dining-room, drawing-room, library, bedroom – wafted out its own contribution to the general stew.[91]

45

In *Orlando*, another 'biography', Flush's *olla podrida* of Victorian life takes the form of a grotesque, magnificent, surrealist erection. It is a Great Victorian Collection, the Albert Memorial as invented by Lewis Carroll's White Knight:

> What was her surprise when, as it struck the earth, the sunbeam seemed to call forth, or to light up, a pyramid, hecatomb, or trophy (for it had something of a banquet-table air) – a conglomeration at any rate of the most heterogeneous and ill-assorted objects, piled higgledy-piggledy in a vast mound where the statue of Queen Victoria now stands! Draped about a vast cross of fretted and floriated gold were widow's weeds and bridal veils; hooked onto other excrescences were crystal palaces, bassinettes, military helmets, memorial wreaths, trousers, whiskers, wedding cakes, cannon, Christmas trees, telescopes, extinct monsters, globes, maps, elephants, and mathematical instruments – the whole supported like a gigantic coat of arms on the right side by a female figure clothed in flowing white; on the left by a portly gentleman wearing a frock-coat and sponge-bag trousers.[92]

In all these fictions Victorian life is thick with things. When Virginia Woolf writes her absurd Victorian play, *Freshwater*, about Julia Margaret Cameron and the Tennysons, with parts for Queen Victoria, Ellen Terry and G.F. Watts, the list of props is a bit like that great 'conglomeration' in *Orlando*:

> Bowls of soapsuds. Copy of *Maud*. Chest containing clothes etc. Tripod camera. Turkeys' wings. Beard for Tennyson. Beard for Watts. Skull cap. Cape for Tennyson. Smock for Watts. Reticule for Mrs Cameron. Donkey to bray. Bags. Luggage. Lens. Clock to strike. Coronet. Paper and Pencil. Order of Merit. Brandy bottle. Record God Save the King. Whiskers. Porpoise. Rocks. Clouds. Curtains for window. Cameron photos.[93]

And when she comes to describe the contents of the cupboards at Hyde Park Gate, where 'three families had poured all their possessions into this one house', they too read like a props list for a play, with the same comical serendipity as her fictional collections of Victoriana:

> One never knew when one rummaged in the many dark cupboards and wardrobes whether one would disinter Herbert Duckworth's barrister's wig, my father's clergyman's collar, or a sheet scribbled over with drawings by Thackeray . . . Old letters filled dozens of black tin boxes.

One opened them and got a terrific whiff of the past. There were chests of heavy family plate. There were hoards of china and glass.[94]

When the objects of the Victorian house, with their 'terrific whiff of the past', have been cleared out, leaving nothing but marks on the wall, and the big extended families which had grown up there die and move out and split up, it ought to be possible for something quite new to begin. Virginia Woolf's lifelong argument with the past took its central images from the leaving, and the memory, of the Victorian house. When, in the 1920s and 1930s, she devises a metaphor for a younger generation of women setting out on their professional lives, it is – famously – of a room. This modern room – a bed-sitting room, a college room, a soundproof room – is the substitute for the rooms which women have lived in in the past: drawing-rooms, nurseries, kitchens, rooms with no privacy, rooms where they have 'sat indoors all these millions of years, so that by this time the very walls are permeated by their creative force'.[95] But the recommendations for modern life – and modern writing – in *A Room of One's Own* can't quite shake themselves free from those old rooms and old houses. The new women have won rooms of their own 'in the house hitherto owned by men'. But this doesn't mean that they should, or can, break their contact with the 'creative force' they have inherited from their mothers and grandmothers. 'The room is your own, but it is still bare. It has to be furnished; it has to be decorated; it has to be shared.'[96] Some of the furniture – mental and physical – which gets into the new room may be left over from the old houses. So, Julia Margaret Cameron's photographs of Julia Stephen are put up on the walls of Bloomsbury houses; and the Victorian family provides the furniture of Virginia Woolf's modernist novels.

When they knew they were dying, Julia, and her mother, and Leslie, all scribbled down lists of bequests to their family. These pathetic inventories of their 'dear things' give off, as Virginia would say, 'a terrific whiff' of the family past in the Victorian house. Maria Jackson leaves almost all her possessions to her daughter Julia: the oval miniature of her mother, her fish-knives, candlesticks, envelope case, Indian miniature, davenport, lying down chair, inlaid ivory desk, clocks, bronze candelabras, invalid table, brooches . . . Leslie gets a pencil drawing of Julia, the Duckworth children get photographs of her. 'All my body linen' goes to Aunt Minna. Stella gets her silver inkstand, Georgie her silver cream jug. Julia Stephen, at her death, leaves equally specific wishes:

Crystal locket – to be buried with me. Opal ring to Virginia . . . All the spoons and forks with Duckworth crest and Duckworth plate to George when he marries . . . Irish lace to Virginia . . . All Mr Lowell's letters in despatch box to Virginia. She is never to have them published . . . Picture of my beloved mother to Mary [Julia's sister] as long as she lives. After her death to Stella . . . Picture of Leslie for Thoby.[97]

Leslie's deathbed list, by contrast, is almost all of letters and books, and is typically self-denigrating. He directs his children round the house like literary executors: to the box under the bureau in the study which 'contains my correspondence with Julia and a book in which I wrote the first account, called "Letter to Julia's children" of our lives' (this was the *Mausoleum Book*); to a box on the study mantelpiece (made of old Trinity Hall wainscoting) containing 'my correspondence with Minny and Anny'; to the pigeonholes in the bureau containing 'all the letters I have kept from anyone . . .' 'My books, as you know, are mangy and worthless – I should sell them for what they would fetch after picking out a few that may interest you.' The only ones of any value, he says, are Darwin's Life of his grandfather, some Pope first editions, and *Vanity Fair*. And he lists a few more, including Chateaubriand's *Mémoires*, Sorel, Pater, Santayana, Hobbes, Bayle, Renan, Sainte-Beuve, Lucian, Mérimée's *Lettres*, and Zola's *Thérèse Raquin*.

The bequests, the furniture, the pictures, the bits and pieces from the nursery cupboards, all ended up somewhere. When the objects came out of the gloom of Hyde Park Gate into the white spaces of Gordon Square, 'things one had never seen in the darkness there – Watts pictures, Dutch cabinets, blue china – shone out for the first time'.[98] Old clothes had a second life: Virginia would have a curious, touching photograph taken of her in one of Julia's dresses; the opal ring Julia gave her becomes a tie-pin for Leonard (and Anne Olivier Bell remembers always seeing it in the bathroom of Monk's House). *The Charleston Bulletin*, a comic family magazine of the 1920s, to which Virginia contributed, describes Duncan Grant rescuing a child from water 'at enormous risk to Sir Leslie's grey tweed coat'. Watts's portrait of Leslie now hangs on a great-niece's wall in a bungalow in Norwich; the table which was supposed to have been given by Marie Antoinette to Julia's glamorous French ancestor, the Chevalier de l'Etang, sits in a descendant's house bearing the family photograph album. The big mirror from Julia and Leslie's bedroom ended up in the spare room at Charleston.

Because this is a literary family, its inheritance is of course dominated by books and memoirs and letters. Hundreds of Leslie's books became mixed up with Virginia's and Leonard's, and when they moved house, their floors were awash with the *Dictionary of National Biography*. Family records –

Leslie's grandfather's memoir, Leslie's *Mausoleum Book* and the 'Calendar of Correspondence' in which he transcribed some of his letters, his mother's diary, his sister's journal, his sister-in-law's memoirs, the correspondence of Leslie and Julia, Leslie and Thoby, Julia's stories – all these were circulated and re-read and handed down. Favourite family stories – usually the most grotesque and gruesome – were regularly exchanged like items of jewellery or furniture. In her unpublished sketch of Sophie Farrell, Virginia described a figure who embodied the family past:

> Her room is hung with photographs. Her mind is like a family album. You turn up Uncle George you turn up Aunt Maria. She has a story about each of them. It is crowded with things people threw away – things they didnt want . . . A glass pig is one of them. There is also an Indian temple in silver . . . She goes back far far into the past. She represents a world that has gone.[99]

This is a pathetic and gloomy figure, but she lingers on in Virginia Woolf's imagination. In her adult life, the memory of the family house fills her with horror, but also with desire. She returns to it repeatedly in her thoughts and in her writing. And though she spends her life strenuously establishing and defining herself as an autonomous and exceptional individual, she recognises to the last day of her life that she is part of the fabric of a family history and character, and carries in her own life traces of 'a world that has gone'.

THREE

Paternal

Inheritance interests Virginia Woolf very much: her fictions are full of it. In *Night and Day*, conflicts over inheritance are only resolved when the daughter can start to feel an attachment to her famous grandfather, not as an ancestor but as a person like herself:

> He might have been her brother, she thought. It seemed to her that they were akin, with the mysterious kinship of blood which makes it seem possible to . . . believe that they [the dead] look with us upon our present joys and sorrows.[1]

Orlando's history plays with the notion that genetic inheritance can be pooled (just as sexual orientations can be crossed) in the identity of one person. So, after living for generations, Orlando is both an exceptional individual, *and* the summation of her whole family's history. But inheritance is not usually as joyously resolved. In the novel of her family, *To the Lighthouse* – a novel split down the middle – the splits between husband and wife, parents and children, past and present, generate a violent sense of conflict and a painful desire for resolution: 'For what happened to her, especially staying with the Ramsays, was to be made to feel violently two opposite things at the same time; that's what you feel, was one; that's what I feel was the other; and then they fought together in her mind, as now.'[2] This 'violent' conflict of feelings is given to the modern, post-war artist, trying to make her peace with her Victorian inheritance by turning it into her material. It is also the conflict of the twentieth-century daughter, torn between the sympathies she feels arising from 'the mysterious kinship of blood', and the quarrel of the generations: 'that's what you feel . . . that's what I feel.'

In her memoirs, Virginia Woolf is divided between two ideas of herself. One is of a distinctive, self-constructed person, who has reacted against her upbringing, and who exists in a world 'made by my own temperament'. The other is of a self formed by a social context and an intellectual inheritance, existing as part of 'the common life of the family'[3] – without which it would be impossible to describe her. The division is unresolved: 'I do not know how much of this, or what part of this, made me feel what I felt.' Childhood feelings of shame, for instance, only partly derive from what happened to her as a child. They are also attributed to an inherited puritanism, or, further back, to some primitive 'ancestral dread'. 'Virginia Stephen was not born on the 25th January 1882, but was born many thousands of years ago; and had from the very first to encounter instincts already acquired by thousands of ancestresses in the past.'[4] (Note 'ancestresses'.) However she accounts for the person called 'Virginia Stephen', she has to describe her as an inheritor:

> Who was I then? Adeline Virginia Stephen, the second daughter of Leslie and Julia Prinsep Stephen, born on 25th January 1882, descended from a great many people, some famous, others obscure; born into a large connection, born not of rich parents, but of well-to-do parents, born into a very communicative, literate, letter writing, visiting, articulate, late nineteenth century world; so that I could if I liked to take the trouble, write a great deal here not only about my mother and father but about uncles and aunts, cousins and friends.[5]

This 'large connection' has tended to be described in terms of 'ancestors' rather than 'ancestresses'. Leslie Stephen's biographer Noel Annan borrowed from an earlier Stephen the phrase 'an aristocracy of intellect' to define Leslie's 'status group', which had taken shape early in the nineteenth century:

> Certain families established an intellectual ascendancy and began to share the spoils of the professional and academic worlds between their children. These children intermarried and formed a class of able men and women who drew into that circle people of intellectual distinction.

This 'status group' was made up of families who had come via business and trade (motivated by Evangelical or Quaker ideals of 'moral purpose') into the professions of law, teaching, writing, or the civil service. Such families were closely, and widely, interconnected. Leslie Stephen's grandfather married into the Venns and Thorntons and Wilberforces of the Clapham Sect. Leslie's first marriage related him to the Thackerays (and thence to the families of Ritchies, Booths, Warre-Cornishes and MacCarthys). His second connected him to the Jacksons, and through them back to Pattles and Camerons, and sideways to Duckworths, Fishers, Vaughans, Maitlands and Symondses. The next interconnected generation were Costelloes and Stracheys and Grants, Pearsall-Smiths and Russells and Marshalls and Garnetts.

In *Our Age*, his book on the 'generation who created post-war Britain', Noel Annan describes a relationship between family, power and belonging. 'How did one get accepted as a member of Our Age? In the same way that most people have always got accepted – by ability, by family connections and knowing somebody.' The success stories of this status group, in his book, are almost all male.[6] But a different reading can be made of the history of the intellectual aristocracy – a reading influenced by Virginia Woolf's own feminist writings – which notes how many 'politically and economically pioneering women came from this group'.[7] Social activists like Beatrice Webb, Ray Strachey, Margaret Llewelyn Davies and Molly Hamilton, educationalists such as Pernel Strachey and Margery Fry, doctors like Octavia Wilberforce and Elinor Rendel, and an ensuing generation of college principals (Janet Vaughan, Mary Bennett, Sally Chilver) belonged to this network of family connections too, and had a great deal of influence on Virginia Woolf's life and writing.

But her own political position came to be one of ironic detachment from what she called 'the procession' – the influential network derived from public school and University education. She wrote often about her dissociation from the 'Administrative Class', and by the 1930s she could no more talk about 'our age' than 'our country': 'What does 'our country' mean to me an outsider?'[8] The advice she gave to the next generation of women was that they should redefine the terms on which they joined the procession. This was the argument of *Three Guineas* (an argument much disliked and derided, then and since, by the male members of 'our age') which concluded that a detached and ironical critique of the 'civilization' should be made by a 'Society of Outsiders'.

Yet Virginia Woolf's thinking about the politics of outsiderism was always defined by concepts of group, inheritance and family. The family was her political blueprint. For instance, in her 'Sketch of the Past', she compared her own autobiography to the memoirs of her distinguished cousin Herbert Fisher, whose life as a teacher, historian, politician and educational administrator was defined entirely through the institutions of school, government and university.

> Most of our male relations were adept at that game. They knew the rules, and attached extraordinary importance to those who won the game. Father for example laid immense stress upon school reports; upon scholarships; triposes and fellowships.[9] The male Fishers went through those hoops to perfection. They won all the prizes, all the honours. What,

I asked myself, when I read Herbert Fisher's autobiography the other day, would Herbert have been without Winchester, New College and the Cabinet? What would have been his shape had he not been stamped and moulded by that great patriarchal machine? Every one of our male relations was shot into that machine at the age of ten and emerged at sixty a Head Master, an Admiral, a Cabinet Minister, or the Warden of a college. It is as impossible to think of them as natural human beings as it is to think of a carthorse galloping wild maned and unshod over the pampas.[10]

This dry tone of voice echoes *Three Guineas*. But when she is mocking the 'patriarchal procession' in *Three Guineas*, she always refers to 'the daughters of educated men'. Her social satire is inextricable from her experience of family life.

She could never let go of the family. She and Vanessa and Adrian took pleasure, of a ghoulish sort, in exchanging news of surviving family members (whom Virginia kept up with, they always joked, in order to entertain Vanessa),[11] or in recycling old family jokes and stories. For instance, there was the one about Julia Stephen's sister Adeline, 'a damaged beauty', unhappily married to an eccentric Oxford professor of history called Halford Vaughan, who had a spurious reputation based on an unwritten great work. Leslie often told this story, partly because he thought Vaughan treated Adeline worse than he treated Julia:

Now begins the part I always like [says Virginia in her notes to herself on the Vaughans] – the history of his great philosophy. This he wrote; then destroyed; went on writing; destroying; at last accused servants of destroying; had a poster offering a reward exhibited; and died leaving – several versions of the first chapter . . . My father looked and groaned.[12]

'Now begins the part I always like.' As with these family stories, so with the family manner: the sisters often imitated the gushing epistolary styles of their Victorian aunts ('Darling, tell me if I can do anything – I will come at any moment')[13] in order to amuse each other. (But Virginia could also re-enact these blackmailing demands for affection in *her* family letters.)

The post-Victorian Stephens pulled out of the family network and made lives which scandalised the older generation. And they satirised the systems of family patronage and networking they had turned their backs on. So, in her memoirs, sifting through her memories of the minor tributaries of her family tree, Virginia Woolf makes an ironical analysis of the way the kinship system worked.

When there was a family crisis, all the rays of family life at once began to ripple across the pond. A marriage brought them circling round . . . There was Aunt Virginia; a snobby Aunt Virginia who had not recognised Herbert Fisher, realised that he was 'one of the family'. Instantly up go her arms, down comes H.F's head. They embrace . . . And does the network still exist? Is it one of the great unseen forces that keep society together – the Kiss of Aunt Virginia and all it implied?[14]

But though Virginia thought of herself and Vanessa as having placed themselves quite outside 'the network', she replayed a version of it in the social organisation of her adult life. It's often observed[15] that Bloomsbury inherited some of the characteristics of the Clapham Sect: a work ethic, a commitment to cultural and social progress, a belief in intellectual honesty, and a complacency. A description of the Clapham Sect by Virginia Woolf's grandfather, the Right Honourable James Stephen, points ahead to this resemblance:

It is not permitted to any Coterie altogether to escape the spirit of Coterie. The [Clapham] commoners admired in each other the reflection of their own looks, and the echo of their own voices. A critical race, they drew many of their canons of criticism from books and talks of their own parentage; and for those on the outside of the pale, there might be, now and then, some failure of charity. Their festivals were not exhilarating.[16]

The 'festivals' at Gordon Square or Charleston may have been more 'exhilarating' than those of the nineteenth-century Clapham philanthropists, but Virginia Woolf and her friends similarly looked askance on 'those on the outside of the pale'. 'Bloomsbury', though reacting against its ancestry, followed an earlier generation's preoccupation with what has been called 'the question of access'.[17] Virginia Woolf may have repudiated her half-brother George Duckworth's craven desire to enter into (and enter her into) the 'best circles', but she and her friends created their own concept of a 'best circle' which remained founded on family allegiances.

Virginia Woolf's social ideas and practice evolved in critical opposition to the bourgeois habits, the internalised 'norms' of previous generations.[18] From her youth, she stood outside these 'norms', looking in on them with a satirical, alien and fearful eye. Much of her writing diagnosed society as a 'miasma', an absurd and illusory spectacle.[19] All the same, a concept of 'status honour', derived from her upbringing, lingered on into adult life. 'Bloomsbury' behaviour (in as much as this was *her* behaviour) looks as if it travesties and sabotages the conventions of Victorian life: the calling card, the morning visit, the marriage market, the polite conversation, the cut, the dressing for dinner, the evening party. But 'Bloomsbury' in its turn developed the social habits, mannerisms and ways of thinking of an excluding network.

Virginia Woolf was 'modern'. But she was also a late Victorian. The Victorian family past filled her fiction, shaped her political analyses of society and underlay the behaviour of her social group. And it was a powerful ingredient, of course, in her definition of her self. Theories of genetic heredity were generally accepted in her circle: Francis Galton's popular treatise on *Hereditary Genius* (1869) cited the Stephen and the Strachey families as examples.[20] And Virginia Woolf (whose god-father James Russell Lowell wrote a poem at her birth hoping she would be a good 'sample of heredity') often described herself in terms of inheritance, whether in reference to her mental condition, her 'genius', or the split in her character between different tendencies.

When she looked back on her family life she thought of it not as a single thing but marked by dramatic splits. Lines of division criss-cross her memoirs. Childhood was cut in two between Cornwall and London. An end to childhood came with the violent division made by her mother's death. The household was fragmented (as in *To the Lighthouse* after Mrs Ramsay's death, 'as if the link that usually bound things together had been cut, and they floated up here, down there, off, anyhow').[21] There was a historical divide between the younger generation – the four Stephen children – and the other people in the house, their father and the Duckworth sons, who were still, she thinks, Victorians: 'We were living say in 1910; they were living in 1860.'[22] The 'fight' between the Victorian and the twentieth-century members of the household was split across, again, by the extreme, absurd contrast between the social life the two girls were being forced into by their older half-brother George, and the reclusive life of the mind going on in their father's study. 'The division in our lives was curious. Downstairs there was pure convention; upstairs pure intellect.'[23] And there was another division between the 'close conspiracy' of the sisters, trying to build a 'private nucleus', a 'standing place' for their own point of view and their own desires in a world of 'many men'.[24] Even the room Virginia grew up in seemed cut into two halves for waking and sleeping life.

From the start, one of the most dramatic splits was the contrast between her father and her mother. Vanessa remembered that the point at which she and her sister began to talk intimately was when Virginia made them choose a parent:

I remember one evening as we were jumping about naked, she & I, in the bathroom she suddenly asked me which I liked best, my father or mother.

55

Such a question seemed to me rather terrible . . . However, being asked, one had to reply and I found I had little doubt as to my answer. "Mother" I said, and she went on to explain why she, on the whole, preferred my father.[25]

The child's choice developed into Virginia Woolf's adult description of herself (partly a self-dramatising joke, partly believed) as formed by two incompatible inheritances: the cold, law-making, rational, depressive Stephens, originating from Scottish Calvinists, and the creative, decorative, intuitive, emotional Pattles, descended from French aristocracy. She often accounted for her resistance to extravagant gestures, emotional claims or social demands by citing the grim, moralising half of her ancestry. So, she backs off from the Argentinian writer Victoria OCampo's exotic tributes (butterflies, flowers) with wry protestations, saying that her disapproving puritan ancestors make her prefer to 'go ungiven': 'That's what comes of having Scotch clergy in my blood – a detestable race.'[26] Pleasure in art, love, colour, emotion, is contrasted with the legacy of the 'detestable' puritans. In a catalogue note to an exhibition of her sister's paintings in 1930, admiring their impersonal but powerful emotions, she ends: 'But is morality to be found there?' In her draft for this essay, she adds (and then cuts out): 'Upon this last question one would like to confront Mrs Bell with her grandfather.'[27]

But Virginia Woolf thought of herself as a family exception, too, and for a particular reason: 'We Stephen's [*sic*] are difficult' (she wrote in 1924 about Adrian, to Jacques Raverat), 'especially as the race tapers out, towards its finish – such cold fingers, so fastidious, so critical, such taste. My madness has saved me.'[28]

When the historian Frederic Maitland wrote the life of Leslie Stephen, his friend, mentor and relation-by-marriage (Maitland's wife was Julia's niece Florence Fisher, whom he had met at Julia and Leslie's house), he described the Stephen family lineage as a family tree of book titles.

Taking one of Leslie's books, for instance, the 'History of English Thought in the 18th Century', and ascending the direct male line, we might say it was the son of 'Essays in Ecclesiastical Biography' which was the son of 'War in Disguise', which was the son of 'Considerations on Imprisonment for Debt'. We might say it was the brother of 'Liberty, Equality and Fraternity', and of the 'History of Criminal Law'; the brother also of 'Quaker Strongholds'.[29]

This mainly patriarchal line of descent was Virginia Stephen's official intellectual ancestry. Leslie's expectation of his writing daughter, from the age of ten or eleven, was that she would join in this family procession: 'She takes in a great deal and will really be an author in time. History will be a good thing for her to take up as I can give her some hints.'[30] When he was dying, he dictated the last of his *Mausoleum Book* to Virginia, and in the notes he left behind him about his effects, he directed her to his 'miscellaneous papers': 'Perhaps some worth preserving – Ginia may do some research work!'[31] And her first publication in book form was her unsigned contribution to Maitland's biography – fulfilling the expected role for the family's woman historian. Leslie's first sister-in-law, Anny Thackeray Ritchie, a well-known and distinctive writer of fiction and memoirs, spent most of her later years happily writing introductions to all her father's novels. Caroline Emelia Stephen edited the letters of her father Sir James Stephen; Dorothea Stephen, the last surviving daughter of Leslie's brother James Fitzjames Stephen, permitted the publication of the *Memoirs* of her (and Virginia's) great-grandfather James Stephen.

Virginia Woolf sabotaged that subservient role and rewrote her family history in her own terms. She made her female inheritance count for just as much as her father's influence, deriving inspiration from her mother (nurse, muse and writer of stories), her great-aunt Julia Margaret Cameron (famous photographer) and two very different women writers, her astounding 'Aunt Anny', and Caroline Emelia, the author of *Quaker Strongholds*. But she did not entirely want to deny her patrilinear inheritance – even if only as a joke. So, in 1934, embarrassed at finding herself in a dress shop without her purse, she wrote to her nephew Quentin: 'It was rather difficult, but then I remembered my grandfathers nose and gave myself such airs they let me go off with three pound ten worth.'[32]

Certainly that Stephen nose – and the ability to look down it – was visible through the generations. The Stephen 'look' was vividly evoked in Leslie's and Caroline Emelia's accounts of their father:

> My father . . . though not handsome . . . had a marked dignity. A very lofty brow was surmounted by masses of soft fine hair, reddish in youth, which became almost white before he died. The eyes, often concealed by [a] nervous trick ['a tremulous motion'] were rather deeply set and of the purest blue. They could flash into visibility and sparkle with indignation or softer emotion. The nose was the nose of a scholar, rather massive though well cut, and running to a sharp point. He had the long flexible lips of an orator, while the mouth, compressed as if cut with a knife, indicated a nervous reserve. The skull was very large, and the whole face, as I remember him, was massive.[33]

Leslie's sister remembered their father talking with 'those blue eyes apparently on the corner of the ceiling, with a dreamy, far-away look, as though all present things and people were forgotten, as he dwelt on some mental vision.'[34] Many of Virginia Woolf's observers noted the same high forehead, the blue and 'glistening' eyes,[35] the straight nose, the nervousness, and the look turned away from her listeners.

In the facts and legends of her paternal ancestors there are also recognisable, recurring characteristics. The seventeenth-century Aberdeenshire farmers and smugglers, with their long-lived Episcopalian wives and large families, come into focus with the eighteenth-century James Stephen, who went south to make his fortune. The famous story about James Stephen, a big strong man, was of his stormy shipwreck in Dorset, in 1752, with a cargo of wine from Bordeaux, and his heroic climb, with four crewmen roped behind him, up a cliff which a cat could not have scaled. (An episode worthy of Walter Scott, as Leslie, a Scott devotee, observed.) The customs officer at Poole helped the shipwrecked James, who rewarded him by running off with his fifteen-year-old daughter Sibella, whom he married without her parents' consent. Sibella had six children and a poetic disposition: her favourite book was Young's *Night Thoughts*. But her husband was a failure. In the 1760s he tried investing some money in a project for a new maritime village and colliery in Poole, which bankrupted him. He was imprisoned for debt in the King's Bench prison, where he wrote a pamphlet on the injustice of such imprisonment, and organised a rowdy jail protest. Later he tried unsuccessfully to work as a lawyer, but sank into drink and died in 1779 with hardly enough to pay his debts. Lurking on the edge of his story are a brother William, who made money in the West Indies by curing, and selling, sick black slaves, and an interesting-sounding sister Mary, who married an officer in the East India Company and was known for her violent temper, her strong masculine understanding, and her hatred of women.

James or Jem, Virginia's great-grandfather, the son of James, born in 1758, was a young boy when his father was in prison; his father's fellow prisoners encouraged him in his reading. One of them – a strange fortuitous connection – was the poet Christopher Smart, who died in the King's Bench prison in 1771. 'Jem' had a difficult hand-to-mouth childhood but emerged from it to become a public figure of influence and importance. The *Memoirs* which he wrote for his children between 1819 and 1825 (as his grandson would for *his* children) have three confessions to make: of his sexual aberrations in youth, of his pleasure in his public success, and of his devout conviction of God's special favour.

The sexual story is dramatic. James fell in love, very young, with a

58

beautiful girl called Nancy Stent, but then betrayed her with 'Maria', whom Nancy's brother was in love with. Maria had James's child, but then Nancy forgave him (so did her generous brother) and Nancy and James married and went to the West Indies together, where James's elder brother was making a living as a planter. Maria married someone else: her first child, James Stephen's illegitimate son William, grew up to be a retiring country vicar in Buckinghamshire whom Leslie remembered 'as a mild old gentleman with a taste for punning'. In the family history with which he began his life of his brother James Fitzjames Stephen, Leslie concealed the scandal about this mild old gentleman, but to Virginia's great pleasure the secret was revealed to her by one of Fitzjames's sons:

> Sir Harry told us the life history of Great Uncle William, who was, in the 18th century the illegitimate son of the first James Stephen. 'I shall call the lady whom he seduced Lucy Waters, though that was not her name,' he said. This chivalry, considering she died 150 years ago struck me very much.[36]

In the Barbados, James was horrified by the treatment of the blacks and resolved 'never to have any connection with slavery'. In this cause, he began to correspond with the leading English abolitionist, William Wilberforce. When he went back to England he became very close to Wilberforce and, after Nancy's death (in childbirth with her seventh child) and his ensuing 'deep dejection', he married Wilberforce's sister Sarah, a pious and eccentric lady who gave all her money away to charity and could be seen going about Clapham dressed in rags.

The group of evangelical reformers (Thorntons, Macaulays, Wilberforces, Venns) which James Stephen joined in the 1790s was, in Quentin Bell's phrase, 'the conscience of the British middle classes and therefore an enormous political power'.[37] Forster described it eloquently in his book on his great-aunt, the educationalist Marianne Thornton, the daughter of one of William Wilberforce's closest friends, Henry Thornton:

> Such was the atmosphere, such the household, into which Marianne Thornton was born: affections, comfort, piety, integrity, intelligence, public activity, private benevolence; and transcending them all an unshaken belief in a future life where the members of the household would meet again and would recognise each other and be happy eternally. It is this belief that makes the 'Clapham Sect' seem remote today.[38]

The involvement of what Forster calls 'the alarming and able Stephen family' in this group was active and energetic from the first. James became an MP and a Master in Chancery and wrote a famous pamphlet, *War in Disguise*, which influenced the 1812 war with America. 'I cannot say that I have found it amusing', said Leslie of his grandfather's pamphlet, 'but it is written with vigour and impressive earnestness.'[39] Judging from his tomb in Stoke Newington, Virginia imagined Jem Stephen as 'large & plain'.[40] But those qualities were mixed with something more vulnerable. This comes out in his account of himself as a child.

> I have reason to believe that few human bodies or minds were ever endued with a keener sensibility than mine ... My imagination also was extremely active and wild. It gave an interest to every flower and leaf and insect ... At the same period, and till mature manhood, I had a strong belief ... of spiritual beings, with which I was surrounded.

His 'apprehension of ghosts' made him sleep with his head under the bedclothes. Later, his guilt about Nancy and 'Maria', his intermittent 'superstitious terrors', his visible emotion when he spoke in the House about slavery, and his thoughts of suicide when his mother died, all point to what Leslie calls the 'irritable and nervous temperament' of the Stephens.

His sons inherited the mixture of irascibility and nervousness and all (apart from the bastard vicar) went into the law. The son who would be Leslie's father and Virginia's grandfather, another James, was born in 1789. He was educated under an evangelical don at Cambridge, became an extremely successful lawyer, and married in his turn into the Clapham Sect – Jane Venn, the daughter of the Rector who provided 'the spiritual food' congenial to the Claphamites.[41] Two of their children carried the Sect's family names, Herbert Venn (who died aged twenty-four) and Frances Wilberforce, who died in infancy. In spite of these tragedies, Leslie described his mother as serene, reserved, commonsensical, competent, cultured, and with 'an entire absence of any morbid tendencies'. She kept an attentive diary (which Virginia would read)[42] of her children's behaviour and, especially after Herbert's death, dedicated herself as attentively – as would her son's wives – to 'cheering and sustaining' her difficult husband.

Virginia's grandfather, the Right Honourable James Stephen, author of *Essays in Ecclesiastical Biography*, became one of the most influential colonial administrators of the nineteenth century, known – only half-admiringly – as 'Mr Over-Secretary Stephen' or 'Mr Mother-Country Stephen'. His life's work, a family inheritance, was to carry out emancipation in the colonies – as Counsel to the Colonial Office and Board of Trade, and Under-Secretary (but in reality the dominant administrator) to the Colonies. It put him into perpetual conflict with the colonial governors; he was an unpopular as well as a powerful figure. Austere, shy, enormously learned and hard-working, he was a complicated person not much understood by those who worked for him. Public hostility to his campaign for emancipation encouraged what he himself described as 'a sort of morbid self esteem'. He was, as Leslie said, a 'thin skinned' man: 'He could not bear to have a looking-glass in the room lest he should be reminded of his own appearance . . . He could not bear that his birthday should ever be noticed.' But when he decided to talk, he 'talked enormously'. Leslie remembered him dictating to wife and daughter (women's work in the Stephen family) at such a speed that they could hardly keep up.

What he could not talk about, though – and neither could his wife – were his innermost feelings. These feelings were painfully sensitive. He would always anticipate the worst, he was often full of self-disgust. He would groan out loud to himself (just as Leslie would) and sink into 'depression and hopeless dejection'. The death of his first son Herbert, his anxiety for Leslie, who was a sickly child, and pressures of work, led to breakdowns, persistent and terrible headaches and the threat of 'brain fever'. His states of mind were alarming to him:

> Alone, I sometimes am oppressed by myself. I seem to come too closely into contact with myself. It is like the presence of some unwelcome, familiar, and yet unknown visitor. This is a feeling for which I have no description in words. Yet I suppose everyone has now and then felt as if he were two persons in one, and were compelled to hold a discourse in which soliloquy and colloquy mingle oddly and even awfully.

As a father, he was severe, and unremittingly vigilant over his children's behaviour, especially their use of language. 'The paternal is not usually an agreeable relation to the child', he wrote, sounding sad. 'How can any man be lovable who is seen with brows habitually overcast with care?' His daughter said it was like being brought up in a cathedral.[43]

It is too simple to describe the Right Honourable James Stephen as a deep-dyed Victorian patriarchal imperialist. A man powered by a social conscience and a rigid sense of justice, 'one of the great colonial administrators of the age',[44] he seems also to have been a casualty of the system into which he was built and which he helped to build. Leslie thought of his father as 'two persons in one'. That double nature – the rigid will and the thin skin – would emerge again in the next generation, particularly in Thoby. The family type is invoked at the beginning of *To the Lighthouse*, where Mrs Ramsay is looking at her son James, who has been given the Stephen family name as well as the Stephen face and destiny:

He had already his private code, his secret language, though he appeared the image of stark and uncompromising severity, with his high forehead and his fierce blue eyes, impeccably candid and pure, frowning slightly at the sight of human frailty, so that his mother, watching him guide his scissors neatly round the refrigerator, imagined him all red and ermine on the Bench or directing a stern and momentous enterprise in some crisis of public affairs.[45]

The 'stern', 'uncompromising' Stephen character was at its most unyielding in Leslie's older brother James Fitzjames, blustering journalist, penalising judge and scourge of liberal opinion. In old age Fitzjames developed senile dementia and died a broken man, overcome by work ('he did a quantity which was appalling – and killed himself by it,' Leslie said) and by the tragic insanity and early death of his brilliant son James Kenneth Stephen (whom he always refused to admit was mentally ill). Virginia was twelve when he died, and remembered her uncle and his wife as a tall, stiff, unapproachable couple. But in Leslie's youth he was the domineering brother, at Eton the big brave bully who learnt that 'to be weak is wretched', guardian to his frail little brother, at Cambridge the roaring British Lion of the Union and – unlike Leslie – the dynamic 'Apostle'. His character as 'a master of the slashing, exuberant, contemptuous' *Saturday Review* style and at the Bar is well vouched for: John Morley called him 'Bill Sikes converted by Jeremy Bentham' and the pioneering feminist doctor Josephine Butler was appalled by his power to hand down harsh sentences for prostitutes and 'fallen women'. He was 'a coarse cynical fellow,' she said, 'who should be the last to cast a stone at a woman'.

Stephen's hostility to feminism was notorious: he tangled in print with Millicent Fawcett and argued against John Stuart Mill over women's rights. A wife, he said, 'ought to obey her husband, and carry out the view at which he deliberately arrives'. But for all his coarse bullying chauvinism, and the disgraceful end to his career (he was asked to retire after a summing-up in which he said that an adulterous woman was likely to commit murder), he should be remembered too as a progressive reformer in the law, who argued that atheists should be allowed to stand as trial witnesses and that insanity could be pleaded in mitigation of offences.

For his niece, though, Fitzjames came to embody empire, chauvinism and patriarchy. When Virginia took her niece Ann ('an odd upstanding unmitigated Stephen') to see the film *Lives of a Bengal Lancer* in 1934 – 'about a handful of Englishmen ruling eighty million natives' – Ann was bored, but Virginia enjoyed it:

You imagine the old Colonel gashing his arm on a wild boars tusks and saying A mere scratch – for the honour of the Regiment. Now I shed a tear; thats what comes of being one generation nearer to Uncle Fitzy.[46]

Leslie grew up with a powerful sense of Fitzjames's superiority, which led in later life to mixed feelings: 'The great Sir James has at last been made a judge'[47] is an equivocal turn of phrase. In his biography of Fitzjames he dissociated himself from his brother's bullying authoritarianism. Still, the fact that he wrote the biography at all, and the difficulties he had with it (what would Boswell have done, he asked despairingly, if he had been Johnson's brother?),[48] suggest the continuing dominance of Fitzjames over his life.[49]

Uncle Fitzy's large family, living in their huge and 'hideous'[50] house in De Vere Gardens, would play a substantial and mostly unwelcome part in Leslie's children's lives. The four daughters, none of whom married – Katherine, who became Principal of Newnham between 1911 and 1920, Helen, who died at forty-six and whom Virginia could just remember playing Beethoven with 'the tramp of a regiment of dragoons',[51] and Rosamond and Dorothea, both fervently religious – were large, solemn, worthy girls, constantly caricatured by Virginia Stephen for their great 'elephantine' carcasses. Virginia came to admire 'old Kate' (photographs of whom at Newnham show the long, massive Stephen face) as a representative of her generation of pioneering single women educationalists. But pompous Dorothea, who became a religious teacher in India and wrote a book called *Indian Thought*, was anathema to her. The cousins' attempts to convert the Stephen girls 'rasped and agonised' them: 'As they were ugly women, who sweated, I conceived a greater hatred for them than ever for anyone.'[52] Dorothea's disapproval of the Stephen girls' later activities (the Dreadnought Hoax, Vanessa's domestic arrangements) met with cold ridicule and a lasting hatred for 'her sheer repulsiveness and obtuseness and stodge'.[53] Something of Virginia's violent feelings for Dorothea may lurk in Mrs Dalloway's repugnance for the pious, intrusive Doris Kilman.

Two of Fitzjames's sons became pillars of the legal establishment; Herbert, 'upright as a dragoon', was a great authority on criminal law, made a late marriage at seventy ('we Stephens mature late')[54] to a cousin called Hermione, another evangelical Cunningham, and wrote his memoirs. Harry, a high court judge in Calcutta from 1901 to 1914, married a niece of Florence Nightingale (a feminist writer whom Virginia admired).[55] Their son, whom Vanessa referred to as a 'super-oaf', became a Roman Catholic and had a severe breakdown.[56] Harry Stephen stayed in touch, providing an image for Peter Walsh in *Mrs Dalloway*, back from India with his pocket knife:

> Harry Stephen . . . who sat like a frog with his legs akimbo, opening & shutting his large knife, & asserting with an egoism proper to all Stephens, that he knew how to behave himself, & how other people ought to behave . . . The impenetrable wall of the middle class conservative was never more stolid . . .[57]

The Fitzjames family stood for that impenetrable wall. An inspired account of a family picnic with the widowed Lady Stephen and her children in 1899 shows that at seventeen, Virginia, writing with acerbic gusto, already had them pinned down as the representatives of the family type.

> They are immensely broad, long & muscular; they move awkwardly, & as though they resented the conventionalities of modern life at every step. They all bring with them the atmosphere of the lecture room; they are severe, caustic & absolutely independent & immoveable. An ordinary character would be ground to a pulp after a weeks intercourse with them. They are distinct & have more character than most of the world, so for that we will bless them & thank them sincerely. After we had rowed for an hour, the two boats came alongside & it was agreed to land in 10 minutes time. So we duly landed; & some of us sat down to make the kettle boil, & the others went for a dreary walk along the river brink. One remarkable sign of character in this race is that they are able to sit speechless without feeling the slightest discomfort while the whole success of the party they have invited depends on them. They acknowledge that it is drizzling & grey, that their guests are depressed & think the whole party a bore; they can bear the knowledge of these facts & support the discovery without turning a hair. I admire this as I should admire a man who could stand on the line immoveable while an express train rushed towards him. This kind of heroism however, is not calculated to smooth a tea party.[58]

The only cousin missing from this 'somewhat grim day of pleasure', the ghost at the picnic, was 'Jim', or 'Jem', who had died in horrible circumstances in 1892, when he was thirty-three. J.K. Stephen had been a brilliantly promising young man, a big handsome blond (Julian Bell would look rather like him, 'only so much saner'), an athletic star at Eton, an 'Apostle' at Cambridge, and author of a popular book of poetic parodies, *Lapsus Calami*, some of whose best jokes are still remembered.[59] There was a more dubious side to his character too. At Cambridge he was tutor to the Duke of Clarence, who was rumoured to be leading a 'dissipated and unstable' life – rumours which involved Jem Stephen. (This, with the evidence of a coarse misogynist streak in some of his poems, has led one historian to surmise that J.K. Stephen could have been the Whitechapel murderer, the legendary 'Jack the Ripper'.)[60] Even if the Stephen family – as seems more likely, given the insubstantiality of the proofs – was not harbouring a schizophrenic, psychopathic woman-killer, Jem's manic-depressive outbursts, which came on in his late twenties after a blow to the head from a windmill sail, did take alarming and violently sexual forms. Leslie described the depressive stage in a letter to his step-son George in 1890:

> We are uncomfortable about Jem. He lies in bed all the morning and seems unable to rouse himself to anything. I got him to come and play billiards on Saturday. We then proposed a walk on Sunday, but when the time came, he could not be roused to come out. It is very sad.

As the letter suggests, Jem was a regular inmate and visitor at his cousins' house, where he came in pursuit of the twenty-year-old Stella, with whom he was in love, and to whom he wrote pathetic, self-pitying letters. Virginia remembered 'this great mad figure with his broad shoulders and very clean cut mouth, and the deep voice and the powerful face – and the very blue eyes' telling them laughing that Dr Savage had said he was going mad, rushing into the nursery and spearing the bread, taking them off to his room in De Vere Gardens to paint Virginia's portrait, and having to be avoided by the back door of the house or told that Stella was away. He seems to have had the run of 22 Hyde Park Gate ('I cannot shut my door upon Jem,' Julia often said), and must have been an extremely disturbing and sexual presence: 'He always brings to my mind some tormented bull.' In the end he had to be sent away: Gerald Duckworth, who was at Clare College when Jem was going mad in Cambridge, described the crisis to Julia:

> The landlady called Humphrey and [Walter] Headlam who found Jem standing at his bedroom window naked and quite mad throwing all his things out of the window and singing. They quieted him down and telegraphed for Herbert and Harry [JKS's brothers] who came and Savage telegraphed to send him to an asylum at Northampton and two men came and with Harry went with him there. He of course did not know where he was going but only thought he was going into the country with Harry.

At the asylum, he alternated between violence and depression, refused food, and within three months of his admission had starved himself to death.[61] Dr Savage, who treated his mania with incarceration, would become Virginia's doctor soon afterwards: and no doubt the family connection was dramatically immediate to him.

This pitiful, violent figure, emanating from the heart of the solid, rational Stephens, was a distressing ingredient in the thick family plot. But there was an alternative and more benign legacy for Virginia from the Stephen line. In his early years at least, Leslie was very much closer to his sister, Caroline Emelia (always the victim of nicknames: Milly in youth, 'The Quaker' and 'Nun' in later life) than to his brother. Caroline Emelia's position as the intelligent only daughter in a family of extremely clever men is like Alice James's, and she made a similar retreat into invalidism.[62] The family version of her character was created by Leslie, and echoed to an extent by Virginia and by her nephew. This was of an ugly, ill, weepy, irritating lady, author of a book called *The Service of the Poor* (1871) which argued that the family depended for its survival on the unpaid labour of its unmarried daughters, dutiful chronicler of her father's life in what Virginia called 'a well worn semi religious vocabulary', helplessly devoted to Leslie and making a hash of looking after him and Laura in between his two marriages:

> Milly has loved me all her life . . . Julia used to say – of course affectionately – that she was altogether silly about me. Yet . . . she was too like me to be helpful . . . if I was sad, she began to weep – a performance which always came too easily to her.

This 'most depressing companion', who had had her heart broken by an unrequited love and her spirits broken by long nursing of her dying mother, and who had found her only consolation in the Quaker faith (a theology which 'leaves out the devil', Leslie said), was there at Leslie's deathbed 'always saying the one wrong thing', 'blowing her great nose louder than ever, and pouring tears down her pendulous cheeks'.[63] When Virginia was staying with her in Cambridge in 1904, to recuperate from the breakdown which followed Leslie's death, her pious memories of him were a source of extreme annoyance: 'Sometimes I can hardly sit still, she irritates me so . . . I cant tell you how she maddens me when she begins to talk about Father.' A few years later, a sentimental outburst from 'Nun' about Vanessa's first pregnancy was just as maddening: 'O Childhood! O Motherhood! O Lamb of Light! O Babe of Purity! O! O! O! Tell me my darling, how you feel this wondrous blessing? Ah God, I would as soon tell the butcher which was my jugular artery, or the thief which was my diamond ring. She hopes to suck blood and bread from me.' When she died, Virginia's 'respectful lamentations' for her in the *Guardian* concealed, she said privately, her true feelings: 'If one could only say what one thinks, some good might come of it.' Her pleasure in getting a legacy from her of £2,500 gross (a legacy which would later be mythologised as the means to a room of her own) was vitiated by the fact that Adrian and Vanessa only got £100 each. Looking back, she retained a distant memory of a 'poor old lady': 'There she sat in grey alpaca, with her geraniums and cyclamen about her, talking and talking. What was it all about, I wonder?' In short, according to Quentin Bell, 'she found her aunt a dreadful bore'.

But there is a more sympathetic way of reading Caroline Emelia's influence on Virginia Woolf's life. Earlier views of her as a friend of the Thackeray girls and a member of the Cameron/Tennyson 'set' at Freshwater suggest a sympathetic person. Violet Dickinson remembered 'Nun', a woman in a grey habit, 'tall and dignified, and a little pompous', becoming an 'object of interest' to her niece at the time of Leslie's last illness. Virginia wrote a 'comic life' of her (which has not survived), and praised the old lady's 'sense of humour'.

Caroline may have staged a quiet private revolution against Leslie's domination: 'The action of the spoilt child in him often had to me the effect of unkindness,' she told Maitland.[64] Quakerism allowed her to turn her back on the precepts of *The Service of the Poor* and to evolve an idea of a spinster's community, 'a nunnery of one'. The tone of *Quaker Strongholds*, certainly, could not be farther from the autocratic bluster of her brother Fitzjames: 'We do not much seek to surround our beliefs with precise verbal outlines . . . We have ever trusted to the influence of the Divine Spirit, rather than to any form of words, for guidance into all truth.'[65] Perhaps the woman who never stopped talking but wrote in praise of silence offered the example of an alternative 'form of words' to that of her brother. Virginia made a point in her obituary of praising her 'wonderful command of language' and her 'scrupulous wish to use it accurately'. Her aunt's peculiar eloquence had made a strong impression:

I have just come back from a Sunday with my Quaker Aunt . . . We talked for some 9 hours; and she poured forth all her spiritual experience, and then descended and became a very wise and witty old lady. I never knew anyone with such a collection of stories – which all have some odd twist in them – natural or supernatural. All her life she has been listening to inner voices, and talking with spirits: and she is like a person who sees ghosts, or rather disembodied souls, instead of bodies. She now sits in her garden, surrounded with roses, in voluminous shawls and draperies, and accumulates and pours forth wisdom upon all subjects . . . she is a kind of modern prophetess.[66]

No wonder that Caroline Emelia Stephen and her 'nunnery of one', as opposed to the 'phallocentric monument' of the *Dictionary of National Biography*, has been suggested as a feminist role-model.[67] But this doesn't allow for Virginia Woolf's distaste for her pieties. She may reappear as the visionary Mrs Swithin in *Between the Acts*, but her benign optimism is treated sceptically there. All the same, when Virginia wrote to Clive Bell after her aunt's funeral that it would have been better to 'dance round' a bonfire in the back garden than to have a conventional family burial service for her, she anticipates the wild party in *Three Guineas*, when the daughters of educated men 'dance round the fire' of the old hypocrisies and the old patriarchal educational institutions, 'and heap armful upon armful of dead leaves upon the flames' while their 'mothers lean from the upper windows and cry "Let it blaze! Let it blaze!" '[68]

Part of Virginia Stephen's irritation with her aunt in 1904 was that she could not bear to hear her lamentations for Leslie. It is a feature of intense mourning to feel proprietory about one's own version of the lost person. Virginia wrote and rewrote her father all her life. She was in love with him, she was furious with him, she was like him, she never stopped arguing with him, and when she finally read Freud in 1939 she recognised exactly what he meant by 'ambivalence'.

Leslie was fifty when she was born and seventy-two when he died. If he had lived to ninety-six – 'like other people one has known' – she imagined that 'his life would have entirely ended mine . . . No writing, no books; – inconceivable.'[69] She almost always wrote about him as an old man: first when she contributed to Maitland's biography, dwelling in the grief of loss on his kindness to them as children, and then, in private memoirs and in fictions, culminating in Mr Ramsay, dramatising him as the tyrannical egoist, the eccentric scholar, the grand, solitary, mournful Alpine stoic. In the 1930s, she wrote an affectionate centenary tribute to him, but she also used him for her politicised arguments against patriarchy in *The Years* and *Three Guineas*. When she began planning *To the Lighthouse*, in which he was at first going to be the central figure, she called it 'The Old Man'.[70]

Because of Mr Ramsay, and because of the well-known sombre, craggy, bearded photographs of Leslie, and because of the notorious stories of bad behaviour in old age, we too think of Leslie Stephen as an awful and comical old man, groaning on his way up to bed: 'Why won't my whiskers grow? Why won't my whiskers grow?' But at the end of her life, she tried to re-imagine him as young, like the children at the end of *To the Lighthouse* following Mr Ramsay 'as he sprang, lightly like a young man, holding his parcel, onto the rock'. In her late fifties, she at last wrote about him as someone separate from her, 'as he must have been, not to me, but to the world at large'. It is a vital moment in laying a parent to rest, and the fact that she did it so late tells us how entangled her feelings were with him all her life.

She had plenty of materials from which she could reconstruct the young Leslie.[71] She knew his biography, his mother's diary, the *Mausoleum Book*, the courtship letters of Leslie and Julia, and his early correspondence (which she had herself typed up for Fred Maitland). She could trace the Old Man back to a delicate, red-headed, bad-tempered 'little early Victorian boy, brought up in the intense narrow, evangelical yet political, highly intellectual, yet completely unaesthetic, Stephen family'. She knew the stories of his 'thin skinned' childhood: his violent temper and 'nervous naughtiness', his passionate reactions to criticism ('A hasty word will make him burst into fits of crying'), his 'morbid' sensitivity ('He hid under the table as if he could not bear to be looked at . . . He feels deeply and acutely, but will not let others observe his feelings'), his pleasure in birds, flowers and drawings, his physical addiction to poetry (lying in bed at night reciting it in a humming noise, which he called 'playing the band', flushing and weeping and trembling when he heard a stirring verse like 'The Last Days of Pompeii'), and the nervous exhaustion which made the doctors talk about the dangers of 'effeminacy' and brain fever and recommend prose and fresh air, so that the whole family had to move to Brighton for his health. She imagined him as a spoilt boy whose treatment in childhood in part led to his outbursts of intolerably self-centred behaviour. But these outbursts created for her the oddities and depths in an otherwise familiar type, 'like a steel engraving, without colour, or warmth or body; but with an infinity of precise clear lines'. The steel engraving outlined the 'obvious' Victorian story of how he was bullied at Eton, how he turned himself at Cambridge into a muscular oarsman, walker and climber, how he lost his faith (and gave up a clerical career) 'with such anguish, Fred Maitland once hinted to me, that he thought of suicide'; how he went to London to write for the papers, and travelled to America, and was 'the very type, or mould, of so many Cambridge intellectuals'.

In her last memoir, she moves about with wonderful imaginative fluency between his different ages, and merges the Victorian boy, the Cambridge intellectual, the tyrannical Old Man whose gloom and rages and deafness overshadowed her life between the ages of thirteen and twenty-two, and the influential man of letters in his middle years. She can just remember him as he was then, convivial, attractive to women, dining out – 'I can see him taking a lady downstairs on his arm; and laughing' – a well-known public and family man, with distinguished looks:

A very striking, indeed a magnificent figure; well dressed in his Hills Brothers' clothes; a swallow tail coat; very lean and tall and bent, with his beard flowing so that his scraggy tie scarcely showed. His chin I think retreated; perhaps his mouth, which I never saw, was a little looselipped; but his forehead rose and swelled; his skull was magnificent, with a little dent over the arch of the brain, that he made me feel once; and though his eyes were very small, with hairy eyebrows hanging over them, they were pure bright forget-me-not blue.

This 'striking figure' was the hero of a devoted group of male admirers: his New England intimates Charles Norton and James Russell Lowell (Virginia's god-father and Julia's adoring admirer), a few great writers such as Hardy, Meredith and James, and literary friends like John Morley and Fred Maitland. To them he was a loyal, truthful, even romantic character, an intellectual of pugnacious integrity who was also a great Alpine climber and the redoubtable leader of the 20-mile Sunday Tramps. The literary world knew him for his rational agnosticism, his 'determination to separate ethics from religion', his scholarly passion for the eighteenth century, his concern to place literary history in its social context, and his commitment to biography as an essential tool for historians and critics. This was not only as editor of the *Dictionary of National Biography* (for which he wrote many of the entries himself, until the work broke him) but also in his own dutiful biographies of his closest Cambridge friend Henry Fawcett and his brother Fitzjames, and his personal, vigorous lives of Johnson, Pope, Swift, Hobbes and George Eliot for John Morley's 'English Men of Letters' series.

Among the big Victorian male sages, Stephen is not much read now (compared with Carlyle, whom he reverenced but whose domestic behaviour – too like his own – horrified him, or Arnold, whose taste for 'Culture' irritated him, or Ruskin, who he felt did not appreciate him enough). It is hard to retrieve the sense of how influential his radical, independent-minded, forcefully-titled essays like 'An Agnostic's Apology' or 'Freethinking and Plainspeaking' or 'The Suppression of Poisonous Opinions' were between the 1870s and the 1890s. For some young men, he paved the way (like his beloved Meredith, like Gissing or Samuel Butler – all hugely influential figures in the death-throes of Victorianism, and now largely unread) for the intellectual revolutions of the next century.

Virginia Woolf's friend Francis Birrell (whose father had known Leslie) told her, while she was writing *To the Lighthouse*, that 'he dominated the 20th century'. 'He made it possible for me to have a decent life,' he said. 'He pulled down the whole edifice, & never knew what he was doing. He never realised that if God went, morality must follow. A remarkable man.' The anti-conservatism of Leslie's early years, which he shared with a 'vociferous group of middle-class radical intellectuals'[72] – his attacks on religion as the breeding-ground of intolerance and hypocrisy, his support for parliamentary and university reform, Irish independence and Church disestablishment – had settled by the time his daughter knew him into a gloomy political scepticism about national affairs and, in literature, a resistance to anything fanciful, what he would call 'morbid', 'humbug', 'sham' or 'sentimental'.

She always found Leslie's sharp strong tone attractive, even though it became a caricature of itself and would itself be caricatured by her. Leslie's voice comes through in his family letters – toe-stubbingly sending back a Christian gift of Coventry Patmore's poems from his pious mother-in-law with the words, 'I like my poetry hot and strong', or complaining to Thoby about the preparations for the Queen's Jubilee ('Nobody talks about anything else; and I am already sick of the whole concern')[73] – and in some of his more personal essays. His *Hours in a Library*, his accounts of the Alps in *The Playground of Europe*, or his picture of himself in 'A Bad Five Minutes in the Alps' hanging by his nails over a precipice and asking himself why he feels that 'this fag end of the game should be fairly played out, come what might' point up a fierce stoicism which she would develop herself. She could derive an intellectual satisfaction from reading him that had nothing to do with being his daughter:

> When I read his books I get a critical grasp of him; I always read *Hours in a Library* by way of filling out my ideas, say of Coleridge, if I'm reading Coleridge; and always find something to fill out; to correct; to stiffen my fluid vision. I find not a subtle mind; not an imaginative mind; not a suggestive mind. But a strong mind; a healthy out of door, moor striding mind; an impatient, limited mind; a conventional mind entirely accepting his own standard of what is honest, what is moral . . . I get a sense of Leslie Stephen, the muscular agnostic; cheery, hearty; always cracking up sense and manliness; and crying down sentimentality and vagueness . . . I admire (laughingly) that Leslie Stephen; and sometimes lately have envied him. Yet he is not a writer for whom I have a natural taste. Yet just as a dog takes a bite of grass, I take a bite of him medicinally, and there often steals in, not a filial, but a reader's affection for him; for his courage, his simplicity, for his strength and nonchalance, and neglect of appearances.

Given the domestic behaviour which could still make her shake with rage in her fifties, this is a remarkably fair-minded tribute, from one writer to another. But it is not, of course, unqualified.

Stephen's crucial weakness, she thought, was that he allowed himself to behave like a genius (badly, that is), whereas he was, as he once told her, 'only a good second class mind'. His obsession with his 'genius' and his reputation (made much of in the character of Mr Ramsay) was one of the things she most disliked in him. But it was also a point of resemblance. Leslie Stephen's daughter behaved like him in noticeable ways (as well as inheriting some of his literary tastes and manners), though we may prefer to account for this by citing influence rather than genetic inheritance.[74] Like her, he was a workaholic who pushed himself beyond his limits (a substitution for sexual appetites, his biographer suggests). She regarded this – only half-jokingly – as part of her family legacy:

> this influenza has a special poison for what is called the nervous system; and mine being a second hand one, used by my father and his father to dictate dispatches and write books with – how I wish they had hunted and fished instead! – I have to treat it like a pampered pug dog, and lie still directly my head aches . . . To think that my father's philosophy and the Dictionary of National Biography cost me this![75]

Like hers, his relation to his work was often self-tormenting. He was afraid of starting: 'The time it takes to screw up my courage to make the plunge is simply monstrous. I am an absolute coward about going into cold water or beginning work or reading reviews of myself.'[76] The big tasks he undertook became burdensome to him and he would 'howl' and 'groan' over them. Often he looked back on his own work with distaste. These fits of self-doubt would be re-enacted by his daughter, as would his symptoms of pressure – prolonged headaches, insomnia, irritability, anxiety. She borrowed his terms: 'fidgets' or 'a fit of the horrors' for a bad attack of anxiety, 'excited' for upset, and – as joke words of childhood – 'tantrums' and 'tantrumical'. She remembered, as a child, 'twisting my hair, imitating him. "Father does it," I told my mother when she objected. "Ah but you can't do everything father does," she said.' But that was exactly what she wanted to do.

And she was shaped too by wanting to do *nothing* that father did. Much of how she lived and wrote was formulated in reaction against him: his philistinism ('he never went to a play; never went to picture galleries; had no ear whatsoever for music . . . never troubled to visit Italy or France'), his emotional hypocrisy, his inability to deal with his own feelings, above all his bullying demands on those closest to him, which gave her her lifelong horror of domination. Two of her most important words come from her feelings about him. One is 'egotism'. She derived from his behaviour 'one obstinate and enduring conception; that nothing is so much to be dreaded as

egotism'. The other is 'sentimentalism'. Leslie Stephen despised 'sentimentalism', and indulged in it. Sentimentalism was effeminate: this was a
posture he had acquired at Cambridge. He and Fitzjames condescended to
Anny Thackeray because they thought her 'a sentimentalist', and he poured
scorn on those who make 'a luxury of grief and regard sympathetic emotion
as an end rather than a means – a need rightly despised by men of masculine
nature'. But his own gushing of needy emotion (the *Mausoleum Book* is
drenched with it) towards his women and his children, made his daughter
extremely self-conscious about sentimentalism. She resented its equation
with femininity, and was terrified of being satirised for it.[77]

Despite his obvious eminence, Leslie read himself as a failure, a 'jack of
all trades' whose name would only be mentioned in the footnotes of 'the
history of English thought in the nineteenth century'. He let out this
chronic self-doubt to his close men friends: James Russell Lowell, for
instance, consoles him well in 1891:

> How can you say that you are a failure? Everyone who has serious object
> in life must feel so. You have done and done it well on the highest levels of
> thought and your value is recognised by those who are the best judges. I
> love you none the worse for your modesty, but you are a swan taking
> yourself for a goose.[78]

But more often it was the women in his life – his mother, sister, wives,
sister-in-law, step-daughter, and daughters – who took the brunt of his
sense of failure, his appeals for reassurance and his anxieties about money.
The letters to Julia are sodden with the kinds of demands for reassurance
which Mr Ramsay is always making. Leslie, unlike Mr Ramsay, knew he
was doing it, but couldn't stop himself; it provided (as *To the Lighthouse*
brilliantly demonstrates) a form of sexual gratification: 'I have a hideous
trick of making myself out miserable in order to coax a little sympathy out of
you, because I enjoy being petted by you so much.' 'It is when something
happens to show me how little I have done, that I feel as if I should like a
little comfort and try to get it by complaining to you. It is a very bad habit.'[79]

Leslie Stephen's very bad habits have become legendary, mythologised.
They provide a wonderful example of the Victorian patriarch on whom
revenge has been taken by the daughter's writing. Readings of the Father as
Monster can easily portray the women in his life as his victims: the sister he
bullied, the backward daughter he drove to imbecility, the young first wife
he dominated, the sister-in-law he exploited, the widow he browbeat into
marrying him and then wore into her grave with his demands, the step-
daughter whose life he ruined with his possessiveness, the daughters whose

youth he darkened with his selfish grief and his assumptions of their servitude to him, and who only escaped to make their own lives by his death.

But Leslie as Bluebeard does not do justice to the extraordinary characters of many of these women. By his two marriages, Leslie became connected to women who would influence his daughter's life quite as much as he did.

Minny Thackeray, Leslie Stephen's first wife, has been embalmed in sweetness.[80] Virginia knew her only through the fluffy, wide-eyed Watts portrait in her father's study, his and 'Aunt' Anny's idealised reminiscences of her, and the difficult presence of Laura. Dead Minny provided a sanctified image of wifely womanhood; Laura the contradictory opposite, an unmanageable aberration from daughterliness.

The birth of Thackeray's pretty golden-haired third daughter (the second had died in infancy) had triggered the psychosis from which Isabella Thackeray never recovered. She was kept in private nursing homes for fifty-four years, until her death in 1894: Julia Stephen went to her funeral, a year before her own death. Harriet, always known as Minny, was petted by her famous, lovable father (who thought of his daughters as his 'two little wives'), and, after his death, mothered by her older sister Anny. Her marriage to Leslie Stephen in 1867 was not surprising: they moved in the same literary circles. Leslie was devotedly adoring: Minny was his little pet, his little flower, his little angel, and his retrospective language for her – sweet, childish, simple, pure – is all diminutive. He makes her sound like David Copperfield's Dora, sanctified for ever by her early death. Minny died awfully, at thirty-seven, in 'convulsions' from the premature birth of her second child, on Leslie's birthday – which he never celebrated again. She left him their five-year-old daughter Laura, a terribly puzzling and problematic charge for a broken-hearted widower incapable of looking after himself, let alone a child whose behaviour, over the next six or seven years, appeared increasingly peculiar and uncontrollable. The family theory was that Isabella Thackeray's 'madness' had skipped a generation; Leslie mentions having had some fears of Minny's 'inheriting' it, and there may be, in his insistence on her childlike nature and simple sweetness, a suggestion that Minny was in some way backward.

But there are hints that Minny was more vigorous than this. A memoir which Anny wrote for Laura in 1877 described Minny in her early twenties as a brilliant actress. Caroline Emelia talked of 'a rare sureness and delicacy in her critical intuitions, whether as to personal or literary qualities'. And Minny's voice, lingering on in a few letters and a diary she wrote for Anny when she and Leslie went to America in 1868, is funny and sharp.

It seems to me that we make life so much uglier and more expensive and uncomfortable than it need be, boxing ourselves up in stuffy streets, keeping a whole family of voracious servants, and bored to death by at least half the people one knows, and for this the poor master of the house has to toil and sweat for eleven months in the year, getting perhaps one month to breathe in.

Never will this country [America] be one at all, until they have learned to dine. It's perfectly monstrous and ridiculous – I now see what it is that makes them so savage against each other and us, it's hunger – and they think it's religious wrath – darling, couldnt you send me over a tin of pork pies or something. They have a horrid habit here of nibbling at some beastly stuff called popped corn, most nasty, exactly like the inside of quill-pens a little burnt – they say it is delicious – I expect I shall soon be nibbling at my boots, and Leslie asked me for a pair of gloves this morning in a very suspicious manner.

The recipient of Minny's lively letters was one of the most significant figures in Virginia Stephen's early life. Anny Thackeray's life was strangely involved with Leslie's – strangely, since no two people could have been less suited for intimacy. Her character – melancholy, energetic, restless, affectionate, optimistic, unworldly – was shaped by her tragic separation from her mother and her responsibility for Minny, her cosmopolitan (and often unhappy) upbringing in London and Europe, and above all by her dedication to her father, as companion, amanuensis, and last as editor. She was often unwell, suffering from frequent depressions, 'overwrought' states of mind (as in 1866, when 'I could see the characters of my story walking in the air very much smaller than life') and a hyperthyroid condition. Her style, in life as in writing, was famously inconsequential and rhapsodic. The books, tender personal novels of women's lives placed in her own childhood settings of France and London (*The Village in the Cliff*, *The Story of Elizabeth*, *Old Kensington*), a fictional life of Angelica Kauffmann, and many 'divagations' and reminiscences, were known for their impressionistic, loosely-structured charm.

Leslie was fond of her, but found her exasperating, and was driven to despair by her inventiveness with facts. They cohabited tolerantly while Minny was alive, but after her death Leslie's attempt to co-opt Anny, with his sister, as a support for himself and Laura was disastrous for both of them. He found her too weak with Laura, and he bullied her about money. Anny escaped, in 1877, by marrying her much younger (but very grave and responsible) cousin Richmond Ritchie, a marriage of which Leslie was furiously jealous – pointing ominously ahead to his behaviour with Stella

75

twenty years later. Anny had two children, whom Virginia thought very boring, and a good marriage. Richmond, to Anny's great anguish, died before her; she found some consolation in her grandchildren, in editing Thackeray, and in her memories.

Anny never abandoned Leslie or his family. She visited Laura regularly, and was a frequent guest at Hyde Park Gate, treated by the Stephen children (under parental guidance) as a figure of fun: 'Aunt Anny came for lunch, and was most amusing – As soon as she was out of the door after lunch, she said to father in a loud voice – "Oh Leslie what a noble boy Thoby is!" ' After Julia's death, at the time of Virginia's first breakdown, the Stephens stayed with Anny at The Porch (her cottage on Julia Margaret Cameron's estate at Freshwater, on the Isle of Wight); after Stella's death, Anny was one of their most consoling visitors: 'the dear little girls ran into my arms.' She was the only person who could make Leslie laugh on his death-bed ('Well Leslie – Damn – Damn – Damn!' she said once, coming in, before he could utter). And she remained attached to the orphaned Stephens and anxious about Virginia's health – though, as Virginia noted gratefully while writing her obituary, unlike the other elderly aunts, she left them alone, and 'had the wits to feel how sharply we differed on current questions'.

Virginia wrote about her 'Aunt Anny'[81] several times, taking a mellow, comic tone about her, whether she was reviewing her, or writing her obituary, or remembering her in the diary, or turning her into Mrs Hilbery in *Night and Day*. ('Everyone will know who it is of course,' Vanessa commented – and Lady Ritchie's children were indeed rather upset.) She always presents her as a writer of 'charm', 'magic' and 'buoyancy', whose prose 'appears to swim and float through the air rather than to march firmly with its feet set upon the ground'. But she always notes, also, her practical qualities and her 'flitting mockery'. Anny Ritchie's 'divagatory', improvising style (to an extent imitated from Thackeray) was an influence on Virginia Woolf. *Night and Day* could be read as a tribute, in mood and setting, to *Old Kensington*. And Anny's Utopian feminism foreshadows *A Room of One's Own* and *Three Guineas*: her interest in women writers like Mme de Sévigné and Jane Austen, her support for 'old maids' in her essay 'Toilers and Spinsters', and remarks such as this, in a letter to Fitzjames (of all people!) in 1870: 'If *all* women set their faces against war, it would do more than all the peace conventions.'

But what Anny Ritchie demonstrated above all to Virginia Woolf was the possibility of writing about the past in a personal and unofficial way, making 'an art of her own' out of her reminiscences. Her memories of Thackeray, Charlotte Brontë, George Sand, Tennyson and all the other great figures who surrounded her in childhood provided 'a transparent medium through which we behold the dead'. 'We feel that we have been in the same room with the people she describes'; her 'tender and radiant' snatches of vivid memory bring the dead back to us more than any 'stout official biography'. Lady Ritchie's benign relation to the past colours Virginia Woolf's own portrait of her. She comes to stand for all that 'old 19th Century Hyde Park Gate world'. As Mrs Hilbery, moving among the memories of the past she wants to bequeath to her daughter, she speaks in a mystical, Sibylline language (one of Lady Ritchie's books was *A Book of Sibyls*) which evokes something of the effect of her personality on the next generation:

'If I could help you, Katharine, by the memory of what I felt – '
'Yes, tell me what you felt.'
Mrs Hilbery, her eyes growing blank, peered down the enormously long corridor of days at the far end of which the little figures of herself and her husband appeared fantastically attired, clasping hands upon a moonlit beach, with roses swinging in the dusk.
'We were in a little boat going out to a ship at night,' she began. 'The sun had set and the moon was rising over our heads . . . It was life, it was death. The great sea was round us. It was the voyage for ever and ever.'
The ancient fairy-tale fell roundly and harmoniously upon Katharine's ears.

Mrs Hilbery also embodies Anny Ritchie's more exasperating qualities of absent-mindedness and fatuous optimism (which she recognised in herself, referring in letters to 'my Mrs Nickleby incoherence'). When Virginia writes about her 'Aunt Anny' she enjoys dwelling on the famous family stories of her eccentricity: 'She lost trains, mixed names, confused numbers, driving up to Down, for example, precisely a week before she was expected, and making Charles Darwin laugh – "I can't for the life of me help laughing," he apologised. But then if she had gone on the right day, poor Mr Darwin would have been dying.' Molly MacCarthy tells similar anecdotes of Anny Ritchie (a relation by marriage) in her memoirs: at Poets' Corner in Westminster Abbey, for instance, gently insisting on having the whiskers on Thackeray's bust, which she had always thought too long and wanted to have clipped, whittled down by a reluctant sculptor: 'Aunt Anny is a little emotional as she gets into the victoria, smiling at her tears, then weeping again; she is triumphant, for it has been a great relief to her mind.'
Virginia Woolf makes a point in her obituary of saying that it is superficial to sum her up as a sentimentalist, as her father so often did. It is as if she is arguing out loud with him. And, at the time she is writing this, she is thinking about eccentricity. A remark in the diary in January 1919 ('I think

one day I shall write a book of "Eccentrics" ') precedes an essay called 'The Eccentrics',[82] written close in time to her obituary for Anny. It begins by saying that if you are known as an eccentric, you are hardly likely to find your monument in the *DNB*. But the lives of the eccentrics – the fantasists, the obsessionals, the misfits – may be of more interest than the 'solid and serviceable', publicly accredited lives which went into her father's *magnum opus*. The examples she gives are almost all women, most of whom she writes about elsewhere: Margaret Fuller, Lady Hester Stanhope, the Duchess of Newcastle – and her own great-aunt, Julia Margaret Cameron. Anny Ritchie is not cited, but she belongs here as a model both liberating and dangerous. Eccentricity – in Anny's case, comical absent-mindedness and optimism, vagueness and inaccuracy – could be a form of defence for a woman writer, allowing her to create her own peculiar style in the teeth of male disapproval. To be considered eccentric – harmless, amusing – might be a protection against being thought mad. But to be called eccentric is also to be laughed at and marginalised, and possibly not to be read. In Virginia Woolf's lifelong enquiry into what it means, in life and writing, not to belong, to be odd and idiosyncratic, Anny Ritchie was an important example.

FOUR

Maternal

For we think back through our mothers if we are women.

And the phantom was a woman, and when I came to know her better I
called her . . . The Angel in the House . . . And when I came to write I
encountered her with the very first words . . . And she made as if to guide
my pen . . . I turned upon her and caught her by the throat. I did my best
to kill her . . . Had I not killed her she would have killed me . . . She died
hard . . . She was always creeping back when I thought I had despatched
her.[1]

These two famous (but not often juxtaposed) quotations from Woolf on
women writers and their mothers are troublingly, troublesomely contradictory. Should we think through our mothers, or kill them? Must we kill the
ghosts for whom we feel (and who feel for us) such a fatal attraction, who are
always creeping back to life when we thought they were dead? And does
'thinking through' mean well or ill: Do we learn from our mothers, or react
against and reject them? Virginia Woolf's feelings about her mother were
powerful, difficult and mixed. They make it hard (for us and for her) to
imagine Julia Prinsep Jackson Duckworth Stephen as herself, not as Mrs
Ramsay, or as the Angel in the House.[2]

The first time Virginia Stephen wrote about her mother, in her
chivalrous portrait of the 1908 'Reminiscences', she drew to a close with a
strange sentence: 'Where has she gone? What she said has never ceased.'
This peculiar grieving formulation of an absence, an interruption and a
continuation would be returned to for the rest of her life. Coming to terms
with this interruption, laying this ghost to rest, is one of the secret plots of
Virginia Woolf's existence.

The usual formulation, which she set up, is that her father's death was a
blessed release (he 'could have been 96 . . . but mercifully was not. His life
would have entirely ended mine')[3] and her mother's 'the greatest disaster
that could happen'. But suppose her *mother* had been ninety-six? She would
have outlived her youngest daughter by a year. And what then? No
departure from Kensington – no shedding of Duckworths – no Bloomsbury

– no Jewish husband – no *To the Lighthouse*. . . ? Or would Virginia and her siblings have discounted Julia's views, left her behind, and visited her occasionally out of a sense of duty (as she and Leonard periodically visited *his* demanding old mother) – a deaf, tiresome, toothless, aged Victorian lady? When she tries to think of her mother in 'the world of the living', she cannot 'see her in that way at all'.[4]

The impossibility of translating her mother from the past into the present is deep inside the story of Lily Briscoe and Mrs Ramsay in *To the Lighthouse*. Virginia Woolf transforms her personal feelings in the novel: Lily is the artist, not the daughter. All the same, Lily is given the daughter's responses to and memories of her mother. After Mrs Ramsay's death, Lily, trying to re-create her, sometimes thinks of her almost condescendingly:

> Oh the dead! she murmured, one pitied them, one brushed them aside, one had even a little contempt for them. They are at our mercy. Mrs Ramsay has faded and gone, she thought. We can over-ride her wishes, improve away her limited, old-fashioned ideas. She recedes further and further from us . . . Life has changed completely. At that all her being, even her beauty, became for a moment, dusty and out of date.[5]

But poor Mrs Ramsay, dusty, defunct and faded in her pre-war past, is also the object of Lily's grief and desire. *To the Lighthouse* is not so much 'about' Virginia Woolf's parents as about what to do with them, how to think them through or 'think through' them. And, for all the father's power, it is above all about how the daughter can bring the mother back and let her go, can go beyond the pain and rage of her loss ('to want and not to have – to want and want') to the possibility of loving but not needing her: 'to stop asking of the mother more than she can give.'[6] Virginia Woolf twice said that she let go of her parents by writing *To the Lighthouse*. First, about a year and a half after finishing the book, in her diary for 1928, when she imagines what would have happened if her father had lived to ninety-six, she says, 'I used to think of him & mother daily; but writing The Lighthouse laid them in my mind'. Second, very much later, in the 'Sketch of the Past', she describes having been 'obsessed' by her mother until she wrote the book at forty-four (Lily Briscoe's age at the end of the novel). Then:

> I ceased to be obsessed by my mother. I no longer hear her voice; I do not see her.
> I suppose that I did for myself what psychoanalysts do for their patients. I expressed some very long felt and deeply felt emotion. And in expressing it I explained it and then laid it to rest.[7]

This is a satisfying and consolatory statement; but it may also be a simplification. There might be other ways of reading the plot of her relationship with her mother's ghost. It seems, for instance, that she goes on to have a more political, less helpless, less internalised debate with her after exorcising her in *To the Lighthouse*. Only then does she embark publicly on the feminist writings where she has the argument with the Angel in the House which Lily is always having, internally, with Mrs Ramsay: 'That's what you feel . . . that's what I feel.' It's possible too that she partly deals with that 'deeply felt emotion' by transferring it to other women, primarily Vanessa (who has a great deal to do with the character of Mrs Ramsay) and, later, Vita Sackville-West. And perhaps she does not exorcise her mother as completely as she tells herself she has. She goes on, after *To the Lighthouse*, calling her death to mind, and is still trying to describe her – and still finding it difficult – at the end of her life.

'What was the problem then? She must try to get hold of something that evaded her. It evaded her when she thought of Mrs Ramsay.'[8] Lily acts out Virginia's own difficulty. When Vanessa wrote to her sister after reading *To the Lighthouse*, she told her that she had raised their mother from the dead: 'It was like meeting her again with oneself grown up and on equal terms.' But twice in the letter Vanessa uses the word 'difficult': making one feel her beauty must have been 'the most difficult thing in the world to do'; portraying father 'perhaps . . . isn't quite so difficult'.

Virginia also uses the word 'difficult' whenever she tries to write about her mother. Like Lily's picture, the portrait of mother in the 'Sketch of the Past' is constantly snagging on questions of difficulty: 'why I find it now so curiously difficult to describe both my feeling for her, and her herself'; 'why it is now so difficult to give any clear description of her'. Her mother has become 'rubbed out and featureless'. She can hardly ever remember being alone with her: 'Someone was always interrupting.'[9]

Why was it so 'difficult' to get Julia back? Obviously, because she died when Virginia was thirteen. But there were other reasons too. She seems to have been reticent and aloof, and her past was kept mysterious. She was – all agreed – very beautiful and very sad, and these two qualities overloaded her image and tended to cancel out other features. She left no diary or autobiography and very few of her very many letters have survived. She spread herself thinly between a great many people: husband first, eight children, hypochondriac mother, aunts, sister, sister's family, brother-in-law's family, endless further relatives, friends, the sick and the poor. Virginia in 1936 is sent some pictures of St Ives: 'my mother sitting on the lawn just as she used to sit surrounded by dogs and children and innumerable visitors and the old postman and the fishermen'.[10] 'Someone was always interrupting.'

When she tries to bring her mother back, she always invokes a few characteristic gestures or attitudes: her 'clear round voice', her vivid manner of speech, her quickness, her swift upright walk, her look, usually direct, or askance in sadness, her way of making people laugh, her own laugh dipping down into 'three diminishing ahs' ('I sometimes end a laugh that way myself'), her square-tipped hands with their rings and silver bracelets, rubbed swiftly together or raised 'in gesticulation as she spoke', her sharp, severe, practical, unaffected manner, and her withdrawals into melancholy: 'behind the active, the sad, the silent'. These features are all meshed together in Mrs Ramsay, whose beauty and sadness is always mixed with 'something incongruous' ('She clapped a deer-stalker's hat on her head; she ran across the lawn in goloshes to snatch a child from mischief').

The quick, competent, sharp side of Julia can be heard in some of the family documents. She seems to speak out loud through some of the phrases in Stella's diaries: the news of a baby 'red in the body but a good face', the return to St Ives ('garden rather a wilderness'), the comments on the new gardener ('young man seems fairly intelligent') or on a friend ('nice little person but I can't help feeling that he does not care enough for her').[11] Her personality is detectable everywhere in the *Hyde Park Gate News*, which is anxious to please her, in references to her matchmaking, her fears for her children's health, her pleasure at the boys' school prizes, and her nursing, or in more detailed glimpses of her coping with burst pipes or evicting an unsatisfactory dog or seeing off a boring visitor: 'She made but a short stay luckily for Mrs Stephen who literally clapped her hands when she was (we hope) out of hearing and out of the door.' And she gets into the children's revealing fictions – about a little girl whose mother hardly ever praises her, or Miss Smith who gives up women's rights because 'no one took much notice of her', and feels the need 'of someone stronger and wiser than herself' so much that she becomes an excellent wife and mother.[12] And in Julia's own stories for children, her brisk speaking voice can be glimpsed: 'What a fidget you seem in' . . . 'That's the use of accounts, Father always says, to tell one how quick money goes' . . . 'She had her bit of soap but you can't do much washing with a dry bit of soap.' And occasionally, a more sombre tone: 'Was there never to be anything but darkness and quarreling?'

But it is hard for us too to extricate this woman from the gaze of her admirers. She has become the deep-socketed, hollow-eyed, far-gazing widow in her aunt Julia Margaret Cameron's intensely romantic shadowy photographs, with her straight, fine, centre-parted hair, and her severe high-necked dark dresses. She is Burne-Jones's Virgin in his *Annunciation* of 1879, one hand to her breasts, one to her frail draperies, a smooth helmet of parted hair, huge eyes, modestly suffering the gaze of a very feathery angel. She is the saint of Leslie Stephen's *Mausoleum Book*, so beatified – for all his agnosticism – with reverential language ('beauty of soul', 'such tenderness as makes my heart tremble') that the wife he fears he may have treated badly in her lifetime evaporates in a cloud of incense. Similarly, she is the anonymous archetype of the lecture he gave shortly after her death on 'Forgotten Benefactors', those obscure heroes and (especially) heroines who surrender their selves in love, learn from their own grief to sympathise with and relieve the sufferings of others, and seem 'formed by nature for ministering angels'. She is the object of idealised memories – such as those of the actress Elizabeth Robins, who told Virginia in 1928 that her mother was 'the most beautiful Madonna & at the same time the most complete woman of the world'[13] – and of devoted love letters, like those of Leslie's courtship, distressed at her melancholy, awed by her beauty. James Russell Lowell's laboriously flirtatious correspondence (did Leslie not realise that one of his best friends was half in love with his wife?) smothers her in devotion, as here, on seeing 'one of Mrs Cameron's large photographs of you with your hair about your shoulders pretending to look the other way but looking at me all the same out of the corner of your eye with a certain severity as who should say, "Though appearances be against me – I am *not* St Mary Magdalene . . . and my hair *is* becoming isnt it?" ' He idolises her: 'I lay my hand on my left breast and there is no palpitation there. Who is the thief? I shan't apply at Scotland Yard.' 'My Pallas Athene.' 'Age can never disfigure a face like yours.'[14] You expect him at any moment to say, as Mr Bankes thinks of saying to Mrs Ramsay, 'Nature has but little clay like that of which she moulded you'.

These are private documents. Literary tributes were paid to Julia Stephen, but she was not a public person. Virginia did not write a published obituary for her (the nearest she came to it was an essay on 'Pattledom' in 1925), as she did for Leslie, Anny Ritchie, Mrs Cameron and Caroline Emelia. In her lifetime Julia Stephen came into the public eye only with a short essay on nursing, *Notes from Sick Rooms*, an entry in the *DNB* on her aunt Julia Margaret Cameron, one or two letters to newspapers, and as a signatory of an *Appeal against Female Suffrage* in the *Nineteenth Century* magazine in 1889. Her family also read her children's stories (illustrated first by Leslie and many years later, by Vanessa) and, possibly, her unpublished essays on the morality and work ethic of 'agnostic women' and on the current debate on domestic service.

The point of view revealed by these writings is decisive, conservative and pragmatic. The children's stories, written in the early 1880s,[15] are family tales with a message. Naughty children make their own punishments, little sisters are devoted to their brothers and want to grow up to be nurses, and over-philanthropic Jellyby-type parents are reproached (as perhaps Julia sometimes reproached herself) for neglecting their own children:

> 'We shall see a great deal more of Mama then than we do now,' said Bob. 'Isn't she all day long among the poor, and doesn't she always say that though she wants to be with us, she must first think of others? Well, now we shall be the poor, we shall be others, and so she will come and look after us. Perhaps she might even teach us. You know she has one crossing sweeper in her night school.'

The stories display the accepted attitudes of their time and class – Jack's parents are 'in India among the blacks, as Nurse had said'; Maggie and Bob sell their possessions to a cunning Jewish pawnbroker, 'a very dirty looking old man with a hooked nose and long fingernails'. But class pretensions are squashed: a family of pigs is mocked for wanting to dine with the aristocratic bears in their castle, and Maggie is horrified at the thought of having to go and live in 'the suburbs'.

Julia's criticisms of social prejudice are echoed in the stories of the *Hyde Park Gate News*, where a mother tells her daughter to put forth all her powers of 'snobsnubbing' against a vulgar suitor, two country ladies pride themselves on living entirely 'among the happier sets' and seeing very little of 'the lowest of the low, the poor working classes', and a middle-class philanthropist who decides to live in the London slums is despised by his aunt for giving his life to 'degraded specimens of mankind, who were always killing someone, or going on strike'. Clearly Julia's children were being brought up *not* to be snobsnubbers. But her stories' pills are nicely sugared with vivid descriptions of London and Cornwall, lots of animals, including marmosets (the magical country of Emlycaunt is 'the place full of all the animals the children have been kind to') and a great deal of satisfyingly detailed food: 'On birthdays, the children always chose their dinners and Tommy had chosen roast turkey and raspberry puffs; then they toasted chestnuts on the hob.'

Her belief in mutual responsibility – children's, parents', servants' – is firmly voiced in the essays on the matriarchal duties of employers towards their live-in domestic staff (there is no shame in dependence, since 'as surely as we know anything we are convinced that dependence on each other is the most unvarying as it is the happiest law of life') and in her defence of agnostic women as nurses and teachers. She makes much of the virtues of sympathy, reserve and self-control. The agnostic woman may be more useful in charity work because 'the very negativeness of her position may possibly help her to sympathise with the various and widely divergent characters with whom she has to deal'. The nurse must learn silence, calm and forbearance, as well as the practical skills (which Julia outlines with experienced exactness) of turning the patient, making sure the milk is good, or getting rid of crumbs in the bed: 'Bathing and drying must be done in silence. The useless remarks in which attendants indulge are absolutely injurious to sick people. The "All right", "Oh, here it is!", "Wait a moment", irritate and take away all the refreshment which the bath would have given.'

These writings have now been published[16] as part of the twentieth-century feminist resuscitation of 'obscure lives': a movement enormously influenced by Julia Stephen's daughter, but which she herself would have viewed with distaste. She was a woman who believed in working for good, in a practical way, in her immediate domestic circle and through benevolent institutions. She seems to have fully endorsed the Victorian models for female behaviour, as found in Dickens's Esther in *Bleak House*, or in the argument of Ruskin's 'Of Queen's Gardens', or in Tennyson's *The Princess*, or – come to that – in Coventry Patmore's *The Angel in the House*. She was opposed to female suffrage and thought women should only be educated for domestic careers. The romantic Pre-Raphaelite image we have of Julia – as virgin, young mother with child, mater dolorosa, muse, beloved – is a political image, embodying the acceptable roles for a beautiful middle-class woman in the nineteenth-century.

Virginia Woolf spent much of her writing life exposing and analysing those roles, but also in looking longingly back to the world which engendered them. There is an extraordinary gap between her satirical repudiation of acceptable behaviour for women in *Three Guineas* or *The Years*, and the affectionate yearning with which she recalls the culture of her mother's generation. When, in *A Room of One's Own*, she compares the kind of 'tune' – 'a sort of humming noise' – arising from a post-war lunchtime conversation in Cambridge and from the Victorian poets (Christina Rossetti, Tennyson's *Maud*) it is the world of her mother's youth she is looking back to.

Why has Alfred ceased to sing

    She is coming, my dove, my dear.

Why has Christina ceased to respond:

My heart is gladder than all these
Because my love is come to me?

Although the whole essay is concerned with changing the assumptions about women which that poetry embodied, she misses the 'old feeling' – what she calls in 'Reminiscences', her first attempt to write about her mother, 'all the golden enchantments of Tennysonian sentiment'. She evokes her mother's family environment – the world of the old feelings – with a mixture of sentiment and affectionate ridicule, making a Victorian genre painting (and in *Freshwater* a Victorian nonsense comedy) out of it:

I think of it as a summer afternoon world . . . Long windows open onto the lawn. Through them comes a stream of ladies in crinolines and little straw hats; they are attended by gentlemen in peg-top trousers and whiskers. The date is round about 1860. It is a hot summer day. Tea tables with great bowls of strawberries and cream are scattered about the lawn. They are 'presided over' by some of the six lovely sisters; who do not wear crinolines, but are robed in splendid Venetian draperies; they sit enthroned, and talk with foreign emphatic gestures – my mother too gesticulated, throwing her hands out – to the eminent men (afterwards to be made fun of by Lytton); rulers of India, statesmen, poets, painters. My mother comes out of the window wearing that striped silk dress buttoned at the throat with a flowing skirt that appears in the photograph. She is of course 'a vision' as they used to say; and there she stands, silent, with her plate of strawberries and cream . . . The sound of music also comes from those long low rooms where the great Watts pictures hang; Joachim playing the violin; also the sound of a voice reading poetry – Uncle Thoby would read his translations from the Persian poets. How easy it is to fill in the pictures with set pieces that I have gathered from memoirs – to bring in Tennyson in his wideawake; Watts in his smock frock; Ellen Terry dressed as a boy . . . But if I turn to my mother, how difficult it is to single her out as she really was; to imagine what she was thinking; to put a single sentence into her mouth! I dream: I make up pictures of a summer's afternoon.

'Do you find any charm in the 1860s?' she wrote to her friend Nelly Cecil in 1915. 'They seem – my mother's family I mean – to float in a wonderful air – all a lie, I dare say, concocted because one forgets their kitchens and catching trains and so on.'[17] That the charm was not entirely illusory is attested to in memoirs galore, celebrating the highly coloured, idiosyncratic, energetically creative, comfortably-off milieu of Julia Jackson's youth, a mixture of Anglo-Indian colonials, Pre-Raphaelite artists, and beautiful girls. Though it seemed to Virginia Woolf to float in the past, it

just overlapped with her own life. Her relatives – Anny Ritchie, her cousin
Herbert Fisher – vividly remembered what Fisher called the 'elysium' of
Little Holland House in Melbury Road, Kensington, where Julia's aunt and
uncle Sarah and Thoby Prinsep had their extraordinary salon, and that
other famous centre of 'Pattledom', Julia Margaret Cameron's 'Dimbola',
(named after her husband's Ceylon tea-plantation), and the neighbouring
cottages, at Freshwater on the Isle of Wight. One of Virginia's strongest
memories of her mother was of going with her to Melbury Road. She gave a
little spring forward, clapped her hands, and exclaimed: 'That was where it
was!' And though Little Holland House had gone, Holman Hunt was still
living in the 'Aladdin's cave' of Number 18, Melbury Road. Virginia was
taken there by George Duckworth in 1905 and heard the old painter (who
had once proposed to her mother), 'dressed in a long Jaeger dressing gown',
sipping cocoa, stroking his flowing beard, and holding forth on *The Light of
the World*.[18]

'Oh the old Pattles! They're always bursting out of their casks.'[19] The
reference is to the sensational end of Julia Jackson's grandfather, James
Pattle, notorious liar and drinker and member of the Bengal Civil Service,
who reputedly drank himself to death and whose body, sent back to
England in a cask of rum, exploded out of its container during a storm. The
shock drove his widow mad and she died on the journey home; the sailors
drank the rum. This Pattle story was always popping up: on a visit in 1918 to
the redoubtable Lady Strachey Virginia and Leonard heard 'how old Pattle
shot out of his tank, & thereby killed his wife, who thought him come to life
again'.[20] There was an even more sensational version of the same story in the
reminiscences of Ethel Smyth, which Virginia read in 1919, long before
they met. Virginia relayed it with relish in her essay on Julia Margaret
Cameron, and it's there again, a family heirloom, in Quentin Bell's
biography – though a less sensational and possibly truer version does not
mention the widow's insanity, and maintains that it was James Pattle's
brother, Colonel William (known as 'Jemmy Blazes', and leader of a famous
charge against the Amirs of Sindh in 1843), who drank himself to death.[21]

What is certain is that the Pattles were conspicuously active and affluent
members of the Anglo-Indian governing classes; James's father Thomas
worked under Warren Hastings and several of his daughters married into
the Calcutta gentry. Colonial society, attitudes and traditions were
embedded in the fabric of Julia Jackson's maternal ancestry, just as the legal
history of colonial government ran as the main thread through the Stephen
family tree. Indian heirlooms litter the family house and the family pages.
One of Julia's stories has a family of children running across Kensington

Gardens to visit their Aunt Lizzie, just back from India, whose rooms are like a 'big curiosity shop': 'Big boxes and tin cases stood, standing half open, with bits of rough yellowish linen peeping out. Great china jars lay on the floor, and odd ebony chairs, carved with strange beasts, were piled up with shawls and bundles of embroidery.'[22] There is even, much to the children's delight, a 'native' servant with a parrot.

These heirlooms of colonial rule spill over into Virginia Woolf's fictions, where they are viewed with a critical, distanced eye. Katharine Hilbery needs to escape from the house that is full of memorials from the uncle who rode to the Relief of Lucknow. Mrs Ramsay's view of the other sex – that they 'negotiated treaties, ruled India, controlled finance' is rendered defunct by the end of the novel. By the time of *The Waves*, the upper-middle-class male destiny of ruling India, for which Percival's education has formed him, seems a comic project:

> But now, behold, Percival advances; Percival rides a flea-bitten mare, and wears a sun helmet. By applying the standards of the West, by using the violent language that is natural to him, the bullock-cart is righted in less than five minutes. The Oriental problem is solved.[23]

Mrs Ramsay is given, as part of her inheritance, 'the blood of that very noble, if slightly mythical, Italian house, whose daughters, scattered about English drawing-rooms in the nineteenth century, had lisped so charmingly, had stormed so wildly'. In the manuscript of the novel, her ancestry is the French house of Clareville – more like the alluring Sally Seton in *Mrs Dalloway*, who 'always said she had French blood in her veins, an ancestor had been with Marie Antoinette, had his head cut off, left a ruby ring'.[24] This alludes to one of Virginia Woolf's favourite pieces of family history. James Pattle of Calcutta made a romantic marriage to a French aristocrat, Adeline de l'Etang, the daughter of the Chevalier de l'Etang, who had been a page – possibly a lover – to Marie Antoinette and an officer of the Garde du Corps of Louis XVI, and had married the Indian-born Thérèse Blin de Grincourt (not, as the family legend had it, one of the Queen's maids of honour). The story went that he was exiled for being too close to the Queen; or (less probably) that he was present at her execution in 1793 and escaped with his wife to India. In any case, that was where 'he survived, an adventurer, turning defeat into opportunity',[25] and cutting a dashing figure in Calcutta society as master of a riding school. His wife returned to Versailles after his death and lived to a great old age. Herbert Fisher, Virginia's cousin, who reconstructed the Chevalier's history in his autobiography, said that his family were always proud of the 'French connexion', and identified with France. Julia gave her son Gerald 'de l'Etang' as his middle name, and Virginia liked to claim her French ancestry:

> If you want to know where I get my (ahem!) charm [she wrote to Ethel Smyth], read Herbert Fisher's autobiography. Marie Antoinette loved my ancestor: hence he was exiled; hence the Pattles, the barrel that burst, and finally Virginia.[26]

The famous Pattle sisters, daughters of James and Adeline, with their legendary beauty (not much admired by Leonard Woolf, who found their portraits insipid and over-feminine)[27] were the toast of Calcutta and Kensington. 'They created some stir in Victorian society', said one of their grandsons, Herbert Fisher, 'by their good looks, warm hearts, and high-spirited and unconventional ways'.[28] 'Wherever you go in India you meet with some member of this family. Every other man has married, and every other woman has been, a Miss Pattle.'[29] Two of the beauties, Virginia (whom Thackeray described as too handsome even to think of falling in love with) and Sophia (who came to be known as 'the improper Monte Carlo Great Aunt')[30] made aristocratic marriages. Snobbish Aunt Virginia put her own daughters through 'torture' to marry them off to the Duke of Bedford and Lord Henry Somerset (a marriage which broke up in disaster because of his scandalous homosexuality; Lady Isabel, publicly disgraced, subsequently committed herself to the Temperance movement). The other Pattle girls – Adeline, who died young, Louisa, Maria (Julia's mother), Julia and Sarah – all married into Anglo-Indian administrative families. The two most interesting and closest sisters, Sarah and Julia, moved to England. One was married to a Director of the East India Company and Persian scholar, Thoby Prinsep, the other to the first lawyer on India's Supreme Council, Charles Cameron (described by Leslie in the *DNB* as 'a man of cultivated intellect, well read in classical and modern literature'). They collected around them a huge circle of Anglo-Indian, literary, artistic, and political friends: Gladstone, Sir Henry Taylor, Jowett, Herschel, Watts, Ellen Terry, Burne-Jones, Joachim, Tennyson, Browning. Thackerays and Stephens crossed paths here: Leslie met and admired Julia at Little Holland House in the mid-1860s, when they were both still single; and felt a pang of jealousy on hearing of her marriage.

Julia Margaret Cameron died three years before Virginia Stephen was born, and Sarah Prinsep when she was five. But their flamboyant, domineering and affectionate characters were vivid to her. The cultural social life of these two 'eccentric' sisters, with their doors always open to talent and distinction, and a great bustle of home entertainments always in play, provided a congenial model for Virginia and Vanessa Stephen. Clapham, so often cited as Bloomsbury's spiritual ancestor, was perhaps not so influential as Freshwater or Little Holland House. Julia Margaret Cameron's impetuous, despotic energies, bursting out in letters and hospitality and (at last, at fifty) in photography, was a rich source of inspiration. Her photographs, taken from Hyde Park Gate to Gordon Square, greatly influenced the tone of *To the Lighthouse*. And the fabulous stories of goings-on at 'Dimbola' ('Is there *nobody* commonplace?' complained Caroline Emelia Stephen) came pouring out in Virginia Woolf's essay on Cameron for the Hogarth Press edition of *Victorian Photographs* in 1926, in her drafts of a nostalgic story called 'The Searchlight'; ('the rooks were crying and calling over Faringford Wood. "Maud, Maud, Maud" they were crying and calling'), and in her play, *Freshwater*.[31] She had noted the subject's comic potential as early as 1919, had drafted the play in 1923, and completed it in 1935 for a production put on for friends in Vanessa's studio in Fitzroy Street, very much in the spirit and tradition of home entertainments at 'Dimbola'. In *Freshwater*, Tennyson recites *Maud* and pronounces on art ('Facts are the death of poetry'), Ellen Terry sits on his knee, poses for her husband 'Signor' Watts as Modesty crouching at the feet of Mammon and then runs away with a sailor, Mr Cameron discourses on Confucius and moonshine. Mrs Cameron orders their coffins for their return to India (Ceylon, in fact, where they spent their last years) and bullies her guests into photogenic attitudes for her notoriously long exposures: 'Sit still, Alfred. Don't blink your eyes . . . Now, keep perfectly still. Only for fifteen minutes.' The jokes in *Freshwater*, especially the 1923 version, set Victorian sentiment ('Take my lens' says Mrs Cameron, 'see that it is always slightly out of focus') against Bloomsbury freedoms and sexual candour: Ellen Terry is running off to Gordon Square from Signor's beliefs ('religion . . . symbolism in art . . . purity, modesty, chastity') and wants to swap veils for trousers. All the same, the moonshiny ideals and raptures of 'Dimbola' exert a powerful attraction.

In actuality, those female relics of the Pattle line who affected Virginia Stephen's childhood were not so enchanting. 'Cousin Mia', daughter of the beautiful Louisa, was a large, nosy and 'petty-minded' old lady who represented for Virginia the constrictive feminine behaviour of a whole age and whose death seemed like the removal of 'an incubus – a giant cucumber'. Her notes on Cousin Mia MacNamara (which did not get into her 'Sketch of the Past') read as an anthropologist's specimen of a tribe threatened with extinction:

Cousin Mia. This relic of the great Victorian age was almost a museum piece. She was massive. Sunday morning was her time . . . Chicks, she would say. The chicks look blooming. There would follow a list of catastrophes . . . Perpetually 'hurt'. This was a Victorian malady. I hurt her by forgetting to thank for a watch . . . Then, Cousin Mia was supposed to be an angel domestically. To remember every birthday, all anniversaries. This set the pace. When one forgot, she was hurt: I could not have believed it possible. I am more surprised than I can say. Strictures on behaviour. 'Sweet' was the prize. Few won it . . . Her face always looked grumpy. Tragedies were the breath of their nostrils. Some small boy died of an operation. This was delightful . . . Then 'unselfishness' was at a premium . . . It seems a morbid life now: choked with draperies and ornaments. I think perhaps . . . dimly foreseeing that the family was not to survive . . . Like cows uneasily aware of the thunderstorm. So historically Cousin Mia has some importance and dignity. She was the mother feeling her office in danger; feeling society coming to an end . . . and of course suffering from the Indian Empire. So history will see those Vn. mothers; doomed; but fighting – under a cloud of ignorance. They could not foretell 1914, let alone Hitler. But looking back I think they had premonitions; and that they grasped teapots so hard because they were to be smashed.[32]

Julia's sister Aunt Mary also came to stand for a rejected model of Victorian womanhood.[33] She married Herbert Fisher, tutor and private secretary to the Prince of Wales, and brought up a gigantic family of eleven children, who were significant and largely unwelcome presences in Virginia's childhood. Virginia liked the lively, animal-loving oldest daughter Florence, who married Fred Maitland – and after his death Francis Darwin – and whose intense, sensitive daughters (for whom their mother was a 'Grecian goddess'), the high-mindedly named Fredegond and Ermengard, would play some part in Virginia's adult life. And she had a grudging respect for Herbert, alias H.A.L., distinguished historian and President of the Board of Education, whom she visited occasionally at Oxford. But most of Aunt Mary's children – emotional Adeline, who married Ralph Vaughan Williams; difficult, unstable Emmeline; poor Hervey, whose spine was injured by being dropped on his head as a child, who had his unsuitable engagement blocked by his mother, and who was incarcerated in an asylum; naval commander William (who was to be outraged by the Stephens's offensive against naval decorum, the Dreadnought Hoax), and their 'poor stuffed beast' sisters, had a depressing effect on their Stephen cousins. Herbert Fisher thought his mother a saint: 'A more selfless being never drew breath.' Precisely these qualities made Aunt Mary anathema to the Stephen children, who saw her as a 'washed-out ghost' and always cited her when a 'creeping Jesus' example of saintly self-sacrifice was required, or when recalling 'the horror of family life, and that terrible threat to one's liberty'. When she was run over by a taxi-cab it seemed, Virginia said heartlessly to Vanessa, 'a positive stroke of genius – I mean the discomfort and self-sacrifice of it'.

Julia's other sister, the melancholy Adeline Vaughan, had died just before Virginia was born, her peculiar husband four years after. But the next generation of Vaughans – Adeline's orphaned daughters, Marny and Emma, and her son William's wife, Madge (daughter of John Addington Symonds) – were quite another matter. Virginia much preferred them to the Fishers, and they counted to her a great deal, for a time. In the huge clan of Stephens, Fishers, Ritchies, Maitlands and Duckworths, only these Vaughan girls, though some years older than Virginia, were friends as well as relatives; and these were not friendships which lasted into adult life.

Julia sustained family links with as much energy as her daughters – especially Vanessa – would put into breaking them off. Of the three Jackson sisters, she was the closest to Maria her mother, who was stiflingly dependent on her. Indeed Virginia remembered Maria Jackson as a literally stifling presence: 'my grandmother who was so beautiful and smelt so delicious but one had to take a deep breath before one kissed her or one would be suffocated – she held one so long in her arms.'[34] Poor clinging Maria, by all accounts the most puritanical and ascetic of the Pattle sisters, married a Calcutta doctor who, according to Leslie, somehow 'did not seem to count' in the family circle. After his death (when Virginia was five) Mrs Jackson spent a great deal of her time at Hyde Park Gate, but long before then she had enlisted her youngest daughter as confidante, helper, and nurse-companion in her perpetual quest for a rheumatism cure. Maria wrote daily to Julia (and to her children), little querulous missives in black-edged envelopes, full of protective endearments (my own Heart, my own Lamb, my Angel Child), of symptoms and medical details ('My inside has been bothering me in the old way, he advised me to increase the dose of Rhubarb . . .' 'She says it is impossible that Gruyère cheese should have remained two years in the bowels and I suppose it is chemically impossible'), of fears and anxieties (to George: 'I hope you *never* eat sausages, they are such dangerous things'; to Stella: 'My darling never be out late in the afternoon alone . . . Never trust to anyone but a Policeman'), and of troubling dreams ('I dreamt last night that I said to you that my hair had so fallen off lately and you said, "Yes what a difference it makes" – as it does!'). Quentin Bell, in the family tradition, calls her a goose. But in one of her letters she exclaims, 'I feel like a female Woodhouse!' The allusion to

Jane Austen's hypochondriachal parent in *Emma* suggests that she half knew what she was like.

Mrs Jackson's dependency suggests the extent of Julia's commitments to duty. Virginia's theory was that she compensated for a profound sense of life's futility by an exhausting investment in useful toil. She had been passionately in love with Herbert Duckworth, her first husband, a handsome and possibly rather dim young lawyer, described by Leslie as a 'thorough country gentleman' with a sweet temper. His sudden death, after four years of marriage, when she was twenty-four and pregnant with their third child, was her life's catastrophe. Stella Duckworth, their daughter, told Virginia that Julia used to lie on his grave, and Mrs Cameron, writing effusively to her sister when Julia engaged herself to Leslie, remembered her saying, after Herbert's death, 'her sweet large blue eyes growing larger with swimming tears Oh aunt Julia only pray God that I may die soon, that is what I most want'.[35] She lost her faith (much to her mother's dismay) and her capacity for happiness: 'I have got so used to a shadow everywhere', she wrote to Leslie, 'that I dont know if light is possible for me.' She turned herself into a deathbed attendant, the person of whom it would always be said (as Leslie said to her): 'If I were dying I should long to have you by my side.' Leslie complained bitterly that she sacrificed herself too much. But it was presumably that very attraction to suffering which drew her towards a morose middle-aged widower for her second husband. She knew him well. Leslie's writings on agnosticism were a powerful influence on her in the years of her bereavement. She had visited him and Minny – and felt excluded by their happiness – the night before Minny died; she supported her good friend Anny Thackeray's choice of husband against Leslie's disapproval, and she had been trying to advise him about Laura for some time. Julia Cameron, with her usual peculiar intuition, saw how it was: 'I have so long felt that Leslie was your fate', she wrote to her 'cherished' Julia: 'I felt of him "the shadow sits and waits for her" . . . I felt that sitting ever close to you – tall, wrapt in gloom, companionless, and silent, he would make an appeal to you which would be powerful because of the vastness of his intellect.'[36]

Julia herself must have seen that it would be a taxing relationship. It seemed, retrospectively, to her children – and to Leslie too – that he wore her out with his demands for support, his 'fits of the horrors', and his anxieties about work and money. ('I was not as bad as Carlyle, was I?' is the question that lurks behind the *Mausoleum Book*. 'If I felt that I had a burden upon my conscience like that which tortured poor Carlyle, I think that I should be almost tempted to commit suicide.') The terrible problem of Laura, Leslie's awkward attempt to father the Duckworth children, his breakdown over the *Dictionary*, all these factors contributed to Julia's exhaustion. But she may, also, have chosen to punish herself and to wear herself out. Mrs Ramsay does not kill herself, we presume, but she has a strong inclination for death.

As a couple the Stephens were a grand and sombre pair. Henry James, though fond of Leslie, was amazed that the charming Julia 'had consented to become, matrimonially, the receptacle of Leslie Stephen's ineffable and impossible taciturnity and dreariness,'[37] but together they seemed to reinforce the 'tragic atmosphere' which Thomas Hardy always sensed around Leslie.[38] One of their close friends, Lucy Clifford, remembered them visiting her husband just before his death: 'They both looked tall and grave and thin, as if they remembered a world of sorrow, and understood ours, and were half ashamed of the happiness they had recovered for themselves.'[39] The social tone of Julia's Sunday afternoons and their occasional dinner parties[40] was bookish, bourgeois, unglamorous, even perhaps a little dowdy. Henry James and Browning came to dinner, but so did Leslie's dingy, learned old Cambridge friends and a stream of gushing ladies – Kitty Lushington and her sisters, the Stillmann girls – all marshalled by Julia into making polite and charming conversation with the men. There was not much showiness, not much brilliant *fin de siècle* badinage – both Leslie and Julia despised flashy *arrivistes* and conspicuous consumption – and the dining-room carpet was faded. Though Leslie was outspoken and often rude, there were clear codes of social conduct, and no sexual explicitness.

Looking back at their courtship letters, their daughter, late in her own life, wrote: 'How beautiful they were, those old people – I mean father and mother – how simple, how clear, how untroubled . . . Nothing turbulent; nothing involved; no introspection.'[41] It is a surprisingly benign reading of what she had, elsewhere, also described as a destructive and dark relationship. But it pays tribute to something dignified and heroic about Julia and Leslie Stephen which is corroborated in other versions of their marriage. They shared a view of life as work ('For the night cometh, in which no man can work'), a refusal of Christian consolations, a great admiration for each other, and passionate literary tastes. It is appropriate that in the best-known photograph of them together, side by side on the sofa in Talland House, they are both reading.

Lurking behind them in the corner of the room in that photograph is Virginia Stephen, aged ten, who is staring at the back of her parents' heads. Perhaps she wanted them to turn round and take notice of her – to 'read' her, instead of their books, as she would in so much of her writing 'read' them. They both died before she had begun to prove herself as a writer, but it is probable that her writer's life was driven by the desire to say 'look at me!' to those two exceptional and critical parents. A passage in *Mrs Dalloway*, where a woman in her fifties is thinking of her dead father and mother, suggests this:

> For she was a child, throwing bread to the ducks, between her parents, and at the same time a grown woman coming to her parents who stood by the lake, holding her life in her arms which, as she neared them, grew larger and larger in her arms, until it became a whole life, a complete life, which she put down by them and said, 'This is what I have made of it! This!'[42]

FIVE

Childhood

When Virginia Woolf researched the novel, *The Years*, which made an X-ray of her childhood as a prototype of Victorian patriarchal repression, she read up the history of her own period. She took twenty-three pages of notes on R.H. Gretton's 1930 *Modern History of the English People 1880–1920*.[1] These were some of her annotations:

1882: Ireland bombs. Parnell. 1883: m. womens property act. Missing Link at Aquarium. Thought reading and table turning looked into. Ballooning. 1885: Fall of Khartoum. Fabian society founded. A summer of most unusual heat – 90 in the shade. 1886: Gladstone comes in – Question of Home Rule. The riot in Traf. Squ. Dogs muzzled. Fencing taken up by women. Newspapers largely occupied with celebration of Queens Jubilee. 1888: The union of match girls. Parachutes from balloons. Electric light in home to home scheme. phonograph. Jack the Ripper. 1890: Parnell. Tate Gallery projected. Gambling by working men. O'Shea case. 1891: The split over Parnell in the Irish Party. Influenza. Man who broke the bank. White man's burden – Kipling. Death of Parnell. 1892: Tararaboomdeeay.[2] Tendency of average man to make more of his own interests. Oscar Wilde. Barrie. Tess. Paderewski. W. suffrage defeated. 1893: Why educate workmen. Home Rule Bill. Second Mrs Tanqueray. Modern girl: bicycles. lawn tennis. The Boer War. Oscar Wilde downfall. Cycling allowed in Hyde Park. 1896: Dr Jameson raid. Incandescent gas – craze for bicycles. 1898: Dreyfus. 1899: The weekend habit. Tremendous entertaining. Womens extravagance. Women for the first time bought papers in the street. 1900: People broke laurel leaves from the Queens wreaths at her funeral.

Through this mixture of sociological data and historical fact (with its telling emphasis on the Irish question and women's issues), she reconstructs the period of her own childhood, which seems almost as distant to her in 1932 as it does to us over sixty years later.

We are sharply cut off from our predecessors [she writes in 1923]. A shift in the scale – the war, the sudden slip of masses held in position for ages –

has shaken the fabric from top to bottom, alienated us from the past and made us perhaps too vividly conscious of the present. Every day we find ourselves doing, saying, or thinking things that would have been impossible to our fathers.[3]

She is talking about books, but she uses the language of family history. The particular, exceptional story of Virginia Stephen's first years was set in a late Victorian milieu which, by the 1920s and 1930s, seemed 'sharply cut off'. We look back as through the end of a telescope at these details of her childhood: visits to the animatograph at the Regent Street Polytechnic, views of the 'scarlet gentlemen' going to the Queen's Levee, diphtheria scares, a penny peep-show at Brighton of the execution of Mrs Dyer the baby-murderer (which broke down because 'something had to be done to the electricity'), or the terrible fire in the Paris charity bazaar which killed large numbers of the French aristocracy and pushed the Graeco-Turkish war off the front pages of the newspapers.

The children's alphabet games in the *Hyde Park Gate News* are as eloquent of their period as bookjackets or newspaper advertisements or theatre playbills:

> A for Prince Albert/ So good and so kind/B for the Black Prince/ Who was never behind/C for Carlyle/ A great author was he/D for Drake/ Who sailed o'er the sea/E for Miss Edgeworth/ Who wrote many books/ F for the Frenchmen/ Who take care of their looks/ . . . S for Leslie Stephen/ Who lives in Hyde Park Gate/T for Mr Thackeray/ Who had a witty pate/U for Fisher Unwin/Who publishes many things/V for Victoria/Descended from many kings . . .

A glance at *The Times* in the 1890s gives us the daily stuff that fed into this middle-class London childhood: the notices for Variety Shows and Madame Tussaud's, for Madame Clara Butt's Grand Morning Concert at the Queen's Hall, and for the *Yeoman of the Guard* at the Savoy (seen by the Stephens), the advertisements for station broughams and electric baths, the appeals for ladies' maids, governesses, travelling companions and gentle-women as companion housekeepers, for houses to let for the season, for Orphan Asylums and Hospitals for Incurables. Most eloquent of all about the jingoism and vulgarity of the *fin de siècle* are the sales of flags and souvenirs and programmes for the Queen's Diamond Jubilee in 1897. The Stephen children (without Leslie) watched it from St Thomas's Hospital: 'troop after troop – one brilliant colour after another. Hussars, & Troopers & Lancers, & all manner of soldiers – then Indian Princes, & at last carriages with the little Princesses & the big ones . . . the Queen . . . smiled & nodded her poor tired head.'[4] *The Times* gave 'heartfelt thanks to heaven for the prolongation of a reign which has brought manifold blessings not upon the British Empire only, but upon the whole race of man'.[5]

That late-Victorian context would be the stuff of satire and subversion in all Virginia Woolf's writings. Nevertheless, the memory of that childhood was so close and clear to her that it felt, all her life, more like a continuing existence than a memory.

> Is it not possible – I often wonder – that things we have felt with great intensity have an existence independent of our minds; are in fact still in existence? And if so, will it not be possible, in time, that some device will be invented by which we can tap them? I see it – the past – as an avenue lying behind; a long ribbon of scenes, emotions. There at the end of the avenue still, are the garden and the nursery. Instead of remembering here a scene and there a sound, I shall fit a plug into the wall; and listen in to the past. I shall turn up August 1890. I feel that strong emotion must leave its trace; and it is only a question of discovering how we can get ourselves again attached to it, so that we shall be able to live our lives through from the start.[6]

Her 1930s technological vision[7] of a wireless of memory which could be tuned into the past – the ghost in the machine, waiting to be received – suggests how powerfully she was haunted by her childhood. She uses the word 'intensity' to describe, not her memory, but the childhood experiences themselves. And from the evidence of anecdotes and memoirs and her own fragmentary memories a childhood of 'great intensity' and 'strong emotion' can be reconstructed.

She was born into a family situation of considerable stress. Julia and Leslie were both at points of great tension. Julia was not a professional nurse, but, at a period when people mostly died at home, and family members with nursing skills were much in demand at relatives' death-beds, she was perpetually 'on call'. Her commitment to nursing conflicted with her attention to her large family. Leslie complained persistently about her absences. Between 1878, the year of her marriage and of Vanessa's conception, and 1892, when her mother died, Julia attended a series of illnesses which taxed her emotionally as well as physically. In the months leading up to her marriage, she was nursing her dying uncle Thoby Prinsep (of whom she was much fonder than she was of her father), and then looking after his distraught widow. She was unwell herself, and 'felt the effort'.[8] When Vanessa (born in May 1879) was six months old, Julia went to Eastnor Castle in the Malvern Hills (the home of her posh aunt Virginia Somers) to nurse her mother's rheumatic fever. Thoby, her next child, was born in September 1880. Seven months later, in April 1881, Julia was away again to her unhappy sister Adeline, dying of heart disease in a gloomy house in Pembrokeshire. Her letters home, Leslie remembered, 'were the saddest she ever wrote to me'.[9] Adeline died on 14 April; Julia's third child by Leslie was conceived as soon as she came home, and named after her dead sister. But 'as Julia did not like to use the name full of painful association', the name Virginia (after Lady Somers – with financial benefits in view?) was added, and the first name, shadowed by death and grieving, was never used.

When Virginia was two and Adrian, born in October 1883, was three months old, Julia was at the death-bed of her old friend Susan Lushington (whose daughter Kitty would play chaperone and mentor to the young Stephen girls). In 1885, her widowed brother-in-law Halford Vaughan died: you mustn't feel remorse, Leslie wrote to her, for not having been able to help him enough. Two years later, when Virginia was five, Julia's father died. She nursed him, and then spent long weeks at Brighton looking after her mother – leaving Stella, aged eighteen, in charge of a resentful Leslie and all the 'little ones'. In 1888 the younger children had severe whooping-cough; then Leslie's health failed; then Jem Stephen broke down; and then, a month after Jem's death, Mrs Jackson died at last, in April 1892, at Hyde Park Gate. Deaths were part of the plot of the first ten years of Virginia Stephen's life.

Throughout Julia's pregnancy with Virginia, Leslie was extremely anxious about her: she was wearing herself out. 'You must get strength for the next child,' he wrote to her three months before Virginia's birth, 'and if possible, you must not have another'.[10] She had had a difficult time with Vanessa's birth three years before, and Thoby was only two. But Adrian, Julia's 'Benjamin', was conceived a year after Virginia's birth, quickly displacing her as the favoured youngest child. After his birth Leslie and Julia must have been more careful.[11] For a woman who had her first baby at twenty-two, whose first husband had died while she was pregnant with their third child, who had taken on the charge of a difficult eight-year-old with her equally difficult second husband, and who then had four children in five years, seven was enough. They thought themselves lucky, in a time of large families and high infant mortality, not to have 'lost' any of their offspring.

Leslie may have been anxious for Julia's health, but he was exhausting her the most. In the year of Virginia's birth, he was labouring with a different kind of gestation. The *Cornhill Magazine* was flagging, and the publisher George Smith suggested that Leslie give up the editorship in order to embark on the *Dictionary of National Biography*. From then on, for nine years, he committed himself to the massive undertaking of marshalling a team of 653 contributors, editing the articles of the first twenty-six volumes, writing 378 entries himself, endlessly proof-correcting (not his *forte*) and corresponding. By the end there would be sixty-three volumes of 29,120 lives: a monument to Victorian industry, a tomb for Leslie Stephen's health.[12] The first volume came out in 1885. Already it seems to have been perceived by the children as a blight: Thoby at five brought Leslie a 'contradictionary box' which he said was 'full of rubbish'.[13]

At the same time Leslie was asked to give the Clark lectures at Trinity College Cambridge. He wrote twenty of them, but thought 'the whole thing was a blunder', 'a waste of time and an excessive burthern upon my strength'.[14] Then his old friend Henry Fawcett died in 1884, and he dutifully wrote the Life. By the mid-1880s Julia was as worried about his health as he had been about hers, and in 1888, when Virginia was six, his mental and physical state was distressing. The *DNB* office was his 'place of torture'. He had 'fits of the horrors', recurring headaches, terrible sleepless nights when only Julia could 'put me off to sleep like a baby' – at the cost, of course, of her own sleep. The family doctor, Dr Seton, diagnosed a sluggish liver and said that the work had to stop. He wrote to Julia: 'If Mr Stephen could be mentally released from the incubus of this Dictionary, he would be much better in health. After all, what benefit to him and his children if his health fail him from the worry and care of this book!' And he prescribed ammoniated tincture of quinine, thirty to sixty drops, in half a wineglass of water three to four times a day. Leslie was sent off to America for a rest: on his way there, he wrote to Julia: 'Someone threw themselves overboard from steerage. After all, it is a cleaner way of committing suicide than most.' In 1891, his assistant Sydney Lee took over, finally freeing Leslie from the 'burthern', but leaving him feeling more than ever a failure. 'I was dreaming all last night,' he wrote to Julia in 1893 from St Ives, 'or so it seemed, about missing a train . . . or rather letting a train go off without me.'[15]

Work, health, and money (about which he was irrational and obsessive, though he had a small private income, was never at risk of poverty and left £15,000 when he died)[16] were grave preoccupations when Virginia was born. But the worst anxiety was Laura, who was twelve in 1882. After Leslie's death, when Virginia was recuperating from her breakdown in Cambridge, and reading through her parents' letters for Fred Maitland, she wrote to Violet Dickinson that 'the history of Laura is really the most tragic thing in his life I think; and one that one can hardly describe in the Life. The letters are full of her.'[17] Her own first years coincided with the most acute phase of this tragedy; the presence of Laura was part of the 'strong emotion' of Virginia's childhood.

Laura had been born prematurely in 1870 – weighing under three pounds, she was wrapped in cottonwool for three months. She was slow to speak and to teethe, but her mother did not notice anything wrong. It was only after Minny's death, when Laura was five, that Leslie began to be anxious. Over the next few years his letters were indeed 'full' of her – her impossible, baffling behaviour and his thwarted attempts to control her. Anny Thackeray and Caroline Emelia Stephen both tried to deal with Laura during that time, but Milly, though she tried to be strict, could not manage her, and Leslie found Anny 'too soft' with her, and preferred to put his faith in a German nurse whom Anny distrusted. (In later years, Anny was the only person Laura responded to with affection or behaved with normally.)[18] He increasingly turned to the widowed Julia for advice; it was one of the main things that drew them together, and in their letters they discuss their views on, for instance, the education of girls, with Laura as their subject. (Leslie wanted Laura educated well enough to earn a living; Julia was quite opposed to his views on 'female education'.)[19] In 1877 he appointed Julia her guardian. Laura was eight when they married, and was moved in with a new mother and a family of children about her own age, who complained loudly about her backwardness.[20] Over the next four years, Leslie and Julia became increasingly distressed by her. Virginia was born into the middle of this anxiety.

What was wrong with Laura? This can only be deduced from the reactions to her, since she is the one member of the family whose voice we cannot hear. (There is one letter thanking Julia for birthday presents, dictated to Leslie when she was nine, which begins, touchingly, 'Happy Mother, You are a very good person; you are too kind to me'.) It was that sort of gratitude and responsiveness which was wanted from her, but which was not usually forthcoming. She was slow to read (though she did manage to, since in 1886 we hear of her reading *Alice in Wonderland* to Thoby), could not learn to write, and could not concentrate. She chattered excessively ('her little tongue is going faster than a pack of hounds'), she had some odd vocal mannerisms ('a queer squeaking or semi-stammering or spasmodic uttering'), she was given to uncontrolled gestures like spitting out or choking on her food, she was accident-prone (did the iron jump out, or did she let it fly from her hand, asked Mrs Jackson in a letter of 1883), and she howled and shrieked, in what Leslie described as 'fiendish' bursts of temper, 'dreadful fits of passion'.[21] 'All in all she was extremely disturbing and extremely pathetic.'[22]

It's been observed that it was a 'sentimental' Victorian habit of mind 'to think of abnormal children as retarded rather than insane, as babyish rather than psychotic'.[23] Leslie treated Laura as backward and wilful, and was upset and enraged by her 'wicked' behaviour, her recalcitrance at her lessons, and what he often called her 'perversity': 'It seems as though she had a dim consciousness that there was something bad in her – as if she had a small mind somewhere almost quenched by her strange perversity.'[24] He lost his temper with her, knew that this was counterproductive, but found her 'obstinacy' 'intensely provoking': 'I long to shake the little wretch.'[25] His irritation and frustration, and his fear that Laura placed an intolerable burden on Julia, reached their peak in 1882.

Julia, too, made a moral reading of Laura's abnormalities (in her stories for children, naughtiness is always a self-inflicted punishment) and tried to discipline her. At one point Leslie felt 'uncomfortable' at her decision to give Laura 'stronger doses' – of sedation, or of punishment?[26] But really they did not know what to do. They tried a kindergarten, a governess, a separate room in the house. Stella agreed with Julia that a 'Rational Corset' would be 'the thing for Laura'; she would get one 'on approval'.[27] In 1884, Leslie did not want to put her in a special school – 'I cannot think that it would be good for her to be with idiots'[28] – but gradually he gave up on her, and she had to be sent away. Exactly when this took place is a little uncertain. Virginia remembered Hyde Park Gate housing the person she referred to not as her half-sister but as 'Thackeray's grand-daughter, a vacant-eyed girl whose idiocy was becoming daily more obvious, who could hardly read, who would throw scissors into the fire, who was tongue-tied and stammered and yet had to appear at table with the rest of us'.[29]

This may have gone on until the early 1890s. The *Hyde Park Gate News* for 1891 suggests that Laura was still living with the other children and coming to St Ives in the summer; they called her 'Her Ladyship the Lady of the Lake' and played teasing games with her. Thoby included her in his letters from school in the early 1890s. But by 1893 she was being 'visited' by Julia at Earlswood, an 'idiot asylum' in Redhill, and Leslie was saying sadly that 'she fills less of my life than she used to do'.[30] Stella reported in 1896 that she was 'just the same – takes no notice. But her talk was less noisy'.[31] Early in 1897 the doctor from Redhill set up his own 'establishment' in Southgate and Laura was moved with him; Leslie and Stella visited her, but 'she is apparently unable to recognise any of us clearly' and 'is only talking to herself all the time'. 'I want you to remember her', Leslie wrote to Thoby in 1897, 'and see she is properly cared for.'[32] He appointed his niece, Katherine Stephen, as her guardian, and in later years she occasionally reported back on Laura's behaviour. In 1921, when Laura was fifty-one, she was apparently 'the same as ever, and never stops talking, and occasionally says, "I told him to go away" or "Put it down, then", quite sensibly; but the rest is unintelligible'.[33]

In the most damaging and sensational reading of Virginia Stephen's family life, Leslie has been criminalised for his intolerance of Laura, and indicted for brutality and sadism. Perhaps Laura was not abnormal at all, but traumatised by the early loss of her mother and the move into the new household. Perhaps Leslie punished and 'imprisoned' her because she refused to obey him. Perhaps he retrospectively developed a belief that she had inherited a mental condition from her grandmother, Isabella Thackeray, in order to deny the possibility that she might have inherited any mental instability from *him*, and to absolve himself from charges of cruelty. Perhaps she was abused by the Duckworth boys, and 'I told him to go away', forty years later, was a message to that effect.[34]

A less inventive view of the case would argue that 'unless biological mechanisms can beyond a reasonable doubt be eliminated as the cause of a child's mental problems . . . blaming the parent is merely a witchhunt masquerading as science'.[35] It is impossible to read this difficult family story without bringing contemporary prejudices about nineteenth-century attitudes to mental illness – and to daughters – into play. My reading of the evidence suggests not a sadistic patriarchal conspiracy, but an unimaginative and disciplinarian response to the dilemma of caring for a child who was suffering from a mental disability, possibly a form of autism, which may have been inherited from either side of the family.[36] Leslie Stephen seems to have been confused, emotional and incompetent, rather than vicious. He followed the standard thinking on mental disorder which equated wickedness and insanity, and called for the exercise of 'self-control'.

Leslie's forceful attempts to educate and normalise Laura may have exacerbated her condition. His own thin-skinned temper and his demanding attitudes to women evidently played a damaging part. There is a great deal of unexamined egotism in his demand for her to be *lovable*, in his constant complaints that she would never be able to make people 'fond of her'.[37] His assumption that she was 'backward', and could be ordered forward, seem only to have frustrated them both. And it is likely that his expectations of proper 'daughterly' behaviour, so painfully thwarted by Laura, were switched with self-consoling intensity – and with powerful effects – on to his other daughters.[38]

Laura matters a great deal, though Virginia Woolf hardly ever referred to her, and she played no active or lasting part in the life of her half-sister. She matters because she was an abnormal daughter of Leslie Stephen who lived in the same house as Virginia, and was 'put away'. How we read her treatment by the family must influence our reading of Virginia's mental breakdowns and her treatment. The same father, the same doctors, the same general attitudes were in play. She is one of the most obvious and tricky examples, in this life-story, of the way that biography changes according to the prejudices of the time and the emotions of the writer. Quentin Bell, committed to describing 'a happy childhood', reported that her half-sisters regarded Laura as 'a joke'. This would have been an entirely characteristic way for them to refer to the 'idiot' in the family. But that tone of voice on madness now seems blithe, even defensive. There is now, by contrast, a tendency to link the two half-sisters – the mad girl in the attic and the suiciding genius – as parallel victims of patriarchal cruelty and oppression. But this is demeaning to the half-sister who repeatedly overcame her condition (which was quite different from Laura's) in order to do her life's work. Virginia Woolf would have been appalled at being identified with Laura. She violently, fearfully distinguishes herself from 'idiocy', as she calls it, as in this notorious observation – made a month before her catastrophic breakdown in 1915:

> On the tow path we met & had to pass a long line of imbeciles . . . everyone in that long line was a miserable shuffling idiotic creature, with no forehead, or no chin, & an imbecile grin, or a wild suspicious stare. It was perfectly horrible. They should certainly be killed.[39]

When she heard of George Duckworth's death in 1934, she wrote to Vanessa, implicitly endorsing the sentiment: 'Leonard says Laura is the one we could have spared.'[40] Quite apart from the unexpected note this strikes about her feelings for George, the remark confirms her ruthless detachment from her 'vacant-eyed' half-sister. Virginia Woolf frequently describes herself as 'mad'; but not as 'unintelligible'. *She* is not an 'idiot' or an 'imbecile'; *she* is not put away; *she* is the daughter who learned to read and write. Laura's influence works through fearful opposition, not identification.

When Adeline Virginia was born on 25 January 1882, in the main bedroom at Hyde Park Gate, the family called her 'Beauty'. She had red hair and green eyes. Her birth was registered on 16 February, three weeks later, in the 'sub-district of Kensington Town': girl's name, 'Adeline Virginia'; father, Leslie Stephen, author; mother, 'Julia Prinsep Stephen, late Duckworth, formerly Jackson'. Adeline Virginia, because of her mother's sadness about the name Adeline, was immediately known as Ginny, or Ginnum, or Ginia. Like her older brother and sister, she was not christened, though she had her secular godfather or 'quasi-sponsor', Julia's admirer the American Ambassador James Lowell. He gave her a natal poem, a silver posset-dish and a bird in a cage, she wrote some of her first letters to him, and he always asked after her. For this, 'Ginia' was much envied by the other children, whose godparents were less impressive. She was weaned very quickly, within three months: Leslie wrote to Julia in April that of course he did not disapprove of her 'bottling' Virginia, and she should only nurse her as long as it did not hurt her health. There is a wonderfully intimate photograph which Leslie said 'made his heart tremble', of Julia with Virginia on her lap, in 1884.[41] A tired and serious Julia is gazing down at the two-year-old, who, fit and plump – 'a very rosy chubby baby', Vanessa remembered her – and dressed in velvet and lace ruffles, is looking round watchfully, with interest, perhaps with apprehension, at the camera. She is ensconced in the place she first remembers, her mother's lap. But there was competition for this place, and for the kind of deep, undivided attention she was receiving at that moment.

The anecdotes of Virginia Stephen's early childhood at the time (as distinct from much later recollections) are competitive and flirtatious, and suggest manipulativeness and a desire to get her own way. Leslie was charmed by her from the start, and describes her being 'most affectionate': 'She sat on my knee to look at Bewick and then said Kiss and put her cheek against mine.' 'Little Ginia is already an accomplished flirt. I said today that I must go down to my work. She nestled herself down on the sofa by me; squeezed her little self tightly up against me and then gazed up with her bright eyes through her shock of hair and said, "don't go, Papa!" I never saw such a little rogue.'[42]

She could be less winning with her siblings. Stella reported to her mother in April 1884: 'This morning Ginia wanted Thoby to give her something which he had, but he wouldn't, so she went up to him and gave him a hug and said, "Please Thoby give it, Darling Sweetheart Boy", but Thoby still said, "No I won't". Then she went up to him and tried to bite him and said "Nasty Pugwash horrid disgusting boy" and afterwards he gave it her.'[43] Vanessa Bell's memoir of Virginia's childhood remembers her as extremely teasable, quick, hot-tempered and cunning.[44] She would blush flame-red with fury and could produce 'an atmosphere of tense thundery gloom'. She could easily enrage and embarrass her sister: Vanessa's memoir makes her sound like the more powerful of the two. It notes too that Virginia was markedly changed by the whooping-cough which attacked her the most seriously of all the children in April 1888, and emerged from it much thinner, and more thoughtful and questioning than before.[45]

She was from very early on a nervous, apprehensive and intensely responsive child. She was afraid at night: the nursery lamps would flare up, or the light of the fire flickering on the wall would alarm her. Stella had to go to her in the night once in the summer of 1893, at St Ives, because she was 'took bad'.[46] The outside world alarmed her: her friend Violet Dickinson remembered talking to Stella in 1893 about how Virginia was 'so nervous at crossing the road and so furtive at being looked at'.[47]

When she tried to re-imagine herself as a 'little creature', 'roaming about, in that space of time which lasted from 1882 to 1895',[48] her most intense memories were of moments of rapture or of shock, cutting through the moments of 'non-being', of everyday life. Only by being turned into writing, she says in her autobiography, can these moments be 'made whole' or lose their power to hurt. This is her whole rationale for writing: all her life she gives herself pleasure by finding the 'revelation of some order' through such 'moments of being'.[49] So she masters her memories by structuring them like fictions.

These memorable moments were of ecstasy but also of fear. She always remembered, from the first ten years of her life, a feeling of desolation she used to have at St Ives, as she saw the clouds darkening over the waves, while she sat at lessons with her mother; a feeling of shame associated with the mirror in the hall and the stone slab outside the dining-room; a feeling of 'hopeless sadness' while she was fighting with Thoby on the lawn, so that she stopped and let him win ('It was as if I became aware of something terrible, and of my own powerlessness'); a feeling of horror in the garden at night, next to the apple tree, after she had overheard her parents talking about the suicide of someone called Mr Valpy. The apple tree seemed connected to the suicide and she could not pass it. 'I seemed to be dragged down, hopelessly, into some pit of absolute despair from which I could not escape.'[50] In London, there was the terrifying moment in the Gardens when 'the idiot boy sprung up with his hand outstretched mewing, slit-eyed, red-rimmed' and she poured her bag of toffees into his hand; and the moment when she could not step across a puddle and felt that 'the whole world became unreal'.[51]

By the time she put them in her memoir, these dark memories had been shaped and controlled by being used in her fiction. They are literary constructions as well as memories of events. But unedited scraps from the time also suggest her susceptibility to shocks. Leslie reports on her 'grave' interest in the 'naughtiness' of Mr Punch at Brighton in 1885; Lowell is anxious that the picture of the 'bugaboo' he has sent the children in his letters 'might not be wholesome for a young creature with so lively an imagination as Virginia seems to have'.[52] One of two surviving letters she wrote to her mother, at five or six, displays an early fascination with the gruesome:

My dear mother . . . Mrs Prinsep says that she will only go in a slow train cos she says all the fast trains have accidents and she told us about an old man of 70 who got his legs caute in the weels of the train and the train began to go on and the old gentleman was draged along till the train caute fire and he called out for somebody to cut off his legs but nobody came and he was burnt up. Goodbye your Loving Virginia.[53]

This shows a relish for narrative, as well as gore. Virginia was slow to learn to speak (she did not talk until she was over two)[54] but she was then extremely vocal and fluent. She liked inventing and combining long new words: Lowell was delighted by her 'annydogs' 'coursing unmuzzled the fields of history' and thought her 'botanical husband' was as good as a 'mobled queen'.[55] The word 'Adirondacks', in one of her child's letters to him, is carefully written out. She quickly learned to use words as a weapon (calling Vanessa 'the Saint' to embarrass her in front of the adults), and she liked fiction. ''Ginia tells me a "story" every night', Leslie reported in 1887. 'It does not change much but she seems to enjoy it.' ''Ginia said she would make a speech tonight. She stood in the window and declaimed a long rigmarole about a crow and a book till her hearers coughed her down. She would have gone on until now.'[56] There is a faint echo here of his early remarks about Laura's rapid chatter: it is quite possible that the contrast struck him between the bright, promising daughter whose 'rigmaroles' suggested strong imagination and quick thinking, and the hopeless case with her unintelligible, spasmodic utterances.

On daily walks and at night in the nursery, the children made up repetitive stories, satisfying in that they 'did not change much' and belonged to specific places and times of day. Like their mother's stories (and like most children's stories) they took familiar materials – a family like their own or the neighbours' – and fantasised with them. So every night in the Hyde Park Gate nursery Virginia and Vanessa would invent a plot about the Dilke family next door, who couldn't pronounce their 'Rs', and who were conspicuously richer than the Stephens, which would begin with 'My dear Clemont' or 'Clemente', in a 'drawling' voice, and go on to imagine 'the discovery under their nursery floor of immense stores of gold', and how in consequence they ' held great feasts and ate fried eggs "with plenty of frizzling".'[57] They took over their mother's imaginary magical country of 'Emlycaunt', home of the frightful Riskodemba.[58] In Kensington Gardens they told 'the Jim Joe and Harry Hoe story' about the three brothers 'with herds of animals'; at St Ives they had a more sinister and more interesting story about 'Beccage and Hollywinks; spirits of evil who lived on the rubbish heap; and disappeared through a hole in the escallonia hedge'.[59]

These early story-tellings developed into the serial narratives of the *Hyde Park Gate News*, which were group efforts. They shared a family tone and sense of humour, recognisable in the playful graffiti of bears, dogs, owls, pigs and monkeys with which Leslie covered his books, or in Thoby's childhood stories, or in Julia's only remaining letter to Virginia, a brutal, energetic report on a conversation in the train between 'two old females'.

> Then she said a Mrs Bright had died so sudden and they said she was 59 but *she* felt sure she was more she remembered her wedding. Indeed no do you – Yes I was just passing here and saw a carriage My what's that I said its young Mrs Bright [?being] married today – you know she killed her first child – No – not on purpose – but she just waltzed it round the room till all the breath was out of its body – so mind you never waltz children round the room . . . Ever your loving old Ma.[60]

Thoby's family stories, written in 1888 under the influence of *Robinson Crusoe*, take a similarly robust pleasure in debunking the sanctities of Victorian family life. The tale of the Tree family who are shipwrecked on their way to America and set fire to an Indian camp with a box of Bryant and May matches, or of Mr and Mrs Parker and their children stranded on board ship and then surviving by shooting buffalo, are forthright and vigorous. The families don't mince their words: 'Come along and help me to cut down a tree,' says Mrs Tree, 'go along and fetch me the hatchet.' Sighting a bear: 'Shoot quick if you are going to shoot at all yes have I shot him mother yes you have said Mrs Tree.' The Parkers are all very rude to each other – 'You're stupid', 'You can shut up' – and the father is always giving his son a terrible 'jaw'.[61]

The *Hyde Park Gate News* – of which editions survive from 1891 to 1892, and from the first months of 1895 – is a mixture, like the childrens' favourite paper *Tit-Bits*, of announcements, stories and a correspondence column. It was written under parental influence, and Virginia's tense anticipation of their response to it – particularly her mother's – set the pattern for her later sensitivity to criticism. Vanessa remembered eavesdropping on the parents to see their reaction to the latest issue. ' "Rather clever, I think," said my mother . . . It was enough to thrill her daughter – she had had approval and been called clever.'[62]

The tone of the *Hyde Park Gate News*, already heard in the accounts of holidays in St Ives, is satirical and ruthlessly anti-emotional. Maternal feelings are travestied ('It must indeed be sad for the Mother to see her sons growing older and older and then to watch them leave the sweet world of childhood behind'), ridiculous adults are mocked (General Beadle, who says things like 'it was almost too hot but that it was pleasant to perspire freely'), and boring visitors are dismissed ('Sir Fred Pollock and his better half arrived. We will not however say much about them as they were not very interesting'). Sibling behaviour is noted unmercifully: 'Miss Virginia had taken in a good supper. But apparently Miss Virginia did not think so for she took another piece of cake as soon as she got home.'

The serial stories make merciless play with romantic love and the 'matrimony market', marital relations, parental tenderness, class sensibilities, master-servant relations, grief and embarrassment. A proposal is made at the monkey-house at the zoo. ('Oh Georgina darling darling.') Love is declared: 'I love you with that fervent passion with which my father regards roast beef but I do not look upon you with the same eyes as my father for he likes Roast Beef for its taste but I like you for your personal merits.' A lover is rejected: 'As I never kept your love letters you can't have them back. I therefore return the stamps which you sent.' Marital advice is given: '*Always* listen to all that your wife says to you as none but the wife can tell how aggravating it is to have to repeat the same thing at least six times over before she can get an answer.' And there is a fascination with horror-stories and the macabre: Miss Virginia Stephen's poetical works describe the Materfamilias hanging over her sick son Adrian like 'the vulture hovering Oer the dieing horse'; in a story of a haunted house, a man sits groaning and pretending to be a magpie, thus frightening the village; in a ghost story of St Ives for the 'Cristmas' number, a young man is murdered by a skeleton hiding under the bed.[63]

One story, running through several episodes, 'A Cockney's Farming Experiences' (and its sequel 'The experiences of a Paterfamilias'),[64] makes a farcical parody of parental sentiments, marital relations, and class-consciousness. It includes a baby hanging in a tree, a bull charging with 'ereck tail' and fiery eyes, a resentful careless father and a wife left stranded on a collapsing dinner-table. These can all be decoded as sinister pointers to an oppressive and sexually threatening childhood. But this sort of relentlessly psychoanalytical reading, which disallows the comic brio and literary indebtedness of the narrative, also doesn't take into account its joint authorship. The story is attributed to 'Miss A.V. and Mr J.T. Stephen' (and is full of Thoby's schoolboy slang): so it is a dangerous exercise to deduce from it Virginia's secret feelings about her parents and her childhood.[65] Certainly it has a brutal and violent streak, common to much Victorian writing for children. The *Hyde Park Gate News* is an escapade for the writers, a licensed outlet for rudeness and aggression, and for a subversion of family sentiments. Its relish for mischief and in-jokes would develop into the Dreadnought Hoax, into *Orlando* and *Freshwater*, and into a lifelong ruthless pleasure in satire and gossip.

There is a lot of laughter written into the *Hyde Park Gate News*, sometimes literally transcribed, as when Julia receives an April Fool from the children: 'She seemed to wonder at the slip of paper on which was printed in large letters "WE FOOLY WE FOOLY WE FOOLY BRER BUZZARD" by which familiar name she is generally known . . . The anxious infants awaited her burst of laughter. At last it came. "Ha ha ha he he he" laughed she with all the good natured vehemence of her nature.'[66] Not all the family's laughter was so 'good natured', but all of it was 'vehement'. Occasions for laughter, the louder and the more prolonged the better, were always being manufactured. Particularly extreme incidences were noted with pride, like some successful family 'tableaus' at St Ives in 1892 which 'set the audience off laughing',[67] or a visit to the Lushington sisters, Kitty and Margaret, in 1897 – 'We sitting screaming with laughter – to sit and laugh was throughout our part: such a stream of talk and laughter never in my life have I heard'.[68]

These laughing sessions might coincide with times of tension or distress, and can read troublingly. Later stories of Virginia making mocking faces behind people's backs, or 'laughing herself silly', always contain an element of childishness or helplessness or extremity. John Lehmann reported an uncontrolled scene when she was telling him the story of *Flush* in 1932: 'She soon became so excited and hysterical with laughter, that . . . she was red in the face and tears were streaming down her cheeks, before she retired incapable of going on.'[69] A more sympathetic report still suggests how wild her laughter could be: Elizabeth Bowen remembered her laughter with affection, as 'entrancing', 'outrageous'. 'She laughed in this consuming, choking, delightful, hooting way', 'almost like a child's laughter'.[70] There is a dangerous, reckless, perhaps also a sexual element to this laughter. And it is related both to her dazzling, unstoppable conversational displays and to the quality of exhibitionistic dandyism in her work. The Stephen family practice, or even family tyranny, of making people laugh, or being made to laugh, underlies Virginia Woolf's need to perform as a comedian. She played up to the entertaining, eccentric, comical version that the family quickly created for her. But she also had a horror of being laughed at, and this may have originated in the ferocious, blush-inducing teasing in the Stephen family nursery. Virginia Woolf's notorious spitefulness is a weapon against humiliation: ridicule others before they can do it to you.

Nicknames, charades, family plays, cartoons, practical jokes, caricature, were all grist to the laughter mill. Virginia's comical eccentricities, as a child, were fixed with the nickname 'the Goat'. 'From the first she was felt to be incalculable, eccentric and prone to accidents', Quentin Bell reports. The nickname set the seal on this character and was then appropriated by its victim: Virginia always signed herself 'Billy[goat]' to Vanessa. Nicknames were as much in use as in any large Victorian family. Their childhood was full of animals, real and imaginary: odd pets, like a squirrel and a marmoset and a pet mouse called Jacobi;[71] the animals at the Regent's Park Zoo, where the children were allowed to hold the chimpanzees; the family dogs, notably Shag, whose death in 1905 was the subject of one of Virginia Stephen's first published essays, a sentimental obituary; the magical animals of Julia's stories; and a whole menagerie of invented creatures for themselves and their friends. Like Leslie, who told Julia during their courtship, somewhat misleadingly, that he would be to her like his old collie Troy, 'a nice kind loving animal who will take what I give and be thankful,'[72] who caricatured himself as a monkey with a pipe and a fez and who named his children 'the ragamice', Virginia and her siblings used animal names as a way of petting and of mocking each other. Long before she wrote the life of Flush the spaniel, Virginia was giving herself a whole repertoire of animal characters. Every relationship was defined by her animal-name for herself – Sparroy or Wallaby for Violet Dickinson, Billy or Ape for Vanessa, Goat for Thoby and Emma Vaughan, and, later, Mandril or Marmoset for Leonard. And everyone she knew would be reinvented and taken possession of by a nickname: Vanessa was Tawny or Maria or Marmot, or, more lastingly, Dolphin; Thoby was Gribbs or Grim or Cresty or Thobs; Stella (a nickname apparently originating with Julia) was 'The Old Cow'. These nicknames would then in turn be nicknamed, and the animals would reproduce by a literary parthenogenesis into yet more beasts. So 'Goat' or 'the Goat' becomes Goatus Esq, Capra, Il Giotto; Emma Vaughan's 'Toad' would be 'dearest Reptile', or Todkins, Toadlebinks, or Todelcrancz; the Ape might be the Apes, or Singe, or the Singes.

The menagerie is demanding, messy, uncontrolled and sexual, often having to be sent back to its basket or ordered down. Like the stories in the *Hyde Park Gate News*, the nicknames give permission for aberrant behaviour, and allow appeals to be made for petting and admiration, as well as creating figures of fun. Virginia's lifelong courtship of Vanessa was licensed by the invention of the pleading, greedy creatures she kept in play all through their correspondence. When Vanessa marries, she receives a painfully facetious 'Address of Congratulation' from 'three Apes and a Wombat', which is rooted in their childhood story-telling:

We have been your humble Beasts since we first left our Isles, which is before we can remember, and during that time we have wooed you and sung many songs of winter and summer and autumn in the hope that thus enchanted you would condescend one day to marry us. But as we no longer expect this honour we entreat that you keep us still for your lovers . . . Her devoted Beasts Billy Bartholemew Mungo and WOMBAT.[73]

A few years later, the beasts are pining: 'I should point out to you, that it is very dangerous to allow these animals to go long uncared for: they are apt to return to their savage ways. At present, I must confess, I never saw a more engaging troop: their fur is in excellent condition – teeth white, and lips inviting. They gibber if I only say "Maria" to them. I think you would be touched. No one kisses them here.'[74] Virginia's love affair with Vita Sackville-West and her sexual life with Leonard would also be rooted in these animal names, and the story 'Lappin and Lapinova', published in 1938, describes the death of a marriage when the erotic, escapist fantasy of the animal names is cruelly killed off by the husband.[75]

'The Goat' also gave herself an alternative, non-bestial nickname in 1897, when she was fifteen. 'Miss Jan' is a character who gets bored at tea parties, is 'bewildered' by the threat of an unwelcome holiday, and is too 'ignorant' to understand her father's lecture on Pascal. She is given to uttering mournful 'Miss Janisms' like 'how is one to live in such a world', and she is the subject of a long work, referred to as 'The History of Ms and Js Grand Tour' and as 'the Eternal Miss Jan'.[76] But she is also an author, who decides whose remarks shall be 'entered' in the diary and says that she cannot claim to be a poet. Miss Jan marks the beginning of Virginia Stephen's sense of herself as a writer; but, as with all the other performances and disguises in her childhood, this characterisation is not kept secret. It too is part of the shared improvisations and games of the family.

There was not much privacy in her childhood. When she tried to think back, she found it impossible to disentangle herself from 'those instincts, affections, passions, attachments . . . which bound me . . . from the first moment of consciousness to other people'.[77] ('Oh the torture of never being left alone!' her mother was supposed to have said when she was widowed; her daughter was moved by the phrase.) Everything was shared: rooms, baths, walks, jokes, lessons, activities like bug-hunting or skating or cricketing or boating expeditions. All story-telling was collaborative. Virginia Stephen was reading avidly, from very early on, under the guidance of her father, and from eleven or twelve reading became her secret life, her 'habit', and her refuge. But in her early years even reading was a communal rather than a private activity. Leslie read out loud to them all ('*Tom Brown's Schooldays* and *Treasure Island* . . . the thirty-two volumes of the Waverley Novels, which . . . when we had finished the last he was ready to begin the first over again', as well as Carlyle's *French Revolution*, Jane Austen, Hawthorne, Shakespeare, and the great English poets, especially Milton).[78] The children swapped and shared notes on their reading from early on: Thoby reported from school in 1891 that 'there is a "Charlie to the Rescue" in the library so I needn't have taken Ginia's'[79] and Adrian told Julia, in his first school term in 1894, to 'tell Ginia that I have not taken any books by Tennyson or Wordsworth or any of the authors she mentioned but I've taken a book called "The World of Adventure" it's got in it about the light brigade at Balaclava – not the poem but a story in which they quote a lot of the poem.'[80] (This is one of the poems which Mr Ramsay intones to himself in *To the Lighthouse*.) All their lives, the Stephens and their close friends would continue these shared family activities. Virginia Woolf's appetite for performance, her vulnerability to criticism and her passionate need for solitude and independence – which were the terms on which she embarked on her marriage – all had their roots in this communal, collaborative family life.

SIX

Siblings

'How little we know even about brothers and sisters.'[1] The Stephen children were for years extremely close. In their early years they had a robust, energetic group life. But they were, also, reserved with each other, and very distinct in character.

The group life of the Stephens was not static; the pattern of the relations between the four was always changing. Thoby was the leader, admired and followed, first by Vanessa, then by both girls. Vanessa 'mothered' and organised the others. The three older children ganged up on Adrian. The two boys, though they went to the same preparatory school and would both go to the same Cambridge college, Trinity, seem not to have been especial friends: possibly James Fitzjames's early dominance over Leslie was re-enacted in Thoby's superiority over the less confident and more withdrawn younger brother. A special literary relationship developed between Virginia and Thoby after he went to school. And, from the first, Vanessa and Virginia were exceptionally close, and remained so all their lives.

The least satisfactory of these sibling 'relations', Virginia's with Adrian, has to be deduced from a scatter of incidental and largely unfriendly remarks. Uniquely in these family papers, no letters from Virginia to Adrian survive, and very few from him to her. She wrote no full portrait of him. Although they lived in the same houses for thirty years, their relationship was always awkward. Her main feelings towards him were negative and critical.

This difficult relationship began in childhood. Adrian was their mother's favourite (and was weaned much later than Virginia had been).[2] The other children bossed him. At four, he is being encouraged (Leslie reports) in 'rampageousness' by Thoby and Ginia's 'thoughtless levity and giggling'; at ten, his success at billiards scandalises the girls: 'I strictly forbad them to say anything about "flukes" '.[3] There are scathing remarks in the *Hyde Park Gate News* about the young 'literary aspirant' Master Adrian Stephen's failure to bring out the first number of his 'little squitty' newspaper called the *Talland Gazette*: 'as we feared he is not blessed with the spirit of punctuality.'[4] As a child he was very short, and then, in his teens, he suddenly shot up. Leslie attributed his lack of success at school to 'his great growth – over 6ft.2in'.[5] Unlike Thoby, he was an unconfident schoolboy, both at their Uxbridge prep school, Evelyns, where he was sent at ten, (and was so 'nervous' that Dr Seton had to be consulted)[6] and at Westminster, where he started as a day boy and was made a boarder in 1901 because Leslie was worried about his progress. When Leslie gave him extra lessons he was often 'frightened or distracted'.[7] The death of his adoring mother when he was twelve, of his father when he was twenty-one, and of his older brother when he was twenty-three were shocking catastrophes for him, and painfully affected his later relationships. Virginia felt protective towards him in their dark years together: 'I feel a great affection for him, poor little boy.'[8] 'Adrian is perfectly charming, and I do want to make a cheerful place for him. It is terrible that he should have no brother.'[9]

But protectiveness was not her strong suit. She told Ottoline Morrell in 1933 that she could not understand having the maternal attitude to grown up people, and that she never felt maternal to grown men or women.'[10] Though their lives were closely involved – the Dreadnought Hoax shows how much – she was exasperated by Adrian's depressive and difficult withdrawal into himself during the years of their enforced intimacy after Vanessa's marriage. 'I think its absurd to call Adrian a bore,' she wrote to Vanessa in 1918, 'he has great distinction; not that I could ever live with him tolerably.'[11] In adult life, his marriage to Karin Costelloe and his profession as a psychiatrist distanced them: their older daughter described her parents, in relation to Virginia, as 'always outsiders'.[12] Virginia thought of Adrian as an unadulterated 'Stephen': 'such cold fingers, so fastidious, so critical, such taste.'[13] He was a depressing companion for her, cold, satirical and passive, and she would always associate with him a 'feeling . . . of utter lackadaisicalness, which plunges me into the mirk of ten November fogs'.[14] Adrian re-entered his childhood through analysis when he was in his forties. Virginia reported derisively on the results to Vanessa: 'I gather that his tragedy – as the dr calls it – is all our doing. He was suppressed as a child.'[15]

Adrian's closeness to his mother and his gloomy adolescence suggest the boy James in To the Lighthouse. But, outside the novel, he remains a shadowy presence in Virginia's life-story. By contrast, the brother she lost was the brother she was always trying to know better. Thoby haunted her: she perpetually remembered and re-imagined him. She wrote three versions of him over twenty years, as 'Jacob' in Jacob's Room, as 'Percival' in The Waves, and as himself in her 'Sketch of the Past'. In all three, she used the same sort of adjectives. Jacob is awkward, distinguished-looking, unworldly, excitable, statuesque, authoritative, healthy, severe, tolerant, regal, childlike, judicious, solid, shy, slow, barbaric, monolithic. Percival (more of a bully and less of an intellectual than Jacob) is upright, inexpressive, pagan, magnificent, heavy, brutal, single-minded, oblivious, silent, a hero. They are both associated with classical Greece. In the 'Sketch of the Past', Thoby attracts the same adjectives. She describes him having an obscure and depressive side, and a reserve which she cannot quite penetrate.

She remembered Thoby as 'a clumsy awkward little boy, very fat, bursting through his Norfolk jacket', who 'dominated and led' and was difficult to manage. He resented his mother's authority.[16] His rages 'were thorough and formidable' and he had a Napoleonic air.[17] But she also remembered, from the first, 'a vein of sensibility',[18] suggested by some of the childhood anecdotes about him: Stella heard him, at thirteen, discussing with Adrian 'whether people went into mourning for dead born children';[19] Leslie told Julia in 1885, when Thoby was five, that 'Thoby said today at dinner that he always felt very odd when he saw wine upon the table; he felt as if he was out of the world and all the inside of his mouth was very hot. I dont know exactly what he could be thinking about but he seemed to have a very decided opinion about it.'[20] His juvenilia and his letters home from school suggest a sturdy, conventional type:

> There was a lecture on Indian music yesterday by an Indian chap, first he read a lot of bosh about Indian notes and then he played on some Indian things . . . It was an awful lark . . . he sang God Save the Queen in Hindustani. I was top in monthly exams. I utterly licked V – by 29 marks. V– is leaving this term (a good riddance of bad rubbish.)[21]

Despite this jovial tone, all was not well at school. He was not a high flyer: he was behind the other boys in Greek in 1891, and when he won a prize in 1892, the Hyde Park Gate journalists observed their father being reprimanded for his low expectations of Thoby by Mrs Stephen, who said: 'What do you think he's got? . . . looking at Mr Stephen as if she had been having an argument with him.'[22] When Thoby was eleven he was stabbed in the leg – or, as Leslie rather oddly phrased it, 'he allowed a playful schoolfellow to stick a knife into his femoral artery', suggesting that it was not an accident.[23] Three years later, after an attack of influenza, he became delirious, and, wrote the teacher to Julia in March of 1894, 'before the nurse could get to him he was half through the window which he had smashed to shivers . . . It is evidently never safe to leave him for a moment when he is ill – one can never tell when these attacks may come on'. In April it seems that the 'attacks' were still going on, as the teacher writes that 'his screams frighten the little boys'.[24] He messed up his entrance exam to Eton, and went to Clifton College instead, where the housemaster had to be warned about the sleepwalking: 'he says that he has a dormitory where any attempt at windows is impossible.'[25] This sounds very much like a suicide attempt. Virginia does not mention it in her reminiscences; perhaps she did not know about it. She thought that as a schoolboy he exacted his rights and bided his time, sure of himself, maturing slowly.

Though there was an active, outgoing, public-school side to the Thoby Stephen who went cubbing and hunting and walking with his friends, he was thoughtful and introverted too. She saw him as a 'melancholy' young man. His early passion for bug-hunting developed into a talent for drawing birds and animals and an enthusiasm for bird-watching (in 1902 he kept a detailed nature notebook, with excellent illustrations). This was his own hobby, not a family tradition: 'It is very funny that he should have developed this thirst for natural history, considering how little encouragement he has had', Leslie observed.[26] His relationship with his younger sister developed through literary enthusiasms. Her most eloquent memory of him is of his coming home from his prep school for the first time and walking up and down the stairs with her, telling her shyly and excitedly about Greek literature. Later he would tell her vivid narratives of his schoolfriends, later still of the brilliant men he was meeting at college. At this time they would argue about Shakespeare, Thoby ruthlessly dominating her with his confident certainties, she feeling the need to oppose and resist his point of view and make her own judgements. They developed an amicably combative intellectual relationship.

In personal matters, though, they were extremely reserved. Thoby's relationship with men was different: Leslie, who became in old age as emotionally dependent on Thoby as Mrs Jackson had once been on Julia, laid all his griefs and complaints on him; and Thoby would tell his Cambridge friends how he felt about Greece or politics or Tintoretto. But with his sisters, sex and death were taboo subjects. He never talked to them about his feelings for women, and he never mentioned the family's losses. He seems to have been of little help to the sisters in the dark years between 1897 and 1904: 'his general attitude was aloof – was he not a man? Did not men ignore domestic trifles? – and judicial . . . he felt generally speaking that we should accept our lot'.[27] In her unpublished memoir of him she cancels this phrase: 'How little he knew.'[28] And his remarks about Virginia in his letters of 1904 suggest, again, 'how little he knew' about her: 'Virginia is going on pretty well but they say her recovery must be rather a long job as she was much run down.'[29] If Thoby had lived, they would no doubt have paid a price for his aloofness. Working through her thoughts about him, their closeness and their distance, at the end of her own life, her manuscript stumbles painfully over what they could not say to each other:

The reserve between –
– Thoby then, was The reserve which –
– We never spoke of this to each other –
– during those unhappy years we never spoke –

and ends up with: 'we never spoke, during those unhappy years, of these scenes'.[30] Both Jacob and Percival are, ultimately, absent, obscure, and silent, fictionally embodying not just Thoby's absence in death but his aloofness in life. In the whole family, there was only one person whom Virginia Stephen could talk to without reserve.

Vanessa Stephen, three years older than her sister, is the central character in Virginia's family story. Their rivalrous, mutually demanding and often critical intimacy was so deep as to be almost indescribable. The individuated 'scenes' through which Virginia usually invoked her memory could not be applied to it: 'My relation with Vanessa . . . has been too deep for "scenes".'[31]

The 'relation' has been much written about.[32] It is in itself extremely interesting, deep and unusual, and feminism has romanticised and heroinised it. Two sisters, a writer and a painter, mutually influencing each other's work, collaborating artistically, sharing friends and 'life-styles', and spending all their years as intimates, confidantes and neighbours: this is a marvellously appealing narrative. Virginia made version after version of her sister, never finalised or conclusive, in letters and diaries, in reminiscences, in family caricatures and in fiction, where Vanessa as a model overlaps and blurs with versions of Julia and with self-portraits: as the wise, maternal Helen Ambrose in *The Voyage Out*, as Katharine Hilbery working out her independence from the family in *Night and Day*, as Mrs Ramsay in *To the Lighthouse*, as the fecund, brooding Susan in *The Waves*, as the reserved Maggie Pargiter in *The Years*. In *Flush* she parodied her own devotion to Vanessa in the guise of the spaniel adoring his mistress. Very often the fictions of Vanessa have a monumental aspect, like the strange figure of the giant grey nurse who appears to Peter Walsh in his dream in *Mrs Dalloway*, metamorphosing as siren, guardian, goddess, mother.[33] Similarly Vanessa shape-shifted through Virginia's life, taking the roles of mother, lover, conspirator and muse, but always characterised as silent, sensual, maternal, powerful, generous and implacable.

There was something grim in their feeling for each other. Passages of estrangement and hostility strained their relationship. Though Vanessa remembered their establishing from very early on that Virginia 'would be a writer and I a painter',[34] there was competition between them, and it would surface at periods of conflict and intensity in their lives. Vanessa was closely involved with Virginia's breakdowns until, and to an extent after, Virginia married Leonard, but she did not necessarily understand them very well. She was racially prejudiced against, and critical of Leonard (and, later, of Vita) and not much in touch with Virginia's feminism and her political thinking. Virginia often found Vanessa unyielding and cold, and Vanessa resisted her emotional demands. Both constructed versions of the other: Vanessa wrote to Clive in 1910 that 'Virginia since early youth has made it her business to create a character for me according to her own wishes and has now so succeeded in imposing it upon the world that these preposterous stories are supposed to be certainly true because so characteristic.'[35] Vanessa's own caricature of her sister as a malicious, mischievous, crazy genius has powerfully affected the posthumous life of Virginia Woolf.

But, to put it simply, Virginia was in love with her sister. And Vanessa depended on her more than she acknowledged. She turned to Virginia in the greatest tragedy of her life, and they were moved by each other's work. When Virginia sent her *The Waves*, Vanessa responded with an emotional letter, recognising the novel as an elegy for Thoby which could be understood only by them, and drawing an analogy between her own recent painting (of a room with a nurse and a mother, two children and toys on the floor) and Virginia's writing: 'It means something of the same sort that you seem to me to mean.' 'Nobody except Leonard matters to me as you matter,' Virginia replied, 'and nothing would ever make up for it if you didn't like what I did . . . I always feel I'm writing more for you than for anybody'.[36]

The first memory of this relationship, for both, was of meeting in the dark secret space underneath the nursery table at Hyde Park Gate. ' "Have black cats got tails?" she asked, and I said "NO," and was proud because she had asked me a question. Then we roamed off again into that vast space.' In the earlier version of this, Virginia adds: 'In future I suppose there was some consciousness between us that the other held possibilities.'[37] And this first memory is suggestive. The sisters confirmed each other's view of life in a secret space below and inside the life of the family. Virginia is characteristically proud of making an impression. There is freedom and space between them as they wander off again.

The stories of Vanessa and Virginia as children do point ahead to their adult lives. They bathed and slept together; Vanessa mothered her and used to rub her with scents and put her to bed.[38] Vanessa was perceived by the others as the helpful, responsible one, truthful and honest to a fault, silent, grave, determined. She was in the burdensome position of the child in charge. When the boys went to school, even before the family catastrophes, Virginia became increasingly intimate with and dependent on her sister. She was jealous, manipulative and needy. She would 'finger her amethyst beads and emumerate with each the name of a friend or relative whose place in Vanessa's affections would arouse her jealousy'.[39] She wanted to sit on her lap and be petted. But they also helped each other. They would have long bathroom conferences and long autumn walks where they would discuss their futures and Vanessa would give encouragement. 'Nessa preaches that our destinies lie in ourselves', Virginia wrote at the end of 1897.[40] Many years later, looking back on their walks and talks and plans together as they grew up, she thought of the two of them as having been marked by destiny, but as having, also, shaped their own destinies: 'So we have made out our lives, she & I, propelled into them by some queer force'.[41]

The Stephen children were 'Explorers and revolutionists'.[42] They made their revolution against the older generation, and this included the Duckworths: the two sons, 'consenting and approving Victorians', the daughter, brought up to conform to her mother's ideal of lives of service for women. Even before George Duckworth's disastrous régime over the Stephen girls, the enforced intimacy of the Duckworth and Stephen children was awkward. When Leslie married Julia and adopted her children, they were, as he put it, 'a little impressed by the fancy that I should come between you and your mother'.[43] It was hard for them 'to feel at ease with a grisly old skeleton like me'.[44] Looking back on his relationship with them after Julia's death, Leslie made a kind of apology for not having been able to feel for the Duckworth children 'the instincts of genuine fathership'.[45]

In 1882, when Virginia was born, George was fourteen, Stella was thirteen and Gerald was twelve. As young fatherless children they had been extremely dependent on their mother. George, the oldest, a sentimental, unintelligent, emotional boy, who lost his father when he was two ('Where's Georgie's Papa?' he kept saying)[46] was excessively devoted to Julia. His schoolboy letters to her from Eton were soppy and protective – 'You must be worn out with all your rushing about this hot weather'[47] – and his returns home would always be dramatic and emotional, with much weeping and kissing, lavishing 'caresses, endearments, enquiries and embraces as if, after forty years in the Australian bush, he had at last returned to the home of his youth and found an aged mother still alive to welcome him'.[48] On religion he was a much more conventional thinker than his mother or his step-father: 'I think my own dear father would really have wished me to be confirmed if he had known that I wish it', he wrote from school.[49] As Virginia described him in an early, satirical, unfinished draft of a novel in which he was the 'hero', he 'was only possessed of a very moderate share of brains . . . Brains were of very little practical use in the world he reflected – They only led to overwork and nervous breakdowns'.[50] He failed his diplomatic exams, but made a career for himself working for ten years with Charles Booth, the social reformer and author of the massive investigation into urban poverty, *Life and Labour of the People in London 1901–3*, for which George acted as secretary, and, from 1902, as Austen Chamberlain's private secretary, on a salary of £250. (He had also inherited a substantial private income.) Conventional, 'sentimental and pompous',[51] and utterly unintellectual (his relief at leaving the second volume of *Middlemarch* on a train provided a detail for *To the Lighthouse*), he was quite alien to the Stephen children. All the same, he makes an unlikely villain. In later years he was always anxious to help his half-sisters, and is remembered by all who knew him well as kind-hearted, benign, and a pillar of the establishment.[52] Certainly in the children's early years, before Julia's death, he seems to have figured as a benevolent figure, providing presents and expeditionary treats. It was not until their teens that George's social climbing, his exploitation of the girls' position, and his lack of emotional and physical control would become oppressive to them, and the piggy-eyed, sexually rapacious tyrant and imbecile of Virginia's later unforgiving caricatures took shape.

Stella too came to have some authority over her half-sisters, especially Virginia, which was resented; but she was not an authoritative person. Retrospectively, she aroused pity and tenderness in Virginia Woolf, though if she had lived it might have been a different story. But Stella's life was difficult and her destiny pathetic. In *To the Lighthouse*, she is imagined as a silent, beautiful, obedient ghost, shadowily companioning her dead mother 'across the fields'.[53] But in *The Years* Virginia Woolf gave her an alternative life, by imagining her, as 'Eleanor', freed from the family and living on into the twentieth century as a wise and independent old lady. In her memoir she examined the oppressive and torturing relationship between Stella and Leslie and expiated her own regrets for having been, herself, a 'burden' to Stella.[54]

Stella Duckworth was a pale, golden-haired, dreamily blue-eyed replica of her mother, meekly under her shadow. Julia treated her much more severely and critically than she treated her sons. Her nickname for her, 'The Old Cow', seems peculiarly uncharitable. As a child she had a bout of the rheumatic fever which afflicted her grandmother and her mother; there is a suggestion in the 'Sketch of the Past' that it may have 'touched' her, and produced 'a stoppage in her mind, a gentle impassivity about books and learning'.[55] But if she was not intellectual, she had to be very efficient. Even before Julia's death she was looking after the household, taking responsibility when Julia was away, worrying about her mother's health ('Mother to Ebury Street in snow w. made me cross', reads one entry in her 1893 diary).[56] Because she could not go about London on her own, Virginia, at six or seven, was her 'chaperone': 'Among my earliest memories is the memory of going out with her perhaps to shop, or to pay some call; and, the errand done, she would take me to a shop and give me a glass of milk and biscuits sprinkled with sugar on a marble table.'[57] Stella's days in service to the family can be traced in all their exhausting detail in her letters and diaries (which Virginia read):

> After your letter [she writes to Julia in 1884, when she was fifteen] I thought perhaps it was better to have curry and rice instead of the Pie as it is so cold here . . . Thoby's cough has quite gone but he has still a little cold in his head . . . We all went out this morning in the gardens except Gerald . . . The little ones have just gone to bed . . . For tomorrow's dinner there is cold beef and chicken and maccaroni . . . I got a rabbit and chicken from the Stores as Elizabeth said it would be cheaper than two chickens. The staining on the nursery floor looks very nice, but the brown is not quite dark enough.

In the *Hyde Park Gate News*, there are glimpses of Stella with the girls, organising them and playing jokes on them, as here, when on a foggy day the music teacher was unable to come and the 'juveniles' were pleased. 'Miss Stella Duckworth met Miss Vanessa and Miss Virginia Stephen on the stairs and asked them if their hands were clean and told them to their great dismay that the object of their fears was downstairs. They went down and were much relieved only to see harmless Mrs Stephen.'[58]

She seems to have been a conventional girl, dismissing, for instance, a production of Ibsen's *Doll's House* as 'raving mad' (evidently its message did not get through to her) and tut-tutting at the scene at St Ives when a bankrupt neighbouring family, faced with the sheriff coming to seize the furniture, threw everything out of the window and bolted the doors, to the cheers of the townspeople: 'Police absolutely powerless – what is the law?'[59] Like her mother, she believed in domestic order as a model for social organisation. As an extension of (perhaps a refuge from) her home duties, Stella became an active member of Octavia Hill's team of middle-class ladies working in the London slums. Hill was the pioneering Victorian woman activist for housing reform and better living conditions for the London poor. Her followers were often drawn from the same large middle-class families: Julia and Caroline Stephen both supported her work, Julia with donations and Caroline with nightschool teaching and establishing a courtyard housing-scheme in Chelsea. Stella's work for her was the female equivalent of her brother's work with Charles Booth. In between her family duties she would go off to Octavia Hill's East End headquarters on 'endless journeys in buses and trams'[60] for strenuous days learning to do accounts, attending cookery and typing and nursing lectures, and providing country 'treats' for the slum-dwellers: 'Met Miss Hill and all my Southwarkers and 150 more and we went to Reading – Miss O's brother provided waggons, beautiful dinner and tea and a lovely garden.'[61] Like many of Octavia Hill's ladies she helped to set up a block of new buildings for the East End poor for which she had complete responsibility. After Stella died, Octavia Hill paid tribute to Miss Duckworth, 'who had worked with us so devotedly' on her six Lisson Grove cottages.[62] In 1897 Virginia frequently reported that Stella was off to her 'slums', or noted that they had thought better of going through some particularly terrifying streets together: 'S. said it was impossible; so we turned and fled straight home again.'[63] 'There is no doubt' (writes Octavia Hill's biographer) 'that working in poor areas was rough for hitherto protected girls, from middle- or upper-class homes. They had to steel themselves to witness horrors of every kind: drunkenness, starvation, the signs of physical abuse on women and children.'[64]

Virginia Woolf is ambivalent all her life about women philanthropists and social activists. She partly admires them. Eleanor in *The Years*, with her duties to her Ladbroke Grove poor and to her houses in 'Peter Street', where the drains are bad, is allowed to go further than Stella did in her reading of the city's political structure. It's as though Stella had, after all, understood Ibsen:

> The grey line of houses jolted up and down before her eyes as the omnibus trundled along the Bayswater Road. The shops were turning into houses; there were big houses and little houses; public houses and private houses. And here a church raised its filigree spire. Underneath were pipes, wires, drains . . . Her lips began moving. She was talking to herself. There's always a public house, a library and a church, she was muttering.[65]

But the ethic of public service, which for Stella's type and generation meant philanthropic social work (though for a feminist it could also have taken the form of working for the vote or for women's higher education), and which for the next generation meant Labour Party activism, or work for the Women's Guild,[66] also filled Virginia Woolf with sceptical reservations. Her private opinion of the women involved in such activities was in sharp contrast to her public appreciation of them in a work such as *Three Guineas*. And for herself such work was anathema, though she was always looking in on it and sniffing at it. The Duckworth commitment to the middle-class social reformism of Charles Booth and Octavia Hill was influential on her lifelong political argument about responsibilities.

Unlike Eleanor in *The Years*, Stella was beautiful, romantic and admired. While Virginia was growing up Stella was also going abroad with George as her escort, to Rome, to Bayreuth – Julia called them 'the wandering Jews'[67] – where she attracted some attention: 'Stella is looking most lovely' (George wrote home to Julia), 'the whole theatre turns round to look at her when she stands up and I dont think she is at all overtired.'[68] She had her suitors, some of whom (including poor Jem Stephen) were unwelcome: when Dick Norton left St Ives in 1893 Stella noted 'I'm afraid he likes me better than I do him and that's a great deal'; and Walter Headlam (a young Cambridge Hellenist who would turn his attention fourteen years later to Virginia) had an even more serious send-off: 'I cannot think of him without a shudder and yet he is much to be pitied – it is awful.'[69] (What can he have done?) Finally, Jack Hills, an Eton friend of George, a country gentleman and solicitor, was successful. Their long, sad romance overhung Virginia's teenage years and greatly affected her feelings about love and sex.

But these feelings were, to an arguable extent, distorted and damaged in early childhood. Gerald de l'Etang, the youngest Duckworth, was the first culprit in the distressing and contentious matter of Virginia Stephen's abuse as a child. Gerald, his mother's favourite before being displaced by the Stephen brood, had been a 'delicate'[70] and petted child, and would write to his mother in baby-language: 'Toothache quite better. Picked up a great lot of Acorns. Nothing else me did. Me little son Gerald de l'Etang Duckworth.'[71] There are unflattering glimpses of him as a young man, as a student at Clare College, Cambridge, not given to hard work, or at home telling tales on the Stephen children, or mocking them with his sneering and his 'teasing and treacherous laughter',[72] making the family laugh at dinner with 'indecent' lavatorial stories,[73] and going off on unsuccesful 'thinning' cures from which he returned 'as fat as ever'. As an adult he was very keen on his food and increased his likeness, Virginia thought, 'to a pampered overfed pug dog'.[74] Gerald Duckworth made some significant positive gestures in Virginia Woolf's life: he was happy to let the Stephens go their own way in 1904, and he was willing to publish her first two novels. Though he always depressed and alienated her in later life, she knew there was more to him than to George.[75] But his reputation as a half-brother has been irrevocably fixed by her memory of one moment in her childhood.

The Stephen children were ignorant about sex and embarrassed by romance. The tone of adult sexual relations was set by their parents' marriage, so difficult in practice and yet so sacred in its origins, so that it seemed almost impermissible for Virginia to say to her mother, 'How did father ask you to marry him?'[76] Julia's matchmakings and Stella's romance seemed to set the agenda for the girls – courtship, marriage, wifehood – an agenda which they did indeed follow, but with notable differences in tone. As children the Stephens were caustic and giggly about love-making, making satirical jokes about 'tying the bow of unison' and 'carrying off prizes in the matrimony market'[77] and sniggering when George Duckworth read out an embarrassing cracker motto that went, 'My heart sweet girl is wholly thine', while Miss Susan Lushington was sitting next to him.[78] Until Virginia was about sixteen, she recalls, her knowledge of sex came entirely from reading about sodomy in Plato. She knew that Stella had to have a 'chaperone', but it was Jack Hills who first informed her and Vanessa about double sexual standards: 'I was incredibly, but only partially, innocent. I knew nothing about ordinary men's lives, and thought all men, like my father, loved one woman only, and were "dishonourable" if unchaste, as much as women.'[79] On the other hand she had had to deal from early childhood with some unexplained realities grossly out of tune with the 'intense', 'rapturous' vision of first love provided by Stella: Jem Stephen's uncontrolled priapic incursions, a man who used to hang about Hyde Park Gate and expose himself to the children[80] (fearfully remembered in *The Years*), and, it seems, a sexual assault by Gerald Duckworth in very early childhood.

Virginia Woolf makes no written reference to this incident until 1939, when she starts her 'Sketch of the Past'. In its first pages, she describes as one of her strongest memories a feeling of shame and guilt when looking in the mirror in the hall of Talland House as a child – a feeling which she calls 'the looking-glass shame' and which 'has lasted all my life'. She attributes this partly to her puritan ancestors and partly to 'another memory':

There was a slab outside the dining room door for standing dishes upon. Once when I was very small Gerald Duckworth lifted me onto this, and as I sat there he began to explore my body. I can remember the feel of his hand going under my clothes; going firmly and steadily lower and lower. I remember how I hoped that he would stop; how I stiffened and wriggled as his hand approached my private parts. But it did not stop. His hand explored my private parts too. I remember resenting, disliking it – what is the word for so dumb and mixed a feeling? It must have been strong, since I still recall it. This seems to show that a feeling about certain parts of the body; how they must not be touched; how it is wrong to allow them to be touched; must be instinctive.[81]

She goes on to attribute these instinctive feelings to her primitive 'ancestresses' as well as to her immediate puritan ancestors, and adds an account of a dream 'which may refer to the incident of the looking-glass': 'I dreamt that I was looking in a glass when a horrible face – the face of an animal – suddenly showed over my shoulder. I cannot be sure if this was a dream, or if it happened.'

Two years later, about a month after her last entry in the 'Sketch of the Past' manuscript (and only a few weeks before her death) she writes to her friend Ethel Smyth congratulating her on the freedom with which she can write about masturbation and sex. She herself, she says, cannot do this:

> But as so much of life is sexual – or so they say – it rather limits autobiography if this is blacked out. It must be, I suspect, for many generations, for women; for its like breaking the hymen – if thats the membranes name – a painful operation, and I suppose connected with all sorts of subterranean instincts. I still shiver with shame at the memory of my half brother, standing me on a ledge, aged about 6, and so exploring my private parts. Why should I have felt shame then?[82]

This incident has been described as a 'life-threatening' act of extreme sadism which froze Virginia Stephen's sexuality and ignited her madness.[83] It may have given rise (it's been maintained) to her eating problems, because it took place outside the dining-room ('Can there be any mystery in why Virginia Woolf had trouble eating later in life?').[84] It may have triggered her panic fear of illness, because it took place after her attack of whooping-cough. It may have provoked the terrifying dreams, related to the horrible face in the mirror, which led eventually to her suicide. Or, it has been argued, the shame associated with Gerald's act arose from her having *enjoyed* the erotic experience. Perhaps the mirror in the hall was also associated with masturbation. Or, she may have displaced her real erotic feelings of attraction to her father on to her memories (or her inventions) of abuse by her half-brothers. Or, one might deduce (by looking closely at the imagery of mirroring in the passage in the 'Sketch') that it is not only the sexual aspect of Gerald's act which was horrifying to her, but its reducing of her to an object, its triggering of her 'deepest depressive fear – that she does not actually exist behind the face in the mirror'.[85]

Only by hypothesising can this childhood incident be made to explain all of Virginia Woolf's mental history. Certainly it was a distressing and disturbing memory which seems to have been buried for many years. But there were many more long-term, problematic and influential features in her childhood than this, and it distorts the thick complexity of her family life to isolate and emphasise this one. It is not possible to say whether the act was repeated: we simply do not know. It is not possible to prove that this act of sexual interference led directly to her mental breakdowns. It is a distortion, though a tempting and easy one, to elide this incident with the much later and much more damaging story of George's sexual activities, and to think of the Duckworth brothers as conspiratorial rapists. And it is a crude misreading of Virginia's letter to Ethel to suppose that Gerald Duckworth 'had broken her membrane . . . had robbed her of her virginity . . . At the age of six or seven, Virginia Woolf [sic] was no longer a virgin.'[86] The associations in the letter to Ethel between masturbation, 'breaking the hymen', and the memory of Gerald are surely more complicated and indirect than this. The letter is as much about the fear of admitting to sexual feelings in autobiographical writing as it is about sexual abuse. 'Breaking the hymen' is her metaphor for losing one's virginity as a writer, for breaking through self-censorship. The sexual shame which Virginia Woolf associates with her childhood is something that until now she has been unable to write about openly.

But certainly this memory of sexual shame in early childhood is a powerful one, and it would be rash to ignore or belittle the damage done to her sense of herself, at this moment, by the much older half-brother's predatory intrusion. Over and over again in her re-creations of the imaginative world of childhood, there is a moment of fear or shame or panic, the image of a safe private world being invaded, often with the strong sense of sexual threat. Jacob, playing on the beach, is shocked by the sudden sight of 'an enormous man and woman'. The children's secret lives in To the Lighthouse are broken into by sudden attacks of helplessness and fear. In The Waves, the children, especially Rhoda, are caught between private loneliness and the tyranny of the group. In The Years the little girl, Rose, is haunted in her dreams by her encounter with the man who 'fumbles' at himself and 'mews' at her in the dark street. And in her first novel, The Voyage Out, closest in time to and most openly connected to her childhood, Rachel's delirium, and her horrible nightmares of being trapped in an underground tunnel 'oozing with damp' with a 'deformed man who squatted on the floor gibbering', with long nails and a pockmarked face, like an animal, merge Virginia's own breakdowns with her childhood fears. It is simplistic to read these fictional passages as specific coded clues, pointing at a series of sexual crimes. But in her transformations of her childhood memories, moments of ecstasy and moments of horror are placed in dangerous proximity.

Virginia Woolf built her political analysis of her culture on her experience of her childhood. The father's dominant needs and demands, the sacrifice of the mother and unmarried daughters to the tyranny of family, the prejudicial economy which spent money on sending boys to school and university and kept the daughters at home, where the system of lessons kept her, as she always said, 'uneducated', the censorious jurisdiction of grandmothers and aunts, the disciplinarian attitudes of the family doctors, the hypocrisy and censorship which kept the daughters ignorant of sex: these would be the items, for life, on her political agenda.

Emerging from 'the shadow of the private house' (as she put it in *Three Guineas*) to view the world 'from the bridge which connects the private house with the world of public life', she would make her own post-Victorian, post-war analysis of her childhood. But the paradox of her writing is that her family life would also give rise to her most passionate, profound and humane art.

With an awful inner crashing and tearing, the sort of noise she always invokes when she talks about the drastic change from Victorian to 'modern' writing, Virginia Stephen's childhood came to an end on 5 May 1895, the day Julia Stephen died. Virginia was thirteen, and Julia was forty-nine. Her death (from rheumatic fever and over-work), and her obsequies, belonged to a Victorian novel. Her daughter was haunted by it all her life; she wanted to call *To the Lighthouse* an 'elegy'. In her writing and re-writing of this death she did two startlingly incompatible things at once. She ruthlessly subverted the conventions of the Victorian death-bed scene, thereby killing off her mother again and everything she stood for. And she engaged with courage and painful honesty in the extremely difficult work of understanding the meaning of her childhood.

SEVEN

Adolescence

[Mr Ramsay stumbling along a passage stretched his arms out one dark morning, but, Mrs Ramsay having died rather suddenly the night before, he stretched his arms out. They remained empty.][1]

That is how we hear about the death of the mother in *To the Lighthouse*. After the strong emotions which have gathered around Mrs Ramsay in the first part of the book, the abrupt parenthesis is shocking. Nothing could be further from the prayers and weepings and solemn family gatherings of the traditional Victorian death-bed. Virginia Woolf goes out of her way in her fictions to avoid the melodramatic, morbid lamentations which filled the darkened rooms of Hyde Park Gate after her mother's death. Though almost all her novels are dominated by a death, in almost all the death is not written in. Rachel, the young heroine of *The Voyage Out*, whose mother died when she was eleven, can barely say what she feels ('I am lonely,' she began. 'I want – ').[2] She misremembers and can hardly mention her mother, who exists in the book as a gap or a silence. When Virginia Woolf does return to the death of the Victorian mother, in *The Years*, where at the start of the novel the Pargiter children are wearily waiting for it to happen (in this plot the mother, who is quite unlike Julia Stephen, has been ill for years), she writes a brilliantly alienated and unfeeling death-bed scene:

She glanced at the portrait of her mother. The girl in white seemed to be presiding over the protracted affair of her own deathbed with a smiling indifference that outraged her daughter.

'You're not going to die – you're not going to die!' said Delia bitterly, looking up at her. Her father, alarmed by the bell, had come into the room. He was wearing a red smoking-cap with an absurd tassel.

But it's all for nothing, Delia said silently, looking at her father. She felt that they must both check their rising excitement. 'Nothing's going to happen – nothing whatever,' she said, looking at him. But at that moment Eleanor came into the room. She was very white.

'Where's Papa?' she said, looking round. She saw him. 'Come, Papa, come,' she said, stretching out her hand. 'Mama's dying . . . And the children,' she said to Milly over her shoulder.

Two little white patches appeared above her father's ears, Delia noticed. His eyes fixed themselves. He braced himself. He strode past them up the stairs. They all followed in a little procession behind. The dog, Delia noticed, tried to come upstairs with them; but Morris cuffed him back. The Colonel went first into the bedroom; then Eleanor; then Morris; then Martin came down, pulling on a dressing-gown; then Milly brought Rose wrapped in a shawl. But Delia hung back behind the others. There were so many of them in the room that she could get no further than the doorway. She could see two nurses standing with their backs to the wall opposite. One of them was crying – the one, she observed, who had only come that afternoon. She could not see the bed from where she stood. But she could see that Morris had fallen on his knees. Ought I to kneel too? she wondered. Not in the passage, she decided. She looked away; she saw the little window at the end of the passage. Rain was falling; there was a light somewhere that made the raindrops shine. One drop after another slid down the pane; they slid and they paused; one drop joined another drop and then they slid again. There was complete silence in the bedroom.

Is this death? Delia asked herself. For a moment there seemed to be something there. A wall of water seemed to gape apart; the two walls held themselves apart. She listened. There was complete silence. Then there was a stir, a shuffle of feet in the bedroom and out came her father, stumbling.

'Rose!' he cried. 'Rose! Rose!' He held his arms with the fists clenched out in front of him.

You did that very well, Delia told him as he passed her. It was like a scene in a play. She observed quite dispassionately that the raindrops were still falling. One sliding met another and together in one drop they rolled to the bottom of the window-pane.[3]

The raindrops, replacing the tears which the daughter can't weep, the procession up to the bedroom, the sobbing nurse, the stumbling father with his outstretched arms and melodramatic cry: these items in the novel's dry re-writing of damp Victorian conventions also call on powerfully charged personal memories.

Julia's premature death – 'the greatest disaster that could happen'[4] – fell into her youngest daughter's life just at the point of 'strain' between childhood and adulthood.[5] She would often describe the death, each time a little differently, but usually reverting to its most distressing aspect: that she could not feel anything.

This is the 29th anniversary of mothers death. I think it happened early on a Sunday morning, & I looked out of the nursery window & saw old Dr Seton walking away with his hands behind his back, as if to say It is finished, & then the doves descending, to peck in the road, I suppose, with a fall & descent of infinite peace. I was 13, & could fill a whole page & more with my impressions of that day, many of them ill received by me, & hidden from the grown ups, but very memorable on that account: how I laughed, for instance, behind the hand which was meant to hide my tears; & through the fingers saw the nurses sobbing.

But enough of death – its life that matters.[6]

The day mother died in 1895 – that 37

$$\frac{5}{42}$$ 42 years

ago: & I remember it – at the moment, watching Dr Seton walk away up Hyde Park Gate in the early morning with his head bowed, his hands behind his back. Also the doves swooping. We had been sent up to the day nursery after she died; & were crying. And I went to the open window & looked out. It must have been very soon after she died, as Seton was then leaving the house. How that early morning picture has stayed with me! What happened immediately afterwards I cant remember.[7]

[On hearing of Roger Fry's death.] I remember turning aside at mother's bed, when she had died, & Stella took us in, to laugh, secretly, at the nurse crying. She's pretending, I said: aged 13. & was afraid I was not feeling enough. So now.[8]

Finally, she returns to the scene in her 'Sketch of the Past', in May 1939, and re-writes it twice, in two separate passages, filling in still more details. In the first of the two passages, she recalls her mother's last words to her as she is led in to say goodbye ('Hold yourself straight, my little Goat'), and the time of day, six o'clock, that Dr Seton left the house. How telling those last maternal words are to the nervous adolescent daughter, and how vividly they demonstrate the practical, critical relationship the mother seems to have had with her! In the second, longer passage, the death-bed scene becomes a kind of ghost story. In both these accounts, she makes her memories into a powerful fictional narrative.

George took us down to say goodbye. My father staggered from the bedroom as we came. I stretched out my arms to stop him, but he brushed past me, crying out something I could not catch; distraught. And George led me in to kiss my mother, who had just died.

[Here she breaks off her memoir, and resumes it three weeks later.] Led by George with towels wrapped round us and given each a drop of brandy in warm milk to drink, we were taken into the bedroom. I think candles were burning; and I think the sun was coming in. At any rate I remember the long looking-glass; with the drawers on either side; and the washstand; and the great bed on which my mother lay. I remember very clearly how even as I was taken to the bedside I noticed that one nurse was sobbing, and a desire to laugh came over me, and I said to myself as I have often done at moments of crisis since, 'I feel nothing whatever'. Then I stooped and kissed my mother's face. It was still warm. She [had] only died a moment before. Then we went upstairs into the day nursery.

Perhaps it was the next evening that Stella took me into the bedroom to kiss mother for the last time. She had been lying on her side before. Now she was lying straight in the middle of her pillows. Her face looked immeasurably distant, hollow and stern. When I kissed her, it was like kissing cold iron. Whenever I touch cold iron the feeling comes back to me – the feeling of my mother's face, iron cold, and granulated. I started back. Then Stella stroked her cheek, and undid a button on her nightgown. 'She always liked to have it like that,' she said. When she came up to the nursery later she said to me, 'Forgive me. I saw you were afraid.' She had noticed that I had started. When Stella asked me to forgive her for having given me that shock, I cried – we had been crying off and on all day – and said, 'When I see mother, I see a man sitting with her.' Stella looked at me as if I had frightened her. Did I say that in order to attract attention to myself? Or was it true? I cannot be sure, for certainly I had a great wish to draw attention to myself. But certainly it was true that when she said, 'Forgive me', and thus made me visualize my mother, I seemed to see a man sitting bent on the edge of the bed.

'It's nice that she shouldn't be alone,' Stella said after a moment's pause.[9]

In this version it is the daughter, not the father, whose arms are stretched out and remain empty. And the memories are of fear and strangeness: the cold iron of the dead face, the seated figure. Virginia is frightened, and she frightens Stella. The shock of the event, and the confusion of her feelings, are mixed up with anxieties about proper death-bed behaviour. George and Stella, Leslie and the nurse are performing in a play in which Virginia wants to play a part ('I had a great wish to draw attention to myself'), but she stays apart. This troubling feeling of dissociation often recurs in her adult life.

If the daughter could not feel enough, that was partly because the father felt too much. All her accounts of what followed emphasise the terrible burden of their father's extortionate, melodramatic grief. Leslie Stephen made them all feel that no one was allowed to mourn for Julia except him, and, at the same time, that they were not coming up to scratch emotionally, not giving him enough sympathy in his bereavement. There were repeated painful scenes, painful because repeated, when he would walk up and down crying out 'that he had never told mother how he loved her', and they would all have to fall into his arms and cry with him and comfort him.[10] The house filled up with a chorus of grieving, sympathetic women relatives ('various ancient females'),[11] Cousin Mia and Aunt Minna and Aunt Mary, Fishers and Stephens and Vaughans (of whom Annie Ritchie was the least oppressive), happy to indulge Sir Leslie in his pitiable histrionics. An atmosphere of 'muffled dulness' and 'stifling gloom' overtook them. All her images of this time are of suffocation.

The Stephen children retreated into an exhausted, embarrassed inhibition about grieving. In Virginia's diary for 1897, Julia is noticeable by her absence, only referred to indirectly: 'Adrian, Thoby and Father went to Highgate.'[12] All of them resented the way their mother was being falsified by their father's interminable obsequies. 'It's silly going on like this,' the schoolboy Thoby said; yet they all felt that there was 'no escape'.[13] They were drawn closer together by the catastrophe of the death, but it also made them more reserved with each other. When Stella's death followed Julia's, 'We never spoke of them. I can remember how awkwardly Thoby avoided saying "Stella" when a ship called *Stella* was wrecked.'[14] It presaged a life-long embarrassment about expressions of emotions.

This excruciating family tension between excessive and inadequate grieving was very damaging. It did 'unpardonable mischief', she says in the 1908 'Reminiscences', 'by substituting for the shape of a true and most vivid mother, nothing better than an unlovable phantom'.[15] Her childhood turned into a macabre ghost story, her feelings about her mother were distorted, and Hyde Park Gate became a haunted house. Like Katharine Hilbery, the daughter in *Night and Day* whose youth is absorbed by the past, she would often feel that she belonged to the world of the dead: 'She seemed to herself to be moving among them, an invisible ghost among the living.'[16] In the last part of *To the Lighthouse*, Lily Briscoe's embarrassment at her own emotions for Mrs Ramsay, her involuntary vacillations between numbness and agony, her inability to give Mr Ramsay the sympathy he demands except at comically inappropriate moments, make sense and shape out of the destructive after-effects of the mother's death.

Even during the dark 'muffled' days of forced mourning, the shock of the death precipitated a peculiarly creative state of mind. Her memories of this period are dramatically lit and shaded. They went to fetch Thoby from Paddington (who, at school at Clifton, had missed his mother's death) and the train steaming into the station in a blaze of colour and light 'exalted' her. She and Vanessa sat in Kensington Gardens on a hot spring evening a few days after the death, with a copy of *The Golden Treasury*, and the poem she read suddenly seemed to become 'altogether intelligible'. She tried to explain this sensation, with some difficulty, to Vanessa ('One seems to understand what it's about'). Trying to explain it again years later, she uses an image of the burning glass as a metaphor for the sudden moments of revelation: 'my mother's death unveiled and intensified; made me suddenly develop perceptions, as if a burning glass had been laid over what was shaded and dormant.'[17] She often uses images of incandescence and transparency as a way of describing how the mind works at its moments of greatest concentration.

Here she is saying that the effect of her mother's death was to make her see and feel with especial intensity. What she omits almost entirely is the mental and physical disturbance which accompanied that intensity. She crosses out a paragraph which describes her first 'breakdown' after her mother's death: a racing pulse, disturbing feelings of anger and terror and excitement, and two years spent in 'a state of physical distress'.

Now Hyde Park Gate became 'a cage', and Virginia the 'nervous, gibbering, little monkey' who inhabited it.[18] After the death, the regular pattern of the family life was broken (as in *To the Lighthouse*). There followed 'the ending of society; of gaiety; the giving up of St Ives; the black clothes; the suppressions; the locked door of her bedroom.'[19] The boys were at school; the Duckworth sons were living at home and going out to work. Vanessa and Virginia began to forge a much closer alliance. But the most striking change in the family after Julia's death was the sudden and entire shift of responsibility to Stella.

> She assumed control of the household; and it was no light job. My mother . . . was leaving a great enterprise unfinished; to fall upon Stella. The Vn. family was a great business. Four children . . . and Laura . . . and father – not poverty but a strain. Not enough money for luxury. Always on the watch – cutting down. The emotional strain . . . My father was one of the most dependent of men . . . Emotionally he fell then upon Stella. It was the way of the time. He couldn't do anything for himself. She had to buy underclothes; bills; every practical question. The weight – we were to feel it – was very heavy.[20]

Stella's actions at her mother's death-bed – her undoing of her mother's nightgown buttons, her response to her half-sister's frightening fantasy, 'It's nice that she shouldn't be alone' (a good answer to give to an extremely distressed and imaginative thirteen-year-old whose mother has just died) show her taking over at the very point of Julia's death. Abjectly devoted to Julia, Stella had been away on holiday when she fell ill, and had not been told until the last minute. She came back to see her die. She was twenty-six;

she had her admirers, her occupations, her interests. People liked her: 'She is full of quiet intelligence and quick to appreciate the least touch of drollery or humour in talk. And oh, she is such a beautiful creature.'[21] Now she had all at once, in the shock of her own deep grief, to take over the care of the children and to deal with her distraught step-father. Twelve-year-old Adrian, who had been his mother's favourite, and who this year was often ill and in a pitiable state about going back to boarding-school, had to be looked after, and a new day school (Westminster) settled on for him. 'Ginia', in an even more nervous state than Adrian, became Stella's responsibility, to be taken to the doctor and minded and exercised. Stella's own work for Octavia Hill at Southwark continued, while she was running the household: everything from hiring a new parlour-maid, ('who I think will do but who lisps!'), to finding a house for the summer, shopping, visiting Julia's grave with the girls (on 7 February they 'planted snowdrops' on it), chasing the children's marmoset, ('little fiend!') and looking after another kind of 'fiend', the 'Old Man': 'Old Man on sofa groaning and grumpy – but his head *is* bad I fear.' 'Took Ginia to see [Dr] Seton and he says she must do less lessons and be very careful not to excite herself – her pulse is 146. Father in a great state.'[22]

The excitable Ginia was a difficult charge. The first time we hear her talking to herself, in the fat little leather-bound, gilt-edged book with a metal clasp in which she kept her private diary for 1897, she frequently complains about Stella's authority. Stella makes her drink beef tea for luncheon – 'most disgusting stuff'. Stella 'insisted upon putting the books in the library tidy, so that it was too late to do anything'. Ginia repeatedly describes herself – clearly echoing Stella – as 'irritable'. She and Stella spent most of the day together, going on walks and errands to relatives or sick friends or to the workhouse or on social calls, often painful and embarrassing occasions for 'Miss Jan':

> Poor Miss Jan utterly lost her wits dropped her umbrella, answered at random talked nonsense, and grew as red as a turkey cock. Only rescued from this by S. proposing to go away.[23]

The main business of the early part of 1897 was the preparation for Stella's wedding. In February Ginia was forced to go for a dreary week to Bognor with Leslie, Adrian, Vanessa, Stella and 'her young man' (who was convalescing from a minor operation). She spent the time trailing about in the rain 'leaving Stella and Jack to wander about arm in arm', reading Scott, taking photographs, and protesting violently: 'Another week of drizzle in that muddy misty flat utterly stupid Bognor (the name suits it) would have driven me to the end of the pier and into the dirty yellow sea beneath.'[24] In March the banns were read in St Mary Abbots, a 'performance' which Virginia writes up mockingly and gloomily in her diary: 'At certain parts we stood, then sat, and finally knelt – this I refused to do.'[25] As the house filled up with presents and a 'whole pack' of visiting and weeping relatives, tensions mounted. Leslie's evenings of reading aloud to the family were frequently cut short in a rage, and Ginia's apprehension increased: 'What will become of us'; 'Oh dear, I wish it was over.'[26] The formal, conventional church wedding was 'half a dream, or a nightmare'. The next day, the family took the left-over flowers to Julia's grave. Then, 'very furious and tantrumical' preparations for a wet, 'gruesome' family holiday in Brighton, and after that the depressing return to a Stella-less house: 'Everything is as dismal as it well can be.'[27] Stella and Jack came back from their honeymoon and moved into their new house a few doors down in Hyde Park Gate. Three months later, Stella was dead.

Both Virginia and Vanessa would come to think of Stella's pathetic story as the epitome of 'all the old abuses' and vices of the family system.[28] Jack Waller Hills's patient courtship of Stella had been unsuccessful for years. Vanessa thought that Stella would never have married him while Julia was alive, so closely involved was she with her mother.[29] After Julia's death he came back, and as late as in March of 1896 she was still sending him away – 'All is over with him'[30] – and having long confidential talks about it with her friend Kitty Maxse. But in August, during the family's second sad post-St Ives holiday, in a house they had borrowed for the summer in Haslemere, he came bicycling up every day (like Richard Dalloway courting Clarissa), and she finally accepted him.

Virginia liked to return to this romantic scene, though she shifted its details over time. Stella and Jack walked for hours in the moonlight, and she and Vanessa 'wandered about the house' waiting for them to come in. Or did they go out moth-hunting, and then go up to bed? A tramp found his way into the grounds and Thoby sent him away. And did he then mistake Stella and Jack for tramps, when they finally came back? And they watched for Stella to return, blushing 'rose-red'; or perhaps it was the next morning that Stella came up to their room and told them. 'And I whispered, "Did mother know?" and she said "Yes".'[31] The scene was for ever hazy with enchantment: 'As she died so soon after, somehow it still seems to me like a real thing, unsmothered by the succeeding years.'[32] Stella's engagement would become an ideal of conventional romance, a 'lyrical', 'musical' vision of first love, a standard of comparison: 'But they're not in love like Stella and Jack.'[33] While Virginia sat 'half-insane with shyness and nervousness' behind the folding doors of the drawing room, glimpses of happiness – a secret love-letter, night-time words of reassurance from a blushing and laughing Stella about the rosy future awaiting Virginia and Vanessa – would give her 'a quiver of ecstasy'.[34]

But these touching remembrances, like scenes from the quietly turned pages of a Victorian photograph album, are out-of-tune with the scratchy, apprehensive, irritated reactions in the fifteen-year-old's diary. At the time, Virginia seems to have been infected by her father's feelings about the marriage, though it was not until later that she realised the full extent of what he had been doing to Stella. After Julia's death Leslie had completely appropriated Stella as a substitute and she had allowed him to do it. 'I do not think that Stella lost consciousness for a single moment during all those months of his immediate need . . . Sometimes at night she spent a long time alone in his study with him, hearing again and again the bitter story of his loneliness, his love and his remorse.'[35] An unnaturally close dependency was forged between the deaf, grieving widower and a step-daughter who had until then been protected from the full blast of his emotions. And Leslie punished Stella for trying to leave. At first he grudgingly accepted her engagement, but he grew increasingly obstructive and emotional – even the name 'Jack' sounded unpleasant to him, like a whip – when it became clear that the young couple, reasonably enough, wanted to live in their own house. His obstructiveness delayed the marriage by months, and right up to the day of the wedding he was groaning and complaining and asserting his rights. His letters to Charles Norton display his emotions:

I am . . . practising for the new position of father-in-law. To tell you a profound secret, I find that it has its difficulties . . . I could do perfectly well without Jack – Why should not she? Is my feeling something abnormal and discreditable to a father, or is it natural – a result, perhaps, of the jealousy wh. makes the man look askance at the devotion of any woman to anybody but himself?[36]

These flashes of self-knowledge did not make him behave any better, and his staggering letters to Stella immediately after the wedding were calculated to provoke remorse during the honeymoon:

Dearest Stella . . . The excitement of parting from you was great and tiring . . . I am afraid that, barring accidents, I shall be a burthen to you for some time to come. Well, I know that you protest against that view of things . . . Various people have dropped in to congratulate (or sympa-thise) . . . My love to – I cannot find a satisfactory name for him yet. Was he never called Waller? My dearest, I have tried to hold my tongue, as I said, though I feel that something may have peeped out. You will forgive me, I know. I wonder whether I shall ever be able to write a cheerful letter – I will, if I can.[37]

'How the family system tortures and exacerbates', Virginia Woolf commented many years later, thinking back to the unacknowledged sexual jealousy which dominated this relationship. 'I feel that if father could have been induced to say "I am jealous", not "You are selfish", the whole family atmosphere would have been cleared and brightened.' (And how much better, she noted, instancing Clive Bell's friendship with Duncan Grant, her generation were at this.) But the Victorians, she added, cannot be blamed for 'concealing their motives'. They did not have 'the truthtelling machinery at hand'.[38]

And so Stella's relationship with Leslie became the basis for Virginia Woolf's analysis of the tyranny and hypocrisy of the Victorian fathers. It established the fundamental framework for her feminism. Whenever she writes about the Victorian family home and its after-effects – in *A Room of One's Own*, in *The Years*, in *Night and Day* (where Mr Hilbery opposes his daughter's choice and then insists on reading Walter Scott to her) – Stella and Leslie provide the blueprint. Writing in *Three Guineas* on the hostile feelings aroused in men by women's attempts to enter the professions, she cites – only half-mockingly – the findings of a Freudian psychologist who attributes these emotions to 'powerful and widespread subconscious motive', which he labels 'infantile fixation' and 'Oedipus complex'. Virginia Woolf laughs at the Freudian terminology,[39] but she pursues with relish the attribution of unconscious motives, citing two famously repressive Victorian fathers, Patrick Brontë and Mr Barrett, who wanted to keep their daughters to themselves. 'Mr Barrett's emotions were strong in the extreme; and their strength makes it obvious that they had their origin in some dark place below the level of conscious thought.' Similarly with Charlotte Brontë's father: 'Her married life – it was to be a short one – was shortened still further by her father's wish.'[40] She argues in *Three Guineas* that the infantile fixation of the Victorian fathers in the private house, which made them resist the departures of their daughters for marriage or – worse still – for a profession, was supported by society: 'Society it seems was a father, and afflicted with the infantile fixation too.' The 'disease' was rampant, and thousands of Victorian biographies bear witness to 'the familiar symptoms'. And 'now' the infantile fixation has been translated to 'the fathers in public, massed together in societies, in professions'. The case is the same in 1937 as it was in 1897: 'aggravated and exacerbated' male emotions towards women who threaten their supremacy are attributable to the patriarchy's threatened conception of its own manhood.

Like Charlotte Brontë, Stella's married life was shortened by her father's wish, though he cannot quite be accused of killing her. Vanessa remembered the whole period as 'a time of horrible suspense, muddle, mismanagement, hopeless fighting against the stupidity of those in power'.[41] Not for the last time, the Stephen family doctors (Seton and Sir William Broadbent) seem to have been incompetent. When Stella got home ill from her honeymoon she was first thought to have 'a bad chill on her innards'.[42] Then peritonitis (an inflammation of the membrane around the intestines) was diagnosed; but no operation was performed for three months. Years later, Virginia gave another version: 'It was appendicitis; she was going to have a baby. And that was mismanaged too.'[43] And in 1942, the aged Violet Dickinson wrote a letter to Vanessa with a further story about Stella's death. She remembered that 'everyone was told she had appendicitis' but that the nurse had said she had an inverted uterus ('something was concave that ought to have been convex, or vice versa', Violet wrote vaguely)[44] and possibly she had been injured by Jack's love-making.[45] Whatever the facts, it is sure that Stella would have been in agonising pain, and probable that she should have been operated on sooner.

During the months of Stella's illness Virginia was herself unwell and 'nervous'. For a little while Stella seemed to be recovering, and Virginia took carriage rides with her when she had to give Stella a full account of her day. This 'inquisitive hour' irritated her; she wished that 'the drives would cease to exist'.[46] She was exasperated, too, by all the attention Stella was getting from their 'respectable dull visitors': 'answered the invariable "How is Stella?" till I hated poor Stella & her diseases.'[47] Yet she went every day to 24 Hyde Park Gate to sit with her, and was dependent on her for company and comfort: 'I sat with her, & we talked of everything'.[48] There is a troubled mixture of resentment, jealousy, and need in this relationship. Adeline Fisher (who was Stella's closest friend and had just got engaged to Ralph Vaughan Williams) remarked on how bad it was 'for Stella to have Ginia always with her'.[49] In the last days of Stella's life Ginia was taken ill. (She did not keep her diary during these days, but filled it in two weeks later.) She stayed at Stella's house, sleeping in Jack's dressing-room opposite their bedroom. On 14 July, a Wednesday, Stella sat up late with her, soothing away 'the fidgets', as she had done many times before. The next morning she came in in her dressing-gown to see how Ginia was; 'She left me, & I never saw her again.' They called to each other from their bedrooms. Then on the Saturday George carried Ginia home, wrapped in Stella's fur cape, and Stella called out 'Goodbye' as they passed her door. The next day Stella was operated on unsuccessfully and in the early hours of Monday morning George and Vanessa came in and told Virginia that Stella was dead. The diary entry ('it is impossible to write of') was blotched and the next page was left blank. Stella was buried next to Julia in Highgate, but none of the children went. The diary for the rest of the year lapses into brief, desolate notes: 'Things are all in a tangle . . . It is hopeless & strange . . . Very strange & unhappy . . . Everything is miserable & lonely . . . One day is so like another that I never write about them . . . And another & another & another yet to come. Oh dear they are very long, & I seem cowardly throughout when I look at them. Still, courage & plod on.'[50]

'Even now it seems incredible.' 'I remember saying to myself after she died: "But this is impossible; things aren't, can't be, like this." '[51] Stella's death seemed to her retrospectively to have struck even more deeply than Julia's. Among the images she used for herself at this time was that of a butterfly emerging from its chrysalis, still quivering, 'apprehensive' and incapable of flight. And then the second blow struck, as if a voice was 'brutally' telling one 'not to be such a fool as to hope for things'.[52] Security was abolished; the unthinking childhood feeling of being protected and 'family surrounded' and of going on 'exploring and adventuring privately while all the family as a whole continued its prosaic, rumbling progress' was removed; instead the family shelter was 'cracked and gashed' and the protected creature was 'tumbled out of the family shelter'.

Looking back, she wonders if there might not have been advantages to having become 'critical and sceptical of the family'[53] at that age. But it was hard at the time to find consolations. Stella's death was catastrophic. Already, with the new authority her engagement had conferred on her, she had begun to suggest ways in which the girls could be made more independent, with a clothes allowance between them of £40 a year. ('Think of the joy of making a pair of boots last a month longer and buying for ourselves books at a 2nd hand bookstall!' Virginia fantasised in her diary. But added soberly that the scheme was 'not yet proposed to father'.)[54] Though conventional and unintellectual, Stella would have managed the 'Greek slave years'[55] (as Virginia bitterly described the time of 'coming out' into society) far better than her brother George. And Jack Hills, the first person to talk to Virginia openly about sex and the sexual double standard, would have been a helpful and liberating brother-in-law, 'the most open-minded and least repressive' of 'all our youthful directors'.[56] Whenever she encountered him in later years (he lived until 1938 and eventually remarried) she remembered why she had liked him – for his 'human sympathies', his trustiness and freshness, his interest in poetry and philosophy.[57] He was generous, too: when Stella died intestate, he gave Leslie the income from her substantial marriage settlement, to be passed on to the Stephen girls when Leslie died.[58] But because Stella died, Jack's potential helpfulness was transformed into another source of pain. In the autumn after her death, there was a 'dreary and terrifying week'[59] visiting him and his mother in Corby Castle – everything 'very stately and uncomfortable'[60] – which the snobbish, worldly Mrs Hills had borrowed from the Howards. Virginia always remembered her boasting about the number of her housemaids and her aristocratic connections and fixing the Stephen girls 'with her little black eyes'. Jack told them later that his mother hated women. Mrs Hills ushered them into their years of being found wanting by upper-middle-class society ladies, and so earned a special little unforgiven place in Virginia Woolf's memoirs. All her life she would resent this kind of patronage.

Three years later in 1900, Jack Hills, still in anguished mourning (which for all his generosity was as much forced upon the Stephen girls as Leslie's mourning for Julia), transferred his feelings to Vanessa, leading to an angry family confrontation and a breach of trust between Vanessa and Virginia. Since it was then scandalously against the law to marry a deceased wife's sister, the Duckworth brothers and the ubiquitous aunts fell into a panic of disapproval (to be satirised in *Night and Day*) and tried to enlist Virginia. She would never forget Vanessa's bitter response – 'So you take their side too' – and her own realisation that if there were sides to take, she was on Vanessa's.[61]

The girls were eighteen and fifteen when Stella died. The difference between their lives and the lives of all the men in the house was marked, and they now evolved the 'close conspiracy' which would bind them together for ever. They had long since decided on their respective professions, but now they had to 'make some standing place' for themselves.[62] Thirty years later Virginia recalled their long walks at the end of the summer holidays, 'talking of what we were going to do – "autumn plans" we called them. They always had reference to painting & writing & how to arrange social life & domestic life better.'[63] And the obstacle to these plans was always their father.

While Adrian struggled unhappily through his time as a Westminster schoolboy (shooting up to a giraffe-like height, irritating everyone by being so forgetful and accident-prone) and Thoby progressed, looking more and more like a Greek God, from Clifton to Cambridge (in 1899); while the Duckworths went out to their jobs, the daughters' days were split in half. There was the life that was thrust upon them of female duties and the life they wanted to make for themselves, of independent habits and passionate absorption in books and art. In the mornings Adrian went to school (Vanessa or Virginia waving him goodbye on the step as Stella used to do),

George left after breakfasting late and chatting to Virginia about his social exploits, and Leslie climbed sadly up to his study. Vanessa's day was more structured and externally motivated than Virginia's. She had to go down to the basement to negotiate with Sophie Farrell about the day's menu, and then she bicycled off to her art classes, first to Mr Cope's school in South Kensington, and from 1901 by bus to the Painting School of the Royal Academy behind Burlington House. There she studied anatomy and perspective, attended the (segregated) life classes with her friend Margery Snowden – of whom Virginia was extremely jealous – came under the powerful influences of Charles Furse and John Singer Sargent, and entered a world quite different from the intellectual and unartistic Stephen milieu.[64]

Virginia took refuge in her secret life in the 'daytime' half of her room, where she studied Greek, and read and wrote, standing up at her high desk.[65] Her reading was addicted, escapist and ambitious. To an extent she was reading under orders: 'I am to reread all the books Father has lent me.'[66] So she prided herself on acquiring a taste for Carlyle (whom she read enormously) and on tackling her grandfather's heavyweight *Essays in Ecclesiastical Biography*. But from the age of fifteen she was increasingly choosing for herself from Leslie's library, and developing her own passions for prose essays, history and biography: for 'my beloved Macaulay',[67] for Lamb's *Essays of Elia*, for Pepys or Montaigne. She read with great relish the little leatherbound set of Lockhart's *Life of Scott* Leslie gave her (where she found 'his diary of a voyage to the lighthouses on the Scotch coast'),[68] and fell in love with the Elizabethan writer Richard Hakluyt's narratives of travel and adventure, which would lastingly influence her writing:

> It was the Elizabethan prose writers I loved first & most wildly, stirred by Hakluyt, which father lugged home for me – I think of it with some sentiment – father tramping over the Library with his little girl sitting at HPG in mind. He must have been 65; I 15 or 16, then; & why I dont know, but I became enraptured, though not exactly interested, but the sight of the large yellow page entranced me. I used to read it & dream of those obscure adventurers, & no doubt practised their style in my copy books.[69]

This taste lasted her for some years:

> When I was 20 I liked 18th century prose; I liked Hakluyt, Mérimée. I read masses of Carlyle, Scott's life & letters, Gibbon, all sorts of two volume biographies, & Shelley.[70]

Idle reading – reading for 'hair doing' times, like Washington Irving,[71] relaxation from the historians, such as godfather Lowell's essays – was mixed with absorbing nineteenth-century novels (these, often, for reading aloud to Vanessa): *Felix Holt, John Halifax, Gentleman, North and South, Wives and Daughters, Barchester Towers, The Scarlet Letter, Shirley, Villette, Alton Locke, Adam Bede*: all this in 1897. 'Reading four books at once,' she noted more than once.[72] It was now that she developed her feelings about reading at random which would form the backbone of her essays on being a self-educated reader. Like all her central preoccupations, the idea of 'the common reader' is rooted in her childhood and adolescence.

Vanessa had art school, Thoby had the classical training of public school and Cambridge, Adrian had lessons and exams. After a two-year gap following Julia's death in which she wrote nothing and had no lessons, Virginia was writing and 'gobbling' up Leslie's books almost faster than he approved. But she felt the need to keep pace with both Thoby and Vanessa, to acquire some disciplines. German lessons with Leslie, though an improvement on his earlier attempts to teach them maths,[73] were not a great success. 'She rushes at her fences,' he wrote revealingly to Thoby, 'and insists upon sticking a meaning into a sentence in defiance of grammar. However, by insisting upon that tenses and genders have some meaning I hope that I am getting her a little into order.'[74]

A less frustrating and more independent pursuit was bookbinding, in which she had a few lessons from a Miss Power – though she never became very proficient at it. Her 1899 diary, in minute handwriting, was bound into the jacket of Isaac Watts's *Logick: Or the Right Use of Reason* 'because its back had a certain air of distinction', and her letters to Emma Vaughan were full of enthusiastic details about the difficulties of lettering and different kinds of covers.[75] Her sensual, fastidious, aesthetic interest in the making of books – the pens she wrote with, the quality of paper, the colours of end papers and bindings, the look of title pages and type-face and illustrations – would be life-long, and would profoundly affect the way she wrote and the way her books were issued and responded to.

But her main study, in these years of lonely self-education, was the classics. So, in the autumn of 1897, she started classes in Greek and Latin with Dr George Warr, translator of Aeschylus and other classical authors and one of the founders of the Ladies Department of King's College, in Kensington. She didn't take the exams. From 1899 she was having private lessons in Greek and Latin (Homer, Plato's *Apologia*, 'dull' Xenophon) with the classics teacher Clara Pater, Walter Pater's sister, who after her brother's death had moved to Number 6, Canning Place, Kensington: 'all blue china, Persian cats, and Morris wallpapers.'[76] The following year she began lessons with Janet Case, a Cambridge-trained classicist who lived with her sister Emphie in Hampstead. Janet Case, with whom she forged a lasting friendship, had a profound intellectual influence on Virginia Stephen. Her vigorous, unsentimental teaching of the plays of Aeschylus and Euripides, her severity and clarity, and her 'fine human sympathy' (sketched in an essay of 1903)[77] were attributes gratefully admired. She gave Virginia ammunition for her discussions with Thoby, a release from the emotional cage of Hyde Park Gate into a more impersonal, good-humoured environment, and an example of the kind of independent woman educationalist whom she would always appreciate.

A Greek notebook, started in Greece in 1906 and continued in the next two years (partly to keep a connection with Thoby), shows how thorough Janet Case had encouraged her pupil to be, and suggests her teaching methods. Sophocles' *Ajax*, Plato's *Symposium*, Aristotle's *The Frogs*, are carefully annotated; and there is an eloquent commentary on the *Odyssey*,[78] concentrating on the style and beauties of Homer's narrative, its human interest, its evocation of place, and its probable effect on the audience:

Odysseus tells of the land of the Cyclops. This is precisely like an Elizabethan voyager writing of his travels. Immense vividness and strength of description. Probably this was what the audience loved. Like the bible, only more sinuous.

The souls of the dead cluster round, but Odysseus will not let them touch the blood, until Tiresias has spoken. Beautiful, beautiful![79]

These notes, charged with emotion, translate her feelings about Thoby – by then among the souls of the dead – into her feelings about Homer. She always associated Thoby with classical Greece, and her Greek lessons were above all a way of keeping pace with him. She was delighted when he respected her literary judgement.[80] But while she was sitting in her room at Hyde Park Gate, Thoby was moving on, challenging her views on Shakespeare, cutting his intellectual teeth on conversations at Cambridge with new friends who were not yet her friends. Virginia Woolf warns herself, in her memories of Thoby, against the 'falsifications' of hindsight: 'Then I never saw him as I see him now, with all his promise ended.'[81] They were often bad-tempered and inhibited with each other, and she sometimes resented his 'always telling me to explain myself clearly, and to say what I mean'.[82] But it is hard not to find her few letters to him extremely touching: for their imaginative energy, for the promise of their relationship, and for her painful sense of isolation:

I shall want a lecture when I see you; to clear up some points about the Plays. I mean about the characters. Why aren't they more human? Imogen and Posthumous and Cymbeline – I find them beyond me – Is this my feminine weakness in the upper region? But really they might have been cut out with a pair of scissors – as far as mere humanity goes – Of course they talk divinely. I have spotted the best lines in the play – almost in any play I should think –

Imogen says – Think that you are upon a rock, and now throw me again! and Posthumous answers – Hang there like fruit, my Soul, till the tree die! Now if that doesn't send a shiver down your spine, even if you are in the middle of cold grouse and coffee – you are no true Shakespearean! Oh dear oh dear – just as I feel in the mood to talk about these things, you go and plant yourself in Cambridge.[83]

I dont get anyone to argue with me now, and feel the want. I have to delve from books, painfully and all alone, what you get every evening sitting over your fire and smoking your pipe with Strachey etc. No wonder my knowledge is but scant. Theres nothing like talk as an educator I'm sure.[84]

EIGHT

Abuses

Apart from intellectual loneliness, Virginia Stephen was subject to other pressures of which Thoby was only dimly aware. These were the years of Greek slavery, as well as of Greek lessons. Mornings were spent very much as she would spend her mornings all her life, at work. But in the afternoons, 'the rules and demands of 'Victorian society'[1] were in force. Leslie Stephen's daughters poured tea and handed cakes and were pleasant to Leslie's old men and their interfering aunts and cousins and tried sometimes to sneak their own friends up to their room. Leslie groaned and fell silent and wished out loud that people would go and had to be shouted at down his ear-trumpet. In the evenings there were incongruous alternatives: either sitting in the dark, oil-lit drawing-room listening to Leslie reading aloud, or being taken out into George Duckworth's branch of 1890s society. It was not a free choice. Within the same house, they were constrained by two very different but equally demanding male authorities. No wonder that in her reading of the *Odyssey* Virginia Stephen admired the passage about Scylla and Charybdis.

The tragedy of Leslie's relationship with his daughters in the last years of his life was that it obscured their affection for him: in Vanessa's case entirely and for ever, in Virginia's confusingly. Unlike Vanessa, she recognised that his encouragement of both their talents was of fundamental importance for their professional lives. And, unlike Vanessa, she had a love for him which survived the worst outrages of his performance as a widower. She found him attractive and compelling.[2] But his treatment of Stella, and his transference of this behaviour towards Vanessa after Stella's death, could never be forgiven.

If she was the gibbering monkey in the cage of Hyde Park Gate, he was the 'pacing, dangerous, morose lion'.[3] There were still moments of affection and admiration – when he would praise her choice of book, or when he refused to participate in the family outrage over Vanessa and Jack ('If she wants to I wont interfere').[4] But mostly, now, she furiously resented his insistence on their sympathy and companionship. Every year between 1898 and 1904 they took annual family holidays in substantial country houses borrowed from friends or rented – the Vicarage at Painswick in Gloucester-shire, near Stroud, close to the Maitlands' home, the Manor House at Ringwood in the New Forest ('a dismal place', she thought, revisiting it with Leonard in 1936),[5] the Rectory at Warboys in Huntingdonshire (in the Fen country which Virginia loved, but too close to Lady Stephen's household), Fritham House in the New Forest for three summers, and, in the last year of Leslie's illness, Netherhampton House, near Salisbury. The 'young people' and their visitors would pass the time with all their usual hobbies: bicycle rides, trips to points of interest, photography and bug-hunting. 'Family life, of a very independent kind, such as suits us four self willed young animals only really flourishes in the country', Virginia wrote in 1903.[6] There were various romps and pranks, like the sinking of a punt in a pond full of duckweed at Warboys, which gave rise to gales of laughter. But Leslie brooded outside this activity in solitary, demanding deafness. In the country it was easier to by-pass him. Virginia vividly remembered a night-time scene at Ringwood, in the summer of 1898, when the children were walking outside in the dark, and Leslie called them in to play whist, and they did not answer his call. At last they went in and found him 'impressive, old, solitary and deserted'. 'Did you hear me call?' he asked; only Vanessa, implacably truthful, had the courage to say yes.[7]

In London the demands were less avoidable, and Vanessa's resistance to them even more marked. Thoby was bullied by Leslie too, but he could escape to school, where he received emotional letters ('Write to me tomorrow, darling . . . I am fonder of you and prouder of you and more anxious for you to do well than I can say, almost as much as your darling mother . . . Not a word from you last week! . . . Goodbye, your loving but very groggy old father').[8] Virginia was not in the direct line of fire: only on the rare occasions when Vanessa went away (to Paris in 1900, for instance) did she have to dread sitting 'at the head of the Table!' or being 'left alone with my Parent'.[9] But Vanessa was expected to replace Stella, and she took the full force of Leslie's demands. 'When he was sad, he explained, she should be sad; when he was angry . . . she should weep'.[10] These demands climaxed in the famous scenes of the Wednesday books, when Vanessa would present the housekeeping accounts (after a few ineffectual attempts at economies or falsifications with Sophie) and Leslie would accuse her of bankrupting him (though he hardly ever had less than £3000 in the bank)[11] and finally sign the cheque with a weary self-pitying flourish. Meanwhile Vanessa, refusing to bend to his will or to accept the role of the dutiful daughter, stood through it all 'like a stone'. Virginia looked on with outrage and helpless fury, unable to express a word of what she felt.

Until she wrote *To the Lighthouse*, the memory of these scenes would continue to obsess her: 'I would find my lips moving; I would be arguing with him; raging against him; saying to myself all that I never said to him.'[12] And for the rest of her life his 'brutality'[13] was the prototype for everything she hated about 'the terrible threat to one's liberty' in family relations.[14] A lifetime later she and her family were still discussing 'father, childhood. Was he utterly bad?' Was he 'Cruel'?[15]

If he had lived on into his nineties, she thought, 'His life would have entirely ended mine'.[16] When she had to be nice to old Mrs Woolf, it was Leslie she thought of, and all the daughters who had had their lives crushed out of them by their parents. When Vanessa, in her grief after Julian's death, lent heavily on Quentin, an image of Leslie leaning on Thoby came at once into her mind.[17] When she met Forster in the London Library in 1935 and he told her that the Committee had decided to go on excluding women, because Sir Leslie had said that the historian's widow, Mrs Green, had been such a nuisance, her outburst of rage (which poured straight into *Three Guineas*) was fired as much by her memory of her father as by the injustice done to women. In her rage she noted that 'Sir L.S. spent his evenings with the widow Green.'[18] (One of his last jobs had been to write a life of the historian John Green.) The inference is not, I think, that he and the widow Green had a liaison, but that his dependency on such adoring ladies, and his role as a public writer of male lives, was so violently at odds with his behaviour to his daughters.

There were two elements in this complicated, lifelong rage against her father. One was the experience of helplessness in the face of an egotistical exploitation of power. It informed her political ideas and her management of relationships. She wrote against it in all her books and she withdrew from any manifestations of that pattern in her friendships. The other was a more practical resentment of the irrational meanness which not only made him a tyrant of the housekeeping books but prevented him from paying for her education as he paid for his sons. 'He spent perhaps £100 on my education.'[19] Of course it was very unusual at this time for daughters as well as sons to go to school and university. Perhaps, too, Leslie did not think Cambridge a possibility for Virginia because of her illnesses and her nervousness. Arguably – as she sometimes argued herself – he gave her a better education from his study than she would have had at school or college. And certainly she would not have been the writer she was, with the subjects she chose, if she had had a formal education. But, with all these provisos, the fact remains that she was uneducated because he did not want to spend the money on her. She would come to resent bitterly the condition of her mind in her late teens, which, like Rachel's in *The Voyage Out*, was 'in the state of an intelligent man's in the beginning of the reign of Queen

Elizabeth: she would believe practically anything she was told, invent reasons for anything she said.'[20]

This knot of feelings would never be untied, though it was loosened by the writing of *To the Lighthouse*. In the novel, Cam, the daughter who both loves and resists her father, expresses Virginia Woolf's unresolvable ambivalence. Her father was the love of her life, 'for no one attracted her more; his hands were beautiful to her and his feet, and his voice, and his words, and his haste, and his temper, and his oddity, and his passion . . . and his remoteness'. And she would never forgive him for 'that crass blindness and tyranny of his which had poisoned her childhood and raised bitter storms, so that even now she woke in the night trembling with rage and remembered some command of his; some insolence: "Do this", "Do that"; his dominance: his "Submit to me".'[21]

The young Stephen girls struck all onlookers by their ravishing beauty, but they also seemed subdued and ill-at-ease. William Rothenstein remembered two graceful girls sitting silently all in white.[22] The two daughters of Florence and Fred Maitland, Ermengard and Fredegond, a few years younger than the Stephen girls, were much in awe of them: 'We used to make up stories about you, and Ermengard used to say When I put up my hair, I'll have a black velvet dress like Vanessa's and shew my breasts.' They saw them often during their summer at Painswick: 'You and Virginia were so beautiful that even the dogs in the road turned round to look again.'[23] But the lively and observant Caroline Reynolds, Lady Jebb, an acquaintance of Stella's, who had always wondered about 'the attitude of the Duckworth children towards the little ones', rightly perceived the awkwardness in the family relations: 'I should not be surprised if they were to part company and make two households.'[24] And Violet Dickinson, who began to be a close friend to the family and especially to Virginia after Stella's death, found an atmosphere of melancholy always hanging over the family.

In 1906 Virginia wrote a story called 'Phyllis and Rosamond' in which two pairs of girls, both in their mid-twenties, encounter each other, rather like the impressionable Maitland girls meeting the Stephens. One pair are resentfully conventional middle-class society girls, who have come to feel that 'all efforts at freedom were in vain: long captivity had corrupted them both within and without'. 'We are daughters, until we become married women,' they say. The other pair, the Miss Tristrams, are liberated Bloomsbury writers and artists, surrounded by friends. It is as if the pre-1904 Stephen girls have never got free, and are encountering their later, alternative selves. Both judge each other. The conventional visitors envy but fear their free-speaking world; the liberated sisters pity and despise their visitors. 'My God,' says the younger Tristram sister, the writer, listening to their story: 'What a Black Hole! I should burn, shoot, jump out of the window; at least do something!'[25]

In 1906 (at exactly the time this story is being written), Virginia tells Violet that they have finally got free of George Duckworth and his family, and exclaims: 'And now we are free women! Any form of slavery is Degrading – and the damage done to the mind is worse than that done to the body!!'[26] It was not only with their father that the Stephen girls were in a 'black hole' of enslavement. This was also the period of the grotesque and intrusive regime of their half-brother George.

Virginia Woolf and Vanessa Bell, by common consent, made a comedy out of George Duckworth. It is impossible now to think of this worthy gentleman – landowner, family man, Christian, public citizen, knight – without characterising him as a piggish, lustful idiot. The caricaturing of George began early. One of Virginia's first notebooks, from September 1902, contained a fragment of a novel, with many pages torn out. It is based on George's unsuccessful courtship of Flora Russell, daughter of Lady Arthur Russell, whose grand evening parties (where guests had to sit where they were placed, so couldn't escape dull neighbours) were black spots in the Stephen girls' social calendar. George features as 'Roger', a handsome Faun, with one pointed ear, and small shifty eyes, 'possessed of a very moderate share of brains' and 'adored by mother and sisters at home'. Lady Hester's rejection of him is very emotional: 'Beloved, I do care for you so much, he said wistfully. It is no use – oh do let me go, she cried. She was almost in tears . . . the temptation to give up the struggle and find peace in his arms was so great.'[27]

This set the tone for the family jokes about George. There was the story of Virginia sending a telegram on hearing the news of George's engagement to Flora Russell, which was meant to read 'SHE IS AN ANGEL' and was signed with Virginia's nickname, and which came through as 'SHE IS AN AGED GOAT.' (This is supposed to have been one of the reasons the engagement was broken off.) There was the story of Virginia, keen to show off her social skills, entertaining some dowagers with frank accounts of Plato;[28] and of the party, later that evening, having to beat a hasty retreat from the theatre in the middle of a *risqué* French bedroom farce. All these anecdotes have the same embarrassing plot: social conformity upset by eccentricity, sexual hypocrisy unmasked. And they were always told with the same boisterous vindictiveness. In 1908: 'Nature, we may suppose, had supplied him with abundant animal vigour, but she had neglected to set an efficient brain in control of it.' In 1940: 'He lived in the thickest emotional haze, and as his passions increased and his desires became more vehement . . . one felt like an unfortunate minnow shut up in the same tank with an unwieldy and turbulent whale.'[29]

Why was George always caricatured in this way? Because what he did to them was too horrifying to speak of without defensive laughter? Or because his duplicitous bourgeois Victorian behaviour provided a perfect target for satire? Whichever is true, the tone leaves room for ambiguity, and the evidence has to be approached with care.

In the photographs of George with the Stephen girls, he looks large, eager and bombastic; they look grave, nervy and withdrawn. He is always standing too close to them. Or perhaps he only seems to be standing too close because of what we know. But certainly after Stella's death, he did, suddenly, get too close. With Leslie in deaf, isolated retreat, the sentimental and conventional George became their unofficial guardian and their passport to the outside world. In her notes for her 1939 memoir she writes, in a suggestively physical phrase: 'He was in a position to press his mould tight upon us.' The objectionable features of this situation were partly financial. He was rich and they were poor: 'He had a thousand pounds a year whereas I had fifty.'[30] He gave them presents: a trip to Boulogne in 1896 (Virginia's first journey abroad, which, judging from the photographs of them huddled on board ship under George's eye, all in black, was not a great success), an Arab horse for Vanessa, jewellery and clothes. They had to be grateful. Meanwhile they were struggling to make themselves presentable on the £50 a year which Leslie had been persuaded to allow them. One story Virginia tells in her memoir, illustrating George's power over them, of appearing before him in a dress which she had had made from cheap fabric, and being told to go and take it off, is particularly humiliating. It would contribute to her 'clothes complex', her horror of dressmakers, her fear of being laughed at for what she was wearing.

When she examines George's motives, she turns them all to viciousness. He wanted his two beautiful half-sisters to look well and go out with him because it reflected well on him and made everyone say how wonderfully kind he was to the poor bereaved girls. He wanted them to make good matches to enhance his own social status. She describes him as a hypocritical social climber who disguised the fact that the Duckworth money came from cotton and was desperate to marry into the aristocracy. (She played down the socially conscientious side of George evident in his letters to Charles Booth[31] and his work for the Royal Commission on Historical Monuments and, in wartime, for the Ministry of Munitions.) And he got what he wanted: marriage to Lady Margaret Herbert,[32] property, children. But at the time when he was courting high society and working as Austen Chamberlain's private secretary, he forced them both –

first Vanessa, and when she became intractable, the more malleable Virginia – to accompany him on punitive seasonal rounds of dinners and dances and weekend visits.

This was a different milieu – of politicians, diplomats, society hostesses, dowagers, debutantes – from the Stephens' more sober literary circles, from the Cambridge society which Thoby was entering, or from the art world Vanessa had begun to make contact with.[33] The houses belonged to the governing and landowning classes, the 'sons and grandsons of the men who built the empire'.[34] Etiquette, social charm, wealth and status, skills in dancing and dressing and small talk, were still paramount in the big houses and marriage-markets of late-imperial England, in what one young Edwardian called 'the glare and rattle of these great suffocating brilliant parties'.[35] Life was plotted through the rituals of dance cards and weekend parties and visits abroad, morning calls and seasonal events (the opera at Covent Garden, for instance, where George took Virginia to the *Ring*). The prejudices and manners of this tribe are parodied in the plays of Oscar Wilde, and there is something Wildean in Virginia Woolf's ridicule of them; Lady Bracknell could well have been one of George Duckworth's hostesses.

Where Vanessa was bored, furious and silent, Virginia was, at least initially, eager to oblige and allured by the social spectacle. There may perhaps have been (though neither of them refers to it) some rivalry felt here. But curiosity rapidly turned into miserable embarrassment. She felt like 'a child who stands at the flap of the tent and sees the circus going on inside'. Inside the tent, she was forced to jump through George's hoops.[36] She could not dance, she did not know the people or pick up the references. Though she had a very beautiful face and a thin body she did not look right: she moved awkwardly, shuffling slightly, not standing straight, and her hair was not well done. In conversation, she would not play the games. She wanted to talk about books and ideas and this was the wrong place. She was a poor fish out of water.

'The truth of it is . . . we are failures', she wrote to Emma Vaughan of the London Season of 1901 – a quiet season anyway as Queen Victoria had died in January, and the whole of London – an amazing sight – was in deep mourning.[37] She picks up the image in her letter: 'Really, we can't shine in Society. I don't know how it's done. We aint popular – we sit in corners and look like mutes who are longing for a funeral.'[38] She wrote some essays on society in 1903 which vividly evoke the excruciating feeling of being 'outsiders where everybody else is intimate' and the awful sight of 'a room full of people none of whom you know.'[39] Whenever she felt she was being looked at scornfully by strangers, it would take her back to these evenings: 'Its partly the old complex which the misery of youth stamped on one – the sense of being with people who laugh at the things one cares about', she wrote to Philip Morrell in 1919. 'George Duckworth's at the bottom of it'.[40] Going to parties out of obligation would call up these memories: 'I used to be dragged by my half-brothers against my will – hence perhaps some latent sense of outrage'.[41]

These memories provided good materials. Virginia Woolf has been underrated as a Wildean satirist of English society. She derives a great deal of sharp comedy from these experiences. She always places someone on the edge, looking in: 'The amusing thing about a party is to watch the people – coming and going, coming and going.'[42] For the watcher, feelings of unreality and horror struggle with 'amusement'. The dancers look 'painfully like flies struggling in a dish of sticky liquid' – 'flies trying to crawl'.[43] Misfits suffer tortures of embarrassment about their looks, as in the story 'The New Dress'. Humiliation goes with envy and scorn for those who are adept at the game:

'Are you going away for Christmas?' said Mr Calthorp.
'If my brother gets his leave,' said Miss Edwards.
'What regiment is he in?' said Mr Calthorp.
'The Twentieth Hussars,' said Miss Edwards.
'Perhaps he knows my brother?' said Mr Calthorp.
'I am afraid I did not catch your name,' said Miss Edwards.
'Calthorp,' said Mr Calthorp.[44]

Virginia Woolf and her friends evolved their adult social life in opposition to everything which that conversation represented. All the same, she would always be half-fascinated by British high society. From the start, though an unwilling participant in the social game, she takes pleasure in its bravado. She likes the way it forces people to suppress their emotions, to be heroically trivial. And she likes the look of it, its light ripple, its shimmer, its stuffs, 'like some French painting'.[45] That shimmer of society is reworked – in the party scenes in *Jacob's Room* and *Mrs Dalloway*, in the socialite Jinny's speeches in *The Waves* – always with a mixture of detachment and desire.

The story of George's social induction of the Stephen girls is mixed up with the story of his sexual interference with them. Virginia's accounts of going out into society between the ages of eighteen or nineteen and twenty two, are loaded with a sexual language of exposure and humiliation. The nights of dressing up and going out with George ended, she says, with George helping her to undress, or coming into the bedroom after she was undressed, lying on her bed and fondling her. In this context, the 'inexplicably' horrid memories of the parties becomes explicable.

George's motives, in obsessively insisting that they go out with him, are always described as hopelessly confused, whether in the broad satire of the Memoir Club papers ('George's mind swam and steamed like a cauldron of rich Irish stew') or in the more analytical terms of the 'Sketch of the Past': 'Some crude wish to dominate there was; some jealousy, of Jack no doubt; some desire to carry off the prize; and, as became obvious later, some sexual urge.'[46] She feared and disliked that confusion of unanalysed, steaming emotions, in others and in herself. In *The Voyage Out*, when Rachel Vinrace is startlingly woken up from her innocent passivity by being kissed by the 'pompous and sentimental' Richard Dalloway (the first and last graphically described heterosexual kiss in all Virginia Woolf's writing), her reaction is muddled. At first she is excited, then horrified, haunted by her loathsome and erotic dream of the little deformed man gibbering at her in an underground tunnel oozing with damp, the dream that recurs in her fever just before she dies. The fiction invites, and has received, all kinds of biographical explanations – for instance, that Virginia Stephen took some pleasure in her half-brother's sexual approaches, and was then tormented by guilt, or that Rachel's death represents her author's inability to sort out 'threatening emotions'.[47] Certainly this novel about the death of childhood and the confused awakening of adult sexuality ends with a sense of loss and grief. But the novel cannot provide a proof of exactly what George Duckworth did to her. And the 'factual' accounts are somewhat ambiguous, too.

George's behaviour features prominently in her account of her life. First, in the 'Reminiscences' written soon after Vanessa's marriage, for Clive Bell and Vanessa to read, she talks of George's 'restraint' seeming to 'burst' after their mother's death, and of his 'sea of racing emotions',[48] but gives no details. These are provided in the two papers she writes for the Memoir Club in 1921 and 1922. In the first of these, '22 Hyde Park Gate', she describes George coming into her room in the dark at night, after their outings: "Don't be frightened", George whispered. "And don't turn on the light, oh beloved. Beloved – " and he flung himself on my bed, and took me in his arms.' The old ladies of Kensington and Belgravia, she adds in her peroration, never knew that George Duckworth was 'lover' as well as 'father and mother, brother and sister to those poor Stephen girls'.[49] In the second, 'Old Bloomsbury', she repeats the description of George 'flinging himself on my bed, cuddling and kissing and otherwise embracing me' and adds the detail that he 'later' explained this behaviour to Dr Savage as a comfort 'for the fatal illness of my father'.[50]

This looks damning and definite – particularly with the implication, in the second passage, that Vanessa told Dr Savage about George's behaviour during Virginia's breakdown in 1904, and that Savage called George to account for it. But although these memoirs celebrate the uncensored outspokenness of Bloomsbury compared with the hypocritical, night-time sexuality at Hyde Park Gate, there is something inconclusive about them.

In her casting and recasting of these papers she picked her way carefully with the subject. In '22 Hyde Park Gate' she cut out this passage about George: 'He dreamt and he desired with great natural lust; but as for giving either to himself or to others an account of his desires that was out of the question.'[51] In her account of their new freedom of speech in Bloomsbury, she cuts out 'Of course George's embraces, and the fact that my father let us read whatever we liked, had taught us all that can be known of sex in theory from very early days'.[52] George could not explain his desires; he taught them about sex 'in theory': both the excised passages might suggest that he was not actually their 'lover'. Was she cutting out the less dramatic versions in favour of something more exciting? The history of these Memoir Club papers might suggest it.

On 18 March 1920 she was deeply embarrassed at having exposed her feelings at the Memoir Club.[53] Nine months later, on 5 December 1920,[54] she reports that she was 'fearfully brilliant' at the Memoir Club meeting of 17 November, when she (presumably) read '22 Hyde Park Gate'. On 26 May 1921,[55] she is mortified when Maynard Keynes tells her that her best writing was 'your Memoir on George. You should pretend to write about real people & make it all up'. But if that is true, and her 'Memoir on George' is really her best work, she thinks, she is 'a mere scribbler'. This does suggest that she turned her back on a more explicit or emotional autobiographical paper in the effort to amuse her peers, to be 'fearfully brilliant'; and that the memoir was perceived, and acknowledged, to be – at least to an extent – a fabrication.

When she is writing a memoir for herself, in her last years, it is noticeable that the whole business of George's sexuality, which one might have expected her to go into in some detail (since it is here that, for the first time, she introduces the memory of Gerald's juvenile abuse), goes unmentioned. She analyses his motives without mentioning his sexual interference. But then the memoir breaks off; and three months later she kills herself. If George's abuse is thought to explain her life and her death, there may be something sinister or telling about her silence at this point.[56] But this can only be guesswork.

More is revealed when she mentions George in letters, less guardedly than in her memoirs. There are two full accounts of 'George's malefactions'. Both take exactly the same form, though written eleven years apart. They are both reports to Vanessa on a conversation Virginia has had with another woman, a woman who knew George Duckworth and had always felt what they felt about him, and now has her opinion confirmed by Virginia's narrative. The passages are written for comic effect, and they take pleasure (as her letters to Vanessa often do) in reclaiming intimacy through the gruesomeness of their shared memories, and in demonstrating how shocking Virginia has been, rocking these elderly women back on their heels with her frank revelations. The first of these reports on a conversation with Janet Case in 1911.

> She has a calm interest in copulation . . . and this led us to the revelation of all Georges malefactions. To my surprise, she has always had an intense dislike of him; and used to say 'Whew – you nasty creature,' when he came in and began fondling me over my Greek. When I got to the bedroom scenes, she dropped her lace, and gasped like a benevolent gudgeon. By bedtime she said she was feeling quite sick, and did go to the W.C., which, needless to say, had no water in it.[57]

(The letter continues with a series of sexual references, ending with the likelihood of Duncan Grant's having by now 'seduced' Adrian: 'I imagine a great orgy on the river tonight.' The whole document makes a show of sexual frankness for Vanessa's approval and amusement.)

The second is of a conversation with Elena Richmond in 1922. She was the wife of Bruce Richmond, editor of the *Times Literary Supplement*, and as Elena Rathbone, she had been a figure in Virginia Stephen's 'society' years. Thoby had been attracted to her, and Virginia too found her rather alluring in her large calm way.

> Well this gigantic mass of purity sat down by my side and I told her the story of George. It is only fair to say that she began it. 'I am going to be perfectly frank about your brother – your half brother – and say that I have never liked him. Nor has Bruce. I never did like him even in the old days.' This being so, I couldn't resist applauding her, and remarking that if she had known all she would have hated him. The queer thing with Elena is that one never knows what penetrates, what slips off. She was shocked at first; but very soon reflected that much more goes on than one realises. [She imagines Elena spreading 'it' and George being publicly disgraced.] . . . Dont you think this is a noble work for our old age – to let the light in upon the Duckworths – and I dare say George will be driven to shoot himself one day when he's shooting rabbits.[58]

She goes on to say that Elena was kept completely innocent of 'improper' literature as a child. The whole letter plays with the theme of censorship and exposure. And yet it is itself somewhat evasive, and doesn't quite tell us what, pruriently, we would like to know. In the context, 'One never knows what penetrates, what slips off', seems a particularly teasing phrase.

Scattered through her letters, there are numerous other passing references to George Duckworth which suggest that, all her life, his doings were a well-known subject for discussion, for jokes, and even for boasting, with her close friends. So, to Violet, in 1925: 'One of these days I hope to see you again; and then we can discuss George, better than on paper.'[59] She often mentions George to Ethel Smyth, when she is writing to her in the 1930s, in this sort of tone: 'expecting my seducing half brother and his wife – why they drive 30 miles to see us I cant imagine.'[60] In 1932 she offers to copy out the memoir she has just found about 'our doings with George Duckworth when we were so to speak virgins. It might amuse you'.[61]

So George Duckworth as incestuous seducer was a regular butt of satire. Yet there are some anomalies. The few surviving letters she wrote to 'my dear old Bar' or 'My dearest Georgie' in 1898 and 1899 read affectionately, even confidingly ('Nessa and I take walks in the evening . . . and discuss the universe'). But this proves nothing – and one of these affectionate letters also makes a point of telling him *not* to come back and look after them.[62] After the separation of the Stephens and the Duckworths, relations were not entirely broken off, even though Vanessa had to tell Margaret Duckworth to stop sending her invitations. Before Virginia's marriage to Leonard in 1912, they went to visit the Duckworths. When Virginia was ill in 1913, Leonard accepted George's invitation for her to be looked after at his house in Dalingridge: a surprising move, if by then Leonard knew the story of her childhood. And when George died in 1934, she makes none of the usual references to incest and seduction in her diary, but thinks of him with a 'genuine glow', and recalls 'how childhood goes with him – the batting, the laughter, the treats, the presents, taking us for bus rides to see famous churches, giving us tea at City Inns, & so on – that was the best which oddly enough of late years returned a little'.[63] A letter to Vanessa is more equivocal:

> As a matter of fact I feel more affection for him now than I did 10 years ago. In fact I think he had a sort of half insane quality – I cant quite make out what – about family and food and so on. But your memoir so flooded me with horror that I cant be pure minded on the subject. I hope to goodness somebody went to the service – I wish I had been able to.[64]

The evidence of outside witnesses also leaves a mixed impression. Vanessa makes less of George's 'malefactions' than Virginia does. When she is staying on a country house visit with him in 1904, she writes to Virginia that 'George embraced and fondled me in front of the company, but that was only to be expected.'[65] When she writes her own Memoir Club reminiscences of this period, however, she talks bitingly about George's social clumsiness and bullying and her resistance to it, but does not mention his sexual interference. And friends of Virginia and Vanessa gave confusing reports. Ottoline Morrell, in her diary for 9 November 1932, recorded a conversation with Virginia who told her that her half-brother used to come into her bedroom at night, help her undress, and paw her all over: '& she said "He sent me mad." '[66] More contradictory evidence comes in a letter from Fredegond Shove to Vanessa, recalling the time when, as a child, she first came to know the Stephen girls in the summer after Stella's death. 'I can dimly see how terrible it must all have been and I would so like to know all the truth about that George affair. I mean do you think it was conscious (the sexual impulse in him?) and was Jack Hills the same? I suppose it was not quite conscious in George people like him are I imagine too sentimental ever to be able properly to analyse their feelings.'[67] The letter – to which unfortunately no answer has survived – suggests that George's abuses were more emotional than penetrative: if the often-repeated stories of his 'malefactions' were stories of sexual intercourse or rape then the 'sexual impulse' would not have been questionable.

It seems clear that whatever the facts, they were turned into running jokes which may have been, in part, a form of competition with people who had more scandalous sex lives, more sensational narratives of damage or desire, than Virginia Woolf. But the jokes seem also to have been a way of talking about events which she herself felt to be the source of lasting pain and harm.

It is impossible to think about this story innocently, without being aware of what has been made of it. The evidence is strong enough, and yet ambiguous enough, to open the way for conflicting psychobiographical interpretations which draw quite different shapes of Virginia Woolf's interior life.[68] But what matters most in this story is what Virginia Woolf made out of what happened. Here the commentator can only point to the gap between the available evidence and the story she drew from it. There is no way of knowing whether the teenage Virginia Stephen was fucked or forced to have oral sex or buggered. Nor is it possible to say with certainty that these events, any more than Gerald Duckworth's interference with the child Virginia, drove her mad. But Virginia Woolf herself thought that what had been done to her was very damaging. And to an extent, her life was what she *thought* her life was. She used George as an explanation for her terrifyingly volatile and vulnerable mental states, for her inability to feel properly, for her sexual inhibition. And yet she also violently resisted simplistic Freudian explanations of a life through childhood traumas, and would have been horrified by interpretations of her *work* which reduced it to a coded expression of neurotic symptoms.

George Duckworth's stupid, bullying, intrusive presence was a grotesque addition to the shocks and griefs of these unhappy years. Julia's and Stella's deaths, Leslie's behaviour, her mental vulnerability: all these contributed to a dark story of the death of childhood. But meanwhile another story was going on in the cracks and gaps left free of family tyrannies. This was a story of female friendships and, closely linked to these, of a rapid and energetic outpouring of writings.

NINE

First Loves

Virginia Stephen had no schoolfriends to confide in, no college girls to become intimate with. But though she felt isolated compared with Thoby, she was not much alone. Her closeness to Vanessa in the 1890s and early 1900s is evident from her early diaries and from letters to others: 'Nessa and I went for a long walk alone this afternoon,' she wrote from Warboys, in 1899, to Emma Vaughan. 'We walked and walked and walked for miles and never met a creature. Then we sat down by the wayside and gossiped; it was quite Divine.'[1] When Vanessa goes away, for instance on a trip to Paris in the spring of 1900, she is bereft: 'Of course I want her' (this to George) 'but . . . after all we see each other every day of our lives.'[2] She is jealous of Vanessa's other friendships and cultivates her own out of rivalry: when Vanessa insists that her friend Margery Snowden's letters should not be read by Virginia, Virginia responds by keeping Violet Dickinson's secret.[3] These rivalries, and other points of tension – over Jack Hills's courtship of Vanessa, perhaps over George's transferring of his social ambitions from Vanessa to Virginia, and, increasingly, over their very different responses to Leslie's illness – marked and scarred, but did not lessen, a profound bond of love, anger, conspiracy and ambition.

It is not clear whether Vanessa was reading Virginia's early writings. The *Hyde Park Gate News* ended, just before Julia's death, with a strange and gloomy account of two women in a bare room overlooking a London roofscape. They are a 'lank female' covered in ink – the writer – scowling disagreeably as she remembers her childhood, and a 'forty to fifty year old' amiable lady, her editor, who 'knows her author very well', and comes in wanting to know why she has chosen poetry as her subject rather than 'History – Philosophy – Womens Suffrage – Vivisection'.[4] Perhaps this was a comic fantasy of herself and her sister in middle age. But though she often said later that she wrote with Vanessa in mind, it was not her sister who drew out her early experiments with writing. These literary ambitions were exposed, outside the family, to a few women friends who were perhaps less competitive and less close.

There was a pattern to these friendships. The women were all unusual, and they were all older. In 1900, when Virginia was eighteen, Janet Case was thirty-eight, Violet Dickinson was thirty-five, Kitty Maxse was thirty-three, Nelly Cecil was thirty-two, Madge Vaughan was thirty-one, and Emma Vaughan was twenty-six. Their effect on Virginia was consolatory and educative, and it could also be erotic. She would often put into her fiction a relationship between a pragmatic, independent woman and a much younger, more confused, middle-class girl, with strong feeling latent between them. Something of Janet Case or Violet Dickinson enters into the scenes between Rachel and the benevolent teacher, Miss Allan, in *The Voyage Out*, Kitty and her tutor Miss Craddock in *The Years*, and, in unpleasant form, between Elizabeth Dalloway and Doris Kilman in *Mrs Dalloway*.

Doris Kilman, jealous and greedy and yearning, is erotically attached to Elizabeth in a repulsive way. But there was a benevolent side to this feeling between older and younger women which Virginia Stephen enjoyed. Many female relationships in the late nineteenth century, evolved in distinction to the segregated educational world of male companionship, were close and emotional without any self-consciousness or feeling of shame. Many of these women had lifelong lesbian attachments, many were partners living in physical intimacy but without sexual involvement.[5] When Virginia told Violet Dickinson, as she frequently did, that she preferred women, she is speaking of the free, private, playful behaviour which such relationships allowed her, as well as of her erotic feelings. Here she could be flirtatious, whimsical, physically demonstrative, demanding hugs and pettings, resting on capable bosoms and occupying maternal laps. And she could speak her mind and show off and talk about herself as she could not with her father or her brothers.

One of the revolutionary achievements on which her circle prided itself was that this friendly intimacy was developed, later, between men and women and between heterosexuals and homosexuals. And most of Virginia Stephen's early friendships with older women were sacrificed to these later relationships. She put them behind her, sometimes ruthlessly. She came to think of her early friendships as of her early writings, something to be grown out of and be somewhat embarrassed by: 'and I dont want immaturities, things torn out of time, preserved, unless in some strong casket, with one key only'.[6]

The most playful and puppyish of these friendships was with Emma Vaughan. Emma and Marny, the orphaned younger daughters of Julia's sad sister Adeline Vaughan, lived nearby in Kensington and went to stay with the Stephens in the country. Virginia used Emma – her 'dearest Toad', her 'Beloved Todelcrancz' – as her 'intimate' correspondent, but her eighteen-

and nineteen-year-old letters to her are so busy with jokes and mannerisms and experiments with styles that it's hard to get a sense of their recipient. Her act with 'Toad' was to be manic and wild. By contrast there are glimpses of a restrained Emma who disapproved of reading other peoples' letters, or didn't write back enough, or liked to play endless games of patience.[7] But they gossiped and giggled a lot and had running family anecdotes, especially about the dreary Fishers. And they belonged to the same class of professional men's daughters without a formal education. Both shared a passionate desire to earn their own money.[8] Virginia enlisted the Vaughan girls as companions in her classics lessons and her bookbinding, though not with much success: Marny gave up her Greek and, when Emma gave the Woolfs her bookbinding tools in 1917 for the Press, Virginia supposed drily that 'she never bound a book'.[9] Emma went to Dresden to study music and did war-work with German POWs; Marny undertook philanthropic work in London. The sisters never married and went on living together in Kensington. Emma became the disappointed person who said to Virginia one summer in Russell Square: 'One always expects something of the summer; but somehow, it never seems to happen.'[10] The friendship was dropped; when Virginia saw 'the poor Vaughans' in her forties she found them banal and chattering and an unwelcome reminder of the Duckworth years. Emma's pet-name lost its charm, and she was offered up to Vanessa for satire, like all the rest of the family incubi: 'She is rather more set, and has a blankness in the eye which is precisely that of a toad glutted with large moths. Do you remember the look – how desperate it made one feel – and then some perfectly banal remark or laugh in the manner of Aunt Virginia.'[11]

Emma was her confidante; Emma's sister-in-law was her heroine. Will Vaughan's marriage to Madge Symonds connected Virginia to another Victorian literary family as intense and difficult as her own, that of her father's friend the writer John Addington Symonds, whose homosexuality was a well-known secret. His daughter Madge Symonds, who had been very distressed by her father's death in 1893, married Will in 1898. She became close to the Stephens – she was one of the witnesses to Leslie's will – and was known as 'The Chief'. To Virginia, at that time, Madge was a romantic figure. She was beautiful, intense, unconventional, dashing, sympathetic and with ambitions as a writer (she had published *Days on a Doge's Farm* in 1893, with description which Virginia thought expressed 'a person of true artistic soul').[12] She wanted talk and adventure and people, and was always behaving 'like an excitable child, working itself into a passion'.[13] But the wildness was quashed. Like Sally Seton in *Mrs Dalloway*, the passionate, outrageous young woman turned into a solid, middle-class matron. Her marriage to Will tied her to a life as a hard-working headmaster's wife. For a little while, when Virginia was fifteen or sixteen, she 'adored' Madge: 'I see myself now standing in the night nursery at Hyde Park Gate, washing my hands, & saying to myself "At this moment she is actually under this roof." '[14] She showed her some of her writing, and took her advice. When Virginia was recovering from her breakdown in 1904, she went to stay with Madge's family at Giggleswick School, where Will was headmaster. But she found Madge leading a 'deadly' life there, much constricted and reduced by what Virginia saw as Will's blundering officiousness. It was an unsatisfactory marriage, and Madge became very depressed; when Virginia met Marny Vaughan in 1917 she said: 'I dont think anything could make Madge really happy; its not in the Symonds nature'.[15] A coolness grew up after Madge took a high moral tone about Vanessa's marital arrangements at Charleston,[16] and though Virginia became friends with her remarkable daughter Janet Vaughan, she lost her affection for Madge. When she died in 1925, she felt nothing: 'Rustling among my emotions, I found nothing better than dead leaves. Her letters had eaten away the reality – the brilliancy, the warmth. Oh, detestable time, that thus eats out the heart & lets the body go on. They buried a faggot of twigs at Highgate, as far as I am concerned.'[17]

More stylish and smart than the Vaughans, and less intimate with Virginia, were the Lushington girls, Kitty, Susan and Margaret, the daughters of Julia's oldest friends, Judge Vernon Lushington (whom Vanessa remembered as 'a preRaphaelite relic')[18] and his wife. Kitty, the oldest daughter, married (under Julia's eye) the political editor Leo Maxse, in 1890. Much liked by Leslie and Julia, who had admired her feminine charm, Kitty felt responsible for the Stephen girls (particularly Vanessa, whom she preferred) and wanted them to make good 'South Kensington' marriages.[19] She was a sharp-edged, elegant woman, blonde and blue-eyed, who liked to talk politics, played the piano well, and was full of social graces and opinionated energy, which Virginia caricatured:

> 'The great thing in life, I'm sure (and so is Leo)' she went on as one sharing a secret of importance, 'is never to lose your interest in things; now when you wake in the morning and see this chart before you – I keep it over the wash stand – you think "Gracious Heavens, I'm alive!" and then you think "Now am I more alive or less alive?" and then you take your temperature.'[20]

But she had a melancholy side too. Virginia appreciated her kindness at the family death-beds, but found her fashionable, brittle and 'unsatisfactory',[21] too dependent on her husband's views and not enthusiastic enough about Virginia's writing. Kitty was appalled by the move to Bloomsbury and the influx of shabby Cambridge young men ('Virginia might marry an *author* and they always talk about themselves!')[22] and, as a result, was dropped by her protégées. But when Virginia heard of her sudden death at fifty-five, falling over her banisters, in what she suspected to be a suicide, she regretted the breach.[23] The news came in October 1922, just as she was developing her ideas for *Mrs Dalloway*. She had already used some of Kitty's qualities for the wifely, conservative Clarissa Dalloway who appears in *The Voyage Out*; now Kitty's death darkened and deepened her idea of the character. But her 'distaste' for her persisted too, and lent Clarissa something of her 'stiff, glittering', 'tinselly' quality.[24]

Leo Maxse's sister married into the Cecil family, and partly by this route Virginia met Lady Eleanor Cecil, an intelligent and interesting woman, who was important to her in the years when she was beginning to be a writer. She was the daughter of the Earl of Durham and the wife of Robert Cecil (son of Lord Salisbury, the Prime Minister), and Virginia first encountered her, in 1903, in the aristocratic company of Katie and Beatrice Thynne, the daughters of the Marquis of Bath. Virginia found these grand ladies appealing and amusing, and called them the 'pagans' (after Matthew Arnold's term for the healthy unintellectual English aristocracy, the 'barbarians'.) She felt 'nimble witted' but 'entirely middle class' and 'literary' in their company.[25] Katie Thynne, who married Lord Cromer, was a big handsome woman with a forthright, eccentric upper-class manner. Virginia always described her as a Greek goddess or a Greek temple. Beatrice was an honest, inarticulate, red-faced girl who chattered and sprawled and smoked cigarettes (and who eventually, after her brother's death in the war in 1918, inherited large amounts of property and a library, and 'has no idea what to make of them').[26] In this company, 'Nelly' Cecil was like a bright-eyed little bird, very alert, and very deaf. Virginia came to know her better in 1905, and used to visit her for tea in her big house in St John's Wood, and write her careful, witty, friendly letters. They commented on each other's work and for a little while, in 1908, they shared a column for the *Cornhill Magazine* called 'The Book on the Table'. Virginia trusted her judgement and confided in her: 'I love this Human Inside' . . . 'really I feel rather hopeless about my writing'.[27] In later years they hardly met, but kept in touch through Virginia's friendship with Eleanor Cecil's nephew David. Eleanor's letters were admirable – sharp, observant and independent. Her characteristic tone can be heard here, in 1927: 'Will you please tell Mr Woolf that Bob so much agreed with something he wrote about modern novels in the Nation some weeks ago that he told me to write and tell him so. But I didn't take it upon myself to do any such thing. I think men ought to write their own letters.'

Eleanor Cecil remembered in one of these later letters that Virginia used to describe her and Violet Dickinson, mischievously, as 'a pair of pumas'.[28] Violet, who was more like a giraffe than a puma, was one of Eleanor's old friends. She was that late-Victorian type: a well-connected, benevolent and helpful single gentlewoman with attachments and visiting rights in a number of stately homes. She was always being taken on yachting trips to Norway or sight-seeing in Spain; in 1905 she went on a world tour with the Cecils, and she was a close friend of the Bath family. Her albums were full of snaps of Longleat (very near her family house at Frome) and signatures of Cecils and Thynnes. She was known for her generosity, her sympathy, her good works and little gestures. One young friend remembered a cheque for £5 because her thank-you letter to Violet for a Christmas present had been so appreciated.[29] She visited the London Hospital and had an interest in mentally ill women with a criminal record: 'poor distorted remnants of humanity'.[30] From 1899 to 1900 she was Mayoress of Bath. All this was the fruit of a respectable, establishment Quaker background. Her father, Edmund Dickinson, was a landowner and magistrate in Frome, her mother Emily was the daughter of Lord Auckland, Bishop of Bath and Wells, and the niece of the novelist Emily Eden, whose letters Violet edited in 1919. (Virginia found them 'amusing and vivacious' and did a kind review.)[31] Her brother 'Ozzie', with whom she lived all her life in their house in Manchester Square and their 'cottage' near Welwyn, was a barrister who became Secretary to the Board of Control (of Lunacy and Mental Deficiency). Violet's philanthropic, independent attitudes come out in the many notebooks she kept – on her visits to the battlefields in Belgium and France in 1919, on the happiness of 'spinsters', or on being treated as a freak because of her height. She suffered from 'nervous apprehension' 'insomnia and worry', but was a great believer in discipline, courage and the love of God.[32] She also believed firmly in heredity and caste, and tended to put people into types, as in this letter to Virginia of 1927, written from Brighton long after their friendship had died: 'They are most curious people in this Hotel – Elderly Jewesses – spinsters nibbling away at their cigarettes showing off the leanest legs with the sauciest garters . . . Don't go to America. The journalists there are such untiring sharks.'[33]

But Violet was not entirely a conventional woman of her class and time. When Virginia first wrote a sketch of her as 'Aunt Maria' in 1902 she warned that an observer who 'put her down as one of those cleverish adaptable ladies of middle age who are welcome everywhere, and not indispensable anywhere' would be 'superficial indeed'.[34] She had not got on well with her father (a very deaf, dull country squire) and had an appetite for intellectual and London life. She looked odd: extremely tall, and plain, badly dressed, and 'ramshackle'.[35] Leslie commented, on first getting to know her, that she was a very intelligent woman, but that 'her only fault is that she is 6 feet high'.[36] Virginia drew her as 'a very highspirited, rather crazy, harumscarum sort of person', dropping her 'g's' and rushing about asking difficult practical questions, never mincing her words, not afraid to look ridiculous, at once comical and wistful.

> You saw her stride across the grass to slap some mournful dowager on the back; or she pulled out her notebook and wrote directions for killing green fly on roses, or the address of the only man in London who can beeswax tiles; or she undertook to interview a specialist, or gave advice on the feeding of infants, the choice of husbands, or the writing of English prose.[37]

In her letters she teased her for her respectability, and played up her own lack of it. So there were lots of running jokes about Violet having an imaginary husband, and about Virginia's comparative immodesty – her underwear dropping off in public, her lack of religious beliefs, and the probability of her having a large number of illegitimate children. Meeting Violet again after a gap in 1919, she found the same 'inconsequent, generous minded, unselfish talk', the same 'unexpectedness' in her mixture of aristocratic friendships and democratic anti-imperialism.[38]

Violet became indispensable to Virginia for about five years, and played a crucial enabling part in her early writing. She came to know the family first as a friend of Stella's (the Duckworth home at Orchardleigh was near to the Dickinsons at Frome, and Thoby refers to meeting a Miss Dickinson as early as 1894). Visiting the house in 1897, she felt sorry for the Stephen girls; she wanted to take over looking after them where Stella had left off. But Virginia adopted her as her particular friend when they met in the summer of 1902. 'She has taken a great fancy to all the girls, specially to Ginia', Leslie observed, 'who went about with her all day and discoursed upon literary and other matters continuously. Miss Dickinson . . . admires Ginia's intelligence greatly.'[39] Violet was sympathetic to Virginia's nervousness, her need for affection, and her craving for attention. 'Her one thought was her future career', Violet remembered in her old age. 'She discussed by the hour her talents, welcoming, asking for criticism and then impatient and resentful when she received it. She was hungry for work, for experience.'[40] 'Poor Violet', the young author wrote, sending her another essay, 'I think literary advice is a very ticklish thing'.[41]

Virginia's letters to Violet (all of which Violet kept, though Virginia kept none of hers from these years), give a strong sense of Violet's character.[42] Virginia compares her to Mrs Carlyle, a 'human woman' who 'gets into just the same queer places as you do', a letter writer who 'writes as she talks'. Increasingly, in the long months between Leslie's operation and his death, Violet became her security: 'the family friend we all cling to when we're drowning', 'a kind of home for the orphaned and widows herself'. She confided in Violet as an alternative to Vanessa's more critical and undemonstrative intimacy: 'I really do wish you were here. I like Nessa very much, but she gets so bored with me (tho' she's very fond of me too).' She told her about everything: her feelings of social incompetence, her judgements on their mutual friends, her painful feelings about her father. She let her know how grim it was in the house – 'a muddle and a chaos . . . and has been for many years' – and confided the plans that were beginning to be discussed, as Leslie's death approached, for splitting the family and moving house. The incompatibility of the Duckworths and the Stephens was made clear to her.

> No talking to Georgie or Gerald; they are a marvelous pair. A dinner with them is something to laugh over ten days later. Character is what amuses me. Lord – they are comic – Gerald a little jealous and Georgie the good boy whose virtue has been rewarded. If ever I write a novel, those two shall go in large as life. 'People always tell me George ought to have been a diplomat,' says Gerald – 'now I think I should have made a good diplomat' – and waits for our answer. Georgie explains very earnestly how one should always get up to open the door for a lady in a diplomatic household![43]

Whether she would ever write a novel was a subject Virginia discussed with Violet as much as she discussed the characters of George and Gerald. She used Violet as her sounding-board for her evolving ideas about how to live, how to talk and how to write. These ideas are all about refusing conventions and getting round formalities – as Virginia and Violet did in their correspondence.

> Life would be so much simpler if we could flay the outside skin all the talk and pretences and sentiments one doesn't feel etc etc etc – [44]

> I'm going to write a great play . . . Im going to have a man and a woman – show them growing up – never meeting – not knowing each other – but all the time you'll feel them come nearer and nearer. This will be the real

exciting part (as you see) – but when they almost meet – only a door between – you see how they just miss – and go off at a tangent, and never come anywhere near again. There'll be oceans of talk and emotions without end.[45]

Virginia's intimacy with Violet was playfully erotic from the beginning of their correspondence. The teasing jokes, the demands for attention, the confiding of secrets, were part of an extortionate appeal for petting and mothering. Violet was her 'woman'. She was also her kangaroo, with 'a pouch for small Kangaroos to creep to', her giant princess, her general, her Sacred Monster.[46] Virginia was the little Wallaby with a soft wet snout, the 'Sparroy' folding Violet 'in her feathery arms, so that you may feel the Heart in her ribs', her slobbering Baby. She wanted 'hot and affectionate' letters. Violet holds her in a 'long embrace', has stirred her to 'hot volcano depths'. 'Put some affection in to your letters,' she is always urging her. 'My food is affection!' In one photograph of them together, a timid, frail-looking Virginia nestles up close on Violet's breast and clasps her hand; Violet looks enormous, friendly and secure.

Violet helped Virginia to start writing; she looked after her after Leslie's death and her breakdown; she went with the family on their disastrous trip to Greece and Turkey in 1906, and was closely involved in the catastrophe that followed it. But she did not approve of their lives in Bloomsbury, invoking Julia's ghost in support of her disapproval. All Virginia's intense emotions of first love for Violet passed away, as she foresaw: 'Supposing we drift entirely apart, in the next 3 years, so that we blush when we meet and remember our ancient correspondence', she wrote to Violet in 1908.[47] Though she went on calling herself 'Sparroy' to Violet, it was always shortened to 'Sp': a gesture of reminiscence and old loyalty. By 1913, when Virginia was ill again, they had 'drifted' considerably, though Leonard kept Violet scrupulously informed about Virginia's state. When, many years later, in an odd moment of reproach or appeal, Violet sent Virginia back all the letters she had written her, Virginia was embarrassed to read again 'those scattered fragments of my very disjected and egotistic youth'. But even then, in 1936, she echoed faintly the appeals for sympathy which had filled those letters:

Do you like that girl? I'm not sure that I do, though I think she had some spirit in her, and certainly was rather ground down harshly by fate . . . But one thing emerges whole and lucid – how very good you were to me, and how very trying I was – all agog, all aquiver: and so full of storms and rhapsodies.

'All I beg of you', she tells Violet, 'is dont let anybody else read those letters.'[48]

Because Violet was dropped (and because Clive and Vanessa thought of her as a dowdy grotesque), she has been treated subsequently as a negligible, comical figure, the benevolent object of a youthful 'crush' and a lingering reminder of Hyde Park Gate days. But what she gave Virginia Stephen at a time of great vulnerability was very important. Violet enabled her to behave freely, childishly, like a daughter or a favourite pet or a sweetheart. She was devoted, interested, and without aggression. She provided a space in which Virginia could curl up or hurl herself about, and be as egotistical and demanding as her dying father. Other older women – her mother, Stella, Kitty Maxse, her aunts and cousins – had tended to reprove Virginia for signs of egotism; as a result she refers frequently and ruefully to the egotism she displays in talking to Violet about her work. But clearly Violet encouraged egotism, turned it into a virtue. She allowed Virginia to cut her writer's teeth on her as ruthlessly as she liked.

It is very tempting, though probably too simplifying, to find a male and a female source of influence in Virginia Stephen's early writing. One is the authoritative, classical and analytic voice derived from her father's work, and from her arguments with Thoby. The other is the fluid, whimsical tone which she associates with her friendships with women. These friendships are closely involved with the writing. 'You remember there is a very fine instinct wireless telepathy nothing to it – in women – the darlings – which fizzles up pretences, and I know what you mean though you dont say it, and I hope its the same with you,' she writes to Violet. In *Friendship's Gallery* she portrays Violet sitting in the garden of the house she has built herself, with her talk 'playing freely' on the writing of women.[49] When she turns their friendship, in this story, into a silly, tender fairy tale of two giant princesses with benign powers, she uses a different kind of language from the essays she is writing at this time on the Earl's Court Exhibition, or Romsey Abbey. Her feeling for women's lives and characters frees her into fantasy and indirection.

But it would be too schematic to read the early writings only for male or female characteristics. A great mass of reading finds its way into her prose, and what strikes one most is the exuberant and careful way in which she works through influences towards her own tone of voice. At first the rapid, energetic, self-engrossed style of the fifteen-year-old's diary gives way to more formal exercises. In the notebooks for 1899 and 1903 there are descriptions of place, local histories, characters and mood pictures (a storm, a dance, a church, a funeral), the equivalent of Vanessa's sketch-books.

(Virginia does some drawing, too, in silver-point: tentative copies of male figures from Blake and female faces from Rossetti.) As she practises, a stiff literary manner ('Monotony, so methinks, dwells in these plains') turns into a looser, more evocative writing. And she is writing all kinds of things:

> I was then [at fifteen or sixteen] writing a long picturesque essay upon the Christian religion, I think; called Religio Laici, I believe, proving that man has need of a God; but the God was described in process of change; & I also wrote a history of Women; & a history of my own family – all very longwinded & El[izab]than in style.[50]

After that came her portraits of women (notably Violet), her comic novel about George, and her ideas for an experimental play. In all these attempts she wants to be impersonal. She watches herself for indulgence and self-exposure, and is sorry for having sent Violet something in a 'nude, really indecent state', written in 'a sentimental mood'.[51] In the letters she is much more rapid and easy, but here too she is practising. The letters to Emma make play with Shandyesque epistolary manners ('O Lord – what Talk we shall have in our bedrooms'), as in this grotesque account of meeting Charlotte Leaf (Madge Vaughan's sister) at a garden party:

> Well my dear Todkins . . . as I stood talking to Clara [Pater] there advanced upon me a tall and middle aged lady in Blue, with a little grocer like man beside her. Good Heavens – who is this I thought – for she was evidently bent on shaking hands with me – Really and honestly, for the moment I did not recognise your beloved Lotta in this apparition! She is *enormous.* As for her body, I never saw such a shape save in those who are doing business with Infants – and surely she can not already be advanced to such a degree. The waist was just under her armpits, and then she became vast – really noticeable. And her face too was quite changed – grown quite fat and rather dusky red. It is not a change for the better by any means.[52]

It goes on with the kind of unstoppable malevolent glee which will be a feature of her later letters. She knows that she is pleasing herself as much as her recipient: 'Heavens! what a long letter this is! But it is Sunday morning, and . . . I cant help writing for the life of me, and you must be my receptacle.'

Even when well wrapped up in comedy, though, she gives a great deal away:

> The world of human beings grows too complicated, my only wonder is

that we don't fill more madhouses: the insane view of life has much to be said for it – perhaps its the sane one after all: and *we*, the sad sober respectable citizens really rave every moment of our lives and deserve to be shut up perpetually. My spring melancholy is developing in these hot days into summer madness.[53]

In the practice books too, there is an undertow of grief and anxiety, as in an account of the woman who drowns herself in the Serpentine, or a description of a Fenland funeral, which makes her dream of looking 'into the womens faces; & the carts passed on & on into the night they were going back to some strange dark land, & they said the only time they saw the light of day was when they came to Warboys to bury their dead'.[54] In the back of her Warboys journal for 1899, she tests her new pens with some fragments and quotations – including the first verse of Tennyson's sad *Tithonus* – several of which strike a melancholy note.[55] And in her country notes of 1903 she writes of her desire for solitude, and her sense that 'If you lie on the earth somewhere you hear a sound like a vast breath, as though it were the very inspiration of earth herself, & all the living things on her'.[56]

That wish to become part of earth life, to be impersonal, is related to her feelings about reading. Every year in early summer she starts putting aside the books she is going to read when they go away. 'I want to read myself blue in the nose', she says to Thoby.[57] In the country she browses steadily, in London she reads fretfully, laying down the book to say, 'what right have I, a woman to read all these things that men have done? They would laugh if they saw me.' In the country, reading history, Shakespeare, Dante, Burke, Euripides, she feels 'as if the physical stuff of my brain were expanding, larger & larger, throbbing quicker & quicker with new blood'.

> I think I see for a moment how our minds are threaded together – how any live mind is of the very same stuff as Plato's & Euripides. It is only a continuation & development of the same thing. It is this common mind that binds the whole world together; & all the world is mind.[58]

That is written in 1903. It is a very early formulation of her life's belief in writing and reading as a way of transcending the self. From the start she struggled between this ideal of transcendence, as part of the 'common mind', and the anxieties of being a woman reader. From the start, too, books are escape and therapy. The sketches written at Netherhampton in the months before Leslie's death, and sent to Violet for criticism, are written for survival. 'Books are such a mercy', she tells her, a few days before Leslie's death.

Leslie Stephen took a very long time to die. He was showing signs of weakness from 1900, when he had a sudden giddy fit (Virginia remembered in 1936 'father falling down, & I thought he was on fire').[59] From this time, Violet observed that Virginia was in a constant state of 'anxiety and apprehension'.[60] In the spring of 1902 his doctors diagnosed bowel cancer (brought on, his biographer suggests, by his guilt at feeling he had not loved Julia enough). But the 'wool-gathering' family doctor, Seton, disagreed with the surgeon, Sir Frederick Treves, on when to operate. Treves did operate in December, but by the following autumn the growth had greatly increased, and a new doctor they called in was furious with Seton for his neglect. 'Great doctors are so queer', Virginia observed (not for the last time) as she witnessed these arguments, and saw the nurses quarrelling too.[61] At Christmas Leslie tried to do his usual reading of Milton's 'Ode on the Morning of Christ's Nativity', but broke down. Growing slowly weaker, at first refusing to accept his fate and hanging on with 'terrible strength', surrounded by 'endless affectionate sentimental' visitors and his exhausted children, gradually beginning to 'want to die', Leslie at last finished the awful job on 22 February 1904.

Virginia did not describe this death (though it gets into the mother's lingering death in *The Years*), but she wrote down her feelings in daily letters to Violet.[62] Her bursts of heartfelt affection for him – 'He is such an attractive creature' – are mixed with terrible outcries at the 'hard work' of it all. 'If only it could be quicker!' 'The waiting is intolerable . . . I shall do my best to ruin my constitution before I get to his age, so as to die quicker!' She dreamed she was a nurse.

The four Stephens made plans, tried to work and to deal with their visitors, but they were entirely taken up with the business of their father's dying: 'the outside world seems to have ceased.' The house, which they intended to leave when the time came, was their prison: '& more & more prison like does it become the longer we live there & wear fetters of association & sentiment, painful to wear – still more painful to break'.[63]

After Leslie's death, Virginia was overwhelmed with the same kind of remorse he had felt about Julia. 'The dreadful thing is that I never did enough for him all those years. He was so lonely often, and I never helped him as I might have done. This is the worst part of it now. If he had only lived we could have been so happy. But it is all gone.' She had 'the curious feeling of living with him every day'; she dreamed that she was telling him 'how one cared'. The family went to Manorbier, in Pembrokeshire, and tried to recover themselves; they made their plans for moving to Bloomsbury (with the threat of George as companion still hanging over them, though Gerald was happy to go his own way). They took a holiday in Italy and Paris, where Virginia wrote strained and miserable letters to

Emma and Violet. But nothing helped her: 'I cant bear to think of his loneliness, and that I might have helped, and didn't.' 'Oh my Violet, I do want Father so.'

During the years of these family deaths, Virginia Stephen evolved a dark but coherent idea of existence which allowed her an almost *proud* sense (inspired by her reading of Greek) of having been singled out for tragedy: 'the Gods (as I used to phrase it) were taking us seriously.'[64] She began to think of life as a narrow strip which had to be ridden, a small space of 'extreme reality' threatened by hostile brutal forces – an 'invisible giant' or 'two great grindstones'.[65] She would give these views to her characters. Rachel in *The Voyage Out* has 'her sense of safety shaken': 'It seemed to her that a moment's respite was allowed, a moment's make-believe, and then again the profound and reasonless law asserted itself, moulding them all to its liking, making and destroying.'[66] Mrs Ramsay thinks of life as a 'little strip of time', and of herself as carrying out 'a sort of transaction' with it. Sometimes she got the better of it; but for the most part 'she felt this thing that she called life terrible, hostile, and quick to pounce on you if you gave it a chance'.[67] And Bernard in *The Waves* is similarly engaged in 'perpetual warfare', 'daily battle', as much with 'life' (in its sinister, hostile embodiment) as with 'Death'.[68]

Out of this image of a narrow, perilous strip of existence, Virginia Woolf developed her sense of herself as a writer. She had already, as a small child, experienced moments of profound horror or desolation. Now these deaths intensified her anticipation of a hidden enemy waiting to deliver a 'sledge-hammer' blow, and the need for some form of fight or resistance. When she came to explain to herself in her late memoir what made her a writer, she described it as a process of *welcoming* or finding valuable these shocks: 'And so I go on to suppose that the shock-receiving capacity is what makes me a writer.' The shock is followed by an immediate desire to explain it. The 'blow' is to become 'a revelation of some order'; 'it is a token of some real thing behind appearances; and I make it real by putting it into words'. This making of 'order' or 'wholeness' out of 'shocks', is, she says, 'the strongest pleasure known to me'. This 'pleasure' leads her to the philosophy of life which she was beginning to evolve in her 1903 notebook: that there is a pattern hidden behind the 'cotton-wool' of daily life and that all individuals, and all individual works of art, are part of the pattern. So the making of art, in reaction to the blows of life, is both an active, controlling process, in which she orders reality by 'putting it into words'; and a passive, self-abnegating process, whereby she recognises that what she is making is part of something pre-existing and universal: 'There is no Shakespeare; there is no Beethoven; certainly and emphatically there is no God; we are the words; we are the music; we are the thing itself.'[69]

This much-quoted but mysterious passage, with its complicated idea of the relation between 'reality' and 'appearances' and its mystical suggestion of a connecting pattern, presents the fundamental impulse of her work as therapeutic or healing. And it attributes this impulse to the blows received in childhood. So, over time, Virginia Woolf evolved a consoling aesthetic in reaction against her sense of horror and powerlessness. But in the months after Leslie's death she could not find consolation. She stopped writing; she 'broke down'; she 'went mad'. She wanted to die. What was happening to her?

TEN

'Madness'

Virginia Woolf was a sane woman who had an illness. She was often a patient, but she was not a victim. She was not weak, or hysterical, or self-deluding, or guilty, or oppressed. On the contrary, she was a person of exceptional courage, intelligence and stoicism, who made the best use she could, and came to the deepest understanding possible to her, of her own condition. She endured, periodically, great agony of mind and severe physical pain, with remarkably little self-pity.

Her illness is attributable to genetic, environmental and biological factors. It was periodic, and recurrent.[1] It was precipitated, but not indubitably caused, by the things which happened to her. It affected her body as much as her mind and raised the insoluble and fundamental question, which she spent a great deal of time considering, of the relation between the two: 'What connection has the brain with the body? Nobody in Harley Street could explain.'[2] Five times in her life (four of them between the ages of thirteen and thirty-three) she suffered from major onslaughts of the illness and in almost all (possibly all) of these attacks she attempted to kill herself. She frequently uses the word 'apprehensive' to describe her states of mind – saying that her mother's death and the subsequent events 'had formed my mind and made it apprehensive', or, in a terribly shaky depression just before the publication of *The Years*, that she feels 'Very lonely . . . Very useless . . . Very apprehensive'.[3] The word is a crucial one: the awful fear which accompanied her breakdowns and the possibility of their recurrence can never be underestimated.

For most of her life she was vulnerable to recurrent episodes whose symptoms might range from weeks of intense depression to a night's anxiety or a sudden faint. Closely associated with her illness were a variety of symptoms which could themselves be diagnosed as specific ailments: a headache or a back-ache, an attack of influenza or a high temperature. Throughout her life, her states of mind could manifest themselves physically as exhaustion or a rapid pulse rate. A reluctance to eat and severe weight loss was one of the most extreme of these physical manifestations. This sounds like anorexia nervosa, a condition first defined in 1873 and associated at the turn of the century with 'morbid mental states' and hysteria in young girls.[4] But anorexia arises from an obsession with one's body. That does not seem to be the case here. She simply could not eat.

Trying to apply the term anorexia nervosa raises the problem of diagnostic labels for Virginia Woolf's 'madness'.[5] Like the 'flu, or a headache, her illness can be given a clinical name and a set of diagnosable symptoms. It conforms to the profile of what is called manic–depressive illness, or bipolar affective disorder, or (more recently) bipolar disorder. (A milder version of bipolar disorder, 'cyclothymia', has also been applied to her condition.)[6] Like all illnesses that have a name, it is not unique to the person who has it. And so the disadvantage of naming it is that this makes her seem unexceptional, just a case conforming to a clinical category. To name the illness is to begin a process of description which can demote her extraordinary personality to a collection of symptoms, or reduce her writing to an exercise in therapy. But the named illness is also 'her' illness in that it took the material of her life as its subject-matter. It, and the treatment she received for it, affected her personality, her behaviour, her writing and her politics. And it is 'her' illness in that much of what we know about it is derived from what she wrote about it. Her illness has become her language.

It has also become inextricably knitted into the readings of her by friends, family, biographers and analysts. All of these have some vested proprietary interest in the language they use for it. Illness is at the mercy of language, and can only be identified and 'treated' (in a clinical and a literary sense) by being named. To choose a language for Virginia Woolf's illness is at once – from the very moment of calling it an illness – to rewrite and re-present it, perhaps to misrepresent it. Do we endorse, or correct, or ignore, her own language for her illness? Do we think she is the best or the worst person to describe it? Do we think she didn't really know what was happening to her? Do we accept the language of those closest to her? And can we sort out exactly what she was experiencing?

The evidence thickens as time goes on, and is, by the end of her life, copious and complex. But it is also contradictory, and has gaps. There are some doctors' letters and a few prescriptions, but there are no doctors' reports. There are no letters or diaries written when she was undergoing the worst of the crises, though there are some close in time to the events. There are no specific first-hand reports of what she said when she was uttering 'gibberish' or talking wildly or experiencing hallucinations, though there are retrospective and fictionalised versions. And there is confusion between the effects of her illness and the effects of her treatment, a confusion which has given rise to violently opposing schools of thought about her mental history.

The first 'breakdown' of 1895, after Julia's death, is the least fully chronicled. (Leonard, in his autobiography, refers to 'a minor breakdown in childhood' before 1895, but there is no other evidence for this.)[7] She wrote nothing that survives from 1895; a shortlived diary from 1896 was lost or destroyed, and we don't hear her voice until 1897. The immediate evidence of her condition comes from remarks in Leslie's letters to George Duckworth in 1897 that he has had 'one very nice little talk with Ginia which makes me rather happier' and to Charles Eliot Norton in 1898 that he is 'still anxious' about Virginia.[8] Stella's diary for 1896 describes several visits with Virginia to the family doctor, Seton, which suggest that her disturbed state had gone on for over a year.[9] Stella also marks what are presumably Virginia's menstrual periods with a cross, starting on 16 October 1896, as though these might be times of particular anxiety. Virginia's irritability in her 1897 journal, her nervousness and her attacks of the 'fidgets', can be read as symptoms of her illness.

The later evidence for the 'breakdown' of 1895–6 is somewhat ambiguous. Leonard Woolf tells us that 'she had a major breakdown after her mother's death in 1895', and that she tried to kill herself during it by jumping out of a window. But Leonard, writing in the 1960s, seems to have confused her childhood 'breakdown' with the crisis which followed Leslie's death in 1904. Quentin Bell said that she could not bring herself to recall her mental symptoms in her memoirs, only her physical ones – racing pulse, painful excitement, nerves, blushing, terror of people – though 'we know she had already heard "those horrible voices".' This is a reference to the 'Sketch of the Past', where she passes over her first illness, but talks about her feelings after her mother's death. Possibly her memory of seeing the figure of a man sitting beside her dead mother could be taken as a hallucination, a precursor to or a symptom of breakdown.

The other specific references to 'hallucinations' cannot be so clearly dated. When she describes her bedroom in her memoir (not when she describes her mother's death), she speaks of a night when she lay awake 'horrified', 'hearing, as I imagined, an obscene old man gasping and croaking and muttering senile indecencies – it was a cat, I was told afterwards'. This incident is not dated. In the next paragraph, she lists some of her memories of events in that room, in no chronological order, ending (after a reference to the death of her father) with 'There I first heard those horrible voices'.[10] It is not quite clear from this that (as Quentin Bell suggests) these 'horrible voices' were heard in 1895, or indeed that there were in this first breakdown any hallucinations or any of the later symptoms like refusal of food or terrible headaches.

There is a more detailed account of her state of mind after her mother's death in her notes for the 'Sketch', made in the summer of 1939. But it says nothing about hallucinations or suicide attempts or 'madness'.

> My mother's death fell into the very middle of that amorphous time. That made it much more broken. The whole thing was strained. This brought on, naturally, my first 'breakdown'. It was found that I had a pulse that raced. It beat so quick I could hardly bear it. No lessons, no excitement: open air, simple life. So I lived the two years between my mother's death and Stella's in a state of physical distress. How again separate the body and the mind? . . . I was terrified of people – used to turn red if spoken to. Used to sit up in my room raging – at father, at George, and read and read and read. But I never wrote. For two years I never wrote. The desire left me; which I have had all my life, with that two years break . . . Perhaps the excitement was too great – the distraction of that racing pulse.[11]

After the 'seven unhappy years' between 1897 and 1904, and the strain of Leslie's long dying, she had a severe breakdown in 1904, during which she made some kind of suicide attempt. But we have very little commentary from her on what happened at this time.

From 1912 onwards, when Leonard Woolf rather than the family became her close observer, her state of mind comes much more fully into focus. Leonard made Virginia's illness one of his life's works. He studied her mind for nearly thirty years, he says, 'with the greatest intensity'. And he documents her illness with the same scrupulous integrity, exhaustiveness and attempt at objectivity that he would apply to the minutes of the Labour Party's Advisory Committee on International Relations. From his minutely kept diaries (where entries on her daily states of mind are coded in Tamil and Sinhalese), from his anxious and responsible letters at the time of her breakdowns, and from his memoirs, which circle repetitively and insistently over the story of her illness, a careful, clinical narrative emerges.

He begins by giving what he calls 'a very summary account' of her breakdowns, dividing them into 'two distinct stages':

> In the manic stage she was extremely excited; the mind raced; she talked volubly and, at the height of the attack, incoherently; she had delusions and heard voices . . . she was violent with her nurses. In her third attack, which began in 1914 [in fact 1913] this stage lasted for several months and ended by her falling into a coma for two days. During the depressive stage all her thoughts and emotions were the exact opposite of what they had been in the manic stage. She was in the depths of melancholia and despair; she scarcely spoke; refused to eat; refused to believe that she was ill and

'The Pattle Family, Paris 1818' by August Cannery. Julia (later Cameron) standing, Maria (Virginia's grandmother), babe-in-arms.

Leslie Stephen and Laura, 1870.

Julia Stephen and Virginia, 1884.

Leslie and Julia Stephen.

Julia Stephen and Stella Duckworth.

The Stephen family at Talland House, St Ives, 1890's.

Julia Stephen at her desk, with portrait of her mother.

The Stephen family: left to right, Leslie, Adrian, Julia, Thoby, Stella, Vanessa, Virginia, c.1892.

The Stephen/Duckworth family: left to right, front row, Adrian, Julia, Leslie; back row, Gerald, Virginia, Thoby, Vanessa, George, c.1892.

Leslie and Julia Stephen; Virginia behind them, 1892.

Stella Duckworth and Jack Hills, 1896.

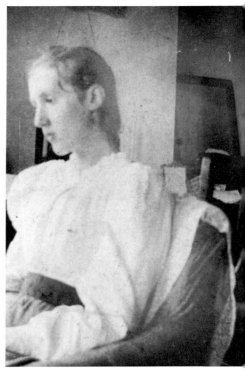

Virginia Stephen, 1896.

George Duckworth with Virginia, 1897.

Virginia with Gerald Duckworth, 1897.

Virginia and Vanessa, 1896.

Vanessa and Thoby, 1900.

George and Thoby, 1900.

Adrian and Virginia, 1900.

Virginia Stephen by Geroge Beresford, 1902.

LEFT INSET *Violet Dickinson.* ABOVE *Violet Dickinson and Virginia, 1902.* RIGHT INSET *Violet Dickinson.*

Virginia reading Hakluyt, 1900.

Portrait of Virginia reading, 1902, by Lisa Stillmann.

Leslie Stephen, 1900.

Portrait of Leslie Stephen by Vanessa Stephen, 1901.

The Stephens riding up Mount Pentelicus in Greece, 1906; left to right, Vanessa, Thoby, Virginia.

Janet Case, Virginia and Vanessa in Firle Park, 1911.

insisted that her condition was due to her own guilt; at the height of this stage she tried to commit suicide.[12]

His view, which he then expounds, was that she passed in these breakdowns across a 'line':

> On one side of this line was a kind of mental balance, a psychological coherence between intellect and emotion, an awareness and acceptance of the outside world and a rational reaction to it; on the other side were violent emotional instability and oscillation . . . a refusal to admit or accept facts in the outside world.[13]

He describes the difficulty of pinpointing that line, for instance when 'echoes' of her 'nightmare' would 'rise to the surface of her mind' while she was 'sane'. He goes on to the 'troublesome' business of her refusal to eat, a refusal he connects with what he calls 'some strange, irrational sense of guilt', and he says that it was difficult to get her to eat, that all their arguments were about eating and resting. And he outlines the programme which he was convinced would keep her sane: 'If she tired herself by walking too long and too far, if she sat up later than 11 two or three nights running, if she went to too many parties, the physical strain would very soon bring on . . . the danger signals.'[14]

When he comes to give a specific account of what happened in 1913 and 1915, he begins again, repeating much of this material. He describes the first stage of suicidal depression and the second stage of excitement and euphoria. For both stages, he repeatedly uses the word 'violent':

> In the first stage she was in the depths of depression, would hardly eat or talk, was suicidal. In the second she was in a state of violent excitement and wild euphoria, talking incessantly for long periods of time. In the first stage she was violently opposed to the nurses and they had the greatest difficulty in getting her to do anything; she wanted me to be with her continually and for a week or two I was the only person able to get her to eat anything. In the second stage of violent excitement, she was violently hostile to me, would not talk to me or allow me to come into her room. She was occasionally violent with the nurses, but she tolerated them in a way which was the opposite of her behaviour to them in the first stage.[15]

He goes on to talk about her beliefs during her insanity, her refusal of food, her unshakable convictions that her symptoms were her own fault, and that her doctors and nurses were conspiring against her. And he describes the uncertain muddles and confusions with the doctors which took them through 1913, up to the point of her near-successful attempt at suicide by taking an overdose of veronal. Then his narrative goes off on to other matters and returns again, when he gets to 1915, to the morning when 'without warning she became violently excited and distressed. She thought her mother was in the room and began to talk to her. It was the beginning of the terrifying second stage of her mental breakdown'. She became 'very violent with her nurses' and 'talked without stopping for two or three days' in what became 'a mere jumble of dissociated words' until 'she fell into a coma'. After which she became calmer, and began to recover.

Leonard's account is at once authoritative and confusing. Her behaviour and her treatment are mixed up, so that it is often impossible to sort out from his account whether events are taking place before or after she is being looked after by nurses or sedated with drugs. His apparently definite division between the first and second stages of the illness and the 'line' between the sane and the insane parts of her mind becomes, with repetition, oddly blurred. The account does not try to work out what it felt to be her during the course of her breakdowns: for instance, it makes no attempt to remember or represent what she was saying during her phases of rapid incoherent speech, or to investigate the 'strange' feelings of shame that made her refuse to eat. Instead, he deals pragmatically with her behaviour, its probable causes, and its treatment. His language makes a deliberate effort to be unemotional, but uses terms like 'raving mad' and 'insanity', 'loss of control', 'incoherent', and above all 'violent', which seem involuntarily to introduce a code of reasonable standards of behaviour versus intolerable lapses. (It is interesting, though, that one of his strongest phrases of this kind, 'gibbering despair', is applied not to the behaviour of the 'insane' person but to her minder, suggesting the enormous strain involved: 'What tends to break one down, to reduce one to gibbering despair when one is dealing with mental illness, is the terrible sanity of the insane.')[16] He makes his convictions quite clear: that she was manic depressive and not 'neurasthenic' as the doctors described her, that her illness could be controlled by a regulated pattern of rest and food, and that it was related to her creative genius, to her intense work-levels and to the stress of finishing a book.

There are other versions of Virginia's 'states' in these years, but all of them, like Leonard's, take up their own positions and make their own self-protecting narratives. The most striking example of this is in Vanessa's letters. Once she had shifted the responsibility to Leonard, she wrote about Virginia (to her husband Clive Bell and her lover Roger Fry) with anxiety but also with a note of cold withdrawal, startlingly different in tone from her affectionate letters to Virginia herself. For instance, to Clive Bell in 1910:

But how utterly incapable the Goat is of taking any care of herself. It is really alarming. Adrian tells me that she had got back into all her old bad ways about eating. I dont know whats to be done. Nothing seems to have any permanent effect.[17]

Three years later:

I saw the Ws off at Paddington. It was all rather wretched as she seems to me to be in just the same sort of state only not so bad, as she was in the very first time. She worries constantly, and she gets rid of one worry only to find that another crops up in a few minutes. Then she also has definite illusions about other people . . . I dont think Woolf can go on for long alone, the strain of always looking after her is so great.[18]

A year later, to Roger Fry:

With Ws to see Craig. C on the whole gave a cheerful account of V. He said she wasnt in a state where she could possibly be certified and that she couldnt therefore be made to go into a home or have nurses. He thought there was a certain amount of risk of suicide but that it must be run. They are going to Cornwall tomorrow. She was very cheerful yesterday at being in London. Of course I think she isnt nearly well yet and it is rather worrying in some ways but there seems to be nothing to be done but go on.[19]

Vanessa tends to speak about her sister as a sad case which has to be managed. Most of her information is taken secondhand from Leonard. There is little inwardness, no attempt to imagine what the 'worries', the 'illusions', the 'incoherence' might consist of. The worries are worrying: and that is as far as Vanessa can go. How far, after all, can an onlooker, however closely related, go into the mind of the ill person? Vanessa's distancing was probably a necessity (her own life at this time was difficult and often painful). All the same, she seems at times impercipient:

Asheham. They have had the most extraordinary adventure here. I cant go into all the details but the almost incredible result was that Virginia took another overdose of veronal by mistake for phenacitin! She took about 25 grains probably – L was away – and the servants didnt understand and eventually she slept it off. Its too odd a story but theres no doubt it was quite an accident. She seems on the whole to be very well.[20]

This sounds as if it might have been another suicide attempt, at some point in 1914, in between Virginia's two gravest episodes of illness. But in lieu of other evidence, we are left with Vanessa's account of an 'accident'. It is an extraordinary example, anyway, of the difficulty of making one's way inside Virginia's experiences from the available reports on her behaviour.

The letters of those in charge of her are, necessarily, just as partial. The 'experts' speak their own language and defend their own corner; they probably do the best they can, but from the few documents remaining their limitations and their biases can be heard. So Jean Thomas, who ran the private home at Burley Park, Twickenham, for ladies with mental problems (helpfully indexed by Quentin Bell as 'a madhouse'), where Virginia went for 'rest cures' in 1910 and 1912, a pious, intense woman who became over-involved with Virginia, wrote fulsomely to Leonard after the suicide attempt in September 1913, 'It must have been terrible, far worse than anything I have ever seen in her. But we felt when she was here, didnt we? there was much more wrong than there had been, and so easily all could grow very bad.'[21] George Savage was openly appalled by the suicide attempt ('I hardly know how or what to write for the mentality of the patient leaves me helpless') and offended by Leonard's decision to consult another, 'younger' doctor.[22] The more impersonal doctors' letters are either reassuringly prescriptive ('must have breakfast in bed, rest before and after meals, only take short walks but lie out in the open air as much as possible taking Robins Hypophosphate after meals') or confidently principled ('I quite agree the time has come to place reliance on your wife's self-control').[23]

During her life she, and Leonard on her behalf, consulted at least twelve doctors. Most of these consultations clustered around the 1913–15 period, when Leonard's growing distrust of Savage, and his desperate search for better advice created some of the tension and confusion leading up to her suicide attempt in September 1913. At this time of maximum danger and stress, it was extremely difficult for them to find anyone sympathetic or advanced. By far their best bet – but not, unfortunately, a major figure in Leonard's consultations – was the distinguished neuropsychologist Henry Head, a pioneering experimenter with the nervous system, a highly intelligent man, a poet, and an informed Freudian. Her other doctors were all more conservative and authoritarian. Leonard's view that the doctors he consulted between 1913 and 1915 'had not the slightest idea of the nature or the cause of Virginia's mental state' and 'no real or scientific knowledge of how to cure her' seems to have been historically accurate. Not until the First World War and the experience of shell shock did 'the era of psychiatric modernism' come to England.[24]

Virginia Woolf's clinical history keeps pace with the developing history of English medicine and attitudes to mental illness. In her childhood she was treated by the affable, 'wool-gathering', old-fashioned Victorian family doctor Seton. From the 1920s her principal doctor was a member of the Strachey family, Elinor Rendel, who held clinical assistant's posts at the Hospital for Heart Diseases in the 1920s and 1930s and was the doctor for a number of the Bloomsbury circle, including her uncle Lytton. And in the last weeks of her life, during the Second World War, Virginia was observed by a pioneering woman doctor, Octavia Wilberforce.[25]

Yet the treatments prescribed for her did not change very much between the 1880s and the late 1930s. All her doctors recommended rest cures, milk and meat diets for weight gain, fresh air, avoidance of excitement and early nights. All prescribed sedatives like bromides. And, indeed, what else could they do? Once Leonard had taken the decision to look after her in the home, thereby (in 1913) averting the horrible prospect of her being incarcerated in a lunatic asylum (horrible even in an 'advanced' institution like the Retreat, where Roger Fry's wife spent most of her life), these sedative measures (before the use of lithium) were all they had available to them.

The authoritarianism of the medical profession at the turn of the century, particularly towards women, is attested to by the medical journals.[26] Here we can read of Sir Maurice Craig's socially corrective diagnosis of insanity as antisocial or non-conformist behaviour, of the hearty T.B. Hyslop's identification, in 1911, of insanity with the 'morbid manifestations' of modern art like symbolism or Post-Impressionism,[27] and of Sir George Savage's belief in the degenerative symptoms of hereditary insanity. Savage treated his 'neurasthenic' or 'hysterical' female patients with 'a combination of entire rest and of excessive feeding'.[28] This popular and respected 'cure' had been pioneered, notoriously, by the American neurologist Silas Weir Mitchell in the United States in the 1870s (and famously satirised there by Charlotte Perkins Gilman in her feminist Gothic horror story, *The Yellow Wallpaper*). The patient had to be 'taken away from her home and deprived of all communication, personal or written, with her family'. The physician was supposed to make her feel that 'her supplications are useless, and that she will revolt in vain against a will that is enlightened and superior to her own'. She was kept in bed and had to have 'absolute rest of the intellect' and 'total inactivity'. Meanwhile she was 'overfed' with a milk diet of four or five pints daily ('taking half a pint at a time every two hours'). After seven or eight days of the milk diet she took a light lunch of a cutlet, and then, progressively, three complete meals with three or four pints of milk a day and with the additions of liquid malt-extract, cod liver oil, and beef tea.[29] Dr Savage's application of this system had a powerful impact on Virginia Woolf's life.

*

The treatment of mental patients is intimately bound up with questions of human rights. There is no doubt that the development of her political position, her intellectual resistance to tyranny and conventionality, derived to a great extent from her experiences as a woman patient. And even before a politics of resistance had been devised, she was very angry and distressed by her treatment. Savage's orders to keep her out of London in 1904 met with furious objections:

> I have never spent such a wretched 8 months in my life . . . I wonder why Savage doesn't see this . . . really a doctor is worse than a husband! . . . never has a time been more miserable . . . I dont expect any doctor to listen to reason . . . If only that pigheaded man Savage will see that this is the sober truth and no excuse![30]

In heartbreaking contrast to this are the subdued, pathetic little notes she is allowed to write to Leonard (in pencil and on one side of the page only) from Burley Park, in the month before her suicide attempt in 1913. 'I want to see you, but this is best . . . I keep thinking of you and want to get to you . . . I have been very good . . . Its all my fault . . . I am grateful and repentant.'[31] These are messages from a deeply depressed and frightened person. More often she was enraged, as here, in 1910, to Vanessa (who she thinks is conspiring against her with Savage to keep her at Burley Park):

> I really dont think I can stand much more of this . . . you cant conceive how I want intelligent conversation – even yours . . . [A caricature of the religious inmates follows]. However, what I mean is that I shall soon have to jump out of a window. The ugliness of the house is almost inexplicable . . . Then there is all the eating and drinking and being shut up in the dark.
>   My God! What a mercy to be done with it!
>   . . . I have been out in the garden for 2 hours; and feel quite normal. I feel my brains, like a pear, to see if its ripe; it will be exquisite by September.
>   . . . I will be very reasonable.[32]

Reading these messages, it is often hard to distinguish the effects of the treatment from the effects of the illness. The neuropsychiatric effects of the drugs she was given need to be considered. We know that during the course of her life she was prescribed veronal, adalin, chloral hydrate, paraldehyde, potassium bromide, and digitalis.[33] Chloral, veronal and paraldehide are sedatives. Like alcohol and the modern benzodiazepines (such as Valium and Mogadon), they are sleep-inducing 'hypnotics' if taken under quiet conditions (though in 1904 we find her complaining that Savage's 'sleeping draught' has given her 'a headache, and nothing else').[34] But taken in large doses in conditions of arousal, they can cause excitement, impaired judgement, euphoria, talkativeness, violent rage, and eventually full-blown delirium. That is, they can produce all the symptoms of mania. In September 1913, during her 'mania', Vanessa writes to Leonard hoping that the violence is 'mainly due to the sleeping draught'. Is this entirely unlikely? In her breakdown in May 1904, Virginia Stephen experienced auditory hallucinations. If, from the start of her breakdown, she was being given large doses of veronal and chloral hydrate, and if the delusions took place some weeks into her breakdown, perhaps at the point when the dosage of drugs was being reduced, then hallucinations could have resulted.

On her prescription forms, dating from 1919, and 1932, she is being given chloral or digitalis (presumably to slow down her rapid pulse and her 'jumping' heart) mixed with potassium bromide (in syrup, as the vehicle). The bromide works differently from the sedatives. In small doses it produced no discernible sedative effect. In large doses, taken regularly, however, it could produce a skin rash, and a stultifying, deadening, torpid effect on the personality. So it is possible that the bromide, too, might have affected her adversely and conduced to moods of despair and depression. Certainly she was extremely susceptible to drugs. In January 1929 on her way back from an exhausting trip to Berlin, she took a sea-sickness drug which Vanessa had given her, called Somnifene (Virginia calls it veronal). She collapsed on board and was ill for three weeks after. 'She was in a kind of drugged state', Leonard wrote to Vita Sackville-West, whom they had been visiting in Berlin, though 'She says she had only taken 20 drops'. A severe headache, jumping pulse and aching back resulted. Elinor Rendel treated her with orders to rest and 'vast draughts of bromide'.[35]

All her life, severe physical symptoms signalled and accompanied phases of agitation or depression.[36] Always in her worst phases of depression she hardly ate, and shed weight frighteningly. Her periods were always disabling, especially on the first day. Terrible headaches always signalled the onset of illness or exhaustion: 'This melancholy,' she wrote in 1929, 'It comes with headache, of course.'[37] Her jumping pulse and high temperatures, which could last for weeks, and which very often came on in the winter months, were usually diagnosed as 'influenza'. At the beginning of 1922 these symptoms got so bad ('my eccentric pulse had passed the limits of reason and was insane')[38] that she consulted a heart specialist in February, who diagnosed a 'tired' heart or a heart 'murmur'.

He said that my old intermittent pulse had rather tired my heart, and the influenza had made this worse, and he wants me not to walk up hill until this has got normal. The temp. is influenza going on, but it is so low that it doesn't matter . . .

What is a 'murmur'? I don't know – but I gather it's not a thing that matters in the least.[39]

Various treatments were tried for the high temperature and the suspect heart. In June 1922 she had three teeth pulled. This was supposed to lower her temperature, on the theory that little nests of germs were clustered in the roots of the teeth. (It was also a recommended treatment for 'insanity'. Savage himself had a theory that neurasthenia might be caused by disorders of the teeth, due to the 'focal sepsis' – those little nests of bacteria – and there were cases of sufferers from dementia praecox having their teeth extracted.)[40] Of course it didn't work, and all that came of it was a vivid essay on having 'Gas' at the dentist's, the wearing of false teeth, and an unnecessary disfigurement of her smile (which might explain her gravity in most of her photographs?)[41] Then, later that year, she went to see a pathologist who decided that her right lung was suspicious. Their own GP and another specialist, Dr Sainsbury, disagreed, and opted for pneumonia microbes. The treatment for this was 'quinine pills, & a box of lozenges, & a brush to varnish my throat with'.[42] Again in February 1923, Leonard reported, 'They found pneumonia germs in her throat and she is now being inoculated once a week with some 50,000,000 of them.'[43] In 1926 an attack of German measles knocked her out for the summer; in 1927 the usual 'flu and headaches put her to bed: 'I get the jumping pulse and pain if I do anything . . . Its so easy with this damned disease, to start a succession of little illnesses, and finally be sent to bed for 6 weeks'.[44] All through the 1930s the symptoms of fevers, faints, headaches, jumping pulses and insomnia increased to danger points. And as usual, she concluded, the doctors 'know absolutely nothing'. Dr Rendel told her that 'in 10 years they'll be able to cure me completely by injecting hormones. At present she says its too risky. Its all the glands in the back of my neck she says'.[45]

But cure her completely of what? Recurrent fever is not a symptom of manic depressive illness; 'flu which lasts for six weeks is uncommon. It is just possible that Virginia Woolf may have had some chronic febrile or 'pyrexial' (tubercular) illness. But this cannot be proved.[46] What is clear is that she did battle throughout her life with physical symptoms and with the restrictions that attended them (both preventive and curative) as well as with violent, constant mood swings. Her emotions struck her physically, in her thighs and her spine and her head. Her moods of despair, some resulting from periods of stress (like the struggle with *The Years*, or the completion of a novel, or the expectation of reviews) but others random and inexplicable, were recorded in terms which intermingled physical and mental terms.

> I know the feeling now, when I can't spin a sentence, & sit mumbling & turning; & nothing flits by my brain which is as a blank window. So I . . . go to bed . . . And what leagues I travel in the time! Such 'sensations' spread over my spine & head directly I give them the chance; such an exaggerated tiredness; such anguishes & despairs; & heavenly relief & rest; & then misery again. Never was anyone so tossed up & down by the body as I am, I think.[47]

> *A State of Mind.*
> Woke up perhaps at 3. Oh its beginning its coming – the horror – physically like a painful wave about the heart – tossing me up. I'm unhappy unhappy! Down – God, I wish I were dead. Pause. But why am I feeling this? . . . Wave crashes. I wish I were dead! I've only a few years to live I hope. I cant face this horror any more – (this is the wave spreading out over me).
> This goes on; several times, with varieties of horror. Then, at the crisis, instead of the pain remaining intense, it becomes rather vague . . . At last . . . I brace myself . . . I become rigid & straight, & sleep again.[48]

Just before the publication of *The Years*:

> I wish I could write out my sensations at this moment. They are so peculiar & so unpleasant. Partly T of L? [Time of Life] I wonder. A physical feeling as if I were drumming slightly in the veins: very cold: impotent: & terrified. As if I were exposed on a high ledge in full light. Very lonely. L. out to lunch. Nessa has Quentin & dont want me. Very useless. No atmosphere round me. No words. Very apprehensive. As if something cold & horrible – a roar of laughter at my expense were about to happen. And I am powerless to ward it off: I have no protection. And this anxiety & nothingness surround me with a vacuum. It affects the thighs chiefly . . . the exposed moments are terrifying. I looked at my eyes in the glass once & saw them positively terrified.[49]

In such passages she is her own analyst and her own doctor. They are some of the most powerful and accurate pieces of prose she ever wrote. But to arrive at this language for illness she had to work past a whole swathe of prescriptive terms, some of which she never quite shed. Her language for mental illness is often brutal and conventional, accepting apparently without irony the current official attitudes. If we want to hear her as the pre-eminent voice speaking for the creativity and singularity of abnormal perceptions, then it is awkward to find her, at times, using exactly the sort of language which her thought-policing doctors, targets of her own satire, might use.

The Darwinian evolutionary psychiatrists of the late nineteenth century roped together lunatics and criminals. Henry Maudsley, writing in the 1870s, warned of the degeneration of the race through hereditary insanity which might end 'finally in the extreme degeneracy of idiocy'.[50] Such fears about inherited degeneration were extremely influential when it came to family planning. Bertrand Russell and his first wife Alys, for example, were persuaded in 1893 that the danger of inherited insanity from both sides of the family should prevent them from having children; Russell read Galton on eugenics and went to see Ibsen's *Ghosts* and said that his family home felt 'like a family vault haunted like the ghosts of maniacs'.[51] It may be that such fears played their part in the advice the Woolfs were given about having children: George Savage wrote in the 1880s that 'an insane patient may have an insane, idiotic, wicked, epileptic or somnambulistic child'.[52]

Virginia Woolf sometimes seems to endorse the language of degeneracy and eugenics. She talks in her notes for the writing of *Mrs Dalloway* of not wanting the 'insane', shell-shocked Septimus Smith to be a 'degenerate' type, and has him in his 'insanity' much preoccupied with Darwinian evolution, the history of civilisation, and his own 'degradation'.[53] And although Septimus Smith's language about madness and doctors, is, like her own, often savagely ironical, there is no indication of ironic distance in his horror at the sight of 'a maimed file of lunatics being exercised or displayed for the diversion of the populace (who laughed aloud)'.[54] This is like Virginia Woolf writing in horror in 1915, 'They should certainly be killed' at the sight of a 'long line of imbeciles' with their idiot grins and wild stares. This violent endorsement of an extreme theory of eugenics, written between two very severe breakdowns, must be understood as expressing her dread and horror of what she thought of as her own loss of control. It may seem to most of us reprehensible and cruel to speak about 'idiots' and 'imbeciles', and it is horrid to find Virginia Woolf doing so. (Similarly, we probably feel squeamish when she calls someone a 'nigger' or says that a woman with a particularly pale complexion 'has the mind of an albino'.) But when she refers to 'a troupe of lunatics', in 1924,[55] we have to remember that these were standard terms. The Lunacy Act of 1890 used the terms 'idiots' and 'imbeciles'. It had only been since the 1850s that institutions (like the new 'idiot asylum' Laura Stephen was sent to in Redhill) had distinguished between the 'mentally defective' and the 'insane' – between 'idiots' and 'lunatics'.[56] The Mental Deficiency Act of 1913 still used the classification of 'idiots', 'imbeciles', 'feeble-minded' and 'moral imbeciles'.[57] It was not until the Mental Treatment Act of 1930 that the terms 'pauper', 'asylum' and 'lunatic' were replaced with the terms 'rate-aided person', 'mental hospital' and 'person of unsound mind'.

As well as the rough-and-ready terminology officially sanctioned by the Lunacy Act, the late-nineteenth-century language of nerves was also built into Virginia Woolf's vocabulary, and hence into her perceptions, of mental illness. The various use of 'nerves' – neurosis, neurasthenia, nervous breakdown, diseases of the nerves – had (for about a century) particularly coloured the approach to women's illnesses. Savage used 'neurosis' to mean any inherited 'disturbance of the nervous system', and 'neurasthenic' to describe any 'hysteric' and sexually deprived young woman given to invalidism, self-starvation, paralysis, masturbation, or eccentricity. Leonard, who like Virginia freely used the standard parlance for mental illness ('raving mad', 'insanity'), quite rightly rejected the diagnosis of 'neurasthenia' in favour of 'manic depression'. But his life-long strategies for controlling her illness had their basis in the old 'cures' for neurasthenia – one of the reasons why he has been implicated with the oppressive procedures of Virginia Woolf's doctors.[58]

But for all her satires on the authority of the law-making doctors, and their unimaginative citings of 'nerve symptoms' or 'nervous breakdown' in *Mrs Dalloway*, Virginia Woolf to an extent incorporated their terminology into her accounts of her own states of mind. As a child she was taught to talk about nerves, and did so in the 1890s with angry impatience: 'I was extremely gruff & unpleasant, which, however, is to be ascribed to the effect of the hot weather on my nerves – Nothing else!'[59] But in adult life she would still invoke 'nerves' – as in 'my poor bunch of nerves at the back of my neck'.[60] 'I've been reading Faber on Newman; compared his account of a nervous breakdown; the refusal of some part of the mechanism; is that what happens to me? Not quite. Because I'm not evading anything.'[61] This interesting remark suggests that she believes her illness to be an illness, not an expression of something repressed or 'evaded'. But she does not like to be too clinically reductive of 'my own queer, difficult nervous system'.[62] When Ethel Smyth robustly decides that everything that Virginia suffers from can be attributed to her liver, she notes, with a fine touch of self-satire, that she has swallowed 'this terrific insult to the celebrated sensibility of my nervous system'.[63]

She also keeps to a family language for depression and stress, which works as a private shorthand. She goes on all her life using Leslie's terms, 'tantrums' and 'fidgets', for anxiety attacks or bouts of insomnia or states of irritation. She has been ill and 'must not work', so the diary is opened (as it often is) for 'an intolerable fit of the fidgets to write away'.[64] But the 'fidgets' also featured as part of the illness: '60 days . . . spent in wearisome headache, jumping pulse, aching back, frets, fidgets, lying awake, sleeping draughts, sedatives, digitalis, going for a little walk, & plunging back into bed again – all the horrors of the dark cupboard of illness once more displayed for my diversion.' 'Fidgets' is a word that hovers between the physical, the mental, and the anti-social (children are told not to fidget). The dark cupboard, too, with its associations of skeletons, ghosts, repressions and domestic mismanagement (horrors pushed to the back and tumbling out pell-mell, as in the old cupboards at Hyde Park Gate) could be a 'bad' place: 'Let me make a vow that this shall never, never, happen again', she says, as though it can be avoided by her own self-discipline; but then goes on to admit that there are compensations: 'the dark underworld has its fascinations as well as its terrors'.[65]

Her language for her illness also, at times, seems to make a guilt-inducing, moral reading of 'madness'. In 1913 Leonard has repeatedly to assure her that what she is suffering from 'is illness & nothing moral'.[66] This distinction has its roots in the history of rational moral management for mental illness.

Under the late-eighteenth-century system of 'moral management' 'lunatics' were turned from animals into children, and, in revolutionary institutions like Tuke's York Retreat, founded in 1796, encouraged to practise responsibility through a system of rewards and punishments. The patient was asked 'to exercise all the self-control of which he is capable'.[67] In the course of the nineteenth century, institutions practising moral management grew larger and the systems used to encourage self-control became more coercive, bearing out Foucault's powerful interpretation of the rational restraint of mental patients as a form of social repression.[68] And long after the concept of the 'moral management' of the 'insane' had given way to the dominance of doctors and psychiatrists, ideas of self-control[69] were still – and still are – bound up with attitudes to mental illness.

Virginia Woolf's reading of her own condition is greatly influenced by the idea of self-control. When she is writing to Vanessa or Leonard from nursing homes, she emphasises, either pathetically or angrily, the need for control. Years later she will still accuse herself of lacking self-control: they could have had children, she thinks in 1926, if she had had 'a little more self-control'; 'my own fault too'.[70]

It's a feature of manic depressive illness that 'mood swings' are frequently confused with 'egotism',[71] and that guilt and self-blame may be ingredients in the suffering. For Virginia Woolf, though, there was also a complex legacy of influences at work in the language of self-control. She had a horror of her father's unbridled domestic egotism, and when she reproaches herself for egotism in her letters, she seems to regard it as a lack of self-control. But she resisted, too, in writing and in life, her mother's programme of self-denial for women. Mixed in with this was the reaction of her generation against Victorian sentimentality and emotionalism,[72] and a fear of self-exposure and of being laughed at. So 'self-control' is opposed to 'egotism', as much in her language for her illness as in her arguments about fiction.

In the course of time her interiorising of the language of nineteenth-century doctors faded away. And the language of her doctors was changing too: her women doctors, Rendel and Wilberforce, did not take a moral tone, and were more forthright with her about the limitations of their profession. Elinor Rendel, advising inoculation for a fever in 1934, was challenged by her patient: 'But have you ever known influenza or any other disease cured that way?' 'To which she . . . being an honest woman, said No.'[73]

Increasingly in the 1930s, she would use terms borrowed from psychoanalysis – repression, complex, suppression, ambivalence. She knew these terms well from conversation and journalism, even though, in spite of her close connections to the British psychoanalytical movement, she did not begin to read the primary texts until the late 1930s. But though she finds psychoanalytical terminology more useful than her repudiations of Freud might lead one to expect, she tends to use it more for political purposes (as when mocking the complexes of the angry patriarchs in *Three Guineas*) than for talking about her illness.

Instead, her response to the competing narratives of mental illness – Darwinian, moralistic, Freudian – was to create an original language of her own, in fiction and in autobiographical writing, which could explain her illness to her and give it value, as in that letter to Vanessa of 1910: 'I feel my brains, like a pear, to see if its ripe; it will be exquisite by September.' This writing recognises the virtue of her illness, the happiness of mania or its creativity, as well as its terror and pain.

> The interesting thing is that one does, normally, keep up a kind of vibration, for no reason whatever. Equally for no reason whatever, the vibration stops. Then one enquires why one ever had it, & there seems no reason why one should ever have it again. Things seem clear, sane, comprehensible, & under no obligation, being of that nature, to make one vibrate at all. Indeed, its largely the clearness of sight which comes at such seasons that leads to depression. But when one can analyse it, one is half way back again. I feel unreason slowly tingling in my veins.[74]

This exciting image of 'unreason', coming back like blood into a limb that has gone to sleep, is a writer's appropriation of an otherwise unmanageable experience. (It takes pretty much the opposite view of Leonard's 'line' between the rational and the incoherent.) She translates her condition into a private language ('vibration', 'unreason', 'tingling') which explains to herself the way her mind feels.

Complaining to E.M. Forster in 1922 about the amount of time in her life she has had to spend in bed doing nothing, she adds, with misleading casualness: 'Not that I haven't picked up something from my insanities and all the rest. Indeed, I suspect they've done instead of religion. But this is a difficult point.'[75] A 'difficult point' which she will come back to:

> Once or twice I have felt that odd whirr of wings in the head which comes when I am ill so often . . . I believe these illnesses are in my case – how shall I express it? – partly mystical. Something happens in my mind. It refuses to go on registering impressions. It shuts itself up. It becomes chrysalis. I lie quite torpid, often with acute physical pain . . . Then suddenly something springs . . . ideas rush in me; often though this is before I can control my mind or pen.[76]

In passages like these, a creative language which describes the value of illness competes with, and overcomes, a clinical or psychoanalytical language for madness. This competition of languages is one of the plots of *Mrs Dalloway*, in which different ways of speaking about mental illness violently confront each other. Her notes to herself in 1922 and 1923 about the book in its planning stages are preoccupied with the structural difficulties of placing 'sanity and insanity' next to each other.[77] From the start she was extremely anxious that she should not be thought just to 'write essays about myself'.[78] 'Egotism' must be countered by narrative 'control'. Septimus should not only be 'founded on me' but 'might be left vague – as a mad person is – not so much character as an idea'.[79] Even so, it was perilous for her to write about him: 'Of course the mad part tries me so much, makes my mind squint so badly that I can hardly face spending the next weeks at it.'[80] In the changes from the manuscript to the finished version, she turns what reads like a direct transcription of her own experience as a 'mental patient' into a less self-referential, more abstracted narrative. But she keeps the 'exasperation' which she says in her notes should be the 'dominant theme' of Septimus's encounters with his doctors.

Dr Holmes, the general practitioner whose only language for mental illness is a virile no-nonsense practical commonsense, and who recommends porridge and outside interests as a cure for 'nerve symptoms' like headaches and sleeplessness, is even more of a buffoon in the manuscript (where he suggests that Septimus should take up golf).

> 'People are asleep when they think they're not asleep. There's no harm in 5 grains of veronal; Dont get into the habit of course. Headaches are often caused by eye strain. As for this palpitation of the heart, there's nothing in that except nerves. Pressure on the top of the head, pains at the back of the neck – why not go and see an oculist?'

On his next visit he tells Septimus: 'There's absolutely nothing whatever the matter with you. But if you lie here, thinking about your own symptoms, you'll only be fit for a lunatic asylum.'[81] Though a little toned down in the final version of *Mrs Dalloway*, Dr Holmes is still a vigorous caricature of the kind of doctor who had been on her case. 'The truth is doctors know absolutely nothing, but as theyre paid to advise, have to oblige', she wrote in 1934, as if speaking in Septimus's 'sceptical' and exasperated voice.[82]

The novel's most outraged satire is levelled against the Harley Street specialist, Sir William Bradshaw, who shuts up his lunatics in his nice 'homes' in the interests of Proportion and of his lucrative bank balance. Her clinical diagnosis of his condition – a political reading, ahead of Foucault, of the conspiracy between social engineering, the restraint of the mentally ill, and the patriarchal self-protection of the establishment – takes revenge on all the diagnoses that his type has made of her. In the manuscript, there is a more direct, ragged confrontation between Septimus and Sir William.

> 'You are the enemy,' he said.
> 'No, no,' said Sir William agreeably.
> Why not speak the truth? Septimus asked, for the last time?
> Why is it for the last time? Sir William enquired, quite casually.
> 'I shan't be here again.'
> 'I hope to see you several times.'
> . . .'Your car must cost a lot to keep up. That *was* your car at the door.'
> 'I have to visit patients all over England . . .'
> Nothing is so profound as vanity. Sir William dealing with a lunatic wished to impress even a lunatic. He was at the top of his tree . . .
> Typhoid fever is a mere joke to this sort of thing, [for] Sir William never underestimated the gravity of a hurt to that complex and mysterious organ the nervous system; about which we know so little he admitted; but in this case it was physical, purely physical.[83]

In the final version, a formal passage on Sir William's dedication to the goddess of Proportion replaces the original confrontation. But the personal note of rage and resistance to medical ignorance and authoritarianism bursts through, and makes a savagely rational caricature of the 'treatment' she herself had received:

> To his patients he gave three-quarters of an hour; and if in this exacting science which has to do with what, after all, we know nothing about – the nervous system, the human brain – a doctor loses his sense of proportion, as a doctor he fails. Health we must have; and health is proportion; so that when a man comes into your room and says he is Christ (a common delusion), and has a message, as they mostly have, and threatens, as they often do, to kill himself, you invoke proportion; order rest in bed; rest in solitude; silence and rest; rest without friends, without books, without messages; six months' rest; until a man who went in weighing seven stone six comes out weighing twelve.[84]

If we decide to name Virginia Woolf's recurrent mental and physical symptoms an 'illness', we immediately fall into the trap of sounding like her fictional doctors. Since in her writing she transforms illness into a language of power and inspiration, it is inviting to think of her illness as a 'gift', not as a disability, and of her fiction-writing as a form of therapy.[85] But to treat her fiction only as therapy[86] is to empty her writing of all content except the curative, to depoliticise it and to narrow its ambitions. Madness is not her only subject. Nor does she write simply in order to make herself feel better (though it's true that she feels worse when she is not writing). A great deal of the process of controlling egotism, or translating personal material into art, is done with laborious painful difficulty. And that strenuous work marks the difference between the illness itself and what she does with it. Septimus and Rhoda (in *The Waves*) are imprisoned alone inside their violent feelings of horror at the human race and their inability to communicate. They act out the frightening solipsism of mental illness. There is a ludicrous, awful gap between Septimus's manic inspiration, and the banal unintelligibility of his utterances and his scribbles.

> She brought him his papers, the things he had written, things she had written for him. She tumbled them out on to the sofa. They looked at them together. Diagrams, designs, little men and women brandishing sticks for arms, with wings – were they? – on their backs; circles traced round shillings and sixpences – the sun and stars; zigzagging precipices with mountaineers ascending roped together, exactly like knives and forks; sea pieces with little faces laughing out of what might perhaps be waves; the map of the world. Burn them! he cried. Now for his writings;

how the dead sing behind rhododendron bushes; odes to Time; conversations with Shakespeare; Evans, Evans, Evans – his messages from the dead; do not cut down trees; tell the Prime Minister. Universal love: the meaning of the world. Burn them! he cried.[87]

Septimus's scribbles[88] about his dead friend and 'the meaning of the world' reflect her own fear of unintelligibility. In all her fictional versions of her illness she expresses the horror of not being able to make sense to others. The fear of incomprehensibility links madness and writing. The voices she hears in her head create a new kind of fictional language. There is a relation between illness and modernism in Virginia Woolf's writing life. It may well be that her extreme apprehension of the reviews of her novels is partly a fear of being thought crazy rather than brilliant. Like the saints of old, poised between interpretations of their voices as daemonic and misleading or as true and angelic, there is always the fear that her 'map of the world' is going to be quite unbelievable and unacceptable. She knows there is a risky connection between originality and incoherence.

> The balance between the outer and the inner is, after all, a terribly precarious business. They depend upon each other with the utmost closeness. If dreams become too widely divorced from truth they develop into an insanity which in literature is generally an evasion on the part of the artist.[89]

Eccentrics require new kinds of biographies, but they may be so 'dishevelled' – 'in such dishabille from their long obscurity and fantastic behaviour' – that they will be illegible.[90] Illness requires a new kind of language – but it may be 'incomprehensible'.[91]

There is a gap between the inner, 'incomprehensible' language of the ill person, and the language of witnesses and retrospect. For example, how should we read one of the best known stories of her illness, her aural hallucination of birds singing in Greek? She recalls these hallucinations in her 1922 memoir 'Old Bloomsbury'. Here she says that in 1904 Vanessa moved the family into Gordon Square 'while I had lain in bed at the Dickinsons' house at Welwyn thinking that the birds were singing Greek choruses and that King Edward was using the foulest possible language among Ozzie Dickinson's azaleas'.[92] Leonard Woolf mentions these Greek-talking birds twice in his autobiography, but gives the impression they might have featured in later breakdowns.[93] Quentin Bell says of her 1904 breakdown that 'it was here that she lay in bed, listening to the birds singing in Greek and imagining that King Edward VII lurked in the azaleas using the foulest possible language'. ('Lurked' peps things up nicely.) And there follows the most notorious sentence in his biography, 'All that summer she was mad'.[94] And so the Greek-talking birds settle in as verified, striking features of her 'mania'. But they don't quite fit the usual pattern of auditory hallucinations in mania, which are usually either grandiose or paranoid. They sound romantic rather than horrifying, like the bird Wagner's Siegfried suddenly finds he can understand, or the talking fish in Yeats's 'The Man Who Dreamed of Faeryland'. But is there, perhaps, something fishy about these birds?

Just before she wrote 'Old Bloomsbury', in 1921, she had again been very ill;[95] she was reading Greek for an essay to be called 'On Not Knowing Greek'; and she was starting work on *Mrs Dalloway*. In the essay, she talked about the impersonality of Greek plays, with their choruses, 'the undifferentiated voices who sing like birds in the pauses of the wind'. No English poets can speak with Aeschylus' intensity about 'the vast catastrophe of the European war'; poets like Wilfred Owen and Siegfried Sassoon could only speak indirectly, while the Greeks could use phrases like: 'Yet being dead they have not died.'[96]

Meanwhile she is working on Septimus's hallucinations. Like Siegfried Sassoon, he has come back from the war shell-shocked, unable to feel anything about the death of his friend Evans. He can hear birds singing 'in Greek words' about death and immortality. And the ghost of Evans appears to him (in the manuscript version) as a 'Greek nightingale'. Septimus is filled with ecstasy by the song of the birds, but with horror and fear at the appearance of Evans. So, by the time she is writing her novel about madness and her memoir of her breakdown in the early 1920s, those Greek-speaking birds have become a very useful, rich, literary hallucination.

Their possible meanings have been much debated. Perhaps they invoke her sexual fears. (After all, George Duckworth interfered with her during her Greek lessons, and the Greek nightingale Philomena is singing of rape.) Perhaps the reference to Edward VII alludes to Sir Leslie Stephen's doctor in his last illness, who was also Edward VII's doctor (this, though ingenious, doesn't quite seem to cover the obscenities in the azaleas).[97] Perhaps the birds are phallic images and 'King Edward,who is a father-figure, stands for Leslie's "incestuous" invasiveness'.[98] Or perhaps, if her hallucination occurred in 1913 rather 1904, it is Thoby (with whom she had such strong Greek associations) who is in her mind.

That her delusions lend themselves to such a variety of readings is almost suspicious. It seems possible that she may have refashioned the frightening, unintelligible mental language of her hallucinations – a language which was, as it were, all Greek to her – into a more meaningful ensemble, either immediately afterwards or long afterwards.[99] And it is possible that these hallucinations may have been the result of toxic withdrawal. Either possibility makes me pause before accepting them as exact narratives of her raw experience, or before attributing to them the kind of coherent biographical meanings which they invite.

The difficulty of knowing exactly what she was experiencing when she was 'mad', and what to make of these experiences, is like the difficulty of explaining dreams. Virginia Woolf would have heard a great deal about Freud's interpretations of the language of dreams.[100] In 1914, years before they were publishing Freud or hearing about Freudian analysis at first hand, Leonard was reviewing a translation of *The Psychopathology of Everyday Life*. He read *The Interpretation of Dreams* for his review, and referred to the connections between the 'dark half' of the mind in Freud's 'theories of dreams and his theories of insanity':

> It is [Freud's] aim to show that it is the 'dark half' of the mind which in the perfectly normal waking man produces all kinds of trivial errors and slips and forgettings and rememberings, and which under other conditions will, following the same laws, produce the absurd fantasies of sleep or the terrible fantasies of madness.[101]

Virginia Woolf was notoriously scathing of psychoanalysis,[102] for reasons bound up with her feelings about Adrian and her resistance to being analysed herself. (Psychoanalysis would not have been an option for her, in any case. It was thought to be dangerous and counterproductive for anyone who had had a major breakdown or attempted suicide.)[103] In her essay on 'Freudian Fiction' of 1920, she mocks 'the new psychology' which cures by undoing repression:

> A patient who has never heard a canary sing without falling down in a fit can now walk through an avenue of cages without a twinge of emotion since he has faced the fact that his mother kissed him in his cradle. The triumphs of science are beautifully positive.

When 'the triumphs of science' are applied to fiction, 'all the characters become cases', and the new key 'simplifies rather than complicates, detracts rather than enriches'.[104] It is a powerful, funny, and self-defensive case against the reductive effect of analysis, which (judging from such comments) she was afraid would stop her writing. But though she held Freudian analysis at arm's length, she would have known all about dream work. She was a vivid dreamer and she often transcribed her dreams. This one occurs in the summer of 1935, when she is writing *The Years*, in deep distress:

> I slept all the evening over the fire, & dreamt of cutting my hand in a theatre, & of a professional mistress of ceremonies who had to entertain people; & somehow Mrs Clifford [Lucy Clifford, a writer friend of Leslie and Julia Stephen] came in, & I woke to find L. standing over me.[105]

What should we do with such dream-narratives (of which there are many others in her diaries)? Can we read them as we would read her books, analysing their manifest content for the 'true' story of Virginia's inner life? In that dream of 1935, perhaps the wound refers to a sexual wound, or the dream has to do with writer's anxiety, or her dread of exposure. But do we need – and do we have the right – to put Virginia Woolf on the couch and make more sense of her than she can make of herself? There may be more interest and significance in the way she tells these dreams, how she shapes them, what she says about how they make her feel, than in their latent meaning.

There is the same gap between a dream as it happens in sleep and a dream as it is retold the next day, as there is between a delusion in psychosis and the shaping or retelling of that delusion. All we have are the narratives.[106] There is a remarkable affinity between the way Virginia Woolf narrates a dream, the way she remembers her childhood, the way she describes her breakdowns, and the way she places images in characters' minds in her fictions.

Take, for example, the incident of the puddle, a puddle as famous to the readers of Woolf's life as those Greek-speaking birds. In *The Waves*, Rhoda, the outcast and suicide, has a moment of self-obliteration when she cannot cross a puddle in the road.

> 'There is the puddle,' said Rhoda, 'and I cannot cross it. I hear the rush of the great grindstone within an inch of my head. Its wind roars in my face. All palpable forms of life have failed me. Unless I can stretch and touch something hard, I shall be blown down the eternal corridors for ever. What, then, can I touch? What brick, what stone? and so draw myself across the enormous gulf into my body safely?'[107]

A few years later, in her 'Sketch of the Past', Virginia Woolf owns this 'moment' as part of her own childhood memories: 'There was the moment of the puddle in the path; when for no reason I could discover, everything suddenly became unreal; I was suspended; I could not step across the puddle; I tried to touch something . . . the whole world became unreal.'[108]

And she leaves this to stand as a 'moment of being' of unexplained helplessness.

The different explanations that have been offered for this moment show that the variant readings of Virginia Woolf's psychic history are as hard to reconcile as the puddle was hard for her to cross.[109] Our versions of her will depend on our own attitudes to feminism, medicine, and mental illness. Interpretations of her life have kept pace with changes or fashions in attitudes to psychiatry as well as with shifts in terminology.[110] But even in the light of these different, and changing, readings, we cannot, I think, be sure what 'caused' Virginia Woolf's mental illness. We can only look at what it did to her, and what she did with it. What is certain is her closeness, all her life, to a terrifying edge, and her creation of a language which faces it and makes something of it. This is a life of heroism, not of oppression, a life of writing wrestled from illness, fear, and pain.

In 1904, three months after her father's death, when the family came back from their journey to Italy and France, Virginia became very ill. (There is an odd, distressing story of her behaviour a few days before they came back to England. The Stephens had been taken by Clive Bell to visit Rodin's studio. Rodin told them they could touch anything except the sculptures which were under wraps. Virginia immediately started to unwrap one of the unfinished works. The English painter Gerald Kelly, who witnessed the scene, said that Rodin slapped her.)[111] 'Oh Lord, how cross I have been, how dull, how tempersome, – and am still' she wrote to Violet Dickinson the day before that incident. 'I *must* work . . . I cant write a word I want to, as I have forgotten everything.'[112]

When they returned to England she became out of control. From May until August 1904, after conferences between Vanessa and Sir George Savage, she was placed under the care of three nurses at Violet Dickinson's home in Welwyn. During this period (according to Quentin Bell and Leonard Woolf) she refused to eat, was violent with her nurses, had hallucinations and appalling headaches, and tried to kill herself by jumping out of a (low) window. She also had a physical illness, scarlet fever. She wrote no letters until September, when she had left Welwyn to join the family on holiday in Nottinghamshire and from there wrote to Violet that 'All the voices I used to hear telling me to do all kinds of wild things have gone – and Nessa says they were always only my imagination.'[113] In her convalescence she was sent to stay with her aunt Caroline Emelia in Cambridge and with the Vaughans in Yorkshire, but she resented being kept away from London and the new house in Gordon Square. Letters from Vanessa Stephen to

Madge Vaughan, asking if Virginia can be sent to stay with them, describe the regulation of her life at this point:

> She is really quite well now – except that she does not sleep very well – and is inclined to do too much in some ways. But she wants no special looking after – except in one way – which might be difficult for you. She ought not to walk very far or for a very long time alone . . . She goes to bed very early as I think you do and she is in all ways absolutely normal in her doings.

> [She has] hot chocolate when she goes to bed, and a cup of tea when she is called. The only difficulty now is sleep. She has been sleeping much too little. She has a medicine to take, and the Dr. says that if she sleeps very badly she is to have mulled wine. This she hates – and wont take it unless it is absolutely necessary . . . You'll think me a fearful old hen! – but now that she is getting better I am very anxious that she should go on getting better and be quite well enough to start London after Christmas. There is no fear of making her think too much about her own health – She never thinks or talks of it unless one makes her. In all other ways she leads a perfectly ordinary life – with as much fresh air as possible – and working all the morning.[114]

These letters, not perhaps as reassuring for Madge Vaughan as they were intended to be, limit themselves to the pattern of curative rests and foods. But through these details come words like 'difficult', 'dependent', 'hates', 'anxious', 'fear', which suggest how perilously borderline her condition was felt to be, and how terribly anxious she had made those closest to her. She was twenty-two. Nobody knew what her future would be now. But her own will, to live and to work, was strong.

PART 2

1904–1919

ELEVEN

Changes

'I am longing to begin work.' 'I know I can write.' After the summer of 1904,
Virginia Stephen urgently wanted to start her life again. A conflict began –
which would recur whenever she was recovering from illness – between her
desire to get back to a full life, and her family's anxiety for her to be quiet
and unexcited. A scurry of letters about her condition went back and forth
between family and friends. In August, Gerald Duckworth paid a visit to
Teversal Manor in Nottinghamshire (where, still with Nurse Traill to look
after her, Virginia joined the others on their holiday) and gave his own
account of 'the Goat' to Violet: 'She really is a different creature and
personally I think much more wholesome in mind than she has ever
been . . . She talked to me so clearly yesterday as to her feelings and what
she thought and had experienced that it made me feel all was clear going
now provided she did not overtax herself.'[1] She may have been 'more
wholesome' – more subdued? – but was, fortunately, not nearly well enough
to make the long train journey to Somerset with Adrian and Vanessa for the
pompous and elaborate wedding of George Duckworth and Lady Margaret
Herbert. (Adrian and Vanessa arrived disgracefully late, having left their
luggage in the third class lavatory at Swindon.)[2]

The wedding removed the threat of George's perpetual presence and
released the orphaned family into its first definite change since Leslie's
death. Virginia's first sighting of Bloomsbury, on a dreary house-hunting
expedition made the previous December, had not been promising: 'It seems
so far away, and so cold and gloomy – but that was due to the dark and the
cold I expect.' 'But it is better to go,' she added sadly.[3] The final decision
was not hers. After some searching, Vanessa had settled on a big house to
rent at 46 Gordon Square, in a district as far away in spirit from Kensington
as she could find. Hyde Park Gate was cleared out and much of the old
furniture was sold to Harrods. The house move took place in early October
– Virginia was brought back to town for a week and the sisters stayed with
the Booths. (Even this exciting moment of liberation took place under the
shadow of more deaths: of the painter Charles Furse, recently married to
Madge Vaughan's sister Katherine, and of poor Jack Hills's young sister-in-

law, hit by a bus on her bicycle, in just the kind of street accident Virginia always feared for Vanessa.)

Virginia wanted to stay in London. There were to be no more nurses, no more voices, no more sleepless nights, no more 'disgusting scenes over food', no more monitoring. But everyone was very anxious to keep her away. It was like the quarrels with Stella over fresh air and exercise all over again, but now she was not a child. The doctor's orders were all that the family had to go by. She was still eating and sleeping badly. And so what seemed to Virginia like a conspiracy between Vanessa and 'that pigheaded man Savage'[4] prevailed, and Virginia was sent off to Aunt Caroline Emelia's house in Cambridge. Then, after a few days in Gordon Square in November, she went to Madge and Will Vaughan in Yorkshire. She noted the frustratedly busy life of the headmaster's wife, played with the children, was driven to despair by the noise of the Giggleswick church bells and took walks from the school buildings, straight up on to the freezing cold grey moors, with their wide, silent views right across to Ingleborough. In December, after another brief London foray, she was sent back to her aunt in Cambridge.

During these autumn months, while Vanessa was decorating the house and writing reassuring letters ('Now my own beloved monkey – Dont go and imagine that I *want* you to stay away'),[5] Virginia took over a job from Thoby which made it possible to transform her grief for Leslie into cathartic work. This was to read through Leslie's correspondence for Fred Maitland, now embarked on the 'Life and Letters' of his friend and mentor, to copy out those she thought worth including, and then to write her own 'Note' on Leslie Stephen for inclusion in Maitland's book. The copying work engrossed her – 'my life here is practically spent with old letters'.[6] (It was now that she realised that 'the history of Laura' had been 'really the most tragic thing' in Leslie's life.) But she also resented the job: 'I am doing what I dislike, against my will at Freds wish.' At the same time she was doing her own writing – copying out the old Warboys punting adventure for Emma, writing 'comic lives' of 'the Quaker' (Aunt Caroline Emelia) and Aunt Mary, and starting her first pieces of journalism. But it maddened her that for ten months, since Leslie's death, she had had no room of her own to do her reading and writing in. She was furious with Vanessa and 'sick of . . . this eternal resting and fussing, and being told not to do this and that'. Her anger spilled over on to the biography. Jack Hills took it upon himself to warn her against including anything too 'intimate'; she hated having her judgement questioned, 'pointing out that I probably cared 10,000 times more for delicacy and reserve where my own Father and Mother are concerned than he could'.[7] Vanessa had to calm her down ('Of course you understood Father better than anyone else did'),[8] but disliked even more than her sister the idea of family exposure: 'I would rather that no one, not even Fred, should see the more intimate bits – I should like them burnt.'[9] It was Virginia Stephen's first brush with the censorious conventions of biography and with the question of who owned a person's posthumous life.

At last, in December 1904, almost a year after Leslie's death, she settled into Gordon Square and began to participate in the changing life of the household. The new house was one of the big tall five-storey terraced houses on the Bedford estate squares, in a district which had been prosperously bourgeois in the nineteenth century but was by 1905 rather shabby and unfashionable. The square was an oasis of green away from the busy life of the big thoroughfares – Tottenham Court Road or Gray's Inn Road or Oxford Street – but she liked being on the edge of what she romantically described as 'the perpetual note of unrest which frets the very shore of the paradise'.[10] In fact it was much noisier than Hyde Park Gate – cabs rattled along the asphalt roads, deliveries came to the kitchen basements all round the square, rival street musicians played all day long.[11]

There was more light and space for them all – though the basement kitchen and bedroom, where the loyal Sophie Farrell had followed them, was still as dark.[12] (As well as Sophie to shop and cook for the family, they still had a maid to open the door to visitors.) On the ground floor there was a dining-room, a living-room, and Thoby's library-study, which they all used as a sitting-room, all with fine ceiling-roses and dados. On the first floor was a double L-shaped drawing-room, and on the three floors above, four bedrooms with their own sitting-rooms – smaller rooms than downstairs, with lower ceilings. The high front windows let in the afternoon sun; Virginia's room at the top of the house looked out on the tops of the huge plane trees in the square gardens, instead of at 'old Mrs Redgrave washing her neck across the way'.[13] All the main rooms had fireplaces, and the house was heated by coal fires – but unlike Hyde Park Gate it had electric lighting. And compared with the old house it had 'an air of great cleanliness & emptiness'.[14] Vanessa distempered the walls and strewed around some coloured Indian shawls which, she said, 'looked rather fine and barbaric against our white walls'.[15] She bought a red carpet for the drawing-room, a dinner table seating eight, a big mirror, a new table for Virginia, and green and white chintzes in the 'Sargent-Furse'[16] manner. The old objects which had been kept from Hyde Park Gate – Dutch cabinets, blue china – 'shone out'[17] in their new pale setting. She hung up Watts' portraits of their parents, and, in the entrance hall, Julia Margaret Cameron's photographs of the great Victorians (Tennyson, Meredith, Browning, Herschel) and of Julia Stephen. She unpacked the books – it took her days.

Virginia settled into her new room with pleasure. She shifted the furniture around to please herself, she made frames for some of the manuscripts Leslie had left (a letter from George Eliot, a Lowell poem) and put them on her mantelpiece. She bought a little bookshelf and a brass coalscuttle, fender and fire irons. She had her books, her typewriter, her pens and papers, her tall desk, her own space for entertaining in. She wrote to Madge Vaughan gleefully:

> I wish you could see my room at this moment, on a dark winter's evening
> – all my beloved leather backed books standing up so handsome in their
> shelves, and a nice fire, and the electric light burning, and a huge mass of
> manuscripts and letters and proof-sheets and pens and inks over the floor
> and everywhere.[18]

The contrast struck her forcibly when she went back to Hyde Park Gate and saw those marks on the wall, vestiges of the last twenty-two years of her life.[19]

Yet the life she began to lead at Gordon Square was in some ways not so different from the life she had led at Hyde Park Gate. That autumn, while Vanessa went to study with the fearsome Henry Tonks at the Slade, Thoby read for the Bar, and Adrian was in his last year at Cambridge, Virginia reconstructed her writer's life. She read and wrote and did some manual work for therapeutic benefit (making 'paper books' to keep her reviews in, printing book plates – a rose design, a copy of Shakespeare's death-mask – from their new silver-point press).[20] She was still being looked after – Violet was making sure that she got enough air, Vanessa was supervising her eating, Nurse Traill was calling regularly to check her. But no one was dying in the house, and no one was forcing her to do things against her will. She could go out when she liked on solitary walks and explore the local bookshops and old furniture shops.

Bloomsbury seemed to her 'a more interesting quarter than Kensington'.[21] The young women of Kensington, visiting the young women of Bloomsbury in 'Phyllis and Rosamond' (1906), are struck by the difference:

> If one lived here in Bloomsbury, she began to theorise waving with her
> hand as her cab passed through the great tranquil squares, beneath the
> pale green of umbrageous trees, one might grow up as one liked. There
> was room, and freedom, and in the roar and splendour of the Strand she
> read the live realities of the world from which her stucco and her pillars
> protected her so completely.[22]

She began, now, her life-long hobby of 'street haunting': 'I like looking at things', she wrote in her diary.[23] Street figures stayed in her mind, such as an old blind woman singing in Oxford Street 'while the traffic went thundering by'.[24] She could take Nessa's sheepdog, Gurth, to Regent's Park; she could go to the zoo, and to concerts. After such expeditions she took pleasure in returning 'home at last to our native Bloomsbury'.[25] By the summer, when they could eat their supper out on the balcony and hear the servant girls chatting up their boy-friends in the street below, Gordon Square 'with the lamps lit and the light on the green' seemed 'a romantic place'.[26]

The romance lay largely in the removal of authority. 'It is really very ideal', Vanessa wrote to Madge Vaughan, 'to have to arrange for a household all of much the same age.'[27] This was unusual for the time. To see Virginia noting in her diary for 23 January 1905 that the 'poor timorous Czar' had gone into hiding after the violent uprising of 'Bloody Sunday', the precursor to the Revolution; or that she had seen Elgar conduct 'Pomp and Circumstance' at the Queen's Hall; or that they all went to Trafalgar Square in January 1906 to celebrate Campbell-Bannerman's huge Liberal landslide – these flashes of history remind us to place the first months of 'Bloomsbury' in the context of an imperial Edwardian culture only just emerging from the nineteenth century. Like their century, the lives of these young upper-middle-class free-thinkers, all in their early twenties, were shaped by overlaps and gradual shifts, as well as by startling moments of change. They were delighted with their freedom, and had great plans, made in definite opposition to what had gone before. Virginia's humorous retrospect on these aspirations deliberately mixes minute domestic details with earth-shaking artistic ambitions.

> We were full of experiments and reforms. We were going to do without table napkins, we were to have [large supplies of] Bromo instead; we were going to paint; to write; to have coffee after dinner instead of tea at nine o'clock. Everything was going to be new; everything was going to be different. Everything was on trial.[28]

The tone implies that everything was not quite as 'new' and 'different' as they thought. Just as their interior decorations mixed objects from the past (notably the Cameron photographs)[29] with the modern colour schemes, so the Hyde Park Gate life mixed – often uncomfortably – with their new friendships. There was much disapproval from the old guard – Kitty Maxse, Aunt Minna, the Duckworths. Henry James was particularly aghast at the shabbiness and bohemianism of Leslie's children. The new Mrs Duckworth had to be dissuaded from including the Stephen girls in

George's invitations, as of old. Vanessa began a policy of cutting off from the Hyde Park Gate network; Virginia would never be so ruthless about this. A cancelled passage from her memoir of this period, 'Old Bloomsbury' (written in the early 1920s for the Memoir Club) describes the conflict:

> When our old family friends and relations made the difficult journey to Bloomsbury – the tube was not yet open I think – they threw up their heads and snuffed the air. They explored the house suspiciously. I can still see the vast bulk of Cousin Mia Macnamara looking in the hall and expressing by the tilt of her bonnet, the heaving of her tremendous bosom, and the glare of her small beady eyes her apprehensions and disapproval. It was not only the green chintz and the white distemper and the lack of table napkins that disturbed her. There was something in the atmosphere; something hostile to the old traditions of the family; something she knew my mother would have disapproved of for her daughters.[30]

Some feared, and rightly so, for their own future as friends. A touching letter written many years later, from Janet Case to Violet Dickinson, thanked Violet for having urged Janet, at this time, to keep in touch with Virginia:

> I remember having tea with you one day after the Greek lesson time was over and done with, and V was established in the new odd Bloomsbury life and I didn't think she'd have any further use for me, and felt shy of going and *you* told me to stick to her. She'd like it – so thank you for that.[31]

But the 'new odd Bloomsbury life' bore strong resemblances to the old Kensington life. Virginia's social behaviour was no less awkward – though, in an excited gesture of emancipation, she took up smoking cigarettes. She was still a failure at dances, on one occasion lurking in a corner reading *In Memoriam* while Vanessa danced all evening.[32] And she was just as much in awe of Thoby. When his friends came to call, she was silent, watchful and anxious for praise. All this would change.

The new friends were not entirely new. Of the young men who now began to become close friends, and who would be, from this year onwards, intimately connected with Virginia for the rest of her life – Saxon Sydney-Turner, Clive Bell, Desmond MacCarthy, Lytton Strachey, and, some time later, Duncan Grant and Leonard Woolf – several had been linked to the Stephen family through their network of family connections, before getting to know Thoby at Trinity College. They became intimates there between

1899 and 1904, some through their membership of Cambridge's most talked-about secret society, the Apostles, some through G.E. Moore's Easter reading parties for his favoured students, and some through the non-Apostolic Clive Bell's 'Midnight Society' (or, from 1902, the 'X society'), for the reading of plays. But the Stephens had been aware for years of the huge, vivid clan of Stracheys at Lancaster Gate, of the extraordinary Lady Strachey, a friend of Leslie's, of Lytton and his brothers James and Oliver, and his odd, clever, ugly sisters, Pernel, Pippa, Marjorie and Dorothy. Before Leslie's death, Lytton had visited 'the Goth's' family and made his own version of them, which he retailed to his friend Leonard Woolf:

> On Sunday I called at the Gothic mansion and had tea with Vanessa and Virginia. The latter is rather wonderful, quite witty, full of things to say, and absolutely out of rapport with reality. The poor Vanessa has to keep her three mad brothers and sister in control. She looks wan and sad.[33]

Desmond MacCarthy, too, who though a few years older than Thoby's generation, came to know Leonard and Lytton on G.E. Moore's Apostolic reading parties, had also visited Hyde Park Gate before Leslie's death,[34] and had formed his impression of the two girls, looking unhappy and oppressed at grand dances. Molly Warre-Cornish, whom Desmond would marry in 1906 (Virginia went to the wedding and subsequently became good friends with Molly) was related to the Stephens via Anny Ritchie. Duncan Grant, whom the sisters did not get to know until about 1908, was Lytton's cousin. And, just as some of these young men were at first indistinguishably part of the world the Stephens had grown up in, so to the young men the Stephen girls just seemed at first like typical Edwardian misses – though exceptionally lovely ones. Leonard Woolf remembered seeing them first in Thoby's Cambridge rooms, up for May Week, being chaperoned by their cousin Katherine Stephen. In their 'white dresses and large hats, with parasols in their hands, their beauty literally took one's breath away'. They seemed to him silent, 'formidable and alarming'.[35] But a more vivid and intimate idea of Vanessa, at least, had begun to be formed by Clive Bell, who had met Thoby and his sisters on their European journey after Leslie's death, had escorted them to the studios of artists he had come to know in his year in Paris, and had observed Vanessa's enthusiasms for new paintings and Virginia's strained and unhappy state of mind.

If some of the new boys who came to Gordon Square for cocoa and biscuits and conversation were slightly known to the sisters, all of them had already been effusively characterised by Thoby during his Cambridge years. Virginia would later satirise the high expectations which these early reports had created: of the 'astonishing fellow called Bell . . . a sort of mixture between Shelley and a sporting country squire'; of Saxon Sydney-Turner, 'an absolute prodigy of learning . . . very silent and thin and odd . . . the most brilliant talker he knew because he always spoke the truth'; of the singular and fascinating 'Strache', exotic, extreme, 'a prodigy of wit' and of dazzling intellectual promise; and of the extraordinary Jew called Woolf who trembled all over because he was 'so violent, so savage; he so despised the whole human race'.[36] These 'prodigies' were extremely nostalgic for their just-ended undergraduate life: they published a little volume of pseudo-classical verse called *Euphrosyne* as a way of keeping together, they still called each other by their student nicknames, and their letters were full of discussions about whether intellectual standards – or levels of depravity – at Cambridge had gone up or down since they left. They were all in on imbroglios such as Lytton's competitive jealousy of Maynard Keynes, but they spoke of homosexuality in Latinate terminology 'without really breaking the conventions of upper-middle-class reticence'.[37] Thoby's friends initially assumed that they would re-create Trinity College at Gordon Square, and, as the Stephens's 'Thursday evenings' took shape (beginning in March of 1905), they were slow to adapt to the presence of the young women. Not all of them were – or would remain – homosexual – but male camaraderie, shared culture and ways of speech shaped their behaviour. Virginia Woolf's fictional versions of these male friendships in *Jacob's Room* and *The Waves* suggest that it was Thoby, in those days, who was the main focus of attention.

All these young men, to differing degrees, felt uncertain or despondent about what they were going to do next. Lytton Strachey had just failed to get a fellowship at Trinity; Clive Bell had given up academic life and taken to French painting and painters; Saxon Sydney-Turner had just entered the Civil Service, but seemed to want to do nothing for the rest of his life except go to the opera; Maynard Keynes was poised between a Cambridge or a Civil Service career; and Leonard Woolf, the most resolute and most depressed of them all, had set off for Ceylon to administer the British Empire in the jungle. Before he left, he had dinner with Thoby and his family on 17 November; Virginia, he noted, was very silent.

In her memoir of 'Old Bloomsbury' of 1905–6 (read out in 1921 or 1922 to a number of the same people who feature in the memoir) Virginia Woolf gave an understandably benign, humorous account of her initial disillusion with Thoby's famous young men. She described them shuffling in, shabby, ugly, ungracious, sitting about for hours in complete silence, entirely lacking in small talk, and firing up only when an issue of truth or beauty was under debate. Her initial nervousness and bemusement changed – she recalled – to a liberated pleasure in talk that could be about ideas and beliefs, talk that was 'astonishingly abstract' and was not restricted to the idiotic social exchanges of the Duckworth social milieu. To illustrate the tone of those early conversations, she describes an exchange with Ralph Hawtrey (a mathematician who became a distinguished Treasury economist) whom she was trying to persuade 'that there was such a thing as atmosphere in literature' by citing George Meredith's *Diana of the Crossways*. That choice of her father's old friend, whose writing was so influential then (E.M. Forster and Desmond MacCarthy, for instance, were devoted Meredith ians), but who looks so mannered and antiquated now, suggests how formal the tone of 'Old Bloomsbury' would seem to us. Meredith's Diana, a scandalously pioneering feminist heroine, renowned as a witty conversationalist, might have been Virginia Stephen's fantasy-model, as she turned herself from a nervous, silent girl into the most idiosyncratic and inspired talker of her group. One of her 1905 reviews was of *Some Famous Women of Wit and Beauty*, where she laments the fact that the conversation of legendary hostesses has vanished, and cites *Diana of the Crossways* as the one example of evanescent 'wit' preserved by a writer's 'genius'.

But Meredith's examples of Diana's witty talk never quite live up to her reputation. Talk – as Virginia Woolf says in 'Old Bloomsbury' – is notoriously elusive: 'It flies up the chimney and is gone.' In later years she would often transcribe conversations, trying to pin down that elusive 'atmosphere'. But for 1905 all we have is her jottings: 'Home & found Bell, & we talked [about] the nature of good till almost one!'[38] But the talk itself has disappeared inside the nostalgic accounts of these years.

The mostly male 'Cambridge' retrospects of those early meetings have established the story of 'Old Bloomsbury'.[39] In this version, an Apostolic, Socratic, analytic debate on the meaning of good and truth, modelled on the teaching methods and thinking of the philosopher G.E. Moore and using the tools of logic and metaphysics, was transferred from Trinity College to Bloomsbury and was civilised, but not much changed, by the presence of Vanessa and Virginia. This kind of talk, goes the story, provided a liberating medium which encouraged her to use her brains and free herself from self-consciousness.[40] The chroniclers of 'Bloomsbury' frequently pour scorn on the idea that it was a formal 'group', but, all the same, list the fraternity of members (as for a football team or a seating plan at High Table), and so perpetuate the image of a coterie.[41]

Of these retrospects, the most eloquent about Virginia Stephen is Duncan Grant's (who was not involved until a couple of years later, and whose memories are of the 1910 to 1912 period):

She appeared very shy and probably was so, and never addressed the company. She would listen to general arguments and occasionally speak, but her conversation was mainly directed to someone next to her . . . there was always something a little aloof and even a little fierce in her manner to most men at the time I am speaking of. To her women friends, especially older women like Miss Pater and Miss Janet Case, who had taught her Greek, she was more open and less reserved. They were alive to her, by remembrance as well as presence, and had already their place in her imagination as belonging to the world she knew and had left – that life with her parents and her half-brothers at Hyde Park Gate . . . I do not think that her new existence had 'become alive' to Virginia's imagination in those first years. She gave the impression of being so intensely receptive to any experience new to her, and so intensely interested in facts that she had not come across before, that time was necessary to give it a meaning as a whole. It took the years to complete her vision of it.[42]

This telling impression of eagerness, fierceness and reserve (very like the character of Rachel Vinrace in *The Voyage Out*) is true to Virginia Stephen's tone at the time. Initially, at least, this 'society of equals' made her feel extremely angry. Throughout 1905 there are irritable references to the dullness of male company. 'Oh women are my line and not these inanimate creatures', she wrote after a satirical account to Violet of Sydney-Turner and another Apostle in Cornwall, who are 'a great trial', sitting absolutely silent and occasionally escaping into a corner and chuckling over a Latin joke.[43] There was more fun to be had from being with women, as in this report of Vanessa's on a visit from Imogen Booth: 'We reached a wild point of hilarity while she was here – The silliest jokes were received with roars.'[44] A (very Meredithian) essay written for the *Guardian* in August 1905 on 'The Value of Laughter' talks of women as the dangerous ministers of 'the comic spirit', 'because their eyes are not clouded with learning nor are their brains choked with the theories of books . . . and it is probably for this reason that women are looked upon with such disfavour in the learned professions.' They are dangerous because it is they who may see that the emperor has no clothes.[45]

In a furious secret review of *Euphrosyne*, heavily scored and unfinished, she pours derision on the vain young men, with every educational privilege, who emerge from 'Oxbridge' 'pale, preoccupied & silent', self-pleased and ineffectual:

They fail to pass their Examinations, because they say, that success is failure & they despise success. It is perhaps because they fear to fall a victim to its snares that they are generally silent, & express for the most

part a serene & universal ignorance; which does not disqualify them
however to pronounce the opinions of others absurd.[46]

Virginia enclosed a copy of *Euphrosyne* in a letter to Eleanor Cecil,
comparing it with 'a real poem' she had just seen in the *Daily Chronicle*,
which she copied out. It was read at the inquest of a charwoman who has
hanged herself: 'Here lies a poor woman who was always tired', it begins,
and ends: 'Dont mourn for me now, dont mourn for me never; /I'm going
to do nothing for ever and ever.'[47] 'The jury said unanimously that she was
mad', Virginia comments. 'However these seven poets have no such mania
in them.' And then: 'Why do I write all about suicide and mad people?' For
the first time, she sets against the product of educated, classical male
culture, the voice of 'anon' and the life of a 'common' woman without
education. And she suggests, too, that the voice of 'mania' – the true voice of
poetry – might have to be a female voice. 'Why do I write all about suicide
and mad people?' Because, the answer might have been, her own appalling
experiences of the previous year gave her a language and a range of feelings
not available to these seven 'melancholy' young men. Far from forming her
writing under the influence of the Cambridge graduates, she forms it in
opposition to them.

In all her writings about Cambridge, there is the same tone – whether it's
in her unpublished caricature of Saxon, 'one of the great men of our time'
who in the end never did anything except crossword puzzles, or her fictional
version of privileged Cambridge life in *Jacob's Room*, or her encounter with
the closed doors of the 'Oxbridge' library in *A Room of One's Own*.[48] She
criticised the closed world of Cambridge Societies all her life for 'rousing
jealousies and vanities'.[49] And she would never forget how the young men
irked her. She wrote to her nephew Julian Bell in 1936:

> at your age [Julian was 28] what with all the family deaths and extreme
> intensities . . . I felt I had lived through all emotions and only wanted
> peace and loneliness. All the horrors of life had been pressed in to our eyes
> so very crude and raw. And then came the burst of splendour, those two
> years at Gordon Square before Thoby died, a kind of Elizabethan
> renaissance, much though I disliked the airs that young Cambridge gave
> itself. I found an old diary which was one violent shriek of rage at Saxon
> and Lytton sitting there saying nothing, and with no emotional
> experience, I said.[50]

Her rage was fuelled by competitiveness. It was *she*, not any of them, who
was going to be the great writer. But she could not say this yet: she hardly
knew it yet. To Violet, she could say: 'No one really takes very much

interest, why should they, in my scribblings. Do you think I shall ever write a really good book?' But it was not a question she could (then) ask Lytton Strachey or Saxon Sydney-Turner. Their little book, so easy and slight, seemed to mock her private struggles. And meanwhile she felt that they patronised her.

This resentment would swell in *The Voyage Out.* When St John Hirst (who looks and talks like Strachey) tells Rachel Vinrace to read Gibbon, but hardly imagines that she will be able to appreciate him, she is violently angry at being condescended to, and has to remind herself, for consolation, how ugly he is. She asks herself of these clever young men 'whether it was necessary that thought and scholarship should thus maltreat their bodies, and should thus elevate their minds to a very high tower from which the human race appeared to them like rats and mice squirming on the flat'. None of them, Rachel concludes, is marriageable.[51]

The Voyage Out is euphemistic but clear about St John's homosexuality; it is eloquent, too, about the way these initially inhibited relationships became eroticised. At first Thoby's young men seemed impossibly – and, to Virginia, reassuringly – asexual. But as they became closer friends, all of them, even Saxon and Lytton, were at least considered as sexual possibilities. The proposals of marriage Virginia would receive in her twenties – there were five, possibly six – all came from the members of this Cambridge group. In spite of their interest in new forms of social behaviour, they all felt the conventional pressure and desire to marry.

At first they all resisted the sexualising of their lives – Vanessa dreaded hearing that Thoby was engaged,[52] and Thoby responded grimly when he heard that Clive had proposed to Vanessa. But the development was inevitable. Virginia, in a description wonderfully evocative of her feelings about Vanessa's more luxurious nature, remembered watching her sister in the big looking-glass 'stretching her arms above her head with a gesture that was at once reluctant and yielding' as she said, 'Of course, I can see that we shall all marry. It's bound to happen'.[53] But it was not until years after that moment that the friends – led on by Strachey – began to discuss their homosexual and heterosexual sex lives with as much thoroughness and glee as they had talked about books or aesthetics. As late as 1908 Clive and Virginia still 'blushed' when she asked him 'to let me pass to go to the lavatory on the French Express'.[54]

In the work Virginia Stephen was beginning to do, which preoccupied her far more than the 'Thursday evenings', she was also encountering inhibitions and frustrations. She wanted to work to give her life meaning, for her own dignity and satisfaction – and simply because she had to: 'I cant help writing – so there's an end of it.'[55] But she also wanted money. The move, and her illness, had cost the family a great deal; their bank 'passbooks' were 'greatly overdrawn'. She was conscious that the 'family coffers' had been emptied by paying for 'those d-d nurses and doctors'.[56] They had their inheritance from Leslie (the equivalent, today, of around £350,000) and their share of Jack Hills's marriage settlement, and they intended to rent out Hyde Park Gate (though it stayed obstinately empty). Vanessa, who although in charge of the household was more sanguine than Virginia about money, thought they ought to have about £300 a year. But they had rent to pay and servants to keep, and none of them was working: 'In fact our income was largely imaginary', Vanessa recalled.[57] In 1906 Thoby made £1,000 ('*one thousand pounds*', Virginia wrote in awe) by selling a page of a Thackeray manuscript to Pierpont Morgan: it paid for his Bar fees and for their trip to Greece.[58] Later, Virginia would get a small inheritance after Thoby's death, and a rather larger one from Caroline Emelia. But when her first cheques for reviews began to come in – £2.7s.6d. from the *Guardian* in January 1905, £5 from the *National Review* in February 1905, the great sum of £9.7s. from *The Times* in July 1906 – she felt extremely pleased at the scent of independence.[59] She never lost this delight at earning her own income, or the (inherited) fear that it would dry up, the 'panics in the middle of the night about money': 'Like my father, I can always conjure up bankruptcy', she wrote to Ethel Smyth in 1941.[60]

Violet set up her first professional commission, to review for Margaret Lyttelton, the editor of the Women's Supplement of an Anglo-Catholic clerical paper called the *Guardian* – which had recently incorporated the *Churchwoman*. 'It takes up the line of a Governess, and maiden Lady, and high church Parson mixed.' An unlikely venue for Virginia Stephen – 'how they ever got such a black little goat into their fold, I cant conceive'[61] – but it paid. Her connections also came into use in a commission from Kitty Maxse's husband's political paper, *The National Review*, and in offers of regular reviewing from Bruce Richmond, the first editor of the *Times Literary Supplement* (who, though she often resented him, would be extremely important in shaping her literary career), and from Reginald Smith, the editor of her father's old magazine the *Cornhill*.[62]

It was not difficult, after all, for Leslie Stephen's daughter to find work in literary journals, even without any experience. But she had to take what they gave her, to knuckle under to editorial pressures, and to write, on the whole, anonymously. The list of books reviewed which she proudly entered at the end of her 1905 diary is a very mixed bag: histories (of the Indian Mutiny, of social life in England, of the Viennese period in music, of 'the American woman'), travel books, memoirs of an American belle, a book on

The Feminine Note in Fiction ('Women, we gather, are seldom artists, because they have a passion for detail which conflicts with the proper artistic proportion of their work')[63] and 'silly'[64] new novels like *The Letter Killeth: a Romance of the Sussex Downs*, by Mrs Stanley Inchbold. She also produced, from the start, short signed personal essays (a popular form at the time) on the subjects of 'street music' or 'laughter' – or on the writing of essays. Here she could express herself more personally than in the reviews ('The Decay of Essay-writing' explored her current preoccupation, the relationship between personal opinions and egotism) but was constrained by a formal idea of what an essayist's manner should be.

'Read your *Guardian* carefully,' she wrote to Violet, 'and see if you find anything about Henry James; the first words, like a coin with a head on it, will tell you who wrote it.'[65] The years of passionate reading and secret writing which preceded these reviews filled them with confidence and perceptiveness. At once she showed a wonderful eye for atmosphere and idiosyncrasy, flashing out wherever she saw her chance with a strong opinion or a dash of style. Her review of Mrs Carlyle's letters, for instance, brilliantly mimicked exactly what she found to admire in them, 'an insight into character and a power of seizing on the essential, which is creative as well as critical'. It could be a description of her own future essays.[66]

She assumed an impersonal, authoritative tone in these first essays, to the point of sounding sometimes absurdly formal: 'That a very dusty little volume dated 1828 should blossom in all the fairness of a new edition at this prolific season of the twentieth century seems a somewhat impudent defiance of the laws of nature.'[67] A novel by the actress Elizabeth Robins (a friend of Leslie and Julia) about a nervous breakdown and a rest cure was firmly admonished for 'morbidity': no self-revelation here.[68] But she had, from the start, the two gifts of the great reviewer. One was of using unpromising material to carve out her own ideas. So, two 'trashy' books on pilgrimages to writers' houses provoked this thought: 'A writer's country is a territory within his own brain; and we run the risk of disillusionment if we try to turn such phantom cities into tangible brick and mortar.'[69] The other was of making the very most of the good material. When Elizabeth Barrett Browning's letters, or Wordsworth's *Guide to the Lakes* fell into her hands, she poured her own experience and her pleasure in the subject into the writing. She liked best books which fired her thoughts with hard factual information, like Walter Raleigh's edition of Hakluyt: 'the more detailed our knowledge of the men and their adventures the more potently they touch our imaginations.'[70]

With sensational rapidity, her journalism began to take on the strong, confident tone of her later essays. Between 1907 and 1910, her pieces on the candid memoirs of the eighteenth-century Lady Fanshawe, or on the shrewd masterful diaries of the great hostess Lady Holland ('What numbers of likenesses she struck off, and with what assurance!'),[71] on Sterne's zest and wilfulness, on Boswell's genius or on Lady Hester Stanhope's eccentricities, are themselves 'struck off' with formidable 'assurance'.

But the work was also frustrating. At first her pieces were liable to be sent back or cut, and she could never stand this. She was furious with 'that fool of a man' Reginald Smith for returning a piece on Boswell's letters, 'without a word, but a printed slip'.[72] Bruce Richmond was more careful with her, but could also be an irritating editor. In March of 1905 he killed a piece, which had been very 'heavy going' to write, on a book about Catherine de Medici, because it was insufficiently 'academic'.[73]

'As usual I groan and struggle',[74] she said of this 'hard work': just like Leslie. She was inordinately conscientious. One of her most difficult first assignments was to review *The Golden Bowl* for the *Guardian*. What a book to be sent as a twenty-three-year-old tyro reviewer! – especially when the author was an old family friend. She took page after page of eloquent reading notes: 'Explains why people say the things they do – which is always a mystery even to the speaker.' . . . 'HJ puts in too much.'[75] She 'wrestled' with him for days – 'the toughest job I have yet had'[76] – and wrote an over-long piece which had to be cut down. 'Literally I cut two sheets to pieces, wrote a scrawl to mend them together, and so sent the maimed thing off – with a curse.'[77] Under the heading 'Mr Henry James's Latest Novel', three respectful and muted paragraphs appeared ('There is no living novelist whose standard is higher, or whose achievement is so consistently great'), with one flash of character, salvaged from her notes: 'The actors remain but so many distinguished ghosts.'[78] Compare this diluted work with the glittering, confident brio, two years later, of her private account of a meeting with Henry James in Rye:

> Henry James fixed me with his staring blank eye – it is like a childs marble – and said 'My dear Virginia, they tell me – they tell me – they tell me – that you – as indeed being your fathers daughter nay your grandfathers grandchild – the descendant I may say of a century – of a century – of quill pens and ink – ink – ink pots, yes, yes, yes, they tell me – ahm m m – that you, that you, that you *write* in short.' This went on in the public street, while we all waited, as farmers wait for the hen to lay an egg – do they? – nervous, polite, and now on this foot now on that. I felt like a condemned person, who sees the knife drop and stick and drop again. Never did any woman hate 'writing' as much as I do. But when I am old and famous I shall discourse like Henry James.[79]

Not until she was older and more famous would she be able to stop thinking of herself as her 'grandfather's grandchild', and to write of James in public as she would in private. Editorial control overlapped with self-censorship. 'At every step I tremble guiltily, & withdraw, to temper my expressions.' 'How I wish I could be brave and frank in my reviews.'[80] When she came to write a retrospect of these first writing years she invented the famous figure of the Angel in the House (named after Coventry Patmore's poem), the Victorian mother/editor who would slip behind her in rustling skirts as she began to review a book by a famous man, and remind her to be charming, tender and polite – and whom the young woman writer had to kill, by throwing the inkpot at her, before she could find her voice. 'She died hard.'[81] This phantom editress (perhaps partly inspired by Margaret Lyttelton's genteel care for her 'Parsons morals')[82] was an inner censor in collusion with paternalistic social attitudes to women writers.

Virginia Stephen's male editors commissioned her as, and expected her to write as, the daughter of Leslie Stephen. So the censorship was both external and internal, a form of control (she writes about Reginald Smith in just the same tone of voice that she writes about Dr George Savage) and a form of inhibition. She couldn't be as rude as she wanted to be: 'My real delight in reviewing is to say nasty things; and hitherto I have had to [be] respectful.'[83] She couldn't speak frankly about sex or religion: Mrs Lyttelton 'sticks her broad thumb into the middle of my delicate sentences and improves the moral tone',[84] and the *Cornhill* wouldn't call 'a prostitute a prostitute, or a mistress a mistress'.[85] And she was terrified of showing sentimentality or egotism, and of being laughed at.

After years of this work, she could be ironical about literary journalism:

> When I read reviews I crush the columns together to get at one or two sentences; is it a good book or a bad? And then I discount those 2 sentences according to what I know of the book & of the reviewer. But when I write a review I write every sentence as if it were going to be tried before 3 Chief Justices: I cant believe that I am crushed together & discounted.[86]

But in her early twenties, establishing herself (she wrote over thirty pieces in 1905, twenty in 1906),[87] she was defensive and proud and avid for praise. Her uncertainty was at its most acute over her 'Note' on Leslie Stephen. 'Oh – for some one to tell me whether it is well, very well, or indifferently done.'[88] Everyone had to comment – Violet, Vanessa, Thoby, Kitty – who, much to Virginia's discomfort, disliked it – before it was sent to Fred Maitland, who thought it 'beautiful'. It was her first contribution to a book, it had to live up to Maitland's standard (which she admired) and it raised more acutely than anything she had yet written the difficult negotiation between private feeling and public writing. She could not tell the whole truth, and she was afraid of sentimentality. And yet the result was the most simple, touching and direct piece of writing of all her early published work.

She knew that her demands for critical attention (both for published and unpublished work) were egotistical, and her letters were full of half-hearted apologies for being someone who (as Vanessa more than once said) 'never gave but always took'.[89] But she could not stop herself. There was a family tradition of appeasing her by calling her a genius: Vanessa's letters at this time often say things like 'You certainly *are* rather a genius'.[90] She does not reject the description: a letter to Madge is at once self-aware and self-regarding: 'I do enjoy flattery! . . . "Genius" is a not a word to be used rashly; it gives me enormous pleasure, and something more than pleasure, that you should find anything of that kind in me. I am no judge'.[91]

But, she went on to say, she veers 'from one extreme to the other' in her judgement on her own work. Sometimes she was fiercely confident of her ability to be 'a writer of such English as shall one day burn the pages'.[92] At other times she was completely unsure, and had to elicit reassurance from Violet just as Leslie once elicited it from Julia: 'Do you feel convinced I *can* write?'[93] She craved approval and detested criticism. When Violet said she preferred the reviews to the occasional essays, or when the Quaker aunt reproved her for selling her soul in her journalism, she flared up. And she responded strongly to accusations that her writing was 'cold-blooded'. She defended (as she often would again) the reality of her own kind of 'feeling':

> My present feeling is that this vague and dream like world, without love, or heart, or passion, or sex, is the world I really care about, and find interesting. For, though they are dreams to you, and I cant express them at all adequately, these things are perfectly real to me.[94]

Her susceptibility to criticism (profoundly related to her feelings for her dead parents and her competitiveness with her two older siblings) continued all her life. But at this stage she was still feeling her way; was she to be a historian, a literary journalist, or a writer of fiction? In August of 1906 she reports to Violet that she has finished forty pages of manuscript during the summer; this may have been the start of *The Voyage Out*. She was certainly embarked on it by 1907; but it would take nine years more for her first novel to emerge. 'George Eliot was near 40 I think' (she reassured herself) 'when she wrote her first novel.'[95]

TWELVE

Thoby

In January 1905, Dr Savage gave Virginia 'a clean bill of health'. ('Aint it a joke!')[1] By the autumn, life was 'in full swing'.[2] Thoby's Thursday evenings were regularised, and Vanessa instituted her 'Friday Club', for the discussion – and later the exhibiting of – new paintings, with a mixture of Slade, Royal Academy, Cambridge and family friends. The meetings were held mostly in Gordon Square; subjects for debate included Thoby on 'the Decadence of Modern Art'.[3] Virginia admired her sister's organisational control over the squabbling artists ('one half of the committee shriek Whistler and French impressionists, and the other are stalwart British').[4] Some new characters, less costive than Thoby's friends, came into Virginia's orbit through the Friday Club. As well as Vanessa's Academy friends such as Margery Snowden, there was Augustus John's disciple Henry Lamb – moody, sexy, clever, and soon to marry Nina Forrest, a *femme fatale* who intrigued and repelled Virginia. (Lamb's fastidious and inhibited brother Walter, a Cambridge classicist friend of Thoby's, was to be one of Virginia's unsuccessful suitors.) Another painter-member of the club was the talented young Gwen Darwin, grand-daughter of Charles.[5] Among the 'lay members' were Ka Cox, who would become, for a time, Virginia's intimate friend, a round-faced, sympathetic, maternal girl, at eighteen about to start at Newnham (where she would fall painfully in love with Rupert Brooke); Beatrice Meinertzhagen, a niece of Beatrice Webb,[6] and Lytton's sister Marjorie Strachey, the 'vivacious & commanding' 'Gumbo',[7] whom Virginia laughed at but admired. So the formation of the Friday Club (which carried on until 1912 or 1913) began some friendships with another Cambridge group, more easy-going and slightly younger. Virginia would call them the 'Neo-Pagans'.

The club's discussions, conversations with Vanessa and visits to galleries meant that Virginia was thinking a great deal about painting. 'Oh Lord, the lucid colour – the harmony – the perfect scheme', she exclaimed of a Whistler exhibition in Regent Street in February 1905. The Watts show at the Academy, by contrast, seemed 'weak and worthless'.[8] She sat for her portrait – to Vanessa early in 1906, to 'little' Francis Dodd the following year.

Many of her private writings took the form of mood pictures; she treated her diary now as the equivalent of a 'sketch book'.[9] Now and always, she measured her work against the work of the painters, and tried to connect their language and hers.

Vanessa was full of energy and activity; Virginia's days, in competition, were filling up. She was learning Spanish, for a trip which she and Adrian were planning to the Iberian peninsula, though she found the verbs hard and could only learn from reading books, not 'out of a grammar'.[10] She resumed her Greek (working hard at Thucydides) and did some Latin as well. She was reading formidably, not at random, and not only for reviewing. Some books were gifts: a copy of James Thomson came from Thoby with the inscription 'There is no God'. By contrast, a book of precepts about selflessness and stoicism from Violet, purporting to be written by 'Anthony Hart', turned out to be by Violet herself.

> In a hard, busy, active life, every hour full almost of work, how much time is given to think on God? . . . Count it a great privilege if it fall to thy lot to see a man stricken with great pain take up his burden bravely, without a murmur, bear it with a cheerful heart and with great courage.[11]

Virginia may have found more use in the pagan precepts in her well-thumbed copy of Mackail's *Greek Epigrams*. At the same time she was reading Pater's *Studies in the History of the Renaissance* (which left its mark on her writing); William Morris; Galton's popular book on 'hereditary genius'; and a great deal of history. She liked to sink her teeth into periods: early in 1905 she wanted books on early Christianity, by the autumn she was filling in her knowledge of the eighteenth century, 'my weak point'.[12] She read a book on town life in the fifteenth century, a six-volume history of the Norman Conquest (on which she took extensive notes), and a book on the legal status of women in the eighteenth century.[13] 'And reading makes me intensely happy, and culminates in a fit of writing always.'[14]

There were vulnerable moments still. As soon as she stopped work she felt 'melancholy'.[15] A long discussion with Vanessa about the 'ethics of suicide' was brought on by a visit from one of her nurses from the previous summer.[16] Her work sometimes came near to obsession: 'I never can get the sound of my own writing out of my head . . . I shouldn't wonder if God struck me deaf and blasted me blind and set my own tunes grinding perpetually through my brain.'[17]

She was volatile, absent-minded, awkward, and bad at looking after herself. Her new glasses (worn at Savage's suggestion) would get twisted, she was very bad at shopping for clothes, she couldn't fasten her own dress or put up her own hair (which came down in great coils, 'sticking feebly with pins'), she forgot sponges and combs on her travels. If on holiday a bird 'performed' (as she put it) on her straw hat and she spilt ink on her skirt, this was typical. People laughed at her in the country when they saw her on her solitary walks; she looked (she thought) 'magnificently eccentric'.[18] She wanted petting and protecting: getting back from the trip to Spain in the spring, she spent 'the whole afternoon on Nessa's lap, in a maudlin condition'.[19] She could be fussy and crusty: Vanessa imagined her 'getting into more and more old-gentlemanly ways and becoming very particular about not having your own special habits disturbed!'[20]

So her emerging relations with the world outside the family – as a social being, as a writer, as a woman – were tense and diffident. She feared mockery and ignominy. But it was a mark of how much stronger she felt in the year after her illness that she took on a completely new kind of public exposure, in the form of voluntary teaching at Morley College. This unpaid work went on, intermittently, for almost two years. It was never a great success, but it provoked some crucial ideas about class and education, and found its way twenty years later into *Mrs Dalloway*.

The Stephens made a great joke of Mary Sheepshanks (inevitably, 'the Sheep'), the Bishop's daughter who invited Virginia to lecture at Morley College. Adrian, in his short-lived diary for 1909, described Virginia 'winking and making horrible grimaces at me' behind her back,[21] and Virginia was snide about her in letters to Violet. And she *was* a difficult, depressive, unapproachable woman, who when she met Virginia in 1905 was grieving bitterly for the death of Theodore Llewelyn Davies,[22] whom she had loved unrequitedly. She developed an unrequited feeling for Virginia, too, though she was critical of her teaching, and was mortified when Virginia dropped her, as she put it, 'down an oubliette'. She was one of the public-spirited women for whom Virginia had such mixed feelings. All Mary Sheepshanks's pacifist, suffragist, left-wing women friends – Molly Hamilton, Lilian Harris, Margaret Llewelyn Davies – brought out the same reaction.[23]

Morley College linked Virginia Stephen to her mother's and Stella's world of late-Victorian good works for women. It had been founded by a friend of Octavia Hill as an evening institute for working men and women in the Waterloo Road, on the premises of the Old Vic. (The classrooms were underneath the stage.) Mary wanted her to teach 'Composition', on Wednesday evenings at 9 p.m. ('She thinks I might combine amusement and instruction')[24] but for the first meeting she agreed to talk about 'English literature'. 'I am rushing off to my workers,'[25] she told Violet importantly. But the class was a mixed experience:

I waited 15 minutes alone in a great dreary room with tables & chairs & flaring gas jets – meditating how on earth to discuss Sir T. Browne under these conditions & two women – nice & intelligent – came finally, but were readier to talk than to listen.[26]

She had to write her lecture out, as she didn't trust herself to speak from memory.[27] In subsequent weeks she talked not about English Literature, but about Venice ('lots of jokes is what they like'),[28] about Florence, Benvenuto Cellini, Greek myths and Greek history. She roped in Vanessa to take the girls to the National Gallery ('How far pictures are intelligible to them – I don't know') and Thoby to teach Virgil to the 'working men'.[29] She began to try to talk from notes rather than lecture. In May they requested 'English History from the beginning'.[30] She took one of the women round the Abbey: 'makes history *so* interesting miss!'[31] She had a class of four women – one a reporter on a religious paper who transcribed sermons in shorthand, and who gave her 'a first view of Grub Street',[32] one whom she tried to get to write her autobiography. As they made their way, perhaps rather haphazardly, through 'Early British, & Romans, & Angles Saxons & Danes, & Normans', she kept wondering 'how is it *possible* to make them feel the flesh & blood in these shadows?' She tried to concentrate their interest on a 'scene', lent them books, gave them sheets of dates.[33] But by the end of the 1905 academic year the college was unhappy with her history lessons and wanted her to resume English Composition, and Virginia wrote a discontented report on her teaching experience. In the autumn she had a larger, mixed-sex group for her 'composition' group – 'the most useless class in the College', with a difficult elderly Socialist and 'anaemic shop girls'.[34] Sheepshanks still criticised her teaching, and in 1906 there was a suggestion – unfulfilled – that she should be the Morley College librarian instead. In 1907 she was timetabled to take a Monday night 'Reading Circle' on Keats, Shelley and Browning,[35] but by now she was fed up with it: the classes took too long to prepare, and the new Monday nights (which she had asked for herself) now clashed with a series of Hans Richter concerts. She gave it up at the end of 1907, making a parting gesture towards a young man called Cyril Zeldwyn who had interested her, a 'degenerate poet' (unstable – or homosexual?) who 'rants and blushes and almost seizes my hand' in his enthusiasm for Keats. She tried to interest Eleanor Cecil in getting a job for 'my good working man – who is a socialist, of a kind, and a poet; but also very clever and enthusiastic'.[36]

This brief relationship between the nervy, conscientious young upper-class amateur teacher and the sensitive working-class older male student was remembered in *Mrs Dalloway*, where Septimus Smith, a 'border case' both socially and psychologically, develops a romantic adulation for Miss Isabel Pole, 'lecturing in the Waterloo Road upon Shakespeare' and Keats.[37] She corrects his love-poems in red ink, and he sees her one evening 'walking in a green dress in a square'. When he goes to war, it is to fight for Miss Isabel Pole and the works of Shakespeare. In the manuscript, the Morley College connection is even clearer: Miss Pole lectures 'at a Working Man's College', and there is more detail on Septimus's self-taught reading of Everyman classics.[38] The placing of Septimus in his social niche recalls Miss Stephen's condescending notes on her working-class students:

> Sometimes they seemed to gape not in mere impotent wonder, but to be trying to piece together what they heard; to seek reasons; to connect ideas. On the whole they were possessed of more intelligence than I expected; though that intelligence was almost wholly uncultivated.[39]

But she felt an affinity, too, with her Morley College workers. The teaching presented her with an insoluble paradox: her conviction of an unbridgeable class gap, and yet her identification with self-educated 'common readers'. Challenged on Bloomsbury's lack of political activism in 1940, she referred to her Morley College years, still with that blend of conscience and condescension, as evidence of her commitment to sharing her imperfect education with 'the working classes'.[40]

'I feel always that writing is an irreticent thing to be kept in the dark – like hysterics',[41] she wrote to Eleanor Cecil, thanking her for sending some chapters of a novel. Feeling that writing was secret, even dangerous, vied with her need for exposure and public experience. From 1905 onwards she wrote continually 'for my own pleasure', trying out possibilities ('I want to learn how to write descriptions without adjectives'),[42] sending out some of her 'masterpieces', keeping others hidden. She kept a book on all her journeys and holidays. In her letters from her trip to Lisbon and Spain with Adrian in the spring of 1905, she caught the dreamy suspension of the 'voyage out', the bright orange-ness of Granada, and the trials of a rough country inn.[43] When the family made their nostalgic return to Cornwall in the summer, she recorded the scenes with a passion of exactness.[44] In 1906, at Easter, she went back to Giggleswick, staying this time in lodgings (to avoid too much of Will and Madge), and wrote up her solitary walks with Gurth the sheepdog. Between them they knocked down a large number of Yorkshire dry stone walls while she imagined the 'great melancholy moors' as Hardyesque tragic scenes or herself as a Brontë heroine, and got some amusement from fitting Bloomsbury and Marble Arch 'on all the hills and valleys'.[45] In August the family rented Blo'Norton, a moated Elizabethan house in Norfolk. This was a fertile writing holiday for her, and she was strongly impressed with the sense of local history.

In her holiday writings she gives a detailed, eloquent sense of Edwardian English life before any thought of war, like the deep Norfolk summer countryside, seen when bicycling to Thetford:

> A very hot August day, a bare road across a moor, fields of corn & stubble – a haze as of wood fire smoke – innumerable pheasants & partridges – white stones – thatched cottages – sign posts – tiny villages – great waggons heaped with corn – sagacious dogs, farmers carts.[46]

Or she notes an old man and his boy holding a flaring gas jet, in the main square at Wells, selling something to a circle of farmers; or 'bent old women, of tremendous age', coming out of their cream-washed cottages in a remote village near Manorbier, in South Wales. She is sometimes sentimental ('Ah, the loneliness of these little distant places!')[47] but she has an acute eye for places and anonymous lives.

Her writing-up of England was not just practice in the picturesque. It was part of the ideas she was evolving now about history and civilisation. Often in her 'descriptive' writings there were moments when feelings of unreality overpowered her. On holiday in 1907, looking at the moon with Adrian, she experienced a feeling of 'dreadful weariness' at the thought of 'wandering not quite alive, nor yet suffered to die, in this pale light'. (She must have been reading Shelley.)[48] When she looked at the stars through a telescope she could imagine 'the earth shrink to the size of a button'.[49] She was intensely conscious (as she would always be) of a pre-history underlying the civilised world which makes it seem fragile and evanescent.

> The sea once came right up to the foot of the Cliff on which this house is built; now it has withdrawn, and instead of bleached bones, and the ribs of ships hung with weed, there are sheep, and cottages, and cornfields.[50]

These deconstructions of the solid world could be risky. Boswell (she wrote in 1909) was possessed of 'some madness' which 'let him see in sudden incongruous flashes, as the scene shifted round him, how strange it all was'.[51] But 'incongruous' ways of seeing allowed for the kind of subversive fictions she was writing now. In the story of the strange disappearing 'Miss V', or in the alternative female medieval history of 'Mistress Joan Martyn', or in the fantastical life of a woman in *Friendship's Gallery*, she was turning solid biography and history into odder stories.

Ideas of female anonymity,[52] of eccentricity,[53] of consciousness not as a solid, clock-measured thing but as a blurred 'centre of innumerable rays',[54] emerge in all the writings of this time. It is extraordinary to find so many of her central preoccupations being formulated so early. At the heart of these ideas was the concept of not belonging, of alienation.

Starting now, in her twenties, she frequently asked herself what it means to belong to a country, to be English. What is the root of emotion for a place: is it merely aesthetic and nostalgic, or is it also moral and patriotic? Staying alone in Wells in 1908 she notices that she feels differently about England when she cannot see the sea, as in Cornwall: 'In Cornwall, I never think of the kingdom, or the population – this view, stands for many I suppose, as a symbol of their mother England'.[55] But for her England is not perceived symbolically, with nationalistic pride. When the family went to Greece in 1906, the idea of England seemed ridiculous:

> we are not patriotic . . . Out here . . . The Times loses its stately proportions: it is the private sheet of a small colony of islanders, whose noise is effectually shut up in their prison.[56]

It is only the *place* they crave for, she adds. The novel she was beginning to write, *The Voyage Out*, looks coldly at the civilisation of the 'small colony of islanders'. The little group of English middle-class travellers to South America bring with them all their constructed rules and traditions. They busy themselves with meetings and expeditions and quarrels and engagements. But in this grand, 'savage' country, with its 'dark races' and its lost civilisations, the English seem feeble and absurd. They are not as civilised as they think: the sea (as in Conrad's *Heart of Darkness*) links their cities to the jungle: 'It was this sea that flowed up to the mouth of the Thames; and the Thames washed the roots of the city of London.'[57]

The vision of an artificial, absurd 'civilisation', liable to revert to jungle and darkness, from which an alienated (female) onlooker can stand apart as in a dream, makes a political application of her personal sense of unreality and melancholy. And it is closely bound up with her strong feelings about religion. The English priest in *The Voyage Out* who justifies their colonial history with the Christian ethic of 'a duty to the natives' is cruelly debunked. All through her twenties she was arguing with Christianity. Her thoughts about public censorship and hypocrisy in her reviews, her quarrel with Violet about egotism versus 'philanthropy',[58] a furious set-to over Tolstoy in 1910 with the devout Jean Thomas in her 'mad-house' in Twickenham ('The self conceit of Christians is really unendurable'),[59] her conviction that art and morality should be separate, and her discussions with Vanessa and their friends on 'the Ethics of Empire' or 'the Ethics of suicide', were all part of this argument. The humanist atheism they had all been brought up with ('There is no God', wrote Thoby in her book, like a family message), now became part of an adult debate about how to live and think in the twentieth century.

There were no religious consolations for the appalling family catastrophe, Thoby's death at the age of twenty-six, which struck into the middle of all this busy, intelligent life. Remarkably, Virginia Stephen was not overcome by the blow; she drew on reserves of stoicism and imagination to deal with it. But it changed her life and fixed the tone of her writing. The death intensified her sense of life as a threatened narrow strip between 'two great grindstones', 'something of extreme reality'. The novels she would now write would almost all be elegiac.

The family made great preparations for their journey to Greece in the autumn of 1906. Vanessa was getting away from an unresolved predicament: this was the second summer in which she refused Clive Bell's offer of marriage. She busied herself reading books on Greek sculpture, and organising travel outfits for herself and Virginia: 'grey felt hats, white linen suits and white boots, and . . . green-lined white parasols'.[60] Violet was coming with them in her role (as she put it) of 'foster-mother'.[61] For Thoby, Greece was the last long holiday before he was called to the Bar. He was full of energy and ambitions, passionately opinionated and enthusiastic. His letters make dogmatic outbursts on the decadence of modern Cambridge, the benefits of the Liberal victory, the joys of hunting, the greatness of Swift, and the absurdity of Christianity. He kept a notebook with careful observations and drawings of birds and animals. He was falling in love – there were rumours of a dancing-girl at Cambridge, and he was drawn to Elena Rathbone and to Irene Noel, whom they visited in Greece.[62] He and Adrian went on ahead: they were going to travel, adventurously, via Trieste, on a boat down the Dalmatian coast, and on horseback through Montenegro. The sisters, who were going out in September, said goodbye to them in Norfolk. They walked with the departing travellers a few miles, discussing religion as usual. Virginia wrote, like a prophecy, in her Norfolk diary: 'So thinking, arguing, and expounding, we tramped along until we reached a crossroads, where the signpost waved in three different directions. Here was the appropriate place to part'.[63]

Her own preparations for Greece were intellectual and imaginative. Before she went, while they pored over maps and itineraries, she tried to work out the relation between 'present Greeks and the classical Greece'. It seemed incongruous to be looking at a railway station called Olympus. She imagined the crowds of 'Turks or barbarians' swarming below the Parthenon, and at night the spirit of the 'Maiden Goddess' reigning supreme once more.[64] This (feminised) vision of the death of the old Gods, much influenced by her reading of Pater, would be the theme of her journey. She wanted to enter into the spirit of Greece (in her Greek notebook she was always trying to 'read Greekly')[65] but recognised that her idea of 'Greekness' might be an illusion. The education of the English literary upper-classes made them think they 'knew' Greek, but their idealised feeling for the 'classic spirit' – learnt through Plato, Sophocles, the *Antigone* – meant that 'Greek' had come to stand for 'all that we dream and desire', 'felt to be beautiful in art and true in philosophy'. When she turns this into a dialogue (between Thoby and Adrian) on the slope of Mount Pentelicus, she resolves it by the appearance of a Greek monk who seems to put the English visitors momentarily and mystically in touch with the unalterable spirit of Greece.[66] But the argument would be resumed in *Jacob's Room* without any such neo-pagan resolution. Jacob sets out with the conviction that 'we are the only people in the world who know what the Greeks mean'. But on his journey (which retraces the Stephens'), he is brought up against the separateness and implacability of the Greek sights, their refusal to accede to 'our sentimental devotions'. 'As for reaching the Acropolis who shall say that we ever do it, or that when Jacob woke next morning he found anything hard and durable to keep for ever?' And – obliterating civilisations as she likes to do – she makes a dark wind blow through Athens, covering the world's great cities in blackness, blurring the features of 'Greek, Levantine, Turkish, English' nationalities. All Jacob comes away with are a few hesitant scribbles on the Ancient Greek model of democracy.[67]

The long Greek section of *Jacob's Room* is poignant with the memory of Thoby, whose ecstatic responses to the experience (in letters to Clive Bell and Leonard Woolf) seemed almost prescient: 'the colour of Athens and Attica by God sir you must come and see it and then your Nunc Dimittis if you like.'[68] But *Jacob's Room* recalls, also, her own strong, confused emotions on this journey. She took her notes, as they travelled by train through Italy to Brindisi, by boat to Patras, by slow train again to Olympia (where they met Thoby and Adrian), then criss-crossing the Peloponnese to the great sights of Corinth, Athens (the Acropolis at sunset, the view from Mount Pentelicus, arrived at on mule-back). Then, Eleusis, Nauplia (the romantic fort overlooking the harbour), Epidaurus (the wonderful country-side, the amphitheatre), and the great, ominous tombs at Mycenae. Then on to Euboea and finally by boat through the Dardanelles to Constantinople and the stupendous sight of St Sophia. And at every place she returned to the same engrossing, insoluble dilemmas.

Nowhere in her diaries does she so often complain of inarticulacy: 'I might as well leave a blank page.'[69] How to make fresh descriptions without falling into the clichés of other tourists or the listings of Baedeker? She frequently resorts to comparisons, and is always saying that Greece reminds her of Cornwall (Athens is 'like' St Ives). When she tries to 'get' the great statues and buildings – the Hermes of Praxiteles, or the head of a boy in the Athens museum, or a Victory at Eleusis – she tries Paterian sublimities: 'There, I think, you have the God; for he looks out and away, as though some serene vistas in the far Heaven drew his gaze.'[70] Meanwhile, modern Greece appalled her. The bugs in the bed in the hotel at Corinth, the beggars, the 'gimcracky' modern bits of Athens, the unAthenian modern Athenians who couldn't understand Ancient Greek, spoilt her attempt to get in touch with 'that supreme Greek image'.

> You must look upon Modern Greek as the impure dialect of a nation of peasants, just as you must look upon the modern Greeks as a nation of mongrel element & a rustic dialect of barbarous use beside the classic speech of pure bred races.[71]

The part of modern Greece she most enjoyed was their visit to the big estate of the Noel family at Achmetaga, in Euboea – where the friendly, respectful but noble peasants (including a romantic group of Wallachian shepherds), and the drama of a local murder, made her feel that 'for the first time Greece becomes an articulate human place'.[72] In Turkey, she was aware that she could not begin to make sense of Constantinople. The evening worship at St Sophia was 'a scene which we shall never understand'.[73] There was no literary entry-point for her to Muslim culture. And she says very little in her diary about the politics of contemporary Greece and Turkey. A passing reference to 'the fall of nations' and a momentary shocked thought of the recent massacre of Armenians is all.[74]

But a great deal of her Graeco-Turkish experience was dominated by sick-rooms, anxiety, and dealings with contradictory foreign doctors. The journey was difficult from the start, even with Violet to look after them. The expenses Virginia kept are mostly for champagne (to revive Vanessa), smelling bottles, doctors' bills and medicines (though they did buy a lot of Turkish Delight, too). Vanessa began to feel ill on the voyage out, and by the time they reached Corinth they had to stop. The party split up: Thoby and Adrian went to Delphi (so Virginia missed that great sight until her return to Greece, many years later), then the three of them went to Euboea while Violet looked after Vanessa in Athens. But when they got back she was worse. One doctor said appendicitis, another 'hysterics', a third recommended ice packs. It *was* appendicitis, but there was also stress and depression. When they got home there was talk of a 'nervous breakdown', of 'general tiredness', and of a rest cure. Two years later Vanessa wrote to Margery Snowden, of her depressions: 'When I really get laid hold of by blue devils it sometimes lasts for weeks or even months.'[75]

Their hotel became a sick-room; Virginia sat reading and making notes on Mérimée's *Lettres à une inconnue* while Thoby and Adrian quarrelled downstairs about whether the Portsmouth to Hindhead road was macadamised.[76] (The boredom, the nervous strain, the irritability and anxieties of waiting by a sick-bed in a foreign country are brilliantly caught in the last pages of *The Voyage Out*.) By the time they reached Constantinople, Vanessa had to be carried, almost fainting. Thoby left for London on 14 October; the others returned on the Orient Express, and got back on 1 November. On the ferry from Ostende to Dover, Violet – herself now beginning to be unwell – lectured Virginia yet again on the need for self-effacement and unselfishness.[77] It was timely advice. They found Thoby at home, seriously ill. He had a high fever and severe diarrhoea. The family doctors had diagnosed malaria, but ten days later they realised he had typhoid. (The two were often confused.) So had Violet, at her home in Manchester Street. Virginia wrote, in her daily bulletins to her, that when their visitors came 'I begin now by saying my brother has typhoid, my sister appendicitis – dont laugh.'[78] She did not fall ill or break down. Clive Bell was in attendance: Vanessa softened towards him in her illness, and Virginia spent a great deal of time discussing bedpans and enemas with him, thereby getting to know him better. The doctors at first told them they could be 'quite happy' about Thoby, but he got worse. He was operated on on 17 November.[79] He was quiet and courageous. And he died – two years after his father – on 20 November 1906.

Old friends of the family were aghast: George Meredith (who would die three years later, aged eighty-one) wrote tremulously to Virginia: 'The loss of this bright young life is felt by me as if it had been part of mine . . . Fortitude you will have inherited from father and mother.'[80] Aunt Milly characteristically transformed her distress into religious comforts, thinking of Thoby 'called upward, like a young Michael, to his own place – somewhere higher up than we are, but not out of reach. He will always shine for us, and the beautiful image will never be dimmed'.[81] Horrified, numbed letters went between 'the Goth's' friends: Lytton, Leonard in Ceylon, Saxon, Clive. All drew closer to the sisters as a result; Lytton, as she would always remember, came at once to see them. And Clive was accepted by Vanessa two days after Thoby's death.

Because Violet was so ill, Virginia could not tell her of the death – or of the engagement. Every day, for almost a month, she wrote her detailed reports on Thoby's progress. He was arguing or flirting with his nurses, he was reading reviews of Fred Maitland's *Life* of Leslie (published almost on the day of Thoby's death), he was having his 'little ups and downs', he was beginning 'to curse a good deal', he was looking forward to jelly and pointing out 'the virtues of a mutton chop'. Only when Violet saw a review of Maitland which mentioned Thoby's death did Virginia end the pretence.[82]

Probably these extraordinary, detailed, inventive letters were making the fact of Thoby's death bearable to her. Certainly they mark the beginning of her *keeping* Thoby by turning him into fiction. The process of literary – as opposed to religious – consolation continued with an essay on Sir Fulke Greville's life of Philip Sidney, published six months later. Greville composed Sidney, she said, 'detached from time and matter, like a Greek statue': and this is how she would always think of Thoby. Had he lived, Sidney would have been a statesman as well as a poet. But some reparation for the loss could be found:

> When Sidney died, at the age of thirty-two, his death was but the final harmony of a life that was too short, but that was complete; indeed, the shortness of such lives seems in some way a necessary part of their perfection.[83]

The essay allowed her to say what she would have thought sentimental in autobiographical terms; it consoled her to write it. And her feeling for Thoby thereafter was not painfully obsessional, as her feelings were for her parents. It was intensely sad, but also calm. 'That queer ghost. I think of death sometimes as the end of an excursion which I went on when he died. As if I should come in & say well, here you are.'[84] She could take this tone for his loss by associating him with, and characterising him through, an ideal of classical stoicism and clarity, which had been at the centre of their friendship. Finishing *Jacob's Room* in the summer of 1922, she wrote in her notebook,[85] as though trying it out for the novel's epigram, Catullus' line of farewell to his brother:

Atque in perpetuum, frater, ave atque vale
Julian Thoby Stephen
(1880–1906)
Atque in perpetuum, frater, ave atque vale.

THIRTEEN

Experiments

Each family death precipitated the loss of a home: Julia's, Talland House; Leslie's, Hyde Park Gate; Thoby's, Gordon Square. 'More bad news', Lytton Strachey wrote to Leonard Woolf, who was desolated to learn of Thoby's death, 'Vanessa and Bell are engaged . . . Poor Virginia! And Adrian! They must set up house together now. The mind recoils.'[1] Virginia was resolute (' "we must make the best of things" as father would have said'),[2] resigned to making a life with Adrian, determined to like Clive as a brother-in-law. Thoby had liked him, he was deeply in love with Vanessa, he was lively and amusing and liked people to have a good time, he cared and was knowledgeable about books and art, and he had been considerate and unselfish during the family ordeal. And Vanessa's recovery was a relief; and her happiness was impressive.

But the death and the engagement were both felt as bereavements. (The 'amount of pain that accumulates for someone to feel'[3] was almost immediately compounded by the news of Fred Maitland's death, just after the publication of his book on Leslie.) Virginia took refuge in the impersonal consolations of Lucretius and Keats ('no d—d humanity . . . cool Greek gods, and amber skies, and shadow like running water, and all his great palpable words – symbols for immaterial things').[4] But 'd—d humanity' pressed in on her. She was dispossessed, and jealous. Frequent references to Adrian's loss of Thoby ('It is terrible that he should have no brother')[5] could as well apply to herself: it was terrible, suddenly, that she should have no sister. 'That is all over, and I shall never see her alone any more.'[6] 'It will be some time before I can separate him from her.'[7] (But that was what she would soon try to do.) She could not stop herself being critical of Clive for his pomposity, his tendency to snub her, 'his nice tastes, and kindness to me, and his slightness and acidity',[8] and his unclassical physique (he was stocky, with a flat, round, high-coloured face and bright yellow hair). A spiteful sketch, drawn for Violet (who, undeceived about Thoby, was once again the recipient of Virginia's true, secret feelings) suggests her sexual distaste at his closeness to Vanessa:

When I think of father and Thoby and then see that funny little creature twitching his pink skin and jerking out his little spasm of laughter I wonder what odd freak there is in Nessa's eyesight.[9]

At the same time her feeling for Vanessa's sensuality and power intensified; she repeatedly described her now in rich colourful terms: 'She had a gauze streamer, red as blood flying over her shoulder, a purple scarf, a shooting cap, tweed skirt and great brown boots. Then her hair swept across her forehead, and she was tawny and jubilant and lusty as a young God.'[10]

A visit in January to the Bells' 'rich and illiterate'[11] family home, Cleeve House, in Wiltshire (where Vanessa was doomed to spend many grimly dutiful days with Squire Bell and his fox-hunting, church-going county family) did not improve Virginia's temper. The family's considerable wealth (Clive got £20,000 on his marriage), made from coal-mines, was loudly reflected in the house, 'a Victorian pile masquerading as a Jacobean baronial mansion'.[12] It brought out the sisters' snobbery and their horror of going back under patriarchal authority. All this was summed up for Virginia by a gigantic inkpot at Cleeve made 'out of the hoof of a favourite hunter',[13] which she never forgot.

'I hate her going away', she wrote to Violet on the night before the wedding, sounding very like Leslie on the eve of Stella's wedding, 'but I really have been quite good-tempered'.[14] The 'troublesome scratching fleasome and fretful' beasts[15] sent their parting lament to their Mistress.[16]

Clive Bell and Vanessa Stephen were married – soon after Virginia's twenty-fifth birthday, which passed without comment (Violet, never defeated, gave her a Bible) – at St Pancras Register Office on 7 February 1907. There were no aunts or cousins; George Duckworth lent his wife's liveried carriage. The couple missed their first train to Manorbier (where the family had stayed immediately after Leslie's death – mournful associations for a honeymoon). Vanessa wrote her first letter to 'Billy' from the railway station; during the honeymoon they corresponded almost daily.

Two days after the wedding, an enormous women's suffrage rally (known as the 'Mud March' because of the weather), organised by Pippa Strachey (with Lady Strachey and Maynard Keynes conspicuous) marched from Hyde Park to Exeter Hall in the Strand. Lytton Strachey mentioned the march ('I suppose I shall find myself in Exeter Hall, waving a banner, with the words "File the Fetters!" or something of the sort') in the same letter to Leonard Woolf which unflatteringly anticipated the Bell wedding: 'She's very intelligent; how long will it be before she sees he isn't?'[17] But the march went unremarked by the Stephens; it was three years before Virginia was drawn into 'The Cause'.

When Vanessa and Clive returned, blissful, energetic, full of plans for Gordon Square ('My God, they are a happy couple!')[18] Virginia felt more than ever excluded. Once she knew, in July, that Vanessa was pregnant, her letters[19] filled up with images of fertility, conception, and babies. Vanessa, still glamorised by her new distance and erotic experience, is described as the embodiment of 'child': not 'great with child', but 'like a great child', 'a wasteful child pulling the heads off flowers'.[20] Maternity seemed to free her from having to recognise Virginia's troubles. 'Nessa comes tomorrow – what one calls Nessa; but it means husband and baby; and of sister there is less than there used to be.'[21] The phrasing momentarily suggests that the pregnant Vanessa is herself the husband's baby. At the same time Virginia presents herself as feeling extremely old; or as an unmothered child; or (after a disturbing visit to the Duckworths, who 'always make her feel 10 years old') as some awkward hybrid, half-child, half-adult; half-related, half-alone. 'What my position among them all is, I dont know.'[22]

She was being increasingly teased about her own marital prospects, and her response was edgy. 'I wish everyone didn't tell me to marry.'[23] In her work, as early as 1905, she was trying out oppositions between writing and marriage: 'The world might, perhaps, be considerably poorer if the great writers had exchanged their books for children of flesh and blood.'[24] The 'Journal of Mistress Joan Martyn' sets the imaginative power of virginal freedom against the warmer constrictions of sex and domesticity. This opposition would reappear in the novels.

O how blessed it would be never to marry, or grow old; but to spend one's life innocently and indifferently among the trees and rivers which alone can keep one cool and childlike in the mist of the troubles of the world! Marriage or any other great joy would confuse the clear vision which is still mine. And at the thought of losing that, I cried in my heart, 'No, I will never leave you – for a husband or a lover,' and straightway I started chasing rabbits across the heath with Jeremy and the dogs.[25]

But to remain a child meant not to have a child. From now on she began to take a wistful, curious tone on the subject: 'Shall I ever bear a child I wonder?'[26] If marriage and children were not for her, her role, as she was acutely aware, was fixed (she wrote to her favourite spinster) as 'a virgin, an Aunt, an authoress'.[27]

It was as 'authoress' that she could compete with marriage and maternity. Writing vied with conception. She described herself to Violet, staying at Rye in August, as 'solitary' (though the rest of the family was there, and they had numerous visitors) 'and fertile as a teapot'.[28] If Vanessa could create a life, so could she (particularly since Vanessa herself was, while pregnant, writing her own account of everything she could remember up to the age of fourteen).[29] *Friendship's Gallery*, the mythologised life of Violet, written at the time of Vanessa's pregnancy, begins with the birth and measuring of a baby, continues with a parody of female upbringing, and develops into the life of a single woman who builds her own house and says 'I'm very happy alone'. Its coda is a story told to make children sleep, of the two Sacred Princesses whose preferred form of worship is to be shown 'your Babies in their Baths', whom they bless.[30] The fantasy, which was shown to the Bells, emphasised her own credentials for maternal feeling, while conceiving a triumphant virgin Life.

The same mixed motives went into her next 'biography', a Life of Vanessa, begun well before Julian Bell's birth on 4 February 1908, and completed in the months after it. Virginia could not bear the baby; he took Vanessa's attention and her place on Vanessa's lap. But she liked the idea of a nephew as an audience for her narratives. 'When I see small boys of 8 or 10 I marvel to think that we shall have one going about the world with us, and asking information. "Who was Cousin Mia? Dont you like Uncle George? Why has Aunt Goat never married? I think you very beautiful Mama!" '[31] The 'Reminiscences' began to answer those kinds of questions. Like Leslie's *Mausoleum Book* (and written as much out of an impulse of mourning), the essay is cast as a letter to the next generation: though not to her own child. But it turns Vanessa into her own child, beginning with her birth, and breaking off, after the death of Stella, at the point when Vanessa becomes a sexual adult. And it is, as a piece of writing, a new conception, a mixture of her own memories, a portrait of their mother, a guarded account of their childhood, and a tribute to her sister's influence, so that it is hard to say whether the essay is biography, autobiography, memoir or love-letter.

It was a competitive gift for the Bells, a way of 'separating her from him'. 'I ask myself why write it at all?' she says to Clive, 'seeing I never shall recapture what you have, by your side this minute.'[32] It was her first bid for Clive's literary attention: he went through the manuscript, deleting frequent occurrences of the word 'painful', and approving its most rational, balanced bits of prose.[33] And it elicited, as it was meant to, a strong response from Vanessa. Her letter about 'Reminiscences' (very like her letter of response to *To the Lighthouse* twenty years later) dealt with it not as a characterisation of herself (she says nothing about that) but as a moving re-creation of their mother, and as a powerfully affecting document which plunged her back into 'all that underworld of emotional scenes and irritations and difficulties again as I read. How did we ever get out of it?'[34] Virginia may have wanted to reclaim her by dragging her back into that 'scene of gloom'. A strong part of her impulse in writing fiction would be to take back Vanessa, to re-enter and to make her re-enter their past shared life.

Like the 'Reminiscences', with which it overlapped, the novel she now embarked on was partly motivated by competitiveness and the need for consolation. There were tentative references to 'trying to begin things' as early as October of 1907, but the first draft of 'Melymbrosia' was definitely underway by the spring of 1908. So its conception coincided with Vanessa's. In its early stages this story of an ominous sea voyage to South America of a young girl, Cynthia Vinrace, her widowed father, and a couple called the Ambroses (with something of Leslie and Julia in them, and something of Vanessa) was steeped in family feelings. She dreamt (she told Clive Bell) that she was 'showing father the manuscript of my novel; and he snorted, and dropped it on to a table, and I was very melancholy, and read it this morning, and thought it bad'.[35] She would have liked his approval; in lieu of his, she wanted theirs. She made it clear to them that the novel was her alternative to their marriage: 'Why should I intrude upon your circle of bliss? Especially when I can think of nothing but my novel.'[36] She made competitive comparisons between her writing and the mother and baby:

> By the way, I have imagined precisely what it is like to have a child. I woke up, and understood, as in a revelation, the precise nature of the pain. Now, if I could only see my novel like that.[37]

> Ah, I'm so excited about my novel! I read 2 pages, and thought them good ... I write as Julian sucks his bottle; a necessary occupation, but not of intense interest to you perhaps.[38]

The analogy between writing and mothering was passed back and forth between them. In December 1910, soon after Vanessa had Quentin, her second child, and when Virginia was resuming what was probably her fifth draft of the novel, Clive wrote to her: 'For you it will be like having a baby.'[39] She involved them in her search for the right name for her heroine, as if looking for a name for a child. 'Cynthia don't do', 'Belinda is perhaps a little too dainty.' Vanessa responded in kind, asking if the name of one of Virginia's characters could be a name for her own daughter ('Do you think Belinda Bell would be quite impossible?'), making wild suggestions, like 'Apricot', for a heroine's name, and imagining them both in twenty years' time, both with daughters, Virginia's 'clever and cranky'.[40] This interplay continued: Virginia later suggested that Vanessa call her daughter Clarissa.

As the novel which would eventually be named *The Voyage Out* took its first steps and began to 'speak',[41] it reflected Virginia Stephen's own journey to this point. 'I sometimes feel surprised,' she wrote mournfully to Vanessa in 1908, 'when I realise that we are all set out on our journey, as human beings, with all our ceremonies, and marriages.'[42] This sense of strangeness would be given to Rachel Vinrace, but only after years and years of rewriting had shaped and objectified her from an autobiographical to a fictional voice.

When Vanessa married, Virginia and Adrian moved out of Gordon Square, ten minutes away across the Tottenham Court Road, to Fitzroy Square. It was a more elegant setting – this was the only London square designed (as a circle within a square) by Robert Adam, built between the 1790s and 1830 – but a seedier environment. Number 29, which they took on a five-year-lease for £120 a year, was on the brick-and-stucco west side of the square, handsome on the outside but somewhat decrepit within. There was electricity, but a bath had to be put in. The last tenants, on the second and third floors, had been George Bernard Shaw and his mother, who had lived there from 1887 to 1898, until his marriage.[43] All around, the square's grand houses had been turned into nursing homes and artisans' workshops. The traffic of carts and railway vans was noisy and continuous (Virginia suffered from the noise even after putting in double windows). 'Fitzrovia', haunt of bohemians and drinkers, did not come into being until the 1930s and 1940s (in Rosamond Lehmann's *The Weather in the Streets* (1936) Olivia takes Rollo to a gay, gin-soaked, cross-dressed party in Fitzroy Square),[44] but the area had been 'artistic' since the nineteenth century. Duncan Grant lived at No. 22, Sargent had his studio in Fitzroy Street, and in 1913 Roger Fry would establish the Omega workshop and studio at No. 33.

Violet was anxious about 'respectability', and did not visit for some time. This marked the beginning of the end of their intimacy: Virginia started to ask if they were drifting apart, to say 'Don't drop me':[45] but it was she who would do the dropping. Irritated by Violet's opposition, she enthused on the charm of the place: 'All the lights in the Square are lighting, and it is turning silver gray, and there are beautiful young women still playing tennis on the grass.'[46]

She had the whole second floor to herself, and filled her sitting-room as usual with 'great pyramids of books, with trailing mists between them; partly dust, and partly cigarette-smoke'.[47] This time she could furnish her own drawing-room – with bright green carpets and red brocade curtains and a pianola. (Later, the room would be curtained in 'flowing purple'.)[48] Competition with Gordon Square was immediate. She told Madge (still a maternal confidante) that Gordon Square was more beautiful – but then the Bells had wedding presents, and Parisian furniture, and mauve curtains with yellow linings, and money to buy 'priceless looking glasses'.[49] She resented Vanessa's new wealth (Adrian recorded her virulently telling the Bells one evening 'how rich they were and how poor she herself was and therefore how much more important it was for her than for them to do work'),[50] her stylishness and her social prowess: 'Nessa and Clive live, as I think, much like great ladies in a French salon; they have all the wits and the poets: and Nessa sits among them like a Goddess.'[51] Years later, she would make family jokes about the aesthetic redecorations at Gordon Square – the leaking chamberpots which ravished the eye 'with their wollops & their scrollops: blue patterns, golden rumps', and the affair of the humble Bryant and Mays matchbox which Clive threw on the fire because it was not colour co-ordinated with the rest of the drawing-room. 'Never mind: Ars Longa; Matchbox brevis.'[52]

These long-running jokes were born of rivalry. Her life with Adrian felt, by contrast, awkward and unaesthetic. Retrospectively, she would see that they were going through a painful, personal version of the transitions of their pre-war society, though this was not exactly evident at the time. For the first time in their lives, for instance, the servants could not quite be taken for granted. Sophie Farrell and Maud the maid had to decide whether to stay at Gordon Square or to move. Sophie felt she needed to go with Miss Virginia, who was so 'harum scarum' that she would otherwise be unable to cope: 'She dont know what she has on her plate.'[53] But Sophie – an illiterate, illegitimate farm-labourer's daughter who had gone into service with Julia as a child, taught herself to read, passed up the chance of marriage and stayed doggedly loyal to the family all her life, a byword for her bad temper and her blunt sayings ('If you don't like it you must loomp it') – was like a piece of furniture from Hyde Park Gate. (The old family servant Crosby, in *The Years*, is always identified with the furniture.) Virginia was not good at dealing with her, and her uncomfortable, embarrassing relationships with her live-in servants dated from this period.

The habits of Fitzroy Square were informal, even messy. Adrian and Virginia did not 'dress', they served up 'herrings and tripe' for dinner at eight, they had a notoriously un-house-trained dog called Hans, their talk was free (and getting free-er), and their hours were late. By 1911, they would have a telephone (Mayfair 797), like most of their friends. And yet the servants continued, indispensably it seemed then, to open the door to visitors, shop for food, cook the meals in the basement, clean the grates, set the fires, wash the clothes, apply for permission to go out, gossip, quarrel, and make everything 'pompous and heavy-footed'.[54] 'Oh Lord – what servants are!'[55] wrote Vanessa, who started to have 'servant problems' immediately after her marriage. All long-term plans for summer holidays and country houses and baby-care came back to the 'insuperable' questions of Sophie and nurse-maids. As early as 1911 Virginia was replying to Vanessa: 'Why we have them, I cant think.'[56]

Years later Virginia Woolf would say that the most interesting story to be gleaned by posterity from her diaries might be that of her relations with her servant Nelly Boxall. Her management of Sophie pointed ahead to those difficulties. It was not snobbishness, but social accuracy, that prompted her in the 1920s to identify the pre-war changes in 'human character' and perceptions with the cook's behaviour.

> The Victorian cook lived like a leviathan in the lower depths, formidable, silent, obscure, inscrutable; the Georgian cook is a creature of sunshine and fresh air; in and out of the drawing-room, now to borrow the *Daily Herald*, now to ask advice about a hat. Do you ask for more solemn instances of the power of the human race to change?[57]

But in 1907 it did not seriously occur to Virginia and Adrian Stephen that they might live without servants. In other ways too their experiments in living were moderate and gradual, even though the insides of the Fitzroy and Gordon Square houses looked and felt so different from Hyde Park Gate.

As she recalled in 'Old Bloomsbury', there *was* 'a great change' in the next two or three years. The removal of Thoby's reserved authority, the growing intimacy with his Cambridge friends after his death, their use of first names and their freeing-up of talk to include the sisters in their sexual plots; the influx of new social groupings (the Neo-Pagans, Augustus John and his painter friends, Ottoline Morrell's salon), the impact of Roger Fry and Duncan Grant, who switched everyone's conversational attention from philosophy to art, Clive Bell's passion for French culture and his appetite for socialising: all these factors made 'Bloomsbury' less 'monastic'. 'We have parties, and discuss the arts', she wrote with some pride and pleasure to Madge Vaughan, out of it in Giggleswick.[58]

But they were not bohemians; Bloomsbury was not a commune. Adrian's diary for the summer of 1909 recorded some adventurous outings, like a fancy-dress party at the Botanical Gardens when Virginia went dressed as Cleopatra (in long flowing robes with her hair down, she looked more like Isolde). There were more conventional outings to plays, operas and concerts: *Aida*, *Electra*, Lillian Nordica at the Queen's Hall, *Orpheus and Eurydice* at Drury Lane, an Arnold Bennett play, Wagner operas, and the première of Ethel Smyth's *The Wreckers*, when the composer took a bow with Thomas Beecham. There were expeditions to the zoo, to Speaker's

Corner, to the Friday Club shows, for ices at Buzzards. Virginia was busy – writing, teaching, taking German lessons, sitting for her portrait, going to soirées, dinners and entertainments, parties, weekends in the country and holidays in Europe, and playing host at the new Fitzroy Square 'Thursday evenings'. It was, viewed externally, an unexceptional, if independent, middle-class young woman's pre-war life. 'The whirl of the London season is upon us', she wrote conventionally – or in a parody of conventions – in June 1909.[59]

But underneath this 'whirl' of activities, Virginia was still extremely vulnerable. She missed Thoby intensely. She walked about London 'engaged with my anguish . . . alone; fighting something alone'.[60] A 'doggerel' line of an elegiac poem by Stevenson kept coming into her head: 'You alone have crossed the melancholy stream.' (She remembered this when Julian Bell, who always reminded her of Thoby, died young.)[61] These young deaths (Stella's too, still painfully remembered) made her feel 'old as a hoary grey tortoise', 'ossified'.[62] The feeling went on for a long time: 'It is just two years since he died, and I feel immensely old, and as though the best in us had gone . . . It is such an odd life without him.'[63] Alone in Cornwall two years later she still found herself thinking of Thoby 'all the time', reminded of him by the birds he used to draw.[64]

In the Fitzroy Square years there were many of these holidays away from London, alone or with the others. In spring 1907 she went with Clive and Vanessa and Adrian to Paris (and was never alone with Vanessa); that autumn the family were all at Playden, near Rye. In April 1908 they went to Cornwall (she would send Clive a postcard in 1936 from the spot where they had quarrelled)[65] and that summer she went alone to stay in lodgings in Wells and then in Manorbier; and then to Italy, and again to Paris, with the Bells. In the spring of 1909, after another trip to Cornwall, she and Adrian made all kinds of plans for Easter, like 'taking a steamer in the middle of the night and landing at St Malo, as the First Cock rises to crow on Easter Day'.[66] In the end she went to Florence with Clive and Vanessa, but the holiday was an unhappy one, and she came home alone. That summer, she and Adrian and Saxon went to Bayreuth; in September she stayed in lodgings near the Bells at Studland, in Dorset; at Christmas she suddenly set off alone to Cornwall. In the spring of 1910, when she was beginning to feel dangerously shaky, she went back to Cornwall with the Bells and then with them to Studland and to Canterbury. Her summer was spent at Burley Park, having a 'rest cure'; after that she went back to Studland with the family. That winter she and Adrian went to Lewes, and it was then that she found a house of her own to rent in Firle and began to 'settle' on Sussex as her country place.

These frequent forays from London into seaside lodgings or European hotels (not unusual for her class at that time, but also part of a programme to keep her from getting exhausted and strained in London) often accentuated her feelings of loneliness. When she was with Clive and Vanessa she felt excluded; when she was away from them, she felt isolated, though she put on a brave front: 'I always want you; but save for that, I haven't been lonely yet.'[67] Alone, she read herself into 'the middle of a world', like 'shutting the doors of a Cathedral'.[68] She took long solitary walks, in all weathers, talking to herself and reciting, 'very lively in my head', and coming close to the edge of behaving like a 'scandalous' eccentric.[69]

> I walked along the Cliff yesterday, and found myself slipping on a little ridge just at the edge of a red fissure. I did not remember that they came so near the path; I have no wish to perish. I can imagine sticking out ones arms on the way down, and feeling them tear, and finally whirling over, and cracking ones head. I think I should feel as though I saw a china vase fall from the table; a useless thing to happen – and without any reason or good in it.[70]

'I have no wish to perish': but she imagines it vividly.[71] There is melancholy and peril, as well as pleasure, in her solitudes. A stranger, seeing her once at a Hans Richter concert at the Queen's Hall, thought she looked so 'lonely and sad' that he followed her home and wrote to her, offering her a ticket for a play. She sat next to him (the play was Galsworthy's *Strife*) but when he wrote again she let it drop.[72]

Her closest companion was Adrian, who was working desultorily towards the legal career which Thoby would have had, and was also grieving for his lost brother. But Virginia and Adrian were no help to each other. Quentin Bell described his uncle as a young man as 'maddeningly lethargic, lamentably silent, unable to find interest in anything except the constant rehearsal of old family reminiscences'.[73] These were 'his weary days'.[74] She felt protective towards him, but they were both irritable, unconfident and self-absorbed. It was one of the family jokes – jokes derived from angry feelings – that they would regularly throw Sophie's butter-pats at each other at breakfast. Virginia looked back years later on many evenings which would end in 'dismal failure': 'Adrian stalked off to his room, I to mine, in complete silence.'[75] Saxon Sydney-Turner – taciturn, pedantic, fussily jocose – was always in attendance, sitting out the other guests, staying on for hours 'talking about good and evil and playing the pianola'. Too inert to go to bed, they would all lie about 'blinking and sleeping'[76] at two in the morning.

Their trip together to Bayreuth in 1909 was trying. (They went to *Parsifal* and *Lohengrin* and possibly *Götterdämmerung* – and then on to Dresden, where she found Strauss's *Salome* 'a new discovery', and fell in love with the Vermeers in the gallery.) Virginia was stirred by Wagner (music which a few years later she would find oppressive and sentimental, and which she would use in *The Years* to illustrate dictatorship and aggression).[77] But Saxon and Adrian snubbed her for her musical ignorance and made her read the libretti in German, and she lost patience with Saxon, 'an ineffectual old cat', 'dormant', 'peevish' and 'shrivelled'. (She would use these characteristics for William Pepper in *The Voyage Out* and for Augustus Carmichael in *To the Lighthouse*.) They made an odd trio. She and Adrian talked a great deal about Leslie, and they all compared their nightmares at breakfast. She longed for Vanessa.[78]

Virginia could not lift Adrian's and Saxon's inertness; she was not an adept hostess, and her brilliant sallies came in jagged bursts. Adrian's grumpy, sardonic diary for the summer of 1909 described Virginia behaving extravagantly or maliciously: making faces behind people's backs, over-praising their hospitality, mockingly flattering an outsider, Miss Cole, until 'she did not know what to do with herself', gossiping in a corner with Lytton about his 'obscene loves', leading people on in argument by 'making the vaguest statements with the intensest feeling' and then agreeing immediately with anyone who refuted her point.[79] His unsympathetic witness began to establish the family version of Virginia as mischievous, untrustworthy and difficult. And his capacity to depress her would never be forgotten; it came back to her years later when she heard that his marriage was breaking up:

> I felt come over me the old despair; the crouching servile feeling which is my lowest & worst; the desire for praise, which he never gets; & the old futile comparisons between his respect for Nessa & his disrespect for me came over me, that made me so wretched at Fitzroy Sqre.[80]

Most of her retrospects on Fitzroy Square were of being wretched. She often used the word unhappiness when she looked back on these pre-war years. When they left Fitzroy Square in 1911 she thought of it as an 'advance towards freedom'.[81]

Yet her memories of this period are also of enfranchisement. This was when they all established a truthful way of speaking, 'a view of life which was not by any means corrupt or sinister or merely intellectual', which would keep her circle together for the rest of their lives, and which she always thought 'creditable'.[82] And this was when they began to talk freely about homosexuality and 'copulation'. They were shedding the inhibitions of the past and turning their gossip – under the tutorship, particularly, of Lytton and Maynard – into what seemed to them daringly erotic scandal. Vanessa especially relished this verbal freedom, and in her letters and talk loved to be as outrageous as she could. If there was a competition between the sisters for erotic bravado, then Vanessa was the out-and-out winner. She typed out Lytton's obscene poems with relish; Lytton wrote to Leonard (in the summer of 1908): 'You see how shockingly advanced we all are now.'[83] At Gordon Square 'there was now nothing that one could not say, nothing that one could not do'.[84]

Virginia Woolf summed up this mixture of restriction and freedom in a 1930 letter to Ethel Smyth:

> And then I set up house alone with a brother, and Nessa married, and I was rather adventurous, for those days; that is we were sexually very free . . . but I was always sexually cowardly . . . My terror of real life has always kept me in a nunnery. And much of this talking and adventuring in London alone, and sitting up to all hours with young men, and saying whatever came first, was rather petty . . . at least narrow; circumscribed; and leading to endless ramifications of intrigue. We had violent rows – oh yes, I used to rush through London in such rages, and stormed Hampstead heights at night in white or purple fury.[85]

Her 1922 reminiscence of 'Old Bloomsbury' takes a similarly equivocal tone. She links together in one paragraph her incompatibility with Adrian – as in a bad marriage – and her growing realisation that she was bored with the young men from Cambridge because they were sexually interested in each other, not in her. She comments on 'the society of buggers' (her circle's accepted word for homosexuals) that women can be at ease with them, but that 'something is always suppressed, held down'. They make it impossible to 'show off', to 'fizz up into some absurd delightful effervescence', which is one of the next best things – and the closest thing – in life to 'copulation'. Only when Lytton Strachey let flow 'a flood of the sacred fluid' by notoriously uttering the word 'semen' in the drawing-room of Gordon Square did 'the love affairs of buggers' become their central topic of conversation, and 'fizzing up' became a possibility. 'A great advance in civilization', she calls it: the illegal, the banned, became the subject of their jokes and gossips, and their private life became a challenge to public conventions.

But what sexual space did this 'liberation' provide for Virginia Stephen in her late twenties? She tells Ethel that 'fizzing up' ('saying whatever came first') was always collapsing into petty rows and intrigue. Perhaps their new freedom of speech (had Lytton 'copulated' with George Mallory? was Duncan dropping him for Maynard? who had been to bed with Rupert Brooke?) was not after all so enfranchising for her, but rapidly became a game in which she had to compete (like learning to read a Wagner libretto in German) but in which her own desires had to be discounted.

'Something is always suppressed, held down.' It is too simple to assume that because she herself maintained all her life that she was emotionally damaged by George Duckworth's sexual interference with her, she was therefore entirely frigid and a-sexual. Virginia's sexual cowardice and ignorance tended, from this time onwards, to be set in contrast to Vanessa, who, after Thoby's death, laid claim to all the heterosexual eroticism in the family (but whose own later relationship with Duncan Grant involved quite as ambiguous sexuality as her sister's). Vanessa and Clive and Lytton, and all Virginia's male admirers (including, eventually, Leonard) now began to construct, by contrast with Vanessa, an image of a chaste, chill, sexually inhibited maiden: Virginia the Virgin. Clive's flirtatious letters to her of 1908 and 1909 described her as a solitary, mystical, aetherial presence:

> You look out over the world with your wild, romantic vision sweeping away beyond the horizon, beautifully fixed and desolate . . . that is how I once saw you, sitting on a bench at Hampton Court, with soft deep eyes, and in their depths the last secrets of things . . . You wore a white muslin dress, and floating over it a long white ghost-like cloak.[86]

When in 1909 Lytton told Clive that he had fallen in love with the handsome George Mallory, he wrote: 'Virginia alone will sympathise with me now – I'm a convert to the divinity of virginity!'[87] His letters to Leonard Woolf about his own interest in Virginia insisted on this characterisation: 'How can a virgin be expected to understand? You see she *is* her name.'[88] Leonard, in response to these advance warnings, would in his courtship idealise Virginia as 'Aspasia',[89] one of the 'Olympians', cold, pure, and remote. The strange, even vengeful, novel which emerged from this idealisation, *The Wise Virgins*, and the version of their marital sex-life put about by Vanessa and Clive, perpetuated the legend of Virginia's frigidity.[90]

But in the years when Virginia Stephen was being set up as a virginal ice-maiden, she expressed strong sensual demands and susceptibilities. Talk and petting, thought and writing, were powerful sources of excitement. Her eroticism expressed itself not as 'copulation', but as demands for comfort and admiration, as 'effervescence' in talk or whimsical animal-play, and as intensely physical apprehensions, both of her own bodily feelings and of the world around her. She had a sensual imagination. A letter to Ethel of 1941, sympathising with her for not being able to write about masturbation (while admiring her usual sexual outspokenness)[91] suggests she too knew how that felt. And her writing, while evasive and indirect about the sexual lives of her characters – in deliberate contrast to Lawrence or Joyce – is full of intensely dramatised sensual feeling. No 'gropings or grapplings',[92] certainly, but her translation of perceptions and emotions into concentrated moments of physical response has its own eroticism – as (famously) in Clarissa Dalloway's attempt to describe her occasional feelings for women:

> It was a sudden revelation, a tinge like a blush which one tried to check and then, as it spread, one yielded to its expansion, and rushed to the farthest verge and there quivered and felt the world come closer, swollen with some astonishing significance, some pressure of rapture, which split its thin skin and gushed and poured with an extraordinary alleviation over the cracks and sores. Then, for that moment, she had seen an illumination; a match burning in a crocus; an inner meaning almost expressed.[93]

But in her twenties Virginia Stephen was sexually confused and uncertain. She could make private jokes in her own letters to Violet or Madge or Vanessa about feeling hot and ready for affection, but there was no acceptable outlet for her erotic feelings about women – as there were accredited ways of behaving for the Apostolic Cambridge homosexuals, or for randy bohemian artists like Henry Lamb or Augustus John with their wives and mistresses. Except as a joke, she did not define herself as a lesbian (or, as she would say, as a 'Sapphist'): it was not a concept for her, or a group for her to join, or a political identity. Instead, she was poised between incompatible identities and roles.

FOURTEEN

Liaisons

She was a young woman of marriageable age, thought by many who knew her to be extremely beautiful. The famous and much-used Beresford photographs, taken in 1902, before her breakdown, when she was twenty, show us how alluring and fragile she could appear. The sensual, down-curved lips, the large sad gazing eyes, the dark lashes and strong eyebrows, the lovely straight nose and delicate curve of the chin, the long elegant neck, the high cheekbones, the soft, loosely-coiled bun, the pretty ear-lobe, and the aetherial lacy dress, were to be crucial items in the making and maintaining of the Virgin Virginia legend. (Less formal snapshots, for instance of her cavorting on the beach at Studland with Clive in striped beach-costume, give her a more vivid, wicked, playful look.) But would-be 'suitors' were also confronted by her history of mental illness, her exceptional family, and her already daunting reputation for satire, wit and learning. She was no ordinary proposition. And no ordinary suitor was likely to get near her. Keeping pace with the *amours* of Lytton & Co, she involved everyone she met in the mechanisms of scandal: reputations exposed, letters opened, gossip exchanged. 'You live in a hornets nest', one of her wary admirers, Walter Lamb, accused her (rightly, as she immediately told Vanessa).[1]

Though most of her male friends were homosexuals, there were nevertheless expectations that she should be looking for someone to marry; and up to a point she had these expectations herself. But her suitors were a kind of joke. Their attentions to her, usually master-minded by Clive, were merely grist for the gossip-shop.

They were, inevitably, Cambridge men. Saxon, to whom she wrote mildly inviting jokes (wanting him to write to her in 'one of the living languages, preferably Romance')[2] was out of the question. 'Turner is certainly not upon the tapis', Lytton wrote to Leonard in 1909.[3] Walter Headlam, a middle-aged Cambridge classicist who had been a family friend since childhood[4] was asking to look at her work and calling for tea in 1906 and 1907. He got as far as writing her a ponderously flirtatious letter after she returned a book ('What I knew I had left behind was not this'). But when he died, unexpectedly, in 1908, she was not much moved, and recalled him as a 'disappointed' man.[5] The other childhood acquaintance who became interested in her was a more likely candidate: an intelligent, conventional friend of Lytton's, the future politician Edward Hilton Young, who is supposed to have proposed to her on a punt in Cambridge in the summer of 1909. But Virginia wrote to Vanessa, 'I don't think he will do', and Vanessa replied, 'I dont think you would really like to marry him, do you?'[6]

Neither Young nor Headlam came close enough to her to cause emotion; Walter Lamb's approaches were slightly more pressing. He was Henry Lamb's older brother and had admired and been frightened of Virginia since Thoby's Cambridge days, upset in 1906 because the Stephen girls were rude to him, admiring her prose style in 1907, finding her distant and mysterious in 1908. After Cambridge he had gone to teach classics at Clifton College, but he kept in with the Cambridge set – Lytton characterised him as short and obsequious – and by 1911 he was being drawn into the hornets' nest. He wrote Virginia emotional letters and declared his love in a roundabout and tentative fashion in Kew Gardens. But Virginia found something pathetic about him, and thought that her falling in love with him was about as likely as her 'growing a beak'. Clive, in any case, was stage-managing the whole business ('I have been talking to Waterlow, and trying to make out what exactly Clive said to him about you', were how poor Lamb's struggling letters went). In the end Clive quarrelled with him – a Bloomsbury Iago with his stooge. If all this touched Virginia at all, it was to make her angry at Lamb's ineffectuality: as far as he was concerned, she did grow a beak. She would always vilify Lamb's unctuousness, the 'placatory manner' with which he 'oiled the wheels of a large institution', as he went on in life to become Secretary of the Royal Academy. The 'perfectly upholstered' Hugh Whitbread in *Mrs Dalloway* caricatures his type.[7]

If Walter Lamb was too much of a sheep for her, Sydney Waterlow, also a friend of Clive (and of Henry James) and a brilliant classicist who became a grand diplomat, ambassador to Sofia and Athens, was too much in the grip of his appetites. When he got to know Virginia in the summer of 1910 he was involved in a dying marriage and a disastrous affair; the day after she refused him in the autumn of 1911 he went out to pick up a 'street-girl'. But this clever, domineering, greedy character was probably the only one of these men to think about her carefully, and to perceive her sensuality:

> I realised for the first time the difference between her [Vanessa] and Virginia: Vanessa icy, cynical, artistic; Virginia much more emotional, and interested in life rather than beauty.[8]

He was the only one who remained a friend. But it was a friendship qualified by her abusive commentary on his pomposity, his pretensions, and his appearance ('if you could have seen him bathing in the river Ouse, which could hardly close above his immense soft pink stomach, belching and bellowing like a walrus. As I say, he has improved').[9] Hearing a story, twenty years later, about his wife's preoccupation with their status, she noted: 'That would have been my fate.'[10]

But what was her fate? She played up these courtships in order to provide gossip for the family circle – so Vanessa obligingly referred to 'your harem'[11] and Adrian always remembered the summer when they all 'rushed to read' Virginia's letters about her rival suitors.[12] But the excitement was artificial. When she refused Sydney Waterlow's proposal, she said he was not her 'idea' of a husband. Nobody she knew was. She told Clive Bell that she could not imagine 'the man to whom I shall say certain things,'[13] and Lytton that 'she wished that earth would open her womb and let some new creature out'.[14] Her intimacy with these two men was made easier, indeed, by their evident unsuitability as husband-material – though both were drawn to her – since one was the most flamboyant homosexual of her circle, and one was her brother-in-law.

Virginia Stephen's initial bids for attention from Clive Bell were self-conscious and guarded: a letter of February 1907 (one of the few letters she rewrote), a pastiche of eighteenth-century epistolary manners, is 'tortuous and angular'[15] with the desire to impress him. They began to be more intimate after the birth of Julian in February 1908. Clive's sexual life with Vanessa was interrupted, and both Clive and Virginia were jealous of Vanessa's intense concentration on the baby and its interference with their conversations on 'marriage, friendship or prose'.[16] In Cornwall that spring, they took long walks together. An essay-fragment called 'A Dialogue on a Hill' suggests her pleasure in talking intimately and alone to an intelligent man, and of finding 'much to say to each other which neither would say to a person of the same sex'.[17] (The only precedent she knew for this kind of relationship was with Jack Hills, and Clive's easy-going openness, good humour and literary passions compared favourably with the earlier brother-in-law.) Her pleasure is reflected in the interchanges between Rachel and Terence in *The Voyage Out*.[18] Because (according to his son and the women he knew) Clive Bell was unable to be interested in a woman without wanting to make love to her, he began to tell Virginia how 'vivid and strange and bewildering'[19] she was to him and to say that he wanted to kiss her. By the time Virginia got her train after two weeks in St Ives, and Clive ran after the train with a book she had left behind, fell and grazed his knee, she was 'moved' by him. From this time – May of 1908 – they began to play a game of intimacy and intrigue which lasted for perhaps two years, until it shifted into the more satirical and distrustful friendship which continued all their lives. Her later portraits of Clive[20] would usually mention his boasting, his silliness, his desire to humiliate her publicly, or his narcissism about his own love-life. She disliked his proprietariness, which began from the moment he thought she might be falling seriously in love with anyone else: he wanted to reserve 'his own little niche'.[21] But she liked talking to him, and was often amused by him; they remained combatively close.

It may be that Clive's later spitefulness towards his sister-in-law arose from her sexual elusiveness. He eroticised the relationship, but within limits. Quentin Bell suggests that he had in mind 'a delightful little infidelity ending up in bed',[22] but he may have perceived this as too riskily taboo. In his letters, he fell in with the whimsical menagerie she created for her initiates – she is a 'dear little squirrel', he is a 'chipmunk', and in one letter he makes her a fantasy world of a limpet paying compliments to a waterfall and 'hares and small rabbits' coming out into a garden at night.[23] He is fondly attentive to her physical needs (recommending winter combinations for a trip to Italy)[24] and takes care of her finances for her (in June of 1910 he is doing her income tax returns).[25] But he also romanticises and aetherialises her; the poem he writes for her in 1909 catches something of the artificiality and sentiment of his 'wooing':

> Do you most dear –
> Sometimes just guessed at, sometimes very near –
> Yet always dear and fairest friend, do you
> Recall the sunlight and the firelight too?
> Recall the pregnant hours, the gay delights,
> The pain, the tears maybe, the ravished heights,
> The golden moments my cold lines commend,
> The days, in memory of which I send
> A book?[26]

The most insistent erotic demands in this relationship passed, via Clive, from Virginia to Vanessa. Clive, who made a habit of showing these letters to his later mistresses, Molly MacCarthy and Mary Hutchinson, told Mary that they presented 'a sadly humiliating picture', since this was the only relationship in which he had ever played 'second fiddle'.[27]

How is my – I dont know what degree of reticence should be between us;

but you can fill up the blank with any figure you like; my balance is boundless. Ah, I often think – was thinking but yesterday, how the best thing one can say of this world is that such a creature can grow there. How she contrives it, how she draws honey and not poison through all the black veins which spout their malevolence into our eyes is proof of her – I hesitate for a word, because I wont attribute such qualities to Heaven . . . Both eyes are to be kissed, the tip of the right ear, and the snout if its wet.[28]

Kiss Dolphins nose – if it isnt too wet – and tap pony smartly on the snout. Whisper into your wife's ear that I love her. I expect she will scold you for tickling her (when she hears the message).[29]

What has been unkindly but understandably called 'the touching and rather odious pathos of this'[30] expressed a complicated mixture of longing and anger. Wooing Vanessa as a magical animal allowed for the nursery language of petting to be retained in adult life. But it also meant that Virginia could get away with reproaching Vanessa for 'malevolence' and 'scolding' and with 'smart taps' which were as revengeful as they were loving. These coyly aggressive erotic messages were attempts to get inside their marriage instead of outside – which, as she told Clive, was where she felt she was: 'Thus I seem often to be only an erratic external force, capable of shocks, but without any lodging in your lives.'[31]

The sisters' relationship now changed, and (according to those who knew them) was never the same again. Vanessa protected herself by making light of whatever jealousy she may have felt. To her husband she now talked of Virginia affectionately but disparagingly, as their mutual responsibility ('I am rather sorry for you having to cheer her up' . . . 'How utterly incapable the Goat is of taking any care of herself'), as a danger-zone for emotional scenes and treacherous gossip, and, at times, as a source of 'bitterness'.[32] To her sister she made uneasy jokes about how her correspondence with Clive excluded Vanessa ('Dont forget to keep my husbands letters for me to see or are they too private?'), and how inferior the two of them made her feel: 'I feel painfully incompetent to write letters . . . as I see the growing strength of the exquisite literary critical atmosphere distilled by you and Clive.'[33]

But this edgy three-way *liaison* did not distance the sisters – rather the reverse. Their feelings towards each other became more explicit, as well as less trusting. Virginia's courtship of Vanessa through Clive freed her to make more direct demands in her own letters to Vanessa: 'Shall you kiss me tomorrow? Yes, Yes, Yes. Ah, I cannot bear being without you.'[34] The tone was reciprocated:

I read your letters over and decided with Clive that when they are published without their answers, people will certainly think that we had a most amorous intercourse. They read more like love-letters than anything else . . . I like love-letters – The more passion you put in the better, Billy – Soon you will know just how to suit my taste in letters – I am greedy for compliments and passion.[35]

The relationship, at this time, was dominated – and changed – by their discussion of how to write to each other. Vanessa would write telling Virginia what kind of letters she liked (ones with lots of flattery and affection, 'but you may write a good deal about your work too – a good deal more than you do').[36] Virginia, in response, made her letters far more emotional than their conversations: 'Writing seems to me a queer thing. It does make a difference. I should never talk to you like this.'[37] So, while she was plunging into new freedom in conversations, and new attempts to write fiction, she was also experimenting with her letters:

The truth is we are too intimate for letter writing; style dissolves as though in a furnace; all the blood and bones come through; now, to write well there should be a perfect balance; and I believe . . . that if I ever find a form that does suit you, I shall produce some of my finest work. As it is, I am either too formal, or too feverish. There, Mistress![38]

With Clive, on the other hand, intimacy *was* 'style'. 'Why do I always feel self-conscious when I write to you?' she wrote to him.[39] He put her on her mettle, as she came under the influence of his vigorously choosy attitudes to literature, art, behaviour and aesthetics. His prejudices did not bring out the best in her:

I would like, just for once, to strip her [Miss Sheepshanks, whose 'stout calves' he is deriding] naked and put her into plaid worsted stocking and broad yellow garters . . . A woman without physical charm or great charm of expression is at a terrible disadvantage, a woman without charm of mind is at best a brood-mare.[40]

Later, she would distance herself from Clive Bell's ideas of 'civilization', and would fear his satire – he was always the person who could most embarrass her about her clothes and her looks. But at this time she admired and learnt from his taste and enthusiasms. These centred on French painting and eighteenth-century French and English literature, and in all these areas Clive encouraged interest and imitation.

In 1909 the friends devised a short-lived and risky letter-game, assuming imaginary names and characters to make an epistolary novel. Virginia wrote to Clive as 'Eleanor Hadyng' writing to 'James Philips', with Vanessa as 'Clarissa', Lytton as 'Vane Hatherly', Saxon as 'Mr Ilchester', and so on. Their disguises allowed for personal attacks (Vane Hatherly could tell Eleanor Hadyng that he suspected a love-affair between her and James Philips, Clarissa could complain that she only ever found out how Eleanor was through James).[41] Under the guise of eighteenth-century pastiche, Virginia could voice some of the self-disgust and vindictiveness which periodically overcame her, as in this account of a dinner-party at Bruce Richmond's:

> We were a dreadful set of harpies; Middle aged writers of mild distinction are singularly unpleasant to my taste. They remind me of those bald-necked vultures at the zoo, with their drooping blood-shot eyes, who are always on the look out for a lump of raw meat.[42]

Perhaps all this came too near the bone; the letter-game was quickly discontinued. But in 1911, the book they were all talking about was, appropriately, *Les Liaisons Dangereuses*, which Virginia read 'with great delight'.[43] And the pleasure they took – in part under Clive's influence – in 'style' as a weapon and a game also informed their play-reading society, which Clive started in December 1907 and which ran until the war.

They began with Vanbrugh's ruthlessly amoral and sexy play, *The Relapse*, with Virginia reading the unscrupulous Berinthia and the gullible Miss Hoyden, and Lytton outstanding as Foppington. Then Jonson's *Every Man out of His Humour*, with everyone taking at least four parts (Saxon noted 'a really admirable performance by myself as the Third Rustic'). Virginia played Dalila in Milton's *Samson Agonistes* and the Lady and Sabrina in his *Comus* (the song summoning 'Sabrina fair' would haunt her, and she put it into *The Voyage Out*). In February 1908, with Vanessa absent for Julian's birth, Virginia was the feminist heroine Rebecca West in Ibsen's *Rosmersholm* (Saxon criticised her lack of 'concentrated nervous force', but acknowledged that this was hard to do). She was praised, though, for tackling the rhyming couplets of Dryden's *Aurangzebe*. In the spring (when Clive and Virginia's flirtation was in full swing) they were reading Swinburne's *Atalanta in Calydon* (Vanessa read the virgin huntress Atalanta, Virginia the hero's mother Althea: Clive, who had taken over the minutes, praised the 'freedom and beauty' of her performance). They read two Congreves, *The Double Dealer* (Virginia was Lady Froth and Lady Plyant, Vanessa was the passionate Lady Touchwood and her rival in love, Cynthia, for Clive's Mellefont), and *Love for Love*. Here Virginia and Clive played the obstacle-ridden lovers Angelica and Valentine – a name she used in *Melymbrosia* – while Vanessa played the character-parts of the Nurse, Jenny, and Mrs Frail, and Lytton, in an inspired piece of casting, played Tattle. In the autumn of 1908 they resumed after a break with Dryden's tragi-comedy *Marriage à la Mode* (Virginia 'whimsical' as Melanctha), *Henry IV Part I* (Adrian repeating a Cambridge success as Falstaff), *both parts* of Dryden's *The Conquest of Granada* (the minutes read: 'What the society needs is more self-control') and an evening of mixed poetry, in which Virginia read Spenser's *Epithalamium*, giving the poem (Clive noted) 'a new loveliness and an added association'. The meetings then broke off until 1914, and when they resumed, Virginia was too ill to participate.[44]

'I like to have a little scene, in which I am the leading lady', Virginia wrote to Vanessa in the summer of 1908.[45] The readings allowed her to be bold with sexual innuendoes and cynical about 'the vices and follies of humankind',[46] to show off and make people laugh. But the restoration comedies they read are as much about the need for plain speech as they are about double dealing. Her relationship with Clive, though preoccupied with 'style', also provoked thoughts about the possibilities of straight-forwardness between men and women. 'Isn't there a kind of talk' (she asked him) 'which we could all talk, without these mystic reservations?'[47]

At his instigation, in the summer of 1908 she read G.E. Moore's *Principia Ethica*, the 'bible' of Clive, Leonard, Maynard and Lytton's Cambridge generation, with some difficulty ('feeling ideas travelling to the remotest part of my brain, and setting up a feeble disturbance, hardly to be called thought')[48] but with admiration for his humaneness.

Moore's optimistic, unworldly insistence on truth and reason, his rejection of original sin and his enshrining of value in 'the contemplation of beauty, love and truth'[49] had delivered Clive Bell and his friends from the 'ugly doctrine' of Utilitarianism.[50] Moore's famous idea of intrinsic good in 'the pleasures of human intercourse and the enjoyment of beautiful objects'[51] may have provided his 'disciples' with an excuse for élitism and cultural superiority. But it also gave them a genuine, life-long, and extremely influential belief in the importance of the arts for society. Retrospectively, Clive Bell doubted if the 'Miss Stephens gave much thought to the all important distinction between "Good on the whole" and "Good as a whole".'[52] But Moore's 'high seriousness' and his 'passion for truth'[53] did make their mark on her life, in the form of a respect for argument and a view of her own about the relation of high culture and the common reader.

Clive Bell followed Moore's precepts, when Virginia showed him her writing, in sympathetically trying to analyse exactly what she had in mind. His willingness to read her was, for her, the most important feature of their relationship. He was the critical male reader (more critical than Violet or Madge or Nelly) which Thoby would have been and which Leonard was to be. By the summer of 1908 she was 'talking of her writing' to him as never before, telling him how she wanted to re-form the novel – 'capture multitudes of things at present fugitive, enclose the whole and shape infinite strange shapes'.[54] In the autumn she gave him 100 pages of *Melymbrosia* and in February showed him eleven rewritten chapters.[55] He responded attentively.

Clive's criticism was inhibiting as well as encouraging. He repudiated her 'excrescences' and her 'feverish prose' in favour of what was 'lucid' and 'harmonious'. He resisted everything that looked like feminism, laying the ground for her life-long horror of being laughed at for shrillness or anger:

> I must tell you again that I think the first part too didactic, not to say priggish . . . To draw such sharp & marked contrasts between the subtle, sensitive, tactful, gracious, delicately perceptive, & perspicacious women, & the obtuse, vulgar, blind, florid, rude, tactless, emphatic, indelicate, vain, tyrannical, stupid men, isnt only rather absurd, but rather bad art, I think.[56]

What he liked was her 'magic', her creation of 'poetic atmosphere', the same kind of chaste aetheriality for which he romanticised her:

> What is Virginia doing now, at half past three o'clock? Moulding one of those delicately tangible sentences which remind me of nothing so much as a live bird in the hand, the heart beating through tumultuously? Or does it climb upwards in ecstatic, tuneful flight; while we stand gazing and listening with empty outstretched hands?[57]

These preferences and embargoes may have been partly what made her first novel so difficult to write and so much revised. When it finally came out in 1915, his private judgement on the novel to Mary Hutchinson was denigrating:

> The first two chapters were very disappointing, costive and rather conventional – quite different from what she read me three or four years ago . . . The book's a good one, but nothing more I'm afraid. The psycology [*sic*] and observation are amazing and amazingly witty; but it's all about life and states of mind.[58]

In later years he would write with the same patronising admiration of her unreliable fantasies, her jealousies, her feminist tantrums, and her cool chaste prose, unappealing to 'the over-sexed'.[59] But for all his mockery, he was right to pride himself on having recognised her potential early on. A letter praising 'Memoirs of a Novelist' as a new departure – 'a new medium particularly suited to your genius' – is very perceptive.[60] His reward was to get one of the most candid, moving and detailed letters she ever wrote about her work, telling him what she wanted her narrative methods to be, and what she thought about feminism and fiction. The tone of the letter is deceptive. It is nervous and grateful, but it is also driven by strong convictions quite different from her current mentor's:

> I wrote it originally in a dream like state, which was at any rate, unbroken. My intention now is to write straight on, and finish the book; and then, if that day ever comes, to catch if possible the first imagination and go over the beginning again with broad touches, keeping much of the original draft, and trying to deepen the atmosphere – Giving the feel of running water, and not much else . . . I never meant to preach, and agree that like God, one shouldn't. Possibly, for psychological reasons which seem to me very interesting, a man, in the present state of the world, is not a very good judge of his sex; and a 'creation' may seem to him 'didactic' . . . The only possible reason for writing down all this, is that it represents roughly a view of one's own. My boldness terrifies me. I feel I have so few of the gifts that make novels amusing . . .
> I want to bring out a stir of live men and women, against a background. I think I am quite right to attempt it, but it is immensely difficult to do. Ah, how you encourage me! It makes all the difference.[61]

Virginia Stephen could not ask for, and would not have received, such encouragement from Lytton Strachey, though she rated his intellect much higher than Clive's. They had grown intimate since Thoby's death. Once she had got used to his silences and his physical peculiarities, his mixture of shyness, vanity and desire to be liked, she found him charming, impressive, affectionate and interesting. She would never be as intimate with him as some of his other women friends (Lytton's letters to Mary Hutchinson, for instance, are much more warmly personal than those to Virginia) and there would always be competitiveness and criticism in her feelings towards him. But from about 1908 he became one of the most important people in her life. Both, in the matter of friendship, were as tenacious as they were treacherous. This was one of several similarities between them.

He was two years older than she was, and she had known his family since childhood. She (and Leonard Woolf, whose Cambridge intimacy with Lytton was being sustained by letters while he was in Ceylon) would give vivid pictures of the huge, noisy, brilliant, peculiar household at Lancaster

Gate and (from 1907) at Belsize Park Gardens – a family life which Lytton was desperate to escape – dominated by the literary, eccentric Lady Strachey, thirty years younger than her husband Sir Richard, the distinguished Anglo-Indian administrator. Virginia would remember her first visit, in about 1903:

> Nobody paid me the least attention. Innumerable Stracheys were seated in silence round the dinner table. Sir Richard wrapped in a shawl sat in the middle. After a time James came in, laid a magazine in front of Sir Richard, who without saying anything produced a sixpenny bit and gave it him. Then Pippa said, 'What will you have, Papa? Cold beef or roast partridge?' 'Partridge', said Sir Richard. Lady Strachey threw up her hands. 'I *knew* he'd say that!' she exclaimed. 'So *I* must have cold beef!' That was the only thing that anybody said I think. All the same I thought it was a very amusing and exciting party.[62]

To observers, this larger-than-life Victorian family seemed as vigorous and comical as the Mad Hatter's tea party. But to Strachey it was the relic of an upper-class tradition 'in a very advanced state of decomposition',[63] an oppressive edifice which he would spend his life trying to get away from – and writing about. This painful allegiance to family resembled Virginia Stephen's, and she recognised within the comedy of the high-pitched Strachey manner something she compared to 'dust in the throat': an atmosphere that lacked 'magnanimity' and 'generosity', an inertia, a bitterness.[64] St John Hirst in *The Voyage Out*, her first and very detailed attempt to render Lytton Strachey as a fictional character, is frequently described as 'bitter and unhappy'. Hirst's pride in being 'one of the three most distinguished men in England', his invalidism, his inability to relax except in 'a cosy, smoky, masculine place', his envious longing for appreciation ('I want people to like me, and they don't'), the 'circles of chalk' he places between people's feet, his loathing of the English middle classes – these are repellent Stracheyan attributes. But with this she mixes something 'jaunty', in his outrageous anti-Christian Neo-Paganism and his pleasure in uncensored talk – which she herself censors in the novel. And she gives him power, too: he seems to 'have a key' to the meaning of things; and it is with his view of life that the novel ends.[65] But later fictions which draw on Strachey, like William Rodney in *Night and Day*, emphasise his weakness. Neville, in *The Waves*, 'excites pity not love', and suffers from self-disgust and a desire for 'sovereignty'. His homosexuality is both secret and vaunted, confining and tyrannical.

In life Strachey became the person she most valued for their talk. Over the years, she would pride herself on their intimacy: 'we sit alone over the fire & rattle on, so quick, so agile in our jumps & circumventions'.[66] 'Well, I can walk & talk with him by the hour.'[67] But in all this affable fluent talk she would always be aware of a little mutual 'craving for applause',[68] of 'something peevish & exacting' in him, and of a superciliousness and expression of superiority which in their early intimacy always 'galled' her.[69] She remembered in a letter to Ottoline Morrell in 1933 that she used to *rage* at Lytton.[70]

At the point when he was first getting to know her, Strachey was extremely unhappy. Having failed to enter academic or civil service careers, he was making his name as a reviewer for the *Spectator* and for Desmond MacCarthy's *New Quarterly*, struggling with long essays on Beddoes, Rousseau, Chinese poetry, and Carlyle. He was reading mostly French literature, writing love poetry, and embarking on a political novel.[71] He was often unwell, and was suffering tortures of jealousy and grief, because Duncan Grant (his object of desire since 1905) had left him for Maynard Keynes. His life was dominated by feelings of frustrated ambition. 'His few accomplishments appeared trivial when set beside his vague and limitless aspirations.'[72]

But he had a talent for finding people to look after him. He had warmed to Virginia Stephen in 1905 at a grand house party they both detested, given by mutual family friends, the Freshfields,[73] and since 1906 the Stephens had become his confidantes. He went on holiday with them, to Cornwall and Rye, and he liked going round to their houses, in spite of Clive Bell. In the early days he wrote to Duncan Grant: 'They *are* nice, and Bell, too, really, if one isnt put off by a rather thick layer of absurdity. Do I gather that you think Virginia more beautiful than Vanessa? Its difficult to say, but I suppose most people would vote for Vanessa.'[74] It was Vanessa he could most easily confide in about his 'obscene loves', but it was Virginia who became a literary confidante.

Presumably he said more to her about his ambitions than she did to him about hers. In *The Voyage Out*, St John's impact is cunningly divided between the characters of Rachel and Helen: one feels snubbed by him, the other encourages his confidences. Virginia with Lytton played both parts at once.[75] Michael Holroyd describes their relationship as one of 'eternal correctives', each bringing out 'a latent feeling of inferiority in the other'. 'He was the hare in the race for fame and she the tortoise.'[76] Certainly she was jealous of him. She read what he was reading (such as Saint-Simon's brilliant court gossip), and she wrote her essays (on Sterne, on Oliver Wendell Holmes, on the Duchess of Newcastle) with an eye to his opinion. Vanessa told Clive of a typical exchange:

Conversation with the Goat. 'I suppose your husband wont give me any criticisms on the Duchess of Newcastle?' 'Well, all I know is that he thought it very interesting.' 'Very interesting! Now what do you suppose that means?' 'Very interesting.' 'Didnt he say more than that?' 'No.' 'Did he just put it down and say that?' 'Yes.' 'Do you think he thinks my brains as good as Strachey's?' 'I dont know what he thinks of either' etc etc. Brains took up a good share of the conversation.[77]

Virginia was only half joking when she told Lytton that she found the idea of his writing fiction hard to bear:

> Why do you tantalise me with stories of your novel? I wish you would confine your genius to one department, it's too bad to have you dancing like some (oh well – I'll drop the metaphor) over all departments of literature – poetry, criticism (both scientific & humane) art – belles lettres – and now fiction. A painstaking woman who wishes to treat of life as she finds it, and to give voice to some of the perplexities of her sex, in plain English, has no chance at all.[78]

There is a plain and heartfelt message here. She *is* painstaking, and she *is* writing about 'the perplexities of her sex': in *The Voyage Out*, St John Hirst is the target for Rachel's most impassioned complaints about women's lives. But the letter also falls in with Strachey's version of her, part of the play of their correspondence. 'Brilliant letters we wrote each other once' (she recalls ten years later) 'partly for the sake of being brilliant, & we were getting to know each other then, & there was a thrill about it (I speak of my own feelings).' They re-invented each other: Strachey turns her into 'a woman of sound and solid common sense', she imagines him as 'an oriental Potentate' or 'a Venetian prince, in sky blue tights'.[79] They exchanged 'adventures': his would be meeting a divine pink-cheeked blond undergraduate called Rupert Brooke, hers would be having a 2-shilling dinner at the Friday Club or encountering 'mild Bohemian society' in Paris. The camp, confiding tone she found so appealing in him comes through clearly in his letters:

> I envy you, talking at Gordon Square. If I could have my way, I should go out to dinner every night, and then to a party or an opera, and then I should have a champagne supper, and then I should go to bed in some wonderful person's arms. Wouldn't you? When one reflects upon one's pallid actual existence one shudders. But I suppose there are always the triumphs of Art.[80]

Part of the pleasure they took in each other was the pleasure of 'tattle' (or what has been called 'tit-for-tattle').[81] Under the current influences of Laclos, Congreve and Saint-Simon, they turned their circle into a court and excited each other with court gossip. They had different motives. For Lytton Strachey, gossip was a lived version of his writing: his minor genius and major influence as a biographer was to bring 'lives' to life with the quality of inspired chatter. For Virginia Stephen, gossip was a form of competition and showing-off, a disguise for her deeper interests.

Competitive scandal became their form of love-making. In her later, sadder version of Strachey, as Neville in *The Waves*, she gives a brilliantly generalised model of gossip and explains its allure, as a safely dangerous form of mutual recognition and reassurance:

> Outside lines twist and intersect, but round us, wrapping us about. Here we are centred. Here we can be silent, or speak without raising our voices. Did you notice that and then that? we say. He said that, meaning . . . She hesitated, and I believe suspected. Anyhow, I heard voices, a sob on the stair late at night. It is the end of their relationship. Thus we spin round us infinitely fine filaments and construct a system.[82]

But if they are spiders constructing a web, they are also flies caught in it. By the end of 1908, Virginia and Lytton themselves were the object of speculation. Virginia to Clive, of Lytton: 'You will be glad to hear that I am not in love with him, nor is there any sign that he is in love with me.' Vanessa to Clive, of Virginia: 'I think that she will most likely have married Lytton in less than 2 years, or at any rate be practically engaged to him.' Lytton to Leonard Woolf: 'Dont be surprised if you hear one day – I dont know that you ever will – that Ive married Virginia!'[83]

Their Proposal Scene is often read as a comic interlude, a 'ludicrous'[84] aberration on both their parts. Since she was keeping no diary at the time, it is Lytton's version which has dominated, as given – significantly – to Leonard Woolf. In the very act of asking to marry her, on 17 February 1909, he realised that 'it would be death if she accepted me'. He was horrified at the misunderstanding, terrified that she might kiss him, ashamed of the 'dreadful hash' he was making, anxious that she might be in love with him and filled with admiration at her 'supremacy'. By the end of the conversation he had managed to get out of it. That night, she always remembered, she had to go out to a dull dinner party at the editor of the *Cornhill's* house.[85] The next day they had a mutual 'eclaircissement': 'She declared that she was not in love with me, and I observed finally that I would not marry her. So things have simply reverted.'[86]

'Reverted' makes a shadowy echo of 'inverted' or 'perverted', words used at the time to diagnose homosexuality. Though Lytton's immediate motives were a desperate bid against family pressures and unhappiness in love, there may (as Holroyd suggests) have been a deeper, self-disgusted attempt to 'renounce' his homosexuality. Her motives, too, have been negatively interpreted by both their biographers: Holroyd suggests an attempt to escape from the shadow of her dead father, Quentin Bell a weariness with spinsterhood and a 'sexual coward's' hope of refuge.[87] She may, more positively, have imagined a famous *salon*, a court centre, a *marriage blanc* whose excitements came from talk and literary success. And the part she envisaged, of confidante and intimate partner to a brilliant homosexual artist, was not so unimaginable. It was to be played by a number of women she knew well, among them Dora Carrington – and Vanessa.

Her reasoning was explained under the thin disguise of a review, written a few weeks later, of the love letters of the Carlyles. Since Lytton was reviewing the same book in the *Spectator* at the same time,[88] the essay can plausibly be read as a continuation of their conversation about marriage. The Carlyles' intellectual relationship in the period of their courtship is eloquently described: 'It was his intellect that she admired, and it was her intellect that she would have him admire . . . He took her genius very seriously, and did his best to draw up a programme for the cultivation of it.' But their meeting of minds did not look like a good basis for an ordinary 'union'. 'They were both people of extraordinary capacity, and it seemed again and again, as the process of development and revelation went on, that it was not tending to marriage.' And the marriage was, as it turned out, a tragedy. The essay concludes: 'How shall we, when "ink-words" are all that we have, attempt to make them explain the relationship between two such people?'[89]

The same question applies to Virginia Stephen and Lytton Strachey. But the essay explains, as clearly as 'ink-words' can, her thoughts about this relationship. She realised, then and later, that though this was one of her life's vital friendships (and it was to both their credits that the friendship did successfully 'revert') the marriage would have been a disaster for her. 'If I'd married him [Lytton], I caught myself thinking, I should have found him querulous. He would have laid too many ties on one, & repined a little if one had broken free.'[90] 'Had I married Lytton I should never have written anything . . . He checks & inhibits in the most curious way.'[91] (Those 'checks' are reminiscent of her criticisms of Leslie; and shortly after the proposal she begins to call Lytton, in jest, 'dearest Papa'.) But though she knew she had been right to back off, the experience was distressing, and forced her to re-examine her own resources. She wrote in 1923:

Years & years ago, after the Lytton affair, I said to myself . . . never
pretend that the things you haven't got are not worth having; good advice
I think. At least it often comes back to me. Never pretend that children,
for instance, can be replaced by other things . . . One must . . . like things
for themselves: or rather, rid them of their bearing upon one's personal
life.[92]

Reconciling herself stoically to a single life, she was unaware what the
proposal had put in motion. Lytton's letters to Leonard Woolf in Ceylon,
about Virginia's availability and desire to marry, played on the exile's
imagination. He hardly knew Virginia Stephen, but the *idea* of her
fascinated him. Lytton's description of his proposal was written *in reply to*
Leonard's own fantasy of marriage to her as 'the only way to happiness'.[93]
From then on until Leonard's return from Ceylon in 1911, Lytton eagerly
encouraged the idea. A few months after his own proposal he wrote an
account of Virginia to Leonard which was a departure from his type-casting
of her as chaste, sensible ice-maiden. Instead he made her sound like the
heroine of one of their restoration comedies – Angelica, perhaps, in *Love for
Love*. This is not the usual version of Virginia Stephen in her late twenties,
but it catches something powerful in her – and something sensual, too.

Your destiny is clearly marked out for you, but will you allow it to work?
You must marry Virginia. She's sitting waiting for you, is there any
objection? She's the only woman in the world with sufficient brains; it's a
miracle that she should exist; but if you're not careful you'll lose the
opportunity. At any moment she might go off with heaven know who –
Duncan? Quite possible. She's young, wild, inquisitive, discontented,
and longing to be in love.[94]

FIFTEEN

'Bloomsbury'

In Virginia Woolf's first three novels (published between the ages of thirty and forty, but all concerned with people in their twenties) the metaphor of a new reading is used for a new way of life. Rachel is taught by Helen that she can 'be a person on her own account' in spite of the pages of 'statesmen and soldiers' whose patriarchal biographies fill the pages of *Who's Who*.[1] Katharine Hilbery imagines the book of traditional wisdom laid open on the laps of mothers, uncles and aunts, full of precepts for women's lives and marriage, and is aware that 'the traditional answer would be of no use to her individually'.[2] She tries to imagine instead another kind of writing for another kind of life – perhaps an abstract set of mathematical formulations, or a disc with rays around it. Jacob, more confidently, defines himself ('I am what I am, and intend to be it')[3] through reading 'Homer, Shakespeare, the Elizabethans', and through resisting 'Wells and Shaw and the serious sixpenny weeklies'. 'Detest your own age. Build a better one', he tells himself. But the war cuts short Jacob's passionate literary optimism.

The changing shapes of the novels these characters are in illustrate the new readings they want to make for their lives. What new work can be done, what kinds of lives and marriages and thoughts are now possible for women, and for the young? What connections are there between conventions in behaviour and conventions in art?

But these urgent questions were not hers alone. They were also the questions of her time, her class, her friends and family, her 'group'. What she does with her life, how and what she writes, has to be read as a feature of the dramatic shifts in English cultural history between the 1880s and the 1930s. And her 'group' has come to stand, for good or ill, as a particularly vivid and influential embodiment of some of those shifts.

The three words 'the Bloomsbury group' have been so much used as to have become almost unusable – and, to some, almost unbearable. Those who 'belonged' to it said that it was a figment, or that it was too diverse to be categorisable, or that by the time it came to be named it had ceased to exist.[4] The origins of the term, as applied to a number of like-minded friends living in a particular area of London and involved mainly with the arts and politics, are disputed.[5] It seems to have started being used, as a joke, in 1910.[6] And it was in 1910, at the height of pre-war cultural activity and excitement, that Virginia Woolf retrospectively identified the crucial break between the 'Edwardians' and the 'Georgians', the point when 'human character changed.'[7]

She herself was referring to the 'group' by 1914, when she told her friend Ka Cox ironically that the 'up to date' north country people she was meeting in Northumberland made 'the Bloomsbury group' seem 'stunted in the chrysalis' by comparison.[8] But who was 'Bloomsbury'? No one was elected (as the Apostles were); there was no manifesto (as for the Vorticists or the Imagists); there was no subscription (as for the Labour Party). Identifications of the 'membership' of the circle have varied considerably, depending on who draws up the lists, and when. Leonard Woolf, in the 1960s, listed 'Old Bloomsbury' as Vanessa and Clive Bell, Virginia and Leonard Woolf, Adrian and Karin Stephen, Lytton Strachey, Maynard Keynes, Duncan Grant, Morgan Forster, Saxon Sydney-Turner, Roger Fry, Desmond and Molly MacCarthy, with Julian, Quentin and Angelica Bell, and David Garnett as later additions.[9] Other lists might include Ottoline Morrell, or Dora Carrington, or James and Alix Strachey.[10] And then there were writers who were at some time close friends of Virginia Woolf, but who were distinctly not 'Bloomsbury': T.S. Eliot, Katherine Mansfield, Hugh Walpole.

Even if 'membership' was arguable, there was such a thing as a Bloomsbury product: publications, art-works, exhibitions, interior decorations, a publishing house, a design-workshop. And Bloomsbury persisted as an organism for over thirty or forty years in the form of little overlapping groups and clubs which, from the time of the Thursday Evenings and the Friday Club, sprang up for the purposes of discussions or play-readings or exhibitions or domestic entertainment.[11] During the war, Bloomsbury had a meeting-place in the 1917 Club in Gerrard Street, Soho, along with 'every kind of progressive: labour politicians, pacifists and communists, vegetarians, freelovers and theosophists'.[12] Clive Bell planned in 1918 to take over *The Egoist* and make it 'a Bloomsbury review';[13] in the 1920s Molly MacCarthy founded the Memoir Club; in 1926 there was an idea for a 'Bloomsbury Bar'; for a few weeks in 1928 Vanessa and Virginia reconvened 'at homes' in the form of 'a most extraordinary series of entertainments on the line of the old Thursday evenings',[14] and, as late as 1939, there was a proposal for a 'Bloomsbury Book Club'.[15]

These clubs and meetings were not activist, like the political organisations to which many of Bloomsbury's members also belonged. When Virginia started to make fictional versions of her 'group', she was satirical and defensive about its prioritising of aesthetics. Evelyn, the breathlessly assertive girl in *The Voyage Out* who presents Rachel Vinrace with an incoherent Utopian agenda, is keen that her 'club' should be more political:

> She sat up, and began to explain with animation. 'I belong to a club in London. It meets every Saturday, so it's called the Saturday Club. We're supposed to talk about art, but I'm sick of talking about art – what's the good of it? With all kinds of real things going on round one? It isn't as if they'd got anything to say about art, either. So what I'm going to tell 'em is that we've talked enough about art, and we'd better talk about life for a change. Questions that really matter to people's lives, the White Slave Traffic, Women's Suffrage, the Insurance Bill, and so on. And when we've made up our mind what we want to do we could form ourselves into a society for doing it . . . My idea is that men and women ought to join in these matters.'[16]

Rachel 'doesn't much believe' in any of this. But silly Evelyn's irritation with her group's ineffectuality recurs in the comical presentation of a literary discussion club in *Night and Day*.

> The room very soon contained between twenty and thirty people, who found seats for the most part upon the floor, occupying the mattresses, and hunching themselves together into triangular shapes. They were all young and some of them seemed to make a protest by their hair and dress, and something sombre and truculent in the expression of their faces, against the more normal type . . . [William Rodney gives a high-pitched, badly-delivered, earnest and somewhat absurd talk to the group on 'the Elizabethan use of metaphor in poetry'.] Through his manner and his confusion of language there had emerged some passion of feeling which, as he spoke, formed in the majority of the audience a little picture or an idea which each now was eager to give expression to. Most of the people there proposed to spend their lives in the practice either of writing or painting, and merely by looking at them it could be seen that . . . they were seeing something done . . . to a possession which they thought to be their own. One person after another rose, and, as with an ill-balanced axe, attempted to hew out his conception of art a little more clearly, and sat down with the feeling that, for some reason which he could not grasp, his strokes had gone awry.[17]

This group has very little impact on the inner life of the novel's heroine. And it's treated with the affectionate dismissiveness which suggests a look back at youthful behaviour.

In the war years Virginia Woolf often said to her friends that Bloomsbury had 'vanished',[18] or described it as something which had begun to have a powerful influence on 'the younger generation'.[19] After the war she spoke of it, frequently, as dead or dying or done with; and by the 1930s the phrase had become to her a journalistic irritation, a term of abuse which made her see red, or a 'long since dead phantom'.[20] 'Old Bloomsbury', written in the early 1920s and looking back on the years 1904 to 1914, is full of such phrases as 'the first chapter [of Old Bloomsbury] came to an end', 'Those [Thursday evenings] were a thing of the past'.[21]

This post-war tone was typical of the way Bloomsbury memorialised itself. As a result, it gives off an oddly contradictory flavour, at once old and new, closed and open, free and choosy, experimental and in love with the past.

The Memoir Club's impulse to recover its own past was nothing new. Thoby's Gordon Square Thursday evenings had consoled his friends for the loss of their Cambridge arcadia. When the play-reading society reconvened in October 1914 (without Virginia), after a break of several years, Clive Bell wrote in the minutes:

> I do not know what relationship, if any, this society stands to that older society which was last heard of on January 15 1909. Perhaps the younger members will prefer to regard it as a new formation and the older as a reformation. Anyway, in these days of storm and darkness, it seemed right that at the shrine of civilization – in Bloomsbury, I mean – the lamp should be tended assiduously. It has been decided, therefore, to read plays, ancient or modern, English or foreign, tragic, comic, or simply bawdy, at 46 Gordon Square, on Thursday evenings, at nine of the clock.[22]

Clive Bell's opposition of 'civilization' to the forces of darkness was an extremely common trope at the start of the war.[23] For him, it was a typical group joke, half-absurd (a group of old friends meeting to read Restoration Comedies was not much of a war effort) and half-serious (works of art and intellectual activity seemed to matter more, not less, in wartime.) But the association has retrospectively, and damagingly, come to dominate the image of 'Bloomsbury'.

From the moment, around 1910, that it began to be perceived as a clique, it inevitably gained its enemies and detractors. After the war, when the Gordon Square friends began to be famous, the execration increased, and the caricature of an idle, snobbish and self-congratulatory rentier class promoting its own brand of high culture began to take shape.

Some of these attacks were largely personal, like Rupert Brooke's violent hostility, in 1911, to the 'rotten atmosphere' in the Stracheys' 'treacherous & wicked' circle.[24] D.H. Lawrence's notorious revulsion from the 'principle of evil', like 'some insidious disease', which he perceived in 1915 in Keynes's circle at Cambridge ('black beetles', 'little swarming selves'), and his later attack on the evangelists of 'significant form' as a masturbatory 'arch-elect' are powerful expressions of Lawrence's own fears of homosexuality, and his need to construct targets against which to work out his own aesthetics.[25]

Like Lawrence's caricature of Ottoline Morrell in *Women in Love*,[26] other fictional versions of Bloomsbury came from those who felt themselves excluded or condescended to. Some of these versions, like Leonard Woolf's *The Wise Virgins* or Marjorie Strachey's *The Counterfeits*, came from within the group. Flora Mayor's *The Rector's Daughter*, with a lively satire on the Friday Club, was published by Leonard and Virginia at the Hogarth Press in 1924. The daughter of a country rector, Mary Jocelyn, spends an evening at a friend's fashionable London flat.

> In the flat a new world was opened to Mary, both of the eye and mind. The rooms were furnished with every new convenience. Nothing, even the books, dated back farther than four or five years. 'Books are like sucked oranges when the vogue is over,' said Miss Kenrick. Besides new books there were many magazines, pamphlets, and organs of small societies. There were, too, various thin volumes with thick pages. They contained poems, essays, short stories that the set was constantly publishing and presenting to itself.
>
> The walls were orange; the paint royal blue. There were foreign posters . . . Cubist studies . . . large cushions on the floor . . . covered in Cubist chintzes . . . The windows were dull with London grime . . . Brynhilda, Dermott, and the rest belonged to the same set. Its members were almost all between twenty and thirty. They came from Hammersmith, Hampstead, Chelsea, Bloomsbury and St John's Wood. Most of them had shaken off their families, and united in light elastic unions with friends . . . The 'set' came in. They hardly greeted one another, and Mary noticed that they made no distinction in their manner to the other sex. But were the sexes really so indifferent to one another? Did they perhaps drawl, smoke languorously, loll and lounge among the cushions, lie in long heaps about the floor, appear too silly to finish their sentences, laugh and ejaculate 'Isn't it?' at random more than they might have done if there had not been another sex present?[27]

Cigarettes are hurled into the fireplace, cooling coffee is passed round, a thin girl called Priscilla Leach discusses her sexual 'adventures', and the talk turns to London. The scene suggests some of the ingredients (the addiction to the new, the modern free liaisons, the precious prose, the love of the metropolis, the exclusion of outsiders) which repeatedly feature in fictional caricatures of the group.

Bloomsbury's public controversies (in the tradition of British cultural debate) were always personalised. When the eminent Slade professor Henry Tonks wanted to deride the Post-Impressionist movement, he circulated a cartoon called 'The Unknown God', with Roger Fry as a bug-eyed wild-eyed prophet on a lecture platform, and a fat little Clive Bell as acolyte, uttering little bubbles of 'Cezannah'.[28] When, many years later, Osbert Sitwell wanted to satirise the 'dark flower' of the 'Bloomsbury junta' in its 1914–18 heyday, he concentrated on personal mannerisms – the favourite phrases '("ex-quisitely civilized", and "How *simply too* extraordinary!")', the incredulous, weirdly emphasised Strachey voice. 'The adoption by an individual of the correct tones was equivalent, I apprehend, to an outward sign of conversion, like giving the Hitler salute or wearing a green turban.'[29] These satires show that 'Bloomsbury' was perceived not just as a set of mannerisms and preferences, but as a coterie conspiracy. This view was most strongly put about by figures who had their own rival agendas for modern culture, like Wyndham Lewis.[30]

Virginia could be as satirical of 'Bloomsbury' as any of its detractors; but she could also be defensive and partisan about the 'group'. She did not entirely endorse the way it used the word 'civilization'. On 12 August 1914, she reported to Ka Cox (in the same letter in which she used the phrase 'the Bloomsbury group') on the talk in London about the outbreak of the war.

> Roger, of course, had private information from the Admiralty . . . and Clive was having tea with Ottoline, and they talked and talked, and said it was the end of civilization, and the rest of our lives was worthless.[31]

The tone is sceptical; and when she looks back at this moment, in her biography of Roger Fry, written during the next war, she admires but does not identify herself with those feelings:

> He had come to believe [in August 1914] that a more civilized period in human life was beginning; now that hope seemed ended . . . 'We were just beginning to be a little civilized and now it's all to begin over again.' . . . [During the war years] it was no longer possible to believe that the world generally was becoming more civilized . . . But civilization, art, personal relationships, though they might be damaged, were not to be destroyed by any war, unless indeed one gave up one's belief in them. And that was impossible. He fought his old battles on their behalf . . .[32]

Yet in 1914 and 1915 she too had felt something of this. She entirely concurred, for instance, with 'Bloomsbury's loathing of jingoism. After the playing of the National Anthem at the Queen's Hall in January 1915, she wrote 'I think patriotism is a base emotion'.[33] And a year later (when she was just beginning to recover from her catastrophic breakdown) she burst out vindictively in a letter to Duncan Grant:

> Shall you escape conscription? The revelation of what our compatriots feel about life is very distressing. One might have thought in peace time that they were harmless, if stupid: but now that they have been roused they seem full of the most violent and filthy passions.[34]

After the war her ambivalence about Bloomsbury and civilisation continued. Although in the 1920s she mocked Clive Bell's identification of 'civilization' with 'a lunch party at Gordon Square',[35] she too was capable of using Bloomsbury as a standard against barbarism. In 1936 she wrote to Julian Bell, wishing that Roger Fry was still alive: 'I sometimes feel that old Bloomsbury though fast dying, is still our bulwark against the tawny flood.'[36]

Our bulwark. Sometimes she spoke with complete conviction about 'our set', sometimes she wanted to escape it. In 1920: 'I see myself now taking my own line apart from theirs . . . One of these days I shan't know Clive if I meet him. I want to know all sorts of other people – retaining only Nessa & Duncan, I think.'[37] Yet she could not escape her involvement in a dense, firmly-rooted group:

> All our Bloomsbury relationships flourish, grow in lustiness. Suppose our set to survive another 20 years, I tremble to think how thickly knit & grown together it will be.[38]

She repeatedly identified with 'our set' in distinction to other sets: Kensington, Mayfair, Chiswick; Rebecca West's set, David Cecil's set. (As in: 'So different from B'y. Theres more body to us.')[39] She defended 'Bloomsbury' all her adult life, whether as individuals, as an achievement in living, or most of all, as a form of friendship:

> if six people, with no special start except what their wits give them, can so dominate, there must be some reason in it . . . Where they seem to me to triumph is in having worked out a view of life which was not by any means corrupt or sinister or merely intellectual; rather ascetic and austere indeed; which still holds, and keeps them dining together, and staying together, after 20 years; and no amount of quarrelling or success, or

failure has altered this. Now I do think this rather creditable. But tell me, who *is* Bloomsbury in your mind?[40]

A young man the other day sent me a book in which he perpetually used 'Bloomsbury' as a convenient hold all for everything silly, cheap, indecent, conceited and so on. Upon which I wrote to him: All the people I most respect and admire have been what you call 'Bloomsbury'. Thus, though you have every right to despise and dislike them, you cant expect me to agree . . . Never come and see me, who live in Bloomsbury, again.[41]

But though she lived in Bloomsbury, she also defined herself in opposition to it. The model for this dual movement – between a struggle for self-definition and a need to belong – is family life. Bloomsbury was rooted in family, and much of its art (painting, decoration, biography, fiction) was about the family. So while as a group it was instrumental in changing the nature of English family life, it also stayed thickly knit and grown together like the family trees it had sprung from. *The Waves*, Virginia Woolf's novel of friendships, her Bloomsbury novel – six people bound together all their lives in a loose affiliation – is the only one of her novels which is not ostensibly concerned with family life or inheritance. Yet it has a family feeling. At the start it isn't clear whether the children in the novel are siblings or companions. As they grow old, their friendship is hostile, rivalrous, repetitive, intimate through past ties, withdrawn yet knowing, in the manner of family relationships.

Almost all the narrative of *The Waves* is speech; all the characters exist through what they say. However, they don't seem to be speaking to each other, but to themselves. The novel is full of references to their conversations, but what we read are their monologues. This, more than anything, suggests Virginia Woolf's paradoxical relationship with the Bloomsbury group. When she describes Bloomsbury, she very often refers to conversation. It is for their intimate talk that she most prizes her relationship with Lytton; it is for his endless amusing anecdotes that she most values Desmond; it is for his social garrulity that she tolerates Clive. Bloomsbury conversations were often compared to 'orchestral concerts', with Virginia Woolf as conductor.[42]

The pleasure and excitement of talk gets into her own writing. Some of her best non-fiction, like *A Room of One's Own*, or the essay on Sickert, takes the form or has the air of conversation. This is what 'Bloomsbury' meant to her. But in all her work, and most of all in *The Waves*, there is also the sense of people alone, talking to themselves, unable to say what they mean or speaking something quite different from what is in their minds. There is loneliness in the diaries, those life-long conversations between the writer and her future self, or an imaginary other. Those conversations are really monologues, like the one at the end of *The Waves*. And with that lonely monologue Bloomsbury had nothing to do.

In 1910 'the Bloomsbury Group' had not yet been mythologised, and visitors would encounter in Gordon or Fitzroy Square a less rarefied conversation than later versions suggest. Ray Costelloe, for instance, who came to know the Stephens through Marjorie Strachey, found her first Bloomsbury party in 1909 (with Virginia, Adrian, Vanessa, and Marjorie's cousin Duncan Grant) less alarming than she expected.

> We sat round the fire in anything but gloomy silence . . . in fact we talked continuously of diseases and shipwrecks and other such frivolous topics. Then we somehow fell to making noises at the dog, and this awe-inspiring company might have been seen leaping from chair to chair uttering wild growls and shrieks of laughter . . . I like Virginia exceedingly . . . She was very friendly and told me about the way she lives and the people she meets and the things that seem important. It is a very fascinating, queer, self-absorbed, fantastic set of people. But they are very interesting, and she is also nice.[43]

Though 'self-absorbed', Virginia Stephen was never closed off from new encounters. Her life in these pre-war years was circumscribed by her vulnerable mental states, which kept pace with the long rewriting of *The Voyage Out*. And the relationships which pressed in on her were those of her family and her 'set'. But she was curious about, and responsive ('also nice') to people. She liked to broach intimacy, to measure herself against others, to find out how far they might go in 'sympathy' (her key to friendship).[44] Every so often she itemised and assessed the 'present condition' of her friendships,[45] as though they were her possessions – some more cherished than others.

Between 1909 and 1911 some of the figures in her landscape came into closer focus. Duncan Grant began to wander into her life, not just as Lytton's obsession or Maynard's lover but as a vague, charming, bohemian presence in his own right, 'a queer faun-like figure, hitching his clothes up, blinking his eyes, stumbling oddly over the long words in his sentences'.[46] All the Stephens would fall in love with him, as he gently infiltrated himself into the centre of their lives. Desmond and Molly MacCarthy also moved into Virginia's London orbit (though to Chelsea, not to Bloomsbury). Desmond, engaging, impecunious, dishevelled – the Mr Micawber of the Bloomsbury group – became Roger Fry's assistant on the first Post-Impressionist exhibition, and Molly (quieter, less self-assured than

Desmond, but witty, unpredictable and attractive) came to know Virginia better in the hot summer of 1910, at Studland: 'Virginia is delightful and interesting; – always rather alarming, but that is fascinating, and she has *so* much more in her than most girls – she is most refreshing . . . we have heaps of conversation. I abuse the mutual admiration of souls of the young Cambridge and she rather agrees.'[47] Molly's growing deafness, and her difficult marriage to the unreliable and unfaithful MacCarthy, would darken her later life; Virginia's letters to her would always have a particular kind of easy tenderness.

From 1909 Maynard Keynes was living with Duncan Grant at 21 Fitzroy Square. By 1911, when Virginia and Adrian left Fitzroy Square for a larger house in Brunswick Square, she knew Maynard well enough to invite him to be one of their lodgers. But they were never close friends; he did not correspond with her as he did (intimately and scurrilously) with Vanessa. Virginia found him 'very truculent', 'very formidable'.[48] Her idea of him was coloured, initially, by Lytton's rivalry with him over Duncan. There was a tinge of anti-Semitism in Keynes's personal attitude to Leonard (though they got on well enough professionally). And Virginia was condescending to his wife, Lydia Lopokova. She would call him sceptical, inhuman, 'sensual, brutal, unimaginative', 'very thick & opulent'.[49] He could make her feel 'flittery & stupid'.[50] His huge success, his wealth (he came to earn the equivalent today of about £80,000 a year for his writing), his brilliance and his worldliness, provoked a mixture of awe, and distaste at something she found coarse and pugnacious. When she started a comic sketch of him, for private distribution, in 1933, as the confidant of governments ('famous in New York, famous on Wall Street, famous in Chicago, famous in Boston'), patron of the arts and pig-breeder, she makes him sound a little bit like one of his own prize pigs.[51] But he was her most intelligent male friend, 'the greatest man she was ever to know intimately',[52] and she respected his judgements. She appreciated his 'remarkable mind', 'fertile', 'adroit', 'full of that queer imaginative ardour about history, humanity', 'immensely amused too by little scenes', with a quality of simplicity and 'innocency'.[53]

She liked to find out people's essential qualities, and, for all her malice and exaggerations, she was good at it. The challenge was particularly intriguing when the person was elusive, like Morgan Forster, whom she also began to get to know in 1910. She had reviewed *A Room with a View* respectfully but lightly in 1908,[54] and she would have read *Howards End* when it came out in October of 1910.[55] In December 1910 she heard Forster talk at the Friday Club on 'the feminine note in literature', maintaining that women in women's novels were always preoccupied with being worthy of another character. She praised him for it.[56] They grew a little closer; he was always 'flitting' through Bloomsbury on his way to catch the last train to Weybridge (where he lived with his mother, until he rented a flat in Brunswick Square in 1925). They met often at the 1917 Club. He liked Leonard Woolf and relied on him for advice. And from 1915 onwards, his reviews of Virginia Woolf's work were perceptive and (apart from his reaction to *Night and Day*) enthusiastic. His opinions were extremely important to her. It was a peculiarity of their relationship that she stood in awe of his judgement while creating a picture of a timorous and hesitant character. He was 'a pale blue butterfly', 'attenuated', 'as timid as a mouse', 'erratic, irregular'.[57] The sketch she made of him in 1919 was typical:

> Morgan is easily drowned . . . He is an unworldly, transparent character, whimsical & detached, caring very little I should think what people say, & with a clear idea of what he wishes. I dont think he wishes to shine in intellectual society; certainly not in fashionable. He is fantastic & very sensitive; an attractive character to me, though from his very qualities it takes as long to know him as it used to take to put one's gallipot over a humming bird moth. More truly, he resembles a vaguely rambling butterfly; since there is no intensity or rapidity about him. To dominate the talk would be odious to him . . . there's a lot to say to him, though I don't yet know how to say it. Its absurd at my age, & I feel very middle aged, to be as easily put out & flustered as I am.[58]

It is an affectionate, perceptive, but also hesitant portrait. His tentativeness made her tentative. Though in 1925 she told herself that he was one of the six people in the world she most minded about,[59] she always found him disconcertingly private. She was less sympathetic to his homosexuality than she was to Lytton Strachey's or Duncan Grant's. And he was wary of her: 'One waited for her to snap', he said of her.[60]

In 1927 they almost quarrelled. She wrote two essays on him, one on *Aspects of the Novel*, and one on his fiction. These pieces, written in the same year as his generous review of *To the Lighthouse*, cast a curious light on their relationship. She had no compunction about reviewing a friend (though she starts the essay on the novels with a note about her 'fear of hurting feelings' – which proved apt). It was one of the characteristics of the 'group' that they all reviewed each other constantly without much embarrassment. In both pieces, she gives a critical, even condescending analysis of Forster's method – his elusive message, his failure to connect the bricks of realism with the inner soul – which seems to incorporate something of her frustration with their relationship. 'We want to make Mr Forster stand and deliver'. 'We feel that something has failed us.' Forster was offended and hurt, and wrote to say so. 'This by return of post in haste. *I don't believe my method's wrong!*[61] At once she compared herself with him.

Here is this self-possessed, aloof man taking every word to heart, cast down to the depths, apparently, because I do not give him superlative rank . . . Had I been asked, I should have said that of all writers he would be the most indifferent & cool under criticism. And he minds a dozen times more than I do, who have the opposite reputation.[62]

The quarrel passed – they joined forces the following year to defend *The Well of Loneliness* against censorship – but he must have felt she did not value his work as highly as he did hers. His tribute to her after her death was respectful but guarded. Two of the most significant novelists of their time, belonging to the same social *milieu*, and dealing in their writings on fiction and their novels with some comparable subjects and characters, they had circled warily around each other all their lives.

Keynes and MacCarthy, Forster and Grant, belonged to the male, mostly homosexual, Cambridge-based society which dominated Virginia Stephen's life. But she wanted friendships with women. Her relationship with Vanessa was now more difficult, and Madge Vaughan and Violet were fading. There was Molly, there was (from the summer of 1910) some uncomfortable adulation from Jean Thomas, and there was soon to be a transient friendship with Ka Cox. But the most remarkable woman who came into her life in these pre-war days of 'Old Bloomsbury', Lady Ottoline Morrell, was not exactly a friend. Rather to their surprise, Virginia and Ottoline would at last, in the 1930s, become close. But they arrived at this condition – to both their credit – through oceans of gossip, bad feeling and misunderstandings.

When they expressed their rediscovered affection for each other in 1933 – 'after all', Ottoline wrote, 'our Lives have been interlaced intertwined for many years . . . haven't they'[63] – they had a suggestive exchange about friendship. Ottoline regretted that she had not had more women friends: 'homosexual men take the place of women in one's life', she said.[64] She had always found women catty, untrustworthy, and insufficiently 'impersonal' in their views on life and art. Virginia disagreed: She told Ottoline that she missed women. Had Ottoline really never met a woman she respected? For her part, Virginia said she got tired of men of genius. But perhaps this was some kink of hers, to feel that men of genius always skewed the emphasis towards matters of suppression or desire; and were always getting furious when their vanity was outraged; and then (referring to Lawrence) they would put Ottoline into their books.[65] A few days later, in another letter, she went on thinking about their different attitudes to women. She refused to accept Ottoline's proposition that Virginia was one of only a small number of women of any worth. They must have had very different experiences, Virginia was sure. She could think of a dozen women, without any difficulty, who would pass Ottoline's test of being able to think about life and art as *impersonally* as Virginia did. And some of these women (like Pernel Strachey) knew more than Virginia did about literature; or (like Janet Vaughan) more about art and science. Some of them were much more uncompromising, too. She could think of women such as Rebecca West or Rose Macaulay who had always been generous and critically fair about her writing, even if she had never praised *them*. True, Katherine Mansfield had been as sharp about Virginia as Virginia had about her. But she felt that (smoothing over her past harsh feelings) Katherine had never been catty or spiteful towards her. And their estrangement had only been because of Katherine's illness.[66]

The exchange is revealing about both Ottoline's preference for eroticised friendships with 'great men' (often homosexual), and Virginia's much greater interest in women. (When they first came to know each other, Vanessa asked, teasingly and inaccurately, whether she should treat Ottoline as a rival: 'You will have a desperate liaison with her I believe, for I rather think she shares your Sapphist tendencies and only wants a little encouragement.')[67] The difference of opinion has an underlying reproach: both Ottoline and Virginia seem to be wondering why *they* did not succeed in being friends when they were young, instead of now, in their fifties and sixties. What had prevented the friendship in their early days was Ottoline's sense that 'Bloomsbury' had turned her into a joke: Virginia herself is one of the reasons why she does not trust women.

Looking back on her behaviour through the medium of Ottoline's memoirs, Virginia defends herself. She guessed that she and her friends had often been *devilish* towards Ottoline in those days. But she now feels sure (to do herself justice) that she was aware of what a difficult and painful time Ottoline had with them all. Really no one was to blame – except for the general inadequacy of human beings and the fact that they are always bound to inflict pain on each other (and themselves) without meaning or wanting to.[68]

In 1909, Ottoline seemed to her a 'fancy-dress'[69] character, an alluring, ridiculous phenomenon. Lady Ottoline, then thirty-six, was unhappily married to Philip Morrell, a Liberal MP. She had a three-year-old daughter, Julian (the survivor of twins), and since 1907 she had been turning herself into a famous hostess for writers and artists at 44 Bedford

Square and at Peppard Cottage, near Henley. (The Garsington years began in 1915). In 1908 she was having an affair with Augustus John; by 1910 she was in love with Henry Lamb, for whom Lytton Strachey also developed a passion. The following year she had a brief, unsatisfactory liaison with Roger Fry, and her dramatic love-affair with Bertrand Russell began. During these years – while suffering from numerous illnesses – she was helping Philip Morrell fight his seat in the elections of January and November 1910, and enthusiastically helping young artists through the Modern Art Association and the Post-Impressionist exhibition.

Ottoline's appearance was legendarily idiosyncratic. She spoke in a weird, nasal, cooing, sing-song drawl. Her amazing looks were at once sexy and grotesque: she was very tall, with a huge head of copper-coloured hair, turquoise eyes and great beaky features. She wore fantastical highly-coloured clothes and hats with great style and bravado, and had pronounced tastes in interior decoration. The general effect was one of dazzling 'lustre and illusion'.

> When indeed one remembers that drawing room full of people, the pale yellows and pinks of the brocades, the Italian chairs, the Persian rugs, the embroideries, the tassels, the scent, the pomegranates, the pugs, the pot-pourri and Ottoline bearing down upon one from afar in her white shawl with the great scarlet flowers on it and sweeping one away out of the large room and the crowd into a little room with her alone, where she plied one with questions that were so intimate and so intense . . . I think my excitement may be excused.[70]

Ottoline's memory, by contrast, was of going shyly to Virginia's Thursday evenings, with all her inaudible pipe-smoking intellectual young men, and of Virginia's 'bell-like' voice leading her guests into 'the lives of any she meet, or the world of poetry'. She described her as 'a strange, lovely, furtive creature'.[71] One of their first outings together was to the fancy-dress 'Artists Revels' in the Botanical Gardens, when Virginia went as Cleopatra ('whose qualities, as I imagined them, were just those that Virginia did not possess') and Ottoline herself wore 'a very full black tafetta dress, with black lace mantilla'. It was entirely appropriate that her intimacy with 'Bloomsbury' should have begun at a masquerade, since the 'lustre and illusion' of Ottoline's performance and settings, particularly at Garsington, always had the effect of a charade or a costume party. On this occasion, however, she was disappointed with the ugly costumes and the general dinginess: 'From behind the dark trees I caught the dark sound of mocking laughter.' Was it, she imagined, from their aristocratic ancestors?

No, the sound came from Virginia Stephen and her friends. Ottoline's grand dramatics were turned by 'Bloomsbury' into low farce.[72] They mocked her for her sexual susceptibility, her intense emotions, her desire to leave her own class 'and find what she wants among artists and writers',[73] her pathetic eagerness to get a 'foot' in their lives,[74] and at the same time her inability to be an artist and stop being an aristocrat: 'try as she will she can never lay aside her coronet',[75] Virginia wrote cruelly. Yet it was her 'coronet' – her grand house, her lavish hospitality – which attracted them, and which they exploited. In the war, when she courageously and generously opened her house at Garsington to the conscientious objectors, she was wickedly satirised for her pains.

From the start Virginia was false with, and to, Ottoline. Her earliest surviving letter to her is all gush:

> Dearest Ottoline,
> What a pleasure to get your letter! It made me very happy. Thank you for writing. If you will have me for a friend, it will be a great joy for me. Shyness, I suppose, makes it difficult to say that it is delightful to know you and like you as I do. I wish I could tell you how much pleasure your letter gave me.
> Your affectionate VS.[76]

At precisely the same time she is caricaturing her in the 'letter-game' of 1909, and describing her to Violet and Madge (partly to elicit jealousy) in terms of mingled fascination, condescension and repulsion: she is like 'an Arum lily; with a thick golden bar in the middle, dropping pollen, or whatever that is which seduces the male bee'; or she has 'the head of a Medusa; but she is very simple and innocent in spite of it, and worships the arts'.[77]

Yet there were moments of sympathy between them. Virginia seems, for instance, to have listened encouragingly to Ottoline's confidences about Henry Lamb's impossible behaviour.[78] And she disliked her own duplicity. Returning from a visit to Garsington, full of spleen and loathing, she wrote: 'What puts me on edge is that I'm writing like this here, & spoke so differently to Ott . . . To sneer like this has a physical discomfort in it.'[79] But it isn't quite possible to turn Ottoline into a misunderstood tragic heroine: there *was* something ludicrous about her. Virginia's mixed feelings are reflected in a recognisable portrait of Ottoline as Mrs Flushing in *The Voyage Out*, with her imperious but nervous manner, vigorous features (pointing 'to many generations of well-trained and well-nourished ancestors behind her'), lavish and colourful wardrobe, and preference for new painters such as Augustus John: 'His pictures excite me – nothin' that's old excites me.'[80]

In the 1920s their relations edged towards mutual dislike. Virginia wanted to put Ottoline's 'despicableness' – dancing attendance on the Prime Minister, for instance – into *Mrs Dalloway*. Ottoline, meanwhile, in her diary, repeatedly characterised Virginia as cold, spiteful and inhuman, with 'such unkind eyes': 'full of mockery and contempt . . . She talked of everyone as if she was *far* above them – as if she sat on a throne and they were like creeping pigmies and savages underneath.' She called her a phantom, a mocking-bird, an Ice-Maiden, 'a child of fantasy with this cruel laughing observation of life'. 'Strange that such a lovely mind should also have such a poisonous human side.'[81] Philip Morrell's sentimental worship of Virginia, and some jealousy over Lytton's friendship, did not help.

Virginia's interest in Ottoline's memoirs created a new warmth between them, made up in part of regrets and nostalgia. In 1932, reading Ottoline's accounts of difficult visits to Fitzroy Square, Virginia was bitterly and vividly reminded of her own ghost. She remembered herself, sitting on the sofa in an atmosphere of cigarette smoke and young men's conversation. Did Ottoline know how unhappy she was then, how much she hated those evenings, how much loneliness and terror she felt? And how when Adrian finally banged shut the door on Lytton or Saxon at two or three o'clock in the morning, she used to stumble off to bed in despair? Probably not, she concluded wrily: we all go through life without knowing much about each other.[82]

Despite their different backgrounds, Virginia and Ottoline were linked through an overlapping group of friends,[83] and connected by their politics. In the war years, Ottoline's pacifism, her husband's courageous stand in the House of Commons against war-fever, her relationship with Bertrand Russell and her hospitality to the conscientious objectors, placed Ottoline, with Virginia Stephen and with Bloomsbury, on one side of a split in British life and language. This split was violently felt in 1910 (the year 'human character changed'), and it widened in the war.

SIXTEEN

Subversives

The Edwardian years polarised conservatives and dissenters.[1] On one side was the rhetoric of the Public Morality crusaders and the eugenicists, *The Times* and the *Daily Telegraph*. ('The Daily Telegraph is discussing the sanctity of marriage', wrote Virginia Stephen in 1908, 'and all the deserted wives and husbands in the country are wondering [how] far the marriage service represents the true word of God. Such a display of imbecility is hardly credible'.)[2] Establishment voices spoke for Christianity, patriotism, the defence of the realm, and women in their place; and against degeneracy, poisonous foreign influences, effeminacy, homosexuality, pacifism, cowardice, modernism, and the weakening of the race. In the war, this conflict between 'liberation and control'[3] turned into the 'home-front wars': 'the war against Modernism, the war against culture, the war against dissent, and the war against the woman's war'.[4]

Virginia Woolf's writing was always explicitly on the radical, subversive and modern side of this cultural divide. Her early novels set the individual development of her young, unconventional characters – Rachel, Katharine, Jacob – against the rhetoric of the Establishment.[5] In her feminist writing and in all her later novels, her strategies of anti-authoritarian ridicule are an essential part of her modernism.

In 1910 these ideas were still being struggled for in *Melymbrosia*. And in many ways Virginia Stephen, and Bloomsbury, were still, politically, in the nursery, astonishingly 'unaware of the disaster so soon to come'. 'We in Bloomsbury' (Vanessa Bell wrote in 1951 of the years between 1910 and 1914) 'had only the haziest ideas as to what was going on in the rest of Europe.'[6] Shaw's Tchekhovian denunciation of pre-war society, *Heartbreak House*, written between 1916 and 1917 (and supposed to have been inspired by his first meeting with Virginia in Sussex) mocks the 'very charming people, most advanced, unprejudiced, frank, humane, unconventional, democratic, free-thinking' who sit and talk in Heartbreak House as 'heart-broken imbeciles', the class who deserve destruction. 'We are useless, dangerous, and ought to be abolished.'[7] Their 'civilization' is a blithe fiddling on the edge of catastrophe.

Yet the pre-war interests and activities of Virginia Stephen and her friends would turn out to have some historical weight. In 1910, she was involved with three events which came to be read as connected expressions of British subversiveness: the suffrage movement, the Dreadnought Hoax, and the Post-Impressionist exhibition.

Virginia Stephen's participation in the Votes for Women campaign did not last for long – a few weeks at the beginning and the end of the year addressing envelopes in a NUWSS suffrage office, reluctant attendance at a couple of mass meetings. She could not throw herself into the work, and in spite of the proud boast she made to Benedict Nicolson in 1940 of 'working for the vote' as a young woman,[8] her involvement was equivocal and half-hearted. All the same, the movement had a lasting effect on her.

Since the 'Mud March' of 1907 there had been a succession of huge marches and demonstrations, all of which Virginia Stephen would have been aware of. She was in London for the big NUWSS procession of 13 June 1908 along the Embankment, and for the WSPU demonstration in Hyde Park a week later on 21 June, and again for the WSPU march of 19 June 1909 which ended in stone-throwing and hunger strikes. Lloyd George went to the country at the end of 1909, after his 'People's Budget' for taxing the rich had been thrown out by the House of Lords. At the beginning of 1910, all the different branches of the suffrage movement[9] were working furiously towards the General Election, sending out enormous amounts of campaign material. 'This must be the last General Election in this country at which women do not vote.'[10] 'Bloomsbury' was involved: Duncan Grant had won the Artists' Suffrage League's election poster competition in 1909,[11] Pernel Strachey was a suffragist and Pippa Strachey was the secretary of the London Society. Most of the women Virginia knew who were involved in social work and politics, like Margaret Llewelyn Davies, were supporters of votes for women. The kind of women who opposed it were Victorian conservatives such as Mrs Humphry Ward, who was on Virginia's 'black list'[12] for her stuffiness and sentimentality. Mrs Ward, of course, was a Stephen family acquaintance; and if Julia Stephen had lived, she too would have been opposing the suffragists. To join them was the first move in killing the Angel in the House.

But many women of that older generation were fighting for the vote. It was Janet Case who influenced Virginia to join in with the pre-election pressure campaign: 'You impressed me so much' (Virginia wrote to her) 'with the wrongness of the present state of affairs that I feel that action is necessary . . . How melancholy it is that conversation isn't enough!'[13] Her offer was accepted; Janet Case put her on to a suffragist who wrote suggesting that 'she could get up the history of the New Zealand franchise movement or make a book of extracts on the position of women and of poor and uneducated people'.[14] (In *Night and Day*, the suffrage committee issues 'a statistical diagram showing the proportion of married women to spinsters in New Zealand.')[15]

A few weeks followed (during which time she also took part in the Dreadnought Hoax) of addressing envelopes with 'names like Cowgill' in an office peopled with 'ardent but educated young women, and brotherly clerks . . . just like a Wells novel.'[16] The Liberals came back with a greatly reduced majority and drew up their 'Conciliation Bill' (which would give votes to about a million women). That summer, while Virginia Stephen was ill and away in the country, the campaign to make the Bill law continued, against Asquith's delaying tactics. When she was back in London, she went to the mass meeting in the Albert Hall on 12 November 1910. She felt she was wasting her time, and was not much impressed. 'About a dozen people spoke, like the tollings of a bell . . . The only amusement was that a baby cried incessantly, and this was taken by some as a bitter sarcasm against woman having a vote.'[17]

A few days later, on 18 November ('Black Friday'), Parliament reconvened (to be almost immediately dissolved), the Conciliation Bill was shelved, and a delegation of women to the House of Commons was treated with extreme brutality. (In the same week, a concerted outcry was going on against the Post-Impressionist exhibition, which opened on 8 November.) The battle for votes continued after the election; Asquith continued to put off the Conciliation Bill and the women continued to march. But the suffrage issue was swamped by the war, and votes (for women over thirty) would not become law until 1918.

At the end of 1910 Virginia wrote a different sort of letter to Janet Case about suffrage work. 'Do you ever take that side of politics into account – the inhuman side, and how all the best feelings are shrivelled? . . . I saw Miss LL. Davies at a lighted window in Barton St with all the conspirators round her, and cursed under my breath.'[18] When she came to use her experience of the suffrage office in *Night and Day* (which is set in 1910/1912) she is still cursing under her breath – the more so since her increased exposure, while *Night and Day* was being written, to the world of committees and agendas and policy-making.

Mary Datchet, who works in the NUWSS office in *Night and Day*, is in love with Ralph Denham, who marries Katharine Hilbery. Katharine admires Mary and looks to her for help and solace, but finds her political work alien and unreal, as if she and her 'conspirators' are 'flinging their frail spiders' webs over the torrent of life which rushed down the streets outside'. The office scenes are busily caricatured: there is enthusiastic, disorganised Miss Seal, with her crucifixes and her newspaper clippings and her Utopian rhetoric ('the great march of humanity', 'pioneers in a wilderness'), and Mr Clacton, a Cockney vegetarian with pretensions to culture. Mary, who believes in 'the cause', can only become engaged in 'the larger view . . . the vast desires and sufferings of the mass of mankind' by renouncing her own individual happiness. Yet Katharine and Ralph, whose painful negotiations are for a new kind of *private* life, look to Mary at the end of the book as to a sibyl. Gazing up at her lighted windows late at night, they imagine her 'working out her plans . . . for the good of a world that none of them were ever to know'.[19]

So suffragism has its use for Virginia Woolf in a novel about progress and optimism, set in the time when 'human character changed'. And the suffragists' tactics of battering on the doors of the excluding establishments worked their way lastingly into her imagination. Trespassing on forbidden ground is one of her favourite images.[20]

In the 1930s she brings the struggle for the vote into her analyses of women's history. Her friendship with Ethel Smyth, who had been a suffragette and a close friend of Emmeline Pankhurst, inspired a more combative political tone, and gave colour to the militant Rose in *The Years*. Her late writing links the old battle for the vote to women's struggle for empowerment in all areas: to earn their living, to escape the sexual double standard and to gain equal opportunities in education. In the first draft of *The Years*, 'The Pargiters', one of the Victorian daughters, Delia, is told by her feminist friend 'Nora' (in 1880) that nothing could be done about women's 'chastity' until they have the vote. So she is taken 'to a queer little society that meets off the Gray's Inn Road', and begins to notice what *Punch* and *The Times* have to say about women's rights.

> Punch was full of pictures of little delicate women in bonnets and crinolines trying to cut off legs and appealing to strong men in whiskers – 'Oh Surgeon, do help me! My wrist is *so* tired!' – to illustrate what would happen if one trusted one's body to a woman doctor.[21]

This passage is cut from the final version of *The Years*. But in *Three Guineas*, the fight for the franchise (along with the fight for the professions) is repeatedly instanced as an example of the caricaturing of and violence against women. The tone is fierce. 'The fight for the vote is still generally referred to in terms of sour deprecation', she observes, noting a reference to the suffragists' 'campaign of burning, whipping, and picture-slashing'. And comments: 'Burning, whipping, and picture-slashing only it would seem become heroic when carried out on a large scale by men with machine-guns.'[22] In the twenty years between *Night and Day* and *Three Guineas*, satire on suffragism has turned to satire on the anti-suffragists; her own 'sour deprecation' of the conspirators has been forgotten. And yet *Three Guineas* is about *not* joining up, making a revolution by staying on the outside.

When the vote for (some) women was won in 1918, and muted rejoicings took place (since England was still at war), Virginia and Leonard Woolf went to a 'Suffrage Rally' at Kingsway Hall. Her account of it, alienated, half-attentive, quick to caricature, unconvinced, yet hoping to be moved, takes what she needs from the event to turn it into her own 'form of art':

> It was a very fine afternoon & through a glass door one could see the day light – a difficult light for speakers to speak down. So prosaic, reasonable, & unconcentrated. The hall was fairly well filled; the audience almost wholly women, as the speakers were too. The pure essence of either sex is a little disheartening. Moroever, whether its a meeting of men or of women, one can't help wondering why they do it. I get one satisfactory thrill from the sense of multitude; then become disillusioned, finally bored & unable to listen to a word. In truth this meeting seemed to beat the waves in vain. The vote being won, only great eloquence could celebrate the triumph. None were eloquent; & yet they had to beat up a froth . . . I watched Mrs Pethick Lawrence rising & falling on her toes, as if half her legs were made of rubber, throwing out her arms, opening her hands, & thought very badly of this form of art.[23]

While Virginia Stephen was working for the suffrage, she took part in 'Bloomsbury's' more frivolous trespass inside the bulwarks of the establishment. The story of the Dreadnought Hoax is the best-known and most sensational of all 'Bloomsbury's' public exploits. It still seems incredible that Adrian Stephen and his practical-joker friend Horace de Vere Cole, who had already had a great success at Cambridge pretending to be the Sultan of Zanzibar, should have fooled the British Navy with a plan of such 'lunatic audacity'[24] as to dress up as the Emperor of Abyssinia and his suite, and to be shown round one of the biggest and newest warships of His Majesty's Fleet. (It seems even more incredible that Adrian's original scheme was for him and Cole to travel to Alsace-Lorraine, dress up as German officers and march a detachment of German troops across the border into France in the hopes of starting an international incident.)[25] Yet it worked.

On 7 February 1910, the conspirators got dressed at Fitzroy Square, courtesy of a theatrical costumiers. Adrian was the (bearded) interpreter, Horace Cole the (deaf) Foreign Office official Herbert Cholmondely, and the Abyssinians were Duncan Grant, Anthony Buxton (an ex-Harrovian athlete), Guy Ridley (a judge's son) and Virginia, as 'Prince Mendax', blacked up, with a moustache, flowing robes and a turban. All the Abyssinians wore what would be described as 'the most complete sets of nigger lips'. On the train from Paddington to Weymouth, they practised their Swahili, which seemed the nearest thing to Abyssinian, from a grammar for the Society for the Propagation of the Gospel. At Weymouth they were met by a guard of honour, a red carpet, a launch to the battleship, and a naval band (playing the Anthem of Zanzibar, as the band-master hadn't been able to obtain the Abyssinian National Anthem). Admiral William May had been forewarned by a telegram from 'Harding' of the Foreign Office (in fact sent by a co-conspirator once the train had left Paddington) which read, 'Prince Makalen of Abyssinia and suite arrives 4.20 today Weymouth. He wishes to see Dreadnought. Regret short notice. Forgot Wire before. Interpreter accompanies them.' Admiral May and the Stephens' cousin, Commander William Fisher, showed them all round the ship (the interpreter improvising in a mixture of broken Virgil, the Abyssinians responding with 'Bunga-Bunga' and – this was Virginia – 'Chuck-a-choi, chuck-a-choi'), offered refreshment which was declined on religious grounds, turned down the request for a 21-gun salute, and escorted the party back to shore. On the train, the FO official insisted that the Abyssinians (by now extremely hungry) be served by waiters wearing kid gloves; one version of the story has it that the express was stopped at Reading for the gloves.

The casualness of the plan was part of its effrontery. As Quentin Bell says, the papers which reported it as a carefully organised scheme had got it quite wrong. Virginia was dragged in at the last moment; it was only by good luck that the one Swahili-speaking member of the crew was absent that day and that Fisher failed to recognise his cousin, the eminently recognisable Adrian. All the dialogue was improvised, and depended to a breathtaking degree on the general ignorance of all things African. At one moment Adrian even had to stick Duncan's moustache back on. The whole affair seems now like nothing so much as the Marx Brothers impersonating the Russian aviators in *A Night at the Circus*, Harpo's long beard coming off as he drinks more and more water in order to avoid making a public speech.

The hoax combined all possible forms of subversion: ridicule of empire, infiltration of the nation's defences, mockery of bureaucratic procedures, cross-dressing and sexual ambiguity (Adrian and Duncan became lovers at about this time, though the Navy didn't know *that*; but the fact that one of the Abyssinians was a woman was the greatest source of indignation). Huge embarrassment was caused when the story came out. Though all the conspirators had agreed to keep silent, Horace Cole told the press, and himself went to the Foreign Office to inform them of the hoax. What followed was like another conspiracy, to turn the incident into the epitome of establishment pomposity versus anti-establishment satire. The Assistant Secretary of the Admiralty, Graham Greene (the future novelist's uncle), alerted by the FO, sent a query to Admiral May, who had to explain about the telegram. Questions were asked in Parliament of the First Lord of the Admiralty, Mr McKenna ('The Honourable and Gallant Gentleman will not ask me to go further into a matter which is obviously the work of foolish persons'). At the Pavilion in Weymouth, the music-hall comedian Mr Medley Barrett was greeted with appreciation when he sang, to the tune of 'The Girl I left Behind Me', the following verse: 'When I went on board a Dreadnought Ship/Though I looked just like a costermonger/They said I was an Abyssinian Prince/Because I shouted "Bunga-Bunga".' The *Daily Mirror* reported that an attempt had been made to cut the record of the Abyssinians' visit out of the ship's log-book. A cartoon in the *Mirror* on 17 February 1910 imagined what would happen when real 'Eastern Princes' wanted to visit a man-of-war. When Virginia Woolf told the story in 1940, she added this coda:

> About a week or two later the real Emperor of Abyssinia arrived in London. He complained that wherever he went in the street boys ran after him calling out Bunga Bunga. And when he asked the first Lord of the Admiralty whether he might visit the Channel Fleet, Mr McKenna replied that he regretted to inform his Majesty that it was quite impossible.[26]

The Navy's attempts at retribution did not go well. Horace Cole (who was ill), when called on by two officers, agreed to be tapped ceremonially six times 'on the hindquarters' on condition he could tap them back. Duncan Grant was abducted, by three large men with canes, from his family house ('I expect it's his friends from the *Dreadnought*', said his father Major Grant, smiling). They took him in a taxi to a field near Hendon, where he refused to fight, received two taps, and went home by Tube, still wearing his slippers. Adrian's attempt to apologise to McKenna was brusquely repudiated.[27]

Above all, it was a family affair, and that was how it most struck Virginia. It was the younger generation of Stephens thumbing their nose at their aunts' and uncles' book of tradition. Commander William Fisher, the cousin on the *Dreadnought*, was outraged: the officers in the Mess, he told Adrian, were saying that Virginia 'is a common woman of the town'. All the

"ONCE BITTEN, TWICE SHY."

Cartoon in *The Daily Mirror*, February 1910.

old Fishers and Stephens came out of the woodwork. H.A.L. Fisher wrote angrily to Virginia to say 'for God's sake keep your name out of it' ('his name he meant'),[28] Herbert Stephen told her that her 'reputation was dragged under the feet of all the blue jackets in the Navy'.[29] Dorothea Stephen took the opportunity for some proselytising, which contained a shrewd grain of truth:

> My views on the Dreadnought . . . I think it was a silly and vulgar performance, but I do not think you either the one or the other. I believe you went into it only because you were bored and lonely at home, which is enough to make anyone do anything . . . anyone without a religious faith [must be bored and lonely] . . . You are now to my mind only muddling your time away on things you do not really care for . . . Do not hold off from the one life that is life, only for want of acknowledging to yourself that you want it.[30]

Even Vanessa, now pregnant with 'Clarissa' (who turned out to be Quentin, born on 19 August 1910), had been dubious about 'the Goat's' involvement. 'If they had been discovered as everyone thought they would be, the sailors would certainly have revenged themselves by some violent practical jokes on them and it would then have been very awkward when it was found that one of them was a woman.'[31]

Only a few paragraphs remain of Virginia's later account of the hoax, written for the Women's Institute in Rodmell in wartime, read again to the Memoir Club in September of 1940, and greeted with roars of mirth. It was certainly a story she loved to tell; William Plomer remembered how she used it to demonstrate 'that high-ranking hearts of oak at Portsmouth [sic] were accompanied by heads of the same material'.[32]

The Dreadnought Hoax's playful cheek and exhibitionism gets into her work indirectly – in *Orlando*'s subversive masquerade (for instance the elaborate reception of Orlando as Ambassador to Constantinople by the British Admiral Sir Adrian Scrope),[33] or in the angry ribaldry about male ceremony and officialdom in *Three Guineas*. But she did make one direct reference to it. The story 'A Society'[34] was written ten years after the hoax. Its immediate inspiration was Arnold Bennett's *Our Women*, and Desmond MacCarthy's support, as 'Affable Hawk' in the *New Statesman*, for Bennett's argument that women are the intellectual inferiors of men. Virginia Woolf was provoked, in a 'temper',[35] into 'making up a paper upon Women, as a counterblast to Mr Bennett's adverse views'.[36] This took two forms, one an angry feminist correspondence with 'Affable Hawk', and one a fictional version of her argument.

In the satirical story, a group of women found 'a society for asking questions', in order to find out whether centuries of child-bearing – while men 'bore the books and pictures' – have produced a valuable civilisation. Each of them infiltrates a male bastion: a court of law, an Oxford college (dressed as a charwoman), the London literary scene (dressed as a man, and so 'taken for a reviewer') and the Royal Academy. One, Rose, has 'dressed herself as an Aethiopian Prince and gone aboard one of his Majesty's ships'. After the 'hoax' is discovered, a Naval Captain insists that honour be satisfied by exchanging several light taps 'upon the behind' with Rose, whom he takes to be 'a private gentleman'. The Captain is much moved by this procedure: ' "The honour of the British Navy is avenged!" he cried, and, raising herself, she saw him with the sweat pouring down his face holding out a trembling right hand ... "For God's sake, man, don't mention your mother's name!" he shrieked, trembling like an aspen and flushing to the roots of his hair.' As war breaks out, the women conclude with laughter and gloom that the future for their daughters is bleak unless a new 'society' can be conceived. 'For Heaven's sake, let us devise a method by which men may bear children! It is our only chance.' In inconclusive form, the arguments of *A Room of One's Own* and *Three Guineas* are anticipated. The Dreadnought Hoax is built into this feminist fable in a way which suggests how profoundly that satirical masquerade influenced her life-long thinking about her 'society'.

The outrage of family and authorities over the Dreadnought Hoax was remarkably similar in tone to the public outrage at an exhibition at the Grafton Galleries called 'Manet and the Post-Impressionists', organised by Roger Fry. It ran from 8 November 1910 to 15 January 1911, and consisted of new French paintings and sculptures which hardly anyone in England had seen before.[37] When Virginia Woolf wrote her biography of Roger Fry nearly thirty years later, she decided to make the exhibition into the major turning-point in the book: 'So to the Post Is. & ourselves. That will make the break in the book. A change of method.'[38] She means that at this point she will change her method in the biography, make it more personal. But 'a change of method' is, also, exactly what the exhibition, and Roger Fry's influence, brought about in British art and, in part, in her own work.

When she uses December 1910, in her 1924 essay, as the point of change between the Edwardians and the Georgians,[39] she doesn't refer explicitly to the Post-Impressionist exhibition, but to the influence of Samuel Butler and Shaw (whose *Misalliance* was playing at that time) and to the difference between Wells, Bennett and Galsworthy, and Forster, Lawrence, Strachey, Joyce and Eliot.[40] But the choice of date acknowledges that from this moment changes in art and changes in writing would seem inextricable to her. Her greatest novel, which describes and embodies the transition from Victorian to post-war England, uses painting, not writing, as its central image. Lily Briscoe's thoughts about her work owe more to Vanessa Bell than to anyone. But without Roger Fry the thoughts would not have taken the shape they did. Apart from *Night and Day* and *Orlando*, Virginia Woolf did not dedicate her books. She told Roger Fry, though, that she would have dedicated *To the Lighthouse* to him, if she had thought it was good enough.

> What I meant was (but would not have said in print) that besides all your surpassing private virtues, you have I think kept me on the right path, so far as writing goes, more than anyone – if the right path it is.[41]

Roger Fry's arrival changed 'Bloomsbury', culturally and emotionally and – to use one of his favourite words – in its 'texture'. When he fell into conversation on a train with Clive and Vanessa Bell in January 1910, he was forty-four. His wife had been diagnosed as incurably insane,[42] he had just failed to be elected for the Slade Professorship at Oxford and was about to be sacked from his post at the Metropolitan Museum in New York.[43] He belonged to an older Cambridge generation (Goldsworthy Lowes Dickinson had been deeply in love with him and he had learnt his Renaissance Italy from J.A. Symonds). 'He looked worn and seasoned, ascetic yet tough':[44] white-haired, deep-voiced, bespectacled, bright-eyed, bushy-eyebrowed. The impression he made on his new younger friends was of vigour, energy, and enthusiasm:

> There they stood upon chairs – the pictures that were to be shown at the Grafton Gallery – bold, bright, impudent almost, in contrast with the Watts portrait of a beautiful Victorian lady that hung on the wall behind them. And there was Roger Fry, gazing at them, plunging his eyes into them as if he were a humming-bird hawk-moth hanging over a flower, quivering yet still. And then drawing a deep breath of satisfaction, he would turn to whoever it might be, eager for sympathy. Were you puzzled? But why? And he would explain that it was quite easy to make the transition from Watts to Picasso; there was no break, only a continuation. They were only pushing things a little further. He demonstrated; he persuaded; he argued . . . So he talked in that gay crowded room, absorbed in what he was saying, quite unconscious of the impression he was making; fantastic yet reasonable, gentle yet fanatically obstinate, intolerant yet absolutely open-minded, and burning with the conviction that something very important was happening.[45]

The passage, though coloured by fond retrospect (it is written in 1940 of 1910), makes it clear that she found him very attractive. In her notes for her biography she writes: 'Was always carrying on a very rich emotional life.'[46] Her encounters with him are always marked by her feeling of his 'seductive magic'. He was 'the centre of a whirlwind to me', always 'generous', 'loose & warm & genuine', bursting with enthusiasms and inventions.[47] Sometimes he irritated her and she found him egotistical or querulous, and for a time they were rivals. When he fell headlong in love with Vanessa in 1911, Virginia made characteristic bids for his attention. Vanessa warned Roger of her dangerousness, and tried to keep the relationship secret from Virginia. (This all sounds more like conventional adultery than a 'Bloomsbury' liaison. Clive became very jealous; how ironic, Vanessa said to Roger, that this didn't happen three years ago when he was 'thinking only of Virginia!')[48] And Virginia was envious of the attention that the painters were getting.[49] When Vanessa fell out of love with Roger, Virginia found her own relationship with him improved.

Fry affected her life in all kinds of detailed ways, domestically and professionally and intellectually.[50] And when she agreed to write his biography, she began a new relationship with him, a ghostly love-affair: 'What an odd posthumous friendship – in some ways more intimate than any I had in life.'[51] Above all, his ideas excited her. Their letters to each other bubble over with their desire to interest each other. Fry says that his writing to her is like Sargent trying to exchange a sketch with Velázquez.[52] All the same, with his passions and his stories he holds his own. She always learnt from him.

I dined with Roger & met Clive ... taking a splendid flight above personalities, we discussed literature & aesthetics.

'D'you know, Clive, I've made out a little more about the thing which is essential to all art: you see, all art is representative. You say the word tree, & you see a tree. Very well. Now every word has an aura. Poetry combines the different aura's in a sequence – ' That was something like it. I said one could, & certainly did, write with phrases, not only words; but that didn't help things on much. Roger asked me if I founded my writing upon texture or upon structure; I connected structure with plot, & therefore said 'texture'. Then we discussed the meaning of structure & texture in painting & in writing. Then we discussed Shakespeare, & Roger said Giotto excited him just as much. This went on till I made myself go precisely at 10 ... I liked it all very much (the talk I mean). Much no doubt is perfectly vague, not to be taken seriously, but the atmosphere puts ideas into one's head, & instead of having to curtail

them, or expatiate, one can speak them straight out & be understood –
indeed disagreed with.[53]

I don't see how to put 3 or 4 hours of Roger's conversation into the rest of
this page ... it was about all manner of things; on growing old; on
loneliness; on religion; on morality; on Nessa; on Duncan; on French
literature; on education; on Jews; on marriage; & on the Lysistrata.
Occasionally he read a quotation from a book by Proust . . . so to Gordon
Square, where first the new Delacroix & then the Cézanne were
produced. There are 6 apples in the Cézanne picture. What can 6 apples
not be? I began to wonder.

And she goes on to describe the 'intricate' account that Roger and Vanessa
gave of this wonderful painting (which Maynard Keynes had just bought),
while 'the apples positively got redder & rounder & greener'.[54]

These conversations show how he influenced her. She is excited, alerted,
and also quizzical: the apples don't mean to her quite what they mean to the
painters. All their lives the sisters were involved in a discussion about the
relationship between their work, summed up by this sentence (in a letter
from Virginia to Vanessa written just after the Post-Impressionist show): 'I
think a good deal about you, for purposes of my own'.[55] This debate is
energised by difference as much as affinity, and the issues it raises of colour,
form, and 'texture' are worked out in a language which owes a great deal to
Roger Fry. He understood very quickly what she was trying to do with new
forms (for instance praising her fluid experimental sketch, 'The Mark on
the Wall', in 1918, for its 'plasticity').[56] When in her biography she cites his
attacks on Sargent and Alma Tadema for their photographic realism, the
link with her own critique of Edwardian materialism is clear. No wonder
that December 1910 seemed to her, retrospectively, the point when she, as
well as the painters, began to think about new forms.

At the time, in fact, her response to the Post-Impressionists was
somewhat sceptical.

I hear a great deal about pictures. I dont think them so good as books. But
why all the Duchesses are insulted by the post-impressionists, a modest
sample set of painters, innocent even of indecency, I cant conceive.
However, one mustn't say that they are like other pictures, only better,
because that makes everyone angry.[57]

This comes in a vivid letter to Violet written in the week of the November
1910 election, in a rainy oppressive London. They are dining out, she says,
'in a little restaurant off Soho, where prostitutes lure young men. The

wickedness of London on a day like this is inconceivable; one imagines vice smelling in stuffy rooms.' It sounds like a Sickert Camden Town painting. And the rest of the letter is full of references to indecency and lunacy and vice. These associations (meant to shock poor Violet) are crowding into Virginia's mind because of the current reaction to the 'indecent' paintings, a reaction which brought together a whole stew of censorious fears and prejudices.

The rhetoric of hostility to the suffrage movement and the Post-Impressionist exhibition was astonishingly similar, and touched Virginia Stephen's life very closely. All the accounts[58] of the 'hubbub' of public outrage at the Post-Impressionists (from the 'cultured' classes as well as from an insular British public) make clear that the shock of the new sprang from fears about sexual identity, racial and national survival. The reactions ran together the defence of the realm, the purity of women and the mental health of the nation, in a confused and emotional alignment. Eminent doctors, Virginia Woolf wrote in *Roger Fry*, agreed with William Rothenstein in detecting signs of insanity in the painters. One of the same doctors who would treat her, T.B. Hyslop, lectured on the pictures as 'the work of madmen'. Wilfred Blunt in his diary called the show 'pornographic'; Robert Ross in the *Morning Post* said that it was only of interest to 'students of pathology and the specialist in abnormality'.

The scandal took a more personal direction when the Stephen girls appeared as 'indecent' Gauguin girls at the Post-Impressionist Ball, half-dressed in brightly coloured stuffs from a firm called Burnetts 'made for natives in Africa with which we draped ourselves'. Vanessa recalled: 'we wore brilliant flowers and beads, we browned our legs and arms and had very little on beneath the draperies.' After the ball, they posed for a picture: 'I have to dress up again as a South Sea Savage', Virginia wrote to Molly, 'Its an awful bore!'[59] This is a frivolous example of the European interest in the 'primitive', which finds many different expressions in the 1910s and 1920s – among them Roger Fry's discovery of African art, London's love-affair with the Russian ballet and *Le Sacre du Printemps*, and Rachel Vinrace's learning, in *The Voyage Out*, of 'primitive' temples and 'prehistoric towns' that existed 'before the dawn of European art'.[60] But to its outraged critics, that primitivism was one of the most sinister features of the Post-Impressionist show.

The idea that the pictures were like a poisonous foreign disease, or invasion, infecting the manhood of the English and the purity of their women, resembled the attacks on suffragism as symptoms of national decline and aberrance. The suffragettes were a 'shrieking sisterhood', not 'womenly women'. The medical profession came out strongly against the movement. 'Militant hysteria' was the product of mental disorder, and the disease might be contagious. Since Virginia Stephen spent much of the year under doctor's orders, angrily submitting to a rest cure in the interests of sanity and good health, the connections struck home.

For her this year, which to Vanessa was 'a sizzle of excitement',[61] was a troubled time. By the summer she accepted the need for a six-week rest cure. When she came out to join the family in Studland, she begged Clive not to irritate her: 'My resolution is to be cautious . . . not walking too far, or exciting the emotions, and taking great care to circumvent headaches.'[62] The policy of self-protection meant retreating to the country as often as possible, away from the 'sizzle' of London. At the end of the year she and Adrian went to stay in Lewes, and, for the first time, she began to explore the Sussex countryside. It filled her with pleasure. She wanted her own place to go to – like St Ives, only within reach of London – and rapidly decided that Sussex would do. She rented a semi-detached cottage in Firle, a small village under the Downs near Lewes, and called it 'Little Talland House'.

This satisfying move seemed to open the way for more changes. The lease on Fitzroy Square was up, and neither she nor Adrian wanted to continue their unsatisfactory partnership. A bigger house, nearer to Gordon Square, was found, and the plan was to make it into a communal household, shared with friends. 'Our new address is 38 Brunswick Square', she told Ottoline in the autumn of 1911. 'Its ever so much nicer . . . so quiet, and a graveyard behind. We are going to try all kinds of experiments.'[63]

Leonard Woolf was to be one of the tenants. Virginia was, scandalously, the only woman in the new house. There had been plans for her new friend Ka Cox to move in, but pressure was brought to bear on her not to join the Bloomsbury hot-house. This conflict came from a group which affected Virginia Stephen's life briefly but challengingly at exactly the same time that Leonard returned from Ceylon.

The dominant personality here was the dazzling and self-dramatising Rupert Brooke, Apostle and Fabian and promising young poet (he was twenty-three in 1910), whose long golden hair, sensual energy and powerful, unsettled personality had made him a schoolboy star at Rugby and a charismatic Cambridge undergraduate. Virginia had known him slightly as a child and she met him again in 1909. Around him orbited a group which, to an extent, attracted her. Its atmosphere was different from that of Gordon or Fitzroy Square, but its emotional entanglements were quite as complicated. For a short time, she became involved, but she had reservations about the circle she christened the 'Neo-Pagans'.

In 1910, Rupert Brooke's emotions were fixed on two independent-minded young women (though James Strachey, Lytton's brother, was hopelessly in love with him, and he would have some homosexual experiences). Since 1908 he had been in love with the very young Noel Olivier, one of the four striking daughters of the Fabian Sir Sydney Olivier.[64] But by 1910 he was beginning a relationship with Katherine Cox, a Newnham student and a young Fabian, the orphaned daughter of a rich stockbroker. Ka Cox was also involved with a dark, clever, Bedales-educated Frenchman called Jacques Raverat (who in 1910 switched from maths at Cambridge to painting at the Slade). Jacques Raverat had wanted to marry Ka but was being rejected by her, and was falling in love with the Slade student Gwen Darwin, whom he married in 1911.

The tone of the 'Neo-Pagans' was set by Bedales and Fabianism and by Rupert Brooke's Shelleyan enthusiasm for the simple life.[65] They went on huge walks with knapsacks, liked to take their clothes off and swim naked at their 'O.B.' (Old Bedalian) summer camps, ate vegetables, believed in socialism, wore socks and sandals and head-scarves and open-necked shirts, and tended towards heterosexuality. The girls were modern, chaste and healthy: they all sound like H.G. Wells's Ann Veronica or Ibsen's Hilda Wangel in *The Master Builder*, energetically striding out towards a new world. The Neo-Pagans were also more racist and anti-Semitic than most of 'Bloomsbury': after Virginia Stephen married Leonard Woolf, Rupert Brooke referred to them as 'the Jew and his wife',[66] and Noel Olivier had to reassure him in 1912: 'You need have no fear of slug-like influences from the people Jacques calls "the Jews": (they comprise the Bloomsbury household and the Stracheys, I believe).'[67] Jacques Raverat told Rupert Brooke that he hated Jews 'because they crucified Christ daily'.[68] Years later Raverat acknowledged to Virginia that 'it's true that things and people that I disliked were Jewish . . . I do like *some* Jews.'[69]

Virginia began calling them the Neo-Pagans some time in 1911,[70] for reasons made clear in her sardonic 1918 retrospect on Rupert Brooke:

He was living at Grantchester; his feet were permanently bare; he disdained all tobacco and butcher's meat; and he lived all day, and perhaps slept all night, in the open air . . . Under his influence the country near Cambridge was full of young men and women walking barefoot, sharing his passion for bathing and fish diet, disdaining book learning, and proclaiming that there was something deep and wonderful in the man who brought the milk and in the woman who watched the cows.[71]

This acerbity is partly a reaction to the posthumous idealising of Rupert

Brooke, but it also echoes her earlier feelings: 'Oh dear, how the Neo-Paganism at that stage of my life annoyed me',[72] she wrote to Jacques in 1924. And yet their bucolic unworldliness, their exhibitionist, innocent sexiness appealed to her. They seemed to provide a contrast with her own more sceptical, intellectual group.

When she first met Ka Cox (on a weekend in Oxford in January 1911 with Ray Costelloe and Marjorie Strachey) she was drawn to her. She found her 'a bright, intelligent, nice creature', and liked the atmosphere of 'clever young women' together, telling each other about their passions and their periods.[73] Her descriptions of Ka make her into a cross between a jolly schoolgirl and a life-force: 'Ka came striding along the road in time for lunch yesterday; with a knapsack on her back, a row of red beads, and daisies stuck in her coat. Her innocent face was brown.' There was a plan for them to go to France together, in the spring of 1911, and for Virginia to escape the 'pallor of headache' and to 'throw myself into youth, sunshine, nature, primitive art. Cakes with sugar on the top, love, lust, paganism, general bawdiness . . .'[74] Virginia was attracted by Ka's solidity and energy, her 'trustiness', her 'stable goodness'.[75] She called her Bruin – 'Bruin oaring her way – with a beaver's tail, and short clumsy paws.'[76] Their intimacy would pass; but Ka acted as a steadfast companion to Virginia during her illness, and remained devoted to her.

Rupert Brooke's death in 1915 seemed to Virginia to be the tragedy of Ka's life: 'Her own happiness, I suppose, went out very completely with Rupert's death.'[77] When she married Will Arnold-Forster ('small', 'fretful', 'peevish')[78] and moved with him to Cornwall, Virginia stayed in touch with her, but became increasingly critical. She didn't like Ka having seen her 'mad'. She felt that Ka's real life had been unreal, a performance, ever since Brooke's death. And in later years she found her irritatingly provincial and bossy, 'as if she always must be impressing me with her busyness, her social standing even among the county families'.[79]

She could never quite forgive Ka for not having made a more romantic marriage. When she became embroiled in the Ka-Jacques-Gwen triangle in 1911, she predicted (to Vanessa) a different future for Ka: 'Ka will marry a Brooke next year, I expect. J. will always be a Volatile Frog. Gwen will bear children, and paint pictures; clearly though, J. and K. would be the proper match.'[80] But J. married G. instead, a match which aroused a peculiarly powerful emotion in Virginia Stephen. There may have been a scene, an eruption of irritation on her part against Jacques and Gwen, as she recalls to Gwen: 'all those years ago, when you used to come to Fitzroy Square, I was so angry and you were so furious, and Jacques wrote me a sensible manly letter'.[81] Her feelings for 'the Volatile Frog' were sharp and memorable. At the time she associated him with Rabelais and sex and the outdoor life; retrospectively she told him he daunted and impressed her, with 'your big nose, your bright eyes, your talking French, and your having such a quick easy way with you, as if you had solved the problems of life'. 'I so much wanted you to admire me.'[82] His marriage to Gwen gave her the same sense of romance and exclusion which she had felt, as a child, about Stella and Jack. In *To the Lighthouse*, Lily Briscoe feels scorched and diminished by Paul Rayley's engagement: 'He turned on her cheek the heat of love, its horror, its cruelty, its unscrupulosity.'[83] And in *The Years*, a dark, acerbic Frenchman called Renny – the only Frenchman in her novels – rouses a surge of emotion in the much older, single, Eleanor Pargiter: 'That is the man, she said to herself, with a sudden rush of conviction . . . that I should like to have married.'[84]

Her strong feelings about Jacques and Gwen Raverat's marriage were connected to the after-effects of her painful triangular involvement with Clive and Vanessa. Here again was a couple whose marriage left her on the outside looking in. The two relationships are linked in her memory: 'I think it was my affair with Clive and Nessa I was thinking of', she told Gwen in 1925, 'when I said I envied you and Jacques at Fitzroy Square. For some reason that turned more of a knife in me than anything else has ever done.'[85] She made sure that much was made at Gordon Square of her forays into Neo-Paganism and her brief friendship – and naked bathe – with Rupert Brooke. The family was happy to oblige. 'I shall see the Goat today,' Adrian wrote to Clive that month 'and hear how her Rupert romance is going on. She told me that he said he did not want to marry for several years at any rate but did want to copulate occasionally and promiscuously. I am afraid that her bathe has not been taken quite seriously enough for her taste but perhaps she will now have gone a step further.'[86]

But Virginia Stephen and Rupert Brooke, both ambitious, difficult and vulnerable, both to be treated by the same doctors with the same cures, both to become posthumously revered and mythologised, were not enchanted by each other. The naked moonlit bathe at Grantchester, where Brooke had lodgings at the Old Vicarage (his party trick was jumping in the water at Byron's Pool and emerging with an instant erection) became legendary. Virginia would retell the story, denying Lytton's claim that Rupert had bandy legs.[87] But the week she spent there was more literary than libidinous. Conversation was incessant, manuscripts were scattered around, and Brooke read his poems to her. She remembered once completing a line for him: 'Virginia, what is the brightest thing you can think of?' 'A leaf with the light on it' – and the line 'was filled in immediately'.[88] She remembered finding him 'all that could be kind and interesting and substantial and goodhearted',[89] but (this was during the national rail strike in August 1911) she was scathing about his attempt to 'work up some Socialist enthusiasm'.[90] And her experience of Camp, later that summer, on the edge of Dartmoor – 'sleeping on the ground, waiting at dawn, and swimming in a river' with a lot of unshaven Neo-Pagans – was not an unmitigated success.[91]

That winter Rupert Brooke turned violently against Bloomsbury. A jealous rage over Ka's flirtation with Henry Lamb developed into a hatred of Lytton Strachey, whom he saw as 'Lamb's dark genius', and a paranoid attack on the whole group. Ka's tentative plan to move into Brunswick Square was met with horror; Gwen Raverat remembered him calling it a 'bawdy house' and thinking of Bloomsbury as 'deadly poisonous'.[92] Some feeling for Virginia survived this obsession. He wrote her a disturbed and disturbing letter during his breakdown in 1912:

> Let me implore you not to have, as I've been having, a nervous breakdown. It's *too* unpleasant – but you're one of the few people who, of old, know what it's like ('Hypersensitive and Introspective' the good doctor Craig said I was.) I feel drawn to you in this robust hard world. What tormented and crucified figures we literary people are! [He continues with stories of life at Rugby.] Church circles are agitated by what happened at Holy Trinity three Sundays ago. In the afternoon there is first a Choral Service, then a children's service, then a service for Men Only. Two fourteen-year-old choirboys arranged a plan during the Choral Service. At the end they skipped round and watched the children enter. They picked out the one whose looks pleased them best, a youth of 10. They waited in seclusion till the end of the children's service. Then they pounced on their victim, as he came out, took him, each by a hand, and led him to the vestry. There, while the Service for Men Only proceeded, they removed the lower parts of his clothing and buggered him, turn by turn. His protestations were drowned by the organ pealing out whatever hymns are most suitable for men only. Subsequently they let him go. He has been in bed ever since with a rupture.[93]

Virginia Stephen (who was in the process of deciding whether to marry Leonard Woolf when she received this) might well have thought that the whole letter should have been marked, 'Men Only'. After Rupert Brooke's death, like everyone else who had known him well, she found it hard to stomach 'the peculiar irony of his canonisation'.[94] His friends, she wrote, reviewing Edward Marsh's 'disgraceful soppy sentimental' 1918 hagiography of Brooke, had not been willing 'to tell the public the informal things by which they remember him best'.[95] The 'choir-boy' letter might have been one of those. 'It must be a wonderful self' she wrote drily in 1919 'when no two people remember the same thing, but all are agreed that he was wonderful.'[96]

As soon as Brooke died, the patriotic and idealistic rhetoric of his war sonnets was echoed in his obituaries.[97] Virginia resisted that rhetoric. If Jacob Flanders, dead in the war, owed something to Rupert Brooke as well as to Thoby Stephen, his novel is like a riposte to Brooke's poetry, speaking not of ideals, but of the waste and pointlessness of all the young men's deaths.

SEVENTEEN

Leonard

Meanwhile, Leonard Woolf, in his late twenties, employee of the Colonial Civil Service in Ceylon, was keeping order with a stick over 40,000 Arab and Tamil pearl-fishers at Marichchukaddi, improving the salt collection rate in Hambantota Province, grappling with outbreaks of rinderpest and the opium trade, learning Tamil and Sinhalese, streamlining the census-taking operations, riding and cycling many miles through the jungle, and experimenting with new methods in ploughing, cotton-growing, and education.[1] But while his maintenance of law and order became increasingly 'severe and unrelenting',[2] he was becoming utterly disillusioned with the colonial system he was administering so effectively. 'I became' (he recalled, over fifty years later) 'more and more ambivalent, politically schizophrenic, an anti-imperialist who enjoyed the flesh-pots of imperialism.'[3]

He put his mixed feelings into his Sinhalese fictions, his first novel *The Village in the Jungle* (1913), which he began to write as soon he left Ceylon, and the three *Stories from the East* (1924). Much indebted to Conrad and to Kipling,[4] they are savagely critical of imperialist complacencies about 'the inferior races', and grimly wedded to the belief (in the words of one wise villager) that life is 'full of evil – nothing but evil and trouble'.

Leonard Woolf's own solution to his political schizophrenia was echoed by the narrator of his story 'Pearls and Swine', who gives his audience 'facts', not 'views', and who survives through discipline: 'One just did one's work, hour after hour, keeping things going.'[5] When he first went out in 1904 he wrote desperate letters to his best friend Lytton Strachey, blackly depressed about losing touch with everything he held dear. The colonial structure and his role in it seemed to him a grotesque illusion. 'I feel as if I were playing the buffoon in a vast comic opera,' he wrote to Strachey in 1904.[6] But as time went on and he prided himself more on his success in the work, he 'hardened his heart against the past', became 'fanatically' absorbed in his tasks, and developed an increasing taste for solitude.[7] England began to feel as unreal to him as Ceylon: 'I shall live and die in these appalling countries now', he wrote to Strachey in 1907 from Kandy. 'And as for happiness – I don't believe in being happy even in England.'[8]

What were the roots of this grimly unflinching character? Leonard Woolf was the child of middle-class assimilated Jews, the fourth – born in 1880 – in a family of nine children. His paternal grandfather Benjamin was a London-born tailor who 'educated his children out of their class' and left a proviso in his will that they could only inherit if they married Jews. His mother's family, the de Jonghs, were Amsterdam Jews – her father was a diamond merchant – who migrated to London in the 1860s. Marie de Jongh was one of ten children; Leonard could remember her parents as a redoubtable old Dutch lady and a rabbinical-looking white-bearded old man.

He thought of his father as hard and his mother as soft. Sidney Woolf, Marie's second husband (her first was a Dutchman called Goldstucker) was a successful barrister who became a Q.C., a liberal Jew, highly intelligent, nervous, driven, emotionally reserved, and intolerant of fools. His crest – a wolf's head with the motto 'Thoroughly' – suited both him and his son Leonard, who derived from him a nervous tremor of the hands, a passion for work, a clear forceful mind and a scorn for stupidity or corruption.

Sidney Woolf established a comfortable bourgeois home in Lexham Gardens, not very far from Hyde Park Gate. (Perhaps Leonard and Virginia passed each other in Kensington Gardens as children.) But in 1892, when he was forty-eight and Leonard was eleven, he died suddenly of TB and heart-failure. He had made no savings, and Marie Woolf and her children had to remove to suburban Putney. Overnight, Leonard Woolf acquired 'an acute and highly conscious sense of complete economic insecurity'.[9] He had, from that time, no private means and nothing to fall back on. This explains the carefulness with money which his critics would attribute to Semitic meanness.[10]

Retrospectively, Leonard admired his mother's courage and good management, but in his teens he became extremely impatient with her mourning, her possessiveness, her piety and her 'dream world': 'a fairyland of nine perfect children worshipping a mother to whom they owed everything, loving one another, and revering the memory of their deceased father.'[11] His own childhood experiences of 'cosmic' melancholy, his loss of faith at fourteen, his intellectual interests, and an early developed sense of fatalism and scepticism, estranged him from Mrs Woolf. 'Half the vileness of men is due to the fact that in childhood their natures are moulded in the hands of women',[12] he wrote coldly in his juvenile commonplace book. When he took his revenge on his mother in *The Wise Virgins*, he portrayed 'Mrs Davis' as parochially snobbish, self-pitying, sentimental and foolish – an embarrassing Jewish mother. Mrs Woolf was bitterly offended. But one of the most intense passages in the novel was the son's lament for his lost filial feelings:

Harry looked at his mother. He tried to recall the vision of what she was . . . The little boy he remembered had known a very tall grown-up, very beautiful, whom he had loved, of course! . . . For twelve, perhaps fourteen years of his life he had been tied to her, and moulded and ruled by her . . . It was strange that no finest strand of that relationship, one could hardly call it love or affection, remained to bind him to her. He wondered whether perhaps he was merely without human feeling.[13]

This betrays strong unresolved emotions. There is shame and self-hate in the novel's caricatures of his family. All his life Leonard would have the mixed feelings of the intellectual, assimilated Jew who has forged a separate life out of his wits and talents, who is alienated by occasions of family solidarity, but who stays in touch with and feels duty and some loyalty ('one could hardly call it love or affection') towards his relations. Virginia would often remark on his 'family complex'.[14]

Leonard Woolf thought of himself as a Jew. At least, he began and ended as one. His childhood Bible was carefully annotated: he knew the reigns of the kings of Judah and who the 'adversaries of the Jews' were in the Book of Ezra and which Psalms 'were sung by the Jews when they went up to Jerusalem after the Babylonian captivity'.[15] As an adult he could still 'sing in Hebrew'.[16] One of his undergraduate poems gives the secret thoughts of a Jewish pawnbroker sentenced to penal servitude for manslaughter:

> You spit upon my face, while I
> A spark of the world's eternity
> A remnant of the old Earth's sons
> In whose veins the dark blood runs
> Of kings and princes of the East
> Feel the wild waves swell in my breast
> Of hate and scorn for the foul thing
> You've made me. O the maddening sting
> Of that tone in the gentile voice
> Hissing out 'Jew!' . . . your seal of shame
> Has stamped in blood the scorned name
> Upon my brow . . .[17]

Around the time this poem was written, the Dreyfus case was affecting him powerfully; it always seemed to him a crucial struggle 'between right and wrong, justice and injustice, civilization and barbarism'.[18] His development as a socialist stemmed, to an extent, from this early identification with Jews as victims.[19]

But he also preferred to identify with classical culture and to operate as a citizen of the world. In his autobiography, he is preoccupied with questions of divided loyalties, and recognises this as typical. 'Nearly all Jews', he writes, 'are both proud and ashamed of being Jews.'[20] In his old age, he came back to some of the Jewishness of his youth. He visited Israel, and invoked in his old man's autobiography traditional 'Jewish' characteristics, notably in his account of his response to Virginia Woolf's death:

> I have my full share of the inveterate, the immemorial fatalism of the Jew, which he has learned from his own history beginning 3,428 years ago – so they say – under the taskmasters of Pharaoh in Egypt . . . down to the lessons of the gas chambers and Hitler. Thus it is we have learned that we cannot escape Fate, because we cannot escape the past, the result of which is an internal passive resistance, a silent, unyielding self-control.[21]

More usually, he accepted the role his friends and his wife gave him, of the exceptional, accepted Jew. There are passages in the autobiography where he describes with pride a successful process of self-concealment as a means to acceptance – by his school-mates, or by the colonial 'sahibs' in Ceylon who took him in as 'one of them' because he had a dog and could play bridge, thereby 'avoiding being condemned as not a good fellow or not a gentleman'.[22] Or, as this oddly contorted sentence does not add, not a gentile. The same anxiety about acceptance is felt in his accounts of the Strachey/Stephen 'intellectual aristocracy', with their unquestioned assumptions and manners so different from his own. The difference, he knew, was as much a matter of class as of tribe:

> I was an outsider to this class, because, although I and my father before me belonged to the professional middle class, we had only recently struggled up into it from the stratum of Jewish shopkeepers. We had no roots in it.[23]

At school (after prep school at Brighton he was a scholarship boy at St Paul's) he had an intensive training in the Classics (as well as in the bullying philistinism of his schoolmates and the need to keep his feelings hidden). He grafted a passion for Hellenism on to his father's Hebraic ethics. He liked to say that his 'rules for life' were rooted in his father's quotation from the prophet Micah ('to do justly, to love mercy, and to walk humbly with thy God') and that his political ideals were inspired by Periclean Greece.[24] His Classics scholarship to Cambridge changed his life (as Cambridge changed the lives of most of the young men he met there: *Jacob's Room* and *The Longest Journey* show how). In his first year he went through some kind of crisis, one of the 'cosmic' apprehensions of life's futility which periodically overtook him. G.E. Moore provided an ethical basis for living in 'a universe without meaning'.[25] Under his influence Leonard developed his liking for Socratic rationalism and for a Greek ideal of friendships, a preferable alternative to family life. Moore's division of life into 'reality' (ideas, relationships, the 'good') and 'phenomena' (the outside material world of careers and money and politics, or in Forster's phrase, of 'telegrams and anger') profoundly affected Leonard Woolf's world-view.

Academically, though, his achievements were second-rate. After a fifth year of cramming, he did poorly in the Civil Service exams, and faced the Colonial Service as the only alternative to teaching. And so he set off for Ceylon in 'a horrible state of mind, & complete despair',[26] with a fox terrier called Charles and a seventy-volume set of Voltaire, to do the work which was, in fact, to be the making of him as a political thinker and worker.

Almost all Leonard Woolf's friends at Cambridge were homosexual or bisexual. The single-sex intimacy of public school and college life provided the context for these relationships. (Leonard always said that his prep boarding school was 'the most corrupt place I have ever been in', and prided himself on having cleaned it up – at the age of twelve! – from a 'sordid brothel'.)[27] But these loves were constructed too out of what Keynes's biographer has called 'cultural commitment':

> Keynes, Lytton Strachey and other Apostles . . . thought that love of young men was a higher form of love. They had been brought up and educated to believe that women were inferior – in mind and body. If from the ethical point of view . . . love should be attached only to worthy objects, then love of young men was, they believed, ethically better than love of women. The Higher Sodomy, as the Apostles jokingly referred to it, was thus an ethical position, not just a sexual or emotional preference.[28]

It is probable that Leonard Woolf, like Adrian Stephen or Maynard Keynes, passed through this phase too, at least emotionally if not physically, even though the accounts of his youth always emphasise his masculinity, his puritanism, and his attraction to women. Lytton Strachey was always teasingly telling him in graphic detail about his sex life and complaining about his prudishness: he should join a 'League for the Advancement of Social Purity'.[29]

But the running joke of Lytton's bawdiness and Leonard's priggishness allowed for some eroticism between them. They would exchange notes on Thoby's physical 'magnificence'; or Leonard would tell Lytton how the college thought they were 'given up to the most abandoned and horrible practices'. He once told Lytton he wanted to do 'nothing but copulate – only, unlike you, I usually want it, when it is that and nothing else, with women. If it wasnt for the paraphernalia and their extraordinary foulness, I should work all the morning and engage a whore for the afternoon and copulate among the ferns.' Not a very convincing manifesto for heterosexual pleasures. He described himself as Lytton's 'love surveyor & expert'. On the boat to Ceylon, he had some sensational stories to tell about attempts at copulation among the homosexual colonial staff. In softer mood, he longed for them to journey together to the Island of Cythera, the Greek isle of love. Lytton lamented, as Leonard left for Ceylon, 'the kisses I never gave you, your embraces that I have never felt'.[30]

Beneath all this teasing, there was tender affection between them. 'Youre the person I turn to first in the world', wrote Leonard. Lytton replied: 'I'm only happy when I write to you,' or 'I implore you – yes, for me, for my sake, – not really to do what you seem to say you will do – despair altogether.'[31] When Virginia accepted Leonard, one of the first things he did was to write a long letter to Lytton containing 'a detailed analysis of friendship', which Virginia advised him to tear up.[32] He was always at his warmest when he spoke of Lytton:

> Do you know Lytton? He is the most particular of the particular in wit, taste, literature, race, music, humour, art, brilliancy. He has an immense and immensely beautiful russet beard, an immense black broadbrimmed felt hat, a suit of maroon corduroys, and a pale mauve scarf for a waistcoat fastened with a Duke's daughter's cameo brooch. He is the most charming and witty of human beings since Voltaire.[33]

All this suggests some androgyneity in Leonard Woolf. And his youthful attitude to women was very confused. His jokes to Lytton about the squalor of copulation and the disgustingness of his whores in Ceylon (to whom he refers with a mixture of boastfulness and evasiveness), alternated with scornful remarks about the 'degradation' of falling in love with a nice colonial girl with 'big cow eyes which could never understand anything which one said'.[34] *The Wise Virgins* (written a year after his marriage) contains some violent expressions of sexual disgust:

> One imagined that 'forked' animal woman – a poor, thin, soft white body, forking out into two long, weedy white legs like one of those white clammy turnips, which you sometimes see forking grotesquely into two legs – one imagined her thrust into that sort of bell-like cover of clothes, like an egg into a ridiculous egg-cosy.[35]

Politically, he was scornful of the battle for women's rights. 'I don't think it really matters a damn whether they have votes or not . . . More women are fools, I believe, than men.'[36] His sister Flora (a supporter of the campaign) told him: 'Your suffrage sentiments are horrible.'[37] It would not be until after his work with Margaret Llewelyn Davies and the Women's Co-operative Guild that he would become an honorary feminist, and, even then, his blank spots over Virginia's work always centred on her politics.

Physically, Leonard was a tense-looking young man, dark, thin, slight, long-faced, with a handsome sardonic mouth, strong blue eyes, and trembling hands. This nervous tremor became much more pronounced in stressful public situations like a formal dinner (when sometimes his cutlery would rattle uncontrollably on his plate) and much less so when he was concentrating alone, writing or printing. He sought medical help for this condition on several occasions (in the 1930s, on Shaw's advice, he tried the Alexander Method). But in 1902 the family doctor he consulted did nothing but talk to him about Plato and Paederasty.[38] Maurice Wright, one of Virginia's doctors, applied for Leonard's exemption from military service in 1916 and 1917 on the grounds of his 'general tremor', which he described as evidence of 'definite Nervous disabilities' – a diagnosis which Leonard disputed.[39] Virginia Woolf thought of the tremor as 'a disease that has, I guess, moulded his life wrongly since he was 5'. Without it, 'all his shyness, his suffering from society, his sharpness, & definiteness, might have been smoothed'.[40]

And he did have a painful sense of life being wrongly moulded. His first feelings for Virginia Stephen were not much more than consolatory fantasies for life's awfulness. He had only met the Stephen sisters three times,[41] and on those occasions had been more drawn to Vanessa's sensuality and resemblance to 'the Goth'.[42] It was Lytton who initiated the suggestion of 'Virginia Stephen and Leonard Woolf' and who played on Leonard's imagination, encouraging him (in the same breath as he described his own proposal to her) in a fantasy of coming home to claim her. 'If you came & proposed she'ld accept you. She really would.'[43]

Leonard Woolf replied to Strachey's 'proposal' letter with a peculiar tirade which mixed together the unreality of his life, his memories of Cambridge as being all that stopped him committing suicide, his realisation that 'the one thing to do would be to marry Virginia', his fears of the 'ghastly complications of virginity & marriage', and an outburst on 'the stupid blind vindictive foulness of everything & of myself'.[44] It was not the letter of someone confident of their own attractions as a husband, or which showed a real interest in Virginia Stephen as anything other than a virginal mystery.

*

When Leonard came back to England on 10 June 1911 for a year's leave, after six-and-a-half years in Ceylon, everything seemed at once familiar and strange.[45] He went to see his family in Putney, and then 'plunged' straight back into Cambridge and Bloomsbury life. He saw Lytton first, and then the Bells and Virginia Stephen at Gordon Square, on 3 July. On 16 September he went to Sussex to spend a weekend with Virginia, Desmond MacCarthy, and Marjorie Strachey in Firle. In October he and Virginia went to hear *Siegfried* together in Covent Garden. That autumn they were meeting at the Russian Ballet (to which 'everyone' in London was going), at Gordon and at Fitzroy Squares. In November Virginia and Adrian moved to Brunswick Square with two tenants, Maynard Keynes and Duncan Grant. Leonard joined the household on 4 December. He was already enthralled by Virginia (though he was also seeing someone else, the daughter of a family friend).[46] 'I see it will be the beginning of hopelessness', he wrote to Lytton on 1 November. 'To be in love with her – isn't that a danger?'[47] But he moved into the Brunswick Square house as a lodger, not as a lover.

No. 38 Brunswick Square was a preferable alternative to the unsatisfactory *ménage à deux* at Fitzroy Square. There was a graveyard behind it, and the Foundling Hospital – occasion for some predictable jokes – next door. Virginia and Adrian as 'boarding house keepers',[48] letting rooms to three male tenants (two of whom were lovers) was not thought desirable by distanced onlookers like Violet or George. But Sophie Farrell and Maud stayed on – the whole arrangement depended on their willingness to cook for the tenants and their occasional guests – and the house was run on business-like terms. This was Leonard's tenancy agreement as drawn up by Virginia in December 1911, very much not a love letter:

Meals are:

Breakfast	9 a.m.
Lunch	1.
Tea	4.30 p.m.
Dinner	8 p.m.

Trays will be placed in the hall punctually at these hours. Inmates are requested to carry up their own trays; and to put the dirty plates on them and carry them down again *as soon as the meal is finished.*

Inmates are requested to put their initials upon the kitchen instruction tablet hung in the hall against all meals required that day before 9.30 a.m . . .

The meals will consist of tea, egg and bacon, toast or roll for breakfast; meat, vegetables, and sweet for lunch; tea, buns, for tea; fish, meat, sweet, for dinner. It is not possible as a general rule to cater for guests as well as inmates. If notice is given, exceptions can sometimes be made. Particular desires will be considered. A box will be placed in the hall in which is requested that inmates shall place their requests or complaints.

It is hoped that inmates will make a special effort to be punctual, for thus the work of service will be much lightened.

The proprietors reserve the right of ceasing to supply service at any time.[49]

Leonard, who had the cheaper upstairs rooms, was charged 35s. a week for rent, light, coals, hot baths, and service. Maynard Keynes, in whose name the lease was taken out, and who lived with Duncan in the larger ground floor (which Duncan decorated with a large mural of London life), paid more like £3 a week. Meals cost 1s. for breakfast, 2s. for lunch, and 2s. 6d. for dinner. Each person's contribution to the servants' wages was about 7s. 6d. a month. Virginia, who collected the rents (even on the eve of her marriage), was on the second floor, with all her books and papers; Adrian, whose room was also decorated by Duncan with a tennis-playing mural, was on the first floor.

Virginia looked back on this communal household as one of her pioneering achievements.[50] Comparing Stracheys unfavourably with Stephens in 1919, she said that they had never had the energy or initiative to bring about any 'new departures': 'an Omega, a Post-Impressionist movement . . . a country cottage, a Brunswick Square, or a printing press.'[51] The house was the site of a rich social life ('Callers come in rather a thick stream', wrote Keynes)[52] and of some of the dramatic events of her life.

When on 11 January 1912 Leonard asked Virginia Stephen to marry him, he was entirely unsure of the outcome. It was two weeks before her thirtieth birthday and the day on which she published a sympathetic essay on Gissing's 'melancholy questionings':

When the man and the woman are to meet for the great scene of passion, let it all be frustrated by one or other of them having a bad cold in the head. [What is the cause of Gissing's gloom? she asks.] His men and women think . . . The great advantage of making people think is that you can describe other relationships beside the great one between the lover and the beloved.[53]

Virginia Stephen was vulnerable to Leonard Woolf's proposal, but she also resisted it. Her feelings about herself were anxious and uncertain after the painful summer of 1910. In 1911 the unsatisfactory proposals she had received, her feelings for Jacques Raverat and Rupert Brooke, her still troubled emotions about Clive and Vanessa, all disturbed her. Vanessa's changing life particularly affected her. In the spring of 1911, Vanessa went to Turkey with Clive, Roger Fry, and Harry Norton; she had a miscarriage there, and then a breakdown. She was looked after with sympathetic efficiency by Roger Fry, and they began to fall in love. At the end of April, Virginia went out to Broussa to help bring her back to England. 'It was the oddest parody of what we did five years ago,' she wrote to Violet.[54] It was one of several occasions when a catastrophe in Vanessa's life brought out her sister's competence and strength. For the next year or more Vanessa was ill with a mixture of mental and physical symptoms which elicited from Virginia the same kind of reassuring letters which Vanessa had written to *her* when she was having her rest-cure. But during this time the devils of depression ('hairy black ones') were attacking Virginia as well. They focussed, often, on comparisons of her state with Vanessa's. 'To be 29 & unmarried – to be a failure – childless – insane too, no writer.'[55] As opposed to having a husband, two children, a promising career as a painter, *and* a lover.

That summer Vanessa Bell and Roger Fry began the affair which Vanessa was anxious to conceal from Virginia: she did not trust her discretion. But Virginia's letters to them both spoke pointedly of 'you and Vanessa' or 'you and Roger'. On 18 January 1912 Vanessa told him that 'V told me last night that she suspected me of having a "liaison" with you. She has been quick to suspect it, hasn't she?'[56] This talk took place in the week of Leonard's proposal, which Virginia had immediately reported to Vanessa. (Vanessa wrote to Leonard: 'You're the only person I know whom I can imagine as her husband.')[57] Virginia's discovery of Vanessa's passionate affair with Roger Fry played its part in her own decision about marrying.

There was considerable pressure on her to say yes. Lytton's influence cannot be underestimated. Clive was being mischievous (Adrian clumsily showed Leonard and Virginia some spiteful letters Clive had written about her, and a row ensued). Vanessa was almost too encouraging. It's been suggested that she was so eager to transfer the responsibility for Virginia to Leonard Woolf that she was not entirely candid with him about the nature and the extent of Virginia's earlier breakdowns. Vanessa's influence on Leonard has been said to have shaped the whole marriage: it was Vanessa who gave him the idea of Virginia as vulnerable, 'mad', in need of close guardianship. Was this, then, 'an arranged marriage', with Lytton and Vanessa as the brokers?[58] These sinister readings of a family plot call for more Machiavellianism on Vanessa's part, less acuteness on Leonard's, and less independence on Virginia's, than seems characteristic. But Vanessa did involve Leonard very quickly in the role of guardian, going with him to consult Dr Savage about Virginia as early as March 1912.

Leonard Woolf's obvious suitability as a husband was both an attraction to Virginia and, perversely, an obstacle. He was the right age. He belonged to her 'family': he had loved Thoby (one of the first things she did after Thoby's death was to send Leonard, via Saxon, a book of Thoby's); and he was the closest friend of her closest friends.

At the same time he was a stranger who had been living a quite different life from anyone else she knew. The figure of the returning colonialist would play an important part in her novels. Peter Walsh in *Mrs Dalloway* and North in *The Years* both derive a kind of cynical strength from their experiences. 'And this has been going on all the time!' thinks Peter as he returns to visit Clarissa, much as Leonard did when he got back to Cambridge from Hambantota. 'All India lay behind him; plains, mountains; epidemics of cholera; a district twice as big as Ireland; decisions he had come to alone.'[59] Leonard Woolf told his stories of Ceylon to Virginia Stephen like Othello wooing Desdemona with tales of the anthropophagoi. 'He spent 7 years in Ceylon, governing natives, inventing ploughs, shooting tigers.'[60] He seemed to her competent, experienced and extremely intelligent. They had the same desire to work, the same friendships, the same pleasure in the countryside. His problematic Jewishness may also have been an incentive. This would be the opposite of the sort of 'Stephen' marriage which either of her parents could have countenanced, and therefore might be worth adventuring on, now that 'human character' had changed. And he was romantically in love with her, always a persuasive ingredient in a courtship, though not necessarily the best circumstances for finding out what someone is like.

The courtship was pressurising and intense. She was still trying to finish her novel, which she read to him. (He was encouraging.) He had to make up his mind whether to return to Ceylon or whether to take his chance in England. However scrupulous he was about this, she must have been made to feel that her decision was bound up with his professional destiny. If he gave up his job he would have very little money. On 14 February, about a month after his proposal in January, he asked for his leave to be extended. At exactly this time, she began to suffer from 'wild dreams' and anxiety, and on 16 February she went back to Twickenham for another rest-cure, and was not allowed to receive 'emotional' letters from him or to see him. She wrote a jagged, alarming letter to him on 5 March about being elected 'king' of 'the lunatics' and hoping to 'escape molestation'.[61] The next day Vanessa wrote to him reassuringly: 'I think V is going on quite well. She says her sleep is much better and she's really, I think, living quietly in the present.'[62]

But it was hard at this point to live quietly in the present. Virginia wrote to Molly that she was a semi-invalid and was thinking intensely about marriage:

> Now I only ask for someone to make me vehement, and then I'll marry him! . . . I feel oddly vehement, and very exacting, and so difficult to live with and so very intemperate and changeable, now thinking one thing and now another.[63]

On 23 April 1912 Leonard was told that his extension of leave was impossible. On the 25th, he told his employers that in that case he would resign. On the 26th he and Virginia 'talked about what we should do if we married'. On the 27th, walking on the cliffs above Eastbourne, he kissed her: 'she was extraordinarily gentle.' On the 28th they talked all morning; he went to see *Götterdämmerung* in the evening. On the 29th he wrote her a long letter about her 'lovableness', saying that she should finish her novel before she decided, that he desired her, that he could never now be content with the second-best, and telling her not to worry. The next morning he received an official letter saying that his leave *could* be extended; he wrote to her at once to say that he had now got to make up his mind about Ceylon. The next day, 1 May, she wrote him a long letter which made his mind up. He went to hear *Tristan* that night, and the next day he wrote to confirm his resignation (which was accepted on the 7th). On 3 May they both went to the inquest on the *Titanic*, which had gone down on 15 April. Her imagination had fastened on the wreck. She wrote inventively to Ka Cox: 'Do you know it's a fact that ships don't sink at that depth, but remain poised half way down, and become perfectly flat, so that Mrs Stead is now like a pancake, and her eyes like copper coins.'[64] The underwater image stayed with her; a few weeks later, while she was still trying to make up her mind *and* finish her book, she wrote to Violet: 'You'll tell me I'm a failure as a writer, as well as a failure as a woman. Then I shall take a dive into the Serpentine, which, I see, is 6 feet deep in malodorous mud.'[65]

She was 'in sight of the end' of the book – and the end of being Virginia Stephen. Throughout May she saw Leonard almost every day; they went on the river to Teddington, to Hampton Court, for walks in Regent's Park. One night Leonard walked alone for hours along the Embankment. By the end of the month he had joined Virginia's menagerie, and they had invented their pet names for each other – she was Mandril (a big ugly baboon) and he was Mongoose (little and fierce). On 29 May they were talking quietly in her room after lunch when she told him that she loved him. They went on a trip to the river at Maidenhead. The next day they began to tell people;

Virginia's letters to her women friends, Violet, Madge, Janet, Ottoline, almost all started with the information that Leonard was 'a penniless Jew'. On 6 June a note went to Lytton Strachey, signed by both of them:

> Ha! Ha!
> Virginia Stephen
> Leonard Woolf.

It is hard not to read the voyage to 'Maidenhead' symbolically. Virginia Stephen's decisive letter to Leonard on 1 May was extremely open about her sexual feelings, and about all the other difficulties of this courtship. The letter, an extraordinary, touching, and admirable document, has to be read in full if she – and the marriage – are to be understood.

> May 1 Asheham
> Dearest Leonard
>
> To deal with the facts first (my fingers are so cold I can hardly write) I shall be back [at Brunswick Square] about 7 tomorrow, so there will be time to discuss – but what does it mean? You can't take the leave, I suppose if you are going to resign certainly at the end of it. Anyhow, it shows what a career you're ruining!
> Well then, as to all the rest. It seems to me that I am giving you a great deal of pain – some in the most casual way – and therefore I ought to be as plain with you as I can, because half the time I suspect, you're in a fog which I don't see at all. Of course I *can't* explain what I feel – these are some of the things that strike me. The obvious advantages of marriage stand in my way. I say to myself. Anyhow, you'll be quite happy with him; and he will give you companionship, children, and a busy life – then I say By God, I will not look upon marriage as a profession. The only people who know of it, all think it suitable; and that makes me scrutinise my own motives all the more. Then, of course, I feel angry sometimes at the strength of your desire. Possibly, your being a Jew comes in also at this point. You seem so foreign. And then I am fearfully unstable. I pass from hot to cold in an instant, without any reason; except that I believe sheer physical effort and exhaustion influence me. All I can say is that in spite of these feelings which go chasing each other all day long when I am with you, there is some feeling which is permanent, and growing. You want to know of course whether it will ever make me marry you. How can I say? I think it will, because there seems no reason why it shouldn't – But I don't know what the future will bring. I'm half afraid of myself. I sometimes feel that no one ever has or ever can share something – Its the thing that

makes you call me like a hill, or a rock. Again, I want everything – love, children, adventure, intimacy, work. (Can you make any sense out of this ramble? I am putting down one thing after another.) So I go from being half in love with you, and wanting you to be with me always, and know everything about me, to the extreme of wildness and aloofness. I sometimes think that if I married you, I could have everything – and then – is it the sexual side of it that comes between us? As I told you brutally the other day, I feel no physical attraction in you. There are moments – when you kissed me the other day was one – when I feel no more than a rock. And yet your caring for me as you do almost overwhelms me. It is so real, and so strange. Why should you? What am I really except a pleasant attractive creature? But its just because you care so much that I feel I've got to care before I marry you. I feel I must give you everything; and that if I can't, well, marriage would only be second-best for you as well as for me. If you can still go on, as before, letting me find my own way, as that is what would please me best; and then we must both take the risks. But you have made me very happy too. We both of us want a marriage that is a tremendous living thing, always alive, always hot, not dead and easy in parts as most marriages are. We ask a great deal of life, don't we? Perhaps we shall get it; then, how splendid!

One doesn't get much said in a letter; does one? I haven't touched upon the enormous variety of things that have been happening here – but they can wait.

D'you like this photograph? – rather too noble, I think. Here's another. Yrs. VS.[66]

Is this the letter of someone who does, or does not, want to marry? The 'noble' photograph she enclosed has her looking up, photographed from below, with her hands behind her back, in a rough tweed skirt, cardigan and floppy hat, looking self-contained, demanding, and apprehensive – like this letter. It might have discouraged a less adamant lover. All the reasons for saying yes are made to sound like no. And she signals with 'brutal' honesty the danger areas: his desire, his Jewishness, her instability. She was truthful and she was right: these *would* be their difficulties. It was brave and honest of her to say that she was angry with his desire, and half wanted to be left alone. If Virginia Stephen was to marry, she would need a great deal of solitude and privacy.

The letter is self-absorbed, but it suggests the freedom and intimacy of the conversation they were having: Leonard, she had found, was 'the one person to talk to'.[67] It is forceful, but uncertain of itself. Its author is not 'the author' 'Virginia Woolf', but a young woman of thirty who felt she had not achieved much, who was still struggling to finish her first novel, and who felt that he was the more successful and superior person. But as she takes her own temperature in the letter, she passes from cold (cold fingers, fog, a rock) to hot (always alive, and always hot). She changes from 'I' to 'we'. She moves towards an idea that the marriage might be possible because they are both capable of creating new terms for it. Like the heroine of a Restoration Comedy laying down her provisos, or the New Woman of an Ibsen play, she is determined that this will be the kind of marriage in which human character has changed. This is to be a pioneering, a 'modern' marriage. The letter ignores material matters of careers, money, or habitats. It is about reshaping the possibilities of marriage, rejecting the standard issue. 'Perhaps we shall get it; then, how splendid!' And perhaps they did.

These arguments and images got into both their writings. The lovers in *The Voyage Out* are full of melancholy bewilderment. Rachel – who is going to die rather than marry – vacillates painfully with Terence between detachment, fear, and a sense of intimacy. She finds peace only when she can think of them not as 'little separate bodies' who 'struggle and desire one another' but as disembodied, impersonal entities:

> So too, although she was going to marry him and to live with him for thirty, or forty, or fifty years, and to quarrel, and to be so close to him, she was independent of him; she was independent of everything else. Nevertheless . . . it was love that made her understand this . . . She wanted nothing else.[68]

In *Night and Day*, instead of dying, Katharine struggles through a period of disturbing confusion with Ralph towards the possibility of a new kind of marriage. The difficulty of finding no satisfactory precedent from previous models is discussed, in this calmer second novel, in more social and comic terms than in *The Voyage Out*, but with the same vacillation between separateness and intimacy. 'She had now to get used to the fact that someone shared her loneliness.'[69] In later novels, the space (or lack of it) that married couples leave each other will be of great importance, as if the experience of her own marriage is being held up against that of her parents.

The letter's image of her as a hill or a rock (re-used in *Night and Day*) was picked up from an odd courtship document written by Leonard, which began 'I am in love with Aspasia'[70] and in which Virginia and her friends were the 'Olympians'. Aspasia (in Greek history a teacher of eloquence in Athens, tutor to Socrates and wife of Pericles) is portrayed as a Greek statue or (like Pater's 'La Gioconda') as a figure made 'of the eternal snow and the rocks'. She is praised for her 'quietness and clearness', her 'fearless mind', the bubbling spring of her fantasy; but perhaps she 'has no heart'. Aspasia reads, and complains that 'you have not made me lovable enough'. (Hence

Leonard's reassurances, in his 29 April letter, of her 'lovableness'.) By contrast, Leonard presents himself as a 'Syrian born at Jericho' with 'a large nose and black hair'. 'There is some taint', he says, in the Syrian blood. He has 'a good brain and a bitter tongue'; and he is afraid that if the other Olympians read this paper he will have to 'take the train to Jericho'.

The romance of Aspasia is reversed in *The Wise Virgins*, where Leonard allows himself to express a sexual and racial anger which must have played some part in his feelings for her. Camilla writes a version of Virginia Stephen's letter to Harry Davis: 'It's the romantic part of life that I want; it's the voyage out that seems to me to matter . . . But I can't give myself; passion leaves me cold.' But Harry Davis, who in the novel misses his chance of marriage to Camilla, responds not with idealised fervour but with bitter anger:

> Harry turned on him . . . 'I'm a Jew.'
> 'Yes, I know. Well?'
> 'You can glide out of a room and I can't: I envy you that! But I despise you . . . I admire your women, your pale women with their white skins and fair hair, but I despise them.'
> 'Do most Jews feel like that?'
> 'All of them – all of them. There's no life in you, no blood in you, no understanding. Your women are cold and leave one cold – no dark hair, no blood in them. Pale hair, pale souls, you know. You talk and you talk and you talk – no blood in you! You never *do* anything.'
> 'Why do you think it's so important to do things?'
> 'Why? Because I'm a Jew, I tell you – I'm a Jew!'[71]

Both were right to perceive that this would be an issue in their marriage. As she told him candidly in her letter, his 'being a Jew' was one of the things she found difficult. In 1930 she told Ethel Smyth: 'How I hated marrying a Jew – how I hated their nasal voices, and their oriental jewellery, and their noses and their wattles – what a snob I was.'[72] As she can see, her racial and class prejudice were indistinguishable.

Upper-class English anti-Semitism was, until well into the 1930s, quite usual. Remarks by Virginia's friends about Hebrews and 'the chosen' were blithely unselfconscious. So Fredegond Shove, a childhood friend, could write to Vanessa in 1917 when the first Hogarth Press publication, 'The Mark on the Wall' and Leonard's 'Three Jews', came out: 'Virginia's story and L's have come. *Three* Jews – is not that rather too much of a good thing?'[73] And Clive Bell jested to Mary Hutchinson in 1915: 'I wonder why the Jews instituted the rite of circumscision [*sic*]. Was there money in it, d'you think, as there is in lambs' tails? Did the Levites traffick in *prepuces*?'[74]

Leonard, as the assimilated, deracinated Jew among upper-class gentiles, was the target of such jokes, but he also accepted them. Vanessa wrote to him in 1913: 'I think I owe you a letter and I'm afraid of getting into trouble if I dont pay what I owe to the Jews.'[75] Virginia would refer to him as 'my Jew', and at meals would say, 'Give the Jew his food.'[76] These marital habits were not cause for offence.

But when it came to his family her prejudices *were* offensive, and may have offended him. The more of them there were, the more Jewish they seemed to her. Whenever she referred to the big ceremonial family gatherings which the Woolfs went in for, she would always (especially in letters to Vanessa or Vita or Ethel) multiply their numbers, as a joke about how Jews do multiply (and 'pullulate' and 'copulate' and 'amass'). 'Here they are, dressed, like all Jews, as if for high tea in a hotel lounge'; '9 Jews, all of whom, with the single exception of Leonard, might well have been drowned without the world wagging one ounce the worse'; 'dine with 22 Jews & Jewesses to celebrate my mother in laws 84th birthday. And we shall play Bridge.'[77] Edgar and his wife Sylvia, Philip, Herbert and Freda, Bella and her second husband, poor unmarried Clara, Flora, Harold and his wife Alice: she thought of them all as suburban stockbrokers, who were either glum, or talked incessantly, ate lots of sweet things, gave terrible presents (like 'a vast sham brass fish slice'),[78] and required demonstrations of affection in return.

Individually, she responded to them rather differently. She was touched by Leonard's wistfulness about the two brothers, Cecil and Philip, who had been inseparable, and moved by their fate in the war: Cecil was killed (they printed a posthumous book of his poems at the Press) and Philip wounded. She liked Philip; and she found Herbert 'gay', less glum than Edgar, and felt sorry for Clara's enslavement by her mother. But all these in-laws were overshadowed by the overwhelming figure of Marie Woolf.

It was one of the comic oddities of Virginia Woolf's life that she found herself lumbered with a caricaturable Jewish mother-in-law, who seemed to her a grotesque antithesis of her own idealised lost mother. From her first kosher tea with Mrs Woolf, which she found 'queer' ('We don't eat Ham or bacon or Shellfish in this house')[79] she was amazed and appalled. Marie Woolf's childish desire for attention and affection (especially from her 'Len'), her lamentations, her family pride, her vanity, her emotionalism ('All was personal'), enraged but also impressed her daughter-in-law. At the worst, she felt, as she hated to feel, endlessly tyrannised by her:

> But there I am pinned down, as firmly as Prometheus on his rock, to have my day . . . made cheap & ugly & commonplace; for the sting of it is that

there is no possible escape . . . that wont make old Mrs Woolf begin to dab her eyes & feel that she is not being welcomed – she who is so 'painfully sensitive' – so fond of cakes, so incapable of amusing herself, so entirely without any interest in my feelings or friends; so vampire like & vast in her demand for my entire attention & sympathy, while she sits over the fire, in her dreary furs & ugly bonnet & large boots, with her pendulous cheeks & red nose & cheap earrings, talking about . . . how she will come to Worthing every year, & will expect to come to tea with us. Lord Lord! how many daughters have been murdered by women like this![80]

But it was she who wanted to do the murder. Yet she will give the old woman her due:

> Then, old Mrs Woolf . . . She has come to wear a charm & dignity to me, unknown before . . . she becomes curiously more humane & wise, as old women are; so pliable; so steeped in life that they seem to become philosophic, & more mistress of the art of living than much cleverer people. So many many things have happened before her; illnesses, births, quarrels, troubles – nothing much surprises her, or long upsets her.[81]

Though Virginia grew no kinder about 'Len's' relations *en masse*, in the course of her life's political reading of British culture she became critical and analytical of her own anti-Semitism. By the 1930s she had become intensely aware of and critical of her own complicity in the prejudices of her class and time. When she says 'How I hated marrying a Jew!' in 1930, she is passing judgement on herself.

Harry Davis, Leonard's anti-hero in *The Wise Virgins*, likes to refer to himself in gentile company not just as a Jew but as an *archetypal* Jew – 'the wandering Jew, the everlasting Jew'.[82] Leonard liked the idea of living a 'nomadic life', and of never settling – 'I hope when I die like a good Jew at 70 I shall still have no home'.[83] Virginia Stephen too found the idea attractive; perhaps it romanticised his Jewishness. She insisted in the month of their marriage that they would never have 'a real house', but would be 'chronically nomadic'.[84] So do Katharine and Ralph in *Night and Day*, who want 'more than anything movement, freedom from security, silence, and the open air'.[85] They are like Ursula and Birkin in *Women in Love* (also a war-time novel about the possibilities of marriage in the early twentieth century) who decide that they will 'wander about on the face of the earth'.[86]

The paradox for Virginia and Leonard was that though they both liked the idea of wandering about on the face of the earth, they were also very responsive to particular places. She was, always, extremely traumatised by house-moves; he insisted in his autobiography that his life was shaped by the places he lived in.[87] Their feeling for Sussex was one of the things which drew them together. Leonard's first romantic vision of Virginia Stephen placed her on the Downs, her face 'no less clear and fresh than the wind'.[88] Though she had visited Sussex before then, the countryside around Lewes was another of the important new discoveries of 1910 and 1911. She and Adrian had stayed in a pub in Lewes at Christmas, and had started to explore, with a view to finding somewhere to rent. After her breakdown of the summer of 1910, her doctors said she needed a quiet alternative to Studland or Giggleswick or Manorbier which was within easy distance of London. And she was also under the influence of the ruralism of the 'OB' campers. 'I am violently in favour of a country life', she wrote to Vanessa.[89]

The walks over the Downs, the wide distant views of the sea on the tops, the great hollows and gulfs below in the flanks of the Downs, the little scattered villages, the emptiness of the landscape, the enormous changing sky-scape, all filled her with intense pleasure. 'The country is so amazingly beautiful, that I frequently have to stop and say, "Good God!" '[90] She liked setting up a country routine, sinking into herself alone there, walking, 'coming back for tea, & finding letters . . . & having tea, & then writing over the fire, or reading a book'.[91] She liked 'looking out places on the map' and planning expeditions. But staying in inns was too expensive, and no good for visitors. Country life in a small cottage was very cheap before the war (and many artists and writers took advantage of this). And renting a house would make her more inward with 'another side of life [which] reveals itself in the country' and 'which I can't help thinking of amazing interest'.[92]

She acknowledged her desire to re-create the atmosphere of her childhood by naming the house she found to rent (for £19.10s a year) Little Talland House. It was an ugly, new, redbrick, semi-detached cottage in the narrow, curving main street of Firle (a pretty, but noisy, village), which she always referred to as an 'eyesore' or a 'horrible suburban villa'. But it had room for six, a bathroom and a lavatory, and so could be used – with Sophie and Maud in attendance – for weekend visitors. Little Talland House, though, was only a stop-gap.

When Leonard Woolf had spent his first weekend in Sussex with her in mid-September, and they went walking out of Firle up across the Downs and down to the Ouse valley, they found the house called Asheham (or 'Asham'). By October she and Vanessa had taken a joint lease on it.[93] (Clive, who was jealous of Vanessa's life at this time, was not enthusiastic.) They had two housewarming parties on freezing cold weekends in January: Leonard came to both. In February, while Virginia retreated again to Burley Park, Leonard helped Vanessa put down carpets. So, from the first,

Asheham was shared between the sisters, and this would be the ground of some practical difficulties and conflicts.[94] Nevertheless, Virginia and Leonard would come to think of it as particularly their own.

Asheham was an odd house, elegant, remote, dark, and rather mysterious. Leonard described it as 'an extraordinarily romantic looking house'.[95] It was set back from a bend of the road between Newhaven and Lewes, and sat 'dropped beneath the Downs'[96] right under the huge high slope of Asheham Down (where there were mushrooms in profusion all through the late summer and autumn). There were no other houses near, only some barns and a shepherd's cottage. It was led up to by a line of big elm trees, and had a long view in front of it. A rough lawn and fields ran straight down to the river Ouse, with Rodmell, their future home, across on the other side of the valley. There was a 'small, dishevelled walled garden'[97] on one side, which Leonard would work on. It had been built between 1820 and 1825 by the owner of Itford Farm (a little way further south, at the river crossing to Southease) and it was a pretty Regency building given character by its windows and its side wings. L-shaped, with two sitting-rooms downstairs, four bedrooms above and a big attic, it had a slated roof and brick floors and was painted yellow outside. On the first floor was a charming row of three double-arched windows and below them, in perfect symmetry, three long narrow french windows opened out on to a small terrace. On either side of the main building were two little single-storey wings each with a pointed roof and a french window. In fact it looked, as has been observed, rather like 'a hunting pavilion'.[98] In winter it could be ferociously cold; in summer it was shady and damp indoors, and rotted all their books. It could be a little 'shut in & dismal', as well as 'dim & mysterious'.[99] It had an underwater feeling: 'the window-panes reflected apples, reflected roses; all the leaves were green in the glass.' It was quiet, except when the new-born lambs were making a racket all night: outside in summer you could hear 'the wood-pigeons bubbling with content and the hum of the threshing machine sounding from the farm'.[100] Visitors, who came in numbers through the summer months, were met by a fly at Lewes station, or walked the five miles or so across the fields. The servants hated Asheham because it was so isolated, and those who lived there were dependent for practical help in all sorts of ways on the neighbouring shepherd's wife, Mrs Funnell, a forceful country character.

Asheham was where Leonard and Virginia spent the first night of their marriage. She would always remember walking outside the house that night, along the path they had christened the Mandril's walk.[101] Between 1912 and 1919 she spent a great deal of time there. She identified Asheham (as she identified London) with her deepest feelings for England and

Englishness. A phrase from Arnold's *Thyrsis*, quoted in her 1917 review of
Edward Thomas's book about English writers in their landscapes, *A
Literary Pilgrim in England*, sums up her feelings about Asheham and the
South Downs: 'I know these slopes; who knows them, if not I?'[102] She
recognised this emotion:

> How I adore the emptiness, bareness, air & colour of this! . . . A relic I
> think of my fathers feeling for the Alps – this ecstasy of mine over the bare
> slope of Asheham hill. But then, as I remind myself, half the beauty of a
> country or a house comes from knowing it. One remembers old
> lovelinesses: knows that it is now looking ugly; waits to see it light up;
> knows where to find its beauty; how to ignore the bad things. This one
> can't do the first time of seeing.[103]

It is like a description of a long marriage.

'A Haunted House', the little story she wrote about Asheham (which *was*
supposed to be a haunted house),[104] is full of that sense of beauty and loss. It
imagines a ghostly couple revisiting the house, half-sensed by the couple
living there.[105] The ghosts go from room to room (like the questing airs in
the 'Time Passes' section of *To the Lighthouse*), looking for their own past,
seeking their 'buried treasure' which seems to lie in the 'pulse of the house'.
As they hang benignly over the sleeping couple, the 'I' of the story wakes up
understanding that the buried treasure is 'the light in the heart'. But the
present inhabitants seem as insubstantial as the ghosts, the ghosts' marriage
more vivid than that of the living sleepers.

EIGHTEEN

Marriage

Twenty years later, she wrote: 'If it were not for the divine goodness of L. how many times I should be thinking of death'.[1] Death and marriage were connected, but as counter-forces. The marriage made a frame and a space for the work, which was life to her. And because 'I married Leonard Woolf in 1912, . . . & almost immediately was ill for 3 years' ('Nevertheless we have nothing to complain of')[2] the marriage very quickly became constructed as a régime. Her provisos for marriage were answered by his (en)treaties for her 'self-control', for behaviour which would save her life. So he too thought of the marriage as an opposing force to death.

Leonard's drive for control and her need for care fell into a consistent life-long shape because of her illness. There were phases when these patterns of behaviour became constrictive to both of them, more of a *folie à deux*, perhaps, than a sensible balancing-act. They had fierce arguments and violent differences of opinions. In the course of their marriage, her emotional life was absorbed by powerful and demanding women. In the last years of her life she became more isolated, more distanced from him, partly for political reasons. But they also came to be like-minded in their social habits and in their public identity as a culturally influential couple. And they both cultivated, in ways quite obscure to outsiders, a private space of play and tenderness. There are eloquent tributes in the diaries to what she calls 'the core of my life'[3] or 'my inviolable centre'.[4] She often marks the places where the 'dailiness' of married life has sprung into a 'moment of great intensity', a process she at one point sums up under the heading 'The Married Relation':

> Life – say 4 days out of 7 – becomes automatic; but on the 5th day a bead of sensation (between husband & wife) forms, wh. is all the fuller & more sensitive because of the automatic customary unconscious days on either side. That is to say the year is marked by moments of great intensity. Hardy's 'moments of vision'. How can a relationship endure for any length of time except under these conditions?[5]

Sometimes these moments seem to have no particular source, but just to emerge from their life together:

> [After a very wet spring holiday driving in France in 1931]: That we retrieved so much from it that was lovely, ravishing, amusing & had so many good hours, spinning along wet roads, under a complete grey cloud, speaks well for the state of our souls. After being married since August 1912
>
> 1931
> 1912
> ————
> 19
>
> nineteen years, how moving to find this warmth, curiosity, attachment in being alone with L.[6]

Sometimes such moments of awareness will come out of a conflict:

> Leonard gave me the blue glass jug today, because he was cross when I slapped his nose with sweet peas, & because I was nice to his mother, & when I went into luncheon I saw it on the table. Indeed, I almost cried. He went to Brighton to get it for me. 'I thought of it just as I was getting into the car' he said. Perhaps I have analysed his motives wrongly.[7]

From these pains taken, compromises and moments of awareness, they built up a space of mutual necessity, which continued to give delight in middle age. When in October 1937 Leonard admitted that he would rather she did not to go off to see Vanessa in Paris, 'I was overcome with happiness. Then we walked round the square love making – after 25 years cant bear to be separate. Then I walked round the Lake in Regents Park. Then . . . you see it is an enormous pleasure, being wanted: a wife. And our marriage so complete.'[8]

This reads like a marriage which is worked at; a working marriage; and a marriage which works. The key to its completeness, she often perceives, lies in its privacy:

> The immense success of our life, is I think, that our treasure is hid away; or rather in such common things that nothing can touch it. That is, if one enjoys a bus ride to Richmond, sitting on the green smoking, taking the letters out of the box, airing the marmots [a private phrase], combing Grizzle [the dog], making an ice, opening a letter, sitting down after dinner, side by side, & saying, 'Are you in your stall, brother?' – well, what can trouble this happiness? And every day is necessarily full of it.[9]

But this private inwardness retains some mystery. For much of the time she keeps it hidden even from the diaries, as though its particular virtue lies in not being too fully analysed. When she describes their 'warmth, curiosity, attachment', she continues: 'If I dared I would investigate my own sensations with regard to him, but out of laziness, humility, pride, I dont know what reticence – refrain. I who am not reticent.'[10]

All marriages are inexplicable; the Woolfs' remarkable and unusual marriage, witnessed by extremely gossipy and watchful types, was much commented on, but not necessarily well understood. The gossip about them started early, and, as stories about Virginia Woolf often did, they became more grotesque in the telling. There was an apocryphal tale, for instance, put about by Lytton, of a botched acceptance:

> There's a story that a week or two before the engagement he proposed in a train, and she accepted him, but owing to the rattling of the carriage he didn't hear, and took up a newspaper, saying 'What?' On which she had a violent revulsion and replied – 'Oh, nothing!'[11]

Eighty years later this was repeated to me by Isaiah Berlin in a rather altered form: that Virginia, alone in a train compartment with Leonard, knew that he was going to propose, and in order to stop him, rolled up her copy of her newspaper (the *Observer*), peed into it, and threw it out of the window. 'That stopped him in his tracks!'[12] From the start, Clive Bell made a mocking version of the marriage, here to Molly MacCarthy:

> Virginia and the Woolf have come to some pretty definite understanding . . . It is really very satisfactory, I suppose; but it would be rather horrible to think that, most probably, people would feel for one's children what none of us can help feeling for Jews. – 'Oh, he's quite a good fellow – he's a Jew you know –'. Don't you think it would be rather painful to get oneself into that plight? And Woolf's family are chosen beyond anything.[13]

But on the honeymoon 'the Woolves' (as they were immediately called) disappeared from such commentary, conventionally enough, into two months of unwitnessed life. The weeks of June and July were spent meeting each other's friends and relations, including the Duckworths at Dalingridge Hall, and Mrs Woolf – 'chosen beyond anything'. They wrote numerous 'engagement' letters, and she rushed towards the end of *The Voyage Out*. In June they had a weekend in Suffolk (Walberswick, Blythburgh and Southwold). But she was not well and spent many days in bed: this was a stressful time. The wedding between Leonard Sidney Woolf, age thirty-one, Bachelor of Independent Means, and Adeline Virginia Stephen, age

LONDON, TUESDAY, AUGUST 13, 1912.

MARRIAGES.

RIDGWAY : BANNATYNE.—On the 7th inst., at St. Peter's Church, Flores, Buenos Aires, by the Rev. Canon Stevenson and the Rev. Jules Dubourg, GEORGE, second son of RICHARD GRUBB RIDGWAY, of Riverview House, Waterford, to AGNES, daughter of the late ANDREW BANNATYNE, of Glasgow and Hamilton.

WOOLF : STEPHEN.—On Saturday, the 10th Aug., at the St. Pancras Register Office, LEONARD SIDNEY WOOLF, son of the late Sidney Woolf, Q.C., and of Mrs. Sidney Woolf, of Lexham, Colinette-road, Putney, to VIRGINIA STEPHEN, daughter of the late Sir Leslie Stephen, K.C.B.

thirty, Spinster (rank and profession left blank) took place at 12.15 on Saturday 10 August 1912 in St Pancras Town Hall, in the middle of a thunderstorm. Vanessa and George Duckworth were the witnesses. The registrar, Edwin Stevens ('half blind and otherwise deformed') mixed up the names Vanessa and Virginia; Vanessa interrupted the matter-of-fact ceremony to ask how she could change her baby's name. Marie Woolf was bitterly slighted at not having been asked. Roger Fry, Duncan Grant in borrowed clothes, Saxon Sydney-Turner, Aunt Mary Fisher, now seventy-odd, and the socially inept painter Fred Etchells, a friend of Roger and Duncan, were the ill-assorted wedding party; not Clive, though he played host afterwards at a small lunch party at Gordon Square. Then Leonard and Virginia Woolf left for Asheham for the weekend, and Clive wrote her a farewell letter: 'I love you very much and I love your lover too.'[14] The next week they came back through London to the Plough Inn at Holford (near Nether Stowey, where Coleridge once lived, as Virginia noted), ate the good food for which the Inn was famous, walked on the Quantock Hills through the mist (the weather was still terrible) and read novels in front of the fire.

On 18 August they left England for Dieppe, first for the South of France (where they took a terrifying bus ride to the top of Mont Serrat), then to Spain (Tarragona, Saragossa and Toledo). In Spain the lavatories were filthy ('you can there distinguish the droppings of Christian, Jew, Latin and Saxon'),[15] the mosquitoes bit, the heat was terrible, and Leonard had a bout of malarial fever, which would recur after their return.[16] But the countryside was magnificent, and the cathedral at Toledo was especially good. On 17 September they took a Hungarian cargo boat from Valencia to Marseilles (Virginia was sick, Leonard managed to eat 'an enormous gherkin' and a huge breakfast) and then on to Pisa. In the Campo Santo she hid behind a pillar in order to avoid being recognised by the Palgraves, old friends of Leslie.[17] They went on to Milan and by the end of September were in Venice (which she detested) in cold rainy weather.

During the honeymoon Virginia read *Le Rouge et le Noir*, *Pendennis* (which she would make rich use of for 'Arthur's Education Fund' in *Three Guineas*), *The Antiquary* (one of her father's favourite novels, and important in the marital story of *To the Lighthouse*), Charlotte Yonge's *The Heir of Redclyffe*, D.H. Lawrence's second novel *The Trespasser* (about a tragic love-affair), and, most important, Dostoevsky's *Crime and Punishment*, which completely absorbed her, and began her long and impassioned involvement with the Russians. She placed more emphasis in her letters home about their travels and their reading than on 'the proper business of bed',[18] though she told Ka Cox that she could not see what the fuss was about: 'I find the climax immensely exaggerated.'[19] Vanessa, meanwhile, was writing aggressively inquisitive and teasing letters:

> As long as the ape gets all he wants, doesnt smell too much and has his claws well cut, he's a pleasant enough bed fellow for a short time. The whole question is what will happen when the red undergrowth sprouts in the winter?
> Are you really a promising pupil? I believe I'm very bad at it. Perhaps Leonard would like to give me a few lessons. But of course *some* people don't need to be so skilful.[20]

On 3 October they returned to face this sort of family curiosity, first to Brunswick Square, and then a week later to rooms at 13 Clifford's Inn.

There was now a degree of estrangement between 'Virginia Woolf' and Vanessa. She had discovered while they were away that Vanessa had broken faith by telling Leonard about Virginia's dealings with Walter Lamb. But the distancing between them had deeper causes. Vanessa had found it 'bewildering and upsetting', initially, to think of Virginia as one of a couple – just as, six years before, Virginia had been unable to bear *her* marriage. 'I shan't see more than I can help of them,' Vanessa wrote to Clive, 'as after all they don't want me now'.[21] She had mixed feelings about Leonard.

> Talking of Woolves [Clive reported to Molly MacCarthy in 1913] I came back on Thursday to find Vanessa in a fine old rage: they had just left. 'Clive, am I an atrocious egoist, and intolerable to live with? Are all Stephens egoists?' Every subject that Vanessa touched, it seems, was made personal forthwith, and a casus belli. Woolf just as bad in his own way: 'I told you so' 'I foresaw' 'I took steps' 'I can make it go' 'I am life's master' . . . if there is to be a drifting apart I shan't touch the rudder much less an oar. It's clear that the young couple are down in the world at present, the feeling seems to be that Virginia + Woolf = 2 [22]

In the early years of the marriage, Vanessa was frequently exasperated by Leonard's intransigence. 'I wish Woolf didnt irritate me so!' she wrote to Roger Fry in 1914.[23] But these outbursts must be set against her respect for his stoicism during Virginia's breakdowns. Vanessa herself was going through a time of great stress at the start of Virginia's marriage. She was unwell – at Christmas 1912 she collapsed with exhaustion – and she was absorbed with her children, her love-affair with Roger, and her painting. In 1913, she made a trip to Italy in the spring with the three men she was closest to, Clive Bell, Roger Fry and Duncan Grant; she was helping Roger Fry set up the Omega workshops in the second half of 1913; and her feelings were shifting, surprisingly but strongly and for ever, towards Duncan Grant. So she had other concerns than Virginia: though Virginia's increasingly alarming state of mind did trouble her.

But the sisters' lives were still closely involved. Helen Ambrose in *The Voyage Out* was built out of Virginia's feelings for Vanessa, and she would draw on them again when she began *Night and Day* in 1916. They were sharing Asheham, and Leonard had come back to work for Roger Fry as secretary of the second Post-Impressionist exhibition at the Grafton Galleries, which ran from October 1912 to January 1913. It may have provoked some envy in Virginia that Vanessa was showing a few paintings here, alongside the Cézannes and the new Russians and the Matisses (including 'The Dance'). Leonard witnessed the reactions to the show at first hand and discussed it with Vanessa. Fry's manifesto ('These artists do not seek to imitate form, but to create form; not to imitate life, but to find an equivalent for life'), the debate on 'significant form' which arose from it, and Clive Bell's 1914 bible on the non-representational sources of aesthetic enjoyment, *Art*, would have a strong influence on Virginia Woolf's work in the late 1910s.[24]

On their return to England the Woolfs set up more like students than like a middle-class married couple, in rooms at the top of an eighteenth-century building between Chancery Lane and Fetter Lane, off Fleet Street. It could have been a Cambridge college (though they had a phone – Holborn 5711) with names on the door and a porter and a charwoman who came in to 'do' (and seemed not to mind finding Leonard in the bathtub). It seemed bohemian and rather dingy to Virginia: the other tenants left their plates and their milk bottles outside their doors, and they could see the love life of the couples opposite. After some failed attempts at cooking mutton cutlets (which tended to burn outside and stay bloody inside) they took all their meals at an old city eating house in Fleet Street, the Cock Tavern, with wooden partitions and a vintage head waiter. This, and the flagged courtyard below, and the ancient, draughty, dirty rooms, made them feel as if Dr Johnson might easily 'come out of his grave for a turn in the moonlight'.[25]

She often wrote about the energy and activity and the weekend desolation of this part of London, under the shadow of St Paul's. She loved the 'unconcerned, business-like look of things', the 'uproar, the confusion, the space of the Strand', the 'vast funeral mass of the Law Courts' with their 'press of people', the need for pedestrians to 'jostle and skip and circumvent each other' on the narrow pavements and jump out of the way of motor-cars. ('It was odd how soon one got used to cars without horses', she writes in the 1914 section of *The Years*, 'they used to look ridiculous'.) She missed all this very much when, because of her health, they moved out to Richmond for nine years. At the same time she felt that the 'brotherhood', the 'procession' of City life was alien to her. For Elizabeth Dalloway in *Mrs Dalloway*, for Sara Pargiter in *The Years*, this is the centre of male energy and business, and they come there as tourists or observers, half-wanting and half-fearing to join the male procession. Out of these few months of living in the heart of the City she added to her political reading of British life.

The main reason they were there, and the reason Leonard was working at the Grafton Galleries, was financial. Virginia Stephen's presentation of Leonard Woolf to her friends as 'a penniless Jew' was meant to shock on two grounds; and those who felt responsible for her reacted accordingly. George Savage wrote to Violet Dickinson: 'I think he is all right though he is a Hebrew without present occupation.'[26] (And added: 'I have warned Mr L.W. of the delicate machine.') George Duckworth asked Leonard: 'Can you and will you settle anything on Virginia?' And if not, 'would you agree to investing say $\frac{1}{10}$th of your income in the purchase of a life assurance in Virginia's favour?' (And, as an afterthought: 'Virginia will be a most adorable wife.')[27]

The prospect of a settlement was unlikely. Leonard had gambled a little in Ceylon, and in 1908 he won £690 in the Calcutta Turf Club Melbourne Cup sweepstakes.[28] When they married, Leonard had £506 to invest, and Virginia had £9013.16s. 9d. inherited capital (from the combined legacies of Leslie, Thoby, Stella, and Caroline Emelia) and an extra £300 which was a third of the sale of Leslie's second house in Emperor's Gate. (In 1928 she also got a third of the sale price of 22 Hyde Park Gate, £4925).[29] Her capital was invested in stocks and shares and would give an income of just under £400 a year. Their annual expenditure in 1914 came to £443; for 1917 it rose to £680. In the next few years it was between £700 and £800 a year: so they needed to earn £400 or £500 a year.[30] Leonard's account of their accounts emphasised three things: that until 1929 they could not possibly live on earnings from their books (*The Voyage Out*, for example, took fifteen years to sell 2,000 copies and in those years earned less than £120); that their expenses went up catastrophically because of her illness (in 1915, for example, they spent £500 on doctors' and nurses' bills); and that Virginia, not he, had attacks of anxiety, like her father, about money.[31]

Leonard was determined to invest their capital, and both would work extremely hard to make up the four or five hundred pounds' income they needed. They started as they meant to go on: 'In the morning we write 750 words each' (Leonard wrote to Lytton from Asheham, in April 1913) 'in the afternoon we dig; between tea and dinner we write 500 words each.'[32] Between 1916 and 1929 Virginia Woolf wrote as many as forty-seven articles a year, and hardly ever fewer than ten. For a few months in 1914 she kept a housekeeping book; then Leonard took it over, and for the rest of his life kept scrupulous annual accounts, balancing their actual against their estimated expenditure at the end of every year.[33] But she was not 'unworldly about money'.[34] The diaries and letters were full of details about her income. Like her parents, she despised and was personally indifferent to conspicuous consumption. But she loved to earn.

At the end of 1912, though, there was no evidence that she would ever become a money-earning professional novelist. The breakdown of 1913 was triggered, in large part, by the pressure she placed on herself to finish *The Voyage Out*. Though a penultimate draft had been completed just before the wedding, she still felt she had work to do on it. It would have been difficult for her not to be threatened by the fact that Leonard's novel *The Village in the Jungle* (which she read respectfully in November 1912) was finished and accepted before hers.[35] She had written at least five drafts of *her* novel, and between 1909 and 1913 she may have had two versions on the go simultaneously. Between December 1912 and March 1913 she retyped and to an extent rewrote it entirely – and she may have been working on still another version. She typed 600 pages in two months, working, according to Leonard, 'with a kind of tortured intensity' and with 'excruciating effort'.[36] Evidently, finishing and letting go of her first book terrified her almost to death.[37]

On 9 March 1913 Leonard Woolf delivered the typescript to Gerald Duckworth's publishing house, and for the rest of the month she was in the unpleasant position of waiting for the half-brother she had never liked to decide whether he would accept it. She stopped herself – or Leonard stopped her – from talking about it: 'My novel – but having said that, I'm now trained to stop short: isn't it wonderful? It's all Leonard's doing',[38] she wrote to Ka. It was the start of a new reticence about work in progress. She distracted herself with an enthusiastic piece on Jane Austen's courage and impersonality:

She possessed in a greater degree perhaps than any other English woman the sense of the significance of life apart from any personal liking or disliking.[39]

But then Edward Garnett wrote a perceptive and enthusiastic reader's report,[40] and *The Voyage Out* was accepted for publication on 12 April. From May to June Virginia Woolf corrected her proofs. It would always be a painful task for her, and this first time, unprepared for, was the worst of all. She would never forget how excruciating her first re-reading of herself in cold print felt. When she was in despair at the proofs of *The Years* in 1936, she wrote: 'I have never suffered, since The Voyage Out, such acute despair on re-reading, as this time.' 'Never been so near the precipice to my own feeling since 1913.'[41] She was staggering on the brink of breakdown. Vanessa, Leonard and Jean Thomas (who had looked after her in 1910 and 1912) all said that ending the book brought on the illness. Because of it, Duckworth decided not to publish the novel until the first year of the war, on 26 March 1915. But when at last *The Voyage Out* was published, weeks after her thirty-third birthday, and Leonard registered her, under the National Registration Act of 1915, as an 'author', she was in the dark cupboard of her mental illness, and did not emerge until the autumn of that year.

Leonard was, of course, working hard too, and from 1912 onwards this work began to take its future shape as a lifetime's commitment to British socialism. In the summer of 1912 Virginia's cousin Marny Vaughan roused Leonard's interest in her work for the Charity Organisation Society in Hoxton, in the East End. What he saw of conditions there, he said later, 'turned me from a liberal into a socialist',[42] though he quickly became impatient with the ineffectual good works of the COS. At the same time, through Janet Case and Virginia, he met Margaret Llewelyn Davies,[43] the chief organiser of the Women's Co-Operative Guild, the women's branch of the Co-Operative Society, which organised working-class women into regional groups based on the principle of consumer control and consumer co-operation. Leonard was drawn to this Owenite workers' movement because it aimed 'to place large sections of the economy in the control of the community organised as consumers'. As soon as he got involved he began to analyse and write about its potential 'as a socialist alternative to the profit-making capitalist system'.[44] He joined forces with Davies in her pressure-goup work to improve the divorce laws for women (a Royal Commission recommended changes in November 1912), writing a paper which argued (among other things) that insanity should be grounds for divorce.[45] He joined the suffrage movement. Davies fired him with the idea that the co-operative movement could be turned into a framework for 'the political education of the working classes'.[46] With this in view, in the spring of 1913 he and Virginia visited provincial Guild centres in what she called 'obscure but enlightened northern towns',[47] talking to working women about the 'social potentialities of co-operation'.[48] That year he planned with Davies the setting up of regional Guild schools. His writing on the Guild brought him to the notice of Sydney and Beatrice Webb; in the summer of 1913 Leonard and Virginia went to their first Fabian Conference. By the time the war started, Leonard had moved on from his WCG work, under the Webbs' influence (or, as Virginia put it, caught in their web) to work for the Fabians and their organ, the *New Statesman*.

Leonard Woolf wrote warmly in his autobiography of Davies as an exhilarating Joan of Arc figure; Quentin Bell characterised her as a battle-axe and a bore. Perhaps she was something of both: her gargantuan correspondence with Leonard on Guild matters evokes dedication, efficiency and a relentless preoccupation with her work. She played an emphatic part in Virginia Woolf's life at this time. While she was finishing the novel, Leonard was working closely with Margaret; when Virginia was ill, Leonard called on Margaret for support, along with Ka Cox and Janet Case. And she was one of the few people who was quite as worried about Leonard's needs as about Virginia's: 'Please tell your landlady to see you have an egg beaten up in milk at 11, and hot milk when you go to bed, and you must take them! I feel sure your meals are often rather failures,'[49] she wrote to him fondly.

It is improbable that Margaret was a rival for Leonard's affections but it would have been hard for Virginia not to imagine them as an impressive political couple, like Sidney and Beatrice Webb. And her reaction to Margaret was like her response to Beatrice (or Lilian Harris, or Molly Hamilton), those vigorous political women who made her feel insignificant, sceptical and lightweight. Margaret 'could compel a steam-roller to waltz', she said.[50] In her illness, latent resentment burst out as rage. 'I cant help feeling she is not sufficiently used to me,' Margaret wrote to Leonard, 'Best not to reply to her letter I think.'[51] But after her recovery, Virginia would be impressed by her sense of Margaret and the pipe-smoking Lilian in Hampstead as being at 'the heart of the woman's republic'.[52]

'Being ignorant doesn't mean that one can't at least appreciate', Virginia wrote in a p.s. on a letter from Leonard to Margaret in June 1913.[53] She quickly took up a position on Leonard's new work, formulating imaginative rather than methodical responses to the lives of working women: 'Why the poor dont take knives and chase us out of our houses, I cant think', she wrote from Manchester to Eleanor Cecil. 'They stand for 8 hours tying up 6 gross of jampots.'[54] She made two profound judgements on this kind of activity. One was that there was an unbridgeable gap between the 'fiery reformers' of the middle classes and the working classes they wanted to re-educate. The other was that philanthropic activity could also be an expression of the desire for power.[55] She was embarrassed, too, at the thought of being mocked for taking an interest in politics. When she was ill, one of her obsessions was that she 'thought people laughed at her'[56] and that 'people were despising' her and Leonard as a couple.[57] Not without reason, as a letter from Clive Bell to Molly MacCarthy suggests:

> How far more admirable are the Woolves who have gone, or are going, to the great industrial centres of the north to study co-operation and found girls' clubs; they do all things well, except one apparently. And talk and write about Socialism and Life and Books, which is far more real, of course, than writing and talking about Art. I wonder why.[58]

Clive would have sneered at the conscientious notes Virginia Woolf took at the Fabian Conference in Keswick, in July 1913. She scribbled on to hotel notepaper: 'Nothing ignoble in being a consumer . . . Man wage-earner can make his power felt, woman consumer very little power. Wage earner's view predominates.'[59] The opposition would sink deep into her mind.

But a few days after this, back in London, she was in such a dangerous state – not eating, not sleeping, terribly anxious – that Leonard obeyed George Savage's advice to take her to a rest cure at Burley Park. She was angry with him and accused him of 'beastliness'; then she became remorseful and subdued, and accused herself of 'vile imaginings'. She came out on 11 August and they went to Asheham. She got worse.

They went to London, and Leonard's consultations – with Savage, with Henry Head – continued. Savage told them to go back to the Plough Inn, where they'd been on their honeymoon. They went down on 23 August. Virginia would not eat or sleep; she was having 'delusions'. Sometimes she said 'she thought everything would come right'; mostly she was beside herself with struggles over food, 'illusions', 'acute worry'. Leonard asked Ka to come and help him. On 7 September Virginia agreed to go back to see Henry Head. On 8 September they went back by train to London and stayed in Adrian's rooms in Brunswick Square. On the 9th, they went to see Maurice Wright and Henry Head, both of whom tried to persuade her that she was seriously ill, and that her condition was not her own fault. Vanessa came round and Virginia became more cheerful, and rested. Vanessa and Leonard went out to arrange a consultation between Head and Savage.

Leonard carelessly left his case of sleeping drugs unlocked. At 6.30 p.m. Ka Cox telephoned him at Savage's consulting rooms from Brunswick Square to say that Virginia had fallen asleep. He rushed back by taxi to find her unconscious. He rang Vanessa and told her to come back with a doctor. She came back with Head, who found that Virginia had taken 100 grains of veronal. Nurses were called. Geoffrey Keynes, then a house surgeon at St Bartholemew's, who was living in Brunswick Square, drove Leonard at full speed through London to the hospital to get a stomach-pump. Head and Keynes and the nurses worked through the night. At 1.30 a.m. on 10 September 1913 Virginia nearly died. By 6 a.m. she was out of danger, though unconscious all day.

In the days after the suicide attempt her symptoms continued. Leonard at this point considered putting her in a home. Clifford's Inn was clearly out of the question now. Then George Duckworth offered them the use of his house, Dalingridge Hall, which was a kind of solution, and in August they went down there for two months, with nurses. In the autumn she was moved back to Asheham, with either Leonard or Ka or Janet in attendance. She spent the winter there, getting a little better. In April they went to Cornwall, but otherwise, until the summer of 1914, Virginia stayed at Asheham. During those months, while Leonard was away 'she took another dose of veronal by mistake for phenacitin' and 'slept it off'.[60] Apart from this 'accident', she seemed to be recovering. In April 1914 they went with Vanessa to see the neurologist Maurice Craig: he said that 'she wasnt in a state where she could possibly be certified and that she couldnt therefore be made to go into a home.'[61]

The beginning of the war in August 1914 was not as immediate to Virginia as her own state of health. In the autumn of 1914 they moved out of London, to lodgings on the Green at Richmond. That autumn and winter Virginia seemed better. She was typing and 'reading Co-op books'[62] for Leonard, and taking cookery lessons. She started a diary, observing some details of the war, half-in half-out of the continuing life of London – the Omega workshops, the Women's Guild, the *New Statesman*. She described suburban life in Richmond, outings to concerts and music-halls, street-scenes, encounters with friends, a treat for her birthday ('I was taken up to town, free of charge, & given a treat, first at a Picture Palace, & then at Buszards . . . I was also given a packet of sweets to bring home')[63] visits from Leonard's family, arguments with Leonard (as when she invented a cunning system for cooking her breakfast in bed) and moments of horror and dismay: 'I begin to loathe my kind, principally from looking at their faces in the tube.'[64] Then, in February 1915, just before the publication of *The Voyage Out*, she became deranged and was ill again for most of the year.

She would not see Leonard for eight weeks, was said to have attacked her nurses, and wrote some violent letters to her friends. When at last she emerged from her life-and-death battle, it was into the middle of the war.

Her 'series of catastrophes' changed the marriage for ever. They survived it and remained a couple, but it reshaped their life together. And, though Leonard Woolf was not the cause of her breakdown, his effect on her partly triggered, and partly provided the material for, the obsessions and anxieties and delusions of its most serious phases.

Witnesses to the marriage had been quick to deduce that it was sexually inadequate. Vanessa rushed to tell Clive about their consultations with her, a few months after the honeymoon, 'on the subject of the Goat's coldness'. Her report was as much about her own sexuality as about Virginia's lack of it. (This was while she was deep in her intensely sensual affair with Roger Fry, begun the previous summer, to which Clive, with his own amorous interests elsewhere, had grudgingly accommodated.)

> I think I perhaps annoyed her but may have consoled him by saying that I thought she never had understood or sympathised with sexual passion in men. Apparently she still gets no pleasure at all from the act, which I think is curious. They were very anxious to know when I first had an orgasm – I couldn't remember. Do you? But no doubt I sympathised with such things if I didnt have them from the time I was 2.[65]

This tone persisted in Clive's later gossip to Mary Hutchinson (his mistress from 1914 to 1927): 'Wolf [sic] fucks her once a week but has not yet succeeded in breaking her maidenhead. They have been married six years. It gives her very little pleasure. Nothing could be more private.'[66] Vita Sackville-West told Harold Nicolson that Virginia had never 'lived with' (meaning had sexual relations with) 'anyone except Leonard, which was a terrible failure, and was abandoned quite soon'; and her son took his cue from her in describing Virginia Woolf as 'sexually frigid'.[67] Stories of her sexual incompetence and Leonard's heroically restrained normal sexual appetites became commonplace; this version, from 1967, is by Gerald Brenan:

> Leonard told me that when on their honeymoon he had tried to make love to her she had got into such a violent state of excitement that he had had to stop, knowing as he did that these states were a prelude to her attacks of madness. This madness was of course hereditary, but her early seduction by her half brother was no doubt a predisposing factor. So Leonard, though I should say a strongly sexed man, had to give up all idea of ever

having any sort of sexual satisfaction. He told me that he was ready to do this 'because she was a genius'. All through his life with her he kept to this, and to avoid upsetting her never even flirted with other women. The only return he asked of her was that she should do the same with other men, and here he had especially in mind Clive Bell, a rather boisterous womaniser, who tried to make up to her and (on one occasion) Ralph Partridge who kissed her naked in the bathroom. Some years later, so I was told, he had an affair with the parlour maid . . .[68]

This kind of evidence, mainly put about by male writers of renowned unreliability and heterosexual energies, was based on standard assumptions about what a full-blooded sexual life needed to consist of. The Woolfs' marriage certainly did not live up to those standards. From early on in their life together they had separate bedrooms. *Mrs Dalloway* famously describes a marriage of sexual incompatibility, in which the wife feels that she has failed her husband and is more erotically aroused by young women. In 1930, Virginia described herself to Ethel Smyth as having always been 'sexually cowardly'.[69] Many of her remarks in letters and diaries about sexually active men expressed distaste: after her ex-suitor Sydney Waterlow had been staying at Asheham she said the house 'stank of dried semen'.[70] That was written to Lytton; she liked to sound bold when she was acting up to her sexually adventurous homosexual friends, but often, instead, sounded queasy.[71]

But Virginia Woolf's sexual squeamishness, which plays a part in the indirections and self-censorship of the novels, is combined with a powerful, intense sensuality, an erotic susceptibility to people and landscape, language and atmosphere, and a highly charged physical life. 'Frigid' seems a ridiculously simplistic description of this complicated, polymorphous self.

The standard image of Leonard Woolf as a full-blooded heterosexual sacrificing himself on the altar of her genius, seems equally simplistic. It would be easy to read his passion for work as a form of sublimation, but it's a demeaning version of a life. It is tempting to see the attention he lavished on his animals as a substitute for an erotic life. Leonard's stories about his South American marmoset, Mitz – how jealous it was, how it never left him, how in order to get it to come down from a tree he would make Virginia stand underneath the tree and kiss her – are open to hostile or ribald interpretation.[72] But the simple view of the Woolfs' marriage as a-sexual and over-controlled, the product of child abuse and madness, with all her erotic feeling directed towards women, and all his compensated for by work and pets, doesn't incorporate, or is embarrassed by, the deep tenderness of those references to 'my inviolable centre', and the evidence of an erotic secret life.

The pet names, the animal games, the 'little beasts', the 'marmots', coming out to play or being given an airing, the cuddling and nuzzling and kisses: these 'antics' are often referred to in the letters and diaries of the early years. When in 1933 she re-reads her diary for 1915, she looks back with tears in her eyes on their days in the Green: 'Our quarrels; how he crept into my bed with a little purse, & so on; how we reckoned our income & I was given tea free for a treat.'[73] But this sort of intimacy is still going on in 1936: 'A great deal of fuss about the marmots. In fact, these weeks of solitude, seeing no one . . . have space & quiet thats rather favourable to private fun.'[74] This is not an a-sexual marriage, but one which thrives on affectionate cuddling and play.

Who played child, who played parent? 'I was given a packet of sweets to take home' sounds as if she was the one who was babied, as she had been with Violet and Madge and Vanessa. But in their secret play Leonard was often the little stringy creature, the mongoose, the 'Servant', and she was the big mandril, goddess or mistress. 'Lappin and Lapinova', written at Asheham (so before 1919) but not published until 1938, sardonically describes the death of the secret fantasy life of a wife who pretends, to keep out reality (her husband's awful family, his boring job), that he is a rabbit and she is a hare, rulers of a wild night-time country. The husband gets bored with the fantasy, and kills it off: 'So that was the end of that marriage.'[75] The story certainly has its roots in the dark side of the Woolfs' marriage. While she was rewriting it in 1938, Virginia told Vanessa that she could not visit her in France because 'the fact is we are so unhappy apart that I cant come'. This, she recognises, is a form of bondage: 'Thats the worst failure imaginable – that marriage, as I suddenly for the first time realised walking in the Square, reduces one to damnable servility. Cant be helped. Im going to write a comedy about it.'[76] In the 'comedy', Queen Lapinova, alias Rosalind Thorburn, is despised by her in-laws, who 'breed' (like rabbits), because she is orphaned and childless. And it is clear that the couple's fantasy life is, for the wife, a form of substitution for children. No doubt the games Leonard and Virginia played in private would have altered if they had had a family.

It is possible that if Virginia Woolf had had children she would have been unable to cope with them, would have broken down, would not have written. All this is unprovable, though it has often been said, for instance by Brenan: 'There could have been no question of her ever having children though she may occasionally have day-dreamed of it. She knew that her bouts of madness put her in a different category from other women.'[77] What *is* known is that she liked and was good at talking to children (there are many witnesses to this), that she often bitterly regretted not having them; and that she never consoled herself with the belief that her books were a substitute or an equivalent. These feelings would surface whenever she was depressed. In her deepest plunges into 'melancholy' or a sense of failure, she always uttered the words 'children': 'Its having no children', it's 'a desire for children'.[78] Though she knew that childlessness left her open to, or created, other kinds of relationships and other sorts of work ('These efforts of mine to communicate with people are partly childlessness'), that perception did not lessen 'the horror that sometimes overcomes me'.[79]

Comparisons with Vanessa were central to these moods. Sometimes, in the 1930s, she would console herself with having earned more money: 'I put my life blood into writing, & she had children.'[80] More often the comparison was to her own detriment. In her struggles with these feelings she was typically ruthless with herself: 'Never pretend that children, for instance, can be replaced by other things.'[81] But she could never avoid an ingredient of self-blame.

> My own fault too – a little more self control on my part, & we might have had a boy of 12, a girl of 10: This always makes me wretched in the early hours.[82]

And she felt Leonard's loss as much as her own, seeing a small boy on a walk talking to his father about his stamp album: 'upon wh. I thought of L. if he had a son'.[83]

But it was 'L' who stopped them having children, and it may be that part of her anger with him during her breakdown, and part of her sense that marriage could be a form of 'damnable servility', was a result of that decision.[84] Her letter of 1 May 1912 made it clear that she would want to have children if she married. When Violet Dickinson, characteristically, sent her a cradle after the honeymoon, her response was embarrassed but positive: 'My baby shall sleep in the cradle', she said; 'my brats to play' on Clifford's Green.[85] As late as April, she was still telling Violet: 'We aren't going to have a baby, but we want to have one, and 6 months in the country or so is said to be necessary first.'[86] But Leonard, anxious about her from the beginning of the year, was consulting all the doctors, and debating the question with Vanessa. In January 1913, he talked to Maurice Craig and to Jean Thomas, who both thought Virginia should not have children. Maurice Wright and George Savage were in favour; Dr Hyslop recommended putting off the decision. Vanessa, who had always wondered what Virginia 'would do with children',[87] seems to have played an ambivalent part. On 20 January she wrote to Leonard, at first agreeing with Craig's opinion ('I had for some time been thinking so more and more definitely myself'), which she assumed to be that 'the risk she runs is that of another bad nervous breakdown & I doubt if even a baby would be worth that'. But she added that if Virginia led a boring life in the country it might be possible and that 'of course I think on the whole almost any amount of temporary boredom *is* worthwhile for the sake of having children'.[88] A few days later she wrote to Virginia: 'I expect on the whole by waiting a bit and being careful enough you could have one with very little risk . . . Jean told me she thought it very likely that a baby would be very good for you.' In her next letter she said: 'I shouldnt worry about the baby question. One can never really settle these matters beforehand . . . I wonder why Leonard has gradually come to think child bearing so dangerous.' And next, after seeing Dr Craig, she wrote: 'I told him what Savage and Hyslop had said and he seemed to think it possible that you could get into a state when the risk would be very much less.'[89] It looks from this as though Vanessa was saying one thing to Virginia and another to Leonard. In any case, it is clear that Virginia's maternity was decided for her.

An angry passage of fiction, written in June 1933, set in 1910, and cancelled from the manuscript of *The Years*, adds to the story of how she felt about her childlessness. This writing was done in a mood of 'grim despair . . . intensity of anguish' and 'desire for death'.[90] It involved her in reading old diaries and sketching memoirs of the past.[91] *The Years* was a history of middle-class life in Britain between 1880 and 1937, which used her own experience and observations for a political diagnosis of her society. The early version, *The Pargiters*, is much more explicit, particularly about sex:

'Look at those wretched little children' said Rose. looking down into the street.
'Stop them, then' said Maggie. 'Stop them having children.'
'But you cant' said Rose.
'Oh nonsense, my dear Rose,' said Elvira. 'What you do is this: you ring a bell in Harley Street. Sir John at home? Step this way ma'am. Now Sir John, you say, casting your eyes this way & that way, the fact of the matter is, ~~my husband~~' whereupon you blush. Most inadvisable, most inadvisable, he says, the welfare of the human race – sacrifice, private interests – ~~three~~ six words on half a sheet of paper. A tip. [In the margin: Three guineas in his left hand]. Out you go – well, ~~that's all~~. What I mean is, in plain language, if ~~that woman~~ Maggie ~~says she wont have a child~~, she wont [have] a child [. . .] 'We wouldnt have children if we didnt want them', said Maggie.
'~~You wouldn't be allowed~~ But you cant say that in public' said Rose.

'You can say that here, to me, in private' [. . .] 'But how is that woman down there going to Harley Street? with three guineas?'

'Well then, publish it in the Times' said Elvira [. . .]

'D'you never take anything seriously Elvira?' said Rose. 'It's against the Law.'

'What law?'

'The law of England . . . You dont seem to realise that we live in England . . . And its the year 1910,' said Rose.[92]

The language applied to the Harley Street abortionist is very like the language used for Septimus's rage with Sir William Bradshaw in *Mrs Dalloway*, so closely based on her own experiences with the doctors between 1913 and 1915. And the sum of money required for an abortion, three guineas, is the symbolic sum used in the essay of that name to demonstrate the relation between domestic and public tyranny. This is a startling censored passage. It suggests that fear of hereditary insanity might have been one of the reasons for their not having children ('most inadvisable, the welfare of the human race'). It suggests that this decision may have been forced upon her in the same way that she felt 'forced' into rest-homes and rest-cures. For 98 days between 6 August and 12 November 1913, the time of her suicidal breakdown in the first year of her marriage, Virginia Woolf had no periods.[93] During this time and again in 1915 she had outbursts of violent rage against Leonard (and hostility towards Vanessa). Her profound depressions always involved thinking of her childlessness. The onset of her periods were always particularly stressful and would often leave her, as she put it, 'recumbent'. It seems possible that at some point in 1913 she might have had a termination. But this is speculation.

'Leonard made me into a comatose invalid', she wrote to Violet, putting off a visit in 1912.[94] It is a suggestive phrase. Though it is unwarranted and extreme to say that Leonard was the cause of her 1913–15 breakdowns (even if the content of her illness had to do with the marriage), there is no doubt that after her suicide attempt he 'made her into an invalid' in order to prevent a recurrence. A playful 'contract' which he drew up, and she signed, when he had to go away in the summer of June 1914, sets the tone for his guardianship:

I, Mandril Sarcophagus Felicissima var. Rarissima, rerum naturae simplex (al. Virginia Woolf) swear that I will on June 16, 17 & 18 1. Rest on my back with my head on the cushions for a full half hour after lunch. 2. Eat exactly as much as if I were not alone. 3. Be in bed by 10.25 every night & settle off to sleep at once. 4. Have my breakfast in bed. 5. Drink a *whole* glass of milk in the morning. 6. In certain contingencies rest on the

sofa, not walk about house or outside, until the return of animal illud
miserrisimus, mongoosius communis 7. Be wise. 8. Be happy. Signed:
Mandril Sarcophagus Felicissima Var.rarissima, r.n.s.V.W. June 16th
1914. And I swear that I have so done in each & every respect. Signed:
Mandril Sarcophagus F.V.R.R.N.S.V.W., June 19th 1914.[95]

There is a narrow line between this careful watchfulness and a desire for
control. The life's programme which Leonard set up for Virginia, of
avoiding excitement, parties, late nights, and too many visitors, of staying
out of London as much as possible and preventing stressful situations, was,
given the advice he received, a reasonable one. But it may have provided an
excuse to hold off visitors whom Leonard disliked (such as Ethel Smyth),
and it certainly turned him, over the years, into more of a guardian than a
lover.

This was the most visible feature of their life together, and was
frequently remarked on and much caricatured. Ottoline, who thought
Leonard mercenary, cold, and 'wicked', often lamented his control of
Virginia in her journal: 'We had just begun to talk when Leonard came in,
which I think *she* felt as a bore – as I did but its important not to offend him.
He is her Guardian – and if I offended him I should never see her.'[96] And
this was always Clive Bell's line: 'She is to come to Garsington some day if
Woolf will let her – but he wont.' 'Virginia has been in a sad scrape with
Leonard for going out at midnight, in a car and on bank holiday . . .
Leonard thought it all so foolish that Virginia "will never again regain her
place in his estimation." '[97]

'Of course Leonard puts a drag on, & I must be very cautious, like a child,
not to make too much noise playing', she wrote in 1929.[98] Leonard did
inhibit her, and his formidable self-discipline profoundly affected her life.
She knew what she gained from it: she told Vanessa, discussing their
respective marriages in 1935, that she had married him because 'she found
Leonard absolutely dependable & like a rock which was what she badly
wanted. She said she could never make up her own mind & must have
someone to do it for her – which L no doubt does – & that he was also very
unselfish – & always ready to plunge into any enterprise she suggested.'[99]

He may have constrained her, but he also provided conditions favourable
for writing. Even if she had not already, like her parents, felt a compulsion
to work, she would have had to learn it in order to keep pace with him. Part
of her compulsiveness was, perhaps, competitive. It is clear how much he
admired her strenuous work habits and how much she would have felt that
admiration.

Neither of us ever took a day's holiday unless we were too ill to work or unless we went away on a regular and, as it were, authorized holiday. We should have felt it to be not merely wrong but unpleasant not to work every morning for seven days a week and for about eleven months a year.[100]

There is something partly appealing and partly appalling in Leonard's pride in his own efficiency. His political vision had a great deal to do with simply getting things better organised. The Leonard Woolf archives at Sussex University demonstrate his rage for order. Every letter, no matter how silly, is replied to. Every item of expenditure is noted. On small cards, every gramophone record in his possession is indexed, with the dates on which that music has been played, and another notebook for what he has listened to on the radio. Every fluctuation in Virginia Woolf's state of mind is recorded.

When Leonard Woolf spoke in his autobiography of doing 'a certain amount of work',[101] he meant a certain amount more than most. Take, for instance, 1917 to 1919. He was participating in celebratory conferences for the Russian Revolution,[102] helping to found the 1917 Club, starting the Hogarth Press, beginning twenty years' work as secretary of the Advisory Committee to the Labour Party on International Questions, actively supporting the Ceylon independence movement, editing *The Framework of a Lasting Peace* for the League of Nations Society, and turning a piece of research for the Fabian Society on international trade (and imperial exploitation of the third world) into *Empire and Commerce in Africa*. Meanwhile he was writing two shorter books, one on *Co-operation and the Future of Industry* and one on *The Future of Constantinople*, doing freelance journalism for the *New Statesman* and the *Nation*, helping to edit a socialist political journal called *War and Peace*, and taking it over as editor when it was reborn as the *International Review*, for which he also wrote a weekly international diary.

This level of work was a way of mastering a fundamental sense of life's futility. Leonard Woolf did think of existence, to a great extent, as being 'downhill all the way'.[103] He had a generally poor opinion of human beings, preferring, like many misanthropes, his gardening, his pets, and music. Summing up his career at the end of his autobiography, he described it, with bitter relish, as having been completely futile:

The world today and the history of the human anthill during the last fifty-seven years would be exactly the same as it is if I had played pingpong instead of sitting on committees and writing books and memoranda . . . I

338

must have in a long life ground through between 150,000 and 200,000 hours of perfectly useless work.[104]

This grim pleasure in the idea of life's futility was something Virginia Woolf came to know well. She would speak of his glooms, his scepticism, his impatience with people. She knew he was difficult to work for (so did he: 'I am not a person who bears even wise men gladly')[105] and that the problems they had in finding a colleague for the Press and in getting on well with their servants arose in large part from his intractability.[106]

Unlike Leslie Stephen, he would not elicit consolation and encouragement from his wife, but retreat into a silence. It is usual to think of Leonard giving Virginia encouragement in *her* work, and of her taking little interest in *his*. She is the 'Mr Ramsay' in this equation. She disliked wifeliness: 'Am I not sitting waiting for L to "come back from the office" like other wives. It annoys me to be like other wives.'[107] But she could be wifely, all the same: 'Its a good thing now & then to read one's husband's work attentively', she wrote in 1920.[108] She often grudged his committees and commitments, felt that his poetic side was buried in blue books,[109] and argued with his politics. But she liked the range they covered together as a couple, her sense of their being at the centre, of becoming 'accomplished, successful, looked up to'.[110] Her thinking was influenced by his anti-imperialism and his conviction that democracy could be improved through information and education. She was impressed by his life's commitment, in spite of his pessimistic realism,[111] to combating war, injustice and tyranny.

Though he could be rigid and grim, he was also truthful and generous. What he admired most – and rarely found – in public men was 'the passionate pursuit of the thing rather than passionate concern with the self'.[112] He disliked oratory, sentimentality and showing-off. To many who knew him, including Virginia Woolf, he seemed a good man. He was always very kind to younger people: his letters to Julian Bell, for instance, who argued with his form of socialism, are models of tolerance and sympathy. Angelica Garnett remembered how impressive he seemed to her when she was a child. She recognised, in contrast with Vanessa's tendency 'to compound and procrastinate in favour of those she loved', and Duncan's ability 'to laugh away and ignore things he didn't like', 'the passion in Leonard's character, which was both convinced and inflexible'.[113] It would be a mistake, fatal to the understanding of the Woolf marriage, to read Leonard Woolf simply as a cold, obstructive disciplinarian. He was a person of deep, articulate, excitable feelings, controlled by fierce self-training.

One story, told differently by Virginia and by Leonard, gives a revealing glimpse of his character and of the reason why – after everything else has been said about their marriage – she *liked* him. In *Downhill All the Way*, Leonard remembers them returning from an evening spent with Vanessa in her studio in Fitzroy Street. (This was in 1930.) A drunk woman was being abused by two passers-by and was then accosted by a policeman who seemed to Leonard to be 'deliberately trying to goad her into doing something which would justify an arrest'. He lost his temper, challenged the policeman in front of a small crowd, and made him let the woman go.

What Leonard omitted to mention in his reminiscence was that he and Virginia had been to a fancy-dress party for Angelica's eleventh birthday. Virginia was dressed as a ('mad') March Hare, with a pair of hare's ears and paws. Roger Fry, at the party, had been a wonderfully characterful White Knight. And Leonard was 'wearing a green baize apron and a pair of chisels as the Carpenter'. But as he tackled the policeman ('Why dont you go for the men who began it? My name's Woolf, and I can take my oath the woman's not to blame'), 'holding his apron and chisel in one hand',[114] he forgot all about his comical fancy-dress in his anger and his determination to see justice done.

NINETEEN

War

'But there had been a complete break; none of them could remember what they had been saying.'[1] That complete break is the air-raid in the '1917' section of *The Years*. It forces the novel's characters underground. 'Like cripples in a cave', they try to carry on their lives while the bombs fall. When the raid stops, they drink to 'the New World'. In the next short section, '1918', as peace comes 'the guns went on booming and the sirens wailed'. Then we jump to the last long 'Present Day' section which ends the novel. All the years between 1918 and 1936 seem to have been swallowed up by the overshadowing war. And the 'New World', it transpires, is still imprisoned by the causes and the after-effects of that war.

The First World War as a catastrophic break, and as the event which shaped the twentieth century, overshadows Virginia Woolf's work. In her novels there is often a violent moment of destruction or obliteration. All the lights go out, there is a roaring blackness and a sense of 'complete annihilation'.[2] Her own apprehension of and attraction to death creates the private psychodrama behind these frightening patterns. But personal feelings are translated into history. Her books are full of images of war: armies, battles, guns, bombs, air-raids, battleships, shell-shock victims, war reports, photographs of war-victims, voices of dictators.

In *Jacob's Room* (1922) the emergence of a young life is obliterated by the war, which is seen as a grotesque mechanical force superimposed on to terrifying chaos. The battleships 'ray out' at sea, and young men are sent out to suffocate uncomplainingly in their submarines. Guns are heard (as she heard them in Sussex) sounding like giant women beating carpets. 'Darkness drops like a knife' over Europe, the great cities of the world go black, and Jacob dies. The novel which celebrates her discovery of new formal possibilities for fiction is also an elegy for the war-dead.

Mrs Dalloway (1925), her most dramatic mixing of autobiography and history, puts to shame the idea of starting afresh in a New World 'now that it was all over, truce signed, and the dead buried'.[3] We see a society divided between those who have profited from the war and those who, like Septimus

Smith, have been destroyed by it. The war lives in dreams, madness, memory. A grey nurse knitting on a park bench becomes, in the dream of one of the characters, a gigantic symbolic shape looming over the book, 'the figure of the mother whose sons have been killed in the battles of the world'.[4]

While she was finishing *Mrs Dalloway*, the structure of *To the Lighthouse* (1927) was taking shape as two halves with a 'complete break' down the middle. In the break, the 'Time Passes' section, she wanted to suggest:

> Hopeless gulfs of misery.
> Cruelty.
> The War.
> Change. Oblivion.

And then, 'human vitality': what survives.[5] At the end of the late-Victorian family story of the first part, 'one by one the lamps were all extinguished'. In a 'night of wind and destruction' come ominous sounds like 'the measured blows of hammers', while the shells explode, the young men are killed, an ashen-coloured ship sails past, and a purplish stain boils on the water. After the break of time, the post-war family have to struggle to piece together and make something of the fragments from the past.

The novel's political argument is translated into *A Room of One's Own* (1929), and here too a 'complete break' is marked:

> Shall we lay the blame on the war? When the guns fired in August 1914, did the faces of men and women show so plain in each other's eyes that romance was killed? Certainly it was a shock (to women in particular with their illusions about education, and so on) to see the faces of our rulers in the light of the shell-fire. So ugly they looked – German, English, French – so stupid.[6]

The narrator is divided between regret and relief that 'the catastrophe . . . destroyed illusion and put truth in its place'.

In *The Waves* (1931), like *Jacob's Room* an elegy for the death of a young man, there is no war in the narrative, but images of war fill the book. An impersonal force which pushes people to their deaths is in control. The machinery of modern life – like the escalator in the Tube station – imitates the force of war. 'Millions descend those stairs in a terrible descent. Great wheels churn inexorably urging them downwards. Millions have died.' The people on the moving stairs are 'like the pinioned and terrible descent of some army of the dead downwards'.[7] The voices of the novel are trying to 'do battle' against the flood, the 'strip of time'. They are like 'relics of an army', coming back every night with their wounds.[8] Those who don't march together – the renegades, the outcasts – are destroyed. The machine collects up the rest, and 'An army marches across Europe'.[9] The last remaining speaker's last words are of the need to fight. The novel deliberately evades a specific historical time, but the presence of the 'Great War' is palpable.

The next two novels, *The Years* (1937) and *Between the Acts* (1941), are set carefully in their historical moment. They deal with the disappointed and ineffectual lives of a family, a class, a country, 'between the acts' of the two World Wars, and re-enact the trauma of the First. So do *Three Guineas* (1938) and *Roger Fry* (1940), which is sliced down the middle by the war which he saw as the end of civilisation. The essays and fiction of the 1930s present a disfigured society with a hypocritical culture and an unbridgeable class gap. They diagnose rigidly constructed gender identities which exclude or oppress the misfits of either sex. They attack tyrannies, war-mongering and the victimisation of those who will not conform. They satirise patriotism, imperialism, Christianity and nationalism. That reading of her social landscape had its roots in her childhood, but it took its force from her experience of the First World War.

In the reviews she began to write again in 1916, she thought a great deal about what art had to do with the war. She reviewed a number of war poets, and had reservations about them all. Siegfried Sassoon[10] impressed and shocked her with his 'realism', which made her feel: 'Yes. This is going on, and we are sitting here watching it.' He brought home to her 'the terrible pictures which lie behind the colourless phrases of the newspapers'. But she drew back from the 'raw stuff' in his work.[11] If poetry had begun to find ways, however 'raw', of registering the war, fiction was going to have more difficulty. 'We do not like the war in fiction', she wrote in March 1917. 'The vast events now shaping across the Channel are towering over us too closely and too tremendously to be worked into fiction without a painful jolt in the perspective.'[12]

There is something squeamish in this. Her aesthetic judgements on wartime art are a mixture of angry radicalism and class-bound fastidious-ness. She disliked war rhetoric – as in the glorification of Rupert Brooke – because it was false and exploitative, but also because it was vulgar. Certainly it should have no place in art: 'Patriotism in literature is an insidious poison', she wrote in 1919.[13] The same applied to painting, she thought, reeling back from Sargent's painting *Gassed!*, the climax of all the fossilised Victorianism in the Royal Academy show of 1919:

In order to emphasise his point that the soldiers wearing bandages round their eyes cannot see, and therefore claim our compassion, he makes one of them raise his leg to the level of his elbow in order to mount a step an inch or two above the ground. This little piece of over-emphasis . . . was the last straw. Suddenly the great rooms rang like a parrot-house with the intolerable vociferations of gawdy and brainless birds. How they shrieked and gibbered! . . . Honour, patriotism, chastity, wealth, success, importance, position, patronage, power – their cries rang and echoed from all quarters. 'Anywhere, anywhere, out of this world!' was the only exclamation with which one could stave off the brazen din . . .'[14]

There was plenty of that brazen din to listen to in the wartime newspapers and the speeches of politicians ('Deep down in every one of us is the urge to give ourselves as fully as possible at the bidding of the ineffable somewhat that we feel has the right to require the sacrifice'),[15] and plenty of opposition to it. When she wrote in her diary that patriotism was 'a base emotion', or told Ka Cox 'For God's sake don't sacrifice anything to your country',[16] she was in company with other dissenting voices. But she was also making her own reading of the language of propaganda, as when she asks what 'Liberty' really stands for: 'Sometimes I try to worry out what some of the phrases we're ruled by mean.'[17]

Her 'outsider' position was bound up with her analysis of sexual roles. When in January 1915 she began to write a (lost) book with a heroine called Effie who argues against *all* forms of activity,[18] or stands off from the political debate where 'Everyone makes the state of the country his private affair,'[19] her disengagement is connected to her feminism. She 'read' the war as 'a preposterous masculine fiction'.[20] 'I become steadily more feminist, owing to *The Times*', she wrote to a sympathetic Margaret Llewelyn Davies. As she says in *A Room of One's Own*, it was the war which hardened women's views about their male rulers. The suffrage movement (which was sidelined by the war) lost its hold on her imagination, and she put her feelings about its irrelevance into *Night and Day*. When the Lords passed the Suffrage Bill in January 1918 she noted, 'I dont feel much more important – perhaps slightly less so'.[21] But it did seem ever more important to subvert the establishment language – of *The Times* or the Royal Academy – on war or sexual roles or art. She made some strong, angry feminist statements now,[22] and those sparks smouldered into the post-war novels, *Jacob's Room* and *Mrs Dalloway*.

Her reactions to the war were a mixture of a pacifist's horror of the glorification of militarism, and alienation from the ordinary combatant or civilian's view. The behaviour of most of her friends in wartime occupied this uneasy space between snobbish detachment and courageous resistance.

Though they were naïvely unprepared for August 1914, when the war came they were in the vanguard of the peace movement, before a wider disillusionment with the war set in in 1916.[23] None of her closest friends fought; many of them did 'alternative service'. They all thought that 'the war which had begun in opposition to militarism, was militarising England and taking away one of the outstanding liberties of the British people.'[24] All the people she knew best were articulately anti-war; even her more equivocating friends, like Maynard Keynes, thought it was disgusting and unnecessary. Duncan Grant summed up their feelings:

> I never considered the possibility of a great European war. It seemed such an absolutely mad thing for a civilised people to do. I had become I suppose in a sense unpatriotic, as most artists must do . . . I think the war utter madness and folly.[25]

While Virginia was ill in 1915, Clive Bell was writing flamboyant anti-war pamphlets, *Peace at Once* and *Art and War*.[26] Vanessa, who had fallen in love with Duncan Grant before the start of the war, was painting in a farm-cottage on the Sussex coast, living in an uneasy triangle with Duncan and his new lover, David (known as 'Bunny') Garnett. She wrote to Virginia that she felt 'completely isolated from our kind' in her reaction to the war.[27] But it was coming closer. That autumn the coalition government began its move towards conscription. First the pressure came from Lord Derby's scheme for able-bodied men to 'attest' their willingness to serve (helped on by the handing out of white feathers and the ubiquitous Kitchener posters, 'Your Country Needs You'). This failed. In December the War Cabinet decided on a vast new Allied offensive for the spring, and hastily accepted the principle of military conscription. On 27 January 1916 the Military Service Act became law. Bachelors between the ages of eighteen and forty-one were enlisted, but could apply for exemption (one of the grounds was conscientious objection) to local tribunals. This measure swelled the ranks of gun-fodder; but it was also a means of controlling and eliminating dissent.[28]

Vanessa was staying with Leonard and Virginia at Asheham when the news broke; the Woolfs, she felt, though anti-conscription, were not very sympathetic. When Duncan and Bunny Garnett arrived, though, conscription became the main subject of conversation. And so it continued to be, for many months. 'The whole of our world does nothing but talk about conscription, and their chances of getting off,' Virginia wrote to Ka Cox in June 1916.[29]

Many of Virginia's friends became involved in the work of the opposition movements.[30] Lytton Strachey and Bertrand Russell were particularly visible opponents; Russell gave an influential series of lectures on pacifism at Caxton Hall in 1916 (which left Virginia, reading them in their published form, with the 'melancholy feeling that this sort of lecturing does me no good').[31] Keynes came under attack from his Bloomsbury friends for staying at the Treasury.[32] But his support proved helpful when the deadline for exemption applications expired on 2 March 1916, and Virginia's family and friends faced their tribunals. He advised Duncan and Bunny and Vanessa to establish themselves at Wissett, a Suffolk fruit farm which belonged to a relative of Duncan's, to show that they were doing useful alternative war-work. ('I rather hope you wont settle at Wissett', Virginia wrote forlornly from Asheham, 'I miss your company very sadly.')[33]

The hearings began. In March 1916, Lytton Strachey, supported by the Morrells and numerous Stracheys, made his notorious appearance before the Hampstead tribunal, and was exempted after a medical examination.[34] But Duncan Grant and David Garnett, supported by Maynard and Adrian, had no success with their local tribunal, whom Vanessa described to Virginia as 'perfectly bovine country bumpkins whose skulls couldnt be penetrated at all'. 'I suppose', she added, 'everyone we know will soon be either in prison or in the army.'[35] After a second application to the Ipswich tribunal, they were granted non-combatant service in the army; Maynard appealed again, and Virginia tried to get Eleanor Cecil to help, since her brother-in-law Lord Salisbury was the Chairman of the Central Appeals Tribunal. Lady Cecil politely refused. In July Duncan Grant and David Garnett were exempted on condition they did work of 'national impor-tance'. There was much discussion about this. They could not stay at Wissett, because they were 'self-employed' there; Vanessa could not contemplate joining the squabbling and conspiratorial company (which included Clive) of Her Ladyship's COs at Garsington. But in May 1916 Leonard had discovered an unoccupied farmhouse four miles from Asheham, with a 'charming garden'[36] (Virginia wrote invitingly to Vanessa) below Firle Beacon, where Duncan and Bunny could work on the land for a tenant-farmer of the owner, Lord Gage, and Vanessa could paint and have room for the children. And so, out of wartime pressures, came the move of Vanessa's household to Charleston in Sussex. It would turn out to be the most important move of Vanessa's life, and it profoundly affected Virginia too.

National hostility to the 'conchies' (especially the socialist and political, rather than religious, objectors) was vociferous: they should all be deported to Germany, wrote the *Daily Express*, 'if we are too mealy-mouthed to hang them'.[37] Their prison treatment drove several of them to suicide. Stories began to circulate of COs being shipped to France for court-martialling and execution. The issue came home to Virginia Woolf in April 1916, when married men became eligible. In retrospect, Leonard said he was 'against the war', but not a CO: 'Once the war had broken out it seemed to me that the Germans must be resisted.'[38] But at the time he wrote to Margaret Llewelyn Davies: 'I feel I am a conscientious objector . . . for I loathe the thought of taking any part in this war.'[39] The emphasis, though, fell on '*this* war': Leonard was never a pacifist in the sense that Lytton Strachey or Bertrand Russell or Aldous Huxley were pacifists. And this was an issue between him and Virginia in both wars.

His shaking hands, Virginia's mental history, and sympathetic statements from their doctors, got him off. But the whole thing had to be done again in October 1917, when the war-machine required another trawl of previously exempted men. There was a humiliating examination at Kingston Barracks, where Leonard was described as having a 'senile tremor', and Virginia registered 'a disagreeable impression of control & senseless determination'.[40]

The war was a defining event in Leonard Woolf's political life. By the time it broke out, he was deeply involved with the Webbs and their Fabian Society, the socialist pressure group with its roots in Victorian Positivism and philanthropy, which drew its pre-war character from the dynamic forces of Shaw and Wells. Leonard set to work on a report for the Webbs (suggested by Shaw) on the possibility of controlling international governments and armaments and preventing future wars. The first part of what would become *International Government* (1916) was published in the Webbs' magazine, the *New Statesman*, in July 1915. This ground-breaking work of Leonard's on international relations made his name; and it would have an important influence on the League of Nations.

At the same time Leonard was getting to know the people in the Independent Labour Party and in the Union of Democratic Control.[41] He was appointed to the Executive Committee of the League of Nations Society, was involved with the movement for Sinhalese independence, and was writing a critique of imperialism for Joseph Rowntree's paper, *War and Peace*. By the end of the war he had freed himself from the Webbs' influence and moved into the Labour Party; in 1918 he began his years of work as Secretary to the party's Advisory Committee on International Questions.

Virginia watched him being swallowed up by blue books and committees with a mixture of respect and dismay. His work profoundly influenced her understanding of the war, but it also provoked her into scepticism. Her reactions could be impatient or superficial – passing references to Leonard's 'darkies' don't suggest much attention paid to the Sinhalese independent movement, for instance.[42] But the Fabians touched her more closely. She 'declared myself a Fabian' after attending their meeting on 'The Conditions of Peace' in January 1915, full of 'earnest drab women' and 'unhealthy & singular & impotent'-looking young men in brown tweed suits.[43] It was her characteristic response: she always found them a bit dingy and puritanical, with some justice. But, also, the Webbs made her feel ignorant and small. Like Margaret, they challenged her valuation of her own life and made her more conscious of the differences between herself and Leonard.

In June 1916, Mr and Mrs Woolf spent a weekend with Mr and Mrs Shaw and Mr and Mrs Webb. Everyone talked incessantly and spoke their minds: Virginia liked that, and she liked Beatrice Webb's impressive open-mindedness, even if she did 'pounce', 'like a moulting eagle, with a bald neck and a bloodstained beak'. Shaw, when he was not falling asleep or reading out the letters he was writing to the newspapers, told long stories about himself. Poor Mrs Shaw 'was completely out of it', and kept taking Virginia aside to tell her about Indian mysticism. 'I think I should be driven to mysticising if I saw much of the Webbs,' she told Vanessa.[44] A weekend visit from the Webbs in the autumn of 1918 aroused the same 'half carping half humorously cynical' reaction. She knew she was doing it, but couldn't help herself. And so, in one of the diary's most brilliant bursts of caricature, she 'did' Beatrice's lack of interest in personality, the 'bright electric torch' she shone on everything, her loud snores while Sidney explained the government of the future Fabian state (in which Virginia would have 'some small office no doubt'), her brisk and definite statements of her aims and priorities: 'Mrs W has a compartment devoted to nature.' 'Marriage was necessary as a waste pipe for emotion.' (Leonard's memory of this visit, and other accounts of Beatrice Webb, suggest that Virginia was scatologising this famous remark, and that it was a waste-paper basket, not a waste-pipe, which Mrs Webb had in mind.)

Her compulsion to satirise the older couple (whose good sense and stoicism she also admired) partly came, she knew, from a need to reassert herself in her own eyes after their visit. Beatrice, especially, gave her a 'curious discomfort of soul' produced by the flattening of her own ego: ' "I" was not exalted; "I" was practically non-existent.'[45] To the Webbs, Leonard was the important person; Virginia's identity was neither interesting nor useful. So she exaggerated Beatrice's grimness, and when she later read her autobiography, she immediately felt the need to set Mrs Webb's dedication to causes against her own less 'integrated' personality.[46]

This comparison connected to her life-long debate with Leonard (and with herself) about the value of different kinds of work. One afternoon in

1922 the issues boiled up into an interesting row (turned into a comic anecdote for Janet Case):

We've been sitting in the Park and listening to the Band and having a terrific argument about Shaw. Leonard says we owe a great deal to Shaw. I say that he only influenced the outer fringe of morality. Leonard says that the shop girls wouldn't be listening to the Band with their young men if it weren't for Shaw. I say the human heart is touched only by the poets. Leonard says rot, I say damn. Then we go home. Leonard says I'm narrow. I say he's stunted. But don't you agree with me that the Edwardians, from 1895 to 1914, made a pretty poor show. By the Edwardians, I mean Shaw, Wells, Galsworthy, the Webbs, Arnold Bennett. We Georgians have our work cut out for us, you see. There's not a single living writer (English) I respect; so you see, I have to read the Russians . . . How does one come by one's morality? Surely by reading the poets. And we've got no poets. Does that throw light upon anything? Consider the Webbs – That woman has the impertinence to say that I'm a-moral: the truth being that if Mrs Webb had been a good woman, Mrs Woolf would have been a better. Orphans is what I say we are – we Georgians – but I must stop.[47]

It is an argument about politics and literature (and also about prose and poetry, English and Russian writing, morality, class and marriage) in which the sides taken are exaggerated for the benefit of the quarrel. She is thinking hard about literary inheritance at this time. These post-war orphans, she says, here and elsewhere, *want* to be orphaned. They have to push away the morality of their high-minded intellectual parents and work out their own. (But they are still sufficiently influenced by those 'parents' to believe that there *is* a relation between literature, morality, and social influence worth arguing about.) The resulting difference between the generations was splendidly shown up, years later, when Beatrice Webb exclaimed after reading *The Years* in 1937: 'What a picture of decadence in the absence of any sense of obligation on the part of *The Family* in the way of public work or personal conduct.' 'No stress is laid on the essential obligation of every individual to promote the welfare of the whole community.'[48] So if the Pargiters had been Fabians, *The Years* would have been a more moral – and a more influential – work. It is a voice from another world.

That post-war argument in the park is also about authority. Since childhood this was a painful issue for Virginia Woolf, and it became increasingly important to her (and her generation) in the war years. Who was in charge, whom should they trust and respect? What allegiance she could give was offered to the anti-war movement. So, though she mocked its social and sexual machinations, she respected the Morrells' pacifist support-system – or 'assemblage of Bloomsbury and crankdom'[49] – at Garsington. To the local authorities Garsington was a nest of German spies; to the establishment end of Virginia's family, like the Duckworths at Dalingridge, it was a refuge for shirkers.[50] To the inhabitants and regulars – Lytton and Clive, Aldous Huxley and Maria Nys, Fredegond and Gerald Shove, Katherine Mansfield and Middleton Murry, Brett and Lawrence, Gertler and Sassoon – it was a steam-bath of gossip, rivalry and misalliance: 'they've brought themselves to such a pass of intrigue & general intricacy of relationship that they're hardly sane about each other', Virginia wrote after her first visit in November 1917. But though she found Ottoline's relations with her protégés and with the local villagers absurd and theatrical, she could see the value (and the beauty) of Garsington: 'to the outsider the obvious view is that O. & P. & Garsington house provide a good deal, which isn't accepted very graciously.'[51]

Ottoline's anti-war causes were to an extent Virginia's. She agreed with the Morrells in admiring Sassoon's open letter of protest against his army service: 'It was a splendid thing to do,' she told Ottoline.[52] Ottoline also raised Virginia's awareness of wartime censorship. She mocked Ottoline's taking-up of the Italian author Rosa Allatini, whose novel *Despised and Rejected* (about a homosexual CO in prison) was 'burnt by the public hangman' in the last month of the war. ('Allatini . . . almost fainted & had to be fed on bath buns, which Ottoline had by her.')[53] And she ridiculed the appeal sent out by D.H. Lawrence and Philip Heseltine, after the banning of *The Rainbow* in November 1915, to start up what Virginia called 'a private indecency press called the Rainbow'. But she was interested (she would always be interested in Lawrence) when Ottoline read her bits of *The Rainbow* in 1917.[54] By then she was aware of the political potential of the privately owned small press. And she knew that 'patriotism' often meant 'censorship'.[55]

Though she was against the war, she was curious about what was going on 'behind the scenes'. She enjoyed being put in the know by Maynard Keynes about the Asquiths' behaviour after Asquith's resignation as Prime Minister in December 1916, or about the country's backing for Lord Lansdowne's peace letter.[56] When her cousin H.A.L. Fisher, President of the Board of Education in Lloyd George's coalition government from 1916 to 1922, gave her the inside story of the end of the war and the prospects for the next one ('No one can face another war. Why in 10 years they could blot out London by their aeroplanes. It cost us £1,000 to kill a German at the battle of the Somme; now it costs us £3,000') she relished the sense of being 'at the centre of things'. But the picture she derived from him of elderly gentlemen sitting in Downing Street with 'wireless messages racing through from all over the world' went straight into one of the most bitter passages of *Jacob's Room*, where the quiet-voiced, balding old men at the Admiralty, deciding that 'the course of history should shape itself this way or that way', send the young men to their deaths.[57]

Her pacifist's war was not entirely insulated – no one's could be – from that slaughter. Two of her Fisher cousins died, and Leonard's brother Cecil was killed by a shell in a messy, wasteful incident at Bourlon Wood.[58] Philip Woolf was wounded by the same shell, and never got over his brother's death. She visited him (and, later, a new friend, Nick Bagenal, seriously wounded in the last month of the war) at the Fishmonger's Hall at London Bridge, which had been turned into a military hospital. The nurses sat knitting, the wounded men stared out of the window or read, and on the river bank below, Lucien Pissarro could be seen painting. She came away with 'a feeling of the uselessness of it all, breaking these people & mending them again'.[59]

But her day-to-day, immediate experience of the war, as for most middle-class British civilians, was compounded of air-raids, rationing, the cost of living, and problems with live-in servants. Leonard looked back on years of *boredom*, nothing happening except 'the pitiless, useless slaughter in France', waiting for change, hearing the guns, being bombed.[60] She always remembered darkness: so much time underground.

Their war was spent in Asheham and Richmond. In January 1915, in the lull between Virginia's breakdowns, while they were living in their rooms overlooking the Green at Number 17, a 'House of Trouble' with an affable Belgian landlady and an erratic boiler, they found the house they wanted to live in. They knew that they would need to stay in the suburbs for her health; and Richmond, even if it couldn't be taken quite seriously, like London, was the 'first of the suburbs by a long way'. And the house they wanted was 'far the nicest house in England'.[61]

It was in fact half a house, the right-hand side of a grand, solid, redbrick Georgian building, with a tiled roof and fine rows of windows, which, when it was built in 1748, would have been 'a medium sized aristocratic country house', with stables and grounds. By 1876 the house, in Paradise Road, Richmond, had been divided into 'Suffield House' and 'Hogarth House', with two porches and two gardens. Hogarth House had a 100-foot garden with apple trees and a long brick wall. It was a few minutes uphill from the shops on Richmond High Street, which leads down to the station. A longer walk in the other direction led up to Richmond Hill, with its wide curving view of the river and Windsor Castle, and the big high spaces of Richmond

Park, where the 'deer exactly match the bracken'.[62] Paradise Road itself, though, did not live up to its name. There was a noisy school next door, a laundry and a municipal mortuary opposite. But inside, the house was spacious and well-proportioned, with a fine main staircase. The basement (where they were going to spend an unexpected amount of time) had very thick walls and a barrel-vaulted ceiling, and was divided into a kitchen, a scullery with a copper and a stone sink, a larder, wine and coal cellars, a lavatory, and the door to the yard. On the ground floor were a light, large drawing-room and dining-room with high ceilings, splendid panellings, and door and window carvings. On the first floor were their two bedrooms and a bathroom with a cast-iron bath and lavatory. The top floor, where the servants would live (and where the panelling ran out) had four smaller bedrooms. From the rear windows there was a view of Richmond chimneys and of the pagoda and the trees in Kew Gardens.

Leonard Woolf leased Hogarth House from Ida Brewer of Bushey Heath on 25 March 1915 for five years, for £150 a year.[63] They would live there for nine years; it would give its name to their Press. The house became their office: the work of the Press spread everywhere and 'crept all over the house',[64] and Virginia described it to Jacques Raverat in 1922 as being 'rather nice, shabby, ancient, very solid & incredibly untidy'.

When they moved in at the end of March 1915, Virginia was extremely ill, they had four nurses living in, and for many weeks she did not see Leonard, and lay in bed – as she recalled nine years later – 'mad, & seeing the sunlight quivering like gold water, on the wall', listening to 'the voices of the dead'.[65] The last of the nurses left in November; only then did she begin to like the house,[66] to entertain in it and to decorate it. She missed London passionately; whenever she went into town it would catch at her, as here in Berwick Street, Soho, in the spring of 1918:

> I walked through a narrow street lined on both sides with barrows, where stockings & ironmongery & candles & fish were being sold. A barrel organ played in the middle. I bought 6 bundles of coloured tapers. The stir & colour & cheapness pleased me to the depths of my heart.[67]

Richmond was dull by comparison. But she always had a great affection for and a feeling of gratitude towards what in leaving she would call 'this beautiful & lovable house'.[68]

For their first four years there, though, there was darkness and deprivation: those years, she would remember, 'when I was creeping about, like a rat struck on the head, & the aeroplanes were over London at night, & the streets dark, & no penny buns in the window'.[69] The war from the air was a tremendous shock. Few people had seen aeroplanes, and no one had had bombs fall on them, before this war. The Zeppelin raids on London began in January 1915. Beatrice Webb, in her diary for 8 October 1915, described the amazement at seeing 'a long sinuous airship high up in the blue black sky, lit up faintly by searchlights', moving slowly with the shells bursting far below it.[70] The wail of descending bombs, the different wail of the sirens, the crackle of anti-aircraft guns, the 'ghostly whistlings' summoning the workers at the Richmond munitions factory, the all-clear bugles sounded by Boy Scouts ('how sentimental the suggestion of the sound was'), became familiar noises. In 1917, aeroplane bombing began; and in the summer of 1917 there were many casualties in London (though nothing like the civilian casualties of the next war).

Virginia noted the jittery anticipation the raids provoked. Taking the walk she would give to Mrs Dalloway, through Green Park to Piccadilly, in February 1915, she saw an explosion bring people running out of their clubs: 'It is really an instinct with me, & with most people, I suppose, to turn any sudden noise, or dark object in the sky into an explosion, or a German aeroplane.' She noted too her curious sense of immunity: 'It always seems utterly impossible that one should be hurt.'[71] In the bitterly cold winter of 1917–18, they spent many nights waking up or interrupting their dinner parties, to go down to the basement with 'clothes, quilts, a watch and a torch', and sit on wooden boxes in the coal cellar, or lie on mattresses in the kitchen, during the bombardments.[72]

These memories are at the dark centre of *The Years*, which places the war in London. But in the country too it came closer to her than the perpetual sound of the guns across the Channel. At Asheham they saw German prisoners; their landlord was using them to work on the farm, guarded by 'absurd little soldiers'.[73] Virginia watched them, sometimes smiled at them, thinking (when Adrian engaged one in conversation) what it would mean to kill someone:

> The reason why it is easy to kill another person must be that one's imagination is too sluggish to conceive what his life means to him – the infinite possibilities of a succession of days which are furled in him, & have already been spent.[74]

She thought of what her own life meant to her, during the air-raids that took place on the clear moonlit nights of September 1917. When the war was coming to an end, this was how she put it to herself: 'One went to bed fairly positive that never again in all our lives need we dread the moonlight.'[75] She was wrong.

353

Both in London and in Sussex the main domestic difficulties of the war were created by shortages and by the servants. Before and after the war, Leonard and Virginia had two live-in servants, Vanessa had four. But girls were becoming dissatisfied with 'the long hours, lack of privacy, and lack of freedom', and many of the women who went into war-work (like munitions) were getting out of domestic service. The newspapers of 1919 were full of advertisements for housekeepers wanted for £35 or £40 a year (scullery-maids got £30, parlourmaids £35), promising them 'no basement', 'good outings', 'half day off each week, alternate Sundays'.[76] 'How hopeless it is,' Mary Hutchinson wrote to Vanessa in 1918, 'there doesnt [sic] seem to be servants anywhere.'[77]

Virginia and Vanessa could not have the same kind of quasi-parental authority over their servants that Julia had had. The dismal story of Sophie Farrell, turned out after Virginia's marriage (like poor old Crosby in *The Years*, pensioned out to Richmond) first to Aunt Minna and then to the George Duckworths at Dalingridge, showed how uncomfortable the traditional relationship made them feel. When Virginia tentatively asked Sophie to return, she refused with offended dignity.[78]

The next generation of servants expected more freedom and more intimacy. Sometimes Virginia wished that 'the old laws of life held good' for servants and 'establishments',[79] and tried to use the same tone as Julia ('Though I pressed all the advantages of going to you, & told them I thought them very foolish, they wouldnt budge')[80] but it hardly ever worked. And yet it still did not seem imaginable to do without them, or to treat them as friends. Clive's feelings about his servants (in a wartime letter to Mary), though more brutal than Virginia's, share some of her assumptions:

> Frankly I dont think one can expect much honesty or sensitiveness or delicacy for twenty-eight pounds a year; but one can escape one's more grievous responsibilities at the price . . . If one can get material comfort and reasonably good manners from one's body-slaves I think one can regard their cheatings as a slight addition to their wages . . . People like you and Vanessa very properly shift your domestic responsibilities. You might spend your lives looking after your children and your houses; but you would be idiots and worse if you did, because you have better things to do.[81]

The mistresses of this generation, even the more bohemian ones like Vanessa, expected a certain performance from the servants: 'I want a house parlourmaid', Vanessa wrote to Virginia when Virginia was trying to help her (with dire results) 'but there is practically no parlour work. She need not wait at table, only bring the courses in when I ring. Otherwise it is all housemaids work . . . wages I suppose about £24.'[82] A great deal of time was spent exchanging 'characters' of their servants (just as the Bloomsbury servants exchanged notes on their employers, through what Virginia called their 'secret society').[83] These mistress-servant relationships were unequal, self-conscious and troublesome: there was, as Quentin Bell put it, 'incomprehension on both sides'.[84]

Nelly Boxall and her friend Lottie Hope came from Roger Fry's house to Richmond on 1 February 1916. Lottie stayed until 1924 (after which she worked for Adrian, then Clive, and then Vanessa). Nelly would stay with the Woolfs until 1934.[85] Lottie was a 'foundling', an emotional and volatile girl; Nelly, a more complicated character it seems, was quieter, but affectionate, moody and demanding. Their lives were closely intertwined; they defended each other, didn't like to be parted, sometimes slept in the same room: perhaps they were lovers. But their story is not told, except in Virginia's words. She recognised that her version had the makings of a novel, and that the story might be told differently by someone else:

> If I were reading this diary, if it were a book that came my way, I think I should seize with greed upon the portrait of Nelly, & make a story – perhaps make the whole story revolve round that – it would amuse me. Her character – our efforts to be rid of her – our reconciliations.[86]

This eighteen-year relationship was one of the most stormy and – in a way – intimate, of Virginia Woolf's life. From the first there were clumsy misunderstandings. The girls did not like going to Asheham. Perhaps, then, they wouldn't do. Virginia tried to pass them on first to Mary Hutchinson, and then, unsuccessfully, to Vanessa, who was expecting another baby in 1918 and badly needed stop-gap servants at Charleston. But misunderstandings and indecisions muddied these negotiations, and Nelly and Lottie stayed put. 'Don't let us quarrel about servants anyhow!' Vanessa begged. 'Theyre too incomprehensible.' Both resented the time they spent thinking and talking about them.[87]

But there was much, much more to come. Both servants complained of the mess made by the Press. In the autumn of 1919 Nelly gave the first of her many notices because her employers were having too many dinner parties. For years these scenes and quarrels continued. In 1924, Virginia made up her mind to 'deliver sentence of death', but though Lottie went, Nelly stayed on, 'too fond' of Mrs Woolf to leave. Again in 1930, when Nelly was away in hospital, she decided to be callous and resolute; again she failed, and only succeeded in the end in March 1934. The relief was tremendous.[88] But that was still not the end – not until the next war – of living with servants.

She disliked being in a position of authority over anyone, she quarrelled with Leonard over how to treat them, and she developed a horror of Nelly's jealousy, spitefulness, chatter and dependency (for which we only have her word).[89] And the whole system on which their relationship was based seemed mutually degrading.

My opinion never changes that our domestic system is wrong . . . the system of keeping two young women chained in a kitchen to laze & work & suck their life from two in the drawing room.[90]

Eleven years later she is still saying it:

It is an absurdity, how much time L. & I have wasted in talking about servants. And it can never be done with because the fault lies in the system. How can an uneducated woman let herself in, alone, into our lives? What happens is that she becomes a mongrel; & has no roots any where. I could put my theory into practice by getting a daily of a civilised kind, who had her baby in Kentish town; & treated me as an employer, not friend. Here is a fine rubbish heap left by our parents to be swept.[91]

The problem gets into almost all the novels. In *To the Lighthouse* the servants are the forces of survival, but are described in chillingly class-bound terms. In wartime, when her relationship with the girls was very new, this tone is much in evidence. The worst thing about the air-raids, she said, was having to make conversation with the servants all night.[92] On the other hand, if *they* were going to take shelter then she thought she and Leonard had better do so too: after all (she wrote to Clive) 'what an irony if they should escape and we be killed'.[93]

Nelly's initially mediocre cooking was not improved by the wartime shortages. In 1914, a shopping-list of a loaf, a pint of milk, 1 lb of beef, a quarter of a pound of tea, six eggs and 1 lb of sugar could be had for today's $12\frac{1}{2}$p.[94] Prices were up and supplies were low from 1917, when Virginia complained one weekend in February of having 'no coal, no milk, no telephone', and asked Vanessa for advice on 'cheap dishes', as she couldn't make her housekeeping books go any lower than 17s. a head. They thought about money[95] and about food every day. Sugar was hard to come by; in July 1917 she was getting it for 9d. a pound and sending it to Vanessa in return for potatoes and greens from Charleston. At Christmas 1917 they were using Nestlés dried milk and dried eggs; they couldn't afford a turkey, and got a chicken for 6s. Cigarettes had to be stockpiled (importation stopped in 1917). Visitors to Asheham in 1918 brought their ration cards for meat, sugar or butter. They made the most of apples, blackberries, mushrooms, and honey from David Garnett's bees at Charleston. By January 1918 everything was 'skimped': no chocolates, margarine or 'nutter' to be had, butter rationed to 1 lb a week, eggs 5*d*. each, a chicken now anything from 10*s*. to 15*s*. She found it hard to remember, looking in the Richmond bakers' windows at the plain biscuits and buns with nothing but 'decoy' plums in them, that a year ago they were still 'allowed' 'iced cakes'.[96]

The false plums in the cakes, like the false words in the papers, fed her thoughts about war and society. There were impassioned debates in the drawing-room of Hogarth House about what kind of 'New World' – Fabian, Communist, Socialist? – should follow the war. One wet evening in January 1918, they had two younger women friends to supper, ex-Newnham girls, Alix Sargant-Florence and Fredegond, one of Virginia's Maitland cousins, a poet who had married the economist and CO Gerald Shove. They talked about money. Gerald Shove had been reading Tolstoi (they were all reading Russian plays and novels now), and thought they should 'give up their capital'.

> 'What's the use of that? L. demanded. Thats the worst of all things to do. We dont want people to live on 30s. a week.'
>   'Psychologically it may be necessary if one is to abolish capitalism' I remarked.
>   . . . L. gave us a great many reasons why we should keep what we have, & do good work for nothing; I still feel, however, that my fire is too large for one person. I'm one of those who are hampered by the psychological hindrance of owning capital.[97]

Leonard remarked more brutally in *his* diary: 'V said we ought to give up all our capital. I said it was nonsense.'[98] Sitting in the garden at Asheham a few weeks after that conversation, Virginia brooded – as her characters in *The Years* would brood Tchekhovianly – on the relation between history and the soul.

> I happened to read Wordsworth; the poem which ends 'what man has made of man'. The daffodils were out & the guns I suppose could be heard from the downs. Even to me, who have no immmediate stake, & repudiate the importance of what is being done, there was an odd pallor in those particular days of sunshine.[99]

The poem she had been reading was 'Lines written in Early Spring, 1798':

To her fair works did nature link

The human soul that through me ran
And much it grieved my heart to think
What man has made of man.

Any optimism about a better post-war future was dispelled by the national tone when peace broke out. Though she experienced at first a feeling of hope and 'lightness',[100] the victorious utterances seemed 'odious'.[101] 'The Northcliffe papers do all they can to insist upon the indispensability and delight of war. They magnify our victories to make our mouths water for more.'[102] Through the autumn of 1918 and the summer of 1919 *The Times* bellowed its patriotic oratory about 'the vast and gallant company of the fallen', 'the immortal dead who gave youth, and manhood, and all the good things of life to save England from the pollution and the blight of German supremacy'.[103]

Those who had opposed the war, like Siegfried Sassoon ('The War had been a loathsome tragedy and all this flag-waving couldn't alter it')[104] detested this chauvinism. Leonard and Virginia 'talked of peace', without illusions:

how the sausage balloons will be hauled down, & the gold coins dribble in; & how people will soon forget all about the war, & the fruits of our victory will grow as dusty as ornaments under glass cases in lodging house drawing rooms. How often will the good people of Richmond rejoice to think that liberty has been won for the good people of Potsdam? I can believe though that we shall be more arrogant about our own virtues. The Times still talks of the possibility of another season, in order to carry the war into Germany, & there imprint a respect for liberty in the German peasants. I think the distance of the average person from feelings of this sort is the only safeguard & assurance that we shall settle down again neither better nor worse.[105]

But she did not feel like 'the average person'. Her war was different from Nelly Boxall's. The celebrations in November 1918 were 'sordid and depressing',[106] and Peace Day, which she described in detail on 19 July 1919, seemed to her 'a servants festival', 'got up to pacify & placate "the people".' 'There's something calculated & politic & insincere about these peace rejoicings.'[107] The war-history of 'the Man in the Street' was *his* history, 'not ours': she could not cross that gulf.[108]

But the war years were also, for her, years of recovery, ambition and discovery. She was thirty-four at the beginning of 1916, when she began to 'creep about',[109] still spending mornings in bed, still only allowed to write for a limited amount of time, much heavier (12 stone instead of her usual 8 or 9), and (as Vanessa told Roger) 'so much changed to look at that it's quite odd talking to her'.[110] When Leonard went away she was anxious, and could not be alone. During his tour of northern cities in October 1917, for instance, she went to Charleston, and then had Saxon to stay at Asheham (a sharp contrast to her 'rapid bold Mon[goose]').[111] Her menstrual cycle, which had now resumed, always made her ill: 'Its very melancholy,' she wrote to Vanessa, 'how life is disposed of by periods.'[112] In dreams and jokes, her body's functions often took control. Just after Vanessa moved to Sussex, when Virginia was dreading that she would say that 'Charleston is better than Asheham', she dreamt she was 'sitting in a kind of portable w.c. at Charleston, painted grey, like a Beehive'.[113] In a letter telling Duncan of a 'terrifically exciting & somehow sexual dream' she had had at the dentist's, joking about spinsters and chamber pots and how she was making her own sanitary towels, she concluded:

> I wish I could stop writing this letter – it is like an extremely long visit to the W.C. when, do what you will, fresh coils appear, and duty seems to urge you to break off, and then another inch protrudes, which must be the last; and it *isnt* the last – and so on, until – However – [114]

There's a mixture of relish and disgust in this stylish comic drama of writing-as-shitting. Disgust was always very close to the surface. In May 1918 she went through the 'horror' of buying a hat. ('Horror' was not too strong a word. Choosing and appearing in new clothes made her rigid with fear and embarrassment.[115] Yet she could be eccentrically insouciante about how she wore them: 'In the street my grey knickers came off', she could remark blithely.) Outside the hat-shop, she saw women's faces 'as senseless as playing cards; with tongues like adders'.[116] The ordinary city street could suddenly turn into a threatening nightmare. And terrible 'fits of melancholy' waited their time to strike – as when she finished *Night and Day* at the end of 1918.

She embarked on therapeutic – and practical – tasks. The most short-lived of these was learning Italian, one of several attempts at a foreign language (German, French and Greek in her youth; Russian, briefly, in 1921; French again, which she read and wrote competently but spoke poorly, in 1928 and 1934). She was always conscientious. Her Italian notebook has 36 pages filled with lists of words taking the subjunctive, rules for pronouns ('After interjection expressing grief the pronoun *may* also be put into the dative'), and some intriguing, though rather limp, exercises in translation: 'Were you not visited by the doctor this morning? Have you taken the remedies which were ordered you? Not yet. The doctor will not be content not to be obeyed.'[117] When she thought back to the war for *The Years*, she also returned to her Italian. She took lessons again, and was reading Dante through 1934 and 1935. A phrase from the *Purgatorio* echoes through *The Years*: 'Chè per quanti si dice più lì nostro/ tanto possiede più di ben ciascuno.'

> For by so many more there are who say 'ours'
> So much the more of good doth each possess.[118]

As a more sustained practical commitment, she agreed to organise and to chair monthly meetings of the Richmond Branch of the Women's Co-operative Guild. She did this for four years. She invited speakers she knew (Forster, Ray Strachey, Bob Trevelyan, Adrian, Molly Hamilton) to talk for about half an hour, on a weekday evening (with dinner first at seven) about social questions, or travel, or labour problems, followed – she hoped – by discussion. About twelve women came. Mostly they were quiet and phlegmatic (unless the subject of food or rationing came up), and she sometimes wondered what they got out of it: 'unless they like sitting in a room not their own, gas & light free, & other women on other chairs.' But she respected their 'good sense' and their desire for 'something beyond the daily life'; and she agreed with their denunciations of the war: 'They would all have peace tomorrow, on any terms, & abuse our government for leading us on after a plan of its own.'[119] Those views were echoed many years later, in a collection of letters by Guild women (edited by Margaret Llewelyn Davies and published by the Press in 1931 as *Life As We Have Known It*, with an introduction by Virginia). One of the letter-writers said:

> I don't think we should have had war if the women could have had the vote before, & a voice in it. There's no mother or wife in England or Germany that would give their loved one to be killed. Now we are working for peace.[120]

Virginia ran into trouble with this book, trouble which echoed the problems she had had with the Guild meetings themselves. When she set up a lecture on venereal diseases in January 1917, some of the audience complained. It was a pity, she thought (sounding in one way very like her mother, and also very unlike) 'that that class shouldn't discuss these questions openly, considering how much more they are affected by them than we are'.[121] Later, they conceded that the talk had been useful, and asked for one on sex education.[122] But she too had her inhibitions in relation to the

Guild. When *Kew Gardens* came out in 1919, with its caricature of the voices of the 'two women of the lower middle class' (intoning 'My Bert, Sis, Bill, Grandad, the old man, sugar, sugar, flour, kippers, greens, sugar, sugar, sugar')[123] some of the Guild members asked her for a copy. But: 'I don't want them to read the scene of the two women. Is that to the discredit of Kew Gardens? Perhaps a little.'[124]

That same unease returned in the publication process of *Life As We Have Known It*. She accepted Margaret's invitation to write the introduction reluctantly, and produced an equivocal personal reminiscence of a 1913 Guild conference at which she had felt alienated from the minds of the women speakers. She could respond to their letters more as revealing documents than as good writing. Margaret (by 1930 a rather forlorn old lady) objected to the highly-coloured accounts of her companion Lilian Harris smoking a pipe, and to such remarks as: 'It is not from the ranks of working-class women that the next great poet or novelist will be drawn.' Virginia, fuming, edited the piece for book publication, but it was too late to censor its appearance in the *Yale Review* in 1930. Virginia was 'appalled', she said, by the conventionality of the Guild women: they were as bad as the middle-classes! It was rather like the row, years before, over the syphilis lecture; but it reflected more on Virginia Woolf than on Margaret or the Guild. In both versions of her honest, uneasy essay, there is a genuine interest in the details of the women's lives, an inability to understand them fully, and a hope for a time – a New World still not in existence in 1930 – when middle-class women would not meet working-class women as 'mistresses or customers', and when 'perhaps friendship and sympathy would supervene'.[125]

TWENTY

The Press

The appearance in 1931 of *Life As We Have Known It* as a Hogarth Press title shows how political the Press had become by then.[1] It also suggests how 'private' the Press had always been, drawing on old friends and family for its publications. In October 1916 Virginia wrote to Eleanor Cecil that they wanted to start a printing press 'for all our friends stories'.[2] She could not have imagined then how this would develop into the publishing of Pamphlets and Letters and Lectures, into a Psychoanalytical Library and Folios of New Writing, into books on economics and empire and disarmament, as well as poetry, fiction, novels and memoirs. Nor could she have foreseen the transformation of an absorbing hobby into a burdensome business.

They first thought of getting a printing press on her thirty-third birthday, on 25 January 1915, and Leonard started making enquiries in February; but then all plans were halted for many months. He said, looking back, that he thought of it as 'a manual occupation which would take her mind completely off her work',[3] and it's often noted that the Press was meant to be a form of therapy for Virginia.[4] But at the time she too was thinking of it as an escape for Leonard from the demands of the Webbs.[5] So perhaps it was meant to be mutually therapeutic. If so, this was basket-weaving with a vengeance. In practice, the Press was a time-consuming occupation which immediately gripped them both, and which at once gave a sense of 'possibilities' opening up.[6]

Their new hobby drew on the likeness, and the liking, in the marriage, both of them excited, obsessional, determined, hard-working, proud, and resistant to criticism. And the story of the Press is, in a way, the story of the marriage: Leonard's anxiety for her health, their mutual interests, their areas of division, and, reflected in the list, their cultural and political life. They instituted themselves as a couple on the title page of their first publication, two stories 'written and printed by Virginia Woolf and L.S. Woolf'. The forms of these names would keep changing: sometimes they printed their full names, sometimes they were linked by an ampersand. On the last page of her first separate publication for the Press, *Kew Gardens*, they put: 'Printed by Leonard & Virginia at the Hogarth Press, Richmond', and had to paste over a colophon correcting this to 'L & V Woolf'.[7] It was as though they had not yet decided if these books were for private or public sale. But from then on (until 1938) their joint names became the sign of a marriage which was also an imprint.[8]

Their beginners' excitement is palpable. Though they had been talking about it for some time, in the end it was an impulse buy. There had been frustrations: the income tax refund they had been waiting for wasn't as large as they had hoped for, and they discovered at St Bride's School of Printing that lessons could only be taken by unionised apprentices. But then, gazing longingly one March afternoon into the window of a small shop in Holborn called the Excelsior Printers' Supply Company, they just decided to go in and buy a small handpress and a teach-yourself-to-print booklet.[9] With some Caslon Old Face roman type (probably in two sizes), and the necessary tools, the initial outlay (as Leonard would characteristically recall) came to £19.5s.5d. It all arrived at Hogarth House on 24 April 1917. A part was broken, and had to be replaced. But immediately both of them became utterly absorbed; Virginia could hardly tear herself away; Leonard cursed the day they had bought it, 'because I shall never do anything else'.[10]

Through the spring and early summer of 1917 Virginia learnt to become a compositor. Leonard's shaking hands made type-setting impossible for him, so he did the machining, and she did the type-setting, the distributing, and the binding. Her first job was to sort the 'great blocks of type', which came wrapped in brown paper by the typefounder, into the wooden type-case, placing each individual piece of type (upper and lower case letters, punctuation marks, numbers and symbols) in its compartment. Then the type was ready for words and lines to be set, or composed. She would put the text they were going to set where she could see it conveniently, next to or above the type-case. She would find each piece of type in the case (this was slow at first, but would get faster) and then place it, face up and upside down, in the composing stick. This was a small tray,[11] which could hold four or five lines of type. Each line, set letter by letter and word by word, had to fill the width of the stick exactly: once a whole page was set, the type had to be compressed together so tightly (packed out with different size pieces of 'spacing') that none of them would fall out when the page was carried to the press. Once she had completed a line, she would place a strip of lead above it and begin the next line, until the stick was full. Then she would transfer the lines from the stick to the galley and then fill the stick again, until she had set enough lines to make up a page. This compositor's work required manual dexterity, patience, vigilance and concentration.

The next job (usually Leonard's) was to 'impose' the type, to place it on a flat surface and arrange the pages so that they would print in the right sequence. Then the type pages would be tightly 'locked up' in a rectangular metal frame, the 'chase'. 'Locked up' and 'knocked down' (levelled, so that, as printers used to say, the page was 'on its feet' and completely flat), the type was ready for printing.[12]

Leonard would then ink the inking disc, and, with what their booklet called 'a simple downward motion of the handle', bring the platen with the paper on it up against the type in its chase overhead. Then he had to turn the sheet over and make sure that the page was 'registered' – that the page on one side was exactly aligned with the page on the reverse side. Because of the size of their first press, machining was excruciatingly slow and laborious work for them.[13] In between each printing of a page (or of two pages if they had enough type for that – and they bought a great deal more in April 1918),[14] Virginia had to inkily distribute the type of each page back into the type-cases, and then go on to set the next pages. No wonder that it took them two-and-a-half months to produce their first book, or that Leonard would look back with amazement on 'our rather eccentric and amusing printing antics'.[15] Then they had to learn, by trial and error, how to print the woodcut illustrations to the stories; how to fold the pages, bind them together, and glue or sew on the coloured bindings. This was her job, and the part of the process she was most familiar with from her bookbinding days. They also had to keep their press 'in good working order, well cleaned and oiled'. ('And', their instructions added, 'do not amuse yourself by taking it to pieces.')[16] And then, last, there was the work of wrapping, addressing, and sending out the packages. Virginia Woolf spent hours and hours of her time – and would for many years to come – doing these various manual jobs, which combined addictive and fiddly attention to detail, aesthetic decisions, and boring mechanical routines.

Like all self-taught beginners, they had considerable teething problems. She mixed up the ns and the hs, the ink came out too thick or too thin, type got spilt, they didn't proof-read, and the first notice they sent out in May had awkward spacings and blotted ink and looked extremely amateurish. But, rather quickly, the amateurs began to transform themselves into professionals. Fifty, sixty orders came in for their first publication, days after the notice went out. *Two Stories* came out in July, costing 1s. 6d., with four (unsigned) woodcut illustrations commissioned from their new acquaintance, the Slade art-student, Dora Carrington (who would earn 15s. from her work). The two stories were Leonard's 'Three Jews', and Virginia's 'The Mark on the Wall'. By publishing together, they signalled that the Press was a joint enterprise and a vehicle for their own writing. For Leonard, the story was a signpost pointing down a road he would not take –

THE HOGARTH PRESS

Telephone
Richmond 496

Hogarth House
Paradise Road
Richmond
Surrey

LIST OF PUBLICATIONS.

NEW PUBLICATIONS.

Stories from the Old Testament. Retold by
LOGAN PEARSALL SMITH, author of
Trivia. 4s. 6d. net.
Paris, a Poem. By HOPE MIRRLEES, author
of *Madeleine.* 3s. net.

TO BE PUBLISHED SHORTLY.

The Story of the Siren. By E. M. FORSTER.
2s. 6d. net.

PREVIOUS PUBLICATIONS.

VIRGINIA WOOLF
The Mark on the Wall. Second edition.
1s. 6d. net.
Kew Gardens. With woodcuts by
VANESSA BELL. Second edition. 2s. net.
KATHERINE MANSFIELD
Prelude. 3s. 6d. net.
T. S. ELIOT
Poems. 2s. 6d. net. *Out of print.*
J. MIDDLETON MURRY
The Critic in Judgment. 2s. 6d. net.
LEONARD & VIRGINIA WOOLF
Two Stories. *Out of print.*

as a fiction writer, as a Jewish writer. But for Virginia it 'marked', as her title suggests, a completely new direction, the beginning of a new form and a new kind of writing. 'We have just started printing Leonards story; I haven't produced mine yet,' she told Vanessa in May 1917. It was a casual remark of the utmost significance: the new machine had created the possibility for the new story.[17]

Two Stories was called 'Publication No. 1' on the title page, and though it didn't develop into a series, their optimism was vindicated. They sold the 134 copies they printed to 91 buyers, raised the price to 2s. for the last few copies (by 1922 it was fetching 25s. in second-hand bookshops),[18] made a profit of £7.1s., and had some enthusiastic responses. They at once began to plan ahead. They would buy a bigger machine. (This, the Minerva treadle press, eventually arrived in October 1921, and was so heavy that they installed it in the basement of Hogarth House in case it went crashing through the floor on to Nelly's head.)[19] They would use a commercial printer for larger operations (though they continued to handprint, as well, for many years, and would, altogether, print 34 books themselves).[20] They would experiment with pictures and illustrations, coloured end papers and bindings. Emma Vaughan gave them all her old bookbinding tools. They would look for young unpublished writers, as well as soliciting their friends.

(In their fifth anniversary notice they described their aims as 'producing works of genuine merit which . . . could scarcely hope to secure publication through the ordinary channels'.)[21] They would start a subscription scheme, as other small presses did.[22] They would have a bronze plaque put on their front door reading 'The Hogarth Press'. And, clearly, they would need an assistant.

They began with the gloomy Alix Sargant-Florence, who tried it for a day (they left her to sort type and went for a walk with the dog; by the time they came back she had had enough). Barbara Hiles, Carrington's jolly, irritatingly talkative, fresh-faced fellow student at the Slade, replaced her from October. There followed, over twenty years, one or two young women (notably the efficient and independent Marjorie Joad) and a succession of ambitious, thwarted, talented young men (Ralph Partridge, Dadie Rylands, Angus Davidson, Richard Kennedy and John Lehmann), all of whom found the work tedious and all of whom rubbed up against Leonard's adamantine proprietariness and perfectionism. There would be many quarrels, in which Virginia would support Leonard but would also try to act as a peace-maker. It was a well-known joke among their friends that working at the Hogarth Press drove you mad.

From the first there were other quarrels and difficult decisions. In the two years after July 1917, when *Two Stories* came out, they did not produce a great deal, but the Press went through dramatic developments. They accepted a long story by Katherine Mansfield, *Prelude*, and spent almost a year printing it by hand – interrupted by the setting of Cecil Woolf's poems, after his death. They planned a book of woodcuts with Vanessa, but she pulled out because Leonard would not let her have 'the final decision aesthetically'.[23] In the spring of 1918 they were offered the manuscript of Joyce's *Ulysses* by Harriet Weaver of the *Egoist Press* and – notoriously – turned it down, principally because of its length. A few months later, Virginia (who all this time was writing her second novel, *Night and Day*) began a story, *Kew Gardens*, for the Press to publish and Vanessa to illustrate with woodcuts. Other short pieces, 'Solid Objects', 'An Evening Party', were in the works. There was much correspondence between them about illustrations. Vanessa provided a frontispiece of two women in a leafy setting and an end-piece of a caterpillar and a butterfly. But she thought the end-product 'very bad', and told Virginia that she would not illustrate any more of her stories 'under those conditions' – 'and went so far as to doubt the value of the Hogarth Press altogether'. Virginia was 'stung & chilled'.[24]

Kew Gardens was offered to their subscribers as one of three books, all published on 12 May 1919. The others were John Middleton Murry's *The Critic in Judgement*, and a book of startling new poems by a young American poet they had just met, T.S. Eliot. On 29 May an enthusiastic review of *Kew Gardens* appeared in the *TLS*. On 4 June 1919 they came back from Asheham to find the doormat of Hogarth House deep in requests from about 150 subscribers. *Kew Gardens* was quickly reprinted by a commercial printer. They had a business, and Virginia Woolf had a name. Five months later she published *Night and Day*, the last book she would publish in England under another imprint.

The Press freed her, but it also led to her being seen as a protected species. And in 1917, though her reviewing was by now enormously confident,[25] and though she was writing her second novel, she was afraid of being thought of as an amateur. She worried at the thought in a piece on Samuel Butler, written while they were printing *Kew Gardens*, in the summer of 1919. *The Way of All Flesh*, she said, had been written very slowly, over twelve years. 'It bears in every part the mark of being a home-made hobby rather than the product of high professional skill.' 'It is a limitation to be an amateur', she went on. 'Butler failed to be a great novelist because his novel writing was his hobby.'[26] She wanted neither her books nor her publishing firm to be considered 'a home-made hobby'.

Even if no one could, in the end, accuse the Hogarth Press of unprofessionalism, they might – and would – accuse it of being too private a private press.[27] The business always mixed the personal and the professional. Friendships with contributors came under threat if the publishers felt betrayed, or if their contributors were dissatisfied. And most of Virginia's intimate relationships (for instance with Vanessa and with Vita) were affected by their involvement with the Press.

The Woolfs published their friends, as they always intended doing. Virginia was always soliciting people she knew for books, particularly her women friends for memoirs. Some of these friends were major figures: Forster and Fry and Keynes would have been first-class contributors to any Press. But personal interest was involved in their publishing of Fredegond Shove's or George Rylands's verse, or in their handsome edition of Julia Margaret Cameron's photographs, or in Clive Bell's witty hedonistic poem *The Legend of Monte Della Sibilla*, with illustrations by Duncan Grant and Vanessa Bell – a stylish and attractive production, but very much in the family.[28]

The social and personal network on which the Hogarth Press drew was inextricable from literary journalism.[29] Once Leonard Woolf became an editor, beginning on *War and Peace* in 1916 and taking on the literary editorship of the *Nation* in 1923 – by which time Virginia Woolf was a major reviewer and well-known author – they were at the centre of the literary power-structures, and had plenty of opportunities for what *Scrutiny* would call 'Clique-Puffery'.[29] In fact, they particularly did not want to be like Middleton Murry, who promoted and employed his wife Katherine Mansfield as editor of the *Athenaeum* from 1918, and, after her death, 'boiled her bones' in his own magazine, the *Adelphi*.[30] Virginia was leery of reviewing her friends, though she did do it sometimes: 'If I review yours' (she wrote to Lytton over *Eminent Victorians* in 1918) 'then why not Clive's, Desmond's, Molly's and Fredegond's, which would be more than I could stand.'[31] She was sorry that Desmond MacCarthy had had his book sent to her for review: 'One cant avoid a certain uneasiness in writing formally of people one knows so well.' And Leonard would as a literary editor be very careful about seeming to promote Hogarth Press books.[32] They did not repeat one unfortunate early piece of 'clique-puffery', when in 1919 they reviewed, anonymously and jointly, two of their own Hogarth Press publications, Eliot's *Poems* and Murry's critical essay. Murry was the editor of the magazine they were writing for, the *Athenaeum*, and had commissioned the piece. As might be expected, the review read somewhat stiffly, and when Virginia referred in it to the 'uncompromising' nature of the Hogarth Press's 'little books' (she used the word twice) she may have been prompted by feeling that this was a compromised review.[33] All the same, when in later years the literary pages of the *Nation* would have a review by Virginia side-by-side with a round-up of the month's books by Leonard, or when its front page would advertise *To the Lighthouse* and Leonard's *Essays* prominently on its 'Just Published' list, it would be hard for the Press not to be perceived as part of a cabal. Virginia Woolf's reputation in her life-time, and after it, has been affected by this.

And affected too, for good and ill, by how her books looked. After their bumpy start, the sisters' collaboration in the decorating and presentation of Virginia Woolf's writing continued for life. In 1921, when she put together all her short pieces as *Monday or Tuesday*, Vanessa provided woodcut illustrations for four of the stories. 'The Mark on the Wall' was reissued in 1921 with Vanessa's woodcuts, and *Kew Gardens* in 1927, with her eloquent illustrations on every page, in their most appealing and complete collaboration.[34] And she would provide endearing end-paper illustrations for *Flush* in 1933. But Vanessa mainly contributed the cover-design. Sometimes these were formalised images, like the flower bowl and window-curtains for *Jacob's Room* (laughed at by the booksellers for its Post-Impressionist vagueness),[35] or the stylish geometric design of cross-hatching and circles and lines for the cover of *On Being Ill*. Sometimes they were elaborate representational set-pieces, like the still life and bottle on the cover of Virginia's essay on Sickert. Sometimes they were simple figures like the clock on the mantelpiece for the cover of *A Room of One's Own*, or the characteristic large, calm, classical woman reading, for 'Mr Bennett and Mrs Brown' (and for other Hogarth Essay covers). Only very rarely would the covers represent the contents (like the portrait of Roger Fry on the cover of the biography). Often, indeed, Vanessa would have only the roughest idea of what the contents were to be.[36] When she did provide a 'literal' cover – a lighthouse, some waves, or stage-curtains for *Between the Acts* – they were impressionistic and decorative rather than explanatory. What she provided was a kind of 'visual underscoring'[37] which gave the books a sympathetic atmosphere – feminine, imaginative, delicate, modern but domestic. The enthusiastic review of *Kew Gardens* in 1919, which boosted its sales so dramatically, praised what it called 'this odd, Fitzroy-square-looking cover' (identifying it thus with Roger Fry's style) as a perfect collaboration between the writer and the artist to create 'a thing of original and therefore strange beauty, with its own "atmosphere", its own vital force.'[38] As Virginia Woolf's writing developed, the decorativeness of the covers became, to an extent, misleading: the heavy dark rose lying over the interlocking circles on the cover of *The Years*, the pretty swagged floral curtain design for *Between the Acts*, make these novels look less powerful and angry than they are.

From the start, practical problems apart, Virginia felt that her new professional relationship with Vanessa confirmed their intimacy:

> I think the book [*Kew Gardens*] will be a great success – owing to you; and my vision comes out much as I had it, so I suppose, in spite of everything, God made our brains upon the same lines, only leaving out 2 or 3 pieces in mine.[39]

It was extremely important to her to claim – however wryly – that identity of vision. Their collaboration, and the beginning of the Press, coincided with a period of intense aesthetic exploration for Virginia, which went much further than looking for beautiful coloured papers or arguing painfully over woodcuts. Styles in painting, dress, interior decoration, stage-sets (as well as in music and writing) were changing rapidly during the war, and she was involved with and highly conscious of those changes. Like everyone else in her London world she was dazzled by the extraordinary experience of seeing the Russian Ballet.[40] Like many of her friends she was buying things from the Omega workshops, Roger Fry's original, unorthodox and hugely influential design centre at 33 Fitzroy Square, committed to inventiveness, spontaneity, and playfulness, vibrant Italianate colours and bold new shapes, in every area of domestic decoration – textiles, ceramics, pottery, woodwork, silkscreening. She was sceptical about the more Utopian arts-and-crafts flavour of the Omega, as embodied in the 'foolish young woman in a Post Impressionist tunic'.[41] She disliked its crude effects on the colour of dresses, especially her sister-in-law's gaudy stripes 'of the vilest kind', which, she told Vanessa, 'almost wrenched my eyes from the sockets'. 'I shall retire into dove colour and old lavender, with a lace collar, and lawn wristlets.'[42] Still, she did buy some Omega clothes (a blue dress was particularly admired), as well as furniture, ceramics and pottery. When she looked back in 1938 on the closing down of the Omega in 1919, it was with affection for those irreplaceable, unique objects: 'a painted table, a witty chair'. 'And if by chance one of those broad deep plates is broken, or an accident befalls a blue dish, all the shops in London may be searched in vain for its fellow.'[43]

The relationship she was investigating now between different types of 'aesthetic emotions' would be essential to her work. But at this time she was still finding out how (and whether) she could write as a painter would paint. In a letter to Vanessa of July 1918 about taste and painting, she asked her sister humbly: 'Do you think this semi-conscious process of coming to dislike one colour very much and liking a picture better and better points to some sort of live instinct trying to come into existence?'[44]

She kept testing her judgements against the painters. She went to the Omega shows and tried to make up her own mind about the paintings under the barrage of Roger Fry's opinions. She listened to him talking about Cézanne to Clive, and compared her own responses to the famous apples. She set her aesthetics against Fry's, when he wrote to praise her for 'The Mark on the Wall': 'I'm not sure that a perverted plastic sense doesn't somehow work itself out in words for me.'[45]

At the same time she was thinking a great deal about interiors (*Night and Day* is full of furnishings and decor) and what they meant. The purchase from the Omega of some bright yellow chair-covers in 'a painful staring check'[46] sparked off a half-serious crisis about her taste. She got into a state about these covers, telling both Clive and Ottoline that she didn't want them to visit because the chairs were so hideous, rushing off to the famous fabric store Souhami's to get some 'pale green & blue Persian cloth' to cover the chairs with, deciding never to buy anything from the Omega again.[47] This fuss coincided with a burst of pleasure at getting a green glass jar from the chemist 'for nothing': 'Glass is the best of all decorations, holding the light & changing it.'[48]

The comparison she kept making between Asheham and Charleston, which Vanessa and Duncan were beginning to paint and decorate in 1917, was not only motivated by sisterly rivalry.[49] It was part of the debate she was having with herself about a whole style of living. Could everything – paintings, furnishings, chair-covers, clothes, forms of social life, domestic arrangements, ways of producing as well as reading and writing books – have a coherent value and represent an attitude to life (even without having very much money to spend)? She often compared her own interiors with Charleston's improvised, colourful workshop, or the theatrical jewelled rooms and formal gardens of Garsington, or the cool modern stylishness of Mary Hutchinson's riverside house at Hammersmith. She always noted other people's interior decoration, whether it was the newly-married Barbara Hiles and Nick Bagenal's Hampstead studio where 'even the black & white cat seemed decorated by the Omega'[50] or the horrid 'acid lemon colours' in Ka and Will's flat,[51] or the plush, 'luxurious sham' of the enormously grand Shelley House on the Chelsea Embankment, where the wealthy printer St John Hornby gave Sunday subscription concerts.[52]

St John Hornby owned the Ashendene Press, strongly influenced by William Morris's Kelmscott Press, which produced luxurious Gothic-style reprints of classics (notably the Ashendene Dante.) This was exactly the sort of private press the Hogarth did not want (and could not afford) to be, any more than she wanted Hogarth House to look like Shelley House. Though she took passionate pleasure in the look and feel of her books (delighting for instance, in one review, in 'the very sight of a book in which the plain paper so generously balances the printed page')[53] she distrusted 'editions de luxe'. The Omega workshop produced some beautiful expensive illustrated books at the time the Hogarth Press was starting, like *Lucretius on Death*, which Virginia owned. They used Roger Fry's list of subscribers,[54] and of course Vanessa worked for them both. But the Hogarth Press was not really like the Omega, or other later 'arts and craft' presses like the Golden Cockerel or the Nonesuch. The Woolfs were not as interested in fine looks as in content.

Though their printing has never been much admired by serious historians of private presses,[55] for historians of twentieth-century thought the Press came to be of enormous importance. Many of its publishing decisions were, as John Lehmann said, 'revolutionary'.[56] Though their titles were often 'highbrow', and sometimes sold only in small numbers, the influence of their publishing choices would eventually filter into a wider market. (Some of their most popular titles, however, like Vita Sackville-West's best-selling *The Edwardians* (1930) have since proved ephemeral.) The Hogarth Press joined the wave of small magazines and presses in the 1910s and 1920s, non-establishment printers of difficult and challenging new work, which were the shapers of the modernist movement: the *Dial*, the *Egoist*, Wyndham Lewis's *Blast*, the *Little Review*, Shakespeare and Company. Their publishing of Eliot's *Poems* and of *The Waste Land* (which first appeared in the *Dial*) put them in this company. *The Waste Land* was the most momentous of their 'modernist' titles (though the 460 copies they printed in 1923 sold only slowly and didn't sell out until 1925). But there were other significant titles: Mansfield's *Prelude*, Fry's 1927 essay on Cézanne and his *The Artist and Psycho-Analysis*, Forster's *The Story of the Siren*, *Pharos & Pharillon*, *Anonymity*, *A Letter to Madan Blanchard*, and Gertrude Stein's *Composition as Explanation* in 1926.

The Press published influential Russian translations in collaboration with 'Kot', the Russian émigré S.S. Koteliansky, including Gorky's *Reminiscences of Tolstoi* (1920), Tchekhov's *Notebooks* (1921), and Bunin's *The Gentleman from San Francisco* (1922), co-translated with Kot's friend D.H. Lawrence, his only connection with the Hogarth Press.[57] Publishing Freud was their boldest and biggest move, instigated by Leonard's decision in the early 1920s to publish translations of the International Psycho-Analytical Library Series founded by Ernest Jones. The series principally consisted of James and Alix Strachey's *Freud*, but also included transations of Melanie Klein, Anna Freud and Sandor Ferenczi.[58]

Other individual titles showed the Press's editorial acumen (mostly, but not entirely, Leonard's). They had some failures of nerve and judgement (over *Ulysses*, over Cyril Connolly, and over Ivy Compton-Burnett)[59] and they published some negligible fiction and poetry. But they also made some bold and intelligent moves in publishing Robert Graves, Herbert Read, Italo Svevo, Rilke, John Crowe Ransom, Edwin Muir, William Plomer, Robinson Jeffers, Isherwood, C.L.R. James, Edward Upward and Henry Green. Their political essays, their feminist titles (Jane Harrison, Ray Strachey, Willa Muir, Viscountess Rhondda) and their intermittent attempts to cut through class, by publishing 'working class' novels like John Hampson's *Saturday Night at the Greyhound* (1933) or Derrick Leon's *Livingstones* (1933), marked their radicalism. Some of their poetry choices were weak (too dependent on the editorial choices of Dorothy Wellesley), but they maintained their commitment to publish poetry of an 'experimental kind', poetry which was 'obviously difficult, that is which has merit, but of an obscure kind, so that other publishers would not take it'.[60] This is reflected in their strong poetry list in the 1930s, made under John Lehmann's influence: Blunden, Day Lewis, Kenneth Allott, Spender, Michael Roberts's *New Signatures*. Virginia Woolf thought hard about modern poetry in those years.

She was not the Press's main editor, but her taste, her decisions, and her influence are part of its history. She wrote some judicious editorial letters to their authors which are as revealing about her own work as about theirs – as here, to Beatrice Howe, a girlfriend of Clive's.

> I think you need greater firmness in your construction: the proportions tend to get too large here, too small there, so that the climax is overshadowed or diminished . . . But all I am saying amounts to the fact that you are still experimenting, and I feel all the time that you are full of the right perceptions: see things your own way; and need only go on, being experimental but at the same time rather more severe, in order to do something really interesting. I think your poetry and your realism are at present tripping each other up; but I remember this (how condescendingly I am writing!) in my own beginnings: two instincts each running away, and seeming to refuse to combine. Both are genuine in you; which is very attractive to me; the poet and the realist; but I am sure that writers thus complicated with two points of view develop more slowly and blunderingly than the simpler sort.[61]

Though she was not an especially generous champion of her women contemporaries, the list shows a taste for an idiosyncratic, humorous fiction by women, like F.M. Mayor's *The Rector's Daughter* (1924) and Julia Strachey's *Cheerful Weather for the Wedding* (1932). Julia Strachey's novella had learnt from Virginia Woolf; so would *Olivia*, by Lytton Strachey's sister Dorothy Bussy, an anonymously-published lesbian story (based on the French teacher Marie Souvèstre, a powerful figure for the Strachey family) and dedicated in 1949 'to the beloved memory of V.W.' Their list influenced Virginia Woolf's own writing, too, from the startling impact of the Russians and, much later, of Freud, to the effect of *The Waste Land* on *Jacob's Room*, or the debt in *A Room of One's Own* to Jane Harrison's Cambridge memoirs, *Reminiscences of a Student's Life* (1925).[62] Of these mutual influences, the first, Katherine Mansfield's, was also one of the most important.

The Press profoundly affected her thinking about writing and reading and the dissemination of literature. Two unpublished texts illustrate this. One was the draft of a lecture which she gave to a girl's school in 1926 called 'How Should One Read a Book?'

> Try to understand what a writer is doing [she advised]. Think of a book as a very dangerous and exciting game, which it takes two to play at. Books are not turned out of moulds, like bricks. Books are made of tiny little words, which a writer shapes, often with great difficulty, into sentences of

different lengths, placing one on top of another, never taking his eye off them, sometimes building them quite quickly, at other times knocking them down in despair, and beginning all over again.[63]

The writer is imagined as a kind of mental compositor, and the reader is invited to think of the book not as a fixed object, but as a process – something like the process that goes into type-setting. In the last year of her life, she wrote about the historical effects of printing:

> It was the printing press that finally was to kill Anon. But it was the press also that preserved him . . . The printing press brought the past into existence. It brought into existence the man who is conscious of the past [,] the man who sees his time, against the background of the past; the man who first sees himself & shows himself to us. The first blow has been aimed at Anon when the author's name is attached to the book. The individual emerges.[64]

So in the two sides of her thinking about writing – how it comes into being, and who the audience is – the Press was an inspiration.

But its most crucial function was that it made her independent as a writer. She saw at once that this could be so, linking (in a letter to Bunny Garnett in July 1917) the possibility of inventing 'a completely new form' and the 'greatest mercy' of being able 'to do what one likes – no editors, or publishers'. 'I dont like writing for my half-brother George', she added, making a significant slip of George for Gerald.[65] She did not want to go on being censored or controlled – in that sense, abused – by her conventional relations.[66] It must have felt uncomfortably demeaning, like being a child and an amateur, to get letters from her publisher addressed to 'Dear Goat', however mildly he asked her to cut the length of her second novel ('but you are the best judge of that'.)[67] Appearing on the Duckworth list,[68] *The Voyage Out* had been respectfully reviewed as a promising and original first novel, and praised (with reservations about its lack of 'vivid' characters or of 'cohesion') by Forster and Lytton Strachey – who called it 'very, very unvictorian'.[69] Now, tentatively, with frequent breaks for resting and printing and reviewing, she was writing a long novel whose traditional structure constrained her. Though *Night and Day* dealt with the struggle between two generations, it was deliberately set before the war and was not formally experimental. When it came out in 1919, as a Duckworth publication, it looked old-fashioned. Already, by then, she had been hoping that Gerald would turn it down, as 'I should have liked to try the other way'.[70]

'The other way' would mean that she could consider herself as 'the only woman in England free to write what I like. The others must be thinking of series' & editors.'[71] 'Why dont you write more short things? Perhaps you will now,' Vanessa asked in July 1917.[72] 'I mean to write a good many short things at Asheham', Virginia confirmed in June 1918.[73] And, in an essay on Coleridge: 'There is a great deal to be said for small books.'[74]

And so, while *Night and Day*, her long, melancholy comedy of the break with Victorianism was taking shape, she was, also, cutting loose. After 'The Mark on the Wall' of 1917, quizzical, domestic, conversational, there was the humming, hazy impressionism of *Kew Gardens* (begun perhaps as early as August 1917), with its spots of colour, its disembodied 'wordless voices', its sense of suspended time, and passing through it, an 'eccentric' elderly man talking to himself about his encounters with the spirits of the dead. In one paragraph, the story dares to touch, as *Night and Day* in all its length could not, on what being deranged had felt like. Through 1918 and 1919, she wrote other sketches for Vanessa to illustrate. In all of them, silence, darkness, death, pull against social conventions. In 'The Evening Party', voices talk about literature, melancholy, the dead, lost childhood, wartime events ('The Armenians die. And penal servitude') and long to escape alone to a dark moor.[75] 'Solid Objects' is a comedy of a man who gives up a brilliant career in Parliament because he becomes obsessed with bits of glass and china. (Her recent meetings with the painter Mark Gertler, darkly self-absorbed, and her current covetous fascination with glass and decorative objects, bore on this story.)[76] 'A Haunted House' makes a ghostly fantasy out of Asheham. In 'Sympathy', the announcement of the death of an acquaintance in the newspaper sets off thoughts about how death 'composes' and reveals: 'So, from an express train, I have looked upon hills and fields and seen the man with the scythe look up from the hedge as we pass, and lovers lying the long grass stare at me without disguise as I stare at them without disguise. Some burden has fallen, some impediment has been removed.'[77]

After the publication of *Night and Day* in October 1919 came a crucial turning point in these writings, a story about an attempt to invent a story, of a woman seen in conversation on the train. This was 'An Unwritten Novel', which suddenly, in January 1920, gave her an idea of further possibilities, of how the 'short things' might be thought of as 'taking hands & dancing in unity'.[78] She would always remember the excitement of seeing how these 'short things' could evolve into her post-Duckworth novels. Looking back in 1930 (for Ethel Smyth), she dramatised that realisation as a victory over illness:

After being ill and suffering every form and variety of nightmare and extravagant intensity of perception – for I used to make up poems, stories, profound and to me inspired phrases all day long as I lay in bed, and thus sketched, I think, all that I now, by the light of reason, try to put into prose (I thought of the Lighthouse then, and Kew and others, not in substance, but in idea) – after all this, when I came to, I was so tremblingly afraid of my own insanity that I wrote Night and Day mainly to prove to my own satisfaction that I could keep entirely off that dangerous ground. I wrote it, lying in bed, allowed to write only for one half hour a day. And I made myself copy from plaster casts, partly to tranquillise, partly to learn anatomy. Bad as the book is, it composed my mind, and I think taught me certain elements of composition which I should not have had the patience to learn had I been in full flush of health always. These little pieces in Monday or Tuesday [sic] were written by way of diversion; they were the treats I allowed myself when I had done my exercise in the conventional style. I shall never forget the day I wrote The Mark on the Wall – all in a flash, as if flying, after being kept stone breaking for months. The Unwritten Novel was the great discovery, however. That – again in one second – showed me how I could embody all my deposit of experience in a shape that fitted it – not that I have ever reached that end; but anyhow I saw, branching out of the tunnel I made, when I discovered that method of approach, Jacobs Room, Mrs Dalloway etc – How I trembled with excitement; and then Leonard came in, and I drank my milk, and concealed my excitement, and wrote I suppose another page of that interminable Night and Day (which some say is my best book).[79]

This is a conflated memory (Night and Day was published by the time she wrote 'An Unwritten Novel') but it catches her excited sense that the 'little pieces' could now be connected to shape the unwritten novels of the future.

TWENTY-ONE

Seeing Life

Between 1917, the year of the Press, and 1920, the year that began with 'An Unwritten Novel', her energy and confidence swelled up. She settled into her stride as a full-time professional writer, working on *Night and Day*, trying out shorter pieces, reading intensively, and formulating her ideas about reading and writing, modern fiction and women novelists.

Though *Night and Day* dissatisfied her, she wrote it quickly compared with *The Voyage Out*. And though she looked back on herself now as a delicate invalid writer, in fact she combined the novel with a big output of literary journalism (mostly for Bruce Richmond at the *TLS*) and with vivid exercises in self-definition, gossip and caricature in the diary (started again in 1917) and in her letters, particularly to Vanessa. She was making regular earnings of 'one hundred pounds a year' as a reviewer,[1] and Richmond was offering her lead pieces. In 1919, for example, he asked her to prepare a major obituary in the event of Hardy's death – which meant that she was rereading and thinking about Hardy between 1919 and 1921, all the time she was writing *Jacob's Room*.

All her journalism referred back in some way to her own work. In her essays on her contemporaries – from confidently dismissive pieces on Galsworthy or Compton Mackenzie to more tentative stabs at Dorothy Richardson or Lawrence ('we always dread originality')[2] – she was carving out her own version of modernism. The war drastically confirmed that there had to be 'new forms for our new sensations'.[3] Novels which realistically described pre-war families, like Galsworthy's *Beyond* or Hugh Walpole's *The Green Mirror*, were reflecting a world which 'the war had done nothing to change'; but those mirrors had been 'smashed to splinters'.[4] By 1920 she felt that there was a case to be made against anyone who read like 'a pre-war writer'.[5]

She was well aware of the contradictions. While she kept saying that new forms were needed, she was herself 'go[ing] on perserveringly, conscientiously, constructing our thirty-two chapters after a design which more and more ceases to resemble the vision in our minds'.[6] The very case she was making against 'pre-war writing' was made against her when *Night and Day* came out in 1919. So in her wartime essays she kept coming back to the question of tradition and change. What made the Russian novelists so different from English writers?[7] What do we need to take from the English 'classics'? Writing, skilfully, on the deep rich pleasure of reading Hakluyt, or on Defoe as 'a great plain writer', or on the self-consciousness and melancholy in George Eliot's generous sympathetic mind ('Everything to such a mind was gain. All experience filtered down through layer after layer of perception and reflection, enriching and nourishing')[8] she was working out her divided feelings.

She was also letting rip, in exuberant character pieces – on Walpole's strange imagination and repressed feelings, on Coleridge's conversation, on Anny Ritchie – with the same gusto that was going into her private writing. Sometimes her sharp ironical talking voice seems to come off the page, as in this account of a member of the Tennant family.

> When he rode a motor-bicycle he was uneasy at the amount of dust that he raised. He wrote therefore, in very large letters, 'Apologies for the Dust', tied the placard to the tail of his machine, and then 'went sweeping through the Southern counties in unparalleled speed.' The impulsiveness, the lack of self-consciousness, the desire that slum children and agitated pedestrians shall smile in his wake, with all that this implies of good fortune, good temper, and the most innocent belief in the goodness of life, are the attractive virtues of an aristocrat. But one has to reflect that it is possible presumably to ride a motor-bicycle slowly, in which case apologies are unnecessary; and that you need not give up the problem of poverty because the sorrows of the poor are not altogether appeased by feeding them on sweets out of a large tin.[9]

These published satires were connected to her increasingly bold private caricatures. She makes Coleridge, endlessly talking ('For how can a man with Coleridge's gifts produce anything? His demands are so much greater than can be satisfied by the spiritual resources of his age,')[10] sound suspiciously like Desmond MacCarthy, who paid a garrulous visit while this piece was being written. She set about describing people she knew with the same relish and attention to style that she brought to the dead. And the odder the better, as this small paragraph suggests, in a letter to Duncan, about a terrible dinner at J.C. Squire's house.

> O my God! what an evening! All the lights went out, dinner an hour late, pheasants bleeding on the plate, no knives, tumblers or spoons; poor Mrs Squire thought to laugh it over, but became distracted; Squire ferocious. Strange figures wandered in and out, among them Mrs Hannay, an

artist – Pike an inventor, Scott a don. Stove smoked, fog thick. Trains stopped. Bed.[11]

The most vigorous rush of her energies went into her diary, which she began to keep again in August 1917. It was partly a sedative, written to appease a 'restless state', to calm an uncomfortable vibration in her mind after too many visitors, or to objectify herself through 'meticulous observation'.[12] To start with, as if a great soloist were getting back into shape with simple exercises, she put down brief, exact nature notes at Asheham, suppressing the 'I' of self ('went mushrooming') and becoming merely a mirror, a recorder, of wartime rural life. So she notes mushrooming and bilberrying, planting the garden, digging up their own potatoes, sawing wood, watching the horse-drawn mowing machines, sighting butterflies, hawks, swallows, snakes and bees, listening to the locals ('An old thatcher thatching the stack behind the house told L that many people die at 4 in the afternoon').[13] As she walks she looks out for things 'to be noticed':

[In a gale]: Swallows flying in great numbers very low and swift in the field . . .

The field full of swallows, & leaves broken off in bunches, so that the trees already look thin.

Found the same caterpillar – dark brown with 3 purple spots on either side of the head – that we found last year. We took him home . . . The caterpillar has disappeared. There is a purple smudge on the window sill, which makes it likely that he was crushed.

[In the rain]: I waited for him [L.] in a barn, where they had cut mangolds which smelt very strong. A hen ate them.[14]

These country notes are unflinching, not idyllic – a chicken is found with its head wrung off, a hawk has dropped a dead pigeon, butterflies feed on dung – but they also communicate an almost trance-like state of mind which is part of her recovery, and feeds her writing.

The days melted into each other like snowballs roasting in the sun.[15]

I remember lying on the side of a hollow, waiting for L to come & mushroom, & seeing a red hare loping up the side & thinking suddenly, 'This is Earth life'. I seemed to see how earthy it all was, & I myself an evolved kind of hare; as if a moon-visitor saw me.[16]

The Diary would always be used for what she called 'seeing life', and for practising her 'concise, historical style'.[17] But as diary-writing took hold, she also plunged avidly into character sketches: Roger talking about art or Ottoline holding forth on emotions, Karin being greedy and crude, or Desmond imitating Joyce's cat's miaow in the early hours of the morning. These sketches often worked off spasms of irritation or anxiety. But through them she was trying out ways of catching personality. She began to collect her friends on paper like possessions (except that 'when people come to tea I cant say to them, "Now wait a minute while I write an account of you" ').[18] That self-consciousness was built into the diary-writing from the start; it became part of her relationships, as she imagined all their diaries lying 'like vast consciences, in our most secret drawers'.[19]

Though she described Pepys's diary as 'the store house of his most private self', his 'intercourse with the secret companion who lives in everybody',[20] her own diary, however rapidly written, was not uncensored. For instance, when Vanessa told her on a May evening at Charleston in 1918 that she was expecting another baby, and that it was Duncan's, Virginia wrote euphemistically of 'possibilities' in her secret book (she kept the secret from Leonard for a time too, and perhaps that's why she didn't put it in the diary)[21] but let her feelings out in a ravishing burst of description:

> Last night at Charleston I lay with my window open listening to a nightingale, which beginning in the distance came very near the garden. Fishes splashed in the pond. May in England is all they say – so teeming, amorous, & creative.[22]

The diary gives eloquent glimpses of her private life, as on a walk with Leonard in London while she's been reading *Moll Flanders*: 'So home with L. walking over Hungerford Bridge on a fine warm evening & thinking of Defoe as I say.' But mostly she sets to work, as strenuously and eagerly as she did everything, to take possession of the stuff she sees outside her, 'seeing life, as I walk about the streets, an immense opaque block of material to be conveyed by me into its equivalent of language'.[23]

There is a great deal about age in these private writings of a woman in her mid-thirties. She anticipates herself as an 'elderly' lady of fifty, rereading her diaries 'for her memoirs', a fantasy (which she often returns to, making her imaginary older self a little older each time) which partly made her thirty-seventh birthday 'robbed of some of the terrors'.[24]

In her reading and her writing, in her social life and in her feelings about herself, she felt pulled between feeling old and feeling young. She was acutely conscious of the relationship between the generations, which was filling *Night and Day*. She matched herself against all the new people she was meeting, members of the overlapping groups which circled around Garsington, or the Slade, or the Omega, or the 1917 Club. ('It's strange how whole groups of people suddenly swim complete into one's life.')[25] Each of these new encounters would be summed up by a judgement of looks, character, and *age*: Aldous Huxley (met at Garsington) was 'a nice youth';[26] Edith Sitwell was 'a very tall young woman, wearing a permanently startled expression, & curiously finished off with a high green silk headdress'.[27]

She watched her old friends and her family moving into new phases, remarking on the strangeness of seeing them 'taking their "fixed shape" ': 'How one can foretell middle age for them, & almost see them with the eyes of the younger generation!'[28] Vanessa was establishing herself as a professional painter (showing at the Omega and the New Movement in Art shows in 1917, painting a big Matisse-like naked figure in 'The Tub'). She was settling into her ramshackle, isolated, intensely domestic life at Charleston, where she set up a small school in 1917, and where her boys were getting bigger and rowdier. She was involved in a tense triangular relationship with Duncan and his lover, and was still being brooded over by a jealous Roger Fry. Duncan's daughter Angelica was born on Christmas Day 1918 (her future husband, her father's lover David Garnett, was there at her birth). At once there was a crisis; the baby nearly died, badly handled by the local doctor. Virginia had offered to look after the boys in Richmond, making all kinds of eager plans for 'things we are going to do': zoo, movies, tea at the Omega, pantomime, Russian dancers, Richmond Park, 'Sliding staircase on the Tube' (a new treat), British Museum, tea at Buzzards. 'But the thing Julian wants to do *almost* most of all is to learn the Greek alphabet! . . . and I hope to persuade Quentin to be a writer and not a painter when he grows up.'[29]

But within a few days she was in bed with a headache, and the nephews had to be moved on – neither sister acknowledging that they had been too much for their aunt. And though Virginia was full of ideas for the new baby's name (her favourite was Clarissa, Leonard's 'Fuchsia': 'he long ago decided to call his daughter that'),[30] she did not see her until March, 'a wistful, patient, contemplative little creature'. On this visit, she recorded a vivid impression of Charleston, 'by no means a gentleman's house', chaotic, good-humoured, busy with family life and somehow working, because of Nessa's 'extreme method & unselfishness & routine'.[31]

Clive, still Virginia's most needling and critical friend ('his personal remarks always seem to be founded on some reserve of grievance'),[32] had introduced Mary Hutchinson, a cousin of the Stracheys and of Duncan, wife of the liberal barrister St John Hutchinson, into the circle, with the usual attendant difficulties of any 'new' arrival. (Keynes's introduction of the Russian dancer Lydia Lopokova created the same sort of problems a few years later.) Mary, worldly, elegantly fashionable, ugly-charming, had a wonderful taste in clothes, painting and interior decoration. She was drawn by Matisse, and was a close friend of Lytton and of T.S. Eliot. A lively letter-writer, a hostess and a mother, sexually adventurous and with a talent for intimacy, she was not much liked by Vanessa and was a threatening and intriguing figure to Virginia.[33] She called Clive and Mary, disparagingly, 'the cockatoos', and was sure that Clive was dreading 'some alliance between Mary & me which shall threaten his position with her'.[34] Clive (perhaps protecting himself against such an alliance) gave descriptions of Virginia to Mary which summed up the worst possible view of her.

> I am most uneasy about your getting in touch with Virginia [he wrote to Mary in August 1917]. Her main object will be to set us by the ears and I daresay she will succeed. She made me quarrel with Lytton and we didnt speak to each other for a year, she embroiled me with Molly, she did her best to upset my relations with Vanessa and to break my friendship with Duncan.[35]

Not surprisingly, with such warnings, and with accusations of Virginia's malicious indiscretions put about by what Virginia furiously described to Vanessa as 'this infernal spy system',[36] Mary was 'suspicious' and 'unconfident' of her.[37] But she was also curious and observant, as a letter to Lytton in July 1918 shows:

> Clive took me to Richmond. I had never been before to Virginia's – I got that clammy sensation when the front door was opened by Lotty – that one has when one begins a Turgeniev novel – of being aware that the surroundings were perfect for seeing the personality which was going to emerge from them. A strange house built all on one side; something palatial about its grand dark staircase, the height of its rooms, its carved doorways; the landing too vast for the size of the house lined to the ceiling with books – a sense of emptiness – of something half aristocratic, half literary – an air of shabby grandeur. The evening was exquisitely reasonable. No one gave himself away – all was oblique – calm – finished – and *au fond* mysterious. I thought V's great charm was that she spoke sentences that one usually only finds written. Perfect literary sentences spoken without hesitation or stumbling. One was compelled to listen even when she only called for more milk. It was strangely like being in a novel.[38]

Gradually, Mary became a more important character in that novel (and would be the main inspiration for the febrile socialite Jinny in *The Waves*.) By the mid-1920s, they had developed a teasingly affectionate, semi-erotic friendship. Virginia's relationship with Vita, Mary's own bisexuality[39] and her falling out of love with Clive in 1927, influenced the terms of their relationship. Virginia called her Weasel and Poll and Flinders, wrote her flirtatious notes ('I like Weasels to kiss; but as they kiss to bite; and then to kiss').[40] 'Mary says I'm the only woman she loves', she noted with pleasure in September 1926.[41] In return Mary imitated her prose style in her short stories[42] and wrote her seductive letters.

> Virginia . . . I think of the pleasures of friendship . . . how delicious to begin such an adventure . . . what discoveries might I not make or what 'spiritual changes' might you not start? Probably, though, with that sharp twist you cannot resist, you will snap my threads; 'put it into a book, Flinders', you will say, so, cracking my heart; or 'you know quite well you are a little popinjay of fashion' – so turning me crusty and uncomfortable. How will you answer me? beware, beware, be very kind . . .[43]

In a passionate outburst ten years later, Mary spoke of her longing for '*you* – all that is you – in any mood you like or chance to be in – I must love – can you bear such hunger – for I believe it is really this that I feel and I pine for you sometimes'.[44] If this was a love-affair it was probably one-sided; Virginia always wrote of Mary with a hostile edge. Yet they were friends also as married couples; when the Hutchinsons moved from Hammersmith to Regent's Park, Leonard and Virginia went for dinner and evening visits to the zoo; and in 1940 Virginia wrote affectionately to Mary of how much the Woolves liked the Hutchinsons: 'Isn't it a satisfaction, liking one's friends better & better as time goes on?'[45]

There was less sympathy between Virginia and Adrian's wife Karin Costelloe, whom he had married in 1914. Karin brought out her most scornful responses; she marked her down as greedy, deaf, American, hyperactive, and bad for Adrian, and was always scathing about her appearance: 'Adrian & Karin dined with us on Sunday; she resolutely artistic in a distressing way; bright green, with sturdy embroidery let in.'[46] She was never very understanding of the difficulties of their marriage, and when they announced in 1919 that they were going to train as psycho-analysts, she was unimpressed.[47] Her prejudice against Freud and psycho-analysis was bound up with her critical disparagement of Adrian and Karin. But Freud was part of the modern post-war air, and was coming at her from all sides. Leonard was extremely interested in Freud, and Lytton was bringing back reports of the 'British Sex Society' on discussions of 'incest between parent & child when they are both unconscious of it'. She noted, in a suggestive joke to herself, 'I am thinking of becoming a member' and continued: 'Lytton at different points exclaimed *Penis*: his contribution to the openness of the debate.'[48]

Lytton's life – if not his fondness for sexual jokes – was changing greatly during the war. The overnight success of *Eminent Victorians* in 1918 (which she had been reading since 1915, as each of the four essays was written, and which affected her thoughts about biography) made him a rival as well as a friend, and – as she told him half-jokingly – 'poisoned her peace'.[49] She was a little jealous of Carrington, too, who had been living with him since the end of 1917 at the Mill House at Tidmarsh, after extricating herself from a tormented relationship with Mark Gertler. 'You like me better, dont you?' Virginia asked him.[50] She was touched by Carrington, with her 'thick mop of golden red hair, & a fat decided clever face, with staring bright blue eyes',[51] her odd, original impulsiveness and her passion for art. But she also found that Carrington made her rather too 'conscious of her admiring & solicitous youth'.[52] She was one of the group that made Virginia feel old.

Her resemblance to Leslie Stephen in this respect was striking. When she exclaimed to Lytton in 1918, 'How fearfully old one's getting!'[53] it was hardly a joke. The women she was now seeing – Mary Hutchinson, Katherine Mansfield, Carrington, Alix Sargant-Florence, Barbara Hiles, Hope Mirrlees, Dorothy Brett, Fredegond Shove – provoked her into 'me and them' comparisons.[54] She looked at their bisexual love affairs and threesomes, more ingenuous and less private than her feelings for Clive or Vanessa's for Duncan, and thought, half-admiringly, that they were 'abolishing private property' in their loves.[55] They cut their hair, wore modern clothes ('It seems to me quite impossible to wear trousers'),[56] went abroad alone, said goodbye in the matter-of-fact 'modern' fashion.[57] They were doing all the things she had not done. And here they were, coming to work at the Press, hanging out at the 1917 Club, and falling in love with her oldest friends (Barbara divided her affections between Nick Bagenal and Saxon, Carrington dedicated her life to an asexual passion for Lytton, and Alix, after a desperate pursuit which irritated Virginia, would marry and work with James Strachey on Freud). At the Club, on the ground floor in Gerrard Street, where the 'Bunnies', or 'cropheads', rubbed shoulders with serious revolutionary socialists, she partly felt that she had found a new family, and partly that she didn't fit in.

She was torn between self-protective condescension and a desire for new intimacy. If I was 'gracious' to Mary, she told Clive in July 1918 (when Mary was twenty-nine and Virginia was thirty-six), it was 'inevitable for one of my age to one of hers'.[58] She got involved with them all, advising (not very helpfully) on Barbara's love-life and feeling drawn to the beautiful Fredegond: 'I feel like her in some fundamental way'. And Fredegond sent her emotional letters from the Temperance Hotel where she was living – an arrangement which Virginia thought of as 'a sign of the times' – 'I might write a passionate letter to you only too easily – but you would be so sarcastic about it if you really realised what I thought of you – for I dont believe you like worship as much as you pretend – you like flattery because you can turn it all into nonsense and fun.'[59] Her 'sarcastic' habit of nicknames caused offence, and provoked a delegation from Carrington, Alix and Fredegond (whom she had named the Turnip, the Owl and the Bat). 'I don't think you ought to be so sure' (Fredegond said) 'that you belong to an older generation than everyone who isnt two years older than yourself.'[60] Alix, writing from her semi-permanent address at the Club, said that in comparison to what 'really *is* your younger generation', she and her friends 'were merely a ghostly interregnum – mere war miscarriages'. But for all these half-joking reproaches, the younger women terribly wanted her to like them, and to have what they 'still persist in fondly imagining to have once been a certain, very unequal, kind of relationship with you'.[61] They were nervous of her. Her first dealings with Carrington and Barbara (and Bunny Garnett), in 1916, pointed to the tone of these relationships. They broke into Asheham without permission,[62] slept there while the Woolfs were in London, stole a book, and then had to ring up in trepidation to apologise. Virginia was half pleased to find that she was so frightening. But she felt, too, that 'the younger generation' was breaking in on her life.

So much of her was still attached to the past, to memories of Thoby on the tenth anniversary of his death, to traces of the old life. She saw Kitty Maxse for what turned out to be the last time; she still wrote to Violet and Janet and heard from the Vaughans and went to see Lady Strachey. Aunt Mary died, Charles Booth died, Dr Seton died, Anny Ritchie died. She thought or wrote about them all: Hyde Park Gate was always, always coming back to her. She was absorbed in the Victorian past she was evoking in *Night and Day*, just as a great part of her reading was of her father's friends, Hardy, Meredith, James, who 'summons back the past and makes us a present of that'.[63] At the same time she was tackling all the modern writers at once – Joyce, Dorothy Richardson, May Sinclair, Eliot, Lawrence, Mansfield – and trying to become one herself. The relationship around which all these oppositions cohered, which most challenged her in the war years, and which deeply influenced the ways she developed her writing in the early 1920s, was her friendship with Katherine Mansfield.

TWENTY-TWO

Katherine

'Friendships with women interest me,' Virginia Woolf wrote in her diary on 28 November 1919.[1] The apparently simple remark came, typically, out of a tangle of thoughts and feelings. She was upset that week by Katherine Mansfield's review of *Night and Day*, which had insinuated that the novel was old-fashioned:

> We had thought that this world had vanished for ever, that it was impossible to find on the great ocean of literature a ship that was unaware of what had been happening. Yet here is *Night and Day*, fresh, new and exquisite, a novel in the tradition of the English novel. In the midst of our admiration it makes us feel old and chill. We had never thought to look upon its like again![2]

Mansfield's reading of her book made Virginia feel like 'a decorous elderly dullard'. Because of it, she had refused to review the new Dorothy Richardson, in case she might – like Katherine? – be swayed by rivalry. At the same time, she was reading Ethel Smyth's memoirs and relishing her 'honesty'. Honesty was exactly what she felt she was not getting from Katherine (and would get, in spades, from Ethel). She had seemed to be a kind of friend, but now she had published a piece in which Virginia detected spite and subterfuge.

So the remark about 'friendships with women' comes out of the heart of her extremely complicated relationship with Katherine. Their friendship was intimate but guarded, mutually inspiring but competitive ('If she's good then I'm not'). It ultimately disappointed her, but it was always tugging at her. She fluctuated between feeling that they had found a particular intimacy of equals, and feeling that Katherine was not really interested in her at all. There were many crucial things about her that Virginia failed to understand, or understood too late – her background, her marriage, her illness. She was often snobbish and unkind about her. And Katherine too was ambivalent and inconsistent. Nevertheless, this relationship affected Virginia powerfully in the years between 1917 and 1920, and would continue to do so after Katherine's death in 1923.

Katherine Mansfield was six years younger than Virginia Woolf, utterly different from her in looks and temperament and experience, but with some strong affinities, like her fierce dedication to her work, her childless marriage, her dangerousness as a friend, and her battle with illness and bereavement (she too lost a loved brother, in the war in October 1915). But her colonialism and her itinerant uprootedness were the opposite of Virginia's ancestral network. She had chosen exile from her prosperous middle-class New Zealand family at the age of twenty, in 1908. Sexually bold and adventurous in ways that Virginia was not, but also vulnerable and manipulative, she had had several lovers, a failed marriage, and at least one miscarriage by the time they met in 1917. Since 1911 she had been living with John Middleton Murry, whom she would marry in 1918. Murry's self-advancing promotion of her writing career was one of the things Virginia found displeasing about her. She had published one book of stories, *In a German Pension*, in 1911, and was writing for the little magazines, Orage's *New Age*, Murry's *Rhythm*, and the short-lived *Signature*, briefly edited by Lawrence and Murry in 1915. She and Murry were closely involved with the Lawrences between 1914 and 1916: Lawrence lent a good deal of Katherine's sensuality, harshness, and troubled, powerful will, to Gudrun in *Women in Love*. It may have been from Lawrence that she caught the tuberculosis she developed in 1917; but she was already ill, since 1910, with an arthritis probably caused by gonorrhea.[3] Her illness became part of her personality. It worked itself into her peculiar evasiveness and self-deception, as her biographer Claire Tomalin says:

> For the rest of her life, Katherine maintained two entirely disparate sets of beliefs in her head: one that she was incurably ill and indeed dying, the other that she would recover, have children, live in the country with Murry and be perfectly happy.[4]

That doubleness was typical. She was defensive, slippery, hard to know. Her most passionate emotional life was fixed on her work. She demanded affection, especially from Murry, who while idealising her also failed her repeatedly in her times of need. She was often impatient and angry with people, especially her most loyal companion, her 'wife', Ida Baker. She could be cynical and sharp; and, out of the other side of her face, ingratiating and flattering. She had a great deal of charm, and could rival Virginia in company as a comedienne. But she did not inspire trusting confidence. She had a mask, like the sister-in-law in *Prelude*, who is aware of the gap between her false self and her 'secret self':

The voice of the letter seemed to come up to her from the page. It was faint already, like the voice heard over the telephone, high, gushing, with something bitter in the sound. Oh, she detested it today . . . Her heart was cold with rage. 'It's marvellous how you keep it up,' said she to the false self.[5]

All too often that false self can be heard in her letters to Virginia (and sometimes in Virginia's letters to her).[6] Virginia was right to be wary of her, especially when she herself was so conscious of the gap between her inner and outward selves. Even so, there were moments when they would speak or write to each other with affection and without affectation.

They knew about each other, of course, before they met. Katherine had met Kot through Lawrence, and in the summer of 1916 she infiltrated Garsington, where Ottoline lent her *The Voyage Out*. Lytton met her, and – as he had with Leonard – it was he who whetted Virginia's interest, reporting back to her that Katherine was 'decidedly an interesting creature . . . very amusing and sufficiently mysterious' with 'an ugly impassive mask of a face – cut in wood, with brown hair and brown eyes very far apart; and a sharp and slightly vulgarly-fanciful intellect sitting behind it.' She had been enthusiastic about *The Voyage Out* and said she wanted to meet Virginia more than anyone.[7] Virginia replied that Katherine had been dogging her steps for years.[8] When they *did* meet seven months later, in February 1917, Lytton's remark about vulgarity lingered on. She thought her unpleasant and unscrupulous.[9] But here was a perfect candidate for the Press, a promising original writer of short stories. She went to see her 'to get a story from her', and then had her to dinner alone. They talked about reviewing and about Katherine's past: 'She seems to have gone every sort of hog since she was 17', Virginia commented fastidiously to Vanessa.[10] But Katherine was wooing her. After another evening at Hogarth House when Vanessa and Murry were there too, she wrote seductively that she was a bit 'haunted' by Virginia, and turned their last meeting into a Mansfield short story:

The memory of that last evening is so curious: your voice & Vanessa's voice in the dark, as it were – white rings of plates floating in the air – a smell of strawberries and coffee . . . My God I love to think of you, Virginia, as my friend. Dont cry me an ardent creature or say, with your head a little on one side, smiling as though you knew some enchanting secret: 'Well, Katherine, we shall see . . .' But pray consider how rare is it to find some one with the same passion for writing that you have, who desires to be scrupulously truthful with you – and to give you the freedom of the city without any reserves at all.[11]

This was compelling. But immediately they were constructing images of each other, Virginia emphasising Katherine's tough rakishness, Katherine playing up Virginia's fragility: after their next meeting she told Ottoline that Virginia was 'still VERY delicate' and that she had felt 'the strange, trembling, glinting quality of her mind'. She seemed to Katherine 'one of those Dostoievsky women whose "innocence" has been hurt – Immediately I decided that I understood her completely.'[12]

In July Virginia promised to publish her story. In August, Katherine wrote to Virginia vividly describing Ottoline's garden at Garsington.[13] A few days later she spent a weekend at Asheham, and wrote in her thank-you letter:

> We have got the same job, Virginia, & it is really very curious & thrilling that we should both, quite apart from each other, be after so very nearly the same thing. We are you know; there's no denying it . . . Yes, your Flower Bed is *very* good. Theres a still, quivering, changing light over it all and a sense of those couples dissolving in the bright air which fascinates me.[14]

It sounds from this that over the week-end Virginia may have shown Katherine a draft of *Kew Gardens* which set Katherine thinking about a 'garden' piece of her own; or that Katherine's description of Ottoline's garden influenced *Kew Gardens*. Either way, the overlap suggests how close they felt they could be.

But at once they were in trouble with each other. Virginia was accused by Clive of 'having come inimitably up to sample' by repeating some spiteful Garsington gossip of his and Maynard's to Katherine. As the sort of remarks Clive made about Katherine were that she reminded him of some cheap thing on a barrow that has been turned over and over and always found not quite good enough,[15] it would not have taken much embellishment to make this sound unpleasant. Virginia got on her high horse with Clive ('I very much want to keep out of these affairs in future')[16] – though Katherine's post-Asheham thank-you letter does suggest that Virginia was implicated: 'Dont let THEM ever persuade you that I spend any of my precious time swapping hats or committing adultery – I'm far too arrogant & proud.'[17] This sort of thing kept happening between them – the atmosphere at Garsington made it almost inevitable.[18] And Katherine's friends, like Kot – who told Virginia that Katherine's 'lies & poses' had proved too much for him[19] – didn't help her reputation. All 'these affairs' confirmed Virginia's tendency to be prudish about Katherine, to read her in rather the way that she was reading *Ulysses*, as a squalid modern artefact not to her taste. 'She stinks like a – well civet cat that had taken to street walking. In truth, I'm a little shocked by her commonness at first sight; lines so hard & cheap.' (But then adds at once, 'she is so intelligent & inscrutable that she repays friendship'.)[20] She often identified Katherine with what she called the 'underworld', by which she meant rootless, seedy metropolitan types like Kot and Gertler and Murry, on the make professionally and sexually, who she imagined spent their time in pubs and tea-shops and boarding houses. Katherine was well aware that she was being sniffed at, and she too was playing a double game, praising 'The Mark on the Wall' to Virginia's face and calling it commonplace behind her back.[21]

But in the autumn of 1917 Katherine Mansfield developed the first symptoms of consumption; she was very ill, and had to leave the country for the first of many lonely winters abroad. She was extremely wretched, and over the winter she began to turn against her patrons in Garsington and Bloomsbury (the Bloomsbury *tangi*, she called them – a Maori word for wailing mourners at a funeral). She had been delighted that Virginia and Leonard wanted *Prelude* (the New Zealand story she had cut down for them from a longer version called 'The Aloe').[22] 'I threw my darling to the wolves,' she told her friend Dorothy Brett, 'and they ate it and served me up so much praise in a golden bowl that I couldn't help feeling gratified.'[23] But it seemed to be taking them a very long time to digest: 'I think the Woolfs must have eaten the Aloe root and branch or made jam of it,' she wrote to Ottoline in February 1918.[24] 'I'm sorry you have to go to the Woolves,' she wrote to Murry in the same week. 'I dont like them either. They are *smelly*.'[25] But at just this time Virginia was thinking of Katherine as one of the few people she could discuss her work with.[26] Inevitably, Katherine was on her mind, since almost every day during these winter months of the war, while she was writing her own novel, she was setting *Prelude*.

The effect on her of *Prelude* – its fragmenting of a whole family history into intense, solipsistic moments of experience, its funny child's eye view, its brilliant tiny coloured details, its fluid movement between banal realities and inner fantasy, its satirical opposition of the female and male point of view, its sexual pain – coincided with her other readings in 'modern fiction'. Between 1918 and 1919, the most intense years of her friendship with (and reading of) Katherine, she was publishing Eliot, trying to make her mind up about the early chapters of *Ulysses*, and reading and reviewing the first books of Dorothy Richardson's long narrative of Miriam Henderson's mind, *Pilgrimage*. All this was interconnected. When the demure, decorous, grey gloved Miss Weaver arrived in the drawing room of Hogarth House in April 1918, with the bombshell of a brown paper parcel on her lap, containing the first chapters of *Ulysses* ('quite out of keeping' with her appearance),[27] the Woolfs turned it down because they could not possibly have printed a whole book themselves on the handpress, and because Leonard could find no printer prepared to be liable in case of an obscenity charge. And at a first glance, she thought it boring and smutty:

> First there's a dog that p's – then there's a man that forths, and one can be monotonous even on that subject – moreover, I don't believe that his method, which is highly developed, means much more than cutting out the explanations and putting in the thoughts between dashes. So I don't think we shall do it.[28]

But this did not mean that Virginia dismissed Joyce unthinkingly. As *Ulysses* appeared in the *Egoist* through 1918, she took careful reading notes on what he seemed to her to be doing,[29] notes which began with references to the novelist May Sinclair's 1918 review of Dorothy Richardson.[30] Sinclair discussed the modern novelist's need to 'plunge in' to the thick texture of reality ('Miss Richardson has not plunged deeper than Mr James Joyce in his *Portrait of the Artist as a Young Man*'), and the 'stream of consciousness' (the first application of the phrase to fiction) of which Richardson's narrative entirely consisted. Virginia Woolf's notes to herself on Joyce, and her review of Richardson in February 1919,[31] wrestled with this problem of the relation between 'reality' and 'consciousness' in modern fictional forms. The issue dominates her piece on 'Modern Novels', written in April 1919 (the first draft of an essay she would be returning to and rewriting for the next two or three years). Her work on Joyce and Richardson, her reading of the Russians, her own division between the kind of writing she was doing in *Night and Day*, and in *Kew Gardens* or 'The Mark on the Wall', pour into that essay. Where should 'the accent' fall, how can we catch 'the essential thing' in fiction?[32]

Katherine was at the centre of this debate about modernism. She too was telling Virginia what she thought of the new writers, finding Eliot 'unspeakably dreary',[33] 'plunging' straight into the question of Dorothy Richardson after not seeing Virginia for many months,[34] praising 'Modern Novels' and reviewing *Kew Gardens* and May Sinclair in the same few weeks.[35] She longed to read *Ulysses*, and when Virginia produced it for her (presumably an early chapter in the *Little Review*), Katherine began by ridiculing it, and then suddenly said: 'But theres something in this'. This scene, Virginia thought, remembering it almost at the end of her life just after Joyce's death, 'should figure I suppose in the history of literature'.[36]

Certainly it figured in the history of her own literature. Katherine's literary interests and methods did influence her: a tiny example shows how. A story by Katherine Mansfield called 'Autumn (II)', first published in *Signature* in 1915 (a few days before her brother's death) and rewritten for the *Athenaeum* in 1920 as 'The Wind Blows', moves between a memory of the childhood of a brother and sister, and of childhood being left behind as a ship sets out to sea and into the dark. Brother and sister, from the deck, see themselves on shore as they once were. Mansfield included it in her collected stories, *Bliss*, because 'so many people admired it . . . Virginia, Lytton'.[37] The story begins with a child's sudden waking in the wind with a sense of dread:

> The wind, the wind. It's frightening to be here in her room by herself. The bed, the mirror, the white jug and basin gleam like the sky outside. It's the bed that is frightening. There it lies, sound asleep . . . Does Mother imagine for one moment that she is going to darn all those stockings knotted up on the quilt like a coil of snakes? She's not. No, Mother. I do not see why I should . . . The wind – the wind![38]

At the start of *Jacob's Room*, which Virginia began to write in 1920, also with thoughts of her brother, the child Jacob takes fright on the beach, hears his mother's voice, hears the wind rushing outside where the ships are out on the dark waves. In the bedroom the silver and white shapes of the furniture take dim shape – as they do again for the children in *The Waves*. The child's eye, the floating fragmented narrative and its ingredients, echo Katherine's story; but *Jacob's Room* has none of the cute sweetness of the child's imaginary dialogue with her mother. The influence is there, but it is also resisted.

Katherine formed part of her inner debate about how a woman writer could write a modern text without giving in to what Virginia Woolf saw as the egotism and self-consciousness of Joyce and Richardson. Both she and Katherine wanted to work through intense short pieces, not on the scale of *Pilgrimage* or *Ulysses*, and to explore consciousness in a more fluid impersonal way than May Sinclair or Dorothy Richardson. And both were concerned with the problem of how solid narrative form could be broken up without losing deep feeling.

She was eager to resume the friendship and the conversation when Katherine came back from her winter away in the spring of 1918. In May, they had 'a most satisfactory & fascinating renewal' of their friendship in Murry's flat in Fulham.[39] Katherine was very ill (she looked 'marmoreal', Virginia said) and was now married to Murry. Virginia could not quite bring herself to sympathise with either of these facts; she sought out only the 'oddly complete understanding between them' that was founded on Katherine's 'love of writing'. They talked about Tchekhov, and *Prelude*, and 'The Mark on the Wall'.[40] For once they felt the same about their meeting: 'She was very nice,' Katherine wrote to Brett. 'She *does* take the writing business seriously and she *is* honest about it & thrilled by it. One can't ask more.'[41] Katherine went to Cornwall for her health and Virginia sent her packs of Belgian cigarettes.

Prelude came out in July to the accompaniment of tiffs and spats. At Garsington the Morrells were fuming about Murry's attack on Sassoon in the *Nation*. Murry and Katherine were cross because the Woolfs disliked their chosen cover design ('To Hell with other peoples' presses!')[42] Virginia felt rivalrous. She defended *Prelude* to Clive, but admitted her jealousy to Vanessa: 'Tell me what you think of it; & should you say that you *dont* like it as much as 'Kew Gardens', I shant think less highly of you; but my jealousy, I repeat, is only a film on the surface beneath which is nothing but pure generosity.'[43] It was almost a relief to her, when the much more brittle, sexy, mannered story 'Bliss' came out in the *English Review*, to be able to dislike it wholeheartedly: 'so hard, & so shallow, & so sentimental.'[44] 'She's done for! . . . I dont see how much faith in her as a woman or writer can survive that sort of story.'[45] That violently personal reading shows how close her liking of Katherine always came to personal and professional disparagement. But at the same time she needed her to talk to: 'at least she cares about writing',[46] she told Vanessa, sounding just like Katherine talking about *her*.

That autumn of 1918 they were at their closest. Virginia often went up to 'the tall ugly villa' in East Heath Street, Hampstead, to have tea with Katherine, and Katherine wrote her tender messages: 'You are immensely important in my world, Virginia.' 'You do not know, Virginia, how I treasure the thought of you.' Sometimes there was a sharp edge to her effusiveness: 'Your brilliant brilliant letter was so captivating that Murry suggests we frame it in a revolving frame.'[47] Virginia's reports to herself of these sessions were mixed. Katherine impressed her unfavourably, then favourably. She was clearly extremely ill, 'husky & feeble, crawling about the room like an old woman'. She talked about illness, how it took away one's privacy, how she hated being watched over by Murry and Ida (whom she unkindly called 'the Monster').[48] Virginia probably recognised that invalid's frustration, though she doesn't say so. She responded to something 'childlike' about her which she found appealing. But with Murry there she was uneasy. Later, when she had come to despise him for his whining treacherousness and fake spirituality, she would remember him 'squirming and oozing a sort of thick motor oil in the background'.[49]

Leonard, too, remembered being uncomfortable with them together ('Katherine seemed to be always irritated with Murry'),[50] though Katherine on her own amused him.

That winter Katherine stayed in England but hid from everyone. Virginia assumed, since she had had no letter from her, that they had quarrelled, and tried to work out, with a mixture of honesty, vulnerability and defensiveness, what this made her feel:

> It is at this moment extremely doubtful whether I have the right to class her among my friends. Quite possibly I shall never see her again. Upstairs I have letters in which she speaks of finding the thought of me a joy, dwelling upon my writing with excitement; I have letters making appointments, pressing for visits, adding postscripts of thanks & affection to visits already paid. But the last is dated December, & it is now February. The question interests, amuses, & also slightly, no, very decidedly, pains me. If it were not that I suspect her of wishing to produce precisely these emotions, save that of amusement, I should be still more put out. As it is – well I should need to write a long description of her before I arrived at my queer balance of interest, amusement, & annoyance. The truth is, I suppose, that one of the conditions unexpressed but understood of our friendship has been precisely that it was almost entirely founded on quicksands.[51]

Immediately after this painfully exact account came another wave of spring friendship. Their talks again seemed to Virginia to have a special charm: 'I find with Katherine what I don't find with the other clever women a sense of ease & interest, which is, I suppose, due to her caring so genuinely if so differently from the way I care, about our precious art.' Katherine gave *Kew Gardens* a kind, if short review ('I can't hope to please you') in the *Athenaeum*. But Murry's appointment to the editorship of that magazine was a galling event (as Leonard was now editor of the *International Review*), and Murry's (and Ida the 'Rhodesian woman''s) appearances at tea were always sticky. Conversation only worked *tête à tête*: 'She gives & resists as I expect her to; we cover more ground in much less time.'[52] But Virginia was still quick to 'feel the acid' in Katherine whenever she didn't write or invite,[53] and still unable to hold back flashes of viciousness. When they went to Hampstead on Easter Monday and found the holiday crowd brutish and detestable, 'We thought she would have enjoyed herself, from the likeness of her prose to the scene'.[54]

By August 1919 Katherine was desperate, almost 'insane' (she told Ottoline) with physical suffering.[55] She made a will, said goodbye to all her London friends, and set off for the Italian Riviera. 'Do not think I am forgetful of you,' she wrote to Virginia. 'You would not believe me if you knew how often you are in my *heart & mind*. I love thinking of you.'[56] 'I like her more & more, & think we have reached some kind of durable foundation', Virginia wrote after their farewell meeting.[57]

But in the autumn of 1919, wretchedly depressed and lonely in her house near San Remo, at Ospedaletti, Katherine sent in her chilling review of *Night and Day* to Murry, and in her letters to him angrily called the novel 'a lie in the soul', a refusal to admit that the war had happened, filled with 'intellectual snobbery': 'so long and so tāhsōme'.[58] Again and again she returned to its 'boundless vanity and conceit'.[59] And at the same time she was turning against the 'Bloomsberries': 'We must be bold & beat these people',[60] she wrote, sounding more and more like her old friend and enemy, Lawrence. There is something intemperate in these attacks; they take the novel as personally as Virginia took Katherine's story 'Bliss'. Their literary judgements of each other were vitiated by feelings they could perceive but not control. Katherine too was jealous of Virginia. Once when Roger Fry was telling her how Virginia was going to 'reap the world', she felt like pinning a paper on her chest with the words 'I, too, write a little'.[61] 'I see Virginia's book is announced in today's Times Literary Supplement' (she wrote to Ottoline in August 1919). 'I expect it will be acclaimed a masterpiece and she will be drawn round Gordon Square in a chariot designed by Roger after a supper given by Clive.'[62] In one of her few conversations with Forster, she told him that 'Virginia's art had no penumbra, wasn't, her metaphor ran, a broken off piece of living stuff, and implied that her own was, or that if one implied that it wasn't the evening would be a failure socially'.[63]

But she felt another kind of envy too. Living so often apart from the unreliable Murry, she compared her personal situation with Virginia's. She had said it pleasantly to her face: 'A husband, a home, a great many books & a passion for writing – are very nice things to possess all at once – It is pleasant to think of you & Leonard together.'[64] But often it wasn't pleasant. A few days after sending her review of *Night and Day* she wrote bitterly to Murry: 'Thats one thing I shall grudge Virginia all her days – that she & Leonard were together.'[65] Soon after: 'How I envy Virginia; no wonder she can write. There is always in her writing a calm freedom of expression as though she were at peace – her roof over her – her own possessions round her – and her man somewhere within call.'[66] Looking back on this mood of bitter self-pity and distress a few months later, she said to Murry: 'I used to feel like Virginia but she had Leonard. I had *no-one*.'[67]

Virginia took no account of Katherine's state of mind, and was mortified by the review. She tackled Murry about it at a dinner party: 'She said she thought your novel reviews showed that you were not interested in novels', Murry reported back to Katherine.[68] A cold little note Katherine sent when she got back to England in May 1920 ('I would be delighted if you'd care to come & see me one afternoon, but I am grown *very* dull')[69] cut her further. 'What does this mean – *she* hurt with *me*?' Virginia exclaimed to herself, understandably bewildered.[70] Their reunion was 'formality & coldness' at first. Katherine's cat-like solitariness struck her more than ever. 'And then we talked about solitude, & I found her expressing my feelings, as I never heard them expressed. Whereupon we fell into step, & as usual, talked as easily as though 8 months were minutes' – until Murry interrupted. Virginia's account of her own behaviour at this meeting shows how well she knows herself: 'pretending I couldn't write', she says (like Leslie eliciting praise from Julia). She even mentioned *Night and Day*, 'though I hadn't meant to speak of it'. 'An amazing achievement,' Katherine at once replied. 'But I thought you didn't like it?' 'Then she said she could pass an examination in it.' And having elicited praise, Virginia is immediately suspicious of it: 'Is she emotional with me?'[71] A few days later she went again and they had two hours of 'priceless talk'. 'To no one else can I talk in the same disembodied way about writing; without altering my thought more than I alter it in writing here. (I except L. from this.)'[72] This kind of talk, she feels, gets through self-consciousness, physical distaste or attraction, and illness, to an essence of intimacy and reality. It is very like what she thinks fiction should do.

From this one-sided account (it is what Katherine could do for her, not what she could do for Katherine, which absorbed her) it seems that she was the more enchanted, the more eager, and the more forgiving. She was 'the simpler, the more direct of the two', she thought, saying goodbye to her again in August before Katherine left for Menton. Her departure would leave 'the blankness of not having her to talk to . . . A woman caring as I care for writing is rare enough I suppose to give me the queerest sense of echo coming back to me from her mind the second after I've spoken.'[73] The phrase gives an almost erotic sense of closeness, like a phrase cut out of *Orlando* a few years later, about the intimacy of love-making between the androgynous lovers: 'when it seemed as if the doors of each mind stood wide open to the other so that they could pass in and out with perfect freedom – he taking the words from her lips, or the other way about.'[74] In their last conversation, they talk about their different ways of perceiving themselves:

> I said how my own character seemed to cut out a shape like a shadow in
> front of me. This she understood (I give it as an example of her

understanding) & proved it by telling me that she thought this bad: one ought to merge into things.[75]

The disagreement is like their relationship: momentarily disembodied, and then conscious of bodies; intermittently merging, and then cut off from each other by their own shadows cast in front of them. 'Strange how little we know our friends,' she added, wondering if Katherine would write. She missed her train because of all this talking, '& what I wanted most in the world was to catch it & travel back with L.' Travel back to Richmond, and travel back into her other closest conversation.

Her memory of these last meetings in the summer of 1920 would be very intense: of how she would go up the stairs and Katherine would get up 'very slowly, from her writing table' and draw herself across the room 'like some suffering animal' to lie on the sofa by the window; of the tidy bright dolls' house room with books and medicine bottles; of Katherine's dog-like, brown, wide-set eyes, her straight-combed fringe like 'a Japanese doll', her thin hard lips, her sharp 'vulgar' nose, her short skirts (she liked 'to have a line round her') – and of their long looks at each other, 'as though we had reached some durable relationship'.[76]

But once abroad, Katherine fell silent again, and by the time *Bliss and other Stories* was published at the end of 1920, Virginia was happy to hear her abused.[77] She had decided not to review it, for obvious reasons, but wrote her what she described as an 'insincere-sincere letter', without reading the book.[78] This did, immediately, elicit a response. Katherine saw through her: 'Please don't talk of a triumph, even in jest. It makes me hang my head.' And she heaped coals of fire:

> I think of you often – very often. I long to talk to you . . . If Virginia were to come through the gate & were to say, 'Well, Katherine' – Oh there are a thousand things I'd like to discuss. I wonder if you know what your visits were to me – or how much I miss them. You are the only woman with whom I long to talk *work*. There will never be another. But leagues divide us . . .[79]

In the early spring of 1921, when Katherine was in Menton, terribly ill, lonely and wretched because Murry had been having an affair with Elizabeth Bibesco, Murry saw Virginia and asked her to write to Katherine. And she did write, a long, funny, gossipy, intimate, excellent letter, the kind of letter she was also writing to the dying Jacques Raverat. She told her what she was trying to do in *Jacob's Room*: 'I'm always chopping and changing from one level to another'. She told her how she'd just lost her temper with Arnold Bennett and written an angry feminist story, how at a dinner at the

1917 Club 'Morgan Forster said that "Prelude" and *The Voyage Out* were the best novels of their time, and I said Damn Katherine! Why can't I be the only woman who knows how to write?' She told her about Lytton's great success with *Queen Victoria*, and how she was trying to learn Russian. She offered her her friendship yet again: 'Please, Katherine, let us try to write to each other.'[80]

There was no reply to this letter, and that, in a way, was the end of it. Virginia did not forgive her silence and did not make allowances for her terrible situation.[81] She hardened her heart against her. She spoke of needing to 'rinse her mind' after reading her stories in September 1921.[82] She rejoiced when Katherine didn't win the Hawthornden Prize in May 1922. She spoke harshly of the volume of stories called *The Garden Party* when they 'burst upon the world in glory' in February 1922,[83] feeling that they were in competition with *Jacob's Room*. She knew perfectly well that she could not bear her to be successful: 'the more she is praised, the more I am convinced she is bad.'[84] When Katherine came back to London for a few weeks, staying in Brett's house in the summer of 1922, while Virginia was in Sussex, she referred to her return callously ('What a joke that the Murry's have turned up again!')[85] and did not think of going to see her.

Then Katherine died, horribly and sadly, at the age of thirty-four, in the Gurdieff commune near Fontainebleau, on 9 January 1923. Virginia heard the news at breakfast on the 16th, from Nelly, who'd seen it in the morning paper. Immediately, she began another relationship with her, which continued, and revised, the unsatisfactory failed living friendship. This posthumous relationship began in memory and remorse. At once she wished she had not let things go, had not taken offence when Katherine didn't write, had not found it all 'too difficult'.[86] For the first time she realised that she had 'never given her credit for all her physical suffering & the effect it must have had in embittering her'.[87] She felt depressed, disappointed, flat: there seemed 'no point in writing any more'. The echo had gone: 'Katherine won't read it. Katherine's my rival no longer.' The loss of the rival was as important as the loss of the friend. 'There's no competitor. I'm cock – a lonely cock whose crowing nothing breaks – of my walk.'[88]

The mixture of rivalry and remorse would always shadow her thoughts of Katherine. When other women writers died she would think of her at once, with the same sense of guilt: 'I go on; & they cease.'[89] But she also continued to match herself against her. Murry's self-dramatising exploitation of her literary remains kept her feelings alive. A paragraph of his in the *Nation*, a few weeks after Katherine's death, would rankle for years.[90] Murry named Katherine and Virginia (and Lawrence) as the best of the younger generation, but said that they hadn't solved the problem of 'story'; they had reached an impasse. Only the short works, like *Prelude*, succeeded; the novels lacked 'constructive solidity' and worked only in brilliant incoherent flashes. This was clearly directed at *Jacob's Room*, and worked in her mind 'after the manner of the jigger insect'.[91] When Murry brought out Katherine's last stories, *The Dove's Nest*, in June of 1923, prefaced by extracts from her journals, she could hardly bring herself to look at them. She explained to Jacques Raverat that she didn't like her writing because although she had the most brilliant powers of observation, as soon as she tried to 'put thoughts, or feelings, or subtleties of any kind into her characters', she became either hard or sentimental.[92] And how did she compare? Katherine talked in her journals about working from deep feeling.[93] Did she too write from deep feeling? 'Am I writing *The Hours* [the working title for *Mrs Dalloway*] from deep emotion? . . . Or do I write essays about myself?' This passage, so often quoted, where she asks herself the crucial questions of her writing life, come directly out of her argument with Katherine. She knew that this was so. Some years later, in a review of the journals which Murry had edited, she paid generous tribute to what Mansfield had been trying to do, in terms which seem to invoke, and revoke, the jealousy she felt:

> No one felt more seriously the importance of writing than she did. In all the pages of her journal, instinctive, rapid as they are, her attitude to her work is admirable; sane, caustic, and austere. There is no literary gossip; no vanity; no jealousy. Although during her last years she must have been aware of her success she makes no allusion to it. Her own comments upon her work are always penetrating and disparaging. Her stories wanted richness and depth . . . Under the desperate pressure of increasing illness she began a curious difficult search.[94]

But Katherine haunted her too, not as a literary rival but as an object of 'deep feeling'. As soon as she heard of her death she went back over her memories of their last meetings, appeasing the shock of the blow, as she always did, by describing her emotions as exactly as she could.[95] She summoned her up, asking herself all over again what their relationship had been: 'Did she care for me? Sometimes she would say so – would kiss me – would look at me as if (is this sentiment?) her eyes would like always to be faithful. She would promise never never to forget.' But now it was up to Virginia never never to forget. A calming image, half-classical and half-late-Victorian, came into her mind of 'Katherine putting on a white wreath, & leaving us, called away: made dignified, chosen.'[96] The image would be saved up for the deaths of Mrs Ramsay and Prue in *To the Lighthouse*. 'For days after she had heard of her death she had seen her thus, putting her wreath to her forehead and going unquestioningly with her companion, a shadow, across the fields.'[97] Its re-use there suggests how deeply Katherine's death called up again all her feelings about the deaths of Julia and Stella.

Virginia was sceptical when she heard that Katherine's ghost had in fact (as it were) been seen, a few days after her death, at Brett's house. (Brett was a superstitious believer in this kind of thing.) How typical of Katherine, she caught herself thinking, to have that sort of 'cheap posthumous life'.[98] Yet, she *was* haunted by that 'faint ghost, with the steady eyes, the mocking lips, & at the end, the wreath set on her hair'.[99] The haunting was partly the result of the long trickle of posthumous publications; when the letters or the journals came out she was struck all over again with a desolating sense of waste and regret.[100] Katherine haunted her as we are haunted by people we have loved, but with whom we have not completed our conversation, with whom we have unfinished business. So she often dreamed of her, and would wake up wondering what dreams are:

> Often evoke so much more emotion, than thinking does – almost as if she came back in person & was outside one, actively making one feel; instead of a figment called up & recollected, as she is, now, if I think of her. Yet some emotion lingers on the day after a dream; even though I've now almost forgotten what happened in the dream, except that she was lying on a sofa in a room high up, & a great many sad faced women were round her. Yet somehow I got the feel of her, & of her as if alive again, more than by day.[101]

Almost fifteen years after their friendship, she was still recalling it to Vita (with whom she began to be intimate soon after Katherine's death), describing her dreams of Katherine, in which their relationship seemed somehow to be continued.[102]

So Katherine Mansfield's effect on Virginia Woolf was not only as a writer or a woman or a friend or a rival, but also as a person who died young. The climax of Virginia's feeling for Katherine comes on the day when she records in her diary in October 1924 the ending of *Mrs Dalloway*, the writing of the last words, 'For there she was'. She immediately thinks about Katherine: there she was, again, in her mind. As usual, mean feelings and deep feeling are inextricable. At last, she thinks, with this novel she has beaten her. 'Yes, if she'd lived, she'd have written on, & people would have seen that I was the more gifted – that wd. only have become more & more apparent.' In her mood of triumph and achievement, she pities 'that strange ghost', 'poor woman, whom in my own way I suppose I loved'.[103] But she also acknowledges what Katherine has meant to her, as, in the novel she has just finished, the living make sense of their life through their thoughts of the dead. 'But I stick to it; K.& I had our relationship; & never again shall I have one like it.'

TWENTY-THREE

Reading

'I can see already that no one else has ever known her as I know her.' This too sums up a relationship with a woman. 'However' (she adds) 'I always think this when I read – don't you?' The remark is a made in a letter to Eleanor Cecil about 'reading through the whole of George Eliot, in order to sum her up'.[1] It's a joke, but she means it. That confident enjoyment of the intimacy which comes from reading is one of the main sources of happiness in Virginia Woolf's life. Reading, quite as much as writing, is her life's pleasure and her life's work. It is separated from the rest of her activities by its solitude and withdrawal, but she is always comparing it to other forms of behaviour and experience – relationships, walking, travelling, dreaming; desire, memory, illness. When she writes about reading she makes it overlap with those other things. 'On Being Ill' (1926), an essay which begins by saying how rarely illness is a subject for fiction, turns into an account of reading in illness – how being ill makes us want 'intensity' or 'incomprehensibility' or 'rashness' in our reading.[2] Often her female character – the narrator of 'The Mark on the Wall' or 'An Unwritten Novel', Mrs Ramsay in *To the Lighthouse* – will look up over the edge of the pages of a book or a newspaper as the beginning of their train of thought. So here, in the essay called 'Reading':

> And somehow or other, the windows being open, and the book held so that it rested upon a background of escallonia hedges and distant blue, instead of being a book it seemed as if what I read was laid upon the landscape not printed, bound, or sewn up, but somehow the product of trees and fields and the hot summer sky, like the air which swam, on fine mornings, round the outline of things.[3]

This interchange between reading and living can be tricky. Her novels are about the difficulties of reading people, of saying of anyone that 'they were this or were that'. She knows all the problems that arise from treating books like people and people like books. People can't be summed up and finished with and returned to at will. ('When people come to tea I cant say to them, "Now wait a minute while I write an account of you".')[4] And there is something alarming about someone who needs to think of people as if they were books. It is a sign of self-defensiveness, perhaps of coldness and fear – but also of interest. Her readings of people after they have gone are like the 'after-readings' that she makes of books once they are closed and settling in the mind. The wary beginnings of new relationships – as, from 1918 onwards, with Eliot – negotiate obscurities as she might with a difficult new book. And her encounters with new writers struggle humanly with incompatibility. In 'How Should One Read a Book?' (1926), she says that 'books are in many ways like people'. The intuitions which colour social encounters ('Its an odd thing but I like you – or I may be wrong, but I'm sure we shant get on/ I shall never be able to stand you') apply just as much to the reading of books. So one must try to override prejudice, and to 'understand'.[5]

Her notes on Joyce's *Ulysses* (made between 1918 and 1919) make that sort of effort, against the grain. She vacillates between an attempt and a refusal to understand. She tries to do justice to 'the undoubted occasional beauty of his phrases', his attempt to 'get thinking into literature'. Then she runs up against the insuperable difficulties of what she perceives as Joyce's 'egotism' and his 'desire to shock'. She reproaches herself for injustice while thinking that all he wants to do is 'show off'. She recognises that his method 'cuts out a lot that's dull'. She considers that he is 'quite right, morally, not artistically' to do what he is doing. And she ends with a moral note which seems to have as much to do with relationships as with reading:

> The necessity of magnanimity & generosity. trying to see as much of other people as possible, & not oneself – almost a school for character. The bane of prejudice.[6]

Books are a school for character, she argues, because they change (like people) as we read them, and change us as we read. Books read us.

The reading and re-reading she does in the transitional years between *Night and Day* and *Jacob's Room* – of Joyce and the Russian writers, Eliot and Hardy, Chaucer and the Elizabethans, the Greeks, and (from 1922 onwards) of Proust – is as important to her life-story as any of her relationships. During this time she evolved a way of writing about her reading somewhere between notebook, diary, fiction and criticism. Just as she was devising her own kind of novel, so she constructed her own kind of essay out of the (still current) belle-lettriste tradition of essays on general literary subjects. The demand for those kind of essays in newspapers and periodicals provided her context, but what she did within that context was idiosyncratic: part polemic, part criticism, part fantasy, part history, part confession. These writings about reading were at the heart of her life's work.

In 1919 and 1920, when she was finishing *Night and Day* and moving into the 'little stories' which opened the way for *Jacob's Room*, she wrote three connected pieces on the relation between reading and writing: 'Reading', written some time in 1919, but not published; 'Modern Novels', in the *Times Literary Supplement* in April 1919, and 'An Unwritten Novel', for the *London Mercury* in July 1920.[7]

In 'Reading', while the reader is sitting with her book in the library of an Elizabethan house, Victorian figures of ladies and gentlemen go in and out of the house, the gardener mows the lawn, and there is a smell of the escallonia hedge. It might be a memory of childhood at St Ives; but the house could also be one of the Elizabethan family houses she had written about before.[8] The author she is reading seems to have behind him 'hosts' of other English authors, going back to Shakespeare and Chaucer and before. Through 'a great depth of time', the reader makes out a procession of English voices (anticipating the pageants of English history in *Orlando* and *Between the Acts*) which began with the 'taciturn' pre-Elizabethan ancestors of the house, and continued with Queen Elizabeth and the 'fine stories' of the Elizabethan colonists. She makes her own contemporary analysis of the uninterpreted stories of the past – for instance of Hakluyt's Elizabethan travel narratives – while trying to 'conjure up' the Elizabethan past,[9] as an 'atmosphere' rather than as facts. This 'illusion' of the past comes out of 'slips and somnolences' on the reader's part, out of inattention as much as attention. She seems to be reading – or remembering reading – almost in her sleep, as if slipping into a 'deep sea' of the past.

By the end of this imagined or remembered day of reading in the big English house, she has reached a point of satiation, where just to draw or slide her hand across the backs of the books in the dark is to invoke 'the fruit of innumerable lives'. As night falls, she moves into a long, eloquent description of children going into a wood to catch moths, and of hearing a tree fall in the depths of the wood. It becomes harder than ever to decide whether this is an essay on reading – or dreaming – or an autobiographical reminiscence. The essay drifts on into the question of 'knowing one's author', and talks of the way authors change as they are read. She compares the readers of Cervantes to the readers of Thomas Hardy. Hardy speaks to us 'separately', as modern individuals. But we misread Cervantes because we are unlike his readers, who were more homogeneous than we are. And do writers know what they are doing? 'Perhaps great writers never do', and that's why they can be read differently by each generation of readers – they leave things open. Certainly we are different kinds of readers now from the Elizabethans – we are not used to hard books like Browne's *Urn Burial*. So what do we do with his writing now? It leaves us wanting to communicate its beauty in some way. With this the essay ends, inconclusively, as if in mid-thought.

'Modern Novels' is much shorter and more direct, and is about the effect on the reader of contemporary writing. But though this essay (or rather its rewritten version of 1925, called 'Modern Fiction')[10] is always cited as her manifesto for the 'new' kind of novel she is now going to write, it is as much about reading as writing. And though it is usually seen as her programme for the future, in fact it mostly talks about the present in terms of our relation to the past.[11] What happens when post-war readers of fiction look back? They tend to assume a model of technological progress: literature must have improved, as have mechanical inventions like the bicycle. (When she revised this 1919 essay in 1925, she changed her example of progress to a motor-car.) But that linear, progressive model is denied: an overview of literary history, she says (anticipating Forster's round table in *Aspects of the Novel*) would see a circular, not a progressive movement. Yet though she maintains there is no such thing as progress in fiction, she also says that we need to move *on*. 'The essential thing has moved off, or on.' She implies a preference for a kind of fiction which will go faster – as a car goes faster than a bicycle – than the old machinery. In this first strike against the male writers of the previous generation, Wells, Bennett and Galsworthy, whom she calls the 'materialists' (lumping them together unfairly for the purposes of her argument), she presents them as the makers of solid, old-fashioned machines, those safe, slow, 32-chapter constructions, whose craftsmanship has not kept pace with 'the essential thing'.

Her attempt to describe that 'essential thing' is purposely impressionistic, fluid, 'modern' and unstable: 'showers of atoms' and 'semi-transparent envelopes' instead of railway carriages, villas and hotels. It is hard to tell, particularly in the 1919 version, whether she is talking about what writers should do, how human beings experience life, or how readers respond to books:

> Is it not possible that the accent falls a little differently, that the moment of importance came before or after, that, if one were free and could set down what one chose, there would be no plot, little probability, and a vague general confusion in which the clear-cut features of the tragic, the comic, the passionate and the lyrical were dissolved beyond the possibility of separate recognition? The mind, exposed to the ordinary course of life, receives upon its surface a myriad impressions – trivial,

fantastic, evanescent, or engraved with the sharpness of steel. From all sides they come, an incessant shower of innumerable atoms, composing in their sum what we might venture to call life itself; and to figure further as the semi-transparent envelope, or luminous halo, surrounding us from the beginning of consciousness to the end.[12]

The essay goes on to make readings of two possible alternatives to 'materialism'. One is of Joyce's *Ulysses* (based on her reading notes), which changes the accent and abandons conventions but is limited by its 'indecency'. The other is of a sad short story by Tchekhov called 'Gusev', which leaves questions 'to sound on and on after the story is ended', making an English reader protest, in the end, that unlike the Russians we prefer 'to enjoy and fight rather than to suffer and understand'. Both writers, she concludes inconclusively, 'flood us with a view of infinite possibilities'. Are we under water, or in the open air? Are we in a room, or on a journey? Are we writers, or readers? The essay is full of these sorts of unanswered questions: so it mimics the inconclusiveness she wants in fiction, both as a reader and as a writer.

'Modern Novels' sets up the terms for the representation of consciousness in fiction; 'An Unwritten Novel', the crucial turning-point between *Night and Day* and *Jacob's Room*, shows how that experiment might work. The 'story' demonstrates how the accent might be made to fall differently, how the 'essential thing' might be pursued, by inventing a hypothetical, never-to-be-written novel about a woman seen on a train.[13]

'An Unwritten Novel' implicitly parodies the 'materialism' of the 'first class railway carriage' English novel she referred to in 'Modern Novels', by setting its encounter on a train going to Eastbourne, by beginning with the narrator reading *The Times*'s report on the Peace Conference, and by constructing the story of 'Minnie Marsh' out of the materials of a pre-war English novel. The classbound details of Minnie's outer life – a patronising sister-in-law, a sick mother, an old dog, cruets, aspidistras, gloves, drapers' shops, commercial travellers, the price of eggs, hatpins, mackintoshes – metamorphose into ideas about 'the soul' or 'the spirit' or 'the self'.

Lifting her eyes from the pages of *The Times*, the narrator tries to read the woman opposite and finds that she is 'gazing into my eyes': the reader is being read. She has a twitch, and the narrator finds herself imitating it. She tries to rub out a mark on the window; the narrator rubs at it too. She begins to become her, as she reads and is read: 'I read her message, deciphered her secret, reading it beneath her gaze.' The story of Minnie's life she starts to tell herself is a rapid reading, full of skippings and dashes, alternative versions quickly discarded, summaries of off-stage events, dead ends, suppressions, false trails, characters who aren't allowed in ('the unborn children of the mind'). As she reads, the narrator finds that 'everything has meaning'. The shells that Minnie peels from her hardboiled eggs are like 'fragments of the puzzle', the glove she darns is like the spinning of the narrator's web.

At the end of the journey and of the story, she concludes that she has 'read her right'. And at once Minnie gets up and walks away from her gaze and out of her reading (she's met by her son at the station), leaving the reader-narrator-biographer to 'start after' her all over again. In the end it's she, not Minnie, who is the dominant character, and who becomes a sibylline prophetess on the sea-shore, opening her arms to the infinite possibilities of life.

Her rhapsody is a far cry from Minnie's hypothetical thoughts about the price of eggs and the awfulness of her sister-in-law. Class-difference gets in the way of the story's ideal of a free union between writer and subject, art and life. In spite of the story's desire to merge into her secret soul, Minnie's world is defined by very specific social markers. It is hard for the narrator to 'read Minnie right' if she locks her inside a caricature of lower-middle-class gentility. But there is another way she can 'become' her, which is by constructing a female narrative to rescue Minnie from 'the man's way' of telling her story.

'An Unwritten Novel' turned Virginia Woolf into a modernist (though this was not a word she used herself). And it raised for her all the perils of modernism. Did she 'deal . . . in autobiography & call it fiction?'[14] she asked while she was writing it. Would a fluid form let self-indulgence and egotism leak in, which she saw as the ruin of Joyce and Richardson? Could she, she asked herself in a peculiar phrase, 'provide a wall for the book from oneself'? The 'unwritten novel' made possible the novels she would now write, but it also opened up possibilities for her non-fiction writing. Its idea of a pursuit, a relinquishing and refinding of the self through the entry into another life, suggested a whole theory of reading.

When she came to describe the workings of her inner life in 1939 in her 'Sketch of the Past', and presented it in terms of response to a shock 'followed by the desire to explain it', to make it 'whole',[15] the account resembles her experience of reading. She often describes its impact as shocks followed by an effort to 'make it whole'. Reading is often a release or an escape for her. But though it is an addiction, it is not an opiate. 'The world which has been made by reading passionately or [laboriously] fiercely, according to the needs of the moment,'[16] can be a violently emotional realm. Reading can be more demanding than writing, especially when she sets herself – as here in the summer of 1918 – such strenuous reading-lists:

> Just back from the Club, & therefore in the restless state most safely to be appeased by writing; reading, though I've Don Juan, the Tragic Comedians, Verrall upon Meredith, Crees upon Meredith, the poems of Heredia & the poems of Laforgue to read, to say nothing of the Autobiography of Tagore, & the life of Macaulay, being out of the question before dinner.[17]

She often asks herself why she so much wants to read, and wants to read so much. It's a 'despotic' desire, she observes, which is 'capable of analysis'. 'Why this sudden passion for Pepys or Rimbaud? Why turn the house upside down to discover Macaulay's *Life and Letters?*' Is it a desire 'to be steeped in imagination' (as when reading Thomas Browne) or to be made 'more aware of ourselves' (as when reading Proust)?[18] It is certainly a desire for sensation. At its most intense, reading produces a direct 'shock of emotion',[19] like the 'shocks' she gets from life. Sometimes the charge can be too powerful. 'Shall I read King Lear? Do I want such a strain on the emotions?'[20] she asks herself, like Keats, 'On Sitting Down to Read *King Lear* Once Again':

> . . . for once again the fierce dispute
> Betwixt damnation and impassioned clay
> Must I burn through . . .[21]

She knows (as Keats knew) what emotion she will provoke by choosing to read *Lear*. And she often writes about the relation between her moods and her readings. One book will suit a certain state of mind: 'What book can I settle to read? I want something that wont colour my morning's mood – something a little severe.'[22] Another – *The Faerie Queen*, for instance – will suddenly become unreadable.

> I have decided to stop reading FQ at the end of the 4th book because I am completely out of the mood. I have read I suppose 2 or 3 large volumes of it since Jan 20th [1935] and it strikes me that I have absorbed that keen desire I had. Now I shall wait and see how long it takes to come back. What has formed is a desire for something particular, which I am gratifying by reading Chateaubriand, Memoirs. It looks to me as if there were a regular cycle of (at any rate) *my* taste. About 6 weeks one taste lasts; the first 2 or 3 are the keenest in sensation. It maybe that the first books of

the FQ are in fact the best. But I think the ebb and flow of my feeling is also at the back of it.[23]

As there, she identifies books with the emotions they produce. In order to argue with Percy Lubbock's theory in *The Craft of Fiction* that a work of fiction *is* its form, deliberately arrived at and consciously responded to by the reader, she examines her own reading of Flaubert's *Un coeur simple*, and looks for the moment when she suddenly arrives at 'a flash of understanding', a conception of what the story is about. This is a recognition, not an analysis: 'Therefore the "book itself" is not form which you see, but emotion which you feel'.[24]

And however difficult or painful the book may be, the essential emotion of reading is pleasure. The richest and best way of reading, she maintains in 1918, is to let oneself 'run on for pleasure'.[25] A life-time of reading later, she is still saying much the same thing. 'What a vast fertility of pleasure books hold for me!' she exclaims, blissfully, in 1933. 'I went in & found the table laden with books. I looked in & sniffed them all. I could not resist carrying this one off & broaching it. I think I could happily live here [in the country] & read for ever.'[26] A year later, again in the country for the summer, she writes to Ethel Smyth:

> I've not read so many hours for how many months. Sometimes I think heaven must be one continuous unexhausted reading. Its a disembodied trance-like intense rapture that used to seize me as a girl, and comes back now and again down here, with a violence that lays me low. Did I say I was flying? How then can I be low? Because, my dear Ethel, the state of reading consists in the complete elimination of the *ego*; and its the ego that erects itself like another part of the body I dont dare to name.[27]

Ethel was the right recipient for this joke about the erotic 'rapture' of reading, which she teasingly opposes to phallic, penetrative, climactic pleasure. This is an erotics of being flooded, fertilised,[28] 'getting full' of a book.[29] It can be vigorous, as when reading Shakespeare:

> Every ounce of energy is used up in realising the perpetual succession of images which coin even the thinnest pencilled thoughts on the borderlands of our consciousness into robust highly coloured shapes (bodies). Merely to throw ourselves this way and that with the emotions of the different speakers gives the illusion of violent physical exercise.[30]

Or it can be a languid rapture. Reading essays is more like sunbathing, 'a trance which is not sleep but rather an intensification of life – a basking, with every faculty alert, in the sun of pleasure'.[31] Different kinds of reading give different pleasures:

> Misc. Reading.
> One grades one's feelings.
> I get intense and deep pleasure from reading that Johnson buffeted his books.
> But the pleasure I get from reading the six lines of Dante seems to me more exalted.
> Still one must admit that all these pleasures are present in the same book sometimes.
> Take Religio Medici as an example.
> The better books universalise/disinfect personality.
> Simply they are dealing with important feelings.
> What I get fr. Johnson or Scotts diary I get from a great many pages, suddenly, but as a climax . . . What I get from Milton or Dante is complete the work done for you.[32]

At the heart of the pleasure of reading is the delight in a free union, like a very intimate conversation or an act of love. That longing for loss of self, entry into an other, is one of the deepest plots of her books. It is often a thwarted plot: the searcher is left loitering, cut off from the object of desire or stuck in the isolation of self. But reading can fulfil the desire for 'a perpetual marriage, a perpetual union'.[33] 'Love is so physical, & so's reading'.[34]

> Proust so titillates my own desire for expression that I can hardly set out the sentence. Oh, if I could write like that! I cry. And at the moment such is the astonishing vibration and saturation and intensification that he procures – theres something sexual in it – that I feel I *can* write like that, and seize my pen and then I *can't* write like that. Scarcely anyone so stimulates the nerves of language in me: it becomes an obsession.[35]

Even as she writes this extraordinary tribute you can see her being taken over by Proust's insidious, manipulative, sensual style – the word 'procures' is especially apt. Reading Proust almost stops her writing; other readings, though, will 'rock oneself back' into writing.[36] The most successful reading is when, as we finish the book, we feel that 'it leaves us with the impulse to write it all over again'.[37] In her notes to the 1926 lecture, 'How Should One Read a Book?' she talks of 'tracking your author down', seeing him 'leaving things out on purpose', or 'using certain words'.[38] She advises the reader to become the writer's 'accomplice'.

She says of her writing that it is a species of 'mediumship' – 'I become the person'.[39] And the same could be said of her reading. Reading is absorption ('absorbing at every pore'),[40] reading is saturation ('the mind is so saturated').[41] To read is to 'snuff the strange smells'.[42] The signs of this 'saturation' are everywhere in her books, from small magpie-stealings to larger schemes. Her work is permeated with her reading, which surfaces not as elaborately displayed layers of reference but in the atmosphere or structure of the novels,[43] as pastiche or rewritings or historical reconstructions,[44] in significant, specific allusions,[45] or in small hoarded details.[46] In her essays, the distinction is eroded between reference, imitation, tribute, and stealing; she works up her subjects out of a tissue of quotation and paraphrase.[47] Her mind is full of echoes.

Virginia Woolf was always monitoring the timetable of her day's work in her diary, congratulating or reproaching herself on how well she has kept to her targets. She called it her 'work account'.[48] She structured her working life by self-imposed routines which were essential to her. Writing (fiction or reviews) was done in the first part of the morning; just before or after lunch was for revising (or walking, or printing). After tea was for diary or letter-writing; the evenings were for reading (or seeing people): 'How great writers write at night, I don't know. Its an age since I tried, & I find my head full of pillow stuffing.'[49]

Her compulsive and compulsory timetables fulfilled her need for order, and stopped her thinking about death.

> One ought to work – never to take one's eyes from one's work; & then if death should interrupt, well it is merely that one must get up & leave one's stitching – one won't have wasted a thought on death.[50]

They gave the kind of steadiness (and hence freedom) necessary for the writer's life, which she remarked on as often as Flaubert: 'Habit is the desirable thing in writing,' 'What one wants for writing is habit.'[51] She liked it very much when the day was like 'a perfect piece of cabinet making – beautifully fitted with beautiful compartments.'[52] Illness, returns from holidays, house moves, disruptions to the day's routine, too many visitors, profoundly disturbed her. She acutely disliked this feeling, for instance (well known to all who write at home): 'Such a good morning's writing I'd planned, & wasted the cream of my brain on the telephone.'[53] Or being 'unable to settle' to her novel, and guiltily writing her diary instead at ten o'clock in the morning, because a visitor was expected at midday.[54] Or

feeling her schedule interrupted ('Alas, for the break in my scheme of work
– but we must make money')[55] when reviewing interfered with fiction.

Her notebooks reflected her timetables. They are her filing system, her
way of keeping her compartments separate. In any given month, she may
have several differently coloured notebooks on the go at the same time: one
(or more) for the novel in progress, one for her current diary, one for
newspaper clippings, one (or more) for her reading notes. These reading
notebooks were her system of annotation. She hardly ever marked her
books, and was satirical about people who did. She imagined annotators as
types. First a peppery old Colonel, denouncing any 'pernicious heresy' he
finds in his books to his wife ('To all of which, Mrs Tallboys answers,
"Certainly dear" '), or taking out his temper on his 'violated margin'. Then
a clergyman 'who feels it incumbent on him as a Christian' to disseminate
his little facts. Then an emotional lady who draws 'thick lachrymose lines'
in books of poetry 'beside all the stanzas which deal with early deaths, &
hopes of immortality', and sends the books back to the library with 'a whole
botanical collection' pressed between the leaves. Last an inserter of errata
and corrector of misprints, a public-spirited officious person who would
'accost a stranger in the underground and tell him that his collar is turned
up'. What all these addicted annotators have in common is that they are
forcing their readings on her.[56]

Instead of annotating, she rules margins in her notebooks, puts the
number of the page she's referring to in the margin, and writes next to it a
quotation or a comment. When she comes to write her review, she will ring
the quotations she wants to use, usually in blue pencil. If she's been reading
without her notebook to hand, and making notes on scraps of paper, she will
stick these scraps into the notebook. Out of this 'reading with a purpose' or
'reading with pen & notebook',[57] she accumulates the many volumes of
notebooks, which tell the story of how her mind works when she is reading.
These notebooks often breach their self-imposed compartments. On the
back of her notes on *The Canterbury Tales*, in 1923, she draws a map of
Green Park and Bond Street: she is planning Mrs Dalloway's walk.[58] The
manuscript of a book she is planning on fiction between 1925 and 1929,
called 'Phases of Fiction', keeps getting mixed up with the manuscript of *A
Room of One's Own*.[59] Her later notebooks are very mixed, stirring together
essays on biography and reviewing, drafts of her last novel 'Pointz Hall', a
story called 'The Searchlight' and the beginnings of a literary history called
'Anon'. By now the very idea of categories in writing had become
antipathetic to her.

Life is always breaking in on her reading. She makes a pencil sketch of a
new bathroom and study addition to Monk's House on the back of some

quotations from Geraldine Jewsbury; she lists the rooms in the house that need painting in the middle of her notes on Henry James's letters.[60] A good many of her notebooks have the marks of animals' paws on them, suggesting that they lay about open in the rooms she worked in, were picked up sometimes at random, and were not tidily put away. But the blurring of compartments in her notebooks doesn't just suggest that she was messy and absent-minded. She *wanted* boundaries to overlap: it was a form of cross-fertilisation. Above all, she wanted reading and writing to infiltrate each other. In 'How Should One Read a Book?', both reading and writing are compared to walking through city streets. Sometimes, she says, we need to move from one kind of book to another (from poetry to biographies, say), 'to skip and saunter, to suspend judgment, to lounge and loaf down the alleys and bye-streets of letters'.[61] This anticipates an essay called 'Street Haunting' (1927), where she describes her roamings and observations in London streets (on her way to buy a pencil) as a form of reading. She becomes 'an enormous eye' which can leave 'I' behind, leave the 'tether' of a 'single mind' and 'the straight lines of personality', and deviate into the 'bodies and minds of others'.[62]

Reading, like street-haunting, is partly passive – you become what you see – and partly active, energising, disturbing. She knows 'how great a power the body of literature possesses to impose itself: how it will not suffer itself to be read passively, but takes us and reads us; flouts our preconceptions; questions principles which we had got in the habit of taking for granted, and, in fact, splits us into two parts as we read, making us, even as we enjoy, yield our ground or stick to our guns.'[63]

Being split into two parts as we read takes the form, often, of what she calls 'making up'. You make up the author as you might make up the person opposite you in the railway carriage: 'as if you took advantage of every hint at life to live more fully yourself.'[64] Much of the art of reading is 'not reading', but a fantasy life carried on behind and during the reading. As she reads, half her mind is on the writer's life, making up the story behind the story. And when she returns to an author – Scott, say – she will 'make him up a little differently at every reading'.[65]

When the book is closed, and the 'after reading' begins, 'making up' turns into 'making whole'. This is not just an interesting part of the process, it is an urgent personal necessity: 'one must, for one's own comfort, have a whole in one's mind: fragments are unendurable.'[66] Over and over again she insists on the need to 'make it whole'. 'A book is all on top of us. Before we can grasp a single detail, we have to possess ourselves [of] the whole.'[67] This is like the way she makes sense of the 'shocks' she receives in life by explaining them, and the way she shapes her novels by retrospective summings-up: 'I have had my vision', says Lily, concluding *To the Lighthouse*; 'Now to sum up', says Bernard in *The Waves*. 'Now to explain to you the meaning of my life.'

'Making whole' is, again, partly a passive process: 'the whole book floats to the top of the mind complete.'[68] But it also involves the effort to communicate, to say what she thinks about the book. And this is when reading turns from a private 'intoxication'[69] to a process of public explanation. The heat of the notebooks cools into the essays, and the intimate 'union' between one reader and one book opens out into comparisons and contexts. Now she needs to consider the different demands made by different kinds of books.[70] She is specially concerned with the painful difference between reading contemporaries and 'old books': the lack of coherence in the moderns, set against the enviable certainties and 'release from the cramp and confinement of personality' in the 'master-pieces of the past'.[71]

When she is putting her reading in order, Virginia Woolf asks a great many questions about canon-formation, and insists that great books must be set in the context of inferior, ordinary, forgotten books: trashy novels, obscure memoirs, especially of women's lives, dust-gathering volumes of letters, mediocre biographies, minor plays. 'A literature composed entirely of good books' would soon be unread, extinct; 'the isolation is too great'. We need 'trivial ephemeral books': 'They are the dressing-rooms, the work-shops, the wings, the sculleries, the bubbling cauldrons, where life seethes and steams and is for ever on the boil.' They fertilise our minds and get them ready for the big masterpieces.[72] We can't always be reading Keats or Aeschylus or *King Lear*;[73] so she defends the pleasures of bad books, the historical importance of the rubbish heap.[74] She argues for serendipitous, random reading from the shelves of second-hand bookshops and public libraries: 'I ransack public libraries & find them full of sunk treasure.'[75] All her life she celebrated the democratic function of the public library as the university of the non-specialist, uninstructed reader; it is the reading room for the common reader.

When she revised and collected the essays she liked best between 1923 and 1924, added some new ones, and published a volume in 1925 called *The Common Reader*, she wanted to make clear, not so much whom she thought her book of essays was for, but how she thought of herself as a reader: non-specialist, adventurous, and open. But her borrowing of that phrase, 'the common reader', from Dr Johnson has been a hostage to fortune. She used the word 'common' as he did, to mean general or ordinary. But because there have been so many attacks on her life and work (especially in Britain) for snobbery, high-brow-ism and a refusal to write for a mass public, the other meaning of 'common' has crept into the discussion. Her life-long identification with the self-educated reader and her passionate interest in anonymous 'obscure' lives has been travestied by mocking attacks on her condescension and élitism.

She digs part of this pit for herself. Her keenness to avoid autobiographical self-exposure makes her refer to her common reader as 'he' (though in the unpublished 'Byron & Mr Briggs' she lets the cat out of the bag when she admits that at least one of her common readers is a woman).[76] So the common reader with whom she means to identify sometimes seems awkwardly remote from her. And – as in 'An Unwritten Novel' – her desire for empathy can be compromised by her pronounced sense of class-difference. So, her common reader, she says, might have read more than 'could be expected of a working man, or any but a very exceptional bank clerk'; if we don't get more than our own emotions back from our reading, it requires 'no more effort than a shop girl makes who dreams as she listens to the band in Hyde Park of making love by moonlight at Margate'.[77] If these figures out of *The Waste Land* aren't capable of being *her* kind of common reader, then the cat is really out of the bag: Virginia Woolf's common reader is in fact very uncommon indeed.

When she wrote 'Byron & Mr Briggs' in 1922, her draft of the first chapter of 'Reading' (with her first mention of the common reader), she ended it by saying that 'the writers of England & the readers of England are necessary to one another. They cannot live apart. They must be forever engaged in intercourse.'[78] So she translated her metaphor of a secret intimacy between the individual writer and reader into a vision of a national, public union, shaped by the demands and compromises of the market-place. Both as a novelist wanting to be read, and as a reader wanting to talk about her books, she found the public relationship as uneasy and frustrating as any private relationship could be. Virginia Woolf is equally hostile to academic appropriations of literature and to 'middlebrow' literary journalism. Her books – especially *A Room of One's Own* and *Orlando* – are full of savage play at the expense of (male) cultural coteries: professors, editors, literary hacks. As her writing life goes on she becomes increasingly scornful and intolerant of what's been fiercely called 'the massive confidence-trick perpetrated by the middlemen of the book trade.'[79] She formulated much of her thinking about modern fiction in angry reaction to pieces of journalism (like Arnold Bennett's critique of *Jacob's Room*).[80] She often had to edit her journalism to make it more acceptable. Sometimes she felt forced to write 'stiffly, without spontaneity', too aware of her audience or her editor. Sometimes she was censored, or censored herself: Bruce Richmond wouldn't let her use the word 'lewd' in a review of Henry James's ghost stories in 1921; she had to be 'discreet' about lesbianism in a piece on Geraldine Jewsbury and Jane Carlyle in 1929.[81] Though in 1931 she said she had learnt to throw the inkpot at the Angel in the House, she did sometimes pull her punches. For these sorts of reasons (reasons which would flare up furiously in her feminist writings), she resented the pressures and constrictions of reviewing for money (particularly in the early 1920s when she was thinking so much about fiction and the market-place),[82] and used *The Common Reader* as a place where she could write about literature to please herself.

Yet she wanted to write – essays as well as fiction – *for* someone. She thought of conversation between like-minded lovers of literature as an ideal model for literary criticism (and tried this out as an essay-structure),[83] but she did not want her criticism to be merely 'random chatter',[84] or just talking to herself. She was keenly concerned, both as a novelist and a critic, with the question 'For whom should I write?' 'To know whom to write for is to know how to write', she said in 1924.[85] If, as a novelist, you were too cut off from your public, too indifferent to it, your art became like some weird, tortured, malformed growth (like Meredith, or late James). If you were too much at one with the public, you became faded and dusty, like a wayside flower. 'Undoubtedly all writers are immensely influenced by the people who read them.'[86] But those readers also had to be resisted, and not always given what they expected. If the 'great British public' was sitting out there saying in its 'vast and unanimous way' that this was what they thought novels should be like,[87] then one of the writer's jobs was to change its expectations. So the mutual need of writer and reader which she so much desires is also a highly problematic union, set about with conventions and hypocrisies.

For the woman reader-critic – as for the woman writer – there was conflict and peril in the literary market-place. Virginia Woolf was right to think of the British literary world of the 1910s and 1920s as a male-dominated culture. Almost all the literary editors, magazine owners, publishers and reviewers were men.[88] So was a woman reader to disguise herself, to suppress her sexual character and inclination in reading, or to read and write *as a woman*?[89] Virginia Woolf partly wanted reading to have nothing to do with sex, to be ungendered and impersonal. But her metaphors for reading as slipping, skipping, loitering, weaving, are all feminised: there *is* a kind of reading as a woman which is different from 'the man's way', she seems to suggest, even while she says that reading should be as androgynous as writing. As a biographer, as a critic, or as a novelist, she felt that there is a distinct way for a woman to read, and write about, other women's lives.[90] *A Room of One's Own* is a history of a woman's reading, and is written in tandem with her history of literature, 'Phases of Fiction'. *Three Guineas* makes a woman's reading of biographies the basis of its attack on her patriarchal culture. So the pleasure of reading was not simple or separate, but bound up with Virginia Woolf's politics and her feminism. As with everything in her life which closely involved her, she also, sometimes, wanted to withdraw from books, to set them aside. In a strange notebook entry, made probably at the end of 1928 or the beginning of 1929, mixed up with the manuscript of 'Phases of Fiction' and a draft of the beginning of *A Room of One's Own*, she suddenly says:

> But I cannot write anything more about fiction.
> What I want to do is to write the first word of [The Moths].
> ~~More~~
>   ~~It was a silent b~~
> No; I am superstitious and will not write another word.

There follows a mysterious, fragmentary description of a garden – Monk's House? – and a churchyard with its tombstones at dusk. And then: 'She was tired of all this . . . All seemed to be writing, & inscriptions, & words, & meanings.'[91] This obscure note seems to be the first conception of *The Waves*, the novel which keeps trying to move through story and language into silence. But it also seems to be a moment of despair, a withdrawal from everything she knows and sees; and from having to know and see everything as a form of reading.

PART III

1919–1929

TWENTY-FOUR

Monk's House

In the summer after the war, the summer of the move to Monk's House, Virginia Woolf was reading the poems of Gerard Manley Hopkins, posthumously published in 1918 by Robert Bridges. She was enchanted by them, and when she wrote in January 1920 to Janet Case, telling her about the landscape around Rodmell and the new house, she enclosed her copy and began her letter with a quotation from 'Heaven-Haven':

> I have desired to go
> Where springs not fail
> To fields where flies no sharp and sided hail
> And a few lilies blow.

'Yes, I should like to have written that myself', she added.[1] She went on to describe a walk on the Downs, with that intense, sensual apprehension of landscape which she shared with Hopkins. She watched this country 'haven' and worked in it, looked up from her book at it and walked through it, for twenty-two years. The landscape and the village were continually written into the diary and the letters – and there were stories and essays set in Sussex too. And though her novels are often urban, they are the most pastoral city novels ever written. In her last novel, *Between the Acts*, she gave a version of rural England, written while she was living permanently in Sussex, which drew on her long experience of the village between the two wars.

Until the Second World War, the Woolfs were seasonal visitors. But their seasons were more like her Victorian parents' split years than the next generation's country cottage weekending. Three or four months in the summers, weeks at Easter and Christmas, frequent spring and autumn weekends, were enough for her to feel rooted there. She anticipated this in 1919: 'Monks House . . . will be our address for ever and ever; Indeed I've already marked out our graves in the yard which joins our meadow.'[2]

Monk's House is haunted by Virginia Woolf's writing. Because she turned it so vividly and lovingly into her words, her readers have the illusion that they can cross the broken bridge into the past[3] and see it as she did. This illusion is the more tempting because the house has been preserved and the village of Rodmell is 'unspoilt'. They seem to have withheld something from the extreme, complex changes of the century. Yet these changes, as drastic in rural as in urban England, were an important part of what Virginia Woolf registered in her Monk's House writings. The Woolfs themselves changed the house substantially in her life-time; meanwhile the life of the village changed greatly, and much more in the next half-century. 'Her' Monk's House, 'her' Rodmell, exist and do not exist.

She did not want to leave Asheham in 1919, but they had no choice: the owner needed it for his farm-bailiff. She forced herself, as Leonard advised, not to 'make a fetish' of the house,[4] and to get interested in house-hunting. In June, walking unhappily into Lewes after her quarrel with Vanessa over the design of *Kew Gardens*, she saw the Round House for sale, an old windmill which had been made into an odd little house in the centre of Lewes, up a steep narrow alley overlooking the city walls. She made a rash offer for it of £300, which was accepted – and blamed Vanessa for her impulsiveness. A fortnight later she took Leonard to see it. He was polite, but thought it cramped. By coincidence, they passed an auctioneer's notice for Monk's House in Rodmell, about two miles south of Lewes, off the Newhaven road. It was a house they knew from the outside. Rodmell was on the other side of the Ouse valley from Asheham, and they had often walked there over the water-meadows. They had looked into the garden of this house, over the wall which ran down the side of the lane to the church, and envied it.

The next afternoon Virginia bicycled in a cold wind to Rodmell to see inside the house. Her account eloquently and humorously relates (as if she is telling someone about it) the start of a passion, and the vain attempt to resist it. By the end of the paragraph she is calling it 'ours':

'These rooms are small, I said to myself; you must discount the value of that old chimney piece & the niches for holy water. Monks are nothing out of the way. The kitchen is distinctly bad. Theres an oil stove, & no grate. Nor is there hot water, nor a bath, & as for the E.C. I was never shown it.' These prudent objections kept excitement at bay; yet even they were forced to yield place to a profound pleasure at the size & shape & fertility & wildness of the garden. There seemed an infinity of fruitbearing trees; the plums crowded so as to weigh the tip of the branch down; unexpected flowers sprouted among cabbages. There were well kept rows of peas, artichokes, potatoes; raspberry bushes had pale little pyramids of fruit; & I could fancy a very pleasant walk in the orchard under the apple trees, with the grey extinguisher of the church steeple pointing my boundary. On the other hand there is little view – O but I've forgotten the lawn smoothly rolled, & rising in a bank, sheltered from winds too, a refuge in cold & storm . . . There is little ceremony or precision at Monks House. It is an unpretending house, long & low, a house of many doors; on one side fronting the street of Rodmell, & wood boarded on that side, though the street of Rodmell is at our end little more than a cart track running out on to the flat of the water meadows.[5]

It is like Leslie reporting on his first sighting of Talland House, excitedly filled with the sense of its potential. She described it to Leonard, 'as quietly as I could', and they both went to look. She saw at once that he would become 'a fanatical lover of that garden'. On 1 July 1919 they bid for it at the auction at the White Hart Hotel in Lewes (an event as 'close packed with sensation' as any in her life) and bought it for £700. In the aftermath of the suspense, they had a brief quarrel about nothing. The Round House, now an embarrassment, was sold for £320 on 16 July.

Monk's House had been neglected[6] and partitioned into little rooms. Not only were there no facilities, but the kitchen was very damp. But it was solid, with weatherboarding and a steep slate roof, good windows and chimneys and oak floorboards. The garden door round the back (they didn't use the front door on to the street) led into a small entrance hall, with an oak-beamed dining-room and drawing-room on the left. There was a large fireplace (with two pointed 'niches' on either side) in the dining-room. On the right of the entrance was a small room to be used at first for guests, later as a dining-room, and next to it the unsatisfactory kitchen, with a small larder. Up the stairs, above the drawing- and dining-room, was a large bedroom, also with oak beams and a fireplace, and a view up the village street. A small box-room opened off it and there was an attic above. For a short time they shared this bedroom in separate beds,[7] then Leonard slept either in the box-room, or in one of the two small bedrooms on the other side of the landing.

So in 1919 Monk's House was a primitive cottage, smaller and less attractive than Asheham. But the garden was richer and bigger, with promising outbuildings, and 'the garden gate admits to the water meadows, where all nature is to be had in five minutes'.[8] Going out in winter through the frosty grass to use 'the romantic chamber', the earth closet with a 'cane chair over a bucket' in one of the outbuildings, was for years one of the features, if not the pleasures, of Monk's House.[9]

They kept its past with some of the house's old furnishings. All the possessions of the previous owner, Old Jacob Verrall, whom Leonard described years later as a Sussex 'character', (but who had neglected the house and had, according to the local doctor, starved himself to death),[10] were hauled out on to the lawn for sale, like the objects from the long-deserted house in *To the Lighthouse*. In the sale catalogue, which Leonard marked up on 14 August 1919, was a whole century of Sussex life: the oak and mahogany chests, the rush-seat elbow chairs, the brass bedsteads, the japanned hip-bath and foot-bath, the crotchet antimacassars and damask crumb cloth, the copper warming pan and kettles, the 'Sheraton sideboard with revolving cellarette on massive bronze feet', the Broadwood cottage pianoforte, the 'stuffed otter in case', the 'pair of bullock horns and fossils', the models of ships in glazed cases. They bought some furniture, some cutlery, a lot of gardening things. Their one indulgence was three nineteenth-century oil-on-wood portraits of the Glazebrook family, the house's previous owners: 4 shillings for the three. 'For myself, I don't ask anything more of pictures. They are family groups, and he began the heads very large, and hadn't got room for the hands and legs, so these dwindle off till they're about the size of sparrows claws, but the effect is superb – the character overwhelming.'[11]

The pictures made them the inheritors of the house's history, which Leonard researched, finding that Virginia's monks and their holy water were, sadly, 'mythological', but that the house since 1707 had been owned first by a family of carpenters, the Clears, then by the Glazebrooks, the local millers whose millstones were in the garden, and then by Old Verrall.[12] The relics of these families now began to be mixed up with dark blue Omega plates on a green kitchen dresser, paintings by Duncan and Vanessa, and strong-coloured wall paints (pomegranate, green, yellow, blue) applied by Virginia. Later they added carpets and china and screens, armchairs and cushions, all designed at Charleston. They bought mirrors in decorated canvas frames, cupboards and tables from Provence. There would be a painted dining table with chairs and a painted music cabinet from the music room designed at the Lefevre Gallery by Duncan and Vanessa in 1932. There would be a gramophone and a wireless, a fish tank, a box of bowls. The style of the furnishings was very similar, in places identical, to the sister house at Charleston. But the walls of Rodmell were left barer, and the effect was starker and plainer, less intense. And where Charleston had the mess of painting and children everywhere, Rodmell had dogs, and piles of books and papers. It was never a tidy or a luxurious house. But it gradually became a more comfortable country home as their spending power increased in the 1920s and 1930s.

The kitchen had to be rebuilt at once.[13] Until they had a proper stove they had their meals cooked for them by the sexton's wife Mrs Dedman next door ('stews and mashes & deep many coloured dishes swimming in gravy thick with carrots & onions').[14] They got a solid fuel oven in the summer of

1920, and their servants managed on that in the dark damp kitchen, interrupted by Leonard coming in to chop up the dogs' food, or to make his morning coffee and Virginia's breakfast, taken to her on a tray, and by Virginia baking her bread and cakes.[15] The installation of an oil stove in 1929 seemed a great advance:

> At this moment it is cooking my dinner in the glass dishes perfectly I hope, without smell, waste, or confusion; one turns handles, there is a thermometer. And so I see myself freer, more independent – & all one's life is a struggle for freedom – able to come down here with a chop in a bag & live on my own. I go over the dishes I shall cook – the rich stews, the sauces. The adventurous strange dishes with dashes of wine in them. Of course Leonard puts a drag on, & I must be very cautious, like a child, not to make too much noise playing.[16]

The stove was one of many improvements to the house which the sales of her books in the 1920s – *Mrs Dalloway* and *The Common Reader, To the Lighthouse*, and above all *Orlando* – made possible. 'I'm out to make £300 this summer by writing, & build a bath & hot water range at Rodmell.'[17] In the spring of 1926, Philcox Bros of Lewes improved the kitchen and put in a hot water range, a bath (a narrow one, with curly feet), a sink and a lavatory, squeezed on either side of the chimney-breast in the little room above the kitchen. She wrote paeans to 'the luxury of water running in torrents, boiling hot'.[18] Now every morning at Monk's House after her breakfast she would take a bath; in later years their servant, Louie Everest, would hear her from the kitchen below (Monk's House was not a sound-proof house) talking out loud the scenes she had written or thought of in the night, as she lay in the bath. 'On and on she went, talk, talk, talk: asking questions and giving herself the answers. I thought there must be two or three people up there with her.'[19]

At the same time, they had the wall between the dining-room and the drawing-room knocked down, leaving wooden support pillars, to make 'a perfect triumph': 'Our large combined drawing eating room, with its 5 windows, its beams down the middle, & flowers & leaves nodding in all round us.'[20] 'It has the makings of a most peculiar and I think comfortable, charming, characteristic, queer resort,' she told Vanessa, asking for advice: 'What curtains? What chair covers? Would I be allowed some rather garish but vibrating and radiating green and red lustres on the mantelpiece?'[21]

A year later, in 1927, they began to make major plans for a new extension: 'we might build a bed sitting room for me in the attic, enlarge L's study, & so have a desirable, roomy, light house': what else, now that they were beginning to have money, should they spend it on, except this house, 'travel, & pocket money'?[22] The money from *Orlando* made the extension possible,[23] and in the spring of 1929, Philcox Bros again began work. The attic was made into a long narrow L-shaped study for Leonard, with a little corner fireplace (its blue and brown flower-patterned tiles were by Duncan) and two windows, one, in the toe of the L, looking over the garden, and one at the far end looking up the quiet street. The room next to the kitchen became the dining-room. A square, brick, two-room extension was built on next to the kitchen.[24] Underneath was a simple garden room (16' by 16') entered by an outside door. The fireplace had tiles decorated by Vanessa in 1930 with a sailing ship and a lighthouse. It had bookshelves on either side, a sink-basin, and a window with 'vast sweeping views' over the fields.[25] Virginia had intended this to be her work room, with a bedroom above, but it became her bedroom, and she went out of the house to it every night, and very often watched the night sky from it when she could not sleep. ('And I shall pull open my curtains & see the stars at night. Really a marvellous spectacle – all for nothing.')[26] In winter, when it was too cold to work in the garden-lodge, she wrote there, though it took a little time to get used to it: 'I cannot yet write naturally in my new room, because the table is not the right height, & I must stoop to warm my hands. Everything must be absolutely what I am used to.'[27] The top half of the new extension, reached by a narrow curved staircase of twelve steps to the right of the bathroom, was a light room with a good fireplace (lilies and fruit bowl tiles designed by Vanessa). It had two large windows, one looking out over the garden and the church, one, like her bedroom below, over the fields. This became their sitting-room, and unless there were a large number of people visiting, they came to use it more often in the evenings than the big downstairs room. (Most of the photographs of Virginia Woolf at Rodmell after 1929 were taken in here.) There are stories of Leonard quietly taking Virginia up to this sitting-room when, with a big party downstairs, she became 'over-excited'.[28]

Leonard, as she had foreseen, fell immediately and fanatically in love with the garden. The first month there, he weeded and planted relentlessly; after tea 'L runs out like a child allowed to get down & go'.[29] She joined in, with 'a queer sort of enthusiasm which makes me say this is happiness', ending the days stiff and scratched with 'chocolate earth in our nails'.[30] But it was really his terrain. As the rampant, straggling $\frac{3}{4}$-acre of garden bent to his will, she took an attentive pleasure in it. She liked their plums and apples, their bees, and their two ponds, one in the formal garden for ailing fish and, later, a big round one on the croquet lawn. She often used them as images of contemplation.[31] She liked the two tall elms they named Leonard and Virginia,[32] the garden statuary they gradually acquired from the village shop in Balcombe, and all the little divisions (edged with brick paths or yew hedges or lonicera hedges) between the flower garden in front of the house, the orchard beyond it, the vegetable plots, and the wide smooth lawn.

She liked the colours: 'Our garden is a perfect variegated chintz: asters, plumasters, zinnias, geums, nasturtiums & so on: all bright, cut from coloured papers, stiff, upstanding as flowers should be.'[33] There would be flowering potted plants in the house. Above all she liked her garden work-lodge and its views, though her first outhouse, a wooden hut half-way down the garden, was not ideal. It had a loft above it, reached by an outside ladder, where Leonard stored the apples, and the noise he made sorting them would irritate her.[34] The dog would come and sit behind her, scratching, on her chair,[35] and it was too cold to work out there in the winter. But it had a large window and a view of the downs',[36] and later improvements made it a 'palace of comfort'.[37] In 1934 it was moved to the bottom of the garden, under the chestnut tree next to the flint churchyard wall. She worked in there, surrounded by papers, writing on a board on her lap, and looking out over towards Asheham and 'across the water meadows to Mt Caburn'.[38] A little brick patio was built in front, with a step down to it from the french windows, and on summer evenings with visitors they would sit there and watch the games of bowls – the Woolfs' extremely competitive Rodmell hobby – on the lawn, with a view of the Downs beyond.

The garden (like the bowls) could also be a source of conflict. They began by timetabling two weekly walks 'to counteract' its 'tremendous draw'.[39] But she would more often walk alone. And they would argue over the expense of heated greenhouses, and of buying more land (though she liked 'our new field' when they got it in 1928), and of a cottage for a regular gardener. Were they to tie themselves to Monk's House for ever as 'the hub of the world', never to travel, to spend all they earned on the garden?[40]

The quarrel was between two strong wills with different priorities, but it also sprang from her competition with Vanessa, who in the 1920s was spending more and more time in France, and with her own ambivalent feelings about English village life. She was interested but wary, and for years did not want to commit herself to Rodmell. The position of Monk's House, down at the end of the long village which straggled on either side of the narrow track off the main road, seemed to symbolise her preference for apartness and seclusion. She had no desire to get involved with the two centres of village life, the nineteenth-century school on the other side of the lane to the church, and the church itself, twelfth-century St Peter's with its grey flint tower.[41] Both were sources of irritation to her. The children stole their apples, and their 'cursed shrill voices' playing cricket in the field or 'saying the multiplication table in unison'[42] distracted her (even, in vulnerable moods, made her think of her own lack of children).[43] She pretended they were 'swifts & martins skirling round the eaves'[44] to stop herself getting annoyed. But she was always irritated by the church bells, ('intermittent, sullen, didactic'),[45] which she disliked as much for what they represented as for their insistence.

But she enjoyed her meetings with the picturesquely unregenerate old rector, the Reverend Hawkesford, who had been there since 1896, an 'old decaying man, run to seed', shabby, dirty, with black wool mittens and a beard like 'an unweeded garden', who smoked endless cigarettes and had a cynical store of old village stories. She liked to think of him leaning on a stile talking to the rector of Iford, Rodmell's next-door village, about the cost of Aladdin lamps.[46] He belonged, Leonard thought, looking back, to 'the ancient English village way of life which in Sussex has completely disappeared . . . I never heard him say a word about religion or his work as a clergyman.'[47] In one of her stories set in Rodmell, 'Miss Pryme', she set the unpresentable Mr Pember, sneaking out to the graveyard for a smoke in the middle of a service, against the suburban forces of reform and progress.[48] Old Sussex appealed to her: the publican called 'Mr Malthouse', the 'muddy & ruddy & obsolete' old farmers who 'drink & lounge about',[49] the two 'draggle tailed' spinster sisters of the vicar at Southease (the tiny village down the Ouse from Rodmell by the bridge). Visiting them, Leonard remembered, was 'like walking into the 16th century.'[50] They were both struck by old Mrs Grey, her face cut into by wrinkles, ninety-two in 1932, wretched with the dropsy: 'I crawls up to bed hoping for the day; & I crawls down hoping for the night.'[51] Virginia noted that Leonard 'liked her despair'.

She (and Leonard) relished poor Mrs Grey for aesthetic reasons, but Virginia did not sentimentalise her: she wrote a bitter sketch about the medicine and good works which prolonged the life of the old creature. She resisted the 'ubi sunt' guide book tone about 'old' Sussex.[52] But she was attracted to the residual bits of past Sussex life. Her fictional versions of Rodmell were ghost stories or histories. 'The Widow and the Parrot' is a comic tale indebted to Flaubert and inspired by the ruins of a burnt-down house in the village. An old lady from Yorkshire, who has come to claim her Rodmell inheritance, is saved from death in the Ouse by a loyal and intelligent parrot who also reveals, after her house has gone up in flames, the site of her hidden inherited treasure. The story ends with the ruins of the house haunted by the parrot and 'an old woman sitting there in a white apron'.[53] A meditation on 'The Fascination of the Pool' sees a lost history of the village in the 'profound under-water life'.[54] And in *Between the Acts*, the

Sussex village on the edge of war is a patchwork of left-over and misunderstood bits of the past.

As in *Between the Acts*, Rodmell, like many small Sussex villages, could be 'read' for layer upon layer of local and national history. Histories of the evolution of the human race – popular reading in the 1920s and 1930s – greatly interested Virginia Woolf, and she liked (as much as Mrs Swithin in *Between the Acts*, absorbed in Wells's *Outline of History*) to imagine palaeolithic man living on the Downs, or iguanodons on the Weald.[55] Rodmell was one of the pre-Conquest Saxon settlements between the river marshlands and the Downs where cattle were grazed, with the great forests of the Weald beyond one horizon and the sea beyond the other. ('It seems from the terrace as if the land went on for ever and ever.' 'Once there was no sea.')[56] Relics of passing civilisations surrounded her there, not only the famous pre-Christian chalk carving of the Long Man of Wilmington, but the Iron Age barrows on the Downs, the traces of the Romano-British fort on Mount Caburn, the supposed line of the Roman Road on the highway. Out in the marshes was the relic of a medieval priory. In the village, the 'Stock Cottages' had replaced the stocks, the 'Poor Cottages' marked where the Elizabethan poor law had been dispensed. Arms of the old families, de Rademelde and de la Chambre, could still be seen; an ice house under a big mulberry tree marked where the big house, Hall Place, had stood; a medieval vineyard, a Dame School, a Hardyesque cello-playing blacksmith who led the church choir, were spoken of as items in the village's history.[57]

When the Woolfs moved there the village had no bus, water, drains or electricity; to get to Lewes they had to walk, ride a bike, or hire a trap. But this was not a backwater of rural calm (as it now seems), nor a feudal village in the shadow of a great house, like Firle. It was a busy, noisy, self-supporting community, with a pub, a mill and a forge (which became their garage) on the main road, and, as well as the church and the school, a village shop, a post office, a bakery, a Club Room (rebuilt as the village hall), a cricket pitch, and several farms. The carter, Mr Thomsett, drove his horses past their house up from the meadows to work and back down in the evening, as he had every day for half a century.[58] The old Sussex game of stoolball (a cross between rounders and cricket) was still played in the field at the bottom of their garden,[59] and the Sussex tradition of smock funerals was only just coming to an end.[60] She complained when a camp of Boy Scouts sang 'Here we are' about a million times daily at the end of the garden,[61] or 'a gospel caravan' of young men pitched tent nearby and chorused 'Washed in the Blood of the Lord' outside her window.[62] But these noisy incursions meant an active society. And, when they were not on her doorstep, she relished her glimpses of community life. Once, in 1927, driving in their new car on a hot summer day near Ripe (over the road from Charleston), they heard hymn singing, and saw 'a middle class "lady" in skirt & coat & ribboned hat, by the cottage door . . . making the daughters of the agricultural labourers sing . . . It strikes me that the hymn singing in the flats went on precisely so in Cromwell's time.'[63] She liked manifestations of continuing community:

> The old whitehaired women sit on the doorstep till 9 or so, then go in; & the light is lit in the upper window & all is dark by ten o'clock . . . last night [going to look for Lottie, who was late back on her bicycle] I went on foot up to the cross roads; thus passing all the men coming back from the public house, & saying more 'Good nights' than in a week of daylight.[64]

> One of the charms of Rodmell is the human life; everyone does the same thing at the same hour: when the old vicar performs erratically on the bells, after churching the women, everybody hears him, & knows what he's up to. Everyone is in his, or their garden; lamps are lit, but people like the last daylight, which was brown purple last night, heavy with all this rain. What I mean is that we are a community.[65]

But more often she was aware of being outside the 'we' of community; as when she saw the wedding of a village carter as 'the heart of England – this wedding in the country: history I felt; . . . as if they represented the unconscious breathing of England & L. & I, leaning over the wall, were detached, unconnected.' (Was it because of their class or their profession that they felt European rather than English? 'Yet I am English in some way'.)[66]

The English country figures whom she would put into *Between the Acts* as villagers with 'names in the Domesday book', or as the old woman who 'never in all her fifty years had been over the hill, nor wanted to',[67] were beginning to vanish. Rodmell was a village in transition, and the sale of Monk's House to the 'detached, unconnected' Woolfs after the death of Old Verrall was part of that transition. She saw this clearly. The old vicar told her that 'thirty five years ago, there were 160 families living here where there are now no more than 80. It is a decaying village, which loses its boys to the towns. Not a boy of them, said the Rev. Mr Hawkesford, is being taught to plough. Rich people wanting weekend cottages buy up the old peasants houses, for fabulous sums.' He had been offered Monk's House for £400, but didn't want it; they had paid £700, and by 1927 could have sold it for £2,000.[68]

She and Leonard were, at least initially, incomers in rural England, who had bought their way in to traditions and landscapes about whose picturesqueness they then became proprietary. Their initial relationship to the village was as employers – as the Stephens had been at St Ives, thirty or forty years before. At first, when Nelly and Lottie did not come down with them, Mrs Dedman, or the carter's wife, Mrs Thomsett ('an old woman who has borne 11 children and has the sagacity of the whole world since the Flood in her')[69] came in to cook. Later, Annie, a Thomsett daughter, lived in one of the two village cottages they bought, and 'did' for them regularly; Louie Everest, a local girl, replaced her in 1934. Percy Bartholemew became Leonard's permanent gardener, housed in the other cottage. His wife Rose helped in the house. He and Leonard quarrelled over every single gardening decision: Virginia, watching them laying out a new bit of garden, called them Uncle Toby and Trim.[70]

Virginia admired and liked these Rodmell women. She did not sew stockings for their little boys or minister to the sick, as her mother would have done, but she was acutely conscious of rural working-class poverty. When the railwaymen went on strike (almost as soon as they moved into Monk's House, in the autumn of 1919) they offered their support to their local signalman and his wife.[71] When Annie Thomsett was being thrown out of her cottage, Virginia Woolf was appalled at the example of 'this terrific high black prison wall of poverty'.[72]

> If I were Mrs Bartholomew I should certainly do something violent . . .
> What though could one do, at the bottom of that weight, with that incubus of injustice on top of one? Annie Thompsett & her baby live on 15s. a week. I throw away 13s. on cigarettes, chocolates, & bus fares. She was eating rice pudding by the baby's cradle when I came in.[73]

Louie Everest remembered the difference her employment made to her standard of living: 'seven shillings and sixpence a week and a cottage rent-free was really a big wage.'[74]

In time they both, Leonard particularly, became more involved in the village lives around them. She liked this in Leonard, that he could talk to the postman 'about the League of Nations',[75] or that he helped the old carter make his Will,[76] or gave advice to a farm worker who wanted to get divorced.[77] What she could not bear was to be involved, or still worse identified with, the middle-class gentry who had moved into (or in some cases inherited) the better houses in the village, who wanted to expand their properties or build on empty land, and whose input into village life was gradually modernising – or suburbanising – it.

Though Virginia Woolf was accurate and prescient about this gentrification of rural England, she was also extremely snooty about it. She reserved her bitterest anathema for such figures as the rich Australian landowner J.M. Allison, who owned the field next to their house and threatened to sell it for building, and who got up cricket games with his friend Jack Squire, the editor of the *London Mercury*, the last person she wanted to meet in the country. She was scathing about them and about Squire's assistant editor Edward Shanks, who lived in the next cottage ('and one hears Mrs Shanks, over the wall, asking Shanks whether he'd like his cocktail mixed')[78] and who, after Mrs Shanks did a bolt with a German, had an affair with the rector's daughter. She wished them all gone: 'and the Woolves be left by themselves in chastity & glory.'[79] But such an ideal of total solitude (only half a joke) was, of course, the opposite of real life in an English village, then as now.

Though Leonard bought the field next to Monk's House in 1928, and preserved their immediate space, they had to watch the unstoppable eruption of building that took place all over Sussex in the 1930s. Neither of them could ever reconcile themselves to the violent alterations to 'their' landscapes, the Sussex they had known before the First World War. They made several efforts to buy up land when views and walks they knew were about to be destroyed; but 'Is it worth saving one crumb when all is threatened?'[80] Her rage against new buildings like 'Hancock's Horror', up on one of her favourite Downs walks, and her distaste for the 'suburban' ribbon villas being built at Peacehaven, was of a piece with her incurable condescension about Lewes and Rodmell 'society' – the sort of people she met at tea with the old rector's discontented genteel wife, who spent her life longing for Kensington:

> I dont think the intelligentzia need fear, either on earth or in Heaven, the competition of these simple natures – for stupidity, buttressing itself with all the conventions & prejudices is not nearly so humane as we free thinkers are.[81]

Not surprisingly, they aroused some animosity themselves in the village, particularly among the conservative Rodmellians suspicious of their Labour Party meetings. In 1938 she spoke of 'the village cabal against us'.[82]

They drew their social life at Rodmell from their visitors: friends from London, family from Charleston. But weekend guests could be an irritant. 'The truth is, I like it when people actually come; but I love it when they go.'[83] She often wanted them to go as soon as they had arrived, or began to enjoy herself just as they were leaving. And her visitors sometimes had reservations, too. Ecstatic thank-you letters (the most heartfelt from

Elizabeth Bowen, in the 1930s) should be set against Clive's wicked note on a reluctant visitor in 1925:

> I think the Woolfs are a little hurt at Lytton not having asked to stay with them during his Sussex tour. They put it down to an unfavourable notice of his play in the Nation; I rather to the fact that there is no bath at Monks House, no wine, and not very nice food.[84]

And against Forster's dissatisfaction as a guest in 1934:

> I was irritated at being left so much 'to myself' . . . Here are Ws, who read, Leonard the Observer, and Virginia the Sunday Times, and then retired to literary studies to write till lunch. At least L has just come out, but I, piqued, continue my letter to you [Isherwood] and he, most displeased, cuts the dead wood out of a Buddleia with a small rusty saw . . . Virginia has now . . . suggested a photograph should be taken of me. L thinks it a good idea, and continues to saw the buddleia. It is 5 minutes to one – no, one, the bell rings, and I must jolly well lock this letter up during lunch, or it'll get read.[85]

The main point of life at Monk's House, though, was not society, but space and seclusion, privacy and thought. Every morning they would work; every afternoon, in all weathers, she would walk with the dog, up on the Downs or along the river. Local people got used to the sight of her: in their eyes, an eccentric, solitary figure, shabbily dressed and talking to herself.[86] To the outside view there might not have been much to choose between her and the old woman who lived up at 'Mount Misery', who 'used to moon over the downs with a dog', and who drowned herself in 1938 when the tide was high in the Ouse.[87]

In letters and diaries, she made a narrative of this contemplative existence in her 'monk's' house. Coming to the end of *To the Lighthouse*, she writes:

> I am extremely happy walking on the downs . . . I like to have space to spread my mind out in. Whatever I think, I can rap out, suddenly to L. We are somehow very detached, free, harmonious. I don't in the least want to hurry up & finish the time here. I want to go to Seaford & walk back over the downs . . . to breathe in more light & air; to see more grey hollows & gold cornfields & the first ploughed land shining white, with the gulls flickering. No: I dont want anyone to come here & interrupt. I am immensely busy.[88]

Walking and looking and 'making up' ('I walk, nosing along, making up phrases'),[89] coming home and writing, seemed a seamless process: 'I slip easily from writing to reading with spaces between of walking – walking through the long grass in the meadows, or up the downs'.[90] The rhythm of walking gets into her sentences, the phrases she thinks of while looking and walking are saved and used. The landscape – 'the old habitual beauty of England'[91] – is entered raw and quickly into her private writings and recomposed in the fiction.[92] (So, during the same years in France, the painter Bonnard would walk through his landscape every day, make little pencil sketches, and then turn what he had seen into his own extraordinary colours.) Days and days of this could give her a kind of rapture; the love-letters she would write to Vita were never more sensuous and intense than when describing her walks, as here, in the winter of 1928:

> I have been walking alone down a valley to Rat Farm, if that means anything to you: and the quiet and the cold and the loveliness – one hare, the weald washed away to vapour – the downs blue green; the stacks, like cakes cut in half – I say all this so excited me; and my own life suddenly became so impressive to me, not as usual shooting meteor like through the sky, but solitary and still that, as I say – well how is the sentence to end?: figure to yourself that sentence, like the shooting star, extinct in an abyss, a dome, of blue; the colour of night: which, if dearest Vita you can follow, is now my condition: as I sit waiting for dinner, over the logs.[93]

Just as she brings this meteor-like rhapsody of a sentence home to a safe and solid conclusion by the fire-side, so these private moments of ecstasy depended on the settled habitual domestic life with Leonard. After Vita's passion and interest had shot through her life, that solid basis remained:

> Back from a good week end at Rodmell – a week end of no talking, sinking at once into deep safe book reading; & then sleep: clear transparent; with the may tree like a breaking wave outside; & all the garden green tunnels, mounds of green: & then to wake into the hot still day, & never a person to be seen, never an interruption: the place to ourselves: the long hours.[94]

Virginia and Julian Bell, 1910.

Clive Bell and Virginia on the beach at Studland, 1910.

ABOVE *Jacques Raverat.*
INSET *Virginia and Rupert Brooke, 1911.*
RIGHT *Roger Fry outside Durbins.*

LEFT *Fitzroy Square.*
ABOVE *Asheham.*

LEFT *Virginia in May, 1912.*
ABOVE *Virginia and Leonard Woolf, July 1912.*

Marie Woolf.

Virginia and Ka Cox at Asheham, 1914.

Leonard in Cornwall, 1916.

Virginia in 1916.

TOP LEFT *Monk's House*.
TOP RIGHT *Charleston*.
MIDDLE *Murals by Duncan Grant and Vanessa Bell for 52, Tavistock Square*.
ABOVE LEFT *The Woolfs' printing press*.
ABOVE RIGHT *Tavistock Square*.

TOP *Virginia Woolf reading by Duncan Grant,*
1918.
LEFT *Virginia Woolf by Duncan Grant, c.1918.*
ABOVE *Virginia Woolf in 1928 or 29 by Richard*
Kennedy, 1972.

Lytton Strachey and Virginia at Garsington, June 1923.

Morgan Forster and Leonard.

ABOVE Katherine Mansfield in 1916.
ABOVE RIGHT Vanessa, Clive and Duncan, c. 1918.
RIGHT Mary Hutchinson and Clive Bell, c. 1916.

ABOVE *Vita Sackville-West by Hoppé.*
BELOW *Virginia Woolf, studio portrait, 1925.*

Vita Sackville-West and Virginia at Monk's House,
1933.

Virginia, Quentin Bell, and Lydia Lopokova.　　　*Virginia in her mother's dress in* Vogue, *1926.*

Virginia at Monk's House, 1932.

TWENTY-FIVE

Post-war

She wrote this happiness down so carefully and persistently because it was fragile. When they first moved to Monk's House she was extremely depressed. The loss of Asheham and the disturbance of the move, the expectation of *Night and Day*'s publication in October 1919, the flourishing of the growing boys and the new baby at Charleston, all contributed. She had, as always, her sharp sense of intimate rivalry with Vanessa. While the rail strike was on, Virginia felt she was having her own 'private strike', numbly cut off from the 'vibration' which connected her to the world.[1] As the 'beaks' of her friends embedded themselves into the new book, she entered on a period of intense vicissitudes.[2] The mixed reactions to the novel excited and distracted her, and a wave of old emotions accompanied its publication. Vanessa responded to her tender, courtly dedication ('But, looking for a phrase, I found none to stand beside your name') by reading the novel as a reminder of their 'particular hell'[3] at Hyde Park Gate. Virginia demurred, but Hyde Park Gate was on her mind: to both Vanessa and Violet she wrote that she could not have 'survived to write' at all without them.[4] And two arguments with figures from the past called up old feelings. Madge Vaughan had a falling-out with Vanessa about renting Charleston for the spring because she had heard rumours about Angelica's parentage; Vanessa, with Virginia's support, haughtily spurned all interference in her private life.[5] Virginia's old mentors, Margaret Llewelyn Davies and Janet Case, also took a high moral line with her; Margaret told her, at tea at Hampstead, that they had decided her novels lacked heart and human sympathy.[6] An intense letter to Janet showed that this had gone deep. Possibly, she argued, the chilly effect of *Night and Day* was the result of 'the things one doesn't say', and of the 'form, which must sit tight'.[7] She was acutely aware of what she had left out in order to write the book at all. And she hated being accused of heartlessness.

At the end of 1919 and the start of 1920 she recorded, almost in the same breath, spasms of anxiety and rushes of confidence. On one day she could do no more than make 'marks' on the page.[8] Then the deep 'well of confidence' would bubble back up.[9] Her edgy reactions to the criticisms of *Night and*

Day, while she was rereading *The Voyage Out* for a second edition in February 1920, alternated with clear, urgent ideas about her future as a writer. Her discovery of a new form for her next novel on her thirty-eighth birthday, filling her with determination and hope ('immense possibilities', 'I've learned my business', 'there must be a path for me there') came in the middle of these 'vicissitudes'.

On the whole – though there were phases of illness and depression too – the confidence and energy was sustained through the writing of *Jacob's Room*, from the spring of 1920 to the summer of 1922. In April 1920, she started a new notebook with the heading 'Reflections upon beginning a work of fiction to be called, perhaps, Jacob's Room', and wrote under it: 'I think the main point is that it should be free.' The first piece of writing in the notebook was the experience of Jacob as a small boy, afraid on the beach, and then asleep in his seaside room. She gives him her first memories of St Ives. Then, when she comes to rewrite, she alters the passage to make it less autobiographical. To be 'free' meant to be structurally adventurous, less weighted down by tradition, shorter, more condensed and fragmentary. But it did not mean to be 'free' of inhibition. *Jacob's Room* is as full of Thoby Stephen as *The Voyage Out* is of Virginia's painful adolescence, and *Night and Day* is of her sister's character, her family past, and her decision to marry. But the formal experiments of the new book work hard to 'provide a wall for the book from oneself'. Any display of naked autobiography is carefully suppressed. 'The damned egotistical self' does battle with her tendency to dissolve into over-abstraction and aetheriality.

There was a dramatic mixture of confidence and self-consciousness in the other work of the early 1920s. She was doing many different kinds of writing now. The little sketches that kept pace with *Jacob's Room*, like 'The String Quartet' or 'Monday or Tuesday', pursued *Kew Gardens*'s success with intense, free-floating word pictures. The diary was growing 'a face of its own',[10] becoming increasingly fluent and rich. The Memoir Club, which Molly MacCarthy set up in March 1920 for their friends to regroup after the war (with the proviso that they should always tell the truth) concentrated her mind on biography and autobiography.[11] At the same time she was writing long masterful review pieces on writers' lives (George Eliot, Austen, Gissing, Horace Walpole, Sterne, Turgenev, Dostoevsky) and giving a great deal of attention to memoirs and 'lives of the obscure'.

Jacob's fictional biography aroused and composed her feelings about Thoby and her memories of Greece, pre-war London, Cambridge, and the early days of 'Bloomsbury': so it was itself a kind of memoir. It was her first novel centred on a young man's life, and its classical mythologising and Greek settings deliberately invoked late-Victorian Hellenism (so often a metaphor or a disguise for homosexuality) to reconstruct the education and the loving friendship of these young Edwardian Englishmen. Women – mothers, girlfriends, wives, students, debutantes, prostitutes, art-models – are placed in Jacob's room as furniture he overlooks or makes use of. The women's voices speak loudly but unheard at the edges of his story, like his mother's eloquent letter, lying unread on the hall table. A scene in the British Museum Round Reading Room sums up their exclusion from Jacob's story. Miss Julia Hedge, 'the feminist', is waiting for her books in the Reading Room, sitting near to Jacob. Next to him, Miss Marchmont's pile of books – random, disorderly – have toppled into Jacob's compartment. On Jacob's other side, Fraser, 'the atheist', reads on irritably, at his task of destroying religion. Jacob reads Marlowe, 'unmoved'. Julia Hedge reads the gilt names round the dome of the Reading Room: the final 'y' in Lord Macaulay's name has just been completed. ' "Oh damn", said Julia Hedge, "why didn't they leave room for an Eliot or a Brontë?" ' Her shoelaces are untied; she wets her pen, in bitterness, and must study statistics on working women. Later that night, Jacob reads on in his room, as 'imperturbable' as his Plato, while stone lies solid 'over the enormous mind' of the British Museum, and outside in the street a drunk woman 'cries all night long: "Let me in! Let me in!" '

Some of these characters would come back in different guises: Julia Hedge as Lily Briscoe, Mr Fraser as Charles Tansley, Miss Marchmont as Lucy Swithin. And their feelings about privilege, education and exclusion would be spelt out in her next 'room', *A Room of One's Own*, whose feminist narrative takes shape in the British Museum Reading Room. The story of Jacob was involved with her current thoughts about women's status[12] and about the construction of sexual difference, thoughts inextricable from her memories of Thoby. One section of the novel in manuscript (later taken out and published separately), 'A Woman's College From Outside', created a night-time fantasy of Newnham College, Cambridge. The girls are imagined, behind their names on their college doors, one thinking about her parents, some laughing and talking, one gazing out of the window feeling she has reached 'light at the end of the tunnel', a brave new world.[13] A 'vapour', or white mist, seems to issue from the rooms where the girls and their teachers slept. It anticipates the wind blowing through the garden of 'Fernham' college, or the 'extremely complex force of femininity which will issue from the rooms where women have lived' in *A Room of One's Own*, which also re-creates, in much more detail, a women's college *from the inside*: a place she herself had never lived in.

The reactions to *Night and Day*, especially Katherine's; the move from

Duckworth's to the Press, the publication of *Monday or Tuesday* in April 1921, the reviewing, and the work on *Jacob*, all intensified a preoccupation with reputation and with fame. Her feeling that she was now on the right path and in the right context for her work was accompanied by a desire to pull back from the market-place, to be more 'free'. A meeting with Lucy Clifford, the widow of an old friend of Leslie's, a woman in her sixties who earned her living as a hack writer, filled her with revulsion ('What an atmosphere of rancid cabbage & old clothes stewing in their old water!')[14] This was not what she wanted to be like in twenty years' time. 'Never write for publishers again anyhow.' She began to cut down on journalism (43 pieces in 1918, 45 in 1919, 31 in 1920, 14 in 1921, 5 in 1922. Then it picked up again.) But she was also extremely concerned with 'the psychology of fame'.[15] Like her father she disliked conversations about how none of them (except possibly Shaw) would be read in a hundred years' time.[16] But she found it hard to say simply: 'I'm to write what I like; & they're to say what they like.'[17] All this came to a head when *Monday or Tuesday* came out (badly printed by McDermott, with woodcuts by Vanessa), was scrappily reviewed, and turned down by the American publisher who had accepted the first two novels.[18] Meanwhile Lytton got three columns of praise in the *TLS* for *Queen Victoria*. A Leslie-like outburst followed: 'I'm a failure as a writer.'[19] How could she control the 'despicable' promptings of vanity, and calmly get at 'something which I want to write; my own point of view'? She told herself she should not mind if that 'point of view' meant low sales and a small, élitist reputation. But her jumpiness showed up in her decision to print, at the back of the first edition of *Jacob*, a collection of hostile (as well as good) reviews of her earlier books. It was a way of 'pulling the sting' of adverse criticism; but it looked defensive.[20]

The stress and concentration of this post-war period let her in for moments of extreme depression. The old feeling of life as a tragic 'strip of pavement over an abyss' could bring her down.[21] An event like the accidental death of a young man, who fell over the edge of the roof at a party at 50 Gordon Square, struck her forcibly.[22] In the summer of 1921 she was very unwell for about two months.[23] Afterwards she was fractious, moody and difficult. But these dark feelings were not just personal. She felt that 'life itself' was for her generation 'so tragic' ... 'Unhappiness is everywhere; just beyond the door.'[24] She shared this sense with one of the writers she now became intimate with, who also felt that their difficult adventurous work was being done 'under conditions that seem unpropitious'.[25]

'I was interrupted somewhere on this page by the arrival of Mr Eliot',

Virginia Woolf wrote in her diary at the end of the war.[26] Mr Eliot –'great Tom', 'the incredible Tom', 'Old Possum', 'dear old ass' as he would by slow stages become – seemed to her at their first meeting 'well expressed by his name': 'a polished, cultivated, elaborate young American'. She was thirty-six, he was thirty. She was all set to be condescending: to his youth of course, to his Americanness, to his literary enthusiasms. But it proved to be a formidable 'interruption', not one to be taken lightly.

When they met, with a view to publishing his poems, Eliot had been living in England since 1914. His marriage to Vivien Haigh-Wood, already in difficulties, was three years old. He had finished his thesis in 1916, and had since 1917 been working, from necessity, at Lloyds Bank, while acting as an editor on the *Egoist*. He was soon to start reviewing on the *TLS*, and he had made a mark with *Prufrock and other Observations*, published by the *Egoist* the year before. He was reserved, watchful, ambitious, arrogant, anxious, and very conscious of his potential and his distinction:

> There is a small and select public [he wrote to his mother in March 1919] which regards me as the best living critic, as well as the best living poet, in England . . . I really think that I have far more *influence* on English letters than any other American has ever had, unless it be Henry James. I know a great many people, but there are many more who would like to know me, and I can remain isolated and detached.[27]

Virginia Woolf immediately detected in him that will and power. She noted his slow, controlled speech, and the peculiar contradiction between his careful manner and his wildly glittering eyes, which seemed to 'escape from the rest of him'.[28] She could see that he wanted both to belong and to remain detached; she found him sinister, insidious, eel-like; also mono-lithic, masked, intensely reserved. They disagreed on literature immedi-ately: his enthusiasm for Pound and Joyce and Wyndham Lewis was the first contentious issue between them: 'Can't his culture carry him through,' she wrote to Roger Fry, 'or does culture land one there?'[29] Pound, whose work she hardly knew but 'hated',[30] was Eliot's great supporter; in a spat in 1920 between Wyndham Lewis and Clive Bell, Eliot would support Lewis, whom Virginia thought detestable. And he was not likely to be sympathetic to her feminism: 'I struggle to keep the writing [in the *Egoist*] as much as possible in Male hands, as I distrust the Feminine in literature', he wrote to his father in 1917.[31] His passion for *Ulysses*, which he admired 'immensely' (he never stopped trying to convince her that it was a great book)[32] was extremely challenging to her. She had to stop herself feeling outdone by the combination of Eliot's intellect and Joyce's epic boldness. She would not have put it so schematically to herself, but it was as if Eliot embodied for her (since she never met Pound or Lawrence or Lewis or Joyce) the male post-war version of modernism, with its egotistic anti-hero adrift in the modern world: Prufrock, Rupert Birkin, Mauberly, Stephen Dedalus. These powerful voices threatened to drown the delicate experimental structure she was now building around her own modern anti-hero in *Jacob's Room*.[33]

Eliot himself was impatient with the 'critical Brahminism' of the London intelligentsia 'which will not have Joyce'.[34] At the same time he was attracted to Bloomsbury and Garsington for 'their nonconformity within a culture to which they nevertheless firmly belonged'.[35] He half wished to belong, too. By the time he met the Woolfs he already knew the Morrells, Bertrand Russell, the wealthy arts patron Sydney Schiff, Herbert Read, Sibyl Colefax, and Mary Hutchinson (with whom he developed a much more tender and intimate friendship than he ever had with Virginia Woolf). Virginia was right to discern that socially, in England, Eliot was at once detached and insinuating, 'a resident alien' as he called himself. When she drew on her sense of him for the voice of Louis in *The Waves*, she emphasised this painful desire to belong and proud sense of not belonging.

Though he may not have appeared, at first, as a very promising candidate for intimacy, he was certainly a very promising candidate for the Press. By the end of November 1918 they had agreed to publish *Poems* (which included 'Sweeney among the Nightingales', 'Whispers of Immortality', 'The Hippopotamus', and 'Mr Eliot's Sunday Morning Service'), and they appeared in May 1919.[36] Virginia observed that the poems, formally brilliant, bristling with obscure sinister violence and disdainful irony, seemed to be fetched up out of 'the depths of silence'.[37]

This professional relationship was immediately vitiated by a 'Blooms-bury' imbroglio, arising from Clive's jealous intuition of a new powerful influence on Mary, and possibly also on Virginia. In the spring of 1919 there was a spate of 'telling'. Clive told Virginia that Tom Eliot had told Mary he didn't like her; Mary told Virginia it wasn't true; Virginia told Vanessa what Mary had told her; the Murrys told Virginia that Tom had told them how much he liked her. Certainly there was jealousy and dislike at this time between Mary and Virginia – 'these women's emotions',[38] Virginia said scathingly, though she felt them too – and Eliot had walked unknowingly into this tangle. As a result of all this, Virginia, to her own amusement, at once found him less pleasant and more intriguing. She determined to 'draw the rat from his hole'.[39] Vivien, already defensive and proprietary about Tom, wrote a wild letter to Mary saying she thought the Woolfs were holding up publication of *Poems* out of vengefulness. 'If a man is sensitive, and an artist, he can't stand these people . . . He hates and loathes all sordid quarreling and gossiping and intrigue and jealousy.'[40] But Eliot's own reaction seems to have been cooler and more quizzical. Standing half-in, half-out, of these plots, he gave a cunning, comic version of them to his cousin Eleanor Hinkley, and commented:

> Think of this sort of thing as going on continually in a society where everyone is very sensitive, very perceptive and very quick and you will see that a dinner party demands more skill and exercises one's psychological gifts more than the best fencing match or duel.[41]

It's as if Prufrock were watchfully picking his way in the room full of quick slippery voices. An odd sentence in Virginia's account of him a few months later confirms this image: 'If anyone asked him whether he meant what he said, he would have to say no, very often.' ('It is impossible to say just what I mean!')[42] She, by contrast, wanted to say what she meant. She preferred, and got into trouble for, speaking out, though when the mood or the need took her she could also lie, gush, flatter and fabricate. She would try to get Eliot to say what he meant, to say 'no' less often.

Eliot paid his first visit to Rodmell in September 1920 (Vivien had also been invited, but he came alone). He had been warned not to 'dress'. (The Woolfs told all their new weekend guests this, but it was especially necessary for Eliot, who usually came to dinner, as Virginia put it, wearing 'a four-piece suit').[43] They sent a pony trap to meet him off the Victoria to Lewes train on the Saturday; he spent one night and left on Sunday after dinner. He was still Mr Eliot after this visit, but she felt an advance in intimacy, and a powerful sense of challenge. She had been writing *Jacob* non-stop for two months, and was in the middle of Chapter Seven, Clara Durrant's party, a scene of fragmentary encounters, scraps of talk and quotation, glimpses of figures – a concentrated attempt to make the social event seem 'semi-transparent'. She was enjoying it enormously: it was her first go at the kind of scene she would often return to, from Mrs Dalloway's party to the pageant audience in *Between the Acts*. But immediately after Eliot's visit she stopped writing, and was thrown off her stride until the end of the month.

On the Saturday they talked socially, about Garsington and publishing and journalism and the 'aristocracy'. She was more impressed with him than Leonard was (who she felt showed up much better than she did in this encounter). Eliot's presence affected her strongly; she wrote, curiously, in her diary on the Sunday morning: 'Eliot is separated only by the floor from me. Nothing in mans or womans shape is any longer capable of upsetting me.'

On the Sunday he began to loosen up and 'laughed more openly'. They talked about his work (not about hers): about his admiration for *Ulysses*, yet his own desire to deal with 'externals' rather than 'internals' as Joyce did. He wanted to write caricature, drama, 'a verse play in which the 4 characters of Sweeney act the parts'. As soon as he had gone she felt overcome. All the things she was trying to do in Jacob, she thought, were being better done by Joyce. And perhaps too (though she doesn't say this) by Eliot himself: the fragmentary, theatrical voices, the shadowy figures, the sinister, vivid urban frieze, with the war behind, unseen.

A few months later, in March 1921, he came to dinner in Richmond and they went to the Lyric Theatre Hammersmith to see *Love for Love*, which she reviewed for the *New Statesman*, finding the production too 'demure' for the 'wildness and rashness and rakishness' of Congreve.[44] (Leonard sat upstairs with the *New Statesman* ticket while they sat in the pit.) Virginia and Tom missed their train from Richmond and had to take a taxi together to the theatre. As they rode together through 'dark market gardens', their conversation became intimate, voices speaking out of the dark interior:

> 'Missing trains is awful' I said. 'Yes. But humiliation is the worst thing in life' he replied. 'Are you as full of vices as I am?' I demanded. 'Full. Riddled with them.' 'We're not as good as Keats'[45] I said. 'Yes we are' he replied. 'No; we dont write classics straight off as magnanimous people do.' 'We're trying something harder' he said. 'Anyhow our work is streaked with badness' I said. 'Compared with theirs, mine is futile. Negligible. One goes on because of an illusion.' He told me that I talked like that without meaning it. Yet I do mean it.[46]

'I do mean it'; as opposed to 'If anyone asked him whether he meant what he said, he would have to say no'. This is a truthful conversation between equals, though also between opposites – Eliot fearful of humiliation, Woolf prepared to be humbled; Eliot cloaked, Woolf open – but both motivated by a formidable sense that they needed to 'try something harder'. Could they, with their 'damned self-conscious susceptibility', become intimate, she now wondered? 'But I plunge more than he does; perhaps I could learn him [*sic*] to be a frog.' A frog, a rat, an eel: not an inviting choice of intimates, and not a creature who could ever be quite fitted into her menagerie. At the play, though, she noticed that he was able, as she was not, to 'laugh out'.

That summer of 1921 when she was ill, Tom Eliot's health also broke down (Vivien, too, was chronically unwell). He stopped work, and went to Margate and to Lausanne. When they met again in Rodmell in September she found, rather to her disappointment, that she was no longer 'afraid of him'.[47] The next summer, June 1922, he came to Hogarth House for dinner on a Sunday (by then she was in the middle of copying out *Jacob's Room*) and read them his new poem:

> He sang it & chanted it rhythmed it. It has great beauty & force of phrase: symmetry; & tensity. What connects it together, I'm not so sure . . . One was left, however, with some strong emotion. The Waste Land, it is called; & Mary Hutch, who has heard it more quietly, interprets it to be Tom's autobiography – a melancholy one.[48]

These three meetings – the conversation about his verse drama at Rodmell, the visit to the play, the reading of *The Waste Land* – all had to do with performances. And it was as an actor that he most impressed her. His face was closed to her, emitting signals of anxiety and repression: 'A mouth twisted & shut; not a single line free & easy; all caught, pressed, inhibited; but great driving power some where – & my word what concentration of the eye when he argues!'[49] Even after years of knowing him, he would still present to her a 'great yellow bronze mask all draped upon an iron framework. An inhibited, nerve drawn; dropped face – as if hung on a scaffold of heavy private brooding; & thought. A very serious face & broken by the flicker of relief, when other people interrupt.'[50]

In over twenty years of friendship there was always some distrust. They hardly ever broke through to the intimacy of that dark taxi ride. She was never cosy with Tom: when he came for a weekend with Morgan Forster in 1922 she noticed how Morgan 'snuggled in' after Tom had left.[51] In her lists of adjectives for him ('sardonic, guarded, precise, & slightly malevolent')[52] she used the word 'suspicious' both for her feelings towards him and for his manner.[53] What was she suspicious of? Vanity, ruthlessness, egotism. And something weird, too, revealed at a time of terrible strain in his life, when Eliot's strangeness flashed through. She noticed on occasion, as others did, that he was wearing make-up.[54] One night in December 1923 they went to a small party he gave, and he was completely drunk – white, slurred, throwing up. He rang the next day apologising horribly. ('Humiliation is the worst thing in life.') She found a sort of comic gruesomeness about him. She felt this when she sat next to him at the Group Theatre production of *Sweeney Agonistes* in 1934. She was acutely aware then of the 'atmosphere' he conveyed: 'something peculiar to himself; sordid, emotional, intense – a kind of Crippen, in a mask'.[55] Acutely, perhaps (given Eliot's married life, and his obsession with the famous wife-murderer Crippen, whom he once chose to dress as at a costume party) she made no distinction here between Tom and his play.

But she couldn't just laugh at Eliot's strangeness. He weighed on her too, and whenever she met him she had to remind herself not to be intimidated by him, not to be 'knocked off my perch'.[56] If in conversation she 'loosed' a figure of speech, Eliot would pounce on it and utterly destroy it.[57] She found him severe, unflattering. Though she had made so much of his youth when they first met, he brought out her daughterly tendency to supplicate or give way before a 'great man'. They tended to talk about *his* writing: she couldn't move 'the heavy stone of his self-esteem' enough to be able to talk about hers.[58] Yet she was aware that behind the mask, under the stone, there was a 'good heart'.[59] She saw that he liked to be teased.[60] And increasingly in the 1930s, as he became freer and happier and more humorous in his letters, she could think of him (although she couldn't begin to understand his religious conversion) with more affection: 'When you are thrown like an assegai into the hide of the world – this may be a definition of genius – there you stick; & Tom sticks. To shut out, to concentrate – that is perhaps – perhaps – one of the necessary conditions.'[61]

Their relationship was complicated, though, by their professional links. In the 1920s, her work and his overlapped within the world of small magazines and new publishing houses, and through what Eliot called, with as mixed feelings as her own, the 'huge journalistic organism' of modern society.[62] They were, almost, colleagues. This was bound to lead to trouble.

Eliot's involvement with the Hogarth Press began well (after Vivien's suspicions over *Poems*). He didn't give them his next two books,[63] but they were the first publishers of *The Waste Land* in book form,[64] and Eliot was pleased with the results. (He blamed the typos on his own abominable proof-reading: in this edition of the poem, a crowd flowed under, not over, London Bridge.)[65]

In between publishing *Poems* and *The Waste Land*, Virginia sent Eliot a story for *The Criterion* ('In the Orchard', a mood piece of a young girl's day-dream written to resemble a post-impressionist painting), asking him to be 'sincere, and severe' as 'I can never tell whether I'm good or bad'.[66] He printed this, and when he took it he made some respectful and perceptive comments to her on *Jacob's Room*:

> You have freed yourself from any compromise between the traditional novel and your original gift. It seems to me that you have bridged a certain gap which existed between your other novels and the experimental prose of *Monday or Tuesday* and that you have made a remarkable success.[67]

But a year later (while they were setting *The Waste Land*) he did not take the more substantial story she sent him, 'Mrs Dalloway in Bond Street'. Instead it appeared in America in *The Dial*. She said nothing about this rejection when she described, in July of 1923, a difficult tea with him and Vivien.[68] But at the time when he told her, equivocally, in May 1924, that he was 'struggling' with *Jacob's Room* for a piece on contemporary fiction for the *Nouvelle Revue Française* ('you do not make it easy for critics')[69] she was again feeling suspicious of him.[70] They went to a performance of *Lear* and 'jeered' at it together; then he wrote a piece in *The Criterion* attacking 'those who jeer & despise'. 'Then what does he mean by what he says? God knows.' But a few weeks later he did seem to mean what he said about her work. In July 1924 she sent him 'Character in Fiction' (he offered her a special rate of £20 for 5,000 words) and he responded with a continuation of their conversation in the taxi three years before, claiming the literary kinship of orphans. The essay, he said, was 'a most important piece of historical criticism':

> It also expresses for me what I have always been very sensible of, the absence of any masters in the previous generation whose work one could carry on, and the amount of waste that goes on in one's own work in the necessity, so to speak, of building one's own house before one can start the business of living. I feel myself that everything I have done consists simply of tentative sketches and rough experiments. Will the next generation profit by our labours?[71]

She wrote at once to thank him.[72] That autumn, when the Press launched its first series of 'Hogarth Essays', hers (now called 'Mr Bennett and Mrs Brown') was published with Eliot's essays on Dryden, Marvell, and the Metaphysical Poets. She probably felt anxious about the conjunction of their two pamphlets, hers so discursive, personal and anecdotal, his so impersonal and authoritative. But he was very sympathetic towards her as a fellow-author:

> One exists most of the time in morose discontent with the sort of work that one does oneself, and wastes vain envy on all others: the worst of it is that nobody will believe one. But no one regrets more that these moods should occur to Mrs Woolf (of all people) than Yr devoted servt. Thos. Eliot.[73]

The balance on their books between credit and debt was complicated by her role as Eliot's would-be benefactor. Virginia had not been involved before in this sort of private fund-raising[74] and she seems to have handled the business, which involved an elaborate dance of 'fine feelings'[75] and some extremely wilful participants, with as much patience, skill and efficiency as the situation would allow.

Ezra Pound, with his unreliable and difficult friend Richard Aldington, had started the 'Bel Esprit' fund in 1920 to rescue Eliot from the toils of the bank for full-time literary work. In July 1922, Ottoline set up 'a complementary scheme', the Eliot Fellowship Fund.[76] Virginia undertook to approach people with money who would give £10 a year. 'It is a great effort,' she told Ottoline, 'and leaves one humiliated.'[77] Eliot, in response, was embarrassed and ambivalent, telling Ottoline he could have nothing to do with it ('Sometimes I simply want to escape from the whole thing and run away')[78] and telling Virginia that he could only leave the bank if he had a sum of £500 a year assured him for life. Meanwhile Ottoline produced a circular, without consulting the rest of her committee, asking for a target of £300 a year for five years. 'An appalling shindy', Virginia described it to Roger Fry: 'Tom's psychology fascinates and astounds . . . why twist and anguish and almost suffocate with humiliation at the mere mention of money? Its on a par with not pump shipping [Bloomsbury's euphemism for peeing] before your wife.'[79]

Much gleeful mockery ensued, of course. Clive told Mary that Charleston had 'formed a league against subscribing to the Tom sustentation fund,'[80] and Virginia received one excellent parody in response to the circular:

> It has been known for some time to Mr Lytton Strachey's friends that his income is in excess of his expenditure, and that he has a large balance at the bank. It is impossible, if his royalties continue to accumulate at the present rate, that he should be in a position to spend them entirely upon himself, without serious injury to his reputation among his more impecunious acquaintances.[81]

Presumably she found this funny, but the fund stirred up the competitive issue of how much money they all had. It never raised more than a hundred pounds or so, and gradually petered out.[82]

Early in 1923, when Maynard Keynes was buying the *Nation*,[83] Virginia made one other effort to help 'poor Tom', to a job as the literary editor, taking considerable time to write efficient letters on his behalf.[84] But again she ran up against Eliot's 'peevish, plaintive, egotistical' indecision: 'He elaborates & complicates, makes one feel that he dreads life as a cat dreads water.' She was aware that she might be allowing herself some of the 'vile & patronising feelings of the benefactor' – and she didn't know that Vivien was strongly resisting the idea of a move from the bank to the paper. But she became, understandably, impatient: 'He seemed "distraught" . . . Whether distraught people can edit the Nation lit. sup. I doubt.'[85] In the end Eliot backed off, and in March the job was offered to Leonard instead. 'Well,' she said to herself ruefully, 'thats unexpected!'[86]

With Leonard at the *Nation* and Virginia as his frequent contributor, and with the Press expanding at the same time, the Woolfs settled, as a couple, into the centre of the London literary network. Virginia's relationships were greatly entangled in this: Katherine couldn't be separated from Murry at the *Athenaeum* and the *Adelphi*; Desmond MacCarthy, as 'Affable Hawk' at the *New Statesman*, was an opponent as well as a friend; Maynard was now Leonard's employer; Vita would be the Press's best-selling author. The painters had limited appetites for these endless literary conspiracies; one can feel for Vanessa's letter to Roger Fry in 1923:

> Talked a great deal about the Nation. It seems to me like a drug. Everyone reads it and discusses it in and out and theres always a lot of gossip about each article or review – one is quite out of it if one hasnt seen it for some weeks as I generally havent. But it really bores me stiff, all this talk about writing no one can possibly remember in a years time or less.[87]

At *The Criterion*, Eliot now played the game of a fellow-sufferer in matters of literary editing ('But seriously, Virginia, how tired I am of being supposed to edit the *Criterion*, how tired of the very word *Criterion*!'). When he was threatened with 'dismemberment' ('like a hero of a Grecian tragedy (rather than a bungalow bride)') for letting Wyndham Lewis have his head, he jokingly blamed her: 'For you are my oracle and counsel in matters journalistic, and did you not advise me . . . that it was in pursuance of the best tradition of British journalism to let one contributor say what he likes about another?'[88]

This style of playful flattery was more difficult to sustain when Eliot (finally) left the bank in 1925 to join the new publishing house of Faber & Gwyer, and became a competitor to the Hogarth Press. He was careful to deny rivalry ('and I dont think it is at all likely . . . judging from our list – unless you go in for Nursing and Indian Education').[89] But he 'poached' Herbert Read (whose first two books the Press had published), and he reprinted *The Waste Land* (which they had wanted to reissue) in his *Poems 1909–1925*, without warning them. 'The queer shifty creature',[90] they called him now. It was an awkward time for Virginia to be sending him, for the *Criterion*, her essay 'On Being Ill'. The mock-formal letter she sent with the essay, addressed to 'Dear Sir', was not entirely a joke.[91] Unfortunately Eliot seemed to have forgotten he had offered her a special rate, and was less than enthusiastic about the essay.[92] Immediately she 'saw wordiness, feebleness, & all the vices in it', and was made afraid of starting her new novel, *To the Lighthouse*: 'I know so little of my own powers. Here is another rat run to earth', she concluded strangely. She meant a rat of her own hidden feelings; but the 'rat' was also one of her images for Eliot ('I think we are in rat's alley . . .') He scrabbled at her confidence. 'On Being Ill' was more personally revealing than she usually allowed her essays to be. And Eliot preferred impersonality: 'I like to feel that a writer is perfectly cool and detached, regarding other people's feelings or his own, like a God who has got beyond them.'[93]

Eliot's opposite in this matter of reserve and impersonality was, notoriously, his wife, who ended a letter in 1921 to Eliot's brother: '*Be personal*, you must be personal, or else its no good. Nothing's any good.'[94] Vivien's outbursts exposed Eliot to all the humiliations he most feared. Mightn't Virginia Woolf have found some appeal in Vivien Eliot's reckless self-exposure? Might she even, as the inside story of the marriage began to be apparent to her, have thought of this ill and wretchedly unhappy woman as a victim rather than as a burden? No, the reverse was the case. Virginia's rare encounters with Vivien filled her with horror and revulsion. 'Mrs Eliot' made me 'almost vomit, so scented, so powdered, so egotistic, so morbid, so weakly'.[95] Perhaps there was a trace of fellow-feeling at first, when they had tea in the summer of 1923, and Vivien resisted Tom's command to put brandy in her tea: 'One doesnt like taking medicine before one's friends', Virginia said, kindly.[96] But in 1925 Vivien fell into a 'fearful abyss' of illness and Tom Eliot became desperate, on the verge of breakdown himself.[97] Ottoline had recommended a German doctor who specialised in starvation diets, bee-sting injections, and quasi-mystical analysis sessions.[98] Eliot was taken with him at first, and recommended him to Virginia. Her response to his account of this Doctor Marten (whom Eliot soon thought so damaging to Vivien that he wanted to sue him) was extremely sceptical:

> Martin the dr. set V. off thinking of her childhood terror of loneliness, & now she cant let him, Tom, out of her sight. There he has sat mewed in her room these 3 months, poor pale creature, or if he has to go out, comes in to find her in a half fainting state.[99]

It is Tom, not Vivien, who is the 'poor pale creature'. She felt so much sympathy for him that she laid her arm on his shoulder: 'not a very passionate caress, but the best I can do.' At this meeting, they all discussed who would be the right doctor for Vivien. Did Virginia know that Tom was writing frequently at this time to Leonard asking for advice? Probably. But she herself resisted any idea that she and Vivien might be thought of as analogous cases, as they are in this correspondence between the two husbands.

> She wants to begin writing again [Eliot wrote to Leonard]: do you think I should encourage this or not, and if so, should she try to write a letter each day or in spells. Should you say that it is good or bad for her to write yet?[100]

> As to the writing [Leonard replied], the difficulty is that it all depends on what is the actual cause of the nervous disturbance. I am convinced myself that, if the real cause is nerve exhaustion, anything which excites or tires the brain is therefore bad and that therefore writing is bad. In these cases you must begin with food and rest which alone begin to produce stability. When the stability begins, then a little work like writing is good, but only at first in minute quantities. When Virginia was recovering from acute nerve exhaustion, she began by limiting her writing strictly to half an hour a day, and only increased it when, after months, she was convinced that she would stand the strain of more. [He added, as though marking the difference between Virginia and Vivien]: Virginia would like to give Vivien a copy of *The Common Reader*, but does not like to do so unless you think that it would be right to do so.[101]

Eliot replied:

> Vivien was (as I mentioned) never trained in regular habits of study. She is naturally immoderate. When she gets an idea she wants to work it out at once. If she postpones *writing*, the idea goes on fermenting in her brain, so that often it has *seemed* better to let her write . . . Would you begin by limiting and regulating her times of writing – or at the other end? Yours gratefully TSE. *Of course* V. would be delighted and flattered to have *The Common Reader*, and would certainly read it! though *slowly*, at present.[102]

As the married life of the Eliots disintegrated, Virginia saw it as 'a vision of misery' for Eliot.[103] She gave a violently vivid account (in her diary and in a letter to Vanessa) of her last sightings of them together, in 1930 and 1932, which have powerfully affected all the versions of the Eliot story.[104] So appalled was she by Vivien's presence that she refused to invite them together again.[105]

> But oh – Vivienne! Was there ever such a torture since life began! – to bear her on ones shoulders, biting, wriggling, raving, scratching, unwholesome, powdered, insane, yet sane to the point of insanity,

reading his letters, thrusting herself on us, coming in wavering trembling
– Does your dog do that to frighten me? Have you visitors? Yes we have
moved again. Tell me, Mrs Woolf, why do we move so often? Is it
accident? Thats what I want to know (all this suspiciously, cryptically,
taking hidden meanings.) Have some honey, made by our bees, I say.
Have you any bees? (& as I say it, I know I am awakening suspicion.) Not
bees. Hornets. But where? Under the bed. And so on, until worn out with
half an hour of it, we gladly see them go. Vivienne remarked that I had
made a signal that they should go. This bag of ferrets is what Tom wears
round his neck.[106]

Virginia understood 'suspicion' very well: the passage makes a frighteningly
close reading of paranoia. (And it echoed a remark she made about herself in
the summer of 1921: 'A wife like I am should have a label to her cage: She
bites!')[107] But it also distanced Vivien by identifying her with all those
biting, stinging animals. When Tom at last decided to throw off his 'bag of
ferrets' in 1933, Virginia was intrigued but unmoved: 'It was a most
interesting process, to one who loves the smell of the rubbish heap as I do, to
watch.'[108] She noted Tom's recovered boyishness after the separation: 'he is
10 years younger: hard, spry, a glorified boy scout in shorts & yellow shirt.
He is enjoying himself very much.'[109] Vivien's fate moved her only a little.
'Yes, Vivienne seems to have gone crazy poor woman,' she wrote to
Elizabeth Bowen (who knew them all by then) in July 1933.[110] But a few days
later she was telling Quentin Bell jokingly that Vivien was on the war path
with a carving knife to skin first Tom, and then her and Ottoline, whom she
believed to be Tom's mistresses. 'As I never had a favour from that man its
rather hard to give my life on the pavement.'[111] Yet Vivien, for all her
suspicions, had registered a possible ally in Virginia Woolf, and made one
appeal to her, before she disappeared into life-long incarceration – the very
fate which Leonard had protected Virginia from in 1913. 'This morning I
had a remarkable letter', Virginia told Ottoline in December 1933, 'from
Vivien Haigh Eliot. Happily she doesn't ask me to do anything. She merely
says that Tom refuses to come back to her, and that it is a great tragedy – so I
suppose I can agree and say no more. She has made Leonard her executor,
but writes sensibly – rather severely, and with some dignity poor woman,
believing, she says, that I respect marriage.'[112]

While Eliot was freeing himself from his marriage, his letters became freer
and more playful, more able to 'laugh out'. As famous writers in the 1930s
Tom and Virginia settled into a teasing friendly affability. Adapting his
manner to his correspondent's needs and character, as he always did, Eliot
sent her funny rhyming thank-yous, satires on America, literary pastiches

(like a wonderful paraphrase of a typical Ibsen play), flattering jokes about the difficulties of writing to her and the difference in their reputations. They are his skilful calling cards to the upper-middle-classes with whom he now so immaculately belonged. And they also read as genuinely affectionate entertainments.

I wish that I might have Seen the Old Year Out with you at Rodmell. As a matter of fact, I wasnt asked to. If I had been, I should have brought a bottle of Champagne, and sung one of my songs, viz.:

> I don't want any Wurzburger –
> I'd sooner drink gasoline.
> I don't care to tarnish
> My throat with such varnish:
> It's allright to oil up a sewing-machine.
> I don't care for Budweiser,
> And Anhauser-Busch I decline;
> The platform I stand on
> Is Moet & Chandon –
> The bubbles that blow off the troubles for mine!

There is another song for the occasion called 'The Miner's Dream of Home'; but I dont remember the words, but the Miner was in Australia, in a red shirt and a widebrimmed hat, and

> the bells
>   were ringing
>   the Old Year OUT
> and the
>   New
>   Year
>   IN.

The bells were in England, of course, and he heard them in imagination, you could tell that from his eye.[113]

You see, I am more terrified of writing to Mrs Woolf than to anybody, because her standard of letter writing is so high – one feels that a letter to Mrs Woolf should compare favourably to, let us say, a letter from Gibbon to Mme du Deffand. But, I, alas, am not so important as Gibbon; and you, alas, are more important than Mme du Deffand.[114]

> Among the various Middle Classes
> (Who live on treacle and molasses)
> A custom has (for want of better)
> Been called the Bread & Butter Letter.
> But Mrs Woolf would not rejoice
> In anything that's so bourgeoise,

So what can poor Old Possum do,
Who's upper-middle through and through?
For centuries and centuries
And under President or King,
He's always told the proper lies
And always done the proper thing.
Still growing longer in the tooth,
He sometimes yearns to speak the truth,
And would express his gratitude
For conversation, bed and food,
And quiet walks on downs and knolls,
And Sunday morning game of bowls.
Whoever gives him their approval –
He only hopes that Mrs Woolf'll.[115]

In the ruins of time, it may be that posterity – or the posterity of some foreign race – will make various conjectures as to the identity of the T S Eliot whose name is associated with the works of Old Possum; and perhaps (the Memoirs of Ottoline having by that time become wholly undecipherable to the most expert paleographers, happily enough), it will be only some passing reference in the journals and correspondence of Mrs Woolf that will lead to the inference that he was the author of a considerable body of writings, some of which enjoyed a limited popularity at that time. Your OP.[116]

Possum now wishes to explain his silence
And to apologise (as only right is);
He had an attack of poisoning of some violence;
Followed presently by some days in bed with laryngitis.
Yesterday he had to get up and dress –
His voice very thick and his head feeling tetrahedral,
To go and meet the Lord Mayor & Lady Mayoress
At a meeting which had something to do with repairs to
                                         Southwark Cathedral.
His legs are not yet ready for much strain & stress
And his words continue to come thick and soupy all;
These are afflictions tending to depress
Even the most ebullient marsupial.
But he would like to come to tea
One day next week (not a Wednesday)
If that can be arranged
And to finish off this letter
Hopes that you are no worse and that Leonard is much
better.[117]

'Neither of them really understood or appreciated the other's writing', Peter Ackroyd decided in his biography of Eliot.[118] Eliot seems, as an editor, to have preferred her essays to her novels, and there is no evidence that he minded what *she* thought of *him*. And though *The Waste Land* made a great impression on her, his religious conversion left her cold.[119] She disliked the work which came after it: *Murder in the Cathedral* in 1935 was 'the pale New England morality murder',[120] *The Family Reunion* was (she was pleased to find, in 1939) a failure, 'no free lyricism . . . nothing grips: all mist'.[121] Yet still his power was a threat to her: still, in December 1940, when Desmond praised *East Coker*, she had to walk out over the marshes telling herself: 'I am I; & must follow that furrow, not copy another.'[122]

When Eliot wrote her obituary in May 1941, Herbert Read was 'shocked by the chilly detachment' of it.[123] Eliot wrote, tortuously, that he felt 'neither regret that an author's work has come to an end nor desolation at the loss of a friend, for the former emotion can be expressed, and the latter one keeps to oneself; but the loss of something both more profound and more extensive, a change to the world which is also a damage to oneself.' He identified her death, in wartime, as the end of 'a whole pattern of culture' of which she was both the symbol and the mainstay.[124] This is formal, but surely not 'chilly'. In private, in a letter to his friend John Hayward, he said that he had not known her work very well, but that his interest in her was 'almost entirely personal'. She had been, he said, 'a kind of pin' which had held people together. He spoke of feeling towards her 'like a member of his family – "at ease with her" – but without that "gene" one feels with one's own family.'[125]

There was distance, conflict, detachment, in this friendship between two of the most influential writers of their generation. But there was 'ease', humour, even silliness too, as this letter of 1927 shows:

I am free for tea on Wednesday or Thursday or for dinner on Wednesday. And if any of those times suited you I should be very glad to show you what little I know about the Grizzly Bear, or the Chicken Strut. I should not dare to bring you any more records without being sure that you have not got them already, but have you got The Memphis Shake? Ever yours affectionately, TSE.[126]

We can allow ourselves this 1920s picture of Virginia Woolf and T.S. Eliot, dancing the Chicken Strut or the Memphis Shake together, with Leonard, pehaps, winding up the gramophone, after tea on a June afternoon.

TWENTY-SIX

Party-Going

In August of 1922, a patchy, cold summer, Virginia Woolf was tussling with 'the exacting claims of egoism'.[1] She was 'wedged' into her work, but there were many interruptions.[2] She felt she was always caught between her interior life as a writer, when at her best she was potent and alive, 'washed by the flood . . . of my own thoughts', and the 'scattered & various & gregarious' identity she had with other people. The lure of solitude, anonymity, countryside, reading, creating, pulled against the desire for fame, society, money, gossip, parties, and involvements. There was no resolution to this conflict. She was forty. It was (Leonard had to remind her) the tenth anniversary of their marriage.[3] It was the fifth anniversary of the Press, now larger and growing more problematic. It was also, never to be forgotten, 'unsmothered by the succeeding years', the twenty-fifth anniversary of Stella and Jack's engagement.[4] It was the summer she began her correspondence with Jacques Raverat, who was dying slowly of disseminated sclerosis, and to whom, over the next three years, she would give one of her most intimate accounts of her life and her work. She was finishing *Jacob's Room*. Leonard read it, and told her he thought it a very interesting and beautiful ghost story and a work of genius.[5] She was writing the first of the Mrs Dalloway stories, which was about to 'usher in a host of others'[6] and which in October, when *Jacob* was published, would turn into a book. She was beginning her 'reading with a purpose' for *The Common Reader*.[7] And she had just heard that the writer 'V. Sackville-West' – 'Mrs Nicolson' – admired her work and wanted to meet her.[8]

She had also been adjusting to the possibility that she might not have much longer to live. She had been very unwell, with all the old symptoms, including even hallucinations, for most of the summer of 1921, and had thought for the first time about making her will.[9] In the bitterly cold spring of 1922, she had had the 'flu, and the GP Dr Fergusson had told her that her pulse was 'insane' and that 'the rhythm of her heart was wrong'.[10] He referred her to a Wimpole Street heart specialist, Dr Sainsbury, who told them she had a heart murmur and must rest and not travel. Eight years later (and with a perfectly sound heart) she recalled 'the agony' produced by these 'entirely false verdicts': 'Once (having a temperature) I was told that my right lung was diseased; then that my heart was inflamed, and L. and I walked away prepared (so the man said) for death in a fortnight.'[11] Vanessa reported to Roger that it sounded as if 'she was going to have to be very careful for a long time'.[12] Her temperature remained high, and in May there followed that pointless drawing of three teeth[13] and more disagreement among the doctors. 'Equanimity – practise equanimity Mrs Woolf', murmured Dr Sainsbury, taking his three guineas, after a 'semi-legal discussion on my body'[14] when it was decided she didn't have consumption but 'pneumonia microbes in the throat'.[15] She seemed to be able to: Clive told Mary that Virginia was taking her visit to the doctor 'very calmly'.[16] But this encounter got into her savage attack on the profession in *Mrs Dalloway*: 'Exasperation should be the dominant theme at the Drs.', she told herself in her notes for Septimus.[17] The novel, which she began to plan in October 1922, was powerfully affected by this brush with mortality. 'Suppose the idea of the book is the contrast between life & death', she noted in November.[18] There would be no more novels centred entirely on a single youthful character or placed entirely in a pre-war world. From now on she would deal more with middle age and growing old, with whole life-spans or histories.

Had she died now, in 1922, as Katherine was to die in 1923, would she have 'beaten' Katherine in her afterlife? Probably not. She would have been remembered as a confident and imaginative essayist, an interesting commentator on the modern movement in fiction, an idiosyncratic feminist thinker, a gifted writer of unusual short sketches, the author of two novels on late-Victorian women's lives, one ambitious and patchy, the other more conventional-seeming, and of one experimental post-war novel: a small but significant posthumous reputation. The work which made her name was to come, now, in an intense rush, one book overlapping with the next, several books coming at once.[19] The writing reflected her acute sense of the pressure of time, and of adult freedom.

Only now did she feel she could really do what she wanted. The diary is full of statements about arrival. 'There's no doubt in my mind that I have found out how to begin (at 40) to say something in my own voice.'[20] 'At forty, I am beginning to learn the mechanism of my own brain.'[21] She was determined not to be drowned by the 'splash' of the reception of *Jacob* in the autumn. She struggled with her uncomfortably obsessional responses to criticism – responses linked to her horror of being laughed at or looked at, her resistance to being put right or put down, especially by men, and her desire to be loved and admired, especially by women; above all perhaps to her fear of being thought mad. Adrian, now undergoing a painful psychoanalysis which she refused take seriously,[22] would have told her that these emotions had their roots in her childhood. But, just as she fought to put her illness to good use (especially in this next novel), so she needed to master these infantile emotions.

She would never not 'mind'. 'Why did one mind what he said', Lily Briscoe thinks to herself of the male chauvinist who has said that women can't paint or write, in the manuscript of *To the Lighthouse*.[23] 'I doubt that I mind very much,' Virginia Woolf said to herself, painfully anticipating the publication of *A Room of One's Own* and the possible attacks on her as a 'feminist' and a Sapphist. ('Minding' is the subject of *A Room of One's Own*, in both senses: women writers minding about being kept out and kept down; women writers finding a mind of their own.) As she began to be better known, with the publication of *Jacob*, she set out to 'make out some rule about praise & blame'.[24] She urged herself not to be forever 'totting up compliments, & comparing reviews'.[25] If her friends praised the novel (and they did) that had to make up for the mixed critical reception. She resigned herself to the fact that it was 'too experimental' to be generally acclaimed or to sell widely.[26] But the criticisms she took deeply to heart (Arnold Bennett saying that she 'couldn't create characters that survive', Murry saying she was one of the new writers who neglected plot or story and had 'brought the novel to an impasse')[27] could be profited from. She would try to incorporate them usefully into her work, as she had incorporated the bad reviews into the back of *Jacob's Room*. That determination made *Mrs Dalloway* a deeper, richer book. And its strong design and adventurousness showed that she had convinced herself she did not need to 'mind' what was said. 'Certainly I'm less coerced than I've yet been', she noted after a year of writing[28] – using the same word for literary pressures as she often did for the treatment of madness. Six months later, at the top of her second manuscript book for *Mrs Dalloway*, she wrote, in brackets: 'A delicious idea comes to me that I will write anything I want to write.'[29]

As if she had been getting ready for it for ten years, she now felt able to write 'the world seen by the sane & the insane, side by side'.[30] 'Sanity & insanity,' she wrote in her first notes for the novel. 'Mrs D. seeing the truth. SS seeing the insane truth.'[31] It was brave, and it rocked and jolted her terrifyingly. In the summer and autumn of 1923, she was writing the mad scene in Regent's Park. Septimus, she wrote in her notebook, was 'falling through into discoveries – like a trapdoor opening'.[32] She felt her mind 'squint' or 'squirt' as she fell into 'the mad part'.[33] In September and October she was writing Septimus's voices, the birds' Greek song, Evans's appearance, Septimus's dismay ('The panic of a child lost in a dark room') and Rezia's horror at his behaviour: 'He pointed at people in the street. He laughed. They stared at him. He said he was an outcast.'[34] On 18 September, while writing this, she fell into a state of rigid panic, fear and horror. She was waiting for Leonard to get back from London on a cold windy night at Rodmell and thought that the time for the last train had passed. She decided she had to get to London, and bicycled to Lewes in the dark and wet, passing people walking together: 'thought, you're safe & happy I'm an outcast'. She bought a ticket, then Leonard came off the last train. 'He was rather cold & angry (as perhaps was natural.) And then, not to show my feelings, I went outside & did something to my bicycle.' They went back talking about reviewing, while she thought, 'My God, thats over. I'm out of that.' The dramatic narrative, written almost a month afterwards in a rapid note-form rather like the style she was using for Septimus's thoughts, told of a narrow escape – from a fall into madness, perhaps even from suicide.[35] When she came to rewrite the book a year later, she told herself that she was 'dreading the madness rather'.[36]

But she did not break down while she was writing this novel, and she wrote it, from its first idea in October 1922 to its last words in October 1924, in almost exactly two years. The outrush of the book sprang from her sense that there seemed terribly little time to do it in. The clocks and bells that structured 'The Hours' (its working title) dramatised her sense of the pressure of time. 'At my age,' she wrote to Carrington, 'life I may say melts in the hand . . . I sit down, just arrange my thoughts, peep out of the window, turn over a page, and its bedtime!'[37]

In life as in writing, she was determined to fill this quick day and not to become, in her forties, acquiescent and habit-ridden. She made up precepts to urge herself forward. Take your fences! Be always on the move! Never settle! She was horrified at the thought of slowing down, of becoming half of an elderly couple weighed down by two houses and the Press and the need to make money. 'We are busy & attach importance to hours. I have my correspondence to finish, says L today. I don't laugh. I take it seriously. But we must not let our hobbies & pleasures become objects of fetish worship.'[38] It seemed to her a decisive moment. 'My theory is that at 40 one either increases the pace or slows down.'[39] To increase the pace meant to plunge in, to want more and more, like the fisherman's wife in the Grimm fairy story which Mrs Ramsay reads to her son in To the Lighthouse. 'And as usual, I want – I want – But what do I want? Whatever I had, I should always say I want, I want.'[40] As always, she matched her desires and needs against Vanessa. Was Vanessa more free, more adventurous, more satisfied? Moving in and out of her sister's life, she saw her as the strong centre of a coloured painting. At Charleston (which would be transformed in 1925 with the addition of a studio), in Gordon Square and at Duncan's studio in

Fitzroy Street, Vanessa created an atmosphere of her own, what Virginia called in 1920 'that astonishing brightness in the heart of darkness'.[41] And she constructed an apparently relaxed, unfussy system ('shabby, loose, easy', Virginia described her in 1923)[42] which managed to balance, just, the claims of the three children (the two boys very big and obstreperous, playing war games and resisting all discipline, Angelica now a dazzling, winning little girl), the anxieties that Duncan would wander off with one of his loves, and the uncertainties about her work, which she sometimes felt was too much under his shadow. (They were collaborating on interior decoration schemes for their friends.) To Virginia she seemed ever more fruitful, glowing, abundant, 'Pagan', and in these terms she both adored and made fun of her: 'dear old Dolphin in her many coloured multiplicity presiding and ladling out scents and spices from the steaming obscenity.'[43] And she never had anything to say against Duncan; her portaits of him are full of amused affection.[44] Virginia involved herself in this coloured ramshackle world in her role as an aunt, which interested her more as Julian reminded her more of Thoby, as Quentin's ambitions to be an artist touched her, and as Angelica began to charm her. She played the spellbinding performer; the plans for *Freshwater*, and the Christmas collaborations with Quentin, were her way of claiming her place in the Charleston menage. As an aunt she was evidently a great success: 'I dont think you need regret your nephew and niece arent your offspring,' Vanessa wrote in the spring of 1924. 'There seems to me to be an added excitement in the fact that you're round the corner and not in the house.'[45]

But Vanessa's attention was turned much more away from England than Virginia's. In the spring of 1920 she had gone to Italy and France with Maynard and Duncan. She spent the winter of 1921–2 and the spring of 1922 in St Tropez. The paintings she showed in her first solo show, early in 1922, had mostly been painted there. And from then on she was often in Paris. Plaintive half-joking appeals went up: 'God knows when I am to see you.' 'I often wake in the night and cry aloud Nessa! Nessa!'[46] Virginia wanted *her*, but she also wanted her life. Her depressions always fed on this as their main food.[47] A particularly painful meeting in February 1922 summed up their conflict. Vanessa spoke of Paris, of the children, of the relative insecurity of her relationship with Duncan. This made Virginia feel 'settled & unadventurous'. Brilliantly transforming this heavy, sad feeling into a light, rapid, stylish joke, she wrote to Vanessa:

Yes, I was rather depressed when you saw me – What it comes to is this: you say 'I do think you lead a dull respectable absurd life – lots of money, no children, everything so settled: and conventional. Look at me now –

458

only sixpence a year – lovers – Paris – life – love – art – excitement – God!
I must be off'. This leaves me in tears.[48]

But when there was a crisis, Virginia was practical and resolute – as she
had been in Greece, and as she would be again in the great tragedy of
Vanessa's life in 1937. In April 1924 Angelica and her nurse were knocked
down by a car; Virginia took the 'phone call and went to the hospital with
Vanessa. For a moment when they arrived they thought Angelica was dead.
Virginia watched on Vanessa's face 'that extraordinary look of anguish,
dumb, not complaining', and even there felt 'half envious' of such great
grief. She prepared herself again for 'death & tragedy'. But Angelica was all
right; 'it was only a joke this time.'[49]

Virginia's longing for a life closer to Vanessa's pulled against Leonard's rule
against too much family and social excitement. When she said to herself 'I
want, I want', what she wanted above all was to move to London. And like
the fisherman wanting to stay in his hut, what Leonard wanted was to stay
in Richmond. It was to keep her safe; also to keep himself separate from
Bloomsbury.[50] His intransigence thwarted her intensely. 'I could not stay at
46 last night, because L on the telephone expressed displeasure. Late again.
Very foolish. Your heart bad – & so my self reliance being sapped, I had no
courage to venture against his will. Then I react.'[51] But 'I love the chatter &
excitement of other peoples houses.'[52] It was one of the great battles of their
marriage, and went on all through 1922 and 1923, finding its way, like her
longing for London, into the novel she was writing. Unusually, too, given
her reticence about Leonard in the diary, she poured it out to herself in an
outcry of frustration:

> L . . . has the old rigid obstacle – my health. And I cant sacrifice his peace
> of mind, yet the obstacle is surely now a dead hand, which one should no
> longer let dominate our short years of life – oh to dwindle them out here,
> with all these gaps, & abbreviations! Always to catch trains, always to
> waste time, to sit here & wait for Leonard to come in, to spend hours
> standing at the box of type . . . when, alternatively, I might go & hear a
> tune, or have a look at a picture, or find out something at the British
> Museum, or go adventuring among human beings. Sometimes I should
> merely walk down Cheapside. But now I'm tied, imprisoned,
> inhibited . . . But then, Lord! . . . what I owe to him! What he gives me!
> Still, I say, surely we could get more from life than we do.[53]

She compared his rigid puritanism and Spartan self-control with her social
side, which she thought of as something in her blood, like a 'piece of

jewellery I inherit from my mother'. And now, for her work, she felt she wanted 'freer intercourse, wider intercourse'. There was a party going on, and she wanted to be at it.

This was one mood, and a very insistent one. But at other times she felt with equal passion that she wanted to withdraw from the 'thousands of people' they saw (even in suburban Richmond). And then, at other times (these 'other times' could coexist within the same hour, on the same page in the diary) she appreciated that they *were* in the swim of things, that they had 'bitten off a large piece of life'.[54]

Leonard's political life was a big part of that bite. As a wife, she respected, endorsed, and to an extent involved herself with his maverick political career. The sound of post-war politics filtered through to her from the other side of the door, and shaped the bitter analysis of post-war society and its class divisions in *Mrs Dalloway*. Though Richard Dalloway's politics (apart from his sympathy for the poor) were the opposite of Leonard's, her fiction of Clarissa Dalloway as an MP's wife drew on some of her own wifely feelings from these years. After the war, Leonard was deeply involved with the League of Nations and increasingly with the Labour Party. In 1920 he was invited to stand as candidate for the 'Seven Universities Democratic Association'.[55] His manifesto, which she admired, spoke for equality of education, international disarmament, anti-colonialism, and co-operation between classes. These beliefs (spelt out in his 1921 book, *Socialism and Co-operation*) were summed up in a letter to Lord Robert Cecil: 'Personally I think that the class war and the conflict of class interests are the greatest curses, and that the first thing that one should aim at is to abolish this . . .'[56]

Between 1920 and 1922 Leonard visited four of the universities he would represent. Virginia went with him in March 1921 to Manchester, and was well aware of her snobbish response to the 'provincial', 'dowdy' academics, sitting silently at dinner 'like two old horses who have been working in the fields all day together', or 'trying to live up to the metropolitan intellect (me, I mean) which they can't do.' 'How supercilious I thought myself.'[57] A holiday in Cornwall followed, perhaps as a reward for this tribulation.

In the run up to the election of 1922[58] she began to wonder, anxiously, if there mightn't be a 'ghastly chance' that he would get in.[59] In the event he came third; though the Labour Party as a whole did much better. She was relieved, but her principal emotion about the election was that it was interfering with the sales of *Jacob's Room*. Leonard gave up the idea of a parliamentary career. By the time the Labour Party came to power under its new leader Ramsay Macdonald (whom Leonard detested) in January 1924, for a brief nine months,[60] he had been appointed literary editor of the *Nation*, and was spending long hours at the office. It was another motive for moving: 'It annoys me to be like other wives', waiting in the suburbs for the husband to come home from work.[61] After the election Leonard's party involvement increased, and he took on the Secretaryship of another Committee, on 'Imperial Questions'. Her own sceptical views on political engagement continued to harden. When Labour was brought down in the autumn of 1924 (by minor scandals which signified a fear of the Party's links with Communism)[62] and gave way to five stolid years of Baldwin's Conservative rule (marked by the return to the gold standard, opposed by Maynard, and the General Strike) her own cynicism and alienation were pronounced: 'Owing to the defeat of the Govt . . . we are now condemned to a dose of lies every morning: the usual yearly schoolboys wrangle has begun. If I were still a feminist, I should make capital out of the wrangle.'[63] This is a very political way of disowning politics; the appearance in *Mrs Dalloway* of the ludicrous figure of the Prime Minister bears out this attitude.

She was watching the world. 'We live in stirring times', she noted in April 1921, at the time of the miners' strike. 'People go on being shot & hanged in Ireland.' Michael Collins's death shocked her, though she didn't understand it.[64] The catastrophic history of Ireland, the terrible unemployment and class injustice after the war, the coalminers' strike, the victorious Allies' behaviour in Europe: she felt these things, yet knew that like most of the middle-classes she could remain immune to them. 'Our cellars will be full; our larders too. Nothing is going to upset us. People in a century will say how terrible it all was. And I walked past Downing St yesterday & saw a few men in cabs, a few men with despatch boxes, orderly public watching, wreaths being laid on the Cenotaph.'[65] The first version of *Mrs Dalloway*, which she began writing in June 1923, started with a procession of the sons of dead officers laying a wreath on the Cenotaph.[66]

The novel was energised by her critical distance from the 'civilization' which had been died for. All the systems and structures in the book – the relics of empire in Lady Bruton's drawing-room, or Hugh Whitbread's courtier's world, the clubs and the monarchy and the 'season' – seem to crumble under the eye of Septimus's apocalyptic vision and the traumatic force of what he has witnessed. The shimmer and movement of 1920s London and its parties, which she so loved, seem to close over the past; but just underneath is terror, grief and catastrophic change. Similarly, a piece written about the British Empire Exhibition at Wembley[67] in June 1924 dismantled the great show of empire in an absurd, chaotic storm (a harbinger of the rapid, gleeful demolishings of history in *Orlando*). Like the debunking of the establishment and the conservative government in *Mrs Dalloway*, the essay blows to bits the solid illusion of Britain trumpeted by

The Times: 'The Empire is perishing; the bands are playing; the Exhibition is in ruins.'[68]

If she kept her distance from Leonard's Labour Party work, she was closely involved with his working methods at the Press. Here there was trouble of a complicated kind, arising from the usual overlap between personal and professional relationships. By 1920 the Woolfs were committing themselves to a full-scale operation which needed proper assistance. Retrospectively, Leonard could see that they were trying to be two things at once, a hobby and a commercial concern.[69] At the time they were eager to find someone who would enthusiastically share their interest and their labours, but not take over.

Lytton had a suggestion. Since the end of the war, and since his huge success with *Eminent Victorians*, he had been settled at the Mill House in Tidmarsh (a little Berkshire village on the Thames) with Carrington. And since 1919 he had been involved in a triangular relationship with her friend, Major Rex (known as Ralph) Partridge, a large, blue-eyed young man, who, after a conventional Anglo-Indian upbringing and education, a heroic war, and great prowess as a rower at Oxford, had now fallen under the spell of Carrington and the loving protection of Lytton. Ralph wanted Carrington to marry him, but Carrington – elusive and evasive in her love affairs – did not want to leave Tidmarsh. Lytton suggested that Ralph should work at the Press. The Woolfs vetted and liked him, and in August of 1920, he joined as a part-timer on £100 a year, which meant that he and Carrington would live in London during the week – and that he became even more insistent about marrying her.[70]

In Virginia's feelings for the *ménage à trois* her affection for Lytton was dominant. This affection was not diminished by the fact that she was jealous (jealous as a joke, and so, also, seriously) of his great success with *Eminent Victorians*, and, in the spring of 1921, with *Queen Victoria*. She was very pleased that it was dedicated to her (and insisted, out of 'vanity',[71] on having her full name on the page). She thought it a historical biography which would change the way people thought about Victoria for ever. But her effusive letter of praise betrayed some reservations: 'Occasionally I think one is a little conscious of being entertained.'[72] Like Forster she also thought it 'flimsy'.[73] But though she criticised Lytton's work, and his passions for his young men made her impatient ('Love is the devil. No character can stand up against it')[74] she always felt tenderly towards him:

> Why not let oneself be content in the thought of Lytton – so true, gentle, infinitely nimble, & humane? I seldom rest long in complete agreement with anyone. But here I think one's feelings should be unqualified.[75]

462

She thought of the other two almost entirely as his protégés. She had become fond of Carrington's 'ardent, robust, scatterbrained, appreciative' ways, but her role had to be that of Lytton's handmaid, or child-bride. There are unpleasant instances of Virginia's condescension to her.[76] Now, at one of the great crises of Carrington's emotional life, and also after Lytton's death, it seems that Virginia did not try to understand her well.[77]

Ralph certainly impressed her in one respect: she referred after their first meeting to his 'superb body'.[78] She began to like, in her forties, to be slightly fallen in love with by younger men (best of all by witty, talented, attractive and gossipy homosexual men). Clive noted drily that she was being paid court to by Raymond Mortimer, or that she couldn't resist Dadie Rylands; Gerald Brenan had 'rather a crush' on her, David Cecil ('a pretty boy') was in awe, and later she would be good friends with Stephen Spender and John Lehmann. (When these 'crushes' became over-insistent, like Stephen Tennant's, she backed off.) Perhaps there was some desire, when she first met Ralph, to find out what Lytton felt. 'I have just kissed Ralph on the nape of the neck – Its these elderly passions that are so dangerous', she boasted (to Vanessa, naturally).[79] Gerald Brenan reported (years later) that Ralph had 'kissed her naked in the bathroom'. But Brenan was an unreliable witness, and may have exaggerated Ralph's story of staying the night in Richmond, and seeing Virginia coming down in her nightdress, with bare feet, looking 'like an angel'.[80]

But Ralph's turbulent sexual life quickly became an irritant, combined with what they perceived as a lack of commitment to the Press. At the first crisis between Ralph and Carrington (who could not bring herself to leave Lytton), in the spring of 1921, Virginia liked being confided in. As with Saxon and Barbara a few years before, she enjoyed, as her mother used to, acting as a match-maker. (This characteristic of Mrs Ramsay's in *To the Lighthouse* derives from her as well as from Julia.) Perhaps carried away by being 'in the thick of it',[81] or working off some smothered jealousy over Lytton's love for Carrington, or not thinking carefully enough about her, she gave Ralph the impression that Lytton did not care much about Carrington and would be quite happy to have her out of his life. Leonard, meanwhile, brutally advised him to 'put a pistol' to Carrington's head.[82] So he did, telling her everything that Virginia had said; and Carrington, very wretched, wrote a poignant letter of renunciation to Lytton, and gave in to Ralph's bullying. Virginia said later that she felt 'slightly responsible for that marriage'.[83]

The marriage and the job both went wrong very quickly. Ralph found Leonard authoritarian and the work unsatisfying. Carrington mildly observed that Virginia and Leonard were 'perfect people to know as friends, but rather difficult as overseers and business people'.[84] A year after he joined, in the summer of 1921 when Virginia was so ill, Carrington and Ralph went to Rodmell to sort out 'the Situation'. Carrington was enchanted by Virginia's friendliness towards her, but 'the Situation' remained unresolved.[85] In the autumn the office rows continued. In a comically self-revealing sentence, Virginia wrote to Vanessa: 'He and Leonard argue incessantly; and then appeal to me, and I have been thinking of something else.'[86]

By 1922 Ralph's marriage was also in trouble. Carrington had become involved with his ex-fellow officer, Gerald Brenan, a romantic and eccentric character who, after the war, had got away from his repressive family to live and write in a remote Spanish village. Brenan had fallen extravagantly in love with Carrington in England in the summer of 1921, and had begun an affair with her in the spring of 1922. Meanwhile Ralph was making love to Valentine Dobrée (wife of the poet and scholar Bonamy Dobrée) whom Carrington was herself very attracted to. Virginia met Gerald at Tidmarsh in May 1922, and liked him immediately,[87] but by June, when the crisis was at its height, she (and Leonard) were both sick of hearing about it. Carrington told Lytton that they were 'slightly worn with poor R's outpourings & Leonard insists it should not be mentioned again until July 23rd.'[88] Ralph's 'outpourings' tipped Virginia from curiosity into revulsion. 'We have had a mad bull in the house – a normal Englishman in love,' she wrote,[89] using the same phrase she would give to crazy Jem Stephen's pursuit of Stella. The 'stupidity of virility' appalled her. On the train to Richmond coming back from one of Roger Fry's lectures, she shouted at him ('You're a maniac'), then immediately thought of 'lusts' speeding along 'the railway lines of convention'.[90] Like Lily Briscoe, backing off from the hot, callous, careless force of Paul Rayley's passion for Minta in *To the Lighthouse*, she disliked having this bullying male sexuality thrust at her. (She tried to work this out some time later in a letter to Jacques Raverat, saying that she was more and more engrossed by friendship, but that '*sexual relations bore me more than they used: am I a prude? am I feminine? Anyhow for two years past, I have been a spectator of I daresay a dozen affairs of the heart – violent and crucial; and come to the conclusion that love is a disease; a frenzy; an epidemic; oh but how dull, how monotonous, and reducing its young men and women to what abysses of mediocrity!*')[91] Also she was irritated with Lytton, who backed Ralph, and seemed to be manipulating his relationship with the Press.[92] So Ralph's role there became hopelessly mixed up with his private life: 'Next time we must stipulate for eunuchs.'[93]

By the autumn of 1922 they had resolved that Ralph (by now 'the gawkish boor')[94] must go. He was not working hard enough and they did not like him. Their dilemma was partly solved by finding – accidentally, at the 1917 Club – a bright, likely young woman (not a 'lady', as Virginia found it necessary to observe) called Marjorie Thomson, who wanted to become a printer. She would stay for two years, 'a nice trusty creature'; and though she too confided in Virginia about *her* problems (an on-off marriage to 'a clever little bounder', C.E.M. Joad, and a search for 'a room of her own') she confirmed Virginia's sense of 'how much nicer young women are than young men'.[95] Ralph stayed grumpily until March 1923 and then left, without a farewell, and unforgiven.[96] At the end of the year another new young man, Dadie Rylands, made a brief appearance at the Press; but he lasted as a friend, not as an employee.

The only beneficial side-outcome of the involvement with Ralph was a journey to visit Gerald Brenan, in April 1923, in Yegen, a primitive Berber village 40 miles south-west of Granada, high in the Alpujarra mountains, the foothills of the Sierra Nevada. It was her first European journey for a long time. 'My eyes are entirely grey with England – nothing but England for 10 years.'[97] She fell on the 'warmth & colour' of the Catholic country with passion. ('Why not bring the children up Roman Catholics?' she wrote to Vanessa. 'I think it induces to warmth of heart.')[98]

They would have had some idea of what to expect of Yegen from Lytton, who had had a strenuous journey on muleback through floods in 1920 ('The roads, ma chère, the roads!' he wrote to Mary, 'Lady Hester wasn't in it!') but had been impressed with the 'wild, violent, spectacular' views across the mountains to the Mediterranean.[99] It had been raining hard, too, before the Woolfs' arrival, and Gerald had equipped himself with 'an umbrella as big as Robinson Crusoe's' for Virginia.[100] But the weather cleared, they talked all day and night – about *Ulysses*, about Ralph and Carrington, about their lives. 'Our tongues wag – mine like a vipers, his like a trusty farmyard dogs.' She found him 'a sympathetic but slightly blurred character, who owing to solitude and multitudes of books has some phantasmagoric resemblance to Shelley.' He was enchanted by her, watching her by the fireside, or eagerly walking, 'as excited as a schoolgirl on holiday', or scribbling in her travel diary (which to his later disappointment did not survive). They travelled to Murcia and Almería and Alicante together (he noticed that Leonard made a fuss over her sleep) and after their return he sent her some romantic poems and intense, literary letters. But this intimacy faded away, partly perhaps because he did not admire her novels.[101]

But a letter she sent him before their visit showed her openness to new relationships. She spoke of her difficult new writing as a painful process of transition: 'This generation must break its neck in order that the next may have smooth going.' And she challenged his impression of her as secure and settled: every ten years she had tried to 'end it all'. Anyone who could 'feel and reflect' must live through these 'recurring cataclysms of horror'.[102] She linked her personal history to world history, as she linked Septimus's madness to the 'cataclysms' of the war. In her notes for *Mrs Dalloway*, she planned for Septimus to be 'partly R, partly me'; and then asks 'Why not have something of GB in him? the young man who has gone into business after the war: takes life to heart: seeks truth-revelations.'[103] It was Ralph who wanted to go into business, and it was Gerald who was a seeker after truth-revelations. But together, these young men out of the war, with their disturbingly intense emotional lives[104] and their uncertainty about the future, seemed to her to represent the post-war trauma of a whole generation.

As in *Mrs Dalloway*, the catastrophe was covered over; it was time to go to the party. Gordon Square, that 'lions house', that 'menagerie without cages' where 'the animals prowl in and out' (or, less impressively, that 'rabbit warren'), was a 'flare and glare' of social intimacy and activity.[105] There were Memoir Club evenings and Apostles dinners; house-warmings and reunions; family parties and fancy dress parties; weekend parties, dancing parties, studio parties, concert parties. There were parties on the river and parties to the zoo (the new Aquarium opened in 1924, and she wrote it up),[106] parties to meet distinguished visitors (Gertrude Stein at Edith Sitwell's)[107] or to see star performers; parties for special purposes (like the one at Richmond to immortalise Desmond MacCarthy's dazzling conversation, which somehow evaporated on the page).[108] There were grand soirées and tea parties in the houses of famous hostesses, with fireworks and fairy lights in the gardens and jazz. There were all-night parties with a great deal of drink. ('Bloomsbury', on the whole, did not take drugs – or gamble.) Frances Partridge (one of the stunning dancers of her day) remembered that 'youth, high spirits, alcohol and gregariousness were the chief ingredients'.[109] It was a long way from cocoa and philosophy at Gordon Square in Thoby's days, twenty years before.

Virginia, under orders or out at Richmond, missed a good many of these parties. (When she couldn't go, she *imagined* it: possibly an even more satisfying form of party going.)[110] But she was there when Vanessa, on her way back from Rome and France, gave a party at no. 50: she kissed Mary, talked about the past with Lady Strachey, and felt open and sensual and excited.[111] She was there, dressed in her mother's lace-edged dress, at a fancy dress party at no. 46, in January 1923, lit up and fizzing, talking to all her old friends (and with especial pleasure to Sickert, so 'workmanlike' and straightforward). Lydia danced, there were charades, and Sickert acted Hamlet. Indeed she felt they were all Shakespearean, mellow, gay and convivial, friendly without having to think about 'copulation'. Copulation, though, was in the air. Later that night, staying at no. 50, she heard a woman's cry in the night, and got out of bed (putting her upper teeth in) to see what was wrong; it was Mary, next door, making love with Clive. (Perhaps they wanted her to hear.)[112] At another Gordon Square party, given by Alix and Marjorie Strachey at no. 50, copulation was enacted on stage, in a performance of Schnitzler's *La Ronde*. Vanessa reported in detail to Roger.

> The whole plot . . . is a copulation scene which at first doesn't come off. It is done on the stage, though at the back, which is in darkness. It seemed to me pointless and rather painful, as they acted very realistically and rather slowly and the audience felt simply as if a real copulation were going on in the room and tried to talk to drown the very realistic groans made by Partridge! . . . It was a great relief when Marjorie sang hymns. But I didn't think it was a very successful party.[113]

Leonard went home, after this, and 'contemplated, seriously, some scientific form of suicide'.[114]

Some of these performances crossed the line (like the Dreadnought Hoax) between home entertainment and public shows. One famous full-scale review at Maynard's house in 1926, based on the scandal of the owner of Pippington Park in Sussex (arrested for 'debauching' one of his servants: sex as farce, again), featured Duncan Grant as a wolfhound, and Maynard and Lydia dancing the can-can, or Keynes-Keynes.[115] Christmas shows at Charleston, scripted by Virginia in collaboration with Quentin (now a fat and funny teenager), turned family legends into pranks and manic in-jokes, like the story of 'Duncan Grant of Bedlam and Bloomsbury, Charleston-cum-Tilton'.[116] *Freshwater*, drafted in 1923 and then set aside, was one of these home entertainments. At the other end of this spectrum were semi-professional public performances, like Lytton's play *A Son of Heaven*, put on in July 1925, or Walton's and Edith Sitwell's *Façade*. Virginia went to the Aeolian Hall in June 1923 and listened 'in a dazed way, to Edith Sitwell vociferating through the megaphone'. She thought it monotonous. All the same, it made her feel that the party was in full swing, and that she wanted to be part of it.[117]

Lady Colefax was at *Façade*, too, in a hat with green ribbons. She did not give the sort of parties where copulation would be realistically mimed or Duncan Grant would play G.F. Watts. Known always as an 'indefatigable' hostess, and married to a dull Yorkshire lawyer and MP who provided the title and the backing, Sibyl Colefax entertained in the very beautiful eighteenth-century Argyll House, at the rural end of the King's Road (known to her guests as the Lions' Corner House). Famous literati mingled (as the society columns would say) with diplomats, prime ministers, and Hollywood stars. She began to pursue Virginia in 1922. Soon her dashingly illegible purple missives became as much a feature of Virginia's social life as Ottoline's rival effusions. Domineering and garrulous ('talking talking in consecutive sentences, like the shavings that come from planes, artificial, but unbroken')[118] 'painted and emphatic',[119] she eventually revealed a more vulnerable side and became an odd kind of friend. But her arbitrary switches from soulful intimacy to compulsive showing-off kept her as a figure of fun. Leonard had no patience with her sort of parties, where people talked through the playing of a famous pianist or sat in feathers and white gloves to hear Valéry recite.[120] Virginia partly hated them too. They reminded her too much of the Duckworth Greek slave years: everyone 'chained to a particular patch of the carpet, which they can't cross for fear of death'.[121] Stupid talk was bad for the mind: 'Aristocrats, worldlings, for all their surface polish, are empty, slippery, coat the mind with sugar & butter, & make it slippery too.'[122] But she was attracted by the 'social sense': she wanted to feel what Proust felt and to see if she couldn't turn this world into something like À La Recherche.[123] She let Sibyl know her ambivalence in her entry in her visitor's book: 'Virginia Woolf, who sometimes spends an hour in Chelsea Town hall, summoning spirit enough to face the blaze of brilliancy, the lights, the voices, the faces of Sibyls friends.'[124] When she faced the blaze, she called it 'taking her fences';[125] not so distant a metaphor from 'jumping through hoops', which was her description of social life under George Duckworth.

High society meant dressing up, and so meant fear and self-consciousness. She put her 'clothes complex', or 'frock consciousness', into a story called 'The New Dress' (written in between *Mrs Dalloway* and *To the Lighthouse*). 'Mabel' goes to Mrs Dalloway's party wearing a dress quaintly designed in the style of her mother's time. She realises at once that it is a failure, she is sneered at by the other fashionable well-dressed guests (including 'Charles Burt' (Clive Bell?), 'malice itself') and retreats in horror, feeling like a fly drowning in a saucer. Her agony is ascribed to 'the sense she had had ever since she was a child, of being inferior to other people'.[126]

Inferior, but also superior. Jokes about her hairpins dropping into the soup at a Sibyl Colefax lunch party suggested some contempt, as well as nervousness, at the world where hairpins mattered.[127] She would have preferred to go out 'in my own clothes, & at my own hours'.[128] Though she had a dress-maker (the gossipy Mme Gravé in Kensington) she knew she would never be fashionable. She took refuge in jokes about her clothes being unsuitable for the aristocracy[129] or about her eccentricity and shabbiness. But it was unbearable if other people – especially Clive – made jokes about her clothes.

Clive, and Mary Hutchinson, loomed large in her feelings about fashion. Mary was to find her a dressmaker 'who would make me look like other people'.[130] She was going to write essays for the *Nation*, perhaps a book for the Press, on 'Dress'.[131] ('Should it be prefaced by an account of a great dress show – of the Clients – mannequins – and frocks – and the buying of a frock?')[132] Mary tried to bring Virginia up to date with the new post-war fashions for make-up and perfume – an opportunity for flirtatious intimacy:

Don't you smell me? I am like a civet. Leonard detests me. I think myself too, too, too lovely. Yes: you've entirely altered my life, and given a new channel for vanity to flow in. As you may have guessed, that inexplicable and most detestable prudery which for 10 years led me to make sanitary towels out of Kapok down rather than buy them, has always prevented me from saying to a powdered shop girl 'I too am a woman . . . I want powder too.' . . .

Tom's dining tomorrow, and I shall be very curious to observe whether rouge on the lips, quickens his marmoreal heart.[133]

In the voices in *The Waves*, Mary was Jinny – seductive, flashy, partying – to Virginia's shy, solitary Rhoda. But there was something of Jinny in Virginia too. She made fun of Mary's gawdiness (she and Clive were 'the parakeets') but she would also have rather liked to be her. At a fashionable party Mary gave to say goodbye to her beautiful house on the river at Hammersmith, before her move to Regent's Park, Virginia was amused (thinking of Proust, and what he would have made of it) by watching the bright young things, Lady Diana Cooper and Elizabeth Ponsonby and Viola Tree and 'all that set', whom she described as 'tubular cropheads'. She thought they showed up poorly, though, beside Vanessa, completely indifferent and independent in her 'old red dress', and Molly MacCarthy, whom she reassured kindly about *her* dress ('I thought it a mixture of snowdrop and viper') and urged not to be 'downed by those pert misses'.[134]

The kind of people who were at Mary Hutchinson's party were always in *Vogue*. *Vogue*, with its reports on the parties and the shows and the upper-class beauties, and its directives on the shorter, straight skirts, the feathers and fringes, the backless evening dresses in metallic colours, the capes and cloches, the shingled (or bingled) hair, the jerseys and the elegant underwear, might seem a far cry from the *Nation* or the Hogarth Press. But they did have links. Between 1922 and 1926 the editor was the remarkable Dorothy Todd, (unflatteringly described, though with some admiration, by Virginia)[135] who tried to bring together fashion, design, theatre, music and literature. For a while *Vogue* was filled with articles by Clive Bell on Brancusi or Paris exhibitions, Raymond Mortimer or Edwin Muir reviewing Virginia Woolf, stories by David Garnett and Aldous Huxley, essays by Desmond MacCarthy, articles on Vanessa and Duncan's interior decorations (including those for 52 Tavistock Square), reviews of *Façade* or of Lytton's play, and examples of the work of Corbusier, Man Ray, Léger, and Cocteau. (Virginia was photographed for *Vogue*, looking ravishing in her mother's dress, in 1926.) Virginia contributed a few pieces and was criticised by the fastidious and catty Logan Pearsall Smith, who 'grieved to see Bloomsbury descend from the heights & scatter its pearls in Mayfair'. At least Todd let you write what you like, Virginia retorted, 'and its your own fault if you conform to the stays and the petticoats'.[136]

Being in *Vogue* was being at the party; by 1926 Virginia was even going to go to a dressmaker recommended by Todd.[137] 'Bloomsbury' was not chic, but it set a fashion of its kind, and its edges overlapped with the beau monde. This is nicely placed by Evelyn Waugh in *Brideshead Revisited*. When Charles Ryder first goes to Oxford, in about 1923, he decorates his rooms with 'a screen painted by Roger Fry with a Provençal landscape, which I had bought inexpensively when the Omega workshops were sold up . . . a poster by McKnight Kauffer and Rhyme Sheets from the Poetry Bookshop . . . Roger Fry's *Vision and Design*, the Medici Press edition of *A Shropshire Lad*, *Eminent Victorians*, some volumes of Georgian Poetry.' Sebastian Flyte's room, by contrast, is decadent and catholic. Sebastian converts him to the Baroque. But then again, the cosmopolitan and homosexual Anthony Blanche is reading *Antic Hay* in preparation for a Sunday at Garsington. Charles Ryder's initial puritan anxieties about joining this set caught an echo of 'Bloomsbury's' queasiness about high society. Virginia was defensive about writing for *Vogue* or dining with 'Coalbox', and irritated by Clive when he teased her for 'wishing to dress like Lady Diana [Cooper]'.[138] 'One rushed back from the squares of Mayfair, from dinners with dukes, parties with princesses, the loops and tendrils of titles catching at one's back, and sank into a chair in Gordon Square. Had one caught something, were spots already breaking out?'[139]

They were all becoming well known, if not all as much in demand as Lytton or Maynard. In the spring of 1925 she anticipated 'a slow silent increase of fame' and 'my value mounting steadily as a journalist'.[140] She could command higher fees now: £50 for a piece for *Harper's Bazaar* by

December 1924, £10 for each 1,000 words from Todd. She was asked to speak in public: at the London School of Economics in December 1923, at the Cambridge Heretics Society in May 1924, where she gave the spoken version of 'Mr Bennett and Mrs Brown', and at the London Group dinner in March 1924 (where Osbert Sitwell witnessed her nervous distress beforehand and her brilliant performance). Her speech, she noted, 'drew tears' – of laughter?)[141] She was becoming a figure, soon to be photographed and caricatured and glamorised. By the end of 1924 she was in a position (as she remembered Leslie wanting to be) 'to know everyone worth knowing'.[142] When she summed up her friends, she judged them by their response to fame and success.

Keynes and Strachey and Fry were at the top of this tree of fame. On holiday with Maynard and Lydia in September 1923 (at Studland in Dorset again, after many years) she noted how 'gross & stout' Maynard had got. But the pages he showed her of *A Tract on Monetary Reform* filled her with awe: 'The process of mind there displayed is as far ahead of me as Shakespeare's.'[143] Lydia, the new arrival, was ridiculed by Virginia for her effusive, naïve, *foreign* eccentricities, and even more by Vanessa, whose intimacy with Maynard she threatened. But when Virginia drew on her for Rezia in *Mrs Dalloway* (so closely that she caught herself calling Lydia 'Rezia') she made a touching, attractive character. Lydia's high spirits and passion for Maynard overrode the hostility of his 'set'. Their marriage in 1925 was certainly a fashionable event: *Vogue* ran a full-page picture with the caption: 'The marriage of the most brilliant of English economists with the most popular of Russian dancers makes a delightful symbol of the mutual dependence upon each other of art and science.'[144]

Virginia's much closer friendship with Roger Fry (whose portrait show in 1923 was judged a failure, but whose London lectures were, she told him, 'a d–d success')[145] flourished. Her tender admiration is nicely expressed in a joke to herself about a cow in the field by Monk's House, a genius of a cow who had 'decided to leave the herd & eat the branches on the fallen tree . . . She is a Roger Fry'.[146] After the sadness of his break-up with Vanessa and the suicide of a French girlfriend (a story he related in intense detail to Virginia), he began a happier relationship with Helen Anrep. (Like Mary and Lydia and Karin, and for some similar possessive reasons, Helen was not popular with the Stephen sisters.) He was still bursting with energy and with new interests, in particular the relation between art and psychoanalysis. Virginia was interested in his views on Forster's new novel, *A Passage to India*. She had been touched that Forster wrote to her first to tell her it was finished, but like Roger Fry she had reservations about it.

I wish he weren't a mystic or that he would keep his mysticism out of his books more . . . The fact is that he is an artist but he despises his art and thinks he must be something more; at least that's what I suspect, but I'm certain that the only meanings that are worth anything in a work of art are those that the artist himself knows nothing about. The moment the artist tries to express *his* ideas and *his* emotions he misses the great thing.[147]

At just this time the Hogarth Press were publishing Fry on *The Artist and Psychoanalysis*, and laying out '£800 in the works of Freud'.[148] Adrian's analysis was placing his marriage under great strain, and in 1923, he and Karin temporarily separated. (Virginia was shocked.) And Freud now became one of the dominant topics of Bloomsbury. James and Alix Strachey were translating the Freud case histories and were about to invite Melanie Klein to London. In her letters to Jacques Raverat, psychoanalysis featured as something Virginia was holding at bay, though the language of her confessions to him was influenced by what she was hearing of Freud. So to Jacques (and to no one else at this time) she explained the layers of her personality: the falsity of her letters, the masks that she put on to avert intimacy, her interest in her own psychology, her vanity, her dependency on her friends, and the egotism that stopped her talking about her writing.

She entertained him, too, with virtuoso accounts of the people she was meeting and the local scandals. 'Whom do you wish me to see in particular?' she asked, charmingly.[149] New figures were crowding in all the time. 'We see too many people for me to describe them, had I the time' became a constant note.[150] In 1923 she got to know the affable, gossipy 'Dadie' Rylands, who would become her special pet (he looked like Rupert Brooke, she told Jacques, and everyone was in love with him). Raymond Mortimer, a clever young ex-Oxford reviewer, 'all angle & polish . . . half a dandy'[151] (shortly to become Harold Nicolson's lover) assiduously paid court. Bunny Garnett became more of a figure to reckon with: he had a fashionable hit with *Lady into Fox*. She got to know, but not intimately, some of the other women writers of her generation, Rebecca West, Rose Macaulay, Edith Sitwell. (The Sitwells, she told Jacques, 'take themselves very seriously. They descend from George the IVth. They look like Regency Bucks.')[152] Hugh Walpole made the first moves towards friendship; at first she was not impressed (he looked like a banker) but he gradually made her into a close confidante.[153] She came to know Sickert; she met Arnold Bennett, and liked him. Old friends to whom she felt affectionately attached – Francis Birrell, Saxon, Charlie Sanger and his wife and nice young daughter – made their claims. Clive was always around, critical, proprietary, teasing and bracing. In the spring of 1922 they had something of a renewed flirtation.

Garsington was in full flight; her occasional visits induced violent swings between curiosity, amusement, and dismayed revulsion.

This party-going mood went into *Mrs Dalloway*.[154] She wrote about pleasure and social excitement, making anticipation and participation float on to the page, like an English, female alternative to Proust:

> Was everybody dining out, then? Doors were being opened here by a footman to let issue a high-stepping old dame, in buckled shoes, with three purple ostrich feathers in her hair. Doors were being opened for ladies wrapped like mummies in shawls with bright flowers on them, ladies with bare heads. And in respectable quarters with stucco pillars through small front gardens, lightly swathed, with combs in their hair (having run up to see the children), women came; men waited for them, with their coats blowing open, and the motor started. Everybody was going out. What with these doors being opened, and the descent and the start, it seemed as if the whole of London were embarking in little boats moored to the bank, tossing on the waters, as if the whole place were floating off in carnival.

At the start of 1924, the Woolfs at last moved back to London. Gradually, Leonard's objections had been worn down: he must have felt that unhappiness at Richmond outweighed the dangers of excitement in London. Virginia began house hunting in the autumn of 1923. A good house at 35 Woburn Square fell through. On 9 January, she signed a ten-year lease[155] of 52 Tavistock Square, one of the tall, four-storey, brick, terraced houses on the south side of the Square. Change of address cards went out:

Mr & Mrs Leonard Woolf
to
52 Tavistock Square,
London,
W.C.1.
Telephone: Museum 2621.
After Thursday, March 13, 1924.

The ground and first floor were let to a firm of solicitors, Dollman and Pritchard. Leonard and Virginia took the basement (with a room for the Press and a large billiard room at the back – the stock room and Virginia's 'studio') and the two top floors.

And the basement, & the billiard room, with the rock garden on top, & the view of the square in front & the desolated buldings behind, & Southampton Row, & the whole of London – London thou art a jewel of jewels, & jasper of jocunditie – music, talk, friendship, city views, books, publishing, something central & inexplicable, all this is now within my reach.[156]

Passionate celebrations of London[157] filled the diaries and letters and spilled over into *Mrs Dalloway*. She determined to make the rooms beautiful, to spend money on furniture and decorations (Vanessa and Duncan charged her £25 for their painted panels). A euphoric description went to Jacques:

L. and I on top looking at all the glories of London, which are romantically, sentimentally, incredibly dear to me. The Imperial Hotel, all pink and blue, in Russell Square: St Pancras Church spire, carved from white plaster – do you know it? These are the things I love.[158]

But she felt haunted. 'I feel as if I were going on with a story which I began in the year 1904', she wrote to Vanessa, 'then a little insanity, & so back.'[159] As in her novel, and as in her letters to Jacques, present life was shadowed and intercut with the past. The novel and those letters would come to an end at the same time: Jacques died in March 1925, *Mrs Dalloway* was published in May 1925. As a writer, she now felt a sense of 'rush & urgency' and for the first time the conviction that 'I might become one of the interesting – I will not say great – but interesting novelists?'[160] So she kept on with her persistent urgent tussle between life and death, her vision of her own existence as a battle-ground between these two forces: 'I meant to write about death, only life came breaking in as usual.' 'But enough of death – its life that matters.' And, hearing at a party of Jacques' death: 'Nevertheless, I do not any longer feel inclined to doff the cap to death. I like to go out of the room talking, with an unfinished casual sentence on my lips.'[161]

TWENTY-SEVEN

A Haunted House

On the day the last words of *Mrs Dalloway* were written in October 1924, Virginia entered a cryptic note in her diary, 'I see already The Old Man'.[1] When *To the Lighthouse* was published in the spring of 1927, she looked back on 'the odd hurried unexpected way in which these things suddenly create themselves – one thing on top of another in about an hour . . . so I made up The Lighthouse in one afternoon in the square here.'[2] The novel may have come to her all at once ('without any premeditation, that I can see', she added in a letter to Vanessa),[3] but its ingredients had been accumulating all her life.

To the Lighthouse began to take clearer shape as *Mrs Dalloway* neared publication. Her first notes for it began with the form of the book, and with an idea of Mrs Ramsay:

All character – *not* a view of the world.
Two blocks joined by a corridor

Topics that may come in:
How her beauty is to be conveyed by the
impression that she makes on all these
people. One after another feeling it without
knowing exactly what she does to them . . .

She feels the glow of sensation – & how they are
made up of all different things – (what
she has just done) & wishes for some bell to
strike & say this is it. It does strike.
She guards her moment.[4]

On 14 May 1925, the day *Mrs Dalloway* was published, she wrote down a slightly different list of ingredients for the next novel:

This is going to be fairly short: to have father's character done complete in it; & mothers; & St Ives; & childhood; & all the usual things I try to put in – life, death &c. But the centre is father's character, sitting in a boat, reciting We perished, each alone, while he crushes a dying mackerel . . .[5]

Before she could get to this, she had some stories to write, which made a bridge from *Mrs Dalloway* to *To the Lighthouse*. They are all set at Mrs Dalloway's party, but the tunes of *To the Lighthouse* are beginning to be played in them. There are memories of childhood seaside holidays, prickly encounters between an egotistical lawyer and an angry woman, a lament for a lost family house. In June and July 1925, she began to build ingredients from these stories into her plans for the novel. She knew by now, that 'the sea' was to be heard all through it; she knew she wanted to call it an 'Elegy' rather than a novel.[6] She was anxious that the theme might be 'sentimental'. How to thicken and enrich it? How to control emotions through form?

> It might contain all characters boiled down; & childhood; & then this impersonal thing, which I'm dared to do by my friends, the flight of time, & the consequent break of unity in my design.[7]

These anxieties over sentimentality and the need for 'thickening' the material were never to leave her. As she came to the end of the first draft, she asked herself if it was 'rather thin',[8] and observed that she was going in dread of 'sentimentality'.[9] On publication day she was still worrying that people would call it 'sentimental'.[10]

She was also gripped by the 'new problem' she was setting herself with the passage of time and the 'break of unity'. By July, she was vacillating between 'a single & intense character of father; & a far wider slower book'.[11] It needed to be 'quiet', but not 'insipid'. She might 'do something' to 'split up emotions more completely'. These questions of balance and construction would be carried into the novel. Lily Briscoe, painting her picture, diagnoses a problem of design which is also the problem of understanding the relation between the Ramsays:

> For whatever reason she could not achieve that razor edge of balance between two opposite forces; Mr Ramsay and the picture; which was necessary. There was something perhaps wrong with the design? . . . She smiled ironically; for had she not thought, when she began, that she had solved her problem?[12]

When she thought about her lecture of 1925, 'How Should One Read a Book?', the problem of design in *To the Lighthouse* was very much in her mind. (A fragment of the lecture is written in the manuscript of the novel.)

She compares the 32 chapters of a novel to 'an attempt to make something as formed and controlled as a building: but words are more impalpable than bricks'.[13] It is like a note to herself on the writing of her new novel. The bricks are being trundled up the little plank, the construction is underway. The building must be 'formed and controlled'. But the pull towards breakage and fragmentation is immense. And the difficulty is compounded because she wanted a strong structural basis and an appearance of fluid translucence (as in Proust, whom she was reading now). Only by this combination could she get what she kept calling a 'central transparency'. Lily Briscoe's images for her work – 'she saw the colour burning on a framework of steel; the light of a butterfly's wing lying upon the arches of a cathedral' – invoke Virginia Stephen's vision of St Sophia on her visit to Constantinople, recorded in her diary of 1906: 'thin as glass, blown in plump curves' and 'as substantial as a pyramid'.[14] That dome shape, at once solid and ethereal, comes into the novel, and was at the heart of the plan for the book.

She began writing *To the Lighthouse* on 6 August 1925, at Monk's House, and wrote '22 pages straight off in less than a fortnight'.[15] But all that summer she was ill, an illness connected (like her state of mind while writing the mad scenes in *Mrs Dalloway*) to the strong emotions the novel was drawing on. 'Cant write', she said to Roger Fry, '(with a whole novel in my head too – its damnable).'[16] She felt dejected and uncertain about the 'personal' aspects of the book ('It will be too like father, or mother')[17] and it was not until January 1926 that she was launched again.

When she went back to it, she wrote the first draft at a rate of about two pages a day, with speed and fluency ('Never never have I written so easily, imagined so profusely')[18] between January and September 1926. She was often unwell; in July she had 'a whole nervous breakdown in miniature'.[19] But she forged ahead – 'close on 40,000 words in 2 months – my record', she wrote to Vita in March 1926[20] – and felt that she was setting herself new targets. She noted to herself on 9 March that she was writing 'exactly the opposite from my other books: very loosely at first . . . & shall have to tighten finally . . . Also at perhaps 3 times the speed.'[21] She loved the dinner party scene;[22] she had trouble with the middle section, 'Time Passes',[23] but she liked her strategy there of 'collecting' all the 'lyric portions' in one place, so that they 'dont interfere with the text so much as usual'.[24] In the last part, moving between Lily painting her picture on the lawn and Mr Ramsay with his two children in the boat, she wrestled, like Lily, with problems of balance, feeling that the material in the boat was not so rich 'as it is with Lily on the lawn'.[25] She wanted to get the feeling of simultaneity: 'Could I do it in a parenthesis? so that one had the sense of reading the two things at the same time?'[26] As she completed the first draft, in September, she went into a period of intense depression. Out of it, in a curious state of mind, she began to see 'a fin passing far out',[27] and the image of 'a solitary woman musing':[28] possible premonitions of the next book.

Between October 1926 and January 1927 she revised the novel, working at the typewriter, and still liking it: 'easily the best of my books'.[29] While she was revising, she and Leonard went for a winter holiday to a house near St Ives, and she wrote ruefully: 'All my facts about Lighthouses are wrong.'[30] On 23 January 1927 Leonard read the novel and called it a 'masterpiece'.[31] Between February and March she revised two sets of proofs for the American and English editions (which meant that the two first editions were considerably different from each other). Even during this drudgery, and anxiety about its reception, she was still pleased with it:

> Dear me, how lovely some parts of The Lighthouse are! Soft & pliable, & I think deep, & never a word wrong for a page at a time.[32]

Retrospectively, she saw it as a successful endeavour to do the two things at once she makes Lily do in the last part of the book: understand her own feelings, and create a structure that worked: 'I . . . got down to my depths & made shapes square up.'[33] And the novel is full of shapes, which vary and change depending on perspective: 'So much depends, she thought, upon distance.'

These shapes hover on the edge of the symbolic. 'I am making some use of symbolism, I observe', she observed drily, and warily, as she reached the end of the first draft.[34] But she backed off from Roger Fry's suggestion that arriving at the Lighthouse 'has a symbolic meaning which escapes me':

> I meant *nothing* by The Lighthouse. One has to have a central line down the middle of the book to hold the design together. I saw that all sorts of feelings would accrue to this, but I refused to think them out, and trusted that people would make it the deposit for their own emotions – which they have done, one thinking it means one thing another another. I can't manage Symbolism except in this vague, generalised way. Whether its right or wrong I don't know, but directly I'm told what a thing means, it becomes hateful to me.[35]

Her version of symbolism is like her process of 'scene making'. 'Always a scene has arranged itself: representative; enduring.'[36] It might be her father 'sitting in a boat, reciting "We perished, each alone" ', or her mother sitting by the window knitting while the children played cricket. These scenes are not codes, they do not 'stand' for something else.

As the novel progressed, some of its intended ingredients were suppressed, others were deepened. Particular images – light, waves, the lighthouse – were developed and thickened. Narrative which began as authorially omniscient was shifted inside the character's inner speech. Some characters were altered a good deal; in general the politics of the novel's first draft were more explicit. Lily's feelings of oppression, sitting opposite Charles Tansley at the dinner table (who seems to her to be saying 'women can't paint, women can't write'), originally took the form of a more extended inner debate, anticipating *A Room of One's Own*:

> Lily Briscoe remembered that [everyone] man has Shakespeare [behind him]; & women have not.[37]

But she doesn't want to express her 'horror & despair; annihilation; nonentity' because she 'could not bear to be called, as she might have been called had she come out with her views a feminist.' There is a line scored through this passage, and the word 'feminist' is censored from the novel. Charles Tansley's scornful and envious class-feeling about the Ramsays becomes more muted too, and so does the endurance of the working-classes, like the charwoman Mrs McNab, putting up in wartime with what the 'kings and kaisers' have brought about. Even so, the political argument of the novel pushes strongly against its tender nostalgia and its rhythmic, fluid patterns.

Behind the Ramsay family is a history of imperialism, the history of the Stephen family. Mrs Ramsay's relatives govern India, and Mr Ramsay, though socially eccentric and not rich, is part of the educational establishment. He has his own empire too, the little island of the family. Mr Ramsay's metaphorical leadership of men is partly a comic fantasy, but it is serious too. He is heroic, but he is also a tyrant. The mixture of courtly veneration and domination with which he treats his wife is a product of the patriarchal system, as well as being characteristic of him. Napoleon, Carlyle, and the French Revolution are mentioned often enough in the men's conversation to make it clear that a male tradition of imperialist despotism is being resisted. Resisted by Mrs Ramsay with an alternative language of matriarchy; by Lily with her painting; by William Bankes with his scientific objectivity; by the homosexual Augustus Carmichael with his mystical, impersonal Persian poetry, and by the children. *To the Lighthouse* re-enacts the 'republic' of the Stephen children resisting the tyranny of their father and half-brothers.[38]

479

When Vanessa read the novel in May 1927, she was deeply stirred by it.

> It seemed to me in the first part of the book you have given a portrait of mother which is more like her to me than anything I could ever have conceived possible. It is almost painful to have her so raised from the dead. You have made one feel the extraordinary beauty of her character, which must be the most difficult thing in the world to do. It was like meeting her again with oneself grown up and on equal terms and it seems to me the most astonishing feat of creation to have been able to see her such a way. – You have given father too I think as clearly, but perhaps, I may be wrong, that isn't quite so difficult. There is more to catch hold of. Still it seems to me to be the only thing about him which ever gave a true idea. So you see as far as portrait painting goes you seem to me to be a supreme artist and it is so shattering to find oneself face to face with those two again that I can hardly consider anything else.[39]

This moved and moving response to the book makes it very tempting to read *To the Lighthouse*, as Vanessa did, as a simple transcription of Virginia Stephen's family life. It is a profoundly autobiographical novel, very close, in places, to the *Mausoleum Book* and to her parents' letters, to the 'Reminiscences', to her early diaries and her memoirs, and to the later 'Sketch of the Past'.[40] It is also, as Vanessa went on to say, 'a great work of art'. Virginia Woolf, in her retrospective story of the Victorian family, diffuses her personal self. She is the child Rose, choosing her mother's jewelry in the parental bedroom. She is the adolescent Nancy, making an empire out of a rock pool and drawing in her skirts at the sight of adult passion. She is Cam in the nursery being talked asleep by her mother, and Cam in the boat adoring and hating her father. She is Lily Briscoe, painting her picture, like Virginia Woolf writing this book. 'The painting bits', which she feared Vanessa would laugh at,[41] are derived from Vanessa and from exchanges with Jacques Raverat and Roger Fry. And Vanessa, with her family of children and her beauty and shabbiness and privacy, also becomes the mother in the novel: 'Probably there is a great deal of you in Mrs Ramsay'.[42] When Virginia goes to a lecture by Tatiana Tolstoi, she turns into Charles Tansley, hating the upper classes and wishing 'to excuse my life to Tolstoi'.[43] The deaths of Prue and Mrs Ramsay, going across the fields in their white wreaths, echo the deaths of Julia and Stella. But in December 1925, she was thinking again about Katherine, 'that faint ghost', whose death two years before had brought into her mind the image of 'Katherine putting on a white wreath, & leaving us, called away; made dignified, chosen'.[44] Lily's erotic desire for physical closeness to Mrs Ramsay is charged up by Virginia's growing feelings for Vita, whom she imagines, while she is writing the novel, as like 'a lighthouse, fitful, sudden, remote'.[45] Mrs Ramsay's dark feelings about solitude and death are also Virginia's.

Of all these complicated connections between the life and the fiction, perhaps the most surprising – and, it may be, the deepest – is between Virginia Woolf and Mr Ramsay. The comic, tyrannical, charismatic father is often described as the enemy in the novel. But his long walks and his declamations of poetry are as much like her. And so are many of his thoughts. When he broods on the relation between Shakespeare and the liftman in the Tube, or is obsessed about his own immortality, it is not only Leslie Stephen's anxieties and egotism she is invoking. 'Murry says my works won't be read in 10 years time', she wrote in the diary for 8 February 1926, next to her joyful exclamation about the easy progress of *To the Lighthouse*.[46] John Middleton Murry's article on 'The Classical Revival', which described *Jacob's Room* and *The Waste Land* as failures that nobody would be reading in ten or fifty years' time was as much the source for Mr Ramsay's wanting to reach R as Leslie Stephen's lamentations in the *Mausoleum Book*.

But the simple reading is also right. *To the Lighthouse* is about her childhood, her relationship with her father as she grew up, her unassuageable grief for her mother and her feelings of rivalrous solidarity with her sister and brothers. She wanted to call it an elegy and not a novel, because it is a memorial of her powerful, loved, dead parents. It has that peculiarly intimate deep feeling which comes out of fictions where childhood memory is being uncovered and appeased, like George Eliot's *The Mill on the Floss*, or Katherine Mansfield's *Prelude*, or Joyce's *A Portrait of the Artist as a Young Man*.

She knew very well (at a time when Freudian analysis was at her door) what she was doing for herself in writing *To the Lighthouse*. She explained it twice, once in the diary for 1928, about eighteen months after finishing the book, and once, many years later, in the 'Sketch of the Past'. Both explanations refer to the writing of the novel in therapeutic terms, but one is about her father and the other about her mother:

1928
Father's birthday. He would have been 1832 96, yes,
96
today; & could have been 96, like other people one has known; but mercifully was not. His life would have entirely ended mine. What would have happened? No writing, no books; – inconceivable. I used to think of him & mother daily; but writing The Lighthouse laid them in my mind.

And now he comes back sometimes, but differently. (I believe this to be true – that I was obsessed by them both, unhealthily; & writing of them was a necessary act.)[47]

It is perfectly true that she obsessed me, in spite of the fact that she died when I was thirteen, until I was forty-four. Then one day walking round Tavistock Square I made up, as I sometimes make up my books, *To The Lighthouse*; in a great, apparently involuntary rush . . . I wrote the book very quickly; and when it was written, I ceased to be obsessed by my mother. I no longer hear her voice; I do not see her.

I suppose that I did for myself what psycho-analysts do for their patients. I expressed some very long felt and deeply felt emotion. And in expressing it I explained it and then laid it to rest.[48]

The writing of *To the Lighthouse* was the closest that Virginia Woolf came, she says, to undergoing psychoanalysis. She invented her own therapy – the narrative – and exorcised her obsession with both her parents. But it also seems, from her repeated choice of words when she describes this process, that she felt the writing of the novel to be a way of pacifying their ghosts. And *To the Lighthouse* is a kind of ghost story, a story of a haunted house. It re-enacts, over twenty years later, the ghostly feelings of the young orphaned Stephens going back to Talland House in 1905, in its return to a Victorian past, and in its echoes of Victorian pastoral elegy. But it is also a twentieth-century post-war novel, concerned with the English class structure and with the social and political legacies of the war as much as with family memory. The savage break of narrative down the middle of the book, like Lily's line down the middle of her painting, is a break with literary tradition as much as with childhood.

The lost safe house and garden are the traditions of writing from which the new writer has to travel, out into formidable space. But the new writing keeps trying to find its way back into the past, so that there is an odd tension in the book between the experimental and the nostalgic. *To the Lighthouse* is about something ending, and it contains a number of endings. Mrs Ramsay finishes her story to James ('And that's the end'), Minta Doyle leaves the last volume of *Middlemarch* on the train, Mr Ramsay reads, after dinner, the end of Scott's story of poor Steenie's drowning. As his journey to the lighthouse ends, he closes his little book (his Plato): 'Mr Ramsay had almost done reading' – and so have we when we read that. The book ends with Lily's 'vision'. It has so much to do with endings because its subject is death, not just people dying and being mourned, but the wish for death. 'If she had said half what he said,' Mrs Ramsay thinks of her husband, 'she would have blown her brains out by now.' She goes into action at the dinner party like a sailor who sets off again wearily, but would almost rather have 'found rest on the floor of the sea'. Mrs Ramsay does not kill herself (though Lily in the manuscript 'had never heard how she had died: only "Suddenly" '),[49] but her deep sense – Virginia Woolf's sense – of the cruelty and sadness of being alive are at the bottom of the whole novel.

As well as endings, though, there are recurrences. A number of things happen twice. There are two dinner parties, the one Mrs Ramsay has in mind in the first section of the novel, and the one we see in full. There are two journeys to the lighthouse, the promised and the actual. There are two lighthouses, too, as seen by James: 'For nothing was simply one thing.' There are two paintings, the one Lily starts in Part I and the one she starts again in Part III. The Ramsays' lives, like the novel, give off 'constantly a sense of repetition'. And Mrs Ramsay returns, as the model for Lily's painting, in the same position she took up in 'The Window'. The ending of the novel is poised between arriving and returning, getting somewhere ('he must have reached it') and being finished. This dark book of loss and grief begins and ends with sentences starting 'Yes'.

TWENTY-EIGHT

Vita

Virginia Woolf sent Vita Sackville-West a dummy copy of the first edition of *To the Lighthouse*, on publication day, 5 May 1927. It was inscribed 'In my opinion the best novel I have ever written.'[1] All the pages were blank. A few nights later she kept herself awake worrying that Vita might not have seen the joke, and sent an anxious note to 'Dearest donkey West': 'Did you understand that when I wrote it was my best book I merely meant because all the pages were empty?' Immediately Vita replied: 'But of course I realised it was a joke; what *do* you take me for? a real donkey?'[2] She followed this with an effusive letter of praise for the 'real' *To the Lighthouse*: 'Darling, it makes me afraid of you. Afraid of your penetration and loveliness and genius.' How could Virginia have thought that she wouldn't like the novel? Vita could say nothing 'illuminating' about it 'but I leave that to your clever friends!' The letter ended: 'Bless you, my lovely Virginia.' Virginia thanked her warmly, explaining that she had feared Vita would find the novel 'too psychological', too full of personal relationships; and was still anxious that Vita might have thought it 'sentimental'. The letter continued with arrangements for a trip they were about to make to Oxford; Vita had agreed to go with her while she lectured on poetry and fiction to undergraduates, but now she was embarrassed at having asked her. She added, 'Why do you think me "lonely"; lovely I understand; not altogether, lonely.'[3]

The blank-paged book, surrounded by all these written pages of protestations and misunderstandings, is a tempting image. It is suggestive both about this relationship and about Virginia Woolf's work. François Mauriac called 'the volume of blank pages, which Virginia Woolf described as her "best book": 'not the product of an author who had nothing more to say (those who have nothing to say, go on for ever saying it) but of one who had too much, and when I say too much, I mean in terms of quality rather than quantity.' He called her one of the writers who 'are moving towards silence'.[4]

The dummy book suggests how close Virginia and Vita had become by 1927 for Virginia to risk this joke, and tells something too about how their intimacy worked. They went in for surprises and gestures and gifts, challenges and refusals. Vita was always giving Virginia things (or being told not to): a miniature garden in a bowl, bottles of Spanish wine, a puppy, her books for the Hogarth Press. Or she would urge her to splash out, to treat herself – on a moleskin coat, or a trip to Spain or France. Virginia always thought of the risks in giving, and receiving. 'The Virginia who refuses is a very instinctive & therefore powerful person', she told herself, in 1926.[5] She was afraid, when they went to France together for a few days in 1928, that they would give themselves away, find each other out.[6] The story of this relationship could be summed up by saying that more was asked (on both sides) than could be given.

Although they didn't 'find each other out', they 'made each other up'. Both these women were professional writers. They cast each other, and themselves, in dramatic roles. Virginia set the terms, but Vita played up. Vita was the mother, Virginia was the child. Virginia was the will o' the wisp, the invalid, the frail virgin, the 'ragamuffin' or 'scallywag', the puritan, the sharp-eyed intellectual with the 'clever friends', the talker, the wit. Vita was the rich, supple, luxurious, high-coloured, glowing, dusky, fruity, fiery, winy, passionate, striding, adventuring traveller; also dumb, dense, a 'donkey'. Virginia was the one with the head, Vita was the one with the legs.

These exaggerated versions of themselves were their routes to intimacy. But they had many misunderstandings. Of all her close relationships, that with Vita made Virginia most aware of how little we know of the people we are closest to:

I'm so orderly am I? I wish you could live in my brain for a week. It is washed with the most violent waves of emotion. What about? I dont know. It begins on waking; and I never know which – shall I be happy? Shall I be miserable. I grant, I keep up some mechanical activity with my hands, setting type, ordering dinner. Without this, I should brood ceaselessly. And you think it all fixed and settled. Do we then know nobody? – only our own versions of them, which, as likely as not, are emanations from ourselves.[7]

This, one of the most intimate accounts of herself she ever wrote to another person, takes the form of a statement about the impossibility of intimacy. She is often struck by how partial her 'own version' of Vita is: 'there may be many parts of her perfectly unillumined.'[8] Like others of Vita's friends, she sensed something 'dense' or 'blank' in her.[9]

There is a great deal of manner and effort in their letters to each other. Narcissism is one of their themes: Vita is aware of this too. Receiving *Orlando*, she falls in love with herself. But the effusions which make their relationship read so artificially were also ways of evading the blanks between them. Virginia turned their secret codes and key words into safety valves, prophylactics against estrangement and quarrels. When their affair began in December 1925, they went shopping together in Sevenoaks, near Long Barn, Vita's house in Kent. Virginia saw Vita striding into the fishmonger's shop, wearing pink and pearls, 'with a candlelit radiance, stalking on legs like beech trees, pink glowing, grape clustered, pearl hung'.[10] It seemed to sum up Vita's colourful, powerful presence, and her distinction from the 'commonplace' scene. The vision in the fishmonger's became a kind of password to intimacy. Virginia cited it whenever she wanted to remind Vita of their first night together, or when she needed to reassert her influence. Eventually it became a nostalgic fixture – an example of how Virginia liked to replay scenes and reclaim the past. 'Aint it odd how the vision at the Sevenoaks fishmongers has worked itself into my idea of you?'[11] When she felt, in 1935, that the friendship was over, this vision remained: 'There she hangs, in the fishmongers at Sevenoaks, all pink jersey & pearls; & thats an end of it.'[12]

Virginia co-opted Vita into her menagerie of imaginary animals. Vita was Towser the sheepdog and Virginia was the little mole in her moleskin coat,[13] the little squirrel nestling up, or a more dangerous creature, 'her soft crevices lined with hooks'.[14] In 1928 she turned herself into a new animal: 'And by the way I'm now called Bosman's Potto, *not* V.W. by arrangement – A finer name, don't you think? More resonant.'[15] Real dogs played a big part in their correspondence, too: the puppy Pinker (or 'Pinka') which Vita gave to the Woolfs in 1926 (the model for Flush), and the Woolfs' dog Grizzle. The dogs allowed for running jokes about sex and disobedience and discipline. How can Virginia face her husband (she asked Vita) with the confession, 'not that I've been seduced, but that Grizzle has.'[16] It's something of a relief to find her saying, in one letter, 'But enough of dogs'.[17]

There is a gap between the tone of their letters, and the drier, more reserved accounts of the relationship in Virginia's diary. While Vita is telling Harold Nicolson how much she loves Virginia and how much Virginia loves her,[18] Virginia is asking herself how much she *does* like her – whether she *is* in love with her. Because she minds so much, in November 1925, when Vita has to go away for months to join Harold in Persia, she concludes 'that I am genuinely fond of her . . . after sifting & filing, much, I am sure, remains'.[19] This is not very effusive. While the letters exaggerate and dress up, the diary censors itself. She never writes any details of their physical intimacy, though she often describes what it feels like to be with her. She is laconic about the effect of the relationship on Leonard. She mostly plays down her jealousy of Vita's other lovers. And so the friendship with Vita, which is extremely well documented,[20] opens up the tricky relationship between evidence and events.

For a reclusive person who disliked vulgarity and 'la populace', Vita Sackville-West has been extremely exposed, both in her life-time (a contested inheritance, a trial, a scandalous lesbian liaison) and after it. Nigel Nicolson's decision in 1973 to publish his mother's secret manuscript of her affair with Violet Trefusis, followed by a television series, books and plays on Vita and Virginia, and a film of *Orlando*, have made Vita's story better known, now, than her works. (In the 1920s, when they became intimate, Vita was a more popular and better-selling author than Virginia.) Few people now read *The Edwardians* or *The Land*, compared with the number who visit Sissinghurst and Knole, or who watched *Portrait of a Marriage* or *Orlando*.

The glamorous and sensational facts of Vita's life, which Victoria Glendinning summed up as 'an adventure story', contrast dramatically with Virginia Woolf's history. Some of it would have been known to Virginia when they were introduced at the end of 1922. And part of the attraction was the story Vita had to tell. Virginia fell on it, dramatised and exaggerated it, long before she wrote *Orlando*. But Vita hardly needed dramatising for her to make a strong impression on Virginia.

First, there was the ancestry. The Sackville family went back to William the Conqueror; they were made Earls of Dorset in the sixteenth century, and granted the vast Kentish house of Knole by Elizabeth I. They were parliamentarians, ambassadors, royalists; Charles Sackville, 6th Earl of Dorset, was a poet and literary patron. Then there was the great house, built over four acres, like a gigantic, palatial Oxford college, with (legend had it) seven courts, fifty-two staircases, and 365 rooms.[21] Knole was Vita's first passion (she grew up there) and her greatest lost love (she could not inherit, as she was a woman). The first gift Virginia received from Vita after their first meeting was a copy of *Knole & the Sackvilles*. And she would always associate Vita with her house and ancestry: it was as much the inspiration for *Orlando* as Vita was herself.

Then there were the family scandals, inextricably tangled up with the inheritance of Knole:[22] the famous family court case over her father's claim to the house, when Vita was eighteen, and then the legal dispute over the fortune which Vita's mother was left by her lover. There was a long and bitter estrangement between Vita's parents, and, most dramatic of all, the destructive and demanding presence of Vita's mother. Lady Sackville ('Bonne Mama', or 'BM') was the dominant figure in Vita's childhood,[23] and Vita's dark personality – her fatalism, her narcissism, her love of solitude, and her susceptibility to passionate relationships – were shaped by her painful love-affair with this self-pitying, temperamental mother.[24]

Vita's family seemed exotic and strange to Virginia Woolf. Her marriage, though, was in some respects comparable to her own. Vita had fallen in love with Harold Nicolson when she was twenty and he was a charming, clever, lively young diplomat. (At the time, typically, she was also involved with two girlfriends, one of them Violet Keppel, the wild, sexy, sophisticated daughter of Edward VII's mistress.) In 1917, when Vita was four years married and had had two sons and a stillborn child, she found out that Harold was homosexual (and had VD). A year later she began a passionate affair with Violet, now Trefusis, culminating in 1920 in the two husbands' dramatic pursuit to fetch their wives back from France.[25] Thereafter the marriage readjusted to a dedicated companionship which would accommodate and survive their homosexual affairs. It worked through long periods of separateness, a habit of affectionate letter-writing, a code of evasion about their sexual activities, a mutual commitment to their two sons, and clearly demarcated professional lives.[26] The structure only worked, Vita thought, because she and Harold had homosexual affairs.

> If you were in love with another woman, or I with another man, we should both or either of us be finding a natural sexual fulfilment which would inevitably rob our own relationship of something. As it is, the liaisons which you and I contract are something perfectly apart from the more natural and normal attitude we have towards each other, and therefore don't interfere. But it would be dangerous for ordinary people.[27]

This letter, written while Vita was in love with Virginia, revealed two assumptions: one, that homosexual love was less 'natural'; two, that she and Harold were extraordinary people. Both assumptions suggest that, though she had no interest in guilt or shame – she didn't think of herself as an 'invert', a stigmatised outcast, as Radclyffe Hall did – she did consider herself as a person apart.

Vita's lesbianism was not a political identity nor a public position. It was both known and hidden. In her fictions, Vita often projected herself as a lonely romantic boy, a darkly Byronic, passionate, cruel character, often involved with a desirable, extremely feminine woman. The love-affairs would be doomed because of age or adultery or some other obstruction. So she both displayed and disguised her lesbianism. Sometimes the disguises slipped: in *Challenge*, a romance based on her affair with Violet, the codes were so easily penetrable that her mother persuaded her to withdraw it. In her book of poems, *King's Daughter*, published by Leonard and Virginia in

1929, the love poems to women were so thinly dressed up as classical-pastoral or exotic orientalism that Harold advised against publication (ostensibly on grounds of literary quality); but both Virginia and Vita thought this ridiculously over-cautious. Mostly, though, like many other queer writers of the time, she kept her explicit lesbian writing in the closet, and in her published work encoded her desires as myth or romance or conventional heterosexual comedy.

That doubleness was acted out in Vita's life as well. From the early 1920s she was well known in her circles as a lesbian, or (as Virginia always said) a 'Sapphist'.[28] She cross-dressed, she had lesbian and homosexual friends, she had figured in a lesbian scandal, and she had a reputation for passionate and predatory affairs, a reputation which lay behind Virginia's comment after their first night together: 'These Sapphists *love* women!' At the same time Vita presented herself as a successful writer of pastoral poetry and conventional fictions, as a home-maker, a mother, a diplomat's wife, and a conservative and traditionalist thinker. She and Harold Nicolson broadcast on women and marriage in 1929 (the producer, ironically enough, was Vita's new lover Hilda Matheson), talks which have been variously interpreted as the display of a highly civilised relationship, a muted expression of her feminist disapproval of marriage, and a defensive public smokescreen.[29] Though they agreed that marriage should be redefined and that women should be more independent, they of course said nothing in public about homosexuality within marriage. And though in her fiction Vita was eloquent about the compromises of a married woman's life, she disliked feminism, and was ill-at-ease with Virginia Woolf's polemical writing about women's lives.

When Virginia Woolf wrote to Vita late in 1925 (and Vita immediately repeated it to Harold) that 'in all London, you & I alone like being married,'[30] it was a complicated remark, part joke, part boast, part warning. The joke about the unconventionality of their circles, where any stable marriage looked eccentric, and the boast that within that context they had both evolved a form of marriage they could 'like', was mixed with a warning to Vita (a few weeks before they spent their first night together) that Leonard was essential to her. In fact their marriages were very different. Virginia and Leonard were much closer, professionally and politically, than Vita and Harold. They spent much more time together. They were less effusive to each other, less flashy and self-marketing. (It's hard to imagine them doing a joint broadcast on their married life, though they did do one on publishing.)[31] Leonard had far greater control over Virginia's social choices and the pattern of her days. The Woolfs had quite different ideas about art and writing, class and society, from Vita and Harold. And their structures of intimacy were different. Their marriage worked through stability and reliance and talk, not through adventures and absences and letters. All the same, Virginia's fictional writings on marriage as a possible space for privacy and independence (especially in *Night and Day* and *Mrs Dalloway*) had something in common with Vita's attitudes. When she came to make up a romantic, parodic version of Vita and Harold's marriage in *Orlando*, she invested it with her own feelings.

As with their marriages, so with their sexual orientation, their imaginations and their politics. Virginia and Vita were more different than they were alike: the difference was part of the attraction. Virginia's remark, 'These Sapphists *love* women; friendship is never untinged with amorosity'[32] places herself apart from Vita. She goes on to say that what she likes about Vita and perceives as different is 'her being in short (what I have never been) a real woman'. As a 'Sapphist', as a 'real woman', as a mother, Virginia felt that Vita eclipsed her.

Virginia's preference for her own sex had been a fact of her life since childhood. She turned it into a joke (especially with Violet and Vanessa), a joke which allowed her to express her strong feelings of need without embarrassment. With all her close women friends she employed a comically demanding, amorous flirtatiousness. Her letters from other women (Mary Hutchinson, Ottoline Morrell, Katherine Mansfield, Fredegond Shove, Sibyl Colefax) often read like love letters. But though kisses and pettings and intimate conversations are asked for and provided, she did not define herself as a Sapphist. She could not bear to categorise herself as belonging to a group defined by its sexual behaviour (just as she didn't want to think of herself as an ordinary 'wife', or as a writer of 'novels'). She wanted to avoid all categories.

When she came into contact with a roomful of homosexual friends, or a lesbian group, she felt critical and ill-at-ease. She laughed at the picture of herself at a party sitting 'hug a mugger in a Sapphists Cosy Corner'.[33] Her friendship with Vita put her in closer touch with lesbian households, like Ethel Sands and Nan Hudson in their tasteful château in northern France, or the odd trio of Edy Craig, Christopher St John and 'Tony' (the painter Claire Attwood) at Smallhythe, their converted theatre. But she thought of herself as an outsider in such set-ups. She detested what she called 'the 2ndrate schoolgirl atmosphere'[34] Vita created with her 'girlfriends' (Dorothy Wellesley, Hilda Matheson, Mary Campbell, and, later, Gwen St Aubyn) and was jealously aghast to think she might be identified with them. With Vita, and then (in a different spirit) with Ethel Smyth, she was the recipient of feelings which she did not identify with her own. She played up to these feelings, but played up, at the same time, her marriedness, her delicate health, and her inviolability.

Yet her relationships with women, beginning with Julia, Stella and Vanessa, shaped her life and her writing. Her life-stories of women and the friendships between them are always set against the limitations of heterosexual and marital relationships. Rachel and Helen in *The Voyage Out*, Katharine and Mary in *Night and Day*, Sally and Clarissa in *Mrs Dalloway*, Lily and Mrs Ramsay in *To the Lighthouse*: these are all love-stories. At the end of 1924, when she and Vita were growing closer, she asked herself (thinking of Mary Hutchinson) about the connection between these friendships in her life and her writing:

> If one could be friendly with women, what a pleasure – the relationship so secret & private compared with relations with men. Why not write about it? truthfully? As I think, this diary writing has greatly helped my style; loosened the ligatures.[35]

Is 'friendly' a euphemism for 'lovers'? Perhaps; but what matters is the idea that a 'secret and private' kind of relationship could be written about in the looser language of secret truthfulness which she has been developing in her diary. And the writing which comes out of the intimacy with Vita does that.

But she did not commit herself as 'a Sapphist'. In her writing, unlike Vita's (or Radclyffe Hall's) there are no romances between Byronic heroes and languid girls, no sadomasochistic erotic scenes, no gloomy doomed transvestites. In almost every book, there are intimate and sensual relationships between women who move fluidly between the roles of mothers and daughters, sisters and friends. But Virginia Woolf is ambiguous in her treatment of these female friendships, just as she is at pains to smooth over her radical, angry feminism in *A Room of One's Own*.

This is not just a matter of avoiding censorship, though that would be one of the themes of *Orlando*, a masterpiece of playful subterfuge. It suggests also her preference for sexual amorphousness and complexity, and for an indeterminate, concealed presence as an author. Simplified readings of Vita 'as' Orlando or of Mrs Dalloway's bisexual and virginal marriage as a straightforward representation of Virginia Woolf's own life won't do. She experiments with possibilities and adventures in the writing, but stops teasingly on the edge of confirming her own sexual identity.

When she wrote to Jacques Raverat at the beginning of 1925, asking his views on 'loving one's own sex', she took a lightly disparaging tone on all forms of queerness. She gave Eddy, rather than Vita, Sackville-West as her main example of same-sex love, thus setting Vita in the context of aristocratic homosexuality which she can't take seriously. *Orlando*'s irreverent high camp is anticipated.

> Have you any views on loving one's own sex? All the young men are so inclined, and I can't help finding it mildly foolish; though I have no particular reason. For one thing, all the young men tend to the pretty and ladylike, for some reason, at the moment. They paint and powder, which wasn't the style in our day at Cambridge. I think it does imply some clingingness – a tiny lap dog, called Sackville West, came to see me the other day (a cousin of my aristocrat and will inherit Knole) and my cook said, Who was the lady in the drawing room? He has a voice like a girls, and a face like a persian cats, all white and serious, with large violet eyes and fluffy cheeks. Well, you can't respect the amours of a creature like *that*. Then the ladies, either in self protection, or imitation or genuinely, are given to their sex too. My aristocrat . . . is violently Sapphic, and contracted such a passion for a woman cousin, that they fled to the Tyrol, or some mountainous retreat together, to be followed in an aeroplane by a brace of husbands . . . To tell you a secret, I want to incite my lady to elope with me next. Then I'll drop down on you and tell you all about it.[36]

Her next letter describes a 'typical' Bloomsbury party:

> The 40 young men began waltzing, and the three lovely girls sat together flirting in corners. Isn't it an odd thing that Bloomsbury parties are always thus composed – 40 young men; all from Oxford too, and three girls, who are admitted on condition that they either dress exquisitely, or are some man's mistress, or love each other. Much preferring my own sex, as I do, or at any rate, finding the monotony of young men's conversation considerable, and resenting the eternal pressure which they put, if you're a woman, on one string, [I]find the disproportion excessive, and intend to cultivate women's society entirely in future. Men are all in the light always: with women you swim at once into the silent dusk.[37]

And then she describes a conversation between the 'horribly bored' Leonard and little Eddy ('all men confide in Leonard – especially such as love their own sex'). Again she makes a point of describing both herself and Leonard as standing as unmoved observers, both in and out of the homosexual scene.

Jacques replied by distinguishing between 'sodomy' ('pefectly natural & normal up to the age of about 20. After that, I don't know why, faintly disgusting to me . . . a state of arrested developement.') He had reproached Gide, he said, for writing 'a dull little, dreary little book in defence of it', telling him that Proust had already done it all. Gide had replied that 'Proust has left out the really fine and noble side of it'. 'Sapphism seems to me much more attractive & understandable, & with all those surplus, unattached women about, they must find, shall we say, some outlet for their passions, poor things.' He added: 'I wonder how you would like the exclusive company of women. Not for long, I suspect. One wants a change.'[38] Probably this detached satirical tone (which she liked in Jacques' letters) had an influence on *Orlando*: she did not want *her* book on sexual identity to be dull or dreary. And Jacques pinpointed her resistance to being just one thing or another. She liked to be 'very mixed'.

'What is the effect of all this on me?' she asked herself after her first night alone with Vita at Long Barn, and replied, 'Very mixed'. She knew that what attracted her in Vita was her 'full breastedness' and 'voluptuousness', her aristocratic manners and her capacity for lavishing the 'maternal protection which, for some reason, is what I have always most wished from everyone'. She knew that she would not stay fixed in her feelings for Vita ('one emotion succeeds another'). 'Then I am – altogether so queer in some ways.'[39]

This is a tantalising sentence. *Queer* was certainly a known code word for homosexuality by the 1930s. Virginia used the word suggestively in 1927, in what she told Vita was 'a nice little story about Sapphism': 'Moments of Being: Slater's Pins have no Points'. The story drew on (and echoed in its title) her memory of Greek lessons with Clara Pater, Walter Pater's sister. In the story, she refers to Julius Craye, the 'famous archaeologist', the late brother of 'Miss Craye', as being spoken of in 'an indescribable tone which hinted at something odd, something queer' in him. (And Pater was known to have had something 'queer' about him.)[40] Perhaps Virginia did not have that meaning of 'queer' in mind when she called herself 'altogether so queer in some ways' in her diary entry for 1925. All the same, the turn of phrase tells us something about her mixed reaction to Vita's Sapphism. She may have been 'queer in some ways', but she was not 'altogether so queer' enough for Vita. If Virginia Woolf was lesbian and Vita Sackville-West confirmed that identity, she accepted it only evasively and ambivalently.

The friendship got off to a hesitant start. Vita Sackville-West, 'Mrs Nicolson', was the 'new apparition' at the very end of 1922, introduced by Clive, and invited to dine at Hogarth House, where she was struck by the shabby bohemian mess of the Press in the dining-room. She appeared at the moment of Katherine Mansfield's death, almost as if she were to replace her in Virginia Woolf's life, or as though the relationship with Katherine had made ready, without satisfying, the emotions which Vita would now arouse.

Initially, though, that seemed unlikely. While Vita was writing humorously to Harold (who had cause to be immediately on the alert at this) 'I love Mrs Woolf with a sick passion',[41] Virginia was noting her first impressions of a 'florid, moustached, parakeet coloured' aristocrat, 'hard, handsome, manly; inclined to double chin', with a confident manner but no 'wit'. Vita made her feel 'virgin, shy, & schoolgirlish'; all the same, after dinner 'I rapped out opinions'. (Desmond MacCarthy was there too, moping 'like a tipsy owl in his corner, affectionate & glad to talk to me').[42] These first impressions, like most first impressions, would persist. Her sense of 'something dense instead of vibrant'[43] about Vita would become a joke, but also a problem: Virginia always thought 'donkey West' rather stupid. And Virginia would always be the one (however 'virgin' and 'shy') to 'rap out her opinions'. She would, also, always fear that Vita could not fit in with her old friends. Some weeks later, in March 1923, at dinner with Vita and Harold at 46 Gordon Square with Vanessa, Leonard, Duncan, Clive and Lytton, 'we judged them both incurably stupid'.[44] But Harold remembered that evening having been put down by Lytton and rescued, kindly, by Virginia: 'So at the bottom of my terror of her glimmers a little white stone of gratitude.'[45]

Their worlds seemed quite at odds: Vita began the friendship by proposing Virginia for membership of PEN, which was not to Virginia's taste.[46] A dinner with Vita, Siegfried Sassoon and Lord Berners, which Virginia described to Clive, summed up the differences between them:

When it comes to sitting tight, 2 feet apart, over the fire from 8 to 11.30 – more brain, O God, more brain! So Meredith cries, in a sonnet which in our youth we quoted . . .

Vita was well laughed at about PEN, but the poor girl has lost her way and dont know which light to turn on next . . . 'Why dont you contribute to the Queen's dolls house, Virginia?' 'Is there a W.C. in it, Vita?' 'You're a bit hoity toity, Virginia.' Well, I was educated in the old Cambridge School. 'Ever heard of Moore?' 'George Moore the novelist?' 'My dear Vita, we start at different ends.' The poor girl looks divinely lovely, a little tousled, in a velvet jacket.[47]

Meredith, Cambridge, lavatorial humour and G.E. Moore – old Bloomsbury staples – are placed, for Clive's benefit, against the literary establishment, royalty, popular fiction, and the attractions of the flesh.

Vita felt ill-at-ease. She hated Bloomsbury's Anglo-European modernism (her first reaction to the new house at Tavistock Square was to note 'panels of inconceivable hideousness by DG and Vanessa').[48] She would lend these feelings to her smart, unhappy heroine Evelyn in her novel *Family History* (1932):

Evelyn felt completely out of her element. The conversation disconcerted her too, for there was none of the small-talk to which she was accustomed; if these people had nothing particular to say they merely remained silent. They did not seem to think it worth while talking for the sake of talking. Neither gossip nor personalities interested them, but only ideas . . . Yet they were not solemn. They flashed and laughed, and were eager and argumentative . . . It was clear that the men, in this universe, would not put themselves out to be conventionally civil to women . . . These people were real; Evelyn owned it, much as she hated them.[49]

Even if, to start with, Vita thought Bloomsbury shabby and difficult, and Virginia thought her and Harold posh and stupid, the Woolfs were quickly interested in Vita as a possible, and profitable, new author for the Press, and as a reviewer for the *Nation*. (Leonard's appointment as literary editor in March 1923 came just as they were getting to know Vita.) As with all Virginia's closest relationships, there was at once an overlap between professional commitments and friendship. One of Virginia's first letters to Vita praised her for her reviews in the *Nation*,[50] and one of Vita's first gestures towards Virginia was to agree to write a story for the Press.

Seducers in Ecuador was a cool, quizzical fantasy, meant to appeal to Virginia's taste. Its central character wears tinted glasses to protect himself against a 'daylight world' of 'realism'. Without them he would 'go mad', but wearing them, he responds to the dangerous fantasies of the people travelling with him on a long sea-voyage.[51] In July 1924 Vita was writing this story and Virginia was working on the first draft of *Mrs Dalloway*. Mixed into the same book were notes on the bombast and violence of Elizabethan plays.[52] On 5 July 1924, Vita took Virginia to Knole and to Long Barn for the first time. They drove there with Geoffrey Scott (a smooth, clever littérateur, whom Virginia had met before on her unhappy visit to Florence in 1909) and Dorothy Wellesley (very rich, poetry-loving, married to the future Duke of Wellington.)[53] Virginia was unaware at the time that both these people were in love with Vita, but she didn't warm to either of them, and felt (as Vita felt at Charleston or Gordon Square) quite outside their 'set': she was the 'scallywag', the 'ragamuffin' in the grand house. (She liked Harold more, 'trusty & honest & vigorous' by the fireside at Long Barn.) Lunching with Vita's father Lord Sackville at Knole, seeing the galleries and tapestries and pictures, the 'chairs that Shakespeare might have sat on', and Vita being casual about her Elizabethan ancestors (while her own mind was full of Elizabethan plays), fixed her sense of Vita as a historical phenomenon. 'All these ancestors & centuries, & silver & gold, have bred a perfect body.' So Vita began at once to be Orlando-ised. Virginia was aware that on this visit she did not keep 'my human values & my aesthetic values distinct'. But, after Vita and her friends had put her on the train ('with the lower middle classes') at Sevenoaks, and she looked out of the window at the slums of London, human and aesthetic values began to come apart:

There is Knole, capable of housing all the desperate poor of Judd Street, & with only that one solitary earl in the kernel.[54]

That simple social (and socialist) observation was crucial to this relationship. Vita brought out the historian in Virginia Woolf as much as the snob, but she was always critical of Vita's class, identifying it with too much immunity and not enough intelligence.

The visit to Knole shifted interest into intimacy. They began to make up their versions of each other. Vita had decided that Virginia was 'an experimentalist in humanity' who had had no *grande passion* in her life.[55] She told Virginia that she looked on everything as 'copy'.[56] Virginia was hurt, but recognised that as 'the first stage of intimacy'.[57] Vita came to Monk's House, in a big car with her smart dressing case, 'a perfect lady', intimidating Nelly, but pleasing her hosts. 'Oh yes, I like her, and could tack her onto my equipage for all time; & suppose if life allowed, this might be a friendship of a sort.'[58] Though with Vita in it, Monk's House looked like 'a ruined barn'.

Virginia liked *Seducers* (she saw her own face in it) and was seduced by having it dedicated to her; she responded with 'childlike dazzled affection'.[59] She was finishing the party scene in *Mrs Dalloway* and beginning the final draft. It was a delicate moment. Leonard was absorbed in the Labour Party and the *Nation* ('he works & works').[60] Vita provided attention and devotion. Virginia's letters to Jacques filled up with Sapphism.

A comical letter to Molly MacCarthy in October 1924 suggested some agitation too. The letter was written alone at Rodmell, sitting by the fire and 'wishing for a companion' (Leonard was in London). It begins with a joke about not having reached the menopause ('the funny time') and runs on into a caricature of Freud's *Collected Papers* (currently filling up the basement of Tavistock Square.)[61] A sidelong glance at the proofs of one case-history has left her with the impression of how 'Mr A B threw a bottle of red ink on to the sheets of his marriage bed to excuse his impotence to the housemaid, but threw it in the wrong place, which unhinged his wife's mind, – and to this day she pours claret on the dinner table.' 'We could all go on like that for hours', she comments, attributing this narrative to German 'imbecility'. After this distorted parody of Freud's lecture on 'The Sense of Symptoms',[62] she comes to the letter's central admission. She tells Molly that she has reviewed her memoir (*A Nineteenth Century Childhood*) in the *Times*

Literary Supplement, and makes play with her own embarrassment at having reviewed a friend, and Molly's embarrassment at being praised. 'I thought I'd better make a breast of it; (clean breast it should be).' Now Molly will be 'squirming . . . like a toad one's half trodden on in the dark'. Then, she asks playfully if she will be 'raped' alone at night in Rodmell; but 'I say, I'm past raping'. And then on to a description of 'Vita Nicolson, more than ever like a Guards officer in bearskin and breeches'. This medley of stained sheets, clean breasts, Freudian slips, squirming things half-trodden underfoot, and jokes about impotence, the menopause, and being past raping, culminating in a manly vision of Vita as dominatrix, suggests – if she were to make a clean breast of it – that she was excited and aroused.

But the flirtatious friendship with Vita might have gone on without acceleration, if not for a crisis in Virginia's life in 1925. The year of the move to Tavistock Square, 1924, was a time of great activity. Though *Mrs Dalloway* gave her some anguish, much of the writing was 'fast & free'.[63] She was getting two books done, the novel and *The Common Reader*, and energetically defining her position on modern fiction. There were moments of depression, of trembling hands, and 'fritter to my nerves' ('Cut me anywhere, & I bleed too profusely. Life has bred too much "feeling" of a kind in me').[64] But there was also a sense of power and achievement. This rushed her on into the spring of 1925. She and Leonard took a pleasurable holiday in France, in the fishing village of Cassis near Marseilles (where Vanessa would soon establish a 'Charleston in France'). She felt happy, in spite of the news of Jacques' death. *Mrs Dalloway* and *The Common Reader* came out to much acclaim, public and private, and she 'got through the splash' by quickly writing some short stories. Though she was constantly 'taking the temperature' of the books' reception, and finding it difficult to 'settle in, contract, & shut myself off',[65] she was excited about her sudden rush of ideas for the next book and wanted to get at it. And she was going about the town, to parties and on outings, much to Leonard's disapproval.

Suddenly in midsummer there was a crash. At a Charleston party in August to celebrate Quentin's fifteenth birthday, 'V. fainted' (as noted baldly in Leonard's diary.) For months afterwards she was very unwell, and deeply frustrated that she could not get on with *To the Lighthouse*.[66] In September, Harold Nicolson was posted to Tehran, and Vita prepared to join him in Persia in the New Year. The combination of Virginia's illness and Vita's impending absence softened their feelings for each other. Their letters became more intimate. Virginia was writing 'On Being Ill', on how illness makes us long for the absent, and how it makes us say things we would not usually say to the people we love.[67]

In her letters, she was saying such things. She fantasised Vita as a pagan creature, 'stamping out the hops in a great vat in Kent – stark naked, brown as a satyr & very beautiful'. Vita was now writing her long Virgilian pastoral poem, *The Land*; Virginia said she was 'old fashioned' in her poetry, and wanted lots of facts, about the 'habits of earthworms'. (This debate about poetry, whether it could be 'old fashioned' rather than modern, and how it differed from prose, was one of their continuing themes.)[68] She told her, strangely, not to go 'striding above my head in the moonlight, exquisitely beautiful though the vision is'.[69] She said she was planning an exotic gala night in London where Vita would appear 'like a lighthouse'.[70] Vita wrote back encouraging and adoring letters, praising her for her remarkable achievements.[71] Lying in her room, Virginia tried to take possession of her through fantasy: 'I try to invent you for myself', she wrote; but Vita kept slipping out of her grasp: 'I find you going off.'[72] By November she felt that illness had 'loosened the earth about the roots' of this affection; she was beginning to mind very much that Vita was going away. She was thinking about death. Gwen Raverat came to see her and they talked about Jacques. Madge Vaughan died – and she felt nothing. But she did not yet count Vita among the six people whose deaths would irrevocably alter her life: these were Leonard, Vanessa, Duncan, Lytton, Clive, and Morgan Forster.[73]

When Vita did not get in touch, in December, she wanted to cry like a child. Witnessing this state of mind, Leonard urged her to invite herself to Long Barn, and put her into Vita's hands with the message: 'I enclose Virginia and hope she will behave.'[74] And so, thanks to Leonard, this 'wounded & stricken year' of 1925 wound up 'in great style'.

Vita picked Virginia up from London in her car (having just got rid of Geoffrey Scott). They drove to Long Barn and spent two days and nights alone. The first evening was 'peaceful', according to Vita's diary. Late that night she wrote reassuringly to Harold saying that she was not going to fall in love with Virginia, nor Virginia with her (nor, for that matter, she with Leonard, or Leonard with her.) The second day was spent shopping in Sevenoaks (where Virginia had her vision of Vita in the fishmonger's). Vita added to her letter to Harold that Virginia liked *The Land*, and liked Vita. 'She said she depends on me. She is so vulnerable under all her brilliance. I do love her, but not b.s.ly.' (This was the code which Harold and Vita used for homosexual love: it stood for 'back-stairs-ly'.) But the second night was 'not peaceful'; they stayed up until 3 a.m., talking, intimate, amorous. The next day Vita added yet more to her letter to Harold: how 'mentally exciting' Virginia was, how their friendship was advancing 'by leaps and bounds': 'I love her, but couldnt fall in love with her, so don't be nervous!' (These protestations aroused Harold's anxieties. He replied from Tehran that he thought Virginia and Vita should be good for each other, but that she had not got 'la main heureuse' with married couples.)[75] Leonard arrived, and Vita drove them both back to London on the Sunday, leaving Tavistock Square without being offered any lunch (an omission which made Virginia wake up trembling with shame in the night).

Virginia's afterword to her diary, on Vita's Sapphic amorosity and fullbreastedness and maternal affection, was full of reservations: 'How much shall I really miss her?' In retrospect, as the weekend became mythologised, they would joke to each other about Virginia's bad behaviour on the sofa, how she had 'snared' and 'surprised' Vita that night.[76] It seems that Virginia was as seductive as she was seduced. She was the one who was teasing and flirting, her sensuality and her will as much in play as Vita's.

The new 'affair' at once attracted Clive's jealous attention. Vita went to Boxing Day lunch at Charleston ('very plain living and high thinking', she described it to Harold).[77] Clive noted that Vita was 'very shy and handsome and doting on Virginia'. He told Mary that the family gave Virginia a rough time in front of her new admirer, raking over old ashes: 'Vanessa was none too merciful. For my part, I told her that I had definitively fallen out of love with her in 1911.'[78] At a New Year houseparty at Dorothy Wellesley's, Clive kept asking Vita in public if she had gone to bed with Virginia. 'I think my NEVER convinced him and everybody else of its truth', Vita wrote, teasingly, to a worried Harold.[79]

In January there was a succesion of farewell scenes in Tavistock Square, with Virginia ill again – 'the iron bed had returned to the drawing room'.[80] Then Vita went to Persia (with Dorothy), and love-making turned into letter-writing. Virginia accurately predicted her feelings to herself: 'I shall want her, clearly & distinctly. Then not – & so on.'[81] Later Virginia would tell Vita that she surprised and alarmed herself by how much she missed her.[82] She missed 'the glow & the flattery',[83] the gratification of being gushed over.

These images of fullness poured into her book. While Vita was away she became deeply, even alarmingly, absorbed in To the Lighthouse.[84] She told herself how profusely she was writing, how she was reaching whatever 'fruit hangs in my soul' (her old favourite image from Cymbeline, that she used to quote to Thoby). 'I am now writing as fast & freely as I have written in the whole of my life.' 'Fertility and fluency' were her new aims: 'I used to plead for a kind of close, terse, effort.'[85] The language she used for the writing of the book was like her language for Vita, who seemed to have fertilised her mind. In an unusually detailed letter about her writing, she told Vita about the importance of rhythm. Rhythm was a wave which could 'dislodge' and release ideas and visions: '& then, as it breaks & tumbles in the mind, it makes waves to fit it.'[86] It was as if the person she was writing to had also 'dislodged' and liberated something previously 'close' and 'terse'. And Lily's longing for Mrs Ramsay in the novel was coloured by her missing Vita. She would put into the later stages of *To the Lighthouse* a passage on 'people going away & the effect on one's feeling for them'.[87]

Vita wrote passionately ('I am reduced to a thing that wants Virginia'), playing down the presence of Dotty, and giving rich, entertaining travel-narratives of India and Egypt and Persia. They now established the conventions of Vita as the exotic gypsy/ambassadress, Virginia as the stay-at-home whom Vita wanted to steal away to some 'absurdly romantic place'.[88] Virginia told wry stories of what Vita called 'Gloomsbury' – of the Press, of Leonard's decision to give up the *Nation* (he went part-time), of an embarrassing dinner at Rose Macaulay's – and countered the dazzle of Asia with panegyrics to the beauty of the English spring.[89]

Absence allowed Virginia to speak more intimately, to air what she called her 'pigmy emotions'. She told Vita about her feelings for Nessa and Duncan – 'who pour out pure gaiety and pleasure in life, not brilliantly or sparklingly, but freely quietly luminously'. She talked about an argument with Eddy Sackville-West over snobbery; she told Vita how her upbringing had produced a character lacking in 'jolly vulgarity': 'No school, mooning about alone among my father's books . . . only rages with my half brothers, and being walked off my legs round the Serpentine by my father.' (Vita replied that she well understood the effect of a peculiar upbringing.) She described, after a visit to some old acquaintances, Walter Leaf and his wife, how she was filled with a powerful feeling of the 'profound natural happiness' of ordinary English family life. All these items were challenges to Vita and her view of life, as well as intimate gifts.[90] She did not, however, describe to her the details of the General Strike. Vita arrived back in the middle of it, in May. Unlike the Woolfs, she was not in sympathy with the strikers.

Virginia knew that her mood was shifting as reunion loomed; there might be embarrassment in seeing each other in the flesh after such intimate writing. ('You have broken down my defences', Vita had written from Trieste – not the other way around.)[91] While Virginia was asking herself, 'Am I in love with her?', she thought that when they saw each other again Vita might be saying: 'Well, is this all?'[92] Was this going to be a love-affair, or would they settle into flirtatious companionship? When they did meet, Vita was tired and shy, Virginia talked to cover their awkwardness.

After Persia, they saw each other often, but were not at the centre of each other's lives: Vita's 'unillumined' side was taken up much more with Dorothy Wellesley; Virginia was deep in *To the Lighthouse*. But she moved pleasurably in and out of the gratifying friendship. In the warm June, Vita came to stay at Monk's House for two nights. She described to Harold Nicolson how proud the Woolfs were of their new lavatory and bathroom ('They both run upstairs every now and then and pull the plug just for the sheer fun of it, and come down and say, "It worked very well that time – did you hear?" rather as the mars might do if their standard of luxury were lower than it is.') Virginia, she said, was embroidering 'a rose, a black lace fan, a box of matches, and four playing cards, on a mauve canvas background, from a design by her sister'. She kept stopping Vita from writing: ' "You have written enough, let us talk about copulation." '[93] The second night Leonard went to London and they were alone together, perhaps doing more than 'talking about copulation': 'I did sleep with her at Rodmell', Vita reported later to Harold.[94] But Virginia wrote to Leonard: 'Lonely day. Longing to see all hearts.'[95] On 16 June, Vita told Harold: 'We did have two very good days, and I like having her friendship – as who wouldn't? Her brilliance is simply amazing. She loves your Mar, and she is so *nice* as well as everything else. I motored her up and restored her safe to Leonard.'[96] But she added that Virginia was not a person she would tell her troubles to.

Through the summer of 1926, Virginia summoned Vita commandingly in notes and letters: 'Anyhow, dine, tea, Friday'; 'Will you come on after your play on Thursday and see me alone'; 'Will you dine with me off radishes alone in the kitchen'. They went to Stravinsky's new ballets at the Haymarket, Virginia wearing an extraordinary outfit:

It was very odd indeed, orange and black, with a hat to match – a sort of top-hat made of straw with two orange feathers like Mercury's wings – but although odd it was curiously becoming, and pleased Virginia because there could be absolutely no doubt as to which was the front and which the back.[97]

After the theatre Virginia shivered with excitement: 'I couldn't get her away from the theatre at all, and we strolled up and down, with the dark blue sky overhead, and groups of well-dressed people talking, and it was all very like Mrs Dalloway.' A 'dwarf on crutches' came past who 'frightened' Virginia. They went on to dinner at the Eiffel Tower with a Hogarth Press author, Viola Tree, and Dorothy Todd. On another June evening they went to see *Façade* at the Chenil Galleries in Chelsea, arriving late and pushing their way through the fashionable audience to seats in the front. (The public behaviour of this striking pair may well have been haughty and intimidating.) Vita observed Virginia getting drunk on the crowd 'as you and I do on champagne'. In the street they met Vanessa ('In the dark in her quiet black hat'); Duncan emerged from a pub carrying a hardboiled egg. They all went to Clive's house (where Clive mocked Virginia's hat and Leonard, who met them there, 'got silent').[98] Virginia went to Garsington, met H.G. Wells and Robert Bridges and Osbert Sitwell, and felt the hourglass of the summer running on 'rapidly & rather sandily'. Vita (with newly fashionable shingled hair) came to a disreputable Bloomsbury party of Vanessa's in July and Virginia 'carried her to the top of the house'.[99] Virginia turned down a fashionable house party at Long Barn, but went to stay there for one night in July after her visit to Hardy. They talked intimately and stayed up very late. ('Thinking about copulation', Virginia wrote tantalisingly afterwards, 'I now remember a whole chapter of my past that I forgot, I think, to tell you.')[100] Vita gave her Pinker, the spaniel, and drove her back to Rodmell, reporting to Harold that evening on how funny Virginia was, how she made her laugh ('& *so* sane, when not mad. And so how [pathetic] about going mad again').[101] And indeed the moment she got back to Rodmell, Virginia collapsed with 'a whole nervous breakdown in miniature', and could do nothing but sit in a chair and sleep. ('Character & idiosyncrasy as Virginia Woolf completely sunk out.')[102] This exciting intimacy took its toll.

That summer Vita was working hard on her travel book on Persia, *Passenger to Tehran*, which she had promised to give to the Hogarth Press. (This was the only 'muddle' she was in over Virginia, she told Harold: she couldn't go on refusing her the book, though her previous publisher would be annoyed.)[103] There were more visits to Rodmell in August: on the first, finding Virginia 'very sunburnt & attractive, with a fortnight's worth of penned-up conversation',[104] on the second feeling sick, while Virginia was walking her down to the water-meadows, but not telling her.[105] In September Vita's poem *The Land* (dedicated to Dorothy Wellesley) was published. When Virginia had read it earlier in the year she had been kind about it.[106] But she also told Vita that it lacked 'a little central transparency: Some sudden intensity'.[107] It was the key to her dissatisfaction with Vita. To herself she complained (jealous of its success?) about its subject and manner: 'so smooth, so mild'.[108] She sent Vita her good reviews and prophesied (correctly) that she would win the Hawthornden Prize. Her reaction hovered between generosity and mockery.

Vanessa (in Venice in June 1926, exhibiting at the London Artists' Association, and at Charleston later in the summer) was wary of Vita; she told Virginia that Vita eyed Vanessa 'as an Arab steed looking from the corner of its eye on some long-eared mule'.[109] Virginia encouraged this frisson of rivalry ('you do your best to stir up jealousy between us', Vanessa wrote). She teased Vanessa: 'But you are bored by Vita, bored by love, bored by me, & everything to do with me'.[110] Vita courted Vanessa, and asked her to paint her a portrait of Virginia. 'So beautiful, so charming,' she said of her to Virginia. This was at once repeated, with the caveat: her 'motives are suspect'.[111] So the sisters united in their dryness and sharpness against Vita's effusions. The triangular jealousy became a running joke between them: 'Has your Vita gone? Dont expend all your energies on letter writing to her. I consider I have first claim.'[112]

Harold Nicolson was getting increasingly anxious. Was there going to be 'a muddle'? It was like 'smoking over a petrol tank'.[113] Vita wrote to reassure him several times, describing the exact nature of her feeling for Virginia this summer of 1926. It was quite unlike her passion for Violet Trefusis, she insisted:

> One's love for Virginia is a very different thing: a mental thing, a spiritual thing if you like, an intellectual thing, and she inspires a feeling of tenderness which I suppose is because of her funny mixture of hardness and softness – the hardness of her mind, and her terror of going mad again. She makes me feel protective. Also she loves me, which flatters and pleases me. Also . . . I am scared to death of arousing physical feelings in her, because of the madness. I don't know what effect it would have, you see; and that is a fire with which I have no wish to play. No, thank you. I have too much real affection and respect. Also she has never lived with anyone but Leonard, which was a terrible failure, and was abandoned quite soon. So all that remains is an unknown quantity . . . Besides, *ça ne me dit rien;* and *ça lui dit trop,* where I am concerned; and I don't want to get landed in an affair which might get beyond my control before I knew where I was. So you see I am sagacious – though probably I would be less sagacious if I were more tempted . . . ! But, darling, Virginia is *not* the sort of person one thinks of in that way; there is something incongruous and almost indecent in the idea . . . I *have* gone to bed with her (twice) but that's all; and I told you that before, I think. Now you know all about it, and I hope I haven't shocked you.[114]

This letter has set the terms for subsequent accounts of the relationship between Vita and Virginia. Vita presents herself as the bold, decisive, highly-sexed adventurer holding off from the delicate invalid for fear of arousing uncontrollable frenzy. Yet Vita's letters to Virginia have a quite different tone, more wooing and placatory. The version she gave Harold may not be the whole truth.

And Harold was not altogether convinced. The intimacy could be 'dangerous' for Virginia and Leonard's marriage. He was jealous: Virginia's effect might be to make Vita less interested in him.[115] Vita reproached him half-jokingly for behaving like Iago, and assured him again: 'I am absolutely devoted to her, but not in love.'[116] Harold wrote to Virginia, explaining to her that he loathed jealousy and was glad that Vita had 'come under an influence so stimulating and so sane'.[117] Virginia immediately told Vita about it: 'Harold writes about us too – wont be jealous he says.'[118]

Leonard's point of view is less apparent, but it seems that by the autumn of 1926 he was finding Vita an irritation, and perhaps a threat – if only as a source of over-excitement. There was some tension between the three of them in September. Vita arrived at Rodmell with an American friend and Virginia told Leonard he had spoiled the visit by 'glooming' (an echo of Vita's word for Bloomsbury). 'He shut up, & was caustic.' Then he told Virginia that 'our relations had not been so good lately'.[119] For a time it became awkward for Virginia to be getting so many love-letters from Vita, so Vita concealed them inside letters that could be read by Leonard – a strategy for which Virginia half-mocked her friend: 'You are a miracle of discretion – one letter in another. I never thought of that.'[120] In November she acknowledged that the 'affair', though 'creditable', was 'rather a bore for Leonard, but not enough to worry him' since 'one has room for a good many relationships'.[121]

As *To the Lighthouse* drew to an end, in the autumn, she became acutely depressed. Strange feelings of unreality overcame her. These had something to do with Vita, but were also entirely private. Words struggled to express these obscure sensations:

> On the mystical side of this solitude; how it is not oneself but something in the universe that one's left with. It is this that is frightening & exciting in the midst of my profound gloom, depression, boredom, whatever it is: One sees a fin passing far out.[122]

It might be, she thought, the dim beginnings of another book; but just now her mind was 'blank & virgin of books'. Vita felt the force of these dark emotions.[123]

The London season cut across that dangerous mood. Virginia involved Vita in plans for a new social venue, 'The Bloomsbury Bar', in Duncan's studio, 'for the furtherance of intelligent conversation in London.'[124] But not all Bloomsbury evenings were so high-minded.

> Oct 22 (1926). We [Vita and Eddy] went to Virginia's. Virginia, Vanessa and Leonard were eating hard-boiled eggs in the kitchen. Virginia had smashed a glass, and the puppy was eating the splinters on the floor. So Leonard was cross. Virginia was cross because I was late, and had brought

Eddy, [and because] Eddy had had an affair with Duncan Grant. I was cross because Virginia was cross.[125]

On another evening Vita and Virginia went to see *The Three Sisters* and then called in on Dotty in her flat in Mount Street, who was lying asleep and 'woke up chattering & hysterical. Virginia Woolf Virginia Woolf My God! Virginia Woolf is in the room. For Gods Sake Vita dont turn the lights on . . . We sat and drank. Dusky shapes of glasses & things, a room I had never seen; a woman I scarcely knew; Vita there between us, intimate wi'both; flattery extravagance, complete inner composure on my part.'[126] There was a stiff evening when Vita lectured on poetry at the Royal Society of Literature, introduced by 'that little dapper grocer' Edmund Gosse, and Virginia sat in the back row grinning at her ironically, surrounded by all 'the red plush curtains of respectability'. Out in the street, she 'put Vita properly in her place'.[127] (And would save up this scene for Orlando's forays into the literary establishment.) Then there was what Vita called a 'highbrow' party at Tavistock Square where Virginia brilliantly described having dinner with Wells and Shaw. There was a weekend at Long Barn, when Leonard stayed one night and 'Virginia remained(!)': they talked until four in the morning.[128] Vita went often to Tavistock Square and sat on the floor by the fire while Virginia talked and stroked her hair. She felt proud of 'having caught such a big silver fish'.[129]

But Virginia's painful moods at this time affected Vita; it may be that the intimacy was as dangerous for her as the husbands feared it would be for Virginia. In November 1926 Virginia wrote her a letter which went beyond their usual gratifying flirtatiousness to a darker analysis of the limits of their intimacy.

But you dont see, donkey West, that you'll be tired of me one of these days (I'm so much older) and so I have to take my little precautions. Thats why I put the emphasis on 'recording' rather than feeling. But donkey West knows she has broken down more ramparts than anyone. And isnt there something obscure in you? There's something that doesn't vibrate in you: It may be purposely – you dont let it: but I see it with other people, as well as with me: something reserved, muted – God knows what . . . It's in your writing too, by the bye. The thing I call central transparency – sometimes fails you there too.[130]

Vita was profoundly affected by this shrewd, cruel overlap between literary and personal criticism; she told Harold that Virginia – 'damn the woman' – had 'put her finger on it'.[131] She wrote an unhappy poem ('Year's End') about her feelings of inadequacy. She too began to think a great deal about death, which Virginia now said to her (ruffling her hair by the fireside) was 'the one experience I shall never describe'.[132] 'I know Virginia will die, and it will be too awful', Vita wrote to Harold, 'I don't mean *here*, over the weekend, but just die young.'[133] Virginia had the power to infiltrate and dominate her feelings; it was Virginia who was the stronger.

After a cold 1926 Christmas (spent by the Woolfs uncomfortably with the Arnold-Forsters at Zennor, by Vita in bed with the 'flu), Virginia came to Knole for the second time. Her two other, deeper relationships were at the front of her mind: Leonard had just read *To the Lighthouse* and called it a masterpiece; Vanessa had had to rush off to France because Duncan was dangerously ill. The sisters parted in the snow: 'We are very intimate – a great solace to me.' Knole, by contrast, was an entertainment, a historical pageant: 'All the centuries seemed lit up, the past expressive, articulate.'[134] It was the beginning of her transformation of Vita, 'quite easily', into a fiction.

Vita went to Persia again for the spring of 1927, increasingly wanting to get Harold back from a diplomatic life to a career in England. She broached a tentative plan that she and Harold and the Woolfs would meet in Greece; could Virginia arrange it? 'For you have a kind heart really, and are rather clever at managing what you want to manage.'[135] Though this wasn't managed, the idea that she and Virginia might go abroad together lingered on. 'My darling, please let this plan come off. I live for it.'[136] Vita wrote eloquent, devoted letters from Tehran and Persepolis and Shalamzar, and other 'exotic' locations. In Tavistock Square, 'I must be fond of her', Virginia told herself. But she felt the lack of Vanessa quite as much.[137] She was uncomfortably involved with Clive's break-up from Mary Hutchinson; she was writing on Gissing and Cowper and planning a book on English fiction for the Press. In a bold, Vita-influenced move, she had her hair shingled. ('I think I preferred the dropping hairpins, that cheerful little cascade that used to tinkle onto your plate,' Vita wrote.)[138] In March Virginia wrote her another devastatingly candid letter:

> Why do I think of you so incessantly, see you so clearly the moment I'm in the least discomfort? An odd element in our friendship. Like a child, I think if you were here, I should be happy. Talking to Lytton the other night he suddenly asked me to advise him in love – whether to go on, over the precipice, or stop short at the top. Stop, stop! I cried, thinking instantly of you. Now what would happen if I let myself go over? Answer me that. Over what? you'll say. A precipice marked V.[139]

Dim ideas of a new kind of book – a mixture of poetry, novel and play – kept coming into her mind. It might be a fantasy, a 'Defoe narrative', written for fun, about two women, perhaps to be written 'as I write letters at the top of my speed'; a mixture of 'satire & wildness'. 'Sapphism is to be suggested'. It might be called 'The Jessamy Brides'. It would be 'an escapade'.[140]

In the spring, just before the publication of *To the Lighthouse*, Virginia and Leonard went to Europe, to Vanessa at Cassis, to Rome and Sicily. She was intensely happy. Rome was wonderful; she loved the aestheticism of Roman Catholicism. 'I am sure Rome is the city where I shall come to die', she told Vanessa (describing to her, incidentally, how they had seen D.H. Lawrence – her only sighting of him – and Norman Douglas at the railway station at Civita Vecchia).[141] She came home to the publication of *To the Lighthouse* and the return of Vita.

That summer of 1927 their relationship changed again. They went to Oxford together so that Virginia could talk to 'the youth of both sexes' (whom she found greatly under the influence of Bloomsbury) about poetry and fiction. During their visit she admired Vita's casual aristocratic habits, 'very splendid and voluptuous and absurd'. This was written to Vanessa in France, who was very much on her mind.[142] Vanessa was reading *To the Lighthouse* and Virginia was waiting anxiously for her response. (A brilliant, funny, affectionate letter, imagining Vanessa and Duncan in France reluctantly settling down to read the book, at once exposed and made light of that anxiety.) Vanessa's emotional responses to the novel made Virginia think about her next book ('The Moths'?). It was Vanessa to whom she was writing her deepest feelings – about motherhood, about their parents, about *To the Lighthouse*.

At the same time her view of Vita was becoming more critical. In May and June, with the sales of *To the Lighthouse* taking off, she was unwell: 'Three weeks wiped out by headache.'[143] Vita wrote effusively, as she always did when Virginia was ill: 'Oh Virginia, I'd do anything to make you well.' She was enchanted by the sight of her, 'so lovely and golden, stretched on two chairs, and more irresistible than ever, with the sparkle gone and only the child remaining.' To Clive she wrote: 'I would go to the ends of the earth for your sister-in-law.'[144] Virginia sent a characteristic thank-you for the lupins she left: 'Enormous trees they look like, and I am a little rabbit running about among the roots. Its odd how being ill even like this, splits me up into several different people.'[145] In bed at Rodmell, she was reading Vita's erotic novel *Challenge*. Vita, on a visit to Dotty Wellesley at Sherfield House in Kent with Clive and Raymond, fantasised a sudden night-time drive to Rodmell. She would arrive in the middle of the night, throw gravel up at Virginia's window, and stay till dawn. 'But, you being you, I can't, more's the pity . . . For a different Virginia I'd fly to Sussex in the night.'[146] Virginia was stung by the double challenge and the clear implication that she could never give Vita the kind of erotic excitement described in her banned novel. 'Come then', she wired – but Vita didn't.

> You see I was reading Challenge & I thought your letter was a challenge 'if only you weren't so elderly & valetudinarian' was what you said in effect 'we would be spending the day together' whereupon I wired 'come then' to which naturally there was no answer and a good thing too I daresay as I am elderly and valetudinarian – it's no good disguising the fact. Not even reading Challenge will alter that . . .
> I was very excited all day.[147]

And at around this time she responded with her own challenge, in a note urging Vita to 'throw over your man': 'and we'll go to Hampton Court and dine on the river together and walk in the garden in the moonlight and come home late and have a bottle of wine and get tipsy, and I'll tell you all the things I have in my head, millions, myriads – They won't stir by day, only by dark on the river.'[148]

These bids for attention marked some tension. Vita was going on to other involvements. In July Virginia made her cry, after seeing her get the Hawthornden Prize: as at the Royal Society of Literature, she thought it 'a horrid show-up . . . infinitely distasteful'. (But she was jealous, too.)[149] A week or so later they travelled by special trains and coaches from Euston to Yorkshire, to see the total eclipse of the sun on Bardon Fell above Richmond. (She wrote it up with brilliant exactness in her diary, and again in 'The Sun and the Fish' and in *The Waves*.)[150] This was very much a party of family and old friends – the Nicolsons and the Woolfs, Eddy, Quentin, Saxon, Ray Strachey. On the way up in the train, Virginia watched the Nicolsons asleep: 'H curled up with his head on V's knee. She looked like Sappho by Leighton, asleep.' She noted, half-affectionately and half-mocking, small details of their behaviour – Harold breaking their china sandwich box (at which Leonard 'laughed without restraint'), the Nicolsons quarrelling over their luggage, Vita's typical interest in a Yorkshire castle and in buying a guinea pig ('Quentin advised a savage'), Harold's kindness in the train on the way back: all the little details of personal and married life which the 'astonishing' moment of the total eclipse seemed to her to wipe out, turning them from individuals into 'very old people, in the birth of the world', like 'druids on Stonehenge'.

That summer of 1927 the Woolfs acquired a motor-car, a second-hand

Singer known as 'The Umbrella', and Virginia became extremely excited by
the idea of driving. Vita met them in Richmond Park.

> Leonard and I watched her start. The motor made little pounces and
> stopped dead. At one moment it ran backwards. At last she sailed off, and
> Leonard and I and Pinker went for a walk at 5 miles an hour. Every five
> minutes Leonard would say, 'I suppose Virginia will be all right' . . . We
> got back to the trysting place and there was Virginia taking an intelligent
> interest in the works of the car.[151]

(The concern was mutual. When Vita suggested an arrangement, a year
later, which involved Leonard meeting them both at Rodmell, Virginia
refused, 'because then Leonard would drive himself down to Rodmell alone
& I should be thinking all the time that he was going to be smashed up'.)[152]
But the driving lessons did not continue so well. Clive reported to Mary
that the Woolfs were getting on badly:

> The other day when Virginia backed smartly into the wall Leonard
> became so agitated and peremptory about her having or not having put in
> the clutch (I think) that she exclaimed with unconcealed acerbity that she
> should never get on if people would stand looking at her.[153]

And very soon after this Virginia gave up driving, possibly as a result of a
small accident: 'I have driven from the Embankment to Marble Arch' (she
told Ethel Sands) 'and only knocked one boy very gently off his bicycle.'[154]
(This would become a family joke: in Quentin and Virginia's comic
collaboration for the *Charleston Bulletin* that summer, Quentin drew a
Thurberesque picture of a decapitated boy and a distant car, with the
caption: 'Mrs Bell drove from Hyde Park Corner to Marble Arch. Mrs
Woolf drove from Marble Arch to Hyde Park Corner. Mrs Woolf knocked a
boy off his bicycle. Mrs Bell killed a cat. The less said the better.') It seems
that driving (one of Vita's skills, as emphasised at the end of *Orlando*) was
one of the challenges which Leonard thought it best for Virginia not to
pursue.

The Woolfs and the Nicolsons had a weekend at Long Barn in July, with
Raymond Mortimer, and with a visit from Lord Sackville and his mistress.
In a political discussion about the empire, Harold the diplomat argued for
the benefits of colonial rule: 'our English genius is for government.'
Raymond opposed him: 'The governed don't seem to enjoy it.' Virginia
supported Raymond, and made a modernist argument for decolonisation
and anti-nationalism: ' "Why not grow, change?" I said. Also, I said,
recalling the aeroplanes that had flown over us, while the portable wireless

played dance music on the terrace, "can't you see that nationality is over? All divisions are now rubbed out, or about to be." '[155] (But they would all spend the next fourteen years seeing the flaws of this argument.)

Fired up by this debate, Virginia observed afresh the opulence at Long Barn, the whiff of ancient Sackville obtuseness and decay produced by Lord Sackville's visit, Vita's conservative taste in 'all the inherited tradition of furnishing', and her lack of 'cutting edge'. As always, her political and aesthetic judgements on Vita were inextricably mixed. The sexual challenge played its part too in this critique. At Long Barn, Vita confessed that she had spent a night with Mary Hutchinson (another woman who rose to challenges and had adventures). The confession provoked Virginia's whole repertoire of satirical jealous jokes. And that summer Vita began a passionate and reckless affair with Mary Campbell, the wife of the writer Roy Campbell (who would take his revenge in a brutal satire on the Nicolsons and Bloomsbury, *The Georgiad*).

Other events in this 'striving working splashing social summer'[156] compounded Virginia's sense of sexual difference. Clive had started a new affair.[157] Virginia made a three-day visit to Ethel Sands and Nan Hudson (Vanessa and Duncan were painting rural scenes for a loggia in their elegant château at Offranville, near Dieppe)[158] and was strongly affected by the atmosphere created by the two women. (An acquaintance, a friend of Beatrice Mayor, seeing her walking quickly along the street in Dieppe, didn't go over and claim acquaintance, for fear that Virginia Woolf would laugh at 'her young man's accent'.)[159] She had an emotional visit, and a sudden burst of amorous letters, from Philip Morrell, who had a notoriously roving eye and had long cherished a *tendresse* for her. The incident was grotesque, and faintly threatening to her: she was reminded of George. She immediately turned this peculiar courtship into a subject of mockery for all her friends. Combined with Vita's defection, these things made her feel (as she told Vanessa) that 'poor Billy isn't one thing or the other, not a man or a woman'.[160] When Vita confided in her about the catastrophic situation she had brought about with the Campbells, Virginia was irritated, jealous, and critical: 'I hate being bored', she said brutally; told Vita her life was a muddle, and made her cry.[161]

But it was just at this moment that she reclaimed Vita for her own purposes, and put to fertile use her sense of 'not being a man or a woman'. Since 1925, she had been trying to write a book on fiction, a development from *The Common Reader*, a personal account of 'the impressions made upon the mind by reading a certain number of novels in succession'.[162] Through the summer of 1927 and 1928 she read and read for it: Austen, Proust, Radcliffe, Ruskin, Sterne, James, Dostoevsky. (She was reading biographies, too, and reviewing Harold's book *Some People*.)[163] But, though the ideas for 'Phases of Fiction' would stream into her next two books, it was a burden to her. She was feeling restless, in an 'odd suspended frame of mind' because she wasn't writing fiction (apart from her Sapphist story). Her mind was 'like a dog going round & round to make itself a bed'.[164]

The idea of *Orlando* came to her suddenly, first as a collection of 'memoirs of one's own times during peoples lifetimes', a new way of writing history and biography, and a relief from 'that intolerable dull Fiction [book]'.[165] 'Vita should be Orlando, a young nobleman'. 'It should be truthful; but fantastic.'[166] With her head full of this idea, she and Leonard went for the day to Long Barn, and saw Vita's son Nigel, dressed up by her as a Russian boy. 'Dont. It makes me look like a little girl', he said.[167] At a fancy-dress party at the Keynes's, photos of 'a pretty young woman who had become a man' were handed around; she was fascinated.[168]

Almost at once the idea of 'Orlando: A Biography' took over from the first concept of a collection of sketches. By October it had turned into 'a biography beginning in the year 1500 & continuing to the present day, called Orlando; Vita; only with a change about from one sex to another.' So, just at the point when Vita was turning her interest elsewhere, Virginia recovered her for her fiction. From the end of 1927, she took control of the relationship in a new form.

TWENTY-NINE

Censors

Virginia Woolf began writing *Orlando* in a great rush of excitement. She felt she was doing something illicit – 'I am launched somewhat furtively but with all the more passion upon Orlando: A Biography' – a feeling which had as much to do with her subject-matter as with her conscience about the 'Fiction' book. ('Illicit' books would continue to interrupt 'task' books: so *Three Guineas* would cut across *The Years*, and the writing of her memoirs and of *Between the Acts* would sabotage the labour of *Roger Fry*.)

The first person she told about the new book was Vita. Would she mind, if Orlando 'turned out to be' Vita? She seemed to be asking permission; but actually, as Vita ('thrilled and terrified') was at once aware, there was no stopping her. Virginia wrote: 'its all about you and the lusts of your flesh and the lure of your mind . . . Also, I admit, I should like to untwine and twist again some very odd, incongruous strands in you'.[1] Vita perceived that there might be some danger for her in being taken in hand like this: 'any vengeance that you ever want to take will lie ready to your hand.'[2] A flurry of teasing, suggestive letters let Vita know how much she was now being 'made up', and how much pleasure this was giving her author: 'Is it true you grind your teeth at night? Is it true you love giving pain?'[3] 'If I saw you would you kiss me? If I were in bed would you – I'm rather excited about Orlando tonight.'[4] She noted to herself how uncannily the book seemed to have 'shoved everything else aside to come into existence'; and how the rapid game-playing of this fake biography seemed to her now, at the age of forty-six, to mark the end of 'novel'-writing: 'I shall invent a new name for them.' 'I will never write a novel again. Little bits of rhyme come in.'[5]

From the outset, Virginia envisaged *Orlando* as an illustrated book (the pictures, with an 'index' and 'acknowledgements', were part of the paraphernalia of the fake 'biography'). There were to be portraits of Sackville ancestors (for Orlando as a young man), photographs of Vita (for Orlando as a woman) and a portrait of Orlando's lost love, the Russian princess 'Sasha'. (This would be Angelica, now a ravishing nine-year-old.) Virginia and Vita went together to Knole to choose obscure Sackville ancestors. Virginia made Vita pose as a voluptuous Lely for the photographer Lenare ('I was miserable, draped in an inadequate bit of pink satin with all my clothes slipping off, but V was delighted and kept diving under the black cloth of the camera to peep at the effect').[6] Vanessa and Duncan then decided to join in, and Vita, even more miserable, and feeling like 'an unfortunate victim', 'was made to sit inside a huge frame while they took endless photographs' and Virginia sat reading and commenting on all the obituary notices in that day's *Times*, and making them all giggle.[7] Vita was indeed being framed.

Her own life was in a state of great turbulence. Her affair with Mary Campbell was a catastrophe, she hated Harold's new posting to Berlin, her father died early in 1928, Knole passed into other hands, and she had some appalling scenes with her mother. Virginia, though jealous of her love-affairs, was sympathetic: 'I've made a discovery', Vita wrote to Clive: 'Virginia has a heart of pure gold. I shall *never* forget her sweetness to me during all this time.'[8] But Virginia's interest in Orlando overrode her feelings for Vita's real life.

Orlando, in its rapid flow, dominated her life in the winter of 1927–8; though there were other events. The early death of Philip Ritchie at twenty-eight (who had been loved by both Lytton and Molly MacCarthy) made her feel like 'an elderly laggard' with 'no right to go on'.[9] That of H.G. Wells's wife Jane, whose funeral she and Leonard attended (with Shaw), reminded her of her father's mourning for Julia.[10] Her father came to mind, too, with the death of his old friend Thomas Hardy in January 1928. The funeral service on the 16th in Westminster Abbey depressed her, made her feel 'the futility of it all'.[11] She 'furbished up' the obituary essay she had been asked to write years before (in 1919) and which she had read for and worked on intermittently ever since. Rereading Hardy, and reading a great deal of her father's other great literary companion, Meredith, for a long essay, brought her down with a headache. She was also reading Michelet's history of France ('Does it strike you', she wrote to Clive, 'that history is one of the most fantastic concoctions of the human brain? . . . Ought it not all to be re-written instantly?')[12] and Yeats's new book of poems, *The Tower*, which greatly excited her.[13] She was beginning to 'woolgather' for some lectures she had been asked to give at Cambridge, on 'Women and Fiction': these thoughts (which she caught herself dwelling on during Hardy's funeral) would interweave themselves with *Orlando*, and eventually take shape, almost two years later, as *A Room of One's Own*.

There were some slight local strains. Leonard was quarrelling with Angus Davidson at the Press. Forster was hurt by the rather cool piece she wrote on his *Aspects of the Novel*, and she had to write to him soothingly and apologetically.[14] Eliot had converted – to her dismay and bafflement – to Anglo-Catholicism, and came to discuss it. ('I was really shocked.')[15] Julian, just up at Cambridge, was importuning her with his poems and plays, which she was giving careful but not entirely encouraging readings. She hoped he would not start writing novels.

Orlando at first provided light relief. But something went wrong with her feeling for it. By the spring of 1928 it had become as burdensome to her as 'Phases of Fiction' (still waiting in the wings of her mind). She found herself, towards the end, 'forcing my book along'. What had begun 'as a joke' now seemed 'rather too long for my liking'.[16] She often found her last chapters difficult. In this case, the game or joke had turned serious. Having taken Orlando through 300 years, several countries and a change of sex, she had trouble making an end of her. The rival claims of satire and fantasy and personal tribute weren't easy to resolve. Her letters to Vita sounded anxious, both about finishing the book and about their friendship; even after all this writing, she could no more take possession of her 'subject' than ever: 'Do you think I know you? Intimately?'[17]

ORLANDO IS FINISHED!
Did you feel a sort of tug, as if your neck was being broken on Saturday last at 5 minutes to one? That was when he died – or rather stopped talking, with three little dots . . . Now every word will have to be re-written [. . .] It is all over the place, incoherent, intolerable, impossible – And I am sick of it. The question now is, will my feelings for you be changed? I've lived in you all these months – coming out, what are you really like? Do you exist? Have I made you up?[18]

Leaving Orlando with his metaphorical neck broken, she and Leonard went for a month to Cassis in the spring of 1928 to be with Vanessa and her family. *Orlando*, on her return, seemed 'wretched' to her.[19]

By an irony of literary history, she took part, just before the proofs of *Orlando* arrived, in the sort of establishment prize-giving which was one of the book's targets of satire. This was the awarding of the Femina Vie Heureuse Prize (in the 'foreign book' category) to *To the Lighthouse*.[20] She called it (to Julian Bell) her 'dog show prize,'[21] though her scornful embarrassment did not quite disguise some pride. The event, though, in the Institut Français in South Kensington, was anathema to her: 'an affair of dull stupid horror.' Hugh Walpole (who would now become a close friend) awarded the prize in front of an audience of 'elderly fur bearing women' (or, as Walpole put it, of glaring old female novelists).[22] They included Elizabeth Robins, the feminist actress and old acquaintance of Julia Stephen, who had an interesting conversation with Virginia about her mother's mixture of

MR. HUGH WALPOLE making the
formal presentation of the *Femina-Vie
Heureuse* prize to Mrs. Virginia Woolf.

[*The Times*, May 3, 1928.]

beauty and wicked satire. Vita, taking her revenge for Virginia's mockery of *her* at the Hawthornden prize-giving, sat in the audience and watched her get her cheque for £40 and make 'a charming little speech of thanks'. She though it 'a very shoddy affair, with a distinct Pen-Club atmosphere about it'.[23] Virginia woke up in the night afterwards, horrorstruck at 'having looked ugly in cheap black clothes'.[24] Vanessa, who saw the photograph of Virginia and Hugh Walpole in *The Times,* said they looked 'a melancholy couple'. 'Do tell us how you behaved – did your drawers drop off?'[25]

Leonard read *Orlando* and called it a 'satire'; he took it more seriously than Virginia had expected.[26] She started to correct the proofs, and as usual hated them. At the same time she felt her friendship with Vita passing on to 'different terms', though Vita was still 'adoring', and they were still taking little trips – to have their ears pierced, for instance.[27] ('Are you making an appointment to be penetrated on Friday?')[28] Vita wanted them to go to France for a week in September, for the vintage.[29] Virginia agreed, then dithered: Leonard said go, then 'somehow conveys without a word the fact of his intolerable loneliness without me – upon which I give it all up; and then suddenly think, what an unwholesome sentimental state this is! I will go. And then visualise myself saying goodbye to him and cant face it; and then visualise a rock in a valley with Vita in an Inn: and *must* go. So it goes on . . . Can you put up with these vacillations?'[30] She finished the proofs of *Orlando*, and went back ('under orders') to 'Phases of Fiction'. *Orlando*'s publication date loomed. Because she had decided to subtitle it 'A Biography', it was being placed on the biography shelves of bookshops, so advance sales were poor.

In mid-September, after many detailed travel plans, many doubts about leaving Leonard for a whole week ('You see, I would not have married Leonard had I not preferred living with him to saying goodbye')[31] and many qualms about the intimacy of holidaying together ('excited, but afraid – she may find me out, I her out') she and Vita at last took their trip abroad.

This holiday in Burgundy, so long anticipated, was in the event not much of an adventure. This was more like companionship than honeymoon. Virginia fantasised their escapade in advance, on *Orlando*-ish lines ('We might go to moonlight ruins, cafés, dances, plays, junketings: converse for ever; sleep only while the moon covers herself for an instant with a thin veil; and by day traipse the vineyards').[32] But the reality was less flamboyant.

Though Virginia bought the tickets (37s. for a first-class cabin-berth – 'stuffy and smelly' – and the train from Newhaven to Paris on Monday 24 September 1928), and booked the hotel at Saulieu which Ethel Sands recommended, it was Vita, with her consummate travelling experience and her good French, who acted as manager and minder.[33] Virginia, though, controlled the mood and the agenda of the holiday. She had 'a small and sudden row' with Leonard, on the morning of the departure, and her anxiety about leaving him dominated the week. They spent a great deal of their time writing letters and going for the post.[34]

In Paris, they bought books (Virginia's was *J'adore* by Jean Desbordes), admiring the bookseller and his customer for their unEnglish discussion of the merits of Proust, and had dinner at a modest restaurant in the Boulevard Raspail. In the Brasserie Lutétia on the Rue de Sèvres, they wrote letters to their husbands on the torn-out fly-sheets of their books. This first day, Virginia wrote to Leonard, was 'completely ruined by parting with you'. On Tuesday 25 September, they were up at six for the taxi through deserted Paris to the Gare de Lyon, to get the train to Saulieu. On the journey they talked about French literature. The food at the Hôtel de la Poste at Saulieu ('the usual small French inn, with farmers lunching') was as good as Ethel Sands had promised: duck paté, trout, gnocchi:, stuffed chicken and spinach, cake, pears, 'Bourgogne mousseaux'. After lunch Virginia bought Leonard a green corduroy coat, and they sat in a field overlooking Burgundy and wrote letters home. Vita wrote: 'I feel amused and irresponsible. I can talk about life and literature to my heart's content – and it amuses me to be suddenly in the middle of Burgundy with Virginia.' Virginia wrote: 'I dont think I could stand more than a week away from you, as there are so many things to say to you, which I cant say to Vita – though she is most sympathetic and more intelligent than you think. At least we can discuss books for hours – perhaps I do most of the talking.' In the evening they went to a fair. There was a girl with a snake and lion cubs and a gypsy woman and 'people firing guns at rabbits'. Virginia was 'delighted'; they had confetti thrown over them.

At breakfast (in Vita's room) on Wednesday morning they argued about 'men and women'. 'Virginia is curiously feminist', Vita wrote in her diary: 'She dislikes possessiveness and love of domination in men. In fact she dislikes the quality of masculinity. Says that women stimulate her imagination, by their grace & their art of life.' After another stupendous lunch they went for a walk; the weather was rather cold. In the evening Virginia read Vita 'Old Bloomsbury', her memoir of early days at Gordon Square, and 'talked a lot about her brother'. They decided to come home a day earlier than planned, as Vita had to broadcast.

On Thursday they went by train from Saulieu to Avallon, which they both found charming. Virginia imagined buying a house there: 'If I am left a widow I shall live here.' At the Poste Restante there were letters from Harold but not from Leonard. Virginia was 'very much upset' (Vita's phrase; Virginia's to Leonard was 'rather melancholy'). They stayed on for the afternoon post. At 3.30 there was still no letter; Virginia was 'rather fidgeted' not to have heard, she wrote to Leonard, balancing her notepaper on her lap on a bench in an avenue in Avallon, while Vita had gone to hire a car. Vita advised her to send a telegram. 'No Letters anxious wire Hotel de la Poste Vézelay.'

They drove in the hired car to Vézelay, the old Italianate hilltown in the wide rolling Burgundian countryside, with its great Romanesque church on the top of the hill, which enchanted them. They sat in a field listening to the crickets, and talking about Vita's past, about Virginia's friends, about poetry – not much about *Orlando*. In the evening Vita wrote to Harold (switching from pen to pencil because Virginia had fallen asleep, and pencil made less noise): 'She is very very sweet, and I feel extraordinarily protective towards her – The combination of that brilliant brain and that fragile body is very loveable – so independent in all mental ways, so dependent in all practical ways.' She sent Virginia to bed at a quarter to ten. 'Vita is a perfect old hen, always rushing about with hot water bottles.' In the night there was a thunderstorm and Vita went to Virginia's room 'thinking she might be frightened'. In the storm, they sat up for an hour and talked about science and religion.

In the morning it was raining and they sat indoors writing letters. A welcome letter arrived from Leonard, who had been at Charleston with Lytton and Raymond Mortimer going over Stephen and Strachey family genealogy. ('It is very dreary without you & the minor animals – I could not live without them despite their curious ways . . . I hope you wont make a habit of deserting me.') Virginia consoled herself for their separation with a bout of noisy chatter (a comical example of the number of voices she could hear in her head) from the whole menagerie of the minor animals:

> We adore dadanka do-do – we want to talk with him; and kiss the poos. Have they really begun to play the violin, daddie? Are you fonder of them than of the marmoteski? Now stop mots; go under the table. I cant hear myself speak for their chatter. How they sobbed when there was no letter from Dinkay at Avallon! Shall you be glad to see us all again?

Mid-morning, the rain cleared, and they walked to the antique shop. Vita took some photographs and they walked in a vineyard and watched village women doing washing by the river. Then Vita made Virginia go and rest. On Saturday, a warm morning, they left Vézelay by car and then train to Auxerre. They looked at the stained glass in St Étienne, had chocolate in a tea-shop (Virginia talked about Edith Sitwell and told Vita the story of one of her 'early loves', Madge Symonds). At the antique shop Virginia bought a mirror. On Sunday they got up early and took the train to Paris and then, after lunch, to Rouen, where Ethel Sands's chauffeur met them and took them to Offranville. Vanessa and Duncan were there, painting the loggia. After a delicious dinner, Virginia read 'Old Bloomsbury' aloud, skimping none of the risqué details. 'The two old virgins bridled with horrified delight', Vita noted. She and Virginia stayed the night at Dieppe and took the morning boat; as it was rough, Vita made Virginia drink 'the best part of a bottle of Burgundy' to knock her out. At Newhaven, Leonard was waiting for them in The Umbrella, to drive them back to Rodmell.

It had been a controlled success. Virginia wrote to Harold: 'Vita was an angel to me – looked out trains, paid tips, spoke perfect French, indulged me in every humour, was perpetually sweet tempered . . . in short, it was the greatest fun.' Vita wrote to Harold: 'I feel I now understand V through and through. She has a sweet and child-like nature, from which her intellect is completely separate. But of course no one believes this, except Leonard & Vanessa.' Virginia wrote in her diary: 'We did not find each other out. It flashed by. Yet I was glad to see Leonard again.'

Four years later, Virginia wrote a revealing letter to Vita about the complicated triangular relationship which that important, uneventful little trip to France exposed.

As usual, the other day I was ashamed of my molly coddling; you'd never consent to such a thing; the fact is, it's my one heroism, letting people think me a coddle, in order to soothe Leonards old maid fussiness. And that reminds me, oughtn't you to be equally unselfish? Harold mumbled to me that *you had been giddy*; and its the duty of the wife to be, as I am, submissive in the extreme about giddiness, or whatever it is. No more room, or I would pitch you a very melancholy story about my jealousy of all your new loves. V.

And when am I going to see you? because you know you love now several people, women I mean, physically I mean, better, oftener, more carnally than me.[35]

The letter underlines the mixture of manipulation and neediness in Virginia Woolf's relationships. She wishes Vita to believe that it is a form of 'heroism' for her to 'submit' to being looked after, in order to assuage Leonard's uxorious guardianship. This leads on to a highly ironical remark about the duties of good wives. But the Burgundy journey showed her transferring that wifely submission to Vita, just as much in order to please *her*. Her submission, in all her close relationships, is a form of control. And her jealousy here about Vita's loves is also a kind of plot. She is being truthful. But the jealousy is part of the flattering formula she has invented for their relationship – as Leonard is the fussy guardian, so Vita is the carnal adventurer. And they have to play up.

By the time of that letter, 1932, her relationship with Vita was less intimate. Vita was taken up with making the house and the garden at Sissinghurst, and with 'all her new loves': Hilda Matheson at the BBC, her sister-in-law Gwen St Aubyn, both of whom Virginia disliked. She thought *The Edwardians*, Vita's more conventional reply to *Orlando*, 'not a very good book,'[36] though it made a great deal of money for the Press. In the 1930s she began to find Vita's increasing reclusiveness and heavy drinking difficult; Vita too felt alienated by Virginia's friendship with Ethel Smyth, and the politics of her writing after *A Room of One's Own*. In 1935, Virginia was talking of the end of their friendship, and it was some years before they found their old intimacy again.

But in the autumn of 1928, when they came back from France, all Virginia Woolf's concerns seemed to centre on that discussion with Vita at Saulieu about preferring women, and the relation of that preference to her writing. She came back to three closely connected events: the publication of *Orlando* (on 11 October), the *Well of Loneliness* trial, and her two lectures on 'Women and Fiction' at Cambridge.

Vita at last read *Orlando* (she had seen no work in progress) and was 'dazzled, bewitched, enchanted'[37] – though she wrote privately to Harold to say she didn't see why Orlando had to marry and have children, and she didn't like the wild goose which flies away with the story at the end.[38] Vita's mother read it and was horrified; she thought it a vicious and hateful book. ('You have written some beautiful phrases in Orlando, but probably you do not realize how *cruel* you have been' she wrote to Virginia.)[39] She put a photograph of Virginia in her copy of the book and wrote next to it: 'The awful face of a mad woman whose successful mad desire is to separate people who care for each other. I loathe this woman for having changed my Vita and taken her away from me.'[40] She covered her own copy with outraged graffiti: every time the word 'sex' occurred it was violently circled and underlined.[41]

Very soon after the publication of *Orlando* and the lectures at Cambridge, at the same time as the *Well* trial, Virginia wrote her evocative essay on the friendship between Geraldine Jewsbury and Jane Carlyle. She created an eloquent, affectionate picture of Geraldine's extravagant love for Jane, and of Jane's mixed feelings about her friend's intensity.

> A crooning domestic sound like the purring of a kitten or the humming of a tea-kettle seems to rise, as we turn the pages of Mrs Carlyle's letters, from the intercourse of the two incompatible but deeply attached women.

Her own arguments in *A Room of One's Own* were foreshadowed by Geraldine's angry, passionate ambitions in her letter to Jane:

> We are indications of a development of womanhood which as yet is not recognised. It has, so far, no ready-made channels to run in, but still we have looked and tried, and found that the present rules for women will not hold us – that something better and stronger is needed . . . There are women to come after us, who will approach nearer the fullness of the measure of the stature of a woman's nature.[42]

But their intimacy – as Geraldine Jewsbury knew – could not be fully written about; it would require some blank spaces on the pages of a biography. Sixty years later, Virginia Woolf was still unable to write candidly about their feelings for each other. She wrote to John Hayward, who praised her for her piece on Geraldine: 'Her relation with Mrs Carlyle was interesting, and I had to be discreet.'

At the beginning of 1929 a large and awkward party met in Berlin. Vita booked rooms in the Prinz Albrecht Hotel for the Woolfs, and for Vanessa, Duncan and Quentin, who were in Germany looking at galleries. Eddy Sackville-West (who was complaining that he could be identified as 'S.W' in *Orlando*) was there too, gay with rings and bracelets and make-up. It was not a good mixture. The 1920s decadent Berlin which interested Eddy – summed up by Christopher Isherwood's phrase ('To Christopher, Berlin meant Boys')[43] – was the Berlin of homosexual bars and 'dance places for inverts' full of 'huge men with breasts like women and faces like Ottoline, dressed as female Spanish dancers', as Eddy wrote to Morgan Forster.[44] Virginia had heard about all this from Vita[45] and from Clive, who described to her the 'young men in low-necked dresses and feathers sing[ing] Carmen' and 'bald-headed bank clerks Charlestoning together and discreetly kissing in corners; it is all very touching . . . professional Lesbiennes – all rather like a German treatise on Vice and Liberty, and in my opinion highly respectable.'[46] However much these images of transvestism appealed to her imagination, this was not the Berlin she and Leonard would be visiting. Nor were they keen on Harold's diplomatic world. (Leonard flatly refused to attend the lunch-parties he had arranged.) Vanessa's letters to Julian and to Roger caustically described the ill-assorted party.

> We dined together and first no table could be found for the whole party and we had to traipse through snow from one restaurant to another . . . Then the film [Pudovkin's *Storm over Asia*] (which I thought very good) was Russian propaganda against the English in Asia. At least some thought it was and some thought it wasn't (I didn't notice particularly) and Harold's feelings ran high on the subject and Leonard was enraged by Vita who asked him six times over whether he thought the people were meant to be English or not.' [She added to Roger:] 'The Nicholsons [*sic*] seem to me such an unnecessary importation into our society that I can only leave Virginia to deal with them.'

She noted Leonard and Virginia's habits abroad:

> They dont of course know quite what to do. They walk miles rather than take a cab and go to the hotel restaurant where one pays about 10 marks for lunch rather than to some far better place where one could feed for a third as much. I think Leonard has already got involved with socialists and Virginia with Vita who has a car and will whisk her about.[47]

At dinner with Vita and the others one night, Virginia made some excited protestations; Vita wrote to her afterwards about the 'feelings to which you gave such startling and disturbing expression' at the Funkturm.[48] The whole trip seems to have been too 'rackety' and stressful for her. On the journey back she took a sea-sickness pill, given to her by Vanessa, and collapsed; at home she was very ill (letters between Leonard and Vita made it clear that he blamed her for this). But, like many of her illnesses, this period of lying in bed gave rise to a burst of 'excited composition'. She made up – all in a rush, like the beginning of *Orlando* – a book based on her Cambridge lectures, called 'Women and Fiction', which would be renamed *A Room of One's Own*. Recovered, she had a few meetings with Vita (for instance to visit Keats's house on 29 May). And she finished 'Phases of Fiction' at last.[49] That summer, Virginia supported the Press's publication of Vita's lesbian love-poems, *King's Daughter*, against Harold's objections:[50] 'Why should you attach any importance to the criticism of a diplomat?'[51] The poems were published in the same month as *A Room of One's Own*. This came out on 24 October 1929, almost exactly a year after *Orlando*. By then Virginia Woolf's mind was on mysticism, solitude, anonymity: the voices of 'The Moths', which would become *The Waves*, were in her ears.[52]

Virginia Woolf's writing and thinking, especially in the 1920s, about the lives and friendships and sexuality of women, about biography and history and class, and about freedom and censorship, were all involved with Vita, who gave her the central relationship of her forties. She came into the emotional mood of *To the Lighthouse*; she played the main role in the theatre of *Orlando*; she provided the impulse for the love stories of 'Slater's Pins', of 'Geraldine and Jane', and of 'Chloe and Olivia' in *A Room of One's Own*.

So Vita kept reappearing; but she kept being written over, too. *Orlando* both was and was not her portrait. Vita's class, her ancestral house, her looks, her sensuality, her resistance to convention, her travels, her unusual marriage, her writing: all that is in the 'biography'. It *is* a knowing, loving, private message (so much so that it alienated some of Virginia Woolf's younger admirers, such as Elizabeth Bowen, later to be herself a close woman friend of Virginia's, who in 1928, at twenty-nine, felt excluded and snubbed by *Orlando*'s coterie air: 'What we had heard of *Orlando* galled us. We were young enough to feel out of it').[53]

Orlando was a joke for Vita, and perhaps too a kind of farewell. But the joke was *on* Vita, as well. Lady Sackville, for all her frantic paranoia, may have been right to accuse the book of cruelty. There is parody in it, as well as affectionate celebration. The manuscript shows that she adjusted the tone a good deal. (Vita read it and called it 'a sort of brouillon').[54] A few of the personal details, private messages for Vita, were added late, like her cheroot-smoking or the secret code she used in letters to Harold Nicolson. But some of Orlando's more riskily recognisable characteristics were cut out: such as a sardonic reference to the indolence of her aristocratic ancestors, who collected books but were too lazy to write them themselves. And Orlando's desire to hurt, her association of love and friendship with pain and whipping, touched on several times in the manuscript ('The chief use of friendship is to inflict pain. Our friends are so many lashes on the great tawse by which we are daily lacerated') was censored in the end.[55]

Yet the desire to inflict pain was not entirely censored out. Vita is made love to, but she is also made over: her characteristics are exploited. Where Vita was romantic, private and gloomy, *Orlando* is showy, glittering, witty and camp. (Intriguingly, Virginia was meeting and liking the young playwright Noel Coward while she was writing it.)[56] Where Vita's taste is conservative and snobbish, *Orlando* is anarchic and socially unsettling. *Orlando*'s (and Orlando's) feminism is – of course – much more Virginia Woolf's than Vita's. And Orlando's biographer, preoccupied with questions of how lives can be written (in a way quite alien to Vita's more conventional preferences in fiction and poetry) ends up dissolving all concepts of a stable 'self'.[57] As Virginia Woolf manipulated Vita Sackville-West, so *Orlando* manipulates its readers. It is a biography which makes a mockery of the very idea of writing biography. It is a blatant account of an intimate friend which is extremely self-concealing about the author's emotions. (In this sense *Orlando* treats real life in the opposite way from *To the Lighthouse*, where she did not want to identify her parents, but exposed her deep feelings about them.) It is a critique of sexual censorship, and of fixed notions of sexual difference, which is also cunningly self-censoring. It covers its tracks, and gets away with murder.

Orlando makes play with Virginia Woolf's life-long interest in the history of the book. She is always writing about the evolution of fiction, especially by women writers. And this was closely bound up with her thoughts about repression and censorship. Increasingly in the late 1920s and early 1930s, her ideas about the function of fiction were involved with her political 'philosophy of anonymity',[58] her detestation of the insistent 'I'-word of Victorian patriarchy or 1930s Fascism. She wanted to move narrative away from 'the damned egotistical self'. So her political position coincided with what could almost be called an aesthetics of inhibition. In 1939 she would write:

> I have been thinking about Censors. How visionary figures admonish us. Thats clear in an MS I'm reading. [Of the memoirs of Elizabeth Robins.] If I say this So & So will think me sentimental. If that . . . will think me Bourgeois. All books now seem to me surrounded by a circle of invisible censors. Hence their self-consciousness, their restlessness.[59]

The Invisible Censor is first cousin to the Angel in the House, that highly audible Censor whom she described in her lecture of 1931, 'Professions for Women', standing over her when she started to write reviews, telling her to be nice to the men. In *Orlando* it takes the form of 'the spirit of the age'. This is an invisible voice over Orlando's shoulder, making sure she doesn't write anything a married lady shouldn't. Orlando, as a woman in the nineteenth century, wonders about 'the effect that her behaviour would have had upon the spirit of the age'. Would getting married (however unconventionally) and wearing a ring allow her to get away with writing as she likes? Or would the spirit, like a customs officer, find something 'highly contraband for which she would have had to pay the full fine'? In the manuscript of *Orlando*, the possibility of 'deceiving' the spirit of the age is more explicit: it's made even clearer that Orlando 'scraped through, but only by the skin of her teeth, as a married woman who wrote almost exclusively about natural objects.' When she gives birth, it's much more emphatic in the manuscript that this too is a subterfuge:

> to propitiate that elderly gentleman who was so mysteriously imposed himself upon the minds of /the/ young of the opposite sex. minds, the bodies, the hearts & the lives of /the/young women. If she could put this old fogy off with the idea that marriage & childbearing were enough for her[. . .]then he would perhaps take himself off to his duties elsewhere. Lying had always seemed to her a dull form of conversation; but after all, lie one must.

Through its fantasy and jokiness, *Orlando* escapes the public suppression which *The Well of Loneliness* notoriously encountered in the same year. Dangerous details (references to Sappho, to Orlando's 'lusts' and her love-affairs with women) are excised from the manuscript. Full though it is of teasing sensuality, the finished version risks being slightly less *risqué*. A joke cut from the manuscript makes mock of just this process, when the biographer admits with some compunction to having torn up and put on the fire Shakespeare's own account of his relations with Mr W.H. and the dark Lady. 'But there was much in those pages of an impure nature [. . .] and there can be no real conflict in an English heart when Truth and modesty conflict.'

The evasiveness in *Orlando* is sexual and also political. There is a bold angry moment where Orlando joins a 'society' of eighteenth-century women of the town and they tell each other their adventures. (Men ask, what can women do without men? Only 'scratch'.) The manuscript is even more scathing at this point: 'Let the gentlemen have the field all to themselves; let them write book after book in dispraise of the other sex; let them adduce every reason they can for thinking vilely of them.' One of the gentlemen she had in mind was Arnold Bennett, who had been reviewing

Woolf critically and making derogatory statements about 'the intellectual status of women'. In the manuscript, she names him as one of the tribe of 'our modern masculinists' ('tho' they flatter us, they despise us'). Virginia Woolf is referred to as a minor writer, a 'poor scribbler', immortalised only by Arnold Bennett's brilliant articles. A pity. 'She would have been forgotten anyhow, & the half hour spent on her might have given us another of his masterpieces.'[60] All this revealingly personal material is excised.

The censorship which the making of Vita into *Orlando* demonstrated, and satirised, was external as well as internal. This connects *Orlando* with *A Room of One's Own*, especially in Chapter 5 of the essay, where the narrator picks up a new novel to see what a woman writer is capable of in October 1929. The book is *Life's Adventure*, by Mary Carmichael. Thinking aloud as she reads, she is taken by surprise:

> I turned the page and read . . . I am sorry to break off so abruptly. Are there no men present? Do you promise me that behind that red curtain over there the figure of Sir Chartres Biron is not concealed? We are all women you assure me? Then I may tell you that the very next words I read were these – 'Chloe liked Olivia . . .' Do not start. Do not blush. Let us admit in the privacy of our own society that these things sometimes happen. Sometimes women do like women.
> 'Chloe liked Olivia,' I read.

She 'breaks off' again to consider what a change this marks and how different Shakespeare would have been if, in *Antony and Cleopatra*, for instance, Cleopatra had liked Octavia. Then she looks down again at the page, continuing to read:'Chloe liked Olivia. They shared a laboratory together . . .' And she continues to reflect that with this change of subject in contemporary literature, something 'of great importance' has happened. The speaker seems to be describing a new inclusiveness, directness, confidence, in women's fiction of the 1920s. But the passage is full of breaks and starts and stops, blushes and suggestive dots. And it is dominated by a powerful image of censoriousness, the 'red curtain' – red for danger, red for sex, red for rage – which may conceal 'the figure of Sir Chartres Biron'.

The draft version of this passage in the manuscript of *A Room of One's Own* was written in mid-March 1929, when the book was still being called 'Women & Fiction'.[61]

> ⟨I read⟩ ~~She said~~ 'Chloe liked Olivia; they shared a ——' ⟨the words came at⟩ the bottom of the page; the pages had stuck; while fumbling to open them there flashed into my mind the inevitable policeman; the summons; the order to attend the court; the dreary waiting; the Magistrate coming in

with a little bow; the glass of water; the counsel for the prosecution; for the defense; the verdict; this book is ~~called~~ obscene; & flames rising, perhaps on Tower Hill, as they consumed ‹that› masses of ~~print~~ paper. Here the pages came apart. Heaven be praised! It was only a laboratory. [IN MARGIN: that was shared].

As she fumbles to unstick the pages of her imaginary novel, an unmentionable word – bed? lover? – hangs in the air, and an imagined scene flashes into her mind of an obscenity trial. This brief fantasy has its foundation in fact. Sir Chartres Biron was the presiding magistrate in the obscenity case brought against Jonathan Cape, publishers of Radclyffe Hall's *The Well of Loneliness*, on 9 November 1928 at Bow Street Magistrate's Court, after the book had been seized and withdrawn by order of the Home Secretary, Sir William Joynson-Hicks.

Virginia Woolf knew about the case from the moment the book was banned.[62] She wrote to Vita in August 1928 about 'Your friend Radclyffe Hall' being banned because of her 'proclivities'.

Leonard and Morgan Forster began to get up a protest, and soon we were telephoning and interviewing and collecting signatures – not yours, for *your* proclivities are too well known.

Vita replied: 'I feel very violently about The Well of Loneliness. Not on account of what you call my proclivities; not because I think it is a good book; but really on principle.'[63] Virginia agreed; 'but what is one to do?' She had agreed to sign 'one rather comic little letter written by Forster and published in the *Nation*, on 8 September 1928. 'Now it appears that I, the mouthpiece of Sapphism, write letters from the Reform Club.' Woolf and Forster protested against the Home Secretary's censorship of the book on grounds of its lesbian subject matter: 'What of the other subjects known to be more or less unpopular in Whitehall, such as birth-control, suicide and pacificism? May we mention these? We await our instructions!'[64] She agreed to stand as a witness, though she thought it a dull book, and didn't care for Forster's reports of Radclyffe Hall's behaviour: 'she screamed like a herring gull, mad with egotism and vanity.' (Forster, talking of this matter on a weekend at Rodmell, 'said he thought Sapphism disgusting: partly from convention, partly because he disliked that women should be independent of men'.)[65]

But, while she committed herself publicly to the protest against censorship which the Radclyffe Hall case aroused, even among intellectuals with no commitment to Sapphism, she carried out a telling piece of self-censorship in those cancelled pages of *A Room of One's Own*. The final emphasis is on Chloe and Olivia as friends who worked together – and she goes on to make the point that one of the two is married and has small children. What interests her about *Life's Adventure*, she insists, is the impersonality of the two women's friendship. So the suggestion that *Life's Adventure* is a lesbian novel, has been as well concealed – she hopes – as the figure of Sir Chartres Biron behind the red curtain. Yet the cancelled suggestion both is and is not there in *A Room of One's Own*. In spite of her camouflage, Woolf was still anxious about its reception: 'I shall be attacked for a feminist and hinted at for a sapphist'.[66]

In November 1928 the Radclyffe Hall case came to trial. Virginia told Quentin that 'Leonard and Nessa say I mustn't go into the box, because I should cast a shadow over Bloomsbury. Forgetting where I was I should speak the truth'.[67] She did go to give evidence on 9 November, and was impressed by 'the reason of the law, its astuteness, its formality'.[68] But Sir Chartres Biron refused to hear the expert witnesses who had agreed to testify on behalf of the book ('we could not be called as experts in obscenity, only in art') and adjourned the case. On 16 November he ruled (in explicitly anti-homosexual terms) that the book was an obscene libel and should be destroyed. Virginia did not go to court on 14 December, when Hall's appeal was disallowed. 'I was very much upset' (Virginia wrote to Vita) 'to think you had been angry that I didn't go to the bloody womans trial.'[69]

Unlike *The Well of Loneliness*, *Orlando*'s ambiguous, androgynous treatment of sexuality was reviewed entirely in terms of its charm, its wit and its idiosyncrasy. (Though Richard Kennedy, the young dogsbody at the Hogarth Press at the time, remembered having trouble with the book when he tried to sell it to an Edinburgh book shop, 'because of the homosexual element'.)[70] Virginia may have felt that she had evaded the issues: 'Of course a very quick brilliant book. Yes, but I did not try to explore . . . I never got down to my depths & made shapes square up, as I did in To the Lighthouse. Well but Orlando was the outcome of a perfectly definite, indeed overmastering impulse. I want fun. I want fantasy. I want (& this was serious) to give things their caricature value. And still this mood hangs about me. I want to write a history, say of Newnham or the womans movement, in the same vein.'[71]

Orlando and *A Room of One's Own* are bids for freedom. Both have Utopian endings. Both set their women free from histories of repressions and limitations. Orlando gets free of 'his' parents very easily (unlike all her other characters) and 'her' marriage is more of a free adventure than a domestic bondage. And she doesn't die. *Orlando* is the only one of her books with no deaths, turning away from the elegiac mood of *To the Lighthouse*, and holding off the contemplation of death in *The Waves*. Only in *Orlando* and *A Room of One's Own* does Virginia Woolf free herself, through the idea of a woman's writing, from the pressures of the family, the doom of fate, the prison of madness. Both books work playfully through literary periods and come out with an idea of a new, modern freedom. Yet in both there are anticipations of the mood of solitary meditation, silence and mysticism which will fill *The Waves*. And in both there are pauses, gaps, silences, things that can't or haven't been said. So, for all its romance and eloquence and high colour, at the centre of *Orlando* (as at the heart of the relationship with Vita) there are blank pages. The leaving of the great blank in the middle of the love-story of *Orlando*, the narrator says, must be taken to indicate that the space is filled with unutterable things.

> And really it would profit little to write down what they said, for they knew each other so well that they could say anything, which is tantamount to saying nothing . . . For it has come about, by the wise economy of nature, that our modern spirit can almost dispense with language; the commonest expressions do, since no expressions do; hence the most ordinary conversation is often the most poetic, and the most poetic is precisely that which cannot be written down. For which reasons we leave a great blank here, which must be taken to indicate that the space is filled to repletion.[72]

And she leaves a blank space on the page.

THIRTY

Selves

For she had a great variety of selves to call upon, far more than we have been able to find room for, since a biography is considered complete if it merely accounts for six or seven selves, whereas a person may well have as many thousand.[1]

Orlando's biographer keeps disassembling and then re-assembling Orlando's 'selves': a reflection of Virginia Woolf's sense of her own 'great variety of selves'. As she began to develop her ideas for *The Waves* – of the author as six different voices speaking in solitude – and as at the same time her public, famous self became increasingly established, her life can be seen as a complicated range of performances. Questions about her 'selves' filled her mind in the late 1920s. Her battle-cry, 'How I interest myself!'[2] was loud in her ears. She knew that she had different ways of presenting her own identity. She kept returning to *Orlando*'s idea of the unstable self. And the old argument persisted about whether the diary should be a record of the soul, or of facts.

And as for the soul: why did I say I would leave it out? I forget. And the truth is, one can't write directly about the soul. Looked at, it vanishes: but look at the ceiling, at Grizzle, at the cheaper beasts in the Zoo which are exposed to walkers in Regents Park, & the soul slips in. It slipped in this afternoon. I will write that I said, staring at the bison: answering L. absentmindedly; but what was I going to write?[3]

To be 'absent minded' is to split off from one's self, to be – as was often said of her – not all there. It was a way of catching herself off-guard. And if *she* could find herself out only by indirection, then it was a great deal harder for other people to pin her down. Most of what went on in her internal zoo was invisible to the outsider. In September 1926, for instance, she had the vision of a fin rising on a wide blank sea, one of those strange interior seeings that seemed to come out of herself and also out of nowhere. It could never be known by others, or explained. A year later she was still thinking about the inscrutability of that sort of 'moment of vision'. 'No biographer could possibly guess this important fact about my life in the late summer of 1926: yet biographers pretend they know people.'[4] Even to herself such a moment could not be 'known' until it had been turned into language: 'What image can I reach to convey what I mean? Really there is none I think.'[5]

She began to try out different methods of catching the self in the diary. She gave headings to her inner life: 'Art & Thought', 'My Own Brain'.[6] 'I played with my mind watching what it would do.'[7] She noted almost imperceptible changes – shifts in feelings for friends[8] or changes in habits – for instance that by 1929 she had gradually stopped doing any printing. 'Habits gradually change the face of ones life as time changes one's physical face; & one does not know it.'[9] She was aware of her see-saws between involvement and withdrawal: 'I have wrapped myself round in my own personality again.'[10] She asked herself constantly whether her solipsism revealed a deeper 'reality', and whether that 'reality' could be written.[11]

Her quarrel with herself over the diary's uses intensified at moments of political crisis. The few days of the General Strike, in May 1926, made her more acutely aware than usual of the relationship between her interior life and the history she existed in. She wanted to keep part of herself – the part that was writing the 'Time Passes' section of *To the Lighthouse* – entirely separate. At the same time she was immersed in, and keenly attentive to, the day-to-day events of the strike. The diary for these few days of crisis displays her doubleness. She keeps asking herself how 'interesting' the external details would be to look back on, and scoffs at the transitory excitement of real things. Yet she feels compelled to record everything she noticed.

This doubleness repeated itself throughout her life and was built into the dynamics of the marriage (part of her response to the strike was a quarrel with Leonard). She maintained the separateness she needed, often by affecting to be less politically observant than she was.[12] At the same time she was drawn in and challenged by what was happening. During the strike she felt excited and bored at the same time: a wearying combination.

She often adopted a tone of disengagement or irritation towards political activity or social inequities, but this didn't mean she was aloof. Her comments, a few years before, on 'Black Friday', April 1921, were as uncertain as most leftist middle-class reactions to this precursor of the General Strike. (After the withdrawal of government control of the coal-mines, and the huge wage reductions that followed, the miners' appeal to the 'Triple Alliance' of railwaymen and transport workers failed, and they had to fight alone and unsuccessfully for better pay and hours.) She dreaded the anticipated discomfort, so reminiscent of the recent war; she thought about her own protected and privileged position; and she assumed that the workers would rather work than not:

> Presumably the miners will have to give in, & I shall get my hot bath, & bake home made bread again; yet it seems a pity somehow – if they're to be forced back & the mine owners triumphant. I think this is my genuine feeling, though not very profound. It is fairly obvious that working people are well enough satisfied to prefer going on working; I remember the pleasure of the railwaymen when they started running about platforms & leaning out of engines again.[13]

This was a limited, but not an unthinking response. Her personal requirements co-existed with a profound dislike for injustice, cant and exploitation.

Her own sceptical resistance to authority, and her horror of being dominated, influenced by Leonard's commitment to socialist democracy and by the anti-establishment liberalism of most of her friends, meant that she was always against coercive government. The Dreadnought Hoax, the anti-conscription movement, the suffrage work, the distaste for victory celebrations, the protests against censorship, and, soon, her thinking against Fascism: in all these public connections, she would not join up, but she was also a political participant. This position was fundamental to her feminism.

She knew that this was not a simple opposition. She observed that her responses to the General Strike infiltrated the writing self which she thought she was preserving against 'real things'.[14] During the strike she was writing the part of *To the Lighthouse* in which, after the war, the charwoman rescues the deserted house from ruin. This passage is about the stoic survival of working people, and also about the alternative life of the 'solitary mystic', the 'visionary', withdrawn from the real world: the self she would half-like to be, but could not quite be, at the time of the strike.[15] The strike reminded her (and many others) of the war. It produced the same feeling of being caught in darkness, of helpless waiting and anxiety, of lack of real information, as wartime had (and would again): 'So we go on, turning in our cage.'[16]

She shared with Leonard and with most of their friends a sense of helplessness and political depression. They all thought the strike was a catastrophe for class-relations and for the economy. Everyone in Keynes's circle was well aware, the year before, of what the restoration of Britain to the Gold Standard would mean: lower wages, huge increases in industrial costs. In 1925 the mining industry was in dreadful straits – 300,000 men out of work, losses of £1 million a month, drastic wage cuts imposed by the mine-owners. The polarisation between Baldwin's Tory government and the mine-owners on one side, and the mine-workers, unions and Labour Party on the other, was clear to all. What was not so clear was how effective the TUC could really be in a strike, and how much support the Labour Party (whose leaders were extremely fearful, with Russia in mind, of the revolutionary implications of a strike) would give to the unions. In the event, the General Strike (according to Kingsley Martin) was 'an unmitigated disaster, not merely for Labour but for England'. Retrospectively, it seemed to ensure the 'crude' class-divisions in English society, and to be the harbinger of the Depression of the 1930s.[17] There was division between the miners, the General Council of the TUC, and the Labour Party. There was uncertainty about who should come out: for example transport workers, printers, builders, but not post-office workers, engineers, electricians. (So, as Virginia Woolf's diary makes clear, the telephone and the bicycle were the two most crucial weapons for both sides.) Baldwin's government organised as for war, energised by a ferociously anti-working-class Churchill (Virginia Woolf saw his armoured tanks on the streets, and heard the rumours about his plans for using tear-gas) and a reactionary Home Secretary, Joynson-Hicks, as hard-line against communists and strikers as he would soon be against a lesbian novel. Harold Laski called them 'pinchbeck Mussolinis'.[18] A large number of middle- and upper-class citizens rallied round the government in the strike-breaking effort: this was a class war.[19] Above all, it was a war for the eyes and minds of the public. The government took control of the BBC, though John Reith, managing director since 1922, tried for neutrality. When the Archbishop of Canterbury joined in on the side of conciliation, his appeal was censored by the BBC; and when the strike was over, the BBC 'obligingly' played Blake's 'Jerusalem'.[20] In lieu of other newspapers, Churchill issued his propaganda-publication, the *British Gazette*, countered by the *British Worker*. Propaganda, the government's good organisation, and confusion on the left, led after a week to the collapse of the strike. The TUC betrayed the miners, settled without consulting them, left them to fight on alone, and was rewarded by the punitive Trades Disputes Act.

Leonard saw it all as clearly and as grimly as usual.

Of all public events in home politics during my lifetime, The General Strike was the most painful, the most horrifying. The treatment of the miners by the government was . . . disgracefully dishonest. If ever there has been right on the side of the workers in an industrial dispute, it was on the side of the miners in the years after the war; if ever a strike and a general strike were justified, it was in 1926. The actions of the mine-owners and of the government seemed to me appalling and when the General Strike came, I was entirely on the side of the workers. There was, of course, really nothing one could do, and one watched appalled the incompetence of those who had called and were conducting the strike.[21]

He was closely involved with the people who knew what was happening – Keynes, Laski, Hubert Henderson, R.H. Tawney, Hugh Dalton. He spent most of the week helping Tawney collect signatures for a petition asking for fair treatment of the miners after the strike was over. Later, he published a number of books at the Press about the conditions of the coal-industry and the miners, including Kingsley Martin's *The British Public and the General Strike*. However, he resisted Keynes's request during the strike to print a pro-strike edition of the *Nation* on the Hogarth Press machine. Virginia disagreed with him. (The strike, of course, put a temporary stop to the publishing of any books that week.)

Tavistock Square was an agitated centre of activity: radio broadcasts, droppers-in with news and rumours, arguments, telephone calls and speech-writing. Meanwhile Virginia tried to go on with *To the Lighthouse*, breaking off continually for news of the latest developments. Madge Vaughan's daughter Janet, a medical student at University College Hospital, remembered it well. With Hilda Matheson, she was organising concerts for working men and women, which attracted large audiences, and she bicycled round London fixing things up. She also went round asking for signatures to the appeal for clemency for the miners (Leonard remembered that the only writer who refused her was Galsworthy). In the evening she parked her bicycle in Virginia and Leonard's hallway, and would 'go upstairs and drink tea or cocoa with them. We would talk politics and Virginia with her endless curiosity would ask about the concerts and what it was like on a bicycle in Piccadilly.'[22]

From their windows Virginia could see the traffic of bicycles and crowded cars and lorries with old men and girls standing up, as in third-class railway carriages, going down Southampton Row. She noted the swarms of scavenging children, people walking long distances to work, the crimson and silver guard at the Cenotaph and men 'bare-heading themselves'. (The war was so recent; so many of the strikers, and the workers who helped to break the strike, had fought for their country.) Also she noted odd details: the distant sound of a barrel organ playing in the unusual quiet of the evening, a policeman smoking a cigarette on one of the armoured cars in Oxford Street. On the Friday she went to write in the British Museum, for the first time for about fifteen years, as it was cold and dark at home: 'Written up are the names of great men; & we all cower like mice nibbling crumbs in our most official discreet impersonal mood beneath.' On the Monday she took a speech which Leonard had written for Hugh Dalton to the House of Commons (travelling by bus, 'with a policeman on the box, and boards up to protect us from stone throwers') and found 'all this humbug of police & marble statues vaguely displeasing'. But mostly she listened and talked, and was above all keenly alert to the political use of language.

The BBC set up five news bulletins a day, starting at 10 and ending at 9.30 p.m. (This was the first occasion in Britain when a national crisis was acted out on the radio. People listened at home and in shops, and the rush to volunteer came directly out of the news bulletins. By the time of the abdication crisis ten years later, and then the war, radio had become accepted as the crucial instrument of information. Like everybody else, Virginia Woolf listened in continually.) She reported on the second day, with a mixture of snobbery, scepticism and helplessness: 'A voice, rather commonplace & official, yet the only common voice left, wishes us good morning at 10. This is the voice of Britain, to wh. we can make no reply. The voice is very trivial, & only tells us that the Prince of Wales is coming back, that the London streets present an unprecedented spectacle.'[23] She noticed how the news instantly created clichés of the strike: how people 'trek to work' was 'the stock phrase'. She noted how everyone had a phrase, a way of speaking which made them sound in control. The dentist said, 'It's red rag versus Union Jack, Mrs Woolf.' Bob Trevelyan said, 'Churchill is for peace, but Baldwin won't budge.' Clive said, 'Churchill is for teargas bombs, fight to the death, & is at the bottom of it all.' J.C. Squire said they shouldn't 'knuckle under'. Hubert Henderson said, 'There is imminent danger of civil war.' Eileen Power, an economic historian, said at dinner, 'This is the death blow of Trades Unionism in England.' And yet everybody ended their sentences with 'Well I dont know'. Leonard attributed this to the lack of newspapers. *His* way of speaking was just as usual: 'L says if the state wins & smashes TUs he will devote his life to labour: if the archbishop succeeds, he will be baptised.'

She listened to Baldwin speaking on the radio – the first time a Prime Minister had addressed the nation in this way. He said:

I am a man of peace. I am longing and working and praying for peace, but I will not surrender the safety and the security of the British Constitution. You placed me in power eighteen months ago by the largest majority accorded to any Party for many, many years. Have I done anything to forfeit that confidence? Cannot you trust me to ensure a square deal to secure even justice between man and man?[24]

Virginia Woolf's diary entry on Baldwin was factually accurate and lethally satirical. She objected to the male political authority which she had been noticing all week in the 'humbug of police & marble statues', and in the men's knowing, helpless talk, and in the names inscribed at the British Museum. This response would go straight into *A Room of One's Own* and, later, *Three Guineas*.

> He rolls his rs; tries to put more than mortal strength into his words. 'Have faith in me. You elected me 18 months ago. What have I done to forfeit your confidence? Can you not trust me to see justice done between man & man?' Impressive as it is to hear the very voice of the Prime Minister, descendant of Pitt & Chatham, still I can't heat up my reverence to the right pitch. I picture the stalwart oppressed man, bearing the world on his shoulders. And suddenly his self assertiveness becomes a little ridiculous. He becomes megalomaniac. No I dont trust him; I dont trust any human being, however loud they bellow & roll their rs.[25]

When the strike ended, she was in the Tottenham Court Road, and heard the news through the loudspeaker of a firm of upholsterers. She rushed home, and they all listened to the announcement: 'They told us to stand by & await important news. Then a piano played a tune. Then the solemn broadcaster assuming incredibly pomp & gloom & speaking one word to the minute read out: Message from 10 Downing Street. The TUC leaders have agreed that the Strike shall be withdrawn.' There was relief, excitement, and gloom. She made a clear-sighted and accurate reading, the next day, of the outcome: 'Labour, it seems clear, will be effectively diddled again, & perhaps rid of its power to make strikes in future . . . In short, the strain removed, we all fall out & bicker & backbite.'

This tone of voice and point of view owed a great deal to Leonard, but during the strike they quarrelled fiercely. Leonard stood for action and disillusionment, Virginia for passive observation and optimism. 'I dislike the tub thumper in him; he the irrational Xtian in me.' What she felt through the crisis was deadlock, helplessness, the unnatural atmosphere of 'great activity but no normal life'. It reminded her of a situation she knew all too well, of 'a house where someone is dangerously ill, & friends drop in to enquire, & one has to wait for doctors' news'. In this state, she found herself 'praying' for God, 'the King or God; some impartial person to say kiss & be friends – as apparently we all desire'. To Leonard, presumably, this longing for a *deus ex machina* to sort everything out seemed feeble and unrealistic.

Meanwhile, at the other end of the spectrum of political involvement, there was Vanessa writing from Venice, accusing her (as her family always did) of exaggerated reports, and happy to be absent herself ('I would rather read your account of the strike than be in it . . . I suppose even I couldn't have escaped a good deal of very tiresome discussion')[26] and Vita in Kent, writing amusingly: 'I am felling an oak to show my rustic independence of the coal strike.'[27]

External conflicts were matched by internal conflicts: not just between the self that wanted to keep apart and write fiction, and the self that avidly noted all the facts, but also between wildly inconsistent feelings about the working-classes. Just before the strike she had been having another row with Nelly, who had given notice, and then apologised: it made her feel furious and horrified. The servant she was writing into *To the Lighthouse* during the week of the strike, Mrs McNab, was being drawn with a strange mixture of dehumanising condescension and admiration for her stoicism. In the middle of the strike, she was visiting her dressmaker and worrying about her dress-sense. A few days after the strike had ended, when it had begun to be very hot and she was on a bus, thinking about those terrible hot May days in London twenty years before, she was suddenly overcome with horror at humanity in the mass. She wrote to Vanessa:

> I have just travelled Kensington High Street – which almost made me vomit with hatred of the human race. Innumerable women of incredible mediocrity, drab as ditchwater, wash up and down like dirty papers against Barkers and Derry and Toms. One was actually being sick or fainting in the middle of the street. All our past – George Gerald Marny and Emma – rose about me like the fumes of cabbage. And I had to sit next to a man in the tube who picked his ears with a large pin – then stuck it in his coat again.[28]

There is no getting round this; there is no reconciling these contradictions.

On Friday 23 July 1926, Virginia and Leonard took a day return train journey to Dorchester, to have tea with Thomas Hardy, then aged eighty-six, and Florence Emily Hardy at Max Gate. She took her copy of *The Mayor of Casterbridge* to read on the train. It was Virginia Woolf's first and last encounter with Hardy, but it came out of a long history of literary knowledge and family connection. Hardy's friendship with Leslie Stephen, who published him in the *Cornhill*, had linked them since her childhood: she had written to thank him in 1915 for his poem about Leslie, 'The Schreckhorn'.

She had been reading and writing about Hardy since 1903, for most of her adult life.[29] After Bruce Richmond had asked her to prepare his obituary in 1919, she worked on this Hardy essay for several years, filling a notebook on his work while writing *Jacob's Room*. In June 1925 Hardy sent Leonard a poem for the literary pages of the *Nation*, and Mrs Hardy wrote to say that Hardy was greatly enjoying *The Common Reader*. And so this visit, made while she was remembering her father for the writing of *To the Lighthouse*, was a kind of return, as well as an adventure. It took her back to her sensations on meeting the 'great men' of her childhood. But it was also a test of how established and secure she felt as a writer.

Mrs Hardy, she noted first, was the entry-point, resigned to yet more visitors, talking with real interest only about their dog Wessex. ('He bites, she told us.') Then:

> in trotted a little puffy cheeked cheerful old man, with an atmosphere cheerful & businesslike in addressing us, rather like an old doctors or solicitors, saying 'Well now –' or words like that as he shook hands. He was dressed in rough grey with a striped tie. His nose has a joint in it, & the end curves down. A round whitish face, the eyes now faded & rather watery, but the whole aspect cheerful & vigorous.

He took his tea, 'extremely affable & aware of his duties', keeping the talk going. Later, Leonard was offered a whisky and water – Hardy was 'competent as a host'. He 'talked of father' and how he had published *Far From the Madding Crowd*. 'We stood shoulder to shoulder against the British public about certain matters dealt with in that novel – You may have heard.' He said he wrote it chapter by chapter, for instalments, which may have been bad for the novel. Mrs Hardy agreed. 'She was leaning upon the tea table, not eating gazing out.' He talked about the London he remembered and how he would never go back there; how he had seen an air raid. She noted his shrewd smile, his lack of doubts, his lack of interest in his novels. He told her how long it took to write the *Dynasts*, but when she pressed him, 'the dog kept cropping up'. She asked if he wrote poems and novels at the same time. 'I wrote a great many poems. I used to send them about, but they were always returned, he chuckled.' They touched on mutual friends, Sassoon and Forster. She tried to get him to say which of his books he would choose to read on a train, 'but he was not going to be drawn'. Of the *Mayor*, he asked: 'And did it hold your interest?' They talked about his fans ('Small boys write to him from New Zealand'), and about de la Mare's disappointing recent stories. Hardy said he was a 'very nice man' who saw a lot of people and who had stopped writing poetry. Did one have to choose between writing poetry and seeing people? 'Its a question of physical strength', Hardy said; but 'clearly preferred solitude himself'.

He mentioned Huxley's new stories, which Mrs Hardy was reading to him as his eyes were so bad, and he chuckled about modern story-telling. 'We used to think there was a beginning & a middle & an end . . . Now one of those stories came to an end with a woman going out of the room.' She found him 'sensible & sincere', 'very active minded; liking to describe people; not to talk in an abstract way.' He described T.E. Lawrence (whom the Hardys had got to know well while he was serving as 'Private Shaw' with a regiment in Dorset) driving over on his motorbike with a broken arm. Mrs Hardy hoped that 'he won't commit suicide'. He had promised Hardy not to fly: 'My husband doesn't like anything to do with the air.' Virginia and Leonard said they had to go; Hardy 'trotted off' to get a copy of *Life's Little Ironies* signed for her, and came back with her name spelt 'Wolff': this must have 'given him some anxiety', she thought. She asked him to pat Wessex, who 'went on wheezing away'.

She noted again his impressive simplicity, 'his freedom, ease & vitality', his 'great Victorian' air, his interest in facts. He showed them an 'awful engraving' which he said was rather his idea of Tess. She asked about an old picture which was meant to have inspired Tess: 'Thats fiction', he said. Outside, he pointed out Weymouth before he 'trotted in again'. She realised that she did not know 'what his secret interests & activities are – to what he trotted off when we left him'.

For the next few weeks she could not stop talking about this visit. Two reported accounts show how her story began to harden into caricature. Vita passed on to Harold what Virginia had felt ('Here's a great man, and I'm only so damned clever') and how she described the meeting: 'She says he is a simple, ugly, insignificant little old man, and almost illiterate; also that literature, as such, has no interest or importance for him at all.' Clive passed *his* version on to Mary Hutchinson: 'She was still full of Hardy, who, she says, is like a very dignified retired country solicitor – but not at all stupid – on the contrary, sharp and intelligent, avid of facts and not at all disposed to talk about his own works. Which is the more real Hardy,' Clive added shrewdly, 'the one Virginia saw, or the one Morgan Forster saw?'[30]

Clive's question suggests the visit to Hardy as a miniature version of biography. 'Thats fiction' might be said of her 'picture' of him, delicately poised between her observation and her interpretations. She knew she was changing it as she retold it:

I was telling myself the story of our visit to the Hardys, & I began to compose it: that is to say to dwell on Mrs Hardy leaning on the table,

538

looking out, apathetically, vaguely; & so would soon bring everything into harmony with that as the dominant theme. But the actual event was different.[31]

After Hardy's death two years later, in January 1928, and the funeral service at Westminster Abbey, which depressed her, she 'furbished up' her old essay on him. It was published in the *TLS*, anonymously, on 19 January. The essay shows how important Hardy was to her in her thinking about English fiction. She called him a 'great unconscious writer'.

> The novels therefore are full of inequalities; they are lumpish and dull and inexpressive; but they are never arid; there is always about them a little blur of unconsciousness, that halo of freshness and margin of the unexpressed which often produce the most profound sense of satisfaction. It is as if Hardy himself were not quite aware of what he did, as if his consciousness held more than he could produce, and he left it for his readers to make out his full meaning and to supplement it from their own experience.[32]

Later that year, in November 1928, she reviewed Mrs Hardy's (or rather Hardy's) memoir.[33] In 1932, Mrs Hardy wrote to say that she had often wished she had asked Virginia Woolf to be Hardy's biographer: surely one of the most intriguing unwritten books in literary history. By 1936, though, she had become less enthusiastic. 'I think he had genius & no talent', she concluded.[34]

Of all Hardy's literary gifts, the one that most moved her was the one that most closely resembled her own. This was his unconscious capacity for 'moments of vision': 'With a sudden quickening of power which we cannot foretell, nor he, it seems, control, a single scene breaks off from the rest.'[35] She took his phrase, 'moments of vision', and used it in her own late autobiography as 'moments of being'. Hardy's work – and her meeting with him – confirmed her sense that in fiction, as in autobiography and biography, it was the 'moments of great intensity' which counted and told all. It was true of life, too, as she noted in the Hardyish account of her marriage, written a few days after the visit, where she spoke of these moments – Hardy's 'moments of vision' – as being all the fuller because of the automatic customary unconscious days on either side.[36]

At the beginning of 1927, Vanessa got news that Duncan had been taken ill with pneumonia in the South of France. Virginia came into the room at Gordon Square and found her white-faced on the telephone. With the nine-year-old Angelica, and her servant Grace, Vanessa left London in a snowstorm, kissing Virginia goodbye in the street. 'I think a left-handed marriage makes these moments more devastating: a sense remains, I think, of hiding one's anguish; of insecurity.'[37] As in other catastrophes, Vanessa drew strength from Virginia. 'I'm afraid I was very tiresome and silly in London,' she wrote from Cassis once Duncan was found to be out of danger. 'As usual in a crisis – and in ordinary life too though you pretend not to think so – I depended on you & Leonard – I hope you didn't worry after I had gone my Billy – you were the greatest help to me . . . Your letters will be a godsend when they come.'[38] 'Do get a little rest,' Virginia wrote, 'I thought you were worn to a shred as Mary Fisher wd. say.'[39] It was an old joke between them, to parody the language of needy affection from the letters of their aunts and parents; but need and affection there still were.

Virginia was acute, though not altogether informed, about the strain of Vanessa's 'left-handed marriage'. The pressures of life with Duncan were considerable. 'Divinely charming',[40] dazzlingly gifted, susceptible, lovable and sexy, completely committed to his work and evasive of other responsibilities, bohemian, idiosyncratic and careless of appearances, the person Vanessa had chosen to love for the rest of her life was the cause of as much pain as pleasure. Since the birth of their daughter Angelica in 1918 they had (probably) not had a sexual life, but instead a companionship of professional, social and domestic collaboration. Duncan stayed in Vanessa's household while having affairs with a series of lovers with whom Vanessa had to make friends, for fear of losing him from her life.

Virginia knew some of these friends of Duncan well, but she seems not always to have been aware of the tensions they caused. When Bunny Garnett and Duncan became lovers during the war, there was an intense triangle of jealousy and attraction.[41] Virginia did not comment on it, though she noticed the friction between them.[42] The latest of Vanessa's rivals was an ex-boyfriend of Lytton's, the Woolfs' unsatisfactory assistant at the Press, Angus Davidson, who was now at Duncan's bedside in Cassis. There would be many others, most threateningly, in 1930, a handsome half-Russian artist called George Bergen. For some time Vanessa feared that Duncan might leave her for George, and her letters to Duncan at this time were full of anguish. But she waited it out, and said nothing to Virginia, whose joking reference (early in 1931 in a letter to Quentin) to Duncan's inexplicable pleasure in the society of his sheep-headed Russian[43] suggested that she was taking Vanessa's predicament rather lightly.

It was an irony of the sisters' lives that Vanessa, whom Virginia had envied all her life for her sensuality and her maternal calmness, should from her late forties onwards be living in a sexually thwarted and emotionally unreciprocated relationship. Virginia could sense its sexual atmosphere; on one visit in 1927 (at the height of her involvement with Vita) she told Vanessa that she and Duncan seemed to her 'marmoreally chaste', having cast out 'the devils that afflict poor creatures like me'.[44] Vanessa, not pleased, replied that 'it is terrible to be thought chaste and dowdy when one would so much like to be neither'.[45] (It had been Virginia whom the family had always caricatured as marmoreally virginal; no wonder that this remark 'rankled' with Vanessa.) Virginia was always aware, too, of Vanessa's possessive maternal emotions, which she found 'destructive and limiting'.[46] She could see that, in her fifties, Vanessa transferred some of her sexual feelings to her three children, especially to Julian and to Angelica, for whom (as Virginia observed to Vanessa, only half-joking) 'you are a mere tool in the hands of passion'.[47]

But Virginia also needed to keep up her version of Vanessa as strong and powerful. When Vanessa spoke to her of the relative insecurity of her own 'marriage' to Duncan, with nothing 'binding' in it, Virginia was made to feel put down, settled and unadventurous.[48] Vanessa's reserve, too, was romanticised by Virginia. The situation with Duncan required great self-control. No one was to know how painfully insecure she felt. And there was still secrecy around Angelica's parentage. Everyone in their immediate circle knew that Duncan was Angelica's father (after all, she looked like him). But the outside world (including Clive Bell's parents) did not – and nor, till she was eighteen, did Angelica herself.[49] This allowed Duncan to be as uncommitted a father to Angelica (to her later distress) as he was a 'husband' to Vanessa. Angelica Garnett, speaking of her mother and her aunt in later life, frequently used the words 'inhibition', 'manipulation', 'formality', and 'coldness'.[50]

Vanessa's reserve began to harden now into habits. (Virginia observed that one's characteristics tended to do this in middle life unless watched out for.) There were family jokes about Vanessa's behaviour, of course, as when she put up a permanent sign at the bottom of the field reading 'To Charleston: OUT'.[51] After Julian's death in 1937 her comic misanthropy would solidify into a dark retreat from the world, in sharp contrast to Virginia's insatiable interest in new and younger people. But Virginia had to idealise Vanessa's reserve: 'You are, fundamentally, mysterious'.[52] She needed too to think of Vanessa and Duncan as 'humming with heat and happiness'[53] and of herself as comparatively insecure. When Vanessa admitted in the summer of 1929 that 'she was often melancholy & often envied me', Virginia thought this 'incredible'. With a characteristic mixture of self-mockery and self-satisfaction, she noted: 'Other peoples melancholy certainly cheers one.'[54]

If Vanessa had stayed with Roger Fry her middle age might have been less 'melancholy'. Though from 1926 he was living with Helen Anrep,[55] Vanessa never lost hold of him: the sisters shared a great retentiveness in their friendships. Vanessa kept her old lovers and friends in her orbit, though she had to adapt to their new relationships. (This was proving particularly difficult in the case of Lydia and Maynard, living across the fields at Tilton in increasing fame, grandeur and stinginess.) Clive, meanwhile, was messily breaking up with Mary (Virginia was dragged in on both sides) and embarking on a series of affairs which he liked to boast of, especially to Virginia. Much of the talk between Virginia and Vanessa in the late 1920s was (as it had been twenty years before, with a difference) about Clive's love-life.

Professionally, Vanessa's partnership with Duncan continued to be active and inventive. Both sisters chose as their life's companion someone they could work with: it was a form of revenge on, and an answer to, their mother's life. But these were different kinds of partnerships. Virginia worked with Leonard at the Press and contributed to his pages on the *Nation*, but her major work was done privately and alone. If Leonard had continued as a novelist after 1914, there would have been terrible problems of competition. Much of Vanessa's work, by contrast, was done under the influence of, or in collaboration with Duncan, and she was often overshadowed by him.[56]

From 1925 to 1931 their careers were jointly developed through the London Artists' Association.[57] Vanessa often showed her work alongside Duncan's, though she had a solo exhibition in 1930. In these years, they became 'famous and fashionable'[58] together, as much for their collaborations in interior decoration as for their paintings and portraits.[59] This work was brought to popular attention by Dorothy Todd and Raymond Mortimer's 1929 book *The New Interior Decoration*, and reached its peak of fashion in their collaboration on the 1932 Lefèvre Gallery Music Room (from which Virginia bought a screen by Vanessa and a carpet by Duncan). But by the time they left the LAA for Agnew's in 1931, they were beginning to be perceived as conventional by younger artists, rather as Virginia Woolf was demoted by some of the new writers of the 1930s.[60]

In the late 1920s, Virginia and Vanessa watched each other's work with attention and emotion. Virginia often defined what she was doing in Vanessa's terms, or as if through Vanessa's eyes. Vanessa did not usually initiate these cross-readings, but responded to them intensely. Virginia's readings of Vanessa's work came out of a mixture of admiration, recognition and rivalry. Her competitiveness was a vice, she knew. In January 1929, when *Orlando* was praised and Vanessa's big new painting at the New Burlington Galleries went unnoticed, she wrote: 'So I have something, instead of children, & fall comparing our lives.'[61] 'Fall', as if it was a lowering habit, something she couldn't help herself doing.

It was always the same. While Vanessa was away looking after Duncan in France, Virginia went to the first LAA show at the Leicester Galleries, and reported with a comically heartfelt mixture of envy ('as you have the children, & the fame by rights belongs to me') and admiration for her 'flashing brilliance', her 'singing' tone, her radiant use of colour. Her criticisms (of occasional 'flat passages', of the problem of 'empty spaces') arose from, and went straight back into, her own struggles with form in *To the Lighthouse* and Lily's analogous difficulties with her painting.[62]

Nine months later, when Vanessa was showing 'a few sketches' at the LAA show in March 1927, Virginia told her that her pictures were 'built up out of flying phrases', and excitedly praised her spontaneity and lyricism. But how could she 'buttress up this lyricism with solidity'? As usual she referred the problem back to herself: 'I think we are now at the same point . . . both . . . concerned with entirely new problems of structure.'[63] Vanessa was 'flattered and interested'.[64] Soon after, they exchanged gifts: Vanessa sent her a description of moths coming into the house at night, which Virginia was haunted by and wanted to turn into a story; Virginia sent her *To the Lighthouse*, with fears that she would be laughed at for 'the painting bits', and invitations for comparisons: 'I made it up one afternoon in the Square . . . How do you make up pictures? Suddenly all in a second?'[65] That summer she thought how their work was keeping pace, both of them come to a late flowering: 'Think of my books, Nessa's pictures.'[66] They would make the same close connections when Vanessa read *The Waves* in 1931 and told Virginia about her painting, 'The Nursery'.[67]

This private interchange was made public in Virginia's preface to Vanessa's 1930 solo show at the Cooling Gallery.[68] It is an outstanding example of how Virginia's working life was part of a 'family business'. Her thoughts about Vanessa's exhibition (which she brazenly puffed) were closely linked to her current thinking, in *A Room of One's Own*, *Orlando*, and 'Professions for Women', about the difficulties for women artists (or writers) and how they could disguise or save themselves through marriage. She began, in the first draft, with a lament for Victorian women artists who could not look at male nude models unless they had (like Orlando) 'a gold ring upon the second finger of the left hand'. In her treatment of Vanessa's paintings themselves, she emphasised her lack of identifiable 'femininity', and the reticent expressiveness of her art, 'which has no truck with words'. 'Mrs Bell' was baffling: Was she 'a mixture of Goddess and peasant, treading the clouds with her feet and with her hands shelling peas?' It was a public version of her feelings about Vanessa, and it was also a rewriting of

Mrs Ramsay. The manuscript ended with a joke about needing to consult Mrs Bell's grandfather about her morality, but this, presumably, was too much of a 'family business' to stay in the published pamphlet.

The family business between Vanessa and Virginia continued to affect all the practical aspects of Virginia's working life. In France in 1927, Vanessa was doing her eloquent illustrations for a new edition of *Kew Gardens*, and she went on illustrating all Virginia's covers, and other Hogarth Press titles.[69] Though Virginia was a reluctant sitter, Vanessa did paint her occasionally in the early 1930s.[70] And the houses, at Tavistock Square and at Monk's House, were filled with Vanessa's and Duncan's carpets, screens, mirrors, wall paintings, fabric designs and tiles, like Vanessa's 1930 lighthouse design for the fireplace tiling in Virginia's bedroom at Monk's House.

Her mid-life relationship with Vanessa, was, as always, complicated by the children. As an aunt, Virginia Woolf had two conflicting feelings. At bottom, there was the painful sense of failure which her childlessness gave her, and which always came on in moments of depression. In the late 1920s, she told herself that time had done its work in assuaging this sense of lack: 'I scarcely want children of my own now . . . I don't like the physicalness of having children of one's own . . . I can dramatise myself as parent, it is true. And perhaps I have killed the feeling instinctively; as perhaps nature does.'[71] But she continued to feel threatened by Vanessa's maternal superiority,[72] and if other people observed this 'family complex' she was defensive.

I was rather shocked that you [Ethel Sands] should think that I didn't care for Nessa's [children]. They are such an immense source of pleasure to me. But I see what it is: I'm always angry with myself for not having forced Leonard to take the risk in spite of doctors; he was afraid for me and wouldn't; but if I'd had rather more self-control no doubt it would have been all right. That's I suppose, why I don't talk of Nessa's children – it's true I never do – whom I adore.[73]

Alongside that fixation about childlessness there was a different feeling, connected to her active – and distinct – relationships with Vanessa's three children. Her 'performance' in this role sometimes disgusted her: 'irritated . . . with myself for being the good fairy Aunt. Lord how that role can bore me – how unreal it is – & why do I act it?'[74] But she was also keenly interested in the characters of her nephews and niece, especially now that the boys were becoming adults and Angelica was turning from indulged, entrancing child into a dramatic adolescent.

She was fascinated by the difference between their childhood and hers. The fact that they had grown up uncensored, running wild and naked at Charleston, used to living as equals with exceptional, creative adults (Julian, for instance, had developed a close friendship with Roger Fry), made them seem to her much more in control of their lives than she had been at their age: 'Nessa's children are terrifyingly sophisticated . . . They have grown up without any opposition: nothing to twist or stunt. Hence they have reached stages at 16 or 17 which I reached only at 26 or 27.'[75] When she made futuristic jokes to Quentin, aged twenty and just off to Rome, about how in half a century more there would be 'methods of circumventing these divisions of Aunt and Nephew' ('by attaching a small valve something like a leech to the back of your neck I shall tap all your sensations')[76] she was partly indulging her pleasure in science fiction – like her prophecies of a telephone that could see or an electric machine that would connect us to the past. But she was also commenting on how extraordinarily *modern* their relationship felt. Being a modern aunt involved, increasingly as the two large boys grew up, feeling like a sister. 'I can't believe theyre not my younger brothers', she would say to Vanessa.[77] Sometimes this was confusing: 'What a mix up we are! – I pretending to be an Aunt and then a contemporary – I never know which.'[78] She flirted with them, took pride in them, and played up to what they expected of her.

She treated the two young men differently. By the late 1920s, Julian was leaving Leighton Park School for a year in France before going to Cambridge (in 1927) to read history; Quentin, a well-travelled European by his teens (he stayed in France in 1924 and in Germany in 1928) left school in 1928 to be a painter. Both were active Labour supporters; in the General Strike, Julian made a school speech on the need for violent revolution in Britain.[79] Julian – pugnacious, big, uncouth, independent, vulnerable, messy, vain – had interested her since, as a child of nine, he had come into her bedroom at Charleston when she was staying the night and talked to her about the war.[80] She had always felt his force and his will; once at a picnic in Firle Park 'he took a bottle of water and smashed it. He stood there in his knickerbockers with long naked legs looking defiant and triumphant . . . I thought This is the victorious male; now he feels himself the conqueror.'[81] She compared him often with Thoby ('sensitive, very quick witted, rather combative')[82] though she always thought Thoby had been more elegant, less rough. Julian was anxious to inherit the Stephen literary mantle. But, as Virginia and Vanessa often observed to each other, there was a great deal of chauvinistic, country-squire Bellishness in Julian as well.

Julian had begun life as her rival, when Virginia was in *her* twenties; and now their relationship again became competitive. From the moment that

Julian began to assert himself as a writer, to send Virginia his work (his first volume of poems was published when he was twenty-two and still at Cambridge), she was sharply critical of him. The advice she sent him was rigorous and even discouraging; he found it 'disquieting'.[83] She knew this, of course: when she was relieved to hear his poems dispraised she struggled to discharge herself from accusations of 'vanity & jealousy'.[84] His politics and his attempts to write greatly affected her thinking and her work in the 1930s; he became a force to be reckoned with in her life. And she was deeply attached to, and interested in him:

> He is growing like a crab [she wrote to Vanessa in the spring of 1929] – I mean he is only half covered with shell; he is very queer; one finds him noticing, and feeling, and taking up what last year was imperceptible to him. We argued about poetry as usual, and he said he has written a long essay on poetry, which he is sending us. The Bell sociability is so odd, mixed with the Stephen integrity. I daresay he'll give you a lot of trouble before he's done – he is too charming and violent and gifted altogether: and in love with you, into the bargain. It is very exciting – the extreme potency of your Brats; they might have been nincompoops – instead of bubbling and boiling and frizzling like so many pans of sausages on the fire.[85]

Her friendship with Quentin, who was eighteen in 1928, was funnier, less complicated, more playful. She had a running joke with him throughout his teenage years in their collaborations, in the *Charleston Bulletin*, a scurrilous and modern family reprise of the *Hyde Park Gate News*. Once Quentin started to write letters to her, they developed a jokey, scandalous epistolary style which evidently gave her huge pleasure. Here he writes to her from his stay with a German family in 1928:

> Munich itself is quite amusing, the women are chaste but pretty, the beer is weak but good, but apropos of the beer I might as well tell you that it was sufficiently strong the other night to make me attempt to climb one of the lesser monuments of Munich, and to crawl up the stairs to the flat on all fours, while . . . another member of the party fell comatose in a state of complete nudity into the bedroom of a student of divinity, about to take holy orders, whose confusion and embarrassment at finding her there in the morning can better be imagined than described. But as a general rule I lead a very staid and sober life, and am, I believe, one of nature's puritans, which is surprising considering my beloved parents isn't it?[86]

'Fancy writing like that about father to the Quaker!' Virginia commented to Vanessa, thinking of their old Aunt Milly, while delightedly returning her own version of his letter to Quentin: 'I was fascinated and appalled . . . climbing the Monument naked, and sleeping with a professor of divinity, who is, unfortunately, but its the way in Germany, of the female sex – such is your way of life, and I tell it at many a merry party, half crying, half laughing.' He was the best letter-writer she knew, and ought to give up painting for writing: 'Think how many things are impossible in paint; giving pain to the Keynes', making fun of one's aunts, telling libidinous stories, making mischief . . . Throw up your career, for God's sake.'[87] She liked the idea of him as a worldly, amusable, observant companion ('We might see life together',[88] she told him, using her childhood phrase for going out and about). She played up to his sexual frankness, his unshockability, and his appetite for eccentricity and gossip, and wrote him some of her freest and funniest letters. Her much appreciated role as crazy aunt Virginia, though, could have its perils; an undated and unpublished note to Quentin read: 'Just to remind you if youve forgotten that human nature is incurably mad. Virginia. Tear Up.'[89]

With Angelica, she was protective, whimsical and girlish. Angelica remembered, as a child, being a pawn in the game between her aunt and her mother: Virginia's 'ingratiating, even abject' demands for kisses and attention from Vanessa would involve the little girl: 'My objection to being kissed was that it tickled, but I was only there to be played off against Vanessa's mute, almost embarrassed dislike of the whole demonstration.'[90] This retrospective account was making a point about Vanessa's reserve. But Virginia did 'play off' daughter against mother, as she had once played off Clive against Vanessa. Her messages ('I have several secrets to tell her, in great private – I have seen three new witcherinas. They sent her their love. I said she had a beautiful tribe of Elves, and also a crested newt but this is *very private*'),[91] her *risqué* jokes about 'raping' Angelica when she grew up,[92] her bid for her affections and interest, were clearly competitive. In her whimsical letters to Angelica, she signed herself 'Jinny' or 'Ginny'. It was her childhood name (so as to turn herself into Angelica's little sister) but it was also the name she gave to the most flirtatious character in *The Waves*, who was in competition with the darkly maternal and Vanessa-like Susan. Her 'pixerina-witcherina' language with Angelica was intended to be exclusive, to shut out everyone else, as Richard Kennedy, a young office boy at the Press in 1928, noticed:

LW and Mrs W drove me to the station to catch my train. Mrs W's little niece came in the car with us and she and Mrs W sat in the back. Mrs W kept up a flow of absolutely absurd conversation with the child in a high pitched voice, using a crazy language made up of unrecognizable sounds.[93]

Looking back, Angelica saw that she was being enlisted in a competition between Rodmell and Charleston, and that she never quite lived up to what was required of her: she felt she had always been rather a disappointment to Virginia. At the time, she echoed the tone set by her aunt, as in this twelve-year-old's letter from boarding-school:

> This afternoon we found 4 birds nests and one was a pheasants nest only a rat had got at it and 2 others were thrushes and another was a funny little queer one made out of leaves and it was about 6 ft from the ground because Im five ft you know!!!! love to everyone from Pixerina.[94]

But though the aunt-niece relationship may have been a whimsical performance on both sides, Virginia did understand the serious feeling between Vanessa and Angelica. When Angelica started going to school (and later when she imagined the scene of Vanessa and Julian's school visit) her response is profoundly sympathetic – as well as self-absorbed:

> Angelica goes to school for the first time today I think; & I daresay Nessa is crying to herself – one of the emotions I shall never know – a child, one's last child – going to school, & so ending the 21 years of Nessa's children – a great stretch of life; how much fuller than I can guess – imagine all the private scenes, the quarrels, the happinesses, the moments of excitement & change, as they grew up. And now, rather sublimely she ends her childhood years in a studio alone, going back, perhaps rather sadly to the life she would have liked best of all once, to be a painter on her own. So we have made out our lives, she & I, propelled into them by some queer force . . .[95]

As they grew up, the children conspired with their parents to create a family image of Virginia Woolf as the batty, playful, malicious, untrustworthy, eccentric genius. The letters between the children about Virginia always strike this note; it lingers on into Quentin Bell's biography, and has greatly influenced the British reading of her life. So Quentin would tell Julian about Virginia's indiscretions and exchange jokes about the Stephens' tendency to 'go barmy' (illustrated with a magnificent drawing of a Victorian lunatic asylum).[96] Julian would report to Quentin on how 'stark, staring mad' her new book was; or would tell him about a 'cracked' party she had given; or would describe a particularly aberrant piece of social behaviour on her part:

Virginia stays in a perpetual rainbow about anything. She dropped a stunning brick at a tea party of Dadie's on Saturday. I was sitting on the sofa between her and Mrs Kenneth Clark – wife of the Gothic revival – to whom both Virginia and I had just been introduced. Virginia deny'd that The White Devil was by Webster – I dont mean said it was by another Elizabethan, but just forgot Webster had written it. I proceeded to laugh at her, on which she turned savagely on Mrs Clark. 'Well, have you read it?' 'Yes.' 'Of course she has,' said I. 'Well, you professional students of literature at Newnham and Girton are taught to count the lines with a feminine ending.' ' . . . ' (The poor woman had never had an education at all, and was about 28, I should think.) 'I thought she was engaged to you,' said my dear aunt, as we left. Really, really. Is it malice, imbecility, or both?[97]

Julian was as caustic about her bad habits as she was severe about his writing. Writing to Vanessa in 1929 and confessing a secret (that he was having an affair at Cambridge with a fellow-student, Anthony Blunt), he begged her not to let it get to Virginia, 'and then one might as well put a notice in the Times.'[98] In 1931: 'I saw Virginia for a moment, she only had time for one story and a mere handful of vicious remarks and to betray one important secret.'[99] Quentin and he exchanged jokes about the craziness of her letters, and she played up to it with a will. This was the tone she adopted to Quentin:

What did you have for breakfast? Where did you dine last night and so on? And are you in love? And are you happy? And do you sometimes write a poem? And have you had your hair cut? And have you met anybody of such beauty your eyes dance, as the waves danced, no it was the stars; when Shakespeare's woman – Lord lord I've forgotten all I ever knew – was born?[100]

In response to this sort of thing, the delighted nephew would write to Julian, oh dear, listen to this, isn't this typical of 'our poor poor aunt'.[101]

Vanessa's settling for part of the year in France, from 1927 onwards, greatly affected Virginia's relationship with her. For one thing it meant more letters. (They had a typical joke that Virginia would exchange a letter for a painting.) Vanessa pointed out that her absence was really preferable for Virginia, since Virginia could re-invent her.[102] For another it made Virginia think more about why she was committed to England. For years friends like Lytton and Roger and Clive had been telling her that France was the greatest civilisation in the world.[103] And France was cheap; it was hot; it was light. So why not live there?

Also, quite simply, she missed her. Repeatedly, in the late 1920s, she spoke of Vanessa's absence like a drought, of being 'watered' by her return.[104] Vanessa, for her part, tried to lure her out there. As she began to re-create in La Bérgère, the house she had found in Cassis, 'another Charleston in France – even nicer in some ways',[105] she tempted the Woolfs with prospects of beautiful walks and cheap villa rentals. They went out three years running, in the spring of 1927 and 1928 and again in the summer of 1929. The month spent in Cassis in the spring of 1928 aroused all Virginia's pleasure in Mediterranean life, and all her most relaxed, wild behaviour. Julian regaled Quentin, who was in Munich, with stories of the Woolfs.

> Leonard had continual quarrels with Nessa and Duncan as to the exact shares each should pay for a litre of petrol. Virginia was quite dotty and asked perpetual questions. Here is a specimen with Clives and my replies. Q: Why are you called Julian? A. Because St Julian is the patron saint of hunting. Q: Why? A: Because he shot a stag with a cherry stone. A: I dont see what that has to do with it.[106]

She sent her own version of their sillinesses to Quentin (from 'your afflicted Aunt') and to Angus Davidson: 'Julian has actually made himself sick laughing at Duncan and me. Our eccentricities seem to flower in the south.'[107] They drove to see Van Gogh's asylum at St Rémy; Vanessa wrote to Quentin: 'We went through St Rémy and saw the asylum where he was shut up for a time. It's a wonderful place and Virginia hoped she'd be shut up there next time she went cracked.'[108] The analogy lingered on in Quentin's mind; writing to Julian two years later he said: 'Some artists have to break away – Something to be said for abandoning commonsense if ones mad like Van Gogh and Virginia.'[109]

On this holiday, she had a row with Clive (who 'slapped' her: verbally rather than actually?) and reproached him afterwards: 'If I ought to remember that you've been unhappy, so ought you to remember that I've been mad.'[110] By contrast, she felt completely devoted to Duncan: 'I often wonder' (she told Vanessa, still rivalrous) 'how we should have done married'.[111] With her real husband, Virginia arrived home after an adventurously puncture-strewn journey in their new Singer, The Umbrella, which she was now not allowed to drive.

In the summer of 1929 they went back, and nearly bought a house in Cassis. Vanessa wrote to Clive:

> The Woolfs are taking a house here! In a rather curious way of course.

They wanted, or rather V wanted, to buy the little house on the hill just opposite, but it turned out to be too expensive. Then they thought of taking it for 3 years and possibly buying it later, but the man refused. Finally they are going to take it for 3 months whenever they want to paying only 300 francs a month but furnishing it and putting in new windows. It may be sold over their heads at any time. Its all very odd and I cant think what will happen. Its certainly in a very nice position and could be made quite an attractive house. At present its not unlike Rodmell in being rather dark with odd-shaped rooms.[112]

Virginia immediately attached herself to the idea of this little house, and vividly imagined a life in France – part idyll, part competition with Vanessa:

And this island means heat, silence, complete aloofness from London; the sea; eating cakes in the new hotel at La Ciotat; driving off to Aix; sitting on the harbour dining; seeing the sardine boats come in; talk with people who have never heard of me & think me older, uglier than Nessa, & in every way inferior to her; that odd intimate, yet edgy, happy free yet somehow restrained intercourse with her & Duncan . . . Leonard in his shirt-sleeves; an Eastern private life for us both; an Indian summer running in & out of the light of common day; a great deal of cheap wine & cigars . . .[113]

But the dream of having three houses proved impractical; Leonard was never very enthusiastic, and the fantasy came to nothing. Though they visited Europe often in the next ten years, they never settled at Cassis again. So she stayed in her island until the end of her life.

In the late 1920s and early 1930s Virginia Woolf thought a great deal about her Englishness, even as she was writing increasingly about her alienated scepticism towards English social structures and English politics.[114] Susan, in the first draft of *The Waves* (written late in 1929) says of a country landscape: 'It was merely England . . . I should never be myself anywhere else.'[115]

England as an island, to which she both belongs and does not belong, is often mentioned in her late forties. In 'Street Haunting', the 1927 essay on roaming through London, she pauses to look at English travel-books: 'So restless the English are, with the waves at their very door. The waters of travel and adventure seem to break upon little islands of serious effort and lifelong industry stood in jagged columns upon the bookshop floor.'[116] She makes another version of what 'washes up' in England from travels and adventures, in her essay on the warehouses of the London docks, where she describes the merchandise which has been brought up the Thames from all over the world – including the tusks of Siberian mammoths. 'If you buy an umbrella or a looking-glass not of the finest quality, it is likely you are buying the tusk of a brute that roamed through Asian forests before England was an island.'[117]

It excited her to imagine her civilisation undoing itself, reverting to prehistory, grass and mammoths re-inhabiting the city streets, the island joining back to the continent. At the same time she increasingly wanted to investigate how the island-empire was constructed and sustained. She was interested in infrastructures: reviewing a book on Victorian England in 1926, for instance, she picks out a detail about the (disgusting) antiquity of London's drainage systems until the mid-nineteenth century; in her essay on the docks she is fascinated by the waste-grounds and rubbish-dumps surrounding the city, the growth from 'whatever we leave on our plates and throw into our dustbins'; in *The Years*, Eleanor, going on a bus down the Bayswater Road, thinks: 'Underneath were pipes, wires, drains . . .'[118] When she and Leonard walked to Greenwich under the Millwall-Greenwich foot tunnel in November 1929, from the kilns on the Isle of Dogs where Vanessa and Duncan were painting tiles for Dorothy Wellesley's house, she thought 'of the pressure of grey water round it; & of the absurd sublimity of errand boys & nursemaids walking on dry land under the river.'[119]

Setting herself critically apart from her island history, she continued to contemplate the two points of the island she knew best, Sussex and London. In both places, her feelings were divided between belonging and repulsion. In the country, her absorption in tradition, seasons and landscapes came up against her violent dismay at 'progressive' transformations of the place she knew – the cement works at Asheham, the villas at Peacehaven. Whose England was it, she kept asking herself as she walked through it, who was to own it, who was it *for*?[120]

In London she was known, social, much invited and inviting: a focus and a participant of London life. That was indoors. Outdoors, she walked about anonymously, looking, collecting, absorbing – 'seeing life', reading the streets. She often called the noise of the streets a kind of language: 'I stop in London sometimes & hear feet shuffling. Thats the language, I think; thats the phrase I should like to catch.'[121] She used her street-hauntings as keys to her reading, her 'selves', and her society.[122] In past novels (*Night and Day*, *Jacob's Room*, *Mrs Dalloway*, *Orlando*), London was a centre for emotions and memories, a site of social satire, and a celebration of 'life itself'. In the late 1920s and 1930s she became increasingly analytical of its political meanings, as in her descriptions of the General Strike. But her pleasure in walking through the city alone never diminished. The more violent and strange the sights, the better pleased she was:

> London itself perpetually attracts, stimulates, gives me a play & a story & a poem, without any trouble, save that of moving my legs through the streets. I walked Pinker to Grays Inn Gardens this afternoon, & saw – Red Lion Square: Morris'es house; thought of them on winter evenings in the '50ties; thought we are just as interesting; saw the Great Ormond St where a dead girl was found yesterday; saw & heard the Salvation Army making Xtianity gay for the people . . .[123]

> A fine spring day. I walked along Oxford St. The buses are strung on a chain. People fight & struggle. Knocking each other off the pavement. Old bareheaded men; a motor car accident, &c. To walk alone in London is the greatest rest.[124]

> [Notes on black and red police cars chasing a thief in Tottenham Court Road.] What does it feel like to be chasing a criminal? What does he say about it when he gets home and takes off his heavy boots and jacket? In all modern fiction there is no account of this that convinces one that the writer knows.[125]

How to read the polyvalent city was always a test case for her. London was her own past, which she traced and retraced, meeting her previous selves as she went. It was her key to the culture. It unsettled identity, turned her from a writer, wife, sister, aunt, friend, woman, into an unobserved observer. And it was a challenge to the writer.

So, *A Room of One's Own*, written in 1929, was as much a book about London as about the history, education and writing of women in England. London illustrates at every street-corner the 'infinitely obscure' and unrecorded lives of women. London provides the possibility of co-operation between the sexes – as when a girl and a young man are seen getting into a taxi-cab and are 'swept on by the current of the city'. But London also brings home to the woman observer who is thinking back through her mothers rather than through her fathers, her separation from the 'current' of public professional city lives. 'If one is a woman one is often surprised by a sudden splitting off of consciousness, say in walking down Whitehall, when from being the natural inheritor of that civilization, she becomes, on the contrary, outside of it, alien and critical.'[126] London – as she says in the draft of *A Room of One's Own* – is 'full with signals'.[127]

Soon after it was published, in October 1929, she wrote a set-piece on 'The Town' in her manuscript of *The Waves*. In the published novel, this became the section when Bernard, newly engaged, is coming into town on the train, thinking about his sense of individuality in opposition to the indifferent roar and 'general impulse' of the city.[128] But in the manuscript this passage is not individualised. Instead, it describes the power and 'vast conglomeration' of the city seen as a whole from the train, and then its fragmentation into separate lives, breaking off into the 'sliding surface' and 'superficial stimulus' of the streets. London is pure process: but human beings need to be fixed and identified through their occupations and professions. Similarly, in the 'enterprise' culture of London's buildings, architecture expresses competition, evolution, the struggle for supremacy of individual energies:

> Hence in the city, or in the in every street, through sheer abundance of personality some flaunt building, domed or pinnacled had risen; some extravagance had forced itself up, had grown & beyond the rest, had in height or breath above the others; with some festoon of stone, or statue in a niche, or motto over the door. There was hardly a street without its exclamation, its claim, its protestation; & which wha already in the winked here & there, lit up in the middle of the day. in letters of coloured light[129]

Neon lights, shop windows, advertising, trade, works, professions: this is the modern 'surface' which stimulates and absorbs her, and yet in which she is 'alien' and 'critical'.[130] Two years later, in her articles on 'The London Scene' for *Good Housekeeeping*, she analyses the city's 'layers' and 'strata',[131] its systems and processes, and makes a slice down through the city to its vaults and tunnels beneath. Everything has its use in the city's evolutionary scale; language itself has 'adapted' to the needs of commerce and trade. (She was writing this piece at the same time that she was starting to read science books by Wells and Heard and Jeans on evolution and physics.)[132] Even the white fungus growing on the arches of the wine-vaults at the dockside Custom houses (she noted accurately) is a 'bye-product': 'It is a fungus, but whether lovely or loathsome matters not; it is welcome because it proves that the air possesses the right degree of dampness for the health of the precious fluid.'[133] London itself was a kind of fungus, a growth of the civilisation evolved out of trade and usage, changing all the time it is observed.

There was nothing insular or complacent about her view of her city. Such patriotism as she had was for places, not people or traditions or beliefs. (This emotion would be increasingly questioned and tested, ten years on, when England came under threat.)[134] And she viewed her English landscape as if it were on the point of dissolution or regression. (You find this in the first chapter of her first novel and on the last page of her last.) Her imagination was always at play with continents she had never visited: 'America which I have never seen,'[135] Africa, India (where Percival goes in *The Waves*, and the others all follow in their fantasies). Towards the end of *The Waves*, Bernard goes to Rome. He realises that 'Rome is the limit of my travelling . . . it strikes me sometimes with a pang that I shall never see savages in Tahiti spearing fish . . .'[136] Even going as far as Rome makes England disintegrate by comparison. London becomes an unreal city; is no longer the centre, is a tiny spot on the map of the world. 'London has also crumbled. London consists of fallen factories and a few gasometers.'[137] But although the writer (and her characters) may fantasise another life for herself in another country or continent, the habits and language and tradition of the island define and surround her. That, as Bernard says in *The Waves*, is 'the penalty of living in an old civilization with a notebook'.[138]

THIRTY-ONE

Money and Fame

'I feel on the verge of some strenuous adventure', she wrote on 28 March 1929. By one of the cheap ironies available to biographers, this would be the day of her death, twelve years later. But this entry, at forty-seven, reads like a setting-out. She felt bold, quick, impatient, capable of cruelty, excited, courageous. And, for the first time in her life, she felt rich. She 'braced' herself from nights of terror, on such spring mornings, by telling herself 'I shall need great courage: after all, I say, I made £1000 all from willing it early one morning. No more poverty I said; & poverty has ceased. I am summoning Philcox next week to plan a room – I have money to build it, money to furnish it.'[1] That same week she wrote in the first draft of *A Room of One's Own* that 'everything depends (if you are a woman) upon ‹having› money ‹of one's own› & a room of your own'.[2]

The new room at Monk's House and the 'room of one's own' of her essay are connected. *A Room of One's Own* could be read as her own disguised economic autobiography. She would say as much to Ethel Smyth: 'I forced myself to keep my own figure fictitious; legendary. If I had said, Look here am I uneducated, because my brothers used all the family funds which is the fact – Well theyd have said; she has an axe to grind; and no one would have taken me seriously.'[3]

The personal history of the essay has its roots in her childhood – the patriarch's cheque-book, the step-daughter's servitude, the daughters' exclusion from schools and university. But it is also being written at the time when her earning-power was suddenly increasing. In June of 1929, when she was finishing the revisions of the essay, she wrote: 'This last half year I made over £1800; almost at the rate of £4000 a year; the salary almost of a Cabinet minister; & time was, two years ago, when I toiled to make £200.'[4] Again, at the beginning of 1930: 'When we made up our 6 months accounts, we found I had made about £3,020 last year – the salary of a civil servant: a surprise to me, who was content with £200 for so many years.'[5] The feeling of pleasure and power in being able to spend money is crucial to *A Room of One's Own*, if only because it insists on what it means to *lack* that power. Wanting too much money is bad for you: she maintains her family's puritan distaste for those who live to 'make money & more money & more money still at the command of the vulture in their breasts'. There are timely jokes in the manuscript about the risks of gambling on the Stock Exchange.[6] But it is essential for women's independence to have 'enough' money. In *A Room of One's Own* that sufficiency takes the form of a legacy (as, in her life, she had the security of an invested inheritance). But the essay says that women should also to be able to *earn* their £500 a year – the equivalent now of an average middle-class salary, about £25,000.[7] She had only been earning this amount since 1926.[8]

Virginia Woolf was never poor. When she married, Leonard invested their capital as 'a strategic reserve',[9] not for living expenses. Before the First World War their investments yielded about £400 a year; between the two wars Leonard's investments gave a return which rose, gradually, from £310 in 1924 to £802 in 1939. (Richard Kennedy, working at the Press in 1928 at the age of sixteen, and noting Leonard's firm financial opinions – 'he says accounts are beautiful and waste is ugly' – ended his humorous and vivid reminiscences of his time there with this: 'A small legacy from my grandmother enabled me to take the course [in journalism]. How right LW was when he told me on one of our walks round the Square that a little capital was one of the most important things in life.')[10]

Leonard's stocks and shares were (in spite of his political convictions) in 'imperial ventures'[11] such as Shell Oil, Federated Selangor Rubber, Ceylon Para Rubber, Venezuelan Oil Concessions, Bajoe Kidoel Rubber & Produce, as well as in tobacco companies, Cable & Wireless, Austin and Ford Motors, Courtaulds, Electric & Musical Instruments, Union Castle Mail Steamship, United Dairies, and Great Southern Railways.[12] This invested, inherited capital made Virginia Woolf – like Forster and Strachey and others of her English friends, and unlike incomers such as T.S. Eliot or Katherine Mansfield – a member of the 'rentier' class. But it did not make her feel rich.

At the start of their marriage, their investments brought in only about half of what they needed to live on and to pay doctors' bills. This was about £800 a year from 1912 to 1927, and thereafter rose to (and held steady at) about £1100 a year. She began writing articles for money in 1904; she began publishing books in 1915. Leonard calculated, looking back on their accounts, that between 1919 and 1924 her earnings from her books came to £228 (£38 per annum, the equivalent now of about £1,900) and her total earnings for those years came to £1019 (£170 per annum).[13] From 1904 to 1919 her only income (apart from the yield from her capital) came from journalism, and until 1928 she was still earning more from her journalism than from her books. Only from 1928 did the larger part of her income come from her books.

Meanwhile, for the first fourteen years of their twenty-nine-year marriage, Leonard's income far outstripped hers.[14] It wasn't until 1926, the year after the publication of *Mrs Dalloway* and *The Common Reader*, that Virginia Woolf's total income began to go over the magic figure of '£500 a year', and she began for the first time – as she would now for the rest of her life – to earn more than her husband.[15] In 1925 her income from books was £164 and her total income (including journalism) was £223. In 1926 her income from books was £356 and her total income was £713. In 1927, the year of *To the Lighthouse*, her income from books was £545 and her total income was £748. And in 1928, in a sudden jump which marked the publication of *Orlando*, her income from books was £1,434 (£556 earned in England, £878 in the USA) and her total income was £1540. Her richest year (total income £2936) was 1929; through the 1930s her annual total income held at between £1300 and £2500, with a dip in 1935–6 when she was ill and working on *The Years*, and a surge again in 1938 (to £2972, the highest year's income of her life) after *The Years* became a best-seller. It is misleading to think of her as indifferent to financial matters, in spite of her capital and her private Press. Like her father, she thought a great deal, probably every day, anxiously and greedily, about how much money she had and how much she could spend. She was intensely conscious of her value in the market-place.

With the increased sales of her books[16] came more success for the Press – though it remained, to the despair of Leonard's employees, his 'shoestring operation'.[17] By 1930 Virginia's income was three times more than the Press profits.[18] But those profits increased greatly, due to the publication of *Orlando*, Leonard's bold and successful move in buying the back-list of the International Psycho-Analytical Library in 1924,[19] and the huge success in 1931 of Vita's *The Edwardians*.

In 1929, they decided to publish a 'Uniform Edition' of the works of Virginia Woolf. They bought the publishing rights to *The Voyage Out* and *Night and Day* from Duckworth; and they republished her subsequent novels from their own first editions. It was a decision which staked a claim for Virginia Woolf's commercial value and, at forty-seven, for the lasting value of her works.[20] From then on, they also developed a practice of publishing some of her essays and short pieces as attractively designed pamphlets or short books: a way of 'maximising income from her minor works'.[21]

The increased sales of her books after 1926, the start of translations of her novels, and the marked increase in her readership was anticipated by her

American publisher Donald Brace in 1924, when he was awaiting *Mrs Dalloway* and *The Common Reader*: 'I feel', he wrote to Leonard from Madison Avenue, 'that Mrs Woolf is now at a point where her work may go far beyond the rather small circle which has admired it here in the past and that these next books may be handled in such a way as to attain a really considerable sale' – which they did.[22] This meant a great increase in the fees she could command from journalism, especially in America.

Up to 1925 she had appeared mainly in the *Times Literary Supplement* (anonymously) and in the *Nation* and the *New Statesman*. From 1925 onwards she increasingly diversified her venues, and wrote more and more for the big, distinguished American magazines and papers (*New Republic, Forum, Yale Review, Atlantic Monthly, New York Herald Tribune, Bookman*). When, by 1924, Dorothy Todd was ordering four articles for *Vogue* at £10 for 1,000 words;[23] when, in 1927, she could tell the editor of the *TLS* that 'I can't always refuse £60 in America for the Times's £10'[24] or boast to Vita that she was being paid £120 to write four reviews for the *Herald Tribune*;[25] when she could risk asking the *Yale Review* for a rise,[26] she rode on a sense of power and independence, and appeased her lifelong anxiety about not having enough to live on.

In the 1930s she did less reviewing and came increasingly to resent the traps and compromises of the literary market-place. But in the late 1920s, at the point of her greatest fame and success, she took pleasure (though she complained about the pressure of work) in making money from articles – particularly in making a double income from the same piece, published once in America and once, or more than once, in England. It's a mark of her satisfaction in her earning power that in 1928 she starts to keep an account book, and does so until 1939. The book frequently notes double sums (about twice or three times more in America than in England) paid for the same piece.[27]

But, now that she could command her price and spend money, how was it to be spent – and whose was it? Looking back on his meticulous account-books, Leonard noted with satisfaction that although their income greatly increased between 1924 and 1934, their basic level of expenditure remained fairly stable: 'In 1924 our income was £1,047 and our expenditure £826, in 1934 our income was £3,615 and our expenditure £1,192.'[28] The rent of Tavistock Square remained at £140;[29] the books show that their weekly housekeeping expenses remained surprisingly constant over forty years.[30] But, unlike Leonard, Virginia *wanted* to spend her money: and this was one of the fierce battles of the marriage. It followed on from the struggle about going back to London, and coincided with tensions over Vita. Virginia was the winner in all these battles, but they caused her great pain. At the end of 1928, when *Orlando* was a best-seller, she wrote:

> For the first time since I married 1912 – 1928 – 16 years – I have been spending money . . . All this money making originated in a spasm of black despair one night at Rodmell 2 years ago. I was tossing up & down on those awful waves: when I said that I could find a way out. (For part of my misery was the perpetual limitation of everything; no chairs, or beds, no comfort, no beauty; & no freedom to move: all of which I determined there & then to win). And so came, with some argument, even tears one night (& how seldom I have ever cried!) to an agreement with Leonard about sharing money after a certain sum; & then opened a bank account; & now, at the lowest shall have £200 to put there on Jan 1st. The important thing is to spend freely, without fuss or anxiety; & to trust to one's power of making more – Indeed, I cannot at this moment very seriously doubt that I shall earn more, this next 5 years, than ever before.[31]

The entry refers back to the autumn of 1926, where the order of events in the diary looks rather different (a good example of how she sometimes censored her diary entries). In early September 1926, there is a muted reference to their agreement. 'Under a new arrangement, we're to share any money over £200 that I make.' But there then *follows* her night of despair, and Leonard's observing that their relations 'had not been so good lately', and her argument with him, in the interests of wifely 'freedom', that they should not tie themselves down so much to the house and the garden, and should be freer to travel and to buy 'rugs, beds or good arm chairs.' She goes on to promise herself that 'by taking pains' she will be 'much more considerate of L's feelings'.[32] It seems as if the decision to share their income precedes, and is then confirmed, by the argument. Unusually, Leonard kept no diary that month. Looking back many years later, he gives a quite different version (which Quentin Bell echoes) of the agreement:

> At the end of the 1914 war I invented a system with regard to our finances which we found both useful and amusing and which we kept going until Virginia's death. At the end of each year I worked out in detail an estimate of expenditure for the coming year. This was to provide for only the bare joint expenses of our common life together; it therefore covered rents, rates, upkeep of houses, fuel and lighting, food, servants, garden, upkeep of car (when we got one), doctors and medicine, an allowance to each for clothes. At the end of the year I worked out what the actual expenditure had been and also the total actual combined income, and then the excess of income over expenditure was divided equally between us and became a personal 'hoard', as we called it, which we could spend in any way we

liked. For instance, when we decided to have a car, I bought it out of my 'hoard', and if Virginia wanted a new dress which she could not pay for out of her allowance, she paid for it out of her hoard. The amount of our hoards varied enormously as time went on ... at the end of 1927 [net income £1313, expenditure £1193] we each got £60, but at the end of 1929 [net income £3137, expenditure £1120] we each got £1,008.[33]

This makes Leonard (as has often been observed) sound like the inventor, the controller, and the banker of this system, and also makes it sound as if the agreement had lasted almost all their married life. But Virginia's diary entries suggest otherwise: that she prompted and urged the scheme, and that it was a 'new agreement' in 1926 – and (though this is not made clear in Leonard's accounts) that the 'hoard' was divided between them only after £200 of *her* annual income had gone into the pool of their basic expenditure.

What is certain is that from the autumn of 1926 onwards her diary fills up with greedy plans for her 'hoard', her 'nest egg'. She talks for the first time of the pleasure of having her own cheque book (a 'great advance in dignity')[34] and refers repeatedly to her spending plans. Annoyed at having had to turn down the offer of writing an American piece on Willa Cather for £30, she says: 'I should have had £70 of my years £200 ready made by October: (my greed is immense: I want to have £50 of my own in the Bank to buy Persian carpets, pots, chairs, &c.)'[35] Again, a few days later: 'I have only to write & stir myself, to make, I wager, quite £50 extra in the year for my own extravagances. No longer shall I let a coat for £3 floor me in the middle of the night, or be afraid to lunch out because "I've no clothes".'[36] Pleasure edges to the brink of obsession: 'I have thought too much, thought on purpose, with my eyes open, of making money; & once we have each a nest egg I should like to let that sink into my sub-consciousness, & earn easily what we need.'[37] But there's no doubt that it pleases her to write in her diary: 'We are very prosperous'[38] or, sending Duncan a cheque for Vanessa's birthday present: 'I am extremely rich.'[39]

She thinks now a great deal about the relation between cash and value, not always in mercenary terms. Turning down a publisher's offer of £2,000 for her to write a life of Boswell (exactly the kind of job her father would have wanted her to do), she thinks, 'I have bought my freedom'.[40] And again in October 1930, when they were talking about selling the Press: 'What's money if you sell freedom?'[41] At the same time, she takes pleasure in planning what she will spend her money on: a bed from Heals, a sofa, a rubber boat for paddling down the river Ouse, clothes, twenty-five volumes of the Waverley novels, first class tickets for the trip to France with Vita, cheques for Vanessa, a champagne party, a contribution towards the income of the impoverished MacCarthys, silk stockings, furniture and carpets for her new room at Monk's House, blue paint to repaint the mantelpiece at Tavistock Square, commissions from Vanessa and Duncan of plates and lampshades and bowls.[42]

But the act of spending itself often made her anxious, worried 'about spending wrongly'. 'The money psychology'[43] interested her. Why, given that it gave her such pleasure to get it, did it not give her more pleasure to spend it? She repeatedly tells herself to get used to having money; to flex or unbend what she calls her 'spending muscles' or (by contrast) her 'penurious muscles'. She has to exhort herself to spend;[44] and to get used to the idea that money had changed its value for her. At a time when for thousands of people in the West, money crashed, and wealth turned into losses and poverty, for her, money changed its dimensions, and became something she could control. She recognised it as one of the most important facts of her life.

> When I offered Miss Rivett-Carnac [a temporary replacement for Nelly Boxall] £50 yesterday it seemed to me nothing, because I was thinking that I can make that by writing 2,000 words. But 5 years ago, £50 was a substantial sum. How money has shrunk in my mind! This is one of the most curious things in my existence – the shrinkage of money.[45]

In this frame of mind, in the summer of 1930, she made her will (which remained unchanged),[46] leaving specific bequests to her family: £100 for Vanessa, £50 to Adrian, Clive, and Duncan, £10 to Nelly Boxall, 'my jewellery of which I may die possessed' to Vanessa, 'the manuscript of one of my books to be selected by my husband' for Vita, and 'all residue – copyrights – entailed property to my husband absolutely'.[47]

The will is symbolic of the finances of the marriage. It would be misleading to suggest that, having won her battle, she then hoarded her money away from Leonard. Their expenditure, from 1928 onwards, enlarged both their lives. She spent on the houses; he bought the car (the second-hand Singer, The Umbrella, replaced in 1929 by an open-top Singer and in 1932 by a much grander Lanchester),[48] the gramophone,[49] more land and cottages at Rodmell. They shared all the benefits of their new prosperity. It seems telling that, giving her a 1927 edition of Rollins's sixteenth-century anthology, *The Paradise of Dainty Devices*, for Christmas 1929, Leonard inscribed it:

> What is, or may be mine,
> That is, & shall be thine.[50]

*

The contrast between social life in London and quiet life in the country was at its most extreme in her late forties: 'Life is either too empty or too full.'[51] She keeps asking herself how can she 'dip' into society, how 'get control' of it and not be drowned by it.[52] The autumn, winter and spring diaries are full of remarks like 'a plethora of parties this week'; 'life a cascade, a glissade, a torrent: all together'; 'We have seen an endless number of people'.[53] These are complaints and boasts in one; she didn't want not to see people, but being continually seen was a pressure. Sometimes her taxing exposure seemed creative to her. 'I use my friends rather as giglamps: Theres another field I see: by your light. Over there's a hill. I widen my landscape.'[54] But she also felt like a target, a fixture: 'I have been for the last 6 weeks rather a bucket than a fountain: sitting to be shot into by one person after another. A rabbit that passes across a shooting gallery, & one's friends go pop-pop.'[55] 'But why I ask "see" people? Whats the point? These isolated occasions which come so often. May I come & see you? And what they get, or I get, save the sense of a slide passing on a screen, I cant say.'[56]

She had begun to be a slide in other people's collections, on view as a famous 'sight'. 'Also the "fame" is becoming vulgar & a nuisance,' she wrote in 1928,[57] the inverted commas around *fame* expressing at once self-regard and distaste. Sightings of her on public occasions – often behaving in a puzzlingly contradictory manner – began to be recorded in people's memoirs. Julien Green remembered meeting her at a literary prize-giving in 1929. 'I asked Virginia Woolf if she wanted to speak before I did. She was very nervous, her hands in constant motion and beating like wings. She threw me the glance of a hunted animal and said: "No. You go first." . . . Virginia spoke next and said insignificant things, but she created a great impression. There was a mixture of disdain and fright in her long face.'[58] Osbert Sitwell similarly looked back, from the 1940s, to a dinner at the London Group of painters when Virginia had to speak, was 'pitiably nervous', and then gave a 'superb display of . . . poetic eloquence'.[59]

There are other less flattering accounts of her as a public performer. Her lectures to the young – on 'How Should One Read a Book?' at Hayes Court School in 1926, on 'Women & Fiction' to the young women of Cambridge in 1928 – had a mixed reception. At Hayes Court, one 'old girl' remembered it as a vivid occasion:

> The lecture was in [the Drawing] Room, in the afternoon. The school sat on the floor, Miss Cox, the distinguished visitors and staff, sat round the fire, and Virginia Woolf sat at a little table near the piano. She wore a bright blue polo-necked jersey, which seemed to accentuate her height;

she made a striking figure, quite coming up to my expectations of what a distinguished writer should look like.

But she added: 'I must admit that her appearance made a much more lasting impression on me than anything she said.' And one of the younger girls wrote in her diary at the time: 'Had a lecture by Mrs V. Woolf – very boring.'[60]

The Cambridge lectures, which she transformed into the fictional occasion and the subject of *A Room of One's Own*, were in reality awkward performances. She gave the lecture twice in one week (soon after she came back from France with Vita and just as *Orlando* was published), first at Newnham College, on 20 October, and then at Girton, on the 26th. For the Newnham visit, Leonard drove her (with Vanessa and Angelica), and they stayed with Pernel Strachey (who had become Principal of Newnham after Katherine Stephen, and was remembered by the girls as a stiff and unapproachable figure). They arrived nearly an hour late, and because she had not warned them that Leonard was coming too, there was an embarrassed rejigging of the seating plans. Afterwards she had coffee with some of the girls; the next day they had lunch in Dadie Rylands's rooms in King's, and out of the contrast was born the drama of *A Room of One's Own*. (Dadie would recall the lunch he provided as much less lavish and opulent than her re-creation of it.) For the Girton talk, she went on the train with Vita, and met Julian in the afternoon (who told Vanessa that he had spent half the next day in 'a frightful chase' after them both).[61] The Girton girls gave Virginia and Vita dinner before the talk.

In her diary, as in *A Room of One's Own*, she fused the two occasions together, and gave a sharp, if condescending, picture of the Cambridge girls as 'starved but valiant young women . . . Intelligent eager, poor; & destined to become schoolmistresses in shoals . . . I felt elderly & mature. And nobody respected me . . . Very little reverence or that sort of thing about.'[62] Their memory was equally mixed. To Kathleen Raine at Girton, Virginia Woolf and Vita Sackville-West seemed like 'goddesses from Olympus', nothing to do with the realities of her own life. She had not given much thought, before the talk, to the problems of women writers. These Cambridge students were bright, energetic college girls, eager for work and careers, who did not think of themselves as disadvantaged, though they were conscious of themselves as pioneers. They found Virginia Woolf formidable and not altogether sympathetic (and when *A Room of One's Own* came out, they were rather discomfited by her version of them). Elsie Phare (who became the Shakespearean scholar Elsie Duncan-Jones) remembered her praising a poem by Stella Gibbons and gossiping about T.S. Eliot's 'marital troubles' at dinner; another girl remembered feeling ill at ease:

> I think I had expected some profound, philosophical remarks, even after prunes and custard; but fixing me with that wonderful gaze, at once luminous and penetrating, what she actually said was, 'I'd no idea the young ladies of Newnham were so beautifully dressed.' The prig in me was chagrined, even if my vanity sat up and purred; but over the years what has persisted has been the quality of her look . . . [it] held the hint of a smile, a hint of compassion, but it was above all an absolutely ruthless look; my pretty frock was no proof against it.[63]

Her lecture did not seem, at the time, the stuff of which legends would be made. Beryl Paston Brown (a scholarship girl who would become Principal of Homerton College) remembered the students – about 200 of them – sitting in Clough Hall after the dinner had been cleared away through the swing doors; but the talk, she said, was inaudible. Her friend Marna Sedgwick remembered the effect it had on her with remorse:

> I was seated beneath the gallery at the far end from the dais on which Virginia Woolf sat, so that the accoustics were probably somewhat impaired. The Hall was in total darkness save from the light of the lamp on the table at which she sat. The effect of this one point of bright light was mesmeric: her mellifluous cultivated voice *reading* from her manuscript added to the lullaby effect and I am deeply ashamed to confess that I slept right through it. If only I had known it was to become A Room of One's Own![64]

Some of the girls had not heard of her before she came. All the same, by 1928 she was justified in thinking of herself as famous. The things that went with fame had begun to happen to her. She was immortalised (in 1930) as Clio in the mosaic Boris Anrep made for the floor of the National Gallery (in which, among other mythologisings, Osbert Sitwell appeared as the God of Music and Greta Garbo as the Muse of Tragedy).[65] She was asked to broadcast, first with Leonard (they gave a talk called 'Are Too Many Books Written and Published?')[66] and then (twice) on her own.[67] She began to be profiled and featured.

Though she affected (and probably in some degree also felt) ironic indifference about what was said in such 'profiles', she minded very much how she looked in the photographs and pictures which accompanied them, and she intensely disliked any sense of intrusion into her privacy. When the French painter Jacques-Emile Blanche met her at Ethel Sands's house in

Normandy and then 'wrote up' his conversation with her as 'Entretien avec Virginia Woolf' in *Nouvelles Littéraires*[68] (her first interview, and the beginnings of her great fame in France), she was off-hand about the interview (in which she mostly talked about Proust) but extremely anxious about which photograph would be used. In the end she was relieved that 'he used an old photograph of me at 19'.[69] Three years later, when Cecil Beaton (whom she had heard of as 'a smart young man . . . notorious as a gate crasher at smart parties', but whose requests to photograph her she had twice turned down),[70] included her without her permission in his collection of famous living ladies, *The Book of Beauty*, with two drawings taken from photographs by others, she was beside herself with annoyance. She had some reason: it was a cheap write-up, half sloppily reverential, half bitchily intrusive, and patronisingly de-sexing. And she may also have been riled by its insistence on her old-fashionedness and its sharp observation of her as both frightening and frightened. And it was published by Gerald Duckworth.

> Mrs Virginia Woolf is one of the most gravely distinguished-looking women I have ever seen. In her we do not find the conventional pink cheeks and liquid eyes and childish lips. Although she would look like a terrified ghost in an assembly of the accepted raving beauties, she would make each one separately appear vulgar and tawdry in comparison with her. She has all the chaste and sombre beauty of village school-mistresses, housekeepers, and nuns, and one cannot imagine her being powdered and painted: the mere knowledge that *maquillage* exists is disturbing in connection with her, for when one sees her so sensitively nervous and with the poignant beauty of the lady in the faded photograph in the oval frame, the lady who is one's grandmother as a girl, one realises that a face can be a reverend and sacred thing. Her fine skin is parchment-coloured, she has timid startled eyes, set deep, a sharp bird-like nose and firm pursed lips. Her lank hair and aristocratic wrists are of a supreme delicacy, and one imagines her spending eternities of dreamy leisure sewing and gazing out of the window. She wears cameo brooches and cotton gloves, and hatpins, and exudes an atmosphere of musk and old lace and the rustle and scratch of stiff ivy-coloured taffeta, but her old-fashioned dowdinesses are but a conscious and literary game of pretence, for she is alertly contemporary, even a little ahead of her time. Many of her confreres see her as a Juno, awe-inspiring and gaunt, but she herself is frightened, a bundle of tentative gestures, and quick nervous glances, as frail and crisp as a dead leaf; and like a sea-anemone she curls up at contact with the outer world.[71]

Sibyl Colefax wrote to him nervously: 'I wish you hadnt put in Virginia –

she will never forgive it – & she's so worth having for a friend.'[72] She was right; before she had even seen the book, Virginia wrote furiously to *The Times*, who wouldn't publish the letter, and then to the *Nation*, who did, that in publishing the drawings without her permission Beaton was making her a 'victim' of a 'questionable' and 'highly disagreeable' form of book-making. Beaton protested, and so did their mutual friend Christabel McLaren, who wrote as 'an admirer of Mrs Woolf', arguing that her 'exquisite' beauty should not be kept in the family but should be more widely known. Virginia repeated her point that she objected to the principle of publishing pictures of people without their consent.[73] It was the pictures she minded, even more than the text.

When a more discreet and admiring public tribute was paid to her in the form of a characterisation in Hugh Walpole's novel *Hans Frost*, where she appears, recognisably, as the novelist Jane Rose (who has just written a novel with a lighthouse in it), she was not irritated, but extremely sardonic about the 'portrait' of her. (It was not the first or the last time she would be a character in someone else's fiction.)[74] This was Walpole's idealised and affectionate version of Virginia Woolf, which has some features in common with Beaton's more superficial and satirical view.

Jane Rose looked like the wife of a Pre-Raphaelite painter, her dark hair brushed back in waves from her forehead, her grey dress cut in simple fashion, her thin pale face quiet and remote. She was, Hans thought, the best living novelist in England. She wrote the most beautiful prose in the most beautiful way . . . Ruth [Hans's wife] didn't like her, because she looked odd and always in conversation (with Ruth at least) answered the last question but one. There was something terrifying in her gentle remoteness . . . [Hans and Jane talk at dinner, and she says]: 'I was lost on my seventh birthday. The nurse went off with a soldier and I followed the man with the balloons. I was lost for a whole afternoon. I sat in the police-station for an hour. I've loved policemen ever since. They were so very kind to me and gave me a piece of seed-cake. But don't you think,' she added, 'that possessions are a pity? Don't you feel sorry for your Manet, that it isn't free, dancing about on its own – a little like the tigers at the Zoo?' 'It shall be free,' he said. 'It shall do whatever it likes. I won't complain if it flies out of the window.' 'No, you wouldn't,' she said, smiling at him. 'You know what freedom means.'[75]

To Vita she wrote that the book was completely unreal and all about Hugh, and she would never be able to bear to read it again. To Hugh she wrote that it was adorable and glittering, but she responded equivocally to her characterisation.

Of course, I don't think it's *my* world. I feel rather like the wife of a Pre-Raphaelite painter who has blundered in among Rubens and Matisse and Cocktails and Champagne and sits in a simple grey dress looking very odd and causing some alarm to her hostess. Poor woman! She is a little out of place I agree, but enjoys herself hugely and trots off home to tell her husband, in their rather austere flat, all about it. Many many thanks; I did enjoy myself hugely she says.[76]

She adopted this pose too for Christabel McLaren (a smart, rich, clever, art-loving society hostess, friend of the Sitwells and Tennants and Hutchinsons, who became Lady Aberconway when her husband, Henry McLaren, Lloyd George's private secretary and a great gardener, inherited his family title in 1934). 'Chrissie', like Sibyl Colefax, was for ever inviting her to smart lunches and dinners. Virginia was always wriggling out of these invitations and inviting her round for tea instead, or pretending that she would come to her grand parties in a humble role: 'I will keep any date to come to you, grey as a mouse & white as a nun, and hand cocktails to the debauched . . . I intend to keep you to your promise to employ me as a waiter – black dress, white apron & cap.' 'I could have crept about in a grey alpaca with a frilled apron.'[77] The joke at once exposed and played up to wealth, class-consciousness and snobbery.

For the 'endless number of people' who came to see her, this quiet timid mouse-like persona was not much in evidence. People went, in great numbers, to the house in Tavistock Square, in various states of eagerness and apprehension, but always in the expectation of an event. Since the Woolfs had moved there in 1924, the house had acquired a strong character. People coming or working there took a vivid impression from it, particularly because of its double and divided nature, the basement for work, the upstairs flat for entertaining. The basement life at Tavistock Square was, evidently, a curious mixture of the ramshackle and the orderly. The Press office at the front of the basement (with the printing room – the treadle machine, the compositor's stone and all the type – in a disused scullery behind it) was divided by a door and a long stone corridor from the huge, sparsely furnished, windowless room at the back, once a billiards room, with a skylight and a rather dim underwater feeling to it. (Occasionally, rats were spotted – which discouraged Virginia from her first plan of sleeping downstairs in the 'studio'.) She wrote there every morning, in what Leonard described as 'the most frightful disorder – even squalor',[78] surrounded by the big brown paper bales of books. These bales contained the less rapid sellers of the Press (the higher-selling and more frequently unpacked books were kept out in the corridor so as not to disturb her more than was necessary). But every so often, the Press employees would have to come in and unpack round her. Richard Kennedy was extremely aware of her presence:

> Sitting in her little space by the gas fire, she reminds me of the Bruce Bairnsfather veterans of the War, surrounded by sandbags. She looks at us over the top of her steel-rimmed spectacles, her grey hair hanging over her forehead and a shag cigarette hanging from her lips. She wears a hatchet-blue overall and sits hunched in a wicker armchair with her pad on her knees and a small typewriter beside her.[79]

John Lehmann, by contrast, remembered her working at a desk, 'stuffed and littered with papers, letters and innumerable half-finished manuscripts'.[80] All the Press employees were struck by her concentration on her work when they had to disturb her: 'I used to slip in as silently as possible,' John Lehmann remembered, more reverentially than Richard Kennedy, 'feeling that I was entering the holiest part of the house, the inmost ark of its presiding deity'.[81] They remembered how she would look through the window of the door between the passage and the Press office, and if the coast was clear would come in to talk to the office staff, make them laugh, and help pack up books. They all remembered her setting type and tying up parcels. Sometimes young authors – who would have loved to meet her – would come in and leave their books, not recognising her and not realising that she was in the office. Elizabeth Hepworth, who worked as a traveller for the Press in the late 1930s, said that her most vivid memory of her was 'her back view, her tall figure bent over the packing-shelf, tying up parcels'.[82] Richard Kennedy, in his affectionate retrospective pretence of a diary kept at the time, also made a comedy out of her absent-minded quirkiness, and her vague intrusions into Leonard's professional systems. It may be that she protected her private thoughts by this performance of scatty impracticality.

It seems a curiously distracting working arrangement for a professional novelist (especially compared with the deep solitude and privacy of the writing-room in the garden at Monk's House). Presumably she could have written in the flat upstairs if she chose to. Perhaps she liked to feel the link between her private thinking, at one end of the corridor, and Leonard's production of printed words for sale at the other.

Friends and visitors went up the stone stairs past the first and second floor let out to Dolman and Pritchards, the solicitors. (The layout of Tavistock Square is vividly described in the party scene at the end of *The Years*.) The solicitors and their staff were on good terms with the Woolfs, and had their own version of them. Mr Pritchard's secretary, Rose Talbot remembered that 'it was evident that Mrs Woolf left all business matters to her husband'; that 'Mr Woolf used to have chats and give them Fortnum and Mason chocolates'; that 'Mr and Mrs Woolf would stroll in the garden every lunch time to exercise the dog and sometimes watched us at tennis, sometimes came over to chat while I did some sketching'. (It was on people like Mrs Shrager's account that Virginia Woolf wrote a letter to the *New Statesman & Nation* in 1933 arguing that the London Squares should not only be for the use of residents, but should be opened during the summer months.)[83] Nelly Boxall would come down and chat to Mrs Shrager, and tell her when 'celebrities' were expected upstairs.[84]

The 'celebrities' – or aspiring celebrities – would be met at the door of the third floor by Nellie, and would enter the stage of Virginia Woolf's indoor social performance. The rooms of the Woolfs' two floors, looking out on to the high trees of Tavistock Square and the churches and buildings beyond, were light and colourful and pretty and Mediterranean-looking, full of books and papers; they looked like the covers of her books. Everyone was struck by the three huge panels which Vanessa and Duncan had painted when the Woolfs first moved in, in reds and browns and blues, each presenting a domestic tableau in a roundel, within a frame of crosshatching: the table and jug and scroll of paper on the left, the piano and guitar in the centre, the bowl of flowers, fan, open book and mandolin on the right.[85] The panels contributed, William Plomer thought, to 'the unsolemn atmosphere of a room not quite like any other'.[86] The tables and chairs in the smaller, low-ceilinged dining-room on the floor above, the carpets and screens and chinaware, the mantelpiece designs, the tiles, and some of the pictures were Vanessa's and Duncan's too. (Virginia's own bedroom was decorated with 'moonrises and prima donna's bouquets'.)[87] It was not a grand or glossy setting, but it had a strong, idiosyncratic, seductive atmosphere.[88] Everyone who sat in the dining-room for tea (honey from Monk's House) or for supper under soft lamp-light, and then in the large drawing-room over the fire, with the dogs, the cigarette smoke, the talk, took away an image of Virginia Woolf. Many of them were writers, and recorded what they saw.[89]

What they saw was not necessarily what she thought they saw. She disliked her looks, for instance ('And now my neck is so ugly . . .')[90] but other people thought she was beautiful. Each observer saw something a little different and a little the same, like photographs taken in different clothes, from different angles, at different ages. Her hair? Her hair was reddish – no, it was greyish – no, it was mouse-coloured. (In 1927 it was shingled and modern: Dorothy Wellesley said she would miss the 'enchanting' gesture 'when you put up your hand to arrange an untidy bit of hair at the back'.[91] Later she grew it back into a bun, swept away from her face.) Her clothes? Eliot's friend Emily Hale, who went to tea at Tavistock Square in 1935, described her as 'a very tall slender woman, dressed in a dark nondescript dress, over which was worn a short dark velvet coat. The simple dark clothes set off to advantage the small head carrying a wealth of greying hair, thick, but soft, which she wears simply off the forehead, and massed in a great Rossetti like coil at the nape of a very long slender neck.'[92] Trekkie Parsons remembered her wearing martial-looking clothes.[93] William Plomer remembered that 'her clothes did [not] suggest a concern with fashion or any effort to defy it. She knew, as people used to say, how to wear her clothes, which were neither simple nor complicated. She was not given to wearing ornaments.'[94] Madge Garland, the fashion editor of *Vogue* in the 1920s, remembered her first sighting of 'this beautiful and distinguished woman wearing what could only be described as . . . an upturned wastepaper basket on her head'. Madge chose some clothes for her in 1925, aware that Virginia wanted to look elegant but did not want to take time thinking about it.[95] Other people remembered her being badly dressed, not caring about her clothes. Isaiah Berlin remembered her wearing a wonderful red dress in the 1930s, at a dinner-party in Oxford. H.A.L. Fisher's daughter Mary was at the same dinner; she remembered her wearing a wonderful green dress.

What everyone agreed on was her thinness, her fine bones, her fragility, her eyes, her voice, her laugh, and her mixture of angularity and awkwardness. Her eyes, everyone said, were very striking, not just because they were large and hooded and greenish-greyish coloured but because they were so bright: they glistened. She would look away when she was talking, look intently at you when she was listening. The look was sharp, magnetic, even unsettling. Edith Sitwell (who looked even more extraordinary herself) called them 'thoughtful' eyes.[96] People sometimes saw pain and tension in the look. Spender remembered 'something about the tension of the muscles over the fine bones of the skin which was like an instrument tautly strung. The greyish eyes had a sometimes limpid, sometimes wandering, sometimes laughing, concentration or distractedness.'[97] Frances Partridge said that her face bore 'the stigmata that are to be seen in many who have been gravely mad – a subtly agonised tautness, something twisted'. She noted something 'awkward' in the way she held herself. 'When she was carried away by her own talk Virginia often hugged herself in her folded arms and rocked her body from side to side.'[98] Angelica Garnett described her as 'never placid, never quite at rest', always 'angular'.[99] Other observers noticed something awkward and odd about the way she held her neck, and that she would always twist her legs around each other when she was sitting.[100] William Plomer, more romantically, spoke of her 'nervous shoulders' and 'creative wrists'.[101] Everyone commented on the deep (even 'sepulchral') voice, and the hooting infectious laugh which could go out of control. Everyone remembered her smoking – rolling her own strong shag tobacco, using a cigarette holder, or smoking cheroots.

She had become a famous talker. With one or two other people she could be very quiet; she could listen intently; and she always asked specific, detailed, interested questions. She was the observer of all observers. But her friends dropped in to hear her as much as to talk to her, to see if she was performing well, and to recommend visits to each other if she was. Clive would tell Mary: 'Virginia on her best form'; 'Virginia in high spirits, fantastical, spiteful, in fact . . . deliciously herself again . . . I strongly advise you to go and see her'; 'Virginia extremely gay and garrulous, mostly about books and people . . . a good Virginianism . . . It was all most enjoyable.'[102] People reported on her talk as they might discuss or review her new book or essay. Gerald Brenan, unreliable but sensitive, made some vivid notes in 1969 on her conversation:

> I believe she could be shy, but in the company of friends she talked fluently in a language that was crystal clear . . . she was never at a loss for a word. She was quiet and simple when one saw her alone . . . but with her Bloomsbury friends she became very animated . . . Absolute frankness was the rule. The general tone of the conversation was light and irreverent, but with a deep underlying seriousness about literature and science. The same topics had a way of coming up every time – the younger generation v the older, painters v writers, women v men, even Bloomsbury v the world – well practised subjects, but leading to different treatment and to sudden flights of fantasy . . . Her tone was nearly always ironical. Thus she could be stimulated into flights of fantasy when her imagination had full scope and these were delightful. But she always jumped at any chance to talk on literature and then she talked seriously and well, without her usual irony. But she easily became over excited. Then she would talk too much from the surface of her mind, which had begun to work too quickly. (~~It was at such times that she could be very indiscreet and even malicious~~) . . . Leonard . . . was what a manager is to a famous actress.[103]

Living up to this reputation as a performer was a pressure as well as a pleasure. At parties she could be dizzy, wild and extravagant – 'over-excited'. Reporting to Lytton on a characteristic party at Tilton in 1927, she sounds high on scandal, snobbery, silliness, wit, and clowning:

> I have come to a time of life when I can help nothing.

572

This was, in fact, what I was saying to Sheppard last night, at Tilton, when we picked the bones of Maynard's grouse of which there were three to eleven people. This stinginess is a constant source of delight to Nessa – her eyes gleamed as the bones went round. We had a brilliant entertainment afterwards in the new Loggia, with a rustic audience. Sheppard half naked, tightly swathed in red silk, shingled as to his head, with coloured garters, was Miss T to perfection: Maynard was crapulous and obscene beyond words, lifting his left leg and singing a song about Women. Lydia was Queen Victoria dancing to a bust of Albert. What did the yokels make of it? I wish you had been there – which reminds me, there was a good deal of talk about you at dinner, some for you, I, of course, against . . .[104]

Vanessa and Virginia initiated some Thursday evenings in 1928 on the lines of 'Old Bloomsbury'; Vanessa reported to Roger Fry that on one of these 'everyone sat and listened while Virginia got wilder and wilder and other people threw bits into the ring more or less successfully'. Angelica's twelfth, masked birthday party in January 1931, was a 'hectic affair'; Virginia 'came as Sappho . . . at any rate a most voluptuous lady casting her eyes up to heaven'.[105]

Stories of her extravagant or odd behaviour turned into little legends, to be endlessly retold: how (according to Igor Anrep) she parted her legs and peed on the lawn on her way out of someone's house; how, sitting alone at a concert, she so definitely seemed (to Stephen Spender) not to want to be talked to that he pretended not to know her; how, sitting next to Harold Laski at a lunch party, she took out a notebook when he said anything interesting and wrote it down: 'It was like watching someone organising her own immortality.'[106] But her immortality was also being organised for her, by (often male) spectators who wanted to fix her strangeness as comic or romantic eccentricity.

Certainly she could behave badly. Stories of her cruelty and malice were notorious. There is much cruelty, and pleasure in cruelty, in the letters. She knew she was like this: 'I can help nothing.' Setting out to meet a young writer, Elizabeth Jenkins, she wrote: 'I am going dutifully, not to snub the female young. But I shall be overpowering I doubt not.'[107] Again: 'How formidable I must be.'[108]

Plenty of people went up the stone steps in a state of fear and anxiety, and came away feeling like fools. Kathleen Raine remembered 'very well going to tea with Virginia Woolf and being dumb with terror'.[109] David Cecil was crushed on his first meeting with her by being told to tell an amusing story.[110] The director John Houseman, who went to Tavistock Square in his early thirties to talk about his first book, arrived terrified, tried to make himself sound more interesting than he was, but remembered her, none the less, as 'talkative, humorous and domestic'.[111] Even people who knew her well could be rebuffed, and go home puzzled or thwarted. Ottoline (easily hurt) recorded, in the summer of 1925, taking her for a drive around London.

> How lovely she looked – with a wisp of hair blown across her face. She is curiously inhuman though – When we left her – she got out of the motor ran up her steps and shut the door upon herself without even looking back once – or giving one wave of her hand – or even a good night – or a smile. She is like an entrancing intellectual Phantom . . .[112]

Against this, there are many stories and proofs of her kindness – just as, in the letters, breathtaking spitefulness runs alongside tender affection and interest. Hope Mirrlees remembered all her life the letter she had from Virginia after the death of her companion, Jane Harrison. 'It was only one line', she told her friend Valerie Eliot, consoling her, years later, for the death of her husband, 'but it was more comforting than all my other letters put together: "But remember what you have had." '[113]

These contradictions, of cruelty and kindness, curiosity and snobbery, sympathy and offensiveness, were inextricably mixed together. They have been noted by witnesses whose own self-centredness necessarily colours their descriptions. When an incident in her life was observed by more than one witness, her complexity is more than ever apparent. One 'legendary' encounter exhibits this with particular force. This is the meeting of Yeats and Virginia Woolf, which took place, with Walter de la Mare, in Ottoline's drawing-room in her house in Gower Street, on 7 November 1930.

When Yeats met Virginia Woolf, he was (she worked out) sixty-five. He was in a period of intense creativity, between the first and second versions of *A Vision*, and had just written *The Words upon the Window Pane*, his play on Swift. She had met him once before, in 1907, but he did not remember her. The play he had written that year used the ideas of *A Vision*, of 'the six states of the soul between the death of the body and rebirth',[114] with its seance invoking the point in Irish history when a great man like Swift could emerge. These themes coloured their conversation.

As usual in her meetings with great men, Virginia gave several versions of the encounter. In the diary she described Yeats's thickness, like 'a solid wedge of oak'. They talked about dreams – '& so on to dreaming states, & soul states; as others talk of Beaverbrook & free trade – as if matters of common knowledge.' She recognised that he had 'worked out a complete psychology'. De la Mare talked about looking at paintings; 'Yeats said he could get nothing from Rembrandt, nothing from El Greco'. He explained the pleasure one got from paintings by an 'elaborate metaphor' which she couldn't quite remember. They discussed Milton, 'and so to modern poetry, & the question of the spade'.

> Yeats said that 'we', de la M. & himself, wrote 'thumbnail' poems only because we are at the end of an era. Here was another system of thought, of which I could only snatch fragments. He said that the spade has been embalmed by 30 centuries of association; not so the steam roller . . . Steam rollers are not covered in symbolism . . . He & de la M. can only write small fireside poems. Most of emotion is outside their scope. All left to the novelists I said . . .

But she felt herself sounding 'crude & jaunty' by comparison with 'the intricacy' of his art, his sense of 'its seriousness, its importance, which wholly engrosses this large active minded immensely vitalised man. Wherever one cut him, with a little question, he poured, spurted fountains of ideas.' (The phrase resembles her responses to reading Shakespeare.) He seemed direct: 'No fluff & dreaminess.' They talked about the necessity of tragedy ('this belongs to another theory about the soul & its antitype, which I vaguely remember in his poems'). He mentioned James Stephens's poverty; Tom Eliot's cleverness in using mythologies; the 'break' in Pound's poetry between beautiful use of myths and 'common objects'. She recorded a remark she had made on how 'we did not talk enough, not easily & equally'. In response he talked about 'men he had met in trains'. She noted and liked 'his transitions to dialect & humour. With men perhaps he might be coarse.' He described his stay with the Masefields, cordially. He struck her as generous and urbane.[115]

In her letters to Vanessa and to Ethel Smyth, she introduced more gossip and personalities: Ottoline's black ear-trumpet, the offstage sound of Philip Morrell talking to a woman, de la Mare's odd charming daftness, and her own indiscretions: 'I said all the wrong things about poetry.' To Vanessa she just kept on the edge of caricature: 'As he believes in the unconscious soul, in fairies, in magic, and has a complete system of philosophy & psychology – it was not easy altogether to understand: at the same time, I agreed with many of his views; & he also is surprisingly sensible.' To Ethel she composed more of a fantasy, with herself at the centre: 'For what do I know of the inner meaning of dreams, I whose life is almost entirely founded on dreams (yes, I will come to the suicide dream one of these days) I mean I know nothing of the spiritual significance of ruby eyes . . . But Yeats said, as it might be a man identifying a rather rare grass, that is the third state of the soul in contemplation (or words to that effect – it will not surprise you if I got them wrong.)' She noted their talk of Milton, and 'Irish life in brogue', and 'the soul's attitude to art', and then introduced Ottoline and her black ear-trumpet as a figure of comic heroism.[116]

Ottoline's version in her own diary did not mention her ear-trumpet, but (perhaps because of her deafness) gave a different emphasis to the encounter. She noticed that Virginia 'was very silent & didn't say much. She seemed rather to shrivel & have the wind taken out of her sails'. Ottoline expanded the remark about not talking enough: Virginia 'wanted to widen her knowledge of people by mixing with the people of the streets', and thought that 'we hide in little sets'. (Ottoline commented to herself: 'You do but I don't.') Because she always criticised Virginia's aloof coldness, she made more of Yeats's remarks on 'men he had met in trains' and 'Irish life in brogue'. Ottoline's version of this part of the conversation was more political and more romantic:

> Yeats said if you came to Ireland you wouldn't get that ['little sets']. There is equality here. If you visit in the cottages you would be free but have your dignity. But this cottage woman would also have her dignity. So you would meet equals – there is no striving to 'better' position as there is in America. [Told by a lawyer in America that he was 'democratic', Yeats replied,] 'In our country there is no such thing.'

Ottoline went on to report that Virginia talked about her introduction to the letters of the Working Women's Guild Co-Operative, and couldn't understand why they were offended by her reference to their 'enormous arms'. 'Well,' Ottoline commented, 'I really don't think it is difficult to understand that it would be very hurting to say that!' And she ended her account with something she often observed. 'Virginia has certain limitations that surprise me . . . I think it is living always amongst intellectuals.' Characteristically, she found Yeats's reactionary romanticism about Irish peasantry more sympathetic than Virginia's equivocal and contradictory attitudes to English social divisions. As for Yeats, the next day, inspired by this meeting, he wrote a quatrain which became the poem 'Spilt Milk', published in 1933:

> We that have done and thought
> That have thought and done,
> Must ramble, and thin out,
> Like milk spilt on a stone.[117]

Both women paid less attention to Walter de la Mare, who was then fifty-seven, and who was, unlike Yeats, at an arid period in his life as a poet (as Hardy had told Virginia), publishing stories and essays rather than poems. But de la Mare, the unnoticed observer, was watching closely, and, with no axe to grind, gave a more humorous and less awed version of the encounter. He was used to 'sitting at Yeats's feet while the brogue monologue chanted on, impressing on himself the while (so he said) "This is *Yeats*: I must remember every word." But each time he got up to leave he found it was the same thing – alas, already nothing whatever remained! He cherished an occasion . . . at the Morrells when Yeats was holding forth about the occult. De la Mare presently stole a glance across the captive audience at the face of Virginia Woolf. She gave no other sign, just let her eyebrows go up – one tiny lift, expressing all.'[118]

The alternation between the public self and the private interior self seems crucial in this life story. It is often commented on, and Virginia Woolf writes about it a great deal herself. *The Waves*, the novel of 1929 to 1931, embodies this kind of contrast, setting the worldly, seductive, gossipy, intimacy-loving selves (Bernard, Neville, Jinny) against the silent, apprehensive, inhibited, mystical selves (Louis, Rhoda, Susan). And as she is moving from the social concerns of *A Room of One's Own* to the beginnings of *The Waves*, she frequently describes herself and her work in terms of these contrasts. The diary entries about the beginnings of *The Waves* speak of 'The Lonely Mind' as the voice of the novel, or of the book forming 'underneath' in silence and solitude.[119] On 11 October 1929, when *A Room of One's Own* was about to be published and *The Waves* was 'forming', she wrote a long passage about her 'inner loneliness', her sense of 'vacancy & silence somewhere in the machine', underlying all her social activity of 'seeing people'. 'What I like is to flash & dash from side to side, goaded on by what I call reality.' In an extraordinary phrase, she sums up the conflict of her 'selves': 'The feeling of the singing of the real world, as one is driven by loneliness & silence from the habitable world; the sense that comes to one of being bound on an adventure.'[120]

But the diary entry, and the novel it is working towards, know that these oppositions between the lonely mind and the habitable world, or between silent thought and a socialised language, are always collapsing and merging. There is no deep, essential silent self, neatly divided off from the superficial, garrulous social self. The 'characters' in *The Waves* exist in the form of written speech; they can have no form except through 'writing, & inscriptions, & words, & meanings'. They *talk* their lives. Virginia Woolf talks to herself, all her life, in the silence of 'the lonely mind'. But that silent, private conversation connects to, and plays its part in, 'the singing of the real world'.

PART IV

1929–1941

THIRTY-TWO

Ethel

Virginia Woolf went to have her eyes tested on a Friday afternoon at the end of May 1929. She was finding that she suddenly needed much stronger spectacles for reading.[1] The oculist said to her, 'Perhaps you're not as young as you were.' She left the optician's feeling like an 'elderly woman' ('putting on a manner of great wisdom & toleration'). Her diary for that week – voting, and waiting for the results of the General Election (Ramsay Macdonald's second, ill-omened Labour Government came in), visiting a more-than-ever demanding Mrs Woolf, calling on the 'divinely' likeable Francis Birrell, dropping Pinker off at Long Barn in preparation for their holiday in France – was coloured by an acute sense of ageing. Watching Leonard's mother, aged seventy-six, greedily and self-pityingly hanging on to 'more life', she wondered whether she would be like this. Suicide would be more dignified; she disliked the thought that 'one will not perhaps go to the writing table & write that simple & profound paper upon suicide which I see myself leaving for my friends'. How best to grow old, how best to die? The mood overcast her; but, writing it in the diary, she became again, not an elderly woman, but simply 'a woman': 'as I always am when I write.'[2]

It was a 'rackety' summer, with too many interruptions. She was upset by her jealousy when Vita went on holiday (and did not tell her) with Hilda Matheson. She was having a series of mutually degrading scenes with Nelly. She was revising *A Room of One's Own*, with anxiety. She was writing too many 'tugging & distressing' little articles. Often at night her feeling of 'worthlessness' overcame her.[3] At the same time, thinking about old age, she was responding minutely to the valuable small moments of ordinary life. She copied out in her diary some lines from Wordsworth's *The Prelude* which she wanted to remember:

> The matter that detains us now may seem,
> To many, neither dignified enough
> Nor arduous, yet will not be scorned by them,
> Who, looking inward, have observed the ties
> That bind the perishable hours of life

Each to the other, & the curious props
By which the world of memory & thought
Exists & is sustained.[4]

In September she was unwell again. She began *The Moths*, thinking about solitude and 'the lonely mind', and about the value of illness for her writing.[5] Leonard put a drag on her excitement about their new oil stove at Monk's House; he was irritated when she changed their travel plans one weekend. The music from the hotel in London was very bad, and he was preparing to take the hoteliers to court. They argued about whether to get rid of Nelly. These minor symptoms overlaid Leonard's uncertainty at this time about whether to stay on at the *Nation*, and her extreme trepidation about the reception of *A Room of One's Own*. A vivid dream, very revealing of their married life, seemed to act out her anxieties:

> I dreamt last night that I had a disease of the heart that would kill me in 6 months. Leonard, after some persuasion, told me. My instincts were all such as I should have, in order, & some very strong: quite unexpected, I mean voluntary, as they are in dreams, & have thus an authenticity which makes an immense, & pervading, impression. First, relief – well I've done with life anyhow (I was lying in bed) then horror; then desire to live; then fear of insanity; then (no this came earlier) regret about my writing, & leaving this book unfinished; then a luxurious dwelling upon my friends sorrow; then a sense of death & being done with at my age; then telling Leonard that he must marry again; seeing our life together; & facing the conviction of going, when other people went on living. Then I woke . . .[6]

Some of the problems in daytime life resolved themselves: *A Room of One's Own* was a success; Leonard decided to leave the *Nation*; they made up their minds, finally, to give Nelly her notice.

But this last was not so easily sorted out. For the next two years, all the time Virginia was writing *The Waves*, getting rid of Nelly Boxall took up much time and emotion. Nelly had often given in her notice, complaining about overwork, the mess of the Press, the endless guests, the difficulties of the Sussex house. Just as often, Virginia complained about her possessiveness, her jealousy, and her gossiping (wherein the cook resembled her mistress) with the claque, or 'click', of Bloomsbury servants. Lottie had left for Adrian's household in 1924, but the two women were still a pair, and Virginia felt too involved with their lives. The relationship produced in her feelings of irritation, guilt, and resentment. She did not want Nelly in her life. She was snobbish about her illiteracy, and what seemed to her Nelly's stupidity. She did not like the sound of her voice. And she detested herself for these detestable emotions, and was moved by Nelly's loyalty and her gestures of affection. She knew that the advantage was all on her side. Nelly had no power, no voice. Instead of power, Nelly used the ploys of dependency: emotional scenes, sulks, self-pity. When Virginia began to write *Flush* in the summer of 1931, as a relief from finishing *The Waves*, she made comic use of that dependency – and also noted the life of the maid, Wilson, as the crucial untold part of Elizabeth Barrett Browning's story.

That autumn of 1929 they tried (Leonard less willingly) to sack her. When she protested again, Virginia, 'weariedly, & disillusionedly' tried a month's compromise – to give her a helper at Tavistock Square.[7] Then, in May 1930, Nelly fell ill, and had to have a kidney operation. Virginia went with her in the ambulance, and visited her while she was convalescing in Surrey.[8] Meanwhile, she was telling everyone what a bore Nelly's illness was, and plotting to get rid of her while she was away. It was a great relief to be without her:

> Partly the silence is so grateful; & partly the absence of lower classes . . . I cannot bring myself to talk to her as I should. I am always seeing myself told to 'leave my room'.[9]

The advertisement she placed in *Time & Tide* for a live-in cook for Tavistock Square only (Annie Thomsett had taken over at Monk's House during Nelly's illness) showed the kind of person she dreamed of employing: 'Woman of intelligence and initiative wanted to do entire work of flat, WC1, for two writers. Live out. Good cooking essential.'[10] She got Miss Rivett-Carnac, the impoverished thirty-five-year-old daughter of an Anglo-Indian family 'who let her live in Wimbledon with her mother on a pound a week'. But Miss Rivett-Carnac, to Leonard's dismay, was a poor cook (though her life-story would be useful ammunition for *Three Guineas*). Nelly kept showing up, suspicious and pleading, and making what was, indeed, a powerful case: 'Why did I not have her back & give her help, seeing that she had been with us for 15 years?'[11] Virginia felt 'rage at our general ineptitude' and dislike of Nelly's 'dependence and defenceless-ness'.[12] In November, 1930, she wrote Nelly a long, careful letter of dismissal, to which she received the reply: 'Dear Mr & Mrs Woolf. Thank you for your cheque; Yrs truly' – as though it was Virginia who was doing the pleading, and Nelly the dismissing. But then she was back, pathetic, demanding: impossible to explain to her that this was 'a psychological strain'. So once more the mistress gave way, and Nelly was reinstated for four more years, when the whole thing had to be gone through all over again.

The Waves was turning into a struggle ('fight, fight!') between life and death. Thoby's death, and thoughts of mortality, were much in her mind. 'What are the arguments against suicide?' she asked in October 1930.[13] Other people's deaths kept happening, as for most people with a large circle of friends, from their late forties onwards. In February 1930 came the death of Charlie Sanger – old Cambridge friend, Apostle, brilliant lawyer, of whom she had been very fond. Since Jacques Raverat, he was the first of their close Cambridge friends to die. D.H. Lawrence's death in March moved her in a different way. Though she disliked some of his work intensely, had never met him, and despised his fictional revenge on Ottoline in *Women in Love*, she felt an affinity with him. All through the early 1930s she kept reading and thinking about him. In August 1930, she heard of the death of a young tutor of the Nicolson boys, killed mountaineering: she vividly imagined the accident.[14] Arnold Bennett, her old adversary, 'drank a glass of water, & died of typhoid'.[15] His death made her 'sadder than I should have supposed', she wrote, in an ironical, somewhat condescending tribute in her diary. 'An element in life – even in mine that was so remote – taken away. This is what one minds.'[16] Bennett's funeral made her think of her own: 'We went home & drew up instruction for silent dispersal in a field', she told Hugh Walpole.[17] In January 1931, as she was working towards the end of *The Waves*, they saw a plane that had crashed near Gatwick, and heard that three men had been killed. 'But we went on, reminding me of that epitaph in the Greek anthology: when I sank, the other ships sailed on.'[18]

But the usual powerful counterforce was at work. At the start of 1930, in her forty-eighth year, other people's old age made her feel her own vigour and energy. A visit from old 'Snow', Margery Snowden, who had made her so jealous over Vanessa thirty years before, and who now seemed to be saying with every breath, 'I have had no life & life is over',[19] allowed her to celebrate her own capacity to 'coerce every minute of my life since I was born!' The pathetic old age of Margaret Llewelyn Davies and Lilian Harris made her determine to escape the sad 'shapelessness' of old age by 'working the mind'.[20]

She was thinking a good deal about caricature. She wanted the characters in *The Waves* to be sharp outlines, 'statues against the sky'.[21] She wrote a comical but not altogether hostile sketch of George Duckworth, who turned up for an unexpected visit, fat and prosperous. She meditated a life of Duncan. She wanted to 'canter her wits' with little satires.[22] She was thinking about starting a broadsheet of opinionated essays. A (now rather rare) visit from Lytton in February 1930 charmed her all over again, with his 'gusto' and irony and 'fantastic amusing' story-telling.[23] She was reading

Byron (thinking how he mixed sentiment and vigorous rhetoric, satire and a deep feeling for nature),[24] Hazlitt (taking pleasure in his energy and fervour and convictions), and Shakespeare, whom she read 'directly I have finished writing, when my mind is agape & red & hot', feeling herself completely outpaced by him.[25] In between the first and second drafts of *The Waves*, in the spring of 1930, she told herself to live 'with energy & mastery, desperately', 'to dispatch each day high-handedly', to do things with decision. Even when she was ill (she fainted on a hot day in September, and had flu and headaches in December), she felt a keen appetite for life. (Two years later she fainted twice, alarmingly, once on a hot night at the Ivy Restaurant, once at Monk's House on the last day of her period. Leonard listed her symptoms. Both she and Leonard noted the 'pounding of the heart and head and the bitter taste in the mouth' which inaugurated these attacks; also the menstrual cramps, the blood rushing to her face and the violent diarrhoea which accompanied the last one.)[26] She imagined, after this 'brush with death', arriving in the divine presence 'with fists clenched & fury on my lips'. ' "I dont want to come here at all!" '[27]

Into this period of contraries – illness and strength, poetry and caricature, mysticism and satire, the lonely mind and the real world, ageing and energy – came Ethel Smyth. Ethel introduced herself because of *A Room of One's Own*. She knew and admired Vita and had heard a great deal about Virginia from her. Then she read *A Room*, and in January 1930 she was asked by the BBC to chair a programme called 'Point of View'. She wrote to ask Virginia if she would participate, telling her how greatly she admired the book.[28] So, from the start of their relationship, Ethel occupied the opposite place, politically, from Vita (now moving to Sissinghurst, and into her absorption with the making of her garden). Unlike Vita,[29] Ethel Smyth greeted *A Room of One's Own* as a heroic addition to the history of the liberation movement. After her fan-letter, and Virginia's delighted response, she arrived promptly at the start of 1930 (or it would have been prompt if Virginia's illness hadn't delayed their first meeting until February, a pattern which would repeat itself), like a loud overture to the decade. 'Let there be banners and music!' was the climactic line of her current work, *The Prisoner*. As her feelings for Virginia rapidly intensified, she liked to quote that line as an illustration of them. But it makes just as good an introit for Ethel herself.

Virginia Woolf was forty-eight and Ethel Smyth was seventy-two. She was a well-known figure whom Virginia had glimpsed all her life, and in her first letter to her she told Ethel that she had often wanted to meet her.[30] In 1909, she had gone to the first London performance of Ethel's Cornish opera, *The Wreckers* (its setting would have interested her).[31] A year later, when Virginia Stephen was addressing envelopes for the suffrage movement, Ethel, then in her early fifties, was throwing stones at a Colonial Secretary's house in Berkeley Square, as part of an orchestrated campaign by Emmeline Pankhurst's militant WSPU. (She had picked this particular MP's window 'because of an infuriating remark he had made to the effect that if all women were as pretty and as wise as his own wife, we should have the vote tomorrow'.)[32] While in Holloway Prison for two months, in the cell next to Emmeline Pankhurst's, she wrote the 'March of the Women', and was seen (according to Sir Thomas Beecham, Ethel's sardonic champion) 'leaning out of her prison window conducting it with a toothbrush'.[33]

Virginia knew too about Ethel's Anglo-Indian family, which had close connections to her own. In 1919, she had read in Ethel's memoirs, *Impressions That Remained*, the story of her great-grandfather Jim Pattle exploding out of his cask.[34] The retelling of this story, rooted in their high-coloured Anglo-Indian family past, was one of the first jokes between them.[35] Ethel too came bursting at Virginia out of an embalmed past. Her memoirs seemed wrapped in a late-Victorian atmosphere. Virginia's generation of friends had spent the last twenty years repudiating that ethos. She wrote to Lytton in 1919 that Smyth's book was, 'of course, the soul of the nineties'.[36] And in a review of the next volume, in 1921, she fixed her firmly in 'the age of Charles Furse and Sargent and Henley and Stevenson and the Boer War'.[37] That Ethel had been drawn by Sargent in 1901 was entirely apt.

But Ethel had herself revolted against the conventions of her time. When Virginia caught sight of her at a concert in 1919, she described (to Lytton) a comic figure, half-pioneer, half-antique: 'striding up the gangway in coat and skirt and spats and talking at the top of her voice. Near at hand one sees that she's all wrinkled and fallen in, and eyes running blue on to the cheeks; but she keeps up the figure of the nineties to perfection.'[38] She reminded Virginia of the world of Susan Lushington, of Kitty Maxse or Violet Dickinson.

Ethel's late-Victorian associations – her attachment to grand old ladies like the Empress Eugénie, widow of Napoleon III, and to Balmoral and the Royal Family, her golf-playing (she would have her ashes scattered on the Woking Golf Links) and her country life with her dogs in Surrey – felt stuffy and antediluvian to Virginia. Though (to start with at least) she tried to be nice about Ethel's literary friendships, she found the tone of voice of her friends the Bensons (the three sons of Archbishop Benson were all novelists and belle-lettristes) 'repulsive'.[39] She was no keener on the Old Etonian, Catholic, aristocratic tone of Ethel's hero Maurice Baring. As for 'H.B.', Henry Brewster, one of the great loves of Ethel's past life, a Jamesian

Europeanised American and dilettantish philosopher-poet whose libretti for *The Wreckers* and *The Prison* had a good deal to do with the lack of success of those works, Virginia had soon heard quite enough of him. She called his poetry for *The Prison* a 'hopeless farrago'.[40]

The whole atmosphere of Ethel's past was summed up in E.F. Benson's novel *Dodo*, a portrait of the young Margot Asquith, née Tennant (once referred to by Virginia as 'that libidinous Ape')[41] which Virginia had read when it was popular in 1893,[42] and which she looked at again after meeting Ethel. Here Ethel featured as the outspoken, eccentric and ardent feminist composer Edith Staines: 'a young lady' (Ethel noted) 'who ate eggs and bacon on the lid of her piano while composing; no mean feat.'[43] Edith Staines whistles, warms her back 'in a gentlemanly manner' by the fire, smokes cigarettes in the drawing-room, devours grilled bones, is an excellent shot, has no desire to marry, strides about in boots, talks in staccato and screams and laughs with her hair sticking on end when she's not composing, and is deadly earnest in everything she does, 'whether it was shooting, or music, or playing lawn-tennis'. She is very Nineties, very New Woman. Ethel didn't want Virginia to type-cast her as 'Edith Staines', and was upset when she made joking allusions to *Dodo* – but there remained some resemblance to that forty-year-old caricature.

'I have only come in time to hear about the past. Everything is past.'[44] Virginia liked this, though it was also rather sad. In the first months of their friendship, she imagined writing Ethel's life-story – a portrait, a fictional memoir, as she had once done for Violet – and of being in some sense Ethel's 'literary executor'. And Ethel's history came pouring out of her, exactly as it did in her autobiographies. Virginia would occasionally try to drive a 'wedge' into this flood, or there would be a pause as Ethel would draw breath with an emphatic '*Well!*' before tearing off again on to the next story. At first this was mutually pleasurable. Listening to Ethel was like reading one of Virginia's favourite kind of memoirs; being listened to, was, for Ethel, a mark of friendship. Too many new friends in old age, she would say bitterly, were not interested in the other person's 'back numbers'.[45]

Ethel did seem a 'back number', not only in her emphatic characteristics but also in her music. It's a striking fact of Virginia Woolf's life that, apart from Vanessa, and Katherine Mansfield, and (soon) Elizabeth Bowen, all her closest women friends were traditionalists and anti-modernists. Violet, Ottoline, Vita and Ethel, for all their pioneering qualities, cherished distinctly old-fashioned ideals of life rooted in the past. Virginia was much the most radical of these women. (That may have been part of their appeal: she did not relish competition.) But she shared with them, too, their emotional connections with Victorianism.

Ethel, though personally unconventional, was not an experimental artist. Her musical inspiration derived from nineteenth-century German and French romanticism and from an English choral tradition. She started composing in the 1870s and much of her work sounded more like Brahms, or Gounod – or Sullivan, whom she greatly admired, and whose example as that rare thing, an English opera-composer, she wanted to follow – than it anticipated Walton or Stravinsky. (She loathed Delius.) Perhaps because she was aware that her work was not avant-garde, she greatly resented the critical terms 'old-fashioned' and 'dated'.[46] But she made up in vigour and boldness what she lacked in originality. The work was highly coloured and energetic. There was her exuberant *Mass in D* (1893), greeted condescendingly on its first performance ('Is a great female composer possible?' *The Star*) which she struggled all her life to have put on again. (Archbishop Benson remarked of it: 'God was not implored, but commanded, to have mercy.')[47] There was the famous 'March of the Women', to whose rousing tune Cicely Hamilton fitted suitable words, and which Vera Brittain called the 'Battle Song of the Suffragettes'.[48] There were two short comic operas, the folksy *Boatswain's Mate* (1916), centring on a comic landlady of a pub called The Beehive, with singing parts for the cats, and a 'post-war comedy', *Entente Cordiale* (1925), by 'Ethel Smyth, Bengal Military Orphan', with Ethel's own Kiplingesque lyrics for the English soldiers in France: 'Of good luck and bad luck we 'as our share/ And life's made up of patches/ But it's the *little* things that is 'ard to bear/ The tiny rubs and scratches.'[49]

The Wreckers, her most lasting work, was written at the turn of the century, first performed in Leipzig in 1906.[50] Its story of grim, godfearing Cornish 'wreckers' casting out and sentencing to watery death the lovers who break ranks and save the ships from harm foreshadows Britten's *Peter Grimes*, in its dramatic opposition between the bigoted community and the outcasts, and in its seascape music. But with its big choral numbers and its dramatic confrontations it feels more like a nineteenth- than an early twentieth-century work. So does *The Prison*, Brewster's mystical, Whitmanesque 'dialogue' between the Prisoner and his Soul, with Voices singing – either *fff* or *ppp* – of 'the indestructibility of human passions'.[51]

The story of the soul bursting its bonds was an apt one for Ethel. What Virginia admired most in her was her narrative of struggle and resistance. When she read Ethel's memoirs, stuffed with valiant stories – of her preference for boy's clothes as a child, her battle to become a musician with her authoritarian father and her difficult mother, her flight to Germany, her struggle to establish herself against bitter setbacks, her suffragette days – she admired Ethel's 'great rush at life'.[52] Ethel transferred the Pankhursts'

Joan of Arc spirit to her professional career, and her memoirs (and letters and conversation) were full of Pankhurstian oratory on women's 'slave habit of mind'.[53] Full, too, of bitter diatribes on what she called the Inner Circle, the Club, the Gang, or the Machine, consisting of 'University Men, rich music patrons, Heads of Colleges, of publishing houses, representative men on big provincial Festival committees, pressmen', 'the Oligarchy that has always ruled Musical England'.[54] She was always 'taking the bull by the horns',[55] and she never stopped dramatising her own isolation, courage and bad treatment. She called herself 'a female Ishmael in the English musical tribes'.[56]

All this was still going strong when they met: Ethel was struggling with arrangements for *The Prison* and trying to get *The Wreckers* put on again, against opposition from one of her 'enemies', Adrian Boult. Virginia was at first roused by the story of these battles and – quite soon – driven to exasperation by them. But she still relished Ethel's energy and candour. What she had said to herself on first reading Ethel in 1919 – 'friendships with women interest me' – was borne out by their relationship. Ethel's outspokenness about her own 'friendships with women' was inspiring. She filled her memoirs with effusive portraits of the exceptional women she had loved. The pattern was that Ethel would embark, immediately, on a passionate pursuit, and then settle for a close, emotional friendship. She used to say that imagination played more part in women's love affairs than sex. For many women, she wrote in her diary in the 1930s, looking back on her overwhelming feelings for Virginia, 'passion is independent of the sex machine'; but for her, she admitted, physical feelings went on into old age.[57] In her memoirs, the tone of her declarations of strong feelings for women is fervid and proud:

> Let me say here, that all my life . . . I have found in women's affection a peculiar understanding, mothering quality that is a thing apart. Perhaps too I had a foreknowledge of the difficulties that in a world arranged by man for man's convenience beset the woman who leaves the traditional path to compete for bread and butter, honours and emoluments . . . the people who have helped me most at difficult moments of my musical career . . . have been members of my own sex. Thus it comes to pass that my relations with certain women, all exceptional personalities I think, are shining threads in my life . . . And I may add that if the world is inclined to scoff or speak ill of women's friendships, this is one of those cheap generalities that will pass muster only as long as women let men do their thinking for them.[58]

There is nothing laughable about that passage. Ethel was an emotional, demanding, self-absorbed person with a great investment in her own feelings, a deep fund of loyalty, and a capacity for intense suffering. When Virginia Woolf used Ethel for fiction – as the battle-scarred suffragette Rose Pargiter in *The Years*, or the lesbian theatre-director Miss La Trobe in *Between the Acts* – she turned her into resilient figures who are also vulnerable, troubled – and ridiculed. Because Ethel was quarrelsome and odd-looking; because in old age she was very deaf (she had had split hearing: music came through a semitone apart in each ear) and used a large cumbersome ear-trumpet;[59] because she had battled her way angrily in a man's world; and because she was a single woman who loved her own sex, she was a figure of fun. She was the joke lesbian-feminist, the absurd Edwardian dyke-composer. The very name Ethel Smyth makes some people smile: she was treated in her lifetime, and has been ever since, as a comic spectacle. Her career was sabotaged in part because she was regarded as a laughable eccentric. She was all too aware of this, and made things worse by insisting on her rights, and at the same time being indecisive about her work.

All the male musicians she worked with thought her absurd and impossible. Henry Wood had stories about her appearance in bicycling bloomers, about her last-minute alterations to the orchestral parts ('Dame Ethel is a law unto herself') and about her vigorous way with a baton: 'She went up to my rostrum, took up my baton and surveyed its length critically. Deciding it was more than she could manage, she calmly snapped it in two, threw away one half and conducted with the other.'[60] Adrian Boult also told impatient stories to illustrate her 'erratic yet obsessive' musical personality, mostly about her frequent changes of mind ('How fast do you want this movement to go *today*, Dame Ethel?'). She attracted rude sniggers: 'Has someone altered your parts, Dame Ethel?' 'Nonsense – nobody has touched my parts since Norwich!' Boult said she used to blow her nose on lavatory paper, Henry Wood's daughter remembered her producing long strips of it at breakfast to write her notes on. (And Ethel was very frank and free, as Virginia noted admiringly, in discussing the WC, and in stopping to pee during country walks. There are heavy-handed jokes about being caught peeing in the bushes in *Female Pipings*: clearly this was a rich source of *risqué* comedy for Ethel's generation.) Her clothes were a joke, too. There were many stories about her battered cardboard suitcases, her tricorne hat and old tweed suits, the same evening dress she always used for conducting, hitched up with safety pins that were extremely visible to the audience. Lady Barbirolli, who played the oboe in a 1930s' revival of *The Wreckers*, remembered her taking the band to tea in a Lyons Corner House after rehearsals, and rolling up her skirts to get her moneybag out from her underwear.[61] Beecham, her supporter and admirer, was also her leading caricaturist:

> There was something militant, belligerent, about Ethel, which differenti-
> ated her from every other member of her sex . . . She was an absolute
> PORTENT of activity, physical and mental. She was on the go from
> morning till night and I suspect in part from night till morning . . . She
> was a stubborn, indomitable, unconquerable creature . . . one of the most
> remarkable people of her time.[62]

Her violent, bellicose energies were legend: 'One has to be very *well* to enjoy you, Ethel', her niece remembered a sick friend remarking.[63] This was a significant note in the relation between Ethel and Virginia, who so often was not very well.

Ethel as a comic performance was of course a gift to Bloomsbury. Virginia had heard stories about her from Vita and Harold, who had met her on his travels. Vita would make great fun of Ethel's grotesqueness: 'Oh, and her deaf aid! Ethel's deaf aid was attached to a wooden box which I suppose contained a battery . . . as conversation progressed she would grow more and more excited . . . would jump up and down, arguing, declaiming, while the box, still attached, trailed round after her.'[64]

Virginia at once gleefully adopted the standard tone about Ethel; it was almost impossible not to. 'An old woman of seventy one has fallen in love with me' she wrote to Quentin. 'It is at once hideous and horrid and melancholy-sad. It is like being caught by a giant crab.'[65] As Ethel turned into a nuisance, Virginia's commentary became ever more lethally satirical, especially in letters to Vita and Vanessa. Vanessa found her impossible: 'Ethel Smyth even followed her [Virginia] to the studio and snorted like an angry bull between me and V., complaining about her operas and women's rights generally.'[66]

But Ethel, unlike Virginia, could cope with being laughed at. She knew (she told Virginia in letters about her harlequinade *Fête Galante*, which Vanessa was designing for Sadler's Wells in 1934), that people said 'O! Dame E.S. is *such a handful!*'[67] And she played up to her comic side. Perhaps she *was* something of a 'juggernaut', she admitted.[68] Possibly her 'celebrated vitality' might end up 'fatiguing' Virginia.[69] One of her longest love-letters, at the end of 1931, broke off at the top of the second page with: 'Pause. To unstiffen buttocks.'[70] Was this entirely unselfconscious?

Ethel's humour wasn't exactly the sort that Virginia Woolf enjoyed and practised. One of her criticisms of Virginia was that 'the only thing she can't do well is laugh.'[71] Although she told Virginia, 'No one's fun makes me laugh as yours does,'[72] Ethel's own 'fun' was of a different kind: pranks, belly-laughs, naughty jokes. Talking to a servant-girl on holiday in the Hebrides, she was told that 'lots of girls have themselves operated nowadays so as not to endure tortures on marriage nights. What a pity you (let alone me) were not thus treated. But principally you – why not try it now? (Its never too late to mend).'[73] (The joke suggests how intimate Virginia's confidences to Ethel were about her sexual history.) In 1938 Ethel told her a story about Lilian Baylis, the formidable theatre manager with whom Ethel had worked more than once. Baylis had put on *A Midsummer Night's Dream* at the Old Vic; a rival producer came to see it, to Baylis's fury: 'I hate that man! He's pinched my Puck and now he'll pinch my Bottom!'[74] This made Ethel laugh, and so did this (in a letter to Vanessa): 'I've just thought of a good name for Professors of Composition at Music Colleges: . . . *Bore-Constrictors!* (Ha!Ha!)'[75]

Ethel's jovial, boisterous tone comes through loud and clear, but what also comes through is her entire lack of irony. This became a great problem. Virginia found herself having to explain *her* kind of rapidly written jokes – exaggerations, teases, caricatures, satires – to Ethel, who took umbrage at everything and took everything literally. Their difficulties were reflected in Ethel's nicknames for Virginia. She called her 'Aunt', but she also called her ' "4d for 9d" because she asks a lot and gives little,' and 'Frozen falcon' because 'someone who sat behind her at a concert said she looked like that – so still, so alert.'[76]

On their first meeting, in Tavistock Square, Virginia swallowed Ethel whole. Virginia was lying down, Ethel came 'tramping' up and 'bursting' in. She was wearing her three-cornered hat, and her suit. She immediately got out a notebook and started asking questions about the Pattles and talking about herself – her career, her musical quarrels, her country life, her love of games, her character – I am an egoist, I am a fighter. She at once established first name terms, as they were going upstairs to tea ('how sensible; how rapid'). They launched into comparisons between orchestration and novel-writing. Virginia noted all the comic physical details – the military air, the reddening cheeks, the vein in her forehead like a big worm, the flashing eyes. She started making up a balance sheet ('There is something fine & tried & experienced about her besides the rant & the riot & the egotism') and turning her into a 'character': ' "I am very strong" which she proved by talking till 7.30; then eating a biscuit & drinking a glass of vermouth & going off to a eat a supper of maccaroni [*sic*] when she got to Woking at 9.'[77] All the ingredients of her admiration for this 'fine old creature' were there, and she spent a good deal of time over the next few months, while Ethel fell vehemently and rapidly in love with her, considering the qualities of the 'game old bird'.[78] She enjoyed the 'fine & curious spectacle'.[79] She liked the attention, and she soon began to think of her as a source of succour, of 'strength and comfort', in the dark waking hours of the night.[80]

It was part of Ethel's quality that Virginia could immediately tell her what she thought of her. In May she went to a private concert where Ethel was conducting. She enjoyed the sight of Ethel at work, and the whole bustle and comedy of the concert. She compared, amusedly, her own 'furtive and sidelong' existence with the 'spontaneity and ruthlessness' of Ethel's career. And she liked trying to write about music, for which she had no language (it was something that interested her in *The Waves*). Altogether she was at her funniest and most charming:

> Now Ethel, please do something for me really generous; and let me contribute my share to the entertainment: Please do. I had a ticket (which I lost) and tea, a very good tea, and I want to write a cheque to give to the gentleman like an enraged frog playing cymbals in the background. He wants a new tie – it is all gone shiny on the left hand side. Please convey this to him with my blessing.[81]

A few weeks later Ethel organised a party for her and Leonard at 'Coign', her house in Woking. This had been carefully set up: Ethel wrote with eager expectation to Leonard, laying out her attractions – a golfing champion, an Italian duchess who had just been through 'Darkest Africa' on a mule ('She is a great go-er'), and one of her literary lions, Maurice Baring. 'But if Virginia is tired, all this *mise-en-scène* can be recreated later on.'[82] It came off, though, and for once Virginia wrote with equal enthusiasm about the occasion in her diary and in her thank-you letter to Ethel. It was like a Jane Austen outing, she thought, 'a real entertainment' with a plot. 'We all had to do this, to do that.' (The sentence suggests some latent resistance.) She liked Ethel's house (red and pink roses, white walls, old furniture) better than she expected. She liked Ethel more as a hostess than as a guest. 'I say Ethel', she wrote affectionately and enthusiastically, 'What a party! What a triumph!'[83] This was Ethel's summer. Virginia went back to Woking in July, talked a lot about herself, and revelled in Ethel's 'benignity and perspicacity'. 'You are, I believe, one of the kindest of women, one of the best balanced, with that maternal quality which of all others I need & adore.'[84]

This was all very good while it lasted. Ethel was the answer to Virginia's desire, as she moved towards her fifties, to try out new things. Should she 'curb' Ethel's letters, she asked herself? No, she should have the adventure, 'adventure wholly'.[85] She was, obviously, not going to fall in love with Ethel, but she could see it was a real relationship, not just a joke, or a self-limiting communication like her friendships with Tom Eliot or Hugh Walpole.

She began to lay claim to her with familiar names. To start with Ethel was a tawny rose, a general's daughter, a lion. As she began to turn into a nuisance, the pet names got more insulting. She was an uncastrated cat, a hedgehog, a rhinoceros. In one fine burst Virginia compared the traces of what has to be left out in letters to 'the finger print in salt of some huge pachydermatous quadruped which no private house could contain', a very good image (in a letter to Ethel, of course) of Ethel herself.[86] But though Virginia thought Ethel funny ('Ethel yesterday in a state of wonderment at her own genius. "Cant think how I happened," she says, putting on my hat, & bidding me observe what a nutshell it is on top of her gigantic brow')[87] she didn't like to see her being laughed at. Five years later, when she had gone through impossible scenes with Ethel, in the same diary entry that described her as a greedy guzzling old woman with an intolerable 'stab of a voice, emphasising, I dont know what, any longer', she still felt protective. She didn't enjoy seeing her in the artists' room at the Queen's Hall, after a concert where Beecham had conducted a piece of *The Wreckers*, being treated by the singers as 'poor old Ethel', 'a well known imposition upon conductors'.[88]

It would have been easy enough for Virginia to think 'poor old Ethel'. The letters she at once began to get from her were astounding. Sheets and sheets arrived by every post, crossed, crowded, rapid, without beginnings or endings. (Ethel took great exception when Virginia once signed a letter 'love'; she thought it false and conventional.) It was an assault on the citadel. Virginia, ringed round by now with the legend of her irony, her illnesses, her genius, her sternly protective husband, her sexual unavailability, her admirers, her witty, mocking group of close friends, might have seemed too daunting a prospect for a rapid invasion. Not to Ethel.

On the morning of Friday 2 May 1930, Virginia, who had just finished the first draft of *The Waves* ('And I think to myself as I walk down Southampton Row, "And I have given you a new book" '), was assuaging her post-partum feelings by tinkering with an idea for a piece on Fanny Burney, and was getting ready to go for a week selling the Press books to bookshops in Devon and Cornwall. But really she wanted at once to be 'back at The Waves' – which she would finally complete the following February.[89] Ethel, meanwhile, who had paid her a noisy visit the day before, sat in bed in her house in Woking and wrote Virginia a twelve-page love-letter. Virginia, at once making a joke of it to Vita, described it as a declaration of 'violent but platonic love'.

Ethel plunged into a long account of what it felt like to set out 'down the strange road which is called Virginia'. She had been in love with Virginia before she met her, she said, because of *A Room*, because of the sense of 'submergence and stupefaction' she had had on reading *To the Lighthouse*. She talked of her painful love for her own dead mother. She dwelt on Virginia's looks, the face on which 'life has written all that you have turned into the gold of your books, the tragedy, the fun, the divination'. She understood that Virginia was often 'worn out', she recognised her courage in illness, her 'need of silence'. She could see that the most powerful relationships were with Leonard and Vanessa. She wanted to know the details of her life – 'your studio, and the basement at 52'. She agonised over whether Virginia was really interested in her or thought her a joke. Were they really going to have a relationship, or was this strange road a cul-de-sac? And so it went on, pages of protestation and emotional analysis, demanding a response. Virginia replied evasively, affectionately, from Cornwall; to Vanessa she said she had written 'kindly and calmly' in response to Ethel's 'mitigated madness'. Her emotions were centred elsewhere, on this return to St Ives, in between her first and second writings of *The Waves*, and it was to Vita she expressed them: 'I saw my Lighthouse, and the gate of my home, through tears – thinking how my mother died at my age; or next year to it.'[90]

Ethel's love-letter set the tone. Over the next two or three years their meetings, their misunderstandings, their arguments, would be followed up with huge accounts of Ethel's feelings. She wrote a long letter on 'the last day of the old year' of 1930 (meanwhile Virginia was writing to Ethel, putting the same phrase on the top of *her* letter), telling Virginia that she had known at once that 'to have met you was to feel oneself in the grip of a force unlike anything I had met before'. Ethel called her difficult, silent, grim; she was afraid of her 'capacity for terrible emotion, when you are most calm & cool & Cambridge'. But she knew that Virginia was 'rather precariously carrying something that only she can win from life'. She, Ethel, knew all about 'the volcano you walk on'.[91] It was a typical mixture of insistent self-absorption, and a shrewd, penetrating assault on Virginia's 'essence'.

Virginia responded with pleasure, mockery, and wariness. She returned the analysis with interest; for a time they became each other's 'psychologists'. 'The trouble is, I'm so at sea with other people's feelings that I very often appear egotistical and unsympathetic because I'm afraid to discharge my sympathy when it is out of place and therefore offensive. That is I think a true note upon my own psychology.'[92] She did 'adore being liked',[93] as she told Ethel, and in return for this attention she provided her life-story. Ethel's self-absorption and enthusiasm inspired a new kind of autobiographical writing in Virginia's letters. These were connected to the lonely soliloquies in *The Waves*, to her lifelong argument about egotism, and to the political questions she was asking about the effects on women's lives and writing of anonymity, silence and repression. For all her absurdity, Ethel gave Virginia Woolf permission to speak out with greater directness about her own life. She wrote to Ethel in a different tone from the dazzling, fragile performance she put on for Vita, or from her edgy intimacy with Katherine. It resembled, more than anything, her youthful 'egotistical' confidences to Violet Dickinson.

'I only want to show off to women', she told Ethel, who agreed; 'women alone stir my imagination'.[94] She *was* showing off to Ethel, but she was also paying her the compliment of giving her the version of her autobiography which, over the years, she had made up for herself. It was a life-history not so much of facts but of patterns and connections. There were no new secrets, but there was a revealingly interwoven method of self-description. As she talked to Ethel about inheritance, childhood, her 'seducing half-brother',[95] becoming a writer, Cambridge, Bloomsbury, marriage, madness, illness, doctors, sexuality, friendship, society, fears, thoughts of suicide, pleasures, desires, hatred of causes and religion, she did not *explain* these stories, but implied that they were all interlinked.

Within a few days of their first meeting she was describing her 'nervous system' and telling the family story.[96] Inheritance – as ever – was treated as a joke, as a boast, and as a curse. Over the next months, in response to Ethel's challenges, she went back over her past, emphasising the 'nervous system' as the key to it all. She thought again about the mixed legacy of Cambridge asceticism. She defended, in response to Ethel's claim to greater frankness, the freedom of speech in the 'bi-sexual conversations' of her group.[97] (The debate about relative freedoms became a recurring one. Virginia admired Ethel's greater outspokenness, but she did not want to seem prim by comparison.) She described her group as having been sexually adventurous for their time, but set herself apart: 'My terror of real life has always kept me in a nunnery.'[98]

Ethel had immediate problems with Leonard, who found her, generally speaking, appalling, and wanted to keep her at bay. (His diary in the early 1930s frequently contains entries like this: 'Ethel Smyth tea. V. headache.'[99] And he would have nothing to do with publishing her work. On holiday in Greece in 1932, Virginia noted: 'L reading, not with sympathy, Ethel Smyth'.[100] Eventually Ethel found a way of liking Leonard – she told Ottoline he was like dried Australian apricots, quite nice when stewed up.[101] But she saw at once how the marriage worked. Virginia felt able to give her a remarkably undefensive, risky account of it. 'I married Leonard Woolf in 1912, I think, and almost immediately was ill for 3 years. Nevertheless we have nothing to complain of.'[102] 'And then I married, & then my brain went up in a shower of fireworks.' In the lava, she still found 'most of the things I write about'.[103]

A great deal of her autobiography for Ethel was about 'the exact poise' of her health,[104] the 'entirely false verdicts' she had had from Harley Street,[105] the perpetual dilemma 'about being too careful, about not being careful enough.'[106] She told her about her sleeplessness, her dreams, her suicide thoughts. In her description of her medical history she emphasised the value of madness, and the lifelong frustration in being a patient.

She wrote to Ethel openly and ruthlessly about her own prejudices (and these tough confessions have been held against her by posterity). Ethel's anti-Semitism allowed Virginia to admit how she had 'hated marrying a Jew', how much she could dislike her Jewish in-laws.[107] But she was outraged when Ethel suggested that if she had not married Leonard she might have had some religious feeling: 'My Jew has more religion in one toe nail – more human love, in one hair' than your sanctimonious Christians, she wrote furiously.[108]

More than in her letters to Vita, she told Ethel about her writing: how difficult *The Waves* was, how it connected back to *To the Lighthouse*,[109] how it felt to wake up with the next bit of a book inside her, and how appalling it was to be interrupted: 'I wake filled with a tremulous yet steady rapture, carry my pitcher full of lucid and deep water across the garden, and am forced to spill it all by – some one coming'.[110] She told her how she couldn't reread her own books, how she would 'shudder past them on the shelf as if they might bite me'.[111] In one long, remarkably open letter, she gave Ethel the whole history of her beginnings and her development as a writer in the 1910s and 1920s, connecting this story with her illness and her marriage, and explicitly presenting this narrative as notes towards the autobiography of a 'writer's life'.[112]

That letter of October 1930 was an impressive proof of how intimate they had become this year. Virginia took pleasure in exposing herself to Ethel: she confessed to her (*à propos* Ethel's being jealous of Vita) her jealousy, her vanity, her horror of intrusions. Though to herself and to others she mocked Ethel's love-making ('the old fires of Sapphism are blazing for the last time'),[113] she entered into serious debate with her on her attitude to same-sex love. 'Perversity', they agreed, was 'silly' (she was particularly hostile to 'buggers' and 'sodomites' at this time); she had hardly ever had physical feelings for a man; both Clive and Vita called her a 'fish'. But she understood jealousy very well, and the need for intimacy with different kinds of people – Vita, Ethel, Leonard, Vanessa. What stimulated her, what she wanted from other people, was not physical love (though physical contact could give her 'exquisite pleasure'), but 'illusion – to make the world dance'. 'There must be this fanning and drumming.' She got it from Leonard; but she got it as much, in another way, from walking about London. 'Where people mistake, as I think, is in perpetually narrowing and naming these immensely composite and wide flung passions – driving stakes through them, herding them between screens.' What was the line, for instance, 'between friendship and perversion'?[114] And she would tell Ethel, in terms at once physical and disembodied, what her mind felt like: 'My mind, this floating glove, or lily or whatever I called it, wants to drift off into some obscure pool, and be shaded by weeds.'[115]

Then in another mood she would resist Ethel's eagerness for analysis: 'I dont think I ever feel anything but the most ordinary emotions . . . By the way, why do you take so much interest in your own character? . . . Why are you so fiercely and savagely aware of what is to me a transient and fitful flame?'[116] 'In fact Virginia is so simple, so simple, so simple: just give her things to play with, like a child.'[117] So she moved in these letters between opening herself up and turning herself away. In a haunting passage, she told her what it felt like to listen to Ethel telling her life-story. As Ethel had sat by the fire talking, Virginia seemed to see her move between different ages, different incarnations. 'And thus pulped, my emotions became like so many strange guests: as if chapter after chapter of your life, panel after panel of your psychology were opening and shutting in the twilight.'[118] This strange image, like a biographer's dream, could be applied to her own 'opening and shutting' of herself to her new, old, friend. In spite of its comic side, this friendship is, all the same, a kind of love-story.

Their 'honeymoon' (as Ethel would wistfully recall it) culminated in a public performance of great significance in the history of twentieth-century feminism and in the story of Virginia Woolf's political thinking. Almost exactly a year after their first meeting, at 8 p.m. on Wednesday 21 January, 1931 (a few days before Virginia's forty-ninth birthday) Mrs Woolf and Dame Ethel appeared together on the platform of the 'London and National Society for Women's Service' (the LNSWS) at Marsham Street in Westminster. The hall they were in had recently been built and named in honour of the suffragette Millicent Fawcett; the society was later renamed the Fawcett Society. It worked to 'obtain economic equality for women by propaganda and non-party political work', and by disseminating information for women's education, economic opportunities, and 'freedom for women in pursuit of their work'. Its headquarters had a reading room, a library, a cheap restaurant and some accommodation. The 'Junior Council', which had invited Virginia and Ethel to speak on 'Music and Literature', 'consisted of some hundreds of younger professional and business women'. They usually had talks on subjects such as pacifism or 'Women's prospects in Commerce today', and debated motions like 'It is in the best interests of women to form associations for women only'.[119]

Virginia went because her old friend Pippa Strachey was the society's secretary; and among the 'distinguished guests to be asked' were 'Mrs Bell', 'T.S. Eliot', 'Mr and Mrs Harold Nicholson' (*sic*), 'Dame Laura Knight', 'Miss Cicely Hamilton' and 'Mr and Mrs Malcolm Sargent'. They had dinner with Pippa first, and then spoke to about 200 'well dressed, keen, & often beautiful young women', Ethel wearing her blue kimono and wig. Leonard came, 'slightly exacerbated', she thought ('an interesting observation if a true one').[120] He had other things on his mind – that very day his new employee, John Lehmann, had started work at the Press, and there was endless talk at Tavistock Square about the *New Statesman* amalgamating with the *Nation*. But he may not have enjoyed this feminist double act, rather different in tone from the talks she had given at Cambridge, two-and-a-half years before (when her companion was Vita) on 'Women and Fiction'. The book which came out of *those* talks was her passport to this Society, and she acknowledged this with a reference to *A Room of One's Own* in her speech: 'You have won rooms of your own in the house hitherto exclusively owned by men.'[121]

This speech would in its turn lead to two books, *Three Guineas* and *The Years*, which she would spend most of the next five years writing. Virginia Woolf did not foresee that long and painful process, but she knew at once she was on to something very important.

> I have this moment, while having my bath, conceived an entire new book – a sequel to a Room of Ones Own – about the sexual life of women: to be called Professions for Women perhaps – Lord how exciting! This sprang out of my paper to be read on Wednesday to Pippa's society.[122]

Looking back on this entry in May 1934, she noted in the margin: 'This is Here & Now I think'. *Here & Now* was the working title for *The Years*, *Professions for Women* was the working title for *Three Guineas*. So, in the evolution of these two books, financial independence for women, and women's 'sexual life', were indivisibly linked.

Of course this knot of associations went back to *A Room of One's Own*. It connected, too, to recent events, like the argument she had been having with Margaret Llewelyn Davies over how frank she could be in her essay on the Women's Co-Operative Guild, her struggles with Nelly, her intense resentment of old Mrs Woolf, and her suspense on coming to the end of *The*

Waves. But Ethel's influence was paramount, and in the speech Virginia paid a fulsome tribute to her as a role-model.[123]

> She is of the race of pioneers, of pathmakers. She has gone before and felled trees and blasted rocks and built bridges and thus made a way for those who come after her. [In her first thoughts for the speech she called her, less romantically, an armoured tank, which 'drew the enemy's fire'.] Thus we honour her not only as a musician and a writer . . . but also as a blaster of rocks and the maker of bridges . . . In my own profession . . . I have no doubt that I owe a great deal to some mute and inglorious Ethel Smyth.[124]

Ethel as heroic pioneer provided the opposing female figure (or alternative mother) to the Angel in the House. In the speech, Virginia argues that once she had become 'herself', the woman writer needed to develop an unchecked and unconscious imagination, but that she was still checked and hindered by male prurience and censorship. (And so the professional career of a woman writer was indivisibly linked to issues of sexuality.) She described herself as having won the first battle with the Angel, but not the other – 'telling the truth about my own experiences as a body'. She compared the 'ghosts' that still had to be fought in the haunted house of her own profession to the 'phantoms and obstacles' which might still dog the career paths of the women in the hall. And she listed these careers in a wonderfully unghostly twentieth-century roll-call of new opportunities for working women:

> He had thought that nature had meant women to be wives, mothers, housemaids, parlourmaids and cooks. Suddenly he discovers that nature – but he did not call it nature – he called it sin – had made them also doctors, civil servants, meteorologists, dental surgeons, librarians, solicitors' clerks, agricultural workers, analytical chemists, investigators of industrial psychology, barristers at law, makers of scientific models, accountants, hospital dieticians, political organisers, store keepers, artists, horticultural instructors, publicity managers, architects, insurance representatives, dealers in antiques, bankers, actuaries, managers of house property, court dress makers, aero engineers, history instructors, company directors, organisers of peace crusades, newspaper representatives, technical officers in the royal airships works – and so on.[125]

It was a strong speech, but somewhat damped down from its first draft. In her notes, she gave a more outspoken version of what she would have preferred not to have had to censor when she began writing for money and for male editors:

> For instance, about the war. If I were reviewing books now, I would say that this was a stupid and violent and hateful and idiotic and trifling and ignoble and mean display. I would say I am bored to death by war books. I detest the masculine point of view. I am bored by his heroism, virtue, and honour. I think the best these men can do is not to talk about themselves anymore.
> Of course, none of this would be printed.[126]

And in fact none of this was uttered. It would take several more years for this argument to get itself into print, in the dangerous and misunderstood pages of *Three Guineas* and *The Years*.

The contrast between Dame Ethel's and Mrs Woolf's speeches was striking. She herself thought Ethel's was much the more expressive, 'rollicking & direct', and that her own was too clogged, because of the 'sudden influx of ideas' which had rushed on her in her bath.[127] Vera Brittain (whose friend Winifred Holtby was beginning to write her book on Virginia Woolf) wrote the occasion up in the *Nation* as a 'delicious entertainment', a 'hilariously serious party' dominated by Dame Ethel's 'superb humour': 'Having expressed in her diary at the age of nine the ambition "to be made a Peeress in my own right because of music," she accepted her DBE with alacrity, "especially as it was all due to an absurd row in the Woking Golf Club." ' Brittain noted that both speakers attributed their success to the possession of a private income. Pippa Strachey, in her notes for the LNSWS, also contrasted them: 'Dame Ethel gave a witty description of the relentless and martial methods whereby she defeated obstacles arising in the course of her musical career. Virginia Woolf charmed them by her personality and account of her literary career.' A review in *The Woman's Leader* drew an effusive comparison, which misleadingly romanticised Virginia's contribution: 'Dame Ethel, grey-haired now, was the youngest there in her vivid alertness, still "ready for a fight" in any good cause. And Virginia Woolf? She "was with us, but not of us." Her eyes are on the stars, as though she listens to some far off song – but a song of which even an audience of modern and practical minded young women can catch an echo when Mrs Woolf speaks.'[128]

A Room of One's Own had looked back on the history of women's silencings and exclusions. Virginia Woolf's speech to the Society looked ahead to a later, twentieth-century world where women would be established in the professions, and began to ask what the implications of this would be for women's independence of mind. As the next decade darkened politically – the Labour Party crisis of this year, 1931, augured far worse things – her buoyant confident tone in this lecture would change. But its energy, so much to do with Ethel's gallant example, did point forward to a shift in Virginia Woolf's writing towards a fiercer and more abrasive manner.

In practical terms, the speech led to a consolidation of her relationship with the Society. She joined it in November 1932, and was committed to supporting it. In 1933 she tried to sell the manuscript of *A Room of One's Own* in order to give the LNSWS the proceeds, to Pippa Strachey's delight. Vita was enlisted, on one of her American tours, to find a purchaser. She nearly struck a deal with the Huntington Library in Pasadena, but – because of the recession – this came to nothing.[129] In 1938 she put her name to, and gave books (especially biographies) for their 'Millicent Fawcett Library appeal', and was warmly thanked by the Committee 'for her great kindness'[130] – activities which, among others in the late 1930s, give the lie to her reputation as a complete non-joiner.

The speech she gave in January 1931 went on and on reverberating in her mind. It was a pointer to which she kept returning. In July, the day after Leonard read and – to her great relief – praised *The Waves*, she wrote in a new notebook, 'Intro for A Knock on the Door? July 20 1931'. She wrote five pages of notes, but then at some point she cut these out of the notebook. She started to write *Flush* instead, and to work on the essays for the second *Common Reader*. But the speech and its meanings were knocking on the door of her mind; in September 1931 she broke off from revising her essay on the Elizabethans to make up 'a whole chapter of my Tap on the Door or whatever it is'.[131] The next page in this mutilated notebook reads '11 October 1932: "*The Pargiters*: An Essay based upon a paper read to the London and National Society for Women's Service".' In the next two or three weeks, she corrected this sub-title to read 'A Novel-Essay' and launched in the notebook on the book which would eventually become *The Years*. But the speech still stayed with her. In the middle of her struggle with *The Years*, in the spring of 1935, she was driven into a rage which set her off again on the idea of an essay about the situation of women in England – 'On Being Despised or whatever it is to be called'. She started to draft something called 'Professions', which began as if it were a speech given to a woman's society. This was set aside – *The Years* had to come first – and was at last written, as *Three Guineas*, in the summer of 1937, six-and-a-half years after the speech she had given on the platform with Ethel.[132]

It's clear from this how much Ethel Smyth influenced her imagination. The feminist material of *Three Guineas* and *The Years* had been central issues for many years. But Ethel's life-story confirmed and enriched that material. She might easily have been used as an example for *Three Guineas*, alongside the stories of Florence Nightingale or Sophia Jex-Blake or Mary Kingsley. And the manner of that essay owed something to Ethel, too. Its movements between satirical polemic and case-histories was not entirely unlike the more random, garrulous structure of Ethel's combative memoirs. The difference was (apart from the quality of the writing) that Ethel's case-histories were always her own, and Virginia Woolf's never were. Where Virginia would disguise her autobiography in her fiction, where she concealed in her literary criticism and her feminist histories the deep private sources of her own interests, Ethel, by contrast, let it all hang out, safety pins, underwear and all. Their argument over egotism was the key reason why the friendship could not be kept up at its initial pitch. Ethel's monomania and narcissism felt to Virginia like a grotesque parody of her own self-absorption. It was one of her kindnesses to Ethel that, at least at first, she helped her with her writing.[133] In doing so, she always suggested to Ethel that she should not air her own grievances, should not write letters to the papers complaining about her reviews, and should not boast. Her defence of her own indirection in these respects tellingly invoked Leonard as her censor and as the better judge, as though he and Ethel were two extremes between which she positioned herself:

I was wound to a pitch of fury the other day by a reviewers attack upon a friend of mine to do a thing I have never yet done – to write to the papers a long letter. 'Yes' said L. when I showed it to him; but itll do more harm than good; its all about yourself. When a fortnight later in cold blood I read it, there was 'I' as large, and ugly as could be; thanks to God, I didn't send it. You will say Oh but I must cite my case because there is no other. But my dear Ethel your case is that there are a thousand others. Leave your own case out of it; theirs will be far far far stronger . . . I didnt write 'A room' without considerable feeling even you will admit; I'm not cool on the subject. And I forced myself to keep my own figure fictitious; legendary. If had said, Look here am I uneducated, because my brothers used all the family funds which is the fact – Well theyd have said; she has an axe to grind; and no one would have taken me seriously, though I agree I should have had many more of the wrong kind of reader; who will read you and go away and rejoice in the personalities . . . because they prove once more how vain, how personal, so they will say, rubbing their hands with glee, women always are; I can hear them as I write.[134]

This much-quoted, revealing passage about how little she wanted to reveal herself, written in 1933, was an implicit commentary on their relationship, as well as a description of her own literary tactics as a feminist writer. The quarrel between them was partly that Ethel was always hot, and claimed that Virginia was always cool; here Virginia was claiming equal passion, but more restraint, strategy and good sense. And by 1933 Ethel's lack of restraint had become unbearable to her. As often happens when an intimacy goes sour, the very things she first liked her for were the same things she ended up disliking.

The spark for their first big row, about a year after they had first met, was Ethel's party after the first night of *The Prison* at the Queen's Hall, at the end of February 1931. Virginia was extremely depressed. It was just over two weeks since she had 'reeled over the last ten pages' of *The Waves*, and ended with the words 'O Death': a perilous, intense moment, making her 'almost afraid, remembering the voices that used to fly ahead'. In great emotion, she had sat thinking of Thoby, and wondering (as she had nine years before on finishing *Jacob's Room*)[135] whether she could write 'Julian Thoby Stephen 1881–1906' on the first page. (True to her policy of self-disguise, she did not.) That climax was instantly followed by the familiar 'back wash', and into the middle of this came Ethel's unsuccessful first night and her 'tawdry' party in Berkeley Square with the likes of Margot Asquith and the Countess of Rosebery, just the sort of posh set-up which reminded her of George's 'outrages'. She had a very violent reaction. She knew it was unfair (after all, it was Ethel's first night, and she might have been more tolerant). But she knew what she could not bear, and anyone who was close to her had to understand this:

> I see of course that it is morbid, that it is through this even to me inexplicable susceptibility to some impressions suddenly that I approach madness and that end of a drainpipe with a gibbering old man. But this is me; and you cant know me and merely brush this aside and disregard it as a fit of temper.[136]

Even in her irrational irritation, she was open and honest. And she made it brutally clear that in this state of mind, only Leonard could help her. 'It would be amusing to see how far you can make out, with your insight' (she wrote cruelly to Ethel on the aftermath of the party) 'the various states of mind which led me, on coming home, to say to L: – "If you weren't here, I should kill myself – so much do I suffer." '[137] Ethel was aghast. But the breach was made, and from now on her complaints about Ethel's egotism would increase. Unfortunately Ethel had little success with *The Prison*, and in May had a fight with Adrian Boult, who refused to conduct it for the

BBC. She came straight round to Virginia to tell her all about it. Virginia described the scene, possibly without much exaggeration, to Vanessa:

> She then went through, with the minuteness and ingenuity of a maniac, the whole history of her persecution for the past 50 years; brought out old letters and documents and read them aloud, beat on my chair with her fists; made me listen, and answer, and agree at every moment; and finally I had to shout that I had such a headache that unless she stopped talking I should burst into flames and be combusted.[138]

Ethel then sent Virginia a protest she had written for the *New Statesman* about her bad treatment; Virginia criticised it robustly, comparing (somewhat insensitively) her own decision to be a self-publishing author with Ethel's failure to 'furnish up some orchestra and run things on your own'. She said that Ethel was a big hoary-skinned Cornish pig and that she was her scratching-post. Not surprisingly, Ethel wrote a furious and hurt reply, which Virginia described as Ethel's indignity 'reaching its sordid and ridiculous climax'. She annotated her 'sentimental & hysterical' sheets and sent them back to her, following this with a careful and intimate letter explaining how intolerable she found Ethel's demands on her sympathy.

> The same thing has happened to me twice before – once with my father whom I adored. But then, he had had a very hard life with his deafness, my mother's death, and his sense of being, as a philosopher, a failure. Thus he demanded and needed perpetual sympathy and was apt to fly into violent rages and despairs in what we thought a most unreasonable way if anyone spoke a careless word about his work, or his life. Hence by degrees one felt that one had always to pick and choose what one said to him . . . And I think this queered the pitch and made us much more formal and cautious with him than was right. And it happened again with a woman who was in love with me, and used to write me reams about not understanding her life and her misunderstood virtues (for she thought herself the greatest psychologist in England) and so we parted.[139]

This woman was Ethel, and she was being warned: the letter is truthful and implacable. Virginia will not – she *cannot*, since and because of her childhood – make herself into a repository for, or a servant to, anyone else's emotions, except, when the need arises, Vanessa's or Leonard's. That was the rule: 'This is me.'

They did not 'part', but the tone of the relationship changed. Virginia continued to confide in her, but she became more ironical and dry with her. She mocked Ethel for thinking that she knew her well. She found her looks, her manners, her greedy eating, increasingly revolting. She greatly objected to her religious feelings. She became irritated when Ethel attempted to simplify 'the celebrated sensibility of my nervous system' to merely physiological sources – liver trouble, perhaps, to be solved by calomel – and eventually made a rule that they would no longer discuss her health.[140] She objected to Ethel's appropriating her – relaying compliments, threatening to publish her letters, discussing her with Vita or Vanessa. In the summer of 1932, Ethel criticised her, with inimitable tactlessness, for seeing too many 'admirers' and 'aspirants for interviews'. Since Virginia spent so much time – which could have been writing time – responding to the demands of friends who could not be put off, this was a red rag. The argument erupted into one of the scenes which Virginia found 'harassing and unnerving and odious to an extent that I dont think you realise'.[141] The trouble was that, essentially, Ethel, like Leslie Stephen (and like Nelly Boxall) *enjoyed* scenes. Yet she always protested that she hated them, that she did not want to make demands, that she understood from the beginning that 'Its not Virginia's job to be like other people in friendship – or probably in any other relation.' In her diary for 1933, Ethel called Virginia vain, arrogant, childlike, moody, violent, courageous, and impossible to be close to: 'The fact is, you take what you can get out of V.'[142]

In time, Virginia would use Leonard as a watchdog to keep a plaintive Ethel at bay. They gave up their early attempts to understand each other's work (a more sympathetic literary confidante, Elizabeth Bowen, was soon to appear). Though Ethel wrote stunned, effusive letters about *The Waves*, she did not really like it, finding it cold and inhuman; and she confided in Vanessa that she couldn't stand *Flush*. (*Three Guineas* would be much more to her taste.) There were no new works for Virginia to listen to after *The Prison*: it was the sadness of Ethel's old age that her deafness stopped her writing. Virginia tried to like *The Wreckers* when she heard it (with Vita) at its revival in October 1931 ('vigorous & even beautiful; & active & absurd & extreme; & youthful: as if some song in her had tried to issue & been choked'.)[143] But when she heard the second act again at the Queen's Hall in 1935, she hated the concert ('How long how little music in it that I enjoyed!').[144] and she did not go to the revival at Sadler's Wells in 1939.[145] In November 1933, when Ethel conducted her 'March of the Women' at Central Hall, Westminster (where Rebecca West was speaking on the right of married women to earn), Virginia was very glad to 'sleep over the fire', reading, 'alone thank God'.[146]

By 1935 Virginia felt they had settled into a comfortable friendship:

It is now precisely four years since you caught me a cuff over the head for telling you – I forget what, but I remember falling flat on the drawing room floor – aint it odd how free and easy we are together.[147]

She still listened to Ethel's troubles (for instance over her income tax returns, which were in a terrible mess), made suggestions for her writing, admired her courage, and flared up at her provocations. But Ethel wrote to Vanessa in 1934 that she never saw Virginia 'nowadays' – 'I rather think she's through with me'[148] – and sadly to Virginia in 1937: 'I want you to know that in my opinion you have got all you want, or can do with from me – that in a way our friendship has run dry.'[149] All the same, she told Henry Wood, after Virginia's death, that 'she was the centre of the one-horse life I have led since music left me in the lurch'.[150] In the end Ethel's emotions moved on, and she turned Virginia into a confidante for her latest 'passionettes'. Virginia was delighted to hear in 1939 that Ethel had now fallen in love with her eighty-one-year-old neighbour, and was lamenting what a pity it was they hadn't met ten years before, when Ethel was only seventy.[151]

Young Poets

Virginia Woolf took Ethel seriously. But she also faced away from her and her past towards the future, towards 'new writing' and 'young poets'. She was as interested in the next generation of writers in their twenties as she was in old Ethel. Her range of sympathies was wide, and she was afraid of being fixed in a circumscribed middle age. Fear, as usual in her case, became a form of courage. In 1931 she was in the last and difficult stages of *The Waves*, the novel which raised in its most pure and acute form one problem of her work: could universal experience be expressed by voices so bound by their class? (She had originally planned to include proletarian voices, but this was abandoned in the revising of the novel.)[1] She was thinking about her range. In June, she and Leonard had ideas of a trip to America (they never did go, though she liked imagining a grotesque 'America which I have never seen') and she instantly fantasised a whole novel of a voyage round the world in the manner of *Orlando*. In July, Ottoline Morrell dropped in after dinner to Tavistock Square to find Leonard and Virginia, Mary Hutchinson, John Lehmann and Stephen Tomlin (who was sculpting Virginia's head, much to her dislike) all sitting around talking about being 'in the cage'. Both Ottoline and Virginia were struck by Mary's furious restlessness ('Why this hedge of telephone calls daily? Why not expose a different self?').[2] Ottoline reported, without sympathy, on Leonard's grim realism ('he was doomed every day for the last 30 years and for the next 30 to go down to his office at 9.30 and walk round the square with his dog') and his fury at feeling he had lost his power of action. Virginia, she noted, did not want change. For her it was a matter of 'mood': one could make one's changes internally. Ottoline found the conversation disagreeable. Leonard, she thought, was only interested in money, Mary only in sex. And she was indignant when 'guffaws of laughter' greeted the idea that religion might help. She went away thinking that Leonard and Virginia were growing to look alike: 'Narrow faces and hard eyes. No humour and love.'[3]

To be in the cage but not to feel caged,[4] meant to respond adventurously to new challenges. The very word 'new' was the signature-tune of the writers who were now coming through the door of Tavistock Square and changing the tone of the Hogarth Press. It was essential for her to be in touch with their thoughts. The challenge was embodied for her most of all in three young men: in her nephew Julian, in his great friend at Cambridge John Lehmann, and in Lehmann's friend Stephen Spender.

In the diary entry which first mentions John Lehmann's arrival, on 10 January 1931, she was feeling sorry for her middle-aged generation. She was reading Dante as a counterforce to the painful hard work of revising *The Waves*. She was preparing to give her lecture, 'Professions for Women', and for a comparison she had been looking back at an earlier talk, given in 1927, on 'Poetry and Fiction', which she found rather stirring. In 'Poetry and Fiction' she had discussed what seemed to her the awkward self-consciousness of contemporary poetry, how it has to represent the 'sceptical and testing spirit' of modern life, and how the writer is on edge because of the conditions of discord and separation, which she summed up in the image of a city street:

> The long avenue of brick is cut up into boxes, each of which is inhabited by a different human being who has put locks on his doors and bolts on his windows to insure some privacy, yet is linked to his fellows by wires which pass overhead, by waves of sound which pour through the roof and speak aloud to him of battles and murders and strikes and revolutions all over the world. And if we go in and talk to him we shall find that he is a wary, secretive, suspicious animal, extremely self-conscious, extremely careful not to give himself away.[5]

Not conditions propitious – in her view – either for lyric or epic poetry. This modern tension between a levelling sameness and a self-conscious solipsism (which would be one of the themes of *The Years*) suggested the need for a fictional prose which would take on some of the attributes of poetry, which would give 'the relation of the mind to general ideas and its soliloquy in solitude'. That was what she had tried to do in the novel she was now finishing. And in the writing of *The Waves*, as all her working notes show, she had been continually thinking about the relationship between poetry and fiction.[6]

She had already been having this debate with Julian, and it moved into a more self-conscious phase with the arrival of John Lehmann. 'A tight aquiline boy, pink, with the adorable curls of youth; yes, but persistent, sharp.' He might 'do', she thought. They were going to publish his poems (Dadie, who knew him well at Cambridge, had recommended them) and were offering him a job at the Press, which had begun to be too much of a burden.[7] Rather like the argument about sacking Nelly, their feeling that the Press was getting too much for them, and their fantasies of shedding it, kept recurring. Then they would have a new plan which made it seem enjoyable again. John Lehmann was going to buy three-quarters of the business with £5,000, and they would let him run it. But he found he could not raise the money. So, though he had been warned, by Julian and by Dadie, what the problems could be in working for Leonard, he agreed to become a manager for a year's probationary period, with the option of buying into a partnership later on.[8]

This sensitive, ambitious blond was a trickier recruit than any of his predecessors. More than Dadie Rylands or Angus Davidson or the boy Richard Kennedy, he was not going to be fobbed off with tying up parcels or setting type. He came as a proud, gifted young writer, an introducer of new work, a fellow-reader, and, prospectively, the Press's partner-manager. For Leonard, this meant that his publisher's judgement was to be questioned. For Virginia, it meant that for the first time since they founded the Press, there was someone other than Leonard reading her work before publication. This could spell trouble: what if the young John Lehmann were *not* to like her next book? She had no reason to bow to his judgement, but she would certainly mind it. At first all went well: in September, convinced that it was 'a failure', she gave him *The Waves* to read in great anxiety, and was generously delighted with his intelligent response: 'You've been so perceptive, and gone so much further and deeper in understanding my drift than I thought possible that I'm immensely relieved.'[9]

She was inclined to like him: not only was he Julian's best friend, but he was an appealing young man who hero-worshipped her. (When he came to know her better, and became more certain of his own qualities, adulation changed to a more critical friendship.) His father had edited *Punch*; two of his sisters were making names for themselves, one as an actress and the other as a novelist. Rosamond Lehmann had made a hit, at twenty-five, with her first novel: Virginia described John to Molly MacCarthy, before she had met him, as 'brother of Dusty Answer'.[10] Virginia had greeted her second, *A Note in Music*, with competitive respect, in August 1930: 'She has a clear hard mind, beating up now & again to poetry; but I am as usual appalled by the machinery of fiction: its much work for little result . . . But she has all the gifts (I suppose) that I lack; can give story & development & character & so on.'[11] She liked Rosamond when she got to know her, and in the end, when the relationship with John inevitably soured, preferred her to him ('Not so much ego in her composition').[12] And Rosamond Lehmann always greatly admired her. But they did not become close.

It was John Lehmann's group of male peers who challenged her. This seems ironic. Having grown up measuring herself against one generation of male thinkers – Thoby, Desmond, Lytton, Rupert Brooke, Roger – and then having felt the pressure of comparison with writers such as Bennett and Wells, she now, at the height of her fame and confidence, again felt threatened by a group of younger male writers.

Lehmann was one of several, who were rushing out of public school and Oxbridge into the literary scene and the publishing houses.[13] They were to dominate British culture in the next decades, and they had all started very young. John had been at Eton with a talented group who included Cyril Connolly, Anthony Powell, Harold Acton, Eddy Playfair, Brian Howard and Alan Clutton-Brook. At Cambridge in the late 1920s, with Julian, he was one of a number of young poets and critics (influenced by I.A. Richards and William Empson) who set up new little magazines such as *The Venture* and who debated with serious intensity what directions modern writing should take. And, at Oxford, Auden, Spender, Day Lewis and MacNeice were forging the tone of 'Thirties poetry'.[14] Virginia Woolf did not get to know Auden or MacNeice (Leonard turned down MacNeice for the Press in 1932) but the Press published Day Lewis, and she became friendly with Spender through John and Rosamond Lehmann. Spender and Lehmann in turn introduced Isherwood to the Woolfs. They did not become intimate, but she was vividly struck by him.

The mood of many of these young writers, though they differed individually, was leftist, groupy, anti-patriarchal, and highly politicised. They needed to reject what the last lot had done (Bloomsbury, Modernism, Eliot) in favour of what they thought of as urgent hard-hitting realism (pylons, industry, the workers, Spain). They all wanted to pick a fight with their predecessors. Julian Bell, for instance, disparaged Eliot's work. They were boys excited by ideas of heroism, action and leadership. This was their theme tune, struck by Stephen Spender in *New Signatures*, the key anthology, published by the Hogarth Press in 1932:

> Oh young men oh young comrades
> It is too late now to stay in those houses
> your fathers built[15]

They were extremely disillusioned by British politics (the crisis of 1931, Ramsay Macdonald's betrayal of the Labour Party, ignited or confirmed this mood). They all wanted to encourage or be involved with working-class writing (John Lehmann and Leonard Woolf saw eye-to-eye on this, at least, at the Press, and Lehmann would always say that Leonard sent him further leftwards on his journey). And they were all debating the rival claims of poetry and prose as 'the' art form for the decade.

There are clear signs of this debate everywhere in Virginia Woolf's correspondence with these young men. Her letters to Julian are full of their argument about the right form for the times. When Julian's first book of poems, *Winter Movement*, was published in 1930, he borrowed a phrase from his aunt's work when he outlined his credo on poetry to John Lehmann: 'I do believe that poetry must interest the common reader by talking about human beings and about events that he is acquainted with . . . I believe we must abandon everything fantastic, distant and otherworldly . . . concentrate on the natural and the reasonable.'[16] But if poetry was to be prosaic, why not write prose? His aunt would advise against it – here, in 1936, at the worst point of her struggle with *The Years*:

> I don't see why you should worry yourself to write a novel. It's such a long gradual cold handed business. What I wish is that you'd invent some medium that's half poetry half play half novel. (Three halves, I see; well, you must correct my arithmetic.) I think there ought to be a scrambling together of mediums now.[17]

A letter to her from Stephen Spender, written in Vienna in 1934, while he is writing a long poem, suggests the same kind of continuing debate:

> I think really I agree with you that prose must be far more difficult as a medium to control than verse. But it seems to me partly a question of subject matter. One reason why poetry can't ever die or be unwanted is that certain generalisations can only be made in poetry . . . Now I write this, I remember that your books – the ones I most like – seem to me to be poetry. Still, poetry is what I want to do, if I can only break away from the dead rut of most contemporary stuff.[18]

It was exciting for an ambitious young poet in his twenties to be able to write like this to Virginia Woolf. (Spender vividly recalled her reading a novel of his for the Press in 1931, and being told to 'scrap it'; it suggested to him how much she had 'scrapped' of her own work.) To these young men, she was both an inspiration and a challenge. They had all read her (and Strachey, and Forster, and Eliot) at school and at college. John Lehmann had read Strachey as a schoolboy and had for years thought of Virginia Woolf's novels as expressing beyond any other books 'the sensibility of our age'.[19] And there were other sons and friends of 'Bloomsbury', at Oxford and at Cambridge, cutting their teeth on her work. Though (according to John Lehmann) Julian Bell liked to speak to his Cambridge peers with the borrowed authority of Bloomsbury, he was also 'made uneasy' by his Aunt Virginia's work.[20] Cyril Connolly was never an admirer, nor she of him. But a little later at Oxford, in the early 1930s, there were a group of young men who were strongly under her influence: Mary Hutchinson's son Jeremy, Vita's son Ben Nicolson, Philip Toynbee, Kenneth Clark. Toynbee remembered how this group (all living in Beaumont Street) reacted to her:

> Certainly Beaumont Street admired Bloomsbury, even if they didn't consciously model themselves on the conversation and behaviour of the older group. Virginia Woolf was their conception of what a writer should be, and art was largely seen through the eyes of Roger Fry. The difference . . . is that the early, left-wing Auden was also a hero; Beaumont Street was heavily touched by the politics which Bloomsbury had rejected.[21]

The opposition he accepts there would surface, at the time of the next war, in a vehement correspondence between Benedict Nicolson and Virginia Woolf on the subject of Bloomsbury's political values, where she took care to distinguish herself from anyone else in the 'group'.

'Bloomsbury', we're told, disliked this new Oxford generation as being 'better travelled, more worldly, more flamboyant, more pleasure-loving and more honestly (and successfully) snobbish than the Bloomsbury Group'.[22] Stephen Spender, looking back, assumed that to 'Bloomsbury' 'there was something barbarous about our generation' – comparing their 'watered-down aristocracy' with his lot proclaiming the end of 'bourgeois civilisation'. Virginia Woolf, he said, 'objected to the way in which our writing was put to the service of our views'.[23]

But her response was more complex than these one-sided retrospects imply. In fact she was extraordinarily eager to join in their debates, and open to the influence of their ideas. But she was irritated by them too. She was acutely conscious of their youth, of their criticisms of her 'group', and of their being, mostly, homosexual. Around this time, at the start of the 1930s, she is particularly derisive about 'buggers'. At a dinner at Raymond Mortimer's in April 1930 with Forster and Strachey, when all the men were avidly discussing various youthful beauties (including the decorative young aesthete/dilettante Stephen Tennant, who was going to try to be friends with her), she had 'a tinkling, private, giggling impression. As if I had gone into a men's urinal'.[24] She told Ethel that she found such 'Buggery Poke' parties trivial and silly, and was always arguing this with her 'sodomite' friends like Eddy Sackville-West.[25] The truth is, 'I cant take Buggerage seriously', she told Clive, referring to Eddy. She wrote humorously to Quentin in December 1933, describing Stephen Spender affectionately but tartly ('he talks incessantly and will pan out in years to come a prodigious bore. But he's a nice poetic youth; big nosed, bright eyed, like a giant thrush. The worst of being a poet is one must be a genius . . . He is married to a Sergeant in the Guards'). She went on to mock the 'Lilies of the Valley' in Maida Vale – Spender, Auden, Plomer, Ackerley, with their working-class lovers: 'Why this passion for the porter, the policeman and the bootmaker?'[26]

This bemused distaste for rough trade and for high camp is one of the difficult contradictions in Virginia Woolf. She had no moral prejudices against homosexuality, she opposed all forms of censorship, she was herself more erotically drawn to women than to men. Two of her dearest friends, Duncan Grant and Lytton Strachey, were queer. She defined her generation's move away from Victorianism by their decision to talk openly about same-sex love. And she took great pleasure, with her homosexual friends, in gossip – that gay art which corresponded so closely with her own desire to make pointed and minute analyses of 'what kinds of people there are to be found in one's world'.[27] But she felt excluded by the cult of silly effeminacy, of queeny camp, which characterised the gay circles she knew. She couldn't step outside her historical moment and perceive the value of feminisation for homosexuals who censored themselves in their public lives, who needed to act effeminate to be accepted in gay circles, and for whom straight, butch, working-class males had the double attraction of danger and of virile authenticity.[28] Like Simone de Beauvoir twenty years later, who spoke with Woolfian disgust about the fluttering pansies she knew, the feminist in her deplored the fact that gay men seemed to want to be women.[29] And she must also have felt that homosexuality was, for the next generation of writers, an exclusive passport for literary success.

John Lehmann linked the Hogarth Press more closely to the new young homosexual writers, though that link was partly in place before his arrival. Contrary to the Woolfs' hopes, his presence seemed to make for more rather than less work. Virginia wrote to Clive:

> Young Mr Lehmann is now installed in the back room behind the W.C. at a small table with a plant which Leonard has given him on the window sill. Far from tending the Press and slipping the burden from our shoulders, we are of course rushed into all sorts of fresh projects . . .[30]

Lehmann would vividly remember those work-quarters:

> The basement was cold and draughty and ramshackle. My own office, as apprentice manager, was a small back room that had once been a pantry and cupboard room – the cupboards were piled high with the dusty files of the activities of the Press ever since it had started in 1917.[31]

He came at a time when the Press was very busy. Leonard's commitment to publishing books by and about the British working classes had led to the discovery of the writer John Hampson (who had been down and out, in prison and in a variety of low-grade jobs, before he became known as a writer) whose novel *Saturday Night at the Greyhound* – a vivid account of life in the industrial Midlands – they published in February 1931. (They turned down his first, openly homosexual novel, though Virginia thought that the best, and they published only one more of his books.)[32] They were publishing Day Lewis's poems and Plomer's poems and novels (one, *The Case is Altered*, based on a horrible murder at his lodgings, which had affected Virginia when he described it to her). (After six titles with the Press, Plomer went to Jonathan Cape: but they stayed friends.) Leonard's publications on British Imperial rule and his political pamphlets continued; so did the International Psychoanalytical Library. Vita was still making money for them with *All Passion Spent* and *Family History* – not novels which Virginia admired. They published a new translation of Rilke's poems by Vita and Eddy Sackville-West. And their own books – Leonard's *After the Deluge*, Virginia's *The Waves*, *The Common Reader* and *Flush* – dominated their list between 1931 and 1933.

Their promotion of women writers was erratic. They had made a bad mistake in turning down Ivy Compton-Burnett in 1929, much to Eddy Sackville-West's and Raymond Mortimer's disgust. ('Yes, I agree that we ought to have done *Brothers and Sisters*,' she acknowledged to Eddy. 'But I'd rather have done Eliot's poems and even Katherine Mansfield's Prelude – There's something bleached about Miss Compton Burnett: like hair which has never had any colour in it.')[33] An even more peculiar decision was her patronage of a sixteen-year-old girl poet called Joan Easdale, who wrote naïve, mystical verses, and whom she described to Hugh Walpole as 'a country flapper, living in Kent, & might be from behind a counter'.[34] A more successful promotion was that of Julia Strachey, the flamboyant and temperamental niece of Lytton, married to Stephen Tomlin, close friend of Carrington and Frances Marshall – whose novella, *Cheerful Weather for the Wedding*, an eccentric and witty story of a single difficult day at a wedding in Dorset, shows us what Virginia Woolf's tastes were in contemporary women's fiction. Another younger woman in whom Virginia showed an interest was Lyn Irvine, a Girton graduate in her early thirties who edited an anthology for the Press and later founded her own magazine, the *Monologue*. But later she was found to have 'no great range poor Lyn'.[35]

John Lehmann built on the interests already in place at the Press – anti-imperialist, working-class or socialist political writings, experimental poetry, unconventional fiction. Stephen Spender had put him in touch with a writer who was to become his very close friend, Christopher Isherwood, and he persuaded the Woolfs to publish Isherwood's second novel, *The Memorial*, in 1932, which to Lehmann seemed to convey 'an exact feeling for the deeper mood of our generation with its delayed war-shock and conviction of the futility of the old pattern of social life and convention'.[36] At the same time he launched two connected projects, one a series of 'Hogarth Letters', the other an anthology of new poets called *New Signatures*, edited by Michael Roberts, which was intended to trace 'a pattern, between a number of young and recently published poets, which had escaped notice before, which was in fact becoming clearer, under the gathering winds of the epoch, all the time'.[37] These poets included Julian Bell, who agreed to contribute only after much persuasion from Lehmann, as he didn't want to be seen to 'belong' with the others, and who provided a long Augustan satire on the British establishment and plea for disarmament, called 'Arms and the Man'.[38] Others were William Empson, Day Lewis, Auden (who had published his *Poems* in 1930), Spender, Richard Eberhart, Lehmann himself, A.S.J. Tessimond and William Plomer. (Some of the same writers would contribute to the next anthology in 1933, *New Country*, which Roberts prefaced with a plea for the intellectual and the novelist to combine with the working classes towards the common aim of abolishing the class structure and overthrowing the capitalist system.) *New Signatures*, with its preface advertising a poetry 'in which imagery taken from contemporary life consistently appeared as the natural and spontaneous expression of the poet's thought and feeling', came to be seen as the 'first attempt to define the Auden Generation', a landmark volume for the poetry of the 1930s, presenting what Spender would describe as a near-unanimous vision of 'a society coming to an end of revolutionary change'.[39] Spender's lines summed up its young men's mood of revolt, disillusion, and fear of what was to come:

Who live under the shadow of a war
What can I do that matters?

For Virginia Woolf, Lehmann's two projects were connected, and they brought together all her feelings about him and about Julian. All this was stirred together in her Hogarth 'Letter to a Young Poet' in 1932. It was the public version of the correspondence she was having with 'young poets', especially Julian, and it raised many of the issues which would press on her mind in the next decade.

The summer the 'Hogarth Letters' were planned was a summer of 'violent political argument'.[40] The events of 1931 have been called 'the watershed of English history between the wars'.[41] The world-wide

616

Depression fuelled the crisis in Britain. In August, Ramsay Macdonald's Labour Government had broken up, in the wake of the General Strike and the crash in America. There was imminent danger of galloping inflation, and the economic crisis had the bankers demanding a restoration of confidence. Nine members of Macdonald's Cabinet couldn't stomach the recipe, which was to reduce unemployment benefits and establish a Means Test, in order to achieve a 'balanced budget'. (Oswald Mosley had resigned, in May 1930, over Labour's unemployment policy, and formed his New Party in February 1931. Harold Nicolson had joined him, and was editing Mosley's magazine, *Action*.) Macdonald, trying to prevent Labour's total collapse, and the Liberal-Conservative coalition that would follow, formed a National Government on 24 August, which was at once seen, in left-wing circles, as a betrayal of the Labour movement (and which did cut the unemployment benefit savagely in the September budget.) Lehmann recalled 'the consternation and gloom that settled on all our circle at the collapse of the Labour Government'.[42] John Strachey's influential Marxist analysis, *The Coming Struggle for Power* (1932) said that the 1931 crisis had exposed Macdonald as 'an ordinary capitalist politician' whose mind worked in the same way as 'the average occupant of, say, a first class carriage in a suburban train, travelling up to business'. That attack on British capitalist complacency was a central theme in the 'Hogarth Letters'.

Leonard was much involved, of course, with these deep divisions in the Labour movement. That year saw the founding of the *Political Quarterly*, of which Leonard became co-editor with W.A. Robson, and in which he would air his views, particularly on foreign policy, the League of Nations, and the need for international disarmament, throughout the 1930s and 1940s. He was caught up, from now on, in what he called 'the intelligent man's way to prevent war', in his activities as secretary of the Advisory Committee on International Questions, through his connection with Kingsley Martin, the new editor of the *New Statesman*, through the *Political Quarterly* and in his use of the Press as an outlet for anti-imperialist, pro-disarmament pamphlets and books. For a settled pessimist and sceptic like Leonard, 1931 confirmed all his worst opinions of the human race, and all his convictions that the intellectual's job was to criticise the Establishment. The League, in which he placed so much faith, was also in trouble at this time. In 1930 and 1931 there was a concerted 'Home and Empire' campaign in the right-wing press, Beaverbrook's *Daily Express* and Rothermere's *Daily Mail*. What Robert Cecil, in his 'Hogarth Letter' on the League, called 'the great 100 per cent British campaign' for independence from Europe (not unlike the Conservative anti-Europe campaign in the 1990s) represented one current aspect of British insularity and chauvinism.

Another side was expressed by Winston Churchill's hostility to disarmament and to Indian nationalism. In opposition to this old spirit of empire, the League stood for anti-imperialism, conciliation and internationalism, and had attracted many left-wing thinkers of the intellectual middle classes. Leonard had described the League's ideals eloquently in 1928, in *Imperialism and Civilization*:

> The League stands for a synthesis instead of a conflict of civilizations, for tolerance and co-operation, for an international society of interrelated rather than warring parts, for the adjustment of relations and the settlement of international disputes by discussion, compromise, and adjudication.[43]

This was the Cambridge language of rational liberal optimism, opposed to tyranny and defending intellectual tolerance, and believing in the possibility of maintaining a free civilisation in the jungle of the modern political world. It's echoed later in Forster's essay of 1939, 'What I Believe' (published as one of the Hogarth Press 'Sixpenny Pamphlets'), with its modest, temperate appeals to 'the holiness of the heart's affections' and its vision of an 'aristocracy of the sensitive, the considerate and the plucky' signalling to each other like little lights in the darkness – a sort of flickering League of Souls.

But this language was under threat. Japan's invasion of Manchuria in September 1931 exposed the ineffectuality of the League, and behind that event was the growing power of Fascism – not amenable, it was rapidly becoming apparent, to words like 'tolerance and co-operation'. The voice of the 'Hogarth Letters' expressed a feeling about culture which was individualist, middle-class, middle-aged, Francophile, anti-war, anti-empire, and which used words like taste, civilisation, beauty and self-discovery without embarrassment. It mixed satires on British imperialism, xenophobia, and insularity with attacks on Hitler and accounts of anti-Semitism in Britain. It was in some ways, by now, a voice of the past. In spite of John Lehmann's involvement, the Letters were not part of the 'Thirties' as represented by *New Signatures*, or by *New Writing* or *New Country* or *New Verse* or the *Left Review* or the Group Theatre or *Tribune* or the Left Book Club. They were (as Harold Nicolson said) 'epistles in which the generation of 1910 confronts the generation of 1932'.

Yet all the contributors were keenly aware of the 'backwash'[44] of political events. The 'Hogarth Letters' were as much involved with the politics of the moment as with the future of British culture. Looking back in the 1950s,

Lehmann felt that the Letters encapsulated 'the moods, the pleasures and the preoccupations of the early thirties'.[45]

Virginia's own letter was a continuation of the discussion she was having with John Lehmann and, especially, with Julian, about politics, art and poetry. She leapt at his suggestion at the same time that she thanked him for liking *The Waves*:

> I think your idea of a Letter most brilliant – To a Young Poet? because I'm seething with immature and ill considered and wild and annoying ideas about prose and poetry. So lend me your name . . . and then I'll pour forth all I can think of about you young, and we old, and novels – how damned they are – and poetry, how dead. But I must take a look into the subject, and you must reply, 'To an old novelist' – I must read Auden, whom I've not read, and Spender . . . The whole subject is crying out for letters – flocks, volleys, of them, from every side. Why not get Spender and Auden and Day Lewis to join in?[46]

In her 'Hogarth Letter', she argued that at a time when the attractions of escapism, solipsism and nostalgia were so strongly felt, it was the writer's job to find 'the right relationship . . . between the self that you know and the world outside', even with 'a thousand voices prophesying despair'. But what happens to the writer's privacy, sensuality, lyricism, dreams – to 'beauty' – when the shocks and jolts of political reality, social conditions, or scientific facts are faced up to? The question could not be avoided or by-passed. She knew all about the lure of nostalgia or escapism. But 'nekrophily induces slumber': it's not good enough to hanker after the great dead. Even so, the wary exploration she makes of modern poetry in the Letter (which noticeably ignores Auden) is an uncomfortable one. The examples she took from Lehmann, Spender and Day Lewis of the inclusion of the 'actual' and 'colloquial' in modern poetry are not the best she might have chosen. Her irritation with their extreme youthfulness shows up, too, in her recommendation to her young poet not to publish until he is thirty (the age she was for *her* first book). And in her criticism of the modern poet's attempt to combine the beauty of nature with 'Mrs Gape' (one of her prototypical charladies), there is something of the priggishness of her earlier resistance to Joyce.

She knew she had cause to be defensive – 'I'm not at all satisfied with the Letter' she wrote to John, when he criticised it; but maintained her argument that 'the young poet is rather crudely jerked between realism and beauty . . . he doesnt reach the unconscious automated state – hence the spasmodic, jerky, self conscious effect of his realistic language. But I may be transferring to him some of the ill effects of my own struggles the other way round – writes poetry in prose.'[47] The Letter (and the surrounding correspondence with Lehmann) anticipated her painful anxieties with *The Years*, in which she wrestled with the relationship between art and polemic. Letter and novel both asked how the writer was to take on 'the world outside'?

The Letter was part of her argument that modern times required new forms from fiction, which could somehow maintain the threatened connection between the private creative self and the catastrophically alien public world. But modern poetry seemed to her more resistant than fiction to 'foreign bodies' – it was half nightingales and half charladies. Lehmann's friend Peter Quennell wrote a 'Letter to Mrs Woolf' in response which described the poetry of the 1930s as necessarily transitional, still struggling to take on board 'the prodigious melodrama of modern Europe', moving through difficulty and harshness to a new kind of beauty. But Virginia was not convinced. In 1940, an essay called 'The Leaning Tower' on England's public-school communist writers showed her still arguing with these modern poets.

This summer also saw the ending of *The Waves*. In July she was nervously anticipating Leonard's verdict. 'It is a masterpiece', he said, coming out to her writing lodge at Rodmell on 19 July, 'And the best of your books.'[48] In relief, she sent off the proofs, and immediately set her mind to other things, so as not to succumb to despair between finishing and publishing the novel. She had an idea for a 'light' book, *Flush*, the story of Elizabeth Barrett Browning's spaniel, at first sight an escapist and playful response to a summer of politics, but also a story of courage and independence, and, crucially, of a move outside and away from the English social system. She was thinking, under Ethel's influence, about ruthlessness, about her capacity for saying what she thought and cutting out unnecessary obligations. In her critical writing, she felt more 'fearless': 'Because of a R. of ones Own I said suddenly to myself last night.'[49] On holiday in France in April (a very satisfactory trip, particularly because of her pleasure in being alone with Leonard after all their years of marriage)[50] they had discussed cutting down the endless social demands to a 'black hole' of one day a week.[51]

Part of the impulse behind *Flush* was the desire to do more 'low life scenes'.[52] When *The Waves* came out in October, Ethel criticised it for its aethereality, for not being Dickensian enough. This, combined with the arguments about realism with the poets, provoked her. She was already using for the episode of dog-stealing in *Flush* a brush she had had with 'low life' – in December 1930 she had had her handbag stolen, and they had to go to the police station to recover it. It made her feel 'admitted to the underworld'.[53] She wrote a strong sketch of Sophie Farrell in October 1931; she did her series of vivid London scenes for *Good Housekeeping*. Her brain was fertile in other directions too. 'A Knock on the Door', her feminist essay, kept rumbling away in her mind. She was beginning to read some popular scientific books – 'as the least like to my own ideas'[54] – Gerald Heard, James Jeans, H.G. Wells, Huxley. All kinds of new ideas about evolution, the development of civilisation, the universe as waves, time as a fourth dimension, were filling her mind. In Gerald Heard's *The Emergence of Man* she found the image of the first species dancing round a magic tree, which she would save up and use in *Three Guineas*. 'The stream of knowledge' (she read in Jeans's *The Universe Around Us*) 'is heading towards a non-mechanical reality; the universe begins to look more like a great thought than a great machine. The old dualism of mind and matter . . . seems likely to disappear.' She noted, in a conversation about this book, the idea that 'Civilisation is the thickness of a postage stamp on the top of Cleopatra's needle; & time to come is the thickness of postage stamps as high as Mont Blanc.'[55] She was beginning to read and revise and write new articles for a second *Common Reader*.

This reflected her, and Leonard's, sense of the substantial, established audience for her work. The publication of *The Waves* frightened her, but, with some reservations from those who found it 'bloodless', it was generally very well received: 'One of the most important novels of our day', 'an authentic and unique masterpiece, which is bound to have an influence on the mind of this generation', 'a literary sensation' (this, however, was Harold Nicolson's partisan view), 'a piece of subtle, penetrating magic', and so on.[56] It sold well: 5,000 in the first week, 10,117 by the end of the first six months.[57] Forster's unsolicited praise particularly pleased her: 'Morgan is the only one . . . that matters.'[58] Goldsworthy Lowes Dickinson wrote one of his eccentrically typed letters from Cambridge, calling it a great poem. She replied with an honest response, at once confident and self-critical, which defined her reasons for continuing to write and her sense of how her life and her fiction connected:

The six characters were supposed to be one. I'm getting old myself – I shall be fifty next year; and I come to feel more and more how difficult it is to collect oneself into one Virginia; even though the special Virginia in whose body I live for the moment is violently susceptible to all sorts of separate feelings. Therefore I wanted to give the sense of continuity, instead of which most people say, no you've given the sense of flowing and passing away and that nothing matters. Yet I feel things matter quite immensely. What the significance is, heaven knows I can't guess; but there is significance – that I feel overwhelmingly. Perhaps for me, with my limitations, – I mean lack of reasoning power and so on – all I can do is to make an artistic whole; and leave it at that. But then I'm annoyed to be told that I am nothing but a stringer together of words and words and words. I begin to doubt beautiful words. How one longs sometimes to have done something in the world.[59]

With *The Waves* being reviewed, she was acutely conscious of her reputation. 'Bloomsbury' was becoming a regular target for satire and denunciation, and this made her defensive. Roy Campbell's embittered personal attack on the Nicolsons and their friends as 'Nancy-boys' and 'Fascists', *The Georgiad*, came out, with a blurb advertising its brilliant ridicule of 'the vast, if vague society of stereotyped literary amateurs and back scratchers, commonly known as Bloomsbury, who more or less regulate the literary journalism of the whole country'.[60] Wyndham Lewis's *The Apes of God*, which called Bloomsbury élitist, corrupt and talentless, caused a stir in October 1930. Raymond Mortimer attacked it, and Lewis wrote a pamphlet returning to the fray, which Virginia described as 'the gossip & spite & bickering of a suburban housemaid who has been given notice & is getting a bit of her own back'.[61] As her tetchy and snobbish phrase suggests, these onslaughts got under her skin. She could see that they would continue, and that she was likely to be pilloried by the younger generation. The new Cambridge critics – anti-establishment, anti-modernist – were setting up their armies. A 'Miss B', writing in the magazine *Scrutiny* (this was the future professor and Mistress of Girton, Muriel Bradbrook) – described by Virginia as 'young, Cambridge, ardent' – called her a 'very bad writer'.[62] Some Cambridge don – called 'something like Leaven?' – had a wife who was criticising her in the same publication.[63] 'It is perhaps true that my reputation will now decline. I shall be laughed at & pointed at.'[64] These sorts of attacks made her increasingly nervous, from now on, whenever she published anything: she knew she could not rely on a good press. Leonard, too, was concerned about his reputation. When the first volume of his book on the psychology of democracy in the eighteenth century, *After the Deluge*, was dismissed in a half a column in the *TLS* in October 1931, he sank into a profound despondency, which Virginia attributed (without, however, making a comparison with her own despairing responses to criticism) to centuries of oppression.[65]

Being sculpted by Stephen Tomlin, too, made her think of herself as an image, a thing: she hated it, even more than sitting for her portrait. (The result, though, which now sits in the studio at Charleston, was eloquent and impressive.) She could not bear to be pinned down and fixed, any more than she could bear the thought of becoming an establishment figure. With wry thoughts of Leslie and how much this would have meant to him, she turned down the offer of giving the Clark lectures at Cambridge in February 1932. ('Think of me, the uneducated child reading books in my room at 22 H.P.G. – now advanced to this glory . . . father would have blushed with pleasure could I have told him 30 years ago, that his daughter – my poor little Ginny – was to be asked to succeed him.')[66] And she was having mixed feelings about the book being written about her by Winifred Holtby. There had already been a long personal study by Jacques-Émile Blanche, in 1927, and two books on her in France and Germany appeared in 1932: 'This is a danger signal. I must not settle into a figure.'[67] But this was the first biographical and critical study to appear in Britain.

Characteristically, she was not at all straightforward in her treatment of Holtby, who, at thirty-two, was a pugnacious, energetic young woman of strong political views, a well-known journalist and socialist feminist (and a great admirer of Ethel Smyth). *South Riding* was still to come (and so was the diagnosis, in April 1932, of Bright's Disease, which would kill her at the age of thirty-seven). Virginia could afford to be condescending towards her, and Holtby was somewhat in awe, using Ethel to smooth her path. (In September 1931, she told her friend Vera Brittain that Ethel had read her biographical chapter 'to see if there was anything wrong with it'. Ethel wrote reassuringly to Winifred: '*I am quite sure* there is nothing in it that would put her teeth on edge.')[68] Vanessa, however, was less helpful, and, in a tone which anticipated all her responses to intruders, refused to talk to Winifred about Virginia: 'It would be rather difficult to me to speak about my sister's life to someone who did not know either of us.'[69] Holtby approached Virginia in March 1931, with an introduction from Ethel. Virginia gave her polite permission, told her it was best for her to write 'impersonally', and said she wished to be treated 'with perfect frankness, like the dead'.[70] To Ethel she wrote, less politely: 'The woman Holtby doesn't altogether attract me on paper, but I take your word for it she is not quite so indiscriminate as she seems.'[71]

In May, Winifred came to ask her questions; Virginia described her to Vanessa as 'a Yorkshire farmer's daughter, rather uncouth, and shapeless'.[72] 'I assure you', she wrote to Winifred after their meeting, 'I do not often talk so much about myself'.[73] In September 1931 she agreed to go through the MS, and answered some more queries. She was pleased to see that Holtby had found a resemblance between her and Julia Stephen's *Notes from Sick Rooms*. But to Ethel she called her a 'donkey', and was particularly irritated by her having approached Ethel for biographical information. Anxious now about the reception of *The Waves*, she sent it to Holtby reluctantly, sounding profoundly depressed about the value of her work: 'I become absorbed and can do nothing else . . . As people say "my appeal is only to a few", I sometimes wonder whether they are worth the time they take me.'[74] But she was pleased by Holtby's enthusiasm for *The Waves* ('It is a poem') and copied her response into her diary.[75] Holtby's book was nearly finished, and Virginia made a kind joke: 'You must be, as I always am, so thankful to be quit of your author and off to something fresh.'[76] Holtby then had trouble with her publishers, and Virginia made sympathetic noises, making it clear, though, that the Press would not touch it. She had recently 'laid down the principle', she said, 'that Virginia Woolf as a publisher can't publish books on Virginia Woolf as a writer.'[77]

When it came to reading Holtby's book she was equivocating. To Ethel she said she had 'just glanced at' it and it made her roar with laughter. She told Hugh Walpole that she hadn't read it, and it was just another kind of 'tombstone', saying that Holtby 'learned to read, I'm told, by minding the pigs'. To Margaret Llewelyn Davies she said she couldn't bring herself to read it. (Was she *pretending* not to have read it?) When she at last wrote to Holtby about it, early in 1933, she made a point of dissociating herself from the 'Virginia Woolf' of the book: 'I think you have made the best of her – only she wasn't quite as nice as you make out; & nothing like so cultivated.' And then, teasingly: 'Of course I suspect a good many things happened to her, by way of life, that she concealed successfully.' Of her novels: 'She was always full of excitement, I think, when she was writing them, but as she never read them after they were written, she cant say much about them now.' Drily, she concluded: 'I felt that you suggested so many extremely interesting points of view that I long to write a book on V.W.myself.' It was a put-down; but it was also a real wish: biography made her think about the possibilities of autobiography.[78]

Her point, as usual, was that the 'tombstone' of critical or biographical writing was utterly remote from the true interior self – or selves – of the writer. But the key to her distancing of herself from Holtby's book may lie in her phrase: 'and nothing like so cultivated'. Holtby, who had taken on Woolf as a subject she felt to be the opposite of herself in class and character, made a great deal (even more so in the manuscript, which Virginia had looked at) of social issues. Her book, written from her own political bias, emphasised 'the conflict between the political and artistic conscience'.[79]

Holtby's reviews are an interesting indication of the way Virginia Woolf was beginning to be treated. Even the publisher's blurb reassured readers that it was not written 'from the narrow viewpoint of a coterie'. While Geoffrey Grigson, cutting his teeth on Woolf in a review of *The Second Common Reader* in *The Bookman*, called her nothing more than a 'delicate sentimentalist', a review of Holtby in the same issue of that magazine criticised Virginia Woolf for being a virtuoso only of minor sensations: 'it has been her undoing'. The *Manchester Evening News*'s review of Holtby said that Woolf's were the sorts of novels only written by 'terrifically sensitive, cultured, invalidish ladies with private means'. Other reviews said she had been too much praised by 'little cliques'. 'There is a reaction against Mrs Woolf' (the *Yorkshire Post* summed up): 'It is now increasingly said that she works on too small a canvas . . . She expresses too exclusively the 'sheltered' point of view; she is too ladylike.' Virginia was affected by these reactions,[80] but she could take them lightly, too. She told Hugh Walpole in February 1932: 'Dont dismiss me as an etiolated, decadent, enervated, emasculated, priggish blood-waterish 'ighbrow.'[81]

THIRTY-FOUR

Loss

Fame, life, writing, were overshadowed at the start of 1932. Lytton Strachey's illness and slow death at the age of fifty-two came as a great shock and a cause of deep grief to Virginia, and also to Leonard. They had not been in constant close touch since Lytton and Carrington began to live at Ham Spray in 1924. They visited the house once, soon after Lytton moved there, and then not again until he was dying. Virginia was rather jealous and wary of Lytton's ménage with Carrington and Ralph Partridge. Though she had of course heard a great deal about the emotional complications of the set-up, from Ralph, from Gerald Brenan and from Lytton himself, she had felt distant from that side of Lytton's life. His last passion, for Roger Senhouse, did not interest her much. She viewed at a distance the developing Ham Spray drama of Ralph falling in love with Bunny Garnett's sister-in-law, Frances Marshall. Strachey's more intimate women friends were Mary Hutchinson and, latterly, Rosamond Lehmann. And Virginia and Leonard sometimes criticised him: Leonard could find him 'ungenerous' and 'selfish', and had come to prefer the company of Forster.[1]

When they met in London or Sussex, however, their friendship continued to be a source of deep pleasure and interest to her. 'If we can meet in solitude, all goes as usual.'[2] And 'as usual' when she saw him, she chose the same words to describe the benign, entrancing, affable feeling that conversation with Lytton gave her: such words as 'lustrous', 'glow', 'luminous', 'soft', 'melodious', 'warm'.[3] To Lytton, too, these meetings were pleasurable: staying at Charleston in the autumn of 1927, he was struck when the Woolfs came over by how 'young and beautiful' Virginia looked, as she was declaring 'that they must all write their memoirs, on an enormous scale, and have them published in volume after volume in ten years' time.'[4] They always found each other's conversation funny, absorbing, amusing; as Virginia described it once to Vita, in February 1927: 'Lytton comes. We sit up talking about Queen Elizabeth, sodomy, love, the *Antigone*, *Othello*'[5] – just as they might have done twenty years before.

When the remarkable Lady Strachey died at last in 1928, both Leonard and Virginia wrote down their memories of her, part comical, part admiring, as notes towards a more formal published obituary. (In her notes, Virginia recalled Lady Strachey's memory of Julia Stephen:' "I remember", she said, "seeing you as a child in an omnibus with your mother." "Which omnibus?" I asked, idiotically. "How can I *possibly* tell you that?" she said scornfully. Yet I did not feel in the least snubbed, she was too majestic.')[6] Lytton was pleased by the obituary, and, in general, they liked each other's essays. As for their books, they were aware of each other's reservations. Virginia was always jealous of Lytton's success; that jealousy meant she felt 'secretly pleased' by what she considered to be the 'superficial meretricious' quality of *Elizabeth and Essex*.[7] But at least she was able to tell him what she felt was wrong with it.[8] And when his essays *Portraits in Miniature* came out in June 1929, she thought they were 'very good', Lytton doing what suited him best: 'the compressed yet glowing account which requires logic, reason, learning, taste, wit order & infinite skill'.[9] On his part, he thought that *To the Lighthouse* was extraordinary but was worried by 'the lack of copulation'; he admired *A Room of One's Own* enormously; and when *The Waves* arrived he was already unwell, and put off reading it: 'I shudder and shiver – and cannot take the plunge.'[10]

But in spite of literary rivalry, sexual differences, and social separations, nothing could alter or diminish this settled friendship. He was one of the people whose death she would most mind and could least bear to imagine.[11] She wrote to him about this feeling at the end of 1931, without knowing he was ill, in what reads with hindsight as an extraordinary moment of telepathic sympathy:

'I arise from dreams of thee' – that's why I write. I have just woken from a dream in which I was at a play, in the pit and suddenly you, who were sitting across a gangway in a row in front, turned and looked at me, and we both went into fits of laughter. What the play was, what we laughed at, I've no notion, but we were both very young (no, for you had your beard) and at the age when we used to write to each other. Why are these dreams more vivid than real life? – Anyhow while it hangs about me, I can't help writing to the bearded serpent . . .

Well this is only a dream letter and needs no answer, unless you can tell me what we laughed at; but when you're in London . . . please come and see your old and attached friend Virginia.[12]

But there was to be no reply, and she would never see him again. Carrington wrote a few days later to say that he was very ill. For the next two months, Virginia was caught up (but still at arm's length) in the long, gruesome, absurd and painful epic of Lytton's slow courageous dying, from a stomach cancer which all his doctors had misdiagnosed. On Christmas Eve, she and

Leonard were both in tears. In mid-January they visited the house of mourning, full of glooming Stracheys, puzzled doctors, a distraught, suicidal Carrington and a weeping Ralph, in the hopes of seeing the patient; but he was too ill. He died a week after their visit, on 22 January; they heard the news at Angelica's fancy-dress party. Virginia struggled, in her diary, to find a way of writing it down, moving awkwardly between 'I' and 'one' ('One knows now how irremediable – but no: I cant think of any words for what I mean').[13] By contrast her letters to the Strachey sisters and to Carrington were models of delicacy and understanding. And she dealt tactfully with the competitive mourning which always arises after the death of someone with a great many intimate friends, gracefully acknowledging Mary Hutchinson's greater intimacy and Ottoline's special claims.[14]

Her fiftieth birthday went almost unnoticed. A huge wave of regret washed over her that she had not seen him more often, that she had not gone to visit him.[15] She thought about the lack of memorials and mausoleums for their generation, in contrast to her father's. (There had been no form of ceremony at Lytton's cremation.) What would remain would not be solemn funeral orations or respectful, hagiographical three-volume 'Lives and Letters' (so they thought); their immortality would be in their books, their letters, their portraits and photographs, the stories of their friends, their posthumous reputations. Immediately her diaries and letters filled up with dialogue and sharp character sketches, as though she were holding her feelings at bay and also writing down the kinds of narratives he would have liked to hear. She felt, beyond anything, 'a longing to speak to him'.[16]

Everyone expected Carrington to kill herself. She had already tried to while Lytton was dying. At the end of January, Oliver Strachey came to dinner with the Woolfs, and talked about this possibility, commenting, as Virginia noted, that 'She says she will kill herself – quite reasonable', and again 'suicide seems to me quite sensible'. (This comment has been attributed, by both Carrington's and Strachey's biographers, to Virginia, but she is clearly quoting Oliver.)[17] In fact, the Woolfs were trying to interest her in doing woodcut illustrations for Julia Strachey's *Cheerful Weather at the Wedding*, and Virginia wrote encouraging Carrington to stay alive. She chose words of great beauty, but words which also confirmed (to herself and presumably to Carrington) her feeling that Carrington's life was less significant, in itself, than Lytton's:

Oh but Carrington we have to live and be ourselves – and I feel it is more for you to live than for any one; because he loved you so, and loved your oddities and the way you have of being yourself. I cant explain it; but it seems to me that as long as you are there, something we loved in Lytton, something of the best part of his life still goes on.[18]

Ordinary life – work, society – carried on. She wrote an essay on the *Arcadia*, full of elegiac feeling for the death of the young Sidney.[19] She finished the 'Letter to a Young Poet', she kept thinking about 'A Knock on the Door'. She began to see 'Mrs Cameron', Elizabeth Bowen, who at first sight struck her as 'stammering, shy, conventional', but who was to grow closer. She had an absurd meeting, arranged by Violet Trefusis and Raymond Mortimer, with Violet's mother Mrs Keppel, the ex-mistress of Edward VII. Both had anticipated having nothing to say to each other, but (Violet remembered) they did find one congenial subject: 'Personally I've always been in favour of six cylinders though I know some people think four are less trouble.' 'My dear Mrs Keppel, you wouldn't hesitate if you saw the new Lanchester with the fluid fly-wheel!' Neither (Violet Trefusis commented) knew a thing about motors, but both thought 'they were on safe ground'.[20] It was just the sort of anecdote Lytton would have enjoyed.

On Thursday 10 March, nearly seven weeks after Lytton's death, on a bright spring day, they went to Ham Spray and tried to amuse Carrington with such stories. But Carrington seemed beyond ordinary life, 'pale, small, suffering silently very calm'. At one point in the long, painful afternoon, Virginia and Carrington went upstairs together and Carrington talked about wanting to keep everything in Lytton's room as it had been. She broke down, and spoke of the pointlessness of life without Lytton.

I did not want to lie to her – I could not pretend that there was not truth in what she said. I said life seemed to me sometimes hopeless, useless, when I woke in the night & thought of Lytton's death. I held her hands. Her wrists seemed very small. She seemed helpless, deserted, like some small animal left. She was very gentle; sometimes laughing; kissing me; saying Lytton had loved his old friends best.[21]

When they left, they asked her to visit them. Early the next morning she shot herself (clumsily: it took her several hours to die). There was the possibility of an inquest, at which the Woolfs might have to appear – upsetting for them, as Vanessa told Clive.[22] But the verdict of an accident was brought in, and they were spared this ordeal.

Did Virginia encourage Carrington to kill herself? And if so, was she to blame for this death? I think not. As the stories and gossip began to accumulate, Gerald Brenan wrote to Alix Strachey that a paper had been found, written a few days before Carrington's death, on which she had copied out the dirge from *The White Devil*, and underlined the word 'wolf' in the line 'But keep the wolf far hence'. But – as Gerald added – 'perhaps there is not much point in these conjectures.'[23] Virginia kept asking herself – could she have said more? Could she have prevented it?[24] Discussing the suicide in one of what Leonard called 'these mausoleum talks', feeling the presence of the dead as ghosts, who changed their shape in her mind, 'like people who are changed by what one hears of them', she felt strongly that she did not approve Carrington's act. She felt angry with Lytton, that he had absorbed her life to the extent that he had 'made her kill herself'. Back at Rodmell for Easter, on another of those lovely spring days, she looked about her, thought about her 'happy life', and took her stand against that desire for death which she understood so well: 'I am glad to be alive and sorry for the dead; cant think why Carrington killed herself & put an end to all this.'[25]

All the same, Lytton's death was a point of change in her life. Other, as painful deaths were to follow: but this was the one that left the greatest silence. It was a closing-down of the past; it made her feel (as she always in any case tended to feel) older, more mortal, part of an age that was past. Much of what she did in her writing from now on would be an energetic, vehement attempt to counter that sense of being closer to the ghosts than to the living. That her first mention of the name of Hitler came in the weeks after Lytton's death seems retrospectively symbolic. Lytton did not live to see the rise of Nazism and the Second World War; it was she, of the two of them – old friends, old rivals, old contemporaries – who had to find a way of dealing in her work with these terrible new forces. Leonard also felt, acutely, that Lytton's death marked a point of no return. 'Things have gone wrong somehow', he said to her, as they walked along their London street on the night of Carrington's suicide. 'I saw all the violence & unreason crossing in the air ourselves small; a tumult outside: something terrifying: unreason.'[26] There could be only one way of dealing with all this, and that was to 'make a book' out of it.

But the first thing needed, after the double shock, was some time away. She put off the publication of the second *Common Reader* to the autumn, and they made plans to go to Greece for a month, with Roger and his sister Margery Fry. (John Lehmann was left in charge of the Press.) They set off on 15 April from Victoria Station. It was an escape, but it was also a return. Some of the feelings which had gone into *The Waves* were being re-enacted: thoughts of Thoby, longings to move out into the world from the confines of London and England, the 'desire to be with friends' that comes after a death.[27] Lytton's death had brought back sharp memories of her lost brother ('I sit thinking of Lytton and Thoby and how Lytton came to me when Thoby died', she wrote to Pippa Strachey on the day of the death.)[28]

And the return to Greece, after over a quarter of a century, inevitably evoked the past. On the Parthenon, 'my own ghost met me, the girl of 23, with all her life to come' – 'And how I pitied her!' she added, to Vita.[29] But this was a different kind of travelling: no uncomfortable carriages, no killing of bugs in hotel bedrooms, or youthful 'sentimentality' over the vanished Gods, or ravings over the Hermes of Praxiteles. (Roger Fry's enthusiasms were all for Byzantine art and architecture, so 'we search out obscure mosaics and mosques and neglect all we used to see with Violet Dickinson'.)[30] This time, they planned to go by air – but as they couldn't fly directly to Greece, they instead took the train to Venice and then sailed down the coast of Yugoslavia to Athens, and covered the Peloponnese by car.

Since 1906 and the ensuing wars – the Balkan wars, the First World War, the war with Turkey – Greece had in some ways changed fundamentally, but to the English tourist it seemed, also, ancient and immutable. But this was the lull before the storm. The barbarians (as Leonard would say) were at the gates. All of Europe was in the grip of the Depression, out of which totalitarian regimes were emerging. In Italy, Mussolini's Fascists were firmly in power. In Austria the Nazis were in the ascendant. In Germany, the National Socialist party had had a big victory in the elections of September 1930. Hitler was currently manoeuvring for power; within a year he would be Chancellor, and by the summer of 1934 he was head of the German state. Greece was a republic at this time (the Prime Minister, Venizelos, was travelling on their ship) but in 1935 it was to become a monarchy again, and to fall under the right-wing dictatorship of General Metaxas. The country was extremely poor, though tourism, particularly from Germany, had hugely increased since her last visit. Virginia remarked unsympathetically on this phenomenon: 'The Germans come out like things hidden in a pocket.'[31] She said nothing about European politics, but she noted the extreme poverty, and was well aware of their own insulation from it as they travelled by car, then back through Yugoslavia on the Orient Express: 'Curious contrasts! Our sufficiency & civilization drawing all compact through want, poverty, desolation, shepherds, sheep, torrents, lonely rivers winding through rocks.'[32]

But, as for many middle-class Greek-loving tourists then and since, poverty had ensured the antique picturesqueness of the landscape. She perceived the irony: 'Poverty & war & misery have prevented any obliteration'.[33] The deepest excitement of Greece for her, below the intense physical pleasures of light and colour and space, smells of thyme and olives and cypress, Byzantine art, white marble, flowers, blue sea, smiling peasants, tinkling goat bells, the 'hot sensuality' of the Greek Orthodox

Easter service, was the sense of an unchanged primitive land. 'This is England in the time of Chaucer.' 'The centuries have left no trace. There is no 18th 16th, 15th century all in layers as in England – nothing between them & 300 B.C., . . . If one finds a bay it is deserted; so too with the hills & the valleys; not a villa, not a tea shop not a kennel anywhere; no wires, no churches, almost no graveyards.'[34] When she and Leonard had been to France the previous spring, to the Loire and the Dordogne, they played a game, which they often did on their trips to Europe, comparing their lunches with English lunches, their hotels with the White Hart at Lewes. 'In this great argument I am always for France; L. for England.'[35] In Greece the comparisons seemed more far-fetched. She could console herself for the huge sheds that were currently disfiguring the view of Asheham by pretending they were Greek temples. But faced with real Greek temples, life in England began to seem remote and irrelevant. She had fantasies of living there always.

Her broodings on civilisation were underlined by her holiday reading – Max Eastman's book *The Literary World: Its Place in an Age of Science*, which attacked modernism, including her own work, for its retreat into unintelligibility in the face of the advance of science; Wells's *The Science of Life*, Lawrence (whom she had also been reading the previous year in France) and Murry's book on him, which provoked thoughts about 'maleness'. (Her 'little book' on women was bubbling in her mind.)[36]

The company of the Frys was satisfactory on the whole, though Leonard was irritated by Roger's chess-playing technique, and Virginia found Margery (instantly nicknamed 'the Yak', though in her real life Principal of Somerville College) solid, clever, well-informed, but suspicious of Bloomsbury and lacking in charm. But Roger, at sixty-six, had unstoppable energy. He 'oozed knowledge', enthusiasms and judgements. He set up his easel everywhere: the scenery, he complained, was 'not very plastic'. He rode mules, talked to Leonard about 'the break up of the atom', picked up Greek informants everywhere they went. In short, he was 'far and away the best admirer of life and art I've ever travelled with.'[37] Roger was equally pleased. In his letters home to Helen Anrep, he remarked on Virginia's quietness, how she seemed 'to get immense pleasure from just having experiences'. To protect herself from the sun (she got badly sunburnt on this holiday) she was wearing a kind of silk hood: 'She always looks incredibly lovely and more distinguished than the Goddesses.'[38]

The effects very quickly wore off. As soon as she came back she could feel herself editing the journey for the purposes of 'visions' and anecdotes. The relief from mourning was short-lived. She went into a summer – the summer of their twentieth wedding anniversary – of profound irritation and depression. A feeling of futility and barrenness overcame her. She was working, of course: she finished the revisions of her essays for the *Common Reader*, and then corrected the proofs, and she went on with *Flush*. But it did not seem so much fun now, 'as I meant it for a joke with Lytton, and a skit on him'.[39] Ethel's troublesome adoration, Leonard's 'goodness and firmness', her affections for Vita and for Vanessa and her family could comfort but not alleviate her feelings. Her 'cage in Bloomsbury'[40] seemed vile and constricting; England all seemed 'spoilt'. She cheered herself up with a vigorous sketch of Shaw, met at a lunch party at the Keyneses ('What life, what vitality! What immense nervous spring! . . . He doesnt much notice who's there').[41] Adrian and Karin's marriage seemed to be breaking up; his 'suicidal face' gave her a nightmare.[42] Goldsworthy Lowes Dickinson died: she felt, again, shock, regret, the sense both she and Leonard had of being potentially 'worms crushed by a motor car'. Francis Birrell, too, was very ill and had to have an operation. 'So people will go on dying until we die, Leonard said.'[43]

But all her relationships with the living seemed quarrelsome. She had an 'odious' scene with Ethel. Clive's boasting and malice were riling her again. She was involved in a silly spat with Eddy Sackville-West, who said she had accused him of behaving cheaply towards Duncan. They made it up, but he irritated her again in September at a reading Vita gave of her poem, *The Land*, at the theatre which belonged to Edy Craig and Christopher St John. Stephen Spender, William Plomer and Eddy sat in a row and giggled at Vita's breeches and the general atmosphere; Virginia was furious with them.[44] John Lehmann – 'God damn it'[45] – was starting to make difficulties, wanting far more changes and control at the Press than Leonard was prepared to allow. One of his complaints was that Virginia didn't help by sitting in her work room 'with a red cross on your door, so that I daren't come in'.[46] The promising new friend turned into 'that egotistical young man with all his jealousies & vanities & ambitions'. In September he walked out on them.[47] That autumn she had another quarrel, an epistolary tiff with the malevolent *littérateur*, Logan Pearsall Smith, over Bloomsbury-Chelsea hostilities. He told her that mockery was her favourite pastime; she invited him to found a society for *open* mockery: 'Why should not Chelsea and Bloomsbury meet and laugh at each other to their faces and quite genuinely enjoy themselves?'[48]

She was unwell again, and fainted twice; Leonard was worried about her heart. 'Its nerve exhaustion they say, and dont know what it means.'[49] 'Society' was galling her. Too many people came to Monk's House in the summer months. And yet, on a good day, she could be enchanting to them.

Frances Marshall wrote a letter to Ralph Partridge (still in deep grief for Carrington) on 31 August, describing a happy afternoon at Rodmell of bowls, tea, and conversation:

> Virginia knows how to be utterly charming if she likes, and today she did. Playing bowls she is the cracked Englishwoman, with an old felt hat on the top of her head and long pointed canvas shoes. She started some way behind the jack, and took a little run and then hurled her bowl with wildly waving arms . . . Two dogs sat about, a good deal in the way . . . The Woolves drove us home [to Charleston]. Virginia sat with me and asked me about Ham Spray and about you. I can't describe to you the *kindness* as well as fascination of everything she said – about the beauty of Ham Spray, about life in the country, about you and how she believed you could write if you wanted to. I got a feeling she was *really* fond of you. She sent you her love and asked us to come and see her whenever we were in London. I felt she meant this. She wants you of course to write something about Lytton . . . I felt she really wanted Ham Spray life not to be altogether lost, and for her own sake. I was bowled over by her irresistible cracked charm . . . She is going to be the newest motor-bicycle addict, for she says Leonard won't let her drive the car and a motor bike is just what she wants.[50]

But, alas, Virginia Woolf did not take to riding about London on a motor-bike. Instead she went back (with a detour to Leicester and the Labour Party Conference) to a London season of more irritations. She disliked the sense of being in the limelight which Holtby's book and the publication of *The Common Reader: Second Series* gave her, and was excessively upset by the fact that Holtby's publishers made use of a photograph of her by Leonard rather than her 1929 photography by Lenare: 'I am revealed to the world . . . as a plain dowdy old woman.'[51] She was enraged by Ethel's accusation that she courted publicity and interviews, and infuriated by hearing J.B. Priestley talking on the radio about 'Highbrows'. In a furious response, she attacked the cultural dominance of the 'middlebrow' or 'broad Brow' writer (like Priestley): 'And of all persuasions the most contemptible and most succesful and most parasitic and best paid in all the state is the broad brow and him I most despise.' Leonard advised her not to publish.[52] She was appalled by the smart society wedding of David Cecil and Rachel MacCartny, Desmond and Molly's daughter: 'Oh but the inadequacy of the service – the sense of its being the entirely obsolete & primitive voice of a defunct tribal magnate, laying down laws for the government of the tribe: & then these civilised sceptical people letting themselves pretend that they obey.'[53] Unwelcome guests kept coming to Tavistock Square, like the bizarre Count Potocki de Montalk, a literary claimant-in-exile to the thrones of Poland and Hungary (though born in New Zealand). He had gone to trial in February for publishing a book of erotic poems, supported by Leonard (with Huxley, Walter de la Mare, and Eliot). Now, on his release from prison, he came to dinner in his flowing purple cloak, with hair down to his shoulders, and turned out to be 'an appalling bore'.[54] (He would turn this occasion into venomous caricature some years later in his privately printed *Social Climbers in Bloomsbury*).[55]

In the middle of all this rasping, uncomfortable time, she had a breakthrough. She was grieving, quarrelling, feeling ill, angry, exposed. But she was also feeling her way towards a new idea, a concept of 'immunity'. The word had come to her in the summer. Why not – now she was fifty – stand apart, be more detached?

> 'Immunity', I said to myself . . . To be immune, means to exist apart from rubs, shocks, suffering; to be beyond the range of darts; to have enough to live on without courting flattery, success; not to need to accept invitations; not to mind other people being praised; to feel This – to sit & breathe behind my screen, alone, is enough; to be strong; content; to let Nessa & D go to Paris without envy; to feel no one's thinking of me; to feel I have done certain things & can be quiet now; to be mistress of my hours; to feel detached from all sayings about me; & claims on me; to be glad of lunching alone with Leonard; to have a spare time this afternoon; to read Coleridge's letters. Immunity is an exalted calm desirable state, & one I could reach much oftener than I do.[56]

The word kept coming back to her in the next years – a difficult word, troublingly close in its meaning to 'indifference', or 'élitism', or 'privacy'. But it was close, too, to 'anonymity' (also a favourite word from now on), and in that sense echoed Bernard's sense of impersonality at the end of *The Waves*, or Flush's escape from England and his rebirth as a nonentity: 'To be nothing – is that not, after all, the most satisfactory state in the whole world?'[57]

All her current preoccupations went into this new mood: her thoughts about women's professional lives, her arguments with the poets over art and politics, her reading of Lawrence's letters, which she hated for being so assertive and systematising and preaching, and by contrast the letters of Joseph Wright (the working class boy who became an editor of a dialect dictionary) which she read in the summer, and whose forceful honesty made her feel even more: 'Why do a single thing one doesn't want to do?'[58] She wanted her writing to be 'free straight & undeflected', like his.[59] She wanted above all to be truthful and detached.

Suddenly, in October, all this gelled into the start of a new book, which would become *The Years*. The new book coincided with, and took fire from, her desire to be immune, detached, 'withdrawn; & concentrated'.[60] It would be a commentary on her world and her history, from 1880 to the 'here & now', taking in 'everything, sex, education, life etc.'. She was going to deal with the tug between 'fact & vision' by alternating factual chapters with fiction. It was to tell the story of a late-Victorian patriarchal family, the Pargiters, but also to be a history of British social politics. (How complex a programme this was for her is suggested by the fact that, in the same few weeks, she was writing a tender, affectionate reminiscence of Leslie, for the centenary of his birth.)

She plunged in, and wrote with extreme rapidity: 60,000 words by December. At Christmas she had to break off to revise *Flush*, which she could see needed more work – it took her another month to finish, but 'the Pargiters', the cuckoo in her mind, kept shoving it out of the way. She was full of excitement. Nothing forewarned her what a long, painful, dangerous endeavour she had embarked on, or how many years *The Years* was to consume. At the end of 1932, her mood was assured, calm, hopeful. It seemed more than ever important to her to make the most of being alive. She wrote on the last day of December:

> If one does not lie back & sum up & say to the moment, this very moment, stay you are so fair, what will be one's gain, dying? No: stay, this moment. No one ever says that enough. Always hurry. I am now going in, to see L. & say stay this moment.[61]

THIRTY-FIVE

Outsider

'Autobiography it might be called', she had noted, when she was starting to write *The Waves* in 1929. 'In fact I sometimes think,' she wrote to Hugh Walpole at the end of 1932, after reading his reminiscences, 'only autobiography is literature – novels are what we peel off, and come at last to the core, which is only you or me.'[1] That sentence seems to mean two things, both very suggestive for her biographer. One is that the fictions she writes are her outer skins, which she has been gradually peeling off in preparation for the 'true' literature of life-writing, which she will come to 'at last'. But another meaning seems to shadow the first: that the novels themselves are covers, outer skins, for the concealed 'core' of the author's identity: autobiographies, they might be called.

The tension between fiction and autobiography is at its fiercest in the novel she now began to write. Its history (which she planned to construct like a series of 'great balloons, linked by straight narrow passages of narrative', going from 1880 to 2012)[2] was the history of her family, her childhood, her war, her life in London, her friends. Its political reading of the culture was derived from her upbringing, and had been developed through all her writing life. In a way *The Years* rewrote her earlier books. The suppressed development of the middle-class girl in *The Voyage Out*; the pressure of Victorian traditions on the next generation (particularly on their sexual choices) in *Night and Day*; the waste and trauma of the war in *Jacob's Room* and *Mrs Dalloway*, and, in *Mrs Dalloway*, the iniquitous social structure that survived the war; the tyrannies of family life in *To the Lighthouse*; the satirical pageant of an empire's history in *Orlando*; the silencing of women, and their outsider's view of England, in *A Room of One's Own*; the isolation, the class-constrictions, and the sense of mortality of the six characters in *The Waves*; the escape from the Victorian home in *Flush*: in *The Years*, these preoccupations found their most subversive, harsh and angry expression.

But also their most generalised and de-centred. There is no 'I', no inward 'stream of consciousness' in *The Years*. She conceals her autobiography through structure and tone. The aim was not to have a heroine or a hero, but

637

to make a broad, synthesising social analysis. She needed to disguise the personal sources of this analysis in a narrative with no sacrosanct private spaces. As, in the early 1920s, she had moved from stories of youth to middle-age (a move re-enacted in the plot of *The Waves*) so now, in the 1930s, she moved from the personal to the social, from individual intensity to group voices. In this novel, unlike *The Waves*, no one can speak their 'selves' fully, either to themselves or to anyone else. The inhibition, fear and self-censorship which have always been a feature of her characters' lives here become symptomatic. These lives are case histories; these forms of frustrated and indecisive behaviour are products of a political system.

She starts by talking about the book as a kind of essay – a 'novel-essay' – and ends up thinking of it as a kind of play. As it developed, it became harder and harder to write. It took her almost two years to complete the first draft. The beginning – the 1880 scene of the Victorian family in a house very like 22 Hyde Park Gate, with the mother dying upstairs – was written at high speed, as a relief from correcting 'that abominable dog' *Flush*, and as a 'heavenly freedom' after the strain and intensity of *The Waves*.[3] They had just bought a new car, an opulent green convertible Lanchester which she immediately nicknamed 'The Deluge', and she felt her mind was working like the car, as if 'a Rolls Royce engine were powering its 70 miles an hour in my brain'.[4] 'The Deluge' could have been a nickname for the novel, too, in its early stages. All through 1933 and into 1934 she was talking to herself about being in 'full flood'.[5] The scenes poured out, moving in jumps from 1880 to the 1930s, between different family groups and generations. None of them took more than about six weeks to write.

But from the start there were warning signs. Her first plan was to alternate fictional 'extracts' from an imaginary longer novel about 'a family called Pargiter',[6] with essays commenting on the difficulties for the woman writer in dealing with such fictional material. So the rival demands of fiction and polemic, fact and vision, would be held in counterweighted balance. But this brilliant idea almost immediately ran aground. As early as February 1933 she was 'leaving out the interchapters – compacting them in the text'.[7] She was anxious to avoid a Lawrentian didacticism, to find a way of fusing argument and atmosphere so as to 'give the whole of the present society – nothing less: facts, as well as the vision. And to combine them both . . . There are to be millions of ideas but no preaching – history, politics, feminism, art, literature – in short a summing up of all I know, feel, laugh at, despise, like, admire hate & so on.'[8] But there was one overriding problem with this ambitious scheme for a 'condition of England' novel, which was, essentially, how to present 'intellectual argument in the form of art'.[9]

One of the symptoms of the difficulty was that she could not settle on a title.[10] She didn't finally decide until September 1935, in her last stages of retyping and correcting. Before that, it was to be *The Pargiters*, then *Here and Now* (so as not to 'compete with the Herries Saga, the Forsyte Saga & so on').[11] Or: *Music, Dawn, Sons and Daughters, Daughters and Sons* (both with a nod to Elizabeth Gaskell rather than Ivy Compton-Burnett), *Ordinary People* (because she had been reading and enjoying E. Arnot Robinson's *Ordinary Families*),[12] *The Caravan, Other People's Houses*. Sometimes she just called it 'the nameless book'.[13]

Even while the first version, *The Pargiters* or *Here and Now*, was pouring out of her, there were signs of anxiety. As always (she liked accounts) she began to try and work out how long the next stages were going to take. In April 1933 she thought she might finish the first draft in four months. In fact it took four months and a year. By September 1933 she was worrying about the word-count: 'It will be the longest of my little brood'.[14]

The painful story of the length of *The Years* – length of time, length of book – is summed up in the correspondence with her American publisher, Donald Brace. In April 1934, she told him that the book would not be ready for a year. At the same time she was telling herself that there was no hurry. 'I've enough money to last a year. If the book comes out in June next year its time enough.'[15] But she was terribly aware by the summer of 1934 how much it would need 'sweating down', and was beginning to refer to it, only half-jokingly, as 'interminable'.[16] The first draft, finished in September 1934, came to about 200,000 words. In November 1934, as she began to revise, she told Brace it would need a lot of work and would now probably not be ready until the *autumn* of 1935.[17] But by autumn she was writing again to say that it was too long, and taking too long, and still needed revising. The following April, 1936, Leonard explained that although the book was now in proof, she was unwell, and publication must be put off until the autumn. Brace, who had now seen proofs of the first part, wrote forbearingly: 'It isn't surprising that this long and carefully planned book should have tired her out.' In July he was asking if he could make November a tentative publication date. But by then it was still not ready to send off, and in the end was not published until March 1937 in England and April 1937 in America.[18]

During the writing of the first draft, excitement and interest outweighed apprehension. It was a completely different kind of process from the writing of *The Waves*. That was part of her difficulty, of course. Not to keep writing the same book, always to push on, to find 'a fresh form of being, that is of expression, for everything I feel & think', required 'constant effort, anxiety, & risk'.[19] The narrative in *The Waves* had tried to be both personal and generic. It described how the self comes into being, how it is socialised, turns into an adult, relates to the body, communicates, does not stay fixed or stable. *The Waves* had taken her method of formalising and acting out the secret unspoken inner life of the self as far as it could go – so far, that there had to be an artificial incongruity between the rhythmic, patterned texture of the characters' speeches (all of which sounded as if uttered by 'the same person'), and the obscure, troubled areas of their personality.

In *The Waves*'s long brooding gestation, the notes she made on the book were all about privacy, subjectivity, and abstraction.[20] It had to 'eliminate', 'saturate', 'submerge'. It was to be 'abstract poetic'. It was written to a rhythm, not a plot, and so 'completely opposed to the tradition of fiction'. In order to write it, she told herself, 'I am going to enter a nunnery'. It was to be the story of 'The Lonely Mind'.[21]

The Years reworked some of the same autobiographical materials. And while she was writing the first draft, she re-read bits of her past. In July 1933 she was 'reading old diaries', writing a memoir (perhaps for the Memoir Club) about her unhappy years at Fitzroy Square, visiting the Burne-Jones centenary exhibition at the Tate, which made her think of 'tea at Hyde Park Gate', and encouraging Ottoline to write her memoirs. At the end of the year, as she was beginning the 1917 air-raid scene, she went back to her old diaries of the days at Richmond after her breakdown. 'How close the tears come, again & again, as I read of L & me at the Green . . . the sense of all that floating away for ever down the stream, unknown for ever: queer sense of the past swallowing so much of oneself.'[22]

The Years revitalised that ghostly past. But this novel, she saw in July 1934, was 'breaking the mould made by *The Waves*'.[23] This time the inner selves of the characters are given only as much weight as their ineffectual social gestures or as the political forces and domestic pressures that press in on them. So, as she was writing it, rather than retreating into a mental nunnery for 'The Lonely Mind', she found that everything she did and read seemed to overlap with it. Often she caught herself behaving or sounding like 'Elvira' Pargiter (the difficult, eccentric, critical 'outsider' in the novel, who would be renamed Sara), or absentmindedly writing a bit of the novel into her diary.

Between giving the 'Professions for Women' speech in January 1931 and starting *The Pargiters* in October 1932 she had started to fill up her reading notebooks with references to 'scores – I might boldly say thousands – of old memoirs'.[24] And it was now that she began to keep scrapbooks of press cuttings from newspapers. She did this all through the 1930s, especially between 1931 and 1933 and between 1935 and 1937. These cuttings, examples of current sexist prejudice and double standards, included a 'Whitehall Storm' over whether a woman should run a labour exchange, and the resignation of eleven members of a library committee when a woman was appointed. Next to these sorts of news-stories she copied remarks from C.E.M. Joad ('Women, I think, ought not to sit down to table with men') or from William Gerhardi on women having 'no position to speak of in literature' – and a hundred other examples, modern and Victorian, of bigotry and repression, and of the connections between patriarchy and militarism. All this fed into the novel and into *Three Guineas*: already by 1932 she had 'enough powder to blow up St Paul's'.[25]

At the same time she was making notes on a history of the English people, and reading Montaigne and the *Antigone*. The roles of wives and daughters in history was uppermost in her mind. She was reading a life of Parnell, and had ideas of writing a play about him, or a life of Mrs Parnell. In April 1933 an American publisher suggested that she write a life of Leslie Stephen: 'Good God!'[26] Later in 1933, despite her dislike for the author, she read Vera Brittain's *Testament of Youth* 'extreme greed'. Brittain's personal, pacificist story, 'told in detail, without reserve', gripped her: she knew that to 'stand bare in public' was something she could never do.[27]

She was also reading religious works – a 'virtuous'[28] study of the Oxford Movement by Geoffrey Faber, the book of Job, the New Testament – with fascination and anger. (The most savage footnotes in *Three Guineas* would be on St Paul, whom she identifies as a member of 'the virile or dominant type, so familiar at present in Germany, for whose gratification a subject race or sex is essential').[29] One evening in April 1934, Eliot (now separated from Vivien, and looking more than ever 'like a great toad with jewelled eyes'), Maynard Keynes, Julian Bell and Elizabeth Bowen were at Tavistock Square talking about Eliot's new book, *After Strange Gods*, and about religion and morality. Maynard maintained that the morality of their generation had owed a great deal to their parents' religion. Julian said that *his* generation had been 'landed' by his parents' scepticism in psychoanalysis and communism. Tom, though challenged by Virginia, 'reserved his idea of God'. But she got it full in the face later that year, when she read *The Rock*, and felt her 'anti-religious bias' rising: 'He seems to me to be petrifying into a priest – poor old Tom.'[30]

Ethel was easier to tease about her faith. (And of course Virginia never stopped teasing her. Writing to her on her holiday in 1933 she ended her letter affectionately: 'Well, what are you doing? – inducing a large penis into a small hole?')[31] Complaining about the noise of the Rodmell church bells in the summer of 1934 (and preferring her own idea of heaven as 'one continuous unexhausted reading'), she told Ethel she was reading a life of one of her Venn ancestors, an eighteenth-century parson. She quoted him on a giddy parishioner: ' "Mercifully," he says, "she swallowed a pin;

which led her to thoughts of death . . . & she became a shining light."
Mercifully she swallowed a pin! How can you belong to such a canting
creed!'[32]

In *Three Guineas*, the 'canting creed' of Christianity would be an agent of
repression. In *The Years* she lets in more mixed feelings. All through the
novel, the symbols of Christianity, 'the lean & twisted figure on the
crucifix', or the gobbledygook of the prayer book, 'the father incomprehensible, the son incomprehensible', are treated with baffled scepticism. But
Eleanor, the older Pargiter daughter, who provides the alternative key voice
in the novel to her cousin Elvira/Sara's, is always trying to work out the
'incomprehensible' relationship between belief and evidence. And Delia,
the angriest of the Pargiter sisters, is enchanted at her mother's funeral
service by the phrase 'I am the Resurrection and the Life', without believing
a word of it. (It's like Mrs Ramsay in *To the Lighthouse* finding herself
repeating, against her better judgement, 'We are in the hands of the Lord'.)
The social injustices carried out in the name of Christianity battle against
the allure of its consolatory language.

Apart from drafting (and reading enormously for) *The Pargiters*, Virginia
did not do much other writing in 1933 and 1934. What she did, though, all
seemed to connect with the book. She was reading Goldsmith through
much of 1933 for an essay she wrote in the autumn.[33] His *Citizen of the
World* appealed to her: she noted his detached satire on the 'parochial
patriotism' of the English, just when she was making her own detached
diagnosis as a citizen of her world. From the summer to the autumn she was
also reading Turgenev, for a piece published in December 1933. This
reading strongly influenced her novel. The way he 'wrote & re-wrote' in
order 'to clear the truth of the unessential', his 'long struggle of elimination'
was a powerful example to her. He combined, as she wanted to, 'the fact &
the vision'. She was inspired by the suppression of the 'I' in Turgenev's
novels, their almost 'impersonal' quality, the way that among his characters
'the individual never dominates; many other things seemed to be going on at
the same time'. That was exactly what she wanted to get in *The Years*, and
what she tried for during her own 'long struggle of elimination'.[34]

While she was reading Turgenev, she also began to take notes on the
paintings of Walter Sickert. In November she went to his retrospective
show and wrote to tell him how much she admired it. He replied: 'Why
don't you do me a serious service? Write on this exhibition. I suggest that
you *saute pardessus* all paint-box technical twaddle about art which has bored
and will always bore everybody stiff. Write about the Humours and Drama
you find in it. You would be the *first to do so. I have always been a literary
painter*, thank goodness, like all the decent painters. Do be the first to say

so.'[35] Clive arranged a convivial dinner party in December, at which Sickert told her that she was right to think of his paintings as 'books'. Duncan reported that 'She told him what she imagined about his works and invented astonishing psychological situations for the figures – which got very wild. However Sickert said she was the only person who had ever understood him and that we were idiotic for not realising that he was an entirely literary artist.'[36]

Sickert inspired a dazzling essay, which used one of her favourite devices, the dinner-party and the conversation as starting-point and plot. Taking off (as she so often 'took off' in conversation) from the recent introduction of three-coloured traffic lights in London, in order to ask how it is we respond to colour, she pursued her old controversy between the story-tellers and the painters. Sickert's paintings offer themselves as biographies or as novels, she said: and she brilliantly imagines the life-stories behind *Ennui* or *Lady in Red* to prove her point. She observes how eloquently he places these English lives of 'desolation' and 'sordidity' in their context, how characters are made to lose their 'separateness' and become 'composed'. How much more suggestive are these 'biographies' than the written ones, tripped up by 'the miserable impediments called facts'! But she acknowledges that her literary interpretations of his paintings can't reach the 'zone of silence in the middle of every art'; perhaps the painters, with their concentration on form and colour, get closer to it. The debate, of course, is unresolved: Sickert is a 'hybrid', she concludes, a 'literary artist'.

Her reading of his paintings infected her novel. Sickert (especially in his Camden Town paintings) presented a grim, seedy, violent urban underlife without any moral or political message. He made imaginary lives seem real through colour and texture. He did portraits of real sitters, too, but in the most startling, revealing and unflattering way. His work seemed 'continually conscious of the passing moment, the unrepeatable instant of certain looks and gestures'. One of his friends said that 'he lived at such a pitch of awareness as if he remembered death all the time'.[37] For all these reasons, he was one of the great influences on *The Years*, with Turgenev, the *Antigone*, history books, memoirs – and a thousand newspaper clippings.

Vanessa and Duncan had always greatly admired Sickert; the essay was written at Vanessa's instigation. The drafting of *The Years* involved an intensive return in memory to their childhood years; and one of the novel's themes was sisters. Meanwhile Vanessa's work and family life were much in Virginia's mind. Just as she began the novel, she and Vanessa gave a big party for the opening of the 'Music Room', an entire room decorated by Vanessa and Duncan, at the Lefèvre Gallery in King Street, St James's.

Virginia was a patron of the show; she guaranteed to spend £100, and for this she got a screen with voluptuous ladies by Vanessa, a big mirror, some cane chairs, and a luxurious carpet by Duncan, which filled her with delight and made her feel like 'a tropical fish swimming in a submerged forest'.[38]

The Music Room displayed to perfection Vanessa's and Duncan's typical – and no longer very modernist-looking – motifs of flowers and fruits and shells, their Provençal and Italianate colourings, their mirrors and screens decorated with scallops and drapes and cross-hatchings, their co-ordinated patterning and prettifying of all domestic objects from pianos to chaircovers. It was a style replicated in Virginia's houses and (increasingly incongruously) on her book-jackets.

The opening, which Virginia warned Ottoline would be 'quite ghastly' (and after which, she told Elizabeth Bowen, she was completely 'knocked up'), was a big social occasion. Asquiths and Hutchinsons, 'Bloomsbury' and 'Mayfair', artists and journalists, all came. Reports spoke of the room 'vibrating to a Debussy solo on the harp'; of the sisters as 'shining stars in the literary and artistic world and uncrowned queens of Bloomsbury'; and of Virginia Woolf 'lighting a cigarette in a manner unhurried, airy, and medieval – a kind of Borgia deliberateness'.[39] She herself described it as 'Us two hussies entertaining the peerage: & boys in white jackets handing blue green yellow drinks'.[40]

There were other parties early in 1933, whose mood got into the family reunions in *The Years*. At a fancy dress party for Angelica's fourteenth birthday in January 1933, Virginia went as Queen Victoria. 'I like masks,' she wrote (brooding in the same breath on Elvira and her thoughts about civilisation), 'I like the disorientation they give my feelings'.[41] (After this birthday, Virginia began to pay an annual dress allowance to Angelica, of £100 a year.)[42] At another party in January, after the opening of Constant Lambert's ballet *Pomona* at Sadler's Wells, with designs by Vanessa ('Fra Angelico against a background of Cassis', Virginia described it),[43] they all went back to the studio at Fitzroy Street and ate 'indecent'-looking hot writhing sausages. Bunny Garnett (who at forty had just published a new novel of which Virginia felt jealous) embraced her, because she said she had dreamt that he took her in his arms. It felt to her like a 'pale phantom of old love – the love of men & women'.[44]

Quentin, later this year, fell ill with TB, and had to be flown to a sanatorium in Switzerland. The Woolfs drove Vanessa and Quentin to the airport at Croydon, and she watched them, for the first time in her life, taking off (and then had to imagine Vanessa flying back, in thick fog) with extreme anxiety: 'This is death I said, feeling how the human contact was completely severed.'[45] Quentin's time in the sanatorium was enlivened by a stream of funny, gossipy London – he had started to app... an anti-war exhibition and joining... was hovering uneasily between the lu... pacifism, writing in pain to John Lehman... politics'.[46]

His confusion, which by 1935 had hardened up... pacifism of his parents' generation and on the side of ... against the brought home the darkening political events. Leonard's work, a... Fascism, reading of the papers, and all their friends' talk of what was taking sh... avid ... Europe, also kept Virginia closely aware of developments. At moments, Europe would be brought dramatically near. In April 1933 they met, through Ethel, the German conductor Bruno Walter, who had left Germany after Hitler came to power in January, and who would go to America in 1939. His 'nearly mad' outpouring on what the 'poison' of Hitler's party was doing to the Germany he had loved made a violent impression on her.

A few days later Virginia and Leonard went for their 1933 spring holiday to Italy, via France. Like their trip to Greece the year before, the journey took her back into her past: she remembered going to Italy after Leslie died, with Violet, in 1904; she remembered hiding behind a pillar in Pisa, on their honeymoon, to avoid old friends of Leslie's. But Italy had changed. Her holiday notes were of encounters in hotels, thoughts of the death of Shelley at Rapallo, and of Lawrence, on seeing his tomb at Vence on their way back. But she wrote in an uneasily light tone to Ethel: 'I dont like Fascist Italy at all – but hist! – there's the black shirt under the window – so no more.'[47]

All that year and the next she watched her own country potentially turning into 'Fascist England' as support gathered for Mosley's party and there were increasingly violent clashes between the Blackshirts and the anti-Fascists. Abroad, the civil war in Austria between the Fascists and the Social Democrats, Hitler's rise to Führer, and in June 1934 his mass slaughter of his opponents, filled her with terror, rage and helplessness: 'these brutal bullies go about in hoods & masks, like little boys dressed up, acting this idiotic, meaningless, brutal, bloody pandemonium.'[48] The emotions went into everything she would write from now on.

But through 1933 and 1934, personal and social events pressed in as urgently as world affairs. Scenes from her life seemed to illustrate or confirm the political diagnosis she was making in her book.

It is an utterly corrupt society I have just remarked, speaking in the person of Elvira Pargiter, & I will take nothing that it can give me &c &c:

– oh dear me what a bore – to the
...ity & say that I refuse to be made a

now, as Virginia Woolf, I
Vice Chancellor of M
Doctor of Letters.[49]

The refusal to '... all that humbug' and 'Mumbo-Jumbo' – awards,
...eships, membership of committees – was mixed up
degrees, publ... snobbery about the provinces and a settled dislike (now
with a goo... considerably) of universities as establishments. The following
hardeni... contributed a piece called 'Why?' to an Oxford women students'
year, m...zine, *Lysistrata* (edited by Robert Graves's niece, Sally), on the
fatuousness of lectures on literature: 'Why not create a new form of society
founded on poverty and equality? Why not bring together people of all ages
and both sexes of all shades of fame and obscurity so that they can talk,
without mounting platforms, or reading papers, or wearing expensive
clothes, or eating expensive food?'[50] Going to the Women's Guild Jubilee
celebrations produced the same response, again written in the words she
was giving to Elvira Pargiter: 'I hate ceremonies – not a word that fits – all
wind blown, gaseous.'[51] One good thing, however, came out of the
Manchester episode – a valuable, if not very intimate, friendship with Lady
Shena Simon, a distinguished educationalist and public figure, married to a
leading Manchester industrialist, whose solid, factual, feminist brains she
would pick for *Three Guineas*.

Quarrels continued with Ethel, who mournfully declared in April 1933
that Virginia was now 'dead' to her. 'I'm amused to be dead', Virginia
responded with glee, ' – one of those ghosts that people talk of
respectfully . . . Yes, I intend to be a dead in future; the dead have so many
rights'.[52] She took Ethel to task again for her egotism in her writing, just
while she was thinking about the need for impersonality in her own writing.
('What would the world be,' thinks one of the Pargiters, as Virginia Woolf's
characters often thought, 'without "I" in it?')[53] And the quarrel with Ethel
over social claims also continued. After the return from Italy, the summer of
1933 was swamped with visitors. 'July was like being a biscuit in the middle
of rats', she told her.[54]

Some of this 'society' was interesting (meetings with Shaw, a weekend
visit from Tom Eliot, tender reunions with Ottoline), some at least
intriguing. Two parties at Mary Hutchinson's this year entertained her.
One was in July, with Mary all in white like a pierrot, when they went on to
the zoo (the summer evening openings were in fashion) and Virginia
watched Mary and Leonard picking up pythons in the reptile house: 'L took
one & it wound itself round his head like a toque, sticking its head out &
flicking its tongue at the side.'[55] The other, a smart dinner, was in

November, when she wore her velvet dress and met Michael Arlen ('a little scraping dingy porous clammy monkey faced man'), Princess Bibesco ('Pasty, podgy') and Victor and Barbara Rothschild, filthy rich and endlessly bickering. By the time she had done with them, they all seemed much like the animals at the zoo.[56]

The summer and autumn of 1933 also involved a spill-over of about fifteen people to tea at Rodmell after a Memoir Club meeting in September, a weekend with Rosamond Lehmann and Wogan Phillips, and a visit to the Fishers, in the Warden's Lodgings at New College Oxford. Here she listened to the stories of smooth, equable, distinguished Herbert Fisher, who represented everything she resented – 'culture, politics, worldly wisdom gilt with letters' – and was introduced to Isaiah Berlin ('a Portuguese Jew by the look of him'), who thought her very beautiful and socially difficult, and who noted her lack of ease with the forty or fifty undergraduates she was introduced to after dinner:

> She looked terribly embarrassed, like a Bishop about to do confirmation. She said: 'Has anyone here read *Jane Eyre*?' 'Yes.' 'Could you tell me the plot?' . . . 'Has anyone here read *Shirley*?' 'Yes.' 'Could you tell me the plot?' And so on. Then Mrs Fisher said, 'It's 10.30 and I'm going to bed.' After that she relaxed.[57]

Sometimes her resistance to 'society' was transparent. In June, visiting 'LeonardsLee', a garden in Sussex, on their way back from Sissinghurst, she saw two old ladies, Nelly Cecil and Violet Dickinson, coming towards her, and was spotted by Lady Cecil taking cover behind a large azalea – though she maintained that she had tried to follow them, and *they* had disappeared.[58] And in September she invited the 'charming' and 'fastidious' Cambridge don Peter Lucas and his 'loveless, beautyless' new young wife to Rodmell, and embarrassingly found they had expected to stay two nights, when she had fixed another engagement for the second night. 'The truth is, I like it when people actually come; but I love it when they go.'[59]

Too many visitors, too much society: she was beginning to write these words almost every week. It was preferable to take Pinker for a walk in the country, or to sit silently with Leonard listening to a Haydn symphony or a Beethoven string quartet before bed, or to go to Sadler's Wells to hear Gluck's *Orpheus*, 'the loveliest opera ever written'.[60] All this time she was trying to think herself into a more detached, less obligated way of living. Society had got to be on her terms, both in private and in public. She needed, both for her writing and her life, to develop 'a philosophy of anonymity'. 'I will not be "famous" "great". I will go on adventuring, changing, opening my mind & my eyes, refusing to be stamped & stereotyped.' The same week she wrote a furious letter to the *New Statesman & Nation* about the need for – and the *duty* of – public figures to protect themselves from journalistic intrusion. She offered to create a new society for the purpose: a society for 'the Protection of Privacy'.

> A badge might be worn. A pledge might be administered. Members of the literary profession, for example, might take an oath not to allow any photograph, drawing or caricature of themselves to appear in the papers with[out] their consent; not to give interviews; not to give autographs; not to attend public dinners; not to speak in public; not to see unknown admirers provided with letters of introduction from friends – and so, and so on.[61]

Like the subversive women's club in her 1920s story 'A Society'; or the society founded on 'poverty and equality' she recommended in 'Why?'; or the 'society of outsiders' she was to invent in *Three Guineas*, this idea of an alternative membership fascinated her. It could be a kind of open university, for people who didn't want lectures, degrees, 'tufts of fur' on their head or their pictures in the paper; a club for people who wanted to be 'entirely private'.[62]

The impulse towards privacy and outsiderism was deeply felt and very contradictory. She liked fame, success and money, but she hated publicity, especially at a time when the personalising of authorship through interviews and publicity was increasing. She wanted to be reviewed for her work, but she didn't want to have her private life known. She wanted to be in the swim, asked out and visited, but – like that iconic film star whom Spender and his friends thought such a joke – she wanted to be alone. She wanted to talk, but she wanted to write and to think. She wanted to be outside, but she was snobbish about where she did belong. And all this was what her characters were talking about in the book. Floundering, hesitating, stammering, they all seem to be asking why they can't find a way to live 'differently, differently'.[63]

In the New Year she was at Monk's House for three weeks, still in 'full flood', writing the long air-raid scene. One of the characters, Elvira/Sara's dearest friend Nicholas, is a homosexual. She told Quentin that she was struggling with the problem of candour (and as she revised, she censored herself increasingly): 'How far can one say openly what is the relation of a woman and a sod? In French, yes; but in Mr Galsworthys English, no.'[64] Back in London she visited the law courts to verify a scene set there: she was still collecting 'ammunition', still sounding like Elvira or Eleanor in her diary ('All men are liars'),[65] still turning down official commitments, like having her portrait painted for the National Portrait Gallery, or going on a committee for the 'inconceivably timid', 'oh so proper' BBC. 'No official positions for me.'[66]

She was fifty-two in 1934; this would be the year her menopause (or 't of l' as she called it), which she had been dreading, would begin, though its symptoms continued for at least two years, 'the swollen veins – the tingling; the odd falling; feeling of despair. Brain not fully blooded. Hot & cold.' 'A physical feeling as if I were drumming slightly in the veins.'[67] Other people's deaths made her feel, as always, guilty and empty, like that of the novelist Stella Benson at forty-one, whom she had hardly known but liked. She thought of Katherine: 'I go on; & they cease. Why?'[68] The death of Leonard's sister Clara, however, involved rather different reactions: 'It was all very interesting, as the Jews dress up in black, wear top hats, and look exactly like Hebrew prophets.' As women are excluded from synagogue funerals, Virginia spent a painful afternoon sitting with her grieving mother-in-law.[69]

But the most powerful emotions of the New Year were once again centred on Nelly. In February they had electricians installing a new 'bath water engine'; in March the Bedford Estate required the Woolfs as its tenants to redecorate Tavistock Square, so the whole house, from top to bottom, was taken over by builders, paint, hammering, book moving, and dust. Nelly complained, and 'suddenly' (Virginia told Ethel) 'I felt this was the end'. There were several weeks of scenes and suspense ('Can I do it? I must. I must'.) She was determined not to discuss it with Leonard. At last, hardening her heart, she told Nelly to go on 27 March. The final scene was not as violent as she had anticipated, but the whole drama (which, as she kept telling herself, need not have happened if she had stuck to her guns three years ago) was extremely demoralising and painful – to both women. As soon as it was over, she felt a 'sense of freedom and calm – no more brooding; no more possessiveness; no more sense of being part of Nelly's world.' Nelly, in a pathetic last gesture of pride and resentment, refused to shake hands, and took all the cookery books. She was replaced in London by an ex-servant of Margery Fry, Mabel Haskins, an easily snubbed and less combative character (rapidly and uncharitably nicknamed 'the Cow'), who would last as their cook for six years, but who was never liked by Leonard. ('She is evidently', Vanessa noted, 'terrified out of her wits by him. The difficulty is to keep L out of the kitchen. He goes in to make coffee for breakfast, to cut up his animals food & to carry out dishes during meals – which to my mind no cook will endure.')[70] But in Rodmell, in July, they hired as 'cook-general' a girl in her twenties called Louie Everest. She was living in Southease with her husband and two small children, and badly needed work; the Woolfs were offering a live-in cottage in Rodmell and seven shillings and sixpence a week. She appealed to them as soon as they met her: 'a merry little brown eyed mongrel who came running to meet us in the road.' And though the hours they required were severe, though not unusually so for the time (eight in the morning until nine at night, with some afternoons off) and the Woolfs looked rather daunting at first sight, Louie became attached to her employers. She was to stay with them for the rest of their lives.[71]

After the disruptions at Tavistock Square, Virginia set *The Pargiters* (now being called *Here & Now*) aside, told Donald Brace she had nothing for him yet, and left for their spring holiday, at the end of April, to Ireland. It was her first and only visit there. They drove through Wales to Fishguard and took the ferry, over a stormy Irish sea, to Cork. They stayed one night with Elizabeth Bowen at Bowen's Court in north-east County Cork; then drove to the little village of Glengarrif on Bantry Bay, then to Kerry and Galway and finally to Dublin. Her literary associations with the country were above all with Yeats (whom she was soon to meet again at Ottoline's) and Swift. She saw the 'tremendous words' of Swift's epitaph in St Patrick's Cathedral ('He lies where furious rage can rend his heart no more'), heard that 'Stella's' brass floor plate had been moved away from his by the previous Dean ('I suspect this was prudery'), and visited 'Vanessa''s sham Gothic Abbey at Celbridge, all this with some feeling. But she did not call Joyce to mind in Dublin. 'Why aren't these people the greatest novelists in the world?' she asked, meeting a famous Irish talker, Mrs Fitzgerald, in the Glenbeigh Hotel, Kerry, the remark indirectly confirming how she had underrated Joyce.

Politically, her sense of Ireland was more detailed than the average English tourist's. She knew Shaw, she had been reading about Parnell, she would have heard Julian talking about his great hero, Michael Collins. But the Ireland she met was mainly that of the Anglo-Irish gentry and the hoteliers. She didn't make contact with Joyce's urban middle-class Ireland, and she was not especially allured by the romance of the Gaelic-speaking West. On the coast of Galway, they picked gentians and were delighted by the scenery, saw people gathering seaweed, and looked across at the Aran Islands; in the city, they visited the Claddagh, 'the original Irish quarter', and observed 'shawled women, coated men, all standing in groups together beside thatched huts'. In Dublin, they coincided at lunch at the Shelbourne Hotel with a group of Aran Islanders (dressed in thick tweeds, singing 'what may be hymns' and talking Irish), who were in the city after helping to publicise Robert Flaherty's great documentary, *Man of Aran*, which had just opened in London (and which they saw on 23 May). The film celebrated a way of life which even now, just as Virginia Woolf observed it in passing, was starting to disappear.

What she noticed most of all – visiting at the time when de Valera's Fianna Fail party was giving a freer rein to the IRA and imposing 'Economic War' and retrenchment on the landowners – was, as in Greece, the emptiness and poverty of the countryside. Everywhere she felt 'a sense that life is receding', and a ubiquitous melancholy (she kept using the word). They both fell in love with Glengarrif ('Its a mixture of Italy Greece and Cornwall') with its soft light and its magical little offshore Italian island-garden. As usual on their holidays, she fantasised about living there. And she was amazed and delighted by the eloquence and sharpness of the talk. She caught it, of course, very well. There was the 'Tchehov innkeeper' at Lismore who said 'Theyre all going away & leaving their houses; nothing's kept up since the war', and the Beckettian old man on Glengarrif island who longed to talk, and who 'crooned & moaned' on the same theme, 'leaning on the rake with which he was heaping up some kind of weed'. And there was the superb, quick-witted, unquenchable Mrs Fitzgerald, who, when she started talking again in the morning, and Leonard slightly put out his hand, immediately said, 'Oh I know that means you wanting to be off.' But in the end all the talk depressed her: if one was to live there, 'all one's mind wd run out in talk'.

Dublin too seemed melancholy: she noted, snootily, its provincialism, its 'air of inferiority' towards Europe (Merrion Square trying and failing to be Bedford Square). But she noted, too, and rightly, the feeling of being 'in the midst of history . . . in an unsettled, feverish place' where 'anything may happen'. Elizabeth Bowen would have entirely agreed with her: 'Dublin exhales melancholy', she wrote in the 1930s; 'an anticlimactic, possibly endless pause hangs over her large squares, long light streets and darkening Georgian façades.' But Virginia Woolf was not yet treating Elizabeth Bowen as a literary equal or a close friend. She hadn't read *The Last September* (1929), Bowen's evocative fiction of the Anglo-Irish during the Troubles. When they got to Bowen's Court she was appalled to find Cyril Connolly and his 'gollywog slug wife Jean' there, bringing in 'the roar of the Chelsea omnibus'. (Connolly, who was not all that keen himself, noted with interest that 'she asked Elizabeth Bowen what "unnatural vice" was and what acts constituted it, and sensed that she was a virginal and shy character'). There were things to enjoy; Bowen's Court had a certain 'character and charm', Elizabeth's husband Alan Cameron wasn't as dull as she had been led to expect, and there were entertaining moments, as when

Leonard, taken to the Bowen's Court wishing-well, wished 'that Pinka might not smell'. But Bowen's Court was, like many of the Ascendancy's Big Houses after the Troubles, a place of dilapidated grandeur. What Bowen called 'brave acting-up' went into the Anglo-Irish gentry's maintaining of hospitality in these Big Houses. Virginia was condescending; she found it, mainly, full of 'desolation & pretension'.

> Elizabeths home was merely a great stone box, but full of Italian masterpieces and decayed 18th century furniture, and carpets all in holes – however they insisted upon keeping up a ramshackle kind of state, dressing for dinner and so on.[72]

Elizabeth Bowen, then in her mid-thirties, with four books of stories and four novels and a good deal of journalism to her name, knew (and liked more uncritically) many of Virginia's friends – Ottoline, Tom Eliot, and, especially, David Cecil. (She had loved the Cecil/MacCarthy wedding which Virginia so detested.) She had been greatly influenced by Virginia Woolf, especially in her own first novel, *The Hotel*, and she treated her still with some 'awe and alarm'. Elizabeth's letters to Virginia were anxious to amuse, like the one she wrote her from Rome later that year, with vivid descriptions of landscapes and politics: 'I was given a seat in a grandstand in the Fascist stadium to watch, a few feet away, Mussolini on a white horse reviewing police-dogs, bands, tanks – that was awful.'[73] But she was writing quite as much as Virginia Woolf in the 1930s about the queasiness and lack of conviction of the English middle classes (for instance in the stories in *The Cat Jumps*, published that year). Clearly, though, Virginia as yet knew little of her writing or of her private life: at this time, Elizabeth was involved in a painful and intense affair, kept separate from her stable marriage. After Elizabeth and Alan moved from Oxford to London, to one of the Regency Terrace houses in Regent's Park, in 1935, the two women would become more intimate and relaxed with each other. (Bowen's letters to Virginia about her house-hunting in the summer of 1935 show their affinities: 'But how very alarming and impertinent – feeling this Order to View, walking into people's lived-in houses is. It is impossible to believe that the people discovered in rooms sitting stiffly about as dolls in dolls-house attitudes are not to be sold with the house, and to remember that it is not necessary to ask oneself whether one likes them.')[74] What Elizabeth Bowen liked most about Virginia Woolf was her comic exuberance. She got very impatient with later versions of her as a tragic, gloomy figure, and always remembered her 'entrancing, outrageous laughter'.[75] What Virginia liked about Elizabeth was her stoicism, her courage, her honesty, something 'sterling & sharp edged'[76] about her. Probably she always simplified Elizabeth, as she had patronised her house: she didn't see the passion and wildness, the pride and secretiveness in her character. But Virginia became more interested in her work; a letter to her about *The House in Paris* (1935) was (equivocatingly) generous:

> I think I like it best of all your books. I think it goes deeper, with less effort, & the cleverness pulls its weight instead of lying to dazzle on the top. It all composes so well – perhaps a little too well. I mean, it has a little the air of being tied at the end into a knot, rather too tight. But I have read it only once, & too quickly. But all the same I had the feeling that your world imposed itself on my world, while I read, which only happens when one is being taken in hand by a work. I mean, I said, This is how Elizabeth sees that flower, not that is my flower . . . As usual, the rightness seemed to me unconscious; something that you didn't notice yourself, & the wrongness when it got cold, & you added with bright but rather steely ink something too exact, too definite for the context. But this is only my old grumble, that we are afraid of the human heart (& with reason); & until we can write with all our faculties in action (even the big toe) but under the water, submerged, then we must be clever, like the rest of the modern sticklebacks.[77]

(Writing to their mutual friend William Plomer, Elizabeth called this 'a very nice letter'.)[78] Characteristically, Virginia suggested that Elizabeth should write a memoir of her family: 'Remember the Lives of the Bowens', she wrote to her after their visit. During the war (when Virginia was writing her own unfinished memoir of her childhood) Elizabeth Bowen did write *Bowen's Court* and *Seven Winters*. But Virginia never read them: they were published in 1942.

Travelling back through England, the 'ancient rich traditional' prosperous complacency of Worcestershire struck her forcibly by contrast: 'Horses rule England, as salmon rule Ireland.'[79] Shakespeare's 'relics' at Stratford, by contrast with Swift's angry, embarrassing remains in Dublin, seemed to her to reflect a figure 'serenely absent-present . . . never to be pinned down . . . all air & sun smiling serenely'.[80] She would read him, on and off, all summer.

While they were in Ireland, Leonard saw the announcement of George Duckworth's death in *The Times*. Her reaction was surprisingly tender. 'Poor old creature . . .' 'How childhood goes with him – the batting, the laughter, the treats, the presents, taking us for bus rides to see famous Churches, giving us tea at City Inns'. She found herself remembering the best of George, the George of early childhood. All the same, a memoir

Vanessa had written, presumably about his later behaviour, still 'flooded' her with so much horror that she could not be 'pure minded' on the subject. And yet in the same breath she wished she had gone to the service. And found it possible, visiting the widowed Margaret Duckworth, to 'sob' with her: 'some sincerity welling up after all these indifferent years.' Yet again, when she found that George had left her £100, she felt snubbed and resentful. These confused responses suggest a memory of a less vicious 'George Duckworth' than she usually presented; but they suggest too the lasting force of unresolved emotions.[81]

After they got back, she had an attack of the 'flu, and found the novel difficult to resume. She had been reading Proust ('Sodom et Gomorrhe') on holiday, and by comparison her own book seemed 'hopeless'. It began to feel impossibly long: 'Oh these long books, what a tremendous effort they are – to hold the entire span on my shoulders . . . you must go on now till you die.'[82] Leonard, perhaps dimly foreseeing now the terrible difficulties she would have over the next two years, said ruthlessly that 'anyhow one could burn it'.[83] As a distraction (and possibly out of the fear that she would not be producing anything for the Press for a very long time) she returned to her old book on fiction, and tinkered with it uneasily throughout the summer. Stephen Spender provided encouragement with an enthusiastic letter about *To the Lighthouse*; but she struggled to finish the last chapter, all too aware that she had written more than 170,000 words.

It was very hot; there was a drought. She had cut down on her cigarette smoking (from six or seven a morning to one.)[84] She changed from an old-fashioned nib to a fountain pen (though she didn't much like it.) She took some French conversation classes with Lytton's niece Janie Bussy. The Glyndebourne opera festival opened, and they went to hear *Figaro*. Louie Everest arrived at Rodmell. And (a much more troublesome arrival) after a visit to the vulgarly rich Rothschilds, Leonard acquired their marmoset as a pet, a small furry pop-eyed gibbering creature called Mitzi, or Mitz, much disliked by all at Charleston. (Vanessa called it 'that horrid little monkey who still thrives however much Leonard treads on him'.)[85] It became Leonard's familiar, attracting attention wherever they went, always sitting on his shoulder or his head, and 'always with the same look, as if the world were a question'.[86]

Mitzi, for Virginia, was as much of an irritant as a delight. There were other irritants this summer. 'Coalbox' – Sibyl Colefax, who now had her own decorating business, her husband's financial troubles one sign of the Depression – was cross with her for cancelling a date, and told Clive (who was happy to pass it on) that she thought Virginia was too self-protective. Ethel had to be put off. They heard that Francis Birrell was very ill again.

Duncan had piles, a 'ridiculous torturing' disease which she couldn't help feeling snobbish about.[87] She was critical of him for turning Nessa into 'Aunt Mary', and of herself for playing 'the good fairy Aunt'. She had toothache, and would have to have two more teeth out.

These were the trivialities that mattered locally; but they were shadowed by world events. All summer there was talk about Hitler and Germany. By the summer of 1934 his ambitions and his methods were fully apparent. What might 'taking part' against this threat involve, she began to ask herself; what could she be doing except just 'reading the newspapers'?[88] The summer's conversations about 'civilisation' and 'barbarity' echoed the talk of the characters in her book. At dinner at the Hutchinsons in July, Leonard argued with all present over what the Labour Party might do to prevent war.[89] At tea with the Keyneses, Maynard held forth dazzlingly on the German economy: 'But I am thinking all the time of what is to end Here & Now.' At a tea-party at Rodmell at the beginning of September, Clive and Quentin, the Keyneses and their guests, Kingsley Martin and his eccentric wife Olga, from whom he was living apart, and the economist Richard Kahn ('the economic Jew, I forget his name'), all talked about the end of civilisation. They talked, she noted, 'as in my book that morning'.[90] Was it time to do more than talk? Julian was the one who was taking action: on 9 September he was involved in a huge anti-war demonstration in Hyde Park.

That same day, at Rodmell, the rest of the family heard the news that Roger Fry had died. He had had a fall on the 7th, had broken his pelvis, and been taken into the Royal Free hospital. Vanessa took a phone call from Micu Diamand, Roger's son-in-law; she came out on to the terrace crying out, 'He's dead'. He had died of heart failure: they all suspected that the doctors had mismanaged it. It was a great and unexpected shock. Only a month before Virginia had had one of his lively, energetic letters from France, wanting her to recommend 'books to read', asking her if she liked *Ethan Frome*, saying how attractive he found the candour of Gide's journal.[91] Though he had been greatly distressed by Goldie's death, and had not been very well, he had been as active as ever in the last year or two, giving the Slade Lectures at Cambridge, translating Mallarmé, showing at Agnew's his recent paintings from his travels in Greece and Spain and France. At once 'the poverty of life' struck her; the world felt lacking in substance, 'a thin blackish veil over everything'. She cried, but was numb, and kept thinking of her mother's death, and how 'I was afraid I was not feeling enough'. She had the intensely visualised mental pictures of the dead person that for her always accompanied the shock of a death.

They went to the service at Golder's Green crematorium on 13

September 1934. It was still very hot. There were no words spoken, only music: a Bach chorale and choral preludes, an anonymous Italian aria, a Fugue by Frescobaldi. 'I liked the wordlessness', she thought. On the Programme, though, were printed three quotations, one from *Comus*, one from Spinoza ('A free man thinks of death least of all things; and his wisdom is a meditation not of death but of life') and one from Fry's *Transformations*, which suggested how much she had influenced him:

> The lighthouses of art do not burn with so fixed and unvarying a luster [as real lighthouses]. The light they give is always changing insensibly with each generation, now brighter, now dimmer, and often enough growing brighter once more. But we sometimes forget that the lights have to be tended or they grow faint and may expire altogether. For them to burn brightly they must be fed by the devotion of some few spirits in each generation.[92]

As she watched the coffin slide in, she had her 'tremendous' feeling of life as a fight against an indifferent outer force, a fight in which we '*must* be vanquished'; and, suddenly and powerfully, a fear of her own death.

There were competing women mourners at the funeral, whose rival claims on Roger's life were to have an effect on Virginia's work in the next few years. Helen Anrep, the companion of his last ten years, and her two children, still felt at odds with 'Bloomsbury'. Not she, but Margery, was the executor. ('Do give up trying to be nice to the Frys', Vanessa advised Helen the day after the funeral.)[93] Roger's daughter Pamela Diamand had quarrelled with her father over her marriage. Vanessa too felt like a widow, and seemed to Virginia frozen with grief, like a statue. In October she began to write down her memories of Roger, but she broke off. Virginia herself felt profoundly bereaved. Though the shock of Lytton's death had been as great, Roger had been more closely knit into her family life: he and Julian, for instance, were especially good friends. Somehow, in the weeks after the funeral, his death seemed 'worse than Lytton's'.[94] Life seemed diminished by the loss of that 'dignified & honest & large –"large sweet soul" – something ripe & musical about him – & then the fun & the fact that he had lived with such variety & generosity, & curiosity'. She told Ottoline she felt 'stupid & depressed & dull. I hate my friends dying'. 'I still find myself thinking I shall tell him something,' she said to Vita, just as she had of Lytton. 'And we all lived so much together. Dear me, why must one's friends die?'[95] By the end of the year, she had been asked (separately, by Helen Anrep and by Margery Fry) to write his Life, a task which intrigued her, but which she could see would be extremely problematic, not least because of the possible conflicts between the guardians of his memory. She immediately began to ask herself how it might be done. Why not have a *group* biography, with different people writing about different aspects of his life?[96] But before she could start thinking about that, she *had* to finish the 'interminable book'.[97] By the end of September, the last words were written of the last long party scene set in the 'present day'. The final paragraph of the first draft, which would mostly be cut after revision, was full of her thoughts of mortality. Eleanor is looking out of the window at the end of the party, as dawn breaks, at the London square:

> She thought how she had walked round it, all those years ago . . . And then she must have been young, almost a girl; and that girl was dead; had vanished. The sleeping street seemed for a moment the grave; and the pigeons were crooning a requiem, for her past; for one of the selves that had been hers; for one of the many million human beings who had walked, who had suffered, who had thought so intensely. And now a new moment was coming into being: made of that past, made of those million lives, made of the dust of generation after generation . . .[98]

'Anyhow,' she told herself, finishing this paragraph, 'if I die tomorrow, the line is there'.[99]

THIRTY-SIX

Failure

In the gloomy time that followed the death of Roger and the finishing of the first draft of *The Pargiters*, Virginia's mood was low. She was mocked by Wyndham Lewis in his slashing critique of his contemporaries, *Men Without Art*, which came out in October. In his chapter on her, which 'took the cow by the horns' by satirising 'Mr Bennett and Mrs Brown', Mrs Woolf was presented as the tremulous 'feminine principle' taking on the 'big beefy brute, Bennett'. Lewis lambasted her for timidity, artificiality, feebleness, for 'peeping' out securely 'from the security of the private mind' at the dangerous outside world, and for ruling over, as an 'introverted matriarch', 'a very dim Venusberg indeed'.[1] It was a typical example of the sort of attacks 'Bloomsbury' was getting now,[2] and it aroused a representative series of emotions in her. First, she felt a violent horror of being laughed at, of being 'hated & despised & ridiculed', and had to struggle not to 'mind'. (She consoled herself with Keats: 'I think I shall be among the English poets after my death'.) Then she had to resist the desire to answer back – as always, backed by Leonard's good and 'dignified' advice – or to rewrite what she was doing: 'fatal to arrange the P.s so as to meet his criticisms'. Then she immediately wanted to write her 'anti-fascist pamphlet'. And also she felt anxiety about whether the criticisms were *true*. A strange prose 'Ode', 'Written on Seeing the Name of Cutbush Above a Butcher's Shop in Pentonville', tried – clearly in response to Lewis's jibes about 'peeping' – to imagine the whole life of a London butcher, from a sign glimpsed in the street, but recognised in some despair the limitations of her view: 'These are semblances of human faces seen in passing/translated from a foreign language.'[3]

She felt unrecognised and put down. The Sickert piece fell flat. An invitation from the editor of the *London Mercury*, R.A. Scott-James, to write a piece on the current state of reviewing aroused ideas on 'why reviewing is so bad and contemporary criticism generally', but the piece, in spite of repeated urgings from the editor, was not submitted.[4] Her feeling that she needed to 'go my ways indifferent' was very strong. She burst out to Ethel about her dread of being inhibited from writing 'at full pressure':

'Thats in fact why I never show my own MSS to anyone; and only let L read them when theyre hard and fast finished.'[5] In the same week, she expressed to Vita (in exactly the tone that might have given ammunition to Wyndham Lewis) her horror at the idea of authors being asked to do signing sessions: 'It seems to me an iniquity; the idea of standing to be milked by any red handed oaf'.[6] Private society, too, seemed thin. Another meeting with 'old Yeats' at Ottoline's was not so impressive as the first, though she was pleased that he said he had been writing about *The Waves*. She admired his 'extreme directness, simplicity, & equality' as much as before, but an hour and a half on the occult was too much for her: 'cant unriddle the universe at tea.' Vita reported to Harold:

> Virginia gave me an imitation of Yeats telling her why he was occult. He had been confirmed in this theory because he saw a coat-hanger emerge from his cupboard and travel across the foot of his bed; next night, it emerged again, clothed in one of his jackets; the third night, a hand emerged from one of the cuffs; the fourth night – 'Ah! Mrs Woolf, that would be a long story; enough to say, I finally recovered my potency.'[7]

It was painfully difficult – a 'horrid plunge' – to go on to the second stage of the writing of *The Pargiters*, 'compacting the vast mass',[8] especially as she now badly wanted to write 'On Being Despised'. But the revising would take her until the following July (mostly retyping, because her hand had begun to tremble, like Leonard's, with too much handwriting). Francis Birrell's stoic, awful death ('a credit to atheism')[9] in January 1935 underlined her feeling of the pressure of time. Her world seemed full of ghosts, and she felt all this winter 'a vast sorrow at the back of life'.[10] All social encounters were shadowed by 'a great desire for Roger'.[11]

Like a flash of bright colour, a new acquaintance made that winter momentarily distracted her. On 26 November 1934 they were invited by McKnight Kauffer (the designer who had done the wolf's head colophon for the Hogarth Press) to a private view of photographs by his fellow American, Man Ray. (This led to a sitting with Man Ray: the photographs he took of Virginia Woolf, made up, hair shining and smoothly centre-parted, elegantly dressed, have become part of her legend. Man Ray placed her in cool, contained attitudes, in one with her right hand raised, looking aside, and in another with hands loosely crossed in front of her, looking up quizzically at the lens. If you didn't know who she was, you would see, from these pictures, a woman of great powers, formidable intelligence and humour, and a daunting social presence.)

At the exhibition she met the Huxleys, back from France and living in

London for a while (he was working on *Eyeless in Gaza*) with their Argentinian friend, Victoria OCampo. This was no coincidence: the Huxleys had promised OCampo that if she came she might very well meet Virginia Woolf. The two women talked avidly, partly in French partly in English, as they stood in the middle of the private view. OCampo was forty-four. In her youth she had been a famous beauty; she was still, as Virginia said, 'very ripe & rich . . . the colour of an apricot under glass'.[12] She was also a writer, a critic, an editor, and a courageous and outspoken feminist, who had quarrelled with her wealthy conservative Buenos Aires family. Since 1931 she had been editing an international literary magazine, *Sur*, and, since 1933, had, like the Woolfs, been running her own publishing house. In 1929 she had been introduced to *A Room of One's Own* by Sylvia Beach in Paris, since when Virginia Woolf had become her heroine. She would publish many of her books in Argentina (*A Room of One's Own* and *Orlando* in translations by Borges, though he did not greatly admire them). When they met, OCampo had recently encountered Mussolini in Rome, Jung in Zurich; and she was full of stories. That winter she paid several visits to Tavistock Square, and would write ecstatically about these pilgrimages.

> Often, after the foggy cold of the street, I entered the comfort of that room, and above all, of that presence. As soon as Virginia was there, all else disappeared. Virginia, tall and slender, wearing a silk blouse whose blues and grays (was it Scottish silk?) harmonized admirably with the silver of her hair. Virginia, made even more slender by a very long, black velvet skirt. Virginia, sitting in an armchair, her dog asleep on the floor . . . [she] was as capable of speaking marvellously as she was of writing marvellously . . . I could not, without effort, leave her side.[13]

She sent Virginia gifts of orchids and 'impetuous' outbursts of veneration: 'If there is anyone in the world who can give me courage and hope, it is *you*.' 'I am a very *voracious* person. And I believe *hunger* is all. I am not ashamed of being hungry. Don't you think love is our hunger to love?'[14] Virginia listened eagerly to her stories, asked endless questions (naturally she wanted her to write an autobiography) and responded kindly but moderately to her advances, attributing her own reserve to her puritan ancestors. Though, at the same time, she used this new devotee for credit with Vita: 'I am in love with Victoria Okampo', she told her.[15] Vita and Victoria would later become friends, and in the 1950s Vita would reassure Victoria: 'I don't think it is in the least true to say that you had no real existence for her, because she often talked to me about you even before I had met you. It is true that there was a certain unreality about her unless one knew her very intimately. One always felt that she might take flight at any moment and disappear.'[16] Even while worshipping at the shrine, OCampo was aware that she might have 'no real existence' for her heroine. Virginia had vague and exotic ideas about South America as 'a land of great butterflies & vast fields', of 'wild cattle and pampas grass'.[17] That it might also be full of potential readers of Virginia Woolf seemed incredible to her: 'Don't try to make me believe they're interested in me in South America!'[18]

This was a brief diversion. Its symbolic moment came the following year, when OCampo sent Virginia, to her delight, a glass box of South American butterflies. But four years later, in the summer of 1939, she was enraged with her for insinuating the photographer Gisèle Freund into the house to take her picture, and wrote to her coldly and furiously. OCampo would regret this memory, when in 1941 she recalled (still romanticising) her last sight of her: 'Virginia, very thin, in black, without powder, without rouge, without jewelry: infinitely lovely, the stamp of all her dreams printed on her face.'[19] In her political work, in her imprisonment under the Perón regime in the 1950s and in her struggle for women's rights in Argentina, OCampo would always remember Virginia Woolf.

The other distraction of this sad winter, intended as light relief for them all, was the performance of *Freshwater* in Vanessa's studio in Fitzroy Street on 18 January, for Angelica's sixteenth birthday party. Even this 'donkeys work' (she was the prompter, and took her bow wearing a donkey's head)[20] required rewritings. In early December she began to redraft her 1923 version, making it less wordy and more dramatic. (This gave her ideas for making her novel more dramatic, too.) There were rehearsals at Charleston over Christmas and the New Year. In many ways *Freshwater* was a benign version of what she was doing in *The Pargiters*: setting Victorian emotions against the next generation's rational attempt to reshape their lives. But the play, unlike the novel, was coloured by an affectionate fondness for those old people.

It gave her the chance for *risqué* gags, in the style of *Orlando*, about bisexuality, lecherous old men, public honours, and Queen Victoria; and, of course, for lots of family jokes.[21] The casting of Vanessa as Julia, Leonard as her husband Charles Cameron, Duncan as Watts (he couldn't learn his lines and had them pinned on his easel), Angelica as a ravishing Ellen Terry, Julian as the handsome sailor who runs off with her, Adrian as Tennyson, Ann and Judith Stephen in the minor parts, Angelica's friend Eve Younger as the Queen, and Mitz as a marmoset, was good for knowing laughs. The audience obliged. It included Bunny Garnett, Elizabeth Bowen, David Cecil, Oliver and Marjorie Strachey, Christabel Aberconway, and Clive and his brother Cory, who laughed too loudly throughout. Adrian told a friend that it was 'great fun'. 'You would have been amazed to see Julian in the part of a young naval lieutenant.'[22]

The casting of Julian as Angelica's lover was *risqué* too. Angelica at sixteen was beginning to come into conflict with an over-dominating Vanessa; in retrospect she saw herself then as sexually repressed, infantile and moody. Julian was her closest and most affectionate family friend. Soon after the play, Vanessa took her out of her last year at school, so that they could spend several months in Rome. Ann Stephen was jealous of Angelica, who always got the best parts in these family plays, and she and Judith, the less favoured Stephen nieces, ended up playing the maid and the porpoise. As she had just played the lead in her school play, this didn't seem fair, but the daughters of Karin and Adrian were always the outsiders in Bloomsbury. It was now, though, that Virginia began to be more interested in these large, awkward, coltish nieces, then eighteen and sixteen, both set for Cambridge and professional careers. They were emerging from difficult childhoods in Gordon Square. Karin, who was often extremely depressed, had spent much of their early years in training as an analyst; when they were thirteen she insisted on their being, in turn, psychoanalysed for three years, which Ann greatly resented. Adrian was much involved with anti-Fascist activities. Virginia was gripped by Ann's stories of their rugged sailing holidays (Adrian's hobby since his youth) and of their home life, 'Karin only seen in bed of a morning, Adrian seldom, the house full of lodgers & patients'.[23]

There were other family wrangles over the play. Clive was huffy about how many guests he could bring; Duncan wouldn't let Dadie Rylands come, as he disliked him.[24] Virginia was irritated at the moment by Vanessa's uncritical overprotectiveness towards her children.[25] At a public dinner in honour of the painter Ethel Walker (who had once offered to paint her naked, as Lilith), at which she, Vanessa and Duncan arrived late, *she* was elevated to the high table, next to old Henry Tonks, where she was 'a success', and *they*, much to her amusement, had to eat their dinner alone.[26] She and Leonard were on edge too: he was cross because she was still smoking too much, she thought he should cancel a very cold weekend at Rodmell. Sometimes she wanted to 'break L of his "habits" '. Very unusually, in April and again in June, she noted his stony resentment of her making holiday arrangements 'in favour of my family', and his unkindness and despotism and 'extreme rigidity of mind' towards Mabel.[27] Vita's friendship seemed lost to her: she was becoming more reclusive than ever at Sissinghurst, and, involved in her lover Gwen St Aubyn's religious quest, was starting work on a book on St Joan ('I could tell you all about her Voices', Virginia offered).[28] She got embroiled in a silly dispute between

Vita and Ethel, who had accused Vita and Gwen of living rotten lives.[29] Several of her friends, including Clive, criticised her tentative involvement in a Cambridge Anti-Fascist Exhibition. And an encounter with Morgan Forster at the London Library in April enraged her.

Forster told her that the committee had confirmed its decision (first taken by Sir Leslie Stephen) not to have women members: 'No no no, ladies are quite impossible.' She imagined that perhaps her name had been suggested and they had said, 'No no no: ladies are impossible.' (The minutes of the committee meeting, however, at which Desmond MacCarthy was present as well as Forster, recorded no such discussion, though the tone of the proceedings can be judged by the decision to close the Library for 'the public holiday appointed for the Silver Jubilee' and to give Lady Hart permission 'to use the unexpired portion of her husband's (deceased) subscription.')[30] She went home in such a rage that her hand trembled too much to write; the incident was like an item from one of the clippings she was collecting. All her feelings about the 'pail of offal' of male exclusion and prejudice raged up. She couldn't stop herself beginning to write 'On Being Despised', which she was now calling her 'anti-fascist pamphlet' – by analogy with the pamphlet Leonard was currently writing about primitivism and autocracy, *Quack, Quack!*

All her arguments (for the novel and the essay) were gathering momentum. Everything seemed to fall in with her world view. There were the 'dutiful perfunctory' preparations for the Silver Jubilee, the twenty-fifth anniversary of George V's accession, all over London – when she had just written a satirical piece on 'Royalty'.[31] There were more arguments with Julian over the inevitability of wars. There were political discussions with the MacCarthys ('Patriotism is the devil – yes').[32] There were Kingsley Martin's monologues on his career and his politics. ('He is suffering from egomania, and the egg is bad', she wrote to Vanessa in Rome.)[33] The dislike she felt for the society she was part of, and for which she was meant to feel 'patriotic', came out in small details, like her vitriolic sketch of Fortnum & Mason's:

> all strewn with luxury objects in the worst most opulent heartless brainless taste: women in black with white pearls & red lips. The atmosphere of a rich princely shop is not sympathetic. A kind of halfway house: a shop not a shop; shop people pseudo gentry: an attempt to seduce & coerce. The chimney lamp was 25/6 instead of 18/9 as at the Stores. Six shillings to pay for lipstick & scent & carpets & the casual gentlemanly manners of Mr Marshall & the strew & the carelessness. I watched a gentleman selling Easter eggs with powder puffs, to the head buyer, who might have been Christabel.[34]

Their holiday this year was timed to miss the Jubilee on 6 May 1935. Before they left, they took advice on whether it was safe for them to drive through Holland and then Germany on their way to see Vanessa in Rome (and then return through France). They were warned that it might not be; and the warnings brought home to her as never before the likelihood of war. She imagined, vividly, Nazis in Bloomsbury. But, in spite of warnings, they set off into Europe. They were away for a month, and though most of her holiday notes were taken up with descriptions of Holland and Italy and accounts of their time with Vanessa, what they saw in Germany sank deep into her mind.[35] 'Holidays are very upsetting', she noted on their return.

When they came back, they found that Pinker had died. It was sad; she had been their dog for eight years, and Leonard was very mournful. They would get another dog in the summer, an affectionate spaniel called Sally; but Pinker had been a friend; her pawmarks were on a lot of her pages, and something of their 'play private life' died with her.[36]

But she had to press on. She had refused, on holiday, the offer of a Companion of Honour from the Prime Minister; she would not go to the International Congress of Writers Conference in Paris 'in Defence of Culture', though urged by Forster to help him 'represent the last utterances of the civilised';[37] she would not let herself start the anti-Fascist pamphlet. She was utterly weary of revising, but she was establishing the variation she wanted between 'different strata of being' by switching from what she called 'upper air scenes' to deeper levels.[38]

Her main anxiety was, always, about polemic and 'preaching'. All her readings during these summer months seemed to illustrate this problem. She was reading Marryat for a piece she would write in the autumn called 'The Captain's Death Bed': his work spoke to her of the disharmony of facts in fiction.[39] Eliot (very much at his ease now – 'success is very good for people', she said of him to Vanessa)[40] sent her *Murder in the Cathedral*: 'the pale New England morality murder', she would call it.[41] (Perhaps the poems of Marianne Moore, which she was reading that spring, provided an antidote.) When they saw the play at the end of the year, she reacted violently against its 'tightness, chillness' and 'deadness'; Leonard had almost to be 'carried out, shrieking'.[42] Stephen Spender very much disliked it too. While she was reading *Murder* in June, she was also reading Spender's book *The Destructive Element*, which 'analysed the deep consciousness of destructive forces threatening our civilisation'. She wrote to him about it, arguing (as in 'Letter to a Young Poet') that 'your desire to teach and help is always bringing you up to the top when you should be down in the depths'. She was thinking of her novel.

Here again my hatred of preaching pops out and barks. I dont think you can get your words to come till youre almost unconscious . . . but then for your generation the call to action in words is so much more strident than it was for mine.

Spender accepted her criticisms modestly and good humouredly: 'Of course one shouldn't preach', he agreed. But 'sometimes things seem so clear to me, that like many other people, I feel I want to shout.'[43] The correspondence sums up all her difficulties as a writer in the 1930s.

That summer, apart from a stiff, formal dinner with Rebecca West,[44] and a weekend with Susan and John Buchan at Elsfield outside Oxford,[45] there were two major disruptions. Packets of Roger Fry's letters were beginning to arrive. In June, Margery Fry persuaded her to go to Bristol and open a retrospective exhibition; it was the first unwelcome chore connected with Fry, and an ominous prelude to the writing of the book. She did not want to break off to write this speech, in which she celebrated Roger Fry affectionately as 'a remarkable man' and evoked – as she would in the biography – his idiosyncratic way of talking about paintings. The opening took place on 12 July, and her presence was celebrated by the local press: 'It was good news for the many admirers of her literary work' (one Bristol paper noted) 'to learn that Mrs Virginia Woolf was to speak at the opening ceremony today. Books by this celebrated authoress are widely read in this neighbourhood, and have been much discussed.'[46] She loathed the event (a stodgy and respectable audience of 'stout burgesses' on a broiling hot day) and was upset because neither Margery Fry nor Pamela Diamand wrote to thank her. 'A curious sense of complete failure' made it hard for her to get back to the book.[47] On the next evening, as she was sitting alone at Tavistock Square (Leonard was out), Julian turned up, to tell her he was going to go to China for three years to teach. They talked alone, 'intimately, I mean about the past & our lives, for the first time'. She knew that this decision would be extremely difficult for Vanessa; and she was sorry too: 'Three years. He will be thirty & I 56 alas.'[48] But, in spite of these interruptions, on the day after Julian broke his news, 17 July 1935, she finished her 'first wild retyping' of her novel. It was 740 pages long. It still wouldn't do. She would immediately have to start again.

This last phase of retyping became unbearable. During the final reworking of the novel, from the summer of 1935 and into 1936, she had to struggle with three overpowering feelings. First, her conviction that the 'impossible eternal book' on which she had now spent three years, was no good at all. Second, her violent desire to get on to *Three Guineas* and *Roger Fry*. Third, her intense consciousness of what was happening around her, which made her increasingly feel that her work might be futile. In August, when she set herself once more to retype and condense, with her mind feeling like 'a pudding', she noted: 'War seems inevitable.'[49]

Something seen in the garden in pouring rain that autumn haunted her, a snake eating a toad: 'It had half the toad in, half out; gave a suck now & then. The toad slowly disappearing. L. poked its tail; the snake was sick of the crushed toad.' That night she dreamed of 'men committing suicide & cd. see the body shooting through the water'.[50] She kept coming back to the sickening, fascinating sight of the half-dead, half-ingested living corpse. She used it as an image of power and violence when she saw Bevin crushing Lansbury at the Labour Party conference in October: he was 'like a snake whos swallowed a toad'.[51] She used it for her own sense of being eaten alive, preyed on, by what she had created: 'My book decays upon me like the body of the albatross' . . . 'My book . . . won't finish; its like some snake thats been half run over but always pops its head up.' In *Between the Acts*, which she began three years later, she brought the thing back in full technicolour, oozing with blood and gore, as an image of a 'monstrous inversion', an emblem for a paralysed civilisation ('the snake was unable to swallow: the toad was unable to die') which the Fascistic male stamps on, covering his white shoes with sticky blood. 'Action relieved him.'[52]

Was that the only alternative – paralysing stagnation, or brutal action? Her private image reflected the national debates she heard on all sides about collective security versus armaments, sanctions versus military action. Italy was invading Abyssinia, 'wh. I cannot spell',[53] and there was a great debate on about whether the League should take strong action. Her part in it was to be 'all in a stew about war & patriotism'. What was 'her country', how could she think in those terms?[54] At the Labour Party conference in Brighton, she watched in horror as the arguments for pacifism and non-resistance were overridden. Could she keep herself 'immune' from these debates? Leonard thought she should: it was he, not she, who argued after the conference, as they walked on the marsh at Rodmell, that 'politics ought to be separate from art'.[55] There was daily talk of the war in Abyssinia, of Mussolini and Hitler, of the League, of what to join and what to sign. Huxley said that all the signing and anti-Fascist debates were 'mere chitter-chatter'.[56] Was he right? At the National Peace Council in Westminster at the end of October, at their Labour Party meetings at Rodmell, during the General Election in November (Baldwin's National Government won easily), which she spent waiting in the rain while Leonard ferried voters around Sussex, she kept her vantage point as critical and ironic as ever.[57] But she was beginning to see that an airing of this outsider's view in her next book ('A Knock on the

Door'? 'Professions'? 'The Next War'?) was going to take 'some courage'.[58] 'All politics be damned', she wrote to Julian in China.[59] This was not as simple a statement as it looked.

Julian was teaching Virginia Woolf and T.S. Eliot to Chinese students on the 'practical criticism' principles of I.A. Richards, and watching events in Europe with increasing agitation. 'It's too late for democracy and reason and persuasion and writing to the New Statesman, and Virginia signing letters saying its all a pity. The only real choices now are to submit or fight,' he would write to Quentin the following year.[60] He was getting domestic news from Vanessa, who rarely mentioned politics in her letters. ('It did suggest a really appalling situation if Nessa had noticed it,' Julian observed to Virginia.)[61] Mostly she told him about things like her dinner party at Charleston where she had provided twice too many grouse (eleven for ten people) and Eliot had told funny stories about the unsuccessful practical jokes – sugar lumps with india-rubber fish inside – he had tried out on previous hosts.[62]

Virginia, she said, was starting work on Roger's papers; there was a suggestion, too, that she might write a Life of Lytton: 'It looks as though V would spend the rest of her life writing lives of her friends if she consents, rather a gloomy prospect perhaps.'[63] Virginia's letters to Julian were also full of gossip and affection: 'Oh dear how I wish television were now installed and I could switch on and see you.' She suggested that he should write something on Roger, a request which would lead to trouble. She told him what it felt like to start dipping into Roger's letters; she was beginning to see that she might enter into an 'odd posthumous friendship' with him.[64] She did not want to commit herself yet, but in effect she had really begun the research, and was already, as biographers must, reading his 'every note with a view to some light or hint'.[65] Her struggle in *The Years* (suddenly, in September, she realised that was the right name, 'dropped like a billard ball into a pocket') between upper-air and lower scenes made her think that a biography too could move between different dimensions in a human life, that it might involve 'new combinations in psychology & body – rather like a painting'.[66] But the difficulty of 'doing' Roger already alarmed her. She wrote to Angelica (away from home for the first time in Paris): 'Do you think it is possible to write a life of anyone? I doubt it; because people are all over the place.'[67]

A peculiar encounter with a palm-reading psychiatrist provoked new ideas about how one's life might be described. Charlotte Wolff was a German-Jewish refugee who had been taken up by the Huxleys. With their help, Dr Wolff became a fashionable reader of palms. (Her clients included Mrs Simpson, and the monkeys at the zoo.) Virginia was 'done' twice, for two guineas, at the Huxleys' flat, and was told that her life had completely changed at age thirty-five – no (the palmist corrected herself) at age thirty. Leonard, of course, thought this was all the most 'disgusting humbug'. Virginia was half-convinced, but when she heard that Wolff was writing up her findings, she nervously asked Ethel to translate the extracts from German. She read that her hand was 'full of real and apparent contradictions . . . a desire to escape reality . . . This overstress of the imagination forces her to adopt a defensive attitude.' The idea that lines on the hand might signify one's history and character intrigued her. 'Why should deaths and other events indent the palm of the hand?' In *The Years*, the young doctor, Peggy, watching the older generation replay their childhood behaviour, thinks:

> Each person had a certain line laid down in their minds . . . and along it came the same old sayings. One's mind must be criss-crossed like the palm of one's hand, she thought, looking at the palm of her hand.[68]

The current lines of her life felt tangled, scrappy. She recorded what she had begun to call 'specimen days', days filled up with distractions and demands. On 4 November 1935, for example ('when we are on the eve of the Duke of Gloucester's wedding; of a general election: of the Fascist revolution in France; & in the thick of the Abyssinian war') she went to the BBC to listen to 'some incomparable twaddle' – a 'soliloquy' they wanted her to emulate, complete with BBC sound effects of 'real railway trains; real orchestras; noises; waves, lions & tigers etc'. (The idea of a speech in which real sound effects intervened lingered on into *Between the Acts*.) She went to dinner parties she had to dress up for and didn't want to go to (with the Bruce Richmonds, with Ethel Sands.) Why were these so awful? 'Its because one changes one's values', Vanessa said wisely, who now refused to go anywhere where she had to 'dress'.[69] All manner of people came to see them every day in London, like the 'Bird of Paradise' Iris Origo, an Anglo-American writer of Italian upbringing, writer who came with news of Fascist Italy, and Tom Eliot's friend Emily Hale, who was dismissed as a 'dull impeccable Bostonian lady', but who made an observant reading of *her*:

> The features are delicately modelled . . . and although the face is lacking in mobility . . . there appeared to me a sense of the mind's attentiveness and colour . . . traceable under the mask-like expression, mask-like except for the eyes, which register the reaction of each moment. A strong impression of cool detachment constantly contradicts itself by an equally strong impression of highly charged concentration. Her manner is not one to place people at ease, quite frankly speaking, though with Tom Eliot

and Spender she was simple, friendly and responsive in an almost girlish way.[70]

Figures from the past reappeared, like Ka Arnold-Foster, always irritating, and old Sophie Farrell, who wrote her annual Christmas thank-you letter, useful for the voice of the old servant Crosby in *The Years*.

> I am 74 & it 50 years on the 8th of next April that I first saw you. it as Past so quickley. I dont feel a bit old & you all seem to me Just the Same Children Just as dear to me as when you had the funerals for the birds & mice at St Ives. Such happy days . . . there is nobody Just Like you all are to me. I shall look forward to seeing you all again one day – I keep all your letters & read them over & over.[71]

She promised to deliver *The Years* by 15 February 1936. By the end of 1935 she thought she had got through the retyping, but knew there was still 'a great deal to do'.[72] She was afraid of sinking into 'acute despair' if she didn't prepare distractions for herself. In the New Year she was panic-struck and horrified. Her fifty-fourth birthday went unremarked. How could she possibly finish this book in six weeks? She must not be 'apprehensive', she told herself; she must hang on to her 'immunity'. Though Brace said she could put off publication until next autumn, Leonard pointed out that she had not earned enough of her 'share' for that year's income. When she re-read the last scene and it seemed to her mere 'feeble twaddle', she went running upstairs from her basement to his room, and he said, 'This always happens.' But she felt it had never been as bad as this.[73]

For the first three months of 1936, she pushed herself frantically. To everyone she wrote to – Elizabeth, Ethel, Mary – she described the work as 'dreary', 'feeble' 'eternal infernal', 'my vomit'. In February she was doing three hours' revision in the morning and two in the afternoon: it was all she could bear. Outside events impinged through the screen of her obsession. She noted with interest how the British public plunged into a 'fit of grief' for the death and funeral of George V, which she described to Julian as 'a curious survival of barbarism, emotionalism, heraldry, ecclesiasticism, sheer sentimentality, snobbery, and some feeling for the very commonplace man who was so like ourselves'. The ceremonials provoked her usual curiosity and fascination about British attitudes to its monarchy.[74] Vanessa and Duncan were embroiled in a row with the establishment over their commission to paint panels for the liner *Queen Mary*, which the chairman of the Cunard company rejected as unsuitable. Vita's mother Lady Sackville died at last ('and I hope the poor old wretch who always reviled me has gathered her ashes together and is having a happy time at last').[75] She was worried about Forster, who was to have a prostate operation, just as his essays, *Abinger Harvest*, were published.

When nobody came to visit, she and Leonard had some moments of 'private fun' with 'a great deal of fuss about the marmots'.[76] She and Vanessa had a nice tipsy evening alone together, comparing their marriages. Vanessa told Julian: 'She found Leonard absolutely dependable & like a rock which was what she badly wanted. She said she could never make up her own mind & must have someone to do it for her – which L no doubt does – & that he was also very unselfish.'[77] And she had spirit for some flights of fancy, like this on Hugh Walpole in Los Angeles:

> You are meanwhile sitting with vast blue plains rolling round you: a virgin forest at your back; a marble city gleaming at your feet; and people so new, so brave, so beautiful and so utterly uncontaminated by civilisation popping in out of booths and theatres with pistols in their hands and aeroplanes soaring over their heads – sometimes you find a bleeding corpse in the street but nobody thinks much of that – Well, I've no space to describe Hollywood to you, and so must leave you to your cocktail.[78]

But March, with Hitler's invasion of the Rhineland, was the worst. Leonard was immersed in feverish political talks. 'I might be the charwoman of a Prime Minister', she told Ethel bitterly.[79] And to Julian: 'Here we never stop facing facts.'[80] The 'bray & drone' of 'tortured voices', of 'c[ommi]ttees in the next room', was incessant.[81] She had a profound sense of darkness: her world was becoming 'a world of horror'.[82] It was like a return to the First World War years.

> Its odd, how near the guns have got to our private life again. I can quite distinctly see them & hear a roar, even though I go on, like a doomed mouse, nibbling at my daily page . . . It all seems in keeping: my drudgery; our unsociability; the crisis; meetings; dark – & what it all means, no one knows.[83]

Her state of mind reminded her terribly of the time when she had been at her most dangerously fragile: 'I have never suffered, since The Voyage Out, such acute despair on re-reading, as this time.'[84] Because she was in such distress, they decided that they would have the book set up straight away in galley proofs by their Edinburgh printers, Clark's, so that she would have the sense of having got nearer to the end, and would be able to correct more quickly.[85] But in fact this strategy seemed to increase the pressure; seeing the book in proof was intensely unpleasant to her.

While she was in the throes of this work, a young Jewish girl fainted on the steps of 52 Tavistock Square. They took her in ('You look like brother & sister, both have long noses', she said; Virginia told her Leonard was Jewish, too.) She was twenty-two, starving, and unemployed. They fed her, gave her money, and watched her go off. There on their own doorstep was a specimen of what she knew was wrong with the society – Fortnum's at one end of the scale, a useless Labour Exchange at the other. 'What a system', she commented. This was no casual response: it fitted into the social diagnosis of her book, her arguments about patriotism, and the essay on her relation to the state ('Two Guineas'?) which she so much wanted to start writing. At times she became so obsessed with the ideas for the essay that she felt herself 'verge on insanity'; 'Find myself walking along the Strand talking aloud.'[86]

But the revisions had to go on. On 8 April she posted the last batch of typescript to Clark's. Leonard began his necessary reading of the novel. Was he perhaps lukewarm? She stopped writing her diary; she collapsed with intense (in part menopausal) symptoms of headaches and drumming blood, faintness and sickness, sleeplessness and anxiety. When she did sleep she dreamt of war. The whole world seemed to her like her own sick room, helplessly sitting and waiting.[87] She had to stop work. Until the autumn she could hardly write, hardly function. She went into the prison of an almost catastrophic illness: 'never so near the precipice to my own feelings since 1913'.[88]

Though she stopped writing her diary, a sure sign of danger, she did not fall completely silent. She wrote a few letters, especially to Julian in China, and to Ethel, whom she didn't want to see, but found the thought of comforting in illness. She told her she needed to stop thinking about the book; she needed 'sleep and silence'.[89] And she wanted to get out of London, which seemed to her as vile as it had during the worst periods of breakdown – 'crowded, arid, sordid, unhuman'.[90] She told people she was writing to that she felt very ill, but she did not write down anywhere until months later what she knew was true, that she felt she might kill herself.[91]

The family was anxious. Vanessa wrote to Julian that Virginia seemed under great strain. Leonard put off visitors, had her consult her doctor, Elinor Rendel, and decided to take her down to Cornwall in May. It was her first visit since 1930. They deliberately sought out the past, as though it might soothe her, stopping at Ringwood ('a dismal place'), where the Stephen family went on holiday in 1898 and which made her think of

Thoby,[92] and at the village in Dartmoor where Leonard stayed with Lytton in 1911, the summer of his return to England. They stayed with Ka and Will at Zennor, and went to all her old places. They walked up to Talland House at dusk, yet once more, and she 'peered through the ground floor windows to see the ghosts of her childhood'. Leonard wondered years later, in a rare flight of fancy, whether Schubert's setting of Heine's poem about the Doppelgänger might have occurred to her. Heine's lines (in the unintentionally comical translation Leonard quotes) don't make it sound as if this experience would have been the best cure for an imminent breakdown: 'Heart, do you remember that empty house? Do you remember who used to live there? Ah, someone comes! Wringing her hands! Terrible! It is myself. I can see my own face. Hi, Ghost! What does it mean? What are you doing, mocking what I went through here all those years ago.'[93]

They left St Ives and its haunted house and drove back to the horrors of London. She could not sleep, she could not work. In the aftermath of a lunchtime visit from Vita she required a large dose of chloral. Ellie Rendel recommended three months in the country with the minimum of work. Her letters to Ethel were reduced to shorthand lists: 'This is my new telegraphic style to save mental strain.'[94] For a few days she tried to keep her diary again, celebrating, after two months' wretched silence, 'the divine joy of being mistress of my mind again'. She read Flaubert's letters, which felt 'consoling, admonishing': 'I heard my own voice cry out Oh art! Patience.'[95] She read an essay by Colette, quite unknown to her, whose writing she at once liked enormously; and she read Vita's book on St Joan, which she did not like, but which prompted thoughts about Joan's voices. Perhaps, she argued, 'the general state of mind was so different from ours that voices, saints, came, not through God, but through a common psychology . . . Perhaps I mean, belief is almost unconscious.'[96]

She started trying, like 'a cat stepping on eggs', to revise her proofs. But at the rate of three-quarters of an hour a day, two pages daily out of 600, that would take, she estimated grimly, 'about 6 years'.[97] And the minute she started, she had to stop. It was 'torture'; she was filled, most mornings, with 'a feeling of complete despair & failure'. 'I'm not very happy', she wrote pathetically to Ethel, 'partly because I worry L.'[98] 'The old demons' were 'out of their lairs', 'the spectres' were coming out on sleepless nights.[99] She had lost half a stone since Easter. 'Never again – never another long book for me', she told Ethel.[100]

Before they went to Rodmell, Julian sent her his long essay on Roger, hoping they would publish it at the Press. She thought it was too personal and too 'discursive', and turned it down rather awkwardly. Julian was mortified, and Vanessa was furious. Bunny Garnett's theory, she told Julian by way of consolation, was that 'V lives so precariously (in nerves and brain) that she can't face any other writer of any real merit . . . The responsibility and strain of accepting them would somehow upset her own balance he thinks.'[101] Virginia would come to regret very much the way she had handled this.

That summer Julian was agog for news of what was happening, especially in Spain, where the Civil War began in July. Virginia spoke of hearing news of 'the latest massacres' on the wireless, but she wrote much more to him of the political activities that surrounded her, and of what she felt her own function to be: 'What can I do but write?'[102] Her most active political involvement, her membership of the Anti-Fascist Committee, Vigilance, ended badly; it was something else she could not cope with at this time, and she resigned from it in June.

Leonard commuted to London for his work for much of the summer, while she stayed in Rodmell, still 'a molly coddle',[103] unable to write in her diary, barely able to work. A note she wrote to the 'Mongoose' shows that she was under orders once more:

> I lunched . . . listened to a little dance music – took half an hour's stroll in the marsh – saw a grass snake – came back – lay in bed . . .
>   The fact is its damned dull without you, dearest M: and if you didn't come back I should have to take to writing by way of fillip. I cant help thinking I can now – if I dandle my brain a bit and have frequent lie downs.[104]

They had, in fact, fallen back on 'old Savage's prescription – dont write or read or do anything you like doing.'[105] She did a very little revising, but it was horrid: 'every morning a headache, & forcing myself into that room in my nightgown; & lying down after a page: & always with the certainty of failure.'[106]

She read a lot (*The Prelude*, and the letters of Bertrand Russell's parents, which they were to publish, gave her special pleasure). She had a mild spat with Ethel about her limited view of 'Bloomsbury', but generally felt affectionately towards her: 'How you grow on me . . . how I adore your broad human bottom'.[107] The only big distraction of the summer was an evening of Charleston theatricals. First there was 'Angelica à la Ruth Draper being a shy female authoress calling on Mrs Woolf to whom she has sent her first MS which is found in the mouth of the marmoset.' Then Duncan appeared wearing a mask, mantilla and fan, and a large naked cardboard female figure tied in front of him. Then Quentin put on a play called *A Guided Tour*, of Charleston in the year 2036, in which he played a very large American lady and Christopher Strachey was a uniformed guide; the other characters were tourists visiting Charleston, all of whom were 'desperately anxious to visit the W.C.'. The audience played the furniture. Maynard Keynes was a safe, and Leonard and Virginia were two bookcases labelled Fact and Fiction.[108]

By August, Clive was describing to Mary (they were now good friends again) how Virginia seemed recovered, 'in high spirits, fantastical, spiteful, in fact herself again'.

> She greeted me with: 'This has been an "annus mirabilis" for me; I picked up sixpence in the High Street today; that makes five and sixpence since January all in shillings and sixpences from floors and pavements.' She never looked back: how Sibyl had explained to her why Leonard reminded her of Arthur; how Cyril Connolly was nothing but a 'smartyboots' – till finally she settled down to the pages or postcards she gets daily from Ethel Smyth . . . 'I spent all yesterday afternoon with her . . ., Once she had got the marmoset locked up in the W.C. she became extremely gay and garrulous, mostly about books and people – Ottoline, Lytton's correspondence, Desmond's love affairs, Bertie's memoirs, Tom and Tom's wife, Roger's remains, Lady Colefax – 'it's many a long day since I had a meat meal in that house' was a good Virginia-ism. It was all most enjoyable.[109]

She had started to do some real work, and as late as September she realised that she could ruthlessly cut out two large chunks of the book in order to make it a manageable length.[110] By the end of September she was writing to Spender, in the past tense, about her 'smash up', as of something that was over.

They went back to London on 11 October and, after four months' silence, she began to keep her diary again. She did not want to tell the story of the summer; she wanted to use it to see if she could still 'write'. So she described the scene of the sale of Sibyl Colefax's possessions at Argyll House, of Lord Cecil's tea-time speeches on the need for rearmament, and, at the end of the year, the whole story of the Abdication Crisis, with an energy and a fascinated eye for detail that showed she was once again in 'full flood'.[111] On 1 November, she made herself start to read through the proofs of *The Years* for the last time. At once, she plunged back into frightful despair. It seemed hopelessly bad. She thought: 'I must carry the proofs, like a dead cat, to L. & tell him to burn them.'[112]

Leonard, aware that if he could not praise the book she would be in danger, began to read the proofs. It took him five days. She watched him reading. In fact he did not think it a very good book, but he lied, and it worked. It was a heroic piece of supportive behaviour. And something in the book did move him. When years later he told the story of his necessary subterfuge, he had perhaps forgotten what an impression the book made on him at the time.

> The miracle is accomplished. L put down the last sheet about 12 last night; & could not speak. He was in tears. He says it is 'a most remarkable book – he *likes* it better than The Waves.' & has not a spark of doubt that it must be published. I, as a witness, not only to his emotion, but to his absorption, for he read on & on, can't doubt his opinion: what about my own? Anyhow the relief was divine.[113]

Though the last days of revising were done with 'terrible suffering', she clung on to his 'verdict', and finished the work at the end of November. She knew she would never look at it again. Other interests, at last, could be allowed to press in: a memoir of her encounter with Sibyl for the Memoir Club ('Am I a snob?'), a contrasting piece for the *Daily Worker* on art and politics, reading Gibbon for an essay, the Abdication, and above all *Three Guineas*. A packet of photographs sent from Spain 'of dead children, killed by bombs', shocked and inspired her.[114]

She was freeing herself. They went to Rodmell for Christmas, and on the last day of the year, she sent the book away. She didn't care what became of it now – though in the weeks before publication in early March, she became extremely apprehensive. But at this moment, at the end of 1936, the fate of the book (and, amazingly, it was to be a big, popular, best-selling success) was not what she was thinking of. 'I hand my compliment to that terribly depressed woman, myself, whose head ached so often: who was so entirely convinced a failure; for in spite of everything I think she brought it off, & is to be congratulated.' Her mind sprang back, 'like a tree shaking off a load'.[115]

Why was *The Years* so difficult, why did it nearly kill her? In the manuscript that she wrote between 1932 and 1934, she had made a radical and explicit 'outsider's' denunciation of a male-dominated, imperialist, war-mongering and class-ridden society. It spelt out, clearly and emphatically, the political opinions of the two central figures, Eleanor and Elvira/Sara. Their arguments for pacifism, for instance, are openly made. As the narrator of *Three Guineas* was about to do, they diagnose, from the vantage point of women outsiders, the links in the 'masculine domain' between education, government and war-making. In the manuscript version of the 1917 air-raid chapter, Eleanor and Nicholas agree that the war has been made possible by the social conditions in which most people live:

'Yes,' said Eleanor, 'I have always thought that . . . in a poor district – up in Notting Hill . . . I've always thought the lives people live there; the women always having children; never enough to eat; & not for three four five years, but all their lives, in rooms where you wouldn't keep a dog; that's far worse and infinitely worse . . . that's why . . . war is possible. It's so much better for most people than the lives they are leading, the women can feed their children. The men get excitement.'[116]

The conversation continues, at length, about the futility of war. Why not say to the Germans, 'come along and take it', since they might find 'there is nothing that you can take'?

'If I were King George, I would say, Fight if you like, but it shall all be done in the dark, without medals.' 'The argument is this,' said Renny, 'if we were to end war, in the present state of human progress, people would be far more unhappy than they are at present. If every man & woman had five hundred a year, they would not know what to do with it. Therefore let us end the war as quickly as possible and then . . .' He sat silent. 'Educate ourselves', Elvira finished the sentence . . . 'And so if I have a vote', said Elvira, 'This is what I shall do with it . . . I shall buy a box of matches, and I shall sit in one of those damp fields outside Oxford or Cambridge and set alight to my vote and burn down all colleges/both for men and for women.' 'But you have not got a vote' said Maggie. 'Thats one mercy' she said.[117]

In the finished version of *The Years*, the question is asked 'Could you allow the Germans to invade England and do nothing?', but almost all that is left of the subsequent debate is Eleanor's unfinished sentence: 'Let's end it as quickly as possible and then . . .'[118] In the published novel, the pacifist position, and the political diagnosis which draws analogies between the family home and public life, is muted and evasively expressed.

Her difficulty was that she had to make sure that *The Years* would avoid the very things it was attacking. So she struggled to keep out what she called, writing about the 1930s poets, 'the pedagogic, the didactic, the loudspeaker strain'.[119] Fiction is crippled, she wrote in her piece for the *Daily Worker*, if it starts to sound like an anti-Fascist pamphlet.

If the *Ode to a Nightingale* were inspired by hatred of Germany, if *Bacchus and Ariadne* symbolized the conquest of Abyssinia; if *Figaro* expounded upon the doctrines of Hitler, we should feel cheated and imposed upon, as if, instead of bread made with flour, we were given bread made with plaster.[120]

Because of her horror of propaganda, her feeling that art should subsume politics, and her fear of being laughed at, a good deal of the book's explicit argument is buried. And so *The Years* is a kind of crippled text, which disables itself while writing about a disabled society. As she rewrote and rewrote, struggling for a language that would 'fit' what she was thinking about, she came to think of it as kind of failure: but as a 'deliberate' failure.[121]

When Spender wrote to congratulate her on the novel in 1937, she told him she thought 'action generally unreal'. 'Its the thing we do in the dark that is more real' – like the character in the manuscript who said, 'it shall all be done in the dark, without medals'.[122] *The Years* perceives the Europeans of her generation living like cripples in a cave in a disabled society; but in that darkness (summed up in the air-raid scene) there is dimly perceived the possibility of some other kind of society. In inarticulate bits and pieces, the idea of resistance to force, laws that 'fit', re-education, some better form of communication, makes itself felt, summed up in the phrase from Dante which Eleanor reads: 'For by so many more there are who say "ours"/So much the more of good doth each possess.'[123]

No one in the novel is allowed to make a speech or complete a statement. Instead of 'preaching', the structure of the novel itself make a gesture against totalitarianism. There is no hero, no tragic or climactic plot, no resolution. Instead there is open-endedness, uncertainty, collective voices. The novel, by the very method of indirection and suggestion which cost her so much to achieve, resists the agents of tyranny. Those figure repeatedly in the book: they are men saying 'I, I, I'; oppressive icons of worship; loudspeakers, searchlights, hectoring voices at Speakers' Corner; law-givers in the law courts; the national anthem; the hammering of the dwarves in Wagner; Creon's law against Antigone; bombs interrupting conversation. Eleanor sees the photograph of an unnamed tyrant, probably Mussolini, in her paper, and tears at it furiously and helplessly: 'the usual evening paper's blurred picture of a fat man gesticulating'. 'Damned – ' Eleanor shot out suddenly, "bully!" '[124]

THIRTY-SEVEN

Fascism

Why did Virginia and Leonard Woolf decide to take part of their annual holiday in April 1935 driving through Germany? They knew what to expect. Because 'Leonards nose is so long and hooked', as she put it (in a rare letter to Violet Dickinson),[1] they took the precaution before they left of consulting a friend in the Foreign Office, Ralph Wigram, who had just been to Berlin with the Foreign Secretary and who gave Virginia a vivid sense of Hitler's power and his intentions towards England.

> Hitler very impressive; very frightening . . . The Germans . . . have enough aeroplanes ready to start to keep us under. But if they do kill us all? Well they will have their Colonies. I want room to move about Hitler said . . . No ideals except equality, superiority, force, possessions. And the passive heavy slaves behind him, and he a great mould coming down on the brown jelly . . . there is some reason I suppose to expect that Oxford Street will be flooded with poison gas one of these days. And what then? Germany will get her colonies.[2]

Wigram advised them to get a letter of protection from Prince Bismarck at the London Embassy, and to avoid Nazi demonstrations. She made light in her letters of the possible dangers ('we might be glad of it should we find an anti Jewish riot on, but there's not much risk of that'; 'I dont think there's much danger, and it will be the greatest fun')[3] and they set out in The Deluge, with Mitz.

But in Bonn they did get caught up in an incident. The roads were lined with flag-waving Nazi supporters and armed stormtroopers, awaiting – Virginia thought it might have been Hitler, but in fact it was Goering. Banners reading 'The Jew is our enemy' stretched across the streets. However, there was no need to use Prince Bismarck's letter. When the crowd caught sight of the marmoset, they cheered delightedly. Leonard remembered: 'Mile after mile I drove between two lines of corybantic Germans, and the whole way they shouted "Heil Hitler! Heil Hitler!" to Mitz and gave her (and secondarily Virginia and me) the Hitler salute with outstretched arm.'[4] 'I raised my hand,' she wrote. So, for all the world like

Charlie Chaplin in *The Great Dictator* (a film they later saw and found 'boring')[5] for a moment Virginia Woolf, as it were, played Hitler.

This bizarre incident invites different readings. Does the trip to Germany in 1935 show a lack of awareness and judgement on their part? Quentin Bell and Isaiah Berlin both found their decision to go there 'amazing'; Berlin attributed it to Leonard's 'arrogance', his conviction that 'all politicians were beneath contempt, fools and knaves'.[6] Some people in England in 1935 still did not fully realise what was happening in Germany. But surely the Woolfs were not among them. More likely, the journey to Germany was made so that Leonard could inform himself at first-hand about the situation. From 1935 onwards his position on rearmament changed and hardened – the cause of prolonged and unresolved debate between them.

The image of Virginia Woolf waving to the Nazi crowd is a useful one to her detractors. The attacks on her in the 1930s as élitist and over-protected began a tradition of abuse which continues to this day. Though for feminist readers of Woolf, particularly in the United States, her anti-Fascist politics have become a central key to her work, in Britain there is still a version of Woolf as politically ineffectual or, even, a quasi-Fascist.[7]

There is evidence for such attacks in the 1930s, even in the years when we find her writing with horrified awareness: 'Jews persecuted, only just over the Channel.'[8] At exactly the same time that her internal resistance to Fascism was being worked out, she wrote the scene in *The Years* in which Sara Pargiter, living in cheap lodgings, speaks of her disgust at having to share her bath with 'the Jew', Abrahamson. ('And tomorrow there'll be a line of grease round the bath' 'He made a noise like 'Pah!'')[9] In the summer of 1937 she wrote a story called 'The Duchess and the Jeweller', and sent it to a New York agent, Jacques Chambrun, who offered to place it for her. But the story of 'Isadore Oliver', a 'little Jew boy' with a hooked nose and a doting mother, who begins life in a 'filthy little alley', and makes his way through Whitechapel and Hatton Garden to become the richest jeweller in England, cheating and being cheated by duchesses, was not acceptable to the American market. 'COULD YOU CHANGE RACE OF JEWELLER SINCE THERE IS TERRIFIC RACIAL PREJUDICE IN AMERICA', Chambrun cabled her. They decided to place the story themselves; but in his own defence Chambrun quoted the letter he had received from a magazine editor: 'This certainly is not for us. And what is more I am sure Mrs Woolf cannot make this a story for us. It is a psychological study of a Jew and as they have distinctive characteristics I dont think she could make it a psychological study of a Scotsman or an Irishman.' The story was published in *Harper's Bazaar* once she had changed some of the details: 'Isadore' became 'Oliver', little

Jew boy became little boy, and so on. But his nose was still 'long and flexible, like an elephant's trunk': the 'jew' in 'jeweller' was still pronounced.[10]

It is hard not to read these as examples of offensive caricature. But by writing such things, Woolf separates herself off from the habitual, half-conscious anti-Semitism of her circle.[11] She spells out her complicity in bigotry and offensiveness by way of self-accusation and social critique. (As in: 'How I hated marrying a Jew . . . what a snob I was.')[12] The Jew in the story is the victim, as well as the exploiter, of the gentile duchess's greed and scorn, just as Sara Pargiter is as much an outsider from acceptable society as the Jew, and his presence intensifies our sense of being beyond the pale. Offensive though the moment is, it belongs in the novel's aghast, disenchanted survey of 'civilized' life. 'In time to come,' Sara says earlier in the book to her sister, 'people, looking into this room – this cave, this little antre, scooped out of mud and dung, will hold their fingers to their noses' – she held her fingers to her nose – 'and say 'Pah! They stink! ' Her sister repeats 'Pah!' to herself with 'a spasm of disgust', acknowledging the truth of Sara's version of human beings as 'nasty little creatures'.[13] It is not just 'the Jew' who 'stinks'.

But even when she is not accused of anti-Semitism, the sight of her waving to the Nazi crowds can provoke another line of attack: derision of an ineffectual 'Mrs Woolf', who wrote irrelevantly and uselessly about women's problems when something had to be done about Fascism. This has been a powerful line on *Three Guineas*, from the moment it was published. But the concerted denigration of the book suggests that it was proposing some very unwelcome ideas.

Out of the 'systematic reading of her culture'[14] Virginia Woolf evolved a radical – and unpalatable – critique of 'Hitler in England', or 'subconscious Hitlerism'.[15] *Three Guineas* drew an analogy between 'the tyranny of the patriarchal state' and 'the tyranny of the Fascist state'.[16] It argued, too, that there is no tyranny without complicity. Woolf turned on its head the common belief that our civilisation had to defend itself against the barbarism of Fascism. Standing on the edge of the debate as an outsider, a self-educated woman reader and writer, she constructed a critical version of British social history. And she gives a portrait of the educated middle classes as either acquiescers in or perpetrators of an ugly system, the inheritors of 'ancestral voices prophesying war' (a quotation which haunts her in the late 1930s). What's left to save, she asks? Nothing, unless through re-education and laws which make for social and economic co-operation, another kind of society can be brought into being.[17] The essay brought into the open the buried interchapters she had abandoned in her work on *The Years*. With a great boiling-up, it splashed over everything that affected her: not just the patriarchal home and 'infantilism' of male society, not just the education and employment of women, but the establishment, the media, the church, psychiatry, science, dress. Her cultural conspiracy theory encompassed them all.

The risks of her strategy were great, and *Three Guineas* did lay itself open to 'sneers' by the gaps and slippages within its arguments. It did not deal with women outside her own class, or with women's capacity for martial belligerence, or with the unlikely possibility of re-educating the next generation in the event of a German invasion. It offered a double approach to masculinity as both essentialist and constructed, which it did not try to resolve. For most of the time she insisted on society's construction of gendered attributes, but sometimes the essay responded to the primitivist and regressive models of behaviour offered by Mussolini and Hitler – 'the atavistic programme of both Fascist regimes', which called for 'a return to absolute sexual divisions'[18] – with the suggestion that masculine qualities were primeval and ancestral.

For all its outspokenness, the odd structure of the essay suggests that she was still disguising and censoring herself. As she had unpicked the more aggressive factual content from the text of *The Years*, so she buried the most startlingly subversive items in *Three Guineas* (like the comparisons between St Paul and Hitler, or between priests and dictators) in the footnotes. 'If I say what I mean in 3 Guineas' (she wrote in 1937) 'I must expect considerable hostility. Yet I so slaver and silver my tongue that its sharpness takes some time to be felt.'[19] In the main text, argument takes the form of ironical rhetorical questions, and is constantly being interrupted by more examples, or dissolving into suggestive images: of a poisoned mulberry tree, a burning pyre, a decorated inkpot, or a gramophone needle stuck in its groove. There are, disconcertingly, no tidy distinctions between facts and dreams. Though some revolutionary alternatives to established social forms are proposed, these oscillate, without much change of tone, between the pragmatic (women should be paid for housework, or refuse to participate in demonstrations and organisations which promote war) and the visionary (women should dance in a ring round the bonfire of 'old hypocrisies'). Just as she worked herself almost to death turning *The Years* into a 'deliberate failure', a novel whose form would reflect its politics, so in *Three Guineas* she devised a deliberately fluid structure to undermine the rigid insistence of propaganda and polemic.

To an extent, what she feared has happened: her political work of this period – *The Years*, *Three Guineas*, and shorter pieces such as 'Why Art Today Follows Politics', 'Thoughts on Peace in an Air Raid', and 'The Leaning Tower'[20] – has tended to be misunderstood and undervalued. This is partly because she deliberately presented herself as an unworldly, even mystical private person with no desire for contact with political life: what Leonard Woolf liked to call a 'silly'. He bore witness to this image, which has been solidly maintained by her family and by many of her critics. She did this especially when writing to people who *were* heavily involved, like Stephen Spender or Julian or Quentin Bell. So, to Spender after the murders in Germany in June 1934: 'Even I am shocked by the last week in Germany into taking part; but that only means reading the newspapers.'[21] To Julian: 'Societies seem wrong for me, as I do nothing.'[22] Even to herself, in the diary, she is always writing resentfully of 'the usual shower of anti-Fascist leaflets'[23] or self-mockingly about not being able to spell 'Abysinnia'.[24] She sums up this position in a letter to Julian in 1935: 'But I gather that politics are best avoided. And in any case my views are likely to be inaccurate and perhaps partial – all politics be damned.'[25]

To say *all politics be damned* is not to be ignorant of politics. But why does she take this line so insistently? Obviously it has to do with Leonard. This is his job. In July 1936 she wrote to Ethel: 'I am badgered by all kinds of politicians at the moment, and have just written a firm letter to resign my only office, on the ground that my husband does all that for two – or even one dozen.'[26] She could not compete on his ground, and it would have made her ridiculous to try to do so. It feels as if, at this time, they began to be more intellectually isolated from each other, each caught up in their different responses to what was happening. She had her own job to do – which in 1936, at the point when the anti-Fascist demands got into their full flurry, was the finishing of *The Years* and the struggle against breakdown.

But, in spite of her sense of voices in the other room, the talk was also on her side of the door (two of the working titles for *Three Guineas* were 'The Open Door' and 'A Knock on the Door'). She was an addicted reader of newspapers, she listened avidly to the radio, she paid close attention. At points of drama like the General Strike her commentary shows how keenly she read her world. The abdication crisis was such a moment. Quentin Bell said that she 'enjoyed it enormously'. (So did others: Evelyn Waugh called it 'a great delight to everyone', Virginia noted how 'gay and excited' London felt when the news broke.)[27] But there was dismay in the excitement. As usual, she tested her own responses against other people's, and in doing so made a representative account of the country's response.

As for many others, the Abdication exposed all her mixed feelings about royalty. This had always been a favourite subject. It was a 'number' she did, playing up to her reputation as a snob and a collector of royal stories.[28] Her paper to the Memoir Club, 'Am I a snob?',[29] a funny satire on her friendship with Sibyl Colefax, was given a few days before the abdication crisis. The essay acknowledged and identified with unforgiving self-mockery what it was to be a snob, 'hungry for coronets'. Her analysis of snobbery paralleled her ironic understanding of how the Royal Family functions in Britain. She saw very well how the old imperial myths were sustained by royalty's 'immunity' from ordinary life.[30] It was that immunity (preserved, until December 1936, by a sycophantic press and by the Establishment) which fascinated even an old left-wing anti-conservative thinker like herself.

The abdication crisis was, as she perceived, the turning point in British attitudes to their royals. Edward VIII and Wallis Simpson had been talked about for some time by those in the know (Harold Nicolson, for instance, was noting it gloomily in his diary in October 1936) though Virginia seems not to have heard the gossip until late in November. She saw at once that 'Things – empires, hierarchies – moralities – will never be the same again.'[31] She plunged avidly into the details of this very English, insular crisis,[32] which from 2 December onwards pushed all the foreign news off the papers ('Spain, Germany, Russia – all are elbowed out'.) She noted the range of views – the 'nobs' like Harold Nicolson all glum (he wrote: 'We are all staggered with shame and distress', and to Vita: 'What a little ass the man is to plunge us into this disorder!')[33] and the ordinary people hovering between sympathy and 'sneering contempt'. She noted with interest and surprise her own participation in the common feeling: 'Walking through Whitehall the other day I thought what a Kingdom! England! And to put it down the sink . . . Not a very rational feeling. Still it is what the Nation feels.'[34]

On the day of the Abdication announcement, 10 December, she decided to go to Whitehall. Opposite the Horse Guards she ran into Ottoline, dressed in black and white. Ottoline noted in her diary: 'We fell into each others arms – both feeling that this was indeed a tragic moment.'[35] They met Virginia's old friend, the poet and classicist Bob Trevelyan, and these three exceptional upper-middle-class citizens, all of whom could remember Queen Victoria's Diamond Jubilee forty years before, walked down Whitehall with the crowd, talking about England. Then Trevelyan went on his way, and Ottoline pointed out to Virginia the window out of which Charles I stepped to be beheaded. Virginia wrote: 'I felt I was walking in the 17th century with one of the courtiers; & she was lamenting not the abdication of Edward . . . but the execution of Charles.' She told Julian in China: 'We felt the pressure of all the Kings of England on our heads; & the glory of the Crown. It was partly the light – yellow-brown; partly Ottoline's faded Stuart splendour.'[36] They shared a taxi to Gower Street, and Ottoline noticed that Virginia immediately asked the taxi-driver what he thought. She got the 'vox pop' answer: 'We dont want a woman that's already had 2 husbands & an American when there are so many good English girls.' (This was the real voice of what *The Times*, where Virginia was following the crisis daily, described as 'a stunned and sorrowing people'.) As they drove, a newspaper van drew up with the word 'ABDICATION' written very large on a placard. Ottoline and Virginia bought the first two papers off the new bale. And then they went home to listen to the wireless. 'We both felt that we were like a chorus at a great tragedy', Ottoline wrote. More ironically, Virginia ended her letter to Julian: 'Now it's over & nobody seems a button the worse.'

Whatever feelings about the 'glory of the Crown' the event aroused, she had no illusions about the individuals concerned. Edward VIII sounded 'a very ordinary young man', she thought, listening to his broadcast the next day. Her own broadcast for the BBC, a few months later, on 'Craftsmanship' – how English words can be used by their writers – knowingly incorporated the Abdication into its argument. English words could not be kept 'pure', she said: 'Royal words mate with commoners', words are 'democratic'.[37] Two years later, asked to write a piece on royalty for *Picture Post*, she pursued her usual identification of royalty and snobbery, and her warning that since the Abdication, the Royal Family were no longer immune, and therefore no longer a suitable object for idolatry. Perhaps royalty-worship could be replaced by studies of more scientific interest – the worship of a new kind of caterpillar, or a panda at the zoo? The editor, Tom Hopkinson, returned the piece regretfully; he could not, in August 1939, publish what would be taken as 'an attack on the Royal family'.[38] These reactions to the British monarchy in the 1930s are those of a person who could not simplify mixed feelings into fixed ideologies. But they are certainly not those of a naïve, other-worldly escapist.

It may be that her disclaimers were a smoke-screen against being laughed at, or being thought to act out of character. At the same time, she certainly felt great irritation (and sometimes a snobbish distaste) at having to spend so much time listening to the political anxieties of someone like Kingsley Martin. She disliked the idea of belonging to a fully paid-up group. She was evolving a position in opposition to the voices she heard through the door.

The pattern was that she would get involved – more actively than is generally supposed – and would then resent and pull back from her involvement. So she was part of (and in her own way typical of) the quarrelsome disunity and splinterism of the Left in the 1930s, the 'mixed shades and ragged divisions' of the anti-Fascist 'front' in Britain.[39]

Joining and then quitting was a repeated tendency. In January 1935 she agreed to go on the committee of and to raise money for an 'Anti-Fascist

684

Exhibition' being organised by the Cambridge Anti-War Council and run by Princess Elizabeth Bibesco.[40] Some of Virginia's friends (particularly Clive) were derisive, warning her that she had got herself involved in a communist organisation. Bob Trevelyan wrote to her to say he would not sponsor it, for reasons typical of the sort of debate going on in 1935:

> I do not believe this is the right way to set about counteracting Fascism . . . It can only irritate Fascists abroad . . . and it may tend to increase mere hatred of Hitlerism, which is worse than useless . . . What is wanted is, not further condemnation of the symptoms, horrible as they may be, but understanding of the causes (for most of which we are ourselves responsible) and the removal of them by international action . . . It seems to me that to expose the evils of Fascism and Nazism, and to say nothing whatever of the similar evils of the Russian régime, is completely wrong-headed . . . I regret very much that I cannot help; for Fascism stands for all that I hate most in human things.[41]

In response to this, Virginia immediately backed off: 'I'm not a politician'.[42] But at the same time she was having an argument about the exhibition which shows how sharp – and how unorthodox – her political position was. Virginia wrote to ask Princess Bibesco why 'the woman question' was being ignored in the show, and Bibesco responded that feminism was out of place here. To which she replied: 'What about Hitler?' 'There will of course be a section dealing with women under the Nazi regime', Bibesco confirmed.[43] But Virginia was right to have insisted. She knew what emphasis the Fascists (including Fascists in England) were placing on the repression and subordination of women. One of the items she clipped for *Three Guineas* was this, from the *Sunday Times* in 1936:

PRAISE FOR WOMEN: THEIR PART IN THE NAZI TRIUMPH. Herr Hitler praised the women's part in enabling the Nazi movement to triumph when he addressed the Nazi Women's League. 'So long as we have a strong male sex in Germany – and we Nazis will see to it that we have – we will have no female hand-grenade throwing squads in our country,' he said. He . . . emphasised that women are most useful to the nation when they bring up large families . . . 'There are two worlds in the life of the nation, the world of men and the world of women . . . The woman's world is, if she is happy in her family, her husband, her children and her home. While our enemies assert that women are tyrannically oppressed in Germany, I may reveal that without the devoted and steady collaboration of German women the Nazi movement would never have triumphed.'[44]

The disagreement with Bibesco was part of the pattern. In June 1935

Forster tried to persuade Virginia to go to Paris as part of the British Delegation to an International Congress of Writers in Defence of Culture, organised by André Malraux. Woolf had signed her name to a letter in the *New Statesman & Nation* on 11 May 1935 supporting the Congress, but refused to go. The Congress, though, led to the setting up of the British section of the IAWDC, the International Association of Writers for the Defence of Culture, in which she was, at least initially, involved.[45] In the autumn of 1935 she refused to join PEN.[46] At the same time she went – 'by way of a joke'[47] – to a conference of the National Peace Council in Livingstone Hall, Westminster, on the relation of colonial issues to peace. In December she was present at a meeting at her brother Adrian's house in Gordon Square to set up a group on the model of *Vigilance*, the French anti-Fascist organisation, with a view to holding a big conference in Paris in January. It was Leonard who would propose to name this organisation 'For Intellectual Liberty' (FIL). Virginia Woolf wrote scathingly to Julian of the 'mass of vociferous nonentities'[48] who were present, and she did not go to Paris. But she was there at the FIL meeting at Gordon Square in February 1936 which worded a recruitment letter describing FIL as an organisation dedicated to 'peace, liberty, and culture'.[49] The secretary, Margaret Gardiner, noted that Virginia Woolf was silent and withdrawn: this was at one of the worst moments of her struggle with the *The Years*, and at the keenest point of her resentment of being, as it were, 'the charwoman of a Prime Minister'.[50] 'Every day almost I get rung up to be asked to sign this, subscribe to that . . . but I sign and I protest and so on.'[51] In June she did not go to the London conference of the IAWDC, and commented on the quarrels within what she called 'The International Writers Society for the Propagation of Truth etc.' In July, in a terrible state of health, she resigned from its committee. There had been divisons within it, which she described colourfully to Ethel: 'a woman called Ellis Williams ran amok',[52] she wrote, referring to the high-powered editor of the *Left Review*, Amabel Williams-Ellis.

But in December 1936 she wrote 'Why Art Today Follows Politics' for the *Daily Worker*, at the request of the Artists' International Association. (This was a pluralist alliance between communist and socialist and liberal artists 'against Fascism, War and the Suppression of Culture', with which the Bells and Duncan Grant were involved.) In the essay she said that it was now impossible for the artist, who is 'besieged by voices', to avoid taking part in politics.[53] In 1936 she also gave her support to the campaign to get the pacifist writer Karl von Ossietsky, condemned to prison by the Nazis for treason, out of a concentration camp, by giving him the Nobel Peace Prize, a campaign with which Adrian Stephen was closely involved.[54] And even after her resignation from FIL, her name stayed on the membership list in 1936 and 1937 of the Association of Writers for the Defence of Culture, with which FIL affiliated. In August 1936 she was among those who signed a letter published in several British newspapers urging the British government to commit itself to supporting the Spanish government in 'a struggle against military despotism and of freedom against fascism'.[55] In June 1937 she went to a meeting to raise funds for Basque refugee children ('Oh what a bore these meetings are!')[56] In February 1938 she was one of 170 signatories to a telegram to the Prime Minister, Neville Chamberlain, reading PROFOUNDLY DEPLORE RAPPROCHEMENT MUSSOLINI BEFORE HIS TROOPS LEAVE SPAIN.[57]

In June 1938 a domestic example of 'blatant Hitlerim' aroused her: she advised Ethel to get in touch with the Council for Civil Liberties, of which she was a member, to protest about the expulsion of women musicians from the Bournemouth Symphony Orchestra.[58] In February 1939, with much protesting about her 'repulsion from societies', she gave her manuscript of *Three Guineas* to raise money for German refugees.[59] And in late 1939 and early 1940 she became closely involved in a successful campaign to get the Austrian-Jewish lawyer Robert Spira, who was doing a degree at the Courtauld, out of internment (with the help of PEN and of Anthony Blunt at the Courtauld). Characteristically, she played down her activity here, writing to Ethel about 'wretched Austrians . . . what can one do for them? . . . Even I have to write letters, trying to be "kind".' In the summer of 1940, when German and Austrian refugees were all being interned (and when Leonard was writing to Attlee to protest against the treatment of Freud's son and grandson), Virginia sent off character references for Robert Spira ('Everything that I know about him has given me the impression that he was an opponent of the Nazi regime, & would be loyal to this country') and wrote encouragingly to Mrs Spira: 'The feeling against the internment laws is growing . . . And I will lose no chance of putting your case before anyone who is able to bring the facts to the authorities.'[60]

These gestures of commitment and withdrawal are made within the context of an argument on the Left going on for most of the 1930s. No one could be immune – everyone had to have a position. 'It is impossible any longer to take no side . . . the equivocal attitude, the Ivory Tower, the paradoxical, the ironic detachment, will no longer do.' So argued the letter which urged writers to take sides on the Spanish Civil War, published in the *Left Review* in June 1937, which Leonard, though not Virginia, signed on the anti-Franco side. Did anti-Fascism necessarily mean communism? How many writers could share Eliot's position ('I still feel convinced that it is best that at least a few men of letters should remain isolated'); or did neutrality really mean covert endorsement of Fascism?[61]

If neutrality was itself an equivocal position, so, from the mid-1930s onwards, was pacifism. The term covered a wide range of responses to the threat of Fascism: isolationism, or internationalism (security through improved international contacts), or war resistance (a General Strike to prevent capitalist war-mongering). After Hitler's rise to power in 1933, the peace movement polarised over whether 'the threat of force, such as sanctions applied through the League, was essential to preserve peace'.[62] Some, like A.A. Milne in 'Peace with Honour' (1934) thought that any form of defence was as bad as aggression.[63] But by 1935 most pacifists were moving towards the idea of collective security, or sanctions.

Pacifism by no means equated with socialism. Virginia Woolf saw the pacifist position being brutally overridden at the 1935 Labour Party conference, when the conflict in the party between pacifism and rearmament reached its head, and the pacifist George Lansbury was (as Leonard Woolf put it) 'battered to political death' by Ernest Bevin.[64]

> It was very dramatic: Bevin's attack on Lansbury. Tears came to my eyes as L[ansbury] spoke. And yet he was posing I felt . . . And what is my duty as a human being? The women delegates were very thin voiced & insubstantial[65] . . . too much rhetoric, & what a partial view: altering the structure of society: yes, but when its altered? . . . My sympathies were with [Alfred] Salter who preached non-resistance. He's quite right. That should be our view. But then if society is in its present state? Happily, uneducated & voteless, I am not responsible for the state of society . . . [L] says politics ought to be separate from art. We walked out in the cold over the marsh, & discussed this. [And a few days later]: I got into wild excitement over The Next War [an early title for *Three Guineas*] . . . The result of the L.P. at Brighton was the breaking of that dam between me & the new book.[66]

Salter's position, with which she agreed, was to make pacifism seem the practical choice. 'Pacifists are told they are not practical people. I want humbly to submit to you that we are the true realists, and we are the only practical people. The world has tried again and again every other method except that method laid down in the Sermon on the Mount.'[67]

During the Spanish Civil War, only a minority of socialists remained pacifists.[68] For some, like Julian Bell, who two years before had been editing a volume of pacifist recollections of the First World War, *We Did Not Fight* (1935), the decision to fight, or to help the fight against Franco, became a simple one. For many other left-wingers, such as Kingsley Martin, or

Victor Gollancz, there was a painful division of feeling between the need to oppose Franco and the desire to maintain some kind of pacifist position. The Peace Pledge Union, (PPU) founded by Canon Dick Sheppard, attracted 150,000 people in 1936 (Huxley was one of its leading members, and Clive Bell wrote 'Warmongers' for the PPU in 1938, recommending appeasement). But within the PPU, as within the Labour Party, there was discord, some members supporting 'war resistance' or even rearmament, others taking the Sermon on the Mount (like Salter) as their model for 'peace-making'. Some of those in the peace movement supported collective security – not through the League, after 1936, but through a collective alliance against Hitler and Mussolini of Britain, France, Czechoslovakia and the Soviet Union. But not all those who backed collective security also backed rearmament. They were reluctant to trust a National Government, which favoured Franco in Spain and was following a policy of appeasement towards Hitler and Mussolini, with the use of arms in an anti-Fascist cause. As for the belief of many on the left (including Virginia Woolf) that we needed to overcome the militarism and Hitlerism in our own society rather than fighting Hitler, this seemed by the end of the decade to have been left too late.[69] 'Damn the Nazis,' wrote Rose Macaulay in 1938, 'they are making pacifism impossible.'

The debate over resistance split the left, split the peace movement – and split 'Bloomsbury'. Frances Partridge's diaries of the war years show the divisions that sprang up within this closely interconnected social group. Quentin Bell, for instance, who had shared his brother's feelings about going to Spain, had little sympathy for Frances's position as a pacifist and Ralph Partridge's as a conscientious objector.

> Talking to Quentin about the war I told him how I envied him his passionate interest in it. He wouldn't have been born at any other time for anything, he finds it so enthralling. I tried to convey the sense of constant disgust I feel weighing on me whenever I think of it, and he looked at me in surprise and said: 'Oh I see, you are a *real* Pacifist.' Why are people so loth to recognise the fact, I wonder. I find no difficulty in recognising their bellicosity.

When Marjorie Strachey visited the Partridges at Ham Spray in 1942, she remarked: 'All conscientious objectors ought to be dropped by parachute in Germany since they wish to be ruled by the Nazis.' Frances thought: 'Does she ever remember that both Lytton and James and most of their closest friends were C.O.s in the last war, and would she have wanted them to be treated likewise?'[70]

Leonard's position within the Labour Party was a long way from pacifism. He watched the party's indecisions and contradictions with mounting exasperation, and viewed with cynicism and gloom (he told Julian in China) 'the complete disintegration of opinion here'. For him, collective security had to mean rearming. Aldous Huxley disagreed with him. For Huxley, pacifism was the only practical position:

> The pacifist does not dream of saying that he will have nothing to do with evil. His policy is to be a realist and to deal with evil in the only way that is effective. To deal with it by means of more evil is demonstrably unpractical.[71]

Huxley's position was like Virginia Woolf's in *Three Guineas*. When he refused to sign a manifesto in March 1936 approving sanctions because he was a pacifist, she said to herself, 'So am I'.[72] But after 1936, Leonard would draw even further away. He was critical of the Labour Party for not facing up to reality. 'If the Party really meant to commit itself to a policy of resisting any further acts of aggression by Hitler, then it committed itself to the corollary that Britain must make itself strong enough on land and sea and in the air to defeat Hitler.'[73] By 1938 he thought that the Labour Party should make a coalition with Churchill and agree to the immediate introduction of conscription and rearmament.

'She is for Peace, Leonard for the war,' Rose Macaulay wrote in 1939, after a meeting with Virginia in the London Library.[74] (Virginia's report on this encounter, according to Angelica, was that 'Rose Macaulay was screeching in the London Library, holding up all passers-by with questions about L's views on the war, until V. had to draw her aside . . . she is all for peace.')[75] Quentin Bell would put it slightly differently: 'She wanted peace, he wanted victory.'[76] It was a distancing difference between them in these years. Virginia Woolf defined her own position in relation to the arguments going on all round her. 'I sat there splitting off my own position from theirs,'[77] she wrote after a discussion in April 1937 with Leonard, Julian, Stephen Spender and Kingsley Martin, who all thought pacifism was now irresponsible. 'All the gents. against me,' she noted, after opposing Eliot, Clive Bell and Saxon Sydney-Turner in February 1940 in their view that the war was the end of their valuable civilisation.[78] She was always trying to establish 'what is really the woman's angle' on the anti-Fascist rhetoric she was hearing and on the 'bunch of scares' which Leonard brought home 'after every Cttee meeting'.[79] Like the imaginary artist she describes in 'Why Art Today Follows Politics', she was 'besieged by voices'.

Covers by Vanessa Bell.
MIDDLE *Carpet by Duncan
Grant, bought by Virginia,
1932.*

Family group at Charleston, 1930: left to right, Leonard, Clive Bell, Julian Bell, Virginia, Auberon Duckworth, Duncan Grant.

ABOVE *Ethyl Smyth conducting, 1930.*
ABOVE RIGHT *Tom Eliot, Virginia, and Vivien Eliot, 1932.*
RIGHT *Ethyl Smyth reading.*

Virginia in the 1930s.

The Woolfs, Roger Fry and Margery Fry on the Acropolis, 1932.

Leonard and Virginia at Bowen's Court, 1934.

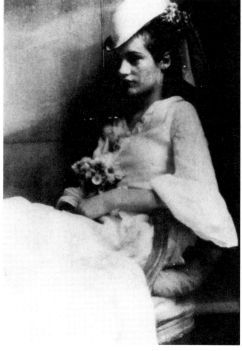

Angelica Bell as Ellen Terry in Freshwater, *1935.*

ABOVE *Virginia Woolf, passport photograph, 1933.*
ABOVE RIGHT *Virginia Woolf by Vanessa Bell, 1934.*
RIGHT *Virginia Woolf by Man Ray, 1934.*

LEFT *Angelica, Vanessa and Quentin Bell, 1938.*
BELOW LEFT *Leonard Woolf, drawing by Vanessa Bell, 1940.*
BELOW RIGHT *Leonard Woolf.*

RIGHT *Virginia Woolf
by Gisèle Freund,
1939.*
BELOW *Virginia and
Leonard Woolf by
Gisèle Freund, 1939.*

Virginia Woolf by Gisèle Freund, 1939.

Three Guineas, far from ignoring those voices, is constructed in response to them. It arises out of her exasperation with what she calls the 'Inquisition'[80] and invents its own manifesto or questionnaire as a pastiche of the inquisitors. The whole of the third section of *Three Guineas* is based on the 1936 recruitment letter of FIL, so often repeating its key phrase 'the defence of culture and intellectual liberty' that it makes a mockery of, and forces a rethinking of, those very terms. 'We can only help you to defend culture and intellectual liberty by defending our own culture and our own intellectual liberty.'[81]

Three Guineas reiterates the debate on the left over peace and war. And it was influenced by a number of the pacifist pamphlets she had been reading. One of these, *The Roots of War*, published by the Hogarth Press in 1936, argued that an imperialist and capitalist society provides 'rich ground for the rapid growth of war psychology'.[82] Bertrand Russell's 1936 pacifist pamphlet *Which Way to Peace* insisted, like her, on the domestic and educational roots of war. 'Mothers and nurses are the first instructors in militarism.' 'There must be no patriotic propaganda, no Empire Day or Flag Day or Fourth or Fourteenth of July . . . Is this Utopian? Perhaps.' His 'way to peace' was 'to abstain from fighting' and to try and persuade others to do so. He made her feel that she too was 'an isolationist', but 'for other reasons'.[83] And Huxley's pamphlet 'What are you going to do about it?' (1936) also made a case for 'constructive peace' with a plan to establish alternative societies of pacifists, affiliations of small groups, like religious orders. Pacifism, he said, was a technique of conflict, a way of fighting without the use of violence.[84]

Bertrand Russell and Aldous Huxley did not get derided for mental instability or ludicrous Utopianism. Yet it's clear from their pacifist pamphlets that *Three Guineas* was not as eccentric as it has been made out to be. Even a contemporary whose political position was completely different from Virginia's, like Harold Nicolson, could share *Three Guineas*' fundamental point of view. Visiting an RAF station in 1940, he wrote:

> Go down to Nether Wallop to lecture to the Air Force about the German character. I do not feel that the young men really like it. They are all fascists at heart and rather like the Germans.[85]

When *Three Guineas* was published, she braced herself for hostile responses from her circle,[86] especially from Keynes ('dear old Hitler'):

> Now the thing to remember is that I'm an independent & perfectly

established human being: no one can bully me; & at the same time nothing shall make me shrivel into a martyr or a bitter persecution maniac.[87]

And she was right to be nervous. Keynes thought it silly, Leonard (though he picked his words with her) thought it her worst book. Most of her friends were embarrassed by it, and few of them passed comment. The next generation of her male readers and friends followed suit. Nigel Nicolson would call *Three Guineas* muddled and unbalanced nonsense.[88] Quentin Bell has always thought the essay's argument was 'wholly inadequate' and that it was wrong to involve 'a discussion of women's rights with the far more agonizing and immediate question of what we were to do in order to meet the ever-growing menace of Fascism and war'.[89] The satire on male uniforms and professional dress seemed silly to him, and he was completely unconvinced by the essay's neglect of female, as well as male, bellicosity.

And there were bellicose reactions from women as well as men. Queenie Leavis in *Scrutiny* was particularly scornful of *Three Guineas*' 'silly and ill-informed' 'dangerous assumptions' and 'nasty attitudes', its 'self-indulgent sex hostility', its recommendations for 'the art of living as conceived by a social parasite': 'like Nazi dialectic without Nazi conviction'. Virginia was able to see this attack calmly as 'all personal'.[90] She was much more incensed by Vita's evasive response to it as 'tantalising', 'provocative', and full of 'misleading arguments'. Dishonest, am I? she retorted. Vita defended herself by pointing out that women could be as bellicose as men, and that she didn't believe any Englishwoman could really believe that 'England is not her country'.[91]

The resistance which *Three Guineas* aroused went beyond rational objections. The essay was a threat. *A Room of One's Own*, charming, witty and urbane, had slipped down deliciously, like the famous lunch in the men's college it described; *Three Guineas*, furious, lacerating, harsh and awkward, stuck in many of its readers' throats. But though there was so much derision and opposition to *Three Guineas* from her close circle, farther afield, especially among women, there was a great deal of rational support and enthusiasm.

She had tapped into some readers' feelings in a very profound and vivid way. Letters came in from all quarters, many enthusiastically greeting her idea of a society of 'outsiders', and some, it must be said, very odd indeed (like the 60-page disquisition on sex and the working classes from Ernest Huxley, of Rock Ferry, Birkenhead.)[92] A self-educated Yorkshire mill-worker, Agnes Smith, wrote from Holmfirth, near Huddersfield, to complain that the essay had not dealt with the problems of working-class women. 'It is true that I have to cook my own dinner while you do not – but that does not make me any more free from the problems which beset women as a whole.'[93] But *Three Guineas* still seemed very important to her, and their correspondence developed into friendly exchanges on education, the importance of public libraries, and the class system. Advising her to continue writing about politics only in her own way, Agnes Smith wrote, conclusively: 'After all, *A Room of One's Own* and *Three Guineas* WERE politics.'[94] Tributes to Woolf's 'politics' circulated among a distinguished cross-section of women. Edith Somerville wrote to Ethel Smyth: 'How *admirable Three Guineas* is!' She had read it 'with ecstasy and fury'; but 'only those of our persuasion will read it. It cuts too deep for men to endure.'[95] Nelly Cecil wrote to Virginia: 'I hope the leading gentlemens get it stuffed down their throats again & again – & the backward gentlewomens too – that is the sad part of the story – if we stuck together as men do – wouldnt we have got everything worth having long ago?'[96] Shena Simon, herself in some dilemma about whether to be a complete 'outsider' or whether (for instance) to train as an air raid warden, felt 'personally grateful' for the book. Once the war started, she thought that 'the truth of *Three Guineas* had been proved over and over again'. The headmistress of Manchester High School for Girls, she told Virginia, was 'going to use *Three Guineas* as her Bible'.[97] Naomi Mitchison, who had greatly admired *The Years*, wrote a long autobiographical letter in response to *Three Guineas*, querying its proposal for 'outsiders' ('one must have contacts with ordinary life') but adding: 'Your book seemed like part of an eternal argument that is bound to go on in one's mind, on and off, the whole time.'[98] Different generations of women who knew her praised it: Judith Stephen, about to read anthropology at Cambridge ('to see how little we are removed from the savages!') liked it, and Pippa Strachey enjoyed the vent for 'evil feelings' it provided.[99] Margaret Llewelyn Davies's praise aroused an eloquent response. 'To sit silent and acquiesce in all this idiotic letter signing and vocal pacifism when there's such an obvious horror in our midst – such tyranny, such Pecksniffism – finally made my blood boil into the usual ink-spray.'[100] The most satisfying tribute came from the grand old lady of the suffrage movement, Emmeline Pethick Lawrence; Virginia's reply to her showed how much she valued her letter:

> None that I have had about *Three Guineas* has given me such pleasure. I was haunted by the fear that those who had a right to judge would think me impertinent – I have had so little experience myself. But no one has more right to judge than you have, & if the book seems to you useful I am greatly relieved. To me, the facts seemed so obvious that I wondered that they had not been stated before. Whether stating them does any good, I

don't know, but it was the only thing I could do, & silence had become intolerable to me.[101]

Three Guineas is evidence (like all her writing of this decade) that she knows it is not possible to be silent or separate. That desire for 'immunity' she had felt so acutely a few years before, at fifty, went on haunting her. In *The Years*, Eleanor Pargiter, underground in an air-raid, thinks of a picture of a landscape in the South of France, and murmurs the word 'immune' over to herself. In July 1940, waiting for reviews of *Roger Fry* and for a possible invasion of England, Virginia still thinks that 'immune' is the right word for her. But in 'Why Art Today Follows Politics' she says that no one can now be 'immune'.[102]

The position on 'immunity' she was taking up against 'all the gents' in the second half of the 1930s, was a complicated version of non-resistance or pacifism. In her interior debate about what resistance can consist in (which mirrored the public debate she was listening to about pacifism) there is a great difficulty over 'action'. 'To be passive is to be active; those also serve who remain outside', she tries to prove in *Three Guineas*.[103] She withdraws from 'action', but she has a horror of passivity. In October 1940 she writes, 'I'm terrified of passive acquiescence. I live in intensity.'[104] She suggests a 'home front' in the form of inner resistance. One of her angriest moments in *Three Guineas* comes when she attacks H.G. Wells for saying that women have not helped to resist Fascism: they may be resisting it, she maintains, in ways not apparent to him.[105] She says to Julian while she is writing *The Years*: 'What can I do but write? Hadn't I better go on writing?' But adds: 'Unfortunately, politics gets between me and fiction. I feel I must write something when this book is over – something vaguely political; doubtless worthless, certainly useless.'[106]

The theme of what 'use' she can be returns again and again in 1938 and 1939. On 6 September 1939, three days into the war: 'For the 100th time I repeat – any idea is more real than any amount of war misery. And what one's made for. And the only contribution one can make – this little pitter patter of ideas is my whiff of shot in the cause of freedom – so I tell myself.' In a letter to her niece Judith Stephen, on 2 December 1939: 'I'm more and more convinced that it is our duty to catch Hitler in his home haunts and prod him if even with only the end of an old inky pen.' And on 15 May 1940: 'Thinking is my fighting.'[107]

This was something she might have said to Julian; and it was the opposite of what he would have said to her. Their argument was crucial in her response to the 1930s. In 1932 it had been a quarrel over poetry's responsibility to the present age, as in 'Letter to a Young Poet'. As part of that debate, she had written a comic spoof of Julian working on a strictly clinical descriptive poem in the style of Hopkins, and asking Vanessa's opinion of it. She replies:

'Why dont you ask your Aunt Virginia? I always ask Virginia about poetry. If she says it's good, I know it's bad, and if she says its bad I know its good. What does Virginia say about your poetry?' 'Oh, it makes her faint.' 'Well then Julian you must be the very greatest poet in the English language.'[108]

Five years on, Julian Bell was no longer interested in poetry but in action, and their argument about what was 'good' and what was 'bad' was over war, not words.

When Julian came back from China in March 1937 (mainly because he wanted to go to Spain, in part because he had been having an affair with a colleague's wife), she could see he was changed.[109] He seemed bitter to her about his life, alienated from his parents' generation, and more resolute. She looked at him with new respect, but also with anxiety on Vanessa's behalf and with irritation at his obstinacy. The memoir she wrote later that year eloquently and honestly describes her feelings for him, in a scene (very revealing about her behaviour with the people close to her) which took place on the afternoon of 18 March.

I never saw him alone, except once, and then only for a short time. I had just come in with the Evening Standard in which *The Years* was extravagantly praised, much to my surprise. I felt very happy. It was a great relief. And I stood with the paper, hoping L would come and I could tell him, when the bell rang. I went to the top of the stairs, looked down and saw Julian's great sun hat (he was amazingly careless of dress always – would come here with a tear in his trousers) and I called out in a sepulchral voice 'Who is that?' Whereupon he started and laughed and I let him in. And he said 'What a voice to hear' or something light; then he came up; it was to ask for [Hugh] Dalton's telephone number. He stood there; I asked him to stay and see Leonard. He hesitated, but seemed to make up his mind that he must get on with the business of seeing Dalton. So I went and looked for the number. When I came back he was reading the Standard. I had left it with the review open. But he had turned, I think to the politics. I had half a mind to say 'Look how I'm praised.' And then I thought No, I'm on the top of the wave: and it's not kind to thrust that sort of thing upon people who aren't yet recognised. So I said nothing about it. But I wanted him to stay. And then again I felt, he's afraid I shall try to persuade him not to go [to Spain]. So all I said was 'Look here, Julian, if you ever want a meal, you've only to ring us up.' 'Yes' he said, rather doubtingly, as if we might be too busy. So I insisted. 'We can't see too much of you.' And followed him into the hall and put my arm round him and said 'You can't think how nice it is having you back' and we half kissed; and he looked pleased and said 'Do you feel that?' And I said yes, and it was as if he asked me to forgive him for all the worry; and then off he stumped, in his great hat and thick coat.[110]

The 'worry' was certainly great. Vanessa spent all the time between his return and his departure trying to stop him going. But his mind was already made up. 'I am proposing to turn myself into a man of action', he wrote in his private 'Prose Reflections: To my bourgeois friends in the Communist Party'.[111] His letters to Quentin from China and the essays he was writing now all argued that what socialism needed was not the liberal optimism of the League, but a level of military discipline which could combat Fascism on its own terms. He wanted to use the Labour Party (where he was asking Leonard to find him some employment) as a cover for an armed revolution, led by a force of 'convinced and disciplined socialists'.[112] He told Quentin he had plans for organising 'an alternative army, police & administration . . . on the Hitlerian model'.[113] Perhaps their childhood war-games were to become a reality. Going to Spain to join the Republican side against Franco was not, he told himself, a romantic gesture (though he did sometimes like to compare himself with Rupert Brooke)[114] but a practical means of getting military experience, which was what the leaders of the socialist revolution were going to need. He wanted to look at battles and dead bodies with the same analytical observant detachment Virginia had teased him for in his poems. But there was also (and quite apparent to her) a strong need to turn his back on the last generation. This was obvious in the way his political agenda was spelt out in the form of messages to 'Bloomsbury'. The article on Roger was all about the need for absolute hardness, 'discipline and impartiality' in art, which Julian saw as 'a form of social propaganda'.[115] His defence of military values ('non-resistance means suffering the full power of fascism') took the form of a letter to Forster attacking his support for the League and 'the liberal inability to think in terms of force'.[116] Virginia (who did not read that essay until after his death, when it helped her to understand his motives) could not accept his reasons for going to Spain, but understood that it was a rejection of the political culture he had been raised in. Her response to that was to defend her pacifism as a form of action:

What made him do it? I suppose its a fever in the blood of the younger generation which we can't possibly understand. I have never known anyone of my generation have that feeling about a war. We were all C.O.'s in the Great war. And though I understand that this is a 'cause', can be called the cause of liberty & so on, still my natural reaction is to fight intellectually: if I were any use, I should write against it: I should evolve some plan for fighting English tyranny. The moment force is used, it becomes meaningless & unreal to me . . . I'm sometimes angry with him; yet feel it was fine, as all very strong feelings are fine; yet they are also wrong somehow; one must control feeling with reason.[117]

Like Vanessa, she tried to stop him. Stephen Spender, who had been travelling through Spain, wrote her in April a very hostile account of the International Brigade headquarters at Albacete, and said he very much hoped Julian would not 'join the Brigade, since to do so required not only courage, but "a terrific narrowness & religious dogmatism about the Communist Party line".'[118] Virginia enlisted Spender and Kingsley Martin to try to dissuade Julian,[119] but it was only Vanessa's desperate anxiety which persuaded him to go not as a soldier in the International Brigade, but as an ambulance driver. He regarded this as a compromise, but it turned out to be just as dangerous.

He left on 7 June: two nights before, at dinner at Clive's, Virginia said she would leave Roger's papers to him in her will. He said, 'Better leave them to the British Museum.' 'I thought "That's because he thinks he may be killed." ' But his parting words to them were 'Goodbye until this time next year'.[120] He and Vanessa wrote to each other often in the next weeks. He told her he was loving it all; she told him (in her next to last letter to him) of a strange moment at Charleston:

I saw a ghost this morning. Really I have never had such a definite illusion. I was standing in the passage outside your room looking at Quentin's room through the open door, thinking vaguely of you I believe, when I saw a figure go across Quentin's room towards the washstand . . . there was no-one . . . of course there was some trick of the light – [121]

On 18 July, during the bloody battle of Brunete, German planes fighting for Franco shelled Julian's ambulance; he was hit in the lung, brought into the hospital at Escorial, and died soon after. He was twenty-nine. From the moment he decided to go, Vanessa and Virginia had both expected that he would be killed. He had anticipated it too. On the boat to China two years before, he had written letters to Vanessa which he had sent to his friend Eddy Playfair, to be given to Vanessa in case of his death (which Playfair now did). In them he said: 'I've had an extremely happy life . . . I love you more than anyone else, and always have done so . . . I owe a great deal to you directly, in having known Roger, Virginia Duncan (and Angelica). If you do hear that I've got involved in a war or a riot, remember that it's the sort of end I should choose.'[122]

A great part of Vanessa's life closed down after his death. (Clive must also have been struck hard, though he 'pretended to a distressing detachment'.) Quentin felt he had lost a limb; Angelica was bereft (her confusion added to by Vanessa choosing this summer to tell her that she was not Clive's but Duncan's daughter).[123] The only people who could really help Vanessa were Duncan and Virginia; Quentin thought of it in later years as 'her finest hour'.

THIRTY-EIGHT

Waiting

She was angry with Julian for what seemed to her the wastefulness of his death, and for what it did to Vanessa. Her anger spilt over on to his contemporaries: when Spender came to dinner she disliked him for not being Julian. And she was angry selfishly, because his death cut across what had seemed, in spite of world events, a period of private relief and pleasure. 1937 could have been a year of profound happiness.[1] At the start of the year there had been a scare over Leonard's health; it seemed he might have diabetes, or an enlarged prostate, or a kidney infection. She prepared herself, as usual, to face up to the worst: 'how to keep cool, how to control myself, if it is a bad report. Work is my only help.'[2] But it was a false alarm, and she had a sense of 'heavenly' relief, as if they had been granted 'another space of life'.[3] In the summer, just before Julian's death, Leonard, on Shaw's advice, tried the Alexander treatment for his trembling hands. She watched this experiment with sympathy and attention, thinking how, if it had not been for his tremor, perhaps 'all his shyness, his suffering from society, his sharpness, & definiteness, might have been smoothed'.[4]

Her relief over his health was followed on 11 March 1937 by another reprieve, the reception of *The Years*. Before its publication she was sick with apprehension, suffering horrible sensations of terror and loneliness, fear of ridicule, conviction of failure. But the reviews were largely excellent and the sales immediately took off; by May it was a best-seller. The 'tight screw' of anticipation and its aftermath led to a bout of headaches, and to a frantic outburst of rage and revulsion at the intrusion of an American journalist with a notebook into the garden of Monk's House. 'Bug bug bug bug bug' she typed savagely, in a kind of furious prose-poem: 'like a bug malodorous glistening . . . as if while he talked he sipped blood, my blood: anybodys blood to make a bugs body blue black.'[5] The 'bug' (for the *New York Times*) wrote in his column, after failing to get his interview, under Leonard's 1932 photograph of her (the one she had not wanted used for the Holtby book):

Virginia Woolf: Kindly and very gracious, but has been known to give you coffee one night and cut you dead in a Bloomsbury 'bus next morning

– all because planning her next novel makes her as absent-minded as any professor. Some readers get a similar effect after reading her books . . . She lives in Tavistock-square with her husband, a large number of cactus plants, a pet monkey and a dog. Her hobby is printing. So is her husband's, but he varies it with gardening . . . Tall and thin, with greying hair, she never speaks unless she has something worthwhile to say. Gossips get no change out of her. Young poets do: she and her husband run a press which has done a great deal for poets . . . And a good number of people forgive her for her books because of this.[6]

This kind of thing affected the tone of her attacks, in the next few years, on journalism and the literary market-place.

But this loathsome intrusion was an exception to the spring's sense of promise. They were talking again about letting go of the Press. She was pouring into *Three Guineas* a great deal of what had been held back from *The Years*. She was writing new pieces, two long essays on Gibbon,[7] her broadcast on 'Craftsmanship', a piece on Congreve which took pleasure in his creation of a 'serene, impersonal and indestructible world of art' out of 'discipline' and 'hard work'.[8] She spoke kindly to herself in her diary about her success with *The Years*, calling herself 'my dear' (as Henry James used to do when he wanted to pat himself on the back).[9] She made a firm resolution that she would never harness herself to a long book again, but would try now to 'invent a new form' for criticism and biography, and to write 'some completely unformal fiction: short: & poetry'. She wanted to go forward: 'Its useless to repeat my old experiments: they must be new to be experiments.'[10] They took a holiday in France in May, avoiding King George's Coronation as they had avoided the Jubilee, and going to the Dordogne and Albi and George Sand's house at Nohant. During this trip, her sense of release after long labour is palpable. (And this even though they were worried now about reports of Maynard having had a heart attack.)

After the holiday there was some minor amusement to be had from the arrival of May Sarton, an eager young Anglo-American with a volume of poems, a first novel on the way, and an adventurous history of working with theatre companies in New York and living alone in Paris. Her long life of writing – self-exposing poems and novels on lesbianism, old age, loneliness – was just beginning. That summer, at twenty-five, she was falling in love with everyone she met in England, most of all Elizabeth Bowen. She was all ready to hero-worship Virginia Woolf too, having read *The Waves*, in Paris, as soon as it came out, and having already glimpsed her in Russell Square, 'leaning on Leonard's arm, under an umbrella'.[11] Virginia met her at Elizabeth's house in Clarence Terrace, and found her pretty, artificial and star-struck: 'Not a type from which I now get much kick.'[12] They had an unsuccessful evening with her at Whipsnade Zoo, near to where May Sarton was living. (At the zoo, Virginia reminded her of one of the giraffes, 'her immense dark eyes, long aristocratic neck, and slightly disdainful, sensitive way of lifting her chin.')[13] The young aspirant came to tea a few times. In May Sarton's recollections, not unlike Victoria OCampo's, these visits glittered with romance, excitement and intimacy: 'I remember that we laughed hilariously, that she teased me about poetry, and told me that it was easy to write poems and immensely difficult to write novels.' Looking back years later, she still cherished her memory: 'She was so charming – just dear. And so funny! She put on a tremendous show for people.' 'I was immensely flattered.'[14] But Virginia referred to May Sarton as 'that goose'.[15] She hated her novel, which she thought was a 'silly clever imitation'[16] of her, and she found her letters gushing – which they were:

> Most conversations seem to me a series of little doors opening and shutting very quickly and by what one sees one guesses at possibilities behind. But with you I think it would be possible sometimes to go to the very end, to go through the little door before it closes.[17]

But Virginia Woolf kept her interior doors closed to this potential intimate. She felt, this summer, inviolable, calm and stable: as if she had arrived at that place of immunity she so desired: 'That is the achievement . . . of my 55 years . . . beyond harm; armed against all that can happen. I have never had this feeling before in all my life; but I have had it several times since last summer.'[18] Even after Julian had gone to Spain she still felt it, viewing Vanessa's despair from the other side of the grass-plot 'on wh. I'm walking with such energy & delight at the moment'.[19]

It was not allowed to continue; the catastrophe of Julian's death broke it all up. And this was not the only grief of the summer of 1937. Old Janet Case, who had been suffering, with dignity, from Leslie's (and Lytton's) disease of abdominal cancer, died on 15 July, taking with her, Virginia felt, a 'great visionary part' of her life. She wrote what she called a 'stiff and mannered' anonymous obituary for *The Times*. The piece oddly echoed, over long years, Leslie's elegy for Julia in 'Forgotten Benefactors'. Her father's Victorian sentiment for the forgotten Angels in the House who dedicate themselves to others is linked to Virginia Woolf's belief in women who are uninstitutionalised and obscure, who – though professionals, not angels in the house – keep themselves apart from the public procession. The obituary for her old teacher (by its anonymity as much as anything) combined her sentiment for the past with the feminist arguments of *Three Guineas*.

In her way she was a pioneer; but her way was one that kept her in the background, a counsellor rather than a champion, listening to the theories of others with a little chuckle of merriment, opening her beautiful veiled eyes with a sudden flash of sympathy and laughter, but for herself she wanted no prominence,no publicity.She was contemplative, reticent, withdrawn.[20]

Virginia herself was acting more like an 'angel in the house' this summer than ever before in her life. All her energies went into looking after Vanessa. No one else could do it. As at earlier times of crisis ('we have been through so much together') she became her sister's strongest support. She went to Vanessa almost every day, wrote her tender love letters, and was not afraid to talk to her about Julian and the past. It gave her a kind of satisfaction, but it also exhausted her, and placed a great strain on both her and Leonard. Vanessa's suffering was terrible to behold and impossible to assuage. 'I shall be cheerful', she told Virginia, 'but I shall never be happy again.'[21] Virginia tried to imagine what this must be like, and to tell Vanessa, with loving subtlety, how close she felt:

Do you think we have the same pair of eyes, only different spectacles? I rather think I'm more nearly attached to you than sisters should be. Why is it I never stop thinking of you . . . ?[22]

But this intimacy was 'very hard work'.[23] Back in London, going round to the studio, she sometimes had to 'make herself' stay on after other people had gone. Often she dreaded being alone with her sister.[24] The old conflicts between them still surfaced. Vanessa's last letter to Julian had a sour note on how Virginia must be enjoying earning so much money for *The Years*, and Virginia was aware that 'she is querulous sometimes about "my success" '.[25] It was typical of Vanessa that she should flash out with some sharpness at her guardian ('I really need not be visited like an invalid now') and that she was only able to tell Virginia indirectly, through Vita, of her gratitude: 'I cannot ever say how Virginia has helped me. Perhaps some day, not now, you will be able to tell her it's true.'[26] Vita at once passed this on, which was the right thing to do. Virginia's response to Vita, halting and obstructed, reflected all the inhibitions and strains in these emotions: 'Nessa's saying that to you . . . meant something I cant speak of. And I cant tell anyone – but I think you guess – how terrible it is to me, watching her . . . But that message gives me something to hold to.'[27] Not until the following February, on Julian's birthday, did Vanessa write to Virginia: 'You do know really dont you how much you help me – I cant show it and I feel so stupid and such a wet blanket often but I couldnt get on at all if it werent for you – so you musnt mind my being or seeming so grumpy.'[28] Not being able to speak out: it was the theme of this catastrophe, as it was the theme of so many of the novels.

Julian's death brought back Thoby's, except that with Thoby 'I felt we were the same age'; now Virginia felt like an old woman who would not see the young again.[29] By an odd coincidence, Violet Dickinson (who had come back to life earlier that year, suddenly returning to Virginia all her youthful letters) had a fall, and Virginia was asked to write to cheer her up. ('How can I cheer up Violet after a 20 years silence? One's jokes grow old.')[30] She wrote concealing the fact of Julian's death, as, thirty years before, she had concealed Thoby's.

And, as her feelings about Thoby had reshaped themselves after his death, so her involvement with Julian went on posthumously. She wrote many letters in response to condolences. She continued her argument with him in *Three Guineas*, in her unpublished memoir of him,[31] and in a story she now revised for *Harper's Bazaar* called 'The Shooting Party'. In this story, two old sisters in an eighteenth-century house sit waiting for the squire to come home after a day's hunting. They call to mind the deaths of the sons of the family, one brought home on a stretcher. In a violent, farcical conclusion, the brutal squire brings the house crashing down over their heads. These family stories seem to linger on into the present, in the mind's eye of an old woman on a train, whose memory, like a ghost, dances over the grave 'of a family, of an age, of a civilisation'.[32] The slaughtered sons of the hunting fathers – caricatures of the Bells – provide analogies for an inherited militaristic chauvinism that destroys its own civilisation, leaving only the old women – malicious and grim – to talk of the past.

Leonard wrote an epigram in a copy he gave her, for their twenty-fifth wedding anniversary, of Peacock's *The Misfortunes of Elphin*. It was a quotation from the book: 'Unlooked for good betides us still/And unanticipated ill.'[33] The phrase referred eloquently to their long companionship and to their present sadness. For her, their work and their marriage were her two most profound resources. At times to come – as at times in the past – she would think of their old inseparability not as an achievement but as a failure, a bondage, a form of 'damnable servility'.[34] But now, not being able to part – when she thought of joining Nessa, who had gone to Paris in October, she then decided she could not go without him – was a great consolation:

Then I was overcome with happiness. Then we walked round the square love making – after 25 years cant bear to be separate. Then I walked round the Lake in Regents Park. Then . . . you see it is an enormous pleasure, being wanted: a wife. And our marriage so complete.[35]

In storm and in calm it endured: in storm, when they saw a great gale smash over the front at Seaford, and she felt the delight of 'the frantic & the unmastered', and Leonard had to restrain her – she said, half-joking, to Ethel – from throwing herself in; in calm, when they sat quietly reading in the evenings, 'L in his stall, I in mine'.[36]

This settledness was threatened again at the end of this 'cursed year' of 1937. Leonard was ill, as he had been the winter before; an enlarged prostate, or kidney disease, was again suspected. He was X-rayed and put on a protein-free diet of 'rice pudding'. He noted the facts baldly in his diary in December and January – 'temperature bed', 'drove Royal Northern Hospital x-ray, went bed on return', and 'in bed' every day from 1 to 11 January. But they were both anxious: the threat of kidney disease or of cancer of the prostate was very alarming, and an operation to remove the prostate would be an extremely painful one. Virginia braced herself, and tried to work. On the 15th his specimens were declared normal. She and Molly MacCarthy, who was in Bart's hospital with suspected gallstones, exchanged cynical views on modern medicine and X-rays, 'a new trifling fashionality', Molly wrote:

> Oh! yes science is overdoing it right and left. Let us die like old women and men in cottages, with crutches and shawls, geraniums and few movements. Then if it must be of cancer, galls, and asthma and kidneys and cerebral growths and what not, just the same.[37]

Leonard, while still in bed, was finalising a new arrangement for the Hogarth Press. Since the summer of 1937, they had both been wanting, more than ever, to shut it down. The death of their manager, Margaret West, in January 1937, had unsettled the running of the business, and Virginia, especially, felt it now as a burden. John Lehmann, meanwhile, had been making a success of his magazine, *New Writing*, which he had launched in 1935 with a manifesto asserting that 'though it does not intend to open its pages to writers of reactionary or fascist sentiments, it is independent of any political party'.[38] Now he needed a new publisher for it, and went back to see the Woolfs, in the summer of 1937, after a five-year silence. Leonard thought that 'the young Brainies' – Auden, Isherwood, Spender, Lehmann – might take the Press and run it as a co-operative company: a plan which would have linked Virginia Woolf in literary history more closely to those writers, and might have had interesting results.[39] But they couldn't afford the £6,000 Leonard was asking. Instead, in January 1938, it was agreed that Lehmann would buy a half share for £3,000, that Virginia would withdraw, and that he would become managing editor in partnership with Leonard. There would be an advisory board of Rosamond Lehmann, Spender, Auden, Isherwood, and Virginia (though it never actually met).[40] *New Writing* would be published by the Hogarth Press. The contract was signed in April. Leonard was brusque, John Lehmann wanted to celebrate, and Virginia wrote appeasingly, inviting him to a dinner: 'You are hereby invited to be the guest of Virginia Woolf's ghost – the Hogarth ghost.'[41] She was proud of the Press and its lasting success: 'Our earnings prodigious. Income last year about £6,000. John much impressed. Press worth £10,000 & all this sprung from that type on the drawing room table at Hogarth House 20 years ago.'[42] But she was relieved to be free of it.

Of course she was not entirely free. As before, things did not go smoothly between the two managers. The Woolfs resented Lehmann's desire to have his own way, and he resisted Leonard's reluctance to delegate his authority. There were immediate problems over the memorial volume for Julian, which Quentin was editing. Everyone involved had different ideas about what should be included, and Vanessa wanted all the tributes to be ideal. The result was something of a botched collection. *New Writing*, too, was a cause of dissent, as John would brook no editorial interference from Leonard.[43] John and Virginia also argued over *New Writing*. He wanted her to write for it; she objected to his 1938 Foreword, which specified that the contributors must be 'in sympathy with its declared character'. 'Why lay down laws about imaginative writing?' she asked fiercely, tempering this with 'Probably I'm an incorrigible outsider. I always want to write only for the Hogarth Press'.[44] He replied with understandable irritation, since the magazine was now part of the Press. 'I think it is very perverse of you to complain about being inhibited by a manifesto when that is just what I was trying to avoid.'[45] But this was part of the old argument with Julian and Stephen Spender over writing and ideology, and would return in her essay 'The Leaning Tower', written in the spring of 1940, and published, in the end, in Lehmann's *Folios of New Writing*.

The sale of her share of the Press to Lehmann confirmed the Press's close relation to the 'gang' of 1930s writers. In the summer of 1937 they had published Isherwood's *Sally Bowles*, and the summer Lehmann joined they published Isherwood's autobiography, *Lions & Shadows* and the influential Marxist novel by Isherwood's friend Edward Upward, *Journey to the Border* (praised, but not much bought).[46] So the Auden-Isherwood-Upward *coterie* was sharply perceptible to her, out of the corner of her eye. Her attitude towards them was at once interested and sceptical, and strongly affected her thinking about war, gender and writing.

She had warmed to Isherwood (and he to her) when early in 1937 they met him with Sally Chilver (Robert Graves's clever, lively niece, whom Virginia found very appealing). He was thirty-three then, and was in the middle of rehearsing *The Ascent of F6* with Auden. She sensed that he was probably 'a real novelist', and liked his bright eagerness; she always thought of him as 'a merry little bird', though 'shifty' and 'inscrutable'.[47] She was pleased when he introduced her to Auden at the big Albert Hall meeting for Spanish refugees in June 1937, and scribbled a quick sketch of the poet as 'a small rough haired terrier man: slits for eyes; a crude face; interesting, I expect, but wire haired, yellowish white.'[48] She was taking note of their work. In her notebook for 'The Leaning Tower' she would copy out some lines from *The Dog Beneath the Skin*: 'Some of you will die without ever knowing what your leaders are fighting for, or even that you are fighting at all.'[49] But reading *Letters from Iceland* in the summer of 1937, she disliked Auden's egotism – 'public scratching', she described it to Ethel, echoing her distaste for Joyce years before.[50] When *On the Frontier* was suppressed in 1938, she was impatient: 'I hope they will no longer pose as the young men to be sacrificed.'[51] In 'The Leaning Tower' she satirised these middle-class boy writers who bit the hand of the culture that fed them and could not escape their own egos. Yet their voices concerned her. When Auden and Isherwood went to America in January 1939, she took a slightly sardonic tone in a letter to Julian's Chinese friend, Sue Ling (to whom she was writing kindly and encouragingly about her possible autobiography).[52] But she did not join in the general war-cry against them as queer traitors. Clive did, and she thought it 'silly'.[53]

She and Leonard, though, had no thoughts of leaving England as war became more and more likely. They kept 'pegging round' in their 'little plot', while Hitler invaded Austria.[54] Ironically, as the general situation grew more threatening, there were some personal gains. Money was pouring in. She sent off *Three Guineas*, having received Leonard's lukewarm approval, and immediately turned to the writing of *Roger Fry*. Towards the end of the 1937 she had started to intuit 'the form of a new novel' – some kind of musical structure, perhaps, with a statement and restatement of 'the same story'?[55] Now, early in 1938, those vague intimations of a new fictional form were taking more coherent shape. She might have a title: 'Summer Night'? 'Pointzet Hall'?[56] By April 1938 she was hovering between two worlds of fact and fiction, while correcting, with her usual horror at this cold process, the proofs of *Three Guineas*. There were some times for mooching and dreaming, 'the unconscious asking for a rise'.

She went walking again through London, soon to be so terribly changed: to Bunhill Fields, to Shadwell and Whitechapel, through the City.[57]

In February 1938 there was a sudden repeat of Philip Morrell's embarrassing love-letters. He had been very ill, and Ottoline was dying; in this extremity he reminisced sentimentally over the dear dead days at Garsington and Hogarth House: 'When I look back over the past . . . I see your image, your lovely familiar image appearing again & again . . . you seem quite unchanged from the Virginia of those remote years.'[58] Virginia responded tactfully, but made a joke of his letters to Vita. Then Ottoline died. There was a dreary memorial service at St Martin's in the Fields ('Oh dear, oh dear the lack of intensity; the wailing & mumbling; the fumbling with bags; the shuffling; the vast brown mass of respectable old South Kensington ladies').[59] She had to agree to Philip's request that she write an obituary, which she greatly disliked doing. 'Lord! when I die, dont ask anyone to write a few words about me in The Times', she told John Lehmann.[60] But beside her resistance to formal obsequies, she had a sharp sense of loss – above all of a house to go to, and of an audience; 'Odd how the sense of loss takes this quite private form: someone who wont read what I write.'[61] Months later, Philip Morrell discovered a death-bed message which Ottoline had prepared two years before her death, to be sent to all her friends. Virginia received this posthumous and highly characteristic 'Farewell Message' in December 1938, which Philip had mounted in a bound cover with a 1903 photograph of Ottoline.

> I should like to write a message to those I love and who love me, to be read to them after I die. Dont mourn for me, dear friends, when you are quiet and alone remember me kindly, and when you are in lovely country . . . and when you walk the streets of London . . . remember I have watched you all and tried to understand what you are like underneath, and when possible I have tried to help you and encourage you to do your best in life. Please do not send any wreaths for my poor dead body, but gladden my soul by giving something for a night shelter or a coffee stall for the poor and destitute – those who have no shelter.[62]

Virginia made no comment on this, but told Philip she was touched. For Ka Arnold-Foster's death in May, she felt very little. She had been impatient with her for years, and admitted now that she had always felt self-conscious with her because 'she had seen me mad'.[63] Her feeling for death was all used up.

In the summer of 1938 she was absorbed in work. She began writing the biography of Roger Fry on 1 April, after three years of intermittent planning and reading. The first notes told herself to 'find out what his qualities were and proceed to illustrate them by events. To be very free with sequence of facts'.[64] But this proved illusory. Plans for an impressionistic and experimental Life quickly got buried in facts and details; her vivid personal sense of him had to be too 'minute & tied down & documented'.[65] Already in May 1938, a month after she began writing, she was describing it as a 'grind', the word she would most often use over the next two years. The making of this life had its pleasures, but it mainly became an unsatisfactory struggle to 'cut loose' from facts, to maintain a vivid portrait against the tyranny of chronology.

There is a scene in the biography where a visitor to Fry's studio in the 1890s looks at his paintings and tells him 'Do not take pains'.[66] This instruction, directed at Fry's 'laboured canvases', might also have been advice to herself over the making of this book. As with the shortest of her articles or the redrafting of any of her novels and stories, she was immensely, exhaustively conscientious. She spent days typing out long extracts from his letters, annotated with her handwritten notes.[67] (Often these rapid notes were more vivid than her final version, like her comment on his letters to Helen Anrep: 'Their state very like music; middle–aged love; ease & intensity.')[68] Her desk was awash with his books and manuscripts and letters and with her annotations and commentaries. Her notes were always in some confusion – especially as she was working at the same time on articles, stories, a new novel, and then her autobiography. 'My books are in a muddle. Yes, at this moment, there are packets of letters to V.B.1910–1916 – packets of testimonials for the Oxford Slade – endless folders, each containing different letters, Press Cuttings, & extracts from books.'[69]

Yet, for all the 'drudgery', she became deeply absorbed, as she followed Roger Fry from his authoritarian Victorian home, through the liberation of Cambridge to the discoveries of Europe, to the point where Fry's life converged with her own in 1910. Rediscovering the history of a person she had been intimate with, she became aware of many points of affinity or connection. Writing it made her 'so in love with him', she told Vanessa.[70] There is vivid, touching, personal feeling in the book, as in her account of Fry's response to his first wife's madness: 'he found . . . that the only way of facing the ruin of private happiness was to work.'[71] The force of his personality comes through strongly when she describes what it was like to be shown pictures by him, or to travel in his company to Greece. When, at the end of 1938 and into 1939, she was writing about Fry's reaction to the 'end of civilisation' in the First World War, and his determination to fight 'Accidia' (the sin of gloominess) with work and with pleasure in life, she felt very close to him. Fry's belief in the value of the unconscious for the artist and his resistance to self-analysis or self-importance ('He detested fixed attitudes; he suspected poses; he was quick to point out the fatal effect of reverence')[72] connected to the work she was sketching now on anonymity and impersonality.

But the writing of *Roger Fry* suffered, not only from the 'grind' of factuality, but from too much pressure from relations and friends. Her relations with Helen Anrep, Roger's 'widow', were especially difficult. In September 1938 she lent Helen £150 to help with her overdraft, but very much resented not being paid back.[73] This resentment was tangled up with her feeling that she was writing the book because she had to, as 'a debt to Roger'.[74] The lost £150, her dislike (and perhaps some jealousy) of Helen, and her sense of the biography as an obligation knotted together uncomfortably in her mind: 'Certainly I owed Roger £150', she wrote in the diary in January, half acknowledging this overlap of feelings.[75] The book was also a consolatory gift for Vanessa (whose 1933 portrait of Roger was to be the cover). And it was a way of making amends to Julian, some of whose rejected letter on Roger she incorporated into her text. But all these loving obligations confined her narrative. She could talk about Roger Fry being beaten by a sadistic paederastic schoolmaster with Stracheyesque freedom, but she didn't feel she could write openly about Cambridge homosexuality. So Lowes Dickinson's passion for Roger is muted, and Fry's discovery of Symonds's circle is euphemistically described. (Even so, she got into trouble with Symonds's daughter Katherine Furse for describing him as 'pornographic'.)[76] As for Roger's affair with Vanessa, all the copious and interesting notes she took on the relationship when she was reading their letters (which had told her a great deal she did not know at the time) had to be suppressed at Margery Fry's insistence. And so the Victorian censorship which had been one of her life-long subjects was re-enacted in this wartime writing, and the book was full of what 'must be left unsaid'.[77]

The frustrating challenge of the biography unlocked alternatives. She counterpointed the work with a commentary on biography's limitations and with a new novel which freed her to write suggestively and lyrically, in dramatic scenes and poetic fragments. As before, with the see-saws between *Mrs Dalloway* and *The Common Reader*, or *Orlando* and 'Phases of Fiction', or *The Years* and *Flush*, these other writings were switches of mood from the main work, but were also connected to what she was doing there. If the unconscious, so necessary in art, had to be explained and rationalised in factual biography, how might it be left to operate freely in other kinds of 'life-writing'? *Pointz Hall*, the new novel, which by the autumn of 1938 she was using as relief from the biography, had at its centre a historical pageant

" The struggle . . . to combine respect and loathing "

From *Time and Tide* June 25 1938—*General Research and Humanities
Division.* The accompanying editorial noted: "Mrs. Woolf's best-seller,
Three Guineas, descending on the peaceful fold of reviewers, has thrown
them into that dreadful kind of internal conflict that leads to nervous
breakdown. On the one hand there is Mrs. Woolf's position in literature:
not to praise her work would be a solecism no reviewer could possibly
afford to make. On the other hand there is her theme, which is not
merely disturbing to nine out of ten reviewers but revolting."

of English literature, set inside the awkward story of a contemporary family
living on the brink of war. Through this double drama, she wanted to work
her way inside the unconscious, communal pool of identity which linked the
audience and the players in this English scene. And the book on literary
history, which she now began to think about (to be called 'Anon', or 'The
Reader') was also to be about the unconscious mind of the reader, as well as
the relation between anonymity and the literary market-place. In addition
to these alternative modes of writing history, her own autobiography, which
she started to draft in 1939, could include everything that *Roger Fry* had to
leave out.

When *Three Guineas* came out in June 1938, she was quietly absorbed in
the novel, in one of her breaks from *Roger Fry.* The publication felt to her
like the end of a six-year stint of work. She felt she was now at the beginning
of something new: 'And now I can be off again, as indeed I long to be. Oh to
be private, alone, submerged.'[78] The reactions to *Three Guineas* made her
think again about what she had meant by it, and about her relation to her
country. 'Of course I'm "patriotic" ', she wrote to Ethel, in response to her
reading of *Three Guineas.*[79] Being patriotic meant feeling English as well as
being an 'outsider'. And what it meant to be English was more than ever in
her mind in the coming months. She was reminded of the beauty of Britain

710

on a journey in June to Northumberland and Skye; the landscape of Hadrian's Wall seemed to her now 'the loveliest in the world', like being in Shakespeare's England.[80] She didn't have that romantic feeling about Rodmell, but village life was, from now on, very much in her eye and her imagination. Its irritations – church bells, Rodmell Labour Party meetings, village hostilities – vied with her enduring passion for her local landscape. And, as always, but now even more acutely, these mixed feelings about being an Englishwoman in an English village co-existed with a critique of living in a xenophobic and parochial old country. All this was going into the new novel.

But her 'little sensation' (the phrase was Roger's, taken from Cézanne, and she often used it while she was writing the biography)[81] was – in the summer of 1938 – up against the force of uncontrollable events. She wanted to get on faster than she could with *Roger Fry*; Leonard said it didn't matter, but time was pressing: 'I'm 56,' she thought urgently in August.[82] And the times, as well as time, were working against her 'petite sensation'. As the Munich Crisis built up in September, she asked herself what the coming war would mean for *her*.

> What would war mean? Darkness, strain: I suppose conceivably death. And all the horror of friends: & Quentin . . . All that lies over the water in the brain of that ridiculous little man. Why ridiculous? Because none of it fits. Encloses no reality . . .[83]

Everyone was waiting; everyone was asking, 'Any news?' That sense of incongruity, helplessness, and threat, filled their lives through August and September. All through the Crisis, she 'blessed' Roger 'for giving me himself to think of – what a help he remains – in this welter of unreality.'[84] The violent gap between world events and private preoccupations filled her diary and letters, as it was filling her new novel. Work seemed to be the one true reality. But at the same time she wrote minutely and dramatically about the Crisis in her diary and her letters to Vanessa (who was, in escapist mode, at La Bergère in Cassis for the autumn). She observed and reported in detail on the national mood, the sights of London, the sense of horrified waiting, the war preparations. Vanessa's family, at Cassis, awaited her letters like news bulletins. 'Life here is most peaceful', Quentin wrote, 'the news in the English papers seems more and more remote, and the family is called into Nessa's room to hear your letters rather as though we were living at Grignan about 1670 – so live up to your reputation and write us some more.'[85]

On Tuesday, 27 September, when all were waiting to hear whether Chamberlain's meeting with Hitler would avert war, Virginia went to the

London Library and sat in the basement reading *The Times'* reports of 1910 on the Post-Impressionist Exhibition. The old man sweeping the library floor said they were all being told to try on their gas masks. Then she walked from the library to the National Gallery to see if she could see Cézanne through Roger Fry's eyes. As she walked along Pall Mall a loudspeaker gave out the announcement about gas masks.[86] London was getting ready for war. But by Friday of that week, Chamberlain was announcing 'peace in our time'. 'I'm doing Roger & PIP [Post-Impressionism]', she ended her notes on these events in her diary, '& must break off this historical note to go back to that.'[87] What the point was of 'going back' to her own work would be much on her mind in the months to come.

A few days before the Crisis, Maynard Keynes had read a paper to the Memoir Club in Sussex on 'Cambridge youth; their philosophy; its consequences; Moore; what it lacked; what it gave.'[88] Virginia was impressed with Keynes's nostalgic and disillusioned account of the pure sweet air of G.E. Moore, that belief in undisturbed individualism, that Utopianism based on a belief in human reasonableness and decency, that refusal to accept the idea of civilisation as 'a thin and precarious crust'. (The younger listeners, like Quentin, were less pleased with Keynes's attack on the current religion of 'Freud cum Marx'). Keynes's fond, elegiac repudiation of his 'early beliefs', in the light of current affairs ('We completely misunderstood human nature, including our own') was, for her, a striking counterpoint to Roger Fry's ideals about 'civilisation'. Were those ideals altogether 'done for' after the First World War – as the Omega workshop and all it represented in new British art and design was 'done for' after 1914? She wasn't sure.

But in these months before the real war, some naïve Utopianism lingered on still. 'Peace for our life time: why not try to believe it?'[89] Perhaps, after all, she was going to be able to get on with her work. Perhaps there might still be what she always called 'the materials for happiness'.[90] She finished the first draft of *Roger Fry* in March 1939, and revised it through the summer and autumn, alternating it with stories and articles, the novel and the autobiography. Even while she was revising, new letters kept turning up: 'Its like making a dress thats always having a new arm or leg let in in the skirt', she wrote eloquently but vaguely to Ethel.[91]

Concentration was fragile. Death seemed extremely close, just at the side of or under the surface of everything, at this time between the acts of the false and true beginnings of the Second World War. In August 1938 a well-known figure around Rodmell, an old woman who lived near Mount Misery, who used to 'moon over the downs with a dog', drowned herself:

the body was found on 'my usual walk'.[92] In September she dreamt of her loved dead: of imploring Julian not to go to Spain, and seeing his wounds; of talking to Roger about Cézanne, as if 'he had not died'. It was as if she 'dreamt away the fact' of their deaths.[93] She and Leonard talked more than usually about mortality. Once, at the end of the year, walking through Russell Square, Leonard told her he had 'taught himself not to think about' death; she told him she 'should not wish to live if he died'.[94] Again, a few months later, in April 1939, they discussed which of them would mind the other's death the more. Leonard thought he would, since 'I lived more in a world of my own'. He hoped he would predecease her.[95]

These thoughts of death were partly aroused by the imminence of war, partly by the sad and complaining terminal old age of Mrs Woolf, who had her eighty-ninth birthday in October 1938. Yeats's death in January, and Auden's elegy for him, made her think of her own: 'I wish someone would write me a poem.'[96] The demise of the marmoset, on the other hand, though sad for Leonard, was turned into a rich comedy for Charleston's benefit: 'V. gave us a magnificent description of the deathbed of Mitz and how she found the corpse on the dining room table and they buried it on one side of the garden wall while church bells and a real funeral were going on on the other.'[97]

But how was she to deal with the onset of her own old age? How hopeful could she be? Could the advent of death be transformed, made interesting? 'Why not change the idea of death into an exciting experience? – as one did marriage in youth?' 'I'm on the qui vive to describe age: to note it.'[98] The desire to write on death and age were involved with the desire to write about her past. Everything pointed her towards this attempt. Jack Hills's death at the end of 1938, unlocking childhood memory again; writing her censored life of Roger; thinking about history and biography; hearing Maynard's memoir and wishing to emulate it; trying to find new ways in the novel of writing about memory, desire, and personality; and feeling that time was short. In January of 1939 she met Freud in Hampstead. He was old and ill, and had been got out of Vienna just in time. They talked about Hitler, and he gave her a narcissus. A few months later she began to read him at last.

Now was the time, if ever, to write her 'Sketch of the Past': if she didn't do it now, as Nessa said, she would soon be too old.[99] At the same time she began to devise a story called 'The Searchlight', which went through a great number of drafts over the next two years, and which would eventually set the searchlight of memory – taking the woman narrator back into a Victorian past – against the searchlights of wartime London.[100] Like Mrs Ivimey in that story, in her 'Sketch of the Past' she switched away from the surrounding darkness and focused on her childhood, re-entering it through intensely visualised scenes. As she returned again in the spring and summer of 1939 to her parents, to St Ives, to Hyde Park Gate, she kept thinking about the need for solitude and for 'private separation'.[101] This violent internal zigzag between living in memories and living in the fractured present ('how one rockets between private & public')[102] brought on some intense moments of depression. She used what she called 'identity' to surmount them: her sense of her own capacities, her will to work, her analysis of her own violent swings of mood: 'Happily I'm interested in depression'.[103]

She veered wildly, at this time of revising her biography and starting her autobiography, between her social and her solitary self. While she was most deeply and privately absorbed in her past, she could seem to the family at her most garrulous, wild and flamboyant. Angelica, who at twenty-one was involved in a love affair with David Garnett which had been greatly distressing Duncan and Vanessa since the spring of 1938, but which Virginia did not yet know about, reported affectionately in her letters to Bunny on Virginia's social behaviour.

[Shopping with Vanessa in Lewes] I heard sharp yelps coming from somewhere behind me. Thinking it might be some dog run over I looked round but saw nothing . . . then louder and more prolonged yelps . . . lo and behold of course it was Virginia, looking more utterly wild & angular & strange than ever.[104]

Tea with the Woolves. Virginia was in a mood where she rambles on and on talking nonsense and making me laugh; then she suddenly asks a question, such as, 'Do you consider your life has been a happy one,' or 'Which of our marriages has been most successful', and very interested when Mummy said that Adrian's had not been. Oh! Why? and what do you think has been the cause of it, and how did you know Nessa dearest *do* tell me, when she really knew perfectly well herself. We played bowls after tea, in which Virginia and Quentin beat Leonard and I by 3. Virginia is extremely good at it. We went indoors and sat by the fire, V. getting out her book-binding and stitching away at the Memoirs of Saint-Simon and carrying on a very one-sided conversation about how good it would be to move house and start a new life in new surroundings . . . She insisted that it was a renovation of one's life to change one's surroundings, and that one ought to have houses all about the country, and directly one has become imbued with the atmosphere of one's house, and indifferent to it, one ought to move to another. That's one of the things that is so nice about Virginia – she is always ready for new feelings and experiences, and she keeps fresh that way, if you see what I mean.[105]

714

On one evening she went to dinner at Charleston and got 'absolutely drunk in about 5 minutes, and shreiked [*sic*] and waved her arms.'[106] On another night she went masked as Cleopatra to a party given by Adrian. (This was when Eliot, whose *Family Reunion*, just out, she very much disliked, went as Crippen.) The 'tipsiness & abandonment' of the party, the liberation of 'not being one's usual self', pleased her very much.[107] Yet, a few days later, walking alone in the City, she climbed down a flight of steps to the muddy banks of the Thames under Southwark Bridge, and saw people staring down at her from the bridge while she made her way in a bitter cold wind (thinking as she walked of the refugees from Barcelona, which had just fallen) along this 'rat haunted, riverine place, great chains, wooden pillars, green slime, bricks corroded'. She called this 'a very sensible day'. But if you had been looking down from the bridge, and had seen this woman walking alone among the debris of London's low tide, perhaps talking to herself, you might have thought her a shabby-genteel vagrant, or a mad person.[108]

The personal disturbances of 1939 pressed in on, but did not hold up, her huge bursts of writing and reading (Dickens, Walpole, de Sévigné, Proust, Freud). The worst local distraction was the threat of a move. Demolitions were going on next to Tavistock Square; a big hotel was being built and the noise was becoming impossible. After fifteen years at No.52, they began to negotiate for a lease on a large house at 37 Mecklenburgh Square, with big rooms and a much quieter and lighter aspect. Leonard wanted to surrender the lease on Tavistock, which was due to run until 1941. But, though he succeeded in getting a nine-and-a-half year lease on Mecklenburgh Square, and Dolman and Pritchard agreed to move with them, so that they could have the same arrangement as before, with the Press in the basement and their own flat at the top of the house, he could not get rid of the existing lease. For all her brave words about giving up old houses, it was all upsetting and distracting: 'House moving causes me extreme distress', she wrote in her autobiography (taken up just then with the memories of two lost houses). 'Shall we ever live a real life again?' she asked Leonard. He replied, 'At Monk's House'.[109]

In the middle of these negotiations, in May and June, they went on holiday to northern France. Her memoir and her biography were both on her mind. As they crossed the Channel and drove around Normandy and Brittany in fine hot weather, thoughts of those English lives were intercut with thoughts about the quality of French life – Catholicism, food, sensuality, drink, places, colours, houses – and what made up a civilisation. But she seems not to have asked herself whether this might be her last journey to Europe. Like her reaction to the Munich Crisis, this trip to France had something ostrich-like about it.

Yet at the same time they saw exactly what was coming. In January Barcelona had fallen; in February Franco triumphed, in March Madrid surrendered: 'And Julian killed for this.'[110] Hitler entered Prague on 15 March. ' "This," says the PM. "is not in the spirit of the Munich meeting." My comment anyhow is superfluous.'[111] On 29 April, sitting on the top of a bus in Cannon Street, she read Hitler's speech demanding Danzig's return to the Reich, and noticed that everyone else was reading it too. Like everyone else, she listened to the news about Poland. 'Private separation', in these circumstances, began no longer to be possible. 'All England thinking the same thing,' she thought, 'this horror of war – at the same moment.'[112]

They came back from France to a summer of personal as well as public stress. They still couldn't shed the lease of Tavistock Square, and the move was upon them. Mark Gertler, Carrington's old lover, whom Virginia had recently consulted about Roger Fry, gassed himself in his studio, at the age of forty-seven; no-one seemed to know why. Victoria OCampo returned with an unwelcome visitor, the photographer Gisèle Freund: the photographs that resulted from this intrusion eloquently show up the subject's resistance and dismay. Freund thought Virginia 'a very reserved woman' who generated 'a captivating atmosphere'. Looking back, she described her as 'shattered' by the prospect of war.[113]

On 28 June 1939, old Mrs Woolf fell and broke two ribs, and was taken to the London Clinic. They watched her dying for four days. 'It was like watching an animal die, L said.'[114] Still, at nearly ninety, the powerful will to live was there. Her daughter-in-law wrote a private tribute to her in her diary, and felt 'regret for that spirited old lady, whom it was such a bore to visit'. For her own family, however, she made a good joke of the gathering of Woolf mourners, nearly 'driving her out of her wits with their entirely inhuman abstracted outlook on life, never for an instant showing a glimmer of real feeling, and thinking it necessary to talk about the new telephone exchange in the Euston Road'.[115] Leonard's own mourning took the outward form of deep gloom over side-issues – a difficulty with Gollancz at the Left Book Club about his new book, *Barbarians at the Gate* (because it was too critical of the Soviet Union for Gollancz's liking); an argument with Virginia, which greatly upset her, about whether or not to build a greenhouse at Monk's House; the practical problems of the move from Tavistock Square.[116] As they looked at their belongings, all packed up in July, and went through the new house planning where things should go, 'a grim thought struck me: wh. of these rooms shall I die in?'[117]

By the middle of August 1939, she was revising the last chapter of *Roger*

Fry. They were moving the Press and their own possessions, between 17 and 24 August, from Tavistock Square to Mecklenburgh Square. On 23 August the German Soviet Non-Aggression Pact was signed, and on the 24th, Parliament was recalled. The mood, she thought, was different from the previous September: less dramatic, more fatalistic: 'patient bewilderment', 'whiffs of despair'.[118] They listened to the news, waited, and attended. Her diary notes, more than ever like the style of her new novel, fragmented into dislocated, jagged headlines, like telegrams from a disaster zone. At Rodmell, writing in her hut at the bottom of the garden on the evening of 28 August, she noted in intense shorthand her own mood, her sense of being part of the world, and her difficulty in writing:

> Will the 9 o'clock bulletin end it all? – our lives, oh yes, & everything for the next 50 years? Everyone's writing I suppose about this last day. I walked on the downs; lay under a cornstack & looked at the empty land & the pinkish clouds in a perfect blue summer afternoon sky. Not a sound. Workmen discussing war on the road – one for it, one against. So to bowls. I bowling am happy: I outside the garden what? Numb I think. Vita says she feels terror & horror early – revives then sinks. For us its like being on a small island. Neither of us has any physical fear. Why should we? But theres a vast calm cold gloom. And the strain. Like waiting a doctors verdict. And the young – young men smashed up. But the point is one is too numbed to think . . . We privately are so content. Bliss day after day. So happy cooking dinner, reading, playing bowls. No feeling of patriotism. How to go on, through war? – thats the question. Of course I have my old spurs & my old flanks. No I cant get at it – so whats the use of staying out? One wanders in; dines; then listens. Sense tells me there'll be no news till tomorrow. Yes, its a lovely still summer evening; not a sound . . . How difficult, unexpectedly to write.[119]

It was necessary, essential, to write; thinking was her fighting. But everything seemed impossible. There was no continuity, instead a 'kind of block & suspension'. The 'killing machine' was about to be set in motion. On 2 September, still in Sussex, she sewed black-out curtains, and argued with Leonard about the consequences of war. On the morning of the 3rd, with the apples shining in the light of a fine late-summer morning, she tried but failed to read a book, and wrote some notes in her diary describing the last two days. At 11.15 a.m. she went in to listen to the news; the Prime Minister announced that Britain was at war with Germany. Three days later, Virginia Woolf wrote in her diary: 'This is the worst of all my life's experiences.'[120]

THIRTY-NINE

War

For the first six weeks of the war, Virginia and Leonard spent most of their time at Monk's House. But in mid-October they went to Mecklenburgh Square for a week – 'an odd morbid week of many disagreeable sensations'.[1] It rained. The house was in cold chaos, books and pictures all over the floor, the 'phone and the oven and the lavatory not working, no carpets, chamber pots in all the wrong places. The kitchen felt too small and the other rooms too large. The disruption of the move seemed unending. They saw a great many people (including the ancient Beatrice Webb, her brain still humming) and talked for 'about 6 hours daily'. London was already utterly changed. Overnight, from being the place that was at the heart of her life, it had become alien and unendurable. So shocked and struck was she by the atmosphere of the city that she described it five times, in letters, in the diary, and on a page of her current 'Pointz Hall' notebook, a page she called 'London in War':

> The sensation of fear very soon evaporates. Everybody is feeling the same thing: therefore no one is feeling anything in particular. The individual is merged in the mob. That is why after the first three nights one's ears become stopped. They were acute the first night. Everyone is on business. Their minds are made up. It is extremely sober. The streets are [un?]lit. They have gone back to the 18th century. Nature prevails. I suppose badgers & foxes wd. come back if this went on, & owls & nightingales. This is the prelude to barbarism. The City has become merely a congerie of houses lived in by people who work. There is no society, no luxury no splendour no gadding & flitting. All is serious & concentrated. It is as if the song had stopped – the melody, the unnecessary the voluntary. Odd if this should be the end of town life.[2]

In these notes, she begins to play the tunes that would repeat in her thoughts all through the next eighteen months (like the insistent repeated tunes in *Between the Acts*): the loss of individuality in the communal life; the regression to barbarism; and the feeling (as in the last war) of blackness and strain, of waiting in the dark. She kept using the word 'distracted' to describe herself in these first weeks of the war: 'rattled & distracted', 'harassed & distracted', 'in fretful useless distraction'.[3] She couldn't settle; she was afraid; nothing felt right; and at the same time nothing was happening. And nothing did happen, for ages. Yet everything felt different. Her experience of 'the phoney war' between September 1939 and March 1940 was, characteristically, both intensely personal and accurately observant. What immediately affected her was the same as for many others, but she made her own version of it.

Blackness was the first impact. The black-out rule began on 1 September, and it wasn't until the end of the month (after many accidents) that dimmed car headlights were allowed. And she noted air-raid warnings, gas masks, and the 'light spotted veil' of barrage balloons over London.[4] The immediate effects of the war on the Woolfs were shortages of sugar, matches and paper, the temporary presence in Rodmell of evacuee children from Bermondsey (Leonard helped them to settle in), and petrol rationing. From now until the end of the war Leonard made a note in his diary of his car mileage, alongside brief entries on the main facts of the war ('Hitler invades Holland and Belgium') and on their day's activities ('Work Garden Drove Lewes Bowls').

But the most serious effects, at first, were limited to minor discomforts, suspense and anxiety. Their petrol limits were quickly augmented by a friend of Clive's, an American art-student, Janice Loeb, who housed her car in the Monk's House garage when she left for the States, and so enabled Leonard to claim a double ration.[5] Food shortages were not grave.[6] And, though Virginia was depressed by the arrival of two of the Hogarth Press clerks (invited by Leonard for a break from London) in the first weekend of the war, and said that the house felt like 'a refugee haunt', they avoided having any 'East End children' billeted on them.[7] (The evacuees soon left again – 'for the country is far worse than a raid', Virginia noted in a letter to her niece Judith Stephen.)[8] The most pressing worry was over money. The rent on Mecklenburgh Square was £250 a year. Tavistock Square was obviously now unsellable. Very likely their books would not do so well now; paper would become increasingly expensive. They sat down to calculate their income. She would have to start writing reviews again, just at the time when she was feeling most alienated from the world of literary journalism. She told Angelica she might have to cut her allowance. Income tax went up to 7s.6d. in the pound. Virginia was acutely conscious of the effect this would have on her income, and, potentially, on the social structure of the country as a whole.

If worrying about money – which she had not had to do for some years – kept her awake at night, personal feeling, as she observed, merged into the general feeling. Like other people, she waited out 'the non-war' in boredom and apprehension, as in a siege. England expected to be next on Hitler's list. 'No raids yet', she wrote on 11 September, 'Poland being conquered, & then – we shall be attended to.' She noted the rejection of Hitler's 'peace plan' in October, and listened to Ribbentrop 'howling' his threats against Britain. In December, she reacted strongly, as everyone did, to Russia's attack on Finland, and was appalled by the excitement over the forced blowing-up of the German battleship, the *Graf Spee*, in Montevideo harbour: 'And journalists & rich people are hiring aeroplanes from which to see the sight . . . the eyes of the whole world (BBC) are on the game; & several people will lie dead tonight, or in agony. And we shall have it served up for us as we sit over our logs this bitter winter night.'[9]

Through that bitter winter she imagined for herself the most dramatic events in this phase of the war, the German U-boat sinking of ships: 'a ship sunk – no survivors – a raft capsized – men rowing for 10 or 12 or 30 hours.' She felt the sense of the 'screw tightening'; it was as though they were sacrificial animals, being helplessly 'led up to the spring of 1940'. Sitting reading and writing in Sussex, she knew she was protected, privileged: 'Now the wind rises; something rattles, & thank God I'm not on the North Sea, nor taking off to raid Heligoland.'[10] But she knew too that there was no chance any more for her, or for anyone, to be immune.

After the first few days of feeling as if she had been hit on the head – days of 'complete nullity' – ideas began to flood back in. The thought of *having* to review made her begin to invent all kinds of articles, and the very end of *Roger Fry* was in sight. She was 'on the buzz' again.[11] Two trains of thought roused her up. One was her reading of Freud. The other was the publication in November of her Hogarth Press Sixpenny Pamphlet, 'Reviewing', which caused a small *furore*.

'Reviewing' contained no new argument, but her obsessions had hardened up in the context of the outsiderism of *Three Guineas*. The link between the compromises of literary journalism and the economic and political injustices of her culture was one of the strong themes of that essay. In a long, furious footnote, she had called reviewing (and academic lecturing, and literary prizes) a form of 'intellectual harlotry'. In the present state of society, however, they were endemic evils:

> Vanity and the desire for 'recognition' are still so strong among artists that to starve them of advertisement and to deny them frequent if contrasted shocks of praise and blame would be as rash as the introduction of rabbits into Australia; the balance of nature would be upset and the consequences might well be disastrous.[12]

The solution was to supplement public criticism by 'a new service based on the example of the medical profession': a panel of critics would practise like doctors and in strictest privacy.

'Reviewing' pursued this theme, but with so much intolerance and bravado that Leonard thought it necessary to print a note at the end, moderating and 'modifying the conclusions' of Virginia's essay. Even so, she had already 'modified' it from its original version, a savage 27-page manuscript containing a caricature of a Hitlerian literary editor with a beard, demanding his article from the servile reviewer, who is like an animal in a cage, dogged by the fear of poverty: 'But then unpaid the bill; unpaid the bill; It is the bill – the bill –.' This is all cut out in favour of a cooler discussion on the uselessness and lack of authority in contemporary criticism. Better for it to be replaced by a 'Gutter' (to précis the work) and a 'Stamp' (to award an asterisk or a cross). So the 'poisoned fang' of the 'louse' reviewer (like her disgusting journalistic 'bug') might disappear in favour of the thoughtful essayist, and the writer could pay – three guineas, of course – for a private 'reader-service', and sink back from fame and ignominy into the 'obscurity' of the workshop. Thus 'his self-consciousness would diminish'.[13]

She was taken aback (even if Leonard was not) by the outraged scorn which greeted this satire. A number of 'tart & peevish' male reviewers leapt in to say how essential reviewing was for the health of the culture. She felt 'rasped & injured', and had to keep telling herself this was what she wanted: it was part of her 'Outsiders' campaign.[14]

The half-desire for obscurity and anonymity, which was at the bottom of 'Reviewing', got into all the pieces she was having to write now. A story about a dog, 'Gipsy the Mongrel', written for American money, harked back to Flush in its preference for the 'vagabond', runaway Gipsy, as opposed to the prim and proper law-abiding pedigree dog. The theme was echoed in one of the tunes in Between the Acts: 'I'm off with the raggle-taggle gipsies, oh!' In an essay on Lewis Carroll, she described him, as an adult, 'passing through the world so lightly that he left no print'. He disappeared inside conventions, and only came into focus when he returned to childhood. An affectionate sketch of Gilbert White emphasised his 'utter lack of self-consciousness': he had no face, no portrait, and his only interest was in the vegetable and animal story of Selborne: 'The gossip is about the habits of vipers and the love interest is supplied chiefly by frogs.' And Walter Scott (in 'Gas at Abbotsford') was 'the greatest of all the ventriloquist' writers, more a playwright than a novelist.[15] That idea of the faceless, hidden writer would culminate in the figure of Miss La Trobe in

Between the Acts, the bossy and demanding author-playwright who is in the end invisible and self-effacing.

She had always liked the idea of being hidden, of escaping self-consciousness through impersonality. But this had always clashed with her desire for recognition and her fascination with her self – or selves. Now, her outsider's campaign for anonymity and obscurity was thrown into violent confusion by reading Freud. While as a writer she increasingly wanted to retreat into the 'darkness of the workshop', and while as an English citizen in war-time she was intensely aware of the dissolving of her private feelings into those of the community, as a new reader of Freud she was thrust dramatically towards the kind of auto-analysis she had always feared and resisted.

She began reading Freud after the outbreak of war (*Moses and Monotheism, Civilisation and its Discontents, Group Psychology & the Analysis of the Ego*, 'Thoughts for the Time on War & Death', *Why War?*)[16] in a deliberate attempt to find something else to think about, to 'enlarge the circumference of her mind', and to make it, in keeping with her current preoccupations, 'more objective'. But that was not the effect. She found Freud immediately 'upsetting'. He seemed to reduce her individual freedom: 'If we're all instinct, the unconscious, whats all this about civilisation, the whole man, freedom &?'[17] But she enjoyed his 'savagery against God', and was at once extremely interested in his idea of the conscience as censor.

She read him through the winter (with Darwin and Gide's journals) while she was working on 'The Leaning Tower', her essay on the 'auto-analytical' young writers who were throwing off the 'suppressions' of the nineteenth century. She was still reading him in June (alongside Coleridge and Wordsworth), by which time she had returned to her autobiography and was writing about her father.

What she read of Freud in this first part of the war affected her profoundly. In his writings on war and civilisation, Freud insisted on the persistence of 'primal' or 'primitive' mental instincts. Aggression, hate and the will to destroy (which is also the desire for self-destruction) are ineradicable instincts of the primitive mind, in the individual as in the society. 'The man of prehistoric times survives unchanged in our unconscious.' 'We ourselves are, like primeval man, a gang of murderers.'[18] Man is naturally cruel and aggressive, a 'savage beast'. Civilisation has to struggle to repress or sublimate these instincts, and the question for the survival of the group, as for the individual, is whether these restraints and repressions can master the instincts of aggression and self-destruction. But, though they may be obliterated, they cannot be eliminated.

We see this in the behaviour of groups, especially in wartime, behaviour which corresponds to 'a state of regression to a primitive mental activity'. (Though Freud acknowledges the possibility of diverting these aggressive instincts into feelings of communality and identity, and though he sees that the group can produce 'high achievements' – for instance the 'creative genius' of 'folksong, folklore and the like' – he dwells much more on the group as 'herd', on its wish to be governed by unrestricted force and its 'passion for authority'.) We see it in the persistence of 'ambivalence', of closely allied love-hate feelings (in individuals as in groups), the desire to merge or unify existing in close alliance with the desire to destroy.[19] Eros (Freud's Platonic term for love in its widest sense), and Thanatos (the death instinct, the desire to destroy) are always joined. Religion, according to Freud, offers only weak and false consolation for this inevitable battle:

> The evolution of civilisation . . . must present the struggle between Eros and Death, between the instinct of life and the instinct of destruction, as it works itself out in the human species. This struggle is what all life essentially consists of, and the evolution of civilisation may therefore be simply described as the struggle for life of the human species. And it is this battle of the giants that our nurse-maids try to appease with their lullaby about Heaven.[20]

At every point, Freud relates these social findings to the mental life of the individual. So, in *Moses and Monotheism*, he argues that the 'forgotten traumata' of mankind's pre-history relate 'to life in the human family'. And pre-history persists in the individual as in the civilisation: 'There probably exists in the mental life of the individual not only what he has experienced himself, but also what he brought with him at birth . . . an archaic heritage.'[21] There is no escape from these primal characteristics, this liability to regress, in the individual as in the group. Mental illness demonstrates this inevitable potential for regression into the primitive:

> In the development of the mind . . . every earlier stage of development persists alongside the later stage which has arisen from it; here succession also involves co-existence . . . The earlier mental state may not have manifested itself for years, but none the less it is so far present that it may at any time again become the mode of expression of the forces in the mind, and indeed the only one, as though all later developments had been annulled or undone . . . the primitive stages can always be re-established; the primitive mind is . . . imperishable. What are called mental diseases inevitably produce an impression in the layman that intellectual and mental life have been destroyed. In reality, the destruction only applies to

later acquisitions and developments. The essence of mental disease lies in a return to earlier states of affective life and of functioning.[22]

This gave flesh to what she had been hearing about, all around her and for many years, of Freudianism and of Freudian analysis.[23] Her argument in *Three Guineas* of the latent Hitlerism in her own society had anticipated some of Freud's arguments. And what she had been writing about her parents, in fiction and in private writings, had taken some of its images from the Freudian theories she had heard generally disseminated in her circle. But now she was presented more directly with a relentlessly determinist diagnosis of civilisation and the individual.

She dealt with this in part by rewriting it, by taking from Freud what fitted her own perceptions and desires. Her novel filled up with ideas about group behaviour, about the indivisible forces of 'Love and Hate', and about an imminent regression to primitive pre-history. But she made a joke of Freud too, turning his solemn insistence on the survival of the primal into Mrs Swithin's whimsical fantasies of dinosaurs on the lawn, and his grim analysis of group psychology into the punning, comical, light communal voices of the audience at Pointz Hall's historical pageant. In her autobiography, she began to uncover the childhood experiences and memories which had formed her, and she applied, with excited recognition, his theory of ambivalence to her feelings about her father. She accepted, too, his belief in the survival of ancestral characteristics, but pointedly changed Freud's 'ancestors' into 'ancestresses'.

In her war-writing, she adopted Freud's belief in the essential aggression and destructive impulses of the human species (a theory which Leonard had been maintaining all his life) but insisted, as she had in *Three Guineas*, on these instincts as *male*. In her notes for 'Thoughts on Peace in an Air Raid' (1940), which she called 'Notes Under Fire', she asked herself 'Hitler. What Hitler means.' and answers 'Aggression. The subconscious desire to impose our will.' Concurrently, in her reading notes on Freud's *Group Psychology and the Analysis of the Ego*, she observed that the fight for liberty in the present war could only be won if 'we destroy the male attributes. Thus the woman's part is to achieve the emancipation of man. In that lies the only hope of permanent peace. Said to be a capitalist war. Capitalism only the result of certain human desires. She has had to suppress them.' That was, in shorthand, the argument of *Three Guineas*, the basis of the analogy between 'the tyranny of the patriarchal state and the tyranny of the Fascist state'.[24]

She had already been appropriating Freud in other ways in *Three Guineas*, where, for instance, she applies the term 'infantile fixation' (by which Freud denotes the son's relation to his mother) to the Victorian father's attitude to his daughter. Her reading of patriarchal power, too, was quite the opposite of Freud's: where, in *Moses and Monotheism*, he laments its decline, in *Three Guineas* she deplores its persistence and its triumph in the form of Fascism.[25] In 'The Leaning Tower', which she began writing in February 1940, she praised Freud for releasing contemporary writers from the 'suppressions of the nineteenth century', thereby completely altering his theory of the *co-existence* of repression and instinct within the unconscious.[26] And her old uneasiness at the idea of analysis is shown in the longing for a cultural era that will go beyond the 'egotism' and 'self-consciousness' of the Leaning Tower poets, when writers will have 'a whole state of mind', 'an unconsciousness which . . . is necessary if writers are to get beneath the surface'.[27]

Reading Freud shocked and disturbed, as well as inspired her. She feared being 'reduced to a whirlpool', losing her power as an individual with choices to make. In the 'Sketch of the Past', she applied Freud's account of ambivalence to her relationship with her father. But in *Between the Acts*, the central experience of ambivalence is between the husband and wife. It may be that reading Freud caused to her think again about the areas of conflict within her marriage, perhaps to imagine the mixture of love and hate that might be felt not only *by* her, but *towards* her.

It was nothing new for her to write about repression and inhibition, but one of Freud's effects was to make her think more dramatically about the close relation of shame and servility to despotism. Here, she couldn't avoid a disturbing comparison between how she had responded to her father and the psychological effects of Nazism. 'Hitlers are bred by slaves', she wrote in 'Thoughts on Peace in an Air Raid'. Her reaction to Hitler – shame, fear, helplessness, rage, a horror of 'passive acquiescence' – was made up of the same emotions she used to have for Leslie. Freud confirmed the relationship she already felt between the daughter's emotion and the political emotion.

Her sense of shame was also historical. It was generally felt by her circle (by Maynard and by Leonard, for example) that Britain was in part responsible, because of the ugly deal made at Versailles after the First World War, for Hitler's rise to power; and it was also felt, then and later, that the Munich agreement's sacrifice of Czechoslovakia was 'peace with dishonour'. During the Munich Crisis she said that she felt 'anger and shame'.[28] This sense of shame was the subject of Virginia Woolf's only conversation with the dying Freud in January 1939. They talked about Hitler. Virginia said that 'we often felt guilty – if we had failed, perhaps Hitler would have not been. No, he said, with great emphasis; he would have been infinitely worse.'[29] So Freud, in this mini-analysis, absolved

Virginia Woolf of guilt. But in his writing he confirmed her judgement that the shaming and shameful voices of Fascism were also primitive 'ancestral voices' prophesying war. That was what she wrote in *Three Guineas*, and her reading of Freud bore it out:

> As we listen to the voices we seem to hear an infant crying in the night, the black night that now covers Europe, and with no language but a cry, Ay,ay,ay,ay . . . But it is not a new cry, it is a very old cry. Let us shut off the wireless and listen to the past.[30]

Borrowing from Tennyson's *In Memoriam*, she turned the voices on her radio into the voices of ancestral urges for domination and suppression, and transcribed them as a world lament which also sounds like the repetition of the male, egotistical, tyrannical 'I'.

The sense of apprehension which filled her writings from 1939 onwards, applied to Europe, but also to herself. Just as civilisation (Freud told her) could not get rid of its aggression, so the individual may not be able to avoid regression into mental illness or self-destruction. It may have been this fear which made her stop writing her autobiography shortly before her suicide.[31]

Freud was one of many insistent voices which troubled and challenged her now. In her mind, as she wrote her autobiography, she heard the inner voices of her past and latent selves, voices she had described in *The Waves* as 'those old half-articulate ghosts who keep up their hauntings by day and night; who turn over in their sleep, who utter their confused cries, who put out their phantom fingers and clutch at me as I try to escape – shadows of people one might have been; unborn selves.' There was the voice, too, as Bernard goes on to say in the novel, of 'the old brute, the savage', visceral, greedy, ape-like, who 'squats in me'.[32] These besieging voices were not just a metaphor but a reality, dominating her life and the lives of everyone else in Europe. As for millions of other people in Britain, the radio, with the voices of Hitler and Mussolini (and, from May 1940, of Churchill) was the most dramatic medium of information.[33] It prevented, as she observed in 'The Leaning Tower', any possibility of 'immunity': 'Jane Austen never heard the cannon roar at Waterloo [or] heard Napoleon's voice as we hear Hitler's voice as we sit at home of an evening.' Virginia Woolf's relationship with Hitler was through his voice. 'Our Master's Voice',[34] she called it, making an angry joke. This was her description of his speech at the Nuremberg Rally on 12 September 1938, when Hitler was threatening Czechoslovakia:

> Hitler boasted & boomed but shot no solid bolt. Mere violent rant, & then broke off. We listened in to the end. A savage howl like a person

excruciated; then howls from the audience; then a more spaced & measured sentence. Then another bark. Cheering ruled by a stick. Frightening to think of the faces. & the voice was frightening.[35]

The voice aroused a violent mixture of feelings. Like Eleanor in *The Years*, shooting out the words 'Damned – bully!' at the tyrant's photograph in the newspaper, it made her feel angry as well as afraid: 'The usual Damn Hitler prayer.' It made her feel scornful, even snobbishly disgusted (a very common reaction to Hitler among the English upper middle classes): 'All that lies over the water in the brain of that ridiculous little man . . . merely a housemaid's dream. And we woke from that dream & have the Cenotaph to remind us of the fruits.' It made her feel helpless: 'All Europe in Hitler's keeping. What'll he gobble next?' 'Whats Hitler got up his sleeve next? – we ask.'[36]

What form could internal resistance take to this fear, shame, anger and helplessness? One could refuse to listen. Leonard Woolf remembered in 1967 listening to 'those ranting, raving speeches.'

> One afternon [in 1939] I was planting in the orchard under an apple tree iris reticulata . . . Suddenly I heard Virginia's voice calling to me from the sitting-room window: 'Hitler is making a speech.' I shouted back: 'I shan't come. I'm planting iris and they will be flowering long after he is dead.' Last March, 21 years after Hitler committed suicide in the bunker, a few of those violet flowers still flowered under the apple-tree in the orchard.[37]

Or resistance could take the minute form of jokes, word–play, inventiveness: quite often in the diaries she makes a wry note to herself of the way the 'voices' have entered her thought-processes, and appropriates the public language of war for her own imaginative uses. So she might call Maynard Keynes 'dear old Hitler'. Or, awaiting unwelcome visitors at Monk's House on 28 July 1940, she says 'our island will be invaded'. She made her own imaginative patterns out of loudspeakers and searchlights, linking the voices on the wireless with the 'crosseyed squint' of the searchlights 'that make a tent over the church at night', and, in her novel, turning that 'criss-cross of lines making no pattern' into an image for the future shadowing the present. Or, reading the work of other writers, she tells herself, 'I want to send out parachutes into these remote places'. Of her desire to read and write during the air-raids, she says, 'I try to let down a fireproof curtain'. And of the critical silence which greeted the publication of *Roger Fry* in July 1940, she wrote drily: ' "One of our books did not return" as the BBC puts it.'[38] So, as she had done all her life for her 'madness', she turned the voices of world madness into fuel for her own imagination. Ideas are 'the only efficient air-raid shelter'.[39]

By the beginning of 1940 the external voices were becoming very insistent. The year had begun gaily with a Charleston celebration for Angelica's twenty-first birthday – Virginia performed her notoriously extended rendition of 'The Last Rose of Summer' and gave Angelica a copy of Mme du Deffand's letters. (Tensions, however, were acute, with Angelica loathing Clive for being drunk and 'getting off with girls', and Vanessa and Duncan increasingly troubled by her affair with Bunny Garnett.)[40] There would still be family meetings, afternoons of gossip, with tiny moments of private pleasure, as at tea-time at Charleston on a snowy day: 'Sally (dog) kissed Leonard. L smiled at me.'[41] But there were to be no more parties. By February the sense of suspense was acute. In March, the real war was 'thought to be beginning',[42] with Hitler's invasion of Norway and Denmark, followed – with savage speed – by that of Belgium, Holland and Luxembourg. Virginia saw the aeroplanes going overhead, heard 'Winston' on 11 April saying that this was 'the first crunch of the war', and listened to Lord Haw-Haw 'having it all his own way' after the Allies' defeat in Norway in May.[43] Chamberlain resigned dramatically and Churchill took over as leader of a national coalition; Virginia (mis)quoted his speech of 13 May to herself: 'I have nothing to offer but blood & tears & sweat.' (Churchill's rhetoric impressed her, much as she distrusted patriotic oratory.) German forces broke through the French defences and marched towards the Channel, taking Amiens and Arras and driving through to Boulogne, with British and French forces in retreat. Then the Belgians surrendered. Virginia listened, in a frame of mind paralysingly compounded of suspense, boredom and horror, to the news of 'the worst week in the war'.[44]

At home, the 'Local Defence Volunteers' were being set up. Leonard was keen to join what would soon be re-named the Home Guard; Virginia – as future historians would too – found them 'slightly ridiculous'. 'An acid conversation' ensued. (Leonard did not join, but later did fire watching and air raid precaution duties in Rodmell.) Her 'war effort', as the summer went on, consisted of going to Rodmell First Aid meetings, where efficient English country spinsters discussed the water supply and the state of the rectory scullery and showed what Leonard called 'the English genius for unofficial organisation'. Once the air-raids had begun, she went to lectures in the village hall on how charcoal absorbed gas and on how to escape from a building (demonstrated by old Miss Green, who, 'shedding her officers cloak, appeared in blue trousers & let herself down from the Rectory window, hanging by her toenails and descending with a jump.') When the call for scrap-metal to make aeroplanes went up, Leonard, to her annoyance, donated all their aluminium saucepans. Virginia, meanwhile, attended the Women's Institute play rehearsals with resentment and impatience. This village 'war-effort' brought out the worst in her: 'My contribution to the war is the sacrifice of pleasure: I'm bored: bored & appalled by the readymade commonplaceness of these plays: which they cant act unless we help. I mean, the minds so cheap, compared with ours, like a bad novel – thats my contribution – to have my mind smeared by the village & WEA mind; & to endure it, & the simper.' She picked up, with lethal accuracy, the WI tone: 'At the moment, the flowers are doing their bit. This jargon from my first aid practice, and the Womens Institute.'[45] But these violent and snobbish refusals of community life were being translated, in her novel, into an idea of the survival of England in the form of a village play.

Whether she liked it or not, she was part of the community. She picked up all the local rumours: warnings of 'clergymen in parachutes', stories of 'the Nun in the bus who pays her fare with a mans hand'. Meanwhile Harold Nicolson was warning Vita that there might be a complete civilian evacuation from Kent and Sussex. Rumour and suspense altered every perception: the sound of a distant thunderstorm was instantly turned, in her mind, into the sound of gunfire at the Channel ports.[46]

Almost everyone she knew, apart from Ethel Smyth (who was completely confident – 'Oh of *course* we shall fight & win')[47] was fairly sure that they were about to be invaded and defeated. This may not have been the national mood, but it was certainly the mood of her circle. Most of their conversations circled round this theme – as when Desmond and the ageing G.E. Moore (less impressive to Virginia than he once was in the days when he wrote 'the book that made us all so wise and good')[48] came for the weekend and ate all the cream and sugar. Leonard remembered the mood of that weekend:

> There we sat in May 1940, Desmond, Virginia, and I in the house and under a hot sun and brilliant sky in the garden, in a cocoon of friendship and nostalgic memories. At the same time the whole weekend was dominated by a consciousness that our little private world was menaced by destruction, by oecumenical catastrophe now beginning across the Channel in France. It was, of course, a week before the capitulation of the Belgians, but the German offensive had been in operation for ten days, the tension was unrelieved and one's memories of unremitting defeat in the terrible first years of the 1914 war left one inevitably with premonition of disaster, so that even hope was a kind of self-indulgence and self-deception.[49]

Like a number of their friends, they began to discuss suicide plans 'if Hitler lands. Jews beaten up. What point in waiting? Better shut the garage doors. This a sensible, rather matter of fact talk.'[50] The Woolfs were well aware that the threats in 'his master's voice' were meant for them, as well as for millions of others. They had good sources of information, and it was known that with the invasion plan for July 1940 the Gestapo had drawn up an 'Arrest List' or 'Black List' for Great Britain, the 'Sonderfahndungsliste G.B.' which ran to 350 pages (and had blank spaces for more names to be added.) On this list, alongside many of their friends and acquaintances, were 'Leonhard Woolf, Schriftsteller, RSHA VIG 1, and Virginia Woolf, Schriftstellerin, RSHA VIG.'[51] No one in 1940 could have been *sure* of being on the list, but they could have taken a reasonable guess, and Leonard and Virginia Woolf were not the only people to make careful, practical suicide plans. In London, these discussions went on with whoever came to call – Kingsley Martin, Rose Macaulay:

> Question of suicide seriously debated among the 4 of us . . . in the gradually darkening room. At last no light at all. This was symbolic. French are to be beaten; invasion here; 5th Coln active; a German pro-Consul; Engsh Govt in Canada; we in concentration camps, or taking sleeping draughts . . . KM gives us about 5 weeks before the great attack on Engld begins.[52]

Meanwhile Harold and Vita were discussing (as were the Brenans and the Partridges) how to get hold of a 'bare bodkin' from their doctor which would be 'quick & painless & private'.[53] Adrian, now working as a psychiatric army doctor, obtained a prescription for morphia for the Woolfs.[54] The war seemed like a 'desperate illness' for which suicide might have to be the only cure.[55]

Bombs and air-raids were getting closer. She watched the aeroplanes go over in their 'wild duck flights'.[56] In June, she listened to the news, and the stories, of Dunkirk. Louie Everest's older brother Harry West was one of the soldiers who got out, and turned up at Louie's cottage in Rodmell after walking all night; she looked out that morning and saw 'a soldier whom she did not recognise at first, hatless, his tunic bloody and full of holes, his boots in rags, lying exhausted outside the front door.' Virginia poured out his Dunkirk story in her diary, in the rapid, fragmented, telegraphic style she used for these times:

> It pours out – how he hadnt boots off for 3 days; the beach at Dunkirk –
> the bombers as low as trees – the bullets like moth holes in his coat – how
> no English aeroplanes fought; how the officer told them to take their

shoes off & go past a pill box on all fours. Then went himself with a grenade & blasted it. At Dunkirk many men shot themselves as the planes swooped. Harry swam off, a boat neared. Say Chum Can you row? Yes, he said, hauled in, rowed for 5 hours, saw England, landed – didnt know if it were day or night or what town – didnt ask – . . . so was despatched to his regiment . . . He saw his cousin dead on the beach; & another man from the street. He was talking to a chap, who showed him a silk handkerchief bought for his joy lady. That moment a bomb killed him. Harry took the handkerchief. Harry has had eno' war, & is certain of our defeat – got no arms & no aeroplanes – how can we do anything?[57]

As the battle for France reached its nadir ('the great battle which decides our life or death', she called it, sounding almost Churchillian)[58] the war-voices grew louder. On the radio, Lord Haw-Haw's propaganda vied with the 'patriotic rhetoric' put out by the new Minister for Information, Duff Cooper, and with Churchill's 'finest hour' speech. Virginia asked herself what all this public talk of patriotism meant to her, and what the relation was between the BBC propaganda and the voice of Harry West, 'the real animal behind the brave, laughing heroic boy panoply which the BBC spreads before us nightly?'[59]

On 11 June, Mussolini came in against Britain and France. On 14 June the Germans entered Paris. That hot summer day, Virginia and Leonard went for a picnic with Vita and Gwen St Aubyn to Penshurst, the great Elizabethan house near Tonbridge in Kent, ancestral home of Philip Sidney's family, and met its present owner, the eighty-seven-year-old Lord de L'Isle, crouched in a 'poky little room', an old snail 'sitting in the corner of his tremendous shell'. Leonard, drinking the Baron's tea, thought about his own ancestors and what was happening that day: 'I felt that in that room history had fallen about the ears of the Sidneys and the Leicesters, the Sackvilles and the Dorsets, while outside, across the Channel, in France, history was falling about the ears of us all.'[60] On Monday 17 June, they went up to London. As they sat down to lunch at Mecklenburgh Square, John Lehmann came in, looking 'white about the gills, his pale eyes paler than usual, and said the French have stopped fighting'. The next day Churchill broadcast: 'Reassuring about defence of England; not all claptrap. Now we're fighting alone with our back to the wall.' She could only think in terms of ending: 'We pour to the edge of a precipice . . . & then? I cant conceive that there will be a 27th June 1941.' Hitler's invasion, it seemed, was planned for mid-July; the battle for Britain began to be fought in the sky above her head, in July and August. Her individual feelings kept being swallowed up in 'the communal feeling': 'We're in for it.'[61]

But she did not want the garage to see the end of her. 'I dont want to go to bed at midday.' She had work to do, even if her writing now seemed a tiny preoccupation hooped round with the circumference of the war, and even if, as a writer, she felt she was living in a world with 'no audience. No echo.'[62]

She was often deeply depressed through this spring and summer, marking in the diary her feelings of emptiness and despair, her need to think of something 'liberating & freshening', her repeated thoughts of suicide. She urged herself along, inducing 'a state of peace & sensation feeling' by writing descriptions or anecdotes or reports of conversations, or copying out helpful quotations: 'There is nothing in the world so much admired as a man who knows how to bear unhappiness with courage. Seneca.' In her letters she made a point of being brisk and stoical. ('I think of Montaigne', she wrote to Ethel, 'let death find me planting cabbages.' To Judith Stephen she referred to Dunkirk as 'a lot of disagreeables'.) The war made her emotional, and she sent warm messages to old friends, Tom, Hugh, Vita and particularly Ethel: 'What a pity there's no wave language – for then you would have gone home with the sound of song in your ears.'[63]

But the sound she could hear most, on her inner air-waves, was that of tears. The air seemed full of it, heard or unheard: 'Not a sound this evening to bring in the human tears. I remember the sudden profuse shower one night just before war wh. made me think of all men & women weeping.'[64] It became one of the dominant tunes of *Between the Acts*: 'Down it poured like all the people in the world weeping. Tears, Tears. Tears . . . All people's tears, weeping for all people.'[65]

She was ill with the 'flu for most of March (when she wrote that diary entry about tears), and at the same time trying to finish the proofs of *Roger Fry* and respond to Margery Fry's many requests for corrections. At this low point, on 10 March, Angelica and Quentin went over to Rodmell for tea. Virginia had a high temperature. That morning, walking on the meadows, Leonard had given her a very severe critique of *Roger Fry*, criticising its method as inert and austere. 'It was like being pecked by a very hard strong beak.'[66] She had to hang on to her sense that he might be out of sympathy with Roger and 'on the wrong track', but it was a painful experience. By the afternoon, when the Bells came, she was feeling extremely low. Angelica told Bunny, in a long letter describing the visit, that 'conversation was sticky'. Virginia worked off her feelings about the morning's attack by caricaturing Leonard's obsession with a rock garden he was making.

Eventually he came in – V. asked him where on earth he had been, rather peevishly so he said, In the garage. What where you doing there? Planting dandelions, he said in his gloomiest tone. Both I & V believed him but it soon turned out that this was a joke to show V what silly questions she asked.

Quentin and Leonard went out again to play bowls, and Angelica and Virginia went upstairs to the sitting room and sat by the fire. They talked about 'vanity' as the bane of the modern world. Virginia said: 'Men are vain of their brains & women of their clothes.' She told Angelica that she minded terribly what people thought of her, and asked her if she was the same. Angelica said no, she only minded what Nessa and Duncan thought. And what Virginia thought? No, Angelica replied, then hastily corrected herself, 'and said that I should mind, but in a different way'. Virginia took her temperature; it was 101. She talked a bit of the biography, and then told Angelica about her dream of Julian: 'how he had come back from some long travels, bounding with joy & laughter & said, of course I wasn't really dead. How could you think so?' 'In return', Angelica told her she had had a similar dream. Then 'she took her temperature again', and Angelica made her go to bed with a hot water bottle. They left, leaving Virginia looking miserable in bed, and Leonard 'cursing influenza, but smiling very kindly at us through the white cinneraria' which he was giving them to take to Vanessa. 'Their garden looked very lovely – no flowers but the grey flint walls & bare trees with the church behind are so beautiful.'[67]

Three days later, Vanessa, who had also been reading *Roger Fry*, wrote a moved and affectionate letter of thanks: 'Now you have brought him back to me.' Virginia replied: 'I never wrote a word without thinking of you and Julian and I have so longed to do something that you'd both like.'[68] She sent off the manuscript on 6 April, and turned her mind to the writing of 'The Leaning Tower', which she gave as a lecture on 27 April to the Women's Institute in Brighton – or to what she called 'the Brighton working classes', '200 betwixt and betweens – you know' (she told Vita) 'how they stare and stick and won't argue'.[69] These comments characteristically undermined the desire she expressed in the lecture for a classless society.

Among the 200, however, were at least two exceptional women, the elderly American actress and feminist Elizabeth Robins (who had known Julia and Leslie, whose memoir on playing Ibsen the Press had published in 1928, and whose autobiography Virginia had just been reading) and her companion Octavia Wilberforce, a doctor in her early fifties, who had fought a pioneering battle to become Head Physician at the New Sussex Hospital for Women in Brighton, who ran a general practice from her Brighton house, and who also superintended a rest-home for women at Elizabeth Robins's Sussex farmhouse. Octavia's and Virginia's family were connected through the intermarriages of the Clapham Sect; so she could jokingly call her 'Cousin Octavia'. Octavia noticed, at the lecture, that Virginia was extremely thin.[70]

A few days after the lecture, in May (just before what she called 'the worst week of the war'), Vanessa told her about Angelica's love-affair with Bunny. It was an indication of Vanessa's reserve that she had not let this out to Virginia until now, though as long ago as last August Angelica had been resentfully sitting through a tea-time conversation at Charleston about early marriages. Vanessa and Virginia had been discussing the Stephen girls (Ann married Richard Llewelyn Davies in 1938, at twenty-two; Judith was engaged to Leslie Humphrey, both in their early twenties). Vanessa and Virginia were agreeing that 'it was a mistake to have children so young'. (This followed a terrible row, which Virginia knew nothing of, between Vanessa and Angelica over what would happen if Angelica became pregnant by David Garnett.) Then Leonard, who had been silent, spoke up: 'He said it was a mistake to lay down the law in this fashion & that no-one could judge for others; that all those he knew who had married late in life seemed to have made no more of a success of it than those who married young, & that anyhow if people made mistakes it was part of their lives & perhaps it was a good thing for them to experience mistakes.'[71]

But now, hearing this news, and understanding at last why Angelica had been so difficult and moody for the last year or so, Virginia could not summon up Leonard's admirable liberal judiciousness. She felt old and sad at the idea of Angelica in love with someone they had all known for years, who had been Duncan's lover, who was married to a dying woman, and who was old enough to be her father. It seemed somehow to 'renew' Julian's death. She wrote strangely and mournfully in the diary, in a voice seeming to come from a distance: 'So the land recedes from my ship which draws out into the sea of old age. The land with its children.' That voice speaks again in her novel, given to the writer who thinks of herself as an outcast: 'From the earth green waters seemed to rise over her. She took her voyage away from the shore.'[72]

'I read myself into a state of immunity', she told Ethel in June. 'My brain hums with scraps of poetry.'[73] She corrected her proofs and resumed 'Pointz Hall'; she started to write an account of her father, strongly coloured by her current reading of Freud. She published a piece on Horace Walpole, celebrating his confident sense of individuality and his vigour and adaptability ('For a self that goes on changing is a self that goes on living') against the ominous prospect of 'whatever ruin may befall the map of Europe in years to come'.[74] An essay on Selina Trimmer, the Quaker

734

governess at Cavendish House, home of the Dukes of Devonshire, gave her the pleasure of thinking her way back into the 1890s. Memory and history created some immunity from the present. A dazzling talk she gave to the Rodmell Women's Institute on 23 July on the Dreadnought Hoax, which made her audience laugh themselves silly, gave her that same pleasure of re-entering the past, and, in the same breath, of satirising uniforms and military dignity.

But not all her writing was a search for escape. She was thinking her way towards an essay on peace, a wartime recapitulation of *Three Guineas*.[75] Her novel, which she was now writing intensively,[76] was dangerously poised between private illusions and desires, and the levelling pressure of history. Scraps of poetry, rhymes, sayings, proverbs, literature, fill its characters' minds and Miss La Trobe's play, surrounded by an exterior language of violent news bulletins, loudspeakers and propaganda. Its figures (homo-sexual, adulterous, frustrated, inhibited, almost all very unhappy) struggle between shameful isolation and self-censorhip, and little thwarted bursts of attempts at communication. They are always being pulled: down into silence and solitude, or out into self-consciousness and social talk, 'gobbets of gossip'. The central battle of the marriage, set inside the life of the middle-class English family, rages in silence, surrounded by voices: fragmented talk of the past, helpless talk of the imminent war 'on a June day in 1939': 'the doom of sudden death hanging over us'. It is a novel about language at a time of stress: 'Words rose, became menacing and shook their fists at you.' The language of the pageant-play struggles against the audience's inattention and inertia, its tendency towards dispersal. The play's author fights against the possibility that her power will desert her and that there will be no way of reaching an audience. 'Beads of perspiration broke on her forehead. Illusion had failed. "This is death," she murmured, "death." ' The writer's struggle to make a version of history exists inside the possibility that history is nothing but meaningless repetition. 'Civilisa-tion' is only a thin crust over the inevitable regression to the primitive. 'History', now, may be coming to an end.

Tick, tick, tick, the machine continued.
'Marking time,' said old Oliver beneath his breath.
'Which don't exist for us,' Lucy murmured. 'We've only the present.'

'You don't believe in history', says one of the voices in the novel to another.[77]

The conflict of voices in *Between the Acts* acted out the battle for supremacy between the voices on her air-waves: Roger Fry's – Freud's –

Hitler's – the BBC's – scraps of poetry – all interrupting each other. One of the voices which added significantly to this war-time chorus of disharmony was that of Coleridge, whose letters and poems she was reading all through the summer of 1940. His voice (and that of other Romantic poets, Keats and Shelley) was, to her, an enchanting alternative to the rest, 'delicate & pure & musical & uncorrupt': 'How lightly & firmly they put down their feet, & how they sing; & how they compact; & fuse, & deepen.' Out of this pleasurable work she wrote two essays, one on Coleridge called 'The Man at the Gate' and one on Sara Coleridge (both published in October 1940).[78]

Her reading of Coleridge was linked to her writing about her father: she re-read Leslie Stephen's essay on him in July, and when she wrote on Sara, she described a daughter's life of posthumous dedication to her father's work: 'She did not copy him, she insisted; she was him.' Virginia Woolf could have dedicated herself to editing her father's work, too: it was what he had expected of her. Instead, she spent her writing life rewriting and subverting him, and was now, in her autobiography, trying to 'find her father' again, to understand from 'my present distance of time' why he had behaved as he had as an old man.

One of the things she was trying to understand in her autobiography was Leslie's 'violent displays of rages'. 'There was something blind, animal, savage in them', she wrote of them. 'Roger Fry said that civilisation meant awareness; he was uncivilised in his extreme unawareness.'[79] Here Leslie is like one of the savage voices of the dictator. But he was *also*, to her, a lovable father, a reader of Coleridge, and a 'civilised' writer. Her 'ambivalence' about him, while she was writing the memoir, was painfully unresolved.

She described Coleridge in her essay as all voice, humming, magical, inspired, rich, various. (Her description is lifted from Keats's wonderful account of how he once walked along with Coleridge and listened to him 'broach a thousand things', from Nightingales and Poetry to Nightmares and Mermaids: 'I heard his voice as he came towards me – I heard it as he moved away – I had heard it all the interval.')[80] She told a story of a little girl who once heard Coleridge talking on and on, and who, 'overcome by the magic of the incantation, burst into tears when the voice ceased and left her alone in a silent world'. She too, coming to the end of rereading his work (an anthology called *Coleridge the Talker*, and the three volumes of his *Poetical Works*) feels 'bereft' when the voice stops. Her description of this emotion resembles her feelings (which she did not get as far as describing in her memoir) on the death of her father.

At the very end of *Three Guineas*, in the last footnote, Coleridge's voice was cited in opposition to the voice of the dictator: 'Man must be *free* or to what purpose was he made a Spirit of Reason, and not a Machine of

Instinct? . . . Whatever law or system of law compels any other service, disennobles our nature, leagues itself with the animal against the godlike, kills in us the very principle of joyous well-doing, and fights against humanity.'[81] So Coleridge's voice, from *Three Guineas* onwards through the war, provided her with a life-line, an alternative to the 'besieging voices' of radio and loudspeaker and manifestos. At the same time, Coleridge's despot, Kubla Khan, who hears 'ancestral voices prophesying war', is invoked in her argument that world aggression has psychological, deeply buried, inherited human sources.

It was typical of the divide she could erect between private feelings and public behaviour that on the same day she had the Rodmell ladies at the village hall in stitches over the Dreadnought, she was anticipating with 'twinges' of apprehension the sneers against Bloomsbury which she thought would greet the publication of *Roger Fry* on 25 July. (Some of that strain did show itself in public, though: at the end of the talk, she left the hall at once and walked off down the village street. The organiser, bossy Mrs Chavasse, told young Diana Gardner, one of Virginia's greatest admirers in the village, to pursue her, thank her, and ask her to come back. Diana ran after her, but, like Miss La Trobe after the success of her play, she would not go back to receive their thanks.)[82] She was as anxious about friends' responses as about the reviews, and felt a sense of responsibility and kinship towards Roger. Any attack on him as a result of the book would feel like an attack on her.

> What a curious relation is mine with Roger at this moment – I who have given him a kind of shape after his death – Was he like that? I feel very much in his presence at the moment: as if I were intimately connected with him; as if we together had given birth to this vision of him: a child born of us. Yet he had no power to alter it. And yet for some years it will represent him.[83]

Publication coincided with other disturbances: the aftermath of a jaded week in London, the death of Ray Strachey at fifty-three (she entered a rapid, affectionate obituary in the diary), and a visit from St John Hutchinson, who was prosecuting an abortionist in Lewes for murder, and who showed them distressing photographs of 'the womans body in the abortionists cupboard: her dead face: long hair: legs trussed up'.[84] She used this image of confinement on the eve of publication:

> All the walls, the protecting & reflecting walls, wear so terribly thin in this

war. There's no standard to write for: no public to echo back: even the 'tradition' has become transparent. Hence a certain energy & recklessness – part good – part bad I daresay. But its the only line to take. And perhaps the walls, if violently beaten against, will finally contain me.[85]

These very troubled notes seemed, initially, borne out by the lack of response to her book. After '2 years hard work' (much more, in fact), she felt it being greeted by 'complete silence'. 'My books only gave me pain, Ch.Brontë said. Today I agree.'[86] Gradually the responses began to come in, and sales were not as bad as she had feared (though the first air-raids in London stopped them short):[87] an enthusiastic tribute from Desmond in the *Sunday Times*, a nice note from Clive, a 'dampening' response from Morgan, a critique from Herbert Read praising her but damning Roger. Forster's and Read's responses summed up alternative ways of writing about 'Bloomsbury' during the war. Forster called the book 'a noble and convincing defence of civilisation'; Read blamed Roger Fry for unrealistic élitism, for retreating into an Ivory Tower 'private world of his own sensibility'.[88]

Read's attack was echoed by Vita's son Benedict Nicolson, a burgeoning art-historian now serving as a gunner private at Chatham. Benedict argued, fiercely (writing during an air-raid), that Roger Fry and his Bloomsbury friends had lived in a 'fool's paradise', and that they could be held partly responsible for the war, for allowing 'the spirit of Nazism to grow without taking any steps to check it'. The artist must join and fight, not retreat into his tower or 'cultivate exquisite sensibilities'.[89] Virginia responded carefully (during her own air-raid), at once defending Roger Fry's social commit-ment and importance, dissociating herself from Bloomsbury, and arguing that she had tried to make her books 'reach a far wider circle than a little private circle of exquisite and cultivated people'.[90] (It was typical of her openness and her kindness to the generation that was challenging her, that she immediately invited him to spend his leave at Rodmell to continue the debate: 'We could argue incessantly in between raids.')

The debate pointed to the heart of her life's meaning in wartime. Had her commitment to Roger during the writing of the book, and, more broadly, her whole way of life and professional achievement, now been rendered meaningless? Was her only value, the value that would outlive her, in having constructed ideas and ways of writing that did not belong to Bloomsbury's – or anybody else's – scheme of things? Thinking about Read, she noted: 'It is essential to remain outside; & realise my own beliefs'.[91]

The strain of publication at once merged into the increasing pressure of the war. 'The Germans are nibbling at my afternoon walks', she wrote in

July. A train was bombed at Newhaven; an RAF Hurricane crashed at Southease, and she walked along the river to see it: 'a little gnat, with red & white & blue bars.' At the beginning of August, gun emplacements were being built on the banks of the River Ouse: 'Great lorries are carrying sandbags down to the river', she told Vita. Every day, as the air battle overhead intensified, they heard 'the wail of the sirens, and then the drone of the German planes flying in from the sea, usually to the east of Rodmell and Lewes'. 'The air saws, the wasps drone; the siren . . . is as punctual as the vespers.'[92] In the week ending 17 August, the battle was at its heaviest, and was fought largely over Kent and Sussex and Greater London. It was very hot. On the 16th, while they were out in the garden, German planes came over very close to the ground, with bombs dropping all around.

> We lay down under the tree. The sound was like someone sawing in the air just above us. We lay flat on our faces, hands behind head. Dont close yr teeth said L. They seemed to be sawing at something stationary. Bombs shook the windows of my lodge. Will it drop I asked? If so, we shall be broken together. I thought, I think, of nothingness – flatness, my mood being flat. Some fear I suppose. Shd we take Mabel to garage. Too risky to cross the garden L said. Then another came from Newhaven. Hum & saw & buzz all round us. A horse neighed on the marsh. Very sultry. Is it thunder? I said. No guns, said L; from Ringmer, from Charleston way. Then slowly the sound lessened.[93]

Two days later, on Sunday 18th, they were sitting down to lunch when three planes roared over them. They could see the swastikas. A cottage in the village was hit: 'The closest shave so far.' (Describing this to Benedict Nicolson a few days later, this became: 'five raiders almost crashing into the dining room'.)[94] Leonard was glad to find (he noted in retrospect) that he was 'perfectly calm and cold, the whole incident seeming to be completely unreal'.[95] On the 28th, they were playing bowls when a plane circled very low above their heads, and there was a spatter of bullets from the searchlight unit above Rodmell. They realised it was an enemy plane, and lay on the grass. The plane circled away and they saw it go down near Lewes. Two British planes came roaring in to circle round it, then made off towards London. 'It wd have been a peaceful matter of fact death to be popped off on the terrace playing bowls this very fine cool sunny August evening.'[96]

She found herself trying to imagine exactly what being killed by a bomb would feel like ('& shant, for once, be able to describe it'.)[97] But she was, mainly, rather 'matter of fact' about the possibility of violent death and the likely imminence of an invasion. In letters to her niece Judith, she took a jokey stoical British tone about the war. 'But the great excitement now, is

the invasion. Its expected tomorrow for some reason. So I am off to Lewes
to get in supplies. Then we go to tea at Charleston, & I wish you were
coming with us . . . Leonard has promised to give 12 lectures on politics this
winter. So we ignore the invasion.'[98] John Lehmann remarked on the funny,
even euphoric tone which she took about the raids, as when inviting him for
the weekend: 'We could have offered you a great variety of air raid alarms,
distant bombs . . . Indeed its rather lovely about 2 in the morning to see the
lights stalking the Germans over the marshes.'[99] In the same spirit she wrote
to Sibyl Colefax in August: 'If you hear that Virginia has disarmed
6 German pilots you wont be in the least surprised, will you?'[100] Somerset
Maugham told a story which suggested insouciance or excitement under
fire, rather than fear. After a dinner-party in Westminster, she insisted on
walking home alone during an air-raid. Anxious for her safety, he followed
her, and saw her, lit up by the flashes of gun-fire, standing in the road and
raising her arms to the sky.[101] She was, even, rather proud of their close calls,
exaggerating them in her letters to Benedict Nicolson, and competing, as
always, with Vanessa's war-damage.

By the time of Benedict's weekend visit she felt acutely that 'they were in
the war'. Kent was harder hit than Sussex, and a 'phone call from Vita at
Sissinghurst in the middle of a raid there made her feel she was 'talking to
someone who might be killed at any moment'. Putting down the 'phone, she
wrote her a kind of farewell love letter, which ended: 'You have given me
such happiness.'[102] She was afraid, intermittently; more, though, she felt a
constant sense of pressure. But in the first week of September Hitler
changed his tactics, and switched from the South Coast to nightly raids on
London. Fighting continued over Sussex: on 11 September they saw a
German plane shot down and fall into the river meadows, sending up
(Leonard remembered) 'a column of smoke absolutely straight into the
windless sky'. Virginia described it, almost elatedly, to Judith:

We had an exciting raid the other evening – a plane came over and was
chased to the same hill as the other. Then it looped the loop, crashed, & a
great tower of smoke sprang up. Not a trace remained of the pilot. This
time they were firing all the way.[103]

But the great damage was now being done to London, and, all through
that autumn, though they were spending the greater part of their time at
Rodmell, her feelings were directed most intensely towards the city. This
split between her emotions for London and her sense of isolation and
constriction at Rodmell became extremely acute. In July she had gone
'street haunting' with Elizabeth Bowen, 'talking in many changing scenes'

as they went up Thames Street to the Tower and to Billingsgate Market, and back on a bus.[104] In August she told Bob Trevelyan that in the autumn they planned to be in London 'every other week'.[105] But from the beginning of September London was under fire. The invasion was thought to be imminent ('Its for the next two weeks apparently if at all' she noted on 11 September). On the 17th, Hitler postponed his plans for taking Britain. Instead, the bombing of London, and then of other cities, went on every night from 7 September to 2 November.

Like many other writers witnessing the city in these weeks (among them Elizabeth Bowen, Rose Macaulay, Henry Green and Graham Greene) Virginia described the destruction of 'her' London eloquently and with strong personal feeling. She wrote about it a little in letters, never in essays or fiction, but mainly to herself in the diary, in a shocked, rapid, jagged, intensely observant language. It was some of her most powerful writing, about some of the most painful things she had ever witnessed.

On Sunday 8 September, there was an air raid over Mecklenburgh Square. John Lehmann was at No.37, and went down to the shelter during the night. By morning some of the houses were destroyed and there was an unexploded time-bomb in the Square, which was cordoned off and evacuated. The Woolfs went up on the Tuesday, 10 September, and saw the house 30 yards from theirs in ruins. The occupants had been in the basement, and had all been killed. The house at No.11 Mecklenburgh Street, where Jane Harrison had lived, was 'a great pile of bricks. Underneath all the people who had gone down to their shelter. Scraps of cloth hanging to the bare walls at the side still standing. A looking glass I think swinging. Like a tooth knocked out – a clean cut.' They drove to Holborn, a shocking sight: 'like a nightmare', she told Ethel. Her sharp, fragmentary prose embodied the scene:

A vast gap at the top of Chancery Lane. Smoking still. Some great shop entirely destroyed: the hotel opposite like a shell. In a wine shop there were no windows left. People standing at the tables – I think drink being served. Heaps of blue green glass in the road at Chancery Lane. Men breaking off fragments left in the frames. Glass falling. Then into Lincolns Inn. To the N.S. office: windows broken, but house untouched. We went over it. Deserted. Wet passages. Glass on stairs. Doors locked. So back to the car. A great block of traffic. The Cinema behind Mme Tussaud's torn open: the stage visible; some decoration swinging. All the R.Park houses with broken windows, but undamaged. And then miles & miles of orderly ordinary streets . . .[106]

She thought of people's wretchedness and exhaustion. She was very glad they were driving back to Sussex and were not staying overnight. On Friday 13th they went up again – 'a strong feeling of invasion' on the roads. At Wimbledon they were caught in an air raid, and took refuge in a shelter. They found a man and a woman and child living there – he was a house-painter, an ex-printer; they were friendly and stoical, and the Woolfs were both impressed by them.[107] They couldn't get in to Mecklenburgh Square, but decided, with John, to move the Press to their printers at the Garden City Press at Letchworth, in Hertfordshire, who agreed to offer the Press two rooms.

The following Wednesday, the 18th, they heard that the time bomb in the square had gone off on the Saturday; all the windows at No.37 were broken and 'part of the ceiling of the basement front room had crashed down, covering everything with dust and lumps of plaster and splinters of wood'. 'Blew out all windows, all ceilings, and smashed all my china – just as we'd got the flat ready! – oh damn.' It was pointless to let herself think, 'Why did we ever leave Tavistock?' All that week in Rodmell she heard about the raids: 'Oxford Street now smashed. John Lewis, Selfridge, B & H, all my old haunts. Also British Museum forecourt . . . A bomb in Gordon Square. All windows at 46 broken.' On Monday the 23rd they went to Mecklenburgh Square to view the damage. It was a terrific mess, 'dark; carpets nailed to windows; ceilings down in patches; heaps of grey dust & china under kitchen table', but there was less structural damage than they had feared. John Lehmann came in and found them 'picking about among the ruins of their flat. Rubble and broken glass were everywhere; and yet I was surprised to see that most of the books were in their shelves and the pictures bright and straight on the walls – perhaps the first task they had undertaken. They both seemed remarkably cheerful in spite of the desolation of their home that surrounded them. Leonard remarked, grinning at me, "Well, really, possessions are such a nuisance, perhaps it will be a good thing to start clear again." '[108] The house was uninhabitable.

A few days later, a bomb fell on the workshop next to Duncan's and Vanessa's studios in Fitzroy Street, and a number of their paintings were destroyed by fire. Virginia had just had a furious quarrel with Vanessa, the first between them for many years. Vanessa had told Helen Anrep that there was a cottage available for rent in Rodmell, and Helen was planning to move there with her two children. This prospect appalled Virginia and she blamed Vanessa. But the news of the fire at the studio was Vanessa's 'Trump Card': 'So I had to pipe low.'[109]

For the rest of September and October Virginia stayed mainly in Rodmell, 'but come up every week or so and see more of Bloomsbury destroyed'.[110] Then, on Wednesday 16 October, 52 Tavistock Square was completely destroyed by a bomb. Because they had been so worried about the rent, she was extremely relieved at the news. But when they went to look at it on the Friday, she had a painful mixture of feelings: relief, release, shock, grief, a sense of loss and unreality; 'Basement all rubble. Only relics an old basket chair (bought in Fitzroy Sqre days) & Penmans board To Let. Otherwise bricks & wood splinters. One glass door in the next door house hanging. I cd just see a piece of my studio wall standing: otherwise rubble where I wrote so many books. Open air where we sat so many nights, gave so many parties.' She wrote to Angelica: 'As for 52 Tavistock – well, where I used to dandle you on my knee, there's Gods sky: and nothing left but one wicker chair and a piece of drugget.'[111] Losing possessions partly exhilarated her, but pained her too: 'how I worked to buy them – one by one.' At Mecklenburgh Square, which was full of litter, glass, dust and powder, she talked to the ladies from Pritchards' the solicitors ('Jaunty jerky talk') and scavenged for what she needed to take away: first of all, her diaries: '24 vols . . . salved; a great mass for my memoirs'. Then, whatever glass and china was left (an Omega plate, 'Duncan's glasses, Nessa's plates', which she packed up in the kitchen with Mabel); her copy of Darwin; her fur coat. 'Now we seem quit of London.'[112]

Two weeks later she went up again and saw the panels that Duncan and Vanessa had painted for them 'still pendant – 3 at least' in the wreck of Tavistock Square. She salvaged a few more books from Mecklenburgh Square, and saw the ruins of St James's Church and Leicester Square. In November, a land-mine fell at the back of the Mecklenburgh house, 'blasting all the rooms that had escaped the damage caused by the time bomb'. Now you could 'stand on the ground floor and look up with uninterrupted view to the roof while sparrows scrabbled about on the joists of what had been a ceiling; bookcases had been blown off the walls and the books lay in enormous mounds on the floor covered in rubble and plaster. In the Press books, files, paper, the printing-machine and the type were in a horrible grimy mess.' The damage to the roof and the pipes meant that there were frequent water-bursts, sending 'a waterfall down the stairs from the third floor to the ground floor'. As a result of this, and the firemen's hose-pipes, 'masses of letters and precious documents were reduced to sodden pulp and lost for ever'.[113] Virginia described this comically and despairingly to Ethel (avoiding in her tone what she called 'the gloomy self consequence of the newly bombed'):[114] 'how we went to London and found mushrooms sprouting on the carpets, pools standing on the chairs, and glass to the right left and then a ceiling fell.'[115]

They decided to move all the books and the furniture to Rodmell, and rented three rooms in Mr Botten's farm, Place Farm House, a little way up the village street, and a storeroom in the Mill House, up at the far end of the village. On 5 December the vans arrived, but Mr Botten panicked at the amount of inflammable stuff pouring into his farm: 'a deluge' of furniture, damp books – and letters. ('Never never keep letters, Ethel. Theyre the devil when it comes to a move.') So half of it had to be brought into Monk's House, followed by the printing press and all the type. In the big downstairs sitting-room, 'the thousands of books which we had had in London' (Leonard remembered) 'were piled on tables, chairs, and all over the floor.' Leslie's books, mixed with their own, 'were piled in grimy, hopelessly jumbled heaps.' From December onwards, there was 'the devil of a hobble and mess'. They had just acquired a new kitten, and from looking at him she drew a phrase for how she felt: 'I cant make a warm hollow for myself.'[116] 'Oh the huddle & hideousness of untidiness – oh that Hitler had obliterated all our books tables carpets & pictures – oh that we were empty & bare & unpossessed.' It was ironic that, having welcomed the destruction of Tavistock Square with brave words on the virtue of losing possessions, she was now more encumbered than ever by what she most disliked, the turmoil of displaced, disarranged, obstructive *things*.

She made very few visits to London that winter, but in January went for a solitary walk to London Bridge, along the river and through the city: 'So by tube to the Temple; & there wandered in the desolate ruins of my old squares: gashed; dismantled; the old red bricks all white powder, something like a builders yard. Grey dirt & broken windows; sightseers; all that completeness ravished & demolished.' Her feeling for London was romantic and heroic: it was her 'only patriotism'. All her sense of English identity, of opposition to the enemy, her respect and sympathy for ordinary citizens and her feeling of being part of a community, cohered around the city. When Churchill spoke about 'our majestic city' she was moved – 'for I feel London majestic'. She wrote to Ethel of 'the passion of my life, that is the City of London – to see London all blasted, that too raked my heart. Have you that feeling for certain alleys and little courts, between Chancery Lane and the City?' 'Why do I dramatise London perpetually? When I see a great smash like a crushed match box where an old house stood I wave my hand to London.'[117]

744

FORTY

Anon

She was waving her hand in farewell as well as in tribute. After the bombing of the two houses, her whole life became fixed in the country. Her violent reaction to the threat of the Anrep 'invasion' (they only stayed two weeks in Rodmell, after all) had as much to do with her feeling that Monk's House, Rodmell and its landscape, was her private island, as with her dislike of Helen and her 'oafish' children. She partly liked this 'queer' 'contraction of life to the village radius',[1] and partly found it alarmingly constricting. Until now she had always had alternatives.

She couldn't hold the life of the village at arm's length any more. The feelings of the community in wartime touched her closely, sometimes dramatically: the admirable stoicism of the mothers sitting 'stolid' through the village play while the sirens sounded; the women rushing screaming into the road when they thought the school bus with all the children on it was being bombed; Louie telling her that at a nearby village, after a German plane came down, 'the country people "stomped" the heads of the 4 dead Germans into the earth'.[2]

Of course many of the Rodmell villagers had been acquaintances – and employees and tenants – for years. She had listened to their stories and been to their funerals and weddings, eaten their cooking, seen them working in the house and the garden, and known about all their closely interconnected families. Frank Dean at the forge often did building jobs in the house as well as looking after the car. Bad-tempered Percy Bartholemew was an immovable fixture in the garden; Mr Fears the intelligent, garrulous, left-wing postman was a regular attender at the Rodmell Labour Party. They had had their disputes with the old Rodmell farmers, Guy Janson of South Farm, Jasper Botten at Place Farm House. Annie Thomsett, now Penfold, had worked for them for years and was fond of Virginia, and they knew all about Annie's family. Her sister Doris looked after the deaf and dumb Thomsett brother, Jack, whose excited reactions to overhead fighting Virginia noted: 'Dumb Thompsett making wild attempts at comment.' Louie Everest's mother, Mrs West (the 'layer out & night watcher to the village') also looked after a retarded son. Virginia referred to him as 'the chattering idiot', and Leonard, telling his story, commented on 'something horrible and repulsive in the slobbering imbecility of a human being.'[3] Leonard, however, spent some time in May 1940 trying to help Mrs West get the boy back into her care and out of a mental home where he was being mistreated. Virginia put 'Albert, the village idiot' into the play in *Between the Acts*: completely at home in the Elizabethan pageant, but causing the audience of local gentry some concern: 'It wasn't nice. Suppose he suddenly did something dreadful?'[4]

It was the connections with the local gentry she minded the most. Arguments over who might have stolen their butter from the kitchen (Leonard got into terrible trouble for accusing the innocent Miss Plumb, the local representative of St Dunstan's),[5] Annie coming round to ask her to be treasurer of the Women's Institute (she said no, then yes: 'If one lives in a village, one had better snatch its offerings'), PC Collins telling her off for 'showing a light' ('the official bully, so "rude", so rasping; the working man male dressed up . . . What a chance to give a lady a bit of his mind!'): these were bearable irritations.[6] But she preferred her involvement with 'the lower village world', she told Shena Simon: 'The gentry dont call.'[7] Most of the gentry thought of the Woolfs, with their literary visitors and bohemian artistic relations and Labour Party meetings, as 'red hot revolutionaries'.[8] But now they began to request her participation. (She told Clive she was 'composing an opera to be performed by the Rodmell musical society so soon as the executants have acquired musical instruments and learned to play on them.')[9] There was Mrs Chavasse, the doctor's widow from Birmingham, in her cottage filled with Jacobean furniture, who spent her money on tight dresses, liked to call herself 'a lone woman', and used to say things like 'Mrs Woolf is the brains'. She was the village boss, in charge of all the activities and president of the WI. There was Miss Emery, who lived in the cottage next to Monk's House with her friend Miss Dicksee and bred the dogs whose barking had irritated Virginia for years, and was so efficient in the First Aid meetings. There was Mrs Ebbs, the parson's unpopular wife (Ebbs had replaced old Hawkesford after he died in 1928), who tried to rouse up patriotic feeling in the village and directed all the plays ('My passion, Mrs Woolf, is for the stage') and who told Leonard that she read his wife's books 'for the beautiful English', but didn't understand them. There was Major Gardner (ex-railway engineer, Malaya) who had lived with his son and daughter in Thatched Cottage since 1934, and whom Virginia described as 'mild eyed' and 'sheep witted'.[10]

The Major's rather brow-beaten young daughter, Diana, a hopeful writer and painter who had just got her first story into *Horizon*, and was a keen supporter of the Rodmell Labour Party, was awed to have Virginia

Woolf living down the road (like 'having the goddess of writing round the corner', she described it) and terribly keen to please her. But she got little return for her youthful enthusiasm. Once when they were on the train together to Brighton, Diana could see that 'she didn't want me in the carriage . . . I was a nuisance'. At the Labour Party meetings, she watched Virginia come in late, sit with her legs wrapped round each other, roll her cigarettes, and listen, looking away, or interjecting in her slow beautiful voice: 'Are we then to believe . . . ?' Diana noted that the house was extremely cold and they were never offered anything to eat or drink at the meetings. Virginia resented the substitution of 'Miss Gardner instead of Elizabeth Bowen' as 'small beer'.[11] 'My old dislike of the village bites at me', she wrote in December. 'I envy houses alone in the fields. So petty so teasing are the claims of Gardners & Chavasses.'[12] In her worst moments the village seemed like a pond full of vampires and leeches, sucking, sucking, sucking at her blood.[13]

The watery image matched what she could see out of her window in the autumn of 1940. On 2 November, her inner feelings of being 'marooned' were dramatically acted out: a bomb had exploded in the river bank, the bank gave way, there was a very high tide and a gale, and the river burst its banks. All of the Ouse valley was flooded; the marshes and meadows were covered, and the water came right up to the bottom of their field. It was an amazingly beautiful sight – Mount Caburn reflected upside-down in the blue water like a cliff, flocks of gulls, leafless trees, a 'haystack in the floods' – seeming, to her delight, to take them back to a prehistoric landscape with no buildings, 'as it was in the beginning'.[14] 'Deluge' and 'island' became her key words: when the damp books and letters and manuscripts poured in from London, she called them a deluge too, and looked at her unpublished life's writing as at a flood: 'All this writing – what a deluge of words I've let loose – on paper only: I mean not printed.'[15]

Her pleasure in the flood was part of the consolation she took, as always, from the visual side of country life. She still took her long walks along the river and up to the Downs: the villagers were all used to seeing her setting off with her stick, alone, or with Sally the dog. The beauty of this countryside she had known for thirty years moved her more than ever in wartime. She went on noting her catalogue of things seen, the 'tune' played in this natural theatre: 'Hills & fields; I cant stop looking. October blooms; brown plough; & the fading & freshening of the marsh.' It all felt to her like a 'Shakespeare song'. Over and over she wrote it down this winter, her sense of being consoled by looking at England. It made her feel she didn't want to die yet.[16] But she also had elegiac feelings about the landscape. In the deep frost of January 1941, looking across at Asheham down, 'red, purple, dove blue grey', she called to mind one of her habitual phrases, 'Look your last on all things lovely'.[17] In this familiar setting, the routine of country days had their delight: picking apples, getting honey from the bees, cycling, helping Louie make butter, 'breakfast, writing, walking, tea, bowls, reading, sweets, bed.'[18]

All that quiet repetitive country feeling, threatened with destruction, went into *Between the Acts*. She finished the first draft in mid-November, and was pleased. Thinking of the butter Louie had just made, she described it to herself as 'more quintessential than the others. More milk skimmed off. A richer pat'.[19] By December she had begun to copy out the manuscript and revise it. But she had a number of other things on her mind, all interconnected. She had begun to write, in November, the '7 unhappy years' between Stella's death in 1897 and Leslie's death in 1904. In December she was talking to Octavia Wilberforce about her feelings for her family; by January she must have broken off her autobiography, as she was beginning then to complain she couldn't write. Through the winter, she was also writing stories, all concerned with family memories, family tensions, and moments of violent death. In October she wrote a black, sardonic story called 'The Legacy', about a widower (a right-wing politician) who discovers from reading his wife's diaries that she had fallen in love with a radical working man and committed suicide. It may have been in part suggested by her visit to Philip Morrell after Ottoline's death in 1938 (from whom her last legacy was an old shawl).[20] But the idea of posthumous enlightenment from the wife's diaries, and the description of the marriage, suggests something nearer home. 'As the years passed . . . he had become more and more absorbed in his work. And she, of course, was more often alone. It had been a great grief to her, apparently, that they had had no children.'[21] Like 'Lappin and Lapinova', and like the battle of Giles and Isa in *Between the Acts*, the story makes a harsh, ironic, exaggerated version of the dark side of her own marriage. *Harper's Bazaar* had commissioned 'The Legacy'; their refusal of it, in January, contributed to her depression.[22]

The day she finished the first version of *Between the Acts*, she started work on another story, 'The Symbol', in which a woman letter-writer in an Alpine resort witnesses the death of a party of climbers, and is obsessed and haunted by the presence of the mountain where they are killed. In the manuscript of 'The Symbol', the woman's feelings are more explicitly – and ominously – expressed than in the final typescript:

> To tell you the truth, I have practically no emotion left. I . . . have not even troubled to clean my nails. I have not done my hair. When I read a book I cannot finish it . . . Vanity of vanities, all is vanity. When the

748

doctor came I assumed a grave expression. Yet he guessed that I had only one wish – I cant even now write that down . . . Always to see that mountain. ~~It drives me mad.~~[23]

The story, which had been brewing for some time, was finally typed up on 1 March.[24] And she was still working on different versions of the story called 'The Searchlight', which was sometimes called 'What the telescope discovered', sometimes 'A Scene of the Past' (echoing her 'Sketch of the Past'), sometimes 'Incongruous' or 'Inaccurate Memories'. Its key scene was set in a lonely farmhouse on the Scottish borders, where a young man is looking at the stars through his telescope (while 'his father and mother were in the sitting room reading and sewing, scarcely speaking', not unlike Leslie and Julia). Turning his telescope to earth, he sees a couple kissing, and runs down from his tower to find the girl. This voyeuristic scene turns out to be an episode in the biography of Sir Henry Taylor, one of Julia Margaret Cameron's habitués at Freshwater, and in another version he is seen at Freshwater telling this story to a young girl. But the book in which this story appears (our narrator says) – perhaps the *Dictionary of National Biography* – has been destroyed by Hitler's bomb. What happens, she asks, to the 'ghosts' of lost stories? In the final version, the Taylor story, much reduced, haunts the memory of Mrs Ivimey, who is telling it as a piece of her family inheritance, while searchlights criss-cross over wartime London.[25]

The many drafts of 'The Searchlight' were mixed up with typed sheets of *Between the Acts* and notes for another book which she began to plan in September, to be called *Reading at Random* or *Turning the Page*. (In these winter months, the interplay of her different notebooks was more complicated and 'random' than ever. This was partly because, with all her notebooks and manuscripts arrived from London, and acutely conscious of the paper shortage, she was writing her notes on the back of old typescripts. She started her diary for 1941 in a cheap ring-bound notebook that had turned up from Mecklenburgh Square.)

Reading at Random was planned as a third *Common Reader*, or a new 'Phases of Fiction': in fact she started by calling it 'a Common History book'. It was to be a collection of essays which would make up a version of English literary history. This would give her an excuse, with the help of Lewes public library, 'to read from one end of lit. including biog; & range at will, consecutively.'[26] The idea was to describe English literature as a 'continuum', but to reverse the usual procedures of the literary criticism of her time, which prioritised the author and the text. This was to be a cultural criticism which (following the cultural and political readings of literary history in *A Room of One's Own*, *Orlando*, and *Three Guineas*) would construct literary history through 'the effect of the country upon writers'. It would insist on the social forces that create a national culture. 'The idea of the book is to find the end of a ball of string & wind out.'[27] One of her ideas was to explain to the painters (i.e. to Vanessa and Duncan) what it meant to be a writer 'thwarted by our society: interruptions: conditions'.[28]

Like *Between the Acts*, this was to be a post-Freudian history, which wanted to search for the prehistoric origins of literature and to pursue 'the continuity of tradition' from those origins to the present. As with her symbolic lily-pond in the novel, with its ancient fish swimming up to the surface, *Reading at Random* was to uncover 'the source of the sunk impulse . . . the hidden spring, the gush of water deep beneath the mud.'[29] So it resembled the difficult work she was undertaking in her unfinishable memoir, of analysing the childhood sources of her life as a writer.

In her notes for and draft of the book's first chapter, 'Anon', the connections with *Between the Acts* were very close. *Reading* was to begin (as *Between the Acts* was to end) with the prehistory of Britain, swamp and forest and wilderness, out of which came sounds, songs, rhythm, folk-tune, and an art whose key word was *anonymity*. As she mapped this first chapter, she enlarged on the romance of an ancient British forest with a voice emerging from its trees, the voice of Anon, with whom (just as in Miss la Trobe's play) the audience joined in as chorus. 'Anon' was a communal, unprinted author, unselfconscious, at one with his audience, who was to be 'killed' by the printing press. Out of these origins, she began to evolve a part-anthropological, part-social, part-psychological reading of literary history. 'Anon' turned into the ornate, public eloquence of Elizabethan prose, whose literature was still close enough to other arts – dress, music – to be unspecialised. With the Elizabethans, we move (as *Orlando* had wittily shown) into the pressures of patronage and social influence. The poet was torn between small aristocratic audiences reading in great rooms (with her visit to Penshurst in mind) and outdoor minstrels, ballads, and players. Gradually, individual personalities began to dominate. The characters in plays became more highly complex, less typical of the community. At last 'the playwright is replaced by the man who writes a book. The audience is replaced by the reader. Anon is dead.'

Her second chapter, 'The Reader' (of which she only wrote rough fragments) followed the death of Anon with the birth of the reader. How does a reader of Shakespeare emerge from an Elizabethan audience? How do we read Shakespeare now? By accumulating impressions? So the best way of describing this would be 'to collect notes, without trying to make them consistent'. The remark suggested that she was moving towards a new critical manner which might resemble the fragmentary method of her novel.

That new kind of criticism is metaphorically described – as she had suggested before in 'Street Haunting' – by a journey through her lost London, on a bus to London Bridge, gazing at the river, walking through the city. In another fragment, the transition of Elizabethan audience to reader is instanced by Nashe's *The Unfortunate Traveller* and by Burton's *Anatomy of Melancholy* – which has at its heart, she says, a man sitting in his study thinking of suicide.[30]

Plans for later parts of *Reading* included chapters on Goldsmith and Mme de Sévigné, whom she was reading now; on Henry James and the nineteenth century as 'the scene from which he took his material'; and on Coleridge. 'Skip present day', she told herself, like Miss la Trobe skipping centuries in her pageant, and come to 'A Chapter on the Future'.

But what was the chapter on the future to consist of? Where was this 'continuous history' of literature going now? She was asking herself perilous questions. If the literary work took its meaning only from its audience or reader, where was her audience now? And if anonymity was really preferable to the self-consciousness of the modern writer, what was the value of her life's work? Perhaps the living writer should make herself disappear completely.

She made some gallant attempts to counter the history book's anxieties by two pieces, written in January and February 1941, not on writers, but on two remarkable women, the actress Ellen Terry and Johnson's friend Mrs Thrale. The piece on Ellen Terry (written on the back of the manuscript of the Restoration Comedy play-scene in *Between the Acts*) celebrated her power as 'something in her that she did not understand; something that came surging up from the depths and swept her away in its clutches . . . It was the voice of her genius'. The essay on Mrs Thrale, published on 8 March, was a tribute to vigour and energy. Mrs Thrale's 'appetite for life was prodigious'. At her eightieth birthday party, 'she led the dance . . . and danced indefatigably till dawn'.[32]

Over the winter, up to the New Year, Leonard remembered thinking of her as contented and calm.[33] He would always maintain that the onset of her depression, in January, was very sudden. But it does seem, from the evidence of her writing and her circumstances, that (like the husband in 'The Legacy') he was no longer paying very close attention to her state of mind. There was so much else, after all, for him to be concerned about.[34] For all the pleasure she took in some aspects of their country life, from the start of the war she had been strained, apprehensive, depressed and on edge. The constant expectation of invasion, the air-raids, the stress of the publication of *Roger Fry*, the bombing of London and of their houses, the withdrawal to Rodmell, her feelings about the war, the challenges she was setting herself in her reading and writing, and her return in her memory to the most unhappy period of her childhood: all these factors were pressing down on her.

As early as November, while she was writing about her father, there is an ominous note in a letter to Ethel. She had gone out to look at the flood: 'Yesterday, thinking to explore, I fell headlong into a six foot hole, and came home dripping like a spaniel, or water rugg (thats Shakespeare.) How odd to be swimming in a field! . . . how I love this savage medieval water moved, all floating tree trunks and flocks of birds and a man in an old punt, and myself so eliminated of human feature you might take me for a stake walking.'[35] An accident, perhaps: but it is an alarming conjunction of wanting to be immersed in the savage water, and wanting to become anonymous and featureless. The next day she notes that Leonard is sitting by the fire with her, so she can't write (because they only lit a fire in the upstairs sitting-room, she often remarks in these winter months of having no room of her own); that the publication of 'The Leaning Tower' in *Folios of New Writing* has given her a feeling of exposure, like 'a gaping raw wound'; that the news of last night's raids on Coventry and London are 'seeping' into her mind. Then she adds, darkly: 'I am a mental specialist now.' She meant she had to watch herself, analyse herself (it was a popular term for an analyst), persuade herself to 'enjoy every single day'.[36]

A month later, in December, she makes a detailed litany of their wartime privations, which is stoical and matter of fact, but gives off an underlying tone of discomfort, and a strong sense of being 'marooned'. She lists the shortages (margarine, sugar, pastry, meat, milk, petrol, clothes), the slowness of the post, the difficulty of feeding visitors or making journeys, the small time-consuming drudgeries of making butter or doing the black-out, eating pickled eggs and pretending 'they dont taste differently', the daily expectation of invasion. 'We dont go hungry or cold. But luxury is nipped off, & hospitality . . . We are of course marooned here by the bombs in London . . . A certain old age feeling sometimes makes me think I cant spend force as I used. And my hand shakes. Otherwise we draw breath as usual.'[37]

It was a terribly cold winter. The house, as well as being still in a mess (she was increasingly frustrated at not being able to get at the books she wanted)[38] was cold and damp. Louie knitted her a warm pullover, but she complained repeatedly of the cold: 'my hands are so cold this bitter morning out in the garden room that I cant move a pen.'[39] The tremor in her hand, which had begun a few years before, now got much worse. In December, Mabel Haskins finally left Rodmell and went to live with her sister. It was a relief, the end at last of live-in servants (though Louie came in every day) but it meant that Virginia was doing more housework and more cooking. Because of this, and because of the food shortages, she thought more about every meal. Gifts of extra food – butter from Vita on Christmas Day, cream and milk from Octavia and Elizabeth Robins's farm, where they kept Jersey cows – were received with comic rapture. The business of bicycling to Lewes to shop or ordering the food from the van which still delivered became more important; trying to invent puddings got harder. 'Food becomes an obsession'; 'I make up imaginary meals.'[40] At the same time, she was eating less and less. Octavia, who began to be a regular visitor at Rodmell from November onwards, was appalled by how 'thin and half-starved' they both looked, but particularly Virginia, 'thin as a razor', her hands always as cold as icicles.[41]

Her anxieties and discomforts became less manageable to her. She was still worrying about money. The intrusion of village life exacerbated her more and more.[42] There were a few visits from the outside world and a few presents from friends (one, very bizarre, a bust of Voltaire sent by limousine from Margot Oxford, who was thinking of her latter end and wanted to leave this object to Virginia in her will). But she felt increasingly isolated. Petrol rationing meant she only saw Vanessa occasionally, Ethel and Vita were mostly out of reach, and Angelica had gone to live with Bunny. (The Woolfs visited them once in November at their rented farmhouse near Selmeston; Virginia thought their relationship 'grotesque', and lamented the loss of her 'old family ease' with Angelica.)[43] Though the concentrated raids and air-battles had ended, incendiary bombs were still going off in Sussex. The war was not being won. The Battle of the Atlantic between destroyers and U-boats continued; the British were fighting the Italians in north-east Africa and the Germans in Greece. But the attempt to form a Southern Balkan bloc of Yugoslavia, Greece and Turkey was to prove a disastrous failure. By mid-March, Hitler was about to attack and invade Yugoslavia, and Rommel was launching his desert offensive. The invasion was thought more likely than ever.[44]

It was at this point, at the turn of the year, as she was revising 'Pointz Hall' again, that she began to feel she could no longer write. She told Octavia at the end of December that she thought it was 'a completely worthless book' and that she had 'lost all power over words, cant do a thing with them.'[45] To herself, the next day, starting her new 1941 diary, she wrote: 'What does it matter, writing too many pages. No printer to consider, no public.'[46] She went to London and wandered through the ruined city. *Harper's* rejected her story. She heard of the death of Joyce, 'about a fortnight younger than I am', and remembered her reactions to

Ulysses, and Katherine and Tom enthusing about it: 'This goes back to a pre-historic world.' Now 'all the gents' would start in with their opinions, '& the books, I suppose, take their place in the long procession'.[47] She could not stop thinking about her family and her childhood. She told Octavia that she was sorting family papers, 'love letters from her father to her mother', and that Leonard was 'tired out by my interest in my family & all it brings back'.[48] She wrote to Ethel about sexual shame and sexual abuse: 'But why should I be writing these sexual speculations now?'[49] It was part of the violent depression and sense of worthlessness that was pouring over her. 'I cant believe in being anyone', she said to Ethel. She felt unable to work and that her work was useless. She decided to take physical exercise instead, and started 'clearing out the kitchen'. She told everyone who came to the house – Diana Gardner, Octavia – about her physical exertions. She felt she was living 'like a moth in a towel'. She read doggedly, 'like a donkey going round & round in a well'. She told herself not to be 'engulfed' in this 'trough of despair'.[50]

In early February there were a few distractions. She took on Desmond's class-critique, made in the *Sunday Times*, of her 'Leaning Tower' essay, arguing (as she had argued against Ben Nicolson's accusation of élitism) that her education gave her the right to say 'we' when she talked to the Workers' Educational Association. They went to Letchworth to look at the Press in its new home, and on the way to see Dadie Rylands and Pernel Strachey in Cambridge. The visit was like 'an oasis', she told Dadie.[51] Elizabeth Bowen came to see her, and they were joking and relaxed together. Vita came with Enid Jones – enough visitors to make her feel 'in a fret', she told Ethel. When Octavia came for tea on 28 February, she was fretting over whether to accept Clive's invitation to lunch with the Hamish Hamiltons at Blackboys. Leonard told her not to go: 'Youd be in their power & Clive once he got talking might go on for hours & you'd not be able to break away & get back.'[52]

On 25 February, she and Leonard went to Brighton for one of his lectures. In the lavatory of the Sussex Grill at lunch-time, she heard a scrap of conversation between 'two common little tarts'; later, in Fuller's tea-shop, she listened to, and then wrote down, a conversation between two women eating cakes, a disgusted and disgusting sketch of two 'fat white slugs'.[53] She began to write something called 'The Watering Place', about a town full of the smell of fish, and the women talking in the lavatory. One cancelled version of the sketch emphasised the smelliness of their talk: 'The words had a strong savour of decaying fish. There was a strong scent of the old rubbish heap . . . For there is a very strong smell about human beings: at watering places. It infects everything.'[54]

Around this time, she wrote other fragments. One had no title:

> The woman who lives in this room has the look of someone without any
> consecutive [?] part. She has no settled relations with her kind. She is like
> a piece of seaweed that floats this way, then that way. For the fish who
> float into this cave are always passing through . . . She inhabits a
> fluctuating water world . . . constantly tossed up and down like a piece of
> sea weed. She has no continuity. The rush of water is always floating her
> up and down.

One was called 'Winter's night':

> It is strange that the sun shd be shining; and the birds singing. For here, it
> is coal black: here in the little cave in which I sit.
> Such was the complaint of a woman who had all her faculties entire.
> ~~She did not not sufficiently. She had no grasp of~~ [55]

Pointz Hall was finished, and renamed *Between the Acts*, on 25 February.
She gave it to Leonard to read. She could not write her history book; she
could not write anything except those revolted, paralysed fragments.
Repeatedly, she noted 'blank space in front of her', the waiting for the
invasion like sitting in a doctor's waiting-room, the feeling of there being no
future, the sense of there being 'no echo . . . only waste air'.[56] She felt as if
everyone had vanished from her life. She tried to rally herself by writing
letters to Stephen and Tom, letters which spoke of her sense of 'how
vanished everyone is', and a letter to Ethel proposing a visit.[57] They went to
Brighton again; there were a few visitors, including Angelica and Bunny.
She told herself to 'observe', not to be sucked in, to do practical things like
planning meals and beating carpets and scrubbing the kitchen floor.[58]

Leonard, by now, was anxious, but did not know what to do, or whether
to do anything. On 12 March, Octavia Wilberforce came to tea, and she and
Virginia talked for a long time. In February Virginia had asked Octavia if
she could write a sketch of her life, perhaps to be called 'English Youth' – to
be written 'anonymously'. This was supposed to be a 'fact-finding' visit for
Octavia's biography, but Virginia talked mostly about herself. She told
Octavia – and it was quite obvious to her – that she was desperately
depressed. Her book was no good; she felt useless. She had asked if she
could do fire-watching duties, like Leonard, but the village 'wouldn't allow
her' to. She talked again to Octavia about her family, how Leslie had
behaved after Julia and Stella's death, how it had affected her whole life,
how 'she had never had any enjoyment of my body'. In the same breath, she
gave Octavia the impression that she had 'adored' her half-brother George

Duckworth. From this conversation, Octavia took the impression that she was 'desperate & scared & haunted by her father'. She too had had a domineering and bullying father, and the only paragraph of 'English Youth' Virginia must have written around now described the father beating his daughter on her bare bottom for saying 'Damn' at the tea-table.[59]

Two days later, on the 14th, they went to London and had lunch with John Lehmann at St Stephen's Tavern, overlooking Parliament Square. John observed that Virginia was extremely tense, and that her hands shook. Leonard told him that she had finished her novel, 'but when I turned to congratulate her she began to talk about the book in great agitation, trying to damp down my enthusiasm and saying that it was no good at all and obviously couldn't be published'. She and Leonard argued over this for some time; John asked to see it. She said she wanted some reading to do, and asked to look at manuscripts submitted to *New Writing*.[60]

That week there were more incendiary bombs near Rodmell. On Tuesday 18th, she went out walking in the rain, and came back dripping wet and shivering. Leonard met her in the garden 'looking ill and shaken', and asked her what had happened, and she said she had slipped and fallen into one of the dykes.[61] It is possible that that day she wrote a letter to Leonard, dated 'Tuesday':

Dearest,
I feel certain that I am going
mad again: I feel we cant go
through another of these terrible times.
And I shant recover this time. I begin
to hear voices, and cant concentrate.
So I am doing what seems the best thing to do. You have
given me
the greatest possible happiness. You
have been in every way all that anyone
could be. I dont think two
people could have been happier till
this terrible disease came. I cant
fight it any longer, I know that I am
spoiling your life, that without me you
could work. And you will I know.
You see I cant even write this properly. I
cant read. What I want to say is that
I owe all the happiness of my life to you.
You have been entirely patient with me &
incredibly good. I want to say that –
everybody knows it. If anybody could [new page]

756

have saved me it would have been you.
Everything has gone from me but the
certainty of your goodness. I
cant go on spoiling your life any longer. I dont think two
people
could have been happier than we have been.
V.[62]

This generous, careful, precise letter, which if written on that day was hidden and kept in reserve, is not the letter of an irrational or mad person, but of a person in despair, with no sense of a future, and suffering from a terrible fear of the possibility of a breakdown with no prospect of recovery. The writing of the letter, and the act it presaged, though an act *in extremis*, was rational, deliberate and courageous.

Leonard was very uneasy after the encounter in the garden, and noted in his diary that Virginia was 'unwell'. On the Thursday, two things happened. Virginia wrote to John Lehmann that she was sure *Between the Acts* was no good – 'Its much too slight and sketchy' – and she had decided, as he had requested at lunch, to send him the typescript for his judgement.[63] And Vanessa, who had been alerted by Leonard that Virginia was not well, came to tea. When she got back to Charleston, she wrote Virginia a characteristically affectionate but ruthless letter, which may have increased Virginia's anxiety over what it would mean to have a complete breakdown in wartime:

I have been thinking over our talk today and I feel as if I hadn't made myself nearly clear enough. You *must* be sensible, which means you must accept the fact that Leonard and I can judge better than you can. It's true I haven't seen very much of you lately, but I have often thought you looked very tired and I'm sure that if you let yourself collapse and do nothing you would feel tired, and be only too glad to rest a little. You're in the state when one never admits what's the matter, but you must not go and get ill just now.

What shall we do when we're invaded if you are a helpless invalid – what should I have done all these last 3 years if you hadn't been able to keep me alive and cheerful. You don't know how much I depend on you. Do please be sensible for that if for no other reason. Do what Leonard advises and don't go scrubbing floors, which for all I care can remain unscrubbed forever. Both Leonard and I have always had reputations for sense and honesty, so you must believe in us. Your VB. I shall ring up some time to find out what is happening.[64]

Vanessa told Clive, who wrote to Mary: 'Virginia seems to be getting into one of her bad phases again. Do you remember, she was in one at the beginning of the last war . . . It seems that war gets on her nerves, which is not surprising and not uncommon. Only her nerves are diseased. It may all blow over . . .'[65]

Soon after Vanessa's letter, Virginia also had one from John, who said that he had unfortunately ignored her protestations at their lunch, and had already advertised *Between the Acts* in the Spring Books number of the *New Statesman & Nation*: 'and it is now too late to reverse the wheels.'[66]

On Friday 21 March, she rearranged Leslie's books, and scrubbed the kitchen floors. Octavia came to tea. She talked again about the worthlessness of her work – how her two 'biographies', *Orlando* and *Roger Fry*, were both 'failures'. How she couldn't write and couldn't do anything useful. Octavia, in her sensible way, said that she ought to stick to her work, and that her obsession with her family – 'all this family business' – was 'all nonsense . . . balderdash.'[67] Virginia asked if she could catalogue her books for her: she wanted a menial job. On Saturday 22nd, she wrote a little note to Vita, ending: 'When shall we come? Lord knows – '.[68] On Sunday 23rd, she wrote one letter, perhaps two. One was to John, saying that her head was too 'stupid' to read the manuscripts she had requested from *New Writing*. She may also have written to Vanessa, telling her that she had 'loved her letter', bidding her goodbye, and saying, as she had (or would) in her letter to Leonard, that she was 'certain' that she was going mad again and was 'always hearing voices'. That Leonard had been 'astonishingly good' – that she wanted Vanessa to assure him of this – that she could no longer think clearly – that she wanted to tell her what she and the children had meant to her. 'I have fought against it, but I cant any longer.' She dated it, Sunday, but she did not send it. She and Leonard went to tea with Mrs Chavasse in the village, and Virginia looked at her from the other end of the room as if across 'an icy sea'. 'And then there was nothing.' This diary entry, written on the Monday, was written in the same short, fragmented, jagged lines as the letter to Leonard, with many crossings out. She added a few notes: on the cold 'sea side' feeling in the air, on Nessa at Brighton ('& I am imagining how it wd be if we could infuse souls'), on how she might write Octavia's story, on letters received but at this moment unanswerable from Shena Simon and Octavia. At the end, written close up under the penultimate line, she scribbled 'L. is doing the rhododendrons'.[70]

Probably on the Monday or Tuesday, she had a letter from Forster, saying that he had been rereading *Jacob's Room* ('These are great times and occasionally one stretches oneself toward being in scale with them, and is helped by work like yours'),[71] and one from John, praising *Between the Acts*. At some point in the early part of this week, Leonard tried to persuade her that she needed a 'real rest cure'.[72] On the Wednesday, Leonard rang Octavia, and said he was extremely worried. He did not know what to do – to get in nurses, to try to insist on a rest cure. Could he make an appointment for Virginia to see Octavia in Brighton? Octavia, who had just gone down with 'flu, agreed, but was anxious and unsure of what she could do.

On the Thursday morning, the 27th, Virginia wrote to John telling him not to publish *Between the Acts* – 'its too silly & trivial'. She would revise it: 'I didnt realise how bad it was till I read it over.'[73] She showed the letter to Leonard, who enclosed it inside one of his own on the Friday morning, telling John that 'she is on the verge of a complete nervous break down and is seriously ill'. He asked him to write to Virginia saying that they would put off publication until the autumn.[74]

On the Thursday afternoon at 3.15 Leonard took Virginia to Octavia's surgery at her house in Montpelier Crescent in Brighton. Virginia was resistant, irritated – '*quite* unnecessary to have come' – but seemed to Octavia to be 'sleep-walking'. Octavia asked her to undress and as she began to obey she asked Octavia to promise not to 'order' her a rest cure. Octavia gave her a physical examination – as usual Virginia's hands were ice-cold, and she was extremely thin, but she was strong and restless – and told her to trust her, to believe that resting and not working were the only cures: she had been ill before, she had been cured before. If she would 'collaborate', Octavia urged her, 'there's nobody in England I'd like more to help'.[75] After the examination Octavia talked to Leonard separately (while they were talking there was an explosion nearby, but they were both too preoccupied to take any notice of it), telling him Virginia should rest and not write. One 'look' she caught from Virginia, before they left, alarmed her terribly. That evening, Leonard listened to a BBC recording of Beethoven's *Appassionata* piano sonata.[76]

On Friday 28 March Virginia went out to the lodge in the morning. It was still cold, but spring was beginning: there was already 'a flood of yellow flowers' in the garden.[77] She wrote another letter to Leonard, similar, but not identical, to the one she had probably written on Tuesday 18th. This one she did not date.

> Dearest,
> I want to tell you that you have
> given me complete happiness. No one
> could have done more than you have done.
> Please believe that.
> But I know that I shall never get over

this: & I am wasting your life. It is this madness.
Nothing anyone says can persuade me.
You can work, & you will be much
better without me. You see I cant
write this even, which shows I am right.
All I want to say is that until this
disease came on we were perfectly
happy. It was all due to you.
No one could have been so good as
you have been. From the very
first day till now.
[She added with fresh ink]: Everyone knows that.
V.

Turning the page, she wrote up the left-hand side:

You will find Roger's letters to the Maurons in the
writing table drawer in the Lodge. Will
you destroy all my papers.[78]

At 11 a.m., Leonard went out to the lodge (she left the letter to him lying
there on the writer's block). She said she was going to do some housework
and then go for a walk before lunch. They went into the house, and Leonard
told her to rest for half an hour. Then he left her, to work in his study.
Louie, who was working in the house, saw her go out to the lodge, return to
the house, put on her fur-coat and take her stick, and go out again. Either
when she went indoors with Leonard, or when she came back again for her
coat, she must have left the earlier letters, in blue envelopes marked
'Leonard' and 'Vanessa', in the upstairs sitting-room, on the table. She
walked out of the garden, through the gate at the end, past the church, down
to the river, and along it a little way towards the bridge at Southease. One of
the villagers, Bert Skinner, working outside, saw her go, but thought
nothing of it. A farm-worker, John Hubbard, who was cleaning out ditches
by an osier bed, saw her walk towards the river at about twenty minutes to
twelve. He had often seen her there before, but usually in the afternoons. He
watched her go for a minute or two, and then went home for his dinner. The
river was running very fast and high – the banks of the Ouse are always bare
because of the speed of the flow. She picked up a large stone from the bank,
put it in her pocket, let go of her stick, and walked or jumped into the river.
She could swim, but she allowed herself to be drowned.

At one o'clock, Louie rang the bell for lunch. Leonard went upstairs to the sitting-room to listen to the news. He saw the two letters, opened his, read it, ran downstairs, looked for her in the house, said to Louie that he thought something had happened to 'Mrs Woolf', and had she seen her leave the house, ran out, looked for her in the garden and lodge, ran down to the river. The tide was on the turn. Almost at once he found her footprints on the bank and her stick floating in the water. Louie went to find Percy, who went for PC Collins at the Rodmell police station. The policeman went down to Southease bridge and found Leonard, about a mile north of the bridge, taking the stick out of the water. Frank Dean and his son came down to the river with ropes and grabs. The policeman 'dived and dived and dived', while Leonard paced up and down on the bank. 'He was a brave man', Frank Dean thought.[79] In a remote hope that she might have gone up to the Downs, Leonard went up to one of her places, the ruined house called 'Mad Misery', and back along the meadows and the river banks. After he got back, Vanessa happened to come over from Charleston. He told her what had happened, and drove her back.[80] By 6.30 he was back in the house; Octavia rang and he told her: 'A dreadful catastrophe has happened.' In his diary, he made one indecipherable mark, and recorded the mileage for the day. He wrote a letter to Vita that evening to tell her what had happened, so that she would not hear it first on the news.[81] The next day, while Frank Dean and the police went on dragging the river with ropes from the forge, he tried to work, and wrote to John Lehmann. Octavia came to see him and they talked, upstairs, about the history of Virginia's breakdowns. As Octavia was going downstairs in front of him, she said, 'Nobody else could have kept her going so long.' Turning at the foot of the stairs, she saw that he was beginning to weep.[82]

The news began to spread. Vita, who had not been in close contact with Virginia for a few weeks, told Harold, greatly distressed, that Vanessa and Leonard had both written to her, explaining that Virginia had been under strain and 'was terrified of going mad again': 'Why, oh why, did he leave her alone knowing all this? He must be reproaching himself terribly, poor man . . . She must have been quite out of her mind or she would never have brought such sorrow and horror on Leonard and Vanessa.' Harold immediately went down to Sissinghurst to be with her, but they spent the evening without making any reference to Virginia's death.[83] Clive wrote to Mary that though 'one hoped against hope for a day or two that she might have wandered off crazily, and might be found sleeping in a barn or buying biscuits in a village-shop', the chances of this seemed increasingly remote. Vanessa, he told her, was withstanding the shock better than could have been expected; Leonard seemed, on the surface, 'perfectly calm'. 'For the rest of us, for you and for me, Duncan, the children, Vita, Desmond, it's an appalling loss . . . For Virginia herself – I dont know . . . If she felt that she was in for another two years of what she had been through before, only to wake up to a world which will be the world another two years of war has made of it, I only wonder at her courage.'[84]

On 1 April, when the body had still not been found, Leonard wrote a letter to the editor of *The Times*, Geoffrey Dawson, telling him what he thought had happened. On 3 April *The Times* carried a report on its main news page, next to the headlines 'Half Abyssinia Conquered', 'Pause in Axis Plans' and 'Italians urging Moderation': 'We announce with regret that it must now be presumed that Mrs Leonard Woolf (Virginia Woolf, the novelist and essayist), who has been missing since last Friday, has been drowned in the Sussex Ouse at Rodmell, near Lewes. We also regret to announce the death of Lord Rockley, who had a long and distinguished career in Parliament and was well known in the City.'[85] On its obituary page, above the obituary of Lord Rockley, it led with five paragraphs on 'Mrs Virginia Woolf: Novelist, Essayist and Critic', summing up her work thus: 'As a novelist she showed a highly original form of sensitivity to mental impressions, the flux of which, in an intelligent mind, she managed to convey with remarkable force and beauty.'[86] That night the BBC announced her death on the evening news. The local press picked up the news, and the Brighton *Southern Weekly News* put this report on its front page:

RIVER OUSE DRAGGED FOR MISSING AUTHORESS: Unavailing search has been made of the countryside around Rodmell for Mrs Virginia Woolf, the authoress, who disappeared from her Rodmell home on Friday last, and the River Ouse in the vicinity has been dragged without result. The river is tidal at the point where Mrs Woolf is believed to have disappeared. Mrs Woolf was very fond of walking alongside the Ouse. Her husband told a reporter on Wednesday: 'Mrs Woolf is presumed to be dead. She went for a walk on Friday leaving a letter behind and it is thought she has been drowned.' Her body has, however, not been recovered.[87]

On the 6th, Desmond MacCarthy wrote a tender tribute in the *Sunday Times*, praising her 'rare and beautiful mind', her lyrical prose, and her 'intensely subjective' response to life. Vita published a poem 'In Memoriam Virginia Woolf', calling her 'Frugal, austere, fine proud . . . Her fluttered spirit, delicate and soft/Yet kept a sting beneath the brushing wing'. On the 9th, Margot Oxford wrote an extravagant, personal 'tribute' in *The Times* ('No woman ever cared less about her appearance . . . an enchanting companion . . . radiant smile . . . untouchable gift of imagination . . . twilight mind.')[88] The next day, Stephen Spender published a tribute in the

Listener, speaking of her irreparable loss, and describing the 'acute nervous tension in her own mind between a too great sensitivity which tended to disintegrate into unco-ordinated impressions, and a noble and sane determination not to lose hold of the central thread'.[89]

Everyone who had known her wrote sad, shocked letters, to each other and to Leonard. Adrian, who had only heard it from the BBC announcement, wrote to Vanessa without expressing any emotion, and moving on to speak of his own war-time life in the same letter.[90] Ethel, who had been ill and had not written lately to Virginia (she had three more years to live) told Vanessa how wise and courageous she thought Virginia had been, and how she had been unable to write a tribute for Raymond Mortimer: 'I had to say *I couldnt*, touched as I was by his suggesting it. Later perhaps – but my god not now. You see it was not only that I loved her; it was that my life [was] literally based on her.'[91] Tom Eliot wrote to his friend John Hayward that, though he had not known her work well, he always felt at ease with her. She was a kind of pin which held a lot people together, and gave them a sense of belonging, of meaning; and that these people would now become separate individuals.[92] Violet Dickinson, in a series of letters to Vanessa, tried her best to understand it: 'I think she was dreadfully bothered by the noise and aeroplanes and headaches. One can understand exactly what she dreaded; turning it all over in her mind during those walks on the downs; she ran down very quickly if nourishment was lacking to her brain . . . Nothing could have been done, and tho' she can spin no more fascinating fairy tales for us one feels that she is out of much misery.'[93] Julian's Chinese friend Sue Ling wrote to ask Vanessa what had happened. Vanessa replied:

> She had been getting ill for some time and felt that she was going out of her mind – I think it was true that she was very near it, but if only one could have kept her safe for a time she would have got better. It had happened so before and she had always recovered. This time I knew nothing and never suspected the danger.[94]

Leonard received over 200 letters. They came from old friends, acquaintances, Rodmell inhabitants, servants, other writers, all praising her and describing her qualities (the word used most often was 'kind') and assuring him he had done what he could. Nelly and Louie wrote: 'We are both very sorry for you.'[95] Someone wrote from a lunatic asylum saying that 'its not madness to take ones life. Its ones right if one cares to use it and that is the sole judgment of the person concerned. the only right we have left.' One of the most perceptive condolences came from Shena Simon, who said that knowing Virginia had made her look at problems – for instance the relations of men and women – from a new angle. 'Her attitude was so much saner and so much more fundamental than any I had met before.' She was struck, reading the tributes, by how little reference had been made to *A Room of One's Own* and *Three Guineas*. 'In war time many people are reluctant to listen to the truth about it but the time will come.'[96]

Leonard replied carefully to each of these letters. But to himself, on a scrap of paper, he wrote:

> They say: 'Come to tea and let us comfort you.' But it's no good. One must be crucified on one's own private cross.
> It is a strange fact that a terrible pain in the heart can be interrupted by a little pain in the fourth toe of the right foot.
> I know that V. will not come across the garden from the lodge, and yet I look in that direction for her. I know that she is drowned and yet I listen for her to come in at the door. I know that it is the last page & yet I turn it over. There is no limit to one's stupidity and selfishness.[97]

Vita went to visit him on the 8th. They had tea; the house was full of Virginia's things. She said, 'I do not like your being here alone like this. He turned those piercing blue eyes on me and said It's the only thing to do.'[98]

On 18 April, a group of teenagers, two girls and three boys, on a cycling trip out from Lewes, decided to stop for lunch by the river near Asheham. They saw what they thought was a log, floating downstream, and threw stones at it to get it ashore. One of the boys waded in, and they realised it was a woman's body in a fur coat. They went for the police. Collins went down, got the body out of the water, and took it to Newhaven Mortuary. He noted that the watch had stopped at 11.45. Leonard went to identify the body, and discovered then that she had weighed her pocket with a stone.[99] The inquest took place the next day, in Newhaven. Leonard went alone, and gave the coroner, Edward Hoare, the suicide notes. The body, it seemed, had not travelled far; it had got wedged either under the piers of the bridge at Southease or in one of the holes dug under the fences on the river banks to prevent cattle getting into the river at low tide. Eventually it had got dislodged, and had floated a little way downstream. The coroner read out some of the 'Tuesday' suicide note, misquoting it, and interrogated Leonard as to the order of events. Leonard's statement gave details of the order of events on 28 March, said that his wife had suffered from 'acute neurasthenia' all her life, and that he had been very concerned about her for some weeks before, but that she had refused to go to bed as he had urged. On the form of the 'Inquisition', the coroner wrote that Adeline Virginia Woolf, authoress, wife of Leonard Sidney Woolf a publisher, was found dead on 18 April in the River Ouse, and that 'the cause of Death was

Immersion in the River on 28 March 1941 by her own act so killing herself while the balance of her mind was disturbed', and 'do further say that death was due to drowning'.[100] The death certificate, which was registered in Lewes on 21 April, repeated these phrases under 'Cause of Death'.

The local reporters were in court, and during the next week wrote up the event in their papers, the *Sussex Daily News* and the *Southern Weekly News*. 'SUSSEX NOVELIST VICTIM OF WAR STRAIN', read one; 'I OWE ALL MY HAPPINESS TO YOU: VIRGINIA WOOLF'S LAST NOTE TO HUSBAND', read another. The reports replicated the Coroner's mistake:

'I feel I am going mad. I cannot go through these terrible times. I hear voices and cannot concentrate on my work.' This is an extract from a note left to her husband by Mrs Adeline Virginia Woolf, aged 59, the authoress, of Monks House, Rodmell, whose body was recovered from the river Ouse at Rodmell early on Saturday. Mrs Woolf disappeared from her home on 28th March. At the inquest at Newhaven . . . Mr Woolf said he saw his wife in the writing room at their house at 11 a.m. on 28th March. In reply to his question she said that after doing some housework she thought she would go for a walk. Mr Woolf said he had been concerned about his wife's health for 2 or 3 weeks. On 2 occasions she had had breakdowns. 3 weeks ago she became depressed and thought she was losing her power to work. In the note addressed to Mr Woolf, in addition to the extract already given, appeared the following: 'I cannot fight any longer. I know I am spoiling your life. You have been perfectly good to me . . .' Recording a verdict of 'suicide while the balance of her mind was disturbed', the Coroner said there was a history of a certain nervous disposition in the deceased's mind. 'We all knew her and her writing,' he said, 'and a responsible person like her must have felt the period of the war and the general beastliness of things more than most people, and it probably brought on a recurrence of the old trouble.' The Coroner expressed sympathy with Mr Woolf.[101]

The same sort of reports appeared in the nationals, the *Guardian* and elsewhere.

The cremation took place at the Downs Crematorium in Brighton; Leonard had asked Frank Dean to arrange it. He went to it alone. Instead of the 'Cavatina' from Beethoven's string quartet opus 130, which they had agreed would be a suitable accompaniment to a cremation, the music played, to Leonard's displeasure, was 'The Dance of the Blessed Spirits' from Gluck's *Orfeo*. He played the 'Cavatina' to himself that evening. The ashes, which, also to his surprise, had been presented to him in a pretentiously elaborate casket, he buried under one of the two great elms in the garden which they had called 'Leonard' and 'Virginia'. He had a tablet made with a quotation from *The Waves* ('Against you I will fling myself unvanquished and unyielding, O Death!') to place over the ashes.[102]

The following week, Leonard went on, in a state of numbness, trying to organise his life. He wrote to Pritchard, the solicitor from Mecklenburgh Square, asking him to deal with the will and with settling the securities and shares Virginia had had in her name, and the two bank accounts, one joint, one of her own at the Midland Bank in Russell Square.[103] But the coroner's report was now creating a distressing aftermath. Leonard had to write to people all over again, explaining that the coroner had misquoted the note and that the newspaper reports 'are completely inaccurate'.[104] He received an anonymous letter which said: 'Sir, Thank the Coroner for being kind in his verdict.'[105] On 27 April, the wife of the Bishop of Lincoln wrote an outraged letter to *The Sunday Times*, responding to the report of the coroner's remark about feeling 'the general beastliness of things more than most people'. 'What right has anyone to make such an assertion? . . . He belittles those who are carrying on unselfishly for the sake of others . . . Many people possibly even more "sensitive" have lost their all and yet they take their part nobly in this fight for God against the devil. Where would we all be if we listen to and sympathise with this sort of "I cannot carry on"?'[106] Leonard wrote to the newspaper (so did Desmond MacCarthy, more intemperately), correcting the misreporting and the Bishop's wife's response to it, and explaining that Virginia Woolf killed herself because she thought she was about to have a mental breakdown. 'Like everyone else, she felt the general strain of the war, and the return of her illness was no doubt partly due to that strain. But the words of her letter and everything which she ever said prove that she took her life, not because she could not "carry on", but because she thought she was going mad again and would not this time recover.'[107] The Bishop's wife wrote to Leonard to apologise, but the story of the feeble, delicate lady authoress giving up on the war-effort began to be built into the posthumous myths of Virginia Woolf. That image of a sensitive, aesthetic, nervous creature, too fragile for her own good, was being processed, in these same few weeks after her death, by the (mostly male) writers who wrote their tributes to her, culminating in the edition of *Horizon* dedicated to her work in May. When *Between the Acts* was published (with minor typographical alterations by Leonard, but otherwise in the form of the final typescript) on 17 July, the respectful reviews which greeted it persisted in the image of a thin-blooded, lyrical, delicate, sensitive, exquisitely imaginative writer, described by one reviewer as 'a war casualty'.[108]

The posthumous publication of *Between the Acts* was agreed by Leonard and John Lehmann as the start of a careful, deliberate campaign to keep

Virginia Woolf in the public's eye. When Leonard went, soon after her death, to look for the final version of her last essay on Mrs Thrale, he found among the 'immense numbers of typewritten sheets lying about her room', 'several revisions of it in the waste-paper-basket' and 'several more revisions in going through her papers'.[109] It was the beginning of his work, for the next twenty-eight years of his life, as Virginia Woolf's executor, archivist and editor. One of his first duties after the inquest was to fulfil the terms of her will in giving one of her manuscripts to Vita: after some debate, she accepted the two volumes of *Mrs Dalloway* (and it took him some time to find the first half).[110] Even before her body had been found, he had started to talk to John Lehmann about how they would deal with the vast amount of unpublished material. He planned to 'husband' it, to bring it out at carefully timed intervals 'over a long period of years'.[111] Leonard would make the decisions which set the terms of her posthumous reception and reputation: that the diary should be produced in severely edited form, as *A Writer's Diary*, in 1953; that the essays should be published in selections without dates or annotations; that the first biography should be written by a member of the family. His 'husbanding' of her posthumous resources controlled our access to Virginia Woolf for many years, for good and ill.

The war continued; millions upon millions of people died violent deaths. Virginia Woolf's death seemed to her contemporaries a part of the darkness of the war, and the war closed over it. In the decade that followed, her writing and her life were, not neglected, but identified with a period of English culture which had passed. It was not until years later, in the 1960s, that she began to be transformed into a heroine, an icon and a myth, for a wider and wider circle of readers. So, from the moment of her death, she 'became her admirers' (as Auden said of Yeats) – and her detractors. She took on another existence in the posthumous life she had so vividly anticipated, for instance in her words on Katherine Mansfield in 1923: 'Do people always get what they deserve, & did KM do something to deserve this cheap posthumous life?'[112] As she had once said of her own dead friends, she went on living and changing after death:

> So we discuss suicide, and the ghosts as I say, change so oddly in my mind; like people who live, & are changed by what one hears of them.[113]

BIOGRAPHER

I was born in February 1948, three years after the end of the war and seven years after Virginia Woolf's death. I grew up in a literary household which had all her books: I can't remember not having heard of her. When I was eight or nine I went away on a visit (this was rather unusual for me) and stayed the night with friends. There was one book on the table by my bed. It was the 1951 orange Penguin edition of *The Waves*, with, on the cover, the price, 1s.6d., the words 'Fiction' in orange letters along the sides, and, on either side of the image of a penguin, the words 'Complete' and 'Unabridged'. On the back was a brief biography of Virginia Woolf underneath the 1929 Lenare photograph. I don't think I was aware of any of these details, but I do vividly remember starting to read the first few pages, without understanding much of what was going on, and feeling as if I had happened on a secret language which belonged to me. It was part of the excitement of being away from home on my own. This was my discovery. I didn't get very far, and I don't remember my subsequent return to the novel. But that sense of a secret discovery remained with me, and left an echo-track in later readings.

As a child growing up in London in the 1950s and 1960s, I lived in South Kensington and Westminster. All through early childhood – almost every day at first, and certainly every weekend – my sister and I were taken by our parents for walks in Kensington Gardens, and visits to the Kensington Museums. Every walk was a choice: the Round Pond *or* the Serpentine, Kensington Palace *or* Peter Pan. Later, in my teens, when I was at my last school, Queen's College in Harley Street (Katherine Mansfield's school, I was proud to know), and we were living near Victoria Street, I used to walk to school every day. I walked past Buckingham Palace, up through Green Park, across Piccadilly, and up Bond Street. I did this for two years, and I knew the contents of every shop window in Bond Street – I used to walk on alternate sides of the street every day. I didn't then know that this was Mrs Dalloway's walk, but by the time I went to Oxford in the mid-1960s I had started to read some of Virginia Woolf's novels. She was not studied in my Oxford English course. At graduate level, she was described to me by my tutor as a minor modernist, not to be classed with Joyce, Eliot or Lawrence, and this was how I thought of her for some years.

While I was a student, Leonard Woolf's collections of her essays began to come out, but it was not until the 1970s that Quentin Bell's biography (1972), the edition of the *Letters* (beginning in 1975), the *Diary* (beginning in 1977), *Moments of Being* (1975) and the first of the edited manuscripts (*The Pargiters*, 1977) were being published. The edited essays would not follow for another ten years, and are still in production. In my first British academic job, in my twenties, I published a short introduction to Virginia Woolf's novels, in 1977, which the publishers thought useful for novice readers of difficult modernist works, 'whose interest has been aroused by the continuing publication of biographical material'. In the twenty years since, I have been reading a Virginia Woolf who has greatly changed. She has changed from the Virginia Woolf who died in 1941, or the Virginia Woolf whose *Writer's Diary* in 1953 seemed so aesthetically intense, so painfully serious and driven, or the Virginia Woolf of Quentin Bell's biography, eccentric genius, brilliant comic aunt, enchanting friend.

She herself, as I've said in this book, was intensely aware, from her own reading and theorising of biography, of how lives are changed in retrospect, and how life-stories need to be retold. 'These facts are not like the facts of science – once they are discovered, always the same. They are subject to changes of opinion; opinions change as the times change.'[1] As she said of Shelley: 'There are some stories which have to be retold by each generation, not that we have anything new to add to them, but because of some queer quality in them which makes them not only Shelley's story but our own.'[2] Posthumously, it feels as if she has generously, abundantly opened herself up to such retellings, as if in an echo of her joking phrase to John Lehmann: 'You are hereby invited to be the guest of Virginia Woolf's ghost.'[3] Virginia Woolf's story is reformulated by each generation. She takes on the shape of difficult modernist preoccupied with questions of form, or comedian of manners, or neurotic highbrow aesthete, or inventive fantasist, or pernicious snob, or Marxist feminist, or historian of women's lives, or victim of abuse, or lesbian heroine, or cultural analyst, depending on who is reading her, and when, and in what context. In the quarter-century since Bell's biography, her status has grown beyond anything that even she, with her strong sense of her own achievements, might have imagined. And the disputes she arouses – over madness, over modernism, over marriage – cannot be concluded, and will go on being argued long after this book is published.

Because of these re-appropriations, she seems to us, now, both a contemporary and a historical figure. This peculiar transitional position, at present occupied by the great early-twentieth-century writers of the modernist movement, makes her seem both close and far. She speaks to us of issues and concerns which are vital to us and are not yet resolved. Her interest in style and her solutions to the formal challenges she set herself still influence contemporary work. But she is, also, a late-Victorian, bringing into her work the concerns and mental habits of a previous century.

When I set out on my biographer's journey in 1991, the paradoxical nearness and distance of Virginia Woolf struck me very strongly. The archives still reflect the early arrangements made after her death, and bear traces of Leonard Woolf's attempt to deal with the complicated chaos of her papers and his piece-by-piece selling-off of her manuscripts and diaries. Manuscripts are scattered between different archives in England and America; there are still unsorted and unedited heaps of materials (for instance the notes towards 'Phases of Fiction' and the drafts of *The Years*) which have been left much as she left them. There are still new letters coming to light. Many of her friends and acquaintances still live (though some have died while I have been working on this book: Stephen Spender, May Sarton, Trekkie Parsons, Janet Vaughan). They have been telling their Virginia Woolf stories for over fifty years, mostly committed to paper and hardened into irrefrangible form. I often felt, as I went on my well-trodden rounds (to be met, on the whole, with kind but wearied civility) how impertinent it was to reduce other people's long histories to their moments of knowledge of this one famous person, as though the rest of their lives counted for nothing. Yet, even so, I felt occasionally that there were new things to hear, a fresh detail to be glimpsed. These interviews made me feel I was moving towards the life of a person which was at once locked in past, distant history, and touchably close.

I have the same kind of feeling about her work. Though much of it is monumentally established in the canon of modernism and feminism, a great part of it, too, is still under-read and under-valued. The early novels, the work of the 1930s, and the essays, are relatively little known. Virginia Woolf as an author will go on changing.

The places she lived in and visited embody my sense of her as at once distant and close. It is still possible to see and do some of what she did. Though her City of London was bombed out of recognition, you can still go to St Paul's, or walk along the river. You can wander through Kew Gardens or up Richmond Hill, or shop at the Army & Navy Stores, or dine at the Ivy, or go to a concert at the Wigmore Hall, or hear Wagner at Covent Garden (at a price). Soon you won't be able to push open the swing doors of the British Museum Reading Room, go to the central catalogue and look up 'Women'. But you can still take Mrs Brown's train from Richmond to

Waterloo, and you are as likely as Virginia Woolf was to see beggar-women with mongrel dogs in Kingsway or the Strand. You can visit Knole and Sissinghurst, or see the grey schoolhouse at Giggleswick, or the Round House in Lewes. The room at King's College Cambridge where the much-mythologised lunch party in *A Room of One's Own* took place still has the same decorations on the walls (and, as I write, the same occupant); the dining room, Clough Hall, at Newnham College, where she gave the talk that became the essay, has been redecorated as it was. The chairs still scrape, the doors still bang and swing.

Her own places have had a mixed afterlife. Charleston has been rescued from decay by the family and the Friends of Charleston and attracts hundreds of visitors; Monk's House is now a neatly kept museum, owned by the National Trust. The ashes are in the garden under the Tomlin bust, the writing lodge is in its place by the church wall. The furnishings and decorations have been carefully and attractively arranged to give the atmosphere of Virginia Woolf's life with Leonard Woolf (though his years after her death, much of them spent in companionship with the painter Trekkie Parsons, who left the house to Sussex University, are also reflected in what is left in the house). Asheham, though, was lived in for a time by employees of the Blue Circle Cement Works and Waste Management, but when methane gas began to leak out of the company's rubbish tip, it was boarded up and left to die, gloomily surrounded by trees and by the workings of the Blue Circle Industries. Despite many protests and a long campaign, it was finally demolished in 1994 to make way for an in-fill site.

Hogarth House, a handsome building in an ugly road, survives as an architect's office, with a blue plaque to mark the presence of the Woolfs and their Press. There is a plaque, too, on the front of 22 Hyde Park Gate (long since divided into flats, with a lift) but it says only that Sir Leslie Stephen lived there. Much of Virginia Woolf's Bloomsbury has changed – a big post-war hotel fills the site of her side of Tavistock Square, the Gordon Square houses are almost all University buildings. The Hotel Russell now has a restaurant called 'Virginia Woolf's', serving Jacob's burgers and Virginia Club Jumbo Sandwiches. Fitzroy Square, however, has been very well preserved. There is a plaque to George Bernard Shaw, as well as to Virginia Woolf, on No 29.

In St Ives, Talland House stands surrounded on all sides by hotels and villas, but with a bit of garden left. It has had an ugly extension added on the roof, and has been converted into holiday flats. The first person to do this, I heard from a St Ives bookseller, was a little unsure of the history of the house, but thought it would be a good move to benefit from it, and so put up a sign which read: 'Talland House, home of Virginia Woolf, wife of the famous novelist.' Then the house was sold to a couple who told me, infuriatedly, that when they bought it they had 'never heard of the bloody woman', but soon realised their mistake: 'Every time you turn round, there's Americans in the living room! Australians in the bathroom!' The owner wouldn't let me into the house (though I could see that the rooms have been subdivided into small spaces) but he did allow me into the grounds. Enough remains of the enclosed strip of garden to suggest the past. There is an escallonia hedge, and there is a view.

I stand in the garden, feeling like a biographer, a tourist and an intruder. It is getting dark. I inspect the stone step below the french window where the Stephen family and their guests were so often photographed. No convenient ghost is going to appear, casting her shadow on the step. However, looking away from the house, over the buildings of the twentieth century, at the distant view from this island look-out, I can allow myself to suppose that I am seeing something of what she saw. My view overlays with, just touches, hers. The view, in fact, seems to have been written by Virginia Woolf. The lighthouse beam strikes round; the waves break on the shore.

NOTES

CHAPTER 1: BIOGRAPHY

1 VW to VSW, 3 May 1938, *L* VI, 3383, p.225.
2 *QB* I, p.1.
3 de Salvo, p.1.
4 Roger Poole, *The Unknown Virginia Woolf*, CUP, 1978, p.1.
5 Stephen Trombley, *All That Summer She Was Mad: Virginia Woolf, Female Victim of Male Medicine*, Continuum, 1982, p.1.
6 Gordon, p.3.
7 Peter F. Alexander, *Leonard and Virginia Woolf: A Literary Partnership*, Harvester Wheatsheaf, 1992, p.1.
8 'Craftsmanship', broadcast in the series 'Words Fail Me', 29 Apr 1937, published in the *Listener*, 5 May 1937.
9 *D*, 2 Apr 1937, V, p.75.
10 *D*, 22 Aug 1922, II, p.193.
11 VW to Stella Benson, 12 Jan 1933, *CS*, 2695a, p.321.
12 *D*, 31 May 1933, IV, p.161.
13 *D*, 19 Feb 1923, II, p.234.
14 *D*, 21 June 1924, II, p.304.
15 *D*, 27 Feb 1926, III, p.62.
16 *D*, 3 Feb 1927, III, p.125. See also *D*, 8 Feb 1926, III, p.58; *D*, 3 May 1931, IV, p.24; *D*, 19 Feb 1940, V, p.269.
17 *D*, 22 Oct 1940, V, p.332.
18 SP, *MB*, 1976, p.80.
19 *D*, 28 July 1940, V, p.307.
20 *Mrs Dalloway*, p.8.
21 Angelica Bell to JB, 7 Sep [1936], King's.
22 'The Genius of Boswell', *TLS*, 21 Jan 1909, in *Books and Portraits*, p.153. She also wrote on Boswell's *Life of Johnson* in the *Nation*, 14 Nov 1925, p.248.

23 e.g. *D*, 21 Aug 1929, III, p.245.
24 *D*, 12 Sep 1922, II, p.201. Cf. *D*, 15, 17 Oct 1934, IV, pp.252, 254.
25 *CE* I, p.126.
26 'And I feel us, compared with Aldous & Maria, unsuccessful.' *D*, 17 Feb 1931, IV, p.11.
27 SP, *MB*, 1976 p.136.
28 Keynes, e.g. *D*, 11 Sep 1923; Eliot, e.g. *D*, 20 Sep 1920; Sickert, 17 Dec 1933; Yeats, 8 Nov 30; Bennett, 2 Dec 1930; Hardy, 25 July 1926; Wells, 29 Jan 37.
29 When she finishes *Orlando* she says to herself: 'I rather like the idea of these Biographies of living people.' *D*, 31 May 28, III, p.185.
30 *Orlando*, p.32.
31 *CE* IV, p.54.
32 'The New Biography', 30 Oct 1927, *CE* IV, pp.231, 230.
33 'The Art of Biography', Apr 1939, *CE* IV, p.222.
34 MS of 'How Should One Read a Book?', Berg.
35 'The New Biography', *CE* IV, p.234.
36 Silver, XLV, p.212, notes but does not quote this entry, Notebooks, Oct 1934, MHP, Sussex.
37 Notebooks, MHP, Sussex.
38 'A Talk about Memoirs', 6 Mar 1920, *CE* IV, p.216.
39 'Stopford Brooke', *TLS*, 29 Nov 1917, *E* II, p.184.
40 'The Humane Art', 8 June 1940, *CE* I, p.104.
41 'The Art of Biography', *CE* IV, p.226.
42 'Not One of Us', Oct 1927, *CE* IV, p.20.
43 *D*, 2 Sep 1929, III, p.250.
44 VW to Hugh Walpole, 25 Aug 1929, *L* IV, 2063, p.83.

45 VW to CB, 21 Feb 1931, *L* IV, 2330, p.294.
46 e.g. *D*, 28 Mar 1937, V, p73
47 *D*, 2 Oct 1934, IV, p.247.
48 *D*, 5 Apr 1935, IV, p.296.
49 In *Tulsa Studies in Women's Literature*, vol. 9, pt 2, 1990.
50 VW to ES, 7/8 Aug 1938, *L* VI, 3428, p.262.
51 *D*, 16 Dec 1935, IV, p.358; 1 Nov 1934, IV, p.258.
52 *D*, 3 May 1938, V, p.138.
53 'Walter Sickert: A Conversation', 1934; new illustrated edition, intro. Richard Shone, The Bloomsbury Workshop, 1992, pp.18, 23.
54 Jane Marcus, 'The Private Selves of Public Women' (*The Private Self: Theory and Practice of Women's Autobiographical Writings*, ed. Shari Benstock, Routledge, 1988, p.116)
55 VW to VSW, 9 Oct [1927], *L* III, 1820, p.429.
56 VW to Eleanor Cecil, 26 Jan? 1919, *L* II, 1010, p.322. 6 Oct [1936], *L* VI, 3178, p.36.
57 VW to Victoria OCampo, 22 Dec 1934, *L* V, 2966, p.356.
58 VW to ES, 24 Dec 1940, *L* VI, 3670, p.453.
59 *WF*, p.195.
60 Carolyn Heilbrun, *Writing a Woman's Life*, Ballantine Books, New York, 1988, p.28.
61 AVS to VD [1 Sep 1907], *L* I, 381, p.308.
62 *Friendship's Gallery*, 1907, *Twentieth Century*, Fall 1979, vol.25.
63 Not AVS's title. *CSF*, pp.33–62.
64 *CSF*, p.74.
65 *CE* III, p.196.
66 *CE* III, p.205.
67 *A Room of One's Own*, p.81.
68 *WF*, p.72.
69 *Three Guineas*, p.202. Also: pp.203, 204, 263
70 *D*, 7 Aug 1939, V, p.229.
71 'Am I a snob?', *MB*, p.182.
72 See Shari Benstock, 'Authorizing the Autobiographical', and Susan Stanford Friedman, 'Women's Autobiographical Selves: Theory and Practice', in *The Private Self*.

73 VW to Hugh Walpole, 28 Dec [1932], *L* V, 2687, p.142.
74 *D*, 28 May 1929, 23 June 1929, III, pp.229, 236.
75 See Patricia Mayer Spacks 'Selves in Hiding', in *Women's Autobiography*, ed. Estelle C. Jelinek, Indiana UP, 1980, pp.112–32.
76 *A Room of One's Own*, pp.47, 72.
77 *WF*, p.184.
78 *D*, 18 Mar 1920, II, p.26.
79 *D*, 5 Dec 1920, II, p.77.
80 SP, *MB*, p.65.
81 'Reminiscences' was set next to the 'Sketch of the Past' when these unpublished writings were at last brought out in *MB* in 1976.
82 'Reminiscences', *MB*, 1976 p.36.
83 See Marcus, op. cit., p.120, on eighteenth- and nineteenth-century examples of 'Women close to great men [who] wrote their lives.
84 *PA*, 30 Jan 1905, , p.230.
85 *D*, 18 Mar 1925, III, p.5.
86 *D*, 17 Dec 1933, IV, p.193.

CHAPTER 2: HOUSES

1 'Cornwall, 1905', *PA*, p.282.
2 AVS to VD [13] Aug 1905, *L* I, 246, p.204.
3 *TL*, p.219.
4 '1903', *PA*, p.186.
5 *MB*, p.73.
6 *Jacob's Room*, p.47.
7 Holograph, vol. i p.5, Berg.
8 *The Waves:Hol* p.6.
9 Ibid., p.400. My ellipses.
10 *The Waves*, pp.3–4.
11 *D*, 23 June 1929, III, p.236.
12 'Ancestors', *CSF*, pp.182–3.
13 Leslie Stephen, letter to Mrs Clifford, 25 July 1884, quoted in Maitland, p.384.
14 Leslie Stephen, letter to Charles Eliot Norton, 23 Oct 1881, Maitland, p.345.
15 From a Mr Bolitho (Maria to Julia, 2 Sep 1893, Sussex,) the great-uncle of Richard Kennedy, who worked in the Hogarth Press. Mrs Ramsay describes the rent of the house in *TL*

as 'precisely twopence halfpenny'.
(*TL*, 1992, p.31.)

16 Leslie to Julia, 10 Apr 1882, Berg.

17 Leslie to Julia, 7 Apr 1882, Berg.

18 Leslie to Julia, 9 Apr 1882, Berg.

19 Name derived from a female saint, St Ia, a fourth-century Irish martyred missionary whose statue is in the medieval parish church.

20 She started a nursing society in St Ives which continued, after her death, as the Julia Prinsep Stephen Nursing Association.

21 Letter from F.E. Halliday to LW, 23 Mar 1964, Sussex.

22 Quoted in *MB*, p.78, from Mrs Helena Swanwick's autobiography, *I Have Been Young* (Gollancz, 1935).

23 Molly MacCarthy had similar memories of her 'whole household, numbering about fifteen souls, with about twenty trunks' being transported 'as a matter of course by rail to our country home in the most remote corner of Devonshire'. Mary MacCarthy, *A Nineteenth Century Childhood*, Hamish Hamilton, 1924, p.18.

24 *Jacob's Room*, p.47.

25 'Cornwall, 1905', *PA*, p.288.

26 Spalding, 1983, p.11.

27 *TL*, p.17.

28 Julia Stephen, 'The Wandering Pigs', in *JDS* p. 148.

29 TL, p. 17.

30 *MB*, pp.74, 141.

31 VW to VD, mid-Apr 1914, *L* II, 704, p.48.

32 Leslie to Julia, 6 Apr 1882; Leslie to Laura, 7 Apr 1882, Berg.

33 Leslie to Julia, 14 May 1883, Berg.

34 Leslie to Mrs Clifford, Maitlands, p. 384.

35 *Mausoleum Book*, p.62.

36 SP,*MB*, pp.141–2.

37 SP,*MB*, 1976, p.111.

38 Marcel Proust, *Remembrance of Things Past*, translated by C.K. Scott Moncrieff and Terence Kilmartin, I, Penguin, 1989, p.51.

39 SP,*MB*, p.148.

40 SP,*MB*, pp.140–1.

41 SP,*MB*, p.148.

42 Ibid.

43 Her accounts of moth-hunting are found in the 'Warboys Diary', 1899, *PA*, p.145; in 'Reading', 1919, *CE* II, p.24; and in *Jacob's Room*.

44 Leslie to Maria Jackson, nd [1882], Berg.

45 Leslie to Julia, 29 July 1893, Berg.

46 Maria Jackson to Julia, 24 Aug [1890], Sussex.

47 Maria Jackson to Julia, 4 Jan 1889, 19 July 1890, to Stella, 25 Aug 1889, Sussex.

48 Stella Duckworth, Diary, 1893, QB. All other references on this page to *HPG*, 1892.

49 *QB* gives a wonderful picture of the train journey to Cornwall, I, p.31.

50 *HPG*, vol.ii, no.41, 24 Oct 1892, BL.

51 *MB*, p.72.

52 Ibid., p.200.

53 *PA*, 11 Jan, 11 Mar, 1897, pp.11, 53.

54 Leslie Stephen, *The Life of Fitzjames Stephen*, 1895, p.66.

55 Anne Thackeray Ritchie, *Old Kensington*, 1854, quoted in Winifred Gérin, *Anne Thackeray Ritchie*, OUP, 1981, p.172; 'A Dream of Kensington Gardens', *From the Porch*, Smith, Elder & Co, 1919.

56 Leslie to Oliver Wendell Holmes, 22 Dec 1867, quoted in Maitland, p.201.

57 Leslie to Charles Eliot Norton, 6 Oct 1876, quoted in Maitland, p.293.

58 SP, *MB*, p.133.

59 *D*, 23 Oct 1918, I, p.206.

60 SP, *MB*, p.133.

61 *HPG*, vol.ii, no.2, 18 Jan 1892.

62 *PA*, 6 Feb 1897, p.30. ABC: Aerated Bread Company (shop and café). For the Underground, see *MB* 134.

63 *MB*, p.134.

64 *PA*, 8 May 1897, p.83.

65 *JDS*, pp.67, 183, 103.

66 *HPG*, vol.ii, no.6, 5 Feb 1892; *PA*, 31 May, 14 May, 1897, pp.93, 85; *MB*, p.87.

67 *The Years*, pp.195–6.

68 Ibid., p.18.

69 'Old Bloomsbury', *MB*, p.198.

70 Leslie to Julia, 7 Oct 1886, Berg.
71 'Old Bloomsbury', '22 Hyde Park Gate', *MB*, pp.199, 179.
72 VB memoirs, 'Adventures in Society' and 'A Brother as Chaperone', QB.
73 'The Cook', MS, MHP, A13D Sussex.
74 *The Years*, p.175.
75 'Great Men's Houses', *The London Scene*, pp.24–5.
76 *The Years*, p.30.
77 SP, *MB*, pp.129–30.
78 *The Years*, p.10.
79 SP, *MB*, p.130.
80 VB, 'Notes on Virginia's Childhood', LW, Sussex.
81 *MB*, p.116.
82 VB, 'Memoir relating to Mrs Jackson', QB.
83 VB, 'Notes on Virginia's Childhood', Sussex.
84 VB, 'Life at Hyde Park Gate', QB.
85 SP, *MB*, p.136.
86 SP, *MB*, pp.131–2; 'Leslie Stephen', 28 Nov 1932, *The Times*, *CE* IV, p.76.
87 SP, *MB*, pp.131, 199.
88 *The Years*, p.173.
89 *Night and Day*, pp.8, 14, 265.
90 *The Years*, p.30.
91 *Flush*, pp.75, 17.
92 *Orlando*, p.160.
93 'Memo Book' for *Freshwater*, MHP Sussex.
94 *MB*, pp.198–9.
95 *A Room of One's Own*, p.79.
96 'Professions for Women', 1931, in *Virginia Woolf: Women and Writing*, p.63
97 Maria Jackson's and Julia Stephen's bequests, QB.
98 'Old Bloomsbury' *MB*, p.201.
99 'The Cook',MHP A13D Sussex.

CHAPTER 3: PATERNAL

1 *Night and Day*, p.271.
2 *TL*, p.111.
3 SP, *MB*, p.94.
4 SP, *MB*, p.77.
5 SP, *MB*, p.73.

6 Annan, p.3, and also Annan, *Our Age:Portrait of a Generation*, Weidenfeld & Nicolson, 1990, p.6.
7 Leonore Davidoff, *The Best Circles*, 1973, Cresset 1986, p.77.
8 *Three Guineas*, p.233.
9 See Charles Tansley and Mr Ramsay in *TL*, talking 'for ever' about 'who had won this, who had won that', who was 'undoubtedly "the ablest fellow in Balliol" ', etc. *TL*, p.11.
10 SP, *MB*, p.167.
11 E.g. VB to VW, 25 June 1916, 'Have you been seeing any of the relics?'
12 'Memoir', Sussex.
13 AVS to VD, 8 June 1903, *L* I, 84, p.79.
14 'Memoir', MHP Sussex.
15 E.g. Annan, p.159, and QB, *Bloomsbury*, 1968, Omega, 1974, p.19.
16 James Stephen, *Essays in Ecclesiastical Biography*, II, 'The Clapham Sect', Longmans, 1849, p.307.
17 This question 'obsessively concerned' the upper-class élite, as it has done all 'status groups'. Davidoff, p.15.
18 Davidoff, describing the social rituals of the late Victorian and Edwardian middle and upper classes, pp.17–18.
19 Ibid. on *Orlando*, p.37.
20 Francis Galton, *Hereditary Genius*, 1869, 1892. Leslie Stephen, in 'Heredity', rejected the 'demoralising fatalism' that would argue that there is no escape from it, but accepts that 'We inherit thoughts as we inherit wealth . . . and indeed our whole mental furniture.' *Social Rights and Duties: Addresses to Ethical Societies*, Macmillan 1896, vol. I, pp.29–30, 54.
21 *TL*, p.160.
22 SP, *MB*, p.161.
23 SP, *MB*, p.171.
24 SP, *MB*, p.157.
25 VB, 'Notes on Virginia's Childhood', Sussex.
26 VW to Victoria OCampo [7 Dec 1934], *L* V, 2959, p.351.

27 *The London Artists' Association:
Recent Paintings by VB*, 4 Feb–8
Mar 1930. MS, 1929, Berg.
28 VW to Jacques Raverat, 8 Mar 1924,
L III, 1450, p.92.
29 Maitland, p.7.
30 Leslie to Julia, 29 July 1893, Berg.
31 Leslie Stephen, 'Memoranda, end
1903', BL.
32 VW to QB, 24 Jan [1934], *L* V, 2850,
p.273.
33 Leslie Stephen, *Life of Sir James
Fitzjames Stephen*, 1895, p.64.
34 Caroline Emelia Stephen, ed., *The
Letters of Sir James Stephen*, 1906,
p.125.
35 Trekkie Parsons, to the author,
1991.
36 Leslie Stephen, op. cit., pp.25–6;
VW to DG [15 May 1918], *L* II, 932,
p.240. [This remark has been incor-
rectly annotated in the *Letters*: the
dates of the James Stephen referred
to are 1758–1832].
37 *QB* I, p.4.
38 E.M. Forster, *Marianne Thornton
1797–1887*, Edward Arnold, 1956,
p.29.
39 Leslie Stephen, op. cit., p.19.
40 *D*, 12 July 1937, V, p.102. For Jem
Stephens *Memoirs* see Annan, p7,
and *The Memoirs of James Stephen*,
ed. Merle Bevington, Hogarth
Press, 1954
41 Leslie Stephen, op. cit., p.35.
42 The diaries descended to Caroline
Emelia and AVS read them while
staying with her after Leslie's death.
AVS to VD, 24 Oct [1904], *L* I, 185,
p.146.
43 For James Stephen (1789–1859) see
Leslie Stephen, op. cit., pp.31–65,
and Caroline Emelia Stephen. op.
cit.
44 Annan, op. cit., p.11.
45 *TL*, p.7.
46 VW to QB, 3 Apr [1935] *L* V, 3007,
pp.382–3.
47 Leslie to Oliver Wendell Holmes, 4
Jan 1879, quoted Maitland, p.324.
48 Quoted Maitland, p.419.
49 For James Fitzjames Stephen
(1829–94) see Leslie, letter to Julia

Stephen, 31 Jan 1895, Berg; op. cit.;
Annan, op. cit.; James Fitzjames Stephen, *Liberty, Equality, Fraternity*,
Smith Elder, 1873; Millicent Fawcett, *Mr Fitzjames Stephen on the
position of Women*, 1873; John Bicknell, 'Mr Ramsay Was Young Once',
Virginia Woolf and Bloomsbury, ed.
Jane Marcus, Macmillan, 1987,
p.65; Barbara Caine, *Victorian Feminists*, OUP, 1992, p.183, K.J.M.
Smith, *James Fitzjames Stephen:
Portrait of a Victorian Rationalist*,
CUP, 1988, reviewed by Rosemary
Ashton, 'Leaving It', *London Review
of Books*, 16 Feb 1989, pp.13–14.
50 *PA*, p.106.
51 VW to VB [7 Aug 1908], *L* I, 428,
p.342.
52 VW to ES, 18 May 1931, *L* IV, 2374,
p.333.
53 VW to VB, 13 Nov 1921, *L* II, 1204,
p.492.
54 *D*, 23 June 1927, III, p.141.
55 VW to MLD, 14 Sep 1930, *L* IV,
2236, p.213, 'I have always liked
what Barbara Stephen has written'.
56 VB to CB, 2 Jan [1938], Tate
Gallery.
57 *D*, 21 Nov 1918, I, p.221.
58 *PA*, 18 August 1899 p.149.
59 'Will there never come a season . . .
When the Rudyards cease from Kip-
ling/And the Haggards Ride no
more.'
60 Michael Harrison, *Clarence: The Life
of H.R.H. the Duke of Clarence and
Avondale (1864–1892)*, W.H. Allen,
1972. De Salvo, pp.46–56, thinks,
'J.K. Stephen's poetry demonstrates
that Jack the Ripper was acting out
the murderous sentiments [against
women] publicly expressed by one
of the highly esteemed and influential young men at Cambridge'. But
her argument for J.K.S's poem 'The
Last Ride Together' (which she does
not recognise as a parody of Browning's poem of that name) as evidence of his anal rape of Stella
Duckworth, does not inspire confidence. For J.K. Stephen see also
Annan, op. cit., p.114; *QB* I; p.35,

MB, p.110, Leslie Stephen, *Mausoleum Book*, p.78; *D*, 12 Aug 1928, III, p.190; Leslie to George Duckworth, 15 Jan 1890, Duckworth family papers; Gerald Duckworth to Julia Stephen, n.d., Sussex.[Adds 1987]; J.K. Stephen to Stella Duckworth, n.d., Berg.

61 Caramagno, pp.101–3, gives a detailed account from the notes at St Andrew's Hospital, Northampton, of JKS's behaviour and treatment.

62 See Jean Strouse, *Alice James*, Cape, 1981.

63 For Caroline Emelia Stephen see *Mausoleum Book*, pp.55–6; Leslie to Julia Stephen, 26 Jan 1893, Berg; VD, 'The Stephen Family', Unpublished Memoir, Sussex; AVS to VD, 24 Aug [1906], [4 June? 1903], [Oct/Nov 1903], 24 Oct [1904], [Dec 1907], *L* I, 283, 83, 109, 185, 397 pp.234, 79, 102, 146, 320; AVS to Eleanor Cecil [13 April 1909], *L* I 480, p.390; VW to Pernel Strachey, 10 Aug [1923], *L* III, 1416, p.63; Adrian Stephen to AVS, 27 Apr 1909, Sussex; *Ritchie Letters*, quoted in Winifred Gérin, *Anne Thackeray Ritchie*, OUP, 1981, p.156.

64 Annan, op. cit., p.129.

65 Caroline Emelia Stephen, *Quaker Strongholds*, Hicks, preface to 3rd ed., 1891.

66 AVS, 'Caroline Emelia Stephen', *Guardian*, 21 Apr 1909, *E* I, pp.267–9; AVS to Madge Vaughan [July 1906], *L* I, 275, p.229.

67 For 'the sisterhood of silence in Caroline Stephen's work', see Jane Marcus, 'Virginia Woolf aslant', *Virginia Woolf: A Feminist Slant*, University of Nebraska, 1983, p.11. For Marcus versus QB on Caroline Emelia Stephen see 'Tintinnabulations', *Marxist Perspectives 2* (Spring 1979) and *Critical Inquiry*, June 1984, vol.10, no.4, and March 1985, vol.11, no.3.

68 *Three Guineas*, p.157.

69 *D*, 28 Nov 1928, III, p.208.

70 *D*, 17 Oct 1924, II, p.317.

71 For Leslie Stephen see Annan, QB,

Maitland, the *Mausoleum Book*, *MB*; *Hours in a Library*, III, p. 338; John Bicknell, 'Mr Ramsay was young once', *Virginia Woolf and Bloomsbury*, ed. Jane Marcus, Macmillan, 1987, p.65, n.26; F.J.M. Korsten, 'The 'English Men of Letters' series: A Monument of Late-Victorian Criticism', *English Studies*, vol.73, no.6, Dec 1992, pp.503–16; *D*, 24 Feb 1926, III p.61.

72 Bicknell, op. cit., p.59.

73 Leslie to Maria Jackson, 8 Feb 1877, Berg; Leslie to Thoby, 20 June 1897, QB.

74 For their resemblance, see Annan pp.134–7, Phyllis Rose, Katherine Hill [cited Annan] p.360, n.50.

75 VW to ES, 27 Feb [1930] *L* IV, 2148, p.145.

76 Leslie to Julia, 3 Oct 1887, 6 Feb 1887, Berg.

77 For Leslie Stephen and sentimentalism, see *Mausoleum Book*, p.13; Annan, pp.39, 75, 127; *Hours in a Library*, III, p.162.

78 James Russell Lowell to Leslie Stephen, 21 June 1891, Berg.

79 Leslie Stephen to Julia Stephen, 21 Apr 1885, 28 Jan 1886, 26 Jan 1893, Berg.

80 For Minny Thackeray, see the *Mausoleum Book*; Gérin; 'For Laura: Written by A.I.R just before her marriage in 1877', memoir in the possession of Mrs Belinda Norman-Butler; Minny Stephen to Fitzjames Stephen, 4 Aug 1870, 16 Dec 1869, QB; 'Letters written to A.I.T. by her sister Minny Stephen from America', 1868, Mrs Norman-Butler.

81 For Anne Thackeray Ritchie, see Leslie to Julia Duckworth, 7 Apr 1877, Berg; *PA*, 6 Jan 1897, p.7; *D*, 5 Mar 1919, I, p.247; *Night and Day*, p.411; *Thackeray and his Daughter*, ed. Hester Ritchie, Harper & Brothers, 1924; Gérin, op. cit.; Boyd, pp.76–93; Mary MacCarthy, op. cit., pp.80–2; Carol Hanbery MacKay, 'The Thackeray Connection: Virginia Woolf's Aunt Anny', in Marcus, ed. pp.68–95; 'Blackstick

Papers', *TLS*, 19 Nov 1908, *E* I, pp.228–9; 'Lady Ritchie', *TLS*, 6 Mar 1919, *E* III, pp.13–20; 'The Enchanted Organ', *N&A*, 15 Mar 1924, *E* III, pp.399–403; letter from Anne Ritchie to VW, 1 Jan 1919, King's; to Jack Hills, n.d., King's.

82 'The Eccentrics', *Athenaeum*, 25 Apr 1919, *E* III, pp.38–41.

CHAPTER 4: MATERNAL

1 *A Room of One's Own*, p.69; 'Professions for Women', 1931.
2 For Julia Stephen see *MB*; Leslie Stephen, *Mausoleum Book* and 'Forgotten Benefactors' in *Social Rights and Duties*, Macmillan 1896, vol.2, pp.225–67; *JDS* (see Ch.2, note 28 above); Letters from James Russell Lowell to Julia Stephen, Berg; Boyd.
3 *D*, 28 Nov 1928, III, p.208.
4 *MB*, MS A5b Sussex.
5 *TL*, p.190.
6 Carolyn Heilbrun, '*To the Lighthouse*: The New Story of Mother and Daughter', in *Hamlet's Mother and Other Women*, Ballantyne Books, New York, 1990, p.161.
7 *D*, 28 Nov 1928, III, p.208; SP, *MB*, p.90.
8 *TL*, p.209.
9 SP, *MB*, pp.90–95.
10 VW to Ka Arnold-Forster, 1 May [1936], *L* VI 3125, p.32.
11 Stella Duckworth, Diary, 1893, QB.
12 *HPG*, 14 Nov 1892, 1 Jan 1895, BL.
13 *D*, 4 May 1928, III, p.183.
14 James Russell Lowell to Julia, Letters, Berg.
15 Cf. enjoyable moral fantasies for children like Mrs Molesworth's stories, George Macdonald's *At the Back of the North Wind*, or Charles Kingsley's *The Water Babies*.
16 *JDS*.
17 *Room*, Ch.1; *MB*, p.97; VW to Eleanor Cecil, 25 Oct [1915], *L* II, 733, p.69.

18 Diana Holman Hunt's *My Grandmothers and I*, Hamish Hamilton, 1960, gives a vivid account of 18 Melbury Road. For AVS's visit see *PA*, 19 Jan 1905, and '22 Hyde Park Gate', *MB*, p.192.
19 VW to VD, [13 Apr 1937], *L* VI, 3235, p.120.
20 *D*, 18 Jan 1918, I, p.107.
21 For the two versions, see Boyd, pp.14, 143.
22 Julia Stephen, 'The Mysterious Voice', *JDS*, p.104.
23 *The Waves*, p.102.
24 *TL*, p.13; *TL:Hol* p.15; *Mrs Dalloway*, p.36.
25 H.A.L. Fisher, *An Unfinished Autobiography*, Oxford, 1940, p.10; see also Boyd, op. cit., pp.144–5.
26 VW to ES, 12 Jan 1941, *L* VI, 3678, p.461.
27 LW, *S*, p.185.
28 Fisher, op. cit., p.9.
29 Hon Frederick Leveson-Gower, *Bygone Years*, John Murray, 1905, p.159, quoted Boyd, op. cit., p.11.
30 AVS to VD, [4 Aug 1906], *L* I, 282, p.234.
31 *Victorian Photographs of Famous Men and Fair Women by Julia Margaret Cameron*, Hogarth Press, 1973; *Freshwater*.
32 'Memoir', typescript, Sussex.
33 For the Fishers, Fisher, op. cit.; Ermengard Shove, *Fredegond and Gerald Shove*, Brookthorpe, 1952; AVS to Emma Vaughan, 19 Apr [1900], 23 Apr [1901], *L* 28, 35, I, pp.30, 41; VW to ES [6 Oct 1932], *L* V, 2640, p.109. *D*, 3 Sep 1928, III, p.194; VW to VB, 10 Sep 1916, *L* II, 784, p.114. For Adeline's character and family, see Ursula Vaughan Williams, *R.V.W.: A Biography of Ralph Vaughan Williams*, Clarendon Press, 1964, p.48: 'Besides her beauty she had a quick wit, a lively intelligence, and an ability to be cruelly critical.'
34 For Maria Jackson, 'Sketch of the Past', cancelled passage, typescript, Sussex; *Mausoleum Book*; Boyd, op.

cit., pp.27–8; Maria Jackson, Correspondence, Sussex, Adds [1987]; Maria Jackson to George Duckworth, 27 Sep 1891, Duckworth family papers.

35 Julia Margaret Cameron to Maria Jackson, 6 Feb 1878, Berg.
36 Julia Margaret Cameron to Julia Duckworth, 5 Feb 1878, Berg.
37 Henry James to Alice James, 17 Feb 1878, Quoted *JDS*, p.12.
38 Quoted Annan, p.113.
39 Quoted Maitland, p.323.
40 Brilliantly described by QB, introduction to *D*, vol. I.
41 *D*, 22 Dec 1940, V, p.345.
42 *Mrs Dalloway*, p.46.

CHAPTER 5: CHILDHOOD

1 Silver, pp.121–2; Holograph Reading Notes, vol.23, Berg.
2 The Stephen children are singing this 'vulgar little ditty' in March of this year: they think it would shock their grandmother.
3 'How It Strikes a Contemporary', *E* III, p.357.
4 *PA*,22 June 1897, pp.104–5.
5 Extracts from *The Times*, 5 May 1897, 21–22 June 1897.
6 SP *MB*, pp.75–6.
7 Cf. VW to QB, 28 Oct 1930, L IV, 2263, p.238.
8 *Mausoleum Book*, p.64.
9 Ibid., p.67.
10 Leslie to Julia, 19 Oct 1881, 9 Apr 1882, Berg.
11 Leslie's money worries, and anxieties about Julia's health and age may have been contributory reasons for Adrian's being their last child.
12 See Annan, pp.82–90, for a detailed account of Leslie's work on the *DNB*.
13 Maitland, p.387.
14 *Mausoleum Book*, p.87.
15 Leslie to Julia, 28 Jan 1886, 23 Jan 1887, 4 Oct 1887, Berg; Maitland, p.373; Dr Seton to Julia, 20 Sep 1889, Berg; *Mausoleum Book*, p.89; *HPG*, vol.1 no.48, 7 Dec 1891;

Leslie to Julia, 6 June 1890, 2 Aug 1893, Berg.
16 Annan, p.343; he calls it 'a decent sum'.
17 AVS to VD, [6 Dec 1904], *L* I, 199, p.164.
18 'There was a pathetic scene once when Anny paid a visit and the child ran to her laughing and beaming to hug the only grown-up whom she could remember had shown her love', Annan, op. cit., p.122.
19 Leslie Stephen, *A Calendar of Correspondence*, BL 57922: Leslie to Julia, 18 July 1877, Julia to Leslie, 19 July 1877.
20 Winifred Gérin, *Anne Thackeray Ritchie*, OUP, 1981 p.195.
21 Leslie to Julia, 7 Dec 1879, Berg; Leslie to Julia, 26 Apr 1886, Berg; Leslie to Julia, 12 Apr 1877, Berg; Leslie to Julia, 21 Oct 1884, Berg; Leslie to Julia, 19 Oct 1884, Berg; *MB*, p.198; *QB* I, p.35; Maria Jackson to Julia, Sussex; Leslie to Julia, 11 Oct 1882, Berg; Leslie to Julia, 28 July 1881, Berg; Leslie to Julia, 11 Oct 1882, Berg.
22 Jean O. Love, *Virginia Woolf: Sources of Madness and Art*, University of California Press, 1977, p.162.
23 Caramagno, p.108.
24 Leslie to Julia, 29 Apr 1881, Berg.
25 Leslie to Julia, 4 Sep 1882, Berg.
26 Leslie to Julia, 29 Sep 1882, Berg.
27 Stella to Julia, 7 Aug [1889?], Sussex.
28 Leslie to Julia, 24 Mar 1884, Berg.
29 'Old Bloomsbury', *MB*, p.198.
30 Leslie to Julia, 1 Aug 1893, Berg. For Redhill see Kathleen Jones, *Lunacy, Law and Conscience 1744–1855*, Routledge, 1955.
31 Stella Duckworth, Diary, 30 Mar 1896, Berg.
32 *Mausoleum Book*, p.103; Leslie to Thoby, 20 Mar 1897, QB. Laura spent the rest of her life at Southgate. A trust fund was set up to pay for her keep from the sale of Hyde Park Gate in 1906. By 1919 this sum had increased from £489 to £1883;

in 1921 they had to raise another £2000 for her keep. (VW to VB, 24 Oct 1921, *L* II, p.487). She died at 74, of stomach cancer, in The Priory, Roehampton, in February 1945 (not in the Retreat at York as Quentin Bell was led to believe). By this time the family was entirely out of contact with her and it took the lawyers, Halsey & Co, over a year to let them know. There was then some discussion between Adrian, Vanessa and Leonard about her estate: she left £7,800 minus death duties. (Adrian to VB, 13 June, 10 July, 13 Aug, 19 Nov 1946, 2 Apr 1947, Sussex.)

33 VW to VB, 13 Nov 1921, *L* II, 1204, p.492.

34 de Salvo, pp.191–239.

35 Caramagno, p.111, in a carefully documented account of the Stephen family genetic history in Ch. 5, opts for a 'biological' interpretation of Laura's case.

36 Caramagno supposes Laura's symptoms to have been more congruent with autism or psychosis than with mental retardation.

37 Leslie to Julia, 28 July 1881 ('no one loves her but me'), 19 Oct 1881, Berg.

38 De Salvo, p.39, claims that Virginia recognised herself and Laura as 'at some deep level . . . sisters under the skin'. The reverse, I would think, is true.

39 *D*, 9 Jan 1915, I, p.13.

40 VW to VB, 4 May [1934], *L* V, 2887, p.300.

41 *Mausoleum Book*, p.32.

42 Leslie to Julia, 10 Oct 1883, 10 Apr 1884, Berg.

43 Stella to Julia, 13 Apr 1884, Berg.

44 'Notes on Virginia's Childhood' by VB, ed. Richard J. Schaubeck, Frank Hallman, New York, 1974, written 'after the death of Virginia Woolf'. Typescript, Sussex.

45 Ibid. Leslie Stephen to Charles Eliot Norton, 20 Apr 1888 (quoted de Salvo, note 19, p.326).

46 *HPG*; *MB*, p.88; Stella Duckworth, Diary, 19 Sep 1893, QB.

47 VD to VB, 16 June 1942, Tate Gallery.

48 SP, *MB*, p.88.

49 SP, *MB*, p.81.

50 *D*, 31 Jan 1920; SP *MB*, pp.77, 78 80.

51 SP, *MB*, p.87.

52 Lowell to Julia, 26 Dec 1886, Berg.

53 AVS to Julia, n.d., QB. Printed (without the last 'and') in *CS*, 1a, p.3. Since Mrs Prinsep died in 1887 this must have been written in 86/87.

54 'Notes on Virginia's Childhood.' Love, VB, pp.216–19, suggests that this slowness may have been related to her 'extraordinarily vivid sense-imagery': she made mental pictures before she made words.

55 Lowell to Julia, 31 July 1889, Berg.

56 Leslie to Julia, 15 Apr 1887, 17 Apr 1887, Berg.

57 *MB*, p.88; and, in a slightly different version, VB, 'Notes on Virginia's Childhood'.

58 Leslie to Julia, 6 Apr 1887, Berg.

59 *MB*, pp.85–6.

60 Julia to AVS, 7 Feb, n.d., Berg.

61 Thoby Stephen, Notebook, QB.

62 VB, 'Notes on Virginia's Childhood'.

63 *HPG*, vol.ii, no.27, 18 July 1892; vol.ii, no.9, 7 Mar 92; vol.ii, no.18, 9 May 1892; vol.i, no.48, 7 Dec 1891; vol.ii, no.21, 30 May 1892; vol.i, no.50, 21 Dec 1891; vol.ii, no.22, 6 June 1892; vol.ii, no.14, 11 Apr 1892; vol.ii, no.12, 28 Mar 1892; vol.i, no.47, 30 Nov 1891; vol.i, no.51, 27 Dec 1891. BL.

64 'A Cockney's Farming Experiences' and 'The Experiences of a Paterfamilias' were extracted from *HPG* and published, ed. Suzanne Henig, by San Diego State UP, 1972.

65 As de Salvo does, concluding that the stories are 'an extremely painful evocation of the experience of child abuse and neglect', pp.150–61.

66 *HPG*, vol.ii, no.13, 4 Apr 1892.

67 *HPG*, vol.ii, no.36, 19 Sep 1892.

68 *PA*, 12 Apr 1897, p.69.

69 John Lehmann, Autobiographical Manuscript, Sep 1932, Texas.
70 *Recollections*, p.62.
71 Stella mentions the marmoset, with irritation, in her 1896 diary; for the mouse see *PA*, 26 May 1897 p. 91.
72 Quoted Annan, p.80.
73 *CS*, 339a, pp.38–9.
74 AVS to VB [19 Aug 1909], *L* I, 504, pp.409–10.
75 'Lappin and Lapinova', *CSF*, pp. 261–68.
76 *PA*, 31 Jan, 4 Feb, 5 Feb, 11 Feb, 20 Apr, 28 Apr, 2 May, 5 Aug 1897. See de Salvo, ' "As Miss Jan Says": Virginia Woolf's Early Journals', in Marcus, pp.96–124.
77 SP, *MB*, p.89.
78 Maitland, pp.474–5; Annan, op. cit., p.109.
79 Thoby to VB, 21 Feb 1891, QB.
80 Adrian to Julia, 2 Feb 1894, QB.

CHAPTER 6: SIBLINGS

1 SP, *MB*, p.77.
2 Leslie to Julia, 9 May 1884, Berg, cited Jean O. Love, *Virginia Woolf: Sources of Madness and Art*, University of California Press, 1977, p.152.
3 Leslie to Julia, 1 June 1887, 2 Aug 1893, Berg.
4 *HPG*, vol.ii, no.46, 28 Nov 1892.
5 *Mausoleum Book*, p.109.
6 Stella Duckworth, Diary, 23 Jan 1896, Berg.
7 Leslie to Mary Fisher, 15 Jan 1898, VB 'Memoir Club Paper', nd, QB.
8 AVS to VD, [27 Nov 1903], *L* I, 122, p.109. Also AVS to VD [22 Dec 1906], *L* I, 329, p.269.
9 AVS to Violet Dickinson, [Feb 1907], *L* I, 341, p.279.
10 Paraphrased from VW to OM, 22 Nov [1933], Goodman family papers.
11 VW to VB, [15 July 1918], *L* II, 951, p.261.
12 Ann Synge, personal communication to the author, 1992.
13 VW to Jacques Raverat, 8 Mar 1924, *L* III, 1450, p.93.

14 VW to VB, 25 May 1928, *L* III, 1895, p.500.
15 VW to VB, 24 May [1923], *L* III, 1395, p.43. Adrian was analysed by James Glover (trained by Karl Abraham) and then by his disciple Ella Sharpe. During analysis he was said to be 'in the most awful condition & threatens to shoot himself'. James to Alix Strachey, 27 Sep 1924, in *Bloomsbury/Freud* p.71.
16 Notes towards 'the HPG chapter', MHP, Sussex.
17 SP *MB*, p.138; *MB*, 1976, p.108.
18 Notebook, MHP, Sussex, MS version of p.100 ff in *MB*, 1976. There are changes in the accounts of Thoby; cf. *MB* 1976 and 1985.
19 Stella Duckworth, Diary, 29 Aug 1893, QB.
20 Leslie to Julia, 18 July 1885, Berg.
21 Thoby to Julia, nd, QB.
22 Leslie to Julia, 25 Oct 1891, Berg; *HPG*, vol.ii, no.49, 19 Dec 1892.
23 Letter from Evelyns School to Julia, 18 May 1891, QB; *Mausoleum Book*, p.84.
24 E.J. Worsley to Julia, 6 Mar, 20 Mar, 4 Apr, 1894, QB.
25 Leslie to Julia, 22 July 1894, Berg.
26 Leslie to Mary Fisher, 23 Mar 1902, QB.
27 SP, *MB*, p.156.
28 Notebook, MHP Sussex, MSS. version of p.157, *MB*, para ending 'It was not right to treat Aunt Mary like that'.
29 Thoby to CB, July 1904, King's.
30 Notebook, MHP, Sussex, MS version of *MB* 1976, p.123; *MB*, p.156.
31 SP, *MB*, p.156.
32 See Dunn and Gillespie.
33 *Mrs Dalloway*, pp.62–4.
34 VB, 'Notes on Virginia's Childhood', Sussex, p.6.
35 VB to CB, 25 June 1910, Tate Gallery, quoted Spalding, pp.129–30.
36 VB to VW, [11] Oct 1931, Tate Gallery; VW to VB [15 Oct 1931], *L* IV, 2451, p.390.
37 SP, 'Reminiscences', *MB*, pp.87, 35.

38 Quoted Love, op. cit., p.235.
39 Spalding, p.13.
40 *PA*, p.134.
41 *D*, 21 Sep 1929, III, p.255.
42 SP, *MB*, p.161.
43 *Mausoleum Book*, p.65.
44 Leslie to Julia, 3 Feb 1886, Berg.
45 *Mausoleum Book*, p.66.
46 Julia to Mrs Vivian, 3 Oct 1870, Duckworth family papers.
47 George Duckworth to Julia, nd, Duckworth family papers.
48 SP, *MB*, p.182.
49 George Duckworth to Julia, nd, Duckworth family papers.
50 'Dramatis Personae', Notebook, probable date Sep 1902, Sussex.
51 The phrase applied by Helen Ambrose to Richard Dalloway in *The Voyage Out* after he has kissed Rachel.
52 The Hon. Mrs Katharine Duckworth, interview with the author, 1991.
53 *TL*, p.197.
54 Memoir, A5c, p.6, MHP, Sussex.
55 SP, *MB*, p.108.
56 Stella Duckworth, Diary, 19 Nov 1893, QB.
57 SP, *MB*, pp.108–9.
58 *HPG*, vol.ii, no.43, 14 Nov 1892.
59 Stella Duckworth, Diary, 11 Mar, 31 Aug 1893, QB. For VW's description of this incident see *MB*, p.93.
60 Stella Duckworth, Diary, 1 Nov 1893, QB.
61 Stella Duckworth, Diary, 30 June 1896, Berg.
62 Gillian Darnley, *Octavia Hill: A Life*, Constable, 1990, p.154.
63 *PA*, 19 Feb 1897, p.38.
64 Darnley, op. cit., p.154.
65 *The Years*, p.83.
66 For MLD's connection with Octavia Hill see Darnley, op. cit., p.56.
67 *HPG*, vol.ii, No. 34, 5 Sep 1892.
68 George Duckworth to Julia, nd [1892], Duckworth family papers.
69 Stella Duckworth, Diary, 27, 22 Sep, 1893, QB.
70 *Mausoleum Book*, p.84.

71 Gerald Duckworth to Julia, nd, in Maria Jackson Correspondence, Sussex.
72 SP, *MB*, pp.114, 116.
73 *PA*, 27 May 1897 p.91.
74 *D*, 18 Mar 1918, I, p.129.
75 *D*, 19 Jan 1940, V, p.259.
76 *MB*, p.101.
77 *HPG*, vol.ii, no.34, 5 Sep 1892; vol.ii, no.21, 30 May 1892.
78 *HPG*, vol.ii, no.42, 31 Oct 1892.
79 *MB*, p.115.
80 *QB* I, p.35, 'private information'.
81 *MB*, p.77.
82 VW to ES, 12 Jan 41, *L* VI, 3678, pp.459–60.
83 See de Salvo, esp. pp.108–11.
84 Ibid. p.105.
85 Caramagno, p.146, disagrees with de Salvo, particularly on her assumption that VW was frigid, or that frigidity could 'cause' manic-depression.
86 de Salvo, p.119.

CHAPTER 7: ADOLESCENCE

1   *TL*, p.140.
2   *The Voyage Out*, p.52.
3   *The Years*, pp.38–9.
4   'Reminiscences'*MB*, p.47.
5   'The years between childhood and maturity . . . are so complex. My mother's death fell into the very middle of that amorphous time. That made it much more broken. The whole thing was strained.' Memoir, A5c, MHP, Sussex.
6   *D*, 5 May 1924, II, pp.300–1.
7   *D*, 4 May 1937, V, p.85.
8   *D*, 12 Sep 1934, IV, p.242.
9   SP, *MB*, pp.102–3.
10 SP, *MB*, p.105.
11 *PA*, 14 June 1897, p.100.
12 *PA*, 6 Jan 1897, p.7.
13 SP, *MB*, p.106.
14 SP, *MB*, p.138.
15 'Reminiscences,' *MB*, p.53.
16 *Night and Day*, p.92. See Mark Spilka, *Virginia Woolf's Quarrel with Grieving* (University of Nebraska,

1980); Jean O. Love, *Virginia Woolf: Sources of Madness and Art*, University of California Press, 1977, p.309, Caramagno, p.132, Gordon, p.39, on VW's obsession with her mother.

17 SP, *MB*, p.103.

18 SP, *MB*, p.128; *Night and Day*, p.406.

19 SP, *MB*, p.137.

20 Memoir, A5c, MHP, Sussex.

21 Caroline Reynolds, Lady Jebb, Letter, 17 June 1888, in May Reed Bobbitt, ed., *With Dearest Love to All; The Life and Letters of Lady Jebb*, Faber, 1960, p.230.

22 Stella Duckworth, Diary, 1896, Berg.

23 *PA*, 19 Jan, 18 Jan, 19 Feb, 1897 pp. 16, 39.

24 *PA*, 13 Feb 1897 p.35.

25 *PA*, 28 Mar 1897 p.61.

26 *PA*, 1 Apr, 5 Apr 1897 p. 64, 66.

27 *PA*, 11, 12, 13, 16, 28 Apr 1897 p. 68–7.

28 VB to AVS, 3 Aug 1907, Tate Gallery.

29 VB, Memoir Club Paper: 'Introduction to Letters from Leslie Stephen to Mary Fisher', deleted passage. QB.

30 Stella Duckworth, Diary, 5 Mar 1896, Berg.

31 The three different versions of the scene are given in 'Reminiscences', *MB*, p.58; SP, *MB*, p.112; and *D*, 22 Aug 1922, II, p.190.

32 *D*, ibid.

33 Memoir, 18 July 1939, A5c, MHP, Sussex.

34 SP, *MB*, pp.116–17.

35 'Reminiscences' *MB*, p.48.

36 Leslie to Charles Eliot Norton, 23 Aug 1896, 10 Jan 1897, Harvard.

37 Leslie to Stella, 10, 13 Apr 1897, Berg.

38 Memoir, 18 July 1939, A5c, MHP, Sussex.

39 *D*, 21 Jan 1918, I, p.110 and Ch.21, note 48.

40 *Three Guineas*, pp.256–65; see also my introduction to *The Years*, OUP, 1992, pp.xii–xiv.

41 VB, 'Life at Hyde Park Gate', QB.

42 *PA*, 28 Apr 1897, p.77.

43 *MB*, p.119. For the 'mismanagement' and different versions of Stella's death, see Love, op. cit., p.193; Stephen Trombley, *All That Summer She was Mad*, Continuum, 1982, p.77, note 5; and de Salvo, *Virginia Woolf, Female Victim of Male Medicine*, who imagines that AVS may have felt 'partly responsible' for Stella's death and that she may have also 'considered Stella's pregnancy her responsibility' if leaving the couple on their own at Bognor had meant that Stella 'engaged in sexual intercourse before her marriage'. 'Virginia Woolf at Fifteen', in *Virginia Woolf: A Feminist Slant*, ed. Jane Marcus, University of Nebraska, 1983, pp.101–3.

44 VD to VB, 6 July 1942, Tate Gallery.

45 A perforated appendix could have led to peritonitis, or a retroverted uterus could have led to a ruptured uterus and thence to peritonitis. And pregnancy would have lent another hazard to peritonitis.

46 *PA*, 12, 20 May 1897, pp.87–8.

47 *PA*, 23 June 1897, p.105.

48 *PA*, 12 July 1897, p.113.

49 *PA*, 7 July 1897, p.112. On Adeline's friendship with Stella, and her 'grief and despair' at Stella's death, see Ursula Vaughan Williams, *R.V.W. A Biography of Ralph Vaughan Williams*, Clarendon Press, 1964, p.49.

50 *PA*, July–Dec 1897, pp.115–34.

51 SP, *MB*, pp.61, 137.

52 SP, *MB*, p.137.

53 SP, *MB*, p.150.

54 *PA*, 30 Mar 1897, p.62.

55 SP, *MB*, p.117.

56 *D*, 1 Jan 1939, V, p.198.

57 *D*, 1 July, 23 July 1918, 9 Jan 1939.

58 Payments continued to 1931 when he remarried; when VW was ill in 1915 LW asked Jack Hills to advance the £100 owing to her so that he could pay the medical bills. In 1938, when he died, the capital

was bequeathed equally to VW, VB and Adrian Stephen, and VW received about £1,300 in securities. *D*, 1 July 1931, IV, p.33; 27 Nov 1939, V, p.247; *L* VI, 3570, p.372; LW to Jack Hills, 7 Mar 1915, Spotts, p.211.

59 SP, *MB*, p.113.
60 AVS to Thoby, 27 Sep 1897, *L* I, 85, p.10.
61 SP, *MB*, p.155.
62 SP, *MB*, p.157.
63 *D*, 21 Sep 1929, III, p.255.
64 Spalding, pp.18, 36–7.
65 See *QB*I, p.73 on her standing at a high desk, perhaps to compete with Vanessa. This desk was handed down to QB and eventually had its legs chopped down.
66 *PA*, 10 Jan 1897 p.10; also AVS to Thoby, July 1901, *L* I, 36, p.42.
67 *PA*, 2 May 1897 p.80.
68 AVS to VD, early 1902, *L* I, 42, p.49.
69 *D*, 8 Dec 1929, III, p.271.
70 *D*, 15 Aug 1924, II, p.310.
71 *PA*, 2 Mar 1897, p.47.
72 *PA*, 25 Mar 1897, p.22.
73 *QB*I, p.26; Love, op. cit., pp.155–6. According to QB, VW always counted on her fingers.
74 Leslie to Thoby, 1 June 1901, QB.
75 *PA*, 18 Sep 1899, p.160; AVS to Emma Vaughan, Oct 1902, *L* I, 53, p.56.
76 VW to William Plomer, 6 Dec 1931, *L* IV, 2478, p.411. Clara Pater inspired a lesbian story written in 1926, 'Slater's Pins Have No Points'. See *CSF*, pp.216–20, 305–6.
77 *PA* 1903, pp.181–4.
78 Greek notebook, MHP A21, Sussex.
79 Ibid.
80 *D*, 15 Feb 1922, II, p.164.
81 SP, *MB*, p.153.
82 AVS to VD, Oct/Nov 1903, *L* I, 110, p.103.
83 AVS to Thoby, 5 Nov 1901, *L* I, 39, p.45.
84 AVS to Thoby, May 1903, *L* I, 81, p.77.

CHAPTER 8: ABUSES

1 SP, *MB*, p.162.
2 See *The Years*, p.282.
3 SP, *MB*, p.128.
4 *D*, 9 Jan 1939, V, p.198.
5 VW to VB, 11 May 1936, *L* VI, 3132, p.38.
6 *PA* 1903, p.178.
7 'Reminiscences', *MB*, p.37.
8 Leslie to Thoby, 13 June 1896; 14 Nov 1896; 22 Nov 1902, 18 Oct 1902, QB.
9 AVS to Emma Vaughan, 27 Sep 1900, *L* I, 33, p.37; 19 Apr 1900, *L* I, 28, p.30.
10 'Reminiscences', *MB*, p.64.
11 VB, 'Life at Hyde Park Gate', QB; Annan, on Leslie's irrationality about his income, p.73.
12 SP, *MB*, p.119.
13 SP, *MB*, p.158.
14 *D*, 3 Sep 1928, III, p.194.
15 *D*, 13 June 1933, IV, p.162.
16 *D*, 28 Nov 1928, III, p.208.
17 *D*, 7 Aug 1937, V, p.108.
18 *D*, 9 Apr 1935, IV, p.298.
19 Annan, p.121.
20 *The Voyage Out*, p.26.
21 *TL*, pp.184–5.
22 VW to CB, 21 Feb 1931, *L* IV, 2330, p.294; William Rothenstein, *Men & Memories*, 1931–2.
23 Fredegond Shove to VB, 4 Dec [1918], n.d. [1918], King's.
24 May Reed Bobbitt, ed. *With Dearest Love to All; The Life and Letters of Lady Jebb*, Faber, 1960, p.240.
25 'Phyllis and Rosamond', *CSF*, pp.17–29.
26 AVS to VD, 29 June 1906, *L* I, 274, p.228.
27 Notebook, Sept 1902, MHP A26, Sussex.
28 '22 Hyde Park Gate,' *MB*, p.190.
29 'Reminiscences', '22 Hyde Park Gate', *MB*, pp.67, 185.
30 SP, *MB*, p.167.
31 George Duckworth's letters to the Booth family are in Senate House.
32 For Margaret as 'stalwart, loyal, loving, kind and sensible' and George Duckworth as 'a man of few

brains but of a happy disposition, good looking and well intentioned ... [his] main misfortune in life was that he was the half-brother of Virginia Stephen, whose brilliant venomous pen has ridiculed him for posterity,' see Margaret Fitzherbert, *The Man Who Was Greenmantle: A Biography of Aubrey Herbert*, John Murray 1983, p.49.

33 The networks overlapped via the Lushingtons, and later, through e.g, Eddie Marsh and Desmond MacCarthy, who went to some of the big Edwardian parties.

34 Fitzherbert, op.cit., p.2.

35 Raymond Asquith to Aubrey Herbert on the 1903–4 London season, quoted Fitzherbert, op. cit., p.42.

36 SP, *MB*, p.167.

37 Leonore Davidoff, *The Best Circles*, 1973, Cresset, 1986, p.56.

38 AVS to Emma Vaughan, 8 Aug 1901, *L* I, 37, p.43.

39 *PA* 1903, pp.167, 170.

40 VW to Philip Morrell, 30 June 1919, *L* II, 1065, p.373.

41 VW to ES, 11 Mar 1931, *L* IV, 2335, p.297.

42 *Jacob's Room*, p.72. Cf. Eliot's *Prufrock*, also a poem about being awkwardly on the edge of society ('In the room the women come and go'). She discussed this poem with Eliot in the week she was writing this scene in the novel. *D*, 17–20 Sept 1920, II, pp.67–8.

43 Cf. *PA*, p.170; and 'The New Dress', *CSF*, p.171.

44 *Jacob's Room*, p.73.

45 *PA* 1903, p.171.

46 '22 Hyde Park Gate' *MB*, pp.186, 168.

47 Caramagno, p.183.

48 *MB*, p.66.

49 *MB*, p.193.

50 *MB*, p.198.

51 MHP A14, Sussex.

52 MHP A16, Sussex.

53 *D*, 18 May 1920 II, p.26.

54 *D*, 5 Dec 1920 II, p.77.

55 *D*, 26 May 1921 II, p.121.

56 Many contemporaneous accounts of sexual abuse argue that inconsistent or missing memories of the abuse, combined with other 'symptoms', can indicate that abuse did take place. (Advertisement from Adult Survivors of Child Abuse, California, 1992). In reaction to numerous accusations in the 1980s and early 1990s of sexual abuse within families, some American parents in 1992 formed the False Memory Syndrome Foundation, defending themselves against charges of abuse which the 'survivors' had been encouraged to remember in the course of therapy. See Lawrence Wright, 'Remembering Satan', *New Yorker*, 17, 24 May, 1993.

57 AVS to VB, 25? July 1911, *L* I, 576, p.472.

58 VW to VB, 20 Feb 1922, *L* II, 1218, p.505.

59 VW to VD, 23 June 1925, *L* III, 1562, p.191.

60 VW to ES, 18 Sep 1931, *L* IV, 2438 p.382.

61 VW to ES, 2 Feb 1932, *L* V, 2519, p.13.

62 AVS to George Duckworth, *L* I, 12, 13, 21, pp.14, 15, 21.

63 *D*, 1 May 1934, IV, p.211.

64 VW to VB, 3/4 May 1934, *L* V, 2887, p.299.

65 VB to AVS, 8 Sep 1904, Berg.

66 OM, Diary, 9 Nov 1932, Goodman family papers. OM gives the half-brother's name as Gerald, not George, but this was probably OM's misrecording (her diaries can be unreliable).

67 Fredegond Shove to VB, 4 Dec 1918, King's.

68 *QB* I, p.44, was the first to describe George's 'nasty erotic skirmish', and to conclude that this 'terrified' Virginia 'into a posture of frozen and defensive panic' about sex. QB was challenged, e.g. by Nigel Nicolson, who claimed that VW was exaggerating in recollection (*L* I, p.xvii), and by Suzanne Henig, in *Virginia Woolf Quarterly*, I, 2, Winter 1972, for

giving no 'satisfactory documentation' except for his mother's reports. Henig suggests that VW 'might have imagined or even wished her elder half-brother's interest to be more than it was'. Others have suggested that VW exaggerated or have found the evidence inconclusive (Spalding, p.19; Jean O. Love, *Virginia Woolf: Sources of Madness and Art*, University of California Press, 1977, p.195; Gordon, p.119; Rose, p.255). More recently, an orthodoxy of VW as a victim of sexual abuse and incest, pioneered by Louise de Salvo, has come to dominate her story. But de Salvo, though influential, is questionable, since she constantly over-interprets or manipulates the evidence. E.g. (i) Speaking of VW's reference in her letter to VB of 3/4 May 1934 (*L* V, 2887, p.299), in which VW says that Vanessa's memoir has flooded her with horror, de Salvo comments (p.72): 'Vanessa sent her sister a memoir of what George had done to her, describing, perhaps, certain events about which her sister had been unaware.' But there is no evidence for the contents of the memoir. (ii) She argues (pp.256–8) that the story of the 'Terrible Tragedy in a Duckpond', written in the Warboys diary for 1899 (in which AVS describes, in mock-dramatic terms, herself, Emma Vaughan and Adrian punting at night in a duck pond covered in duckweed, capsizing and drowning), is a coded cry for help and an accusation against the Duckworths. And she links this to the 'seemingly innocuous' Swinburne quotation, in *Between the Acts*, of 'Swallow, my sister, O sister swallow', and concludes: 'Women who have been sexually abused often refer to their feelings of being smothered, of not being able to breathe. In many case these images become connected to having been forced into oral sex.' These examples suggest that linguistic evidence is being distorted to

fit a theory: there is no proof from VW's writing that she was forced into swallowing George's semen. De Salvo's reading has been challenged by e.g.'A Question of Evidence', Ray Longtin, *The Charleston Magazine*, Winter/Spring 1991–2, pp.30–2, and by Caramagno, pp.7–8, 144, arguing against the claim that abuse and incest necessarily lead to breakdown and suicide.

CHAPTER 9: FIRST LOVES

1   AVS to Emma Vaughan, 11 Sep 1899, *L* I, 27, p.29.
2   AVS to George Duckworth, 22 Apr 1900, *L* I, 29, p.31.
3   AVS to VD, 19? Sep 1903, *L* I, 101, p.94.
4   *HPG*, 14 Apr 1895.
5   See Caroll Smith-Rosenberg, 'The Female World of Love and Ritual: Relations between Women in Nineteenth Century America', *Signs*, 1, no.1, Fall 1975, and Lillian Faderman, *Surpassing the Love of Men: Romantic Friendships between Women from the Renaissance to the Present* (New York, Morrow, 1981) for such friendships.
6   AVS to Eleanor Cecil, 16 Aug 1907, *L* I, 377, p.304.
7   AVS to Emma Vaughan, 11 Sep 1899, *L* I, 27, p.28; 17 June 1900, *L* I, 31, p.33; 1 Nov 1904, *L* I, 187, p.149.
8   AVS to Emma Vaughan, 27 Nov 1904, *L* I, 195, p.160.
9   *D*, 9 Oct 1917, I, p.57.
10 *D*, 30 Mar 1922, II, p.174.
11 VW to VB, 22 May 1917, *L* II, 837, p.156.
12 AVS to Emma Vaughan, 12 Aug 1899, *L* I, 26, p.27.
13 AVS to VB, 18 May 1909, *L* I, 488, p.396.
14 *D*, 2 June 1921, II, p.122.
15 VW to VB, 9 Dec 1917, *L* II, 894, p.202.
16 Spalding, p.181.
17 *D*, 27 Nov 1925, III, p.46.

18 VB, Memoir, QB.
19 *D*, 16 Nov 1921, II, p.144.
20 'Friendship's Gallery', 1907, *Twentieth Century*, Fall 1979, vol.25, p.283.
21 AVS to VD, [Autumn 1903], *L* I, 118, p.107.
22 AVS to Eleanor Cecil, 10 Nov 1905, *L* I 252, p.212.
23 *D*, 8, 14 Oct 1922, II, pp.206–7.
24 *D*, 15 Oct 1923, II, p.272; 18 June 1925, III, p.32.
25 AVS to VD, [June 1903], *L* I, 86, p.81.
26 *D*, 16 May 1919, I, p.274.
27 AVS to Eleanor Cecil, 10 Nov 1905, *L* I, 252, p.212; 18 Apr 1906, *L* I, 267, p.223.
28 Eleanor Cecil to VW, 24 Oct 1928, 15 June 1938, 31 Dec 1927, MHP Sussex.
29 Joy Burden to NN, 7 Sep 1974, Sussex.
30 VD, Notebooks, 1918, Longleat.
31 'Real Letters', *TLS*, 6 Nov 1919, *E* III, p.122.
32 VD, Notebooks, Longleat.
33 VD to VW, 24 Sep [1927?], Berg.
34 Notebook, MHP, A 26, Sussex.
35 VW to VB, 22 May 1917, *L* II, 837, p.156.
36 Leslie to Mary Fisher, 14 Sept 1902, VB memoir, QB.
37 *Friendship's Gallery*, p.284.
38 *D*, 16 May 1919, I, p.278.
39 Ibid.
40 VD, 'The Stephen Family', unpublished memoir, MHP Sussex.
41 AVS to VD, 30 June? 1903, *L* I, 88, p.82.
42 Quotations in the next two paragraphs are taken from AVS to VD, 1902–4, *L* I, nos 43–164, pp.49–128.
43 AVS to VD, 11? Oct 1903, *L* I, 107, p.99.
44 AVS to VD, 2 Oct 1903, *L* I, 105, p.97.
45 AVS to VD, Oct/Nov 1902, *L* I, p.60.
46 The kangaroo joke was in many of the letters; the other images are in *Friendship's Gallery*.
47 AVS to VD, 30 Aug 1908, *L* I, 447, p.367.

48 VW to VD, 8 Dec 1936, *L* VI, 3197, p.101. VD's bound volumes of her copies of the letters, interspersed with photographs of the Stephens and a few of Virginia's drawings (copies of Blake and Rossetti) are headed, in VD's writing, with the line 'Not for publication'.
49 AVS to VD, 2 Oct 1903, *L* I, 105, p.98; *Friendship's Gallery*, p.291.
50 *D*, 8 Dec 1929, III, p.271.
51 AVS to VD, 30 June? 1903, *L* I, 88, p.82.
52 AVS to Emma Vaughan, 17? June 1900, *L* I, 31, p.33.
53 AVS to Emma Vaughan, 23 Apr 1901, *L* I, 35, p.42.
54 *PA*, 4 Sep 1899, p.156.
55 *PA*, Appendix E.
56 *PA*, 1903, p.203.
57 AVS to Thoby, July 1901, *L* I, 36, p.42.
58 *PA*, 1903, pp.178–9.
59 *D*, 16 Mar 1936, V, p.18.
60 VD, Memoir.
61 VW to ES, 1 July 1936, *L* VI, 3148, p.51.
62 Quotations in the next two paragraphs are taken from *L* I, 123–183.
63 *PA*, 1903 p.208.
64 SP, *MB*, p.150.
65 SP, *MB*, p.151, and alternative version, BL.
66 *The Voyage Out*, p.249.
67 *TL*, p.66.
68 *The Waves*, p.228.
69 SP *MB* p.81.

CHAPTER 10: 'MADNESS'

1 The ratio of genetic influence, biochemical factors, and environmental factors in manic-depressive-illness (MDI) is still unprovable; so is the *causative* influence of 'life events'.
2 *D*, 15 Jan 1933, IV, p.143.
3 MS fragment, 'The teatable was the centre', Berg. *D*, 1 Mar 1937.
4 For anorexia see Elaine Showalter, *The Female Malady: Women, Madness and English Culture, 1830–1980*,

NOTES TO PAGES 176–82

Virago, 1987, pp.127–9; A.J. Dunning, *Extremes: Reflections on Human Behaviour*, trs. Johan Theron, Secker, 1993, p.163.

5 Cf. Anne Sexton: 'An overview of her case would distinguish at least three different possible sources: biological, psychological, and sociological . . . Anecdotal evidence of breakdowns on both sides of her family suggests a genetic predisposition to a biologically based illness, a supposition reinforced by Sexton's extreme physiological symptoms: wildly alternating moods, anorexia, insomnia, waves of suicidal and other impulses, rages, rapid heartbeat, Diane Wood Middlebrook, *Anne Sexton*, Virago, 1991, p.37.

6 The specialist territory of diagnostic terminology is daunting to a literary critic with no medical training. But shifts in psychiatric taxonomy in accordance with prevailing social ideologies are part of this story. E.g. (i): '**Neurosis**': *The Diagnostic and Statistical Manual of the American Psychiatric Association*, 3rd ed. revised (DSM IIIR), uses the word 'disorder' rather than 'neurosis'. For those who reject the concept of mental illness as a disease, 'neurosis' avoids using terms like 'psychosis'. But for many psychiatrists 'neurosis' continues to be a distinct category (separable from 'psychosis', 'dementia' or 'personality disorder') to mean a condition involving troublesome thoughts, fear, mental discomforts or habits, or bodily discomforts with no neurological basis, but without hallucinations or self-deceptions. E.g. (ii): '**Schizophrenia**': until the mid-1970s the diagnosis of schizophrenia was much broader in the States than in Europe, incorporating almost any case of mental illness involving delusions or hallucination. (Richard Warner, *Recovery from Schizophrenia: Psychiatry and Political Economy*, Routledge, 1985, p.7.) So, though VW's hallucinations might conform to a diagnosis of MDI, there is still a lingering unprovable hypothesis that she might have been 'a little' schizophrenic. Eg.(iii): '**Cyclothymia**' DSM IIIR defines it as a condition involving 'numerous Hypomanic Episodes and numerous periods of depressed mood or loss of interest or pleasure of insufficient severity to meet the criteria for a Major Depressive or Manic Episode'. Professor Kay Jamison (Psychiatry, Johns Hopkins) cites numerous cases of writers and artists (from Melville, Lamb, Balzac and Hemingway to Goethe, O'Neill and Woolf) who have suffered from what she calls 'extreme cyclothymia' (Kay Redfield Jamison and Frederick Goodwin, *Manic-Depressive Illness*, OUP, 1990, p.347); and argues that the condition can be beneficial as well as destructive for the artist. But some doctors regard cyclothymia as a dubious term, whose symptoms could just as well fall under the label of mild bipolar disorder, but which provides a less alarming name.

7 LW, *BA*, p.76.

8 Leslie to George Duckworth, 5 Sep 1897, Duckworth family papers; Leslie to Charles Eliot Norton, 26 June 1898, Norton papers, Harvard University MS AM 1088(7024).

9 Stella Duckworth, Diary, 13 Oct 1896, 21 Oct 1896, Berg.

10 SP *MB*, p.136.

11 MHP A5c, Sussex.

12 LW, *BA*, p.77.

13 Ibid., p.78.

14 Ibid., p.81.

15 Ibid., p.161.

16 Ibid., pp.163–4.

17 VB to CB, nd, [1910], Tate Gallery.

18 VB to CB, 23 Aug 1913, Tate Gallery.

19 VB to RF, 7 Apr 1914, Tate Gallery.

20 VB to RF, [1914], Tate Gallery.

21 Jean Thomas to LW, 11 Oct 1913, MHP, Sussex.

22 George Savage to LW, 25 Oct 1913, Sussex.

23 E.g. letters to LW from George

Savage (28 Aug 1915), Sydney Belfrage (5 Feb 1914), Maurice Craig (8 Apr 1918), Maurice Wright (15 Sep 1913). MHP Sussex.

24 In pre-war English psychiatry 'resistance to Freudian theories and hostility to feminist protests . . . seemed to have reached an intellectual impasse.' Showalter, op. cit., p.164.

25 *Octavia Wilberforce: The Autobiography of a Pioneer Woman Doctor*, ed. Pat Jalland, Cassell, 1989.

26 See Showalter, op. cit., pp.121, 137, on 'a moralistic, domineering, and masculinist generation of doctors' in the late nineteenth century; she and argues that AVS was a victim of a war between men and women masquerading as negotiations between doctors and patients: 'English psychiatric treatment of nervous women [in the nineteenth century] was ruthless, a microcosm of the sex war intended to establish the male doctor's total authority.'

27 Stephen Trombley, *All That Summer She Was Mad*, Continuum, 1982, pp.192, 209.

28 Showalter, op. cit., p.134; Trombley, op. cit., pp.135–7. Showalter traces (p.172) the presentation of 'neurasthenic' symptoms in First World War shell-shocked soldiers, and the descriptions of war neuroses as exhibiting 'a feminine kind of behaviour in male subjects'. Cf. the doctors' treatment of Septimus Smith in *Mrs Dalloway*.

29 Details of the Weir Mitchell system from A. Proust and G. Ballet, *The Treatment of Neurasthenia*, 1902, pp.182–91.

30 VW to LW, Sept to Nov 1904, *L* I, 186–189 pp.147–53.

31 VW to LW, Aug 1913, *L* II, 675 to 683, pp.32–6.

32 AVS to VB, 28 July [1910], *L* I, 533, pp.431–2.

33 Digitalis was often given by mistake for heart complaint when hyperthyroidism had been missed.

34 AVS to VD, 30 Oct [1904], *L* I, 186, p.147.

35 Jan–Feb 1929, *L* IV, 1986–2002, pp.7–24.

36 Caramagno, p.13, quotes Emil Kraepelin in 1921 reporting on the frequency of headaches in manic-depressive patients, and an article by Leo Hollister on 'Treating Depressed Patients with Medical Problems', which lists the physical manifestations of depression as including 'fatigue, headache, gastrointestinal disturbances . . . anorexia and weight loss, bad taste in the mouth, chronic pain, loss of interest, inactivity, reduced sexual desire, and a general feeling of despondency'. The conclusion is that 'anxiety-depression *can mimic many diseases or disorders*'. (my italics).

37 *D*, 15 Aug 1929, III, p.241. These kind of crushing occipital headaches had been diagnosed by the nineteenth-century French expert on hysteria, Jean-Martin Charcot, as 'neurasthenic headaches': the 'casque neurasthenique.' A. Proust and G. Ballet, op. cit., p.36.

38 *D*, 14 Feb 1922, II, p.160.

39 VW to VD, 1 Mar 1922, *L* II, 1224, p.511.

40 Henry Upson, *Insomnia and Nerve Strain*, Putnams, 1908, pp.28–32.

41 *D*, 7 Jan 1923, II, p.225, on 'thrust[ing] in my upper teeth' when getting up in the night.

42 *D*, 16 August 1922, II, p.189.

43 LW to MLD, 22 Feb 1923, Sussex.

44 VW to VSW, 7 June 1927, *L* III, 1771, p.390.

45 VW to ES [25 June 1936], *L* VI, 3146, p.49.

46 Dr James Durham suggested to me the possibility of a tubercular infection, or of mild chronic disseminated lupus erythematosus (though none of the other symptoms was present), or even chronic brucellosis.

47 *D*, 11 Feb 1928, III, 174.

48 *D*, 15 Sep 1926, III, p.110.

49 *D*, 1 Mar 1937, V, p.63.

50 Henry Maudsley, *Responsibility in*

Mental Disease, 1874, cited in Vieda Skultans, *Madness and Morals: Ideas on Insanity in the Nineteenth Century*, Routledge, 1975, p.208.

51 Skultans, op. cit., p.22; Caroline Moorehead, *Bertrand Russell*, Sinclair-Stevenson, 1992, p.64.

52 George Savage, 'Alternation of Neuroses', 1887, quoted Trombley, op. cit., p.116.

53 Holograph Notes for '*Mrs Dalloway*', 9 Nov 1922–2 Aug 1923, Berg; *Mrs Dalloway*, p.100.

54 *Mrs Dalloway*, p.98.

55 *D*, 9 Jan 1924 Vanessa writes to her when she is at the Retreat at Burley Park that she expects to see her leading a 'troup of lunies'. VB to AVS, 17 July 1910, II, p.283, Marler, p.94.

56 Kathleen Jones, *Lunacy, Law and Conscience 1744–1855*, Routledge 1955, p.201.

57 John and Samuel Wormald, *A Guide to the Mental Deficiency Act, 1913*, P.S. King, 1913, p.8.

58 LW, *BA*, pp.161–2. It is possible that since VW's symptoms differed so much from 'neurasthenia' and were so evidently those of 'manic-depressive' illness that the doctors, by describing her as neurasthenic, were trying to avoid the stigma of 'mania' and the probability of her having to be incarcerated in an asylum as a case of MDI. 70 per cent of those committed to asylums under the 1890 Lunacy Act by 1900 were for suicide attempts.

59 *PA*, 16 May 1897, p.86.

60 *D*, 14 Sep 1925, III, p.40.

61 *D*, 12 Aug 1933, IV, p.172.

62 *D*, 5 Sep 1925, III, p.39.

63 *D*, 2 June 1931, IV, p.29.

64 *D*, 18 Aug 1921, II, p.132. For fidgets, see also *D*, 22 Aug 1922, 14 Sep 1940, II, p.191, V, p.320.

65 *D*, 8 Aug 1921, II, p.125.

66 LW to LS, 14 Sep 1913, Spotts, p.191.

67 Warner, pp.102–3; Anne Digby, *Madness, Morality and Medicine: A Study of the York Retreat 1796–1914*, CUP, 1985, p.72.

68 Michel Foucault, *Madness and Civilization: A History of Insanity in the Age of Reason* 1961, trans. Richard Howard, Random House, 1965. Digby, op. cit., observes that Foucault's theory about moral management was impossible for him to prove, since there was no first-hand evidence of the patients' state of minds.

69 The case notes of admissions to the Retreat in York are still full in the early twentieth century of the language of self-blame and guilt: 'Patient had asked her to chop her head off, as she could do quite well without it' (1913), 'Signs of mental disorder first appeared [in] a lack of interest in her household work and a fear she could not get through the usual spring cleaning' (1914), 'She thinks she is a source of evil, and is harmful to others' (1915), 'Believes that God is talking to her and telling her that she has done a great wrong' (1926). Admission Registers, The Retreat, York.

70 *D*, 5 Sep 1926, 15 Sep 1926, III, pp.107, 111.

71 Caramagno, p.10.

72 See Alison Light, in *Forever England: Femininity, Literature and Conservatism between the Wars*, Routledge, 1991, p.210, on middle-class femininity after the First World War taking on 'what had formerly been regarded as distinctly masculine qualities: in particular the ethics of a code of self-control and a language of reticence'.

73 VW to ES, [31 May 1934], *L* V, 2899, p.307.

74 *D*, 14 Sep 1919, I, p.298.

75 VW to EMF, 21 Jan 1922, *L* II, 1210, p.499.

76 *D*, 16 Feb 1930, III, p.287.

77 Notes for '*Mrs Dalloway*', 16 Oct 1922, in *Jacob's Room*, Holograph Vol III, Berg.

78 *D*, 19 June 1923, II, p.248.

79 '*Mrs Dalloway*', *Holograph Notes*

Nov 9 1922 – Aug 2 1923, Berg, 19 Nov 1922.

80 *D*, 19 June 1923, II, p.248.

81 'Mrs Dalloway', Vol I, p.117, BL, ADD 1961; ADD 50484–53708.. cf. *Mrs Dalloway*, p.100.

82 VW to ES [31 May 1934], *L* V, 2899, p.307. In the MS of 'Mrs Dalloway' Septimus is described by one of the doctors as 'skeptical, suicidal . . . a difficult case'. 'Mrs Dalloway', BL, p.138.

83 'Mrs Dalloway', BL, ADD 1961; vol.I, pp.131, 133. cf. *Mrs Dalloway*, p.128.

84 *Mrs Dalloway*, p.108.

85 Caramagno reads VW in this way: p.148 on MD as 'a gift'.

86 E.g. the characters in *The Waves* 'comprise various aspects of Woolf's manic-depressive states', or *TL* is an exploration of 'the relationship of her bipolar illness to her childhood'. Caramagno, pp.214, 245.

87 *Mrs Dalloway*, pp.161–2.

88 In the manuscript, his messages are even more random and inept; in her plans for the scene, she writes 'The table drawer full of nonsense'. 'Mrs Dalloway', vol.III, p.19, BL.

89 'Madeleine', *TLS* 9 Oct 1919, *E* III, p.109.

90 'The Eccentrics', *Athenaeum*, 25 Apr 1919, *E* III, p.40.

91 Her essay 'On Being Ill', a mixture of literary criticism, autobiography and fairy-tale, moves from the isolation of illness to the 'incomprehensible' 'new language' to which illness connects one. *New Criterion*, Jan 1926, *CE* IV, pp.194, 200.

92 'Old Bloomsbury', *MB*, 1975, p.162; A16, MHP, Sussex. The king's obscenities sound very like the terrifying old man she thought she heard outside her bedroom and who turned out to be a cat; but for this hallucination no 'rational' explanation is provided.

93 LW, *BA*, pp.77, 164.

94 *QB I*, p.90.

95 VW to ES, 1 July [1930], *L* IV, 2199, p.183.

96 'On Not Knowing Greek', *CE* I, pp.1–13. The quotation is from J.W.Mackail, *Select Epigrams from the Greek Anthology* (Longman's Green & Co, 1908), III, Epitaphs, ii, 'On the Lacedaemonian Dead at Platea, Simonides, p.45. The reference to the nightingale is from Sophocles, *Oedipus Colonus*, trans. Jebb. References from *E*, vol.IV. She had reviewed Sassoon in 1917 and 1918 and knew him; he may be a model for Septimus Smith.

97 Trombley, op. cit., p.8.

98 Caramagno, p.47.

99 LW does not say when it was that VW told him about the birds singing in Greek.

100 On dreams expressing 'the power of unconscious thought' in an analogous way to 'neurotic, and especially hysterical, illness'; see 'Delusions and Dreams in Jensen's *Gravida*', 1907, trs. 1917, in *The Pelican Freud Library*, vol.XIV.

101 LW, 'Freud's *Psychopathology of Everyday Life*', *New Weekly*, June 1914, reprinted in Rosenbaum, *A Bloomsbury Group Reader*, Blackwell, 1993.

102 E.g. 'I doubt if family life has all the power of evil attributed to it, or psychoanalysis of good,' *D*, 12 May 1923, II, p.242; 'Last night I dined with the Wolves . . . Virginia made a more than usually ferocious onslaught upon psycho-analysis and psychoanalysts, more particularly the latter.' James Strachey to Alix Strachey, 14 May 1925, *Bloomsbury/Freud*, p.264.

103 Frances Partridge, personal communication to the author, 1992.

104 'Freudian Fiction', *TLS*, 25 Mar 1920, *E* III, p.197.

105 *D*, 16 June 1935, IV, p.323.

106 See Masud Khan, 'Beyond the Dreaming Experience', *Hidden Selves*, Hogarth 1983, pp.42–50, quoted by Adam Phillips in *On Kissing, Tickling and Being Bored*, Faber, 1993, p.67: 'The dream as

text, and therefore as available for interpretation, is replaced by the dream as experience, formative by virtue of being unknowable. The dream becomes a virtual synecdoche for the True Self of the patient, who is not an object to be deciphered . . . If the dream, as Freud showed, is the way we tell ourselves secrets at night about our desires, it also represents the impenetrable privacy of the Self.

107 *The Waves*, p.120.

108 SP, *MB*, 1976, p.78.

109 de Salvo, p.105, reads it sexually: 'The act of opening her legs wide enough to stretch across a puddle of water was horrifying to her possibly because she would be able to see in the puddle a reflection of her legs, open wide, which she might have associated with her abuse.' Caramagno, p.147, pours scorn on this 'simplistic Freudian interpretation' and links the puddle with the mirror, to describe 'the manic-depressive's search for a therapeutic mirroring "Other"'.

110 E.g. Laingian readings of Woolf in the early 1970s; attributions of her lifelong trauma to childhood sexual abuse in the 1980s. The language used for VW will echo the speaker's acceptance or rejection of medical terminology. If, like Kate Millett (quoted by Jonathan Miller, BBC 2, 3 Nov 1991), you believe that it is an abuse of scientific language to apply the terms of 'illness' to mental states ('pretty soon homelessness will be a disease') then the use of the word 'illness' for Virginia Woolf will offend you. But if resisting the definition of illness necessitates attributing her 'depressions' or 'breakdowns' to repressed sexual guilt or to the trauma of sexual violation, then she is imprisoned in a determinist reading which makes her a lifelong victim of oppression. Arguments will continue over whether her breakdowns were caused by 'life-events' whose effects

might be slow to manifest themselves, or whether she suffered from an illness for which the predisposition could have been inherited.

111 Mrs Valerie Eliot, communication to the author, 1992.

112 AVS to VD, [6? May 1904], *L* I, 178, p.140.

113 AVS to VD [22? Sep 1904], *L* I, 181, p.142.

114 Vanessa Stephen to Madge Vaughan, 28 Oct [1904], 18 Nov [1904], Sussex, and Marler, p.24.

CHAPTER 11: CHANGES

1 Gerald Duckworth to VD, nd. [Aug 1905], Dickinson papers, Longleat.

2 'Scenes from the Life of Mrs Bell', *The Charleston Bulletin*, [1923], QB.

3 AVS to VD, 31 Dec 1904, *L* I 145, p.119.

4 AVS to VD, 8 Nov 1904, *L* I, 189, p.153.

5 Vanessa Stephen to AVS, 25 Oct 1904, Berg.

6 Quotations from letters in this paragraph, autumn 1904, *L* I, 188 to 200, pp.151–64.

7 AVS to VD, Nov 1904, *L* I, 188, p.151.

8 Vanessa to AVS, 25 Oct 1904, Berg.

9 Vanessa to AVS, 5 Dec 1904, Berg.

10 'A London Square', MHP Sussex.

11 See 'Street Music', *E* I, p.30.

12 See *Deceived*. pp.48.

13 'Old Bloomsbury', *MB*, p.201.

14 *PA*, 4 Jan 1905, p.217.

15 Vanessa to AVS, 29? Oct 1904, Berg.

16 'Old Bloomsbury', *MB*, p.201.

17 Ibid. *MB*, p.201.

18 AVS to Madge Vaughan, mid-Dec 1904, *L* I, 202, p.167.

19 *PA*, 30 Jan 1905, p.230.

20 *PA*, 7 Jan 1905, pp.217–18.

21 *PA*, 4 Mar 1905 p.246, misremembered in *MB*, p.201.

22 'Phyllis and Rosamond', *CSF*, p.24.

23 *PA*, 22 Feb 1905 p.243.

24 *PA*,11 Jan 1905 p.220.

25 *PA*,11 Mar 1905 p.251.

26 AVS to VD, July 1905, *L* I, 237, p.197.

27 Vanessa Stephen to Madge Vaughan, [25 Mar 1905], quoted *QB* I, p.96.

28 *MB*, p.201.

29 The Cameron photographs which, a generation later, Angelica Garnett would hang in the passage at Charleston: *Deceived*, p.12.

30 'Old Bloomsbury', MS, MHP Sussex, A16.

31 Janet Case to VD, 19 Apr 1937, Longleat.

32 AVS to VD, 16 Jan 1906, *L* I, 259, p.217.

33 LS to LW, 21 Dec 1904, quoted Holroyd, 1971, p.19.

34 Hugh and Mirabel Cecil, *Clever Hearts: Desmond and Molly MacCarthy, A Biography*, Gollancz, 1990, rev. 1991, p.42.

35 LW, *S*, pp.182–3.

36 'Old Bloomsbury' *MB*, p.205.

37 Holroyd, 1971, p.237.

38 'Old Bloomsbury' *MB*, pp.203, 202. *PA*, 8 Mar 1905 p.219, gives 'talked the nature'; *MB* has 'talked about'.

39 Accounts of Bloomsbury have been largely written by men, beginning with Maynard Keynes, LW and CB and continuing with QB, J.K. Johnstone, Leon Edel, S.P. Rosenbaum, Michael Holroyd, Paul Levy and Richard Shone. VW and Frances Partridge are the exceptions.

40 E.g. 'Virginia Woolf's development owed much to Bloomsbury . . . As an artist or as an individual she could scarcely have found a more suitable milieu than she did in this society of equals.' J.K. Johnstone, *The Bloomsbury Group*, 1954, pp.10, 17.

41 Spater, p.39, lists Strachey, Sydney-Turner and Bell, R.G. Hawtrey, Desmond MacCarthy, Robin Mayor, Theodore Llewelyn Davies, C.P. Sanger, H.J.T. Norton, James Strachey, Maynard Keynes, J.T. Sheppard, Duncan Grant, Walter Headlam, Sydney Waterlow, Walter Lamb, Hilton Young, Jack Pollock. In *Bloomsbury*, 1968, Omega,

1974, QB adds to this list E.M. Forster, David Garnett, Roger Fry, Molly MacCarthy, Adrian Stephen, Gerald Shove, James and Marjorie Strachey, and Francis Birrell.

42 DG, 'Virginia Woolf', *Horizon*, III (June, 1941), pp.402–6, reprinted in SPR p.65.

43 *PA*, 20 Jan 1905, pp.225; AVS to Violet Dickinson, 1 Oct 1905, *L* I, 250, p.208. The other Apostle is either Hawtrey or Strachey.

44 Vanessa Stephen to Meg Booth, 24 Sep 1905, Booth Papers, Senate House, University of London, I/6063. Imogen Booth was the daughter of George's employer Charles Booth and the sister of Meg Booth, who married Anny Ritchie's son William in 1906.

45 *E* I, p.60.

46 'Effect of Oxbridge on Young Men', MHP, A 13B, Sussex, printed in Bell, I, Appendix C, pp.205–6, as 'Virginia Woolf and the Authors of *Euphrosyne*'.

47 AVS to Eleanor Cecil, Aug 1905, *L* I, 245, pp.202–3. The poem is in fact a well-known anonymous 'epitaph for a tired housewife', in a Bushey churchyard. See *Oxford Dictionary of Quotations*, 3rd ed., 1979, 'Anon', p.5.

48 See Angela Ingram, ' "The Sacred Edifices": Virginia Woolf and some of the Sons of Culture', in Marcus.

49 VW to JB, 11 Mar 1936, *L* VI, 3111, p.20.

50 VW to JB, 21 May 1936, *CS*, 3136a, p.372.

51 *The Voyage Out*, pp.141, 188.

52 Spalding, p.54.

53 *MB*, p.209.

54 *MB*, p.213.

55 AVS to Madge Vaughan, 1 Dec 1904, *L* I, 198, p.162.

56 AVS to VD, 11 Nov, 14 Nov 1904, *L* I, 191, 192, p.156.

57 VB, 'Old Bloomsbury', 1951, QB.

58 AVS to VD, 22 July 1906, *L* I, 279, p.232.

59 Andrew McNeillie estimates that

for her total contributions to the *Guardian* between 1905 and 1907 she was paid £17. *E* I, p.xviii.

60 VW to ES, 2 July 1934, *L* V, 2907, p.312; 12 Jan 1941, *L* VI, 3678, p.459.

61 AVS to VD, mid-Feb 1905, *L* I, 217, p.178.

62 For details of all AVS's early reviewing from 1905 to 1912, see *E* I.

63 *E* I, p.16.

64 AVS to Madge Vaughan, 11 Dec 1904, *L* I, 201, p.166.

65 AVS to VD, 4 Aug 1906, *L* I, 282, p.234.

66 E, p.54.

67 Ibid., p.75.

68 Ibid., p.43.

69 Ibid., p.35.

70 Ibid., p.121. Hakluyt would strongly influence *The Voyage Out*.

71 *E* I, p.237.

72 AVS to VD, Jan 1905, *L* I, 206, p.171.

73 *PA*, 16 Mar 1905, pp.252–3.

74 *PA*, 8 Mar 1905, p.272.

75 *E* I, Appendix III.

76 *PA*, 12 Feb 1905, p.236.

77 AVS to VD, mid-Feb 1905, *L* I, 217, p.178; *PA*, 15 Feb 1905, p.237.

78 *E* I, pp.22–4.

79 AVS to VD, 25 Aug 1907, *L* I, 380, p.306.

80 *PA*, 1 May 1905, p.270.

81 'Professions for Women', 1931, in *Virginia Woolf: Women and Writing*,

82 AVS to VD, 27 Aug 1905, *L* I, 248, p.206.

83 AVS to Madge Vaughan, mid Dec 1904, *L* I, 202, p.166.

84 AVS to VD, 3 Dec 1905, *L* I, 254, p.214.

85 AVS to VB, 7 Aug 1908, *L* I, 428, p.343.

86 *D*, 18 Feb 1922, II, p.169.

87 In a notebook, end 1905, she adds a tally of the total number of words she has written for her reviews. Silver, XXXV, 36, p.176.

88 *PA*, p.226. 'Impressions of Sir Leslie Stephen' is reprinted in *E* I, pp.127–9.

89 AVS to CB, 25 Dec 1908, *L* I, 462, p.376.

90 Vanessa Stephen to VS, 7 Dec 1906, Berg.

91 AVS to Madge Vaughan, 1 Dec 1904, *L* I, 198, p.162.

92 AVS to VD, 7 July 1907, *L* I, 369, p.299.

93 AVS to VD, July 1905, *L* I, 244, p.202.

94 AVS to Madge Vaughan, June? 1906, *L* I, 272, p.227.

95 Ibid.

CHAPTER 12: THOBY

1 AVS to VD [11 Jan 1905], *L* I, 211, p.175.

2 AVS to Eleanor Cecil, 10 Nov 1905, *L* I, 252, p.211.

3 AVS to Madge Vaughan, 27 Apr 1906, *L* I, 269, p.225.

4 AVS to VD [July 1905], *L* I, 243, p.201. For the Friday Club, see Spalding, p.56; Shone *BP*2, p.26.

5 Gwen later married the French painter Jacques Raverat.

6 Beatrice (Bobo) was a member of a large, talented family. She would marry one of Thoby's Cambridge friends, Robin Mayor, and have an affair with CB.

7 *D*, 10 Apr 1919, I, p.262.

8 *PA*, 23 Feb 1905, 7 Jan 1905, pp.241, 218.

9 *PA*, 1903, p.186.

10 *PA*, 17 April 1905, p.239.

11 'Anthony Hart', [VD], *These Thoughts Were Written by Anthony Hart*, nd. Inscribed 'A Tract for the Sp. from VD, 1905'. In *Leonard and Virginia Woolf: Books* at Washington State University.

12 *PA*, p.233; AVS to VD [1 Oct 1905], *L* I, 250, p.209.

13 *PA*, p.279.

14 AVS to VD [Jan 1905], *L* I, 206, p.172.

15 *PA*, 26 Feb 1905 p.243.

16 *PA*, 30 April 1903 p.269.

17 AVS to VD [4 Jan 1909], *L* I, 465,

p.379. The idea is reminiscent of the fate of Ajax, struck mad by the gods and haunted by voices, in one of the Greek plays AVS had read by 1908. [Greek notebook, MHP Sussex.]

18 *PA*, 2 Feb 1905, p.234; *L* I 431, 492, 493, 411, 442.

19 AVS to VD [24 Apr 1905], *L* I, 224, p.187.

20 Vanessa Stephen to AVS, 16 Apr 1906, Berg.

21 Adrian Stephen, Diary, 1909, MHP, Sussex.

22 Brother of MLD.

23 For Mary Sheepshanks, see Sybil Oldfield, *The Life and Times of F.M. Mayor and Mary Sheepshanks*, Virago, 1984.

24 AVS to VD [early Jan 1905], *L* I, 206, p.172.

25 AVS to VD [Jan 1905], *L* I, 212, p.175.

26 *PA*, 18 Jan 1905, p.224.

27 *PA*, 17 Jan 1905, p.223.

28 AVS to VD [Feb 1905], *L* I, 216, p.177.

29 *PA*, 4 Mar 1905 p.246. She also involved Adrian, Emma Vaughan, and Ka Cox.

30 *PA*, 22 Mar 1905 p.245.

31 AVS to VD, [18 June 1905], *L* I, 230, p.192.

32 *QB* I , p.106.

33 'Report on Teaching at Morley College', *QBI*, pp.202–4.

34 AVS to VD [9 Nov 1905], *L* I, 251, p.210.

35 Morley College Magazine, Sep–Oct 1907, quoted in Lindsay Martin, 'Virginia Woolf [*sic*] at Morley College', *The Charleston Magazine*, Winter/Spring 91/2, pp.21–6.

36 AVS to Eleanor Cecil [Dec 1907], *L* I, 398, p.321.

37 *Mrs Dalloway*, p.93. Leonard Bast in Forster's *Howards End*.

38 *Mrs Dalloway*, MS, ADD ADD 1961 BL.

39 *QB* I, p.203.

40 VW to Ben Nicolson, 24 Aug 1940, *L* VI, 3633, p.419. The reference to Morley College was in the draft, not the final version of the letter.

41 AVS to Eleanor Cecil [July 1905], *L* I, 235, p.196.

42 AVS to VD [27 Aug 1905], *L* I, 248, p.206.

43 AVS to VD, 10 Apr [1905], *L* I, 223, p.185;Cf. 'An Andalusian Inn', *Guardian*, 19 July 1905, *E* I, pp.49–52.

44 *PA*, 1905, p.291.

45 *PA*, 1906, p.303.

46 *PA*, 1906, p.315.

47 *PA*, 1908, p.380.

48 *PA*, 1908, p.374.

49 *PA*, 1907, p.368.

50 AVS to Eleanor Cecil (from Playden, Sussex), [16 Aug 1907], *L* I, 377, p.303.

51 *E* I, p.252.

52 *E* I, p.213, 'Scottish Women': 'It is due to this modesty, perhaps, that so many of the beautiful Scottish ballads are without the name of their author, and we may attribute some of them at least to rustic poetesses.'

53 *E* I, p.325, 'Lady Hester Stanhope'. In *L* I, 513, p.417, VB to CB, she presents herself, like Lady Hester, as an eccentric, 'ridiculous in the daylight'.

54 *E* I, p.169, 'The Memoirs of Sarah Bernhardt'.

55 *PA*, p.379.

56 *PA*, p.345.

57 *The Voyage Out*, pp.224, 218, 100, 194.

58 AVS to VD [30 Aug 1908], *L* I, 447, p.367: 'You call me an egoist – a woman who doesn't love her kind! I think of becoming a philanthropist.'

59 AVS to VB, Christmas Day 1910, *L* I, 546, p.442.

60 Spalding, p.58; QBI, p107.

61 'When I foster-mothered them all to Greece, she wrote fascinating little essays about all those places, not published.' VD, letter, 24 June 1942, Longleat.

62 SP, *MB*, p.153.

63 *PA*, 1906, p.311.

64 'A Vision of Greece', 27 June 1906, MHP A23, Sussex.

65 Greek notebook, MHP A21, Sussex.

66 'A Dialogue upon Mount Pentelicus', *CSF*, pp.66, 68.
67 *Jacob's Room*, pp.130, 141, 142.
68 Thoby to CB, 17 Sep 1906, King's.
69 This is a carefully written diary, with
essays in mind. But because of Thoby's death she published nothing
about Greece until *Jacob's Room*.
PA, 1906, p.331.
70 *PA*, 1906, p.319.
71 Greek diary, 1906, Berg, mistran-
scribed in *PA*, p.340.
72 *PA*, 1906, p.335. For Irene Noel,
and her relations with Desmond
MacCarthy, Hilton Young, and
Thoby, and her marriage to Phillip
Baker, See *D* 8 June 1925 III, p.29
and *Clever Hearts*, Chs 6, 12.
73 *PA*, p.356.
74 *PA*, p.357.
75 Adrian to CB, 24 Oct 1906, King's;
AVS to VD [8? Nov 1906], *L* I, 287,
p.240; VB to Margery Snowden, 26
Sep 1908, CP Sussex.
76 *QB* I, p.109.
77 AVS to VD [14 Nov 1906, 13? Dec
1906], *L* I, 295, 320, pp.244, 261.
78 AVS to VD [14 Nov 1906], *L* I, 295,
p.243.
79 A common complication of typhoid
was a perforation of the bowels. If
untreated, it could lead to a fatal
peritonitis. The operation was
extremely hazardous; either way the
risk of death was high. Thoby was
being treated for malaria (i.e. with
quinine) for the first weeks of his
illness, so, until the operation, he
had *untreated* typhoid. But one cannot be sure that if typhoid *had* been
diagnosed earlier he would have
survived, since there was then no
cure for typhoid except nursing and
general support.
80 George Meredith to AVS, 22 Nov
1906, Berg.
81 Caroline Emelia Stephen to VD, 20
Dec 1906, Longleat.
82 AVS to VD, *L* 307–326.
83 *E* I, p.142.
84 *D*, 26 Dec 1929, III, p.275.
85 Silver, p.237.Cf *D*, 7 Feb 1931, IV,
p.10.

CHAPTER 13: EXPERIMENTS

1 LS to LW, 16 Nov 1906, Berg.
2 AVS to Madge Vaughan, 17 Dec
1906, *L* I, 325, p.265.
3 AVS to VD, 23 Dec 1906, *L* I, 330,
p.270.
4 AVS to VD, 30? Dec 1906, *L* I, 333,
p.273.
5 AVS to VD, Feb 1907, *L* I, 341,
p.279.
6 AVS to VD, 3 Jan 1907, *L* I, 336,
p.276.
7 AVS to VD, 15? Oct 1907, *L* I, 389,
p.316.
8 AVS to VD, 7 July 1907, *L* I, 369,
p.299.
9 AVS to VD, 30? Dec 1906, *L* I, 333,
p.273.
10 AVS to VD, 3 Jan 1907, *L* I, 336,
p.275.
11 AVS to VD, 2 Jan 1907, *L* I, 335,
p.274.
12 Spalding, p.67.
13 *QB* I, p.113.
14 AVS to VD, 6 Feb 1907, *L* I, 339,
p.278.
15 AVS to VD, Feb 1907, *L* I, 349,
p.286.
16 AVS to Vanessa Stephen, 6 Feb
1907, *CS*, p.38.
17 LS to LW, 6 Feb 1907, Berg. For
the Stracheys and the march, see
Elizabeth French Boyd, *Bloomsbury
Heritage*, Hamish Hamilton, 1976
p.74.
18 AVS to Violet Dickinson, 22 Sep
1907, *L* I, 383, p.311.
19 There is no diary for 1907.
20 AVS to VD, 7 July 1907, *L* I, 369,
p.298.
21 AVS to VD 25 Aug 1907, *L* I, 380,
p.307.
22 *L* I, 369, 299.
23 AVS to VD, 31 Dec 1906, *L* I, 334,
p.274.
24 Review of *Nancy Stair*, *Guardian*,
10 May 1905, *E* I, p.40.
25 *CSF*, p.52.
26 AVS to VD, 1 Sep 1907, *L* I, 381,
p.308.
27 AVS to VD, 22 Sep 1907, *L* I, 383,
p.311.

28 AVS to VD, 25 Aug 1907, *L* I, 380, p.308.

29 VB to AVS, 6 Aug 1907, Berg, Marler, p.57.

30 *Friendship's Gallery*, pp.290, 296.

31 AVS to VB, 4 Aug 1908, *L* I, 427, p.342.

32 AVS to CB, 15 Apr 1908, *L* I, 406, p.325.

33 CB annotated the ms., approving all the most formal, unemotional and classical bits. MHP, Sussex.

34 VB to AVS, 20 Apr 1908, Berg, Marler, pp.62–3.

35 AVS to CB, 15 Apr 1908, *L* I, 406, p.325.

36 AVS to VB [Oct? 1907], *L* I, 390, p.316. But this date is hypothetical – it could be later.

37 AVS to VB, 10 Aug 1908, *L* I, 432, p.348.

38 AVS to VB, 11 Aug 1908, *L* I, 433, p.350.

39 CB to AVS, 30 Dec 1910, Berg.

40 VB to AVS, 11 Aug 1908, Berg, Marler, p.67.

41 AVS to VB, 4 Aug 1908, *L* I, 427, p.341: 'Cynthia will not speak.'

42 AVS to VB, 29 Aug 1908, *L* I, 444, p.363.

43 Shaw, who 'wrote his first seven plays, his finest literary, music and theatre criticism and [did] his most active political campaigning' in what he called 'this most repulsive house', worked upstairs in conditions of incredible squalor while his mother, neglecting all housework, communicated with the dead with her planchette and ouija board. Michael Holroyd, *Bernard Shaw*, Chatto, 1988, I, pp.192, 451, 458.

44 Rosamond Lehmann, *The Weather in the Streets*, Collins, 1936, pp.199–206.

45 AVS to VD, Dec 1908, *L* I, 463, p.377.

46 AVS to VD, 7 July 1907, *L* I, 369, p.299.

47 AVS to Eleanor Cecil, 12 Apr 1909, *L* I, 480, p.390.

48 AVS to Madge Vaughan, 2 Apr 1907, *L* I, 356, p.290; AVS to

Eleanor Cecil, 13 Apr 1909, *L* I, 480, p.390.

49 VB to AVS, 22 Mar 1907, Berg; AVS to Madge Vaughan, Apr 1907, 6 Nov 1907, *L* I, 358, 395, pp.292, 318.

50 Adrian Stephen, Diary, 4 July 1909, MHP, Sussex.

51 AVS to Madge Vaughan, 6 Nov 1907, *L* I, 395, p.319.

52 'The Messiah', *The Charleston Bulletin*, Christmas 1925, QB.

53 'The Cook', MHP A13 d, Sussex.

54 AVS to VB, 22? Aug 1911, *L* I, 581, p.475.

55 VB to AVS, 8 Aug 1907, Berg.

56 AVS to VB, 22 Aug 1911, *L* I, 581, p.475.

57 'Character in Fiction', 1924, *E* III, p.422.

58 AVS to Madge Vaughan, 28 June 1908, *L* I, 420, p.336.

59 AVS to LS, 4 June 1909, *L* I, 492, p.398.

60 *D*, 11 Oct 1929, III, p.260.

61 *D*, 12 Oct 1937, V, p.113.

62 AVS to VD, 26 Jan 1909, *L* I, 467, p.380; 8 Aug 1907, *L* I, 376, p.303. The editors of *L* assume AVS is referring to Thoby's death in *L* 376. But more probably VD has written on the 10th anniversary of Stella's death (19 July 1897): 'It is so odd the way you remember that', AVS writes back; there would be nothing 'odd' about remembering Thoby's death eight months before.

63 AVS to Madge Vaughan, 19 Nov 1908, *L* I, 455, p.374.

64 AVS to CB, 4 Sep 1910, *L* I, 534, p.434.

65 VW to CB, 14 May 1936, *L* VI, 3135, p.41.

66 AVS to Violet Dickinson, Mar 1909, *L* I, 478, p.389.

67 AVS to VB, 20 Aug 1908, *L* I, 439, p.357.

68 AVS to CB, 26 Dec 1909, *L* I, 573; p.416; Mar 1911, *L* I, 558, p.453.

69 AVS to CB, 26 Dec 1909, *L* I, 513, p.416.

70 AVS to VB, 20 Aug 1908, *L* I, 439, p.358.

71 Cf. 'The Duke and Duchess of Newcastle', (1911)with a fantasy-story in which 'the hero is for ever thinking about the dead', and finally, 'outraged by contact with unreal fugitive flesh-encumbered live people, he draws his razor and departs.' *E* I, p.345.

72 'Anon' to AVS, Mar 1909, MHP, Sussex; *QB* I, p.142.

73 *QBI*, p.117.

74 *D*, 30 Apr 1937, V, p.83.

75 'Old Bloomsbury', *MB*, p.211.

76 Adrian Stephen, Diary, June 1909. King's.

77 The family addiction to Wagner began with the big Covent Garden seasons of 1907–8. There are frequent refs. in the 1908 *Letters* to emerging 'bewildered' from hours of opera. 'The Opera' (1909) describes her mixed feelings for Wagner. (*E* I, pp.269–72) But in 1923 *Tristan* bored her. *L*, 1410.

78 *E* I, pp.292–3; VS to VB, *L* I, 499, 502, 505, pp.404, 407, 410; Saxon Sydney Turner to CB, 9 Aug, 1909, King's.

79 Adrian Stephen, Diary, 1 July 1909, quoted *QB* I, pp.146–7.

80 *D*, 3 Dec 1923, II, p.277.

81 *D*, 18 Nov 1929, III, p.266.

82 VW to Gwen Raverat, 1 May 1925, *L* III, 1550, p.181.

83 LS to LW, 8 Aug 1908, Berg.

84 'Old Bloomsbury' *MB*, p.214.

85 VW to ES, 22 June 1930, *L* IV, 2194, p.180.

86 CB to AVS, 14 Feb 1909, MHP, Sussex.

87 LS to CB, 21 May 1909, QB.

88 LS to LW, 19 Feb 1909, Sussex. Quoted by Holroyd, 1971, p.405, but omitted, oddly, by Spotts, in his excerpt from this letter, p.147.

89 The name perhaps derived from Samuel Johnson's chaste heroine *Aspasia*, who 'resists the heathen blandishments of the Sultan Mahomet' in his blank verse tragedy *Irene*. [Richard Holmes, *Dr Johnson and Mr Savage*, Hodder & Stoughton, 1993, p.11].

90 See Holroyd (1971, pp.24–6) on 'the aseptic, vestal texture of her fiction', her 'peculiarly bloodless and trivial' curiosity about life, her 'wraith-like spirit', the delvings of her novels into 'the sick, neurasthenic depths of her nature'. C.f. *QB* II, p.6 and *L* II, p.xiii. Elsewhere, her 'sexual coldness' is linked to her 'low self-esteem' (Edel, p.178); her 'neurotic attachment to older women' is an index of frigidity (Spilka, pp.18, 6, 8, quoted Caramagno, p.25); her revulsion from 'the fact (rather than the idea of sex)' shows that 'the connection between sex and dirt in her mind was very strong.' (Alexander, *Leonard and Virginia Woolf*, Harvester, 1992, p.37.) But dissenting voices have re-examined the mythology of her a-sexuality. (Dunn, p.187; Caramagno, p.25); See also Blanche Wiesen Cook, 'Women Alone Stir My Imagination', *Signs*, 1979, pp.718–39.

91 VW to ES, 12 Jan 1941, *L* VI, 3678, p.459.

92 *QB* II, p.6.

93 *Mrs Dalloway*, pp.34–5.

CHAPTER 14: LIAISONS

1 AVS to VB, 21 July 1911, *L* I, 574, p.470.

2 AVS to Saxon Sydney-Turner, 13 June 1910, *L* I, 526, p.427.

3 LS to LW, 19 Feb 1909, MHP, Sussex.

4 *QB* I, p.119, suggests he was interested in 'little girls'.

5 *QB* I, p.119; Walter Headlam to AVS, nd, King's; AVS to VB, *L* I, 318, 347, 354, 336.

6 Holroyd, 1971, p.409; AVS, *L* I, 432, p.348; VB to AVS, 16 Aug 1908, Berg; *QB* I, p.131; Fredegond Shove to VB, 1918, CP, Sussex; VW to VB, *L* II, 1171, p.480.

7 Holroyd, 1971, p.169; Walter Lamb to CB, 1906–11, King's; Walter Lamb to AVS, 1911, MHP, Sussex; *QB* I, pp.152, 172; Keith Clements,

Henry Lamb: The Artist and His Friends, Redcliffe, 1985, Ch. IV.

8 Sydney Waterlow, Diary, 8 Dec 1910, Berg.

9 VW to Ka Arnold-Forster, 23 Aug 1922, *L* II, 1276, p.549.

10 VW to ES, 1 May 1931, *L* IV, 2368, p.326.

11 VB to AVS, Aug 1908, Berg.

12 Adrian Stephen to VB, 20 Oct 1941, CP, Sussex.

13 AVS to CB, 4 Sep 1910, *L* I, 534, p.434.

14 AVS to LS, 6 Oct 1909, *L* I, 508, p.413.

15 AVS to CB, Feb 1907, *L* I, 345, p.282.

16 AVS to LS, 28 Apr 1908, *L* I, 409, p.328.

17 MHP, A24c, Sussex.

18 E.g., *The Voyage Out*, Ch.16.

19 AVS to CB, 6 May 1908, *L* I, 410, p.329.

20 e.g. Like the fondly satirical sketch 'The Messiah of Bloomsbury' for the entertainment of Charleston at Christmas 1925. QB.

21 CB to AVS, 3 Apr 1911, MHP, Sussex.

22 *QB* I, p.133.

23 CB to AVS, 27 June 1910, 30 July 1908, MHP, Sussex.

24 CB to AVS, 23 Aug 1908, MHP, Sussex.

25 AVS to VB, 24 June 1910, *L* I, 529, p.429.

26 CB, 'To AVS with a book', *Poems*, 1921.

27 CB to MH, 24 Nov 1914, Texas.

28 AVS to CB, 18 Aug 1907, *L* I, 378, p.305.

29 AVS to CB, 28 Aug 1908, *L* I, 442, p.362.

30 John Bayley, 'Pretending to be the Parlour-Maid', *London Review of Books*, 2 Dec 1993, p.20.

31 AVS to CB, May 1908, *L* I, 416, p.334.

32 VB to CB, June 1910, Sep 7, 8 1910, Tate Gallery.

33 VB to AVS, 7, 27 Aug 1908, Berg.

34 AVS to VB, 14 Aug 1908, *L* I, 437, p.355.

35 VB to AVS, 25 Aug 1908, Berg, Marler, p.71.

36 VB to AVS, 13 Aug 1908, Berg.

37 AVS to VB, 16 Aug 1909, *L* I, 503, p.408.

38 AVS to VB, 7 Aug 1908, *L* I, 428, p.343.

39 AVS to CB, 31? Dec 1909, *L* I, 515, p.418.

40 CB to AVS, 7 Aug 1908, MHP, Sussex.

41 AVS to LS, 1 Feb 1909, *L* I, 470, p.382; VB to AVS, 7 Feb 1909, Berg.

42 AVS to CB, 19 Feb 1909, *L* I, 474, p.386.

43 AVS to VB, 11 Apr 1911, *L* I, 563, p.458.

44 CB, *Minute Book*, King's.

45 AVS to VB, 7 Aug 1908, *L* I, 428, p.343.

46 Congreve, *The Double Dealer*, 1694, 'Epistle Dedicatory'.

47 AVS to CB, May 1908, *L* I, 416, p.334.

48 AVS to CB, 19 Aug 1908, *L* I, 438, p.357.

49 QB, *Bloomsbury*, p.25.

50 CB, *Old Friends*, Cassell, 1956, p.133.

51 G.E. Moore, 'The Ideal', *Principia Ethica*, 1903.

52 CB, *Old Friends*, p.133.

53 QB, *Bloomsbury*, p.33; LW, *S*, p.135.

54 AVS to CB, 19 Aug 1908, *L* I, 438, p.356.

55 For a detailed though schematically-interpreted description of the early drafts of *The Voyage Out*, see Louise de Salvo, *Virginia Woolf's First Voyage*, Macmillan, 1980.

56 CB to AVS, Oct 1908, ?5 Feb 1909, in *QB I*, pp.207-9.

57 CB to AVS, 12 Aug 1908, MHP, Sussex.

58 CB to MH, Mar 1915, 29 Mar 1915, Texas.

59 CB, *Old Friends*, pp.98, 102, 116.

60 CB to AVS, 27 Oct 1909, MHP, Sussex.

61 AVS to CB, 7? Feb 1909, *L* I, 471, p.383.

62 Memoirs of Lady Strachey [1928], MHP AD 25, Sussex. VW's published account of Lady Strachey is in *Books and Portraits* and *E* IV, p.573. cf LW, *S*, p.191.
63 Holroyd, 1971, p.67, 1994, p.20.
64 *D*, 24 Jan 1919, I, p.235.
65 *The Voyage Out*, pp.140, 143, 147, 205, 290, 352.
66 *D*, 15 Nov 1919, I, p.312.
67 *D*, 15 Sep 1920, II, p.65.
68 *D*, 16 May 1919, I, p.273.
69 *D*, 15 Sep 1920, II, p.65.
70 Paraphrased from VW to OM, 23 Nov 1933, Goodman family papers.
71 See Holroyd, 1971, pp.400–1; 1994, p.198.
72 Holroyd, 1971, pp.364, 394; 1994, p.190.
73 The Freshfield house was a centre of late-Victorian social and cultural life visited by Stracheys and Stephens. She would associate her feelings about LS in 1909 with Mrs Freshfield (*D*, 2 Jan 1923, II, p.221.).
74 LS to DG, 12 Apr 1907, King's.
75 St John Hirst's friendship with Helen is also derived from LS's with VB.
76 Holroyd, 1971, p.403.
77 VB to CB, nd ['Saturday'], Tate Gallery.
78 AVS to LS, 28 Jan 1909, *L* I, 469, p.381.
79 *D*, 22 Jan 1919, I, p.235.
80 LS to AVS, 27 Jan 1909, *VW/LS*, p.28. This edition was censored for the sake of living feelings, with initials, blanks and false names.
81 Christopher Ricks, 'The Ottoline Empire', Review of Miranda Seymour, *OM*, *New Yorker*, 9 Aug 1993, p.84.
82 *The Waves*, p.136.
83 AVS to CB, Christmas Day, 1908, *L* I, 462, p.377; VB to CB, 29 Nov 1908?, Tate Gallery; LS to LW, 19 Nov 1908, Berg.
84 Holroyd, 1971, p.406; 1994, p.64.
85 *D*, 7 Nov 1922, II, p.211.
86 LS to LW, 20 Feb 1909, Spotts, p.147.

87 Holroyd, 1971, p.407, 1994, p.65; *QB* I, p.142.
88 In the *Spectator*, 10 Apr 1909; Holroyd 1994, p.205.
89 *E* I, pp.257–61.
90 *D*, 15 Nov 1919, I, p.311.
91 *D*, 14 Dec 1929, III, p.273.
92 *D*, 2 Jan 1923, II, p.221.
93 LW to LS, 1 Feb 1909, Spotts, p.145.
94 LS to LW, 21 Aug 1909, Berg. Spotts, pp.148–9.

CHAPTER 15: BLOOMSBURY

1 *The Voyage Out*, p.75.
2 *Night and Day*, p.265.
3 *Jacob's Room*, p.28.
4 Desmond MacCarthy, 'Bloomsbury: An Unfinished Memoir' (1933) *Memories*, McGibbon & Kee, 1953, p.173: 'By the time the world heard of "Bloomsbury", "Bloomsbury" as a group had ceased to exist.' Spalding, p.180: 'By 1919 Vanessa was convinced that the term "Bloomsbury" no longer had any meaning, yet it was now constantly employed in the press to label a loose conglomeration of artists and writers.'
5 LS speaks of the 'departure of Bloomsbury for Studland' in his Diary for 26 Mar, 1910. *LS by Himself*, ed. Michael Holroyd, Heinemann, 1971. SPR p.4, calls this the 'first recorded use of the word "Bloomsbury" to stand for the Bloomsbury Group', but quotes VB ('Notes on Bloomsbury', 1951, SPR p.78) and CB (*Old Friends*, 1956, SPR) p.86) attributing the first coinage to Molly MacCarthy, in 1910 or 1911.
6 Richard Shone dates the start of Bloomsbury in 1910. Shone, *BP 2*, p.11.
7 'Character in Fiction', July 1924, reprinted as 'Mr Bennett and Mrs Brown', 1924, *E* III, pp.420–38.
8 VW to Ka Cox, 12 Aug 1914, *L* II, 709, p.51.

9 LW, *BA*, pp.21–6.
10 Or Francis Birrell, Mark Gertler, Lydia Lopokova, Marjorie Strachey, Gerald Shove, Barbara Bagenal, Gerald Brenan, Dadie Rylands, Frances Partridge, Raymond Mortimer.
11 E.g. Molly McCarthy's Novel Club of 1915 or the Aristotelian Society; See *Clever Hearts*, pp.127–8. Holroyd, 1971, pp.522–3.
12 P.N. Furbank, II, p.56: The club was founded by Ramsay Macdonald and others on the left 'in honour of the Russian Revolution and as a place in which to talk freely without fear of DORA, [the much hated *Defence of the Realm Act*].'
13 *D*, 28 Jan 1918, I, p.115.
14 *D*, 28 Nov 1928, III, p.208; cites VB to RF, 19 Nov 1928.
15 For 'the Bloomsbury Bar', see VW to GB, 3 Oct 1926, *L* III, 1677, p.297. For the book club, see *D*, 29 Nov 1939, V, p.247.
16 *The Voyage Out*, p.235.
17 *Night and Day*, p.42.
18 VW to Ka Cox, 19 Mar 1916, *L* II, 746, p.83: 'So you see, Bloomsbury is vanished like morning mist.'
19 *D*, 9 Jan, 14 Jan 1918, I, pp.103, 105.
20 VW to QB, 14 Oct 1933, *L* V, 2806, p.234.
21 'Old Bloomsbury', *MB*, pp.209–18.
22 CB, 'Play-Reading Book', King's.
23 'One finds it in Parliamentary debates, in newspapers, in private diaries and letters, in reported conversations. Civilization is threatened, is toppling, is mutilated or destroyed; the clock of civilization has been put back.' Hynes, p.4.
24 *Song of Love: The Letters of Rupert Brooke and Noel Olivier*, ed. Pippa Harris, Bloomsbury, 1991, p.176. See also Paul Delany, *The Neopagans: Friendship and Love in the Rupert Brooke Circle*, Macmillan, 1987, pp.138, 154.
25 See 'Introduction to these Paintings' (1929) in *Phoenix*, Heinemann, 1936, pp.551–84; Paul Delany, *D.H. Lawrence's Nightmare*, Harvester,

1979, pp.82–6, 225, on DHL's reaction to Cambridge and his 'panic and hysteria at any intimacy with homosexuals'; SPRI, pp.361–70, on David Garnett's account of DHL's attack on Bloomsbury.
26 See Keith Sagar, *D.H. Lawrence: Life into Art*, Viking, 1985, p.88, and Delany, pp.253, 274–6, for OM's reaction to DHL's portrait of her as Hermione.
27 F.L. Mayor, *The Rector's Daughter*, Hogarth Press, 1924; Penguin, 1973, pp.60–6 and see Sybil Oldfield, *Spinsters of this Parish: The Life and Times of F.M. Mayor and Mary Sheepshanks*, Virago, 1984, p.236.
28 VW, *Roger Fry*, Ch.7, says that CB is supposed to be St Paul.
29 Osbert Sitwell, *Laughter in the Next Room*, 1949, quoted SPRI, pp.250–1. VW was irritated by the identification of Bloomsbury with specific words, such as 'important'. VW to ES, 13 Aug 1936, *L* VI, 3160, p.63.
30 For Wyndham Lewis's quarrel with RF, the 'Ideal Home Rumpus', in which he accused RF of appropriating a commission for the Omega workshop meant for Spencer Gore, and of preventing Frederick Etchells from exhibiting in another Post-Impressionist exhibition, see VW, *Roger Fry*, Chapter 8; Spalding, *Fry*, pp.185–7; SPR, pp.331–61. For Lewis's attacks on Bloomsbury, see especially *Men without Art*, Ch.V, 1934, and *The Apes of God*, 1930. Cf. the 1922 Shaw-Bell conflict: VW to Lytton Strachey, 23 Feb 1922, *L* II, 1220, p.507; SPRI, pp.370–9; Garnett, *Carrington*, p.202.
31 VW to Ka Cox, 12 Aug 1914, *L* II, 709, p.51.
32 VW, *Roger Fry*, Ch 9, p.213.
33 *D*, 3 Jan 1915, I, p.5.
34 VW to DG, 15 Nov 1915, *L* II, 736, p.71.
35 *QB* II, p.137, 'private information'; QB, *Bloomsbury*, p.64.
36 VW to JB, 28 June 1936, *CS*, 3146a, p.377.

37 *D*, 19 Dec 1920, II, p.81.

38 *D*, 21 Dec 1924, II, p.326.

39 *D*, 2 June 1932, IV, p.105. C.f., *D*, 23 Oct 1918, 5 June 1921, 24 Feb 1926, 27 June 1935, *L* 2376, *L* 2658.

40 VW to Gwen Raverat, 1 May 1925, *L* III, 1550, p.181.

41 VW to ES, 13 Aug 1936, *L* VI, 3160, p.63. (The young man has not been identified.)

42 GB, *South from Granada*, in SPR, p.293; William Plomer, *At Home*, Cape, 1958, p.44.

43 Ray to Mary Costelloe, 11 Nov 1909; Ray to Mary, 15 Nov 1909, in *Remarkable Relations: The Story of the Pearsall Smith Family*, Barbara Strachey, Gollancz, 1981, pp.247, 248. Ray was the daughter of Frank Costelloe and Mary (née Pearsall Smith), the American Quaker who left her husband for Bernard Berenson. Mary's brother, Logan Pearsall Smith, would have literary quarrels with VW; her sister Alys married Bertrand Russell. Ray's sister Karin married Adrian; Ray married Lytton's brother Oliver Strachey.

44 His 'sympathy' made her think of Desmond MacCarthy as her dearest old friend: *D*, 31 Jan 1919, I, p.238.

45 *D*, 20 Jan 1919, I, p.234.

46 'Old Bloomsbury' *MB*, p.215.

47 Molly MacCarthy to her mother-in-law, 10 Oct, 10 Aug 1910, in *Clever Hearts*, p.115.

48 *MB*, p.216.

49 *D*, 20 Jan 1915, I, p.24; 26 Sep 1920, II, p.69; 15 Aug 1924, II, p.311.

50 *D*, 12 Sep 1938, V, p.169.

51 AEFR, vi pt ii, 1933. Berg.

52 *QBI*, p.175.

53 *D*, 21 April 1928, III, p.181; 7, 12 Aug 1934, IV, pp.235, 237. Robert Skidelsky, Keynes's biographer, thinks that VW understood him well, though they were not close.

54 *E* I, p.221.

55 *Howards End* has not survived in her library of Forster's books, which included signed copies of *A Passage to India*, *Goldsworthy Lowes Dickinson*, and *The Eternal Moment*.

56 Furbank, I, pp.192–3.

57 *MB*, pp.215–16; VW to LS, 21 May 1912, I, 617, p.499; VW to MLD, 31 Aug 1915, *L* II, 726, p.63.

58 *D*, 24 July 1919, I, p.295.

59 *D*, 25 Nov 1925, III, p.48.

60 Furbank, II, p.18: 'She liked him a good deal – rather more, than, in his heart, he liked her. Throughout their friendship, which lasted till her death, he felt the need to be on his guard with her.'

61 EMF to VW, 28 June 1927, MHP, Sussex.

62 *D*, 10 Aug 1927, III, p.152. Her reviews of EMF were collected as 'The Art of Fiction' *CE* II, pp.51–5 (published as 'Is Fiction an Art?' in the *New York Herald Tribune*, 16 Oct 1927) and 'The Novels of E.M. Forster', *CE* I, pp.342–51 (sent in draft to Forster in June of 1927 and published in the *Atlantic Monthly*, Nov 1927 and the *Saturday Review of Literature*, 17 Dec 1927). EMF's response is in Furbank, II, pp.145–6, and in Sussex.

63 OM to VW, 9 Nov 1933, MHP, Sussex.

64 OM, Diary, 23 Nov 1933, Goodman family papers.

65 Paraphrased from VW to OM, 20 Nov 1933, Goodman family papers.

66 Paraphrased from VW to OM, 23 Nov 1933, Goodman.

67 VB to VS, 16 May 1909, Berg, Marler p.84.

68 Paraphrased from VW to OM, 6 Nov 1933, Goodman.

69 *D*, 16 May 1919, I, p.272.

70 'Old Bloomsbury', *MB*, p.217.

71 OM, *The Early Memoirs*, ed. Robert Gathorne-Hardy, Faber, 1964, pp.178–81, in SPR, pp.245–8.

72 Her biographer, who valiantly salvages OM from Bloomsbury's version of her, says that 'with her bizarre clothes, her singular voice, her reverence for creative people and, above all, her religious faith [she] was God's own gift to the quick

and witty minds of Bloomsbury.'
Miranda Seymour, *Ottoline Morrell:
Life on the Grand Scale*, Hodder &
Stoughton, 1992, p.78.
73 'Old Bloomsbury', *MB*, p.217.
74 *D*, 16 Aug 1918, I, p.183.
75 *D*, 25 Feb 1919, I, p.245.
76 AVS to OM, 16 Jan 1909, *L* I, 468,
p.381.
77 AVS to VD, 13? May 1909, *L* I, 486,
p.394; AVS to Madge Vaughan,
May 1909, *L* I, 487, p.395.
78 Seymour, op. cit., p.105.
79 *D*, 4 June 1923, II, pp.244–5; VW to
OM, 7 June 1923, *L* III, 1398, p.45.
80 *The Voyage Out*, p.182.
81 OM, Diary, 2 Nov 1927, 10 June
923, Dec 1930, 11 Mar 1931, Goodman.
82 Paraphrased from VW to OM, 6
Nov 1932, Goodman.
83 Among their mutual friends were
Charles and Dora Sanger. He was a
brilliant barrister, kind, generous,
and an old friend of Thoby's. VW
described him looking like 'one of
the dwarfs in the Ring' (VW to VB,
22 Apr 1916, *L* II, 754, p.90). She
did not seek him out, partly because
she found his wife Dora awkward
and clumsy (VW to OM, 10 June
1918, *L* II, 942, p.249), but she felt
strongly about his death in 1930 (*L*
2498, *D*, 10 Feb 1930, III, p.286.)
Another connection between OM
and VW was Jane Harrison, the
classical anthropologist, whose work
on 'the nurturing values of matriarchy' in primitive societies interested
VW, and whom she invoked in
Room. For Harrison's life, work and
Cambridge milieu see *Jane Ellen
Harrison: The Mask and the Self*,
Sandra Peacock, Yale UP, 1988.

CHAPTER 16: SUBVERSIVES

1 See Samuel Hynes, *The Edwardian
Turn of Mind*, Princeton UP, 1968,
esp. p.287.
2 AVS to Saxon Sydney-Turner, 14
Aug 1908, *L* I, 435, p.353.

3 Hynes, p.348. See also Jose Harris
Private Lives, Public Spirit, OUP,
1993, pp.252, 255.
4 Hynes, *A War Imagined*, Bodley
Head, 1990 p.95.
5 E.g. her satire on the Dalloways'
praise of Empire in *The Voyage Out*
('Think of the light burning over the
house, Dick! . . . Aren't you glad to
be English!' *The Voyage Out*,
pp.42,60) which has, ironically, been
used against VW to demonstrate her
conservatism.
6 Hynes, *The Edwardian Turn of
Mind*, p.354; VB, 'Notes on Bloomsbury', 1951, in SPR, p.82.
7 See Hynes, *A War Imagined*,
pp.141–4. GBS said to VW (10 May
1940, Sussex) that he 'conceived' the
play after meeting her.
8 VW to Benedict Nicolson, 24 Aug
1940, *L* VI, 3633, p.419. This detail
was only in the draft letter.
9 I.e. the 'suffragettes' of the militant
Women's Social and Political
Union, founded by Emmeline Pankhurst, and its splinter group the
Women's Freedom League; and the
'suffragists' of the constitutional
National Union of Women's Suffrage Societies under Millicent Fawcett, and its offshoots, the Artists'
Suffrage League and the London
Society for Women's Suffrage.
10 The *Vote*, 16 Dec 1909, in Lisa
Tickner, *The Spectacle of Women:
Imagery of the Suffrage Campaign
1907–1914*, Chatto, 1987, p.110.
11 Tickner, ibid., p.16, reproduces the
design for Grant's 'Handicapped'
and acknowledges Richard Shone
for the information.
12 AVS to VD, Dec 1907, *L* I, 397,
p.320.
13 AVS to Janet Case, 1 Jan 1910, *L* I,
516, p.421.
14 Rosalind Nash to AVS, 19 Jan 1910,
MHP, Sussex.
15 *Night and Day*, p.137.
16 AVS to VD, 27 Feb 1910, *L* I, 518,
p.422.
17 AVS to VD, 14 Nov 1910, *L* I, 540,
p.438.

18   AVS to Janet Case, Dec? 1910, *L* I, 545, p.441.

19   *Night and Day*, pp.75, 221, 431.

20   Rebecca West, reviewing *Room*, observed its debt to the pamphleteering tradition of the suffragists. 'Autumn and Virginia Woolf', *Ending in Earnest*, 1931, pp.208–13. (See Marcus, p.146).

21   *The Pargiters*, p.58.

22   *Three Guineas*, p.295.

23   *D*, 9 Mar 1918, I, p.125.

24   QB, introduction to *The 'Dreadnought' Hoax* by Adrian Stephen, Chatto, 1983; see also QB's funny account of the hoax in *QB* I, pp.157–61 [documents in Appendix E].

25   Stephen, pp.22–3.

26   'The Real Emperor', Berg.

27   My account of the hoax is drawn from QB, Adrian Stephen, and from: *Daily Mirror*, 16, 17, 18 Feb, 1910; *Daily Express*, 12 Feb 1910; R.K. Massie, *Dreadnought: Britain, Germany and the Coming of the Great War*, Cape, 1992, pp.489–90; 'Horace Cole, King of Jokers', Joseph Hone, *The Listener*, 4 Apr 1940, pp.674–5; 'The Battleship that was taken for a ride', Christopher Hawtree, *Daily Telegraph*, 24 Feb 1990 (who corrects the date of the Hoax from 10 Feb, in *QB* I, to 7 Feb.)

28   VW to ES, 6 Oct 1932, *L* V, 2640, p.109.

29   VW to VD, 3 Feb? 1927, *L* III, 1713, p.324.

30   Dorothea Stephen to AVS, 3 Mar 1910, Berg.

31   VB to Margery Snowden, 13 Feb 1910, CP, Sussex.

32   William Plomer, *At Home*, Cape, 1958, p.52.

33   *Orlando*, p.91.

34   Published in *Monday or Tuesday*, 1921, not reprinted until *CSF*, pp.124–36, note p.300. One of its characters, the pregnant Castalia, bears a strong resemblance to Vanessa, whose daughter Angelica was two when the story was written;

it is partly a private joke about how she should be educated.

35   VW to KM, 13 Feb [1921], *CS*, 1167a, p.128.

36   *D*, 26 Sep 1920, II, p.69.

37   The exhibition had numerous Cézannes, Gauguins, Manets (including *Un Bar au Folies-Bergère*), and Van Goghs; three Matisses (and some of his sculptures), two Picassos, two Seurats, and paintings by other French artists including Signac, Rouault, Derain, and Redon. For a complete list see Hynes, *The Edwardian Turn of Mind*, pp.410–17.

38   *D*, 7 Aug 1938, V, p.160.

39   Edward VII died on 6 May 1910, George V was crowned on 22 June 1911.

40   *E* III, p.421.

41   VW to RF, 27 May 1927, *L* III, 1764, p.385.

42   Helen Fry was committed to The Priory, Roehampton (where Laura Stephen would end her life) and later to The Retreat in York. VW was told that the cause was 'an incurable thickening of the bone of the skull'. But Spalding (Introduction, VW, *Roger Fry*, Hogarth Press, 1992) later ascertained that she suffered from paranoid schizophrenia and inherited syphilis.

43   Spalding, *Fry*, p.123.

44   VW, *Roger Fry*, Ch.7 p.149.

45   VW, *Roger Fry*, Ch 7., p.152.

46   Notebook, B 17, Sussex.

47   See *D*, 8 Apr 1918, I, p.134; 21 Feb 1921, II, p.94, VW to CB, 18 Jan 1930, *L* IV, 2127, p.128.

48   VB to RF, 15 Nov [1911], Tate Gallery.

49   VB, 'Notes on Bloomsbury', SPRI, p.82.

50   She and Leonard inherited their servants Nelly Boxall and Lottie Hope from RF. They decorated their houses with objects from his Omega workshops. Vanessa's bookjackets were influenced by Omega designs. The Woolfs published RF,

he found VW a French translator, and in 1932 they went to Greece together.

51 *D*, 29 Dec 1935, IV, p.361.

52 RF to VW, 19 July 1931, *Letters of Roger Fry*, ed. Denys Sutton, Chatto, 1972, II, p.659.

53 *D*, 22 Nov 1917, I, p.80.

54 *D*, 18 Apr 1918, I, pp.140–41.

55 VW to VB, 22? Aug 1911, *L* I, 581, p.475.

56 VW to RF, 21 Oct 1918, *L* II, 981, p.285; in response to RF to VW, 18 Oct 1918.

57 AVS to VD, 27 Nov 1910, *L* I, 542, p.440.

58 See LW, *BA*, pp.93–9; Desmond MacCarthy, 'Roger Fry', 1945, in *Memories*; Roger Fry, 'Retrospect', 1920, in *Vision and Design*; VW, *Roger Fry*, Ch.7; Hynes, *The Edwardian Turn of Mind*, pp.206–7, 325–35; Spalding, *Fry*, p.139; Lisa Tickner, op.cit., pp.194–7.

59 *QB* I, p.170; VB, 'Memories of Roger Fry'; AVS to Molly MacCarthy, March 1911, *L* I, 559, p.455.

60 *The Voyage Out*, p.224.

61 VB, 'Memories of Roger Fry', QB.

62 AVS to CB, 4 Sep 1910, *L* I, 534, p.434.

63 AVS to OM, 9 Nov 1911, *L* I, 590, p.480.

64 One of Noel's sisters Brynhild, would marry Hugh Popham, later Keeper of Prints and Drawings at the British Museum. (These were the parents of Anne Olivier Bell, the editor of VW's diaries.)

65 For the Neo–Pagans, see Paul Delany, T*he NeoPagans*, 1987 (p.xv: 'If Bloomsbury were fundamentally ironic and classical, the Neo-Pagans were euphoric and romantic'); Pippa Harris, ed., *Song of Love: The Letters of Rupert Brooke and Noel Olivier*, Bloomsbury, 1991; Gwen Raverat, *Period Piece*, Faber, 1952, and Christopher Hassall, *Rupert Brooke*, Faber, 1972.

66 Delany, p.187.

67 Harris, p.216.

68 Delany, p.187.

69 Jacques Raverat to VW, Sep 1924, MHP, Sussex.

70 She did not invent the term: it had been applied to the Pre-Raphaelites, and the homosexual guru Edward Carpenter had been using it in his lectures on the simple life.

71 *E* II, p.279.

72 VW to Jacques Raverat, 4 Sep 1924, *L* III, 1496, p.130.

73 AVS to CB, 23 Jan 1911, *L* I, 551, p.450.

74 AVS to CB, 18 Apr 1911, *L* I, 566, pp.460–1; AVS to VB, 19 Apr 1911, *L* I, 567, p.462.

75 *D*, 25 May, 1938, V, p.143.

76 Ibid.

77 *D*, 24 June 1918, I, p.160.

78 *D*, 3 Nov 1918, I, p.212. Arnold-Forster trained as a painter, and worked all his life in the Labour Party in the cause of internationalism.

79 *D*, 25 May 1938, V, p.143.

80 AVS to VB, 19 Apr 1911, *L* I, 567, p.463.

81 VW to Gwen Raverat, 11 Mar 1925, *L* III, 1541, p.171.

82 VW to Jacques Raverat, 3 Oct 1924, 24 Jan 1925, *L* III, 1501, 1524, pp.136, 156.

83 *TL*, p.111.

84 *The Years*, p.241.

85 VW to Gwen Raverat, 22 Mar 1925, *L* III, 1542, p.172.

86 Adrian to CB, 25? Aug 1911, CP, Sussex.

87 Delany, p.133; Holroyd, 1971, p.282.

88 See *E* II, p.280; LW, *BA*, p.19; *QB* I, p.174.

89 VW to Gwen Raverat, 8 Apr 1925, *L* III, 1547, p.178.

90 VW to VB, 22? Aug 1911, *L* I, 581, p.476.

91 'On her first evening she walked eight miles from the station with Ka, found no one there on arrival, and ate rotten blackberry pudding by mistake in the dark. A picture shows her sitting on the ground with Rupert, Noel and Maitland Radford in front of a five-barred gate; her hair

is tied in the approved Neo-pagan gipsy scarf and her expression is, reasonably enough, quizzical.' The nude photographs which were taken on this camp have not survived. Delany, p.134.

92 Holroyd, 1971, p.471; Gwen Raverat to VW, 22 Mar 1925, MHP, Sussex.

93 Rupert Brooke to AVS, 9 Mar 1912, King's.

94 *E* II, p.203.

95 *E* II, p.278.

96 *E* III, p.135.

97 See Hynes, *A War Imagined*, pp.109–10.

CHAPTER 17: LEONARD

1 'Even as a lowly trainee, [he] served as administrator, policeman, customs authority, judge, veterinarian, agronomist and examining magistrate.' Spotts, p.60.

2 LW, *G*, p.221.

3 LW, *G*, p.159.

4 See LW, *G*, p.46.

5 LW, 'Pearls and Swine', in *Stories from the East*, reprinted in *Diaries in Ceylon*, Hogarth Press, 1963, pp.272, 275; *The Village in the Jungle*, Hogarth Press, 1961, p.262.

6 LW to LS, 16 Dec 1904, Spotts, p.67.

7 LW, *G*, pp.24, 172, 173, 120.

8 LW to LS, 17 Nov 1907, Spotts, p.134.

9 LW, *S*, p.37.

10 His annual accounts were fussily meticulous, he was said to have used proof-sheets for lavatory paper, his letters were written on the back of discarded typescripts, etc.

11 LW, *S*, p.33.

12 LW, Notebook, LW, I N, Sussex.

13 LW, *The Wise Virgins*, p.169.

14 *D*, IV, pp.300, 322.

15 LW's Bible, notes on endpapers, Washington State University.

16 VW to MLD, 27 Mar 1916, *L* II, 748, p.85.

17 LW, 1901 poems, LW Sussex.

18 LW, *S*, p.161.

19 In 1936 he argued with the editor of *Quack, Quack!* about whether to omit the appendix on anti-Semitism; LW gave way reluctantly. Spotts, p.408.

20 LW, *S*, pp.196–7.

21 LW, *JNAM*, p.128.

22 LW, *G*, p.36.

23 LW, *BA*, p.74.

24 LW, *JNAM*, pp.166–7.

25 Spotts, p.7.

26 LW to G.E. Moore, 14 Oct 1904, Spotts, p.48.

27 VW to VB, 2 Sep 1928, *L* III, 1919, p.525; LW, *Sowing*, p.67.

28 Skidelsky, I, pp.128–9.

29 Holroyd describes Woolf as 'repressively fastidious', 1971, pp.143–3.

30 LS to LW, 1902, Texas; LW to LS, 26 Dec 1902, Texas; LW to LS, 9 Aug 1903, Spotts, p.33; LW to LS, 25 June 1904, Texas; LW to LS, 10 Nov 1904, Spotts, p.51; LW to LS, 11 Feb, 1905, Spotts, p.77; LW to LS, 12 Dec, 1904, Spotts, p.67; LW to LS, 16 Oct 1905, Spotts, pp.103–4; LS to LW, 2 Feb 1905, Texas; LW to LS, 26 Jan 1905, Spotts p.75; LS to LW, 1904, Spotts, p.52.

31 LW to LS, 2 June 1912, Spotts, p.176; LW to LS, 11 Oct 1904, Spotts, p.48; LS to LW, 1903, Texas; LS to LW, 8 Jan 1905, Texas.

32 LW to LS, 25 Apr 1913, Spotts, p.182.

33 LW to Janet Case, 29 Dec 1914, Sussex.

34 LW to LS, 17 Nov 1907, Spotts p.134.

35 LW, *The Wise Virgins*, p.155.

36 LW to LS, 3 Mar 1907, Spotts, p.125.

37 Flora Woolf to LW, 18 Dec 1908, Spotts, p.143.

38 LW to LS, 31 July 1902, Spotts, p.26.

39 Maurice Craig, 10 May 1916; Maurice Wright, 2 June 1916. LW, Sussex. LW, *S*, p.178.

40 *D*, 19 July 1937, V, p.103.

41 Spater, p.58.
42 LW to LS, 30 July 1905; LS to LW, 31 Aug 1905, Spotts, p.98.
43 LS to LW, 19 Feb 1909, Spotts, p.147.
44 LW to LS, 14 Sep 1909, Spotts p.149.
45 LW, *BA*, p.17.
46 Spater, p.59.
47 LW to LS, 1 Nov [1911], Spotts p.167.
48 AVS to OM, 13 Nov 1911, *L* I, 591, p.480.
49 AVS to LW, 2 Dec 1911, *L* I, 595, p.485.
50 The Brunswick Square 'system' would be the model for unmarried Bloomsbury life at 41, 46 and 50 Gordon Square from then on.
51 *D*, I, 24 Jan 1919, p.236.
52 AVS to LW, ibid.; MK, Account Book, 1909–13, King's; Skidelsky, *Keynes*, I, pp.270–1.
53 *E*, I, pp.358–9.
54 AVS to VD, 25 May 1911, *L* I, 569, p.465.
55 VS to VB, 8? June 1911, *L* I, 570, p.466.
56 VB to RF, 18 Jan 1912, Tate Gallery.
57 VB to LW, 13 Jan 1912, Spotts, p.170.
58 Trekkie Parsons to the author, 1992; Dunn, pp.125, 184; Poole, p.97; Alexander, p.70.
59 *Mrs Dalloway*, p.53.
60 AVS to Madge Vaughan, June 1912, *L* I, 628, p.503; also to Eleanor Cecil, June 1912, *L* I, 629, p.504.
61 AVS to LW, 5 Mar 1912, *L* I, 606, p.491.
62 VB to LW, 6 Mar 1912, LW, Sussex.
63 AVS to Molly MacCarthy, Mar 1912, *L* I, 608, p.492.
64 AVS to Ka Cox, Apr 1912, *L* I, 613, p.495. The editor W.K. Stead was killed in the *Titanic*, but his widow survived.
65 AVS to VD, 22 May 1912, *L* I, 618, p.499.
66 AVS to LW, 1 May 1912, *L* I, 615, p.496. Quoted almost in entirety by

QB I, pp.185–6. I have quoted the MS of the letter, MHP, Sussex.
67 AVS to Madge Vaughan, June 1912, *L* I, 628, p.503.
68 *The Voyage Out*, p.298.
69 *Night and Day*, pp.403, 419.
70 LW, 'I am in love with Aspasia', LW, Sussex; extract quoted in Spater, pp.61–2.
71 LW, *The Wise Virgins*, pp.51–2.
72 VW to ES, 2 Aug 1930, *L* IV, 2215, p.195.
73 Fredegond Shove to VB, 19 July 1917, King's.
74 CB to Mary Hutchinson, 21 Jan 1915, Texas.
75 VB to LW, 25 May 1913, LW, Sussex.
76 E.g.: VW to Ka Cox, Nov? 1912, *L* II, 651, p.11; and QB, to the author.
77 *L* IV, 2244, p.222, 2274, p.249, V, 2811, p.239.
78 VW to VB, 29 Dec 1930, *L* 2295, IV, p.267.
79 AVS to Janet Case, June 1912, *L* I, 627, p.502.
80 *D*, 29 Sep 1930, III, p.321.
81 *D*, 25 Sep 1929, III, p.258.
82 LW, *The Wise Virgins*, p.194. He planned a book on the Wandering Jew in 1921 (*D*, 17 Apr 1921, II, p.111).
83 LW, VW to Molly MacCarthy, 28 Sep 1912, *L* III, 647, p.9.
84 VW to Janet Case, 17 Aug 1912, *L* II, 643, p.4; to Molly MacCarthy, 28 Sep 1912, *L* II, 647, p.9.
85 *Night and Day*, p.528.
86 D.H. Lawrence, 'A Chair', *Women in Love* (first published in England 1921).
87 LW, *BA*, p.62.'In my experience what cuts the deepest channels in our lives are the different houses in which we live.'
88 LW, Notebook, LW, Sussex.
89 AVS to VB, Christmas Day 1910, *L* I, 546, p.443.
90 AVS to VB, 8 Apr 1911, *L* I, 563, p.458.
91 Ibid.
92 AVS to Clive Bell, 29 Dec 1910, *L* I, 548, p.446.

93 Eric Gill, who knew VW, found it first. He lived at Ditchling, near Lewes, and in 1910 he and Jacob Epstein had proposed building a modern Stonehenge – 'immense human figures standing like gods and giants in the Sussex landscape' – in the grounds of Asheham. (Spalding, p.104; Fiona MacCarthy, *Eric Gill*, Faber, 1989, p.103.)

94 While they were on their honeymoon in 1912, VB took it over, redecorated it and began work on the garden. Asheham was also where Adrian in 1914 first introduced Karin Costelloe into his family circle, and where Carrington in 1915 fell suddenly in love with LS. VB was irritated with VW for wanting to let Asheham in summer 1913 without telling her first, and wrote to her coldly about this when VW was falling ill. In autumn 1914 VB was offended because LW and VW offered her Asheham for £60 a year 'provided they may have it for 6 weekends in the year and 2 or 3 weeks in the spring. Considering a good deal of the furniture is ours we think that too much.' (VB to RF, Sep/Oct 1914, Tate Gallery.)

95 LW, *BA*, p.56.

96 'A Haunted House', *CSF*, p.123.

97 LW, *BA*, p.57.

98 Spalding, p.104.

99 *D*, 28 Sep 1919, I, p.302.

100 'A Haunted House', *CSF*, p.122.

101 *D*, 30 Sep 1931, IV, p.46.

102 *E* II, p.162.

103 *D*, 14 Aug 1928, III, p.192.

104 See LW on the noises at Asheham ('as if two people were walking from room to room, opening and shutting doors, sighing, whispering'), and on the house's strong character: 'romantic, gentle, melancholy, lovely'. *BA*, p.57.

105 Cf. her 1916 piece on Sussex in wartime: The old traditional ghosts of the Downs ('ghostly riders and unhappy ladies forever seeking their lost treasure') are now joined, she says, by wartime phantoms and myths 'hovering on the borderland of belief and scepticism, not yet believed in, but not properly accounted for'. *E* II, p.40. 'A Haunted House' was first published in *Monday or Tuesday* (1921) but may date from 1916.

CHAPTER 18: MARRIAGE

1 *D*, May 28 1931, IV, p.27.

2 VW to ES, 15 Mar 1930, *L* IV, 2157, p.151.

3 *D*, 14 June 1925, III, p.30.

4 *D*, 30 Oct 1938, V, p.183.

5 *D*, 2 Aug 1926, III, p.105.

6 *D*, 11 Apr 1931, IV, pp.17–18.

7 *D*, 3 Sep 1928, III, p.194.

8 *D*, 22 Oct 1937, V, p.115.

9 *D*, 14 June 1925, III, p.30. cf. 'together in our stall', 30 Nov 37, V, p.120.

10 *D*, 11 Apr 1931, IV, p.18.

11 Holroyd, 1971, p.491.

12 Isaiah Berlin to the author, 18 Feb 1992.

13 CB to Molly MacCarthy, 14 May 1912, CP, Sussex.

14 Spalding, p.106; *L*, II, p.1.

15 VW to LS, 1 Sep 1912, *L* II, 644, p.5.

16 VW to DG, 8 Sep 1912, *CS*, 645a, p.76.

17 *D*, 12 May 1933, IV, p.156.

18 As note 16.

19 VW to Ka Cox, 4 Sep 1912, *L* II, 645, p.6.

20 VB to VW, 19 Aug 1912, Berg, Marler p.125.

21 VB to VS, 2 June 1912, Berg; to CB, June 1912, Tate Gallery.

22 CB to Molly MacCarthy, 'Friday night' [Mar 1913], CP, Sussex.

23 VB to RF, July 1917, 17 Sep 1917, Aug 1914, Tate Gallery.

24 See Spalding, *Fry*, 1980, pp.159–65.

25 *Night and Day*, p.57. See also *L* 659, 668; LW, *BA*, p.84.

26 George Savage to VD, 5 June 1912, Longleat.

27 George Duckworth to LW, 8 Aug

1912, MHP, Sussex. When Vanessa married CB, George had enthused to VD on 'the solid comfort of £.s.d., for with the prospect of several thousands one can well afford the simple life'. It was a comfort to feel 'that his collars and shirts are clean and that he has a good seat on a horse'. (George Duckworth to VD, 23 Dec 1906, Longleat.) He could not have the same confidence about Leonard (though he *did* have a good seat on a horse, and tried to teach Virginia to ride, until she fell off one weekend on the Downs.) (VW to Molly MacCarthy, 28 May 1913, *L* II, 671, p.29.)

28 Some of which he gave to his family. Spotts, p.127.

29 *CS*, p.328; VW to VB, 25 May 1928, *L* III, 1895, p.499; LW, Diary, 1927, LW Sussex.

30 In 1916 the rent for Asheham was £12.10s. quarterly; their year's spending on food was £220; in 1917 Leonard spent £15, Virginia about £75, on clothes and their servants' wages were £78 for the year. LW, Diary, LW, Sussex; Spater, p.76.

31 LW, *BA*, pp.87–93; *ATW*, p.142; LW, Account Books, LW, Sussex; Housekeeping Book, Sussex; VW's Residuary Estate, 1940, Sussex; Paul Delany, ' "A Little Capital: The Financial Affairs of Leonard and Virginia Woolf', *Charleston Magazine*, Summer/Autumn 1993, pp.5–9.

32 LW to LS, 25 Apr 1913, Texas.

33 LW itemised expenditure under headings such as Baker, Butcher, Fish, Milk, Nelly (which became Mabel in 1933) and Wash (which became Laundry in 1934).

34 Delany, op.cit., p.8.

35 VW to LW, Nov 1912, *L* 652, II, p.12.

36 LW, *BA*, p.148.

37 de Salvo (pp.11, 61, 65, 102, 105, 156–9) argues that in her painful rewritings of *The Voyage Out* she was exposing, then disguising, and

then half-admitting, to a sexual history of incest and to a guilty preference for death over marriage. 'Each time she revised Rachel's death scene, she herself slipped into insanity.'

38 VW to Ka Cox, 18 Mar 1913, *L* II, 660, p.20.

39 *E* II, p.14.

40 de Salvo, p.105; *QB* II, p.11.

41 *D*, 16 Mar, 11 June 1936, V, pp.17, 24.

42 LW, *BA*, p.100.

43 MLD, fifty in 1911, had worked for the Co-Operative Movement since 1886. She was the daughter of a Christian Socialist clergyman who had known Leslie Stephen; she was a Cambridge graduate. After her father's death in 1916 she lived in Hampstead with her companion and colleague Lilian Harris. She formed the WCG into a major pressure group, supporting suffrage, minimum wages, and the rights of working women. By the time she retired in 1921 she had built up the Guild's membership from 1,800 to 52,000. She was a pacifist and a supporter of the Russian Revolution.

44 LW, *BA*, 105, 111.

45 VW to Eleanor Cecil, 28? May 1913, *L* II, 672, p.30.

46 Wilson, p.51.

47 VW to Ka Cox, 16 May 1913, *L* II, 668, p.27.

48 LW, *BA*, p.111.

49 MLD to LW, nd, Sussex.

50 VW to Eleanor Cecil, 18? May 1913, *L* II, 672, p.30.

51 MLD to LW, nd, [Oct 1913], LW, Sussex.

52 *D*, 3 May 1918, I, p.147.

53 LW to MLD, 13 June 1913, LW, Sussex.

54 VW to Eleanor Cecil, 11 Mar 1913, *L* II, 659, p.19.

55 VW to Ka Cox, 18 Mar 1913, *L* II, 660, p.19.

56 LW, Diary, 24 Aug 1913, LW, Sussex.

57 Ka Cox to LW, 18 Mar 1914, LW, Sussex.

58 CB to Molly MacCarthy, Apr 1913, CP, Sussex.
59 VW, Notes taken at Fabian Conference, Keswick, July 1913, MHP, Sussex.
60 VB to RF, nd [1914], Tate Gallery.
61 VB to RF, 7 Apr 1914, Tate Gallery.
62 VW to LW, 14 Mar 1914, L II, 699, p.44.
63 D, 25 Jan 1915, I, p.28.
64 D, 3 Jan 1915, I, p.5.
65 VB to CB, 27 Dec 1912, Tate Gallery, Marler, p.132.
66 CB to MH, 7 May 1919, Texas.
67 VSW to HN, 17 Aug 1926, in Nigel Nicolson, *Portrait of a Marriage*, 1973, pp.209, 212.
68 GB to Rosemary Dinnage, 4 Nov 1967. Quoted Spotts, pp.162-3. There was also a slight rumour of an affair between Leonard and Molly Hamilton (Spotts, p.163). But Trekkie Parsons, LW's companion after VW's death, assured me that he had never been unfaithful to VW because 'it would have upset her too much'.
69 VW to ES, 22 June 1930, L IV, 2194, p.180.
70 VW to LS, 22 Oct 1915, L II, 732, p.67.
71 See a letter about copulation, chamber pots, spinsters, excretion and sanitary towels, VW to DG, 6 Mar 1917, L II, 825, p.144-6.
72 E.g. Alexander, pp.131-2.
73 D, 17 Dec 1933, IV, p.193.
74 D, 29 Feb 1936, V, p.13.
75 CSF, p.268.
76 VW to VB, 24 Oct 1938, L VI, 3460, p.294.
77 Gerald Brenan, to Rosemary Dinnage, 4 Nov 1967. Quoted Spotts, pp.162-3.
78 D, 25 Oct 1920, II, p.72; 2 Jan 1923, II, p.221; 15 Sep 1926, III, p.110.
79 VW to Gwen Raverat, 11 Mar 1925, L III, 1541, p.172.
80 D, 30 Nov 1937, V, p.120.
81 D, 2 Jan 1923, II, p.221.
82 D, 5 Sep 1926, III, p.107. Also VW to Ethel Sands, 8 Feb 1927, L III, 1716, p.329.
83 D, 8 Mar 1937, V, p.66.
84 Other versions of this story, all blaming LW for the decision, are given by Dunn, Mepham, and Alexander. Alexander argues that LW did not want to have children at all and that his decision drove her mad. James King, *Virginia Woolf*, Norton, 1994, p.92, argues from a late letter from VD to VB that 'Violet tried to get Virginia a baby', but this is guesswork.
85 VW to VD, 9?, 29? Oct 1912, L II, 648, 649, pp.9, 10.
86 VW to VD, 11 Apr 1913, L II, 665, p.23.
87 VB to Margery Snowden, 10 May 1909, CP, Sussex.
88 VB to LW, 20 Jan 1913, Sussex, first paragraph only in Spotts, pp.181-2.
89 VB to VW, 22 Jan, 26? Jan, 2 Feb 1913, Berg.
90 D, 8 June, 10 July 1933, IV, pp.162, 167.
91 D, 30 July 1933, IV, p.170.
92 Holograph Draft, *The Years*, Berg.
93 Recorded in LW's Diaries and noted by Spater, p.69.
94 AVS to VD, June 1912, L I, 625, p.502.
95 LW to VW, MHP, June 1914, Sussex. The terms resemble those which Richard Dalloway imposes on Clarissa.
96 OM, Diary, 4 July 1931, 7 Apr 1933, 26 Feb 1936, Goodman family papers.
97 CB to Mary Hutchinson, 5 May 1917, 7 Aug 1925, 20 Aug 1936, Texas.
98 D, 25 Sep 1929, III, p.257.
99 VB to Julian Bell, 4 Mar 1936, QB.
100 LW, *DATW*, p.156.
101 LW, *BA*, p.166.
102 On LW's support for the Resolution and later criticism of Soviet Communism, see *BA*, pp.208-9.
103 Spotts, (p.9) emphasises: 'the studies not pursued, the colonial governorship never sought, the political

career spurned, the publishing venture kept small, the editorship resigned.'

104 LW, *JNAM*, p.158.

105 LW, *DATW*, p.173. His brother Edgar told him, late in life, that as a child he had been a bully. LW, *S*, p.80; Spotts, pp.493–4.

106 E.g. *D*, 18, 19, 21 Jan 1915, I, pp.23–5, on his lack of confidence about his work. For LW as an employer see Kennedy, p.85, and Lehmann. Colleagues on the *New Statesman* described him as a lovable person of great integrity: see Kingsley Martin, *Editor*, Hutchinson, 1968, p.8, and C.H. Rolph, *Kingsley*, Gollancz, 1973, p.200.

107 *D*, 11 May 1923, II, p.241.

108 *D*, 7 Jan 1920, II, p.5.

109 *D*, 31 Jan 1915, I, p.32.

110 *D*, 2 Apr 1919, 29 Oct 1922; VW to VB, 1 Apr 1923, *L* III, 1376, p.26.

111 See Raymond Williams on his 'honourable' work in 'The Significance of "Bloomsbury" as a social and cultural group', in *Keynes and the Bloomsbury Group*, ed. D. Crabtree and A.P. Thirlwall, Macmillan, 1980, p.49.

112 LW, *BA*, p.220.

113 *Deceived*, pp.108–9.

114 VW to CB, 18 Jan 1930, *L* IV, 2127, p.129. LW, *DATW*, pp.122–3.

CHAPTER 19: WAR

1 *The Years*, p.235.

2 *Mrs Dalloway*, p.63.

3 Ibid., p.95.

4 Ibid., p.63.

5 *TL*, Holograph, MS, Appendix B, p.51, quoted Penguin, p.251.

6 *A Room of One's Own*, p.14.

7 *The Waves*, p.148

8 Ibid., p.178.

9 Ibid., p.189.

10 She reviewed Sassoon twice, 'The Old Huntsman' on 31 May 1917 (*E* II pp.119–22) and 'Counter-Attack' on 11 July 1918 (*E* II pp.269–72.) The second review embroiled her in

a row between the Morrells, who admired Sassoon, and Murry, who reviewed him scathingly in the *Nation*. *D*, 29 July 1918, I, pp.173–4.

11 She also criticised Geoffrey Dearmer's war poems for being too slack and vague (*E* II, p.269); Maurice Hewlett for not being 'vehement' enough (12 Sep 1918, *E* II, p.293); and she praised Charles Sorley's posthumous collection for showing a mind 'naturally incapable of a dishonest or sentimental conclusion'. [1 Aug 1919, *E* III, p.75].

12 1 Mar 1917, *E* II, p.87.

13 3 Apr 1919, *E* III, p.29.

14 22 Aug 1919, *E* III, pp.92–3. EMF satirised the same painting as 'obscene' in 'Me, Them and You' (1926), in *A Bloomsbury Group Reader*, ed. S.P. Rosenbaum, Blackwell, 1993, p.231.

15 *Sunday Herald*, 5 Nov 1915, advertisement for the Rev. R.J. Campbell's articles.

16 *D*, 3 Jan 1915 I, p.5; VW to Ka Cox 12 Jan 1916, *L* II, 739, p.75.

17 *D*, 13 Apr 1918, I, p.138.

18 *D*, 18 Jan 1915, I, p.22.

19 *D*, 27 June 1918, I, p.161.

20 VW to MLD, 23 Jan 1916, *L* II, 740, p.76.

21 *D*, 11 Jan 1918, I, p.104.

22 E.g. In a post-war argument in the pages of the feminist *Woman's Leader* about the Plumage Bill (brought in to stop the importation of bird-feathers), she attacked the male assumption that frivolous ostrich-flaunting women were responsible for the Bill's defeat, and used the debate to say that it was the men, not the women of the country, who had blood on their hands. [23 July 1920, *E* III, p.241.]

23 "Bloomsbury" was 'from the war's beginning . . . a demonstration of the fact that opposition to the war – continuous, principled opposition – was a possible attitude for intelligent English men and women.' Hynes, op.cit., p.84.

24 David Garnett, *The Flowers of the Forest*, Chatto, 1955, p.104.
25 DG, letter to his father, 1916, quoted Skidelsky, *Keynes*, p.326.
26 Hynes, pp.84–5; Spalding, p.147. *Peace at Once* was burnt by order of the Lord Mayor of London.
27 VB to VW, 22 Aug 1915, Marler, p.187.
28 See Skidelsky, *Keynes*, I, p.315; Moorehead, *Bertrand Russell*, Sinclair-Stevenson, 1992, p.241; Hynes, p.145.
29 VW to Ka Cox, 25 June 1916, *L* II, 770, p.102.
30 E.g. the No-Conscription Fellowship, the Union of Democratic Control, the Council for Civil Liberties.
31 VW to MLD, 29 Dec 1916, *L* II, 812, p.133.
32 Skidelsky says MK felt this was the best way to help his friends. *Keynes*, I, Ch.13.
33 VW to VB, 16 July 1916, *L* II, 774, p.106.
34 Holroyd, 1971, pp.627–9, 1994, pp.345–73, for a lively account of the event.
35 VB to VW, 10 May 1916, Berg, Marler, p.196.
36 VW to VB, 14 May 1916, *L* II, 757, p.95.
37 Moorehead, op.cit., p.246.
38 LW, *BA*, p.177.
39 Spotts, pp.214–15.
40 VW to VB, 17 Oct 1917, *L* II, 880, p.187; *D*, 14 Oct 1917, I, p.59.
41 A politically influential anti-war grouping of dissident Liberals and Labour supporters, which he joined in November 1915.
42 *D*, 4 Mar, 11 Apr 1918, I, pp.122, 137.
43 *D*, 23 Jan 1915, I, p.26.
44 VW to Ka Cox, 25 June 1916, *L* II, 770, pp.102–3; VW to VB, 28 June 1916, *L* II, 771, p.104. The visit was at the Webbs'.
45 *D*, 18, 23 Sep 1918, I, pp.193–7.
46 *D*, 27 Feb, 11 Apr 1926, III, pp.62, 74. Holroyd wrote definitively on the contrast between them in 'Mrs

Webb and Mrs Woolf', *LRB*, 7 Nov 1985, pp.17–19.
47 VW to Janet Case, 21 May 1922, *L* II, 1250, p.529. Evidently a disapproving remark by Beatrice Webb about VW had been passed on.
48 Beatrice Webb to VW, 9 Nov, 12 Nov 1937, MHP, Sussex.
49 Holroyd, 1971, p.631.
50 Information to the author, Belinda Norman-Butler, 1992.
51 *D*, 19 Nov 1917, I, p.79. See also *D*, 29 July 1918, I, p.175.
52 VW to OM, 15 Aug 1917, *L* II, 850, p.174.
53 *D*, 25 Feb 1919, I, p.246. See Hynes, op.cit., pp.232–4, on the Allatini case.
54 VW to LS, 28 Feb 1916, *L* II, 745, p.82; VW to VB, 27 Nov 1917, *L* II, 893, p.198). *The Rainbow* was banned and burnt on 13 Nov 1915; two days later VW wrote to Duncan that she was 'distressed' by 'what our compatriots feel about life'. [VW to DG, 15 Nov 1915, *L* II, 736, p.71].
55 VW to MLD, 26 Jan 1917, *L* II, 819, p.139.
56 VW to MLD, 29 Dec 1916, *L* II, 812, p.133; *D*, 7 Dec 1917, I, p.86.
57 *D*, 15 Oct 1918, I, p.204; *Jacob's Room*, p.151.
58 LW, *BA*, pp.181–2.
59 *D*, 14 Dec 1917, 7 Mar 1918, I, pp.91–2, 123; VW to Nick Bagenal, 12 May 1918, *L* II, 930, p.238; VW to DG, 15 May 1918, *L* II, 932, p.240.
60 LW, *BA*, p.197.
61 *D*, 28 Jan, 30 Jan 1915, I, p.29, 31; VW to MLD, 22 Feb 1915, *L* II, 721, p.60.
62 *D*, 19 Jan 1915, I, p.23.
63 It proved to be a good investment. When the lease was not renewed in December 1919, LW bought both houses for £1,950. (They now considered turning the other half of the house into a bookshop). Two years later, he sold Suffield, which had a sitting tenant, for £1,400. When they left the house in 1924 they rented it (still for £150) to Saxon

Sydney–Turner's family, who ran a private asylum (an irony not lost on VW). In 1926 LW sold the house for £1,350. With the sale of Suffield and the rent, he made over a thousand pounds. LW, II H, Sussex; Notes on Hogarth House, Library Services No.13, Richmond, Jan 1976; Chancellors' Auction Land & Estate Office's Report on Suffield and Hogarth House, 2 Dec 1919. I am grateful to Tony Osborn for showing me over the house in 1992.

64 *D*, 9 Jan 1924, II, p.283.
65 *D*, 9 Jan 1924, *D* II, p.283.
66 VW to Ka Cox, 14? Nov 1915, *L* II, 735, p.71.
67 *D*, 8 Apr 1918, I, p.135.
68 *D*, 12 Mar 1924, II, p.297.
69 *D*, 9 Jan 1924, II, p.283.
70 Beatrice Webb, *Diaries*, 1912–24, ed. Margaret Cole, Longmans, 1952, p.47.
71 *D*, 1 Feb 1915, I, p.32.
72 *D*, 6 Dec 1917, I, pp.84–5; *L* 896, 905, 906, 907, 912.
73 VW to Ka Cox, 18 July 1917, *L* 849, p.165.
74 *D*, 27 Aug 1918, I, p.186.
75 *D*, 18 Oct 1918, I, p.206.
76 Gail Braybon, *Women Workers in the First World War*, Croom Helm, 1981, Ch.2; *The Times*, 15 July 1919.
77 MH to VB, 10 Mar [nd], CP, Sussex.
78 VW to VB, 25 Aug 1916, *L* II, 781, p.112.
79 *D*, 1 Nov 1919, I, p.308.
80 VW to Mary Hutchinson, 1917, Texas.
81 CB to MH, 14 Jan 1916, Texas.
82 VB to VW, 24 Sep 1917, Berg.
83 VW to VB, 3 July 1917, *L* II, 842, p.160.
84 See *QB* II, pp.55–8.
85 She later became Charles Laughton's cook. Christopher Driver, obituary of Hope Chenhalls, *Guardian*, 15 Jan 1996.
86 *D*, 15 Dec 1929, III, p.274.
87 *QB* II, pp.55–8; *L* 944, 945, 947 etc; *D*, 27 June 1918, I, p.160; VB to VW, 27 June 1918, Berg.

88 *D*, 28 Nov 1919, I, pp.313–14; *D*, 3 Jan 1924, II, p.281; *D*, 2–5 Nov, 12 Nov 1930, III, pp.327, 333; *D*, 2 Feb, 27 Mar, 11 Apr 1934; VW to ES, 29 Mar 1934, *L* V, 2867, p.284.
89 Examples, *D*, 5 June 1925, III, p.27, *D*, 11 Apr 1934, IV, p.207, *D*, 19 Mar 1934, IV, p.205.
90 *D*, 28 Nov 1918, I, p.314.
91 *D*, 13 Apr 1929, III, p.220.
92 VW to VB, 29 Jan 1918, *L* II, 905, p.214.
93 VW to CB, 19 Feb 1918, *L* II, 906, p.217.
94 2p in 1994 was worth £1 in 1914; inflation has risen 50-fold. ('Cost of Living Index', Central Statistical Office, April 1994).
95 *QB* II, pp.40–1. In 1917, the servants cost £78; the rates at Hogarth and at Asheham were about £4 a month each; the rent for Asheham was £145, for Hogarth £150; medical expenses, £25; LW's clothes bill, £15; Virginia's (for 'brooches, stays, stockings, shoes, combinations, boots, comb, and misc.') £78.46; the food bill came to £232. (LW Diary, LW, Sussex).
96 *L* 842, 862, 898, 916, 917, 968; *D*, I, 30 Oct 1917, Christmas 1917 [Berg], 5 Jan 1918, 12 Jan 1918, 23 Jan 1918. 'Nutter': 'a butter substitute made from nuts.' [AOB].
97 *D*, 6 Jan 1918, I, p.101.
98 LW, Diary, 6 Jan 1918, LW, Sussex.
99 *D*, 5 Apr 1918, I, 131.
100 *D*, 3 Sep 1918, I, p.189.
101 *D*, 15 Oct 1918, I, p.202.
102 *D*, 12 Oct 1918, I, p.200.
103 *The Times*, 18, 19, 26 July 1919.
104 Siegfried Sassoon, *Siegfried's Journey, 1916–1920*, Faber 194, p.98.
105 *D*, 30 Oct 1918, I, pp.211–12.
106 VW to VB, *L* II 986, 987, pp.290–4.
107 *D*, 19 July 1919, I, p.292.
108 'The War from the Street', *TLS*, 9 Jan 1919, *E* III, p.3.
109 VW to Margery Olivier, 13 Jan 1916, *CS*, 739a, p.89.
110 VB to RF, Nov 1915, Tate Gallery.
111 VW to LW, 31 Oct 1917, *L* II, 888, p.193.

112 VW to VB, 26 Dec 1917, *L* II, 897, p.204.
113 VW to VB, 19? Oct 1916, *L* II, 797, p.123.
114 VW to DG, 6 Mar 1917, *L* II, 825, p.146.
115 See 'The New Dress', probably 1925, *CSF*, pp.170–7.
116 *D*, 9 Jan 1918, I, p.103–4; 6 May 1918, p.149.
117 *L* 742, Italian Notebooks, BL, Smith College Library Rare Book Room.
118 *The Years*, p.171; *D*, 17 Feb 1933, IV, p.147; 25 Apr 1933, IV, p.151.
119 *D*, 14 Nov 1917, 23 Jan, 18 Apr, 10 July 1918, I, pp.76, 112, 141, 165; *L* 831, 838, pp.151, 157.
120 MLD, *Life As We Have Known It*, with introduction by VW, Hogarth Press, 1931, p.65.
121 VW to MLD, 26 Jan 1917, *L* II, 819, p.139.
122 VW to Nick Bagenal, 12 May 1918, *L* II, 930, p.238.
123 *CSF*, p.93.
124 *D*, 18 June 1919, I, p.284.
125 *Life As We Have Known It*, *CE*, IV, pp.134–48; Rosenbaum, *A Bloomsbury Group Reader*, pp.152–64; *L* 2252. See Jane Marcus attacking LW's decision to print the *Yale Review* version in *CE*. ('No More Horses', *Art and Anger: Reading like a woman*, Ohio State UP, 1988, pp.118–19.)

CHAPTER 20: THE PRESS

1 For the history of the Hogarth Press, see Willis; Donna Rhein, *The Hand-printed Books of Leonard and Virginia Woolf at the Hogarth Press, 1917–1932*, Ann Arbor, 1985; Woolmer; LW, *BA*, pp.231ff; *QBII*, p.38ff; Spotts, pp.268–72. For accounts of working there, see Lehmann, and Kennedy; for the collaboration between VW and VB at the Press, see Dunn, Spalding, and Gillespie; for the Press's publishing of Freud see *Bloomsbury/Freud*; for insights into the role of the Press in

VW's writing life, see Mepham, p.53; Gordon, p.91.
2 VW to Eleanor Cecil, Oct 1916? *L* II, 791, p.120.
3 LW, *BA*, p.223.
4 LW says this first in *BA*; it is echoed by e.g.: Lehmann, VW, pp.40–1; *QBII*, p.38; Dunn, p.159; Shone, *BP2*, p.164; Tomalin, p.161.
5 VW to MLD, 22 Feb 1915, *L* II, 721, p.59.
6 *D*, 17 Dec 1918, I, p.229.
7 Rhein, p.15.
8 In Apr 1938 JL replaced VW's side of the management of the Press, and 'The Hogarth Press', simply, replaced the two names on all publications. The last Press books to carry the names of LW and VW, published Mar 1938, were Isherwood's *Lions and Shadows* and Edward Upward's *Journey to the Border*.
9 The Excelsior Printers' Supply Company at 36 and 41 Farringdon Street had taken over the Model Printing Press Co, and reissued that company's 44 page 1909 booklet, *How to Print*, under their own name, in 1914. This is probably the booklet from which they learnt to print. The 'Model' printing press was a table-top press like the one LW remembers as 'the Eclipse' in *BA*, p.234. No such name occurs in the Excelsior lists, but in another booklet the firm issued in 1902 (*Everyone his own printer!*) there is a table-top press, a 'platen-jobber', called the 'Excelsior',
10 VW to VB, 22 May 1917, *L* II, 837, p.155; VW to MLD, 2 May 1917, *L* II, 831, p.151.
11 Usually held in the left hand, Kennedy's illustrations, facing pp.44, 62, show her as if left-handed. But these illustrations were made many years after the event, and there is no other evidence for her left-handedness.
12 It looks from their early work as though 'the Woolfs did not bother to correct set type from their proof sheets'. Rhein, p.5.
13 Their press, LW said, could only

print one demi-octavo page (5⅝" × 8¾") or two crown octavo pages (5" × 7½") at a time. To print 134 copies of each page of *Two Stories*, a 32-page booklet would have involved a minimum of 4,154 pulls (as against just over 1,000 if they had been able to print four pages at a time, as they would be able to with their next press.)

14 For her satisfying visit to the Caslon Foundry in Chiswell Street to get more type in April 1918, see *D*, 18 Apr 1918, p.141.

15 LW, *BA*, p.239.

16 'Description of the Improved Model Press', *How to Print*, Exelsior Printers' Supply Company, 1914.

17 VW to VB, 22 May 1917, *L* II, 837, p.155–6.

18 'The Hogarth Press', 1922 notice to subscribers, LW, Sussex.

19 NN, *Charleston Magazine*, no.13, Dec 1985, p.42, reviewing Rhein, notes that they had *three* presses, the Excelsior or Model (remembered by LW as the 'Eclipse'), the second-hand Minerva platen machine, which was given to VSW in 1930 and is still at Sissinghurst, and 'a better platen machine' which LW acquired in 1930. 'Where is that third machine now? And where is the first, the handpress that stood on the dining room table at Hogarth House?'

20 For LW's farcical dealings with their first commercial printer, McDermott of Prompt Press, see LW, *BA*, pp.237–40, and Willis, pp.37, 389; Woolmer, Appendix III.

21 'The Hogarth Press', 1922 notice to subscribers, LW Sussex.

22 Willis, pp.48–9, on LW's scheme for A and B subscribers

23 VB to RF, Sep 1917, Tate Gallery. The book was published by Omega, expensively and beautifully, as *Original Woodcuts by Various Artists*, in December 1918.

24 *D*, 9 June 1919, I, p.279; VW to VB, 18 June 1919, *L* II, 1061, p.369.

25 Several of the pieces she wrote

between 1916 and 1919 (on Defoe, Addison, Charlotte Bronte, George Eliot, 'modern fiction') she reprinted in *CR*, 1925.

26 *E* III, pp.58–9.

27 The 1922 Press notice, seeking new subscribers, poised itself between describing the Press as a thriving business employing the services of professional printers, and as 'work-...carried on by amateurs, in their spare time, in the somewhat cramped conditions of a private house.'

28 Woolmer, p.17, queries DG's contribution.

29 Quoted in Cunningham, pp.145–6, in a passage on the network of literary influence in the 1930s.

30 Tomalin, p.241.

31 VW to LS, 15 [in fact 18] Mar 1918, *L* II, 914, p.224. At various times she reviewed or wrote on the work of EMF, RF, VB, and *D*, 18 Apr 1918, I, p.142.

32 See James Strachey to Alix Strachey, 16 Jan 1925: 'Leonard ... is afraid of being suspected of favouring Hogarth Press publications.' *Bloomsbury/Freud* p.186.

33 *E* III, p.54.

34 Gillespie, pp.123–39, gives a very full account of VB's illustrations for VW,

35 LW, *DATW*, p.76.

36 VB to JL, 2 Aug 1932[?], But nb. VW to VB, 26 Nov 1918, *L* II, 990, p.299, where she describes the story 'Solid Objects' for VB to illustrate.

37 Gillespie, p.161.

38 'Kew Gardens', *TLS*, 29 May 1919, CH, pp.66–7.

39 VW to VB, 7 Nov 1918, *L* II, 985, p.289.

40 *D*, 30 Nov 1918, p.222, on the 'flat blue wall' behind the ballet. See Shone, *BP2*, p.96, for the impact of the ballet on DG.

41 *D*, 7 Jan 1915, I, p.11.

42 VW to VB, 16 Aug 1916, *L* II, 778, p.111.

43 *Roger Fry*, Ch.10, p.218.

44 VW to VB, 15 July 1918, *L* II, 951,

pp.258–61; cf VW to VB, *L* 771, 890, 949.

45 VW to RF, 21 Oct 1918, *L* II, 981, p.285.

46 *D*, 9 July 1918, I, p.164.

47 *L* II, 942, 948, pp.249, 255.

48 *D*, 23 July 1918, I, p.170.

49 *L* II, 797, 821, pp.123, 140.

50 *D*, 7 April 1918, I, p.134.

51 VW to VB, 11 Nov 1918, *L* II, 986, p.291.

52 *D*, 21 Nov 1918 *L* I p.220, *L* II, 986, p.290.

53 *E* II, p.252; see also *E* III, p.439.

54 VW to RF, 10 Sep 1916, *L* II, 785, p.115.

55 E.g. 'the Woolfs continue to divert themselves, from time to time, with efforts at typographic self-expression.' Douglas McMurtrie, *The Book, The Story of Printing and Bookmaking*, Pitman, 1938, p.473, [mis]quoted in Rhein, p.59.

56 Lehmann, *VW*, p.43.

57 Also Dostoevsky's hitherto unpublished chapter of *The Possessed*, *Stavrogin's Confession* (a perverse narrative of the abduction and suicide of a young girl) with his plan for an unwritten novel, *The Life of a Great Sinner*, Countess Tolstoi's *Autobiography* and Tolstoi's *Love Letters*.

58 See Willis, p.319.

59 *Ulysses* alarmed other publishers too. The *Egoist* printer refused it, and Pound cut its 'indecency' when it first appeared in the *Little Review*, Mar 1918. (Carpenter, *Pound*, p.321.) For the HP's refusal of Connolly's *The Rock Pool* (published by the Obelisk Press in Paris for fear of prosecution), see Alec Craig, *The Banned Books of England*, p.98, & Jack Kahane's *Memoirs of a Booklegger* (Michael Joseph, 1939, pp.265–6). Raymond Mortimer wrote scathingly to CB on the Hogarth Press's rejecting Ivy Compton-Burnett's *Brothers and Sisters*, 19 Apr 1929, CP, Sussex.

60 VW to Gathorne-Hardy, 4 Jan, 28 Jan, 1934, Lilly.

61 VW to Beatrice Howe, 31 May 1926, MHP, Sussex. In *Charleston Magazine*, Winter/Spring 91/2, p.6.

62 Jane Harrison, *Reminiscences of a Student's Life* (1925). The concluding quotation on death, 'Nox est perpetua una dormienda' is used in *The Years*.

63 'How Should One Read a Book?', MS, Berg. In *Yale Review*, Oct 1926; *CR* II, *CE* II, p.2. Her fascination with the details of printing was still strong when Evelyn Irons showed her, LW and VSW round the printing presses of the *Daily Mail* in 1933. 'When I asked her if she was tired, she said, rather sharply, "I want to see it all – I'm interested in exactly how things are done here." ' Evelyn Irons, 'An Evening with Virginia Woolf', *The New Yorker*, 30 Mar 1963, p.117.

64 'Anon' and 'The Reader', ed. Brenda Silver, *Twentieth Century Literature*, Fall 1979, pp.384–5.

65 VW to David Garnett, 26 July 1917, *L* II, 853, pp.167–8.

66 Virginia Blain, 'Dinner is served: The Hogarth Press, Sexual Abuse, and the Ritual Site of the Dining Room', *Virginia Woolf Miscellany*, no.42, Spring 1994, p.5, suggests that they put the press on the dining room table because the slab outside the dining room door at St Ives was 'the site of the young Virginia's early traumatic experience of sexual abuse at the hands of her half-brother Gerald' who would now 'no longer be the dubious purveyor to the 'table' (of public consumption) of Virginia's most intimate parts. The dining room in Hogarth House presented an ideal site for the exorcism of the past', etc. It seems more likely that she did not want to be at the mercy of Gerald's editorial opinions, which were not worth much, according to Anthony Powell, who worked for him. (*Messengers of Day*, vol.II, Heinemann, 1978, pp.5–6: 'His interest in books, anyway as a medium for reading, was as slender

as that of any man I have ever encountered.')

67 Gerald Duckworth to VW, 29 Feb 1919, MHP, Sussex.

68 Edward Garnett, Duckworth's reader, created a brilliant list including James, Strindberg, Ibsen, Gorki, early Galsworthy (as John Sinjohn), Belloc, Edward Thomas, and Ford. *VO* was published in the same year as Dorothy Richardson's first volume of *Pilgrimage* and D.H. Lawrence's *The Prussian Officer. Fifty Years: 1898–1948*, Gerald Duckworth & Co, 1948.

69 *CH*, pp.49–65. Lawrence, sent it by Forster, did not think much of it (Delany, p.51, note 13). VW to Ka Cox, 19 Mar 1936, *L* II, 746, p.84, said she she had sold 2,000 copies of *VO*.

70 VW to VB, 4 May 1919, *L* II, 1042, p.353.

71 *D*, 22 Sep 1925, III, p.43.

72 VB to VW, 23 July 1917, Marler, p.207.

73 VW to VB, 25 June 1918, *L* II, 247, p.255.

74 *E* II, p.223.

75 *CSF*, p.96, mentioned *L* 953.

76 See *D*, 29 July 1918, I, p.176, on Gertler.

77 *CSF*, p.110.

78 *D*, Jan 26 1920, II, pp.13–14.

79 VW to ES, 16 Oct 1930, *L* IV, 2254 p.231.

CHAPTER 21: SEEING LIFE

1 *D*, 3 Nov 1918, II, p.212; LW, *BA*, p.231, says she earned £95.9s.6d. in 1917 and £104.5s.6d. in 1918.

2 *E* III, pp.271–2.

3 30 Nov 1916, *E* II, p.60. See also *E* II, pp.112, 163.

4 24 Jan 1918, *E* II, pp.214–17. The review preceded her close friendship with Walpole.

5 17 June 1920, *E* III, p.228. A review of Elizabeth Robins, a friend of Julia Stephen.

6 'Modern Novels', 1919, *E* III, p.33; the first version of the later essay 'Modern Fiction'.

7 *E* III, p.113.

8 *CR* I, p.166.

9 *E* III, p.127.

10 *E* II, p.224.

11 VW to DG, 17 Dec 1916, *L* II, 809, p.131.

12 *D*, 12 July, 2 July, 7 Aug 1918; II, pp.165, 163, 179.

13 Asheham Diary, 30 Aug 1918, Berg. AOB omits the Asheham diaries for Oct 1917, Dec 1917, Mar-Apr 1918, and July-Oct 1918 from *D* I, pp.68, 93, 130 and 179. Published in *The Charleston Magazine*, 9, 1994, pp.27–35.

14 *D*, 6 Sep 1917, I, p.48; 26, 27 Aug 1917, I,p.45; 1 Sep 1917, I p.47; 4 and 6 Aug, 1918, 30 Mar 1918, Berg.

15 *D*, 2 Mar 1918, I, p.120.

16 *D*, 8 Sep 1918, I, p.190.

17 *D*, 1 May, 5 Jan 1918; II, pp.144, 100.

18 *D*, 18 Apr 1918, I, p.139.

19 *D*, 3 Jan 1918, I, p.95.

20 *E* II, pp.236–7.

21 VW to VB, 30? May 1918, *L* II, 936, p.245.

22 *D*, 28 May 1918, I, p.151.

23 *D*, 4 Nov 1918, I, p.214.

24 *D*, 20 Jan 1919, I, p.234.

25 *D*, 12 Oct 1918, I, p.202.

26 *D*, 17 Oct 1917, I, p.62.

27 *D*, 12 Oct 1918, I, p.202.

28 *D*, 17 June 1918, I, p.155.

29 VW to VB, 31 Dec 1918, *L* II, 1000, p.312.

30 VW to VB, 12 Feb 1919, *L* II, 1020, p.330.

31 *D*, 5 Mar 1919, I, p.249.

32 *D*, 27 July 1918, I, p.172.

33 For MH and Matisse see Richard Shone, 'Matisse in England and two English sitters', *The Burlington Magazine*, July 1993, pp.479–84.

34 *D*, 27 July 1918, I, p.173.

35 CB to MH, 20 Aug 1917, Texas.

36 VW to VB, 27 Oct 1918, *L* II, 983, p.287. See *QB* II, pp.59–60.

37 MH to VB, 22 Oct 1918, CP, Sussex.

38 MH to LS, 11 July 1918, Texas.

39 CB to MH, 20 Oct 1922, Texas,

refers to an affair she may have been having with a woman.

40 VW to MH, 6 May 1929, *CS*, 2026a.
41 *D*, 5 Sep 1926, III, p.107.
42 *Fugitive Pieces* (1927) are full of crepuscular dusks and Piccadilly omnibuses and housewives shopping in Kensington High Street reminding one of 'wasps crawling up a jar of honey'.
43 MH to VW, 10 Sep 1924, MHP, Sussex.
44 MH to VW, 7 Sep [1934], MHP, Sussex.
45 VW to MH, pc, 11 July 1940, MHP, Sussex.
46 *D*, 6 June 1918, I, p.152.
47 *D*, 18 June 1919, I, p.282. For reactions to Karin Stephen see eg. 27 July 1918, p.173.
48 At this meeting of the British Society for the Study of Sex and Psychology, Ernest Jones gave a paper attributing psychosexual impotence to 'infantile fixations in early sexual life.' Minutes of the BSSSP, 18 Jan 1918, Wellcome Institute.
49 VW to LS, 24 May 1918, *L* II, 935, p.244.
50 *D*, 12 Dec 1917, I, p.89.
51 *D*, 19 Aug 1918, I, p.184.
52 *D*, 23 July 1918, I, p.171.
53 VW to LS, 12 Oct 1918, *L* II, 978, p.282.
54 VW to OM, 24 Jan 1918, *L* II, 904, p.213.
55 VW to VB, 29 Jan 1918, *L* I, 905, p.214.
56 VW to MLD, 9 Sep 1917, *L* I, 867, p.178.
57 *D*, 18 Mar 1918, I, p.129.
58 VW to CB, 16 July 1918, *L* II, 952, p.262.
59 *D*, 9 Jan 1918, I, p.104; Fredegond Shove to VW, nd, MHP, Sussex.
60 Fredegond Shove to VW, nd [1918], MHP, Sussex.
61 Alix Sargant-Florence to VW, nd [1918], MHP, Sussex.
62 VW to Carrington, 15 Oct 1916, *L* II, 795, p.122.
63 *E* II, p.173.

CHAPTER 22: KATHERINE

1 *D*, 28 Nov 1919, I, p.315.
2 KM, Review of *Night and Day*, *Athenaeum*, 21 Nov 1919, in *CH*, pp.79–82. The same edition also contained a review by VW.
3 Tomalin, pp.73–5, makes this case persuasively.
4 Tomalin, p.167.
5 'Prelude', Anthony Alpers, *The Stories of Katherine Mansfield*, OUP, 1984, pp.257–8.
6 Tomalin, p.48, beautifully compares their letters: 'The personality that appears in [VW's] letters is a rigorous one; she may be playful, but she is not fluid like Katherine. Where Katherine lets her pen run on, trailing emotion, Virginia's phrases shine like thin ice over dark water.'
7 LS to VW, 17 July 1916, *VW:LS*, p.61.
8 VW to LS, 25 July 1916, *L* II, 775, p.107.
9 VW to VB, 11 Feb 1917, *L* II, 824, p.144.
10 VW to VB, 26 April 1917, *L* II, 829, p.150; 27 June 1917, *L* II, 841, p.159.
11 KM to VW, ?24 June 1917, I, p.313.
12 KM to OM, 3 July 1917, *KM* I, p.315.
13 VW to OM, 15 Aug 1917, *L* II, 860, p.174.
14 KM to VW, c.23 Aug 1917, *KM* I, p.327. Quoted Antony Alpers, *The Life of Katherine Mansfield*, OUP, 1982, pp.250–1, who notices this connection, and argues for Mansfield's influence on Woolf rather than the other way around.
15 CB to MH, early 1917, Texas.
16 VW to CB, 17 Sep 1917, *L* II, 869, p.180.
17 KM to VW, 23 Aug 1917, *KM* I, p.327.
18 KM to OM, 22/29 Oct 1917, *KM* I, p.332; *D*, 12 Nov 1917, I, p.75; VW to VB, 27 Nov 1917, *L* II, 893, p.198.
19 *D*, 18 Jan 1918, I, p.108.
20 *D*, 11 Oct 1917, I, p.58.

21 KM to VW, mid August 1917, *KM* I, p.324; CB to MH, 25 July 1917, Texas.
22 Dorothy Alpers, *Stories of Katherine Mansfield*, 558.
23 KM to Brett, 11 Oct 1917, *KM* I, pp.330–1.
24 KM to OM, 22 Feb 1918, *KM* II, p.87.
25 KM to JMM, 16 and 17 Feb 1918, *KM* II, p.77.
26 *D*, 2 Mar 1918, I, p.120, records a conversation with VB and DG who said there were no painters in England 'worth discussing one's business with' 'like K.M. or Forster even'.
27 *D*, 10, 18 Apr 1918, pp.136, I, pp.139–40.
28 VW to LS, 23 Apr 1918, *L* II, 924, p.234. Also *L* 925.
29 'Modern Novels (Joyce)', Sussex.
30 'The Novels of Dorothy Richardson', May Sinclair, *Little Review*, Apr 1918, pp.55–9 [Silver, p.156] in *The Gender of Modernism*, ed. Bonnie Kyme Scott, Indiana 1990, pp.442–8.
31 *E* III, pp.10–12.
32 *E* III, pp.30–6.
33 KM to VW, c.12 May 1919, *KM* II, p.318.
34 *D*, 22 Mar 1919, I, p.257.
35 KM to VW, c.10 Apr 1919, 4 June 1919, to OM, 10 June 1919, *KM* II, pp.311, 324, 327.
36 *D*, 15 Jan 1941, V, p.353.
37 KM to JMM, 6 Apr 1920, *KM* III, p.274.
38 Alpers, *The Stories of Katherine Mansfield*, pp.193, 555.
39 VW to DG, 15 May 1918, *L* II, 932, p.241.
40 *D*, 28 May 1918, I, p.150; KM to VW, 14 May 1918, *KM* II, p.170.
41 KM to Dorothy Brett, 12 May 1918, *KM* II, p.169.
42 KM to JMM, 29 May 1918, *KM* II, p.203. The cover design by John Fergusson, which VW was very rude about [*L* 934,938] was used only for a few copies of 'Prelude'.

43 VW to VB, 15 July 1918, *L* II, 951, p.259.
44 VW to Janet Case, 20 Mar 1922, *L* II, 1229, p.514.
45 *D*, 7 Aug 1918, I, p.179.
46 VW to VB, 13 Nov 1918, *L* II, 987, p.293.
47 KM to VW, 7, 10, 27 Nov 1918, *KM* II, pp.288, 289, 293.
48 *D*, 9 Nov 1918, I, p.216.
49 VW to VSW, 8 Aug 1931, *L* IV, 2418, p.366.
50 LW, *BA*, p.204.
51 *D*, 18 Feb 1919, I, pp.242–3.
52 *D*, 22 Mar 1919, I, p.258; 17 Apr 1919, I, p.265.
53 *D*, 19 Mar 1919, I, p.257.
54 *D*, 24 Apr 1919, I, p.268.
55 KM to OM, 17 Aug 1919, *KM* II, p.350.
56 KM to VW, 13 Aug 1919, *KM* II, p.347.
57 *D*, 12 July 1919, I, p.291.
58 KM to JMM, 13, 16, 17 Nov 1919, *KM* III, pp.91, 97, 100.
59 KM to JMM, 26/27 Nov 1919, *KM* II, p.122.
60 KM to JMM, 9 Nov 1919, *KM* III, p.81.
61 KM to OM, 25 June 1919, *KM* II, p.333.
62 KM to OM, 21 Aug 1919, Texas.
63 EMF to Sydney Waterlow, 5 Jan 1921, King's.
64 KM to VW, late Apr 1919, *KM* II, p.314.
65 KM to JMM, 20 Nov 1919, *KM* III, p.105.
66 KM to JMM, 30 Nov 1919, *KM* III, p.127–8.
67 KM to JMM, 22 Jan 1920, *KM* III, p.191.
68 JMM to KM, *KM* III, p.124.
69 KM to VW, May 1920, Sussex.
70 *D*, 26 May 1920, II, p.43.
71 *D*, 31 May 1920, II, p.44–5.
72 *D*, 5 June 1920, II, p.45.
73 *D*, 25 Aug 1920, II, pp.61–2.
74 *Orlando: Hol.* p.31.
75 *D*, 25 Aug 1920, II, p.61.
76 *D*, 16 Jan 1923, II, p.226.
77 *D*, 12 Dec 1920, II, p.78.
78 *D*, 19 Dec 1920, II, p.80.

79 KM to VW, 27 Dec 1920, Sussex.
80 VW to KM, 13 Feb 1921, *CS*, 1167a.
81 VW to Dorothy Brett, 2 Mar 1923, *L* III, 1365, p.17.
82 *D*, 15 Sep 1921, II, p.138.
83 *D*, 14 Feb 1922, II, p.161.
84 *D*, 22 Mar 1922, II, p.171.
85 VW to Sydney Waterlow, 24 Aug 1922, *L* II, 1279, p.553.
86 VW to OM, 21? Jan 1923, *L* III, 1350, p.8.
87 *D*, 16 Jan 1923, II, p.227.
88 *D*, 28 Jan 1923, II, p.228.
89 *D*, 7 Dec 1933, IV, p.192.
90 *CH*, p.109; *D*, 2 Aug, 17 Oct 1924.
91 *D*, 19 June 1923, II, 249.
92 VW to Jacques Raverat, 30 July 1923, *L* III, p.59.
93 E.g. 'All must be *deeply felt*', KM, *Letters and Journals*, ed. C.K. Stead, Allen Lane, 1977, July 1921, p.225.
94 *E* IV, p.448.
95 *MB*, p.81.
96 *D*, 16 Jan 1923, II, p.226.
97 *TL*, p.197.
98 *D*, 6 Mar 1923, II, p.237.
99 *D*, 7 Dec 1925, III, p.50.
100 VW to OM, 15 Oct 1928, *L* III, 1941, p.546.
101 *D*, 7 July 1928, III, p.187.
102 VW to VSW, 8 Aug 1931, *L* IV, p.366.
103 *D*, 17 Oct 1924, II, pp.317–18.

CHAPTER 23: READING

1 VW to Eleanor Cecil, 25 Jan? 1919, *L* II, 1010, p.321.
2 *E* IV, pp.317–29.
3 *E* III, p.142.
4 *D*, 18 Apr 1918, I, p.139.
5 *E* IV, pp.388–99.
6 'Modern Novels (Joyce)', Reading notes, MHP, Sussex.
7 *E* III, pp.141–62, 30–6; *CSF*, pp.112–21.
8 In 'Lady Fanshawe's Memoirs', 1907, *E* I, pp.143–7, and in 'The House of Lyme', 1917, *E* II, pp.96–101 She reworked some of this material in 'The Elizabethan Lumber Room' and 'The Pastons and Chaucer', *CR*.
9 Rachel Bowlby, introduction to 'The Crowded Dance of Modern Life', in *Virginia Woolf: Introductions to the Major Works*, ed. J. Briggs, Penguin, 1994, p.291.
10 'Modern Novels', *TLS*, Apr 1919 (*E* III, pp.30–7), developed into an essay, 'Mr Bennett and Mrs Brown', *New York Evening Post*, Nov 1923 (*E* III, pp.384–9) and a lecture called 'Character in Fiction', given to the Cambridge Heretics Society, May 1924 (*E* III, pp.501–17) and revised for *CRI* as 'Modern Fiction', 1925 (*E* IV, pp.157–65). The 1924 lecture was reworked again, first as an essay also called 'Character in Fiction', *The Criterion*, July 1924 (*E* III, pp.420–38), and then as a Hogarth Press pamphlet, also called 'Mr Bennett and Mrs Brown', Oct 1924 (*CE* I, pp.319–37).
11 For an excellent repositioning of 'Modern Fiction' in its context, see Mepham, pp.67–76.
12 *E* III, p.33. cf. this passage in 'Modern Novels', 1919, with the much more often quoted version in 'Modern Fiction', 1925, *E* IV, p.160.
13 Cf. an unpublished 1922 essay called 'Byron & Mr Briggs', supposed to be a review of a book called 'The Flame of Youth', which never gets written; and *A Room of One's Own*, meant to be a lecture on 'Women and Fiction', which she never begins writing.
14 *D*, 14 Jan 1920, II, p.7.
15 *MB*, p.81.
16 Ibid., p.492.
17 *D*, 12 July 1918, I, p.165.
18 'Sir Thomas Browne', 1923, *E* III, p.369.
19 'Mr Byron & Mr Briggs', *E* III, p.487.
20 *D*, 16 Nov 1921, II, p.143.
21 Keats, 'On Sitting Down to Read *King Lear* Once Again', 1818, *John Keats: The Complete Poems*, ed. John Barnard, Penguin, 1973, p.220.
22 *D*, 15 Apr 1920, II, p.31.

23 Notebook, MHP, B2m, Sussex. cf. D, 27 Feb 1935, IV, p.283.
24 'On Re-Reading Novels', 1922, E III, p.340.
25 D, 10 Sep 1918, I, p.192.
26 D, 24 Aug 1933, IV, p.173.
27 VW to ES, 29 July 1934, L V, 2915, p.319.
28 'That pleasure is so . . . immensely fertilising to the mind of anyone who enjoys it', 'How Should One Read a Book?', 1926, E IV, p.399.
29 D, 7 Aug 1918, I, p.180.
30 'Byron & Mr Briggs', E III, p.496.
31 'The Modern Essay', 1922, E IV, p.216.
32 Notebook, MHP, B2q (Silver, XLIX), Sussex.
33 'The Modern Essay', 1922, E IV, p.224.
34 VW to VSW, 29 Dec 1928, L III, 1976, p.570.
35 VW to RF, 6 May 1922, L II, 1244, p.525.
36 D, 22 Aug 1922, D II, p.193. See Gordon, p.179.
37 'A Character Sketch', 1920, E III, p.257.
38 Holograph Reading Notes, vol.18 (Silver XVIII), Berg.
39 D, 11 July 1937, V, p.101.
40 'The Pastons and Chaucer', CR I, p.17, E IV, p.31.
41 'Notes on an Elizabethan Play', CR I, p.54, E IV, p.67.
42 'The Elizabethan Lumber Room', 1925, E IV, p.53.
43 E.g. T.S. Eliot in Jacob's Room, Joyce in Mrs Dalloway, Russian fiction in The Years.
44 E.g. Orlando, Flush, Freshwater, Between the Acts.
45 E.g. Shelley in The Voyage Out, 'Fear no more th' heat o' the sun' in Mrs Dalloway, Cowper's 'The Castaway' in TL.
46 E.g. A joke about Manx cats in an early short story by Aldous Huxley ('No tails, no tails, like men. How symbolical everything is!'), reviewed in 1920, will be saved up for nine years for the manx cat seen on the college lawn in A Room of

One's Own. An unintelligible Russian song heard at a party, in a novel by Hugh Walpole which sounds like 'Boshe, boshe, meely moi/ Kreek – ibushna/ Boshe, boshe, meely moi/ Ibushna – la', ('What did it mean? What every other song in the world meant') is borrowed for the song of the caretaker's children in The Years ('Etho passo tanno hai, Fai donk to tu do'), similarly perceived as unintelligible but 'beautiful'. (Hugh Walpole, Hans Frost, 1929, pp.172–3; The Years, p.345.)
47 E.g. Reading the weekly essayists like J.C. Squire or E.V. Lucas, she says, 'one feels that a common greyness silvers everything.' Browning's line invokes his whole discussion in 'Andrea del Sarto' of the relationship between patronage and the market-place and artistic mediocrity. ('The Modern Essay', 1925, E IV, p.223.)
48 D, 11 May 1923, II, p.242.
49 D, 17 Mar 1923, II, p.240.
50 D, 15 Nov 1921, II, p.142.
51 D, I June 1935, IV, p.318; VW to ES, 22 Apr 1930, L IV, 2168, p.159.
52 D, 22 Aug 1922, II, p.191.
53 D, 20 Apr 1920, II, p.32.
54 D, 17 Aug 1920, II, p.57.
55 D, 17 Mar 1923, II, p.240.
56 'Writing in the Margin', nd, MHP, Sussex.
57 D, 4 Oct 1922, II, p.205; D, 28 July 1923, II, p.259.
58 Notebooks B2q (Silver, p.240), Sussex. Other examples of Mrs Dalloway overlaps: A few pages of Peter Walsh thinking about Clarissa are interspersed with notes on reading Shakespeare, (Notebooks MHP, B20, Sussex) and the first thoughts for Mrs Dalloway, between 1922 and 1923, are written on the back of an old notebook from 1907 on Aeschylus (Silver XXVIII, HRN, 9 Nov 1922-2 Aug 1923, p.147, Berg.)
59 Notebooks MHP, B6d, Sussex.
60 HRN, vol.13 (Silver, XIII) Berg; Notebooks, MHP, B2k, Sussex.
61 E IV, pp.388–99.

62 'Street Haunting', 1927, *E* IV, pp.480–91. See Rachel Bowlby, 'Walking, women and writing: Virginia Woolf as *flâneuse*', in *New Feminist Discourses*, ed. Isobel Armstrong, Routledge, 1992, pp.26–47.
63 'Notes on an Elizabethan Play', 1925, *E* IV, p.62. *TLS* printed 'rends us' for 'reads us'.
64 'Byron & Mr Briggs', *E* III, p.483.
65 'The Antiquary', 1924, *E* III, p.456.
66 'Byron & Mr Briggs', *E* III, p.483.
67 *AEFR* vol.II, on *Robinson Crusoe*, 1926, Berg. Cf. the common reader who creates 'some kind of whole' in the preface to 'The Common Reader', *E* IV, p.19; her reading notes on Wordsworth's *The Prelude*, (1928?) where she quotes 'to him . . . who sees the parts/As parts, but with a feeling of the whole', and adds: 'This should be true of criticism'. (Notebooks, MHP, B20, Sussex.)
68 'How Should One Read a Book?', *E* IV, p.397.
69 Ibid., p.396.
70 E.g. in 'On Not Knowing Greek', 1925, *E* IV, p.42; 'The Pastons and Chaucer', 1925, *E* IV, p.33.
71 'How it Strikes A Contemporary', 1923, *E* III, p.357.
72 'Lives of the Obscure', 1925, 1st version, *E* IV, p.140.
73 'On Being Ill', 1926, *E* IV, p.325.
74 'Bad Writers', 1918, *E* II, p.328; 'How it Strikes a Contemporary', 1923, *E* III, p.325.
75 *D*, 9 Aug 1921, II, p.126.
76 *E* III, p.482.
77 'Byron & Mr Briggs', *E* III, pp.481, 488.
78 Ibid., p.499.
79 Gordon, p.282, who writes powerfully about VW and the marketplace. See also Bowlby, 'A Woman's Essays', in Briggs, pp.249–77.
80 18 May 1924, *E* III, p.503.
81 *D*, 19 Dec 1921, II, p.152; *E* III, pp.324–5; VW to John Hayward, *L* 2007, 4 Mar 1929, *L* IV, 2007, p.30.
82 E.g. *D*, 8, 15 Sep 1920, II, pp.63, 65.
83 E.g. in 'Byron & Mr Briggs', *E* III,

p.494; 'Mr Conrad: A Conversation', 1923, *E* III, pp.376–80.
84 'How Should One Read a Book?', 1923, *E* III, p.354.
85 'The Patron and the Crocus', 1924, *E* IV, p.214.
86 'Reading', 1919, *E* III, p.157.
87 'Byron & Mr Briggs', *E* III, p.514; 'Character in Fiction', *E* III, p.433.
88 Exceptions were Harriet Weaver, Sylvia Beach, Dorothy Todd.
89 See Kate Flint, *The Woman Reader 1837–1914*, OUP 1994, esp. pp.35, 43, 273, 327, and Gordon, pp.181–2, on reading as a woman.
90 A marvellous example of a woman's reading of a woman's life is 'Miss Ormerod', 1924, *E* IV, pp.131–40.
91 Notebooks, MHP, B6d, Sussex. In *The Waves*: Appendix A.

CHAPTER 24: MONK'S HOUSE

1 VW to Janet Case, 5 Jan 1920, *L* II, 1112, p.415.
2 VW to Ka Arnold-Forster, 12 Aug 1919, *L* II, 1073, p.382.
3 Richard Holmes, *Footsteps*, Hodder & Stoughton, 1985, Penguin, 1986, p.27.
4 *D*, 5 Mar 1919, I, p.248.
5 *D*, 3 July 1919, I, pp.286–7.
6 VW to LW, 11 Sep 1919, *L* II, 1080, p.388.
7 Leonard woke them both one night because he had a mouse in his bed; when he went back to sleep, Virginia told Vanessa, he had a wet dream: 'you can't think what his sheets are like this morning'. This is revealing about the sisters' sexual jokes, as well as the sleeping arrangements seven years into the marriage. VW to VB, 11 Apr 1920, *L* II, 1127, p.428.
8 VW to Janet Case, 5 Jan 1920, *L* II, 1112, p.416.
9 *D*, 23 Nov 1940, V, p.341. *D*, 7 Jan 1920, II, p.3.
10 LW, *BA*, p.63; *D*, 17 Aug 1921, II, p.131.
11 VW to MLD, 17 Aug 1919, *L* 1075,

II, p.384. Also *L* 1076, 1078; LW, *DATW*, p.15, Spater, p.173.

12 LW, *DATW*, pp.12–13.
13 *D*, 26 May 1920, II, p.42.
14 *D*, 7 Jan 1920, II, p.3.
15 *D*, 2 Aug 1920, II, p.53; 6 Aug 1923, II, p.260; 25 Sep 1929, III, p.257.
16 *D*, 25 Sep 1929, III, p.257.
17 *D*, 19 Apr 1925, III, p.9.
18 VW to VB, 2 June 1926, *L* III, 1644, p.270. Also 'The water closets gush & surge (not quite sufficiently though).' (*D*, 9 June 1926, III, p.89.)
19 *Recollections*, p.189.
20 *D*, 9 June 1926, III, p.89.
21 VW to VB, 13 June 1926, *L* III, 1647, p.273.
22 *D*, 10 Aug 1927, III, p.152.
23 VW to VSW, 29 Dec 1928, *L* III, 1976, p.569.
24 Philcox estimated £386.10s. and two months for the extension; but the work went over the estimated cost and time. VW and LW divided the cost, VW paying £454.12s.7d. for the house extension and a garden WC, LW £80.18s.7d. for a new pond. (LW, Sussex.) Further improvements to Monk's House were electric fires in 1931, the doing up of the old garage, and connection to the water mains in 1934.
25 *D*, 8 Dec 1929, III, p.270.
26 *D*, 23 Sep 1933, IV, p.180.
27 *D*, 26 Jan 1930, III, p.285.
28 NN to the author, 1992.
29 *D*, 28 Sep 1919, I, p.302.
30 *D*, 31 May 1920, II, p.43.
31 E.g. in 'The Fascination of the Pool', *CSF*, and in *Between the Acts*.
32 One blew down (1943), one got Dutch elm disease (1985).
33 *D*, 14 Sep 1921, II, p.138.
34 *D*, 7 Jan 1920, 15 Sep 1921, 3 Sep 1922, 8 Dec 1929; II pp.3, 138, 196; III p.270.
35 VW to Janet Case, 23 Sep 1922, *L* II, 1288, p.560.
36 VW to VB, June 1921, *L* II, 1182, p.475. [in *L*, 'windows' should read 'a window'.]
37 An oil stove in 1924, a WC in 1929. VW to Pernel Strachey, 24 Aug

1929, *L* III, 1492, p.126; *D*, 5 Aug 1929, III, p.238.
38 VW to Ka Arnold Forster, 23 Aug 1922, *L* II, 1276, p.549.
39 *D*, 14 Sep 1919, I, p.298.
40 *D*, 28 Sep 1926, III, p.112.
41 'A very hidden away little church in a rough field full of cow-pats ... with the proper village smell of eld and oil lamps.' (Esther Meynell, *Sussex*, Robert Hale, 1947, p.134.) It had yew trees and elms, a lych-gate, an ancient Saxon font, brasses, and a millstone over the miller's grave.
42 'In the Orchard', *CSF*, p.149.
43 *D*, 8 Aug 1928, III, p.188.
44 *D*, 1 Oct 1920, II, p.70.
45 'In the Orchard', *CSF*, p.149.
46 *D*, 25 Sep 1927, III, p.159.
47 LW, *BA*, p.64.
48 *CSF*, p.232.
49 *D*, 9 Aug 1921, II, p.127.
50 LW, *BA*, p.66.
51 *D*, 16 Sep 1932, IV, p.124; 'Old Mrs Grey', *CE* IV, p.149.
52 Eg: 'Gone, too, is every trace of Caesar's legions, who laid out Ermine Street where now these marshes are.' (Arthur Mee, *The King's England: Sussex*, Hodder & Stoughton, 1937, p.309.) 'In the old days Sussex country people tended to long and contented lives, as many a record and many a memory of still surviving gaffers and gammers show. But these old people are rapidly disappearing ...' (Meynell, op.cit., p.309.)
53 *CSF*, 169.
54 *CSF*, p.227.
55 In 1923 she is having conversations about palaeolithic man (*D*, 5 Sep, 11 Sep 1923, II, p.264,267); in the 1920s and 1930s she is reading Wells, Darwin, James Jeans. In Lewes High Street there is a plaque to Dr Gideon Mantell (1790–1852) who discovered the fossil bones of the prehistoric iguanodon in the Sussex Weald.
56 *Between the Acts*, p.20.
57 Jim Bartholemew, 'Guide to Rodmell', 1985; Maire Mcqueeney,

58 LW, *BA*, pp.67–8.
59 *D*, 11 Aug 1921, II, p.129; 5 Aug 1929, III, p.238.
60 *D*, 20 Aug 1920, II, p.60.
61 VW to VB, 10 Aug 1922, *L* II, 1269, p.544.
62 VW to Pernel Strachey, 10 Aug 1923, *L* III, 1416, p.64; *D*, 6 Aug 1923, II, p.260.
63 *D*, 21 Aug 1927, III, p.153.
64 *D*, 17 Aug 1920, II, p.59.
65 *D*, 1 Oct 1920, II, p.71.
66 *D*, 22 Sep 1928, III, pp.197–8.
67 *Between the Acts*, p.21.
68 *D*, 25 Sep 1927, III, p.158.
69 VW to MLD, 3? Jan 1920, *L* II, 1109, p.413.
70 *D*, 24 Sep 1930, III, p.320.
71 *D*, 1 Oct 1919, I, p.303.
72 *D*, 21 Sep 1929, III, p.255.
73 *D*, 23 June 1929, III, p.236.
74 *Recollections*, p.188.
75 *D*, 15 Sep 1924, II, p.314.
76 *D*, 5 Sep 1938, V, p.167.
77 *D*, 7 Feb 1938, V, p.128.
78 VW to LS, 29 Aug 1921, *L* II, 1187, p.478.
79 *D*, 3 Aug 1922, II, p.188.
80 *D*, 16 Sep 1932, IV, p.124.
81 *D*, 17 Aug 1920, II, p.59.
82 *D*, 22 Aug 1938, V, p.162.
83 *D*, 23 Sep 1933, IV, p.179.
84 CB to MH, 12 Sep 1925, Texas.
85 EMF to Christopher Isherwood, 7 Apr 1934, King's.
86 See Dirk Bogarde, *A Postillion Struck by Lightning*, Penguin 1988, pp.112–4, for a version of his Sussex childhood encounters with a tall thin lady, 'with a long woolly, and fairish hair which looked rather wispy as if she had just washed it', considered 'a bit do-lally-tap' by the local boys.
87 *D*, 17 Aug 1938, V, p.161.
88 *D*, 5 Sep 1926, III, p.107.
89 VW to VSW, 17 Feb 1926, *L* III, 1621, p.241; *D*, 31 May 1940, V, p.291.
90 *D*, 11 June 1922, II, p.176.

91 *D*, 16 Sep 1932, IV, p.124.
92 E.g. *D*, 7 Jan 1920, II, p.4; *D*, 17 Aug 1920, II, p.58.
93 VW to VSW, 29 Dec 1928, *L* III, 1976, p.570.
94 *D*, 13 June 1932, IV, p.109.

CHAPTER 25: POST-WAR

1 *D*, 21 Oct 1919, I, p.306.
2 *D*, 21 Oct 1919. CB and OM praised it; EMF preferred *The Voyage Out* ('None of the characters in N. & D. is lovable', *D*, 6 Nov 1919, I, p.310); RF seemed not to like it (*D*, 20 Jan 1920), LS wanted 'more tupping' (VW to LS, 28 Oct 1919, *L* II, 1087, p.394). Some reviews were appreciative ('a book full of wisdom', *TLS*, *CH*, p.76; 'amazing sensitiveness', *The English Review*; 'her sincerity, her power, her vision are challenging and remarkable', *Cambridge Magazine*.) Others, like KM, or 'The Wayfarer' in the *Nation* (H.W. Massingham, 29 Nov 1919) thought there was too much tea drinking between the 'Four Impassioned Snails'.
3 Dedication to *Night and Day*; VW to VB, 27 Oct 1919, *L* II, 1086, p.393.
4 VW to VD, 27 Nov 1919, *L* II, 1098, p.402.
5 VB to Madge Vaughan, 16 Mar 1920, Marler, pp.236–7.
6 *D*, 15 Nov 1919, I, p.313.
7 VW to Janet Case, 19 Nov 1919, *L* II, 1095, p.400.
8 *D*, 21 Jan 1920, II, p.11.
9 *D*, 11 Oct 1919, I, p.305.
10 *D*, 28 Dec 1919, I, p.317.
11 See *D*, 6 Mar 1920, II, p.23, n.9., for its beginning; See *QB* II, p.83, for its membership; see S.P. Rosenbaum, *A Bloomsbury Group Reader*, Blackwell, 1993, Part IX, 'Memoirs', for some examples; and *Clever Hearts*, pp.201–3, for the club's first meetings.
12 *Jacob's Room*, pp.93–4; and see her correspondence on the Plumage Bill

in Ray Strachey's *Women's Leader* (*E* III, pp.241–5).

13 *CSF*, pp.145–8,301. The chapter was published in Nov 1926 in the *Atalanta's Garland* by the Edinburgh University Women's Union.

14 *D*, 24 Jan 1920, II, p.12.

15 *D*, 10 Jun 1919, I, p.280.

16 *D*, 25 Nov 1921, II, p.145.

17 *D*, 18 Feb 1922, II, p.168.

18 George Doran. Harcourt Brace took *Monday or Tuesday*.

19 *D*, 8 Apr 1921, II, p.106.

20 *D*, 15 May 1921 II, p.118; 'Books by the same author: Some Press Opinions', *Jacob's Room*, 1st ed, 1922. These were two of the critical reviews (of *Monday or Tuesday*): 'Mrs Woolf has a disorderly mind and does not know how to write. She gushes drivel ... Mrs Woolf, like the mathematician, does not know whether what she is saying is true; neither do we, nor do we care. In her own style, we retort: Lobatchevsky! Guru!! Miaow!!!' (*The New Age*). 'The leading papers speak of the genius of the writer, but I must confess that the product of that genius is unintelligible to me. It marks an altogether new method of indicating thought and emotion ... I fear that I cannot wax very enthusiastic about this work. It is not of specific Jewish interest.' (*The Zionist Record*).

21 *D*, 25 Oct 1920, II, p.72.

22 *D*, 29 June 1920, II, pp.50–1.

23 *D*, 8 Aug 1921, II, p.125.

24 *D*, 25 Oct 1920, II, p.73.

25 T.S. Eliot, 'East Coker', Section V, *Four Quartets*.

26 *D*, 15 Nov 1918, I, p.218.

27 *TSE*, ed. Valerie Eliot, Faber, 1988, vol.I, p.280.

28 *D*, 19 Sep 1920, II, p.67.

29 VW to RF, 18 Nov 1918, *L* II, 988, p.296.

30 VW to OM, 24 Sep 1923, *L* III, 1422, pp.70–1.

31 *TSE*, p.204.

32 *TSE*, p.251; *D*, 16 Aug 1922 II,

33 Eliot wrote in 1927 about her removal of the Conradian 'Strong Man', the 'lonely European' from her novels, and the melancholy sense her work gives of 'something *left out*'. *Nouvelle Revue Française*, May 1927, *CH*, pp.191–2.

34 *TSE*, p.314.

35 Peter Ackroyd, *T.S. Eliot*, Hamish Hamilton, 1984, p.74.

36 See Willis, pp.29–30: all seven poems had appeared in the *Little Review*; the edition of about 200 sold well; LW paid Eliot £4.17s.4d. in 1920. Gordon, *Eliot's Early Years*, OUP, 1977, p.85, notes: 'It was a gesture of faith which helped strengthen Eliot's position.'

37 *D*, 3 Dec 1918, I, p.223.

38 *D*, 22 Mar 1921, II, p.104.

39 VW to DG, 17 Apr 1919, *L* II, 1039, p.350.

40 *TSE*, p.288.

41 *TSE*, p.305.

42 *D*, 20 Sep 1920, II, p.68; 'The Love Song of J. Alfred Prufrock', *Collected Poems 1909–1962*, Faber, 1974, p.16.

43 Quoted Gordon, op. cit., p.84, from CB, *Old Friends*, 1956, Cassell, 1988, p.120, as told to him by VW.

44 *E* III, p.296.

45 She was reading Keats's *Letters*. Silver, p.194.

46 *D*, 22 Mar 1921, II, pp.103–4.

47 *D*, 28 Sep 1921, II, p.140.

48 *D*, 23 June 1922, II, p.178. She told David Garnett that she liked 'the sound of it'.

49 *D*, 5 Dec 1920, II, p.77.

50 *D*, 16 Feb 1940, V, p.268.

51 *D*, 27 Sep 1922, II, p.204.

52 *D*, 3 Aug 1922, II, p.187.

53 *D*, 5 May 1924, II, p.302.

54 *D*, 27 Sep 1922, II, p.204; *D*, 12 Mar 1922, II, p.171.

55 *D*, 12 Nov 1934, IV, p.261.

56 *D*, 23 Sep 1935, IV, p.344.

57 VW to RF, 18 May 1923, *L* III, 1390, p.38.

58 *D*, 10 Sep 1933, IV, p.178.

59 VW to VB, 27 Apr 1924, *L* III, 1162, p.103.
60 *D*, 5 Dec 1920, II, p.77.
61 *D*, 10 Sep 1933, IV, p.179. The image of the 'assegai' is used in *The Waves*, where Louis embodies some of Eliot's vulnerable alienation. (She mentions here that Eliot is from St Louis).
62 *TSE*, pp.355–6.
63 *The Sacred Wood* was too long for the Press, and *Ara Vos Prec*, which would have suited them, went to the American publisher of the Ovid Press. Willis, pp.70–1.
64 It had appeared in the first issue of Eliot's new magazine, *The Criterion*, in Oct 1922, and in the American magazine *The Dial* in Nov.
65 Eliot to VW, [nd], 1923, Berg.
66 VW to Eliot, 14 Apr 1922, *L* II, 1238, p.521. The editors of *L* note that the long story she is now writing is 'Mrs Dalloway in Bond Street', but it is 'In the Orchard' which is the story of 'less than 5,000 words' she promises to send him 'by Aug 15th'. She did not send him 'Mrs Dalloway in Bond Street' until 4 June 1923.
67 Eliot to VW, 4 Dec 1922, *TSE*, pp.606–7.
68 VW to Eliot, 4 June 1923, *L* 1397, III, p.45; *D*, 17 July 1923, II, p.256. Possibly Eliot passed it on to his friend Scofield Thayer, the *Dial*'s American editor.
69 Eliot to VW, 1 May 1924, Berg.
70 *D*, 5 May 1924, II, p.302.
71 Eliot to VW, 22 May 1924, Berg.
72 VW to Eliot, 23 May 1924, *L* III, 1472, p.110.
73 Eliot to VW, 27 Aug 1924, Texas.
74 She would be again for Desmond and Molly MacCarthy in 1927. *Clever Hearts*, p.221; VW to Molly MacCarthy, 24 Mar 1927, *L* III, 1736, p.354.
75 VW to VB, 3 Oct 1922, *L* II, 1294, p.565.
76 Ackroyd, pp.128–9;, Gordon, p.124.
77 VW to OM, 19 June 1923, *L* III,

1400, p.43; also, *D*, 13 June 1923, II, p.247.
78 *TSE*, p.554.
79 VW to RF, 22 Oct 1922, *L* II, 1303, p.572.
80 CB to MH, 7 Sep 1922, Texas.
81 LS to VW, Dec 1922, Berg.
82 Eliot to VW, 4 Dec 1922, *TSE*, p.606; Ackroyd, p.130; VW to Richard Aldington, 12 Oct 1923, *L* III, 1429, p.74.
83 *D*, 28 Jan 1923, II, p.229.
84 E.g. VW to MK, 24 Feb 1923, *L* III, 1362, p.16. Also to LS, 23 Feb 1923, *L* III, 1360, p.14.
85 *D*, 6, 17 Mar 1923, II, pp.237–9. Ackroyd, pp.132–3.
86 *D*, 23 Mar 1923, II, p.240.
87 VB to RF, 29 Dec [1923], Tate Gallery.
88 Eliot to VW, 7 May 1924, Berg.
89 Eliot to VW, 5 Sep 1925, Berg.
90 *D*, 30 Sep 1925, III, p.45.
91 VW to Eliot, 13 Nov 1924, *L* III, 1597, p.220.
92 Eliot to VW, 11 Feb 1926, Berg; *D*, 7 Dec 1925, III, p.49.
93 Eliot to Mary Hutchinson, 1917; *TSE*, p.197.
94 *TSE*, p.466.
95 *D*, 21 June 1924, II, p.304.
96 *D*, 17 July 1923, II, p.256.
97 Ackroyd, p.149.
98 Seymour, p.332, Ackroyd p.134.
99 *D*, 29 Apr 1925, III, p.15.
100 Eliot to LW, nd [Apr 1925], Berg.
101 LW to Eliot, 30 Apr 1925, Spotts, p.228.
102 Eliot to LW, nd (1925), Berg. Eliot also wrote asking for the name of 'the best MD there is with psychoanalytical knowledge – if there is one? Would you say Wright or someone else? This is obviously *not* for V but for myself if anyone.' nd, Berg. See Gordon, *Eliot's New Life*, pp.58–9, on Eliot's asking LW for advice.
103 *D*, 29 Apr 1929, III, p.223.
104 VW to VB, 8 Nov 1930, *L* IV, 2274, p.250; *D*, 8 Nov 1930, III, p.331; *D*, 2 Sep 1932, IV, p.123.
105 VW to OM, 22 June 1932, *L* V, 2600, p.71.

106 *D*, 8 Nov 1930, III, p.331.
107 *D*, 18 Aug 1921, II, p.133.
108 VW to Francis Birrell, 3 Sep 1933, *L* V, 2787, p.222.
109 *D*, 10 Sep 1933, IV, p.178.
110 VW to EB, 20 July 1933, *L* V, 2765, p.205.
111 VW to QB, 26 July 1933, *L* V, 2767, p.207.
112 VW to OM, 31 Dec 1933, *L* V, 2841, p.266. In 1936 CB reported that VW now maintained that 'the true inspiration of Tom was Vivien. He was one of those poets who live by scratching, and his wife was his itch.' (CB to MH, Sep 1936, Texas.)
113 Eliot to VW, Twelfth Night 1935, Berg.
114 Eliot to VW, 9 Jan 1935, Berg.
115 Eliot to VW, October 1937, Berg.
116 Eliot to VW, 12 Oct 39, Berg.
117 Eliot to VW, 3 Feb (1938), Berg.
118 Ackroyd, p.96; also, p.207, notes that Eliot made a fierce attack on Woolf in a 1934 lecture to an Anglo-Catholic seminary.
119 Ackroyd, p.161.
120 *D*, 4 Dec 1935, IV, p.356.
121 *D*, 22 Mar 1939, V, p.210.
122 *D*, 29 Dec 1940, V, p.347.
123 Ackroyd, p.188.
124 Eliot, *Horizon*, May 1941, *CH*, pp.429–31.
125 Eliot to John Hayward, 21 Apr 1941, Mrs Valerie Eliot.
126 Eliot to VW, 2 June 1927, Berg.

CHAPTER 26: PARTY GOING

1 *D*, 22 Aug 1922, II, p.192.
2 *D*, 3 Sep, 4 Oct 1922, pp.197, 205.
3 VW to VB, 10 Aug 1922, *L* 1269, II, p.545.
4 As note 1.
5 *D*, 26 July 1922, II, p.186.
6 *D*, 16 Aug 1922, II, p.189.
7 *D*, 4 Oct 1922, II, p.205.
8 *D*, 3 Aug 1922, II, p.187; VW to VB, *L* 1269, 10 Aug 1922, II, p.545.
9 *D*, 11 Aug 1921, II, p.129.
10 LW to MLD, 9 Mar 1922, LW,

Sussex. *L* 1214, 1215, 1216.
11 VW to ES, 8 Oct 1930, *L* IV, 2249, p.227.
12 VB to RF, 2 Mar 1922, Tate Gallery.
13 *D*, 11 June 1922 II, p.176; VW to Janet Case, 21 May 1922, *L* II, 1250, p.529.
14 *D*, 16 Aug 1922, II, p.189.
15 LW to MLD, 16 Aug 1922, LW, Sussex; *D*, 22 July 1922.
16 CB to MH, 8 Aug 1922, Texas.
17 *Mrs Dalloway*, notebook, 2 Aug 1923, Berg.
18 Ibid., 9 Nov 1922.
19 E.g. the first notes for *Mrs Dalloway* are made immediately after the last MS entry for *Jacob* (*Jacob's Room*, Holograph, vol.III, Berg); the 'Old Man' is 'seen' as she is finishing *Mrs Dalloway* (*D*, 17 Oct 1924); the themes of *Room* are in the MS of *TL*.
20 *D*, 26 July 1922, II, p.186.
21 *D*, 4 Oct 1922, II, pp.205–6.
22 *D*, 12 May 1923, II, p.242.
23 *To the Lighthouse*: Hol., ed Dick, 1983, p.136.
24 *D*, 15 Apr 1920, II, p.29.
25 *D*, 29 Oct 1922, 7 Nov 1922, II, pp.209, 210.
26 Willis, p.61, notes a discrepancy (as with *Monday or Tuesday*) between her account of *Jacob's Room*'s sales and the Hogarth Press accounts. The book sold slowly; LW printed a second 1,000 copies soon after publication. About 1,000 copies were sold by Apr 1923. LW closed the account on 17 Mar 1924, 'with a total of 1413 copies sold for a press profit of £42.4.6 and a payment "To author" of a modest £14.1.5.'
27 For Bennett's attack in *Cassell's Weekly*, 28 March 1923, see *D*, 19 June 1923, II, p.248; *E* III, pp.437, 388; for Murry's in the *N&A*, 10 Mar 1923, see *D*, 2 Aug, 17 Oct 1924.
28 *D*, 15 Oct 1923, II, p.272.
29 'Mrs Dalloway', MS, written under this heading: 'The Hours or Mrs

Dalloway, Good Friday, 18 April 1924', BL, ADD. 1961.

30 *D*, 14 Oct 1922, II, p.207.

31 'Mrs Dalloway', MS, BL. cf *D*, 19 June 1923, II, p.248: 'life & death, sanity & insanity.'

32 'Mrs Dalloway', notebook, 2 Aug 1923, Berg.

33 *D*, 19 June 1923, II, p.248. AOB reads the word as 'squint'; it could be 'squirt'.

34 'Mrs Dalloway', [1 Oct 1923], p.56, MS, BL.

35 *D*, 15 Oct 1923, II, pp.270–1.

36 *D*, 7 Sep 1924, II, p.312.

37 VW to Carrington, 24 Aug 1922, *L* II, 1278, p.552.

38 *D*, 28 July 1923, II, p.258; 29 Oct 1922, p.210; 2 Jan 1923, p.222.

39 *D*, 28 July 1923, II, p.259.

40 *D*, 13 June 1923, II, p.247.

41 *D*, 10 Nov 1920, II, p.73.

42 *D*, 13 June 1923, II, p.246.

43 VW to VB, 2 Apr 1920, *L* II, 1126, p.426.

44 E.g. VW to Jacques Raverat, 4 Nov 1923, *L* III, 1432, p.77.

45 VB to VW, 28 Apr 1924, Berg.

46 VW to VB, mid Sep 1921, *L* II, 1194, p.483; 10 Aug 1922, II, 1269, p.543.

47 E.g., *D*, 4 Feb 1922, II, p.159.

48 VW to VB, 20 Feb 1922, *L* II, 1218, p.506.

49 *D*, 5 Apr 1924, II, p.299.

50 LW, *DATW*, p.118.

51 *D*, 2 Jan 1923, II, p.222.

52 *D*, 6 Mar 1923, II, p.237.

53 *D*, 28 June 1923, II, p.250.

54 *D*, 29 Oct 1922, II, p.210.

55 Spotts, p.390: 'Until 1948 English Universities were represented in Parliament, with two seats each for Cambridge, London and Oxford and two for the remaining seven. It was the combined-universities constituency for which LW was asked to be a candidate ... Reckoning his chances of election to be nil, he spoke at only four of the universities.'

56 Spotts, p.391.

57 *D*, 18 Mar 1921, II, pp.101–3. VW to VB, 17 Mar 1921, *L* II, 1169, pp.457–9.

58 On 15 Nov 1922. The outcome was a solid conservative majority under Bonar Law (and after his resignation from ill health, Stanley Baldwin) and a transformation of the Labour Party into an electable, more middle-class and less union-dominated party. Taylor, pp.253–68. Also Arthur Marwick, *The Explosion of British Society, 1914–62*, Pan, 1963, Ch.7.

59 *L* 1249, 1309, 1310, 1323, on her dread of this prospect, and *L* II, p.586, for the voting figures.

60 For the election on 6 Dec 1923 and the ineffectual Labour government of 1924 see Taylor, pp.271–81.

61 *D*, 11 May 1923, II, p.241.

62 Taylor, pp.281–90; Marwick, p.71.

63 *D*, 17 Oct 1924, II, p.318.

64 VW to Carrington, 24 Aug 1922, *L* II, 1278, p.552.

65 *D*, 12 Apr 1921, II, p.109.

66 This scene was later moved to the middle of the novel, *Mrs Dalloway*, pp.56–7.

67 The exhibition which had been postponed from 1915 covered 216 acres of grounds. It included a Palace of Engineers, a Palace of Industry and of Arts, a Stadium, the Domes of India, a Gas exhibition, motor-cars, electrical machinery, and many new inventions like Pyrex glass and fountain pens. 200,000 visitors went on the first day (Elgar conducted 'Jerusalem'). *The Times* said: 'Millions of British subjects will ascend the heights of Empire. Spread before them is the wondrous reality of Britain's might and magnitude – her grandeur and her glory.'

68 'Thunder at Wembley', *E* III, June 1924, p.413.

69 LW, *DATW*, pp.77–8.

70 LW, *DATW*, pp.69,72; *D*, 10 Aug 1920, II, p.56. For these affairs see Holroyd; Garnett; Gerzinga, *Carrington*, OUP, 1990; Frances

Partridge, *Memories*, Gollancz, 1981; Brenan, *Personal Record 1970–72*, Cape, 1974; Xan Fielding, ed., *Best of Friends: The Brenan-Partridge Letters*, Chatto, 1986; Jonathan Gathorne-Hardy, *Gerald Brenan*, 1993.

71 *D*, 25 Jan 1921, II, p.87.
72 VW to LS, 17 Apr 1921, *L* II, 1174, p.465.
73 *D*, 6 Nov 1923, II, p.276; 15 Sep 1921, II, p.139.
74 *D*, 7 Jan 1923, II, p.224.
75 *D*, 4 June 1923, II, p.243.
76 'Ralph, Carrington and I went to hear Roger lecture on Cézanne. On the way home, Virginia and Leonard overtook us, and as we walked along Carrington invited them down to Ham Spray. Virginia: 'Ah, but do you know if you *may* ask us, Carrington; hadn't you better ask the old man?' It was ungraciously, or rather maliciously said, as if to relegate Carrington to her position as Lytton's housekeeper – instead of the mistress of the house.' Frances Partridge, Diary, 31 Oct 1927, in *Memories*, Gollancz, 1981.
77 Mary Ann Caws in *Women of Bloomsbury*, Routledge, 1990, pp.60–8, gives a more positive reading of their relationship.
78 *D*, 31 Aug 1920, II, p.62.
79 VW to VB, Jan 1921, *L* II, 1162, p.454.
80 Brenan, Letter to Rosemary Dinnage, 1967; Jonathan Gathorne-Hardy, interview with Frances Partridge.
81 VW to VB, 22 May 1921, *L* 1179, p.470.
82 *D*, May 15 1921, II, pp.118–19; LW, *DATW*, p.72.
83 VW to VB, 22 Dec 1922, *L* II, 1335, p.595. A hostile reading of this episode is given by Holroyd, 1971, p.817; a defence is made by *QB*II, p.80; Holroyd, 1994, pp.484–5 is much toned down.
84 Quoted Gerzinga, p.193.
85 Gerzinga, pp.175–6.

86 VW to VB, 13 Nov 1921, *L* 1204, p.492.
87 Gerzinga, p.193; Jonathan Gathorne-Hardy, p.179.
88 Carrington to LS, 22 June 1922, quoted Gerzinga, p.193.
89 *D*, 23 June 1922, p.177.
90 *D*, 23 June 1922, p.178.
91 VW to Jacques Raverat, 3 Oct 1924, *L* III, 1501, p.135.
92 In July 1922 he suggested taking over the *English Review* with Ralph as his business manager; in Dec he seemed to be bribing them to keep Ralph on with promises of his own work for publication; in Feb 1923 he floated a rival 'Tidmarsh Press'.
93 *D*, 22 July 1922, II, p.185.
94 *D*, 7 Nov 1922, 15 Dec 1922, VW to RP, 10 Nov 1922; II, pp.211, 216–17: *L* 1317, p.583.
95 VW to Jacques Raverat, 29 Nov 1924, *L* III, 1515, p.145; 24 Jan 1925, *L* 1524, p.155; *D*, 19 Apr 1925, III, p.11.
96 By the end of the year he was in love with Frances Marshall, sister-in-law of Bunny Garnett, who was working at his and Francis Birrell's Bloomsbury bookshop. Another complex situation then developed between Frances, Ralph, Carrington and Lytton.
97 VW to GB, 25 Dec 1922, *L* II, 1337, p.597.
98 VW to VB, 1 Apr 1923, *L* III, 1376, p.26; to RF, 16 Apr 1923, *L* III, 1380, p.29.
99 LS to MH, 11 Apr 1920, Texas; part-quoted Holroyd, 1971, p.797.
100 GB to Ralph Partridge, 27 Mar 1923.
101 GB, *Personal Record*; Gathorne-Hardy, *Gerald Brenan*, pp.188–9; VW to MH, 18? April 1923, *CS* 1380a, p.162; GB to Carrington, not sent, 16 April 1923, BL? GB to David Garnett, 31 Mar 1957: 'Virginia, as a novelist, I regard as a dead end . . . when she abandoned delineation of character she abandoned the shock and drama which are the life of novelising and produced

something stagnant and eventless like an impressionist picture.'

102 VW to GB, 25 Dec 1922, *L* II, 1337, p.597.

103 'Mrs Dalloway', notebook, 19 Nov 1922, Berg.

104 See LW, *DATW*, p.72, and Jonathan Gathorne-Hardy, p.257 for Partridge's and Brenan's instability.

105 VW to J.T. Sheppard, 5 Jan 1920, *L* IIII, II, p.414; VW to Barbara Bagenal, 23 Dec 1920, *L* II, 1160, p.451; *D*, 6 Mar 1920, II, p.23; VW to RF, 22 Oct 1922, *L* II, 1303, p.573. See Holroyd, 1971, p.784.

106 *E* III, p.404.

107 *D*, 9 June 1926, III, p.89.

108 *D*, 23 May 1921, II, p.120. *Clever Hearts*, p.205.

109 Frances Partridge, *Memories*, p.92.

110 VW to Marjorie Joad, 15 Feb 1925, *L* III, 1537, p.168.

111 VW to RF, 1 Aug 1920, *L* II, 1139, p.438. *D*, 2 Aug 1920, II, p.54.

112 *D*, 7 Jan 1923, II, p.225. VW to Molly MacCarthy, 19 Jan 1923, *L* III, 1348, p.6.

113 VB to RF, 22 June 1924, Tate Gallery, Marler, p.277.

114 *D*, 21 June 1924, II, p.304.

115 Partridge, *Memories*, p.92; *Clever Hearts*, p.215.

116 'The Dunciad', *Charleston Bulletin*, QB.

117 Holroyd, 1971, pp.898–9; *D*, 13 June 1923, II, p.246. VSW was there too. It was reviewed in *Vogue*: 'Hidden behind a curtain painted by Frank Dobson, Edith Sitwell half sang, half shouted her musical poetry through a Sengerphone.' Georgina Howell, *In Vogue: Sixty Years of Celebrities and Fashions from British Vogue*, Penguin, 1978, p.6. VSW and VW went again to *Façade* in 1926 and Vita gave a full acount to HN, *V & H*, pp.151–2.

118 *D*, 13 June 1923, II, p.246.

119 *D*, 16 Nov 1923, II, p.275.

120 LW, *DATW*, p.104, & VW to OM, 1 Nov 1922, *L* II, 1311, p.579.

121 VW to RF, 18 May 1923, *L* III, 1390, p.39.

122 *D*, 3 July 1924, II, p.305.

123 VW to RF, 18 May 1923, *L* III, 1390 p.39. See 'Am I a Snob?', MB.

124 Kirsty McLeod, *A Passion for Friendship: Sibyl Colefax & her Circle*, Michael Joseph, 1991, p.105.

125 E.g. *D*, 11 May 1923, II, p.241.

126 *CSF*, pp.170–7.

127 Kirsty McLeod, p.84.

128 *D*, 29 Oct 1922, II, p.210.

129 VW to Eleanor Cecil, 12 Nov 1922, *L* II, 1320, p.585.

130 VW to RF, 17 Oct 1921, II, 1196, p.485.

131 VW to MH, 18 Apr 1923, *CS*, 1380a, p.162.

132 MH to VW, 26 May 1924, MHP, Sussex.

133 VW to MH, 15 Feb 1924, *L* 1442a, VI, p.505.

134 VW to Molly MacCarthy, 22 Nov 1924, *L* III, 1513, p.143.

135 *D*, 18 Feb 1928, III, pp.175–6.

136 Logan Pearsall Smith to VW, 26 Jan 1925, MHP, Sussex; VW to LPS, 28 Jan 1925, *L* III, 1527, p.157. His reply was even cattier: 'I didnt realise the noble & unmercenary motives for writing in the fashion papers which you allege.' See VW to Jacques Raverat, 24 Jan 1925 *L* 1524. p.154.

137 *D*, 6 May 1926, III, p.78.

138 *D*, 23 Jan 1924, II, p.289.

139 Shone, *BP2*, p.178.

140 *D*, 19 Apr 1925, III, p.9.

141 *D*, 5 Apr 1924, II, p.300; Osbert Sitwell in *SPR*, p.252; *E* III, p.449.

142 *D*, 17 Oct 1924, II, p.319.

143 *D*, 11 Sep 1923, II, p.266.

144 *Vogue*, Nov 1925.

145 VW to RF, 6 May 1922, *L* II, 1244, p.525.

146 *D*, 15 Sep 1921, II, p.139.

147 RF to VW, 2 July 1924, Sutton, II, p.555.

148 VW to RF, 22 Sep 1924, *L* III, p.133.

149 VW to Jacques Raverat, 8 June 1924, *L* III, 1479, p.115.

150 *D*, 23 Nov 1920, II, p.75.

151 *D*, 22 July 1923, II, p.257.

152 VW to Jacques Raverat, 30 July 1923, *L* III, 1414, p.60.
153 *D*, 16 Nov 1923, II, p.275; *L* 1505.
154 'A loathing overcomes me of human beings – their insincerity, their vanity . . . [in my book] I want to bring in the despicableness of people like Ott.' *D*, 4 June 1923, II, pp.243–4; *Mrs Dalloway*, pp. 179–80.
155 *D*, 12, 23 Jan 1924, II, pp.284 (n.8, 11) and 288.
156 *D*, 9 Jan 1924, II, p.283.
157 *D*, 3 Nov 1923, II, p.273; *D*, 5 May 1924, II, p.301: 'London is enchanting . . .'; VW to Ethel Sands, 28 May 1924, *L* 1474, III, p.111–12: 'as for the beauty of London at all hours, and its oddity and character and quality and romance, never mention Richmond to me again, to compare with it . . .'
158 VW to Jacques Raverat, 8 Mar 1924, *L* III, 1450, p.92.
159 VW to VB, 27 Apr 1924, *L* III, 1462, p.104.
160 *D*, 20 Apr 1925, III, p.12.
161 *D*, 17 Feb 1922, II, p.167; 5 May 1924, II, p.301; 8 Apr 1925, III, p.7.

CHAPTER 27: A HAUNTED HOUSE

1 *D*, 17 Oct 1924, II, p.317.
2 *D*, 14 Mar 1927, III, pp.131–2.
3 VW to VB, 8 May 1927, *L* III, 1750, p.370.
4 *To the Lighthouse; Hol.*, Appendix A, pp.44, 47, 48–50.
5 *D*, 14 May 1925, III, pp.18–19.
6 *D*, 27 June 1925, III, p.34.
7 *D*, 20 July 1925, III, p.36.
8 *D*, 5 Sep 1926, III, p.106.
9 *D*, 13 Sep 1926, III, p.110.
10 *D*, 5 May 1927, III, p.134.
11 *D*, 30 July 1925, III, p.37.
12 *TL*, p.209.
13 *CE*, II, p.2.
14 Quoted and noted, Gordon, p.112.
15 *D*, 5 Sep 1925, III, p.39.
16 VW to RF, 16 Sep 1925, *L* III, 1583, p.208.
17 *D*, 7 Dec 1925, III, p.49.
18 *D*, 8 Feb 1926, III, p.58.

19 *D*, 31 July 1926, III, p.103.
20 VW to VSW, 16 Mar 1926, *L* III, 1624, p.249.
21 *Hol*, p.3.
22 VW to VSW, 13 May 1927, *L* III, 1754, p.373.
23 VW to OM, 15 May 1927, *L* III, 1757, p.378.
24 *D*, 5 Sep 1926, III, p.107. See *Hol*, p.51, for her 'outline' for 'Time Passes'.
25 *D*, 13 Sep 1926, III, p.109.
26 *D*, 5 Sep 1926, III, p.106.
27 *D*, 30 Sep 1926, III, p.113.
28 *D*, 30 Oct 1926, III, p.114.
29 *D*, 23 Nov 1926, III, p.117.
30 VW to Angus Davidson, Christmas Day, 1926, *L* III, 1697, p.310.
31 *D*, 23 Jan 1927, III, p.123.
32 *D*, 21 Mar 1927, III, p.132.
33 *D*, 28 Nov 1927, III, p.203.
34 *D*, 13 Sep 1926, III, p.109.
35 VW to RF, 27 May 1927, *L* III, 1764, p.385.
36 SP, *MB*, 1976, p.122.
37 *Hol*, p.136.
38 SP, *MB*, 1976, pp.126–7. On p.105, she describes the Stephen children as a 'republic'.
39 VB to VW, 11 May 1927, Marler, p.317, *QBII*, p.128.
40 VW to VSW, 7 Jan 1926, *L* III, p.227: saying that she had left her diary for 1905 either at Long Barn or Charleston. So she must have been rereading it. It described the Stephen children's return to St Ives that summer.
41 VW to VB, 8 May 1927, *L* III, 1750, p.372.
42 VW to VB, 25 May 1927, *L* III, 1762, p.383.
43 VW to VSW, 31 Jan 1926, *L* III, 1617, p.236.
44 *D*, 16 Jan 1923, II, p.226; 7 Dec 1925, III, p.50.
45 VW to VSW, 23 Sep 1925, *L* III, 1588, p.215.
46 *D*, 8 Feb 1926, III, p.58.
47 *D*, 28 Nov 1928, III, p.208.
48 *MB*, p.81.
49 *Hol*, p.303.

CHAPTER 28: VITA

1 See VSW/VW, 10 May 1927, *VW/ VSW*, p.217; VW to VSW, 9 May 1927, *L* III, 1752, p.372. Copy in possession of NN.

2 *VSW/VW*, 10 May 1927, p.217.

3 VW to VSW, 13 May 1927, *L* III, 1754, pp.373–4.

4 François Mauriac, *Mémoires Interieurs*, trans. Gerard Hopkins, Eyre & Spottiswoode, 1960, p.101.

5 *D*, 9 May 1926, III, p.81.

6 *D*, 22 Sep, 27 Oct 1928, III, pp.197, 199.

7 VW to VSW, 1 Mar 1926, *L* III, 1622, p.245.

8 *D*, 25 May 1926, III, p.88.

9 Victoria Glendinning prefaced *Vita* with a remark by the architect Edward Lutyens: '. . . Vita has got blanks in herself and these blanks are blank'. *Vita*, p.xi.

10 *D*, 21 Dec 1925, III, p.52.

11 VW to VSW, 5 Feb 1927, *L* III, 1714, p.325; VW to VSW, Xmas Day 1926, *L* III, 1696, p.309. Also in VW to VSW, 7 Jan 1933, *L* V, 2694, p.148; 14 Feb 1933, *L* V, 2703, p.157; 13 Dec 1933, *L V*, 2834, p.260.

12 *D*, 11 Mar 1925, IV, p.287.

13 VW to VSW, 22 Nov 1927, *L* III, 1837, p.440.

14 VW to VSW, 4 July 1927, *L* III, 1780, p.395.

15 VW to VSW, 9 Feb 1928, *L* III, 1857, p.456; VSW to VW, 8 Feb 1928, p.269. 'Potto' was a West African lemur, or sloth, first noted in *Bosman's Guinea* (1705) (he calls it 'the sluggard') and later named after him. The joke was presumably about VW's invalidism and lying on sofas.

16 VW to VSW, 15 Sep 1926, *L* III, 1670, p.291.

17 VW to VSW, 11 Aug 1938, *L* 3431b. From one of four letters found at Sissinghurst in 1994, printed in *Virginia Woolf Miscellany*, ed. Joanne Trautmann Banks, Special Issue, Summer 1994, no.43 and in *Charleston Magazine*, 10, Aut/Winter 1994.

18 VSW to HN, 26 Dec 1925, *V&H*, p.135. 19 Jan 1926 and in *Charleston Magazine*, 10, Aut/Winter 1994.

19 *D*, 27 Nov 1925, III, p.47.

20 The letters between VW and VSW their diaries, VSW's letters to Harold, his to VSW's, VW's fictional version of VSW, and VSW's fictions of herself, and many later versions.

21 VSW, *Knole & the Sackvilles*, Ernest Benn, 1922, 1958, p.19.

22 See *Vita*, pp.20, 55, 57–8.

23 See *Vita* for a full and vivid account of VSW and 'Bonne Mama'; see Suzanne Raitt, *Vita & Virginia*, Clarendon Press, 1993, p.86, for a discussion of how mother and daughter battled 'over femininity: who has it, and who has got it right.'

24 *Vita*, p.50.

25 See W.H. Auden, February 1947, who attaches the story to the wrong person: 'What a spectacle it was when Virginia Woolf and Stella Benson decided to run off together and their husbands pursued them to the airport. Oh, they finally persuaded them to come home. But what a wonderful scene for a movie!' *The Table Talk of W.H. Auden*, ed. Alan Ansen, Faber, 1991, p.28.

26 See *Vita*, pp.190, 281, on her selfishness and lack of interest in HN's career.

27 VSW to HN, *V&H*, 31 May 1926, p.145.

28 Sapphist began to be used in 1890, lesbian in 1908. OED, cited Catherine Stimpson, 'The Lesbian Novel', *Critical Inquiry*, 8, 1981–2, p.365. See Raitt, p.79.

29 Respectively by NN, *Portrait of a Marriage*, Weidenfeld & Nicolson, 1973, Futura, 1974, p.197, *Vita*, pp.209, 215, and Raitt, p.92.

30 VW to VSW, 16 Nov 1925, *L* III, 1599, p.221.

31 VW and LW, 'Are Too Many Books Written and Published?' broadcast 15 July 1927. See Kate Whitehead, 'Broadcasting Bloomsbury', *The*

Yearbook of English Studies, vol.20, 1990, MHRA, p.124.

32 *D*, 21 Dec 1925, III, p.51.

33 VW to VB, 25 Jan? 1927, *L* III, 1708, p.318.

34 *D*, 25 Nov 1929, III, p.267.

35 *D*, 1 Nov 1924, II, p.320.

36 VW to Jacques Raverat, 24 Jan 1925, *L* III, 1524, p.155.

37 VW to Jacques Raverat, 5 Feb 1925, *L* III, 1534, p.164.

38 Jacques Raverat, to VW, Feb 1925, Sussex.

39 *D*, 21 Dec 1925, III, p.51–3.

40 Raitt, pp.105–6, notes that OED gives Auden's use of 'queer' to mean homosexual in 1932 as a first use, but that Vita used it meaningfully in *The Edwardians* in 1930, suggesting that she 'knew of the connotations of the word'.

41 VSW to HN, 10 Jan 1923, *V&H*, p.119.

42 *D*, 15 Dec 1922, II, p.217.

43 *D*, 20 Jan 1924, II, p.287.

44 *D*, 17 Mar 1923, II, p.239.

45 HN to VSW, 17 Dec 1926, *V&H*, p.177.

46 VW to VSW, 30 Mar 1923, *L* III, 1375, p.24, seems to accept the invitation; but *L* 1378, 1379, turns it down.

47 VW to CB, 23 Jan 1924, *L* III, 1440, p.85. The doll's house was designed by Lutyens, a family friend of VSW's, for Queen Mary; VSW accepted, VW refused, invitations to contribute a miniature MS.

48 VSW, Diary, 19 Mar 1924, in NN, *Portrait of a Marriage*.

49 VSW, *Family History*, 1932, Virago, 1986, pp.162–3.

50 VW to VSW, July 1923, *L* III, 1412, p.57.

51 *Seducers in Ecuador*, 1924; *Vita*, p.141.

52 *Mrs Dalloway*, MS, BL; 'Notes on an Elizabethan Play', *TLS*, 5 Mar 1925, *CR*, *E* IV, pp.62–70.

53 Scott had wrecked his marriage out of love for Vita, who shed him soon after this; he died in 1929. Dorothy would employ VB and DG to decorate her house [Spalding, p.234] and would finance and edit the Hogarth Living Poets series from 1928 to 1932, including her own poems [Willis, pp.143–4]. But VW disliked her 'pecking & exacting ways with Vita' [*D*, 9 Dec 1928, III, p.211] and Dorothy thought VW perverse, intellectually intolerant, and teasing: 'She always asked any member of the upper class or aristocracy innumerable questions about the manners and customs of these mysterious beings: since she was herself extremely well born, and sprang from the intellectual aristocracy, this was often embarrassing.' (*Far Have I Travelled*, 1952, p.153.)

54 *D*, 5 July 1924, II, pp.306–7.

55 VSW, Diary, 22 Feb 1924, misdated 23 in Nicolson *Portrait*, p.208.

56 VSW to VW, 16 July 1924, *VSW/VW*, p.54.

57 VW to VSW, 19 Aug 1924, *L* III, 1491, p.125.

58 *D*, 15 Sep 1924, II, p.313.

59 VW to VSW, 15 Sep 1924, *L* III, 1497, p.131.

60 *D*, 15 Sep 1924, II, p.313.

61 Just taken over by LW from the International Psycho-Analytical Library. Willis, Ch 8.

62 Abel, p.18, explains that Freud 'recounts the case of a woman whose obsessional habit of running into the dining room, summoning the housemaid and standing by a table with a big stain on its tablecloth, corrects, rather than repeats, the behaviour of her impotent husband, who on their wedding night poured red ink on the sheets to protect himself from the housemaid's scorn.' Freud shows that 'symptoms have meaning'; VW reduces his case history to a story of 'meaningless repetition'.

63 *D*, 26 May 1924, II, p.302.

64 *D*, 9 Feb 1924, II, p.291.

65 *D*, 14 May, 14 June, 27 June 1925, III, pp.18, 29, 34.

66 VW to RF, 16 Sep 1925, *L* III, 1583, p.208.

67 *E* IV, pp.318–20.
68 VW to VSW, 24 Aug 1925, *L* III, 1572, p.198.
69 VW to VSW, 1 Sep 1925, *L* III, 1573, p.200.
70 VW to VSW, 23 Sep 1925, *L* III, 1588, p.215.
71 *VSW/VW*, Sep 1925, p.74.
72 VW to VSW, 7 Sep 1925, *L* III, 1578, p.204.
73 *D*, 27 Nov 1925, III, p.48.
74 LW to VSW, 16 Dec 1925, Berg, Spotts, p.228.
75 *V&H*, p.136.
76 VW to VSW, 29 Dec 1928, *L* III, 1976, p.568.
77 VSW to HN, 26 Dec 1925, *H&N*, p.135.
78 CB to MH, 27 Dec 1926, Texas.
79 VSW to HN, 1 Jan 1926, Lilly. CB's innuendoes would persist.
80 VSW to HN, 13, 19, Jan 1926, Lilly.
81 *D*, 19 Jan 1926, III, p.57.
82 VSW to HN, 9 Nov 1926, *V&H*, p.169.
83 *D*, 23 Feb 1926, III, p.59.
84 VW to VSW, 17 Feb 1926, *L* III, 1621, p.241. On 24 Jan 1926 she was writing Part I; by 30 Apr she was writing part 2; on 31 May, after VSW's return, she began Part III.
85 *D*, 23 Feb 1926, III, p.59.
86 VW to VSW, 16 Mar 1926, *L* III, 1642, p.247.
87 *D*, 11 Dec 1926, III, p.119.
88 VSW to VW, 23 Feb 1926, *VSW/VW*, p.117.
89 VW to VSW, *L* III, 1622, 1624, 1626, 1628.
90 *L* III 1617, 1624, 1626, 1628.
91 VSW to VW, 21 Jan 1926, *VSW/VW*, p.98.
92 *D*, 20, 25 May 1926, III, pp.87, 88.
93 VSW to HN, *V&H*, p.146.
94 VSW to HN, *V&H*, p.150.
95 VW to LW, 14 June 1926, *L* III, 1648, p.275.
96 VSW to HN, 16 June 1926, Lilly. 'Mar' was their pet word for each other – it had been Vita's childhood nickname and meant 'little'.
97 VSW to HN, 26 [misdated 16] June 1926, *V&H*, p.147.
98 VSW to HN, 1 July 1926, *V&H*, p.151–2. *D*, 30 June 1926, III p.91.
99 VSW to HN, 3 July 1926, Lilly.
100 VW to VSW, 18 Aug 1926, *L* III, 1660, p.285.
101 VSW to HN, 27 July 1926, *V&H*, p.155.
102 *D*, 31 July 1926, III, p.103.
103 VSW to HN, 6 July 1926, Lilly.
104 VSW to HN, 13 Aug 1926, Lilly.
105 VSW to HN, 27 Aug 1926, Lilly.
106 'She says it is a contribution to English Literature, and is a solid fact against which one can lean up without feeling that it will give way . . . I really do think she likes it.' VSW to HN, 26 Jan 1926, Lilly.
107 VW to VSW, 1 Mar 1926, *L* III, 1622, p.243.
108 *D*, 23 June 1927, III, p.141.
109 VB to VW, 16 June 1926, Berg, quoted *Vita*, p.163.
110 VW to VB, 13 June 1926, *L* III, 1647, p.275.
111 VW to VB, 18 June 1926, *L* III, 1650, p.277.
112 VB to VW, 31 Jan 1927, Berg.
113 HN to VSW, 7 July 1926, *V&H*, p.211.
114 VSW to HN, 17 Aug 1926, *V&H*, pp.158–9.
115 HN to VSW, 17 Dec 1926, p.176.
116 VSW to HN, 21 Dec 1926, p.179.
117 HN to VW, 17 Dec 1926, Berg.
118 VW to VSW, 4 Jan 1927, *L* III, 1705, p.316.
119 *D*, 28 Sep 1926, III, p.111.
120 VW to VSW, 19 Nov 1926, *L* III, 1687, p.302.
121 *D*, 23 Nov 1926, III, p.117.
122 *D*, 30 Sep 1926, III, p.113.
123 VSW to HN, 4 Aug 1926, Lilly.
124 VSW to HN, 8 Oct 1926, Lilly.
125 VSW to HN, 22 Oct 1926, Lilly.
126 *D*, 30 Oct 1926, III, p.115–16.
127 *D*, 30 Oct 1926; VSW to HN, 26 Oct 1926, *V&H*, p.167.
128 VSW to HN, 8 Nov 1926, Lilly.
129 VSW to HN, 10 Nov, 1926 *V&H*, p.169.
130 VW to VSW, 19 Nov 1926, *L* III, 1687, p.302.

131   VSW to HN, 20 Nov 1926, *V&H*, p.173.
132   *D*, 23 Nov 1926, III, p.117.
133   VSW to HN, 30 Nov 1926, *V&H*, p.175.
134   *D*, 23 Jan 1927, III, pp.124–5.
135   VSW to VW, 19 Feb 1927, *VSW/VW*, p.193.
136   VSW to VW, 30 Mar 1927, *VSW/VW*, p.209.
137   *D*, 28 Feb 1927, III, p.129.
138   VSW to VW, 11 Mar 1927, *VSW/VW*, p.205.
139   VW to VSW, 23 Mar 1927, *L* III, 1735, p.352.
140   *D*, 14 Mar 1927, III p.131.
141   VW to VB, 9 Apr 1927, *L* III, 1742, p.361.
142   VW to VB, 22 May 1927, *L* III, 1760, p.381.
143   *D*, 18 June 1927, III, p.138.
144   VSW to VW, 31 May, 2 June 1927, *VSW/VW* pp.224, 226; VSW to CB, June 1927, in *Vita*, p.177.
145   VW to VSW, 5 June 1927, *L* III, 1767, p.388.
146   VSW to VW, 11 June 1927, *VSW/VW*, p.229.
147   VW to VSW, 14 June 1927, *L* III, 1774, p.391.
148   VW to VSW, 1927?, *L* III, 1777, p.393.
149   *D*, 18 June 1927, III, p.139.
150   *D*, 30 June 1927, III, pp.142–4; *E*, IV, p.324.
151   VSW to HN, 22 July 1927, *V&H*, p.182.
152   VSW to HN, 27 June 1928, Lilly.
153   CB to MH, 8 Aug 1927, Texas.
154   VW to Ethel Sands, 22 July [1927], *L* III, 1788, p.400. There was much rivalry, between the Woolfs' cars and VB and DG's, and many rude and anthropomorphic jokes about them.
155   *D*, 4 July 1927, III, p.145.
156   *D*, 4 Sep 1927, III, p.153.
157   With an actress, Valerie Taylor, who then fell for Vita, and then for Raymond Mortimer.
158   VSW to HN, 2 Oct 1928, *V&H*, p.204.

159   Beatrice Mayor to CB, 3 Aug 1927, King's.
160   VW to VB, 23 July 1927, *L* III, 1789, p.401.
161   *Vita*, p.184; *D*, 20 Nov 1927, III, p.162; VSW to VW, 11 Nov 1927, *VSW/VW*, p.256; VSW to HN, 16 Nov 1927, Lilly.
162   'Phases of Fiction', *CEII*, p.56. See *D*, 18 June 1927, III, p.139; VW to Saxon Sydney-Turner, 21 Aug 1927, *L* III, 1800, p.410. The Press announced the book in Feb 1928 as forthcoming: Woolmer, Appendix IV, no.17; Willis, p.374.
163   'The New Biography', 1927, *E* IV, pp.473–80.
164   *D*, 5 Sep 1927, III, p.156.
165   *D*, 22 Sep 1927, III, p.161.
166   *D*, 20 Sep 1927, III, p.157.
167   *D*, 20 Sep 1927, III, p.157.
168   *QB* II, p.132.

CHAPTER 29: CENSORS

1   VW to VSW, 9 Oct 1927, *L* III, 1820, p.429.
2   VSW to VW, 11 Oct 1927, *VSW/VW*, p.252.
3   VW to VSW, 13 Oct 1927, *L* III, 1821, p.430.
4   VW to VSW, 5 Dec 1927, *L* III, 1840, p.443.
5   *D*, 18 Feb, 18 Mar 1928, III, pp.175, 176.
6   VSW to HN, 3 Nov 1927, Lilly; *Vita*, p.182.
7   VSW to HN, 11, 16 Nov 1927, Lilly; *Vita*, p.185.
8   VSW to CB, 8 Feb 1928, King's.
9   *D*, 20 Sep 1927, III, p.156.
10   *D*, 22 Oct 1927, III, pp.163–4.
11   *D*, 17 Jan 1928, III, pp.173–4.
12   VW to CB, 31 Jan 1928, *L* III, 1854, p.453.
13   'Thomas Hardy's Novels', *TLS*, 19 Jan 1928; *E* IV, pp.507–19; 'The Novels of George Meredith', *TLS*, 19 Feb 1928, *E* IV, pp.525–36; 'Mr Yeats', *N&A*, 21 Apr 1928, *E* IV, pp.544–5.

14 'The Art of Fiction', 1927, *E* IV, pp.599–603.
15 VW to CB, 7 Feb 1928, *L* III, 1856, p.455; to VB, 11 Feb 1928, *L* III, 1858, p.457.
16 *D*, 18 Mar, 22 Mar, 1928, III, p.177.
17 VW to VSW, 6 Mar 1928, *L* III, 1868, p.469.
18 VW to VSW, 20? Mar 1928, *L* III, 1873, p.474.
19 VW to VB, 19 Apr 1928, *L* III, 1884, p.485.
20 The Prix Femina (which gives an annual prize to a French book and the Prix Femina Étranger to a non-French book), was founded in 1904 by 22 *collaboratrices* on a magazine called the *Vie Heureuse*. 'They were incipient feminists. They took a look at the new Académie Goncourt, saw that there were no women judges, concluded that there would be no women laureates, either, and started giving their own prizes. They ended up giving two-thirds of them to men.' Jane Kramer, 'Letter from Europe', *The New Yorker*, 22 Feb 1988, p.90. The president was the Comtesse de Noailles and the judges included Alphonse Daudet.'. *TL* was not translated into French until 1929, as *La Promenade au Phare*.
21 VW to JB, 2 May 1928, *L* III, 1888, p.491.
22 In *Hugh Walpole*, Rupert Hart Davis, 1952, p.289.
23 VSW to HN, 3 May 1928, Lilly.
24 VW to VB, 9 May 1928, *L* III, 1893, p.495; *D*, 4 May 1928, III, p.183.
25 VB to VW, early May 1928, Berg.
26 *D*, 31 May 1928, III, p.184.
27 VSW to HN, 16 May 1928, Lilly; *D* 7 July 1928, III, p.187.
28 VW to VSW, 27 May 1928, *L* III, 1897, p.503.
29 VSW to HN, 14? July 1928, Lilly.
30 VW to VSW, 30 Aug 1928, *L* III, 1918, p.520.
31 VW to VSW, 16 Sep 1928, *L* III, 1924, p.531.
32 VW to VSW, 8 Sep 1928, *L* III, 1922, p.529.
33 For instance, she had a permit from the Foreign Office which got them through Customs without a check. And she mocked Virginia for her erratic spoken French: 'Est-ce que la mer est brusque?' VW to VSW, 9 Aug 1930, *L* IV, 2217, p.197, note 2.
34 References to 24 Sep–1 Oct: VSW 'Diary', Berg; VSW to HN, 27 Sep 1928, Lilly; VSW to HN, 25 Sep, 2 Oct 1928, *V&H*, pp.203–5, & Lilly; *D*, 27 Oct 1928, III, p.199; VW to LW, *L* III, 1927, 1930, 1932; LW to VW, 26, 27 Sep 1928, Spotts, pp.234–5; VW to HN, 7 Oct 1928, *L* III, 1935, p.541.
35 VW to VSW, 24 Aug 1932; *Virginia Woolf Miscellany*, Summer 1994.
36 See *Vita*, p.232; *D*, 16 June 1930, III, p.306; VSW to VW, 18 May 1933.
37 VSW to VW, *VSW/VW*, 11 Oct 1928, p.304.
38 VSW to HN, 12, 13 Oct 1928, Lilly.
39 Lady Sackville to VW, 14 Oct 1928, King's.
40 Quoted in Michael de-la-Noy, *Eddy: The Life of Edward Sackville-West*, 1988, p.132.
41 Lady S's resentment of VW became a settled feature of her attacks on VSW. In 1931 HN wrote to her: 'I know that there is a side of Vita which Virginia understands better than I could . . . Virginia's influence on her has been nothing but admirable . . . Virginia is in no sense the sinister figure of your imagining.' HN to Lady Sackville, 2 May 1931, Lilly.
42 'Geraldine and Jane', *TLS*, 28 Feb 1929, *CE* IV, pp.27–39; VW to John Hayward, 4 Mar 1929, *L* IV, 2007, p.30.
43 Christopher Isherwood, *Christopher and his Kind*, Methuen, 1977.
44 *Eddy*, de-la-Noy, pp.121–5.
45 VSW to VW, 12 Jan 1929, *VSW/VW*, p.324.
46 CB to VW, 3 Feb 1928, MHP, Sussex.
47 VB to JB, 22 Jan 1929, Marler, p.341; VB to RF, 22 Jan 1929, Tate Gallery.

48 VSW to VW, 25 Jan 1929, *VSW/ VW*, p.325.

49 'Phases' was published in the *Book-man*, in New York, between Apr--June 29; by LW in 1958 in *Granite and Rainbow*. Willis, p.374: 'The failure of Woolfs to publish as planned remains a mystery.' Some of the work for it went into *CRII*.

50 HN to VSW, 26 Aug 1929, Lilly.

51 VW to VSW, 1 Sep 1929, *L* IV, 2065, p.85.

52 See *D*, 22 Dec 1927, 7 Nov 1928, for early symptoms of *The Waves*.

53 EB, Preface to *Orlando*, 1960, in Hermione Lee, ed. *The Mulberry Tree*, Virago, 1986.

54 VSW to HN, 7 Dec 1928, Lilly.

55 *Orlando: Hol*, p.81

56 VW to VSW, 12 Mar 1928, *L* III, 1870, p.471.

57 VW was thinking about the cinema in 1926, and *Orlando*'s techniques are often cinematic. *E* IV, Appendix II.

58 *D*, 29 Oct 1933, IV, p.186.

59 *D*, 7 Aug 1939, V, p.229.

60 *O:Hol*, pp.227, 257, 219, 72, 177, 169, 252.

61 *WF*, p.114.

62 Also the MS of 'Phases' contains a passage (cut out) on the distorting effect on the Victorian novelists of the 'harm done by suppression'. MHP, B7e, Sussex. Raymond Mortimer had written a 'defence of homosexuality' in 1926 which the press was advised not to publish. VSW to VW, 4 Aug 1926, *VSW/ VW* p.152.

63 VSW to VW, 31 Aug 1928, *VSW/ VW*, p.296.

64 Quoted Furbank, II, p.154.

65 'She wont have any letter written about her book unless it mentions the fact that it is a work of artistic merit – even genius. And no one has read her book; or can read it, VW to VSW, 30 Aug 1928, *L* III, 1918, p.520. Furbank; *D*, 31 Aug 1928, III, p.193.

66 *D*, 23 Oct 1929, III, p.262. See Jane Marcus, 'Sapphistry: Narration as Lesbian Seduction in *A Room of One's Own* in *Virginia Woolf and the Languages of Patriarchy*, Bloomington Indiana UP, 1987, 163–88.

67 VW to QB, 1 Nov 1928, *L* III, 1954, p.555.

68 *D*, 10 Nov 1928, III, pp.206–7.

69 It was then published in France and became an underground bestseller. VW to VSW, 14 Dec 1928, *L* III, 1969, p.563.

70 Quoted de-la-Noy, *Eddy*, p.133, from 'Richard Kennedy in conversation with the author'.

71 *D*, 7 Nov 1928, III, p.203.

72 *Orlando*, pp.175–6.

CHAPTER 30: SELVES

1 *Orlando*, p.213.

2 *D*, 2 Apr 1937, V, p.75.

3 *D*, 27 Feb 1926, III, p.62.

4 *D*, 4 Sep 1927, III, p.153; cf. VW to Hugh Walpole, 25 Aug 1929, *L* IV, 2063, p.83.

5 *D*, 30 Sep 1926, III, p.113.

6 *D*, July 1926, III, pp.102–3.

7 *D*, 27 Mar 1926, III, p.72.

8 *D*, 9 Feb 1924, II, p.291.

9 *D*, 13 Apr 1929, III, p.220.

10 *D*, 11 Apr 1926, III, p.74.

11 *D*, 10 Sep 1928, III, p.196.

12 Labour M.P. Philip Noel-Baker said that in the many years he worked with LW on the Labour Party Advisory Committe of International Affairs, he never remembered Virginia taking 'any interest in what we did together'. Philip Noel-Baker to NN, 5 Oct 1973, Sussex.

13 *D*, 17 Apr 1921, II, p.111.

14 VW to VSW, 13 May 27, *L* III, 1754, p.374.

15 *TL, Hol*, pp.211, 215.

16 *D*, 6 May 1926, III, p.78.

17 Kingsley Martin, *Father Figures*, Hutchinson, 1966, p.160. For the General Strike, see also Kingsley Martin, *The British Public and the General Strike*, Hogarth Press, 1927; Julian Symons, *The General Strike*, Hutchinson, 1957; Arthur Marwick,

The Explosion of British Society 1914–1962, Pan, 1963; Michael Newman, *Harold Laski: A Political Biography*, Macmillan, 1993; A.J.P. Taylor, *English History 1914–1945*, OUP, 1965; LW, *DATW*, pp.217–18; Patrick Wright, *On Living In An Old Country*, Verso, 1985; Kate Flint, 'Virginia Woolf and the General Strike', *Essays in Criticism*, 36 (1986), pp.319–34.

18 Newman, p.93.
19 Symons, p.67.
20 Ibid., p.184; Wright, p.105.
21 LW, *DATW*, p.217.
22 Janet Vaughan to Nigel Nicolson, 2 Aug 1976, Sussex.
23 VW on the Strike: *D*, 5–13 May 1926, pp.77–86; VW to VB, 12 May 1926, *L* III 1635, pp.260–1.
24 Symons, p.180.
25 *D*, 9 May 1926, III, p.81.
26 VB to VW, 15 May 1926, Berg.
27 VSW to VW, 29 May 1926, VSW/ VW, p.139.
28 VW to VB, 19 May 1926, *L* III, 1639, p.265.
29 Her first notes on *Tess* were made in a diary of 1903, her Macmillan editions of his novels dated from 1908, her three-volume edition of *The Dynasts* from 1909, her copy of *Time's Laughingstocks* from 1910; 'Virginia Stephen' was written in all of them. For VW's visit see *D*, 25 July 1926, III, pp.96–102.
30 CB to MH, 12 Aug 1926, Texas. EMF, who had been visiting Max Gate since 1922, found Hardy boring to talk to, eager to please, and preoccupied with his dog. He gave a funny account to his mother of Hardy showing him the graves of his pets, 'all of whom seemed to have come to violent ends'. Furbank, II, p.111.
31 *D*, July 1926, III, p.100.
32 *TLS*, 19 Jan 1928, *CE* I, p.258.
33 *E* IV, pp.567–72.
34 *D*, 7 Jan 1936, V, p.5.
35 *E* IV, p.509.
36 *D*, July 1926, III, p.105.
37 *D*, 23 Jan 1927, III, p.124.

38 VB to VW, 26 Jan 1927, Berg.
39 VW to VB, 25 Jan 1927, *L* III, 1708, p.318.
40 *D*, 15 June 1929, III, p.233.
41 Spalding, p.172.
42 *D*, 16 Aug 1918, II, p.182.
43 VW to DG, 5 Jan 1931, *L* IV, 2307, p.276.
44 VW to VB, 14 Apr 1927, *L* III, 1743, p.363.
45 VB to VW, 23 Apr 1927, Marler, p.313.
46 VW to VB, 21 Apr 1927, *L* III, 1745, p.366.
47 Ibid.
48 *D*, 9 Feb 1922, II, p.159.
49 Eg, a conversation reported by VB about Mendelism 'based partly on Angelica's being said to be so much more Stephen than Bell, while Julian and Quentin are evidently a mixture.' VB to VW, 29 Apr 1929, Berg.
50 Angelica Garnett, in conversation with the author, July 1991.
51 VB to RF, 4 Sep 1927, Marler, p.322.
52 VW to VB, 29 Sep 1927, *L* III, 1815, p.423.
53 VW to RF, 16 Sep 1925, *L* III, 1583, p.209.
54 Cf. De la Rochefoucauld: 'Dans l'adversité de nos meilleurs amis, nous trouvons toujours quelque chose qui ne nous déplaît pas.' *D*, 19 Aug 1929, III, p.243.
55 Helen Anrep thought VW was self-centred and unapproachable. Marler, p.290. She and her children, Igor and Anastasia, inspired some of VW's unkindest descriptions. She may have been jealous of Helen's centre of artistic and social activities in Charlotte Street. (Igor Anrep, in conversation with the author, Oct 1993.)
56 See Dunn pp.216, 251; Gillespie, p.108; Spalding, p.212.
57 Founded by Maynard, Samuel Courtauld and other wealthy art patrons to promote the work of 'promising painters', it had its first show at the Leicester Galleries in 1926, and from 1928 moved to the

Cooling Galleries in New Bond Street. Spalding, p.211, Shone, *BP2*, pp.217–19.

58 Spalding, p.211.

59 For Raymond Mortimer in 1926, Mary Hutchinson in 1927, Ethel Sands in 1927, Dorothy Wellesley in 1929–30.

60 Shone *BP2*, p.219; Shone, introduction to 'Duncan Grant and Vanessa Bell: Design and Decoration 1910–1960', Spink 1991, p.9.

61 *D*, 4 Jan 1929, III, p.217.

62 VW to VB, 2 June 1926, *L* III, 1644, pp.270–1.

63 VW to VB, 5 Mar 1927, *L* III, 1725, p.341.

64 VB to VW, 17 Mar 1927, Berg.

65 VW to VB, 8 May 1927, *L* III, 1750, p.370.

66 *D*, 23 June 1927, III, p.141.

67 VB to VW, 15? Oct 1931, Marler, p.368. See Spalding, pp.250–2. VW to VB, 15 Oct 1931, *L* IV, 2451, p.390.

68 'The London Artists' Association: Recent Paintings by Vanessa Bell, with a Foreword by Virginia Woolf, Feb 5 to Mar 8 1930', Berg. Cf. 'Catalogue of Recent Paintings by Vanessa Bell, Lefevre Galleries, 1934', for which VW wrote a short introduction which also emphasised the 'austerity' of VB's work. Berg.

69 VW to VB, 8 June? 1927, *L* III 1773 p.391, for 'truthful' *TL* cover.

70 VB did a 1931 drawing of her in Stephen Tomlin's studio to get her to sit for Tomlin; VW reported that she was sitting for VB in 1932 (*L* V, 2533, p.22, 2564, p.30) and in 1933 (*D* IV, pp.191, 200). In 1934 VB did a water-colour sketch for, and then a full-length portrait, of VW; see illustrations between pp.690–1. In 1933 VB and DG did a series of dinner plates with heads of famous women for Kenneth Clark; one was of VW. (Gillespie, p.199.)

71 *D*, 20 Dec 1927, III, p.167.

72 E.g., *D* 22 Dec 1927, III, p.168; *D* 15 June 1929, III, pp.232–3.

73 VW to Ethel Sands, 9 Feb 1927, *L* III, 1716, p.329.

74 *D*, 26 Aug 1934, IV, p.239.

75 *D*, 20 Sep 1927, III, p.158.

76 VW to QB, 28 Oct 1930, *L* IV, 2263, p.238.

77 VW to VB, 29 Apr 1926, *L* III, 1633, p.259.

78 VW to VB, 24 Apr 1929, *L* IV, 2020, p.43.

79 Spalding, p.207.

80 *D*, 2 Nov 1917, I, p.70.

81 'Reminiscences of Julian', 30 July 1937, MHP, Sussex.

82 *D*, 2 Aug 1924, II, p.308. cf. *L* 1269, 1633.

83 E.g. *L* 1836, 1887, 1888; JB to QB, 4 May 1928, King's.

84 *D*, 5 Nov 1930, III, p.329.

85 VW to VB, 24 Apr 1929, *L* IV, 2020, p.41.

86 QB to VW, 12 Apr 1928, QB.

87 VW to VB, 9 May 1928, *L* III, 1893, p.496; VW to QB, 6 May 1928, *L* III, 1891, p.493.

88 VW to QB, 22 Nov 1928, *L* III, 1964, p.560.

89 VW to QB, nd, BL.

90 *Deceived*, p.107.

91 VW to VB, 14 Apr 1927, *L* III, 1743, p.363.

92 VW to VB, 12 May 1928, *L* III, 1894, p.497.

93 Kennedy, p.54.

94 AB to VW, in letters from VB to VW, 10, 14 May 1931, Berg.

95 *D*, 21 Sep 1929, III, p.254–5.

96 QB to JB, 29 Nov 1929, King's.

97 JB to QB, Feb 1931, King's. See VW to CB, 16 Feb 1931, *L* IV, 2329, p.292. 'I enjoyed myself more than I expected . . . Julian full of violence and spirit . . . also there was a young Mrs Roger [!] Clark whom I took for Helen Soutar and addressed accordingly.'

98 JB to VB, 14 May 1929, King's.

99 JB to VB, 22 June 1931, King's.

100 VW to QB, 17 Feb 1930, *L* IV, 2145, p.142.

101 QB to JB, 10 June 1930, King's.

102 VW to VB, 9 Apr 1927, *L* III, 1742, p.360; VB to VW, 9 Mar 1929, Berg.

103 E.g. RF to VW, 3 Nov 1928, on France as the chief hope of resistance to Americanisation. Sutton *op.cit.*, II, 630–1.
104 *L* 1852, *D* 31 May 1928, *D* 20 June 1928.
105 VB to CB, 17 Feb 1928, Tate Gallery. See Spalding, 218–24, on VB at Cassis.
106 JB to QB, 22 Apr 1928, King's.
107 VW to Angus Davidson, 7 Apr 1928, *L* III, 1878, p.482.
108 VB to QB, 17 Apr 1928, Marler, p.332.
109 QB to JB, 20 Feb 1930, King's.
110 VW to CB, 21 Apr 1928, *L* III, 1885, p.486.
111 VW to VB, 29 Apr 1928, *L* III, 1887, p.490.
112 VB to CB, 12 June 1929, Tate Gallery.
113 *D*, 15 June 1929, III, pp.231–2.
114 See Gillian Beer, 'The Island and the Aeroplane: the Case of Virginia Woolf', in *The Nation and Narration*, ed. Homi Bhabha, Routledge, 1990, and in Bowlby, *Virginia Woolf*, Longman Critical Readers, 1992, on VW's treatment of her 'island story'.
115 *The Waves, Hol*, Graham, p.184.
116 *E* IV, p.488.
117 'The Docks of London', *Good Housekeeping*, Dec 1931, in *The London Scene*, Random House, 1975.
118 *E* IV, p.340; *The London Scene*, pp.9–10; *The Years*, p.83.
119 *D*, 30 Nov 1929, III, p.269.
120 E.g. *D*, 5 Sep 1927, III,p.156; *L*, 1803, 1807, 1895, 2330.
121 *The Waves*, ed. Graham, p.658. In *The Waves*, p.183, this becomes: 'I begin to long for some little language such as lovers use, broken words, inarticulate words, like the shuffling of feet on the pavement.'
122 E.g. 'Notes of a Days Walk', 1928?, MHP, B7e, Sussex.
123 *D*, 31 May 1928, III, p.186. Morris and Birne–Jones had a studio at 17, Red Lion Square.
124 *D*, 28 Mar 1930, III, p.298.
125 MS, nd, Berg.

126 *A Room of One's Own*, p.91.
127 *WF*, p.139.
128 *The Waves*, p.84.
129 *The Waves*, ed. Graham, p.214.
130 See Bowlby, as Ch.23, n.62.
131 *The London Scene*, p.29.
132 VW to ES, 6 Dec 1931, *L* IV, 2476, p.409; *D*, 30 Jan 1932, IV, p.65.
133 *The London Scene*, p.13. The information she recorded in this essay about the gas-jets keeping the temperature up to mellow the wine and the fungus as an index of moisture was correct. Jancis Robinson to the author, 1995.
134 'Of course, I'm not in the least patriotic'. *D*, 29 Aug 1939, and see Beer, pp.281–3, on VW's wartime feelings for her island.
135 The title of an unpublished fragment, nd, Berg.
136 *The Waves*, ed., Graham, p.609; *The Waves*, p.142.
137 *The Waves*, p.142.
138 *The Waves*, p.141.

CHAPTER 31: MONEY AND FAME

1 *D*, 28 Mar 1929, III, pp.219–20.
2 *WF*, p.167. (Words in brackets were interpolated in the original MS).
3 VW to ES, 8 June 1933, *L* V, 2746, p.195.
4 *D*, 30 June 1929, III, p.237.
5 *D*, 26 Jan 1930, III, p.285. Prime Minister Asquith earned £5,000 in 1914.
6 *WF*, pp.59–60.
7 If, on a rough estimate, pre-war money is multiplied by 50, this was worth about £450,000 today. But attempts to provide equivalents are complicated by differences in how people spent their money, in living standards, in amounts spent on food (60 per cent of a family budget in 1914, now less than 15 per cent), in rates of income tax (22p in the £ between 1921 and 1930) and by the fact that the 50-fold inflation between 1914 and 1994 is outstripped by average earnings.

8 Keynes was earning, for his journalism alone, the equivalent today of £80,000 a year.

9 Paul Delany, 'A Little Capital: The Financial Affairs of Leonard and Virginia Woolf', *The Charleston Magazine*, Summer/Autumn 1993, p.6.

10 Kennedy, p.100. Quoted by Delany, p.6.

11 Delany, p.6.

12 All these companies were listed under VW's investment assets at her death, producing value for probate of between £10 and £1000. (VW's Estate, MHP, Sussex.)

13 LW, *DATW*, p.63.

14 In 1919, when she earned a total of £153, all from journalism, he earned a total of £578 from journalism and royalties and from his income (£250 per annum) as editor of the *International Review*. (Mepham, p.64). In 1920 and 1921 he earned £250 per annum from the *Contemporary Review*, and over £200 from other journalism. (*D*, 28 Nov 1919, I, p.314). In 1923 he became literary editor at a salary of £400 and kept that salary for three years until he reduced his hours and his pay (to £250). In 1922 he got £120 from being on the staff of the *Nation* (*D*, 6 Mar 1923, II, p.237). In 1924 his total income was £569 (Virginia's was £165); in 1925 his was £565, hers was £223.

15 LW, *DATW*, pp.141–2; Mepham, pp.64–5, quotes LW saying that if she had had to earn her living before 1922 she would probably never have written a novel.

16 For sales figures see Mepham, Table 7, p.130.

17 Willis, p.165.

18 Willis, p.167, Mepham, p.131.

19 Flugel's *Psychoanalytical Study of the Family* (1921) and Freud's *Collected Papers* were the most successful Hogarth Press issues. Willis, pp.299–301.

20 The Uniform Edition was of small crown octavo volumes in jade green cloth-boards lettered in gold on the spine, priced at 5s: 'an inexpensive standard trade edition' for the common reader. Willis, p.155. They established a pattern of 'putting each successive book of VW's into the cheaper Uniform Edition after several reprintings of the first edition'.

21 Mepham, p.146, who instances 'On Being Ill' (Hogarth Press, 1930), 'Walter Sickert: A Conversation' (Hogarth Press, 1934) and 'Street Haunting' (The Westgate Press, San Francisco, 1930) as examples. Others are 'Beau Brummell' (Rimington and Hooper, New York, 1930), 'A Letter to a Young Poet' (Hogarth Letters, 1932), and 'Reviewing' (Hogarth Sixpenny Pamphlets, 1939).

22 Donald Brace to LW, 16 Dec 1924, Berg.

23 *D*, 17 Oct 1924, II, p.319.

24 *D*, 23 July 1927, III, p.149.

25 VW to VSW, 2 Sep 1927, *L* III, 1805, p.416.

26 VW to Helen McAfee, 29 June 1928, *L* III, 1907, p.511.

27 Eg, in 1928, for a piece on Sterne's *A Sentimental Journey*, she made £30 from the *New York Herald Tribune*, and £15.15s. from Oxford University Press, when they published it as an introduction to a World's Classics edition. In 1929 she was offered four articles by the *Tribune* (on Cowper, Beau Brummell, Mary Wollstonecraft and Dorothy Wordsworth) for £50 each, which she also published in the *Nation* for £21. In 1930 she published an essay on Hazlitt in the *Tribune* for £50 and in *The Times* for £28; in 1931, 'All About Books' in the *New Statesman* for £3.10s and in the *New Republic* for £15. (Kirkpatrick, A15, pp.45–6; Virginia Woolf's Account Book, Washington State University.)

28 LW, *DATW*, p.177.

29 LW, *DATW*, p.118.

30 Totals for the weeks of 1917 are around £4; for the weeks of 1934,

around £5; for the weeks of 1941, between £3 and £6. [LW, Diary, LW, Sussex; Housekeeping Book, LW, Sussex.]

31 *D*, 18 Dec 1928, III, p.212.
32 *D*, 15, 28 Sep 1926, III, pp.110–12.
33 LW, *DATW*, pp.142–3.
34 *D*, 18 Feb 1928, III, p.175.
35 *D*, 15 Sep 1926, III, p.109.
36 *D*, 30 Sep 1926, III, p.113.
37 *D*, 23 July 1927, III, p.149.
38 *D*, 16 June 1930, III, p.305.
39 VW to DG, 27? May 1928, *L* III, 1896, p.502.
40 *D*, 1 Mar 1930, III, p.295.
41 *D*, 27 Oct 1930, III, p.327.
42 *L*, 1736, 1896, 1902, 1913, 1915, 1916, 1920, 1922, 1959, 1976, 1976, 2016, 2020, 2026, 2031; *D*, 18 Feb 1928.
43 *D*, 20 Nov 1927, III, p.164.
44 *D*, 18 Dec 1928, III, p.212; *D*, 13 Apr 1929, III, p.221.
45 *D*, 24 Sep 1930, III, pp.319–20.
46 VW to ES, 1 July 1930, *L* IV, 2199, p.184.
47 The Will (private ownership); 27 July 1930, witnessed Helen Anrep and Roger Fry. Estate of AVW, 1940, LW, Sussex.
48 LW, *DATW*, p.145.
49 For gramophone see VW to Eddy Sackville-West, 8 Aug 1927, *L* III, 1600, p.222. Also VW to Gathorne-Hardy, 19 July, 14 Aug, 8 Sept 1925, on the purchase of an 'Algraphone' for £11 18s., and on their plans to join the National Gramophone Society in order to collect records and 'plunge into music', Lilly.
50 Inscribed copy, Washington State.
51 *D*, 21 Apr 1928, III, p.180.
52 *D*, 22 July 1927, III, p.117.
53 *D*, III, pp.146, 167, 183, 211.
54 *D*, 12 Sep 1930, III, p.316.
55 *D*, 22 Mar 1928, III, p.177.
56 *D*, 9 Dec 1928, III, p.211.
57 *D*, 4 May 1928, III, p.183.
58 Julien Green, 26 Nov 1954, *Diary 1928–1957*, Collins/Harvill, 1964, p.258.
59 Osbert Sitwell, *Laughter in the Next Room*, Macmillan, 1949, pp.16–23; see *D*, 5 Apr 1924, II, p.124.
60 *Hayseed to Harvest: Memories of Katherine Cox and Hayes Court School* ed. Roma Goyder, Fletcher & Fletcher, Colchester, 1985, p.80.
61 JB to VB, 27 Oct 1928, QB.
62 *D*, 27 Oct 1928, III, p.201.
63 *A Newnham Anthology*, ed. Ann Phillips, CUP, 1979, p.175, in Stape, p.14; Elsie Duncan-Jones, to the author, 4 Mar 1996.
64 Beryl Paston Brown to the author, 1992; Marna Sedgwick, letter to the author, 26 Nov 1992.
65 VW to QB, 14 May 1930, *L* IV, 2181, p.170.
66 VW to VSW, 15 July 1927, *L* III, 1782, p.396. This joint broadcast was not published. See Kate Whitehead, 'Broadcasting Bloomsbury', *Yearbook of English Studies*, vol.20, 1990, p.124, for a summary of the talk (taken from a transcript summary in the National Sound Archive). LW complained that publishing had become over-mechanised and shoddy; VW welcomed a more 'egalitarian' expansion of publishing, and suggested that 'books should self-destruct after three months and should be as cheap and easy to purchase as a packet of cigarettes'.
67 A talk on Beau Brummell, broadcast 20 Nov 1929, printed in the *Listener*, 27 Nov 1929; 'Words Fail Me', broadcast 29 Apr 1937, printed in the *Listener*, 5 May 1937.
68 13 Aug 1927, reprinted in *CH*.
69 VW to VSW, 22 Aug 1927, *L* III, 1801, p.412.
70 VW to ES, 'perhaps' 6 July 1930, *L* IV, 2201, p.186.
71 Cecil Beaton, 'Mrs Virginia Woolf', *The Book of Beauty*, Duckworth, 1930, p.37.
72 Sibyl Colefax to Cecil Beaton, nd [Nov 1930], quoted in Hugo Vickers, *Cecil Beaton: The Authorised Biography*, Weidenfeld & Nicolson, 1985.

NOTES TO PAGES 567–73

73 Letters to the Editor, *Nation*, 29 Nov, 20 Dec 1930.

74 E.g. an offstage appearance in Marjorie Strachey's *The Counterfeits* (1927); included as a target for Roy Campbell's scorn in *The Georgiad: A Charlotade* (1931); satirised by Count Potocki de Montalk; in Wyndham Lewis's *The Roaring Queen* (written 1936, published Secker & Warburg, 1973) as Rhoda Hyman, 'the patronising queen of the highbrow world'. (p.80).

75 Hugh Walpole, *Hans Frost*, Macmillan, 1929; her copy dedicated 'For Virginia from her friend Hugh Walpole. With a bow to Leonard: Sep 1929'. Texas.

76 VW to Hugh Walpole, 18 Sep 1929, *L* IV, 2069, p.89.

77 VW to Christabel McLaren, 1 Nov 1929, nd [1929], nd [1930]; Supplementary Aberconway Papers, 70775, BL.

78 LW, 'Virginia Woolf: Writer and Personality', *Listener*, 4 Mar 1965, in Stape, p.148.

79 Kennedy, p.39; Angus Davidson, *Recollections*, pp.69–70.

80 *Recollections*, p.33.

81 JL, *Listener*, 13 Jan 1955, pp.60–2, reprinted in Stape, p.125.

82 *Charleston Newsletter*, 1986, in Stape, p.118.

83 'London Squares', Letter to *NSN*, 24 June 1933.

84 Mrs Shrager [née Rose Talbot] to Trekkie Parsons, 17 July 1973, Sussex.

85 Gisèle Freund's 1939 photographs of VW posed her (as her visitors must often have seen her) in a chair in front of the left-hand panel.

86 William Plomer, *At Home*, Cape, 1958, p.44.

87 Spater, p.174, VW to Janet Case, 12 Apr 1924, *L* III, 1456, p.97.

88 The ambience of Tavistock Square was under threat in 1929 because the new hotel which had been built between Tavistock Square and Russell Square, the Imperial, had jazz music playing very loudly every night from its ballroom. After protesting, LW took them to law (with no help from his neighbours) and the case was settled out of court in 1930. After that the hotel was supposed to close its windows whenever it had a dance. But often this was not done, and LW would write – every time – to protest again. In March 1930 he even offered to sell the house to the hotel, but they refused. [LW, *DATW*, pp.124–6; LW, II H 3, Sussex; *D*, 12 Dec 1929, III, p.272.]

89 For accounts of visiting VW, see eg. Spender, *World within World*, Readers' Union, 1953, pp.130–7; William Plomer, op.cit., pp.42–56; Kennedy; JL in *Recollections*, pp.33–41; Spater, p.174. There are collections of reminiscences in *Recollections*; Stape; SPR.

90 *D*, 21 Mar 1927, III, p.132.

91 Dorothy Wellesley to VW, 18 Mar 1927, MHP, Sussex.

92 Emily Hale to Ruth George, 6 Dec 1935, Denison Library, Scripps College, Claremont.

93 Trekkie Parsons to the author, 1992.

94 William Plomer, unpublished article, c.1969, quoted Peter Alexander, *William Plomer*, OUP, 1989, p.150.

95 *Recollections*, pp.208–9.

96 Edith Sitwell, *Taken Care Of*, Hutchinson, 1965, p.93, in Stape, p.38.

97 Spender, *World.*, p.130.

98 Partridge, *Memories*, Gollancz, 1981, p.79, in Stape, pp.92–4.

99 *Recollections*, pp.105.

100 Trekkie Parsons, Diana Gardner, to the author, 1992, 1994.

101 *Recollections*, p.131.

102 CB to MH, 12 Aug 1926, 12, 20 Aug 1936, Texas.

103 Gerald Brenan, Notes written for a talk on the BBC, 1969, Texas.

104 J.T. Sheppard, Cambridge classicist; Miss T: Dorothy Todd. VW to LS, 3 Sep 1927, *L* III, 1807, p.418.

105 VB to RF, 19 Nov 1928, Tate

Gallery; VB to QB, 26 Jan 1931, Marler, p.357.

106 Spender, to the author, 1992; Anrep, to the author, 1993; Laski, quoted in Lyttelton-Hart-Davis *Letters*, vol.I, London 1978, p.4.

107 *D*, 4 May 1928, III, p.182.

108 *D*, 10 March 1932, IV, p.81.

109 Kathleen Raine to NN, 5 July 1978, Sussex.

110 *Recollections*, p.150.

111 Stape, p.116.

112 OM, Diary, Summer 1925, Goodman family papers.

113 Hope Mirrlees to Valerie Eliot, 5 Jan 1964. Valerie Eliot.

114 Peter Ure, *Yeats and Anglo-Irish Literature*, Liverpool UP, 1974, p.54.

115 *D*, 8 Nov 1930, III, pp.329–31.

116 VW to VB, 8 Nov 1930, *L* IV, 2274, p.250; to ES, 14 Nov 1930, *L* IV, 2277, pp.253–4.

117 W.B. Yeats, 'Spilt Milk', in *The Winding Stair & Other Poems*, 1933.

118 OM, Diary, 8 Nov 1930, Goodman family papers; Theresa Whistler, *Imagination of the Heart: The Life of Walter de la Mare*, Duckworth, 1993, p.210.

119 *D*, 4? Sep 1929, III, p.251.

120 *D*, 11 Oct 1929, III, pp.259–60.

CHAPTER 32: ETHEL

1 *D*, 16 Sep 1929, III, p.254.

2 *D*, 31 May 1929, III, p.231.

3 *D*, 5 Aug 1929, III, p.238; VW to VSW, 18 Aug 1929, *L* IV, 2057, p.80.

4 *D*, 22 Aug 1929, III, p.247; *The Prelude*, 1850 version, Book VII, ll.458–66. She had written this out before in a notebook while writing *Mrs Dalloway*, and added 'Good quotation for one of my books.' (Silver, p.30; Gillian Beer, introduction, *The Waves*, OUP, 1992, p.xx.)

5 *D*, 16 Sep 1929, III, p.254; 16 Feb 1930, III, p.287.

6 *D*, 2 Nov 1929, III, p.264.

7 *D*, 8 Dec 1929, III, p.270.

8 Years later, the doctor who treated Nelly, Alan McGlashan, had a distant and presumably confused memory of treating *her* for influenza in a workman's cottage in a hamlet near Shamley Green. 'She was extraordinarily frail at that time, like an autumn leaf on the point of dropping off its branch.' Alan McGlashan to NN, 1 Oct 1976, Sussex.

9 *D*, 16 June 1930, III, p.305.

10 *D*, 8 Sep 1930, n, p.317.

11 *D*, 15 Oct 1930, III, p.323.

12 VW to ES, 16 Oct 1930, *L* IV, 2254, p.230.

13 VW to ES, 30 Oct 1930, *L* IV, 2265, p.242.

14 *D*, 28 Aug 1930, III, p.314.

15 *D*, 2 Dec 1930, III, p.334.

16 *D*, 28 Mar 1931, IV, p.16.

17 VW to Hugh Walpole, 12 Apr 1931, *L* IV, 2350, p.311.

18 *D*, 26 Jan 1931, IV, p.7.

19 *D*, 20 Feb 1930, III, p.289.

20 *D*, 11 Mar 1930, III, p.297.

21 *D*, 9 Apr 1930, III, p.300.

22 E.g. *D*, 16 Jan 1930, III, p.283.

23 *D*, 22 Feb 1930, III, p.293.

24 *D*, 16 Feb 1930, III, p.287.

25 *D*, 13 Apr 1930, III, p.300.

26 *D*, 2 Sep 1930, III, p.315; 8 July 1932, IV, p.114; 17 Aug 1932, IV, p.121; LW, 'Account of a Fainting Attack', 11 Aug [1932], LW, Sussex.

27 *D*, 2 Sep 1930, III, p.315.

28 Louise Collis, *Impetuous Heart: The Story of Ethel Smyth*, William Kimber, 1984, p.174.

29 VW to VSW, 22 Oct 1929, *L* IV, 2083, p.101.

30 VW to ES, 30 Jan 1930, *L* IV, 2129, p.130.

31 VW to ES, 6? May 1930, *L* IV, 2174, p.164.

32 Vera Brittain introduces Dame Ethel Smyth, BBC Radio, 1937.

33 From a 1938? recording, in *A Portrait of Dame Ethel Smyth* by Mary Jean Hasler, BBC3, Sunday 31 July 1994, interval of Proms broadcast of *The Wreckers*.

34 ES, *Impressions That Remained*, vol.II, Longmans, 1919, p.251.

35 VW to ES, 30 Jan 1930, *L* IV, 2129, p.131.

36 VW to LS, 30 Nov 1919, *L* II, 1100, p.405.

37 Review of *Streaks of Life*, *NS*, 23 Apr 1921, *E* III, p.298.

38 VW to LS, 30 Nov 1919, *L* II, 1100, p.405.

39 VW to Molly MacCarthy, 7? June 1923, *L* III, 1399, p.46.

40 VW to VB, 23 May 1931, *L* IV, 2375, p.334.

41 VW to Nicholas Bagenal, 12 May 1928, *L* II, 930, p.238.

42 She refers to *Dodo* in a review, with a joke about its 'up-to-date' ladies. *E* III, p.96.

43 ES, *As Time Went On . . .*, Longmans, 1936, p.204; E.F. Benson, *Dodo*, Methuen, 1893, p.66.

44 *D*, 23 Oct 1930, III, pp.325–6.

45 ES, *As Time Went On . . .*, Longmans, 1936, p.136.

46 ES, *A Final Burning of Boats*, Longmans, 1928, p.138.

47 Collis, p.64.

48 Vera Brittain on ES, BBC, 1937.

49 ES, *A Final Burning of Boats*, p.187.

50 The Leipzig 1906 production was cut, to ES's fury, so she removed all the orchestral parts after the first night, and had difficulty in getting it put on again.

51 ES and Henry Brewster, *The Prison*, 1930.

52 *D*, 28 Nov 1919, I, p.315; Review of *Streaks of Life*, 1921, *E* III, p.295.

53 ES *Female Pipings in Eden*, Peter Davies, 1933, p.129.

54 Ibid., p.17, and *A Final Burning of Boats*, pp.19–20.

55 Ibid., p.20.

56 ES, *Impressions*, I, pp.94, 124; *As Time Went On . . .*, p.309.

57 Ronald Crichton, Programme Notes, BBC Proms, 31 July 1994, pp.8–9; Christopher St John, *Ethel Smyth*, Longmans, 1959, p.222.

58 *Impressions*, II, pp.6–7.

59 Deafness also affected Eleanor Cecil, Molly MacCarthy and Karin Stephen.

60 Henry Wood, *My Life of Music*, Gollancz, 1938, pp.366–8.

61 Lady Barbirolli to the author, July 1994.

62 Beecham, recorded 1958, in *A Portrait of Dame Ethel Smyth*.

63 Ethel stories from *A Portrait of Dame Ethel Smyth*, and from Crichton, Programme Notes, and 'Stormy Petrel', Diana McVeagh, *BBC Proms 1994*, p.100.

64 VSW on ES, in 1958, in *A Portrait of Dame Ethel Smyth*.

65 VW to QB, 14 May 1930, *L* IV, 2181, p.171.

66 VB to CB, 14 June 1931, Marler, p.364. The family tone is heard in *QB*: '[Ethel] fumbled and blustered and bawled her way through life . . . She was absurd – grotesque even . . . As was usual – in any matter which concerned Ethel, things went on at a thundering pace.' (*QB* II, pp.152–3.) But cf. Gordon, p.255, who gives an excellent account of how ES liberated VW into a new way of writing.

67 ES to VW, 13 Jan 1933, Berg.

68 ES to VW, 2 May 1930, Berg.

69 ES to VW, 13 Aug 1930, Berg.

70 ES to VW, 'Last day of the old year 1931', Berg.

71 St John, p.224.

72 ES to VW, 20 Sep 1931, Berg.

73 ES to VW, 26 Aug 1933, Berg.

74 ES to VW, 20 Dec 1938, Berg.

75 ES to VB, 9 Sep 1932, Sussex.

76 St John, pp.223–4.

77 *D*, 21 Feb 1930, III, pp.291–2.

78 *D*, 16 June 1930, III, p.306.

79 *D*, 23 Oct 1930, III, p.326.

80 VW to ES, 4 Sep 1930, *L* IV, 2230, p.208.

81 ES to VW, III, 2183, 26 May 1930, p.172.

82 ES to LW, 29 June 1930, Berg.

83 *D*, 6 July 1930, III, p.308; VW to ES, 6 July 1930, *L* IV, 2201, p.184.

84 VW to ES, 16 July 1930, *L* IV, 2204, p.188.

85 *D*, 20 Aug 1930, III, p.312.

86 VW to ES, 10 Aug 1931, *L* IV, 2419, p.367.

87 *D*, 23 Nov 1930, III, p.334.

88 *D*, 4 Mar 1935, IV, p.284.

89 *D*, 29 Apr, 1 May 1930, III, pp.302–3; VW to VSW, 1 May 1930, *L* IV, 2172, p.162.

90 ES to VW, 2 May 1930, Berg; VW to ES, 6? May 1930, *L* IV, 2174, pp.163–4; VW to VB, 7 May 1930, *L* IV, 2175, pp.164–5; VW to VSW, 8? May 1930, *L* IV, 2176, p.165.

91 ES to VW, 31 Dec 1930, Berg.

92 VW to ES, 19 Sep 1930, *L* IV, 2238, p.217.

93 VW to ES, 28 Aug 1930, *L* IV, 2224, p.205.

94 VW to ES, 19 Aug 1930, *L* IV, 2222, p.203.

95 VW to ES, 18 Sep 1931, *L* IV, 2438, p.382.

96 VW to ES, 27 Feb 1930, *L* IV, 2148, p.145.

97 VW to ES, 22 Apr 1930, *L* IV, 2168, p.159.

98 VW to ES, 22 June 1930, *L* IV, 2194, p.180.

99 LW, Diary, 20 May 1931, LW, Sussex. Also *L* IV 2238, 2282; *D*, 28 Mar 1930.

100 *D*, 8 May 1932, IV, p.95.

101 ES to OM, 18 July 1934, in Collis, op.cit., p.190.

102 VW to ES, 15–17 Mar 1930, *L* IV, 2157, p.151.

103 VW to ES, 22 June 1930, *L* IV, 2194, p.180.

104 VW to ES, 19 Sep 1930, *L* IV, 2238, p.216.

105 VW to ES, 22 June 1930, *L* IV, 2194, p.180; 8 Oct 1930, IV 2249, p.227.

106 VW to ES, 26 Oct 1930, *L* IV, 2259, p.234.

107 VW to ES, 2 Aug 1930, *L* IV, 2215, p.195; 28 Sep 1930, *L* IV, 2244, pp.220–1.

108 VW to ES, 8 Aug 1934, *L* V, 2916, p.321.

109 VW to ES, 11 July 1930, *L* IV, 2203, p.187.

110 VW to ES, 21/22 Sep 1930, *L* IV, 2239, p.218.

111 VW to ES, 2 Aug 1930, *L* IV, 2215, p.195.

112 VW to ES, 16 Oct 1930, *L* IV, 2254, p.231.

113 *D*, 16 June 1930, III, p.306.

114 VW to ES, 15 Aug 1930, *L* IV, 2218, p.200.

115 VW to ES, 2 Aug 1930, *L* IV, 2215, p.196.

116 VW to ES, 13/14 May 1930, *L* IV, 2179, pp.168–9.

117 VW to ES, 19 Aug 1930, *L* IV, 2222, p.203.

118 VW to ES, 28 Aug 1930, *L* IV, 2224, p.205.

119 London & National Society for Women's Service, Report to the Secretary, Jan 1931; Membership Form, 1932; 'What is this Society?', April 1935. Fawcett Library.

120 *D*, 23 Jan 1931, IV, pp.6–7.

121 'Professions for Women', in *Virginia Woolf: Women and Writing*, p.63.

122 *D*, 20 Jan 1931, IV. p.6.

123 The notes of the speech and the manuscript of the speech are in Berg; Leaska prints the speech at the front of *The Pargiters*, and the notes as an Appendix. 'Professions for Women', much edited from the speech, was published in *The Death of the Moth* and again in *Virginia Woolf: Women and Writing*.

124 *Pargiters*, pp.xxvii, 165.

125 The list is omitted in the published essay. *Pargiters*, pp.167, xliii.

126 *Pargiters*, p.164.

127 VW to ES, 24 Jan 1931, *L* IV, 2314, p.280; *D*, 23 Jan 1931, p.7. VW suggested to ES that they should publish her speech, but presumably LW refused.

128 Pippa Strachey, Report to the LNSWS Junior Council, vol.VII, 1927–39, p.8, Fawcett Library; Vera Brittain, *The Nation*, 31 Jan 1931, quoted in *Pargiters*, p.xxxv; *The Woman's Leader*, 30 Jan 1931, Fawcett Library.

129 For this attempted transaction see VW to ES, 18 Dec 1932, 2682; VW to VSW, 14 Feb 1933, 2703, where she hopes VSW might successfully

sell the MS to collectors in 'Pineap-
popolis'; VSW to VW, 28 Mar 1933,
VSW/VW, p.389; and *WF*, p.iii, on
the failure of this attempt and how
the MS was eventually given to the
Fitzwilliam Library, Cambridge,
where it remained unedited until
1992.

130 Minutes of the LNSWS Finance
Committee, May 1938, Fawcett
Library; Pippa Strachey to VW, 17
May 1938, thanking her for her
'glorious offers of collaboration in
our Library Plans', MHP, Sussex.

131 *D*, 3 Sep 1931, IV, p.42.

132 MS of 'Professions', MS of 'Pargiters', vol.1, Berg; Pargiters, intro,
p.xvi.

133 VW to ES, 16 Nov 1930, *L* IV, 2278,
p.255.

134 VW to ES, 8 June 1933, *L* V, 2746,
pp.194–5. LW often advised her
against sending intemperate letters
(*D*, 20 Mar 1935, IV, p.289).

135 Silver, p.237; D, 7 Feb 1931,
IV, p.10; cf. Ch12, n.85.

136 VW to ES, 11 Mar 1931, *L* IV, 2335,
p.298.

137 VW to ES, 29 Mar 1931, *L* IV, 2341,
p.302.

138 VW to VB, 23 May 1931, *L* IV,
2375, p.334.

139 VW to ES, 4 July 1931, *L* IV, 2400,
p.353.

140 *D*, 2 June 1931, IV, p.29; VW to ES,
6 Sep 1931, *L* IV, 2429, p.375.

141 VW to ES, 28 July 1932, *L* V, 2614,
p.81.

142 ES to VW, 3 Aug 1931, 11 Sep 1931,
Berg. ES, Diary, 1933, Ann Arbor.

143 *D*, 15 Oct 1931, IV, p.49. [AOB
queries 'choked'.]

144 *D*, 4 Mar 1935, IV, p.284.

145 *D*, 28 Apr 1939, V, p.216.

146 *D*, 14 Nov 1933, IV, p.189.

147 VW to ES, 10 Aug 1935, *L* V, 3056,
p.423.

148 ES to VB, 28 June 1934, CP, Sussex.

149 ES to VW, 18 Jun 1937, Berg.

150 ES to Henry Wood, 25 Apr 1941,
quoted Collis, *op.cit.*, p.204.

151 VW to ES, 26 Sep 1939, *L* VI, 3553,
p.359.

CHAPTER 33: YOUNG POETS

1 Gillian Beer, Introduction, *The
Waves*, OUP, 1992.

2 *D*, 1 July 1931, IV, p.34.

3 OM, Diary, 4 July 1931, Goodman
family papers.

4 See Valentine Cunningham, *British
Writers of the Thirties*, OUP, 1988,
Ch. 4, on 'in the cage' as a theme
tune of the 1930s.

5 *E* IV, pp.432–3. This lecture was
reprinted as 'The Narrow Bridge of
Art'.

6 See Gillian Beer, p.xvii, on how VW
is looking for 'the possibility of
detachment and feeling at once, an
assaying of those experiences ordi-
narily reserved for poetry'. See also
J.W. Graham, Introduction, *The
Waves*, *Hol*, p.19, on her notes now
on how prose had got to 'take over
some of the duties which were once
discharged by poetry'.

7 *D*, 27 Oct 1930, III, p.327.

8 Willis, pp.184–5, for details; LW to
JL, Spotts, p.303; LW, *DATW*,
pp.172–6, Lehmann.

9 VW to JL, 17 Sep 1931, *L* IV, 2437,
p.381.

10 VW to Molly MacCarthy, 30 Jan
1931, *L* 2319, IV, p.284.

11 *D*, 28 Aug 1930, III, p.315.

12 VW to QB, 18 Nov 1933, *L* V, 2821,
p.247.

13 See Cunningham, pp.106–7.

14 See Stansky for a vivid account of JB
and JL at Cambridge; see JL, *The
Whispering Gallery*, Longmans,
1955, for his account of these years.

15 Quoted Stansky, p.73.

16 JB to JL, quoted Stansky, p.70.

17 VW to JB, 21 May 1936, *CS*, p.374.

18 Stephen Spender to VW, nd [1934],
MHP, Sussex.

19 Ibid., p.169.

20 JL, *The Whispering Gallery*, pp.141,
146.

21 Philip Toynbee, *Friends Apart: A
Memoir of the Thirties*, McGibbon &
Kee, 1954, p.50.

22 Clive Fisher, *Cyril Connolly: A Nostalgic Life*, Macmillan, 1995, p.129.

23 Stephen Spender, *World within World*, Readers' Union, 1953, pp.121, 136.

24 *D*, 4 Apr 1930, III, p.299.

25 VW to ES, 15 Aug 1930, *L* IV, 2218, p.200.

26 VW to QB, 21 Dec 1933, *L* V, 2837, p.261. Spender was sharing a flat in Maida Vale with Jimmy Younger, ex-Army.

27 Eve Kosovsky Sedgwick, *Epistemology of the Closet*, University of California Press, 1990, p.23, on gossip as a form of 'nonce taxonomy', comparable to what goes on in the fiction of James and Proust, 'of the making and unmaking and remaking and redissolution of hundreds of old and new categorical imaginings concerning all the kinds it may take to make up a world'.

28 See Edmund White on this phase of gay life and on its changes after 1960s liberation in *The Burning Library*, Chatto & Windus, 1994, p.78.

29 White, p.310.

30 VW to CB, 28 Jan 1931, *L* IV, 2318, p.283.

31 Lehmann, *The Whispering Gallery*, p.166.

32 Willis, pp.188–9.

33 VW to ESW, 23 Sep 1929, *L* IV, 2092, p.92.

34 VW to HW, 12 Apr 1931, *L* IV, 2350, p.311. e.g.: 'Mosquitoes sing their tune around her head, / She knows by that it's time to go to bed. / But no, she wanders to the cliffs And leaps into the sea. / People cry, "O, is she dead?" / She answers "No, sirs, I've leapt into eternity."' 'Song of Nobody', *A Collection of Poems, written between the ages of 14 and 17*, Hogarth Press, 1931, Texas.

35 *D*, 27 Aug 1934, IV, p.240.

36 Lehmann, *The Whispering Gallery*, p.181.

37 Ibid., p.173.

38 Ibid., pp.172–4; Stansky, pp.80–4.

39 Willis, p.200–2; Cunningham, p.23; Spender, *World within World*, p.118;

40 VW to Lyn Irvine, 2 Sep 1931, *L* IV, 2427, p.373.

41 Taylor, p.374. He gives a detailed account of the crisis in Ch.8.

42 Lehmann, *The Whispering Gallery*, p.178.

43 LW, *Imperialism and Civilization*, 1928.

44 Peter Quennell, 'A Letter to Adolf Hitler', *The Hogarth Letters*, ed Hermione Lee, Chatto & Windus, 1985.

45 Lehmann, *The Whispering Gallery*, p.192. See also on the format of the Letters, Lehmann, *Thrown*, p.29.

46 VW to JL, 17 Sep 1931, *L* IV, 2437, p.381.

47 VW to JL, 31 July 1932, *L* V, 2615, p.83.

48 *D*, 19 July 1931, IV, p.36.

49 *D*, 3 May 1931, IV, p.25.

50 *D*, 11 Apr 1931, IV, p.18.

51 *D*, 19 May 1931, IV, p.27.

52 *D*, 16 Nov 1931, IV, p.53.

53 *D*, 23 Dec 1930, III, p.339.

54 VW to ES, 6 Dec 1931, *L* IV, 2476, p.409.

55 Gerald Heard, *The Emergence of Man*, Cape, 1931; James Jeans, *The Mysterious Universe*, CUP, 1930; *D*, 30 Jan 1932, IV, p.65.

56 Quotations from review of *The Waves* in *CH*, pp.263–94.

57 Willis, p.199.

58 *D*, 17 Nov 1931, IV, p.54.

59 VW to Goldsworthy Lowes Dickinson, 17 Oct 1931, *L* IV, 2460, pp.397–8.

60 Roy Campbell, *The Georgiad*, 1931, jacket cover.

61 *D*, 15 Oct 1930, III, pp.323–4.

62 *D*, 17 May 1932, IV, p.101.

63 VW to William Plomer, 22 Feb 1932, *L* V, 2532, p.22.

64 *D*, 17 May 1932, IV, p.101.

65 *D*, 23 Oct 1931, IV, p.51.

66 *D*, 29 Feb 1932, IV, p.79.

67 *D*, 24 Mar 1932, IV, p.85.

68 WH to Vera Brittain, Sep 1931, *Selected letters of Winifred Holtby and Vera Brittain*, ed. Vera Brittain

& Geoffrey Handley-Taylor, A. Brown, Hull, 1960; ES to WH, 5 Sep 1931, WH Collection, Hull Local Studies Library.
69 VB to WH, nd, Hull.
70 VW to WH, 16 March 1931, Hull.
71 VW to ES, 1 Apr 1931, *L* IV, 2342, p.302.
72 VW to VB, 14 May 1931, *L* IV, 2373, p.331.
73 VW to WH, 31 May 1931, Hull.
74 VW to WH, 14 Sep 1931, Hull.
75 *D*, 22 Sep 1931, IV, p.45.
76 VW to WH, 29 Sep 1931, Hull.
77 VW to WH, 3 Jan 1932, Hull.
78 VW to ES, 29 Sep 1932, 2640; VW to Hugh Walpole, 26 Oct 1932, *L* V, 2651, p.114; VW to MLD, 10 Nov 1932, *L* V, 2664, p.124; VW to WH, nd [Jan 1933], Hull.
79 WH, MS of *Virginia Woolf*, p.50, Hull.
80 Reviews of Holtby, Hull. VW quotes some of the phrases from Holtby's review by *The Manchester Evening News* in 'Middlebrow', her letter (not sent) to the *NS&N* of Nov 1932, published in *The Death of the Moth*, pp.176–86.
81 VW to Hugh Walpole, 28 Feb 1932, *L* V, 2537, p.25.

CHAPTER 34: LOSS

1 *D*, 7 Dec 1925, III, pp.49–50.
2 *D*, 2 Sep 1930, III, p.316.
3 *D*, 27 Nov 1925, III, p.48; 22 Feb 1930, III, p.294.
4 Holroyd, 1971, p.930.
5 VW to VSW, 16 Feb 1927, *L* III, 1717, p.330.
6 VW, 'Lady Strachey', 1928, MHP, Sussex. Her published obituary of Lady Strachey was in the *N&A*, 22 Dec 1928. *E* IV, pp.573–77.
7 *D*, 28 Nov 1928, III, p.208.
8 *D*, 15 June 1929, III, pp.233–4.
9 *D*, 19 May 1931, IV, p.26.
10 LS to Roger Senhouse, 11 May 1927, Holroyd, 1994, p.569; Holroyd, 1971, pp.986, 1051.

11 *D*, 27 Nov 1925, III, p.48; VW to VSW, 6 Jan 1932, *L* V, 2503, p.3.
12 VW to LS, 10 Dec 1931, *L* IV, 2481, p.412.
13 *D*, 22 Jan 1932, IV, p.65.
14 VW to OM, 14 Feb 1932, *L* V, 2526, p.18.
15 *D*, 22 Jan 1932, VW to Carrington, 28? Feb 1932, *L* 2538, V, p.25; VW to Carrington, 2 Mar 1932, *L* V, 2542, p.28.
16 *D*, 25 May 1932, IV, p.102.
17 *D*, 30 Jan 1932, IV, p.66. See Gerzinga, *Carrington*, OUP, 1990, p.297, and Holroyd, 1994, p.691.
18 VW to Carrington, 2 Mar 1932, *L* V, 2542, p.28.
19 'The Countess of Pembroke's Arcadia', *CE* I, p.27.
20 Violet Trefusis, *Don't Look Round*, Hutchinson, 1952, p.108.
21 *D*, 12 Mar 1932, IV, p.81.
22 VB to CB, 13 Mar 1932, Marler, p.372.
23 Quoted Gerzinga, p.301.
24 VW to OM, 15 Mar 1932, *L* V, 2553, p.34; VW to ES, 21 Mar 1932, *L* V, 2560, p.38.
25 *D*, 24 Mar 1932, IV, p.85.
26 *D*, 25 May 1932, IV, p.103.
27 *D*, 22 Apr 1932, p.88.
28 VW to Pippa Strachey, 21 Jan 1932, *L* V, 2511, p.8.
29 *D*, 21 Apr 1932, IV, p.90; VW to VSW, 8 May 1932, *L* V, 2582, p.62.
30 VW to VB, 2 May 1932, *L* V, 2578, p.56.
31 *D*, 21 Apr 1932, IV, p.91.
32 *D*, 10 May 1932, IV, p.99.
33 *D*, 8 May 1932, IV, p.98.
34 *D*, 22 Apr, 8 May, IV, pp.92, 94.
35 *D*, 27 Apr 1931, IV, p.23.
36 *D*, 2 May, 8 May, IV, pp.95–6.
37 VW to QB, 1 May 1932, *L* V, 2577, p.54; VW to VB, 19 Apr 1932, *L* V, 2573, p.49; VW to ES, 4 May 1932, *L* V, 2579, p.59.
38 RF to Helen Anrep, 4 May 1932, *Letters of Roger Fry*, II, p.670.
39 VW to JL, 31 July 1932, *L* V, 2615, p.83.
40 VW to OM, 22 June 1932, *L* V, 2600, p.71.

41 *D*, 3 June 1932, IV, p.107.
42 *D*, 21 July 1932, IV, p.118.
43 *D*, 5 Aug 1932, IV, p.120.
44 VW to Eddy Sackville-West, 2591, 2598; VW to VSW, 3142; *Vita*, p.251; de la Noy, *Eddy*, p.154. Spender and Plomer were used to provoking this sort of reaction. That same month they, Auden and Isherwood laughed their way through Garbo's new film; a woman sitting in front of them turned round and said bitterly, 'Can't you stop sniggering for five minutes?' Alexander, *William Plomer*, OUP, 1989, p.186.
45 VW to ES, 9 June 1932, *L* V, 2596, p.69.
46 *D*, 18 June 1932, IV, p.110.
47 *D*, 2 Sep 1932, IV, p.123.
48 VW to Logan Pearsall Smith, 6 Nov 1932, *L* V, 2658, p.119.
49 VW to ES, 21 Aug 1932, *L* V, 2627, p.97.
50 Frances Partridge, *Memories*, Gollancz, 1981, pp.236–7.
51 *D*, 16 Sep 1932, IV, p.124.
52 There were three versions of this essay: one, the unpublished letter to the *NS&N*, 'Middlebrow' (*D*, 2 Nov 1932, IV, p.129) published in *The Death of the Moth*,, pp.176–86; two, 'Three Characters', MS, MHP, Sussex, published in *Adam International Review*, 1972; and three, 'Portraits', published in, *CSF*, p.246, which Dick dates 1937.
53 *D*, 13 Oct 1932, IV, p.127.
54 VW to ES, 20 Nov 1932, *L* V, 2667, p.128.
55 The chapter ('Quack, Quack') is full of anti-Semitic jeers against Leonard and a caricature of Virginia Woolf, cigar between her virginal lips, defending in upper-class tones the Jewish race ('You knoo-oo, Count Potocki, Aie always think may husband's race is soo-oo merch more civilayzed than ahs') and the reality of life in London slums ('Virginia Woolf thinks that those people live the *re-arl layfe*. She describes the back rooms of shops in Marsham Street – it is the-ah that the re-arl

layfe is lived.') Count Potocki de Montalk, *Social Climbers in Bloomsbury*, privately printed, 1939. Texas.
56 *D*, 14 July 1932, IV, p.116–17.
57 *Flush*, p.87.
58 *D*, 13 July 1932, IV, p.115.
59 *D*, 2 Oct 1932, IV, p.125.
60 *D*, 2 Oct 1932, IV, p.125.
61 *D*, 31 Dec 1932, IV, p.135.

CHAPTER 35: OUTSIDER

1 VW to Hugh Walpole, 28 Dec 1932, *L* V, 2687, p.142.
2 Holograph, vol.I, Berg; *D*, 5 Jan 1933, IV p.142.
3 *D*, 3 Jan 1933, IV, p.139.
4 *D*, 5 Jan 1933, IV, p.142. LW ordered the 18hp Lanchester, bought from Salmons & Sons in New Burlington Street, to be upholstered in special green leather to tone with the Italian green paintwork on the lower body (the upper part of the car was painted grey.) LW, Sussex.
5 *D*, 13 June, 20 July 1933, 16 Jan 1934.
6 Holograph, vol. I, Berg. See *The Pargiters*.
7 *D*, 2 Feb 1933, IV, p.146.
8 *D*, 25 Apr 1933, IV, pp.151–2.
9 *D*, 31 May 1933, IV, p.161.
10 This was usual: it was only due to late changes of mind that we don't have novels by VW called *Melymbrosia*, *The Hours*, *The Moths*, or *Pointz Hall*.
11 *D*, 2 Sep 1933, IV, p.176.
12 VW to QB, 15 Aug 33, *L* V, 2777, p.213.
13 *D*, 27 Aug 1934, IV, p.240.
14 *D*, 2 Sep 1933, IV, p.176.
15 VW to Donald Brace, 20 Apr 1934, *L* V, 2880, p.294; *D*, 22 May 1934, IV, p.221.
16 VW to ES, 24 Sep 1934, *L* V, 2935, p.334.
17 VW to Brace, 2 Nov 1934, *L* V, 2947, p.343.
18 VW to Brace, 29 Sep 1935, *L* V, 3065, p.428; Brace to LW, 27 Apr 1936, 31 July 1936, Berg.

19 *D*, 28 July 1934, IV, p.233.
20 *The Waves* was in her mind from 1927 to early 1929, drafted from March 1929 to Apr 1930, and redrafted from June 1930 to Feb 1931.
21 *D*, 21 Feb 1927, III, p.128; *D*, 28 Nov 1928, III, p.209; *D*, 31 May 1928, III, p.185; VW to ES, 28 Aug 1929, *L* IV, 2224, p.204; *D*, 28 Mar 1929, III, p.219; *D*, 4 Sep 1929, III, p.251.
22 *D*, 7 July 1933, IV, p.167; *D*, 30 July 1933, IV, p.170; VW to QB, 26 July 1933, *L* V, 2767, p.206; *D*, 17 Dec 1933, IV, p.193.
23 *D*, 28 July 1934, p.233.
24 Silver, p.67.
25 *D*, 16 Feb 1932, IV, p.77; Silver, p.255, 3G file, MHP, Sussex.
26 VW to VSW, 1 Apr 1933, *L* V, 2723, p.174.
27 *D*, 2 Sep 1933, IV, 177.
28 VW to Francis Birrell, 3 Sep 1933, *L* V, 2728, p.221.
29 *Three Guineas*, Ch.2, n. 38, p.300.
30 *D*, 19 Apr 1934, IV, p.208; VW to Stephen Spender, 10 July 1934, *L* V, 2910, p.315.
31 VW to ES, 18 May 1933, *L* V, 2738, p.187.
32 VW to ES, 29 July 1934, *L* V, 2915, p.320.
33 The *Yale Review* turned it down, saying their readers were not much interested in Goldsmith.
34 *D*, 16 Aug 1933, IV, p.172; 'The Novels of Turgenev', *CE* I, pp.248–251.
35 *D*, 25 Nov 1933, IV, p.190; Sickert to VW, nd, MHP, Sussex; also VW to QB, 26 Nov 1933, *L* V, 2826, p.253; Shone, Introduction to VW, *Walter Sickert: A Conversation* (*Yale Review* Sep 1934, Hogarth Press, Oct 1934), Bloomsbury Workshop, 1992, pp.5–10.
36 DG to Angus Davidson, quoted Shone, Introduction, p.7.
37 Richard Shone, *Walter Sickert*, Phaidon, 1988, p.110.
38 Shone, *BP2*, p.228, figs 160–62. VW to DG, 24 Nov 1932, *L* V, 2669,

p.129; VW to VB, 16 Jan 1933, *L* V, 2693, p.147.
39 Quoted Shone, *BP2*, p.228.
40 *D*, 4? Dec 1933, IV, p.131.
41 *D*, 3 Jan 1933, IV, p.139.
42 Angelica, in *Deceived*, p.111, remembered it as £15 a quarter. But letters suggest it was £100 a year, paid via VB until Sep 1938 [*L* VI, 3439], after which £25 a quarter was paid direct to Angelica, until Dec 1939, when VW had to cut it down to £60 a year. [*L* VI, 3555, 3577.]
43 See Andrew Motion, *The Lamberts*, Chatto & Windus, 1986, pp.184, 195, for the details of *Pomona*.
44 *D*, 19 Jan 1933, IV, p.144.
45 *D*, 12 Nov 1933, IV, p.187; VW to ES, 8 Nov 1933, *L* V, 2816, p.243; VW to QB, 10 Nov 1933, *L* V, 2818, p.244.
46 Stansky, p.111; pp.106–20 for a full account of JB's political confusion in the early to mid-1930s.
47 VW to ES, 18 May 1933, *L* V, 2738, p.187.
48 *D*, 2 July 1934, IV, p.223.
49 *D*, 25 Mar 1933, IV, p.147.
50 'Why?', 1934, in *A Woman's Essays*, p.151.
51 *D*, 20 June 1933, IV, p.165.
52 VW to ES, 19 Apr 1933, *L* V, 2728, p.178.
53 *The Years*, p.195.
54 VW to ES, 7 Aug 1933, *L* V, 2772, p.211.
55 *D*, 21 July 1933, IV, p.168.
56 *D*, 23 Nov 1933, IV, pp.189–90; VW to QB, 26 Nov 1933, *L* V, 2826, pp.252–3.
57 Isaiah Berlin to the author, 18 Feb 1992.
58 VW to Eleanor Cecil, 4 June 1933, *L* V, 2742, p.190, 8 June 1933, *L* V, 2747, p.195; *D*, 8? June 1933, IV, p.162.
59 *D*, 23 Sep 1933, IV, pp.179–80.
60 VW to QB, 12 Dec 1933, *L* V, 2833, p.259.
61 *D*, 29 Oct 1933, IV, p.186; VW to *NS&N*, 28 Oct 1933, *L* V, 2810, pp.237–8.
62 *D*, 29 Nov 1933, IV, p.191.

63 *The Years*, p.314.
64 VW to QB, 24 Jan 1934, *L* V, 2850, p.273.
65 *D*, 14 Feb 1934, IV, p.201.
66 For BBC, see *L* 2615, 2829, 2861, 2895, 3247; *D*, 4 Mar 1934, IV, p.204.
67 In July 1936 she told ES that her menopause had happened 'as gently and imperceptibly as a lamb, 2 years ago'. VW to ES, 25 July 1936, *L* VI, 3156, p.60; but for symptoms, *D*, 24 Nov 1936, V, p.35; 1 Mar 1937, V, p.63.
68 *D*, 7 Dec 1933, IV, p.192. She was touched, too, by WH's tragic early death two years later.
69 *D*, 16 Jan 1934, IV, p.199; VW to QB, 10 Jan 1934, *L* V, 2845, p.268.
70 VB to JB, 4 Mar 1936, QB.
71 For Nelly's departure, *D*, Feb–Apr 1934; VW to ES, 29 Mar 1934, *L* V, 2867, pp.284–6; for Mabel, e.g., *D*, 21 Aug 1934, IV, p.238, 25 Apr 1935, IV, p.306; for first encounter with Louie Everest (later Mayer), *D*, 11 July 1934, IV, p.224; 'Louie Mayer', in *Recollections*, pp.187–98.
72 For VW and Ireland, *D*, 30 Apr–8 May 1934, IV, pp.208–18; *L* V, 2883–90, pp.296–302; 3141, VI, p.45; Elizabeth Bowen, 'Dublin', in *The Mulberry Tree*, Virago, 1986, pp.143–9; J.C. Beckett, *The Anglo-Irish Tradition*, Faber, 1976, p.52; Clive Fisher, *Cyril Connolly: A Nostalgic Life*, Macmillan, 1995, p.129; Victoria Glendinning, *Elizabeth Bowen*, Weidenfeld, 1977; Mark Bence-Jones, *Twilight of the Ascendancy*, Constable, 1987, pp.258, 260.
73 EB to VW, nd, MHP, Sussex.
74 EB to VW, 31 July 1935, in *The Mulberry Tree*, p.211.
75 EB, from *A Night's Darkness, A Day's Sail*, BBC, in *Recollections*, pp.60–5.
76 *D*, 12 Apr 1938, V, p.134.
77 VW to EB, 26 Sep [1935], private collection.
78 EB to William Plomer, [Nov 1935], private collection.
79 *D*, 8 May 1934, IV, p.218.

80 *D*, 9 May 1934, IV, p.219.
81 For George Duckworth's death, *D*, 1 May 1934, IV, p.211; *L* V, 2887, p.299; *D*, 17 July 1934, IV, p.299.
82 *D*, 19 July 1934, IV, p.227.
83 VW to ES, 21 May 1934, *L* V, 2894, p.305.
84 *D*, 18 Apr 1934, IV, p.207.
85 VB to JB, 15 Aug 1936, QB.
86 VW to Victoria OCampo, 28 Dec 1934, *L* V, 2969, p.358.
87 *D*, 21 July 1934, 12 Aug 1934, IV, pp.229, 237.
88 VW to Stephen Spender, 10 July 1934, *L* V, 2910, p.315.
89 *D*, 24 July 1934, IV, p.230.
90 *D*, 2 Sep 1934, IV, p.241.
91 RF to VW, 3 Aug 1934, Sutton, vol.II, pp.692–3.
92 Roger Fry Memorial Service Programme, MHP, Sussex; quoted in Spalding, *Roger Fry*, p.274, who says that these quotations were read out in the service. But VW said there were no words.
93 VB to Helen Anrep, 14 Sep 1934, Marler, p.382.
94 *D*, 17 Oct 1934, IV, p.253.
95 VW to OM, 21 Sep 1934, *L* V, 2933, p.332; VW to VSW, 23 Sep 1934, LV, p.332.
96 *D*, 1 Nov 1934, IV, p.258.
97 VW to ES, 24 Sep 1934, *L* V, 2935, p.334.
98 *The Pargiters*, MS, 27 Sep 1934, Berg.
99 *D*, 30 Sep 1934, IV, p.245.

CHAPTER 36: FAILURE

1 Wyndham Lewis, *Men without Art*, Cassell, 1934, pp.158–71. See Ch. 31, n.74.
2 Eg, Frank Swinnerton, *The Georgian Literary Scene* (1935), *CH* pp.356–8 ('VW's work seems very clever, very ingenious, but on the whole creatively unimportant'), and Prince Dmitry Mirsky, *The Intelligentsia of Great Britain* (1935), *CH* pp.346–50: 'The sufferings with

which VW deals are . . . the sufferings of the parasitic cream of the
bourgeois.'

3 For her reactions to these attacks, *D*,
14, 15, 16, 17 Oct 1934, IV,
pp.251–5; 11, 18 March 1935, IV,
pp.287–9; 'Ode', *CSF*, pp.236–41.

4 Scott-James wrote again in 1935,
1936, and 1938, to ask if she would
write this piece (Scott-James to VW,
Texas); in the end she wrote 'Reviewing' (1939) as an HP pamphlet.

5 VW to ES, 18 Nov 1934, *L* V, 2952,
p.347.

6 VW to VSW, 20 Nov 1934, *L* V,
2954, p.348.

7 Harold Nicolson, *Diaries & Letters*,
vol.I, 1930–1939, Collins Fontana
1971, pp.183–4; quoted *L* V, p.341,
note 1. See also *L* 2994 and *D*, 26 Oct
1934, pp.255–7.

8 *D*, 15 Nov 1934, IV, p.261.

9 *D*, 18 Dec 1934, IV, p.266.

10 *D*, 5 Feb 1935, IV, p.277.

11 *D*, 25 Mar 1935, IV, p.290.

12 *D*, 26 Nov 1934, IV, p.263.

13 Quoted Doris Meyer, *Victoria
OCampo*, University of Texas, 1979,
1990, p.124.

14 Meyer, pp.125, 126.

15 VW to VSW, 19 Dec 1934, 2965, *L*
V, p.355.

16 VSW to OCampo, July 7 1954,
Quoted in Meyer, p.128.

17 VW to OCampo, 22 Jan 1935, *L* V,
2977, p.365; 29 Oct 1935, *L* V, 3075,
p.439.

18 Meyer, p.238, from OCampo, 'Virginia Woolf in My Memory', Apr
1941, *Testimonios II*, Sur, 1941.

19 Meyer, p.240.

20 *D*, 11 Jan 1935, IV, p.273; VW to
OCampo, 22 Jan 1935, *L* V, 2977,
p.365.

21 VW to Virginia Isham, 17 Dec 1935,
L V, 3089, p.454.

22 Adrian Stephen to Wyn Henderson,
10 Feb 1935, private collection.

23 Ann Synge, to the author; *D*, 2 Feb
1935, IV, p.276; Barbara Strachey,
Remarkable Relations, Gollancz,
1980, p.298.

24 *D*, 1 Jan 1935, IV, p.271; VW to QB,
27 Feb 1935, *L* V, 2992, p.373.

25 E.g. *D*, 16 Mar 1935, IV, p.288.

26 *D*, 6 Mar 1935, pp.285–6.

27 *D*, 15 Apr 1935, IV, p.300; 25 June
1935, IV, p.326.

28 VW to VSW, 15 Feb 1935, *L* V,
2986, p.370.

29 *D*, 11 Mar, 31 Mar 1935, *L* V 3003,
3004, 3008; VSW to VW, 28 Mar
1935, VSW/VW, pp.419–20.

30 Minutes of the London Library
Committee, 8 April 1935, chaired by
the Earl of Ilchester. The first
woman elected was Professor Eileen
Power, in 1936. London Library.

31 'Royalty', *Time and Tide*, 1 Dec
1934, mocked Queen Victoria's
inability to write a sentence, and
broached the dangerous republican
possibilities of the royal family taking to self-revelations: 'Can we go on
bowing and curtseying to people
who are just like ourselves? . . . Will
the British Empire survive? Will
Buckingham Palace look as solid
then as it does now?'

32 *D*, 26 Mar 1935, IV, p.291.

33 VW to VB, 28 Apr 1935, *L* V, 3013,
p.387.

34 *D*, 18 Apr 1935, IV, p.302.

35 See Ch.37.

36 *D*, 1 June 1935, IV, p.318.

37 Furbank, II, pp.192–4; VW to VB,
21 June 1935, *L* V, 3031, p.403; *D*,
13 June 1935, IV, p.321.

38 *D*, 1 Nov 1934, IV, p.258; 13 June
1935, IV, p.321.

39 *CE* I, p.178.

40 VW to VB, 21 June 1935, *L* V, 3031,
p.404.

41 *D*, 4 Dec 1935, IV, p.356.

42 VW to JB, 1 Dec 1935, *L* V, 3085,
p.448.

43 Spender, *World within World*, p.122;
Cunningham, pp.43, 58; VW to
Spender, 25 June 1935, *L* V, 3037,
pp.407–8; Spender to VW, 19 July
1935, MHP, Sussex.

44 *D*, 27 June, 28 June 1935, IV,
pp.326–7.

45 Susan Buchan had known VW as a
child; her husband, the writer, was

about to go to Canada as Governor-General. They were close friends of Elizabeth Bowen, and invited her that weekend: Susan Buchan's daughter remembered EB and VW both dressed 'in misty-silvery dresses'. Glendinning, *Elizabeth Bowen*, p.57; VW to VB, 3 July 1935, *L* V, 3040, p.411; Susan Buchan to Elizabeth Bowen, 1952, in *A Winter Bouquet*, Duckworth, 1954, pp.77–84.

46 'Blackboys Diary', *Bristol Evening World*, July 1935.

47 *L* V, 3031, 3044, 3046, 3047, *D*, 15, 16 July 1935, IV, pp.330–31; *CE* IV, pp.88–92.

48 *D*, 17 July 1935, IV, p.332.

49 *D*, 21 Aug 1935, IV, p.334; 29 Aug, p.336.

50 *D*, 4 Sep 1935, IV, pp.337–8.

51 VW to JB, 14 Oct 1935, *L* V, 3069, p.432.

52 VW to JB, 1 Dec 1935, *L* V, 3085, p.448. *Between the Acts*, p.61.

53 *D*, 31 Aug 1935, IV p.337.

54 *D*, 5 Sep 1935, IV, p.338.

55 *D*, 2 Oct 1935, *L* IV, p.346.

56 *D*, 1 Nov 1935, IV, p.351.

57 Eg, on Harold Nicolson's election as a National Labour M.P.: 'What a tribute to a good heart and the upper class manner!' [VW to ES, 16 Nov 1935, *L* V, 3081, p.443.]

58 *D*, 21 Nov 1935, IV, p.354.

59 VW to JB, 25 Oct 1932, *L* V, 3072, p.436.

60 JB to QB, 21 Oct 1936, King's.

61 JB to VW, nd, MHP, Sussex.

62 VB to JB, 19 Sep 1935, Tate Gallery, *D*, 20 June 1935, IV, p.324.

63 VB to JB, 17 Oct 1935, Tate Gallery.

64 VW to JB, 14 Oct 1935, *L* V, 3069, p.432; *D*, 30 Dec 1935, IV, p.361.

65 VW to ES, 18 Sep 1935, *L* V, 3063, p.427.

66 *D*, 15 Sep 1935, IV, p.342; 18 Nov 1935, p.353.

67 VW to Angelica Bell, 18 Nov 1935, *L* V, 3082, p.445.

68 For Wolff and Woolf, see Sybille Bedford, *Aldous Huxley*, I, p.314; *D*, 14 Dec 1935, IV, p.357; VB to JB, 21

Dec 1935, Tate Gallery; VW to JB, 17 Dec 1935, *L* V, 3088, p.452; VW to OM, 5 Jan 1936, *L* VI, 3094, p.3; VW to ES, 13 Jan, 16 Jan 1936, *L* VI, 3097, 3098, p.5. *L* VI, p.5, note 1; *The Years*, p.288. Dr Wolff went on to practise psychiatry and to write books on palmreading, the study of hands, and bisexuality.

69 *D*, 20 Dec 1935, IV, p.359.

70 VW to ES, 26 Nov 1935, *L* V, 3084, p.446; Emily Hale to Ruth George, 6 Dec 1935, Denison Library, Scripps College, Claremont. Quoted Gordon in *Eliot's New Life*, OUP, 1988, pp.162–4.

71 Sophie Farrell to VW, 27 Dec 1935, 29 Dec 1936, MHP, Sussex.

72 *D*, 27 Nov 1935, IV, p.355; 29 Dec 1935, IV, p.360.

73 *D*, 4 Jan, 7 Jan, 10 Jan, 16 Jan 1936, V, pp.4–8.

74 VW to JB, 30 Jan 1936, *L* VI, 3101, p.9; *D*, 21–28 Jan, V, pp.10–12.

75 VW to Hugh Walpole, 8 Feb 1936, *L* VI, 3104, p.12.

76 *D*, 29 Feb 1936, V, p.13.

77 VB to JB, 4 Mar 1936, Tate Gallery.

78 As note 75. Cf. 'America which I have never seen' 1938, Berg.

79 VW to ES, 10 Mar 1936, *L* VI, 3110, p.18.

80 VW to JB, 11 Mar 1936, *L* VI, 3111, p.21.

81 VW to ES, 25 July 1936, *L* VI, 3156, p.60; 3 Aug 1936, *L* VI, 3159, p.62.

82 VW to ES, 27 Mar 1936, *L* VI, 3115, p.24.

83 *D*, 13 Mar 1936, V, p.17.

84 *D*, 16 Mar 1936, V, p.17.

85 *D*, 11 Mar 1936, V, p.15; LW, *DATW*, p.153.

86 *D*, 24 Mar 1936, V, p.20.

87 VW to JB, 2 May 1936, *L* VI, 3126, p.33.

88 *D*, 11 June 1936, V, p.24.

89 VW to ES, 26 Apr 1936, *L* VI, 3124, p.30.

90 VW to Sibyl Colefax, 6 May 1936, *L* VI, 3130, p.36.

91 VW to ES, 20 July 1936, *L* VI, 3154, p.57.

92 VW to VB, 11 May 1936, *L* VI, 3132, p.38.
93 LW, *DATW*, p.154.
94 VW to ES, 11 June 1936, *L* VI, 3143, p.47.
95 *D*, 11 June 1936, 21 June 1936, V, pp.24, 25.
96 VW to VSW, 29 June 1936, *L* VI, 3147, p.50.
97 VW to VSW, 9 June 1936, *L* VI, 3142, p.46.
98 VW to ES, 4 June 1936, *L* VI, 3139, p.43.
99 VW to ES, 8 July 1936, *L* VI, 3151, p.52; 20 July 1936, *L* VI, 3154, pp.56–7.
100 VW to ES, 14 July 1936, *L* VI, 3153, p.55.
101 *D*, 22 Jan 1937, V, p.51; VW to JB, June 28 1936, 3146a, *Modern Fiction Studies*, Summer 1984, vol 30, no.2, pp.175–202. VB to JB, 10 Oct 1936, Tate Gallery.
102 VW to JB, as note 101.
103 VW to ES, 3 July 1936, *L* VI, 3149, p.52.
104 VW to LW, 14 July 1936, *L* VI, 3152, p.55.
105 VW to OM, 9 Oct 1936, *L* VI, 3175, p.76.
106 *D*, 10 Nov 1936, V, p.32.
107 VW to ES, 22 Aug 1936, *L* VI, 3164, p.66.
108 VB to JB, 5 Sep 1936, Tate Gallery; Spalding, pp.290–1; QB, 'Charleston Revisited', *Charleston Newsletter*, no.17, Dec 1986, pp.7–8.
109 CB to MH, 12, 20 Aug 1936, Texas.
110 VB tells JB about this in a letter of 18 Sep 1936, Tate Gallery. See Grace Radin, ' "Two Enormous Chunks": Episodes Excluded during the Final Revisions of *The Years*', *Bulletin of the New York Public Library*, 80/2, 1977, pp.222–51 The two cut sections are reprinted there, and in my edition of *The Years*, OUP, 1992.
111 *D*, 30 Oct 1936, V, p.26; *D*, Nov-Dec 1936.
112 *D*, 3 Nov 1936, V, pp.28–9.
113 *D*, 5 Nov 1936, V, p.30.
114 VW to JB, 14 Nov 1936, *L* VI, 3189, p.85.
115 *D*, 30 Nov 1936, V, p.39; 30 Dec, p.44.
116 Quoted in Grace Radin, *Virginia Woolf's The Years: The Evolution of a Novel*, University of Tennessee Press, 1981, p.70.
117 Holograph of *The Pargiters*, vol.5, Berg; *The Years*, pp.230–1.
118 *The Years*, p.272.
119 'The Leaning Tower', 1940, *CE* II, p.175.
120 'Why Art Today Follows Politics', 1936, *CE* II, p.231.
121 *D*, 7 Mar 1937, V, p.65.
122 VW to Stephen Spender, 30 Apr 1937, *L* VI, 3240, p.122.
123 *The Years*, p.171.
124 Ibid., p.265.

CHAPTER 37: FASCISM

1 VW to VD, 18 Apr 1935, LV. p.385.
2 *D*, 22 Apr 1935, IV, p.304.
3 VW to VB, 28 Apr 1935, *L* V, 3013, p.387; to MLD, 28 Apr 1935, *L* V, 3014, p.388.
4 *D*, 9 May 1935, IV, p.311; LW, *DATW*, p.191. 'Corybantic': like worshippers of the goddess of nature, Cybele.
5 *D*, 7 Feb 1941, V, p.355.
6 QB and Isaiah Berlin, to the author.
7 See Tom Paulin, *J'accuse*, Channel 4, January 1991, and John Carey, *The Intellectuals and the Masses*, Faber, 1992, p.80; Alexander, p.66, for representations of VW as racist, anti-Semitic.
8 *D*, 14 Nov 1938, V, p.186.
9 *The Years*, p.273.
10 Drafts of 'The Duchess and the Jeweller', Berg; *CSF*, p.309; Sandra Kemp, ed., *Selected Short Stories*, Penguin, 1993, notes, pp.121–3; LW correspondence, Sussex. VW referred to it as the story of the Jew and the Duchess.
11 E.g. VSW to HN, 3 Aug 1938, on how she likes LW in spite of his being 'tiresome and wrong-headed and sometimes Jewish', meaning tight with money. This is quoted,

and glossed, in *Vita*, p.294, but silently omitted in *V & H*, p.304.

12 VW to ES, 2 Aug 1930, *L* IV, 2215, p.194.

13 *The Years*, p.153.

14 Silver, p.22.

15 'I let fly a few, guarded hints as to my own attitude [to Forster]. We must attack Hitler in England': *D*, 24 May 1938, V, p.142. 'Let us try to drag into consciousness the subconscious Hitlerism that holds us down.' 'Thoughts on Peace in an Air Raid', *New Republic*, 21 Oct 1940 [written August 1940], *CE* IV, p.174.

16 *Three Guineas*, pp.227–8.

17 See Abel, p.91, for VW's re-situating of 'the battlefield in the British family and workplace'.

18 Zwerdling, p.264.

19 *D*, 30 Apr 1937, V, p.84.

20 'Why Art today follows Politics', written for the *Daily Worker*, Dec 1936 (*CE* II, pp.230–2 retitled 'The Artist and Politics'); 'Women Must Weep – Or Unite Against War', a 'summary' of *Three Guineas* in the *Atlantic Monthly*, May and June 1938; 'Thoughts on Peace in an Air Raid' (*New Republic*, 21 Oct 1940, *CE* IV, pp.173–7), and 'The Leaning Tower' (read to the Workers' Educational Association in May 1940 and published by John Lehmann in *Folios of New Writing*, Nov 1940, *CE* II, p.162.)

21 VW to Stephen Spender, 10 July 1934, *L* V, 2910, p.315.

22 VW to JB, 28 June 1936, 3146a, *CS*.

23 *D*, 30 Oct 1935, IV, p.350.

24 *D*, 31 Aug 1935, IV, p.337.

25 VW to JB, 25 Oct 1935, *L* V, 3072, p.436.

26 VW to ES, 1 July 1936, *L* VI, 3148, p.51; to ES, 7 Mar 1937, *L* VI, 3224, p.112: 'Why does everyone bother me about politics?'

27 *QB*II, p.189; Fri 4*n* Tues 8 Dec 1936, *The Diaries of Evelyn Waugh*, ed. Michael Davie, Weidenfeld & Nicolson, 1976, p.415.

28 Stephen Spender said she was 'fascinated' by royalty. CB reported VW 'boasting' about getting a letter from a duchess. (CB to MH, 7 Aug 1931, Texas.)

29 'Am I a Snob?', *MB*, pp.219–39.

30 'Royalty', *CE* IV, p.215.

31 *D*, 7 Dec 1936, V, p.40.

32 So described by Taylor, p.495.

33 HN, *Diary*, I, p.276; *V&H*, 10 Dec 1936, p.289.

34 *D*, 10 Dec 1936, V, p.41.

35 OM, Diary, 10 Dec 1936, Goodman family papers.

36 *D*, 10 Dec 1936; VW to JB, Christmas Day 1936, *Modern Fiction Studies*.

37 'Craftsmanship', *CE* II, p.250. Broadcast 29 Apr 1937.

38 'Royalty', *CE* IV, p.215; Tom Hopkinson to VW, 11 Aug 1939, Sussex.

39 Cunningham, p.33.

40 Bibesco, writer, daughter of Margot Asquith, was married to a Rumanian diplomat, had been the lover of Middleton Murry, and had known VW since the 1920s.

41 R.C. Trevelyan to VW, 17 Feb 1935, Sussex.

42 VW to R.C. Trevelyan, 27 Feb 1935, *L* V, 2993, pp.374–5.

43 *D*, 6 Jan 1935, IV, p.273.

44 *Sunday Times*, 13 Sep 1936; clipped and dated by VW in *Three Guineas* file, Sussex. cf. the deputy director of the British Union of Fascists in 1934: 'We definitely prefer "women who are women, and men who are men." ' Quoted in Brian Harrison, *Separate Spheres: The Opposition to Women's Suffrage in Britain*, Croom Helm, 1978, p.231.

45 David Bradshaw, in his forthcoming papers, 'The Bray and Drone of Tortured Voices: British Writers and Anti-Fascism in the 1930s' (*Woolf Studies Annual*, 3, 1997) and 'Under the Hawk's Wing: British Writers and Anti-Fascism in the 1930s' (*Woolf Studies Annual*, 4, 1998), sorts out VW's involvement with the IAWDC and FIL. I am much indebted to him for showing me these papers, which have greatly influenced me.

46 Herman Ould, president of PEN, asked her to sign a plea for freedom of expression for Spain, for the PEN Conference in Barcelona in October 1935. Texas.

47 *D*, 30 Oct 1935, IV, p.349.

48 VW to JB, 1 Dec 1935, *L* V, 3085, p.449.

49 Bradshaw, II, MS, p.27.

50 VW to ES, 10 Mar 1936, *L* VI, 3110, p.18.

51 VW to JB, 11 Mar 1936, *L* VI, 3111, p.21.

52 VW to ES, 1 July 1936 and 3 Aug 1936, *L* VI, 3148, 3159. Also on this resignation, VW to JB, 28 June 1936, *CS*, 3146a, pp.375–6, and VW to JB, 28 July 1936, 3156b, *Modern Fiction Studies*, Summer 1984, p.192.

53 *CE* II, pp.230–2. For AIA see Margot Heinemann, 'The People's Front and the Intellectuals', in *Britain, Fascism and the Popular Front*, ed. Jim Fyrth, Lawrence and Wishart, 1985, p.165.

54 VW to JB, Xmas Day 1936, 3203a, *Modern Fiction Studies*, p.196: 'Adrian is off to Berlin to rescue Ossivitsky [*sic*].' See also W.J. McCormack, ed.,'Communicating with Prisoners', *In the Prison of His Days*, Lilliput Press, 1988, pp.84–6.

55 *The Times*, 19 Aug 1936. Quoted Bradshaw, II, MS, pp.14–15.

56 VW to Janet Case, 26 June 1937, *L* VI, 3264, p.139.

57 Quoted Bradshaw, II, MS, p.29.

58 VW to ES, 7 June 1938, *L* VI, 3395, p.234.

59 For the American Guild for German Cultural Freedom. May Sarton to VW, 15 Jan 1939, Berg; VW to May Sarton, 2 Feb 1939, *L* VI, 3485, p.314; also to Elizabeth Bowen, *L* 3493.

60 VW to ES, 24 Jan 1939, *L* VI, p.311; VW to the Home Office, 13 Aug 1940; VW to Mrs Spira, 23 July, 13 Aug 1940. Spira correspondence, Smith College Library.

61 Valentine Cunningham, 'Neutral? 1930s Writers and Taking Sides', in F. Gloversmith, ed., *Class Culture and Social Change*, Brighton, 1980, pp.45–69.

62 Martin Ceadel, *Pacifism In Britain 1914–1945*, OUP, 1980, p.147.

63 Quoted Zwerdling, p.285, who gives some details of how 'many pacifist writers of the period echoed or helped to shape Woolf's satiric attacks on militarism and nationalism' in his excellent chapter, 'Pacifism without Hope'.

64 LW, *DATW*, p.245. VW described it to QB as a big frog squashing a smaller frog.

65 E.g. 'Miss Lucy Cox, prospective Labour candidate for Pudsey and Otley, opposed sanctions. She did not think any conference delegate would be prepared to starve Italian women and babies, much less to drop bombs on them. What was wanted, she suggested, was not war, but an international lunatic asylum.' *The Times*, 2 Oct 1935.

66 *D*, 2, 15 Oct 1935, IV, pp.345–6.

67 Ceadel, p.191.

68 Ibid., p.196.

69 Zwerdling, pp.285–6; Cunningham, p.69; Ceadel, p.278.

70 Frances Partridge, *A Pacifist's War*, Robin Clark, 1983, 7 June 1941, p.95; 17 August 1942, p.142.

71 Aldous Huxley, 'Notes on the Way', *Time & Tide*, 7 Mar 1936, in *The Hidden Huxley*, ed. D. Bradshaw, Faber, 1994, p.208. The essay sets up LW as its adversary.

72 *D*, 13 Mar 1936, V, p.17.

73 LW, *DATW*, p.243; 'Arms & the Peace', 1937, 'Politics & the Intellectual', 1940, quoted Wilson, pp.191, 193.

74 Rose Macaulay, *Letters to a Sister*, 3 Oct 1939, Collins, 1964, p.90.

75 Angelica Bell to David Garnett, 11 Oct 1939, King's.

76 *QB*II, p.122; quoted Zwerdling, p.273.

77 *D*, 15 Apr 1937, V, p.79.

78 *D*, 16 Feb 1940, V, pp.267–8.

79 *D*, 20 Apr 1935, IV, p.303.

80 *Three Guineas*, p.304.

81 Ibid., p.214.

82 *The Roots of War*, Hogarth Press, 1936, pp.41–2. I am grateful to Jim Fyrth for his discussion with me of this and other mid-1930s pacifist pamphlets. See also Zwerdling, 'Pacifism without Hope', for the reading of pacifist literature.

83 *D*, 11 Nov 1936, V, p.33. Bertrand Russell, 'Which Way to Peace?' Michael Joseph, 1936, pp.122, 141, 180, 188, 223.

84 Huxley, 'What are you going to do about it?', Chatto & Windus, 1936, pp.14, 31.

85 Harold Nicolson, *Diary*, vol.II, p.129, 20 Dec 1940.

86 Zwerdling, p.299, calls the essay 'both a product and a further cause of her growing sense of isolation'.

87 *D*, 23 Aug 1938, V, p.163; 27 May 1938, V, p.145; 28 Apr 1938, V, p.137; 22 Aug 1938, V, p.163.

88 *L*, V, 'Introduction', pp.xvi–xvii.

89 *QB* II, p.205; correspondence with the author, 1994; *Elders and Betters*, John Murray, 1995, pp.212–20. The criticism continues. Mepham, p.171, calls *Three Guineas* a serious lapse of judgement. Cunningham in *British Writers of the Thirties*, p.70, dismisses it as 'skittishly wayward' and 'vexingly round about'.

90 Q.D. Leavis, review of *Three Guineas*, *Scrutiny*, Sep 1938, in *CH*, pp.409–19. *D*, 1 Sep 1938, V, p.165.

91 VSW to VW, 23 July 1938, *VSW/VW*, pp.442–3; VW to VSW, 22, 23, 25 July 1938, *L* VI, 3421, 3422, 3423, pp.256–8; *D*, 16 June 1938, V, p.151.

92 Letters re *Three Guineas*, MHP, Sussex.

93 Agnes Smith to VW, 7 Nov 1938, MHP, Sussex.

94 Agnes Smith to VW, 8 Nov 1940, MHP, Sussex.

95 Edith Somerville to ES, 21 Oct 1938, Berg.

96 Eleanor Cecil to VW, 15 June 1938, MHP, Sussex.

97 Shena Simon to VW, 12 June, 5 July, 25 July 1938, 8 Jan 1940, MHP, Sussex.

98 Naomi Mitchison to VW, nd [1938], MHP, Sussex.

99 Judith Stephen to VW, nd, MHP, Sussex; Pippa Strachey to VW, 30 May 1938, Sussex.

100 VW to MLD, 4 July 1938, *L* VI, 3412, p.250.

101 VW to Emmeline Pethick Lawrence, 4 July 1938, Trinity College Cambridge.

102 *The Years*, p.236; *CE* II, p.231.

103 *Three Guineas*, p.245.

104 *D*, 12 Oct 1940, V, p.329.

105 *Three Guineas*, pp.165, 245.

106 VW to JB, 28 June 1936, 3146a, *Modern Fiction Studies*, p.189, CS.

107 'Thoughts on Peace in an Air Raid', *CE* IV, p.173; *D*, 15 May 1940, V, p.285.

108 'JB discovered with a male siskin under a microscope', MHP, Sussex.

109 *D*, 15 Apr, 4 May 1937, V, pp.79–80, 86.

110 'Reminiscences of Julian', 30 July 1937, typescript, MHP, Sussex, final version in *QB*II, pp.255–59.

111 JB, *Essays*, King's.

112 JB, 'Military considerations of a socialist policy', *Essays*, King's.

113 JB to QB, 3 Nov 1936, King's.

114 JB to Lettice Ramsey, 27 Dec 1935, in *Julian Bell: Essays, Poems and Letters*, ed. QB, Hogarth Press, 1938.

115 JB, 'On Roger Fry – A Letter to A', *Essays*, pp.258–305.

116 JB, 'War and Peace: A letter to E.M. Forster', *Essays*, pp.355–90.

117 *QB* II, pp.258–9, quotes part of this; the rest quoted in Stansky p.399, and in Hugh Thomas, *The Spanish Civil War*, 1961, Pelican 1968, p.611. Thomas: 'The answer to VW's question was that men such as Bell saw the Spanish war as a microcosm of European discontents, a way of fighting fascism . . .'

118 Stephen Spender to VW, 2 Apr [1937], Sussex.

119 Stansky & Abrahams, p.396.

120 'Reminiscences of Julian', typescript, MHP, Sussex.

121 VB to JB, 20 June 1937, Tate Gallery.
122 JB to VB, 25 Sep 1935, *Essays*, pp.196–8.
123 *Deceived*, p.132, 134.

CHAPTER 38: WAITING

1 *D*, 26 Sep 1937, V, p.111.
2 *D*, 12 Feb 1937, V, p.54.
3 *D*, 15 Feb 1937, V, p.55.
4 *D*, 19 July 1937, V, p.103.
5 *QB* II, p.254.
6 Clipping [nd] in *Three Guineas* file, MHP, Sussex.
7 'The Historian and 'The Gibbon'', *TLS*, 24 Apr 1937, *CE* I, pp.115–23; 'Reflections at Sheffield Place', *NS & N*, 19 June 1937, *CE* I, pp.124–30.
8 'Congreve', *TLS*, 25 Sep 1937, *CE* I, pp.76–84.
9 *D*, 12 Mar 1937, V, p.67.
10 *D*, 1 June 1937, V, p.91; 22 June, p.96.
11 May Sarton, *I Knew a Phoenix*, 1954, Women's Press, 1994, p.201.
12 *D*, 16 June 1937, V, p.93.
13 Sarton, pp.219–21.
14 Interviews with May Sarton, Claire Messud, *Guardian*, 11 Jan 1995; Natasha Walter, *Independent*, 31 July 1993.
15 VW to EB, 9 Oct 1937, *L* VI, 3321, p.181.
16 *D*, 9 May 1938, V, p.139.
17 May Sarton to VW, 16 May, nd, Berg; 15 Jan 1939, Berg; 22 June nd [1937?], MHP, Sussex.
18 *D*, 9 Apr 1937, V, p.78.
19 *D*, 12 July 1937, V, p.102.
20 'Miss Janet Case', *The Times*, 22 July 1937.
21 VB to VW, 6 Aug 1937, *L* VI, p.106.
22 VW to VB, 17 Aug 1937, *L* VI, 3294, p.158.
23 *D*, 11 Aug 1937, V, p.106.
24 *D*, 30 Nov 1937, V, p.119.
25 VB to JB, 7 July 1937, Tate Gallery; *D*, 1 Nov 1937, V, p.118.
26 VB to VSW, 16 Aug 1937, Marler, p.439.

27 VW to VSW, 1 Oct 1937, *L* VI, 3315, p.175.
28 VB to VW, 4 Feb 1938, Berg. Quoted *L* VI, p.211.
29 *D*, 12 Oct 1937, V, p.113.
30 VW to VB, 12 Aug 1937, *L* VI, 3292, p.157.
31 *D*, 17 Aug 1937, V, p.108; VW to VB, 17 Aug 1937, *L* VI, 3294, p.159; *QB*, *Elders and Betters*, 1995, p.214, on *Three Guineas* as a continuation of an argument with JB.
32 *CSF*, p.260 (note, p.309).
33 Signed copy, private collection.
34 VW to VB, 24 Oct 1938, *L* VI, 3460, p.294. At this time she seems to have rewritten an old story about the failure of a marriage, 'Lappin and Lapinova', *CSF*, p.310.
35 *D* 22 Oct 1937, V, p.115.
36 *D*, 30 Nov 1937, V, p.120.
37 Molly MacCarthy to VW, 19 Jan 1938, MHP, Sussex.
38 JL, *The Whispering Gallery*, p. 236. For the reunion of JL and the Press, see Willis, pp.294 ff.
39 *D*, 22 Oct 1937, V, p.116; Willis, pp.295–6.
40 LW to JL [written by VW], 2 Jan 1938, *L* VI, 3345, pp.200–1.
41 VW to JL, 22 Apr 1938, *L* VI, 3381, p.224.
42 *D*, 28 Apr 1938, V, p.137.
43 Lehmann, *The Whispering Gallery, I am my Brother*, and *Thrown to the Woolfs* for his version of what Willis calls an 'uneasy alliance', p.336; LW, *JNAM*, pp. 102–26, for his version of how the partnership worked from 1938–46 and was dissolved, initially by JL, in 1946, when Chatto & Windus took over JL's 50 per cent of the Press.
44 VW to JL, July 1938, *L* VI, 3414, p.252.
45 JL to VW, 14 July 1938, MHP, Sussex and Texas.
46 The Press also published in 1938 and 1939, *New Writing*, Isherwood's *Goodbye to Berlin*, Spender and Lehmann's edition of *Poems for Spain* (contributors included Auden), Kenneth Allott's *Poems*, Spender

and Leishman's translations of Rilke's *Duino Elegies*, Henry Green's novel *Party Going* and Tom Hopkinson's *The Man Below*.

47 *D*, 21 Feb 1937, V, p.59; 29 June 1937, V, p.100; VW to VB, 2 Nov 1938, *L* VI, 3464, p.299.

48 *D*, 25 June 1937, V, p.99.

49 Notes for 'The Leaning Tower', Berg.

50 VW to ES, 19 Sep 1937, *L* VI, 3309, p.170. Also *D*, 17 Aug 1937, V, p.107.

51 *D*, 3 Oct 1938, V, p.179. She saw, and disliked, its only London performance: VW to VSW, 19 Feb 1939, *L* VI, 3490, p.317.

52 VW to Ling Su Hua, 17 Apr 1939, *L* VI, 3506, p.327.

53 *D*, 28 July 1940, V, p.307.

54 *D*, 10, 12 March 1938, V, pp.128–9.

55 *D*, 30 Nov 1937, V, p.119; 19 Oct 1937, p.114.

56 *D*, 26 Apr 1938, V, p.135.

57 *D*, 10, 22, 31 Mar 1937, V, pp.128–33.

58 Philip Morrell to VW, 6 Feb 1938, MHP, Sussex.

59 *D*, 27 Apr 1938, V, p.135.

60 VW to JL, 22 Apr 1938, VI, p.224.

61 *D*, 27 Apr 1938, V, p.136.

62 OM, 'Farewell Message', Texas.

63 *D*, 25 May 1938, V, p.143.

64 Notebook, 1935, MHP, Sussex.

65 *D*, 7 July 1938, V, p.155.

66 *Roger Fry*, Ch.4, p.84.

67 When Spalding started work on her biography of RF in the 1970s, she found his letters still done up in VW's packets with her annotations, *Roger Fry*, preface, p.ix.

68 Sussex; Silver, p.339.

69 *D*, 22 Sep 1938, V, p.173.

70 VW to VB, 8 Oct 1938, *L* VI, 3454x, p.285.

71 *Roger Fry*, Ch.4, p.104.

72 *Roger Fry*, p.291.

73 VW to VB, *L* VI, 2 Nov 1938, 3464, p.298; *D*, 1 Dec 1938, V, p.190.

74 *D*, 14 Nov 1938, V, p.186.

75 *D*, 18 Jan 1939, V, p.200.

76 'Virginia Woolf and Katherine Furse: An Unpublished Correspondence', *Tulsa Studies in Women's Literature*, vol.9, pt 2, 1990.

77 *Roger Fry*, p.96.

78 *D*, 3 June 1938, V, p.148.

79 VW to ES, 7 June 1938, *L* VI, 3395, p.235.

80 VW to ES, 26 June 1938, *L* VI, 3408, p.246.

81 *D*, 30 Oct 1938, V, p.182.

82 *D*, 17 Aug 1938, V, p.161.

83 *D*, 5 Sep 1938, V, p.166.

84 *D*, 10 Sep 1938, V, p.167.

85 QB to VW, nd [Sep 1938), QB.

86 *D*, 28 Sep 1938, V, p.174; VW to VB, 1 Oct 1938, *L* VI, 3447, p.276.

87 *D*, 30 Sep 1938, V, p.176.

88 *D*, 12 Sep 1938, V, p.169. This paper, given on 11 Sep 1938, was printed as 'My Early Beliefs' in 1949; in SPR, pp.48–64.

89 *D*, 6 Oct 1938, V, p.179.

90 *D*, 3 Mar 1939, V, p.207.

91 VW to ES, 14 Apr 1939, *L* VI, 3505, p.326.

92 *D*, 17 Aug 1938, V, p.161.

93 *D*, 17 Sep 1938, V, p.172.

94 *D*, 11 Dec 1938, V, p.190.

95 *D*, 28 Apr 1939, V, p.216.

96 VW to VSW, 19 Feb 1939, *L* VI, 3490, p.318.

97 Angelica Bell to David Garnett, 28 Dec 1938, King's.

98 *D*, 18 Jan 1939, V, p.202; *D*, 24 Jan 1939, V, p.202; 7 Aug 1939, V, p.230.

99 SP, *MB*, p.72.

100 *CSF*, pp.310–11; see John Graham, 'The Drafts of VW's "The Searchlight" ', *Twentieth Century Literature*, 22: 4 (Dec 1976) pp.379–93

101 *D*, 15 Apr 1939, V, p.215.

102 *D*, 11 Apr 1939, V, p.213.

103 *D*, 15 Apr 1939, V, p.215.

104 Angelica Bell to David Garnett, nd, Mar? 1939, King's.

105 Angelica Bell to David Garnett, 17 Apr 1939, King's.

106 Angelica Bell to David Garnett, 25 Dec 1939, King's.

107 VW to EB, 29 Jan 1939, *L* VI, 3483, p.312; *D*, 30 Jan 1939, V, p.202.

108 *D*, 31 Jan 1939, V, p.203.

109 SP, *MB*, 19 July 1939, p.109.
110 *D*, 28 Feb 1939, V, p.206.
111 *D*, 16 Mar 1939, V, p.208.
112 *D*, 15 Apr 1939, V, p.215.
113 Gisèle Freund, *The World in My Camera*, The Dial Press, NY, 1974, p.129.
114 *D*, 3 July 1939, V, p.223.
115 Ibid.; Angelica Bell to Duncan Grant, nd [July 1939], King's.
116 *D*, 23 June 1939, V, p.220; *D*, 28 July 1939, V, p.227.
117 *D*, 13 July 1939, V, p.226.
118 *D*, 25 Aug 1939, V, p.231.
119 *D*, 28 Aug 1939, V, pp.231–2.
120 *D*, 6 Sep 1939, V, p.234.

CHAPTER 39: WAR

1 *D*, 22 Oct 1939, V, p.243.
2 'London in War', page from *Between the Acts* notebook, MHP A20, Sussex.
3 *D*, 22 Oct 1939, V, p.242.
4 *D*, 11 Sep 1939, V, p.236.
5 *D*, 1 Nov 1939, V, p.244.
6 Taylor, *English History 1914–1945*, notes, pp.566–8, that the government was slow to introduce rationing, and food subsidies went on all through the war.
7 LW, *JNAM*, p.30.
8 VW to Judith Stephen, 15 Sep [1939], private collection.
9 *D*, 25 Oct 1939, V, p.243; *D*, 17 Dec 1939, V, p.251.
10 *D*, 2 Feb 1940, V, p.263; *D*, 8 Feb 1940, V, p.265; *D*, 9 Feb 1940, V, p.266. Heligoland was a German North Sea naval base, target for RAF bombing during the war.
11 VW to ES, 12/13 Sep 1939, *L* VI, 3552, p.358. *D*, 7 Oct 1939, V, p.241.
12 *Three Guineas*, p.308.
13 'Reviewing', Hogarth Press Pamphlet, 1939, pp.23,25.
14 'Reviewer or Gutter?' *TLS*, 4 Nov 1939; Robert Lynd, in *NS&N*, 4 Nov 1939; VW to Lynd in *NS&N*, 11 Nov 1939, *L* VI, 3566, p.369;

Malcolm Elwin in *TLS*, 11 Nov 1939; *Sunday Times* review, 19 Nov 1939; *D*, 9 Nov 39, V, p.245; 2 Dec 39, p.248; *L*, VI, 3567, 3569. She confirmed her 'outsider' status in November 1940 by refusing the invitation which at last arrived from Forster to be on the London Library committee.

15 'Gipsy, the Mongrel' was sold to Chambrun for £170 but not published; *CSF*, p.311; *D*, 20 Mar 1940, V, p.272; 'Lewis Carroll', 9 Dec 1939, *CE*, I, pp.254–5; 'White's Selborne', 20 Sep 1939, *CE* III, pp.122–6; 'Gas at Abbotsford', Jan 1940, *CE* I, p.138.

16 Both Abel, p.165, note 44, and Mepham argue that VW must have read John Rickman's edition of Freud's *Civilisation, War and Death*, containing these essays, Hogarth Press, 1939. See also Zwerdling, pp.295–6; Gillian Beer, 'VW and Pre-History', in *VW: A Centenary Perspective*, ed. E. Warner, Macmillan, 1984; Jan Ellen Goldstein, 'The Woolfs' response to Freud', *Psychoanalysis and Literature*, eds E. Kurzweil & W. Phillips, Columbia UP, 1983.

17 *D*, 9 Dec 1939, V, p.250.
18 'Thoughts For the Time on War and Death', 1915, The Pelican Freud Library, vol. 12, pp.85–6.
19 'Group Psychology and the Analysis of the Ego', 1921, vol.12, p.155, p.111, p.160, p.130.
20 'Civilisation and its Discontents', vol.12, p.314. The phrasing is echoed in VW's account of Mrs Swithin's 'nurse-maid' attempts at unifying consolation in *Between the Acts*.
21 See Beer, pp.105, 118.
22 'Thoughts on War and Death', p.73. See Mepham, p.200, on this as extremely alarming reading for VW.
23 These Freud texts had been published by the Hogarth Press since 1922; 'Group Psychology' was their second title from the International Psychoanalytical Library.

24 'Thoughts on Peace in an Air Raid', *CE* IV, p.174; Holograph Reading Notes, XXI, Berg. Summarised in Silver, p.116; *Three Guineas*, pp.227–8.

25 See Abel, p.105, p.110.

26 See Rachel Bowlby in *A Woman's Essays*, Penguin, 1992, p.203, on 'this passage as a fascinating transposition of Freud into Woolf's own terms . . . for Woolf unconciousness goes with the absence of division; for Freud it is the reverse.'

27 'The Leaning Tower', *A Woman's Essays*, p.175.

28 VW to ES, 3 Oct 1938, *L* VI, 3448, p.278; See also VW to Jacques-Émile Blanche, 5 Oct 1938, *L* VI, 3451, p.282.

29 Peter Gay, *Freud: A Life for our Time*, Dent, 1988, p.640; LW, *DATW*, p.168; *D*, 29, 30 Jan 1939, V, p.202.

30 *Three Guineas*, pp.160–1.

31 de Salvo, p.130, argues that what drove VW to suicide in her reading of Freud was the possibility of 'false memory', that she had invented her memories of incest as a cover for her *desire* for an incestuous relationship with her father.

32 *The Waves*, p.222.

33 Peter Hennessy, *Never Again*, Cape, 1992, pp.110, 176, on radio as '*the* medium of communication in the home and on the battlefield in World War II': there were 9 million sets in British homes by 1939.

34 'The Leaning Tower', *CE* II, p. 164; *D*, 31 Jan 1939, V, p.203.

35 *D*, 13 Sep 1938, V, p.169.

36 *D*, 15 Sep 1940, V, p.321; *D*, 5 Sep 1938, V, p.166; *D*, 22 Sep 1938, V, p.173; *D*, 19 Dec 1940, V, p.345.

37 LW, *DATW*, p.254.

38 *D*, 23 Aug 1938, V, p.163; *D*, 9 Nov 1939, V, p.246; *Between the Acts*, p.103; *D*, 29 May 1940, V, p.289; VW to ES, 20 Sep 1940, *L* VI 3646, p.432; *D*, 2 Aug 1940, V, p.308.

39 'Thoughts on Peace in an Air Raid', *CE* IV, p.173.

40 Angelica Bell to David Garnett, 8 Jan 1940, King's.

41 *D*, 19 Feb 1940, V, p.269.

42 *D*, 20 Mar 1940, V, p.272.

43 *D*, 6 May 1940, V, p.283. Lord Haw Haw, William Joyce, was the Nazi propagandist who broadcast from Germany through the war and was executed for treason in 1946.

44 *D*, 25 May 1940, V, p.286.

45 *D*, 29 May 1940 V, p.288; *D*, 12 July 1940, V, p.302; *D*, 29 May 1940, V, p.288. *D*, 12 July 1940, V, p.302; VW to VSW, 6 Aug 1940, *L* VI, 3622, p.409.

46 *D*, 14 May, 25 May, 29 May 1940; HN to VSW, HN p.84.

47 *D*, 20 June 1940, V, p.297.

48 VW to Judith Stephen, 29 May [1940], private collection.

49 LW, *JNAM*, p.49.

50 *D*, 15 May 1940, V, p.284.

51 RSHA: The Reichssicherheitshauptamt: Nazi Central Security Agency (i.e. the Gestapo). VIG: North-West (i.e. Great Britain). The list included Margery Fry, Duff Cooper, Nancy Cunard, Hugh Dalton, (the late) Sigmund Freud, Victor Gollancz, Aldous and Julian Huxley, Harold Laski, Harold Macmillan, Naomi Mitchison, Harold Nicolson, Paderewski, Sylvia Pankhurst, Paul Robeson ('Negersanger'), Bertrand Russel [*sic*], Emanuel Shinwell, C.P.Snow, 'Steffan Spender', (the late) Lytton Strachey, Sylvia Townsend Warner, Beatrice Webb, Rebecca West, and Stefan Zweig. See David Lampe, *The Last Ditch*, Cassell, 1968, for the Arrest List.

52 *D*, 7 June 1940, V, p.292.

53 VSW to HN, 28 May 1940, *HN*, p.87; Jonathan Gathorne-Hardy, *The Interior Castle: A Life of Gerald Brenan*, Sinclair-Stevenson, 1992, p.333, quotes Frances Partridge: '[Suicide pills] were a common topic of conversation. One saved up sleeping pills, looked at them years later and they had melted and were useless.' Victor Gollancz, during the

week in 1940 when invasion seemed most likely, carried a lethal opium pill.

54 *D*, 20 June 1940, V, p.297. In 1941 he was promoted to Major and posted to a big psychiatric hospital near Taunton. See Barbara Strachey, *Remarkable Relations*, Gollancz, 1980, p.308, and Adrian Stephen to VB, 4 Apr 1941, Sussex.

55 *D*, 20 May 1940, V, p.285.

56 *D*, 30 May 1940, V, p.289.

57 *D*, 20 June 1940, V, p.297; LW, *JNAM*, pp.54–6, calling him 'Percy'.

58 *D*, 7 June 1940, V, p.292.

59 *D*, 22 June 1940, V, p.298.

60 LW, *JNAM*, p.58; *D*, 14 June 1940, V, p.296.

61 SP, *MB*, p.119; *D*, 20 June 1940, V, p.297; *D*, 27 June 1940, V, p.299; *D*, 12 July 1940, V, p.302.

62 *D*, 13 May 1940, V, p.284; *D*, 9 June 1940, V, p.293.

63 *D*, 20, 26 Jan, 29 Mar 1940, V, pp.259, 260, 276; *D*, 29 Mar 1940, V, p.276; *D*, 25 Apr 1940, V, p.282; VW to ES, 17 May 1940, *L* VI, 3609, p.399; VW to J Stephen, 19 May 1940, *L* VI, 3610, p.400; VW to ES, 30 June 1940, *L* VI, 3614, p.403.

64 *D*, 24 Mar 1940, V, p.274.

65 *Between the Acts*, p.107.

66 *D*, 20 Mar 1940, V, p.271.

67 Angelica Bell to David Garnett, 11 Mar 1940, King's.

68 VB to VW, 13 Mar 1940, Berg; VW to VB, 15 Mar 1940, *L* VI, 3589, p.385.

69 VW to Hugh Walpole, 23 Apr 1940, *L* VI, 3601, p.394; VW to VSW, 28 Apr 1940, *L* VI, 3602, p.394.

70 *Wilberforce* p.161.

71 AB to DG, 6 Aug 1939, King's.

72 *D*, 6 May 1940, V, p.283; *Between the Acts*, p.125.

73 VW to ES, 9 June 1940, *L* VI, 3612, p.402.

74 'The Humane Art', June 8 1940, *CE* I, pp.104–5.

75 Silver suggests this might have become a whole book on women and war.

76 She would finish it in Nov, and revise it between Dec and Feb 1941, when she would finally name it *Between the Acts* instead of 'Pointz Hall'.

77 *Between the Acts*, pp.47, 70, 38, 84, 51, 104.

78 *D*, 22 June 1940, V, p.298; 'The Man at the Gate', *NS&N*, 19 Oct 1940, *CE* III, pp.217–26; 'Sara Coleridge', *NS&N*, 26 Oct 1940, *CE* III, p.222–6. She was reading *The Poetical Works of STC*, 3 vols, ed. Pickering, bought 22 Apr 1940 (*D*, V, p.298), *Coleridge the Talker: A Series of Contemporary Descriptions and Comments*, ed. R.W. Armour and R.F. Hower, OUP, 1940 (Silver, p.124) and *The Friend*, 1818 edition, quoted *Three Guineas*, Ch.3, n.49, p.322.

79 SP, *MB*, p.160.

80 Keats, *Letters*, ii, 88–9.

81 *Three Guineas*, pp.322–3, quoting *The Friend*, 1818 ed., vol. I, pp.333–5.

82 Diana Gardner, to the author, 1992.

83 *D*, 25 July 1940, V, p.305.

84 *D*, 20 July 1940, V, p.302.

85 *D*, 24 July 1940, V, p.304.

86 *D*, 16 Aug 1940, V, p.311.

87 VW to Ruth Fry, 28 Aug 1940, *L* VI, 3637, p.423.

88 *CH*, pp.425, 421.

89 Benedict Nicolson to VW, 6, 18 Aug 1940, Sussex.

90 *D*, 7 Sep 1940, V, p.316; VW to Benedict Nicolson, 24 Aug 1940 [not sent], *L* VI, 3633, p.419; 24 Aug 1940, 3634 [sent]; VW to Benedict Nicolson, 2 Sep 1940, *L* VI, 3693, p.424.

91 *D*, 18 Nov 1940, V, p.340.

92 *D*, 5 July 1940, V, p.300; VW to VSW, 6 Aug 1940, *L* VI, 3622, p.409; LW, *JNAM*, p.37; *D*, 28 Aug 1940, V, p.313.

93 *D*, 16 Aug 1940, V, p.311.

94 *D*, 19 Aug 1940, V, p.312; VW to BN, 24 Aug 1940, *L* VI, 3634, p.422. Altogether nine German bombers, Dornier 17s, of Staffel 9/KG76 passed over Rodmell. *Virginia*

Woolf's Rodmell, Rodmell Village Press, p.11.

95 LW, *JNAM*, p.32.
96 *D*, 28 Aug 1940, V, p.313; LW, *JNAM*, p.26.
97 *D*, 2 Oct 1940, V, p.326.
98 VW to Judith Stephen, 16 Sep [1940], private collection.
99 VW to JL, 29 July 1940, *L* VI, 3620, p.408, quoted Lehmann, pp.97–8.
100 VW to Sibyl Colefax, 14 Aug 1940, *L* VI, 3628, p.416.
101 Ted Morgan, *Maugham*, Cape, 1980, Granada, 1981, p.478 quoted from Michael Swan, *Ilex and Olive*, 1949.
102 *D*, 31 Aug 1940, V, p.314; VW to VSW, 30 Aug 1940, *L* VI, 3638, p.424.
103 LW, *JNAM*, p.37; VW to Judith Stephen, 16 Sep [1940].
104 *D*, 5 July 1940, V, p.301.
105 VW to R.C. Trevelyan, 12 Aug 1940, *L* VI, 3626, p.412.
106 *D*, 10 Sep 1940, V, p.316–17.
107 *D*, 13 Sep 1940, V, p.319; LW, *JNAM*, pp.60–1.
108 Lehmann, p.92; VW to ES, 20 Sep 1940, *L* VI, 3646, p.432; *D*, 18 Sep 1940, V, p.322; *D*, 19, 21 Sep 1940, V, p.323. B&H was Bourne & Hollingsworth; Lehmann, p.93.
109 *D*, 26 Sep 1940, V, p.325.
110 VW to Hugh Walpole, 29 Sep 1940, *L* VI, 3649, p.435.
111 VW to Angelica Bell, 26 Oct 1940, *L* VI, 3657, p.442.
112 *D*, 20, 22, Oct 1940, V, pp.330–2; *L* 3679. Mabel Haskins, who had been their maid-of-all-work and cook since 1934, went down with them to Rodmell, did not like the air-raids in Sussex and left for London at the start of September.
113 LW, *JNAM*, pp.62–3; Lehmann, p.92.
114 *D*, 29 Oct 1940, V, p.334.
115 VW to ES, 6 Dec 1940, *L* VI, 3664, p.449.
116 LW, *JNAM*, pp.65–6; *L* VI, 3664, 3666, 3670.
117 *D*, 15 Jan 1941, V, p.353; VW to ES, 12 Jan 1941, VI, 3678, p.460; *D*, 11 Sep 1940, V, p.317; VW to ES, 11

Sep 1940, *L* VI, 3644, p.431.; VW to ES, 25 Sep 1940, *L* VI, 3648, p.434.

CHAPTER 40: ANON

1 *D*, 12 Oct 1940, V, p.329.
2 VW to ES, 11 Sep 1940, *L* VI, 3644, p.430; VW to AB, 26 Oct 1940, *L* VI, 3657, p.442; *D*, 23 Nov 1940, V, p.341.
3 *D*, 26 Mar 1940, V, p.275; *D*, 9 Jan 1941, V, p.351; *D*, 17 Nov 1940, V, p.339; *D*, 26 Mar 1940, V, p.275; *D*, 30 May 1940, V, p.290; LW, *JNAM*, p.52.
4 *Between the Acts*, p.54.
5 CB to MH, 3 Dec 1940, Texas, who reported gleefully that 'the scandal has spread like wildfire through the village of Rodmell'.
6 *D*, 1 Nov 1940, V, p.335; 3 Nov, p.336; 17 Nov, p.339. Diana Gardner, who was then secretary of the WI, says that LW did all VW's work as treasurer.
7 VW to Stephen Spender, 25 Jan 1941, *L* VI, 3683, p.464.
8 VW to MLD, 6 Apr 1940, *L* VI, 3597, p.391.
9 CB to MH, 8 Apr 1940, Texas.
10 *D*, 17 Nov 1940, V, p.339; Diana Gardner to the author; VW to Angelica Bell, 1 Oct 1940, *L* VI, 3650, p.436; *D*, 22 Oct 1940, V, p.332; VW to ES, 7 Feb 1940, *L* VI, 3584, p.382.
11 Diana Gardner to the author; *D*, 12 July, 21 Sep 1940, 9 Jan 1941.
12 *D*, 16 Dec 1940, V, p.344.
13 *D*, 21 Sep 1940, V, p.324; VW to Shena Simon, 25 Jan 1941, *L* VI, 3683, p.464; *D*, 29 Nov 1940, V, p.342.
14 LW, *JNAM*, p.34; *D*, 3, 5 Nov 1940, V, pp.335–6; *L* VI, 3659, 3660, pp.445–6.
15 *D*, 6 Dec 1940, V, p.342.
16 *D*, 12 Oct 1940, V, p.329; VW to ES, 9 June 1940, *L* VI, 3612, p.402; *D*, 2 Oct 1940, V, p.326; 24 Dec 1940, p.346.

17 *D*, 9 Jan 1941, V, p.351; the phrase from Walter de la Mare.

18 *D*, 12 Oct 1940, V, p.329.

19 *D*, 23 Nov 1940, V, p.340.

20 *D*, 12 May 1938, V, p.140.

21 'The Legacy', *CSF*, p.284.

22 *D*, 26 Jan 1941, V, p.354; VW to *Harper's*, 23 Jan 1941, *L* VI, 3681, p.463.

23 Untitled draft of 'The Symbol', Berg.

24 *CSF*, p.312.

25 Sussex, MHP, B9 j & k; *CSF*, p.272.

26 *D*, 12 Sep 1940, V, p.318; VW to ES, 1 Feb 1941, *L* VI, 3685, p.466.

27 This quote from 'Reading at Random', and for subsequent quotes, from ' "Anon" and 'The Reader': Virginia Woolf's Last Essays', ed Brenda Silver, *Twentieth Century Literature*, Fall, 1979, pp.356-435. I am indebted to Silver's commentary.

28 *Reading*, pp.374, 376.

29 *Reading*, p.433.

30 Silver notes that this is in the typescript, not the MS, of *Reading*, p.435.

31 'Ellen Terry', *NS&N*, 8 Feb 1941, *CE* IV, p.70.

32 'Mrs Thrale' [review of *Hester Lynch Piozzi (Mrs Thrale)* by James Clifford], *NS&N*, 8 March 1941, *CE* III, p.161. This was the last piece published in VW's lifetime.

33 LW, *JNAM*, p.77.

34 He was now the sole editor of the *Political Quarterly* in addition to his writing, his work for the Labour Party, and his concerns for the Press in war-time. He was going regularly to London in early 1941. (LW's Diary notes 13, 24, 30 Jan; 11, 13, 19, Feb; 14, 19 Mar.)

35 VW to ES, 14 Nov 1940, *L* VI, 3658, p.444.

36 *D*, 15 Nov 1939, V, p.339.

37 *D*, 19 Dec 1940, V, pp.344-5.

38 VW to VSW, 4 Feb 1941, *L* VI, 3689, p.470.

39 VW to Eddy Sackville-West, 1 Dec 1940, *L* VI, 3663, p.448. Also *L* 3675; *D*, 16 Dec 1940, V, p.343.

40 Diana Gardner to the author on food delivery van. *D*, 29 Dec 1940, V, p.347; 26 Feb 1941, V, p.357.

41 *Wilberforce*, 23 Dec 1940, p.167.

42 VW to ES, 1 Mar 1941, *L* VI, 3695, p.475.

43 *D*, 23 Nov 1940, V, p.341.

44 See Harold Nicolson, 26 Jan 1941, 'We know that the Great Attack is impending'. *Diary*, p.138.

45 VW to Octavia Wilberforce, 31 Dec 1940, *L* VI, 3674, p.456.

46 *D*, 1 Jan 1941, V, p.351.

47 *D*, 15 Jan 1941, V, p.353.

48 Octavia Wilberforce to Elizabeth Robins, 23 Dec 1940, *Wilberforce*, p.166.

49 VW to ES, 12 Jan 1941, *L* VI, 3678, p.460.

50 VW to ES, 1 Feb 1941, *L* VI, 3685, p.467. *D*, 26 Jan 1941, p.354.

51 VW to Dadie Rylands, 19 Feb 1941, *L* VI, 3693, p.473.

52 Octavia Wilberforce to Elizabeth Robins, 28 Feb 1941, Sussex. (repunctuated in *Wilberforce*, p.174).

53 *D*, 26 Feb, V, p.357.

54 MS, 'The ladies lavatory', Berg.

55 MS, Berg.

56 Octavia Wilberforce to Elizabeth Robins, 28 Feb 1941, Sussex, not quoted in *Wilberforce*.

57 VW to Stephen Spender, 7 Mar 1941 (misdated and misplaced in *L* VI as 3587, 7 Mar 1940, p.384); VW to T.S.Eliot, 8 Mar 1941, *L* VI, 3698, p.477; VW to ES, 10 Mar 1941, *L* VI, 3699, p.478. Isaiah Berlin remembered receiving a letter from her at this time, inviting him to 'please knock on my little grey door'.

58 *D*, 8 Mar, p.357, *L* VI, 3699.

59 Octavia Wilberforce to Elizabeth Robins, 14 Mar 1941, MHP, Sussex; *CSF*, p.338.

60 Lehmann, pp.99-100.

61 LW, *JNAM*, pp.90-1; Lehmann, p.101.

62 As in MS, BL. VW to LW, 18? Mar 1941, *L* VI, 3702, p.481; NN argues for this dating in Appendix A. But the letter might have been written the following Tuesday, 25 March.

63   VW to JL, 20 Mar 1941, *L* VI, 3703, p.482. JL argues that her 'Tuesday' letter to LW must have been written *after* this letter to him, i.e., on 25 March. JL to Nigel Nicolson, 25 July 1979, Sussex.

64   VB to VW, 20 Mar 1941, Marler, pp.473–4.

65   CB to MH, 25 Mar 1941, Texas.

66   Lehmann, p.101.

67   Octavia Wilberforce to Elizabeth Robins, 22 Mar 1941, *Wilberforce*, p.180.

68   VW to VSW, 22 Mar 1941, *L* VI, 3706, p.484.

69   VW to VB, 23? Mar 1941, *L* VI, 3709, p.486.

70   *D*, 24 Mar 1941, V, p.359.

71   EMF to VW, 23 Mar 1941, MHP, Sussex.

72   LW to Margaret Llewelyn Davies, 1 Apr 1941, Spotts, p.254.

73   VW to JL, 27? Mar 1941, *L* VI, 3709, p.486.

74   LW to JL, 28 Mar 1941, Spotts, p.250. Lehmann, p.101.

75   Octavia Wilberforce to Elizabeth Robins, 27 Mar 1941, *Wilberforce* [misdated 26 Mar], p.181.

76   LW, music diary, 27 Mar 1941, LW, Sussex.

77   VW to Elizabeth Robins, 13 Mar 1941, *L* VI, 3700, p.479; *D*, 3 July 1939, V, p.223.

78   VW to LW, 28? Mar 1941, *L* VI, 3710, pp.486–7; BL; holograph reproduced, *L* VI, facing p.489.

79   Frank Dean, *Strike While the Iron's Hot*, Susan Rowland, Lewes, 1995, p.58.

80   VB to Jane Bussy, 24 Apr 1941, Marler, p.477.

81   LW to VSW, 28 Mar 1941, Spotts, p.250.

82   Octavia Wilberforce to Elizabeth Robins, 29 Mar 1941, *Wilberforce*, p.183. Details of VW's death: LW, *JNAM*, pp.92–4; Louie Mayer, *Recollections of VW*, pp.194–6; *Wilberforce*, pp.182–3; LW, Diaries, Sussex; NN, Letters VI, Appendix A; Inquest reports.

83   VSW to HN, 31 Mar 1941, *V&H*, pp.336–7; *Vita*, p.314.

84   CB to MH, 31 Mar 1941, Texas.

85   *The Times*, 3 Apr 1941, p.4, part quoted Spotts, p.254.

86   *The Times*, 3 Apr 1941, p.7.

87   Brighton *Southern Weekly News*, 5 Apr 1941, p.1.

88   VSW, 'In Memoriam Virginia Woolf', 6 Apr 1941; 'Virginia Woolf: Lady Oxford's Tribute', *The Times*, 9 Apr 1941, p.7.

89   Stephen Spender, 'Virginia Woolf: A Tribute', *Listener*, 10 Apr 1941, p.533; *CH*, pp.426–8; typescript, Texas.

90   Adrian Stephen to VB, 4 Apr 1941, CP, Sussex.

91   ES to VB, Good Friday 1941, CP, Sussex.

92   Eliot to John Hayward, 21 Apr 1941, Valerie Eliot.

93   VD to VB, 26 July 1942, Tate Gallery.

94   VB to Sue Ling, 27 May 1941, Berg.

95   Nelly Boxall, Apr 1941, LW, Sussex.

96   Shena Simon to LW, Apr 1941, LW, Sussex.

97   LW, note, LW, Sussex; in Spotts, p.165.

98   VSW to HN, 8 Apr 1941, Lilly.

99   Julian Bell, "Monk's House and the Woolfs", *Virginia Woolf's Rodmell*, Rodmell Village Press, 1991, p.27. She had also been wearing wellington boots, which had filled with water, and a hat, which had not been found floating because it was held on by an elastic band. VSW to HN, 8 Apr 1941, Lilly.

100 Coroner's report, LW, Sussex.

101 *Southern Weekly News*, 26 Apr 1941, p.11.

102 LW, *JNAM*, pp.95–6; VB to VSW, 29 Apr 1941, Marler, p.479; Spotts, p.256. One of the elms blew down in 1943, the other died years later. The ashes and the tablet were moved to the centre of the garden, under the Tomlin bust of VW.

103 LW to George Pritchard, 24 Apr 1941, LW, Sussex.

104 E.g., LW to Shena Simon, 22 Apr 1941, LW, Sussex.
105 21 Apr 1941, Sussex. This note, and the difficulties of dating the suicide notes, have led some critics of LW to imply that he may have been in some way responsible for her death. (See Phyllis Grosskurth, Review of *Letters*, vol. VI, *TLS*, 31 Oct 1980; Susan Kenney, *University of Toronto Quarterly*, Summer 1975.)
106 Kathleen Hicks, 27 Apr 1941, *Sunday Times*.
107 LW to *Sunday Times*, 4 May 1941, LW, Sussex.
108 Malcolm Cowley, *New Republic*, 6 Oct 1941, *CH*, p.449.

109 LW, nd, LW, Sussex.
110 LW to VSW, 29 May 1941, Spotts, p.260.
111 Lehmann, pp.104–5; Willis, p.358.
112 *D*, 6 Mar 1923, II, p.238.
113 *D*, 17 Mar 1932, IV, p.83.

BIOGRAPHER

1 'The Art of Biography', 1939, *CE* IV, p.226.
2 'Not One of Us', 1927, *CE* IV, p.20.
3 VW to JL, 22 Apr 1938, *L* VI, 3381, p.224.

SHORT BIBLIOGRAPHY AND ABBREVIATIONS

Titles listed here are referred to in brief in the Notes: other sources cited in the Notes are given in full in the first reference in each relevant chapter, and thereafter referred to by short title or author's name.

WORKS BY VIRGINIA WOOLF

All references to Virginia Woolf's fiction and to *A Room of One's Own* and *Three Guineas* are to the Penguin editions.

Fiction, essays, drama, biography

The Voyage Out, Duckworth, 1915, Penguin, 1992
Night and Day, Duckworth, 1919, Penguin, 1992
Monday or Tuesday, Hogarth Press, 1921, in *Selected Short Stories*, Penguin, 1993
Jacob's Room, Hogarth Press, 1922, Penguin, 1992
CR: The Common Reader, Hogarth Press, 1925, Penguin, 1992
Mrs Dalloway, Hogarth Press, 1925, Penguin, 1992
TL: To the Lighthouse, Hogarth Press, 1927, Penguin, 1993
Orlando: A Biography, Hogarth Press, 1928, Penguin, 1993
A Room of One's Own, Hogarth Press, 1929, with *Three Guineas*, Penguin, 1993
The Waves, Hogarth Press, 1931, Penguin, 1992
CRII: The Common Reader: Second Series, Hogarth Press, 1932 [forthcoming in *E*]
Flush: A Biography, Hogarth Press, 1993, Penguin, 1983
Freshwater: A Comedy, ed. Lucio Ruotolo, Hogarth Press, 1976
The Years, Hogarth Press, 1937, Penguin, 1994
Three Guineas, Hogarth Press, 1938, with *A Room of One's Own*, Penguin, 1993
Roger Fry: A Biography, Hogarth Press, 1940, 1991
Between the Acts, Hogarth Press, 1941, Penguin, 1992

AEFR: Articles, Essays, Fictions, Reviews, in the Berg Collection.
' "Anon" and "The Reader": Virginia Woolf's Last Essays', ed. Brenda Silver, *Twentieth Century Literature* 25 (1979, pp.356–441)
Melymbrosia: An Early Version of 'The Voyage Out', ed. Louise de Salvo, New York Public Library, 1982
Orlando: The Holograph Draft, ed. Stuart N. Clarke, S.N. Clarke, 1993
The Pargiters: The Novel-Essay Portion of 'The Years', ed. Mitchell A. Leaska, Hogarth Press, 1978
Pointz Hall: The Earlier and Later Typescripts of 'Between the Acts', ed. Mitchell A. Leaska, John Jay Press, 1982
To the Lighthouse: The Original Holograph Draft, ed. Susan Dick, Toronto University Press, 1982, Hogarth Press, 1983
The Waves: the two holograph drafts, ed. J.W. Graham, Hogarth Press, 1976
WF: Women & Fiction: The Manuscript Versions of *A Room of One's Own*, ed. S.P. Rosenbaum, The Shakespeare Head Press, 1992

Collections

Books and Portraits, ed. Mary Lyon, Hogarth Press, 1977
The Captain's Death Bed and Other Essays, Hogarth Press, 1950
CE: Virginia Woolf, *Collected Essays*, ed. Leonard Woolf, 4 vols, Chatto & Windus, 1966–7
Contemporary Writers, Hogarth Press, 1965
The Crowded Dance of Modern Life: Selected Essays, vol. II, Penguin, 1993
CSF: The Collected Shorter Fiction of Virginia Woolf, ed. Susan Dick, Hogarth Press, 1985, 1989
The Death of the Moth and Other Essays, Hogarth Press, 1942
E: The Essays of Virginia Woolf, ed. Andrew McNeillie, 6 vols, Hogarth Press, 1986
Granite and Rainbow, Hogarth Press, 1958
The Hogarth Letters, Hogarth Press, 1933, ed. Hermione Lee, 1985
The London Scene: Five Essays by Virginia Woolf, Random House, 1975
The Moment and Other Essays, Hogarth Press, 1947
Mrs Dalloway's Party, ed. Stella McNichol, Hogarth Press, 1973
Virginia Woolf: Women and Writing, ed. Michele Barrett, Women's Press, 1979
A Woman's Essays: Selected Essays, i, ed. Rachel Bowlby, Penguin, 1992

Letters and Diaries

CS: Congenial Spirits: The Selected Letters of Virginia Woolf, ed. Joanne Trautmann Banks, The Hogarth Press, 1989
D: The Diary of Virginia Woolf, ed. Anne Olivier Bell and Andrew McNeillie, 5 vols, Hogarth Press, 1977–84
L: The Letters of Virginia Woolf, ed. Nigel Nicolson and Joanne Trautmann, 6 vols, Hogarth Press, 1975–80
PA: A Passionate Apprentice: The Early Journals of Virginia Woolf, ed. Mitchell A. Leaska, Hogarth Press, 1990
Silver: Virginia Woolf's Reading Notebooks, ed. Brenda Silver, Princeton University Press, 1983
SP, MB: 'Sketch of the Past', in *Moments of Being*, ed. Jeanne Schulkind, Sussex University Press, 1976, revised 1985. The 1985 edition of *Moments of Being* transcribes the revised typescript of 'Sketch of the Past', including a hitherto unpublished section on pp.119–37. The 1976 edition transcribes the manuscript version of 'Sketch of the Past'. I am using the 1985 edition unless otherwise noted.
VW/LS: Virginia Woolf & Lytton Strachey: Letters, ed. Leonard Woolf and James Strachey, Hogarth Press, 1956
A Writer's Diary, ed. Leonard Woolf, Hogarth Press, 1953

OTHER WORKS CONSULTED

Abel: Elizabeth Abel, *Virginia Woolf and the Fictions of Psychoanalysis*, Chicago, 1989
Alexander: Peter F. Alexander, *Leonard and Virginia Woolf: A Literary Partnership*, Harvester Wheatsheaf, 1992
Annan: Noel Annan, *Leslie Stephen: The Godless Victorian*, Weidenfeld and Nicolson, 1984
Bloomsbury/Freud: *Bloomsbury/Freud: The Letters of James and Alix Strachey, 1924–1925*, ed. Perry Meisel and Walter Kendrick, Basic Books Inc, 1985
Caramagno: Thomas Caramagno, *The Flight of the Mind: Virginia Woolf's Art and Manic-Depressive Illness*, University of California Press, 1992
CH: *Virginia Woolf: The Critical Heritage*, ed. Robin Majumdar and Allen McLaurin, Routledge & Kegan Paul, 1975

VIRGINIA WOOLF

Clever Hearts: Desmond and Molly MacCarthy; *A Biography*, Hugh and Mirabel Cecil, Gollancz, 1990, rev. 1991
Cunningham: Valentine Cunningham, *British Writers of the Thirties*, OUP, 1988
Deceived: Angelica Garnett, *Deceived with Kindness: A Bloomsbury Childhood*, OUP, 1984
de Salvo: Louise de Salvo, *Virginia Woolf: The Impact of Childhood Sexual Abuse on her Life and Work*, The Women's Press, 1989
Dunn: Jane Dunn, *A Very Close Conspiracy: Vanessa Bell and Virginia Woolf*, Jonathan Cape, 1990
Furbank: P.N. Furbank, *E.M. Forster: A Life*, 2 vols, Secker & Warburg, 1977–8
Garnett: David Garnett, *Carrington: Letters and Extracts from Her Diaries*, Cape, 1970
Gillespie: Diane Filby Gillespie, *The Sisters' Arts: The Writing and Painting of Virginia Woolf and Vanessa Bell*, Syracuse University Press, 1988
Gordon: Lyndall Gordon, *Virginia Woolf: A Writer's Life*, OUP, 1984
Holroyd 1971, 1994: Michael Holroyd, *Lytton Strachey: A Biography*, Penguin, 1971 [revised from *Lytton Strachey: A Critical Biography*, Heinemann, 1967–8]; *Lytton Strachey: The New Biography*, Chatto & Windus, 1994
HPG: *Hyde Park Gate News*, British Library
Hynes: Samuel Hynes, *A War Imagined: The First World War and English Culture*, Bodley Head, 1990
JDS: *Julia Duckworth Stephen: Stories for Children, Essays for Adults*, ed. Diane F. Gillespie and Elizabeth Steele, Syracuse U.P., 1987
Richard Kennedy, *A Boy at the Hogarth Press*, The Whittington Press, 1972, Penguin, 1978
B.J. Kirkpatrick, *A Bibliography of Virginia Woolf*, 3rd ed., The Soho Bibliographies, Clarendon Press, Oxford, 1980
KM I–III: *The Collected Letters of Katherine Mansfield*, ed. Vincent O'Sullivan and Margaret Scott, Clarendon Press, 1984–93
Lehmann: John Lehmann, *Thrown to the Woolfs: Leonard and Virginia Woolf and the Hogarth Press*, 1978, Holt, Rinehart and Winston, 1979
Lehmann, *VW*: John Lehmann, *Virginia Woolf*, Thames & Hudson, 1975
Love: Jean O. Love, *Virginia Woolf: Sources of Madness and Art*, University of California Press, 1977
LW, S, G, BA, DATW, JNAM: Leonard Woolf, *Sowing, Growing, Beginning Again, Downhill All the Way, The Journey not the Arrival Matters*, Hogarth Press, 1960–9
Maitland: F.W. Maitland, *The Life and Letters of Leslie Stephen*, Duckworth, 1906
Marcus: *Virginia Woolf and Bloomsbury*, ed. Jane Marcus, Macmillan, 1987
Marler: *Selected Letters of Vanessa Bell*, ed. Regina Marler, Bloomsbury, 1993
Mausoleum Book: *Sir Leslie Stephen's Mausoleum Book* ed, Alan Bell, Clarendon Press, 1977
Mepham: John Mepham, *Virginia Woolf: A Literary Life*, Macmillan, 1991
QB I and *QB* II: Quentin Bell, *Virginia Woolf: A Biography*, 2 vols, Hogarth Press, 1972
Recollections: Recollections of Virginia Woolf, ed. Joan Russell Noble, 1972, Penguin, 1975
Rose: Phyllis Rose, *Woman of Letters: A Life of Virginia Woolf*, Routledge & Kegan Paul, 1978
Shone, *BP*2: Richard Shone, *Bloomsbury Portraits*, Phaidon, 2nd ed., 1993
Robert Skidelsky, *John Maynard Keynes* I, Macmillan, 1983
Spalding: Frances Spalding, *Vanessa Bell*, Weidenfeld & Nicolson, 1983
Spalding, *Fry*: Frances Spalding, *Roger Fry*, Granada, 1980
Spater: George Spater and Ian Parsons, *A Marriage of True Minds*, Jonathan Cape and the Hogarth Press, 1977
Spotts: *Letters of Leonard Woolf*, ed. Frederic Spotts, Weidenfeld & Nicolson, 1989
SPR: *The Bloomsbury Group*, S.P. Rosenbaum, ed., Croom Helm, 1975
Stansky: Peter Stansky and William Abrahams, *Journey to the Frontier: Julian Bell and John Cornford: Their Lives and the 1930s*, Constable, 1966
Taylor: A.J.P. Taylor, *English History 1914–1945*, Pelican, 1965, 1975
TSE: *The Letters of T.S. Eliot*, ed Valerie Eliot, Faber, 1988

Tomalin: Claire Tomalin, *Katherine Mansfield: A Secret Life*, 1987, Penguin, 1988
Vita: Victoria Glendinning, *Vita*, 1983, Penguin, 1984
V&H: Vita and Harold, ed. Nigel Nicolson, Weidenfeld & Nicolson, 1992
VSW/VW: The Letters of Vita Sackville-West to Virginia Woolf, ed. Louise de Salvo &
    Mitchell Leaska, Hutchinson, 1984
Stape: *Virginia Woolf: Interviews and Recollections*, ed. J.H. Stape, Macmillan, 1995
Wilberforce: Octavia Wilberforce: The Autobiography of a Woman Doctor, ed Pat Jalland,
    Cassell, 1989
Willis: J.H. Willis, Jr, *Leonard and Virginia Woolf as Publishers: The Hogarth Press
    1917–1941*, University Press of Virginia, 1992
Wilson: Duncan Wilson, *Leonard Woolf: A Political Biography*, Hogarth Press, 1978
Woolmer: J. Howard Woolmer, *A Checklist of the Hogarth Press 1917–1946*, St Paul's
    Bibliographies, 1986
Alex Zwerdling: *Virginia Woolf and the Real World*, University of California Press, 1986

ABBREVIATIONS FOR SOURCES

AG: Angelica Garnett
AOB: Anne Olivier Bell
QB: Quentin Bell
Berg: The Henry W. and Albert A. Berg Collection at the New York Public Library
BL: Department of Manuscripts, British Library
Houghton: The Houghton Library, Harvard University
King's: Modern Archive, King's College Library, Cambridge
Lilly: The Lilly Library, Indiana University
Reading: The Library, University of Reading
Smith: Rare Book Room, William Allen Nielsen Library, Smith College, Northampton
Sussex: University of Sussex Library Manuscript Collections
    CP: Charleston Papers, University of Sussex
    LW: Leonard Woolf Papers, University of Sussex
    MHP: Monk's House Papers, University of Sussex
Tate Gallery: Modern Collection, Tate Gallery Archive
Texas: Harry Ransom Humanities Research Center, The University of Texas at Austin
Washington State: Manuscripts, Archives, and Special Collections, Holland Library,
    Washington State University

ABBREVIATIONS IN THE NOTES

AOB: Anne Olivier Bell
AVS: Virginia Stephen
CB: Clive Bell
DG: Duncan Grant
EB: Elizabeth Bowen
EMF: E.M. Forster
ES: Ethyl Smyth
GB: Gerald Brenan
HN: Harold Nicolson
JB: Julian Bell
JL: John Lehmann
JMM: John Middleton Murry
KM: Katherine Mansfield
LRB: London Review of Books
LS: Lytton Strachey
LW: Leonard Woolf

MH: Mary Hutchinson
MK: Maynard Keynes
MLD: Margaret Llewelyn Davies
N&A: Nation & Athenaeum
NN: Nigel Nicolson
NS & N: New Statesman & Nation
NS : New Statesman
OM: Ottoline Morrell
QB: Quentin Bell
RF: Roger Fry
TLS: Times Literary Supplement
VB: Vanessa Bell
VD: Violet Dickinson
VSW: Vita Sackville-West
WH: Winifred Holtby

A NOTE ON THE TEXT: Virginia Woolf's punctuation and spelling have been followed in all
quotations from her diaries, letters, and manuscripts.

ACKNOWLEDGEMENTS

I owe a particular debt of gratitude to the following: Quentin and Olivier Bell, for their generous permission, their patience, and their critical benevolence; Angelica Garnett, for her permission and her great kindness; my agent Pat Kavanagh and my original publisher, Carmen Callil, for making it possible for me to write this book; Bet Inglis at the University of Sussex, for her unstinting helpfulness and her unparalleled archival knowledge; my husband John Barnard, to whom this book is dedicated; and Jenny Uglow, best of biographers, best of editors, best of friends.

I am grateful to the University of York for allowing me an extended period of leave in order to work on this book, and to the British Academy for awarding me a small personal research grant in 1992 which enabled me to carry out research in archives in the USA.

I am indebted to the following individuals for help, advice, inspiration and encouragement of many kinds: Mulk Raj Anand, Lord Annan, Igor Anrep, Steve Baarendse, Joanne Trautmann Banks, Julian Barnes, Mary Bennett, Sir Isaiah Berlin, Paul Berry, Jacques Berthoud, John Bicknell, John Bodley, Mark Bostridge, Treva Broughton, Dame Beryl Paston Brown, David Bradshaw, Tony Bradshaw, Lord Bullock, Jonathan Burnham, Belinda Norman Butler, John Carey, Hugh Cecil, Sally Chilver, Caroline Cuthbert, Paul Delany, Susan Dick, The Hon. Katharine Duckworth, Elsie Duncan-Jones, James Durham, Valerie Eliot, Matthew Evans, Roy Foster, Diana Gardner, Henrietta Garnett, Jonathan Gathorne-Hardy, Diane Gillespie, Victoria Glendinning, Adrian and Shena Goodman, Alistair Gordon, Warwick Gould, Lesley Hall, Miss K.M. Halpin, Rupert Hart-Davis, Hugh Haughton, Christopher Hawtree, Tom Heacox, Peter Hennessy, Howard Hodgkin, Michael Holroyd, John House, Roger Howe, Lord Hutchinson, Q.C., Rosalind Ingrams, Benjamin Lee, Josephine Lee, Mark Lefanu, Paul Levy, Jeremy Lewis, Amanda Lillie, Jean McGibbon, Andrew McNeillie, Regina Marler, Justin Mead, Peter Miall, Naomi Mitchison, Richard Morphet, Jamie Muir, Christopher Naylor, Virginia Nicholson, The Hon. Nigel Nicolson, Dottie Owens, the late Trekkie Parsons, Frances Partridge, Sir Edward Playfair, Anthony Powell, Kathleen Raine, Robert Reedman, Diana Reich, Jancis Robinson, George Rylands, Marna Sedgwick, Miranda Seymour, Fiona Shaw, Marion Shaw, Richard Shone, Brenda Silver, Lord and Lady Robert Skidelsky, Frances Spalding, Lady Natasha Spender, the late Sir Stephen Spender, Jill Sutcliffe, Ann Synge, Theresa Thompson, Jeremy Treglown, Ursula Vaughan Williams, the late Sandy Viner, Natasha Walter, Jack Willis, Roma Woodnutt, Philip Zeigler, the late Lord Zuckerman.

I would like to thank the following librarians, archivists and academics at these institutions for their help: Alan Bell at the London Library; Helen Bickerstaffe at Sussex University Library; Jennifer Booth at the Tate Gallery; Sally Brown at the British Library; Michael Bott and David Sutton at Reading University Library; Rebecca Campbell Cape, Saundra Taylor and Heather Munro at the Lilly Library, Indiana University; Jacky Cox at the Modern Archive, King's College; Stephen Crook, Francis O. Mattson and Philip Milito at the Berg Collection; Jill Crowther at Hull Central Library; Michael T. Dumas at the Harvard Theatre Collection, Harvard University; Anna Greening and David Doughan at the Fawcett Society; Elizabeth Falsey at the Houghton Library, Harvard University; Kate Harris at Longleat House; Cathy

ACKNOWLEDGEMENTS

Henderson and Michael Winship at the Harry Ransom Humanities Research Center at Austin; Elizabeth van Houts at Newnham College Library, Cambridge; Leila Luedeking at the Modern Literary Collections, Holland Library, Washington State University; David McKitterick at Trinity College Cambridge; the late Ruth Mortimer, Sarah Black and Karen Kukil at the Mortimer Rare Book Room, the William Allen Nielsen Library, Smith College; Judy Harvey Sahak at The Ella Strong Denison Library, Claremont College; Chris Webb at the Borthwick Institute, York.

The author and publishers are grateful to the following for permission to quote materials in copyright: Quentin Bell (for Virginia Woolf, Clive Bell, Julian Bell, Quentin Bell, Vanessa Bell); The Virginia Woolf Manuscripts at the Henry W and Albert Berg Collections; Paul Berry, Marion Shaw, and the Hull Local Studies Library (for Winifred Holtby); The British Library; The Syndics of Cambridge University Library (for Jacques Raverat); Hugh Cecil (for Molly MacCarthy); The Ella Strong Denison Library (for Emily Hale); The Hon. Katharine Duckworth (for Duckworth materials); Faber & Faber (for Rupert Brooke); Faber & Faber on behalf of Mrs Valerie Eliot (for unpublished and published texts by T.S.Eliot); The Fawcett Library (for LNSWS materials); Mary Fedden (for R.C. Trevelyan); Angelica Garnett (for Angelica Garnett and Vanessa Bell); Henrietta Garnett (for Duncan Grant); Adrian Goodman (for Ottoline Morrell); Carolyn Heilbrun (for May Sarton); David Higham Associates (for John Lehmann and Ethel Smyth); The Houghton Library, Harvard University (for Leslie Stephen to Charles Eliot Norton); Lord Hutchinson (for Mary Hutchinson); The King's College Modern Archive Centre, Cambridge (for E.M. Forster); Amanda Hopkinson (for Tom Hopkinson); Henry Lessore (for Walter Sickert); Baroness Llewelyn Davies (for Margaret Llewelyn Davies); The London Library (for London Library minutes); The London School of Economics (for Beatrice Webb); The University of Michigan Special Collections Library (for Ethel Smyth); Nigel Nicolson and the Lilly Library at Indiana University (for Harold Nicolson and Vita Sackville-West); Francis Noel–Baker (for Philip Noel–Baker); Mrs Belinda Norman Butler and the University of London Library (for Booth Papers); The Mortimer Rare Book Room, Smith College (for VW manuscripts); Lynda Pranger (for Gerald Brenan); The Harry Ransom Humanities Research Center at the University of Texas at Austin; The Royal United Kingdom Beneficent Association (for Octavia Wilberforce); Lord Salisbury and Ann Lambton (for Lady Eleanor Cecil); Baron Simon of Wythenshawe (for Lady Shena Simon); The Society of Authors; Lady Natasha Spender (for Stephen Spender); The Strachey Trust (for Lytton, Pippa, and Alix Strachey); The University of Sussex Library Manuscript Collections; Ann Synge (for Adrian Stephen); The Library of Leonard and Virginia Woolf, Washington State University Libraries; A.P.Watt Ltd on behalf of Michael Yeats (for W.B.Yeats, 'Spilt Milk'); The Virginia Woolf Estate.

For illustrative material, thanks are due to the following:

Passport photograph: property of Robert Reedman. End papers: Diary, Berg; MSS page of *Mrs Dalloway*, Manuscripts Department, BL.
Plates from; QB: 11, 12, 15, 16, 17, 18, 21, 23, 25, 28. Berg: 8, 9, 13, 14, 20. Beck & Macgregor ©, The Condé Nast PLC – *Vogue*: 59. AG and QB: 26, 44, 61, 62, 64, 65, 66, 74, 76, 79. Henrietta Garnett for The Duncan Grant Estate 44, 47, 48, 63. Guildhall Library, Corporation of London: 83. Harvard Theatre Library: 2, 10, 31, 35, 38, 39, 40, 41, 42, 50, 51, 53, 54, 56, 57, 58, 60, 69, 72, 73, 76, 77, 78, 84, 85. Lilly Library: 71. Longleat: 22. Nigel Nicolson: 45, 55. Property of: QB, 11, 12, 15, 16, 17, 18, 21, 23, 25, 28; Bloomsbury Workshop, 75; Estate of Gisèle Freund, 81, 82, 86; Wendy Gimbel, 47; Alberto de Lacerda, 48; the author, 49, reproduced by permission of Mrs Richard Kennedy; private ownership: 1, 26, 27, 63, 79. Smith College Library: 3, 4, 5, 6, 7. Tate Gallery Archive, VB photos: 29, 30, 67. Texas: 46.

INDEX

For name abbreviations of correspondents within entries, see p 872